The 116th Congress, January 3, 2019–January 3, 2021

United States House of Representatives

Democrats: 233 | Republicans: 199 | Undecided: 3 | 2018 Election Results: Democrats gained control of the House*

Democrat
Republican
Undecided

United States Senate

Democrats: 45   Republicans: 53   Independents: 2   **2018 Election Results: Republicans retained control of the Senate***

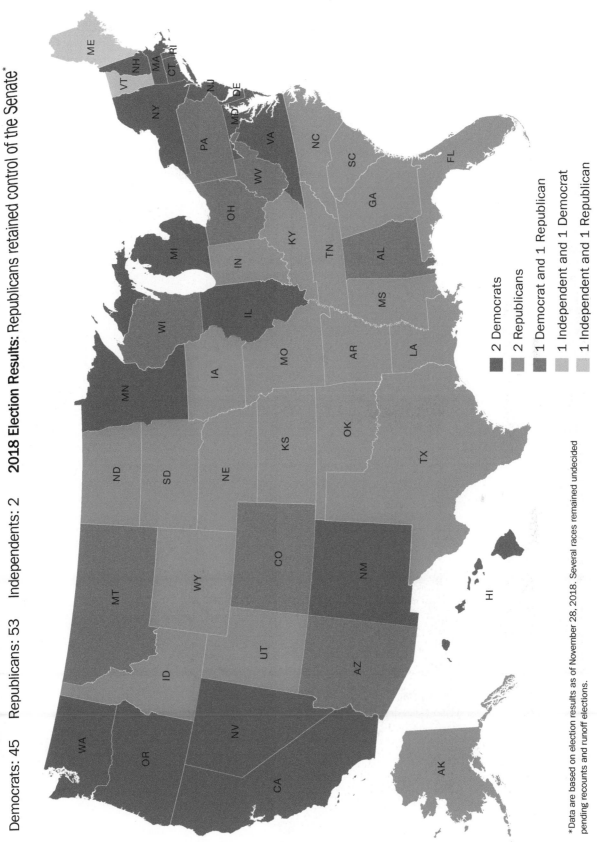

2 Democrats

2 Republicans

1 Democrat and 1 Republican

1 Independent and 1 Democrat

1 Independent and 1 Republican

*Data are based on election results as of November 28, 2018. Several races remained undecided pending recounts and runoff elections.

College of the Canyons
Department of Political Science
26455 Rockwell Canyon Road
Santa Clarita, CA 91355

Dear Political Science Student,

Welcome to Political Science 150: Introduction to American and California Government. This textbook has been customized by the Department of Political Science in collaboration with the publisher, W. W. Norton & Company. The faculty members of the Department of Political Science have collectively decided to adopt this textbook exclusively for Political Science 150. The chapters and content contained herein are well suited to ensure the requirements of the course outline are satisfied.

The initial pages of this textbook include information compiled by the Department of Political Science to assist you with your studies in political science at College of the Canyons. The following four introductory pages of this custom textbook will provide you information on the following:

- *The Discipline of Political Science*
- *Political Science course offerings at College of the Canyons*
- *Information on the Political Science Associate of Arts Transfer Degree*
- *Considerations for students interested to learn more*

We strongly encourage you to utilize this textbook to meet success in your study of the course material. Proper instruction requires an integration of a comprehensive textbook along with the particular instructor's expertise, lecture and focus. Utilizing this textbook, and the accompanying W. W. Norton resources, will ensure you have the necessary means to learn at the highest level.

Thank you for enrolling in Political Science 150. The Department wishes you the best of luck throughout your semester.

College of the Canyons
POLITICAL SCIENCE

Definition

Political science is the study of governments and how they function and interact. Students studying political science will learn about:

- International and national governmental institutions
- Political participants and groups within countries
- Formal and informal aspects of governmental activity
- The formal aspects of government include such things as constitutions; the legislative, executive, and judicial branches of government; and the distribution of power and procedures within a government. Aside from analyzing how a government should work, political scientists also study the informal and behavioral aspects of government, looking at such phenomena as public opinion and voting behavior, political parties and interest groups, and the political socialization process.

Program Description

Public authority, responsibility, and acquisition of power are studied in the discipline of political science. Introductory courses are for students interested in learning about American government, politics in general and relationships with other political systems in the world. Students majoring in political science who are pre-law will particularly profit from the more advanced courses in the department. Students interested in foreign service, international relations, and/or communications will enjoy participating in the Model United Nations program offered by the department. A major in political science is of benefit to students seeking careers in law, the military, economics, law enforcement, business, and public administration. An associate degree is not available in political science.

Career Opportunities

- Congressional aide
- Attorney
- City manager
- Diplomacy or foreign service
- FBI/CIA agent
- Peace Corps/Vista worker
- Political researcher
- Urban/regional planner
- Teacher: humanities/social sciences
- Journalist Campaign adviser
- Lobbyist
- Public relations specialist
- U.S. military officer
- International marketing/trade representative
- International banker
- Businessperson
- Specialist for federal, state, or local government

College of the Canyons
POLITICAL SCIENCE

Department Course Offerings

POLISC 150 INTRODUCTION TO AMERICAN GOVERNMENT AND POLITICS

Units: 3.00 UC:CSU 54.00 hours lecture Examines the institutions, activities, and issues of American and California Governments while presenting an overview of the major ideas and forces that shape the use of public power in American society. The Constitution, the three branches of government, political parties, interest groups, and the media are among the major topics covered. Satisfies the Title V U.S. Constitution requirement and the California State and Local Government requirement.

POLISC 150H INTRODUCTION TO AMERICAN GOVERNMENT AND POLITICS - HONORS

Units: 3.00 UC:CSU 54.00 hours lecture Recommended Preparation: ENGL-101 or ENGL-101H Examines the institutions, activities, and issues of American and California governments, including an overview of the major ideas and forces that shape the use of public power in American society, the Constitution, the three branches of government, political parties, interest groups, and the media. Additional reading, writing, and research techniques are required.

POLISC 200 INTRODUCTION TO POLITICAL SCIENCE

Units: 3.00 UC:CSU 54.00 hours lecture Introduces the nature, scope, and methodology of political science, including basic concepts, terms, contending theories, institutions, and sub-fields in the discipline. This course does not meet the Title V American Institutions requirement in U.S. Constitution, California state and local government.

POLISC 210 MODEL UNITED NATIONS

Units: 3.00 CSU 54.00 hours lecture May be taken three times for credit Examines the norms, rules, and procedures of the United Nations leading to participation in a United Nations simulation. Emphasizes parliamentary procedure, international advocacy, the role of the United Nations, and extemporaneous speaking. Field trip required.

POLISC 230 POLITICAL THEORY

Units: 3.00 UC:CSU 54.00 hours lecture Explores the major political concepts and theories from the early Greeks to modern day political philosophers, including the origins of government, state power, justice, and the distribution of political and economic resources that impact our conceptions of the "good life."

POLISC 250 COMPARATIVE GOVERNMENT AND POLITICS

Units: 3.00 UC:CSU 54.00 hours lecture Provides a comparative, analytical, and theoretical study of political cultures, government institutions, and political processes from selected regions of the world.

POLISC 270 INTERNATIONAL RELATIONS

Units: 3.00 UC:CSU 54.00 hours lecture Analyzes the basic historical, geographical, economic, ideological, and strategic factors which underlie conflict and cooperation among nations, including between international actors and structures of the international system.

POLISC 290 ETHNIC AND GENDER POLITICS

Units: 3.00 UC:CSU 54.00 hours lecture Examines the history, issues, and political processes that affect the status and power of ethnic and gender groups which have traditionally been politically and economically disadvantaged in the United States, including issues of inclusion and exclusion; otherness and scapegoating; and, barriers of inequality among politically marginalized groups.

College of the Canyons
POLITICAL SCIENCE

Department Course Offerings

GLST 101 INTRODUCTION TO GLOBAL STUDIES

This course is an introduction to the interdisciplinary field of Global Studies, including the history of globalization, and economic, political, social, cultural, and ecological developments related to the process of globalization.

GLST 102 GLOBAL ISSUES

This course introduces students to the origins, current status, and future trends of major transnational issues confronting the global community. Topics can include population trends, economic development and inequality, basic human needs (for food, water, health care), human rights, international conflict and security concerns, and environmental problems. The course also focuses on global governance, including the study of collective global responsibilities.

College of the Canyons

POLITICAL SCIENCE

Student Considerations

Why should I study political science?

Most occupations today require a college-educated individual who can write and speak well, solve problems, learn new information quickly, and work well with others on a team.

There is a growing demand for consulting to political campaigns, government regulatory agencies, nonprofit organizations, and international businesses.

Excellent opportunities are available for those who possess sound statistical and analytical skills.

What kind of student studies political science?

Political science students usually have an interest in community activities, a sense of responsibility about government programs and policies, and a desire to make our community, country, and the world a better place to live.

What will you learn and experience?

In political science, you'll learn about:

- how our society and others make political decisions
- the challenges that are inherent in developing public policy
- the fundamental ideas and choices that must be understood and addressed for any society and its citizens to achieve success
- human relations
- critical thinking and developing positions and viewpoints about the way our society and other societies should be
- how political events affect the world we live in

Is there a Political Science Club?

Yes, there is a student Political Science club. For more information please contact Professor Deems Morrione at deems.morrione@canyons.edu

If you have further questions who should you contact?

If you have further questions, please contact Professor David C. Andrus at (661) 362-3052 or david.andrus@canyons.edu. Or, you may visit the Department of Political Science website at http://www.canyons.edu/departments/POL_SCI/

PROGRAM OF STUDY

Political Science Associate in Arts for Transfer (AA-T)

The Student Transfer Achievement Reform Act (Senate Bill 1440, now codified in California Education Code sections 66746-66749) guarantees admission to a California State University (CSU) campus for any community college student who completes an "associate degree for transfer," a newly established variation of the associate degrees traditionally offered at a California community college. The Associate in Arts for Transfer (AA-T) or the Associate in Science for Transfer (AS-T) is intended for students who plan to complete a bachelor's degree in a similar major at a CSU campus. Students completing these degrees (AA-T or AS-T) are guaranteed admission to the CSU system, but not to a particular campus or major. In order to earn one of these degrees, students must complete:

1. Completion of 60 semester units or 90 quarter units that are eligible for transfer to the California State University, including both of the following:
    a. The Intersegmental General Education Transfer Curriculum (IGETC) or the California State University General Education – Breadth Requirements.
    b. A minimum of 18 semester units or 27 quarter units in a major or area of emphasis, as determined by the community college district.
2. Obtainment of a minimum grade point average of 2.0.

Associate Degrees for Transfer also require that students must earn a C or better in all courses required for the major or area of emphasis.

This degree may not be the best option for students intending to transfer to a particular CSU campus or to university or college that is not part of the CSU system. Students should consult with a counselor when planning to complete the degree for more information on university admission and transfer requirements. At the time of catalog publication, a student may earn an AA-T in Political Science. Additional majors are being developed. Please see a counselor or visit http://www.canyons.edu for more information.

Student Learning Outcome:
Students will be able to evaluate and analyze the basic institutional structures of competing governments, various theories of political science and thought, the framework of international relations, and public policy as well as social factors influencing government.

Program Requirements:		**Units**
POLISC 150	Introduction to American Government and Politics	3 - 0
	or	
POLISC 150H	Introduction to American Government and Politics - Honors	3 - 0

Plus nine units from the following:		**Units**
POLISC 230	Political Theory	3 - 0
POLISC 250	Comparative Government & Politics	3 - 0
POLISC 270	International Relations	3 - 0

Plus a minimum of six units from the following:		**Units**
POLISC 200	Introduction to Political Science	3 - 0
POLISC 210	Model United Nations	3 - 0
POLISC 290	Ethnic & Gender Politics	3 - 0
MATH 140	Introductory Statistics	4 - 0
	or	
MATH 140H	Introductory Statistics - Honors	4 - 0

Total Units	**18**

Major Code: NULL

Associate in Arts for Transfer Degree: Global Studies

The Student Transfer Achievement Reform Act (Senate Bill 1440, now codified in California Education Code sections 66746-66749) guarantees admission to a California State University (CSU) campus for any community college student who completes an "associate degree for transfer," a newly established variation of the associate degrees traditionally offered at a California community college. The Associate in Arts for Transfer (AA-T) or the Associate in Science for Transfer (AS-T) is intended for students who plan to complete a bachelor's degree in a similar major at a CSU campus. Students completing these degrees (AA-T or AS-T) are guaranteed admission to the CSU system, but not to a particular campus or major. In order to earn one of these degrees, students must complete:

1. Completion of 60 semester units or 90 quarter units that are eligible for transfer to the California State University, including both of the following:
     a. The Intersegmental General Education Transfer Curriculum (IGETC) or the California State University General Education – Breadth Requirements.
     b. A minimum of 18 semester units or 27 quarter units in a major or area of emphasis, as determined by the community college district.
2. Obtainment of a minimum grade point average of 2.0.

Associate Degrees for Transfer also require that students must earn a C or better in all courses required for the major or area of emphasis.

This degree may not be the best option for students intending to transfer to a particular CSU campus or to university or college that is not part of the CSU system. Students should consult with a counselor when planning to complete the degree for more information on university admission and transfer requirements. At the time of catalog publication, a student may earn an AA-T in Global Studies. Additional majors are being developed. Please see a counselor or visit http://www.canyons.edu for more information.

Degree Student Learning Outcome:

Identify major and emerging global issues and trends, and the definition of globalization.

Program Requirements:

Units Required: 21 - 25

		Units:
GLST-101	Introduction to Global Studies	3.0
GLST-102	Global Issues	3.0

Take five courses from the following for a minimum of 15 units, at least one course from four of the following five sections:

Culture and Society Area

ANTHRO-103	Cultural Anthropology	3.0
OR		
ANTHRO-103H	Cultural Anthropology – Honors	3.0

Economic Area

ECON-201	Macroeconomics	3.0
OR		
ECON201H	Macroeconomics – Honors	3.0
ECON-202	Microeconomics	3.0
OR		
ECON-202H	Microeconomics – Honors	3.0

Geography Area

GEOG-102	Human Geography	3.0
GEOG-104	World Regional Geography	3.0

Humanities Area

ENGL-273	World Literature I	3.0
ENGL-274	World Literature II	3.0
FRNCH-201	Intermediate French I	5.0
FRNCH-202	Intermediate French II	5.0
SPAN-201	Intermediate Spanish I	5.0
SPAN-202	Intermediate Spanish II	5.0

Politics Area

POLISC-250	Comparative Government and Politics	3.0
POLISC-270	International Relations	3.0

★ *edition* ★
12

We the People

An Introduction to American Politics

★ *edition* ★
12

We the People

An Introduction to American Politics

Includes Governing California, Seventh Edition

COLLEGE OF THE CANYONS CUSTOM EDITION

★ **BENJAMIN GINSBERG**
THE JOHNS HOPKINS UNIVERSITY

★ **THEODORE J. LOWI**
LATE OF CORNELL UNIVERSITY

★ **MARGARET WEIR**
BROWN UNIVERSITY

★ **CAROLINE J. TOLBERT**
UNIVERSITY OF IOWA

★ **ANDREA L. CAMPBELL**
MASSACHUSETTS INSTITUTE OF
TECHNOLOGY

 W. W. NORTON & COMPANY
NEW YORK   LONDON

W. W. Norton & Company has been independent since its founding in 1923, when William Warder Norton and Mary D. Herter Norton first published lectures delivered at the People's Institute, the adult education division of New York City's Cooper Union. The firm soon expanded its program beyond the Institute, publishing books by celebrated academics from America and abroad. By mid-century, the two major pillars of Norton's publishing program—trade books and college texts—were firmly established. In the 1950s, the Norton family transferred control of the company to its employees, and today—with a staff of four hundred and a comparable number of trade, college, and professional titles published each year—W. W. Norton & Company stands as the largest and oldest publishing house owned wholly by its employees.

Editor: Peter Lesser
Project Editor: Christine D'Antonio
Assistant Editor: Anna Olcott
Manuscript Editor: Lynne Cannon
Managing Editor, College: Marian Johnson
Managing Editor, College Digital Media: Kim Yi
Production Manager, College: Ashley Horna
Media Editor: Spencer Richardson-Jones
Associate Media Editor: Michael Jaoui
Media Editorial Assistant: Tricia Vuong
Ebook Production Manager: Danielle Lehmann
Marketing Manager, Political Science: Erin Brown
Art Director: Rubina Yeh
Text Design: Jen Montgomery

Photo Editor: Stephanie Romeo
Photo Researcher: Elyse Rieder
Director of College Permissions: Megan Schindel
Permissions Associate: Elizabeth Trammell
Information Graphics: Kiss Me I'm Polish LLC, New York
Composition: Graphic World, Inc.
Manufacturing: TransContinental
Custom Editorial: Susan Brennan, Katie Hannah, Hannah Bachman, Alexandra Gakos, and Kaushika Suresh
Custom Production: Jeremy Burton and Lindsay Fischer
Photo Permissions Manager: Aga Millhouse

Permission to use copyrighted material is included in the credits section of this book, which begins on page A83.

ISBN: 978-0-393-43204-6

Library of Congress Cataloging-in-Publication Data:
Names: Ginsberg, Benjamin, author.
Title: We the people : an introduction to American politics / Benjamin
   Ginsberg, The Johns Hopkins University, Theodore J. Lowi, Cornell
   University, Margaret Weir, Brown University, Caroline J. Tolbert,
   University of Iowa, Andrea L. Campbell, Massachusetts Institute of
   Technology.
Description: Twelfth Edition. | New York : W.W. Norton & Company, [2018] |
   Includes bibliographical references and index.
Identifiers: LCCN 2018046033 | **ISBN 9780393644326** (hardcover)
Subjects: LCSH: United States--Politics and government--Textbooks.
Classification: LCC JK276 .G55 2018 | DDC 320.473--dc23 LC record available at https://lccn.loc
   .gov/2018046033

W. W. Norton & Company, Inc., 500 Fifth Avenue, New York, NY 10110
wwnorton.com
W. W. Norton & Company Ltd., 15 Carlisle Street, London W1D 3BS

1 2 3 4 5 6 7 8 9 0

Custom Contents

To:

Sandy, Cindy, and Alex Ginsberg

David, Jackie, Eveline, and Ed Dowling

Dave, Marcella, Logan, and Kennah Campbell

Contents

3 ★ Federalism   76

4 ★ Civil Liberties 114

5 ★ Civil Rights 158

PART II POLITICS

8 ★ Political Participation and Voting 294

9 ★ Political Parties 334

10 ★ Campaigns and Elections 378

11 ★ Groups and Interests 428

PART III INSTITUTIONS

12 ★ Congress 466

15 ★ The Federal Courts 590

PART IV   POLICY

Appendix

Preface

This book has been and continues to be dedicated to developing a satisfactory response to the question more and more Americans are asking: Why should we be engaged with government and politics? Through the first eleven editions, we sought to answer this question by making the text directly relevant to the lives of the students who would be reading it. As a result, we tried to make politics interesting by demonstrating that students' interests are at stake and that they therefore need to take a personal, even selfish, interest in the outcomes of government. At the same time, we realized that students needed guidance in how to become politically engaged. Beyond providing students with a core of political knowledge, we needed to show them how they could apply that knowledge as participants in the political process. The "Who Participates?" and "What You Can Do" sections in each chapter help achieve that goal.

As events from the last several years have reminded us, "what government does" inevitably raises questions about political participation and political equality. The size and composition of the electorate, for example, affect who is elected to public office and what policy directions the government will pursue. Hence, the issue of voter ID laws became important in the 2016 election, with some arguing that these laws reduce voter fraud and others contending that they decrease participation by poor and minority voters. Charges of Russian meddling in the 2016 election have raised questions about the integrity of the voting process. Fierce debates about the policies of the Trump administration have heightened students' interest in politics. Other recent events have underscored how Americans from different backgrounds experience politics. Arguments about immigration became contentious during the 2016 election as the nation once again debated the question of who is entitled to be an American and have a voice in determining what the government does. And charges that the police often use excessive violence against members of minority groups have raised questions about whether the government treats all Americans equally. Reflecting all of these trends, this new Twelfth Edition shows more than any other book on the market (1) how students are connected to government, (2) why students should think critically about government and politics, and (3) how Americans from different backgrounds experience and shape politics.

To help us explore these themes, Professor Andrea Campbell has joined us as the most recent in a group of distinguished coauthors. Professor Campbell's scholarly work focuses on the ways in which government and politics affect the lives of ordinary citizens. Among her contributions are new chapter introductions that focus on stories of individuals and how government has affected them. Many Americans, particularly the young, can have difficulty seeing the role of government in their everyday lives. Indeed, that's a chief explanation of low voter participation among younger citizens. The new chapter openers profile various individuals and illustrate their interactions with government, from a rock band that gets its controversial name approved by the Supreme

Court (Chapter 4), to a young mother who realizes the tap water in her Flint, Michigan, home is poisoning her children after local officials switched the source (Chapter 14), to teenagers protesting the end of net neutrality and the internet as they have known it (Chapter 7). The goal of these stories is to show students in a vivid way how government and politics mean something to their daily lives.

Several other elements of the book also help show students why politics and government should matter to them. These include:

- **A twenty-first-century perspective on demographic change** moves beyond the book's strong coverage of traditional civil rights content with expanded coverage of contemporary group politics.

- **"Who Are Americans?" infographics**—many new and updated for the twelfth edition—ask students to think critically about how Americans from different backgrounds experience politics. These sections use bold, engaging graphics to present a statistical snapshot of the nation related to each chapter's topic. Critical-thinking questions are included in each infographic.

- **"Who Participates?" infographics at the end of every chapter** show students how different groups of Americans participate in key aspects of politics and government. Each concludes with a "What You Can Do" section that provides students with specific, realistic steps they can take to act on what they've learned and get involved in politics. The InQuizitive course includes accompanying exercises that encourage students to engage with these features.

- **"America Side by Side" boxes** in every chapter use data figures and tables to provide a comparative perspective. By comparing political institutions and behavior across countries, students gain a better understanding of how specific features of the American system shape politics.

- **Up-to-date coverage**, with more than 20 pages and numerous graphics on the 2016 and 2018 elections, including a 12-page section devoted to analysis of these momentous elections in Chapter 10, as well as updated data, examples, and other information throughout the book.

- **"For Critical Analysis" questions** are incorporated throughout the text. "For Critical Analysis" questions in the margins of every chapter prompt students' own critical thinking about the material in the chapter, encouraging them to engage with the topic.

- **"What Do We Want" chapter conclusions** step back and provide perspective on how the chapter content connects to fundamental questions about the American political system. The conclusions also reprise the important point made in the personal profiles that begin each chapter that government matters to the lives of individuals.

- **This Twelfth Edition is accompanied by InQuizitive**, Norton's award-winning formative, adaptive online quizzing program. The InQuizitive course for *We the People* guides students through questions organized around the text's chapter learning objectives to ensure mastery of the core information and to help with assessment. More information and a demonstration are available at digital. wwnorton.com/wethepeople12.

We note with regret the passing of Theodore Lowi as well as Margaret Weir's decision to step down from the book. We miss them but continue to hear their voices and to benefit from their wisdom in the pages of our book We also continue to hope that our book will itself be accepted as a form of enlightened political action. This Twelfth Edition is another chance. It is an advancement toward our goal. We promise to keep trying.

Acknowledgements

We are pleased to acknowledge the many colleagues who had an active role in criticism and preparation of the manuscript. Our thanks go to:

First Edition Reviewers

Sarah Binder, Brookings Institution
Kathleen Gille, Office of Representative David Bonior
Rodney Hero, University of Colorado at Boulder
Robert Katzmann, Brookings Institution
Kathleen Knight, University of Houston
Robin Kolodny, Temple University
Nancy Kral, Tomball College
Robert C. Lieberman, Columbia University
David A. Marcum, University of Wyoming
Laura R. Winsky Mattei, State University of New York at Buffalo
Marilyn S. Mertens, Midwestern State University
Barbara Suhay, Henry Ford Community College
Carolyn Wong, Stanford University
Julian Zelizer, State University of New York at Albany

Second Edition Reviewers

Lydia Andrade, University of North Texas
John Coleman, University of Wisconsin at Madison
Daphne Eastman, Odessa College
Otto Feinstein, Wayne State University
Elizabeth Flores, Delmar College
James Gimpel, University of Maryland at College Park
Jill Glaathar, Southwest Missouri State University
Shaun Herness, University of Florida
William Lyons, University of Tennessee at Knoxville
Andrew Polsky, Hunter College, CUNY
Grant Reeher, Syracuse University
Richard Rich, Virginia Polytechnic
Bartholomew Sparrow, University of Texas at Austin

Third Edition Reviewers

Bruce R. Drury, Lamar University
Andrew I. E. Ewoh, Prairie View A&M University
Amy Jasperson, University of Texas at San Antonio
Loch Johnson, University of Georgia

Mark Kann, University of Southern California
Robert L. Perry, University of Texas of the Permian Basin
Wayne Pryor, Brazosport College
Elizabeth A. Rexford, Wharton County Junior College
Andrea Simpson, University of Washington
Brian Smentkowski, Southeast Missouri State University
Nelson Wikstrom, Virginia Commonwealth University

Fourth Edition Reviewers

M. E. Banks, Virginia Commonwealth University
Lynn Brink, North Lake College
Mark Cichock, University of Texas at Arlington
Del Fields, St. Petersburg College
Nancy Kinney, Washtenaw Community College
William Klein, St. Petersburg College
Dana Morales, Montgomery College
Christopher Muste, Louisiana State University
Larry Norris, South Plains College
David Rankin, State University of New York at Fredonia
Paul Roesler, St. Charles Community College
J. Philip Rogers, San Antonio College
Greg Shaw, Illinois Wesleyan University
Tracy Skopek, Stephen F. Austin State University
Don Smith, University of North Texas
Terri Wright, Cal State, Fullerton

Fifth Edition Reviewers

Annie Benifield, Tomball College
Denise Dutton, Southwest Missouri State University
Rick Kurtz, Central Michigan University
Kelly McDaniel, Three Rivers Community College
Eric Plutzer, Pennsylvania State University
Daniel Smith, Northwest Missouri State University
Dara Strolovitch, University of Minnesota
Dennis Toombs, San Jacinto College–North
Stacy Ulbig, Southwest Missouri State University

Sixth Edition Reviewers

Janet Adamski, University of Mary Hardin–Baylor
Greg Andrews, St. Petersburg College
Louis Bolce, Baruch College
Darin Combs, Tulsa Community College
Sean Conroy, University of New Orleans
Paul Cooke, Cy Fair College
Vida Davoudi, Kingwood College
Robert DiClerico, West Virginia University
Corey Ditslear, University of North Texas
Kathy Dolan, University of Wisconsin, Milwaukee
Randy Glean, Midwestern State University
Nancy Kral, Tomball College
Mark Logas, Valencia Community College
Scott MacDougall, Diablo Valley College
David Mann, College of Charleston
Christopher Muste, University of Montana
Richard Pacelle, Georgia Southern University
Sarah Poggione, Florida International University
Richard Rich, Virginia Tech
Thomas Schmeling, Rhode Island College
Scott Spitzer, California State University–Fullerton
Robert Wood, University of North Dakota

Seventh Edition Reviewers

Molly Andolina, DePaul University
Nancy Bednar, Antelope Valley College
Paul Blakelock, Kingwood College
Amy Brandon, San Jacinto College
Jim Cauthen, John Jay College, CUNY
Kevin Davis, North Central Texas College
Louis DeSipio, University of California–Irvine
Brandon Franke, Blinn College
Steve Garrison, Midwestern State University
Joseph Howard, University of Central Arkansas
Aaron Knight, Houston Community College
Paul Labedz, Valencia Community College
Elise Langan, John Jay College, CUNY
Mark Logas, Valencia Community College
Eric Miller, Blinn College
Anthony O'Regan, Los Angeles Valley College
David Putz, Kingwood College
Chis Soper, Pepperdine University
Kevin Wagner, Florida Atlantic University
Laura Wood, Tarrant County College

Eighth Edition Reviewers

Brian Arbour, John Jay College, CUNY
Ellen Baik, University of Texas–Pan American
David Birch, Lone Star College–Tomball
Bill Carroll, Sam Houston State University
Ed Chervenak, University of New Orleans

Gary Church, Mountain View College
Adrian Stefan Clark, Del Mar College
Annie Cole, Los Angeles City College
Greg Combs, University of Texas at Dallas
Cassandra Cookson, Lee College
Brian Cravens, Blinn College
John Crosby, California State University–Chico
Scott Crosby, Valencia Community College
Courtenay Daum, Colorado State University, Fort Collins
Peter Doas, University of Texas–Pan American
John Domino, Sam Houston State University
Doug Dow, University of Texas–Dallas
Jeremy Duff, Midwestern State University
Heather Evans, Sam Houston State University
Hyacinth Ezeamii, Albany State University
Bob Fitrakis, Columbus State Community College
Brian Fletcher, Truckee Meadows Community College
Paul Foote, Eastern Kentucky University
Frank Garrahan, Austin Community College
Jimmy Gleason, Purdue University
Steven Greene, North Carolina State University
Jeannie Grussendorf, Georgia State University
M. Ahad Hayaud-Din, Brookhaven College
Alexander Hogan, Lone Star College–CyFair
Glen Hunt, Austin Community College
Mark Jendrysik, University of North Dakota
Krista Jenkins, Fairleigh Dickinson University
Carlos Juárez, Hawaii Pacific University
Melinda Kovas, Sam Houston State University
Boyd Lanier, Lamar University
Jeff Lazarus, Georgia State University
Jeffrey Lee, Blinn College
Alan Lehmann, Blinn College
Julie Lester, Macon State College
Steven Lichtman, Shippensburg University
Fred Lokken, Truckee Meadows Community College
Shari MacLachlan, Palm Beach Community College
Guy Martin, Winston-Salem State University
Fred Monardi, College of Southern Nevada
Vincent Moscardelli, University of Connecticut
Jason Mycoff, University of Delaware
Sugmaran Narayanan, Midwestern State University
Anthony Nownes, University of Tennessee, Knoxville
Elizabeth Oldmixon, University of North Texas
John Osterman, San Jacinto College–Central
Mark Peplowski, College of Southern Nevada
Maria Victoria Perez-Rios, John Jay College, CUNY
Sara Rinfret, University of Wisconsin, Green Bay
Andre Robinson, Pulaski Technical College
Susan Roomberg, University of Texas at San Antonio
Ryan Rynbrandt, Collin County Community College
Mario Salas, Northwest Vista College
Michael Sanchez, San Antonio College
Mary Schander, Pasadena City College
Laura Schneider, Grand Valley State University

Subash Shah, Winston-Salem State University
Mark Shomaker, Blinn College
Roy Slater, St. Petersburg College
Debra St. John, Collin College
Eric Whitaker, Western Washington University
Clay Wiegand, Cisco College
Walter Wilson, University of Texas at San Antonio
Kevan Yenerall, Clarion University
Rogerio Zapata, South Texas College

Ninth Edition Reviewers

Amy Acord, Lone Star College–CyFair
Milan Andrejevich, Ivy Tech Community College
Steve Anthony, Georgia State University
Phillip Ardoin, Appalachian State University
Gregory Arey, Cape Fear Community College
Joan Babcock, Northwest Vista College
Evelyn Ballard, Houston Community College
Robert Ballinger, South Texas College
Mary Barnes-Tilley, Blinn College
Robert Bartels, Evangel University
Nancy Bednar, Antelope Valley College
Annie Benifield, Lone Star College–Tomball
Donna Bennett, Trinity Valley Community College
Amy Brandon, El Paso Community College
Mark Brewer, The University of Maine
Gary Brown, Lone Star College–Montgomery
Joe Campbell, Johnson County Community College
Dewey Clayton, University of Louisville
Jeff Colbert, Elon University
Amanda Cook-Fesperman, Illinois Valley Community College
Kevin Corder, Western Michigan University
Kevin Davis, North Central Texas College
Paul Davis, Truckee Meadows Community College
Terri Davis, Lamar University
Jennifer De Maio, California State University, Northridge
Christopher Durso, Valencia College
Ryan Emenaker, College of the Redwoods
Leslie Feldman, Hofstra University
Glen Findley, Odessa College
Michael Gattis, Gulf Coast State College
Donna Godwin, Trinity Valley Community College
Precious Hall, Truckee Meadows Community College
Sally Hansen, Daytona State College
Tiffany Harper, Collin College
Todd Hartman, Appalachian State University
Virginia Haysley, Lone Star College–Tomball
David Head, John Tyler Community College
Rick Henderson, Texas State University–San Marcos
Richard Herrera, Arizona State University
Thaddaus Hill, Blinn College
Steven Holmes, Bakersfield College
Kevin Holton, South Texas College
Robin Jacobson, University of Puget Sound

Joseph Jozwiak, Texas A&M–Corpus Christi
Casey Klofstad, University of Miami
Samuel Lingrosso, Los Angeles Valley College
Mark Logas, Valencia College
Christopher Marshall, South Texas College
Larry McElvain, South Texas College
Elizabeth McLane, Wharton County Junior College
Eddie Meaders, University of North Texas
Rob Mellen, Mississippi State University
Jalal Nejad, Northwest Vista College
Adam Newmark, Appalachian State University
Stephen Nicholson, University of California, Merced
Cissie Owen, Lamar University
Suzanne Preston, St. Petersburg College
David Putz, Lone Star College–Kingwood
Auksuole Rubavichute, Mountain View College
Ronnee Schreiber, San Diego State University
Ronald Schurin, University of Connecticut
Jason Seitz, Georgia Perimeter College
Jennifer Seitz, Georgia Perimeter College
Shannon Sinegal, The University of New Orleans
John Sides, George Washington University
Thomas Sowers, Lamar University
Jim Startin, University of Texas at San Antonio
Robert Sterken, University of Texas at Tyler
Bobby Summers, Harper College
John Theis, Lone Star College–Kingwood
John Todd, University of North Texas
Delaina Toothman, The University of Maine
David Trussell, Cisco College
Ronald Vardy, University of Houston
Linda Veazey, Midwestern State University
John Vento, Antelope Valley Community College
Clif Wilkinson, Georgia College
John Wood, Rose State College
Michael Young, Trinity Valley Community College
Tyler Young, Collin College

Tenth Edition Reviewers

Stephen P. Amberg, University of Texas at San Antonio
Juan F. Arzola, College of the Sequoias
Thomas J. Baldino, Wilkes University
Christina Bejarano, University of Kansas
Paul T. Bellinger, Jr., University of Missouri
Melanie J. Blumberg, California University of Pennsylvania
Matthew T. Bradley, Indiana University Kokomo
Jeffrey W. Christiansen, Seminole State College
McKinzie Craig, Marietta College
Christopher Cronin, Methodist University
Jenna Duke, Lehigh Carbon Community College
Francisco Durand, University of Texas at San Antonio
Carrie Eaves, Elon University
Paul M. Flor, El Camino College Compton Center
Adam Fuller, Youngstown State University

Christi Gramling, Charleston Southern University
Sally Hansen, Daytona State College
Mary Jane Hatton, Hawaii Pacific University
David Helpap, University of Wisconsin–Green Bay
Theresa L. Hutchins, Georgia Highlands College
Cryshanna A. Jackson Leftwich, Youngstown
    State University
Ashlyn Kuersten, Western Michigan University
Kara Lindaman, Winona State University
Timothy Lynch, University of Wisconsin–Milwaukee
Larry McElvain, South Texas College
Corinna R. McKoy, Ventura College
Eddie L. Meaders, University of North Texas
Don D. Mirjanian, College of Southern Nevada
R. Shea Mize, Georgia Highlands College
Nicholas Morgan, Collin College
Matthew Murray, Dutchess Community College
Harold "Trey" Orndorff III, Daytona State College
Randall Parish, University of North Georgia
Michelle Pautz, University of Dayton
Michael Pickering, University of New Orleans
Donald Ranish, Antelope Valley College
Glenn W. Richardson, Jr., Kutztown University of Pennsylvania
Jason Robles, Colorado State University
Ionas Aurelian Rus, University of Cincinnati–Blue Ash
Robert Sahr, Oregon State University
Kelly B. Shaw, Iowa State University
Captain Michael Slattery, Campbell University
Michael Smith, Sam Houston State University
Maryam T. Stevenson, University of Indianapolis
Elizabeth Trentanelli, Gulf Coast State College
Ronald W. Vardy, University of Houston
Timothy Weaver, University of Louisville
Christina Wolbrecht, University of Notre Dame

Eleventh Edition Reviewers

Maria J. Albo, University of North Georgia
Andrea Aleman, University of Texas at San Antonio
Juan Arzola, College of the Sequoias
Ross K. Baker, Rutgers University
Daniel Birdsong, University of Dayton
Phil Branyon, University of North Georgia
Sheryl Edwards, University of Michigan–Dearborn
Lauren Elliott-Dorans, University of Toledo
Heather Evans, Sam Houston State University
William Feagin, Jr., Wharton County Junior College
Glen Findley, Odessa College
Heather Frederick, Slipper Rock University
Jason Ghibesi, Ocean County College
Patrick Gilbert, Lone Star–Tomball
Steven Horn, Everett Community College
Demetra Kasimis, California State University, Long Beach

Eric T. Kasper, University of Wisconsin–Eau Claire
Mary Linder, Grayson County College
Phil McCall, Portland State University
Carolyn Myers, Southwestern Illinois College–Belleville
Gerhard Peters, Citrus College
Michael A. Powell, Frederick Community College
Allen K. Settle, California Polytechnic State University
Laurie Sprankle, Community College of Allegheny County
Ryan Lee Teten, University of Louisiana at Lafayette
Justin Vaughn, Boise State University
John Vento, Antelope Valley College
Aaron Weinschenk, University of Wisconsin–Green Bay
Tyler Young, Collin College

Twelfth Edition Reviewers

Craig Albert, Augusta University
Alexa Bankert, University of Georgia
Nathan Barrick, University of South Florida
Jeff Birdsong, Northeastern Oklahoma A&M College
Sara Butler, College of the Desert
Cory Colby, Lone Star College
Anthony Daniels, University of Toledo
Dennis Falcon, Cerritos College
Kathleen Ferraiolo, James Madison University
Patrick Gilbert, Lone Star College, Tomball
Matthew Green, Catholic University of America
Matt Guardino, Providence College
Barbara Headrick, Minnesota State University, Moorhead
Justin Hoggard, Three Rivers Community College
John Patrick Ifedi, Howard University
Cryshanna Jackson Leftwich, Youngstown State University
Douglas Kriner, Boston University
Thom Kuehls, Weber State University
Jennifer Lawless, American University
LaDella Levy, College of Southern Nevada
Timothy Lim, California State University, Los Angeles
Sam Lingrosso, Los Angeles Valley College
Mandy May, College of Southern Maryland
Suzanne Mettler, Cornell University
Michael Miller, Barnard College
Joseph Njoroge, Abraham Baldwin Agricultural College
Michael Petri, Santa Ana College
Christopher Poulios, Nassau Community College
Andrew Rudalevige, Bowdoin College
Amanda Sanford, Louisiana Tech University
Elizabeth Saunders, George Washington University
Kathleen Searles, Louisiana State University
Matthew Snyder, Delgado Community College
Steven Sylvester, Utah Valley University
Linda Trautman, Ohio University Lancaster
Donald Williams, Western New England University
Peter Yacobucci, Buffalo State College

We are also grateful to Melissa Michelson, of Menlo College, who contributed to the "Who Are Americans?" and "Who Participates?" infographics for this edition; Holley Hansen, of Oklahoma State University, who contributed to the "America Side by Side" boxes.

Perhaps above all, we thank those at W. W. Norton. For its first five editions, editor Steve Dunn helped us shape the book in countless ways. Lisa McKay contributed smart ideas and a keen editorial eye to the Tenth Edition. Ann Shin carried on the Norton tradition of splendid editorial work on the Sixth through Ninth Editions and on the Eleventh Edition. Peter Lesser brought intelligence, dedication, and keen insight to the development of this Twelfth Edition. For our InQuizitive course, Coursepack, and other instructor resources, Spencer Richardson-Jones has been an energetic and visionary editor. Ashley Horna, Michael Jaoui, Tricia Vuong, and Anna Olcott also kept the production of the Twelfth Edition and its accompanying resources coherent and in focus. Lynne Cannon copyedited the manuscript, and our superb project editor Christine D'Antonio devoted countless hours to keeping on top of myriad details. We thank Elyse Rieder for finding new photos and our photo editor Stephanie Romeo for managing the image program. Finally, we thank Roby Harrington, the head of Norton's college department.

Benjamin Ginsberg
Caroline J. Tolbert
Andrea Campbell

October 2018

★ *edition* ★
12

We the People

An Introduction to American Politics

American Political Culture

WHAT GOVERNMENT DOES AND WHY IT MATTERS Meet two of the nation's youngest elected officials. Saira Blair became the youngest member of West Virginia's House of Delegates when she won election as an 18-year-old college freshman. The day after her victory party in November 2014, she was back in class at West Virginia University. In May 2017, Prairie View A&M senior Kendric D. Jones similarly achieved electoral victory, becoming the youngest city council member in the state of Texas. What got Blair and Jones involved in politics? Both had sources of political inspiration. Blair followed in the footsteps of her father, a

West Virginia state senator, who she had accompanied at political events since childhood. Jones was inspired by the long history of activism at Prairie View, which was founded in 1876 during Reconstruction by some of the first African American members of the Texas state legislature. A further spur to action was President Obama's call in his 2017 farewell address to "grab a clipboard, get some signatures, and run for office yourself." Both also had strong commitments to issues. Saira Blair believes in limited government, lower taxes, and Second Amendment gun rights. Kendric Jones has a long history of working in the community, serving in student government,

While Americans share a belief in the values of liberty, equality, and democracy, debates rage about how to live up to those values. To advocate for their beliefs, Republican Saira Blair (left) and Democrat Kendric Jones (right)—both college students—ran for office and won. What is the citizen's role in America's democratic system?

and founding a mentoring program for middle-school boys. Many Prairie View students also have concerns about police relations. Sandra Bland, the 28-year-old who hanged herself in jail after being arrested in a traffic stop, was an alumna of Prairie View.

Both Blair and Jones also believe deeply in political participation, especially that of young people. As Jones said, "The students of Prairie View A&M University's voices have not been heard. Since I have been here, the city has been stagnant and has not made any progression—outside of the university. I feel as though a young, innovative mind can push this city forward." After participating in a mock

government program in high school, Blair saw that young people were just as capable as lawmakers decades older: "When I saw how capable the students were of creating...legislation and really getting work done, it really made me realize that we really didn't need to wait."[1]

Saira Blair's and Kendric Jones's experiences show that citizens are at the center of democratic government. They ran for office because they care about public issues and want to have a hand in shaping policy outcomes. What are you passionate about? How does government affect your everyday life and that of your family, friends, and community? And how are differences in political views adjudicated in the political realm? There are some core values that Americans hold dear, including liberty, equality, and democracy. But there are also disagreements about what those values mean and what the role of government should be. Not everyone has to run for political office as Blair and Jones did. But all of us are affected by government in ways small and large every day. The purpose of this book is to show what government does, how, and why—and what you can do about it.

CHAPTER GOALS

★ Define government and forms of government (pp. 5–10)

★ Describe the role of the citizen in politics (pp. 10–13)

★ Show how the social composition of the American population has changed over time (pp. 13–22)

★ Analyze whether the U.S. system of government upholds American political values (pp. 22–29)

★ Explore Americans' attitudes toward government (pp. 29–33)

Government

Define government and forms of government

Government is the term generally used to describe the formal institutions through which a land and its people are ruled. A government may be as simple as a town meeting in which community members make policy and determine budgets together or as complex as the vast establishments found in many large countries today, with their extensive procedures, laws, and bureaucracies. In the history of civilization, governments have not been difficult to establish. There have been thousands of them. The hard part is establishing a government that lasts. Even more difficult is developing a stable government that is true to the key American political values of liberty, equality, and democracy.

government institutions and procedures through which a territory and its people are ruled

Most Americans find it easy to affirm these three values in principle. In practice, however, these values mean different things to different people, and they often seem to conflict. This is where politics comes in. **Politics** refers to conflicts and struggles over the leadership, structure, and policies of governments. As we will see in this chapter and throughout this book, much political conflict concerns policies and practices that seem to affirm one of the key American political values but may contradict another.

politics conflict over the leadership, structure, and policies of governments

IS GOVERNMENT NEEDED?

Americans have always harbored some suspicion of government and have wondered how extensive a role it should play in their lives. Thomas Jefferson famously observed that the best government was one that "governed least." Indeed, a desire for limited government has also been a central feature of American political culture and history since the nation's founding. Generally speaking, a government is needed to provide those services, sometimes called "public goods," that all citizens need but are not likely to be able to provide adequately for themselves. These might include defense against foreign aggression, maintenance of public order, a stable currency, enforcement of contractual obligations and property rights, and a guarantee of some measure of social justice. These are goods that benefit everyone but that no individual or group on its own can afford to supply. Government, with its powers to tax and regulate, is typically viewed as the best way to provide public goods. However, there is often disagreement about which public goods are essential and how they should be provided. The precise extent to which government involvement in American society is needed has been debated throughout the nation's history and will continue to be a central focus of political contention.

Much of what citizens have come to depend on and take for granted as somehow part of the natural environment is in fact created by government. Take the example of a typical college student's day, throughout which that student relies on a host of services and activities organized by national, state, and local government agencies. The extent of this dependence on government is illustrated by Table 1.1 on page 6.

FORMS OF GOVERNMENT

Governments vary in their structure, their size, and the way they operate. Two questions are of special importance in determining how governments differ: Who governs? And how much government control is permitted?

TABLE 1.1

The Presence of Government in the Daily Life of a Student at "State University"

TIME OF DAY	SCHEDULE
7:00 A.M.	Wake up. Standard time set by the national government.
7:10 A.M.	Shower. Water courtesy of local government, either a public entity or a regulated private company. Brush your teeth with toothpaste whose cavity-fighting claims have been verified by a federal agency. Dry your hair with an electric dryer manufactured according to federal government agency guidelines.
7:30 A.M.	Have a bowl of cereal with milk for breakfast. "Nutrition Facts" on food labels are a federal requirement, pasteurization of milk required by state law, freshness dating on milk based on state and federal standards, recycling the empty cereal box and milk carton enabled by state or local laws.
8:30 A.M.	Drive or take public transportation to campus. Air bags and seat belts required by federal and state laws. Roads and bridges paid for by state and local governments, speed and traffic laws set by state and local governments, public transportation subsidized by all levels of government.
8:45 A.M.	Arrive on campus of large public university. Buildings are 70 percent financed by state taxpayers.
9:00 A.M.	First class: Chemistry 101. Tuition partially paid by a federal loan (more than half the cost of university instruction is paid for by taxpayers), chemistry lab paid for with grants from the National Science Foundation (a federal agency) and smaller grants from business corporations made possible by federal income tax deductions for charitable contributions.
Noon	Eat lunch. College cafeteria financed by state dormitory authority on land grant from federal Department of Agriculture.
12:47 P.M.	Felt an earthquake! Check the U.S. Geological Survey at www.usgs.gov to see that it was a 3.9 on the Richter scale.
2:00 P.M.	Second class: American Government 101 (your favorite class!). You may be taking this class because it is required by the state legislature or because it fulfills a university requirement.
4:00 P.M.	Third class: Computer Science 101. Free computers, software, and internet access courtesy of state subsidies plus grants and discounts from Apple and Microsoft, the costs of which are deducted from their corporate income taxes; internet built in part by federal government. Duplication of software prohibited by federal copyright laws.
6:00 P.M.	Eat dinner: hamburger and french fries. Meat inspected for bacteria by federal agencies.
7:00 P.M.	Work at part-time job at the campus library. Minimum wage set by federal, state, or local government; books and journals in library paid for by state taxpayers.
8:15 P.M.	Go online to check the status of your application for a federal student loan (FAFSA) on the Department of Education's website at studentaid.ed.gov.
10:00 P.M.	Go home. Street lighting paid for by county and city governments, police patrols by city government.
10:15 P.M.	Watch TV. Networks regulated by federal government, cable public-access channels required by city law. Weather forecast provided to broadcasters by a federal agency.
10:45 P.M.	To complete your economics homework, visit the Bureau of Labor Statistics at www.bls.gov to look up unemployment levels since 1972.
Midnight	Put out the trash before going to bed. Trash collected by city sanitation department, financed by user charges.

Some nations are governed by a single individual—a king or dictator, for example. This state of affairs is called **autocracy**. Where a small group—perhaps landowners, military officers, or the wealthy—controls most of the governing decisions, that government is said to be an **oligarchy**. If citizens are vested with the power to rule themselves, that government is a **democracy**.

Governments also vary considerably in terms of how they govern. In the United States and a small number of other nations, governments are limited as to what they are permitted to control (substantive limits) and how they go about it (procedural limits). Governments that are limited in this way are called **constitutional governments**, or liberal governments. In other nations, including some in Latin America, Asia, and Africa, the law imposes few real limits. The government, however, is nevertheless kept in check by other political and social institutions that it is unable to control and must come to terms with—such as autonomous territories, an organized religion, organized business groups, or organized labor unions. Such governments are generally called **authoritarian**. In a third group of nations, including the Soviet Union under Joseph Stalin, Nazi Germany, perhaps prewar Japan and Italy, and North Korea today, governments not only are free of legal limits but also seek to eliminate those organized social groups that might challenge or limit their authority. These governments typically attempt to dominate or control every sphere of political, economic, and social life and, as a result, are called **totalitarian** (see Figure 1.1).

Americans have the good fortune to live in a nation in which limits are placed on what governments can do and how they can do it. Many of the world's people do not. By one measure, just 40 percent of the global population (those living in 86 countries) enjoy sufficient levels of political and personal freedom to be classified as living in a constitutional democracy.[2] And constitutional democracies were unheard of before the modern era. Prior to the eighteenth and nineteenth centuries, governments seldom sought—and rarely received—the support of their subjects. The available evidence strongly suggests that ordinary people often had little love for the government or for the social order. After all, they had no stake in it.[3]

Beginning in the seventeenth century, in a handful of Western nations, two important changes began to take place in the character and conduct of government. First, governments began to acknowledge formal limits on their power. Second, a small number of governments began to provide ordinary citizens with a formal

autocracy a form of government in which a single individual—a king, queen, or dictator—rules

oligarchy a form of government in which a small group—landowners, military officers, or wealthy merchants—controls most of the governing decisions

democracy a system of rule that permits citizens to play a significant part in the governmental process, usually through the election of key public officials

constitutional government a system of rule in which formal and effective limits are placed on the powers of the government

authoritarian government a system of rule in which the government recognizes no formal limits but may nevertheless be restrained by the power of other social institutions

totalitarian government a system of rule in which the government recognizes no formal limits on its power and seeks to absorb or eliminate other social institutions that might challenge it

Who governs	Type of government
One person	Autocracy
Small group (e.g., landowners, military officers, or wealthy merchants)	Oligarchy
Many people	Democracy

Limits on government	Type of government
Codified, legal substantive and procedural limits on what government can or cannot do	Constitutional
Few legal limits; some limits imposed by social groups	Authoritarian
No limits	Totalitarian

FIGURE 1.1

Forms of Government

America's Founders were influenced by the English thinker John Locke (1632–1704). Locke argued that governments need the consent of the people.

voice in public affairs—through the vote. Obviously, the desirability of limits on government and the expansion of popular influence were at the heart of the American Revolution in 1776. "No taxation without representation," as we shall see in Chapter 2, was fiercely asserted from the beginning of the Revolution through the Founding in 1789. But even before the Revolution, a tradition of limiting government and expanding participation in the political process had developed throughout western Europe.

LIMITING GOVERNMENT

The key force behind the imposition of limits on government power was a new social class, the bourgeoisie, which became an important political force in the sixteenth and seventeenth centuries. *Bourgeois* is a French word for "freeman of the city," or *bourg*. Being part of the bourgeoisie later became associated with being "middle class" and with involvement in commerce or industry. In order to gain a share of control of government, joining or even displacing the kings, aristocrats, and gentry who had dominated government for centuries, the bourgeoisie sought to change existing institutions—especially parliaments—into instruments of real political participation. Parliaments had existed for centuries but were generally aristocratic institutions. The bourgeoisie embraced parliaments as means by which they could exert the weight of their superior numbers and growing economic advantage over their aristocratic rivals. At the same time, the bourgeoisie sought to place restraints on the capacity of governments to threaten these economic and political interests by placing formal or constitutional limits on governmental power.

Although motivated primarily by the need to protect and defend their own interests, the bourgeoisie advanced many of the principles that would define the central underpinnings of individual liberty for all citizens—freedom of speech, freedom of assembly, freedom of conscience, and freedom from arbitrary search and seizure. The work of political theorists such as John Locke (1632–1704) and, later, John Stuart Mill (1806–73) helped shape these evolving ideas about liberty and political rights. However, it is important to note that the bourgeoisie generally did not favor democracy as we know it. They were advocates of electoral and representative institutions, but they favored property requirements and other restrictions so as to limit participation to the middle and upper classes. Yet once these institutions of politics and the protection of the right to engage in politics were established, it was difficult to limit them to the bourgeoisie.

ACCESS TO GOVERNMENT: THE EXPANSION OF PARTICIPATION

The expansion of participation from the bourgeoisie to ever-larger segments of society took two paths. In some nations, popular participation was expanded by the Crown or the aristocracy, which ironically saw common people as potential political allies against the bourgeoisie. Thus, in nineteenth-century Prussia, for example, it was the emperor and his great minister Otto von Bismarck who expanded popular participation in order to build political support among the lower orders.

In other nations, participation expanded because competing segments of the bourgeoisie sought to gain political advantage by reaching out to and mobilizing the support of working- and lower-class groups that craved the opportunity to take part in politics—"lining up the unwashed," as one American historian put it.[4] To be sure,

John Stuart Mill (1806–73) presented a ringing defense of individual freedom in his famous treatise *On Liberty*. Mill's work influenced Americans' evolving ideas about the relationship between government and the individual.

excluded groups often agitated for greater participation. But seldom was such agitation by itself enough to secure the right to participate. Usually, expansion of voting rights resulted from a combination of pressure from below and help from above.

The gradual expansion of voting rights by groups hoping to derive some political advantage has been typical of American history. After the Civil War, one of the chief reasons that Republicans moved to enfranchise newly freed slaves was to use the support of the former slaves to maintain Republican control over the defeated southern states. Similarly, in the early twentieth century, upper-middle-class Progressives advocated women's suffrage because they believed that women were likely to support the reforms espoused by the Progressive movement.

INFLUENCING THE GOVERNMENT THROUGH PARTICIPATION: POLITICS

Expansion of participation means that more and more people have a legal right to take part in politics. *Politics* is an important term. In its broadest sense, it refers to conflicts over the character, membership, and policies of any organization to which people belong. As Harold Lasswell, a famous political scientist, once put it, politics is the struggle over "who gets what, when, how."[5] Although politics is a phenomenon that can be found in any organization, our concern in this book is narrower. Here, politics will be used to refer only to conflicts and struggles over the leadership, structure, and policies of governments. The goal of politics, as we define it, is to have a share or a say in the composition of the government's leadership, how the government is organized, or what its policies are going to be. Having a share is called having **power** or influence.

Participation in politics can take many forms, including blogging and posting opinion pieces online, sending emails to government officials, voting, lobbying legislators on behalf of particular programs, and participating in protest marches and even violent demonstrations. A system of government that gives citizens a regular opportunity to elect the top government officials is usually called a **representative democracy**, or **republic**. A system that permits citizens to vote directly on laws and policies is often called a **direct democracy**. At the national level, the United States is a representative democracy in which citizens select government officials but do not vote on legislation. Some states and cities, however, have provisions for direct legislation through popular initiatives and ballot referenda. These procedures allow citizens to collect petitions requiring an issue to be brought directly to the voters for a decision. In 2018, 169 initiatives appeared on state ballots, often dealing with hot-button issues. Five states considered measures legalizing medical or recreational marijuana. Eight states considered restrictions on taxes, 3 considered initiatives on abortion access and funding, and 21 voted on elections policies such as redistricting, voting requirements, and campaign finance. In 2017 voters in Maine decided to expand Medicaid under the Affordable Care Act after the governor had vetoed expansion multiple times, becoming the first state to decide the issue by direct democracy.[6]

Groups and organized interests also participate in politics. Their political activities include providing funds for candidates, lobbying, and trying to influence public opinion. The pattern of struggles among interests is called group politics, or **pluralism**. Americans have always been ambivalent about pluralist politics. On the one hand, the right of groups to press their views and compete for influence in the government is the essence of liberty. On the other hand, Americans often fear that

power influence over a government's leadership, organization, or policies

representative democracy (republic) a system of government in which the populace selects representatives, who play a significant role in governmental decision-making

direct democracy a system of rule that permits citizens to vote directly on laws and policies

pluralism the theory that all interests are and should be free to compete for influence in the government; the outcome of this competition is compromise and moderation

Politics sometimes involves direct action. People often hold public rallies or protests to draw attention to issues. These concerns can range from inequality in police practices (left), animal rights (center), taxes and government spending (right).

organized groups may sometimes exert too much influence, advancing special interests at the expense of larger public interests. (We return to this problem in Chapter 11.)

Sometimes, of course, politics does not take place through formal channels at all but instead involves direct action. Direct action politics can include either violent politics or civil disobedience, both of which attempt to shock rulers into behaving more responsibly. Direct action can also be a form of revolutionary politics, which rejects the system entirely and attempts to replace it with a new ruling group and a new set of rules. In recent years in the United States, groups ranging from animal rights activists to right-to-life advocates to the Tea Party to Black Lives Matter protesters have used direct action to underline their demands. Many forms of peaceful direct political action are protected by the U.S. Constitution. The country's Founders knew that the right to protest is essential to the maintenance of political freedom, even where the ballot box is available.

Citizenship: Participation, Knowledge, and Efficacy

> **Describe the role of the citizen in politics**

Citizen participation is the hallmark of the democratic form of government. "Government by the people" depends on lively citizen involvement in public discussion, debate, and activity designed to improve the welfare of one's community. The very legitimacy of democratic government depends on political participation, which takes a variety of forms, from the conventional—voting, contacting elected officials, working on a campaign, making political donations, attending political meetings—to the unconventional—protesting, boycotting, and signing petitions.

One key ingredient for political participation is **political knowledge** and information. Democracy functions best when citizens are informed and have the knowledge

political knowledge possessing information about the formal institutions of government, political actors, and political issues needed to participate in political debate. Indeed, our definition of **citizenship** derives from the ideal put forth by the ancient Greeks: *enlightened* political engagement.[7] Political knowledge means more than having a few opinions to offer a pollster or to guide your decisions in a voting booth. It is important to know the rules and strategies that govern political institutions and the principles on which they are based, *and* to know them in ways that relate to your own interests. If your street is rendered impassable by snow, what can you do? Is snow removal the responsibility of the federal government? Is it a state or municipal responsibility? Knowing that you have a stake in a clear road does not help much if you do not know that snow removal is a city or a county responsibility and if you cannot identify the municipal agency that deals with the problem. Americans are fond of complaining that government is not responsive to their needs, but in some cases, it is possible that citizens simply lack the information they need to present their problems to the appropriate government officials.

citizenship informed and active membership in a political community

Without political knowledge, citizens cannot be aware of their stakes in political disputes. For example, during the debate in 2017 about whether to repeal the Obama health care reform, one-third of Americans did not know that "Obamacare" and the "Affordable Care Act" are the same thing.[8] That meant that some Americans who had enrolled in "Obamacare" did not realize their access to health insurance would be affected if the ACA were repealed. Citizens need knowledge in order to assess their interests and to know when to act on them.

The internet can greatly facilitate acquisition of knowledge about politics. A 2015 Pew survey found that over the previous year, 65 percent of Americans had used the internet to find data or information about government, including visiting a local, state, or federal government website.[9] Such **digital citizenship**—the ability to participate in society online—benefits individuals and provides advantages to society as a whole. Digital citizens are more likely to be interested in politics and to discuss politics with friends, family, and coworkers than individuals who do not use online political information. They are also more likely to vote and participate in other ways in elections. A lingering concern is that lower-income and less-educated Americans,

digital citizenship using the internet, social media, and other information technology to engage in society and government rural residents, racial and ethnic minorities, and the elderly are all less likely to have internet access. This digital divide (which we discuss further in Chapters 7 and 8) exacerbates inequalities in political participation.

Even though the internet has made it easier than ever to learn about politics, the state of political knowledge in the United States today is spotty. Most Americans know little about current issues or debates, or even the basics of how government works. For example, in 2017 only 26 percent of those surveyed could identify all three branches of the federal government and only 54 percent knew that Congress has the power to declare war. During the summer before the 2016 presidential election, just 22 percent of the public could identify the Democratic vice-presidential candidate and 37 percent could identify the Republican vice-presidential candidate. On the other hand, more than three-quarters of those surveyed knew that Congress has the power to raise taxes and cannot establish an official religion for the nation (see Table 1.2). Those of you who make the effort to become more knowledgeable will be much better prepared to influence the political system regarding the issues and concerns that you care most about.

Another ingredient in political participation is **political efficacy**, the belief that ordinary citizens can affect what government does. The feeling that you can't affect government decisions can lead to apathy, declining political participation, and withdrawal from political life. Why bother to participate if you believe it makes no difference? Americans' sense of political efficacy has declined over time. In 1960, only 25 percent felt shut out of government. In 2015, 74 percent of Americans said that elected officials don't care what people like them think.[10]

political efficacy the ability to influence government and politics

TABLE 1.2

What Americans Know about Government

RESPONDENTS WHO	PERCENTAGE
Could identify all three branches of government	26
Knew Congress has the power to declare war	54
Knew Congress has the power to raise taxes	83
Knew Congress cannot establish an official religion of the United States	77
Could not name any of the rights guaranteed by the First Amendment	37
In 2016, could name the Republican vice-presidential candidate (Mike Pence).	37
In 2016, could name the Democratic vice-presidential candidate (Tim Kaine)	22

SOURCES: Annenberg Constitution Day Civics Survey, July 14–18, 2016, cdn.annenbergpublicpolicycenter.org/wp-content/uploads/Constitution_Day_2016_Civics_Appendix.pdf; and Annenberg Constitution Day Civics Survey, August 9–13, 2017, www.annenbergpublicpolicycenter.org/americans-are-poorly-informed-about-basic-constitutional-provisions/ (accessed 2/17/18).

An Increasingly Diverse Nation

Since the Founding, the American people have become increasingly diverse. This diversity and the changes in the population have frequently raised challenging questions in American politics.

Race

	1790*	1900*	2015

1790*
- White 81%
- Black 19%

1900*
- White 88%
- Black 12%
- Other 1%

2015
- White 62%
- Black 12%
- Hispanic 17%
- Asian 5%
- Native American 1%
- Other 0.4%
- 2 or more races 2%

= 1 million people

TOTAL POPULATION =
- 3,929,214
- 75,994,575
- 323,127,513

Geography

	1790	1900	2015

1790
- 50%
- 50%
- Northeast 50% South 50%

1900
- 28%
- 35%
- 5%
- 32%
- Northeast 28% Midwest 35%
- South 32% West 5%

2015
- 18%
- 21%
- 24%
- 38%
- Northeast 18% Midwest 21%
- South 38% West 24%

Age

1900
- 0–19 44%
- 20–44 38%
- 45–64 14%
- 65 + 4%

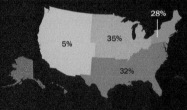

2015
- 0–19 26%
- 20–44 34%
- 45–64 26%
- 65 + 14%

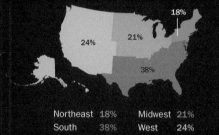

FOR CRITICAL ANALYSIS

1. In 2015, the U.S. Census Bureau estimated that the population of the South and the West continued to grow more rapidly than the Northeast and Midwest. What are some of the political implications of this trend?

2. Today, Americans over age 37 outnumber Americans under 37—and older adults are more likely to participate in the political process. What do you think this means for the kinds of issues and policies taken up by the government?

*The 1790 census does not accurately reflect the population because it only counted blacks and whites. It did not include Native Americans or other groups. The 1900 census did not count Hispanic Americans.

SOURCE: U.S. Census Bureau, 2011–2015 American Community Survey 5-Year Estimates, https://factfinder.census.gov (accessed 8/27/16).

In the 1900s many immigrants entered the United States through New York's Ellis Island, where they were checked for disease before being admitted. Today, individuals hoping to immigrate to the United States often apply for a visa at the U.S. consulate in their home country before traveling to the United States, where the U.S. Customs and Border Protection checks their identity and legal status.

hoped to turn back the clock and revert to an earlier America in which northern Europeans dominated. The new system set up a hierarchy of admissions: northern European countries received generous quotas for new immigrants, whereas eastern and southern European countries were granted very small quotas. These restrictions ratcheted down the numbers of immigrants so that by 1970 the foreign-born population in the United States reached an all-time low of 5 percent.

IMMIGRATION AND RACE

Official efforts to use racial and ethnic criteria to restrict the American population were not new but had been used to draw boundaries around the American community from the start. The very first census, as just mentioned, did not count Native Americans; in fact, no Native Americans became citizens until 1924. Although the Constitution infamously declared that each slave would count as three-fifths of a person for purposes of apportioning representation among the states, most people of African descent were not officially citizens until 1868, when the Fourteenth Amendment to the Constitution conferred citizenship on the freed slaves (see Chapter 2).

Over half a century earlier, the federal government had sought to limit the non-white population with a 1790 law stipulating that only free whites could become naturalized citizens. Not until 1870 did Congress lift the ban on the naturalization of nonwhites. In addition to the restrictions on blacks and Native Americans, restrictions applied to Asians. The Chinese Exclusion Act of 1882 outlawed the entry of Chinese laborers to the United States. These provisions were not lifted until 1943, when China became America's ally during World War II. Additional barriers enacted after World War I meant that virtually no Asians entered the country as immigrants until the 1940s. People of Hispanic origin do not fit simply into the American system of racial classification. In 1930, for example, the census counted people of Mexican origin as nonwhite but reversed this decision a decade later—after protests by the Mexican-origin population and the Mexican government. Only in 1970 did the census officially begin counting persons of Hispanic origin, noting that they could be any race.[19] As this history suggests, American citizenship has always been tied to "whiteness" even as the meaning of "white" shifted over time.

TWENTY-FIRST-CENTURY AMERICANS

Race and Ethnicity By the year 2000 immigration had profoundly transformed the nation's racial and ethnic profile once again. The primary cause was Congress's decision in 1965 to lift the tight restrictions of the 1920s, allowing for much-expanded immigration from Asia and Latin America (see Figure 1.2). One consequence of the shift has been the growth in the Hispanic, or Latino, population. Census figures for 2016 show that Hispanics, who can be of any race, constitute 17.8 percent of the population. The black, or African American, population is 12.7 percent of the total population, while Asians make up 5.4 percent. Non-Hispanic white Americans account for 61 percent of the population—their lowest share ever. Moreover, 3.2 percent of the population now identifies itself as of "two or more races," a new

FIGURE 1.2

Immigration by Continent of Origin

Where did most immigrants come from at the start of the twentieth century? How does that compare with immigration in the twenty-first century?

*Less than 1 percent not shown.

SOURCE: Department of Homeland Security 2016 Yearbook of Immigration Statistics Table 2, November 2017, www.dhs.gov/immigration-statistics/yearbook/2016 (accessed 2/16/18). Figure shows those who have obtained "lawful permanent resident status" by continent of origin.

PERCENTAGE OF IMMIGRANTS*

Legend: Not specified, Oceania, Africa, Americas, Asia, Europe

X-axis: 1900s 1910s 1920s 1930s 1940s 1950s 1960s 1970s 1980s 1990s 2000s 2010s

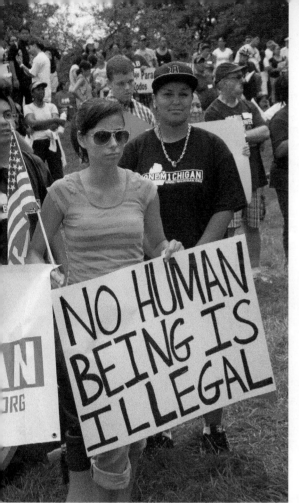

Immigration remains a controversial issue in the United States. While many believe we should do more to protect our borders, others call for comprehensive immigration reform, including an easier pathway to citizenship for the country's nearly 12 million undocumented immigrants.

category that the census added in 2000.[20] Although it is only a small percentage of the population, the multiracial category points toward a future in which the traditional labels of racial identification may be blurring, marking a major shift in the long-standing American tradition of strict racial categorization. The blurring of racial categories poses challenges to a host of policies—many of them put in place to remedy past discrimination—that rely on racial counts of the population.

Large-scale immigration means that many more residents are foreign-born. In 2016, 13.5 percent of the population was born outside the United States, a figure comparable to foreign-born rates at the turn of the previous century.[21] About half of the foreign-born came from Latin America and the Caribbean—almost 1 in 10 from the Caribbean, just over one-third from Central America (including Mexico), and 1 in 15 from South America.[22] Those born in Asia constituted the next-largest group, making up 31 percent of foreign-born residents.[23] In sharp contrast to the immigration patterns of a century earlier, fewer immigrants came from Europe. By 2016 just 10.9 percent of those born outside the United States came from Europe.[24]

One contemporary feature of American society is the large number of immigrants who live in the country without legal authorization. Estimates put the number of undocumented immigrants at 11.4 million, the majority of whom are from Mexico and Central America.[25] The large unauthorized population became a flashpoint for controversy as states and cities passed a variety of conflicting laws regarding illegal immigrants' access to public services. Some states have offered driver's licenses to undocumented immigrants, while others have sought to bar them from public services, such as education and emergency health care, both of which are constitutionally guaranteed to unauthorized immigrants.[26] In 1982 the Supreme Court ensured access to education when it ruled in *Plyler v. Doe* that Texas could not deny funding for undocumented students.[27] In 1986, Congress guaranteed emergency medical care to all people regardless of immigration status when it passed the Emergency Medical Treatment and Active Labor Act (EMTALA).

Religion The new patterns of immigration combined with differences in birth rates and underlying social changes to alter the religious affiliations of Americans. In 1900, 80 percent of the American adult population was Protestant; by 2016 only 44 percent of Americans identified themselves as Protestants.[28] Catholics made up 20 percent of the population, and Jews accounted for 2 percent. A small Muslim population had also grown, with nearly 1 percent of the population. One of the most important shifts in religious affiliation during the latter half of the twentieth century was the percentage of people who professed no organized religion: in 2017, 23 percent of the population was not affiliated with an organized church. These changes suggest an important shift in American religious identity. Although the United States thinks of itself as a "Judeo-Christian" nation—and indeed was 95 percent Protestant, Catholic, or Jewish from 1900 to 1968—by 2016 this number had fallen to under 70 percent of the adult population.[29]

Global Diversity

The United States has become an increasingly diverse country over time particularly in regard to its racial and ethnic makeup. How does the racial and ethnic diversity of the United States compare to that of other countries around the world?

As a "nation of immigrants," the United States is more diverse than many Western countries, but some former colonies are even more diverse than the United States. Racial and ethnic diversity stem not only from immigration but also geography, historical legacies, and whether the government has favored certain groups over others. Many countries in sub-Saharan Africa were colonized by multiple empires, whose governments often drew borders that encompassed multiple ethnic groups in the region. State-building and nationalism are also very new to these regions, meaning that local identities remain stronger than national ones.

In contrast many western European and Asian countries have histories of past conflict and strong state-building efforts, resulting in less diversity either by eliminating rival groups or forcibly assimilating them. For example, Japan's geographic isolation has created a racially homogeneous society, which was reinforced by the government's use of isolationism as a means to consolidate power.[a] Modern policies limiting immigration continue these historic trends. To take another example, France has historically pursued both political and cultural assimilation, using its schools as tools to socialize its citizens into a common "republican" identity. More recent waves of immigrants, however, have highlighted potential problems with this policy.[b]

How might the degree of diversity shape political values in specific countries? What types of values and policies would we expect to see in countries with a high degree of diversity versus those with less diversity?

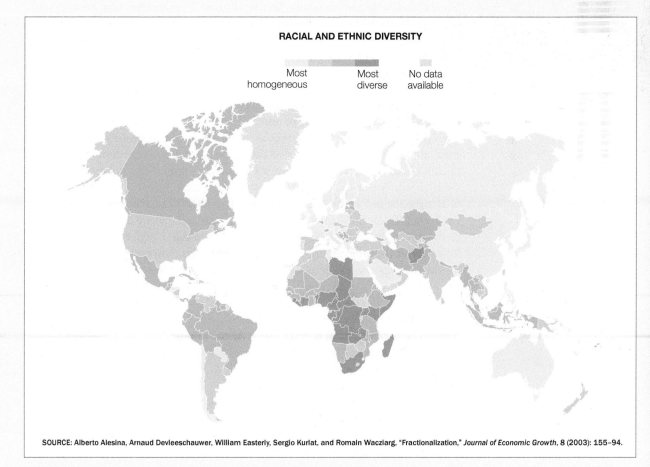

RACIAL AND ETHNIC DIVERSITY

Most homogeneous   Most diverse   No data available

SOURCE: Alberto Alesina, Arnaud Devleeschauwer, William Easterly, Sergio Kurlat, and Romain Wacziarg, "Fractionalization," *Journal of Economic Growth*, 8 (2003): 155–94.

[a]Benedict Anderson, *Imagined Communities: Reflections on the Origin and Spread of Nationalism* (London: Verso, 2006), 94–99.
[b]John R. Bowen, *Why the French Don't Like Headscarves: Islam, the State, and Public Space* (Princeton, NJ: Princeton University Press, 2007).

Age As America grew and its population expanded and diversified, the country's age profile shifted with it. In 1900 only 4 percent of the population was over age 65. As life expectancy increased, the number of older Americans grew with it: by 2016, 15.2 percent of the population was over 65. Over the same period, the percentage of children under the age of 18 fell, from 40.5 percent of the American population in 1900 to 22.8 percent in 2016.[30] Even though the population is aging, Americans tend to be younger than citizens of many industrialized countries, mainly because of the large immigrant population in the United States. The share of the population aged 65 and over is 20 percent in the European Union and 27 percent in Japan.[31] But an aging population poses challenges to the United States as well. As the elderly population grows and the working-age population shrinks, questions arise about how we will fund programs for the elderly such as Social Security.

FOR CRITICAL ANALYSIS

What trend in America's changing population has had the biggest influence on politics? Increasing racial and ethnic diversity? Aging? Increasing urbanization? Increased economic inequality? Why?

Geography Over the nation's history, Americans have changed in other ways, moving from mostly rural settings and small towns to large urban areas. Before 1920 less than half the population lived in urban areas; today 82 percent of Americans do.[32] Critics charge that the American political system—created when America was a largely rural society—underrepresents urban areas. The constitutional provision allocating each state two senators, for example, overrepresents sparsely populated rural states and underrepresents urban states, where the population is far more concentrated. In addition to becoming more urban over time, the American population has shifted regionally. During the past 50 years especially, many Americans left the Northeast and Midwest and moved to the South and Southwest. As congressional seats have been reapportioned to reflect the population shift, many problems that particularly plague the Midwest and Northeast, such as the decline in manufacturing jobs, receive less attention in national politics.

Socioeconomic Status Americans have fallen into diverse economic groups throughout American history. For much of American history most people were relatively poor working people, many of them farmers. A small wealthy elite, however, grew larger in the 1890s, in a period called "the gilded age." The top 1 percent and the top 10 percent of earners accounted for a growing share of the national income. By 1928 nearly one-quarter of the total annual income went to the top 1 percent of earners; the top 10 percent took home 46 percent of total annual income. After the New Deal in the 1930s, a large middle class took shape and the share going to those at the top dropped sharply. By 1976 the top 1 percent took home only 9 percent of the national annual income. Since then, however, economic inequality has once again widened as a tiny group of super-rich has emerged. By 2015 the top 1 percent earned 20.3 percent of annual income and the top 10 percent took home 48.8 percent of the total national income.[33] At the same time, the incomes of the broad middle class have largely stagnated.[34] And 12.7 percent of the population remains below the official poverty line.[35] As the middle class has frayed around the edges, the numbers of poor and near poor have swelled to nearly one-third of the population.[36] (See Figure 1.3.)

Population and Politics The shifting contours of the American people have regularly raised challenging questions about our politics and governing arrangements. Population growth and shifts have spurred politically charged debates about how the population should be apportioned among congressional districts and how those

FIGURE 1.3

Income in the United States

The top graph shows that while the income of most Americans has risen only slightly since 1975, the income of the richest Americans (the top 5 percent) has increased dramatically. The lower graph shows the portion of all income in the United States that goes to each group, with an increasing share going to the richest Americans in recent years. What are some of the ways that this shift might matter for American politics? Does the growing economic gap between the richest groups and most other Americans conflict with the political value of equality?

*Dollar values are given in constant 2016 dollars, which are adjusted for inflation so that we can compare a person's income in 1975 with a person's income today.

SOURCE: U.S. Census Bureau, "Income and Poverty in the United States: 2016" Table A-2, www.census.gov/content/dam/Census/library/publications/2017/demo/P60-259.pdf (accessed 4/16/18).

HOUSEHOLD INCOME (IN DOLLARS)*

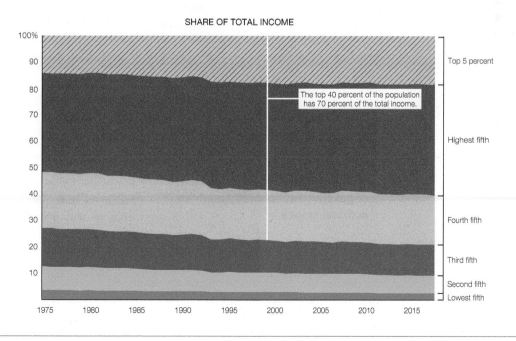

SHARE OF TOTAL INCOME

The top 40 percent of the population has 70 percent of the total income.

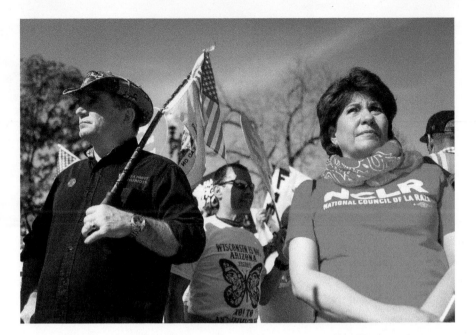

America continues to become more racially and ethnically diverse. These changes have sparked controversy over political issues. Here, Gregg Cummings, a Tea Party conservative from Iowa supporting strong immigration policy, stands outside of the Supreme Court next to Janet Murgu'a, the head of the National Council of La Raza, a large Latino rights advocacy organization.

districts should be drawn. These conflicts have major implications for the representation of different regions of the country—for the balance of representation between urban and rural areas. The representation of various demographic and political groups may also be affected, as there is substantial evidence of growing geographic sorting of citizens by education, income, marriage rates, and party voting.[37] In addition, immigration and the cultural and religious changes it entails sparks passionate debate today as well, just as it did 100 years ago. The different languages and customs that immigrants bring to the United States trigger fears among some that the country is changing in ways that may undermine American values and alter fundamental identities. The large number of unauthorized immigrants in the country today makes these anxieties even more acute. Yet a changing population has been one of the constants of American history. Indeed, each generation has confronted the myriad political challenges associated with answering the question anew, "Who are Americans?"

American Political Culture

Analyze whether the U.S. system of government upholds American political values

Underlying and framing political life in the United States are agreements on basic political values but disagreements over the ends or goals of government. Most Americans affirm the values of liberty, equality, and democracy. Values shape citizens' views of the world and define their sense of what is right and wrong, just and unjust, possible and impossible. If Americans shared no values, they would have difficulty communicating, much less agreeing on a common system of government and politics. However, sharing broad values does not guarantee political consensus. We can agree on principles but disagree over their application or how they are to be balanced.

Much of the debate over the role of government has been over what government should do and how far it should go to reduce the inequalities within our society and political system while still preserving essential liberties.

Even though Americans have disagreed over the meaning of such political ideals as equality, they still agree on the importance of those ideals. The values, beliefs, and attitudes that form our **political culture** and hold together the United States and its people date back to the time of the founding of the Union.

The essential documents of the American Founding—the Declaration of Independence and the Constitution—enunciated a set of political principles about the purposes of the new republic. In contrast with many other democracies, in the United States these political ideals did not just remain words on dusty documents. Americans actively embraced the principles of the Founders and made them central to the national identity. Let us look more closely at three of these ideals: liberty, equality, and democracy.

political culture broadly shared values, beliefs, and attitudes about how the government should function; American political culture emphasizes the values of liberty, equality, and democracy

LIBERTY

No ideal is more central to American values than liberty. The Declaration of Independence defined three inalienable rights: "Life, Liberty and the pursuit of Happiness." The preamble to the Constitution likewise identified the need to secure "the Blessings of Liberty" as one of the key reasons for drawing up the Constitution. For Americans, **liberty** means both personal freedom and economic freedom. Both are closely linked to the idea of **limited government.**

liberty freedom from governmental control

limited government a principle of constitutional government; a government whose powers are defined and limited by a constitution

The Constitution's first 10 amendments, known collectively as the Bill of Rights, above all preserve individual personal liberties and rights. In fact, the word *liberty* has come to mean many of the freedoms guaranteed in the Bill of Rights: freedom of speech and writing, the right to assemble freely, and the right to practice religious beliefs without interference from the government. Over the course of American history, the scope of personal liberties has expanded as laws have become more tolerant and as individuals have successfully used the courts to challenge restrictions on their individual freedoms. Far fewer restrictions exist today on the press, political speech, and individual moral behavior than in the early years of the nation. Even so, conflicts persist over how personal liberties should be extended and when personal liberties violate community norms. For example, a number of cities have recently passed "sit-lie" ordinances, which limit the freedom of individuals to sit or lie down on sidewalks. Designed to limit the presence of the homeless and make city streets more attractive to pedestrians, the ordinances have also been denounced as infringements on individual liberties.

Patrick Henry's famous "Give Me Liberty or Give Me Death" speech demanded freedom at any cost and has resonated with Americans throughout the nation's history.

The central historical conflict regarding liberty in the United States was about the enslavement of blacks. The facts of slavery and the differential treatment of the races have cast a long shadow over all of American history. In fact, scholars today note that the American definition of freedom has been formed in relation to the concept of slavery. The right to control one's labor and the right to receive rewards for that labor have been central elements of our definition of freedom precisely because these freedoms were denied to slaves.[38]

In addition to personal freedom, the American concept of liberty means economic freedom. Since the Founding, economic freedom has been linked to capitalism, free markets, and the protection of private property. Free competition, unfettered movement of goods, and the right to enjoy the fruits of one's labor are all essential aspects of economic freedom and American capitalism.[39] In the first century of the

laissez-faire capitalism an economic system in which the means of production and distribution are privately owned and operated for profit with minimal or no government interference

Republic, support for capitalism often meant support for the doctrine of *laissez-faire* (literally, "leave alone" in French). **Laissez-faire capitalism** allowed very little room for the national government to regulate trade or restrict the use of private property, even in the public interest. Americans still strongly support capitalism and economic liberty, but they now also endorse some restrictions on economic freedoms to protect the public. Today, federal and state governments deploy a wide array of regulations in the name of public protection. These include health and safety laws, environmental rules, and workplace regulations.

Not surprisingly, fierce disagreements often erupt over what the proper scope of government regulation should be. What some people regard as protecting the public, others see as an infringement on their own freedom to run their businesses and use their property as they see fit. For example, many business leaders opposed the Affordable Care Act, the health care reform legislation informally known as Obamacare, because it required businesses with over 50 employees to provide health coverage for their employees and establishes standards about which health services should be covered by the insurance. In addition, the law required that insurers pay for access to contraceptive care. From the perspective of the law's supporters, this provision simply ensured that women have access to basic health care. Many businesses, however, opposed the law as unwanted government intrusion. And some businesses strongly denounced the requirement to cover contraception, in particular, as a violation of their fundamental liberties to run their businesses as they see fit. In fact, in 2014 a company called Hobby Lobby successfully challenged this provision of the act when the Supreme Court ruled that family firms could be exempted on the basis of religious objections.[40]

Concerns about liberty have also arisen in relation to the government's efforts to combat terrorism and protect the nation's security. These concerns escalated in 2013 when Edward Snowden, a former National Security Agency (NSA) contractor, leaked top-secret documents from the NSA to the press. The NSA is the agency charged with protecting the United States by monitoring electronic data flows—including radio, email, and cellular telephone calls—for foreign threats. The leaked documents revealed that the American government was listening in on the private communications of foreign governments, including many American allies, such as Germany and Brazil. The leaks also revealed information about domestic surveillance: the NSA had access to Americans' Facebook, Google, Apple, and Yahoo! accounts, among many other electronic data sources. It was using these "metadata" to track the connections among people, searching for suspicious ties. The revelation that the NSA had been collecting this information for three years without public knowledge set off a storm of controversy since the NSA is supposed to monitor foreign communications, not track Americans. The controversy reinforced the tech companies' commitment to privacy. In 2016, Apple refused an FBI order to unlock the iPhone used by a terrorist who killed 14 people in San Bernardino, California. The FBI dropped the case after it was able to open the phone without Apple's help. However, a new court order to Apple related to an iPhone used in a drug conspiracy case made it clear that the tension between privacy and security will continue.[41]

Concerns about terrorism leave us with an extraordinary dilemma. On the one hand, we treasure liberty; but on the other hand, we recognize that the lives of thousands of Americans have already been lost and countless others are threatened by terrorism. Can we reconcile liberty and security? Liberty and order? In previous national emergencies, Americans accepted restrictions on liberty with the understanding that these would be temporary. But because the threat of terrorism has no clear end point, doubts have grown about whether special government powers that infringe on liberties should be continued.

EQUALITY

The Declaration of Independence declares as its first "self-evident" truth that "all men are created equal." As central as it is to the American political creed, however, equality has been an even less well-defined ideal than liberty because people interpret "equality" in different ways. Few Americans have wholeheartedly embraced the ideal of full equality of results, but most Americans share the ideal of **equality of opportunity**—that is, the notion that each person should be given a fair chance to go as far as his or her talents will allow. Yet it is hard for Americans to reach agreement on what constitutes equality of opportunity. Must a group's *past* inequalities be remedied in order to ensure equal opportunity in the *present*? Should inequalities in the legal, political, and economic spheres be given the same weight? In contrast to liberty, which requires limits on the role of government, equality implies an *obligation* of the government to the people.[42]

Americans do make clear distinctions between political equality and social or economic equality. **Political equality** means that members of the American political community have the right to participate in politics on equal terms. Beginning from a very restricted definition of political community, which originally included only propertied white men, the United States has moved much closer to an ideal of political equality that can be summed up as "one person, one vote." Broad support for the ideal of political equality has helped expand the American political community and extend to all the right to participate. Although considerable conflict remains over whether the political system makes participation in it harder for some people and easier for others and whether the role of money in politics has drowned out the public voice, Americans agree that all citizens should have an equal right to participate and that government should enforce that right.

In part because Americans believe that individuals are free to work as hard as they choose, they have always been less concerned about social or economic inequality. Many Americans regard economic differences as the consequence of individual choices, virtues, or failures. Because of this, Americans tend to be less supportive than most Europeans of government action to ensure economic equality. Yet when

equality of opportunity a widely shared American ideal that all people should have the freedom to use whatever talents and wealth they have to reach their fullest potential

political equality the right to participate in politics equally, based on the principle of "one person, one vote"

Americans struggle to define how equality of opportunity can be provided at the same time as individual liberty. One area of debate is in education. Does the fact that New York (left) spends on average $21,206 per student each year while Utah (right) spends on average $6,575 per student, mean that there is not an equality of opportunity for schoolchildren? (*Data from www.census.gov.*)

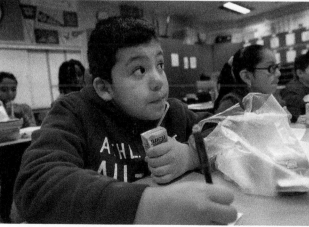

major economic forces, such as the Great Depression of the 1930s, affect many people or when systematic barriers appear to block equality of opportunity, Americans support government action to promote equality. Even then, however, they have endorsed only a limited government role designed to help people get back on their feet or to open up opportunity.

Because equality is such an elusive concept, many conflicts have arisen over what it should mean in practice. Americans have engaged in three kinds of controversies about the public role in addressing inequality. The first is determining what constitutes equality of access to public institutions. In 1896 the Supreme Court ruled in *Plessy v. Ferguson* that "separate but equal" accommodation for blacks and whites was constitutional.[43] In 1954, in a major legal victory for the civil rights movement, the Supreme Court's decision in *Brown v. Board of Education* overturned the "separate but equal" doctrine (see Chapter 5).[44] Today, new questions have been raised about what constitutes equal access to public institutions. Some argue that the unequal financing of public schools in cities, suburbs, and rural districts is a violation of the right to equal education. To date, these claims have not been supported by the federal courts, which have rejected the notion that the unequal economic impacts of public policy outcomes are a constitutional matter, leaving the issue to the states.[45] Lawsuits arguing a right to "economic equal protection" stalled in 1973 when the Supreme Court ruled that a Texas school-financing law did not violate the Constitution even though the law affected rich and poor students differently.[46]

A second debate concerns the public role in ensuring equality of opportunity in private life. Although Americans generally agree that discrimination should not be tolerated, people disagree over what should be done to ensure equality of opportunity (see Table 1.3).[47] Controversies about affirmative action programs reflect these disputes. Supporters of affirmative action claim that such programs are necessary to compensate for past discrimination in order to establish true equality of opportunity today. Opponents maintain that affirmative action amounts to reverse discrimination and that a society that espouses true equality should not acknowledge gender or racial differences. The question of the public responsibility for private inequalities is central to gender issues. The traditional view, still held by many today, takes for

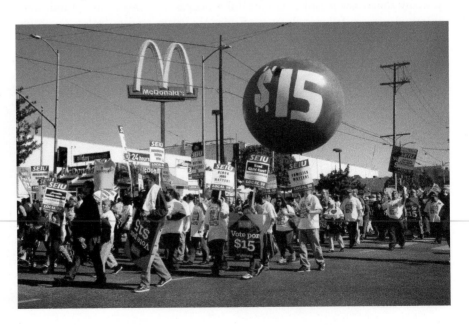

The Fight for $15—a nationwide effort to increase the minimum wage to $15 an hour—first gained traction in 2013, increasing public awareness of income inequality in the United States. In November 2015 fast food workers in hundreds of cities around the country went on strike to rally for higher pay and the right to unionize.

TABLE 1.3

Equality and Public Opinion

Americans believe in some forms of equality more than others. How do these survey results reflect disagreement about what equality means in practice?

STATEMENT	PERCENTAGE WHO AGREE
It is very important that women have the same rights as men in our country.	91
Our society should do what is necessary to make sure that everyone has an equal opportunity to succeed.	86
Our country should have laws that protect gay, lesbian, bisexual, and transgender people against discrimination in jobs, public accommodations, and housing.	69
It should be legal for gay and lesbian couples to get married.	62
The fact that some are rich and some are poor is an acceptable part of the economic system.	52
Our country needs to continue making changes to give blacks equal rights with whites (according to whites).	54
Our country needs to continue making changes to give blacks equal rights with whites (according to blacks).	88
The country hasn't gone far enough when it comes to gender equality (according to women).	57
The country hasn't gone far enough when it comes to gender equality (according to men).	42

SOURCE: Pew Research Center, www.pewresearch.org/. See endnote 47 for specific reports.

granted that women should bear special responsibilities in the family. In this perspective, the challenges women face in the labor force due to family responsibilities fall outside the range of public concern. In the past 30 years especially, these traditional views have come under fire as advocates for women have argued that private inequalities *are* a topic of public concern.[48]

A third debate about equality concerns differences in income and wealth. Unlike in other countries, income inequality has not been an enduring topic of political controversy in the United States, which currently has the largest gap in income and wealth between rich and poor citizens of any developed nation. Americans have generally tolerated great differences among rich and poor citizens, in part because of a pervasive belief that mobility is possible and that economic success is the product of individual effort.[49] This tolerance for inequality is reflected in America's tax code, which is more advantageous to wealthy taxpayers than that of almost any other Western nation.

FOR CRITICAL ANALYSIS

Economic inequality among Americans has been widening since at least the 1970s. Many politicians and news commentators say that inequality is threatening the middle class. Is there any evidence that the American public is worried about the growth in inequality?

Since the Great Recession, however, income inequality has risen on the political agenda. During the 2016 presidential race, Democratic candidates Hillary Clinton and Bernie Sanders discussed economic inequality, as did Republican candidates such as Donald Trump and Marco Rubio, although their proposed solutions differed. Public opinion polls revealed concerns about inequality as well. In 2015 two-thirds of Americans said the distribution of wealth and money is not fair and should be more evenly distributed; in 2017, 63 percent of Americans said upper-income people pay too little in taxes, and 67 percent said corporations pay too little.[50] Nonetheless, the tax bill passed by the Republican-led Congress and signed by President Trump at the end of 2017 lowered taxes on corporations and wealthy households, raising concerns among some critics about lack of responsiveness to public opinion.

DEMOCRACY

The essence of democracy is the participation of the people in choosing their rulers and the people's ability to influence what those rulers do. In a democracy, political power ultimately comes from the people. The idea of placing power in the hands of the people is known as popular sovereignty. In the United States, **popular sovereignty** and political equality make politicians accountable to the people. Ideally, democracy envisions an engaged citizenry prepared to exercise its power over rulers. As we noted earlier, the United States is a representative democracy, meaning that the people do not rule directly but instead exercise power through elected representatives. Forms of participation in a democracy vary greatly, but voting is a key element of the representative democracy that the American Founders established.

American democracy rests on the principle of **majority rule** with **minority rights**. Majority rule means that the wishes of the majority determine what government does. The House of Representatives—a large body elected directly by the people—was designed in particular to ensure majority rule. But the Founders feared that popular majorities could turn government into a "tyranny of the majority" in which individual liberties would be violated. Concern for individual rights has thus been a part of American democracy from the beginning. The rights enumerated in the Bill of Rights and enforced through the courts provide an important check on the power of the majority.

Despite Americans' deep attachment to the *ideal* of democracy, many questions can be raised about our *practice* of democracy. The first is the restricted definition of the political community during much of American history. Property restrictions on the right to vote were eliminated by 1828; in 1870 the Fifteenth Amendment to the Constitution granted African Americans the vote, although later exclusionary practices denied them that right; in 1920 the Nineteenth Amendment guaranteed women the right to vote; and in 1965 the Voting Rights Act finally secured the right of African Americans to vote. The Twenty-Sixth Amendment, ratified in 1971 during the Vietnam War, gave 18- to 20-year-olds the right to vote.

Just securing the right to vote does not end concerns about democracy, however. The organization of electoral institutions can have a significant impact on access to elections and on who can get elected. During the first two decades of the twentieth century, states and cities enacted many reforms, including strict registration requirements and scheduling of elections, that made it harder to vote. The aim was to rid politics of corruption, but the consequence was to reduce participation. More recently, voter ID laws requiring government identification to register or to vote have been enacted for similar reasons and with similar consequences. Other

popular sovereignty a principle of democracy in which political authority rests ultimately in the hands of the people

majority rule, minority rights the democratic principle that a government follows the preferences of the majority of voters but protects the interests of the minority

FOR CRITICAL ANALYSIS

In the United States, do citizens make the decisions of government, or do they merely influence them?

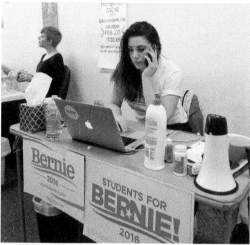

While levels of participation in politics are relatively low for young Americans, the presidential primary campaigns of 2008 and 2016 saw the highest levels of youth turnout—to volunteer and to vote—in decades. What factors might have energized young people to become involved in these particular campaigns?

institutional decisions affect which candidates stand the best chance of getting elected (see Chapter 10).

A further consideration about democracy concerns the relationship between economic power and political power. Money has always played an important role in elections and governing in the United States. Many argue that the pervasive influence of money in American electoral campaigns and lobbying activities today undermines democracy. With the decline of locally based political parties that depend on party loyalists to turn out the vote and the rise of political action committees, political consultants, and expensive media campaigns, money has become the central fact of life in American politics. Money often determines who runs for office; it can exert a heavy influence on who wins; and some argue that it affects what politicians do once they are in office.[51]

Low turnout for elections and a pervasive sense of apathy and cynicism characterized American politics for much of the past half-century. The widespread interest in the 2008 election and the near-record levels of voter turnout, which, at 61.6 percent, was the highest turnout since 1968, reversed this trend.[52] Nine million voters registered and voted for the first time in 2008, including near-record numbers of voters under the age of 24.[53] Despite strong engagement in the presidential primaries and in the general election campaigns, lower turnout in the 2012 and 2016 elections suggested that public disengagement remains a challenge for American democracy.

What Americans Think about Government

Explore Americans' attitudes toward government

Since the United States was established as a nation, Americans have been reluctant to grant government too much power, and they have often been suspicious of politicians. But over the course of the nation's history, Americans have also turned to government for assistance in times of need and have strongly supported the government in periods of war. In 1933 the power of the

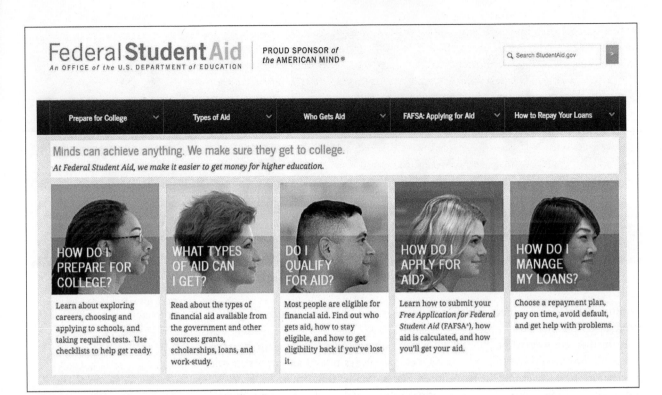

The federal government maintains a large number of websites that provide useful information to citizens on such topics as loans for education, civil service job applications, the inflation rate, and how the weather will affect farming. These sites are just one way in which the government serves its citizens.

government began to expand to meet the crises created by the stock market crash of 1929, the Great Depression, and the run on banks of 1933. Congress passed legislation that brought the government into the businesses of home mortgages, farm mortgages, credit, and relief of personal distress. More recently, when the economy threatened to fall into a deep recession in 2008 and 2009, the federal government took action to shore up the financial system, oversee the restructuring of the ailing auto companies, and inject hundreds of billions of dollars into the faltering economy. In 2017 federal government funds helped fight wildfires in the American West and provide hurricane relief in Texas and Florida. Today the national government is enormous, with programs and policies reaching into every corner of American life. It oversees the nation's economy, it is the nation's largest employer, it provides citizens with a host of services, it controls the world's most formidable military, and it regulates a wide range of social and commercial activities. Americans use government services, benefits, and infrastructure every day and are simultaneously skeptical about the role of government in society. We might consider these contradictory feelings and low government trust additional aspects of contemporary American political culture.

CONSERVATIVE IN THEORY, LIBERAL IN PRACTICE

The Constitution lays out a system of limited government, which largely reflects the preferences of the majority of Americans. When asked questions about the role of government in general, the majority of Americans give answers on the conservative side of the political spectrum. More Americans consider themselves politically conservative than liberal (36 versus 26 percent in 2017; 40–21 in 2009).[54] In 2017, 55 percent of Americans said "the federal government has too much power," and 56 percent said that the "government is almost always wasteful and inefficient."[55]

At the same time, however, when asked about specific government programs, majorities offer strong support. In 2017, 86 percent of Republicans and 95 percent of Democrats wanted federal spending on Social Security to be kept the same or increased; 91 percent of Republicans and 92 percent of Democrats wanted spending on highways, bridges, and roads to be the same or higher; and 61 percent of Republicans and 93 percent of Democrats wanted spending on economic assistance to needy people kept the same or increased.[56] Thus many Americans prefer small government in the abstract, but very much like what government does in some specific issue areas. They are simultaneously "abstract conservatives" and "operational liberals."[57] That both sentiments are prevalent in American public opinion helps explain why there can be calls both for more government action and for less, depending on the situation.

TRUST IN GOVERNMENT

Another characteristic of contemporary political culture is low trust in government. Ironically, even as popular dependence on the government has grown, the American public's view of government has turned sour. In the early 1960s three-quarters of Americans said they trusted government most of the time or always. By 2017 only 18 percent of Americans expressed such trust in government[58] (see Figure 1.4). Different groups vary somewhat in their levels of trust: African Americans and Latinos express slightly more confidence in the federal government than do whites. But even among the most supportive groups, considerably more than half only trust the government some of the time.[59] These developments are important because politically engaged citizens and public confidence in government are vital for the health of a democracy.

Trust spiked higher after the September 11 terrorist attacks, but fell to pre-attack levels within three years, and the trend has continued its downward path. Distrust of government greatly influenced the primary elections in 2015 and 2016, when a

With a few upticks, trust in government has been on the decline since the 1960s. What factors might reverse the trend? Have high-profile populist presidential candidates like Donald Trump and Bernie Sanders helped to raise or lower trust in government?

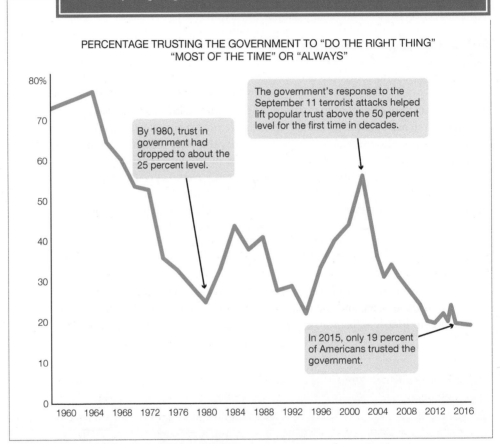

FIGURE 1.4

Public Trust in Government, 1958–2017

Since the 1960s, general levels of public trust in government have declined. What factors might help to account for changes in the public's trust in government? Why has confidence in government dropped again since September 11, 2001?

SOURCE: The American National Election Studies, 1958–2004; Pew Research Center, www.people-press.org/ 2017/05/03/public-trust-in-government-1958-2017/ (accessed 12/27/17). The Pew data after 2004 represent a "three survey moving average."

PERCENTAGE TRUSTING THE GOVERNMENT TO "DO THE RIGHT THING"
"MOST OF THE TIME" OR "ALWAYS"

By 1980, trust in government had dropped to about the 25 percent level.

The government's response to the September 11 terrorist attacks helped lift popular trust above the 50 percent level for the first time in decades.

In 2015, only 19 percent of Americans trusted the government.

number of "outsider" candidates, critical of government, attracted wide support. This trend was especially pronounced in the Republican primaries, in which candidates known for their strong anti-government rhetoric, such as Ted Cruz, and candidates with no government experience, notably Donald Trump, unexpectedly attracted wide support. Among Democratic primary voters, strong support for Bernie Sanders, a democratic socialist, also indicated a desire to depart from business as usual in Washington. Sanders vigorously faulted the government for failing to take more forceful action against corporate misconduct and growing inequality.

Does it matter if Americans trust their government? For the most part, the answer is yes. As we have seen, most Americans rely on government for a wide range of services and laws that they simply take for granted. But long-term distrust in government can result in public refusal to pay the taxes necessary to support such widely approved public activities. Low levels of confidence may also make it difficult for government to attract talented and effective workers to public service.[60] The weakening of government as a result of prolonged levels of distrust may ultimately harm the United States' capacity to defend its national interest in the world economy and may jeopardize its national security. Likewise, a weak government can do little to assist citizens who need help in weathering periods of sharp economic or technological change.

FOR CRITICAL ANALYSIS

What recent events have affected Americans' trust in government? What might it take to restore Americans' trust in the federal government?

American Political Culture
WHAT DO WE WANT?

Americans express mixed views about government. Almost everyone complains about government at one time or another, but in the past three decades, general trust in government has declined significantly. Despite mounting distrust, when asked about particular government activities or programs, a majority of Americans are more than likely to support the activities that government undertakes. These conflicting views reflect the tensions in American political culture: there is no perfect balance between liberty, equality, and democracy. In recent years, finding the right mix of government actions to achieve these different goals has become especially troublesome. Some charge that government initiatives designed to promote equality infringe on individual liberty, while others point to the need for government to take action in the face of growing inequality. Sharp political debate over competing goals alienates many citizens, who react by withdrawing from politics. Yet, in contrast to totalitarian and authoritarian forms of government, democracy rests on the principle of popular sovereignty. No true democracy can function properly without knowledgeable and engaged citizens. The **"Who Participates?"** feature on page 35 shows which Americans voted in the 2016 presidential election.

The remarkable diversity of the American people represents a great strength for American democracy as well as a formidable challenge. The shifting religious, racial and ethnic, and immigration status of Americans throughout history has always provoked fears about whether American values could withstand such dramatic shifts.

Demographic changes will continue to raise thorny new questions in the coming decades. For example, as the American population grows older, programs for the elderly are expected to take up an increasing share of the federal budget. Yet to be successful, a nation must invest in its young people. And, as any college student knows, the cost of college has risen in recent years. Many students drop out as they discover that the cost of college is too high. Or they graduate and find themselves saddled with loans that will take decades to pay back. Yet, in a world of ever-sharper economic competition, higher education has become increasingly important for individuals seeking economic security. Moreover, an educated population is critical to the future prosperity of the country as a whole. Are there ways to support the elderly and the young at the same time? Is it fair to cut back assistance to the elderly, who have worked a lifetime for their benefits? If we decrease assistance to the elderly, will they stay in the labor market and make the job hunt for young people even more difficult?

As these trade-offs suggest, there are no easy answers to the demographic changes that will unfold in the coming years. Undoubtedly, these questions will provoke heated political conflict as politicians and interest groups propose different strategies for supporting the young in an aging country. Informed participation of the American public, especially the participation of young people, is the only way to ensure that the steps taken to address these challenges best reflect the will of the people. The young politicians mentioned at the beginning of the chapter, Saira Blair and Kendric Jones, have become engaged in a particularly deep way, by running for office. But there are many ways to become informed and involved, and the goal of this book is to show you how and why it matters.

WHO PARTICIPATES?

Who Voted in 2016?

Age

- 46% — 18–29
- 59% — 30–44
- 67% — 45–64
- 71% — 65+

Income

- 55% — <$50,000
- 69% — $50,000–$99,999
- 78% — $100,000+

Race / Ethnicity

- 65% — White
- 48% — Hispanic
- 59% — Black
- 49% — Asian

Sex

- 59% — Male
- 63% — Female

Education*

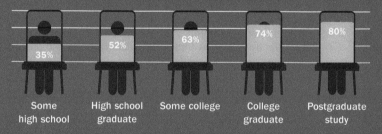

- 35% — Some high school
- 52% — High school graduate
- 63% — Some college
- 74% — College graduate
- 80% — Postgraduate study

*Highest level attained

SOURCE: U.S. Census Bureau, Current Population Survey November 2016, census.gov (accessed 11/20/17).

WHAT YOU CAN DO

Vote

 Register to vote. See page 329.

 Find out what's on the ballot in upcoming elections in your state and district by entering your address at **www.vote411.org** (a website from the League of Women Voters).

 Cast your vote on Election Day. Consider encouraging others to vote too. Research shows that people are more likely to turn out to vote if a friend or family member asks them to.

Government

Define government and forms of government (pp. 5–10)

Government is needed to provide those services, sometimes called "public goods," that citizens need but are not likely to be able to provide adequately for themselves. There are many different kinds of government. Prior to the modern era, governments accepted almost no limits on their behavior and provided citizens with few opportunities to participate in public affairs. Today, numerous countries, including the United States, are constitutional democracies. America's democracy provides citizens with the chance to elect top officials at all levels of government and even allows them to vote directly on laws in many states and localities.

Key Terms

government (p. 5)

politics (p. 5)

autocracy (p. 7)

oligarchy (p. 7)

democracy (p. 7)

constitutional government (p. 7)

authoritarian government (p. 7)

totalitarian government (p. 7)

power (p. 9)

representative democracy (republic) (p. 9)

direct democracy (p. 9)

pluralism (p. 9)

Practice Quiz

1. Services that citizens need but are unlikely to provide for themselves, such as national defense, maintenance of public order, and a stable currency, are called
   a) laissez-faire goods.
   b) pluralist goods.
   c) provisional goods.
   d) public goods.
   e) private goods.

2. What is the basic difference between an autocracy and an oligarchy?
   a) the extent to which average citizens have a say in government affairs
   b) the means of collecting taxes and conscripting soldiers
   c) the number of people who control governing decisions
   d) the size and political influence of the military
   e) there are no differences between autocracies and oligarchies

3. A government that is formally limited in what it can control and how it controls it is known as
   a) a totalitarian government.
   b) a authoritarian government.
   c) a constitutional government.
   d) a autocracy.
   e) a oligarchy.

4. A system of government that allows citizens to vote directly on the law through popular initiatives and ballot referendums is called a
   a) republic
   b) representative democracy
   c) direct democracy
   d) pluralism
   e) laissez-faire capitalism

Citizenship: Participation, Knowledge, and Efficacy

Describe the role of the citizen in politics (pp. 10–13)

Citizenship requires political knowledge. When citizens know about politics, they are better able to understand their interests and to identify the best way to act on those interests. Most Americans, however, do not know much about politics. While the internet has made it easier to learn about and participate in politics, many Americans still do not go online to find information about government. Internet access and digital literacy are increasingly important for full participation in American politics.

Key Terms

political knowledge (p. 10)

citizenship (p. 11)

digital citizenship (p. 11)

political efficacy (p. 12)

5. What is *digital citizenship*?
   a) a new government initiative to expand online voter registration
   b) the ability to vote online
   c) an online certification program that allows immigrants to become American citizens
   d) the ability to participate in society online
   e) a new government initiative to provide daily legislative updates online

6. *Political efficacy* is the belief that
   a) government is wasteful and corrupt.
   b) government operates efficiently.
   c) government has grown too large.
   d) government cannot be trusted.
   e) ordinary citizens can influence what government does.

Who Are Americans?

Show how the social composition of the American population has changed over time (pp. 13–22)

The United States is defined, in part, by its ever-growing and changing population. During the last 200 years, America has become more racially, ethnically, geographically, and religiously diverse. Immigration has been an important reason for the country's shifting demographics, and it has frequently sparked intense debate about the nature of American identity and American democracy.

Practice Quiz

7. In 1910 residents who traced their origin to Latin America or Asia each accounted for
   a) less than 1 percent of the U.S. population.
   b) approximately 5 percent of the U.S. population.
   c) approximately 10 percent of the U.S. population.
   d) approximately 15 percent of the U.S. population.
   e) more than 20 percent of the U.S. population.

8. Which of the following statements best describes the history of income inequality in the United States?
   a) The top 1 percent has never earned more than 10 percent of the nation's annual income.
   b) The top 1 percent has never earned less than 10 percent of the nation's annual income.
   c) Income inequality has remained fairly constant since the late 1970s.
   d) Income inequality has increased considerably since the late 1970s.
   e) Income inequality has decreased considerably since the late 1970s.

American Political Culture

Analyze whether the U.S. system of government upholds American political values (pp. 22–29)

Most Americans express strong support for liberty, equality, and democracy. Agreement on these basic values does not mean, however, that political debate in the United States is without conflict. Questions about how to apply and balance the different elements of American political culture have motivated disagreements throughout the country's history.

Key Terms

political culture (p. 23)
liberty (p. 23)
limited government (p. 23)
laissez-faire capitalism (p. 24)
equality of opportunity (p. 25)
political equality (p. 25)
popular sovereignty (p. 28)
majority rule, minority rights (p. 28)

Practice Quiz

9. "Life, Liberty and the pursuit of Happiness" are the three inalienable rights mentioned in
   a) the Constitution.
   b) the Declaration of Independence.
   c) the Bill of Rights.
   d) the Articles of Confederation.
   e) the Pledge of Allegiance.

10. Which of the following is *not* related to the American conception of liberty?
    a) freedom of speech
    b) economic freedom
    c) freedom of religion
    d) freedom of assembly
    e) All of the above are related to the American conception of liberty.

11. The principle of political equality can be best summed up as
    a) "equality of results."
    b) "equality of opportunity."
    c) "one person, one vote."
    d) "equality between the sexes."
    e) "leave everyone alone."

12. Which of the following is *not* part of American political culture?
    a) belief in equality of results
    b) belief in democracy
    c) belief in personal freedom
    d) belief in economic freedom
    e) belief in equality of opportunity

13. Which of the following restrictions on voting have been repealed over the last 200 years in the United States?
    a) property, gender, and race
    b) gender only
    c) race only
    d) property only
    e) race and gender only

What Americans Think about Government

Explore Americans' attitudes toward government (pp. 29–33)

While Americans have always been hesitant about granting government too much power, they have frequently relied on it during times of national crisis and have become increasingly dependent on it to provide important services. Over the last few decades, Americans' trust in government has declined significantly. Low levels of trust and efficacy may threaten American democracy by weakening the government and reducing the public's willingness to participate in political life.

Practice Quiz

14. What does it mean to say that Americans are "abstract conservatives" and "operational liberals"?
    a) The majority of Americans have no opinions about government in general or about the specific programs government implements.
    b) The majority of Americans prefer large government in the abstract and are very supportive of most specific government programs.
    c) The majority of Americans prefer large government in the abstract but are very opposed to most specific government programs.
    d) The majority of Americans prefer small government in the abstract but are very supportive most specific government programs.
    e) The majority of Americans prefer small government in the abstract and are very opposed to most specific government programs.

15. Americans' trust in their government
    a) rose significantly between 1964 and 1980.
    b) increased immediately following September 11, 2001, but declined shortly thereafter.
    c) declined immediately after the September 11 attacks but has risen dramatically since 2004.
    d) reached its highest point ever in the fall of 2011.
    e) has remained the same over the last 50 years.

For Further Reading

Dahl, Robert. *How Democratic Is the American Constitution?* New Haven, CT: Yale University Press, 2002.

Dalton, Russell. *The Good Citizen: How a Younger Generation Is Reshaping American Politics*, 2nd ed. Washington, DC: CQ Press, 2015.

Delli Carpini, Michael X., and Scott Keeter. *What Americans Know about Politics and Why It Matters*. New Haven, CT: Yale University Press, 1996.

Fischer, Claude S., and Michael Hout. *A Century of Difference: How America Changed in the Last One Hundred Years*. New York: Russell Sage Foundation, 2006.

Hetherington, Marc J., and Thomas J. Rudolph. *Why Washington Won't Work: Polarization, Political Trust, and the Governing Crisis*. Chicago: University of Chicago Press, 2015.

Hibbing, John R., and Elizabeth Theiss-Morse. *Stealth Democracy: Americans' Belief about How Government Should Work*. New York: Cambridge University Press, 2002.

Hochschild, Jennifer L. *Facing Up to the American Dream: Race, Class, and the Soul of the Nation*. Princeton, NJ: Princeton University Press, 1995.

Huntington, Samuel. *Who Are We? The Challenges to America's National Identity*. New York: Simon & Schuster, 2004.

Lasswell, Harold. *Politics: Who Gets What, When, How*. New York: Meridian Books, 1958.

McCarty, Nolan, Keith T. Poole, and Howard Rosenthal. *Polarized America: The Dance of Ideology and Unequal Riches*. Cambridge, MA: MIT Press, 2008.

Mettler, Suzanne. *The Submerged State: How Invisible Government Policies Undermine American Democracy*. Chicago: University of Chicago Press, 2011.

Page, Benjamin I., and Lawrence R. Jacobs. *Class War? What Americans Really Think about Economic Inequality*. Chicago: University of Chicago Press, 2009.

Putnam, Robert. *Making Democracy Work: Civic Traditions in Modern Italy*. Princeton, NJ: Princeton University Press, 1993.

Tocqueville, Alexis de. *Democracy in America*. Translated by Phillips Bradley. New York: Knopf, Vintage Books, 1945. First published 1835.

Winters, Jeffrey A. *Oligarchy*. New York: Cambridge University Press, 2011.

Recommended Websites

American Democracy Project
www.aascu.org/programs/adp
> This is an effort by the American Association of State Colleges and Universities to increase political engagement among college students. See what opportunities are available for you to become politically active.

Americans for Informed Democracy
www.aidemocracy.org
> A nonpartisan organization that promotes democracy and seeks to build a new generation of globally conscious leaders. Find out how you can be politically active and coordinate a town hall meeting on campus, attend a leadership retreat, or publish your opinions on democracy.

DiversityInc
http://diversityinc.com
> This site is dedicated to the promotion of American diversity and education. Here you can read about the issues that directly affect American minorities.

Future of Freedom Foundation
www.fff.org
> This organization promotes individual liberty, free markets, private property, and limited government. Find out how some people are trying to protect freedom in the United States.

Mobilize.org
http://mobilize.org
> This all-partisan network is dedicated to educating, empowering, and energizing young people. Find out how politics affects America's youth and what they are doing about it by being engaged and active.

Pew Research Center, U.S. Politics and Policy
www.people-press.org
> A nonpartisan "fact tank" that provides public opinion data about a wide range of topics related to American government and society. This site covers current issues as well as provides analyses of change over time in American politics and demographics.

The Youth Participatory Politics Research Network
http://ypp.dmlcentral.net
> A network of researchers and writers supported by the MacArthur Foundation. The network conducts studies of youth participation and contains short videos, blogs, and links to other resources about youth participation. The website provides many resources for understanding the impact of digital media on youth engagement in politics.

U.S. Census Bureau
www.census.gov
> The website for the Census Bureau offers a statistical look at our country's population and economy. Check out some of the statistics to get a better idea of American diversity.

The Founding and the Constitution

WHAT GOVERNMENT DOES AND WHY IT MATTERS Often we are barely aware of the many ways the U.S. Constitution shapes Americans' lives every day, but at some moments, its features leap dramatically into view, highlighting the framers' views about the nature of government. One of their worries was the concentration of government powers and the possible infringement of individual liberties. One solution was to divide the executive, legislative, and judicial powers of government across different institutions with separate powers, each checking the other. Governmental power was further divided across the levels of government in the federal system, between the national and state governments.

Sometimes, this constitutional system and its effect on average Americans come vividly to life.

Jim Obergefell was a real estate agent and IT consultant in Cincinnati, Ohio, in 1992 when he met and fell in love with John Arthur.[1] Although their relationship would last for decades, they were unable to marry. In 1996, Congress passed and President Bill Clinton signed the Defense of Marriage Act (DOMA), a federal law defining marriage as between one man and one woman. States could still permit same-sex marriage, but the marriages would not be recognized for federal purposes such as filing taxes or earning Social Security survivor benefits. The law also permitted states to refuse to recognize same-sex marriages

From America's founding to today, debates over the role of the government in citizens' lives have persisted. After the historic decision to rule same-sex marriage a right guaranteed by the Constitution, Jim Obergefell holds a photo of his late husband on the steps of the Supreme Court to celebrate his bittersweet victory.

performed in other states. Then the state of Ohio enacted its own DOMA in 2004, which prohibited same-sex marriage and refused to recognize those performed elsewhere.

Thus Obergefell and Arthur were unable to marry due to the actions of two branches of the federal government—the executive and legislative—and their state. The issue became more acute when Arthur was diagnosed with ALS, or Lou Gehrig's disease— a progressive debilitating disease. Obergefell served as Arthur's primary caregiver, and the couple traveled to Maryland in 2013 and wed on the airport tarmac. Then they filed a lawsuit with the state of Ohio for Obergefell to be recognized as the surviving spouse

on Arthur's imminent death certificate. "We decided to stand up for our marriage and to no longer accept being treated as second-class citizens."[2] Arthur passed away three months later.

The case made it to the Supreme Court, the top of the judicial branch of government. In 2015 the high court ruled in *Obergefell v. Hodges* that the fundamental right to marry is guaranteed to same-sex couples by the due process and equal protection clauses of the Fourteenth Amendment to the U.S. Constitution. The ruling secured a right to marry on the same terms and conditions as opposite-sex couples nationwide.[3] Thus the Court secured a civil right that the executive and legislative branches and a number of states had denied. Obergefell said, "Some have called me a hero; I'm not comfortable with that term, and I doubt I ever will be. But I can now accept it from others because I see what this fight means to them."[4]

The U.S. Constitution lays out the purpose of government: to promote justice, to maintain peace at home, to defend the nation from foreign foes, to provide for the welfare of the citizenry, and, above all, to secure the "blessings of liberty" for Americans. It also spells out a plan for achieving these objectives, including provisions for the exercise of legislative, executive, and judicial powers and a recipe for the division of powers among the federal government's branches and between the national and state governments. Jim Obergefell's quest to marry the love of his life intersected with all three branches and both levels of government.

His story also shows that although many Americans believe strongly in the long-standing values of liberty, equality, and democracy, how those values are defined and implemented by the political institutions that the Constitution created are a source of considerable controversy. The framers believed that a good constitution created a government with the capacity to act forcefully. But they also believed that government should be compelled to take a variety of interests and viewpoints into account when it formulates policies. Sometimes the deliberation and compromise encouraged by the constitutional arrangements of "separated institutions sharing powers" can result in policymaking that is slow or even gridlocked.[5] Public policy is always a product of political bargaining. But so was the Constitution itself. As this chapter will show, the Constitution reflects high principle as well as political self-interest and defines the relationship between American citizens and their government.

CHAPTER GOALS

★ Describe the events that led to the Declaration of Independence and the Articles of Confederation (pp. 43–46)

★ Analyze the reasons many Americans thought a new Constitution was needed, and assess the obstacles to a new Constitution (pp. 47–53)

★ Explain how the Constitution attempted to improve America's governance, and outline the major institutions established by the Constitution (pp. 53–60)

★ Present the controversies involved in the struggle for ratification (pp. 60–65)

★ Trace how the Constitution has changed over time through the amendment process (pp. 65–69)

The First Founding: Interests and Conflicts

> **Describe the events that led to the Declaration of Independence and the Articles of Confederation**

Competing ideals and principles often reflect competing interests, and so it was in Revolutionary America. The American Revolution and the American Constitution were outgrowths and expressions of a struggle among economic and political forces within the colonies. Five sectors of society had interests that were important in colonial politics: (1) New England merchants; (2) southern planters; (3) "royalists"—holders of royal lands, offices, and patents (licenses to engage in a profession or business activity); (4) shopkeepers, artisans, and laborers; and (5) small farmers. Throughout the eighteenth century, these groups were in conflict over issues of taxation, trade, and commerce. For the most part, however, the southern planters, the New England merchants, and the royal office and patent holders—groups that together made up the colonial elite—were able to maintain a political alliance that held in check the more radical forces representing shopkeepers, laborers, and small farmers. After 1760, however, by seriously threatening the interests of New England merchants and southern planters, British tax and trade policies split the colonial elite, permitting radical forces to expand their political influence and seting in motion a chain of events that culminated in the American Revolution.[6]

BRITISH TAXES AND COLONIAL INTERESTS

During the first half of the eighteenth century, Britain ruled its American colonies with a light hand. Evidence of British rule was hardly to be found outside the largest towns, and the enterprising colonists had found ways of evading most of the taxes levied by the distant British regime. Beginning in the 1760s, however, the debts and other financial problems confronting the British government forced it to search for new revenue sources. This search rather quickly led to the Crown's North American colonies, which, on the whole, paid remarkably little in taxes to their parent country. The British government reasoned that a sizable fraction of its debt was, in fact, attributable to the expenses it had incurred in defense of the colonies during the French and Indian War, which ended in 1763, driving France from North America. The British also considered the cost of the continuing protection that British forces were giving the colonists from Indian attacks and that the British navy was providing for colonial shipping. Thus, during the 1760s, Britain sought to impose new, though relatively modest, taxes on the colonists.

Like most governments of the period, the British regime had limited ways in which to collect revenues. The income tax, which in the twentieth century became the single most important source of governmental revenues, had not yet been developed. In the mid-eighteenth century, governments relied mainly on tariffs, duties, and other

British colonists in America shipped many goods back to England, such as furs obtained by trading with Native Americans. The British government claimed that the colonists should pay more in taxes in light of the protection their shipments received from the British navy and the expenses Britain incurred defending the colonies.

taxes on commerce; and it was to such taxes, and to the Stamp Act, that the British turned during the 1760s.

The Stamp Act, and other taxes on commerce such as the Sugar Act of 1764, which taxed sugar, molasses, and other commodities, most heavily affected the two groups in colonial society whose commercial interests and activities were most extensive—the New England merchants and the southern planters. United under the famous slogan "No taxation without representation," the merchants and planters sought to organize opposition to these new taxes. In the course of the struggle against British tax measures, the planters and merchants broke with their royalist allies and turned to their former adversaries—the shopkeepers, small farmers, laborers, and artisans—for help. With the assistance of these groups, the merchants and planters organized demonstrations and a boycott of British goods that ultimately forced the Crown to rescind most of its hated new taxes.

From the perspective of the merchants and planters, this was a victorious conclusion to their struggle with the mother country. In contrast to the shopkeepers, small farmers, laborers, and artisans whom they had helped mobilize initially, merchants and planters were now anxious to end the unrest they had helped arouse; and they supported the British government's efforts to restore order. Indeed, most respectable Bostonians supported the actions of the British soldiers involved in the Boston Massacre—the 1770 killing of five colonists by British soldiers who were attempting to repel an angry mob gathered outside the Town House, the seat of the colonial government. In their subsequent trial, the soldiers were defended by John Adams, a pillar of Boston society and a future president of the United States. Adams asserted that the soldiers' actions were entirely justified, provoked by "a motley rabble of saucy boys, negroes and mulattoes, Irish teagues and outlandish Jack tars." All but two of the soldiers were acquitted.[7]

Despite the efforts of the British government and the elite members of colonial society, it proved difficult to bring an end to the political strife. The more radical forces continued to agitate for political and social change. These radicals, whose leaders included Samuel Adams, a cousin of John Adams, asserted that British power supported an unjust political and social structure within the colonies and began to advocate an end to British rule.[8]

POLITICAL STRIFE AND THE RADICALIZATION OF THE COLONISTS

The political strife within the colonies was the background for the events of 1773–74. In 1773 the British government granted the politically powerful East India Company a monopoly on the export of tea from Britain, eliminating a lucrative form of trade for colonial merchants. To add to the injury, the East India Company sought to sell the tea directly in the colonies instead of working through the colonial merchants. Tea was an extremely important commodity during the 1770s, and these British actions posed a serious threat to the New England merchants. Together with their southern allies, the merchants once again called on their radical adversaries for support. The most dramatic result was the Boston Tea Party. In three other colonies, antitax Americans succeeded in blocking the unloading of taxed tea, which then had to be returned to Britain. The royal governor of Massachusetts, however, refused to allow three shiploads of unsold tea to leave Boston Harbor. Anti-British radicals seized this opportunity: on the night of December 16, 1773, a group led by Samuel Adams, some of them hastily "disguised" as Mohawk Indians, boarded the three vessels and threw the entire cargo of 342 chests of tea into the harbor.

The British helped radicalize colonists through bad policy decisions in the years before the Revolution. For example, Britain gave the ailing East India Company a monopoly on the tea trade in the American colonies. Colonists feared that the monopoly would hurt colonial merchants' business and protested by throwing East India Company tea into Boston Harbor in 1773.

This event was of decisive importance in American history. The merchants had hoped to force the British government to rescind the Tea Act, but they did not support any further demands and did not seek independence from Britain. Samuel Adams and the other radicals, however, did hope to provoke the British government to take actions that would alienate its colonial supporters and pave the way for a rebellion. This was precisely the purpose of the Boston Tea Party, and it succeeded. By dumping the East India Company's tea into Boston Harbor, Adams and his followers goaded the British into enacting a number of harsh reprisals, including closing the port of Boston to commerce, changing the provincial government of Massachusetts, providing for the removal of accused persons to Britain for trial, and, most important, restricting movement to the West—further alienating the southern planters, who depended on access to new western lands. These acts of retaliation confirmed the worst criticisms of British rule and helped radicalize Americans. Radicals such as Samuel Adams had been agitating for more violent measures against the British for some time, but ultimately they needed Britain's political repression to create widespread support for independence.

Thus, the Boston Tea Party set in motion a cycle of provocation and retaliation that in 1774 resulted in the convening of the First Continental Congress—an assembly of delegates from all parts of the country—that called for a total boycott of British goods and, under the prodding of the radicals, began to consider the possibility of independence from British rule. The eventual result was the Declaration of Independence.

THE DECLARATION OF INDEPENDENCE

In 1776, more than a year after open warfare had commenced in Massachusetts, the Second Continental Congress appointed a committee consisting of Thomas Jefferson of Virginia, Benjamin Franklin of Pennsylvania, Roger Sherman of Connecticut, John Adams of Massachusetts, and Robert Livingston of New York to draft a statement of American independence from British rule. The Declaration

FOR CRITICAL ANALYSIS

Conflicts over taxes did not end with the American Revolution. Why is tax policy almost always controversial? What differences and similarities are there between the debates over taxes in the 1760s and today?

The Declaration of Independence held that government could not curtail certain rights and helped to inspire national unity. Every year, Americans celebrate the signing of the Declaration on the Fourth of July.

Articles of Confederation America's first written constitution; served as the basis for America's national government until 1789

confederation a system of government in which states retain sovereign authority except for the powers expressly delegated to the national government

of Independence, written by Jefferson and adopted by the Second Continental Congress, was an extraordinary document both philosophically and politically. Philosophically, the Declaration was remarkable for its assertion that certain rights—the "unalienable rights" that include life, liberty, and the pursuit of happiness—could not be abridged by governments. In the world of 1776, in which some kings still claimed to rule by divine right, this was a dramatic statement. This philosophical view was heavily influenced by the works of the philosopher John Locke, one of England's foremost liberal theorists of the seventeenth century. In his treatises on government, widely read by educated colonists, Locke asserted that all individuals were equal and possessed a natural right to defend their own lives, liberties, and possessions. Individuals created governments to help them protect these rights, and if a government failed in its duties, the citizenry had the right to alter or abolish it. Politically, the Declaration was remarkable because, despite the differences of interest that divided the colonists along economic, regional, and philosophical lines, it focused on grievances, aspirations, and principles that might unify the various colonial groups. The Declaration was an attempt to identify and articulate a history and set of principles that might help forge national unity.[9]

THE ARTICLES OF CONFEDERATION

Having declared their independence, the colonies needed to establish a governmental structure. In November 1777 the Continental Congress adopted the **Articles of Confederation**—the United States' first written constitution. Although it was not ratified by all the states until 1781, it was the country's operative constitution until the final months of 1788.

The first goal of the Articles was to limit the powers of the central government. The relationship between the national government and the states was called a **confederation**; as provided under Article II, "each state retains its sovereignty, freedom, and independence." The central government was given no president or any other presiding officer. The entire national government was vested in a Congress, with execution of its few laws to be left to the individual states. And the Articles gave Congress very little power. Its members were not much more than delegates or messengers from the state legislatures: their salaries were paid out of the state treasuries; they were subject to immediate recall by state authorities; and each state, regardless of its size, had only one vote. All 13 states had to agree to any amendments to the Articles of Confederation after it was ratified.

Under the Articles of Confederation, Congress was given the power to declare war and make peace, to make treaties and alliances, to coin or borrow money, and to regulate trade with the Native Americans. It could also appoint the senior officers of the U.S. Army, but the national government had no army for those officers to command because the nation's armed forces were composed of the state militias. Moreover, the central government could not prevent one state from discriminating against other states in the competition for foreign commerce. These extreme limits on the power of the national government made the Articles of Confederation hopelessly impractical.[10]

The Second Founding: From Compromise to Constitution

> **Analyze the reasons many Americans thought a new Constitution was needed, and assess the obstacles to a new Constitution**

The Declaration of Independence and the Articles of Confederation were not sufficient to hold the new nation together as an independent and effective nation-state. A series of developments following the armistice with the British in 1783 highlighted the shortcomings of the Articles of Confederation.

First, many of the new country's leaders worried that the Articles of Confederation would not allow the United States to conduct its foreign affairs successfully, as the federal government was unable to enforce existing treaties and there was no national military. Furthermore, competition among the states for foreign commerce allowed the European powers to play the states off one another, which created confusion on both sides of the Atlantic. At one point during the winter of 1786–87, John Adams of Massachusetts, a leader in the independence struggle, was sent to negotiate a new treaty with the British, one that would cover disputes left over from the war. The British government responded that since the United States under the Articles of Confederation was unable to enforce existing treaties, it would negotiate with each of the 13 states separately. At the same time, the United States faced a threat from Spain, which still held vast territories in North and South America. Without a national military, the nation's borders were difficult to protect against this potentially hostile foreign power.

Second, the Articles of Confederation allowed for only a weak federal government, with state governments retaining most of the powers of government. This situation became alarming to well-to-do Americans, in particular New England merchants and southern planters, when "radical" forces began to exert considerable influence in a number of state governments. As a result of the Revolution, one key segment of the colonial elite—the royal land, office, and patent holders—was stripped of its economic and political privileges. And although the prerevolutionary elite was weakened, the prerevolutionary radicals were better organized than ever and now controlled such states as Pennsylvania and Rhode Island, where they pursued economic and political policies that struck terror in the hearts of the prerevolutionary political establishment. In Rhode Island, for example, between 1783 and 1785, a legislature dominated by representatives of small farmers, artisans, and shopkeepers had instituted economic policies, including drastic currency inflation, that frightened business and property owners throughout the country. Of course, the central government under the Articles of Confederation was powerless to intervene. Similarly, the Pennsylvania government engaged in land redistribution, to the chagrin of property owners.

However, the Articles of Confederation were by no means a complete failure. The Congress of the Confederation agreed upon two laws that helped to shape American history. These were the Land Ordinance of 1785 and the Northwest Ordinance of 1787. The Land Ordinance established the principles of land surveying and landownership that governed America's westward expansion. Under the Northwest Ordinance, the individual states agreed to surrender their western land claims, which opened the way for the admission of new states to the Union.

These legislative successes were not adequate to sustain the fledgling federal government, however. During the 1780s, the political and economic position of the new American states deteriorated. Europe's great powers—Britain, France, and Spain—hurt colonial commerce by adopting policies that excluded American trade. At the same time, political unrest within the 13 new states further undermined trade and investment. Something had to be done.

THE ANNAPOLIS CONVENTION

The continuation of international weakness and domestic economic turmoil led many Americans to consider whether their newly adopted form of government might not already require revision. In the fall of 1786, many state leaders accepted an invitation from the Virginia legislature for a conference of representatives of all the states, to be held in Annapolis, Maryland. Delegates from only five states actually attended, so nothing substantive could be accomplished. Still, this conference was the first step toward what is now known as the second founding. The one positive result that came out of the Annapolis Convention was a carefully worded resolution calling on the Congress to send commissioners to Philadelphia at a later time "to devise such further provisions as shall appear to them necessary to render the Constitution of the Federal Government adequate to the exigencies of the Union."[11] But the resolution did not necessarily imply any desire to do more than improve and reform the Articles of Confederation.

SHAYS'S REBELLION

It is quite possible that the Constitutional Convention of 1787 in Philadelphia would never have taken place at all except for a single event that occurred during the winter following the Annapolis Convention: Shays's Rebellion.

Daniel Shays, a former army captain, led a mob of farmers in a rebellion against the government of Massachusetts. The purpose of the rebellion was to prevent foreclosures on their debt-ridden land by keeping the county courts of western Massachusetts from sitting until after the next election. A militia force organized by the Governor of Massachusetts and privately funded by a group of prominent merchants dispersed the mob, but for several days in February 1787, Shays and his followers terrified the state government by attempting to capture the federal arsenal at Springfield, provoking an appeal to the Congress to help restore order. Within a few days, the state government regained control and captured 14 of the rebels. Later that year, a newly elected Massachusetts legislature granted some of the farmers' demands.

The effects of the incident lingered and spread. George Washington summed it up: "I am mortified beyond expression that in the moment of our acknowledged independence we should by our conduct verify the predictions of our transatlantic foe, and render ourselves ridiculous and contemptible in the eyes of all Europe."[12]

The Congress under the Confederation had been unable to act decisively in a time of crisis. This provided critics of the Articles of Confederation with precisely the evidence they needed to push the Annapolis resolution through the Congress. Thus, the states were asked to send representatives to Philadelphia to discuss constitutional revision. Seventy-four delegates were chosen. Of these, 55 would actually attend the

Daniel Shays's rebellion proved the Articles of Confederation were too weak to protect the fledgling nation.

convention, representing every state except Rhode Island, and 39 would eventually sign the newly drafted Constitution.

THE CONSTITUTIONAL CONVENTION

The delegates who convened in Philadelphia in May 1787 had political strife, international embarrassment, national weakness, and local rebellion fixed in their minds. Recognizing that these issues were symptoms of fundamental flaws in the Articles of Confederation, the delegates soon abandoned the plan to revise the Articles and committed themselves to a second founding—a second, and ultimately successful, attempt to create a legitimate and effective national system of government. This effort would occupy the convention for the next five months.

A Marriage of Interest and Principle For years, scholars have disagreed about the motives of the Founders in Philadelphia. Among the most controversial views of the framers' motives is the "economic interpretation" put forward by the historian Charles Beard and his disciples.[13] According to Beard's account, America's Founders were a collection of securities speculators and property owners whose only aim was personal enrichment. From this perspective, the Constitution's lofty principles were little more than sophisticated masks behind which the most venal interests sought to enrich themselves.

Of course, the opposite view is that the framers of the Constitution *were* concerned with philosophical and ethical principles—that, indeed, they sought to devise a system of government consistent with the dominant philosophical and moral principles of the day. But in fact these two views belong together: the Founders' interests were reinforced by their principles. The convention that drafted the American Constitution was chiefly organized by the New England merchants and southern planters. Although the delegates representing these groups did not all hope to profit personally from an increase in the value of their securities, as Beard would

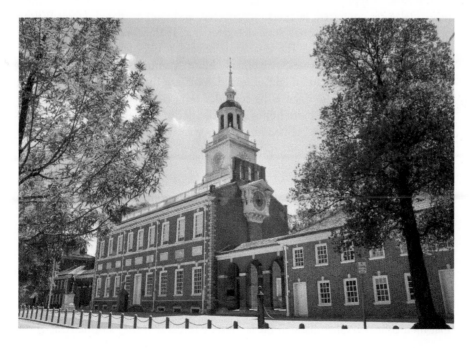

The Constitutional Convention took place from May to September 1787 at Independence Hall in Philadelphia, where the Declaration of Independence had been signed 11 years prior. In order to keep their deliberations secret, the delegates voted to keep the hall's windows shut throughout the hot summer.

have it, they did hope to benefit in the broadest political and economic sense by breaking the power of their radical foes and establishing a system of government more compatible with their long-term economic and political interests. Thus, the framers sought to create a new government capable of promoting commerce and protecting property from radical state legislatures and populist forces hostile to the interests of the commercial and propertied classes.

The Great Compromise The proponents of a new government fired their opening shot on May 29, 1787, when Edmund Randolph of Virginia offered a resolution that proposed corrections and enlargements in the Articles of Confederation. The proposal, which showed the strong influence of James Madison, was not a simple motion. Rather, it provided for virtually every aspect of a new government.

Virginia Plan a framework for the Constitution, introduced by Edmund Randolph, that called for representation in the national legislature based on the population of each state

The portion of Randolph's motion that became most controversial was called the **Virginia Plan**. This plan provided for a system of representation in the national legislature based on the population of each state or the proportion of each state's revenue contribution to the national government, or both. (Randolph also proposed a second chamber of the legislature, to be elected by the members of the first chamber.) Since the states varied enormously in size and wealth, the Virginia Plan was thought to be heavily biased in favor of the large states.

New Jersey Plan a framework for the Constitution, introduced by William Paterson, that called for equal state representation in the national legislature regardless of population

While the convention was debating the Virginia Plan, opposition to it began to mount as more delegates arrived in Philadelphia. William Paterson of New Jersey introduced a resolution known as the **New Jersey Plan**. Its main proponents were delegates from the less populous states, including Delaware, New Jersey, Connecticut, and New York, who asserted that the more populous states—Virginia, Pennsylvania, North Carolina, Massachusetts, and Georgia—would dominate the new government if representation were to be determined by population. The smaller states argued that each state should be equally represented in the new regime regardless of the state's population.

The issue of representation threatened to wreck the entire constitutional enterprise. Delegates conferred, factions maneuvered, and tempers flared. James Wilson of Pennsylvania told the small-state delegates that if they wanted to disrupt the union, they should go ahead. The separation, he said, could "never happen on better grounds." Small-state delegates were equally blunt. Gunning Bedford of Delaware declared that the small states might, if forced, look elsewhere for friends. "The large states," he said, "dare not dissolve the confederation. If they do the small ones will find some foreign ally of more honor and good faith, who will take them by the hand and do them justice." These sentiments were widely shared. The union, as Luther Martin of Maryland put it, was "on the verge of dissolution, scarcely held together by the strength of a hair."[14]

Great Compromise the agreement reached at the Constitutional Convention of 1787 that gave each state an equal number of senators regardless of its population but linked representation in the House of Representatives to population

The outcome of this debate was the Connecticut Compromise, also known as the **Great Compromise**. Under the terms of this compromise, in the first chamber of Congress—the House of Representatives—the representatives would be apportioned according to the population in each state. This, of course, was what delegates from the large states had sought. But in the second branch—the Senate—each state would have equal representation regardless of its size; this provision addressed the concerns of small states. This compromise was not immediately satisfactory to all the delegates. Indeed, two of the most vocal members of the small-state faction, John Lansing and Robert Yates of New York, were so angered by the concession that their colleagues had made to the large-state forces that they stormed out of the

Who Benefits from the Great Compromise?

The Great Compromise attempted to balance power between large and small states in the new Congress. The figure shows the difference in representation for states in the House and Senate in the first Congress (1789–91). In the Senate each state has equal representation, which in the first Congress meant each had 1/13 of all seats. In the House the number of seats apportioned to each state is based on population; thus, the larger states have more representation.

Representation in the First Congress

House of Representatives seat

Senate seat

State Populations, 1790*

1.	Virginia	747,610
2.	Pennsylvania	433,373
3.	North Carolina	393,751
4.	Massachusetts	378,787
5.	New York	340,120
6.	Maryland	319,728
7.	South Carolina	249,073
8.	Connecticut	237,946
9.	New Jersey	184,139
10.	New Hampshire	141,885
11.	Georgia	82,548
12.	Rhode Island	68,825
13.	Delaware	59,096

* These numbers represent the total number of persons in each state according to the 1790 census (including free white males, free white females, "all other free persons," and slaves). For the purpose of representation in the first Congress, the framers calculated the number of representatives per state in 1787 based on population estimates, which counted each slave as three-fifths of a person. This calculation is why the representation in the first Congress does not match perfectly with the total population counts reported here.

SOURCE: U.S. Census Bureau, www.census.gov (accessed 8/16/12); U.S. House of Representatives, www.history.house.gov/Institution/Apportionment/Apportionment (accessed 4/11/14).

FOR CRITICAL ANALYSIS

1. At the Constitutional Convention, large states supported the Virginia Plan, which would have made the whole Congress look like the House. Small states supported the New Jersey Plan, which would have made the whole Congress look like the Senate. How would each group have benefited from its favored plans?

2. What are the advantages of equal representation by states? What are the drawbacks? In your opinion, do the advantages outweigh the disadvantages?

convention. In the end, however, most of the delegates preferred compromise to the breakup of the Union, and the plan was accepted.

The Question of Slavery: The Three-Fifths Compromise Many of the conflicts that emerged during the Constitutional Convention were reflections of the fundamental differences between the slave and the nonslave states—differences that pitted the southern planters against the New England merchants and would almost destroy the Republic in later years. Even in the midst of debate over large versus small states, James Madison observed that "the great danger" lay in the opposition of "southern and northern interests."[15] More than 90 percent of the country's slaves resided in five states—Georgia, Maryland, North Carolina, South Carolina, and Virginia— where they accounted for 30 percent of the total population. In some places, slaves outnumbered nonslaves by as many as 10 to 1. Were they to be counted in as part of a state's population even though they had no rights, thereby giving slave states increased representation in the House? If the Constitution were to embody any principle of national supremacy, some basic decisions would have to be made about the place of slavery in the general scheme. Madison hit on this point on several occasions as different aspects of the Constitution were being discussed. For example, he observed,

> It seemed now to be pretty well understood that the real difference of interests lay, not between the large and small but between the northern and southern states. The institution of slavery and its consequences formed the line of discrimination. There were five states on the South, eight on the northern side of this line. Should a proportional representation take place it was true, the northern side would still outnumber the other: but not in the same degree, at this time; and every day would tend towards an equilibrium.[16]

Whatever they thought of the institution of slavery, most delegates from the northern states opposed counting slaves in the distribution of congressional seats. James

Despite the Founders' emphasis on liberty, the new Constitution allowed slavery, counting three-fifths of all slaves in apportioning seats in the House of Representatives. In this 1792 painting, *Liberty Displaying the Arts and Sciences*, the books, instruments, and classical columns at the left contrast with the kneeling slaves at the right—illustrating the divide between America's rhetoric of liberty and equality and the reality of slavery.

Wilson of Pennsylvania, for example, argued that if slaves were citizens, they should be treated and counted like other citizens. If, on the other hand, they were property, then why should not other forms of property be counted toward the apportionment of representatives? But southern delegates made it clear that they would never agree to the new government if the northerners refused to give in; William R. Davie of North Carolina, for example, heatedly asserted that the people of North Carolina would never enter the Union if slaves were not counted as part of the basis for representation. Without such agreement, he asserted ominously, "the business was at an end."

Northerners and southerners eventually reached agreement through the **Three-Fifths Compromise**. The seats in the House of Representatives would be apportioned according to a "population" in which only three-fifths of slaves would be counted. The slaves would not be allowed to vote, of course, but the number of representatives would be apportioned accordingly.

The issue of slavery was the most difficult one faced by the framers, and it nearly destroyed the Union. Although some delegates believed slavery to be morally wrong, an evil and oppressive institution that made a mockery of the ideals and values espoused in the Constitution, morality was not the issue that caused the framers to support or oppose the Three-Fifths Compromise. Indeed, northerners even agreed to permit a continuation of the odious slave trade in order to keep the South in the Union. But in due course, the disparate interests of the North and the South could no longer be reconciled, and a bloody civil war was the result.

Three-Fifths Compromise the agreement reached at the Constitutional Convention of 1787 that stipulated that for purposes of the apportionment of congressional seats only three-fifths of slaves would be counted

The Constitution

> **Explain how the Constitution attempted to improve America's governance, and outline the major institutions established by the Constitution**

The political significance of the Great Compromise and the Three-Fifths Compromise was to reinforce the unity of the mercantile and planter forces that sought to create a new government. The Great Compromise reassured those in both groups who feared that a new governmental framework would reduce the importance of their own local or regional influence. The Three-Fifths Compromise temporarily defused the rivalry between the merchants and planters. Their unity secured, members of the alliance supporting the establishment of a new government moved to fashion a constitutional framework consistent with their economic and political interests.

In particular, the framers sought a new government that, first, would be strong enough to promote commerce and protect property from radical state legislatures such as Rhode Island's. This became the constitutional basis for national control over commerce and finance and for the establishment of national judicial supremacy and the effort to construct a strong presidency. (See Table 2.1 for a comparison of the Articles of Confederation to the Constitution.)

Second, the framers sought to prevent what they saw as the threat posed by the "excessive democracy" of the state and national governments under the Articles of Confederation. This led to such constitutional principles as a **bicameral** legislature, **checks and balances**, staggered terms in office, and indirect election (selection of the president by an electoral college rather than directly by voters and election of senators by state legislatures).

bicameral having a legislative assembly composed of two chambers or houses; distinguished from *unicameral*

checks and balances mechanisms through which each branch of government is able to participate in and influence the activities of the other branches; major examples include the presidential veto power over congressional legislation, the power of the Senate to approve presidential appointments, and judicial review of congressional enactments

Bill of Rights the first 10 amendments to the U.S. Constitution, ratified in 1791; they ensure certain rights and liberties to the people

separation of powers the division of governmental power among several institutions that must cooperate in decision making

federalism a system of government in which power is divided, by a constitution, between a central government and regional governments

Third, the framers, lacking the power to force the states or the public at large to accept the new form of government, sought to identify principles that would help secure support. This became the basis of the constitutional provision for direct popular election of representatives and, subsequently, for the addition of the **Bill of Rights** to the Constitution.

Finally, the framers wanted to be certain that the government they created did not pose an even greater threat to its citizens' liberties and property rights than did the radical state legislatures they feared and despised. To prevent the new government from abusing its power, the framers incorporated principles such as the **separation of powers** and **federalism** into the Constitution. In Table 2.1, we assess the major provisions of the Constitution's seven articles to see how each relates to these objectives.

If the Declaration of Independence drew its philosophical inspiration from John Locke, the Constitution drew upon the thought of the French political philosopher Baron de La Brède et de Montesquieu (1689–1755). In Montesquieu's view,

TABLE 2.1

Comparing the Articles of Confederation and the Constitution

MAJOR PROVISIONS	ARTICLES OF CONFEDERATION	CONSTITUTION
Executive branch	None	President of the United States
Judiciary	No federal court system. Judiciary exists only at state level.	Federal judiciary headed by Supreme Court
Legislature	Unicameral legislature with equal representation for each state. Delegates to the Congress of the Confederation were appointed by the states.	Bicameral legislature consisting of Senate and House of Representatives. Each state is represented by two senators, while apportionment in the House is based on each state's population. Senators are chosen by the state legislatures (changed to direct popular election in 1913) for six-year terms and members of the House by popular election for two-year terms.
Fiscal and economic powers	The national government is dependent upon the states to collect taxes. The states are free to coin their own money and print paper money. The states are free to sign commercial treaties with foreign governments.	Congress given the power to levy taxes, coin money, and regulate international and interstate commerce. States prohibited from coining money or entering into treaties with other nations.
Military	The national government is dependent upon state militias and cannot form an army during peacetime.	The national government is authorized to maintain an army and navy.
Legal supremacy	State constitutions and state law are supreme.	National Constitution and national law are supreme.
Constitutional amendment	Must be agreed upon by all states.	Must be agreed upon by three-fourths of the states.

the powers of government must be divided in order to prevent any one group or institution from exercising tyrannical control over the nation. Montesquieu recommended a tripartite division, placing the executive, legislative, and judicial powers in different governmental bodies. He claimed that such a tripartite division had worked very well in the Roman Republic and in Britain. The delegates to America's Constitutional Convention referred frequently to Montesquieu's writings in devising America's new governmental structure.

THE LEGISLATIVE BRANCH

In Article I, Sections 1–7, the Constitution provides for a Congress consisting of two chambers: a House of Representatives and a Senate. Members of the House of Representatives were given two-year terms in office and were to be elected directly by the people. Members of the Senate were to be appointed by the state legislatures (this was changed in 1913 by the Seventeenth Amendment, which instituted direct election of senators) for six-year terms. These terms were staggered so that the appointments of one-third of the senators would expire every two years. The Constitution assigned somewhat different tasks to the House and Senate. Though the approval of each body is required for the enactment of a law, the Senate alone is given the power to ratify treaties and approve presidential appointments. The House, on the other hand, is given the sole power to originate revenue bills.

The character of the legislative branch was related to the framers' major goals. The House of Representatives was designed to be directly responsible to the people in order to encourage popular consent for the new Constitution and to help enhance the power of the new government. At the same time, to guard against "excessive democracy," the power of the House of Representatives was checked by the Senate, whose members were to be appointed by the states for long terms rather than elected directly by the people. The purpose of this provision, according to Alexander Hamilton, was to avoid "an unqualified complaisance to every sudden breeze of passion, or to every transient impulse which the people may receive."[17] Staggered terms of service in the Senate, moreover, were intended to make that body even more resistant to popular pressure. Since only one-third of the senators would be selected at any given time, the composition of the institution would be protected from changes in popular preferences transmitted by the state legislatures. Thus, the structure of the legislative branch was designed to contribute to governmental power, to promote popular consent for the new government, and at the same time to place limits on the popular political currents that many of the framers saw as a radical threat to the economic and social order.

The issues of power and consent are important throughout the Constitution. Section 8 of Article I specifically lists the powers of Congress, which include the authority to collect taxes, borrow money, regulate commerce, declare war, and maintain an army and navy. By granting Congress these powers, the framers indicated very clearly that they intended the new government to be far more influential than its predecessor. At the same time, by defining the new government's most important powers as belonging to Congress, the framers sought to promote popular acceptance of this critical change by reassuring citizens that their views would be fully represented whenever the government exercised its new powers.

As a further guarantee to the people that the new government would pose no threat to them, the Constitution implies that any powers not listed were not

expressed powers specific powers granted by the Constitution to Congress (Article I, Section 8) and to the president (Article II)

elastic clause The concluding paragraph of Article I, Section 8, of the Constitution (also known as the "necessary and proper clause"), which provides Congress with the authority to make all laws "necessary and proper" to carry out its enumerated powers

granted at all. This is what Chief Justice John Marshall named the doctrine of **expressed powers**: the Constitution grants only those powers specifically expressed in its text. But the framers intended to create an active and powerful government, so they also included the necessary and proper clause, sometimes known as the **elastic clause**, which declares that Congress could write laws needed to carry out its expressed powers. This clause indicates that the expressed powers could be broadly interpreted and were meant to be a source of strength to the national government, not a limitation on it. In response to the charge that they intended to give the national government too much power, the framers included language in the Tenth Amendment stipulating that powers not specifically granted by the Constitution to the federal government were reserved to the states or to the people. As we will see in Chapter 3, the resulting tension between the elastic clause and the Tenth Amendment has been at the heart of constitutional struggles between federal and state powers.

THE EXECUTIVE BRANCH

The Articles of Confederation had not provided for an executive branch, and the framers viewed this omission as a source of weakness. Accordingly, the Constitution provides for the establishment of the presidency in Article II. As Alexander Hamilton commented, the presidential article aims toward "energy in the Executive."[18] It does so in an effort to overcome the natural tendency toward stalemate that was built into the bicameral legislature and into the separation of powers among the three branches. The Constitution affords the president a measure of independence from the people and from the other branches of government—particularly the Congress.

In line with the framers' goal of increased power to the national government, the president is granted the unconditional power to accept ambassadors from other countries—this amounts to the power to "recognize" other countries—as well as the power to negotiate treaties, although their acceptance requires the approval of the Senate by a two-thirds vote. The president is also given the unconditional right to grant reprieves and pardons, except in cases of impeachment, and the powers to appoint major departmental personnel, to convene Congress in special session, and to veto congressional enactments. The veto power is formidable, but it is not absolute since Congress can override it by a two-thirds vote, reflecting the framers' concern with checks and balances.

The framers hoped to create a presidency that would make the federal government rather than the states the agency capable of timely and decisive action to deal with public issues and problems—hence the "energy" that Hamilton hoped to impart to the executive branch. At the same time, however, the framers sought to help the presidency withstand excessively democratic pressures by creating a system of indirect rather than direct election through a separate electoral college.

THE JUDICIAL BRANCH

In establishing the judicial branch in Article III, the Constitution reflects the framers' preoccupations with nationalizing governmental power and checking radical democratic impulses while preventing the new national government itself from interfering with liberty and property.

Under the provisions of Article III, the framers created a court that was literally a supreme court of the United States and not merely the highest court of the national government alone. The most important expression of this intention is granting the Supreme Court the power to resolve any conflicts that might emerge between federal and state laws. In particular, the Supreme Court is given the right to determine whether a power is exclusive to the national government, concurrent with the states, or exclusive to the states. In addition, the Supreme Court is assigned jurisdiction over controversies between citizens of different states. The long-term significance of this provision was that as the country developed a national economy, it came to rely increasingly on the federal judiciary, rather than on the state courts, for the resolution of disputes.

Federal judges are given lifetime appointments to protect them from popular politics and from interference by the other branches. This, however, does not mean that the judiciary remains totally impartial to political considerations or to the other branches, for the president is to appoint the judges and the Senate to approve the appointments. Congress also has the power to create inferior (lower) courts, change the jurisdiction of the federal courts, add or subtract federal judges, and even change the size of the Supreme Court.

No explicit mention is made in the Constitution of **judicial review**—the power of the courts to render the final decision when there is a conflict of interpretation of the Constitution or of laws between the courts and Congress, the courts and the executive branch, or the courts and the states. The Supreme Court eventually assumed the power of judicial review. Its assumption of this power, as we shall see in Chapter 15, was based not on the Constitution itself but on the politics of later decades and the membership of the Court.

Article I of the Constitution establishes the structure of Congress and lists certain specific powers of Congress. The language of the Constitution reflects the framers' desire to create government that was powerful enough to be effective but not so powerful that it would threaten individual liberty.

judicial review the power of the courts to review and, if necessary, declare actions of the legislative and executive branches invalid or unconstitutional; the Supreme Court asserted this power in *Marbury v. Madison* (1803)

NATIONAL UNITY AND POWER

Various provisions in the Constitution addressed the framers' concern with national unity and power, including Article IV's provisions for comity (reciprocity) among states and among citizens of all states. Each state is prohibited from discriminating against the citizens of other states in favor of its own citizens. The Supreme Court is charged with deciding in each case whether a state had discriminated against goods or people from another state. The Constitution restricts the power of the states in favor of ensuring enough power to the national government to give the country a free-flowing national economy.

The framers' concern with national supremacy was also expressed in Article VI, in the **supremacy clause**, which provides that national laws and treaties "shall be the supreme Law of the Land." This means that all laws made under the "Authority of the United States" would be superior to all laws adopted by any state or any other subdivision and that the states would be expected to respect all treaties made under that authority. The supremacy clause also binds the officials of all governments—state and local as well as federal—to take an oath of office to support the national

supremacy clause Article VI of the Constitution, which states that laws passed by the national government and all treaties are the supreme law of the land and superior to all laws adopted by any state or any subdivision

Constitution. This means that every action taken by the U.S. Congress has to be applied within each state as though the action were in fact state law.

AMENDING AND RATIFYING THE CONSTITUTION

The Constitution establishes procedures for its own revision in Article V. Its provisions are so difficult that, as we shall see below, Americans have successfully availed themselves of the amending process only 17 times since 1791, when the first 10 amendments were adopted. The rules for the ratification of the Constitution are set forth in Article VII. Nine of the 13 states would have to ratify, or agree to, the terms in order for the Constitution to be formally adopted. Even if all the states did not ratify the Constitution it would take effect for those that did once the threshold of nine had been crossed.

CONSTITUTIONAL LIMITS ON THE NATIONAL GOVERNMENT'S POWER

Although the framers sought to create a powerful national government, they also wanted to guard against possible misuse of that power. To that end, the framers incorporated two key principles into the Constitution—federalism and the separation of powers. A third set of limitations, in the form of the Bill of Rights, was added to the Constitution in the form of 10 amendments proposed by the first Congress and ratified by the states. Most of the framers had thought a Bill of Rights to be unnecessary but accepted the idea during the ratification debates that took place when the new constitution was submitted to the states for approval.

FOR CRITICAL ANALYSIS

How does the separation of powers limit the national government's power? What are the consequences for the ability of the federal government to govern?

The Separation of Powers No principle of politics was more widely shared at the time of the 1787 Founding than the principle that power must be used to balance power. As noted earlier, the French political theorist Montesquieu believed that this balance was an indispensable defense against tyranny. His writings, especially his major work, *The Spirit of the Laws*, "were taken as political gospel" at the Philadelphia Convention.[19] Although the principle of the separation of powers is not explicitly stated in the Constitution, the entire structure of the national government was built precisely on Article I, the legislature; Article II, the executive; and Article III, the judiciary (see Figure 2.1).

However, separation of powers is nothing but mere words on parchment without a method to maintain that separation. The method became known by the popular label "checks and balances" (see Figure 2.2). Each branch is given not only its own powers but also some power over the other two branches. Among the most familiar checks and balances are the president's veto power over Congress and Congress's power over the president through its control of appointments to high executive posts and to the judiciary. Congress also has power over the president with its control of appropriations (the spending of government money) and (by the Senate) the right of approval of treaties. The judiciary has the power of judicial review over the other two branches.

Another important feature of the separation of powers is the principle of giving each of the branches a distinctly different constituency. Theorists such as Montesquieu called this a "mixed regime," with the president chosen, indirectly, by electors; the House, by popular vote; the Senate (originally), by state

FIGURE 2.1

The Separation of Powers

LEGISLATIVE	EXECUTIVE	JUDICIAL
Passes federal laws	Enforces laws	Decides constitutionality of laws
Controls federal appropriations	Commander in chief of armed forces	Reviews lower court decisions
Approves treaties and presidential appointments	Makes foreign treaties	Decides cases involving disputes between states
Regulates interstate commerce	Proposes laws	
Establishes lower court system	Appoints Supreme Court justices and federal court judges	
	Pardons those convicted in federal court	

legislatures; and the judiciary, by presidential appointment. By these means, the occupants of each branch would tend to develop very different outlooks on how to govern, different definitions of the public interest, and different alliances with private interests.

Federalism Compared with the confederation principle of the Articles of Confederation, federalism was a step toward greater centralization of power. The delegates agreed that they needed to place more power at the national level, without completely undermining the power of the state governments. Thus, they devised a system of two sovereigns—the states and the nation—with the hope that competition between the two would be an effective limitation on the power of both.

The Bill of Rights Late in the Philadelphia Convention, a motion was made to include a list of citizens' rights in the Constitution. After a brief debate in which hardly a word was said in its favor and only one speech was made against it, the motion was almost unanimously turned down. Most delegates sincerely believed that since the federal government was already limited to its expressed powers, further protection of citizens was not needed. The delegates argued that the states should adopt bills of rights because their greater powers needed greater limitations. But almost immediately after the Constitution was ratified, a movement arose to adopt a national bill of rights. This is why the Bill of Rights, adopted in 1791, comprises the first 10 amendments to the Constitution rather than being part of the body of it. (We will have a good deal more to say about the Bill of Rights in Chapter 4.)

FIGURE 2.2

Checks and Balances

Executive over Legislative
Can veto acts of Congress
Can call Congress into a special session
Carries out, and thereby interprets, laws passed by Congress
Vice president casts tie-breaking vote in the Senate

Legislative over Judicial
Can change size of federal court system and the number of Supreme Court justices
Can propose constitutional amendments
Can reject Supreme Court nominees
Can impeach and remove federal judges

LEGISLATIVE

Legislative over Executive
Can override presidential veto
Can impeach and remove president
Can reject president's appointments and refuse to ratify treaties
Can conduct investigations into president's actions
Can refuse to pass laws or to provide funding that president requests

Judicial over Legislative
Can declare laws unconstitutional
Chief justice presides over Senate during hearing to impeach the president

JUDICIAL

Executive over Judicial
Nominates Supreme Court justices
Nominates federal judges
Can pardon those convicted in federal court
Can refuse to enforce Court decisions

Judicial over Executive
Can declare executive actions unconstitutional
Power to issue warrants
Chief justice presides over impeachment of president

EXECUTIVE

The Fight for Ratification

Federalists those who favored a strong national government and supported the Constitution proposed at the American Constitutional Convention of 1787

Antifederalists those who favored strong state governments and a weak national government and who were opponents of the Constitution proposed at the American Constitutional Convention of 1787

> **Present the controversies involved in the struggle for ratification**

The first hurdle faced by the proposed Constitution was ratification by state conventions of delegates elected by the people of each state. This struggle for ratification was carried out in 13 separate campaigns. Each involved different people, moved at a different pace, and was influenced by local and national considerations. Two sides faced off throughout the states, however, calling themselves **Federalists** and **Antifederalists** (see Table 2.2). The Federalists (who more accurately should have called themselves "Nationalists," but who

Comparing Systems of Government

All democracies possess some form of an executive, a legislature, and a judiciary; however, the amount of power that each branch has varies. In the United States, the Founding Fathers sought to prevent any one branch from becoming too powerful by creating the system of checks and balances, as described in this chapter and outlined in Figure 2.2. Fearing monarchic dominance, the writers of the U.S. Constitution preferred limited government power in all branches rather than risk an overly powerful central government. In contrast, France's Fifth Republic has an extremely powerful president, so much so that the office has sometimes been referred to as the "republican monarchy."[a] Written during a period of intense upheaval and political violence, France's 1958 constitution created a strong executive who could act decisively (if not always democratically) in the midst of crisis.

However, what is "on paper" in a constitution does not always define the true balance of power in daily political life. Through usage and reinterpretation, constitutional provisions may take new shape over time. For example, as written in the U.S. Constitution (and shown below), the presidency is less powerful than Congress. Over time, however, presidential power has grown as Congress has delegated significant powers, such as the war power, to the president, Even constitutions that are less open to interpretation, such as India's 146,385-word constitution, have seen significant shifts in power over time. India's past prime ministers, especially when faced with a crisis, have sometimes reinterpreted their constitutional powers in ways that have benefited the power of their office.

COUNTRY	WRITTEN CONSTITUTION?	FEDERAL OR UNITARY SYSTEM	STRENGTH OF EXECUTIVE	STRENGTH OF LEGISLATURE	JUDICIAL INDEPENDENCE
BRAZIL	Yes	Federal	High	Medium	High
FRANCE	Yes	Unitary	High	Low	Low
INDIA	Yes	Federal	Medium	Low	Medium
ISRAEL	No	Unitary	Low	Low	Medium
SOUTH AFRICA	Yes	Unitary	Medium	Low	High
TUNISIA	Yes	Unitary	High	Medium	Low
UNITED STATES	Yes	Federal	High*	Medium	High*
UNITED KINGDOM	No	Unitary	Low	Low	Medium

*Although the Comparative Constitutions Project classifies the formal powers of both the American presidency and the judicial branch, as originally provided for in the Constitution, as relatively *weak*, we have classified both here as strong, based on the greater powers that have developed over time.
SOURCE: Comparative Constitutions Project, "CCP Rankings," http://comparativeconstitutionsproject.org/ccp-rankings/ (accessed 4/6/18).

[a]Catherine Field, "France's 'Republican Monarchy': When the President Is Treated Like a King," *New York Times*, September 1, 2004, www.nytimes.com/2004/09/01/opinion/frances-republican-monarchy-when-the-president-is-treated-like-a.html (accessed 4/6/18).

TABLE 2.2

Federalists versus Antifederalists

	FEDERALISTS	ANTIFEDERALISTS
Who were they?	Property owners, creditors, merchants	Small farmers, frontiersmen, debtors, shopkeepers, some state government officials
What did they believe?	Believed that elites were most fit to govern; feared "excessive democracy"	Believed that government should be closer to the people; feared concentration of power in hands of the elites
What system of government did they favor?	Favored strong national government; believed in "filtration" so that only elites would obtain governmental power	Favored retention of power by state governments and protection of individual rights
Who were their leaders?	Alexander Hamilton, James Madison, George Washington	Patrick Henry, George Mason, Elbridge Gerry, George Clinton

took their name to appear to follow in the revolutionary tradition) supported the Constitution and preferred a strong national government. The Antifederalists opposed the Constitution and preferred a federal system of government that was decentralized; they took their name by default, in reaction to their better-organized opponents. The Federalists were united in their support of the Constitution, whereas the Antifederalists were divided over possible alternatives to the Constitution.

During the struggle over ratification of the Constitution, Americans argued about great political issues and principles. How much power should the national government be given? What safeguards would most likely prevent the abuse of power? What institutional arrangements could best ensure adequate representation for all Americans? Was tyranny of the many to be feared more than tyranny of the few?

FEDERALISTS VERSUS ANTIFEDERALISTS

During the ratification struggle, thousands of essays, speeches, pamphlets, and letters were presented in support of and in opposition to the proposed Constitution. The best-known pieces supporting ratification were the 85 essays written between the fall of 1787 and the spring of 1788 under the name of "Publius," by Alexander Hamilton, James Madison, and John Jay. These *Federalist Papers*, as they are collectively known today, defended the principles of the Constitution and sought to dispel fears of a national authority. The Antifederalists published essays of their own, arguing that the new Constitution betrayed the Revolution and was a step toward monarchy. Among the best of the Antifederalist works were the essays, usually attributed to the New York State Supreme Court justice Robert Yates, that were written under the name of "Brutus" and published in the *New York Journal* at the same time the *Federalist Papers* appeared. The Antifederalist view was also ably presented in the pamphlets and letters written by a former delegate to the Continental Congress and future U.S. senator, Richard Henry Lee of Virginia, using the pen name "The Federal Farmer." These essays highlight the major differences of opinion between

Federalist Papers a series of essays written by Alexander Hamilton, James Madison, and John Jay supporting ratification of the Constitution

Federalists and Antifederalists. Federalists appealed to basic principles of government in support of their nationalist vision. Antifederalists cited equally fundamental precepts to support their vision of a looser confederacy of small republics.

Representation One major area of contention between the two sides was the question of representation. The Antifederalists asserted that representatives must be "a true picture of the people... [possessing] the knowledge of their circumstances and their wants."[20] This could be achieved, argued the Antifederalists, only in small, relatively homogeneous republics such as the existing states. In their view, the size and extent of the entire nation precluded the construction of a truly representative form of government. As Brutus put it, "Is it practicable for a country so large and so numerous... to elect a representation that will speak their sentiments?... It certainly is not."[21]

Federalists, for their part, saw no reason that representatives should be precisely like those they represented. In the Federalist view, one of the great advantages of representative government over direct democracy was precisely the possibility that the people would choose as their representatives individuals possessing ability, experience, and talent superior to their own. In Madison's words, rather than serving as a mirror or reflection of society, representatives must be "[those] who possess [the] most wisdom to discern, and [the] most virtue to pursue, the common good of the society."[22]

Tyranny A second important issue dividing Federalists and Antifederalists was the threat of **tyranny**—unjust rule by the group in power. Both opponents and defenders of the Constitution frequently affirmed their fear of tyrannical rule. Each side, however, had a different view of the most likely source of tyranny and, hence, of the way in which to forestall the threat.

From the Antifederalist perspective, the great danger was the tendency of all governments—including republican governments—to become gradually more and more "aristocratic" in character, wherein the small number of individuals in positions of authority would use their stations to gain more and more power over the general citizenry. In essence, the few would use their power to tyrannize the many. For this reason, Antifederalists were sharply critical of those features of the Constitution that divorced governmental institutions from direct responsibility to the people—institutions such as the Senate, the executive, and the federal judiciary. The last, appointed for life, presented a particular threat: "I wonder if the world ever saw... a court of justice invested with such immense powers, and yet placed in a situation so little responsible," protested Brutus.[23]

The Federalists, too, recognized the threat of tyranny, but they believed that the danger particularly associated with republican governments was not aristocracy but majority tyranny. The Federalists were concerned that a popular majority, "united and actuated by some common impulse of passion, or of interest, adverse to the rights of other citizens," would endeavor to "trample on the rules of justice."[24] From the Federalist perspective, it was precisely those features of the Constitution that the Antifederalists attacked as potential sources of tyranny that actually offered the best hope of averting the threat of oppression. The size and extent of the nation, for instance,

tyranny oppressive government that employs cruel and unjust use of power and authority

Article VII of the Constitution required 9 of the 13 states to ratify the Constitution in order for it to be adopted. In this image from January 1788, the pillars represent the first five states that ratified the Constitution, with Massachusetts as the likely sixth.

THE FEDERAL PILLARS.

UNITED THEY STAND—DIVIDED FALL.

Debates over how much power the national government should have continue today. After the San Bernardino shooting in 2015, the FBI demanded Apple unlock the perpetrator's iPhone for details into his criminal activity. Here, a group protests the FBI's infringement on the right to privacy.

limited government a principle of constitutional government; a government whose powers are defined and limited by a constitution

FOR CRITICAL ANALYSIS

Do you agree with Rutledge that a power that can do no harm can also do no good? How can a system of government maximize the ability of government to do good while minimizing the possibility of harm?

was for the Federalists a bulwark against tyranny because a majority would have difficulty uniting in a large and populous nation.

Governmental Power A third major difference between Federalists and Antifederalists was the issue of governmental power. Both opponents and proponents of the Constitution agreed on the principle of **limited government**. They differed, however, on the fundamentally important question of how to place limits on governmental action. Antifederalists favored limiting and enumerating the powers granted to the national government in relation both to the states and to the people at large. To them, the powers given the national government ought to be "confined to certain defined national objects."[25] Otherwise, the national government would "swallow up all the power of the state governments."[26] Antifederalists bitterly attacked the supremacy clause and the elastic clause of the Constitution as unlimited and dangerous grants of power to the national government.[27] Antifederalists also demanded that a bill of rights be added to the Constitution to place limits on the government's exercise of power over the citizenry.

Federalists favored the construction of a government with broad powers to defend the nation against foreign foes, guard against domestic strife and insurrection, promote commerce, and expand the nation's economy. Antifederalists shared some of these goals but still feared governmental power. In reply, Federalists such as Hamilton acknowledged that every power could be abused but argued that the way to prevent misuse of power was not by depriving the government of the powers needed to achieve national goals but by adopting the Constitution's internal checks and controls. As Madison put it, "the power surrendered by the people is first divided between two distinct governments (state and national), and then the portion allotted to each subdivided among distinct and separate departments. Hence, a double security arises to the rights of the people. The different governments will control each other, at the same time that each will be controlled by itself."[28] The Federalists' concern with avoiding unwarranted limits on governmental power led them to oppose a bill of rights, which they saw as nothing more than a set of unnecessary restrictions on the government.

Federalists acknowledged that abuse of power remained a possibility but felt that the risk had to be taken in order to achieve essential goals. "The very idea of power included a possibility of doing harm," said the Federalist John Rutledge during the South Carolina ratification debates. "If the gentleman would show the power that could do no harm," Rutledge continued, "he would at once discover it to be a power that could do no good."[29] This aspect of the debate between Federalists and Antifederalists, perhaps more than any other, continues to reverberate through American politics. Should the nation limit the federal government's power to tax and spend? Should Congress limit the capacity of federal agencies to issue new regulations? Should the government endeavor to create new rights for minorities, the disabled, and others? Though the details have changed, these are the same great questions that have been debated since the Founding.

REFLECTIONS ON THE FOUNDING

The final product of the Constitutional Convention was an extraordinary victory for the groups that had most forcefully called for the creation of a new system of government to replace the Articles of Confederation. While Antifederalist criticisms did force the Constitution's proponents to accept the addition of a bill of rights designed to limit the powers of the national government, overall it was the Federalist vision of America that triumphed. The Constitution adopted in 1789 created the framework for a powerful national government that for more than 200 years has defended the nation's interests, promoted its commerce, and maintained national unity. In one notable instance, the national government fought and won a bloody war to prevent the nation from breaking apart. And despite this powerful national government, the system of internal checks and balances has functioned reasonably well, as the Federalists predicted, to prevent the government from tyrannizing its citizens. The national unity created under the Constitution also gradually helped America become a great world power—as many of the framers had hoped.

Although they were defeated in 1788, the Antifederalists present us with an important picture of an America that might have been. Would Americans in the eighteenth century have been worse off if they had been governed by a confederacy of small republics linked by a national administration with severely limited powers? Were the Antifederalists correct in predicting that a government given great power in the hope that it might do good would, through "insensible progress," inevitably turn to evil purposes?

The Citizen's Role and the Changing Constitution

> **Trace how the Constitution has changed over time through the amendment process**

The Constitution has endured for more than two centuries as the framework of government. But it has not gone unchanged. The Constitution assigns citizens an indirect but important role in this process of change. Figure 2.3 outlines the ways in which the Constitution might be amended, all of which involve citizens through the election of members of Congress and state legislatures or, hypothetically, through the election of delegates to national and state constitutional conventions. Amending the Constitution may be difficult, but it is ultimately controlled by institutions elected by the people. Of course, the federal courts, whose judges are not elected by the people but appointed by the president with the consent of the Senate, also interpret the Constitution and adapt it to changing circumstances. Many voters are aware that their presidential ballots may also help to shape the character of the Supreme Court and other federal courts.

AMENDMENTS: MANY ARE CALLED; FEW ARE CHOSEN

The inevitable need for change was recognized by the framers of the Constitution, and provisions for **amendment** were incorporated into Article V. Four methods of amendment are described:

amendment a change added to a bill, law, or constitution

1. Passage in House and Senate by two-thirds vote, then ratification by majority vote of the legislatures of three-fourths (now 38) of the states

2. Passage in House and Senate by two-thirds vote, then ratification by conventions called for the purpose in three-fourths of the states

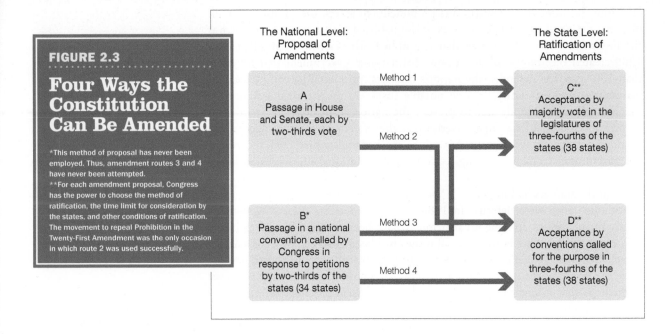

FIGURE 2.3

Four Ways the Constitution Can Be Amended

*This method of proposal has never been employed. Thus, amendment routes 3 and 4 have never been attempted.
**For each amendment proposal, Congress has the power to choose the method of ratification, the time limit for consideration by the states, and other conditions of ratification. The movement to repeal Prohibition in the Twenty-First Amendment was the only occasion in which route 2 was used successfully.

The National Level:
Proposal of
Amendments

The State Level:
Ratification of
Amendments

A
Passage in House and Senate, each by two-thirds vote

Method 1

Method 2

C**
Acceptance by majority vote in the legislatures of three-fourths of the states (38 states)

B*
Passage in a national convention called by Congress in response to petitions by two-thirds of the states (34 states)

Method 3

Method 4

D**
Acceptance by conventions called for the purpose in three-fourths of the states (38 states)

3. Passage in a national convention called for by Congress in response to petitions by two-thirds of the states, then ratification by majority vote of the legislatures of three-fourths of the states

4. Passage in a national convention (as in method 3), then ratification by conventions called for the purpose in three-fourths of the states

Figure 2.3 illustrates each of these possible methods. Since no amendment has ever been proposed by national convention, however, methods 3 and 4 have never been employed. And method 2 has been employed only once (the Twenty-First Amendment, which repealed the Eighteenth Amendment, or Prohibition). Thus, method 1 has been used for all the others.

The Constitution has proved to be extremely difficult to amend. Since 1789, more than 11,000 amendments have been formally offered in Congress. Of these, Congress officially proposed only 29, and 27 of these were eventually ratified by the states. Two of these—Prohibition and its repeal—cancel each other out, so for all practical purposes, only 25 amendments have been added to the Constitution since 1791.

FOR CRITICAL ANALYSIS

It is very difficult to amend the Constitution. Should the amendment process be made easier? Would the American system of government be more democratic if the Constitution could be revised more easily?

WHICH WERE CHOSEN? AN ANALYSIS OF THE 27

There is more to the amending difficulties than the politics of campaigning and voting. It would appear that only a limited number of changes can actually be made to the Constitution. Most efforts to amend the Constitution have failed because they were simply attempts to use the Constitution as an alternative to legislation for dealing directly with a specific public problem.

The 25 successful amendments, on the other hand, are concerned with the structure or composition of government (see Table 2.3). This is consistent with the

TABLE 2.3

Amendments to the Constitution

AMENDMENT	PURPOSE	YEAR PROPOSED	YEAR ADOPTED
I	Congress is not to make any law establishing a religion or abridging free exercise of religion, speech, press, assembly, or petitioning the government for redress of grievances.	1789	1791
II, III, IV	No branch of government may infringe on the right of people to keep arms (II), is not arbitrarily to occupy homes for a militia (III), and is not to engage in the search or seizure of evidence without a court warrant swearing to belief in the probable existence of a crime (IV).	1789	1791
V, VI, VII, VIII	The courts* are not to hold trials for serious offenses without provision for a grand jury (V), a petit (trial) jury (VII), a speedy trial (VI), presentation of charges (VI), confrontation of hostile witnesses (VI), immunity from testimony against oneself (V), and immunity from more than one trial for the same offense (V). Neither bail nor punishment can be excessive (VIII), and no property can be taken without just compensation (V).	1789	1791
IX, X	All rights and powers not enumerated are reserved to the states or the people.	1789	1791
XI	Limited jurisdiction of federal courts over suits involving the states.	1794	1795
XII	Provided separate ballot for vice president in the electoral college.	1803	1804
XIII	Eliminated slavery and eliminated the right of states to treat persons as property.	1865	1865
XIV	Asserted the principle of national citizenship and prohibited the states from infringing upon the rights of citizens of the nation, no matter that they happened to live in that state. Also prohibited states from denying voting rights to male citizens over the age of 21.**	1866	1868
XV	Extended voting rights to all races.	1869	1870
XVI	Established national power to tax incomes.	1909	1913
XVII†	Provided for direct election of senators. This diminished the power of the state legislatures and underscored the idea of a direct connection between Americans and the government of the United States.	1912	1913
XIX	Extended voting rights to women.	1919	1920
XX	Eliminated "lame-duck" session of Congress.	1932	1933
XXII	Limited presidential term.	1947	1951
XXIII	Extended voting rights to residents of the District of Columbia.	1960	1961
XXIV	Extended voting rights to all classes by abolition of poll taxes.	1962	1964
XXV	Provided presidential succession in case of disability.	1965	1967
XXVI	Extended voting rights to citizens aged 18 and over.	1971	1971††
XXVII	Limited Congress's power to raise its own salary.	1789	1992

*These amendments also impose limits on the law-enforcement powers of federal, state, and local executive branches.
**In defining *citizenship*, the Fourteenth Amendment actually provided the constitutional basis for expanding the electorate to include all races, women, and residents of the District of Columbia. Only the "18-year-olds' amendment" should have been necessary since it changed the definition of citizenship. The fact that additional amendments were required following the Fourteenth suggests that voting is not considered an inherent right of U.S. citizenship. Instead, it is viewed as a privilege.
†The Eighteenth Amendment, ratified in 1919, outlawed the sale and transportation of liquor. It was repealed by the Twenty-First Amendment, ratified in 1933.
††The Twenty-Sixth Amendment holds the record for speed of adoption. It was proposed on March 23, 1971, and adopted on July 5, 1971.

dictionary, which defines *constitution* as the makeup or composition of something. And it is consistent with the concept of a constitution as "higher law" because the whole point and purpose of a higher law is to establish a framework within which government and the process of making ordinary law can take place. Even those who would have preferred more changes to the Constitution have to agree that there is great wisdom in this principle. A constitution ought to enable legislation and public policies to be enacted, but it should not determine what that legislation or those public policies ought to be.

Private property is an excellent example. Property is one of the most fundamental and well-established rights in the United States; but it is well established not because it is recognized in so many words in the Constitution but because legislatures and courts, working within an agreed-upon constitutional framework, have made it a crime for anyone, including the government, to trespass or to take away property without compensation. A constitution is good if it produces the cause of action that leads to good legislation, good case law, and appropriate police behavior. Its principles can be a citizen's dependable defense against the abuse of power.

And ordinary citizens, including students, can influence America's constitution. Take the case of the Twenty-Seventh Amendment, which declares that no congressional pay increase can take effect until the next Congress is elected. This idea was proposed in 1789 along with the 10 amendments that became the Bill of Rights. This proposed amendment was ratified by several states but never achieved the three-fourths needed to be added to the Constitution. The idea was forgotten until a University of Texas undergraduate, Gregory Watson, wrote his class term paper on the subject in 1982. Watson proposed a campaign to complete the ratification process. His professor awarded Watson a C grade, asserting that the proposal was unrealistic. Watson, however, was undeterred and launched a student-led campaign to complete the ratification process. In 1992 the Twenty-Seventh Amendment was added to the Constitution, more than two centuries after it was proposed.

THE SUPREME COURT AND CONSTITUTIONAL CHANGE

Although the process of constitutional amendment outlined in Article V has seldom been used successfully, another form of constitutional revision is constantly at work in the United States: judicial interpretation of the Constitution and its amendments by the Supreme Court as it reviews cases. In some instances, the Court may give concrete definition to abstract constitutional principles. For example, the Constitution's Fifth Amendment asserts in general terms that individuals accused of crimes are entitled to procedural rights. The Supreme Court, in a series of decisions, established principles giving effect to those rights. Every viewer of television crime programs knows that, upon being arrested, individuals must receive Miranda warnings informing them of their right to refuse to speak and their right to counsel. These required warnings are the result of a 1966 Supreme Court decision interpreting the meaning and implications of the Fifth Amendment.

In some instances, the Supreme Court does more than interpret or flesh out constitutional provisions: it seems to modify or augment the text itself. For example, in decisions in 1965 and 1973 on birth control and abortion,

The Twenty-Sixth Amendment addressed an issue of representation that came to the fore when 18-, 19-, and 20-year-olds were drafted to serve in the Vietnam War but could not vote for Congress or the president who enacted the policies that affected their lives and deaths.

respectively, the Court said that Americans were constitutionally entitled to a right of privacy. The Constitution does not explicitly mention the right to privacy; it is derived from the Fourteenth Amendment and several provisions in the Bill of Rights.

As we examine in more depth later in the book, much of the Supreme Court's power is itself based on constitutional interpretation rather than on the text of the document. The Supreme Court claims the power of judicial review—the power to render the final decision when there is a conflict of interpretations of the Constitution or federal law among the courts, Congress, the executive branch, or the states. Nowhere does the Constitution mention this power. In a number of early cases, however, the Supreme Court asserted that the Constitution gave it the power of judicial review; and this interpretation has prevailed, enhancing the Court's power. Some commentators denounce this as constitutional amendment by the judiciary and demand that judges limit themselves to "strict construction" of the Constitution, adhering closely to the words of the document's text. Proponents of the idea of the *living Constitution*, on the other hand, assert that the Constitution is subject to change as conditions warrant; and they argue that the judiciary is the institution best qualified to adjust the Constitution's principles to new problems and times.

The Equal Rights Amendment (ERA) is an example of an amendment that almost succeeded. The proposed amendment guaranteed equality under the law for women and made gender discrimination illegal. The ERA was ratified by 35 state legislatures but failed to get the 38 necessary to equal three-fourths of the states.

The Constitution
WHAT DO WE WANT?

The Constitution's framers placed individual liberty ahead of all other political values, a concern that led many of the framers to distrust both democracy and equality. They feared that democracy could degenerate into a majority tyranny in which the populace, perhaps led by rabble-rousing demagogues, trampled on liberty. As for equality, the framers were products of their time and place; our contemporary ideas of racial and gender equality would have been foreign to them. The framers were concerned primarily with another manifestation of equality: they feared that those without property or position might be driven by what some called a "leveling spirit" to infringe on liberty in the name of greater economic or social equality. Indeed, the framers believed that this leveling spirit was most likely to produce demagoguery and majority tyranny. As a result, the basic structure of the Constitution—separated powers, internal checks and balances, and federalism—was designed to safeguard liberty, and the Bill of Rights created further safeguards for liberty. At the same time, however, many of the Constitution's other key provisions, such as indirect election of senators and the president and the appointment of judges for life, were designed to limit democracy and, hence, the threat of majority tyranny.

By championing liberty, however, the framers virtually guaranteed that democracy and even a measure of equality would sooner or later evolve in the United States. Liberty promotes the growth of political activity and the expansion of political participation, as in James Madison's famous phrase "Liberty is to faction as air is to fire."[30] The "**Who Participates?**" feature on the facing page traces the expansion of the right to vote in the United States from the Founding to today. Where they have liberty, more and more people, groups, and interests will engage in politics and gradually overcome whatever restrictions might have been placed on participation. They will fight for their rights and interests, and in doing so, may achieve greater equality, as Jim Obergefell did in securing marriage equality for same-sex couples. By granting citizens the freedom to exercise voice, liberty over time is conducive to democracy.

Who Gained the Right to Vote through Amendments?

Adult Citizens Eligible to Vote in National Elections*

27.9%	31.7%	92.6%	99.9%

1789	**1869**	**1920**	**1971**
The Founding: White men of property, age 21+	15th Amendment: All men, age 21+	19th Amendment: All men and women, age 21+	26th Amendment: All men and women, age 18+

*Percentages are of the adult (18+) population. These figures are approximate for 1789 and 1869. The voting rights of convicted felons are restricted in some states, and of noncitizens in all states.
SOURCES: U.S. Census of Population and Housing, 1790–2010, www.census.gov/prod/www/decennial.html (accessed 9/28/15); United States Elections Project. www.electproject.org/national-1789–present (accessed 9/27/15).

WHAT YOU CAN DO

Know Your Constitutional Rights

- ✓ Review your rights as outlined in the Constitution, a copy of which is reproduced in the appendix of this book.

- ✓ Find out what voting rights are retained by individuals who have been convicted of a felony. Go to **www.ncsl.org** and search "felon voting rights" for more information.

- ✓ Find out what voting rights are retained by individuals with mental illness. Go to **www.bazelon.org** and search "voting" for more information.

- ✓ Should noncitizens (such as longtime permanent legal residents) have the right to vote? Go to **www.latimes.com/citizenship** to read more and to join the conversation online.

The First Founding: Interests and Conflicts

Describe the events that led to the Declaration of Independence and the Articles of Confederation (pp. 43–46)

Dissatisfaction with tax and trade policies, coupled with discontent over retaliatory acts of political repression, radicalized many colonists during the 1770s to push for independence from British rule. The Declaration of Independence helped forge a sense of national unity among diverse elements in colonial society by identifying a widely shared set of grievances, goals, and principles. The first written constitution of the United States, the Articles of Confederation, placed strong limits on the powers of the national government and left most power in the hands of the states.

Key Terms

Articles of Confederation (p. 46)

confederation (p. 46)

Practice Quiz

1. How did the British attempt to raise revenue in the North American colonies?
   a) income taxes
   b) tariffs, duties, and other taxes on commerce
   c) expropriation and sale of Native American lands
   d) licensing fees for the mining of natural resources
   e) requests for voluntary donations

2. In their fight against British taxes, such as the Stamp Act and the Sugar Act of 1764, New England merchants and southern planters allied with which of the following groups?
   a) shopkeepers, small farmers, laborers, and artisans
   b) shopkeepers only
   c) laborers only
   d) artisans only
   e) shopkeepers and laborers only

3. The first governing document in the United States was
   a) the Declaration of Independence.
   b) the Articles of Confederation.
   c) the Constitution.
   d) the Bill of Rights.
   e) the Virginia Plan.

4. Who was responsible for executing laws passed by the national government under the Articles of Confederation?
   a) the presidency
   b) the Congress
   c) the states
   d) the federal bureaucracy
   e) the federal judiciary

The Second Founding: From Compromise to Constitution

Analyze the reasons many Americans thought a new Constitution was needed, and assess the obstacles to a new Constitution (pp. 47–53)

International weakness, domestic economic problems, and the national government's inability to act decisively in response to Shays's Rebellion led to a constitutional convention to replace the Articles of Confederation. The convention's delegates were deeply divided on the issues of representation in the national government and slavery. The Great Compromise and the Three-Fifths Compromise temporarily reconciled these divisions and allowed the Founders to move forward with creating a new constitutional framework for the United States.

Key Terms

Virginia Plan (p. 50)

New Jersey Plan (p. 50)

Great Compromise (p. 50)

Three-Fifths Compromise (p. 53)

Practice Quiz

5. Which of the following was *not* a reason that the Articles of Confederation seemed inadequate?
   a) the lack of a national military
   b) the inability of the federal government to enforce treaties
   c) the persistent economic turmoil among states

d) the growing power of radical forces in state legislatures

e) the Congress of the Confederation's strict control over state governments

6. Which event led directly to the Constitutional Convention by providing evidence that the government created under the Articles of Confederation was unable to act decisively in times of national crisis?
   a) the Boston Tea Party
   b) the Boston Massacre
   c) Shays's Rebellion
   d) the Annapolis Convention
   e) the War of 1812

7. The draft constitution that was introduced at the start of the Constitutional Convention by Edmund Randolph showed the strong influence of
   a) William Patterson.
   b) Benjamin Franklin.
   c) James Madison.
   d) George Clinton.
   e) Thomas Jefferson.

8. Which state's proposal embodied a principle of representing states in the Congress according to their size and wealth?
   a) New Jersey
   b) Maryland
   c) Rhode Island
   d) Virginia
   e) Connecticut

9. The agreement reached at the Constitutional Convention that determined how slaves would be counted for the purposes of taxation and representation in the House of Representatives was called the
   a) Connecticut Compromise.
   b) Three-Fifths Compromise.
   c) Great Compromise.
   d) Virginia Plan.
   e) New Jersey Plan.

The Constitution

Explain how the Constitution attempted to improve America's governance, and outline the major institutions established by the Constitution (pp. 53–60)

The Founders sought to create a stronger national government than existed under the Articles of Confederation. In particular, they hoped that the new constitution would promote commerce, protect private property, and secure popular support while also avoiding the perils of "excessive democracy." The Founders' concern with national power was expressed most clearly in the supremacy clause of Article VI. The national government, however, did not have unlimited power; and there were significant constraints placed on it through the separation of powers, federalism, and the Bill of Rights.

Key Terms

bicameral (p. 53)

checks and balances (p. 53)

Bill of Rights (p. 54)

separation of powers (p. 54)

federalism (p. 54)

expressed powers (p. 56)

elastic clause (p. 56)

judicial review (p. 57)

supremacy clause (p. 57)

Practice Quiz

10. Which of the following mechanisms were instituted in the Congress to guard against "excessive democracy"?
    a) bicameralism
    b) staggered terms in office
    c) checks and balances
    d) selection of senators by state legislatures
    e) all of the above

11. Which of the following best describes the Supreme Court as understood by the Founders?
    a) the principal check on presidential power
    b) the arbiter of disputes within the Congress
    c) the body that would choose the president
    d) a figurehead commission of elders
    e) the highest court of both the national government and the states

12. The ability of the president to veto a bill passed by Congress is a good example of
    a) federalism
    b) the system of checks and balances
    c) the supremacy clause
    d) civil liberties
    e) bicameralism

The Fight for Ratification

Present the controversies involved in the struggle for ratification (pp. 60–65)

Before the Constitution could go into effect, it had to be ratified by 9 of the 13 states. In the debate over ratification, the Federalists supported the Constitution and the Antifederalists opposed it. The three major areas of disagreement between Federalists and Antifederalists were the question of representation, the threat of tyranny, and the extent of government power.

Key Terms

Federalists (p. 60)

Antifederalists (p. 60)

Federalist Papers (p. 62)

tyranny (p. 63)

limited government (p. 64)

Practice Quiz

13. During the debate over ratification, the Federalists were
    a) those who opposed the new constitution because it created a stronger national government than existed under the Articles of Confederation.
    b) those who opposed the new constitution because it created a weaker national government than existed under the Articles of Confederation.
    c) those who opposed the new constitution because it did not end slavery.
    d) those who supported the new constitution because it created a stronger national government than existed under the Articles of Confederation.
    e) those who supported the new constitution because it ended slavery.

The Citizen's Role and the Changing Constitution

Trace how the Constitution has changed over time through the amendment process (pp. 65–69)

The amendment process outlined in Article V of the Constitution creates significant hurdles to change that have rarely been cleared in American history. Attempts to solve specific social problems through the use of a constitutional amendment have been particularly unsuccessful at winning the support required to change the country's basic governing document. The Supreme Court, however, has provided new meaning and new substance to the Constitution on countless occasions during the last 200 years through decisions on important cases.

Key Term

amendment (p. 65)

Practice Quiz

14. Which of the following best describes the process of amending the Constitution?
    a) It is difficult and has rarely been used successfully to address specific public problems.
    b) It is difficult and has frequently been used successfully to address specific public problems.
    c) It is easy but has rarely been used successfully to address specific public problems.
    d) It is easy and has frequently been used successfully to address specific public problems.
    e) It is easy, but it has never been used for any purpose.

For Further Reading

Ackerman, Erin, and Benjamin Ginsberg. *A Guide to the United States Constitution*, 4th ed. New York: W. W. Norton, 2019.

Amar, Akhil Reed. *The Constitution Today: Timeless Lessons for the Issues of Our Era*. New York: Basic Books, 2016.

Beeman, Richard. *Plain, Honest Men: The Making of the American Constitution*. New York: Random House, 2010.

Dahl, Robert A. *How Democratic Is the American Constitution?* 2nd ed. New Haven, CT: Yale University Press, 2002.

Ellis, Joseph. *The Quartet: Orchestrating the Second American Revolution*. New York: Knopf, 2015.

Ferling, John. *The American Revolution and the War That Won It*. New York: Bloomsbury, 2015.

Gerstle, Gary. *Liberty and Coercion: The Paradox of American Government from the Founding to the Present*. Princeton, NJ: Princeton University Press, 2015.

Hamilton, Alexander, James Madison, and John Jay. *The Federalist Papers*. Edited by Isaac Kramnick. New York: Viking, 1987.

Jensen, Merrill. *The Articles of Confederation*. Madison: University of Wisconsin Press, 1963.

Keller, Morton. *America's Three Regimes*. New York: Oxford University Press, 2009.

Lewis, Anthony. *Freedom for the Thought That We Hate: A Biography of the First Amendment*. New York: Basic Books, 2008.

Main, Jackson Turner. *The Social Structure of Revolutionary America*. Princeton, NJ: Princeton University Press, 1965.

Paulson, Michael S. and Luke Paulson, *The Constitution: An Introduction*. New York: Basic Books, 2017.

Stewart, David O. *Madison's Gift: Five Partnerships That Built America*. New York: Simon & Schuster, 2015.

Storing, Herbert, ed. *The Complete Anti-Federalist*. 7 vols. Chicago: University of Chicago Press, 1981.

West, Thomas. *The Political Theory of the American Founding: Natural Rights, Public Policy, and the Moral Conditions of Freedom*. New York: Cambridge University Press, 2017.

Recommended Websites

The American Civil Liberties Union
www.aclu.org
> The ACLU is committed to protecting, for all individuals, the freedoms found in the Bill of Rights. This sometimes controversial organization constantly monitors the government for violations of liberty and encourages its members to take political action.

Archiving Early America
www.earlyamerica.com
> Revolutionary Americans were motivated by a variety of competing ideals, principles, and interests. Visit this website to learn more about the early colonists and the founding of our government.

Constitution Finder
http://confinder.richmond.edu
> Is the American Constitution a model for the world? Explore the constitutions of many different nations and see what elements of the U.S. Constitution can be found in the governing documents of other countries.

FindLaw
http://findlaw.com/casecode/state.html
> The FindLaw website provides all 50 states' constitutions. Click on your state and try to identify such constitutional principles as bicameralism, staggered terms of office, checks and balances, and separation of powers.

The National Archives
www.archives.gov
> This government site provides information about and actual digital images of such founding documents as the Declaration of Independence, the U.S. Constitution, and the Bill of Rights.

The National Constitution Center
www.constitutioncenter.org
> The National Constitution Center in Philadelphia maintains a website that provides in-depth instructional analysis of the U.S. Constitution. Check out the Interactive Constitution function and follow the document from its Preamble through the Twenty-Seventh Amendment.

Oyez
www.oyez.org
> This website for U.S. Supreme Court media has an excellent search engine for finding information on Supreme Court cases. See how the Court has interpreted the Constitution over time.

The PBS *Liberty!* Series
www.pbs.org/ktca/liberty
> The PBS *Liberty!* series on the American Revolution offers an in-depth look at the Revolutionary War and includes information on historical events such as the Constitutional Convention.

The Supreme Court of the United States
www.supremecourtus.gov
> The website for the U.S. Supreme Court provides information on recent decisions. Take a moment to read some oral arguments, briefs, or opinions.

Federalism

WHAT GOVERNMENT DOES AND WHY IT MATTERS Decades of work as a commercial fisherman and long-haul truck driver left Larry Harvey with severe pain. The 70-year-old grandfather found one thing that helped: medical marijuana, which was legalized in the state of Washington in 1998. He and his wife included cannabis among the many herbs they grew on their property outside a little town some 80 miles north of Spokane.

One hot August day in 2012, armed federal agents stormed the Harveys' home. Larry was handcuffed and sent to jail, despite his poor health and advanced age. Prosecutors said guns had been found along with the marijuana. A judge released him 17 days later, but the lack of health care in jail left him unable to walk more than short distances.[1]

Washington state, along with 32 other states and the District of Columbia, protects qualified medical marijuana patients from arrest and prosecution (as of 2018, 10 states permit the use of recreational marijuana as well).[2] Yet under federal law marijuana is classified as a Schedule I controlled substance, in the same category as heroin, LSD, and MDMA ("ecstasy"). Users are subject to arrest and prosecution by the federal Drug Enforcement Administration. Thus medical marijuana patients like Larry Harvey

Federalism is at the center of a national debate over marijuana policy: while marijuana remains illegal under federal law, some states permit marijuana for medicinal or recreational use. Larry Harvey, pictured here, was prosecuted under federal law for growing marijuana though Washington state allowed the practice.

are caught in a clash between state and federal law. States can legalize medical marijuana, and medical marijuana defenses can be mounted in state courts, but federal law considers marijuana a dangerous drug with no medical value; evidence about the medical necessity of marijuana for patient-defendants cannot even be admitted in federal court.[3]

The federal response to the states has shifted over time. As state laws began to loosen restrictions on marijuana starting in the late 1990s, the federal government at first sought to assert its authority, raiding marijuana clinics and individual homes like Larry Harvey's. In 2005 the Supreme Court ruled that

these federal actions were constitutional. By 2013, however, the Justice Department under President Obama, stated that it would not challenge state laws so long as the states maintained a close watch over their marijuana markets. Instead the federal government would focus its enforcement efforts on specific issues, including trafficking by gangs, sales to minors, and selling across state lines. Washington's governor, Jay Inslee, issued a joint statement with the state's attorney general noting that the decision "reflects a balanced approach by the federal government that respects the states' interests in implementing these laws and recognizes the federal government's role in fighting illegal drugs and criminal activity."[4] It remains to be seen whether marijuana will be a focus of a possibly renewed War on Drugs in the Trump administration.[5]

Larry Harvey's situation and the debates about marijuana policy engage some of the oldest questions in American government: What is the responsibility of the federal government, and what is the responsibility of the states? When should there be uniformity across the states, and when is it better to let states adopt their own laws based on the needs and desires of their population, which may result in a diverse set of laws across the country? Which approach serves the common good?

The United States is a federal system, in which the national government shares power with lower levels of government. Throughout American history, lawmakers, politicians, and citizens have wrestled with questions about how responsibilities should be allocated across the different levels of government. Some responsibilities, such as international relations, clearly lie with the federal government. Others, such as divorce laws, are controlled by state governments. In fact, most of the rules and regulations that Americans face in their daily lives are set by state and local governments. However, many government responsibilities are shared in American federalism and require cooperation among local, state, and federal governments. The debate about "who should do what" remains one of the most important discussions in American politics.

CHAPTER GOALS

★ Describe what the Constitution says about the powers of the national government and of the states (pp. 79–84)

★ Consider how the relationship between the federal and state governments evolved during the nation's first 140 years (pp. 84–88)

★ Trace developments in the federal framework leading to a stronger national government (pp. 89–94)

★ Analyze the changing role of the states in the federal framework (pp. 94–102)

★ Analyze contemporary relationships among national, state, and local governments (pp. 102–7)

Federalism in the Constitution

> **Describe what the Constitution says about the powers of the national government and of the states**

The Constitution has had a profound influence on American life through **federalism**, the division of powers and functions between the national government and the state governments. Governments can organize power in a variety of ways. One of the most important distinctions is between unitary and federal governments. In a **unitary system**, the central government makes the important decisions and lower levels of government have little independent power. In such systems, lower levels of government primarily implement decisions made by the central government. In France, for example, the central government was once so involved in the smallest details of local activity that the minister of education boasted that by looking at his watch he could tell what all French schoolchildren were learning at that moment because the central government set the school curriculum. In a federal system, by contrast, the central government shares power or functions with lower levels of government, such as regions or states. Nations with diverse ethnic or language groupings, such as Switzerland and Canada, are most likely to have federal arrangements. In federal systems, lower levels of government often have significant independent power to set policy in some areas, such as education and social programs, and to impose taxes. Yet the specific ways in which power is shared vary greatly: no two federal systems are exactly the same.

The United States was the first nation to adopt federalism as its governing framework. With federalism, the framers sought to limit the national government by creating a second layer of state governments. By granting a few "expressed powers" to the national government and reserving all the rest to the states, the original Constitution recognized two sovereigns: state governments and the federal government. Table 3.1 indicates which level of government has responsibility for some of the actions that affect our everyday lives.

> **federalism** a system of government in which power is divided, by a constitution, between a central government and regional governments

> **unitary system** a centralized government system in which lower levels of government have little power independent of the national government

THE POWERS OF THE NATIONAL GOVERNMENT

As we saw in Chapter 2, the **expressed powers** granted to the national government are found in Article I, Section 8 of the Constitution. These 17 powers include the power to collect taxes, coin money, declare war, and regulate commerce. Article I, Section 8 also contains another important source of power for the national government: the **implied powers** that enable Congress "to make all Laws which shall be necessary and proper for carrying into Execution the foregoing Powers." Not until several decades after the Founding did the Supreme Court allow Congress to exercise the power granted in this **necessary and proper clause**, but as we shall see later in this chapter, this doctrine allowed the national government to expand considerably the scope of its authority, although the process was a slow one. In addition to these expressed and implied powers, the Constitution affirmed the power of the national government in the supremacy clause (Article VI), which made all national laws and treaties "the supreme Law of the Land."

> **expressed powers** specific powers granted by the Constitution to Congress (Article I, Section 8) and to the president (Article II)

> **implied powers** powers derived from the necessary and proper clause of Article I, Section 8 of the Constitution; such powers are not specifically expressed but are implied through the expansive interpretation of delegated powers

> **necessary and proper clause** Article I, Section 8 of the Constitution, which provides Congress with the authority to make all laws "necessary and proper" to carry out its expressed powers

TABLE 3.1

The Presence of Federal, State, and Local Government in the Daily Life of a Student at "State University"

TIME	SCHEDULE	LEVEL OF GOVERNMENT
7:00 A.M.	Wake up. Standard time set by the national government.	Federal and state
7:10 A.M.	Shower. Water courtesy of local government, either a public entity or a regulated private company.	Local
7:18 A.M.	Brush your teeth with toothpaste whose cavity-fighting claims have been verified by a federal agency.	Federal
7:30 A.M.	Have a bowl of cereal with milk for breakfast. "Nutrition Facts" on food labels are a federal requirement, pasteurization of milk required by state law, freshness dating on milk based on state and federal standards.	Federal and state
7:57 A.M.	Recycle the empty cereal box and milk carton.	State or local
8:30 A.M.	Drive or take public transportation to campus. Airbags and seat belts required by federal and state laws. Roads and bridges paid for by state and local governments, speed and traffic laws set by state and local governments, public transportation subsidized by all levels of government.	Federal, state, and local
8:45 A.M.	Arrive on campus of large public university. Buildings are 70 percent financed by state taxpayers.	State
9:00 A.M.	First class: Chemistry 101. Tuition partially paid by a federal loan (more than half the cost of university instruction is paid for by taxpayers), chemistry lab paid for with grants from the National Science Foundation (a federal agency) and smaller grants from business corporations made possible by federal income tax deductions for charitable contributions.	Federal
2:00 P.M.	Second class: American Government 101 (your favorite class!). You may be taking this class because it is required by the state legislature or because it fulfills a university requirement.	State
4:00 P.M.	Third class: Computer Science 101. Free computers, software, and internet access courtesy of state subsidies plus grants and discounts from Apple and Microsoft, the costs of which are deducted from their corporate income taxes; internet built in part by federal government. Duplication of software prohibited by federal copyright laws.	Federal and state
6:00 P.M.	Eat dinner: hamburger and french fries. Meat inspected for bacteria by federal agencies.	Federal
7:00 P.M.	Work at part-time job at the campus library. Minimum wage set by federal government; some states and cities set a higher minimum. Books and journals in library paid for by state taxpayers.	Federal, state, local
8:15 P.M.	Go online to check the status of your application for a federal student loan (FAFSA) on the Department of Education's website at studentaid.ed.gov.	Federal
10:00 P.M.	Go home. Street lighting paid for by county and city governments, police patrols by city government.	Local
10:15 P.M.	Watch Netflix. Broadband internet service regulated by federal government. Check app for tomorrow's weather. Weather forecast provided by a federal agency.	Federal
10:45 P.M.	To complete your economics homework, visit the Bureau of Labor Statistics at www.bls.gov to look up unemployment levels since 1972.	Federal
Midnight	Put out the trash before going to bed. Trash collected by city sanitation department, financed by "user charges."	Local

THE POWERS OF STATE GOVERNMENT

One way in which the framers sought to preserve a strong role for the states was through the Tenth Amendment to the Constitution. The Tenth Amendment states that the powers the Constitution does not delegate to the national government or prohibit to the states are "reserved to the States respectively, or to the people." The Antifederalists, who feared that a strong central government would encroach on individual liberty, repeatedly pressed for such an amendment as a way of limiting national power. Federalists agreed to the amendment because they did not think it would do much harm, given the powers of the Constitution already granted to the national government. The Tenth Amendment is also called the "**reserved powers** amendment" because it aims to reserve powers to the states.

reserved powers powers, derived from the Tenth Amendment to the Constitution, that are not specifically delegated to the national government or denied to the states

The most fundamental power that the states retain is that of coercion—the power to develop and enforce criminal codes, to administer health and safety rules, and to regulate the family via marriage and divorce laws. These issues touch closely on state and local values, which the Founders saw as appropriately differing from state to state (see Figure 3.1). States also have the power to

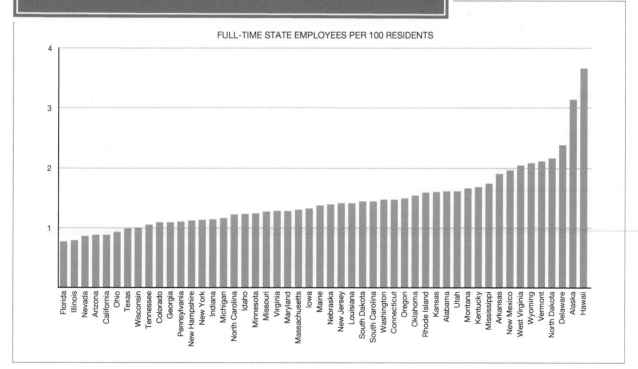

FIGURE 3.1

The Size of State Governments

The Founders believed that local needs and values varied from state to state and thus left many powers and responsibilities to state governments rather than the national government. State governments vary substantially in their relative size (how many state employees per 100 residents). How might these differences reflect differing needs and values?

SOURCES: U.S. Census Bureau, "2016 Annual Survey of Public Employment and Payroll," October 19, 2017, factfinder .census.gov/faces/tableservices/jsf/pages/productview.xhtml?src=bkmk/ (accessed 6/8/18); U.S. Census Bureau, "Annual Estimates of the Resident Population for the United States, Regions, States, and Puerto Rico: April 1, 2010 to July 1, 2017," May 8, 2018, www.census.gov/data/tables/2017/demo/popest/state-total.html (accessed 6/8/18).

regulate individuals' livelihoods; if you're a doctor or a lawyer or a plumber or a barber, you must be licensed by the state. Even more fundamentally, the states have the power to define private property—private property exists because state laws against trespass define who is and is not entitled to use a piece of property. If you own a car, your ownership isn't worth much unless the state is willing to enforce your right to possession by making it a crime for anyone else to drive your car without your consent. These are fundamental matters, and the powers of the states regarding these domestic issues are much greater than the powers of the national government.

police power power reserved to the state government to regulate the health, safety, and morals of its citizens

A state's authority to regulate these fundamental matters is commonly referred to as the **police power** of the state and encompasses the state's power to regulate the health, safety, welfare, and morals of its citizens. Policing is what states do—they coerce you in the name of the community in order to maintain public order. And this was exactly the type of power that the Founders intended the states, not the federal government, to exercise.

concurrent powers authority possessed by *both* state and national governments, such as the power to levy taxes

In some areas, the states share **concurrent powers** with the national government, whereby they retain and share some power to regulate commerce and affect the currency—for example, by being able to charter banks, grant or deny corporate charters, grant or deny licenses to engage in a business or practice a trade, regulate the quality of products or the conditions of labor, and levy taxes. Wherever there is a direct conflict of laws between the federal and the state levels, the issue will most likely be resolved in favor of national supremacy.

STATES' OBLIGATIONS TO ONE ANOTHER

The Constitution also creates obligations among the states. These obligations, spelled out in Article IV, were intended to promote national unity. By requiring the states to recognize actions and decisions taken in other states as legal and proper, the framers aimed to make the states less like independent countries and more like components of a single nation.

Article IV, Section 1 calls for "Full Faith and Credit" among states, meaning that each state is normally expected to honor the "Public Acts, Records, and Judicial Proceedings" that take place in any other state. So, for example, if a person has a restraining order placed on a stalker or batterer in one state, other states are required to enforce that order as if they had issued it.

full faith and credit clause provision from Article IV, Section 1 of the Constitution requiring that the states normally honor the public acts and judicial decisions that take place in another state

Notwithstanding, some courts have found exceptions to the **full faith and credit clause:** if a law is against the "strong public policy" of a state, that state may not be obligated to recognize it—even if it has been sanctioned by other states.[6] A look at the history of interracial marriage, for example, offers some perspective on how much leeway states have to recognize marriages performed in other states. In 1952, 30 states prohibited interracial marriage. Many of the states that prohibited interracial marriage also refused to recognize such marriages performed in other states.[7] For example, in the 1967 *Loving v. Virginia* case, which successfully challenged the ban on interracial marriage, the Lovings (a black woman and a white man) were married in the District of Columbia. However, when they returned to their home state of Virginia, which prohibited interracial marriage, the state refused to recognize them as a married couple.[8]

Until recently, same-sex marriage was in a similar position to interracial marriage half a century ago. Thirty-five states had passed "Defense of Marriage Acts" or had adopted constitutional amendments that defined marriage as a union between one man and one woman. Anxious to show its disapproval of gay marriage, Congress passed the Defense of Marriage Act in 1996, which declared that states would not have to recognize a same-sex marriage from another state. The act also said that the federal government would not recognize same-sex marriage—even if it were legal under state law—and that same-sex marriage partners would not be eligible for the federal benefits, such as Medicare and Social Security, normally available to spouses.[9] In 2013, however, the Supreme Court in *United States v. Windsor* struck down the Defense of Marriage Act in part, requiring that same-sex married couples receive equal treatment on issues relating to taxes, inheritance, and other federal laws.[10] After *Windsor*, many state courts struck down the state bans on same-sex marriage.

Previously a state-level policy, same-sex marriage was declared a fundamental right nationwide by the Supreme Court in 2015. The decision prompted a brief backlash when clerks in some states, such as Kim Davis from Kentucky, pictured here, refused to issue marriage licenses to same-sex couples.

On the second anniversary of the *Windsor* ruling, the Supreme Court, in a historic and long-awaited decision, ruled that the Fourteenth Amendment guaranteed a fundamental right to same-sex marriage. The case, *Obergefell v. Hodges*, combined four lawsuits by same-sex couples challenging their home states' refusals to grant same-sex marriage licenses or recognize same-sex marriages performed out of state.[11] While 37 states recognized same-sex marriage on the eve of the *Obergefell* announcement, the Court's 5–4 decision immediately required that number to jump to 50: all states must offer marriage licenses to two people of the same sex and recognize same-sex marriages licensed out of state. In one stroke, same-sex marriage turned from a state-level policy choice to a nationally recognized right. In the aftermath of the *Obergefell* decision, several of the 13 states that were mandated to lift their bans on same-sex marriage protested the ruling. Ken Paxton, the attorney general of Texas, for example, called the decision "unlawful" and pledged to provide legal assistance to local officials who refused to carry out the new law.[12] However, such resistance ebbed as it became clear that the courts would enforce the constitutional right to same-sex marriage.

Article IV, Section 2, known as the "comity clause," also seeks to promote national unity. It provides that citizens enjoying the **privileges and immunities** of one state should be entitled to similar treatment in other states. What this has come to mean is that a state cannot discriminate against someone from another state or give special privileges to its own residents. For example, in the 1970s, when Alaska passed a law that gave residents preference over nonresidents in obtaining work on the state's oil and gas pipelines, the Supreme Court ruled the law illegal because it discriminated against citizens of other states.[13] The comity clause also regulates criminal justice among the states by requiring states to return fugitives to the states from which they have fled. Thus, in 1952, when an inmate escaped from an Alabama prison and sought to avoid being returned to Alabama on the grounds that he was being subjected to "cruel and unusual punishment" there, the Supreme Court ruled that he must be returned according to Article IV, Section 2.[14]

privileges and immunities clause provision, from Article IV, Section 2 of the Constitution, that a state cannot discriminate against someone from another state or give its own residents special privileges

States' relationships with one another are also governed by the interstate compact clause (Article I, Section 10), which states that "No State shall, without the Consent of Congress . . . enter into any Agreement or Compact with another State." The Court has interpreted the clause to mean that states may enter into agreements with one another, subject to congressional approval. Today compacts are used for a wide range of issues from adult offender supervision to pest control, but are especially important in regulating the distribution of river water, addressing

TABLE 3.2

90,107 Governments in the United States

TYPE	NUMBER
National	1
State	50
County	3,031
Municipal	19,519
Townships	16,360
School districts	12,880
Other special districts	38,266

SOURCE: U.S. Census Bureau, www2.census.gov/govs/cog/g12_org.pdf (accessed 11/2/13).

home rule power delegated by the state to a local unit of government to manage its own affairs

environmental concerns, and operating transportation systems that cross state lines.[15]

LOCAL GOVERNMENT AND THE CONSTITUTION

Local government occupies a peculiar but very important place in the American system (see Table 3.2). In fact, the status of American local government is probably unique in world experience. First, it must be pointed out that local government has no status in the U.S. Constitution. *State* legislatures created local governments, and *state* constitutions and laws permit local governments to take on some of the responsibilities of the state governments. Thus local governments are subject to ultimate control by the states. This imbalance of power means that state governments could legally dissolve local governments or force multiple local governments to consolidate into one large locality. Most states amended their own constitutions to give their larger cities **home rule**—a guarantee of noninterference in various areas of local affairs.[16] In recent years, as discussed below, some local governments have passed laws making policy on matters from minimum wage to public broadband, only to have state legislatures preempt, or remove, that authority, illustrating the degree to which local governments are creations of the state.

FEDERALISM IN PRACTICE

The formally enumerated powers of the national and state governments in the Constitution represent only part of the story. What makes the federal form of government relevant for the nature of American democracy is its shifting practice over time. As we'll see, the states dominated for the nation's first 140 years or so, with the federal government becoming much more important after the New Deal in the 1930s. Over the last 80 years, even as the trend has been toward centralization of government power, the states have asserted themselves at certain times and in certain policy areas, sometimes aided by the courts. But then at other moments a crisis shifts power toward the national government again, as during the Great Depression, the September 11, 2001, terror attacks, and the fiscal crisis that began in 2008. Federalism creates a complex, flexible form of government whose workings shift over time.

The Traditional System of Federalism

> Consider how the relationship between the federal and state governments evolved during the nation's first 140 years

At the time of the Founding, the states far surpassed the federal government in their power to influence the lives of ordinary Americans. In the system of shared powers between the states and the federal government, the states were most active in economic and social regulation, while the federal government took a much more hands-off approach. Even so, the federal government gradually expanded its powers in the wake of important Supreme Court decisions. However, it was not until the New Deal in the 1930s that the federal government gained vast new powers.

RESTRAINING NATIONAL POWER WITH DUAL FEDERALISM

As we have noted, the Constitution created two layers of government: the national government and the state governments. The consequences of this **dual federalism** are fundamental to the American system of government; they have meant that states have done most of the fundamental governing. For evidence, look at Table 3.3, which lists the major types of public policies by which Americans were governed for the first century and a half under the Constitution. We call it the "traditional system" because it prevailed for much of American history.

Under the traditional system, the national government was quite small compared with both the state governments and the governments of other Western nations. It was also very narrowly specialized in the functions it performed. The national government built or sponsored the construction of roads, canals, and bridges (internal improvements). It provided cash subsidies to shippers and shipbuilders and distributed free or low-priced public land to encourage western settlement and business ventures. It placed relatively heavy taxes on imported goods (tariffs), not only to raise revenues but also to protect "infant industries" from competition from the more advanced European enterprises. It protected patents and provided for a common currency, which encouraged and facilitated enterprises and expanded markets.

What do these functions of the national government reveal? First, virtually all the functions were aimed at assisting commerce. Second, virtually none of the national

dual federalism the system of government that prevailed in the United States from 1789 to 1937 in which most fundamental governmental powers were shared between the federal and state governments

---

TABLE 3.3

The Federal System: Specialization of Governmental Functions in the Traditional System, 1789–1937

NATIONAL GOVERNMENT POLICIES (DOMESTIC)	STATE GOVERNMENT POLICIES	LOCAL GOVERNMENT POLICIES
Internal improvements	Property laws (including slavery)	Adaptation of state laws to local conditions
Subsidies	Estate and inheritance laws	Public works
Tariffs	Commerce laws	Contracts for public works
Public land disposal	Banking and credit laws	Licensing of public accommodation
Patents	Corporate laws	Zoning and other land-use regulation
Currency	Insurance laws	Basic public services
	Family laws	
	Morality laws	
	Public health laws	
	Education laws	
	General penal laws	
	Eminent domain laws	
	Construction codes	
	Land-use laws	
	Water and mineral laws	
	Criminal procedure laws	
	Electoral and political party laws	
	Local government laws	
	Civil service laws	
	Occupations and professions laws	

In 1815, President James Madison called for a federally funded program of "internal improvements," which was one of the few policy roles for the national government during the first half of the nineteenth century. By improving transportation through the construction of roads and canals, the government fostered the growth of the market economy and boosted federal power.

government's policies directly coerced citizens. The emphasis of governmental programs was on assistance, promotion, and encouragement—the allocation of land or capital to meet the needs of economic development.

Meanwhile, state legislatures were also actively involved in economic regulation during the nineteenth century. In the United States, then and now, private property exists only in state laws and in state court decisions regarding property, trespass, and real estate. American capitalism took its form from state property and trespass laws and from state laws and court decisions regarding contracts, markets, credit, banking, incorporation, and insurance. Laws concerning slavery were a subdivision of property law in states where slavery existed, though Article I, Section 2 of the Constitution (known as the fugitive slave clause) ensured that slavery would be protected even in free states. This clause obliged free states to return runaway slaves to the state from which they escaped (although it was rendered moot by the Thirteenth Amendment abolishing slavery). Even today, states control many policy areas, including the licensing of professions such as law and medicine, requirements for children's education, and, until recent decades, virtually all criminal laws— regarding everything from trespass to murder.

All this (and more, as shown in the middle column of Table 3.3) demonstrates that in the United States' first 150 years, most of the fundamental governing was done by the states. The contrast between national and state policies, as shown by Table 3.3, demonstrates the difference in the power vested in each. The list of items in the middle column could actually have been made longer. Moreover, each item on the list is a category of law that fills many volumes of statutes and court decisions.

By allowing state governments to do most of the fundamental governing, the Constitution saved the national government from many policy decisions that might have proven too divisive for a large and very young country. And the state and regional variation in policy the federal framework allows continues to facilitate governance in this large and diverse nation. The most fundamental impact of federalism on the way the United States is governed comes not from any particular provision of the Constitution but from the framework itself, which has determined which level of government does what and, through that, the political development of the country. As we shall see, some important aspects of federalism have changed, but the federal framework has survived two centuries and a devastating civil war.

FOR CRITICAL ANALYSIS

Which level of government had the most influence over citizens' lives when the country was founded? Why did this allocation of responsibilities make sense at the time?

FEDERALISM AND THE SLOW GROWTH OF
THE NATIONAL GOVERNMENT'S POWER

As the nation grew, disputes arose about the powers of the federal government versus the powers of the states. In the first several decades after the Founding, the Supreme Court decided several critical cases that expanded federal powers and facilitated trade across the states. These decisions removed barriers to trade in the new nation and laid the groundwork for a national economy. However, by the end of the nineteenth century, as reformers began to enact laws regulating businesses through such measures as child labor restrictions, the Court took a much more restrictive view of federal power. Not until well into the New Deal in 1937 did the federal government gain the expansive powers it exercises today.

The Supreme Court's early decisions to expand federal power rested on its pronational interpretation of Article I, Section 8 of the Constitution. That article enumerates the powers of Congress, including the power to tax, raise an army, declare war, establish post offices, and "regulate commerce with foreign nations, and among the several States and with the Indian tribes." This **commerce clause** would later form the basis for expansive federal government control over the economy, but its scope initially remained unclear.

The Court's early decisions began to define national power by favoring federal control over the economy when there was a conflict between the states and the federal government. The first and most important such case was *McCulloch v. Maryland* (1819), which involved the question of whether Congress had the power to charter a national bank—an explicit grant of power nowhere to be found in Article I, Section 8.[17] Chief Justice John Marshall answered that this power could be "implied" from other powers that were expressly delegated to Congress, such as the "powers to lay and collect taxes; to borrow money; to regulate commerce; and to declare and conduct a war." Marshall's decision rested on the necessary and proper clause of Article I, Section 8, which gave Congress the power to enact laws "necessary and proper" for executing its substantive powers.

By allowing Congress to use the necessary and proper clause to interpret its delegated powers expansively, the Supreme Court created the potential for an unprecedented increase in national government power. Marshall also concluded that whenever a state law conflicted with a federal law (as in *McCulloch*), the state law would be deemed invalid since the Constitution states that "the Laws of the United States...shall be the supreme Law of the Land." Both parts of this great case are pro-national, yet Congress did not immediately seek to expand the policies of the national government.

Another major case, *Gibbons v. Ogden* (1824), reinforced this nationalistic interpretation of the Constitution. The important but relatively narrow issue was whether the state of New York could grant a monopoly to Robert Fulton's steamboat company to operate an exclusive service between New York and New Jersey. Chief Justice Marshall argued that New York State did not have the power to grant this particular monopoly, so Marshall had to define what Article I, Section 8 meant by "commerce among the several states." He insisted that the definition was "comprehensive," extending to "every species of commercial intercourse." However, this comprehensiveness was limited "to that commerce which concerns more states than one." *Gibbons* is important because it established the supremacy of the national government in all matters affecting what later came to be called "interstate commerce."[18] But the precise meaning of interstate commerce would remain uncertain during

commerce clause Article I, Section 8 of the Constitution, which delegates to Congress the power "to regulate commerce with foreign nations, and among the several States and with the Indian tribes"; this clause was interpreted by the Supreme Court in favor of national power over the economy

In 1916 the national government passed the Keating-Owen Child Labor Act, which excluded from interstate commerce all goods manufactured by children under age 14. The act was ruled unconstitutional by the Supreme Court, and the regulation of child labor remained in the hands of state governments until the 1930s.

several decades of constitutional discourse. Backed by the implied-powers decision in *McCulloch* and by the broad definition of "interstate commerce" in *Gibbons*, Article I, Section 8 was a source of power for the national government as long as Congress sought to facilitate commerce through subsidies, services, and land grants.

Later in the nineteenth century, though, any effort of the national government to *regulate* commerce in such areas as fraud, the production of substandard goods, the use of child labor, or the existence of dangerous working conditions or long hours was declared unconstitutional by the Supreme Court as a violation of the concept of interstate commerce. Such legislation meant that the federal government was entering the factory and the workplace—local areas—and was attempting to regulate goods that had not yet passed into interstate commerce. To enter these local workplaces was to exercise police power—a power reserved to the states. No one questioned the power of the national government to regulate businesses that intrinsically involved interstate commerce, such as railroads, gas pipelines, and waterway transportation. But well into the twentieth century the Supreme Court used the concept of interstate commerce as a barrier against most efforts by Congress to regulate local conditions.

Thus, federalism, as interpreted by the Supreme Court for 70 years after the Civil War, made it possible for business to have its cake and eat it, too: entrepreneurs enjoyed the benefits of national policies facilitating commerce and were protected by the courts from policies regulating commerce by protecting the rights of consumers and workers.[19]

All this changed after 1937, when the Supreme Court issued a series of decisions that laid the groundwork for a much stronger federal government. Most significant was the Court's dramatic expansion of the commerce clause. By throwing out the old distinction between interstate and intrastate commerce, the Court converted the commerce clause from a source of limitations to a source of power for the national government. The Court upheld acts of Congress protecting the rights of employees to organize and engage in collective bargaining, regulating the amount of farmland in cultivation, extending low-interest credit to small businesses and farmers, and restricting the activities of corporations dealing in the stock market.[20] The Court also upheld many other laws that contributed to the construction of the "welfare state." With these rulings, the Court decisively signaled that the era of dual federalism was over. In the future, Congress would have very broad powers to regulate activity in the states.

Federalism in the Modern Era

Trace developments in the federal framework leading to a stronger national government

The economic crisis of the Great Depression and the nature of the government response signaled a new era in the age-old question of the meaning and operation of federalism in the United States. In this section we will look at how the balance of state and federal power has shifted since the 1930s, with growth in the size and scope of the federal government. We will examine the changing nature of federalism and the tools the federal government has used both to elicit state effort and to shape resultant state policy.

THE NEW DEAL AND WORLD WAR II: NEW ROLES FOR GOVERNMENT

The door to increased federal action opened when states proved unable to cope with the demands brought on by the Great Depression of the 1930s. Before this national economic catastrophe, states and localities took responsibility for addressing the needs of the poor, usually through private charity. But the extent of the depression quickly exhausted local and state capacities. By 1932, 25 percent of the workforce was unemployed. The jobless lost their homes and settled into camps all over the country, called "Hoovervilles," after President Herbert Hoover. Elected in 1928, the year before the depression hit, Hoover steadfastly maintained that the federal government could do little to alleviate the misery caused by the depression. It was a matter for state and local governments, he said.

Yet demands mounted for the federal government to take action. In Congress, some Democrats proposed that the federal government finance public works to aid the economy and put people back to work. Other members of Congress introduced legislation to provide federal grants to the states to assist them in their relief efforts. Most of these measures failed to win congressional approval or were vetoed by President Hoover.

When Franklin Delano Roosevelt took office in 1933, he energetically threw the federal government into the business of fighting the depression through a number of proposals known collectively as the New Deal. He proposed a variety of temporary measures to provide federal relief and work programs. Most of the programs he proposed were to be financed by the federal government but administered by the states. In addition to these temporary measures, Roosevelt presided over the creation of several important federal programs designed to provide future economic security for Americans. The New Deal signaled the rise of a more active national government.

FROM LAYER CAKE TO MARBLE CAKE: COOPERATIVE FEDERALISM AND THE USE OF CATEGORICAL GRANTS

For the most part, the new national programs that the Roosevelt administration developed did not directly take power away from the states. Instead, the national government

The New Deal expanded the scope of the federal government. One of the largest and most effective New Deal programs, the Works Progress Administration (WPA) employed millions of Americans in projects such as constructing highways, bridges, and public parks.

grants-in-aid programs through which Congress provides money to state and local governments on the condition that the funds be employed for purposes defined by the federal government

typically redirected states by offering them **grants-in-aid**, whereby Congress appropriates money to state and local governments on the condition that the money be spent for a particular purpose defined by Congress (see Figure 3.2). Franklin Roosevelt's New Deal expanded the range of grants-in-aid into social programs, providing grants to the states for financial assistance to poor children. Congress added more grants after World War II, creating new programs to help states fund activities such as providing school lunches and building highways. Sometimes the national government required state or local governments to match the national contribution dollar for dollar, but in some programs, such as the development of the interstate highway system, the congressional grants provided 90 percent of the cost of the program.

FIGURE 3.2

Historical Trend of Federal Grants-in-Aid,* 1950–2019 (in billions of dollars)

Spending on federal grants-in-aid to the states and local governments has grown dramatically since 1990. These increases reflect the growing public expectations about what government should do. What has been the most important cause of the steady increase in these grants?

*Excludes outlays for national defense, international affairs, and net interest.
**Estimate.
†Data in constant (fiscal year 2009) dollars.

SOURCE: Office of Management and Budget, U.S. Budget for Fiscal Year 2019, "Historical Tables: Table 12.1, Summary Comparison of Total Outlays for Grants to State and Local Governments: 1940–2023," www.whitehouse.gov/omb/historical-tables/ (accessed 6/8/18).

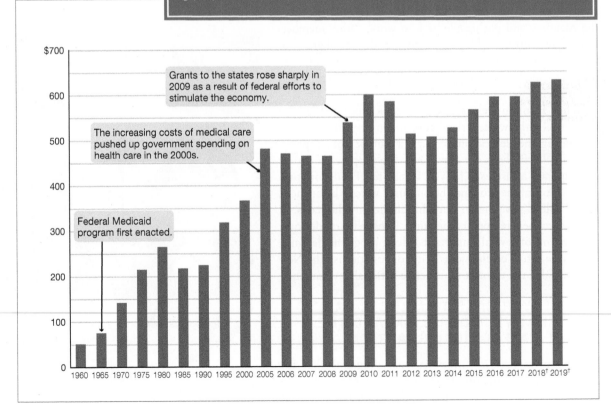

Grants to the states rose sharply in 2009 as a result of federal efforts to stimulate the economy.

The increasing costs of medical care pushed up government spending on health care in the 2000s.

Federal Medicaid program first enacted.

These types of federal grants-in-aid are called **categorical grants** because the national government determines the purposes, or categories, for which the money can be used. For the most part, the categorical grants created before the 1960s simply helped the states perform their traditional functions.[21] During the 1960s, however, the national role expanded and the number of categorical grants increased dramatically.[22] The grants authorized during the 1960s announced national purposes much more strongly than did earlier grants. One of the most important—and expensive—was the federal Medicaid program, which provides states with grants to pay for medical care for the poor, the disabled, and many nursing home residents. Over time the *value* of categorical grants has risen dramatically, increasing from $2.3 billion in 1950 to an estimated $675 billion in 2017.

The growth of categorical grants created a new kind of federalism. If the traditional system of two sovereigns performing highly different functions could be called dual federalism, historians of federalism suggest that the system since the New Deal could be called **cooperative federalism**. The political scientist Morton Grodzins characterized this as a move from "layer cake federalism" to "marble cake federalism,"[23] in which intergovernmental cooperation and sharing have blurred a once-clear distinguishing line, making it difficult to say where the national government ends and the state and local governments begin (see Figure 3.3). Figure 3.4 demonstrates the financial basis of the "marble-cake" idea.

As important as the states were in this new system of grants, some new federal grants, particularly during the War on Poverty of the 1960s, bypassed the states and instead sent money directly to local governments and even to local nonprofit organizations. The theme heard repeatedly in Washington was that the states simply could not be trusted to carry out national purposes.[24]

One of the reasons that Washington distrusted the states was the way African American citizens were treated in the South. The southern states' forthright defense of segregation, justified on the grounds of states' rights, helped tarnish the image of the states as the civil rights movement gained momentum. The national officials who planned the War on Poverty pointed to the racially exclusionary practices of the southern states as a reason for bypassing state governments. The political scientist James Sundquist described their thinking: "In the drafting of the Economic

categorical grants congressional grants given to states and localities on the condition that expenditures be limited to a problem or group specified by law

cooperative federalism a type of federalism existing since the New Deal era in which grants-in-aid have been used strategically to encourage states and localities (without commanding them) to pursue nationally defined goals; also known as *intergovernmental cooperation*

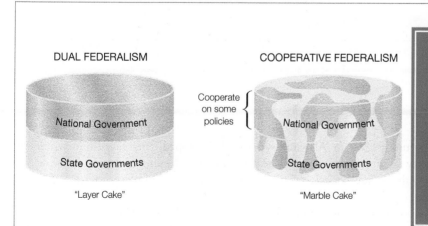

DUAL FEDERALISM

National Government

State Governments

"Layer Cake"

Cooperate on some policies

COOPERATIVE FEDERALISM

National Government

State Governments

"Marble Cake"

FIGURE 3.3

Dual versus Cooperative Federalism

In layer-cake federalism, the responsibilities of the national government and state governments are clearly separated. In marble-cake federalism, national policies, state policies, and local policies overlap in many areas.

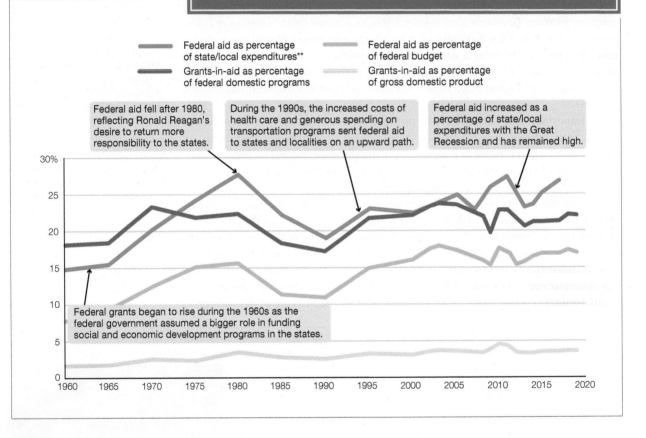

FIGURE 3.4

The Rise, Decline, and Recovery of Federal Aid, 1960–2019*

The level of federal aid has varied over the past several decades as program costs and politics have affected the role the national government plays in funding state and local services. The data in this figure show the rise, decline, and recovery of federal aid. What factors contributed to each of these trends?

*Excludes national defense, international affairs, net interest, and undistributed offsetting receipts. Data for 2018 and 2019 are estimated.
**Estimates for state and local expenditures in 2018 and 2019 are not available.

SOURCES: Office of Management and Budget, U.S. Budget for Fiscal Year 2019, Analytical Perspectives, Table 14-2, "Trends in Federal Grants to State and Local Governments," www.whitehouse.gov/wp-content/uploads/2018/02/spec-fy2019.pdf (accessed 6/8/18). Government Publishing Office, Budget of the United States Government, www.gpo.gov/fdsys/browse/collectionGPO.action?collectionCode=BUDGET (accessed 4/13/16).

Federal aid as percentage of state/local expenditures**

Grants-in-aid as percentage of federal domestic programs

Federal aid as percentage of federal budget

Grants-in-aid as percentage of gross domestic product

Federal aid fell after 1980, reflecting Ronald Reagan's desire to return more responsibility to the states.

During the 1990s, the increased costs of health care and generous spending on transportation programs sent federal aid to states and localities on an upward path.

Federal aid increased as a percentage of state/local expenditures with the Great Recession and has remained high.

Federal grants began to rise during the 1960s as the federal government assumed a bigger role in funding social and economic development programs in the states.

Opportunity Act, an 'Alabama syndrome' developed. Any suggestion within the poverty task force that the states be given a role in the administration of the act was met with the question, 'Do you want to give that kind of power to [then–Alabama governor] George Wallace?'"[25]

Yet even though many national policies of the 1960s bypassed the states, other new programs, such as Medicaid—the health program for the poor—relied on state governments for their implementation. In addition, as the national government expanded existing programs run by the states, states had to take on more responsibilities. These new responsibilities meant that the states were playing a critical role in the federal system.

NATIONAL STANDARDS, REGULATION, AND PREEMPTION

Giving policy responsibilities to states introduces the possibility of variation and raises questions about how different things should be when one crosses a state line, or in what policy areas it is acceptable for states to differ. Supreme Court decisions about the fundamental rights of American citizens have provided important answers to these questions, typically pushing for greater uniformity across the states. But in other policy areas, national government has at times provided incentives or imposed rules in order to create greater uniformity.

Federal grants, as we have seen, are one such tool: Congress provides an incentive by giving money to state and local governments if they agree to spend it for the purposes Congress specifies. But as Congress in the 1970s began to enact legislation in new areas, such as environmental policy, it resorted to another tool: regulations on states and localities. Some political scientists call this a move toward **regulated federalism**.[26] The national government began to set standards of conduct or to require the states to set standards that met national guidelines. The effect of these national standards is that state and local policies in the areas of environmental protection, social services, and education are more uniform from coast to coast than are other nationally funded policies.

Some national standards require the federal government to take over areas of regulation formerly overseen by state or local governments. Such **preemption** occurs when state and local actions are found to be inconsistent with federal requirements. In some cases, federal laws and regulations are more stringent than state laws. In the 1970s, preemptions required the states to abide by tougher federal rules in policies as diverse as air and water pollution, occupational health and safety, and access for the disabled. The regulated industries often oppose such laws because they increase the cost of doing business. After 1994, when Republicans retook control of Congress, the federal government used its preemption power in business's favor, limiting the ability of states to tax and regulate industry. For example, the Internet Tax Freedom Act, first enacted by Congress in 1998 and subsequently renewed, prohibits states and localities from taxing internet access services.

Congress is not the only federal body that can preempt the states; federal regulatory agencies can also issue rules that override state law. One controversial case involved a 2006 Food and Drug Administration drug-labeling rule preempting state laws that allow individuals to sue drug companies in state courts. Opponents—many of them trial lawyers—charged that such rules amounted to "stealth preemption" that "will deprive consumers of their right to hold negligent corporations accountable for injuries caused by defective products."[27] Supporters claimed that the rules were a proper use of federal authority.

State and local governments often contest federal preemptions. For example, in 2001, Attorney General John Ashcroft declared that Oregon's law permitting doctor-assisted suicide was illegal under federal drug regulations. The state, a physician, a pharmacist, and several terminally ill state residents challenged Ashcroft's rule, and in January 2006 the Supreme Court ruled in a 6–3 vote that the attorney general did not have the authority to outlaw the Oregon law.[28] Individuals have also challenged federal preemption. In 2009 the Supreme Court ruled against a drug manufacturer and in favor of a woman whose arm had to be amputated after she was improperly

regulated federalism a form of federalism in which Congress imposes legislation on states and localities, requiring them to meet national standards

preemption the principle that allows the national government to override state or local actions in certain policy areas; in foreign policy, the willingness to strike first in order to prevent an enemy attack

FOR CRITICAL ANALYSIS

When is federal preemption of local laws desirable? Is preemption justified for some issues more than for others?

injected with a drug designed to counter nausea.[29] Although the drug company knew that such complications could arise, it argued that it was not responsible for the amputation because federal regulations did not require it to warn against this danger in labeling the drug. The Court, however, found the company liable for the damage. In its decision, the Court made it clear that federal regulations could not preempt state consumer protections and that states had the power to adopt stricter protections than those of the federal government.

In 2009, after only a few months in office, President Obama reversed the George W. Bush administration's use of federal regulations to limit state laws. Under the new policy, federal regulations should preempt state laws only in extraordinary cases. The president directed agency leaders to review the regulations that had been put in place over the previous 10 years and consider amending them if they interfered with the "legitimate prerogatives of the states."[30] But as we will see, the Obama administration did use its power of preemption to challenge state immigration laws, charging that states were making laws in a domain reserved for federal authority. The Trump administration has moved in the opposite direction. California has long had more stringent vehicle emissions and mileage targets than the federal government, but a Trump administration proposal would revoke the ability of any state to set rules different from federal levels.[31] In May 2018, California and 16 other states sued the Trump administration to keep the stricter regulations in place.

Evolving Role of the States

> **Analyze the changing role of the states in the federal framework**

The federal government's fluid strategies vis-à-vis the states—from cooperating with them to regulating them—raise the question of the appropriate role for the states in the federal system. Do some divisions of responsibility between states and the federal government work better than others? Might states be sources of experimentation and innovation, the "laboratories of democracy" that Supreme Court Justice Louis Brandeis suggested?[32] Which responsibilities are states administratively and fiscally capable of carrying out? And what are the implications of the variation across the nation that might result from having states determine policy? States are sovereign actors in the federal system. In addition to receiving funding from the national government, they raise their own revenues. They make policy in a number of areas and decide which policy areas lower levels of government such as cities and counties can control. Forty-nine states have to balance their budgets, unlike the federal government, which can run budget deficits. Hence states embody both the promise and the constraints of a federal form of government.

FOR CRITICAL ANALYSIS

How have Supreme Court decisions affected the balance of power between the federal government and the states? Has the Supreme Court favored the federal government or the states?

STATES' RIGHTS

states' rights the principle that the states should oppose the increasing authority of the national government; this principle was most popular in the period before the Civil War

The Tenth Amendment, which reserves to the states the powers the Constitution does not specifically delegate to the national government, has been used over the decades by different groups, for different purposes, to bolster the role of the states in the federal system. For much of the nineteenth century, when federal power remained limited, the Tenth Amendment was used to argue in favor of **states' rights**, which in their extreme version claimed that the states did not have to submit to national laws whenever they believed the national government had exceeded its authority. Prior to the Civil War, sharp differences between the North and the South over tariffs and slavery gave rise to arguments supporting nullification. Most fully articulated by John C. Calhoun, vice president under Andrew Jackson and later a senator from South Carolina, the doctrine of nullification proposed that states were not bound by federal laws that they considered unconstitutional. Such arguments were voiced less often after the Civil War, but the Supreme Court continued to use the Tenth Amendment to strike down laws that it thought exceeded national power, including the Civil Rights Act passed in 1875, which would have eliminated discrimination against African Americans in public accommodations and transportation.

By the late 1930s, although the Supreme Court had struck down some national regulations limiting the power of large corporations and preserving the health and welfare of citizens, the overall direction of the Court's decisions expanded federal power. Indeed, so much so that the Tenth Amendment appeared irrelevant. In 1941, Justice Harlan Fiske Stone declared that the Tenth Amendment was simply a "truism," that it had no real meaning.[33]

Yet the idea that some powers should be reserved to the states did not go away. One reason is that groups with substantive policy interests often support states' rights as a means for achieving their policy goals. For example, in the 1950s, southern opponents of the civil rights movement revived the idea of states' rights to support racial segregation. In 1956, 96 southern members of Congress issued a "Southern manifesto" in which they declared that southern states were not constitutionally bound by Supreme Court decisions outlawing racial segregation. They believed that states' rights should override individual rights to liberty and formal equality. With the eventual triumph of the civil rights movement, the slogan of "states' rights" became tarnished by its association with racial inequality.

The 1990s saw a revival of interest in the Tenth Amendment and important Supreme Court decisions limiting federal power. Much of the interest in the Tenth Amendment stemmed from conservatives who believed that a strong federal government encroached on individual liberties. They believed such freedoms were better protected by returning more power to the states through the process of devolution, as we'll see later.[34] The Supreme Court's 1995 ruling in *United States v. Lopez* fueled further interest in the Tenth Amendment.[35] In that case, the Court, stating that Congress had exceeded its authority under the commerce clause, struck down a federal law that barred handguns near schools. This was the first time since the New Deal that the Court had limited congressional powers in this way. In 1997 the Court again relied on the Tenth Amendment to limit federal power in *Printz v. United States*.[36] The decision declared unconstitutional a provision of the Brady Handgun Violence Prevention Act that required state and local law-enforcement officials to conduct background checks on handgun purchasers. The Court declared that this provision violated state sovereignty guaranteed by the Tenth Amendment because it required state and local officials to administer a federal regulatory program.

Thus, the expansion of the power of the national government since the 1930s has not left the states powerless. State governments continue to make important laws. No better demonstration of the continuing influence of the federal framework can be offered than that in the middle column of Table 3.3, which is still a fairly accurate characterization of state government today. In each of these domains, however, states must now share power with the federal government.

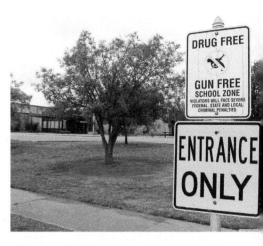

In 1995 the Supreme Court ruled that the Gun-Free School Zones Act was an unconstitutional application of the commerce clause, leaving this area of regulation to the states. In striking down a federal law, the Supreme Court ruled that regulating guns near schools is a state prerogative.

John C. Calhoun, one of the most prominent advocates of states' rights, argued that states should have the right to veto any federal law they found to be unconstitutional.

DEVOLUTION

devolution a policy to remove a program from one level of government by delegating it or passing it down to a lower level of government, such as from the national government to the state and local governments

diffusion policy decisions in one political jurisdiction are influenced by choices made in another jurisdiction

block grants federal grants-in-aid that allow states considerable discretion in how the funds are spent

New Federalism attempts by presidents Nixon and Reagan to return power to the states through block grants

general revenue sharing the process by which one unit of government yields a portion of its tax income to another unit of government, according to an established formula; revenue sharing typically involves the national government providing money to state governments

Since the 1970s, as states became more capable of administering large-scale programs, the idea of **devolution**—transferring responsibility for policy from the federal government to the states and localities—has become popular. Proponents of devolution champion states' potential as innovators and experimenters, whose good ideas might spread horizontally to other states and even vertically to the federal government through policy **diffusion**. Devolution's supporters also assert that government closer to the people can better tailor policies to local needs than can the federal government in far-off Washington, D.C. Political conservatives have been the chief proponents of such views, but as we will see later, there is some expedience to views about federalism that depend on which party controls which levels of government.

Block Grants as a Tool of Devolution Proponents of more state authority have looked to **block grants** as a way of reducing federal control. Block grants are federal grants that allow the states considerable leeway in spending federal money. President Nixon led the first push for block grants in the early 1970s, as part of his **New Federalism**. Nixon's approach consolidated programs in the areas of job training, community development, and social services into three large block grants. These grants imposed some conditions on states and localities as to how the money should be spent, but not the narrow regulations contained in categorical grants. In addition, Congress provided an important new form of federal assistance to state and local governments, called **general revenue sharing**. Revenue sharing provided money to local governments and counties with no strings attached; localities could spend the money as they wished. (see Figure 3.5)

In his version of the New Federalism in the 1980s, President Reagan also looked to block grants to reduce the national government's control and return power to the states. But unlike Nixon, he used them to cut federal spending as well. General revenue sharing ended—members of Congress never liked it because they couldn't claim credit for projects implemented by state and local officials—and the 12 new

FIGURE 3.5
Regulated versus New Federalism

Regulated Federalism			New Federalism		
National government sets policy for the states			National government provides funding		
National standards	Conditional grants	Unfunded mandates	Block grants	Revenue sharing	Devolution
State governments help pay for and administer programs			State governments have flexibility to make policy and administer programs		

Cooperative Federalism: Competition or a Check on Power?

While the United States has evolved into a system of cooperative federalism, some democracies began that way. Germany's constitution, adopted in 1949, was designed to use a cooperative federal system to help prevent the abuses of central government power seen in Hitler's Germany. For example, the upper house of the German parliament comprises delegates from the *Länder* ("states") governments, giving the states an official check on all national policy.

The most interesting blending of power, however, is in taxation and spending. Unlike U.S. states, German states and local governments have no taxation powers, making them fully dependent on federal funding. However, German states are responsible for implementing most government policy. As a result, almost two-thirds of German government spending is carried out by states and local governments, compared to less than half of U.S. spending. This emphasis on local spending includes the running of Germany's extensive social security program, a complex system carried out at the national, state, and local levels. In the United States, comparable social spending is both carried out and financed by national, state, and local government or is left to Americans to pay out of pocket.

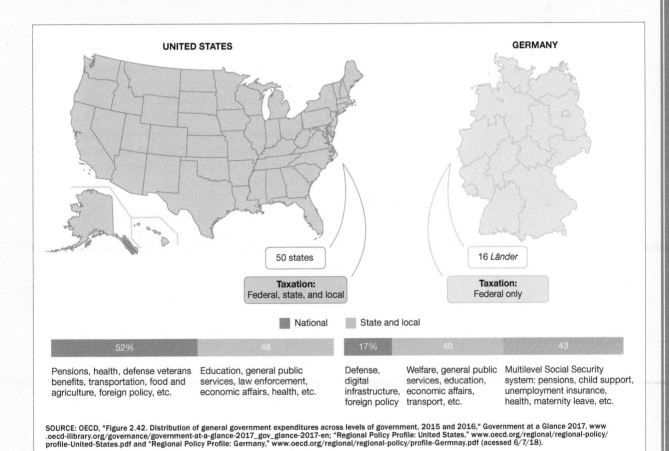

UNITED STATES

GERMANY

50 states

Taxation:
Federal, state, and local

16 *Länder*

Taxation:
Federal only

■ National   ■ State and local

52%	48

17%	40	43

United States		Germany		
Pensions, health, defense veterans benefits, transportation, food and agriculture, foreign policy, etc.	Education, general public services, law enforcement, economic affairs, health, etc.	Defense, digital infrastructure, foreign policy	Welfare, general public services, education, economic affairs, transport, etc.	Multilevel Social Security system: pensions, child support, unemployment insurance, health, maternity leave, etc.

SOURCE: OECD, "Figure 2.42. Distribution of general government expenditures across levels of government, 2015 and 2016," Government at a Glance 2017, www.oecd-ilibrary.org/governance/government-at-a-glance-2017_gov_glance-2017-en; "Regional Policy Profile: United States," www.oecd.org/regional/regional-policy/profile-United-States.pdf and "Regional Policy Profile: Germany," www.oecd.org/regional/regional-policy/profile-Germnay.pdf (acessed 6/7/18).

block grants enacted between 1981 and 1990 cut federal spending in those areas by 12 percent.[37] Reagan's view was that states could spend their own funds to make up the difference if they chose to do so.

The Republican Congress elected in 1994 attempted to take the devolution strategy even further, continuing to support block grants and proposing substantial cuts in federal programs. Their biggest success was the 1996 welfare reform law, which delegated to states important new responsibilities. Most of the other major proposed block grants or spending reductions, however, failed to pass Congress or were vetoed by President Clinton.[38]

Trade-Offs of State Control Neither block grants nor reduced federal funding have proven to be magic solutions to the problems of federalism. For one thing, there is always a trade-off between accountability—that is, whether the states are using funds for the purposes intended—and flexibility. If the objective is to have accountable and efficient government, it is not clear that state bureaucracies are any more efficient or more capable than national agencies. In Mississippi, for example, the state Department of Human Services spent money from the child care block grant for office furniture and designer salt and pepper shakers that cost $37.50 a pair. As one Mississippi state legislator said, "I've seen too many years of good ol' boy politics to know they shouldn't [transfer money to the states] without stricter controls and requirements."[39] Even after block grants were created, Congress reimposed regulations in order to increase the states' accountability.

At times the federal government has also moved to limit state discretion over spending in cases where it thinks states are too generous. For example, in 2007, President Bush issued regulations that prevented states from providing benefits under the State Children's Health Insurance Program (SCHIP) to children in families well above the poverty line. The Bush administration also barred states from providing chemotherapy to undocumented immigrants, who are guaranteed emergency medical treatment under Medicaid.[40] These new rules embroiled states and the federal government in sharp conflicts over state discretion in spending decisions, once the hallmark of New Federalism.

Innovation and Diffusion Sometimes states have been important sources of policy innovations that have in some cases diffused to other states or to the federal government. For example, Minnesota first created charter schools in 1991; now 44 states and the District of Columbia permit them.[41] In 2004, Utah became the first state to allow guns to be carried on college campuses; now 12 states have such provisions.[42] Policy ideas tend to diffuse geographically to neighboring states or ideologically to states with similar political environments. Diffusion can also proceed through the layers of the federal system. In 1990, San Luis Obispo, California, became the first city to ban smoking in bars and restaurants. The State of California followed with a statewide ban on smoking in enclosed workplaces in 1995, and the federal government banned smoking on commercial flights in 1998. The Massachusetts health care reform of 2006 became the template for the federal Affordable Care Act of 2010. With so many jurisdictions in the American federal system having significant policy responsibilities, the possibilities for generating and disseminating new ideas are endless.

States and Fiscal Constraint One reason states have been such important sources of innovation is the creativity spurred by fiscal constraint. The states raise their own revenue, in addition to receiving federal funds, and operate under stringent fiscal constraints. Forty-nine states have legal or constitutional provisions requiring their proposed budgets to balance; most are also prohibited from carrying deficits into the next fiscal year.[43] Both the growth of national standards and devolution have created fiscal challenges for states and heightened questions about which level of government should pay for various public priorities.

One problem that emerged in the 1970s and especially in the 1980s was the increase in **unfunded mandates**—the product of a Democratic Congress that wanted to achieve liberal social objectives and Republican presidents who opposed increased social spending. For example, the 1973 Rehabilitation Act prohibited discrimination against the disabled in programs that were partly funded by the federal government. The new law required state and local governments to make public transit accessible to disabled people with wheelchair lifts in buses, elevators in train stations, and special transportation systems where needed. These requirements were estimated to cost state and local governments $6.8 billion over 30 years.[44] But Congress did not supply additional funding to help states meet these new requirements; the states had to shoulder the increased financial burden themselves. Between 1983 and 1991, Congress mandated standards in many policy areas, including social services and environmental regulations, without providing additional funds to help the states meet those standards. Altogether, Congress enacted 27 laws that imposed new regulations or required states to expand existing programs.[45]

States and localities quickly began to protest the cost of unfunded mandates, complaining that they were unable to set their own priorities due to the unreimbursed costs. These burdens became part of a rallying cry to reduce the power of the federal government—a cry that took center stage in 1994 when a Republican Congress was elected. One of the first measures the new Congress passed was an act to limit the cost of unfunded mandates, the Unfunded Mandates Reform Act (UMRA). Under this law, the Congressional Budget Office must assess the cost of any mandate that it believes would exceed the threshold established in UMRA ($76 million in 2014 adjusted for inflation). Bills that would impose sizable costs on the private sector must also be assessed. The goal is to ensure that Congress knows how much it is expecting of state and local governments and the private sector. Congress must identify funding sources for bills that exceed the threshold established in UMRA. Of all public laws enacted since 1996, fewer than 5 percent have included private-sector mandates with costs estimated to exceed the threshold, while fewer than 1 percent have contained intergovernmental mandates (mandates on state or local governments) with such costs.[46]

Recently, concern about unfunded mandates has arisen around health care reform. The major health care reform enacted under President Obama, the Affordable Care Act of 2010, called for a major expansion of Medicaid. Because Medicaid is partly funded by the states, any major increase in the number of Medicaid recipients could impose a significant fiscal burden on the states. Although the ACA provided additional federal aid to support the new requirements, the Medicaid provisions became a target for state challenges to the health care law. One of the central claims in the 26 states' lawsuits charged that the federal government did not have the power to withhold Medicaid funds from states that did not implement the new expansions.[47] The Supreme Court ultimately ruled that states could decline to expand Medicaid coverage without losing their existing Medicaid funds. After the Court's decision, 25 states, all led by Republican governors, announced that they would not implement the expanded coverage. Some began to reconsider this decision. By late 2018, 36 states plus the District of Columbia had decided to expand Medicaid, and 14 had decided to not expand.[48] It is clear that in programs where the national and state governments share responsibility, the question of who pays remains acute.

The federal government frequently passes laws that impose mandates on the states, such as the 1990 Americans with Disabilities Act, which protects against discrimination based on disability. States were required to pay for changes to meet federal standards for accessibility in public transportation and public facilities.

unfunded mandate a law or regulation requiring a state or local government to perform certain actions without providing funding for fulfilling the requirement

FOR CRITICAL ANALYSIS

Should states be required to implement unfunded mandates? How much of the funding should the federal government provide for policies or standards that it sets?

DEVOLUTION: FOR WHOSE BENEFIT?

As Figure 3.6 indicates, federalism has changed dramatically over the course of American history. Finding the right balance among states and the federal government is an evolving challenge for American democracy, and since the expansion of the national government in the 1930s, questions about "who does what" have frequently provoked conflict. Why does such an apparently simple choice set off such highly charged political debate? One reason is that many decisions about federal-versus-state responsibility have implications for who benefits from government action.

Let's consider the benefits of federal control versus devolution in the realm of **redistributive programs**—programs designed primarily for the benefit of the poor. Many political scientists and economists maintain that states and localities should not be in charge of redistributive programs. They argue that since states and local governments have to compete with one another, they do not have the incentive to spend their money on the needy people in their areas. Instead, they want to keep taxes low and spend money on things that promote economic development.[49] In this situation, states might engage in a "race to the bottom": if one state cuts assistance to the poor, neighboring states will institute similar or deeper cuts both to reduce expenditures and to discourage poorer people from moving to their states. As one New York legislator put it, "The concern we have is that unless we make our welfare system and our tax and regulatory system competitive with the states around us, we will have too many disincentives for business to move here. Welfare is a big part of that."[50]

In 1996, when Congress enacted major welfare reform, it followed a different logic. By changing welfare from a combined federal–state program into a block grant to the states, Congress gave the states more responsibility for programs that serve the poor. Supporters of the change hoped to reduce welfare spending and argued that states could act as laboratories of democracy by experimenting with many different approaches in order to find those that best met the needs of their citizens. As states altered their welfare programs in the wake of the new law, they did indeed design diverse approaches. For example, Minnesota adopted an incentive-based approach that offers extra assistance to families that take low-wage jobs, while six other states imposed very strict time limits on receiving benefits, allowing welfare recipients less than the five-year limit in the federal legislation. After the passage of the law, welfare rolls declined dramatically. On average, they declined by more than half from their peak in 1994. In 12 states the decline was 70 percent or higher. Politicians have cited these statistics to claim that the poor have benefited from greater state control of welfare, yet most studies have found that the majority of those leaving welfare remain in poverty.

More broadly, devolution and state control in areas such as redistributive policy has resulted in substantial interstate variation in program rules. As of 2018

redistributive programs economic policies designed to transfer income through taxing and spending, with the goal of benefiting the poor

FIGURE 3.6

The Changing Federal Framework

New Federalism 1970s–

1789 — 1937 — 1960 — 1970 — 2000

Dual Federalism 1789–1937

Cooperative Federalism 1937–60

Regulated Federalism 1960s–1970s

cash welfare benefits for a family of three are $714 in California, $462 in Colorado, and $290 in Texas.[51] The lifetime limit for receiving welfare benefits is 60 months in most states, but 48 months in Michigan, 21 months in Connecticut, and 12 months in Arizona.[52] Under federal Medicaid rules, dental and vision services are required for children but optional for adults. In most states Medicaid does not cover eyeglasses for adults, but in Texas it does. Utah provides eyeglasses only to pregnant Medicaid recipients, while Tennessee provides them only after cataract surgery. Most Medicaid adults do not have dental care coverage; they can get cavities filled in Massachusetts, but only in the front twelve teeth, not in the molars.[53] Whether one is eligible, under what criteria, and for which benefits vary widely across states; the same person could be eligible in one state but not another, or could receive a differing level of assistance depending on where they live. These differences in policy parameters arise from differences in state wealth and political environment.[54]

In some decisions about federalism, local concerns are overridden in the name of the national interest. The question of speed limits, traditionally a state and local responsibility, provides an example. In 1973, at the height of the oil shortage, Congress passed legislation to withhold federal highway funds from states that did not adopt a maximum speed limit of 55 miles per hour in order to reduce fuel consumption. Although Congress had not formally taken over the authority to set speed limits, the power of its purse was so important that every state adopted the new speed limit. As the crisis faded, concern about energy conservation diminished. The national speed limit lost much of its support, even though it was found to have reduced the number of traffic deaths. In 1995, Congress repealed the penalties for higher speed limits, and states once again became free to set their own speed limits. Many states with large rural areas raised their maximum to 75 miles per hour; Montana initially set unlimited speeds in its rural areas during daylight hours. Research indicates that the number of highway deaths has indeed risen in the states that increased the limits.[55]

Because the division of responsibility in the federal system has important implications for who benefits, few conflicts over state-versus-national control will ever be settled once and for all. New evidence about the costs and benefits of different arrangements provides fuel for ongoing debates about what are properly the states' responsibilities

The debate over national-versus-state control of speed limits arose in 1973, when gas prices skyrocketed and supplies became scarce. Drivers nationwide were forced to wait in long lines at gas stations. The federal government responded to the gas crisis by instituting a national 55-mile-per-hour speed limit. In 1995, Congress removed its speed limit restrictions and allowed states to raise the limit above 55 miles per hour without losing federal highway funds.

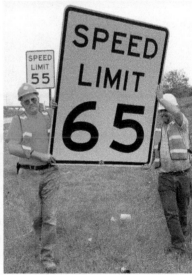

and what the federal government should do. Likewise, changes in the political control of the national government usually provoke a rethinking of responsibilities as new leaders seek to alter federal arrangements for the benefit of the groups they represent.

The Politics of Federalism Today

> **Analyze contemporary relationships among national, state, and local governments**

Since the year 2000, the political polarization between Republicans and Democrats that has characterized national politics and divided states has been played out through the federal system as well. Not all decisions about federalism have divided along political lines. But many of the most controversial issues in American politics—including the appropriate amount of public social spending, the rights and benefits of immigrants (legal and undocumented), government response to global climate change, and questions about whether and how government should regulate business and moral behavior—have been fought through the federal system. Politicians of all stripes have regularly turned to the federal government to override policies they don't like that were made at the state level. The reverse is also true: when the federal government proves unable or unwilling to act, activists and politicians instead try to achieve their goals in states and localities. Sometimes, states seek to go their own way regardless of federal law. It is often then up to the courts to decide which level of government should have the final say. In many cases, the federal government has succeeded in advancing its policy agenda through the states. However, the era since 2000 has been marked by a considerable amount of back-and-forth between the states, the federal government, and even localities as debates over federalism have become politically prominent.

EXPEDIENCY VERSUS IDEOLOGY IN FEDERALISM

FOR CRITICAL ANALYSIS

The role of the national government has changed significantly from the Founding era to the present. Do you think the framers of the Constitution would be pleased with the current balance of power between the national government and the state governments?

Although conservatives proclaim their preference for a small federal government and their support for more state autonomy, in fact they often expand the federal government and limit state autonomy. During the presidency of George W. Bush, the growth of government; the activist, free-spending Republican Congress; and a series of Supreme Court rulings supporting federal power over the states made it clear that conservatives do not always support small government, nor do they always favor returning power to the states. Once in power, many conservatives discovered not only that they needed a strong federal government to respond to public demands but also that they could use federal power to advance conservative policy goals.

For President Bush, the importance of a strong federal government dawned with force after the terrorist attacks in 2001. Aware that the American public was looking to Washington for protection, Bush worked with Congress to pass the USA PATRIOT Act, which greatly increased the surveillance powers of the federal government. A year later he created the enormous new federal Department of Homeland Security. Democrats supported the president in both initiatives. President Bush, with the support of Democrats, also expanded federal control and increased spending in policy areas far removed from concerns about security. The 2001 No Child Left Behind Act introduced unprecedented federal intervention in public education, traditionally a state and local responsibility. New, detailed federal testing requirements and provisions stipulating how states should treat failing schools were major expansions of federal authority in education. When a number of states threatened to defy some of the new federal requirements, Bush's Department of Education relaxed its tough stance and became more flexible in enforcing the act. President Obama later released the states from the federal NCLB mandates and in 2015 enacted a new education law called Every Student Succeeds, returning power to the states to evaluate schools, a move that might be expected more from a conservative president.

In the Supreme Court, too, many decisions began to support a stronger federal role over the states. This was surprising to many observers because in the 1990s it had appeared that the Court then was embarked on a "federalism revolution" designed to return more power to the states. Instead, in several key decisions, the Court reaffirmed the power of the federal government. Decisions to uphold the federal Family and Medical Leave Act and the Americans with Disabilities Act asserted federal authority against state claims of immunity from the acts. In one important 2005 case, the Court upheld the right of Congress to ban medical marijuana, even though 11 states had legalized its use. Overturning a lower-court ruling that said Congress did not have authority to regulate marijuana when it had been grown for noncommercial purposes in a single state, the Supreme Court ruled that the federal government did have the power to regulate use of all marijuana under the commerce clause precipitating the type of raid that Larry Harvey of the chapter opener experienced.[56] Even so, by 2018, 33 states and the District of Columbia had legalized medical marijuana (see Figure 3.7). Amid this legal confusion, a medical marijuana industry began to flourish. In 2012, Colorado and Washington went further by legalizing recreational marijuana soon followed by eight more states even though it is a prohibited substance by federal law. The federal government has not endorsed these laws, and while it made prosecution of marijuana in these states a low priority during the Obama administration, the Trump administration's first attorney general, Jeff Sessions, vowed to increase such prosecutions.

FIGURE 3.7

Marijuana Laws across the States

SOURCE: The National Organization for the Reform of Marijuana Laws, State Laws, norml.org/laws; "33 Legal Medical Marijuana States and DC," November 7, 2018, https://medicalmarijuana .procon.org/view.resource.php?resourceID=000881 (accessed 11/7/18).

CREDIT: State Marijuana Laws in 2018 Map, originally published by Governing.com, March 30, 2018. Reprinted by permission of Governing.

Legend:
- Medical marijuana broadly legalized
- Marijuana legalized for recreational use
- No broad laws legalizing marijuana

Who Benefits from Federal Spending?

Federal Grants to State and Local Governments, 2016

| Health $397 billion | | | | Income security $105 billion | Education $61 billion | Transportation $64 billion | Other $35 billion |

Although Americans often think they pay a lot in federal taxes, they receive much in return in the form of federal money for state and local programs. Federal outlays for grants to state and local governments have grown from $51.5 billion in 1960 to $593.5 billion in 2016 (in constant dollars).

Fiscal Transfers between the States and the Federal Government, 2015

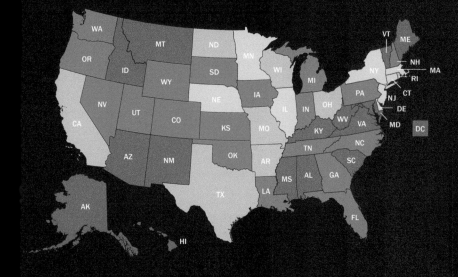

Federal spending per tax dollar

- $1.50+
- $1.01–1.50
- —————————————— $1.00
- $0.80–1.00
- < $0.80

Every U.S. state contributes to the federal government through the federal taxes paid by the state's citizens, and every state receives money from federal spending. Federal spending is a broad category that includes the federal grants described above as well as spending on military bases and federal procurement. Not every state receives the same amount from the federal government, however. The map above shows how much federal spending each state received for each dollar paid in federal taxes in 2015.

SOURCES: Federal Grants to State and Local Governments: A Historical Perspective on Contemporary Issues, https://fas.org; Federal Spending in the States, 2015, http://knowledgecenter.csg.org; IRS 2015 Data Book, https://www.irs.gov, (accessed 3/16/18).

FOR CRITICAL ANALYSIS

1. What are some of the benefits of federal grants to state and local governments?

2. What is the rationale behind transfers from one state to another? Is it fair that some states pay more in federal taxes than they receive? What might explain why some states are net recipients and some net contributors?

POLARIZATION AND NATIONAL GRIDLOCK: STATES STEP IN

The move to a stronger federal role has not been uniform. In some cases the Supreme Court has granted more authority to the states. One closely watched federalism case in 2006 was the challenge to Oregon's "right to die" law, discussed earlier, which allows doctors to prescribe lethal doses of medicine for terminally ill patients who request it. Challengers claimed the law was illegal because Congress has the right to outlaw such use of drugs under the Controlled Substances Act, which regulates prescription drugs. In a 6–3 decision, the Court ruled in Oregon's favor.[57] Washington State, Vermont, Montana, California, and Colorado followed in Oregon's footsteps to make physician-assisted suicide legal.[58]

States have also responded to gridlock at the national level by taking action themselves. On some issues, the majority of the states have pressed the federal government to act, but it has not responded. One issue on which most states would like the federal government to establish uniform law is internet sales. Current law requires internet retailers to collect sales tax on online purchases only when the business has a physical presence in the buyer's state. This has become a major issue for states, most of which rely on sales taxes for a significant part of their revenue. One study estimated that states lost $23 billion in 2012 from internet sales on which no taxes were collected.[59] In 2013 the Senate—with support from both Democrats and Republicans—passed the Marketplace Fairness Act, which would require online retailers to collect state sales taxes. However, in the House, some Republicans opposed the measure as a tax increase. By 2016, with the issue still unresolved in Congress, officials in 13 states had begun to impose taxes on out-of-state internet sales. Frustrated by congressional inaction, the states aimed to push Congress to act or to throw the matter into the courts, where they hoped for a decision that would support them.[60]

STATE-FEDERAL TUG OF WAR

The long-standing tug-of-war between the federal and state governments has continued in recent years. Indeed, immigration policy has been a center of federal-state conflict. Frustrated by congressional inaction on immigration reform, President Obama issued executive memoranda in 2012 that would provide temporary legal status and work permits to those who had been brought to the United States as children, termed the "Dreamers." However, when Obama moved to expand this Deferred Action for Childhood Arrivals program (DACA) in 2014 and extend legal status to some parents of U.S. citizens and legal residents (called Deferred Action for Parents of Americans, or DAPA), 26 states led by Texas challenged the executive order in court. They charged the expansion exceeded executive authority and would impose unreasonable costs on states, which would bear additional costs such as issuing driver's licenses. The expansion was never implemented because the Supreme Court, in the wake of the death of Justice Antonin Scalia, deadlocked in a 4–4 decision, leaving in place lower-court decisions that sided with the states.[61] The Trump administration began a six-month phaseout of the DACA program in September 2017, giving Congress until March 2018 to devise a legislative solution.[62] Congressional action failed, but as of late 2018 DACA remained in place due to two federal judges' rulings.

Whether states and localities have to enforce federal immigration laws has been a particular center of controversy. For example, the Secure Communities program, launched in 2008, required state and local authorities to check the fingerprints of people being booked into jail against a Homeland Security database. The policy led to a record number of deportations in 2009 and 2010, leading several states and

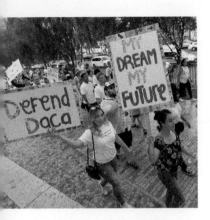

Since the Trump administration's announcement of the six-month phaseout of the DACA program put in place by the Obama administration, the legislative branch on the federal level has failed to implement a solution. State-level challenges to the termination of the policy, however, have been successful in protecting those covered by the program.

localities to pull out of the agreement with the federal government on the grounds that the law was detaining too many undocumented immigrants who had never committed a crime. The Obama administration softened its deportation policy in 2011 but sustained opposition, as well as federal court decisions that challenged the constitutionality of elements of the policy, ultimately led the government to end the program in late 2014. In its place, the Obama administration launched the Priority Enforcement Program in July 2015, which adopts a more limited deportation policy than the one formerly mandated by Secure Communities.[63]

President Donald Trump campaigned on promises for more rigorous immigration enforcement. In January 2017 he signed an executive order increasing the number of immigrants considered a priority for deportation, from those convicted of serious crimes such as felonies or multiple misdemeanors (as under Obama) to those accused or convicted of minor crimes as well.[64] In response, a growing number of cities, counties, and states declared themselves "sanctuaries" that limit cooperation with national government enforcement of immigration law. President Trump pledged to cancel funding for sanctuary cities and states, but in 2017 a federal judge blocked the Trump administration from withholding federal grants from these jurisdictions because of sanctuary policies.[65] In January 2018, the Justice Department began considering whether state and local officials could be subject to criminal charges if they implement sanctuary status, which opponents say would be illegal.[66]

The 2010 Affordable Care Act has also been the object of contestation between the federal and state governments. As we have seen, one controversial part of that legislation required states to expand their Medicaid programs to cover more low-income residents. The Court's 2012 ruling in *National Federation of Independent Business v. Sebelius* that the federal government could not impose all-or-nothing conditions on the states—implement the expansion or lose all Medicaid funding—represented a sharp departure from the past.[67] The ruling has far-reaching potential to change the federal government's power to impose conditions on the states when it supplies the funds. The other controversial provision of the Affordable Care Act was the "individual mandate," the requirement that individuals without health care insurance be required to purchase such insurance. The 26 states suing the federal government charged that Congress had no power to force individuals to purchase a product and that it had exceeded its power under the commerce clause. In defending the law, the federal government argued the opposite: that the complex interactions of the health care market made the individual mandate constitutional under the commerce clause.[68] Everyone is part of the health care economy. Even if a person does not have health insurance, federal law requires that hospitals provide treatment in an emergency, costs which are borne by all of the people who do pay for health insurance. The Court rejected this argument on the grounds that the federal government cannot regulate economic inactivity, that is, the failure to purchase health insurance. Instead, it found that the Affordable Care Act could be justified by Congress's power to tax. The law required individuals who do not receive insurance from their employers or their parents and who are not eligible for Medicaid to purchase insurance or pay a penalty. The Court reasoned that the penalty could be considered a tax and, in that sense, passed constitutional muster. The complex and surprising decision marked a new era in American federalism. The Court placed limits on two of the key powers that have expanded the reach of the federal government since the New Deal—the power to regulate commerce and the power to spend for the general welfare. The decision will surely invite challenges to federal power in diverse areas, possibly including education programs, the drinking age, and environmental regulations.

The Affordable Care Act law survived another challenge in 2015 when the Supreme Court ruled that federal subsidies to help pay for insurance should be available to residents in states that offered insurance through the federal exchange as well as in states that had formed their own state insurance marketplaces. The outcome of *King v. Burwell* ensured that subsidies would be available in all states.[69] The ACA also survived a repeal attempt after the 2016 election, when Republicans took control of Congress and the Presidency. However, the Tax Cuts and Jobs Act passed in late 2017 did repeal the individual mandate requiring Americans to have health insurance.

FOR CRITICAL ANALYSIS

Why was the 2010 Affordable Care Act controversial? How did the Supreme Court's decisions about the law reflect the principles of federalism?

STATE PREEMPTION OF LOCAL GOVERNMENT POLICY

Another notable development in the recent politics of federalism has been the willingness of state governments to preempt local policy. Just as states sometimes seize the initiative and make policy in areas where the federal government has failed to do so, so too have cities made policy in areas of state inaction or where policy preferences differ in the city compared to the state at large. In recent years some cities have set higher minimum wages than their surrounding state; implemented paid sick leave regulations on employers; regulated the "sharing economy" of car- and home-sharing; passed laws prohibiting discrimination in public facilities such as bathrooms; and attempted to establish public broadband services. In each of these cases, some state legislatures that disagreed with the direction of municipal policy have responded with preemption, passing laws nullifying municipal law or authority. As of 2017, 25 states preempt local minimum wage ordinances, 17 preempt local paid leave ordinances, 37 limit local authority to regulate ride sharing, and 3 limit local authority on home sharing. Michigan banned cities from banning plastic bags; Texas banned cities from banning fracking. Seventeen states prohibit localities from establishing municipal broadband service, and three—most famously North Carolina—preempt local anti-discrimination ordinances.[70]

In February 2016, the Charlotte City Council passed an ordinance prohibiting sex discrimination in public facilities. The following month the North Carolina legislature passed HB2, the Public Facilities Privacy and Security Act. The "Charlotte bathroom bill," as it came to be known, eliminated local authority to regulate access to public facilities and required people to use the bathroom of their designated gender at birth. The state faced strong objections to the law, which was viewed by opponents as a violation of transgender rights, and the state lost nearly $400 million in investment as plans for new jobs and events such as the NBA all-star game, NCAA championship, and business conferences were canceled.[71] Other preemption laws similarly unmake local provisions. In St. Louis, the minimum wage rose to $10 an hour in May 2017. Two months later, the Missouri legislature nullified the law. Some business owners pledged to keep the new higher wage, but other owners of fast food restaurants and grocery stores reset wages to the state's minimum of $7.70 an hour ($7.85 as of January 1, 2018).[72]

Like struggles between the federal and state governments since 2000, the more recent episodes of municipal preemption reflect the era's political polarization, with conservative state legislatures preempting the authority of more liberal municipal governments. Although conservatives have historically extolled the virtues of local control, views on federalism can depend more on party control of government than traditional ideological stances.

Despite the Charlotte City Council's ordinance prohibiting sex discrimination in public facilities, state preemption allowed for the North Carolina legislature to pass the "Charlotte bathroom bill," which undid the provisions originally set out by the city council. Opponents to this legislation saw the bill as a clear violation of transgender rights, and protested its passage.

Federalism
WHAT DO WE WANT?

In recent years, sharp differences in Americans' views on many economic and social issues have been reflected in the federal system. Until 2015, when the Supreme Court ruled that state-level bans on same-sex marriage were unconstitutional, 37 states allowed same-sex marriage and 13 did not. Today, over half of the 50 states have legalized medical marijuana, while 10 and Washington, D.C., have gone further and legalized recreational marijuana.[73] More states are likely to change their laws on marijuana, but differences across the states are likely to persist for many years. Half of the states welcomed the expansion of Medicaid, the program that provides medical assistance to the poor. The other half, concerned about costs and the growing role of government in the economy, initially declined to implement the expansion. Some states actively welcome immigrants and seek to opt out of restrictive federal laws; other states go beyond the federal government in enacting restrictive immigration laws. Yet while states have the authority to devise their own laws on a variety of important issues, Americans' participation in state and local politics remains low (see the "**Who Participates?**" feature on the facing page).

As described in the opening of this chapter, Larry Harvey's arrest for using medical marijuana, legal in his state but illegal under federal law, raises questions about the promise, conflict, and ambiguity inherent in a federal system of government. Our history of federalism means that we are comfortable with the idea that states should have the freedom to enact laws that best serve their residents, within the bounds set by Congress and the courts. We expect states to act as "laboratories of democracy" that try out new policies. But the great variation across the states today poses questions that will have to be answered in the coming decades. Is the federal government endangering people by allowing states to legalize marijuana? Or is the federal government endangering critically ill people by prosecuting medical marijuana use even in states with legalization? Is it fair that a transgender person in California can legally change the sex on her birth certificate, but a transgender person in Tennessee would be denied the same? Is it reasonable that a gun owner can openly carry a handgun in Georgia but not in Florida? Each generation confronts a different set of questions about how much variation across the states is appropriate. Are some of the issues on which the states differ fundamental rights that should be uniform across the country? Is it important to preserve state choice on most matters? As today's youth help to answer these questions in the coming decades, they will be remaking American federalism.

Thus, American federalism remains a work in progress. As public problems shift and as local, state, and federal governments change, questions about the relationship between American values and federalism naturally emerge. The different views that people bring to this discussion suggest that federalism will remain a central issue in American democracy.

Who Participates in State and Local Politics?

Turnout in Recent Gubernatorial Elections

Percentage of voting-eligible population*

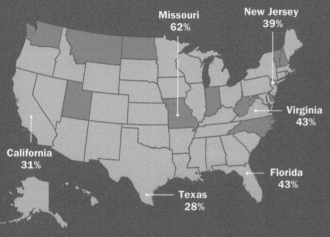

Missouri 62%

New Jersey 39%

Virginia 43%

California 31%

Florida 43%

Texas 28%

Median % of voters to turn out in the following years:

Non-presidential, non-congressional	Non-presidential congressional	Presidential
2015, 2017	2014	2016
39%	**40%**	**65%**

Turnout in Most Recent Municipal Election

Percentage of voting-age population in selected cities*

Seattle 43%

Washington, D.C. 38%

Chicago 33%

Detroit 27%

Denver 24%

Houston 22%

San Antonio 10%

New York City 7%

*The voting-eligible population excludes noncitizens and people who are institutionalized or not allowed to vote in some states because they are ex-felons. The voting-age population includes everyone over 18.

NOTE: Oregon had an additional election in 2016 to fill a vacancy.

SOURCES: Elect Project, electproject.org; Voter Turnout, elect.ky.gov; Post Election Statistics, electionstatistics.sos.la.gov; 2017 Results, state.nj.us; 2017 Results Report, elections.virginia.gov (accessed 3/10/18).

★ WHAT YOU CAN DO ★

Get Involved in State and Local Politics

 Attend a board of supervisors, city council, planning commission, or other local government meeting. Agendas and minutes will usually be available on county and city websites.

 Visit the state capitol. If you make an appointment, you might be able to meet with your local representative. Committee meetings and hearings are generally open to the public, as are meetings of the legislature.

 Attend a session of your local or state judiciary. Cases on the docket are available online, as are rules for attendance and behavior when the court is in session.

★ STUDY GUIDE ★

Federalism in the Constitution

> **Describe what the Constitution says about the powers of the national government and of the states (pp. 79–84)**

While the Founders wanted a national government that was stronger than it had been under the Articles of Confederation, they also wanted to preserve the autonomy of the states. The necessary and proper clause, the supremacy clause, and the specific powers granted to Congress in Article I demonstrate the nation-centered focus of the Constitution. The Tenth Amendment, which grants all undelegated powers to the states, shows the state-centered focus of the Constitution. The Constitution also creates obligations among the states and includes some concurrent powers that are shared by both the federal government and state governments.

Key Terms

federalism (p. 79)

unitary system (p. 79)

expressed powers (p. 79)

implied powers (p. 79)

necessary and proper clause (p. 79)

reserved powers (p. 81)

police power (p. 82)

concurrent powers (p. 82)

full faith and credit clause (p. 82)

privileges and immunities clause (p. 83)

home rule (p. 84)

Practice Quiz

1. Which term describes the division of powers between the national government and the state governments?
   a) home rule
   b) separation of powers
   c) federalism
   d) checks and balances
   e) unitary system

2. Which amendment to the Constitution stated that the powers not delegated to the national government or prohibited to the states were "reserved to the states"?
   a) First Amendment
   b) Fifth Amendment
   c) Tenth Amendment
   d) Fourteenth Amendment
   e) Twenty-Sixth Amendment

3. A state government's authority to regulate the health, safety, and morals of its citizens is frequently referred to as
   a) the reserved power.
   b) the police power.
   c) the expressed power.
   d) the concurrent power.
   e) the implied power.

4. Which constitutional clause requires that states normally honor the public acts and judicial decisions of other states?
   a) privileges and immunities clause
   b) necessary and proper clause
   c) interstate commerce clause
   d) preemption clause
   e) full faith and credit clause

5. Many states have amended their constitutions to guarantee that large cities will have the authority to manage local affairs without interference from state government. This power is called
   a) home rule.
   b) devolution.
   c) preemption.
   d) states' rights.
   e) New Federalism.

The Traditional System of Federalism

Consider how the relationship between the federal and state governments evolved during the nation's first 140 years (pp. 84–88)

The relative importance of states and the federal government has changed significantly over time. For the first 140 years of American history, the national government was small, reluctant to directly coerce citizens, and focused primarily on assisting commerce. Most of the fundamental governing in the United States during this period was done by the states. Beginning in the 1930s, the Supreme Court dramatically expanded the power of the federal government through its expansive interpretation of the commerce clause.

Key Terms

dual federalism (p. 85)

commerce clause (p. 87)

Practice Quiz

6. The relationship between the states and the national government from 1789 to 1937 is known as
   a) unitary government.
   b) New Federalism.
   c) dual federalism.
   d) cooperative federalism.
   e) regulated federalism.

7. In which case did the Supreme Court create the potential for increased national power by ruling that Congress could use the necessary and proper clause to interpret its delegated powers broadly?
   a) *United States v. Lopez*
   b) *Printz v. United States*
   c) *Loving v. Virginia*
   d) *McCulloch v. Maryland*
   e) *Gibbons v. Ogden*

8. In 1937 the Supreme Court laid the groundwork for a stronger federal government by issuing a number of decisions that
   a) dramatically narrowed the definition of the commerce clause.
   b) dramatically expanded the definition of the commerce clause.
   c) struck down the supremacy clause.
   d) struck down the privileges and immunities clause.
   e) struck down the full faith and credit clause.

Federalism in the Modern Era

Trace developments in the federal framework leading to a stronger national government (pp. 89–94)

The Great Depression effectively ended the traditional system of dual federalism in which the states and the federal government performed very different functions and instituted a new system of cooperative federalism. Under this new system, the size and scope of the national government grew dramatically. As Congress began to enact legislation in previously unregulated areas during the 1970s, the national government began to set an increasingly large number of standards that required states to meet national guidelines. This more recent trend is often referred to as regulated federalism.

Key Terms

grants-in-aid (p. 90)

categorical grants (p. 91)

cooperative federalism (p. 91)

regulated federalism (p. 93)

preemption (p. 93)

Practice Quiz

9. The value of categorical grants
   a) increased from $2.3 billion in 1950 to approximately $31 billion in 2016.
   b) increased from $2.3 billion in 1950 to approximately $675 billion in 2016.
   c) decreased from $31 billion in 1950 to approximately $2 billion in 2016.
   d) decreased from $667 billion to approximately $2 billion in 2016.
   e) remained the same between 1950 and 2016.

10. The principle that allows the federal government to take over areas of regulation formerly overseen by states or local governments is called
    a) regulated federalism.
    b) preemption.
    c) devolution.
    d) "layer cake" federalism.
    e) exemption.

Evolving Role of the States

Analyze the changing role of the states in the federal framework (pp. 94–102)

Throughout the history of American federalism, questions about "who does what" have provoked intense political conflict. Despite the national government's expansion since the 1930s and more recent attempts to enhance state authority through block grants and revenue sharing, both the federal and state governments remain important players in American democracy. Most of the important public policy issues in recent years, including controversies about government spending, immigration, climate change, health care, and economic regulation, are debated and addressed through the United States' unique system of federalism.

Key Terms

states' rights (p. 94)
devolution (p. 96)
diffusion (p. 96)
block grants (p. 96)
New Federalism (p. 96)
general revenue sharing (p. 96)
unfunded mandates (p. 99)
redistributive programs (p. 100)

Practice Quiz

11. The process of returning more of the responsibilities of governing from the national level to the state level is known as
    a) devolution.
    b) diffusion.
    c) incorporation.
    d) home rule.
    e) preemption.

12. To what does the term *New Federalism* refer?
    a) the era of federalism initiated by President Roosevelt during the late 1930s
    b) the national government's regulation of state action through grants-in-aid
    c) the type of federalism that uses categorical grants to influence state action
    d) efforts to return more policy-making discretion to the states through the use of block grants
    e) the recent emergence of local governments as important political actors

13. When state and local governments must conform to costly federal regulations or conditions in order to receive grants but do not receive reimbursements for their expenditures it is called
    a) states' rights.
    b) block grants.
    c) general revenue sharing.
    d) unfunded mandate.
    e) redistributive programs.

The Politics of Federalism Today

Analyze contemporary relationships among national, state, and local governments (pp. 102–7)

Since the year 2000, the political polarization between Republicans and Democrats has been played out through the federal system as well as in national politics. Sometimes, states seek to go their own way regardless of federal law, and the federal government has succeeded in advancing its policy agenda through the states. It is often up to the courts to decide who gets the final say. However, the era since 2000 has been marked by a considerable amount of back-and-forth between the states, the federal government, and even localities as debates over federalism have become politically prominent.

14. The Supreme Court's decision in *National Federation of Independent Business v. Sebelius* was significant because
    a) it affirmed the federal government's absolute power to impose all-or-nothing conditions on state governments attempting to receive federal funding.
    b) it limited the federal government's power to impose all-or-nothing conditions on state governments attempting to receive federal funding.
    c) it struck down the individual mandate of the Affordable Care Act as a violation of the interstate commerce clause.
    d) it eliminated the federal government's ability to provide subsidies for health insurance coverage.
    e) it invalidated the educational standards and testing requirements imposed by the 2001 No Child Left Behind Act.

For Further Reading

Derthick, Martha. *Keeping the Compound Republic: Essays on American Federalism*. Washington, DC: Brookings Institution Press, 2001.

Elazar, Daniel. *American Federalism: A View from the States*. 3rd ed. New York: Harper & Row, 1984.

Feiock, Richard C., and John T. Scholz. *Self-Organizing Federalism: Collaborative Mechanisms to Mitigate Institutional Collective Action Dilemmas*. New York: Cambridge University Press, 2009.

Gerston, Larry N. *American Federalism: A Concise Introduction*. Armonk, NY: M. E. Sharpe, 2007.

Grodzins, Morton. *The American System*. Chicago: Rand McNally, 1974.

Johnson, Kimberly S. *Governing the American State: Congress and the New Federalism, 1877–1929*. Princeton, NJ: Princeton University Press, 2007.

Karch, Andrew. *Democratic Laboratories: Policy Diffusion among the American States*. Ann Arbor: University of Michigan Press, 2007.

Kettl, Donald. *The Regulation of American Federalism*. Baltimore: Johns Hopkins University Press, 1987.

Mettler, Suzanne. *Dividing Citizens: Gender and Federalism in New Deal Public Policy*. Ithaca, NY: Cornell University Press, 1998.

Michener, Jamila. *Fragmented Democracy: Medicaid, Federalism, and Unequal Politics*. New York: Cambridge University Press, 2018.

Pierceson, Jason. *Same-Sex Marriage in the United States: The Road to the Supreme Court*. Lanham, MD: Rowman and Littlefield, 2013.

Robertson, David Brian. *Federalism and the Making of America*. New York: Routledge, 2011.

Van Horn, Carl E. *The State of the States*. 4th ed. Washington, DC: CQ Press, 2005.

Recommended Websites

Constitution Finder
http://confinder.richmond.edu
Governments can organize power in either a unitary or a federal system. Examine the constitutions of different countries throughout the world, and try to identify how those governments organize power.

Council of State Governments
www.csg.org
This organization provides information on a variety of state–federal policy areas. See what current issues concerning federalism are of prime importance to the state governments on this site.

Governing.com
www.governing.com
See what state–federal issues are important to your local government officials on the website for *Governing* magazine.

National Conference of State Legislatures
www.ncsl.org

National Governors Association
www.nga.org
These are two of the largest organizations dedicated to representing state and local government interests at the federal level.

Oyez: U.S. Supreme Court Media
www.oyez.org
Read here about one of the most important U.S. Supreme Court decisions regarding the division of federal and state power in the case of *McCulloch v. Maryland*.

Pew Charitable Trusts Stateline
www.pewtrusts.org/en/research-and-analysis/blogs/stateline/about
This nonprofit site provides news coverage in the states, focusing on four issues: fiscal and economic issues, health care, demographics, and the business of government. It also offers a weekly newsletter that includes the highlights of its reporting.

Supreme Court of the United States Blog
www.scotusblog.com
Supreme Court of the United States blog provides independent scholarly analysis of court rulings. The site provides timely discussion of pending and recent court decisions including *Obergefell v. Hodges*, the decision that made same-sex marriage legal in all states.

U.S. Census Bureau
www.census.gov
The Census Bureau maintains one of the largest collections of data about social and economic conditions of the nation's 50 states.

World Federalist Movement
www.wfm.org
This international organization is dedicated to the division of power and authority among all local, state, and international governmental agencies. Generally, it promotes federalism and constitutional democracy throughout the world.

Civil Liberties

WHAT GOVERNMENT DOES AND WHY IT MATTERS In Portland in 2006, Simon Tam founded what *Oregon Music News* called the first and only all Asian American dance-rock band, or "Chinatown Dance Rock," as the band prefers. The various members of the band are of Chinese, Taiwanese, Vietnamese, and Filipino descent. In addition to playing at anime conventions and cultural festivals, they are known for their community involvement battling Asian stereotypes and supporting young Asian people.[1]

They are also known for a First Amendment case over the band's name, the Slants. The name has

three sources. The first two reference the members' "slant" on life and the guitar chords they use: "It actually sounds like a fun, 80s, New Wave kind of band. And it's a play on words. We can share our personal experiences about what it's like being people of color—our own slant on life, if you will. It's also a musical reference. There are slant guitar chords that we use in our music," Tam said. The third source was a reclaiming and repurposing of the old ethnic slur about Asian people. "We grew up and the notion of having slanted eyes was always considered a negative thing," Tam said. "Kids would pull their eyes back in a slant-eyed gesture to make fun of

The First Amendment protects Americans from government infringement on their right to free speech. In the case of the Slants, they used the First Amendment as grounds to re-appropriate a term deemed offensive for themselves and their cultures.

us.... I wanted to change it to something that was powerful, something that was considered beautiful or a point of pride instead."

The U.S. Patent and Trademark Office had a different view. Tam's application for a trademark on the band's name was rejected as a violation of the Disparagement Clause of the Lanham Act of 1946, which prohibits trademarks that disparage a racial or ethnic group. The denial stated that although the "applicant, or even the entire band, may be willing to take on the disparaging term as a band name, in what may be considered an attempt ... to wrest 'ownership' of the term," that "does not mean that

all [Asian Americans] share the applicant's view." The case ultimately went to the Supreme Court, which in 2017 ruled unanimously that the disparagement clause violated the First Amendment's free speech clause. The band could keep the name.

But in a further twist, the band's victory inadvertently undermined legal challenges to the name of the Washington Redskins football team. A group of Native Americans who found the "Redskins" name offensive had filed a petition to revoke the team's trademark, using the Lanham Act's disparagement clause. Once the Court declared the clause unconstitutional, they lost the legal basis for their argument, and the team was able to keep the name. "There's no more challenge to make," said their attorney. Thus the Slants' successful effort to reclaim what had been an epithet to their group meant that a moniker offensive to another group remains in use. The Slants' free speech was protected to their joy, but so was the Redskins' free speech to the disappointment of Native American groups.

Free speech, along with the freedoms of assembly, religion, and privacy, are among the civil liberties contained in the Bill of Rights and elsewhere in the Constitution. Thomas Jefferson said that a bill of rights "is what people are entitled to against every government on earth." Note the wording: *against government*. Civil liberties are *protections from* improper government action. Today in the United States, we often take for granted the liberties contained in the Constitution. But these freedoms raise difficult questions. Do the cases of the Slants and the Redskins strike you as different or the same? Under what circumstances can the government restrict Americans' liberties, especially in the realms of speech, assembly, and privacy? Do freedoms for some people, such as free speech, threaten other people? How should contrasting views be reconciled, or can they? And how should we think about possible trade-offs, as between the right of privacy from surveillance and national security?

CHAPTER GOALS

★ Explain the origins and evolution of the civil liberties in the Bill of Rights as they apply to the federal government and the states (pp. 117–22)

★ Describe how the First Amendment protects freedom of religion (pp. 123–27)

★ Describe how the First Amendment protects free speech and freedom of the press (pp. 127–36)

★ Explore whether the Second Amendment means people have a right to own guns (pp. 136–38)

★ Explain the major rights that people have if they are accused of a crime (pp. 138–46)

★ Assess whether people have a right to privacy under the Constitution (pp. 146–51)

Civil Liberties and the Constitution

Explain the origins and evolution of the civil liberties in the Bill of Rights as they apply to federal government and the states

Civil liberties are related to but different from civil rights. Civil rights, which we will discuss in Chapter 5, are obligations (what the government must do) to guarantee equal citizenship and to define how people will be treated by the government. The foundations of civil liberties as well as civil rights are to be found in the state and federal constitutions which guarantee free speech, freedom of the press, freedom of assembly and so forth. The federal Constitution's Bill of Rights includes both liberties and rights. However, because civil liberties are limits on government power, the evolution and expansion of civil liberties in the United States is mainly a story of judicial action to overturn state and federal government policies that placed limits on liberty. Civil rights, on the other hand, were shaped as much or more by the actions of the Congress and state legislatures as by the decisions of the courts. Thus, in Chapter 5 we will consider such pieces of federal legislation as the Voting Rights Act and the 1964 Civil Rights Act.

Why might the actions of the federal and state governments threaten civil liberties? There may be a variety of reasons, but the fundamental problem is the clash between the basic duty of governments to protect the public's health, safety, and general welfare from such dangers as crime, environmental hazards, and terrorism, and the freedom of citizens to go about their own business without governmental interference. Most Americans wish to be protected against violent criminals, but few would say there should be no restraint on police conduct in conducting investigations and interrogations. Most Americans want to be protected against terrorist plots, but few approve of unrestricted government surveillance and intrusions into their own communications. How do we balance safety and freedom? Where do we draw the line between anarchy and a police state?

In the United States, the federal and state constitutions establish the basic limits on government action and the decisions of the courts, interpreting constitutional principles, attempt to balance public safety and individual freedom. This balance is never carved in stone but needs to constantly be reexamined and revisited in light of changing circumstances.

A BRIEF HISTORY OF THE BILL OF RIGHTS

When the first Congress under the newly ratified Constitution met in late April of 1789, the most important item of business was the consideration of a proposal to add a bill of rights to the Constitution. Such a proposal had been turned down with little debate in the waning days of the Philadelphia Constitutional Convention in 1787, not because the delegates were against rights but because, as the Federalists, led by Alexander Hamilton, later argued, it was "not only unnecessary in the proposed Constitution but would even be dangerous."[2] First, according to Hamilton, a bill of rights would be irrelevant to a national government that was given only delegated powers in the first place. To put restraints on "powers which are not granted" could provide a pretext for governments to claim more powers than were in fact granted: "For why declare that things shall not be done which there is no power to do?"[3] Second, the Constitution was to Hamilton and the Federalists a bill of rights in itself, containing provisions that amounted to a bill of rights without requiring

TABLE 4.1

Rights in the Original Constitution (Not in the Bill of Rights)

CLAUSE	RIGHT ESTABLISHED
Article I, Section 9	Guarantee of habeas corpus
Article I, Section 9	Prohibition of bills of attainder
Article I, Section 9	Prohibition of ex post facto laws
Article I, Section 9	Prohibition against acceptance of titles of nobility, etc., from any foreign state
Article III	Guarantee of trial by jury in state where crime was committed
Article III	Treason defined and limited to the life of the person convicted, not to the person's heirs

habeas corpus a court order demanding that an individual in custody be brought into court and shown the cause for detention

additional amendments (see Table 4.1). For example, Article I, Section 9 included the right of **habeas corpus**, which prohibits the government from depriving a person of liberty without an open trial before a judge. Many of the framers, moreover, saw the very structure of the Constitution, including checks and balances, as protective of citizens' liberties.

Despite the power of Hamilton's arguments, when the Constitution was submitted to the states for ratification, Antifederalists, most of whom had not been delegates in Philadelphia, picked up on the argument of Thomas Jefferson (who also had not been a delegate) that the omission of a bill of rights was a major imperfection of the new Constitution. The Federalists conceded that to gain ratification they would have to make an "unwritten but unequivocal pledge" to add a bill of rights that would include a confirmation (in what would become the Tenth Amendment) of the understanding that all powers not expressly delegated to the national government or explicitly prohibited to the states were reserved to the states.[4]

Bill of Rights the first 10 amendments to the U.S. Constitution, ratified in 1791; they ensure certain rights and liberties to the people

"After much discussion and manipulation...at the delicate prompting of Washington and under the masterful prodding of Madison," the House of Representatives approved 17 amendments; of these, the Senate accepted 12. Ten of the amendments were ratified by the necessary three-fourths of the states on December 15, 1791; from the start, these 10 were called the **Bill of Rights** (see Table 4.2).[5] The protections against improper government action contained in the Constitution and the Bill of Rights represent important **civil liberties.**

civil liberties areas of personal freedom constitutionally protected from government interference

NATIONALIZING THE BILL OF RIGHTS

The First Amendment provides that "Congress shall make no law. . . ." But this is the only amendment in the Bill of Rights that addresses itself exclusively to the national government. For example, the Second Amendment provides that "the right of the people to keep and bear Arms, shall not be infringed." And the Fifth Amendment

TABLE 4.2

The Bill of Rights

Amendment I	Congress cannot make any law establishing a religion or abridging freedoms of religious exercise, speech, assembly, or petition.
Amendments II, III, IV	No branch of government may infringe upon the right of the people to keep arms (II), cannot arbitrarily take houses for militia (III), and cannot search for or seize evidence without a court warrant swearing to the probable existence of a crime (IV).
Amendments V, VI, VII, VIII	The courts cannot hold trials for serious offenses without provision for a grand jury (V), a trial jury (VII), a speedy trial (VI), presentation of charges and confrontation by the accused of hostile witnesses (VI), and immunity from testimony against oneself and immunity from trial more than once for the same offense (V). Furthermore, neither bail nor punishment can be excessive (VIII), and no property can be taken without "just compensation" (V).
Amendments IX, X: Limits on the national government	Any rights not enumerated are reserved to the state or the people (X), and the enumeration of certain rights in the Constitution should not be interpreted to mean that those are the only rights the people have (IX).

says, among other things, that "no person shall...be twice put in jeopardy of life or limb" for the same crime. Since the First Amendment is the only part of the Bill of Rights that is explicit in its intention to put limits on Congress and therefore on the national government, a fundamental question inevitably arises: Do the remaining provisions of the Bill of Rights put limits only on the national government, or do they limit the state governments as well?

The Supreme Court first answered this question in 1833 by ruling that the Bill of Rights limited only the national government and not the state governments.[6] This meant that the actions of state governments were restricted only by their own constitutions as interpreted by their own courts. But in 1868, when the Fourteenth Amendment was added to the Constitution, the question arose once again. The Fourteenth Amendment reads as if it were meant to impose the Bill of Rights on the states:

> No State shall make or enforce any law which shall abridge the privileges or immunities of citizens of the United States; nor shall any State deprive any person of life, liberty, or property, without due process of law; nor deny to any person within its jurisdiction the equal protection of the laws.

This language sounds like an effort to extend the Bill of Rights in its entirety to all citizens, wherever they might reside.[7] Yet this was not the Supreme Court's interpretation of the amendment for nearly 100 years. Within five years of ratification of the Fourteenth Amendment, the Court was making decisions as though the amendment had never been adopted.[8]

The only change in civil liberties during the first 50-odd years following the adoption of the Fourteenth Amendment came in 1897, when the Supreme Court held that the due process clause of the Fourteenth Amendment did in fact prohibit states from taking property for a public use without just compensation.[9] However, the Supreme Court had selectively "incorporated" into the Fourteenth Amendment only the property protection provision of the Fifth Amendment and no other clause of the Fifth or any other amendment of the Bill of Rights. In other words, although according to the Fifth Amendment "due process" applied to the taking of life and liberty as well as property, only property was incorporated into the Fourteenth Amendment as a limitation on state power.

No further expansion of civil liberties via the Fourteenth Amendment occurred until 1925, when the Supreme Court held that freedom of speech is "among the fundamental personal rights and 'liberties' protected by the due process clause of the Fourteenth Amendment from impairment by the states."[10] In 1931 the Court added freedom of the press to that short list of freedoms protected by the Bill of Rights from state action; in 1939 it added freedom of assembly.[11]

But that was as far as the Court was willing to go. In the 1937 case of *Palko v. Connecticut*, the Court gave its blessing to the preservation of a legal framework in which the states had the power to determine their own laws on a number of fundamental issues. In that case, a Connecticut court had found Frank Palko guilty of second-degree murder and sentenced him to life in prison. Unhappy with the verdict, the state of Connecticut appealed the conviction to its highest court, won the appeal, got a new trial, and then succeeded in getting Palko convicted of first-degree murder. Palko appealed to the Supreme Court on what seemed an open-and-shut case of double jeopardy, which is prohibited by the Fifth Amendment. Yet, although the majority of the Court agreed that this could indeed be considered a case of double jeopardy, they decided that double jeopardy was *not* one of the provisions of the Bill of Rights incorporated into the Fourteenth Amendment as a restriction on the powers of the states. It took more than 30 years for the Court to nationalize the constitutional protection against double jeopardy. Because Frank Palko lived in the state of Connecticut rather than in a state whose constitution included a guarantee against double jeopardy, he was eventually executed for the crime.

selective incorporation the process by which different protections in the Bill of Rights were incorporated into the Fourteenth Amendment, thus guaranteeing citizens protection from state as well as national governments

The *Palko* case established the principle of **selective incorporation**, by which the provisions of the Bill of Rights were to be considered one by one and selectively applied as limits on the states through the Fourteenth Amendment. In order to make clear that "selective incorporation" should be narrowly interpreted, Justice Benjamin Cardozo, writing for an 8–1 majority, asserted that although many rights have value and importance, some rights do not represent a "principle of justice so rooted in the traditions and conscience of our people as to be ranked as fundamental."[12] *Palko* left states with most of the powers they had possessed even before the adoption of the Fourteenth Amendment, such as the power to engage in searches and seizures without a warrant, to deprive accused persons of trial by jury, and to prosecute accused persons more than once for the same crime.[13] Few states chose to use these kinds of powers, but some did.

So, until 1961 (see Table 4.3), only the First Amendment and one clause of the Fifth Amendment had been clearly incorporated into the Fourteenth Amendment as binding on the states as well as on the national government.[14] After that, one by one, almost all the provisions of the Bill of Rights were incorporated into the Fourteenth Amendment and applied to the states. Table 4.3 shows the progress of this revolution in the interpretation of the Constitution. Before we leave the topic, it is worth mentioning that one element of the Fourteenth Amendment is being called into question today. This is the idea that all persons "born or naturalized" in the United States are citizens. Some politicians and public figures, most notably Donald Trump, have argued that the children of undocumented immigrants should not be considered U.S. citizens and might be subject to deportation. Though we are

TABLE 4.3

Incorporation of the Bill of Rights into the Fourteenth Amendment

These cases are significant because they represent the first instance that the Supreme Court acknowledged that the selected provision or amendment was binding on the states. In some cases this meant the Supreme Court overturned the state or local law under contention. In other cases the Court held that the law did not violate the Constitution, so the law was upheld.

SELECTED PROVISIONS AND AMENDMENTS	INCORPORATED	KEY CASE
Eminent domain (V)	1897	*Chicago, Burlington, and Quincy R.R. v. Chicago* The city of Chicago was required to compensate a railroad company for seizing its property for the purpose of widening a city road.
Freedom of speech (I)	1925	*Gitlow v. New York* Upheld Gitlow's conviction for "criminal anarchy" for publishing a left-wing manifesto. The Court held the First Amendment allowed the states to suppress speech directly advocating the overthrow of the government.
Freedom of press (I)	1931	*Near v. Minnesota* Overturned Minnesota's permanent injunction against those who created a "public nuisance" by publishing, selling, or distributing a "malicious, scandalous and defamatory newspaper, magazine or other periodical" as an infringement on freedom of the press.
Free exercise of religion (I)	1934	*Hamilton v. Regents of the University of California* Students filed suit to protest mandatory military training at the University of California on religious grounds. The Court upheld the right of California to mandate that its students receive military training as permissible under the First Amendment's free exercise of religion clause.
Freedom of assembly (I) and freedom to petition the government for redress of grievances (I)	1937	*DeJonge v. Oregon* DeJonge's conviction for addressing a meeting of the Communist Party was overturned as an infringement on freedom of assembly.
Free exercise of religion (I)	1940	*Cantwell v. Connecticut* State governments may not prohibit the dissemination or expression of religious views.
Nonestablishment of state religion (I)	1947	*Everson v. Board of Education* Applying the establishment clause, the Court found that using taxpayer money to bus students to private religious schools did not constitute establishing a religion because busing was a "separate" function from the school's religious purpose.
Freedom from warrantless search and seizure (IV) ("exclusionary rule")	1961	*Mapp v. Ohio* The Court overturned the conviction of Dollree Mapp for possession of obscene materials because the evidence was obtained in violation of the Fourth Amendment's requirement of a warrant for conducting a search.

Continued

TABLE 4.3

Incorporation of the Bill of Rights into the Fourteenth Amendment—cont'd

SELECTED PROVISIONS AND AMENDMENTS	INCORPORATED	KEY CASE
Freedom from cruel and unusual punishment (VIII)	1962	*Robinson v. California* The Court overturned a California law imposing a 90-day jail sentence on persons found guilty of "addiction to the use of narcotics" as cruel and unusual punishment for what amounted to illness.
Right to counsel in any criminal trial (VI)	1963	*Gideon v. Wainwright* Gideon requested a lawyer at his trial for a felony crime but was denied under Florida law. The Supreme Court held the right to counsel in the Sixth Amendment applied to the states, so Gideon got a new trial with counsel.
Right against self-incrimination and forced confessions (V)	1964	*Malloy v. Hogan* Malloy was imprisoned for contempt after refusing to answer questions about gambling activities on grounds it might implicate him. The Supreme Court held the Fifth Amendment secures defendants against self-incrimination, so Malloy could not be forced to testify.
Right to remain silent (V)	1964	*Escobedo v. Illinois* Police denied repeated requests by Escobedo to see his lawyer during interrogation; Escobedo eventually incriminated himself in a murder. The Court held Escobedo's Sixth Amendment rights to counsel and to the right to remain silent were violated.
Right to counsel and to remain silent (V)	1966	*Miranda v. Arizona* Miranda was questioned by police and signed a statement of confession without being informed of his right to counsel and protection from self-incrimination. The Court held defendants in police custody must be informed of their rights.
Right against double jeopardy (V)	1969	*Benton v. Maryland* Benton was tried twice for the same crime of larceny. The Supreme Court held "double jeopardy" as impermissible under the Fifth Amendment.
Right to bear arms (II)	2010	*McDonald v. Chicago* The Supreme Court struck down a Chicago firearms ordinance making it extremely difficult to own a gun within city limits as violating the Second Amendment.

a nation of immigrants, struggles over who may lawfully engage in the opportunities provided by American democracy can become bitter.

The best way to examine the Bill of Rights today is the simplest way: to take the major provisions one at a time. Some of these provisions are settled areas of law; others are not. The Court can reinterpret any one of them at any time.

The First Amendment and Freedom of Religion

Describe how the First Amendment protects freedom of religion

Congress shall make no law respecting an establishment of religion, or prohibiting the free exercise thereof; or abridging the freedom of speech, or of the press; or the right of the people peaceably to assemble, and to petition the Government for a redress of grievances.

The Bill of Rights begins by guaranteeing freedom of religion, and the First Amendment provides for that freedom in two distinct clauses: "Congress shall make no law [1] respecting an establishment of religion, or [2] prohibiting the free exercise thereof." The first clause is called the "establishment clause," and the second is called the "free exercise clause."

SEPARATION BETWEEN CHURCH AND STATE

The **establishment clause** and the idea of "no law" regarding the establishment of religion could be interpreted in several possible ways. One interpretation, which probably reflects the views of many of the First Amendment's authors, is that the government is prohibited from establishing an official church. Official state churches, such as the Church of England, were common in the eighteenth century and were viewed by many Americans as inconsistent with a republican form of government. Indeed, many American colonists had fled Europe to escape persecution for having rejected state-sponsored churches. A second possible interpretation is the view that the government may not take sides among competing religions but is not prohibited from providing assistance to religious institutions or ideas as long as it shows no favoritism. The United States accommodates religious beliefs in a variety of ways, from the reference to God on U.S. currency to the prayer that begins every session of Congress. These forms of religious establishment have never been struck down by the courts. The third view regarding religious establishment, the most commonly held today, is the idea of a "wall of separation" between church and state—Jefferson's formulation—that cannot be breached by the government. For two centuries, Jefferson's words have had a powerful impact on our understanding of the proper relationship between church and state in America.

Despite the seeming absoluteness of the phrase "wall of separation," there is ample room to disagree on how high the wall is. One area of contestation over the appropriate boundary between church and state is in public education. For example, the Court has been consistently strict in cases of school prayer, striking down such practices as Bible reading,[15] nondenominational prayer,[16] a moment of silence for meditation, and pregame prayer at public sporting events.[17] In each of these cases, the Court reasoned that school-sponsored religious observations, even of an apparently nondenominational character, are highly suggestive of school sponsorship and therefore violate the prohibition against establishment of religion.

For decades, the Court has faced cases involving government financial support for religious schools. In 1971 the Court attempted to specify some criteria to guide its decisions and those of lower courts, indicating the circumstances under which

establishment clause the First Amendment clause that says that "Congress shall make no law respecting an establishment of religion"; this law means that a "wall of separation" exists between church and state

FOR CRITICAL ANALYSIS

Despite the establishment clause, the United States still uses the motto "In God We Trust" and calls itself "one nation, under God." Do you think its reference to God is a violation of the separation of church and state?

state financial assistance to religious schools was constitutionally permissible. In its decision in *Lemon v. Kurtzman*, the Supreme Court established three criteria to guide future cases. Collectively, these came to be called the **Lemon test**. The Court held that government aid to religious schools would be accepted as constitutional if (1) it had a secular purpose, (2) its effect was neither to advance nor to inhibit religion, and (3) it did not entangle government and religious institutions in each other's affairs.[18]

Although these restrictions make the *Lemon* test hard to pass, imaginative authorities are finding ways to do so, and the Supreme Court has demonstrated a willingness to let them. For example, in 1995 the Court narrowly ruled that a student religious group at the University of Virginia could not be denied student activities funds merely because it was a religious group espousing a particular viewpoint about a deity. The Court called the denial "viewpoint discrimination" that violated the free speech rights of the group.[19]

In 2004 the question of whether the phrase "under God" in the Pledge of Allegiance violated the establishment clause was brought before the Court. Written without any religious references in 1892, the pledge had long been used in schools. But in 1954, in the midst of the Cold War, Congress voted to change the pledge in response to the "godless Communism" of the Soviet Union.

Ever since the change was made, there has been a steady murmuring of discontent from those who object to an officially sanctioned profession of belief in a deity as a violation of the establishment clause of the First Amendment. In 2003, Michael A. Newdow, the atheist father of a kindergarten student, brought suit against the local California school district, arguing that the reference to God turned the daily recitation of the pledge into a religious exercise. The case was appealed to the Supreme Court,

The First Amendment affects everyday life in a multitude of ways. Because of the amendment's ban on state-sanctioned religion, the Supreme Court ruled in 2000 that school-sponsored prayer in public schools is illegal. Requiring pregame prayer at public schools violates the establishment clause of the First Amendment.

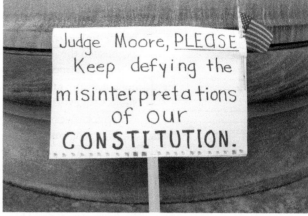

which ruled that Newdow lacked a sufficient personal stake in the case to bring the complaint. This inconclusive decision by the Supreme Court left "under God" in the pledge while keeping the issue alive for possible resolution in a future case.[20]

Another realm of contestation over the meaning of the establishment clause is in public displays of religious symbols, such as city-sponsored nativity scenes in commercial or municipal areas. This realm remains contested, in part because the Supreme Court's rulings on such cases have been inconclusive, as demonstrated by two 2005 cases involving displays of the Ten Commandments. In *Van Orden v. Perry*, the Court decided that a display of the Ten Commandments outside the Texas state capitol did not violate the Constitution.[21] However, in *McCreary County v. American Civil Liberties Union of Kentucky*, the Court determined that a display of the Ten Commandments inside two Kentucky courthouses was unconstitutional.[22] Justice Stephen Breyer, the deciding vote in the two cases, said that the display in *Van Orden* had a secular purpose, whereas the displays in *McCreary* had a purely religious purpose. The key difference between the two cases is that the Texas display had been exhibited in a large park for 40 years with other monuments related to the development of American law, whereas the Kentucky display was erected much more recently and initially by itself, suggesting to some justices that its posting had a religious purpose. But most observers saw little difference between the two cases. Clearly, the issue of government-sponsored displays of religious symbols has not been settled.

In 2001, Alabama Supreme Court chief justice Roy Moore had a large granite statue of the Ten Commandments installed in the Alabama Supreme Court building. Despite a court injunction requiring Justice Moore to remove the statue, citing a violation of the Establishment Clause, the statue remained until the building manager was compelled to remove it.

FREE EXERCISE OF RELIGION

The **free exercise clause** protects the right to believe and to practice whatever religion one chooses; it also protects the right to be a nonbeliever. The precedent-setting case involving free exercise is *West Virginia State Board of Education v. Barnette* (1943), which involved the children of a family of Jehovah's Witnesses who refused to salute and pledge allegiance to the American flag on the grounds that their religious faith did not permit it. Three years earlier, the Court had upheld such a requirement and had permitted schools to expel students for refusing to salute the flag. But the entry of the United States into a war to defend democracy, coupled with the ugly treatment to which the Jehovah's Witnesses' children had been subjected, induced the Court to reverse itself and to endorse the free exercise of religion even when it may be offensive to the beliefs of the majority.[23]

free exercise clause the First Amendment clause that protects a citizen's right to believe and practice whatever religion he or she chooses

Although the Supreme Court has been fairly consistent and strict in protecting the free exercise of religious belief, it has taken pains to distinguish between religious beliefs and *actions* based on those beliefs. The 1940 case of *Cantwell v. Connecticut* established the "time, place and manner" rule. The case arose from the efforts of two Jehovah's Witnesses to engage in door-to-door fund-raising. Americans are free to adhere to any religious beliefs, but the time, place, and manner of their exercise are subject to regulation in the public interest.[24]

In recent years, the principle of free exercise has been bolstered by statutes prohibiting religious discrimination by public and private entities in a variety of realms including hiring, land use, and the treatment of prison inmates. Three recent cases illustrating this point are *Holt v. Hobbs*,[25] *Equal Employment Opportunity Commission v. Abercrombie & Fitch Stores, Inc.*,[26] and *Burwell v. Hobby Lobby Stores*.[27] The *Holt* case involved a Muslim prisoner in an Arkansas jail. The prisoner, Gregory Holt, asserted that his religious beliefs required him to grow a beard. Thus, according to Holt, an Arkansas prison policy prohibiting beards was a violation of his ability to exercise his religion. The Court held that the prison policy was a violation of the free exercise clause and violated a federal statute designed to protect the ability of prisoners to worship as they pleased. In the second case, the Equal Employment Opportunity Commission brought suit against Abercrombie & Fitch for refusing to hire a Muslim woman who wore a head scarf in violation of the company's dress code. The Court held that the store's actions amounted to religious discrimination in hiring, a violation of Title VII of the U.S. Code, which prohibits employers from hiring discrimination based upon race, color, religion, gender, and national origin.

The Hobby Lobby case involved the owners of a chain of craft stores who claimed that a section of the Affordable Care Act (ACA or Obamacare) requiring employers to provide their female employees with free contraceptive coverage violated their religious beliefs as protected by the Religious Freedom Restoration Act (RFRA). This law, enacted in 1993, requires the government to prove a "compelling interest" for requiring individuals to obey a law that violates their religious beliefs.

Does religious freedom lead to discrimination on the basis of religion? Here, senior counsel for Hobby Lobby stores speaks to supporters after the Supreme Court ruled that businesses were not required to provide free contraceptive coverage if they find it in violation of their religious beliefs.

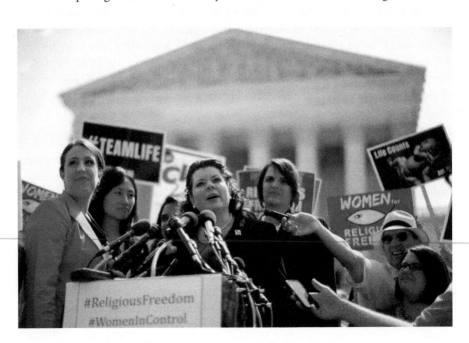

The Supreme Court ruled in favor of Hobby Lobby. Currently, members of the LGBTQ community are concerned that RFRA will be used as the basis for discrimination in hiring or other realms against gay or transgender individuals by individuals claiming that such practices violate their own religious beliefs. In 2017 the Trump administration affirmed the Court's decision by declaring that under ACA employers who had religious or moral objections would no longer be required to provide birth control benefits.

The First Amendment and Freedom of Speech and of the Press

Describe how the First Amendment protects free speech and freedom of the press

Congress shall make no law...abridging the freedom of speech, or of the press.

Freedom of speech and freedom of the press have a special place in American political thought. To begin with, democracy depends on the ability of individuals to talk to one another and to disseminate information. It is difficult to conceive how democratic politics could function without free and open debate. Such debate, moreover, is seen as an essential mechanism for determining the quality or validity of competing ideas. As Justice Oliver Wendell Holmes said in 1919, "The best test of truth is the power of the thought to get itself accepted in the competition of the market... That at any rate is the theory of our Constitution."[28] What is sometimes called the "marketplace of ideas" receives a good deal of protection from the courts. In 1938 the Supreme Court held that any legislation that attempts to restrict speech "is to be subjected to a more exacting judicial scrutiny...than are most other types of legislation."[29] This higher standard of judicial review came to be called "strict scrutiny."

The doctrine of strict scrutiny places a heavy burden of proof on the government if it seeks to regulate or restrict speech. Americans are assumed to have the right to speak and to broadcast their ideas unless some compelling reason can be identified to stop them. But strict scrutiny does not mean that speech can never be regulated. Over the past 200 years, the courts have scrutinized many different forms of speech and constructed different principles and guidelines for each. According to the courts, although virtually all speech is protected by the Constitution, some forms of speech are entitled to a greater degree of protection than others.

POLITICAL SPEECH

Political speech was the activity of greatest concern to the framers of the Constitution, even though some found it the most difficult form of speech to tolerate. Within seven years of the ratification of the Bill of Rights in 1791, Congress adopted the infamous Alien and Sedition Acts (long since repealed), which, among other things, made it a crime to say or publish anything that might tend to defame or bring into disrepute the government of the United States.

The first modern free speech case arose immediately after World War I. It involved persons who had been convicted under the federal Espionage Act of 1917 for opposing U.S. involvement in the war. The Supreme Court upheld the

Espionage Act and refused to protect the speech rights of the defendants on the grounds that their activities—appeals to draftees to resist the draft—constituted a **"clear and present danger"** to national security.[30] This is the first and most famous, though since discarded, "test" for when government intervention or censorship can be permitted.

It was only after the 1920s that real progress toward a genuinely effective First Amendment was made. Since then, political speech has been consistently protected by the courts even when it has been deemed "insulting" or "outrageous." In the 1969 case *Brandenburg v. Ohio*, the court ruled that as long as speech falls short of actually inciting action, it cannot be prohibited, even if it is hostile to or subversive of the government and its policies. This decision came in the case of a Ku Klux Klan leader, Charles Brandenburg, who had been arrested and convicted of advocating "revengent" action against the president, Congress, and the Supreme Court, among others, if they continued "to suppress the white, Caucasian race." Although Brandenburg was not carrying a weapon; some of the members of his audience were. Nevertheless, the Supreme Court reversed the state courts and freed Brandenburg while also declaring Ohio's Criminal Syndicalism Act unconstitutional because it punished persons who "advocate, or teach the duty, necessity, or propriety [of violence] as a means of accomplishing industrial or political reform" or who publish materials or "voluntarily assemble...to teach or advocate the doctrines of criminal syndicalism." The Supreme Court argued that the statute did not distinguish "mere advocacy" from "incitement to imminent lawless action."[31] It would be difficult to go much further in protecting freedom of speech.

Another area of political speech that has recently received much attention is the First Amendment status of monetary contributions to political campaigns. Campaign finance reform laws of the early 1970s, arising out of the Watergate scandal, sought to put severe limits on campaign spending. In the 1976 case *Buckley v. Valeo*, a number of important provisions were declared unconstitutional on the basis of a new principle that spending money by or on behalf of candidates is a form of speech protected by the First Amendment.[32] (For more details, see Chapter 10.)

The issue came up again in 2003 with passage of a new and still more severe campaign finance law, the Bipartisan Campaign Reform Act (BCRA). In *McConnell v. Federal Election Commission*, the 5–4 majority seriously reduced the area of speech protected by the *Buckley v. Valeo* decision by holding that Congress was well within its power to put limits on campaign spending. The Court argued that "the selling of access...has given rise to the appearance of undue influence [that justifies] regulations impinging on First Amendment rights...in order to curb corruption or the appearance of corruption."[33] In the *McConnell* case, the Court also upheld BCRA's limitations on "issue advertising." The act prohibited political advocacy groups from running ads that mentioned a candidate within 30 days of a primary election and 60 days of a general election. This ban was justified with the argument that wealthy special interests could affect election outcomes with last-minute ad campaigns. However, in its 2007 decision in the case of *Federal Election Commission v. Wisconsin Right to Life*, the Court reversed itself, declaring that such ads were protected speech and could not be prohibited so long as they focused mainly on issues and were not simply appeals to vote for or against a specific candidate.[34]

Even more recently, in the 2010 case of *Citizens United v. Federal Election Commission*, the Supreme Court declared that the First Amendment prohibited BCRA's

During the 2008 presidential primaries, the conservative organization Citizens United released a documentary criticizing Hillary Clinton. A lower court found that ads for the film violated the BCRA's ban on corporate funding of ads for or against a particular candidate. In 2010 the Court declared the BCRA ban unconstitutional under the First Amendment.

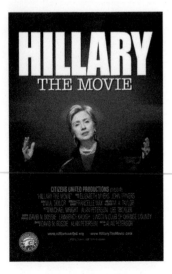

ban on corporate funding of independent political broadcasts aimed at electing or defeating particular candidates.[35] In its 5–4 decision, the Supreme Court ruled that the Constitution prohibits the government from regulating political speech and that therefore the government could not ban this type of political spending by corporations. In 2014 the Court again expanded its protection of campaign expenditures under the First Amendment by overturning aggregate limits restricting how much money a donor may contribute.[36] As a result of this decision several wealthy donors contributed more than $10 million to presidential candidates in 2016. The Court's decisions in both cases have been controversial. Republicans hailed the decisions as a victory for free speech, while Democrats denounced the decisions. President Obama called *Citizens United* "a major victory for big oil, Wall Street banks, health insurance companies, and the other powerful interests that marshal their power every day in Washington to drown out the voices of everyday Americans."[37]

FIGHTING WORDS AND HATE SPEECH

Freedom of speech does have limits, however. Speech can also lose its protected position when it moves toward the sphere of action. "Expressive speech," for example, is protected until it moves from the symbolic realm to the realm of actual conduct—to direct incitement of damaging conduct with the use of so-called **fighting words**. In 1942 a man called a police officer a "goddamned racketeer" and "a damn Fascist" and was arrested and convicted of violating a state law forbidding the use of offensive language in public. When his case reached the Supreme Court, the arrest was upheld on the grounds that the First Amendment provides no protection for such offensive language because such words "are no essential part of any exposition of ideas."[38] This decision was reaffirmed in the important 1951 case of *Dennis v. United States* when the Supreme Court held that there is no substantial public interest in permitting certain kinds of utterances: the lewd and obscene, the profane, the libelous, and the insulting or "fighting" words—those which by their very utterance inflict injury or tend to incite an immediate breach of the peace.[39] Since that time, however, the Supreme Court has reversed almost every conviction based on arguments that the speaker had used "fighting words."

> **fighting words** speech that directly incites damaging conduct

In recent years, the increased activism of minority and women's groups has prompted a movement against words that might be construed as offensive to members of a particular group. Scores of universities have attempted to develop speech codes to suppress utterances deemed to be racial or ethnic or gender slurs. The drafting of such codes has been encouraged by the Department of Education's Office of Civil Rights (OCR) which has also interpreted Title IX of the Higher Education Act to require colleges to vigorously prosecute charges involving racial or sexual harassment. Critics have charged that the procedures encouraged by OCR ignore the rights of the accused and have led, on some campuses, to the creation of tribunals that assume the guilt of anyone charged with an offense. This issue is currently being fought out on college campuses across the country.[40] In 2017, Education Secretary Betsy Devos rescinded the department's previous guidelines, declaring they were unfair to those accused of sexual misconduct, and said new rules would soon be promulgated that would provide justice to all parties involved in a sexual misconduct case.

Similar issues have arisen in large corporations, both public and private, with many successful complaints and lawsuits alleging that the words of employers or their supervisors created a "hostile or abusive working environment." The Supreme Court has held that a "hostile working environment" results from "sexual harassment," including "unwelcome sexual advances, requests for sexual favors, and other *verbal* or physical conduct of a sexual nature [emphasis added]."[41] A fundamental free speech issue is involved in these regulations of hostile speech.

Many jurisdictions have drafted ordinances banning hate speech—forms of expression designed to assert hatred toward one or another group, be they African Americans, Jews, Muslims, or others. Such ordinances seldom pass constitutional muster. The leading Supreme Court case in this realm is the 1992 decision in *R.A.V. v. City of St. Paul*.[42] Here, a white teenager was arrested for burning a cross on the lawn of a black family in violation of a municipal ordinance that banned cross burning. The Court ruled that such an ordinance must be *content neutral*—that is, it must not prohibit actions directed at some groups but not others. The statute in question prohibited only cross burning, which is typically directed at African Americans. Since a statute banning all forms of hateful expression would be deemed overly broad, the *R.A.V.* standard suggests that virtually all hate speech is constitutionally protected.

The issue of hate speech has arisen on a number of college campuses. Some students and faculty at several colleges have demanded that (usually) conservative and far-right speakers be banned from campus on the grounds that they promote hatred. Student protesters have forced the cancellation of speeches by conservatives like Ann Coulter and Milo Yiannopoulos, disrupted talks by such prominent conservative scholars as Charles Murray, and have unsuccessfully sought to prevent "white nationalist" Richard Spencer from speaking. There seems little doubt that the right of all these individuals to speak is protected by the Constitution. The conflict arises when that Constitutional right comes up against university policies to emphasize safety. It is important to remember that not so long ago speakers on the political left were banned from campuses in the name of safety. Perhaps people of all political persuasions should think about the words of Supreme Court Justice Oliver Wendell Holmes, who said, "if there is any principle of the Constitution that more imperatively calls for attachment than any other, it is the principle of free thought—not free thought for those who agree with us but freedom for the thought that we hate."[43]

FOR CRITICAL ANALYSIS

Is there speech that should be banned because it does not contribute to the exchange of ideas? How do we determine what speech should be protected because it contributes to this exchange and what speech does not?

STUDENT SPEECH

One category of conditionally protected speech is the speech of high school students in public schools. In 1986 the Supreme Court backed away from a broad protection of student free speech rights by upholding the punishment of a high school student for making a sexually suggestive speech. The Court opinion held that such speech interfered with the school's goal of teaching students the limits of socially acceptable behavior.[44] Two years later the Supreme Court took another conservative step by restricting students' speech and press rights even further, defining them as part of the educational process and not to be treated with the same standard as adult speech in a regular public forum.[45] A later case involving high school students is the 2007 case of *Morse v. Frederick*.[46] This case dealt with the policies of Juneau-Douglas High School in Juneau, Alaska. In 2002 the Olympic torch relay had passed through Juneau on its way to Salt Lake City for the opening of the Winter Olympics. As the torch passed Juneau-Douglas High, a senior, Joseph Frederick, unfurled a banner reading "BONG HITS 4 JESUS." The school's principal promptly suspended Frederick, who then brought suit for reinstatement, alleging that his free speech rights had been violated. Like most of America's public schools, Juneau-Douglas

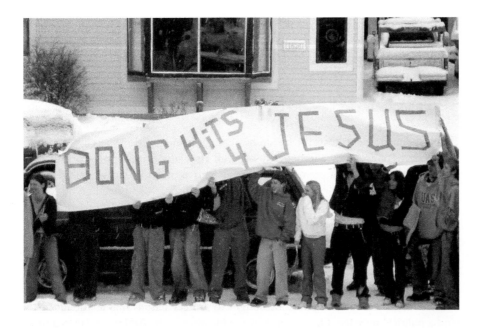

The Supreme Court has ruled that high school students' speech can be restricted. In a 2007 case involving a student who displayed the banner above, the Court found that the school principal had not violated the student's right to free speech by suspending him.

High prohibits assemblies or expressions on school grounds that advocate illegal drug use, saying that some federal aid is contingent on this policy. Civil libertarians, of course, see such policies as restricting students' right to free speech. Speaking for the Court's majority, Chief Justice Roberts said that the First Amendment did not require schools to permit students to advocate illegal drug use.

COMMERCIAL SPEECH

Commercial speech, such as newspaper or television advertisements, does not have full First Amendment protection because it cannot be considered political speech. Initially considered to be entirely outside the protection of the First Amendment, commercial speech today is subject to limited regulation. For example, the prohibition of false and misleading advertising by the Federal Trade Commission is an old and well-established power of the federal government. The Supreme Court has upheld city ordinances prohibiting the posting of all commercial signs on public property (as long as the ban is total so that there is no hint of selective censorship).[47]

However, the gains far outweigh the losses in the effort to expand the protection of commercial speech under the First Amendment. "In part, this reflects the growing appreciation that commercial speech is part of the free flow of information necessary for informed choice and democratic participation."[48] For example, in 1975 the Supreme Court struck down a state statute making it a misdemeanor to sell or circulate newspapers encouraging abortions; the Court ruled that the statute infringed on constitutionally protected speech and on the right of the reader to make informed choices.[49] On a similar basis, the Court reversed its own earlier decisions upholding laws that prohibited lawyers, dentists, and other professionals from advertising their services. For the Court, medical service advertising was a matter of health that could be advanced by the free flow of information.[50] And in a 2001 case, the Court ruled that a Massachusetts ban on all cigarette advertising violated the First Amendment right of the tobacco industry to advertise its products to adult consumers.[51] These instances of commercial speech, significant in themselves, are all the more significant because they indicate the breadth and depth of the freedom existing today to direct appeals to a large public, not only to sell goods and services but also to mobilize people for political purposes.

SYMBOLIC SPEECH, SPEECH PLUS, AND THE RIGHTS OF ASSEMBLY AND PETITION

The First Amendment treats the freedoms of religion and political speech as equal to the freedoms of assembly and petition—speech associated with action. For this reason, the long record of Supreme Court cases largely protects an individual's right to symbolic speech, assembly, and petition. Freedom of speech and freedom of assembly are closely related by the "public forum doctrine." In the 1939 case of *Hague v. Committee for Industrial Organization*, the Court declared that the government may not prohibit speech-related activities such as demonstrations or leafleting in public areas traditionally used for that purpose, though, of course, the government may impose rules designed to protect the public safety so long as these rules do not discriminate against particular viewpoints.[52]

Generally, the Supreme Court has sought to protect actions that are designed to send a political message. One example is the burning of the American flag as a protest. In 1984, at a political rally held during the Republican National Convention in Dallas, Texas, a political protester burned an American flag, thereby violating a Texas statute that prohibited desecration of a venerated object. In a 5–4 decision, the Supreme Court declared the Texas law unconstitutional on the grounds that flag burning was expressive conduct protected by the First Amendment.[53] Since 1995 the House of Representatives has seven times passed a resolution for a constitutional amendment to ban this form of expressive conduct, but each time the Senate has failed to go along.[54]

In the 2011 case of *Snyder v. Phelps*, the Court sought to protect another form of symbolic speech. Members of the Westboro Baptist Church had frequently demonstrated at military funerals, claiming that the deaths of the soldiers were a sign that

Should the First Amendment's protection of free speech apply even when that speech is seen as offensive? In 2011 the Supreme Court ruled 8–1 that members of the Westboro Baptist Church had a right to picket soldiers' funerals to demonstrate what they take as a sign of God's disapproval of homosexuality.

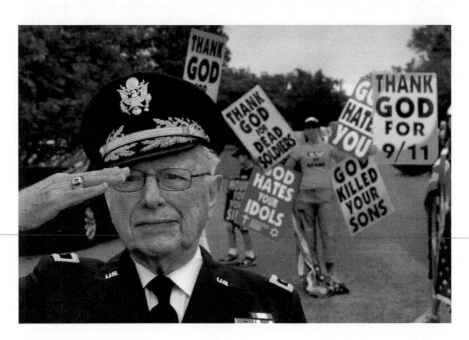

God disapproved of the acceptance of homosexuality in the United States. The father of a soldier killed in Iraq brought suit against the church and its pastor, claiming that the demonstrators had caused him and his family severe emotional distress. The Supreme Court ruled, however, that the First Amendment protected free speech in a public place against such suits.[55]

Closer to the original intent of the assembly and petition clause is the category of **"speech plus"**—following speech with physical activity such as picketing, distributing leaflets, and other forms of peaceful demonstration or assembly. Such assemblies are consistently protected by courts under the First Amendment; state and local laws regulating such activities are closely scrutinized and frequently overturned. But the same assembly on private property is quite another matter and can in many circumstances be regulated. For example, the directors of a shopping center can lawfully prohibit an assembly protesting a war or supporting a ban on abortion. Assemblies in public areas can also be restricted under some circumstances, especially when the assembly or demonstration jeopardizes the health, safety, or rights of others. This condition was the basis of the Supreme Court's decision to uphold a lower-court order that restricted the access that abortion protesters had to the entrances of abortion clinics.[56]

"speech plus" speech accompanied by conduct such as sit-ins, picketing, and demonstrations; protection of this form of speech under the First Amendment is conditional, and restrictions imposed by state or local authorities are acceptable if properly balanced by considerations of public order

FREEDOM OF THE PRESS

For all practical purposes, freedom of speech implies and includes freedom of the press. With the exception of the broadcast media, which are subject to federal regulation, the press is protected under the doctrine against **prior restraint.** Beginning with the landmark 1931 case of *Near v. Minnesota*, the U.S. Supreme Court has held that, except under the most extraordinary circumstances, the First Amendment of the Constitution prohibits government agencies from seeking to prevent newspapers or magazines from publishing whatever they wish.[57] Indeed, in the 1971 case *New York Times Co. v. United States* (the so-called Pentagon Papers case), the Supreme Court ruled that the government could not block publication of secret Defense Department documents furnished to the *New York Times* by an opponent of the Vietnam War who had obtained the documents illegally.[58]

prior restraint an effort by a governmental agency to block the publication of material it deems libelous or harmful in some other way; censorship; in the United States, the courts forbid prior restraint except under the most extraordinary circumstances

Should individuals be prosecuted for leaking classified information to the press? Then-Pfc. Bradley Manning and Edward Snowden were charged for the crime of leaking classified information related to government surveillance.

Another press freedom issue that the courts have often been asked to decide is the question of whether journalists can be compelled to reveal their sources of information. Journalists assert that if they cannot ensure their sources' confidentiality, the flow of information will be reduced and press freedom effectively curtailed. Government agencies, however, aver that names of news sources may be relevant to criminal or even national security investigations. More than 30 states have "shield laws," which, to varying degrees, protect journalistic sources. There is, however, no federal shield law and no special constitutional protection for journalists. The Supreme Court has held that the press has no constitutional right to withhold information in court.[59]

In addition to prosecuting journalists for refusing to reveal their sources, the government may seek to prosecute individuals who leak information to the press. During the Obama presidency, seven individuals were charged or prosecuted for disclosing classified information. These cases included Pfc. Bradley Manning, an army intelligence analyst sent to prison for providing classified documents to WikiLeaks, which published many of the documents, and Edward Snowden, an employee of the National Security Agency (NSA) who fled the country to escape arrest after revealing the details of NSA domestic spying operations. Manning, who took the name Chelsea after undergoing gender reassignment surgery, was released from prison in 2017.

Libel and Slander Some speech is not protected at all. If a written statement is made in "reckless disregard of the truth" and is considered damaging to the victim because it is "malicious, scandalous, and defamatory," it can be punished as **libel**. If such a statement is made orally, it can be punished as **slander**.

Most libel suits today involve freedom of the press, and the realm of free press is enormous. Historically, newspapers were subject to the law of libel, which provided that newspapers that printed false and malicious stories could be compelled to pay damages to those they defamed. In recent years, however, American courts have greatly narrowed the meaning of libel and made it extremely difficult, particularly for politicians or other public figures, to win a libel case against a newspaper. In the important 1964 case of *New York Times Co. v. Sullivan*, the Court held that to be deemed libelous, a story about a public official not only had to be untrue but also had to result from "actual malice" or "reckless disregard" for the truth.[60] In other words, the newspaper had to print false and malicious material deliberately. In practice, it is nearly impossible to prove that a paper *deliberately* printed maliciously false information, and it is thus especially difficult for a politician or other public figure to win a libel case. Essentially, the print media have been able to publish anything they want about a public figure.

However, the Court has opened up the possibility for public officials to file libel suits against the press. The Court has held since the 1970s that the press was immune to libel suits only when the printed material was "a matter of public concern."[61] In other words, a newspaper would have to show that the public official was engaged in activities that were indeed *public*. This principle has made the press more vulnerable to libel suits, but it still leaves an enormous realm of freedom for the press. President Trump has said that stricter libel laws are needed to prevent what he likes to call "fake news," though no action or policies have changed.

With the emergence of the internet as an important communications medium, the courts have had to decide how traditional libel law applies to internet content. In 1995 the New York courts held that an online bulletin board could be held responsible for the libelous content of material posted by a third party. To protect

libel a written statement made in "reckless disregard of the truth" that is considered damaging to a victim because it is "malicious, scandalous, and defamatory"

slander an oral statement made in "reckless disregard of the truth" that is considered damaging to the victim because it is "malicious, scandalous, and defamatory" internet service providers, Congress subsequently enacted legislation absolving them of responsibility for third-party posts. The federal courts have generally upheld this law and declared that service providers are immune from suits regarding the content of material posted by others.[62]

Obscenity and Pornography If libel and slander cases can be difficult because of the problem of determining the truth of statements and whether those statements are malicious and damaging, cases involving pornography and obscenity can be even trickier. Not until 1957 did the Supreme Court confront this problem, and it did so with a definition of obscenity that may have caused more confusion than it cleared up. In writing the Court's opinion, Justice William Brennan defined obscenity as speech or writing that appeals to the "prurient interest"—that is, whose purpose is to excite lust, as this appears "to the average person, applying contemporary community standards." Even so, Brennan added, the work should be judged obscene only when it is "utterly without redeeming social importance."[63] In 1964, Justice Potter Stewart confessed that, although he found pornography impossible to define, "I know it when I see it."[64]

The vague and impractical standards that had been developed meant ultimately that almost nothing could be banned on the grounds that it was pornographic and obscene. An effort was made to strengthen the restrictions in 1973, when the Supreme Court expressed its willingness to define pornography as a work that (1) as a whole, is deemed prurient by the "average person" according to "community standards"; (2) depicts sexual conduct "in a patently offensive way"; and (3) lacks "serious literary, artistic, political, or scientific value." This definition meant that pornography would be determined by local rather than national standards. Thus, a local bookseller might be prosecuted for selling a volume that was a best-seller nationally but that was deemed pornographic locally.[65] This new definition of standards did not help much either, and not long after 1973, the Court began again to review all such community antipornography laws, reversing most of them.

In recent years, the battle against obscene speech has targeted pornography on the internet. Opponents of this form of expression argue that it should be banned because of the easy access children have to the internet. The first major effort to regulate the content of the internet occurred in 1996, when Congress passed the Telecommunications Act. Attached to it was an amendment, called the Communications Decency Act (CDA), designed to regulate the online transmission of obscene material. The constitutionality of the CDA was immediately challenged in court by a coalition of interests led by the American Civil Liberties Union. In the 1997 case of *Reno v. American Civil Liberties Union*, the Supreme Court struck down the CDA, ruling that it suppressed speech that "adults have a constitutional right to receive" and that governments may not limit the adult population to messages that are fit for children. Supreme Court justice John Paul Stevens described the internet as the "town crier" of the modern age and said that the internet was entitled to the greatest degree of First Amendment protection possible.[66] In 2003, Congress enacted the PROTECT Act, which outlawed efforts to sell child pornography via the internet. The Supreme Court upheld this act in the 2008 case of *United States v. Williams*, in which the majority said that criminalizing efforts to purvey child pornography did not violate free speech guarantees.[67]

In 2000 the Supreme Court extended the highest degree of First Amendment protection to cable (not broadcast) television. In *United States v. Playboy Entertainment Group*, the Court struck down a portion of the 1996 Telecommunications

Act that required cable TV companies to limit the broadcast of sexually explicit programming to late-night hours. In its decision, the Court noted that the law already provided parents with the means to restrict access to sexually explicit cable channels through various blocking devices. Moreover, such programming could come into the home only if parents decided to purchase such channels in the first place.[68]

Closely related to the issue of obscenity is the matter of violent broadcast content. Can a state or the federal government prohibit broadcasts or publications deemed to be excessively violent? Here, too, the Court has generally upheld freedom of speech. For example, in the 2011 case of *Brown v. Entertainment Merchants Association*, the Court struck down a California law banning the sale of violent video games to children, saying that the law violated the First Amendment.[69]

The Second Amendment and the Right to Bear Arms

> **Explore whether the Second Amendment means people have a right to own guns**

A well regulated Militia, being necessary to the security of a free State, the right of the people to keep and bear Arms, shall not be infringed.

The point and purpose of the Second Amendment is the provision for militias; they were to be the backing of the government for the maintenance of local public order. "Militia" was understood at the time of the Founding to be a military or police resource for state governments, and militias were specifically distinguished from armies and troops, which came within the sole constitutional jurisdiction of Congress. Many individuals, though, have argued that the Second Amendment also establishes an individual right to bear arms.

The judicial record of Second Amendment cases is far sparser than that of First Amendment cases, and for almost 60 years the Court made no Second Amendment decisions. In the absence of a ruling that would apply to the entire country, localities across the country have very different gun ownership standards, the result of a patchwork of state and local laws. For instance, in Wyoming, there is no ban on owning any type of gun, there is no waiting period to purchase a firearm, and individuals are not required to obtain a permit for carrying a concealed weapon. In California, in contrast, the possession of assault weapons is banned, there is a 10-day waiting period to purchase a firearm, and a permit is required to carry a concealed weapon. Figure 4.1 shows the background check requirements to purchase a firearm across the country.

The Court's silence on the application of the Second Amendment ended in 2008, when the Supreme Court made the first of two rulings in favor of expansive rights of gun ownership by individuals. In the case *District of Columbia v. Heller*, at issue was a strict Washington, D.C., law that banned handguns. In a 5–4 decision, the Court ruled that the Second Amendment provides a constitutional right to keep a loaded handgun at home for self-defense, a view that had long been subject to debate. In the majority opinion, Justice Antonin Scalia stated that the decision was not intended to cast doubt on all laws limiting firearm possession, such as the prohibition on gun ownership by felons or the mentally ill.[70] In his dissenting opinion, Justice Stevens asserted that the Second Amendment only protects the rights of individuals to bear arms as part of a militia force, not in an individual capacity. The District of Columbia

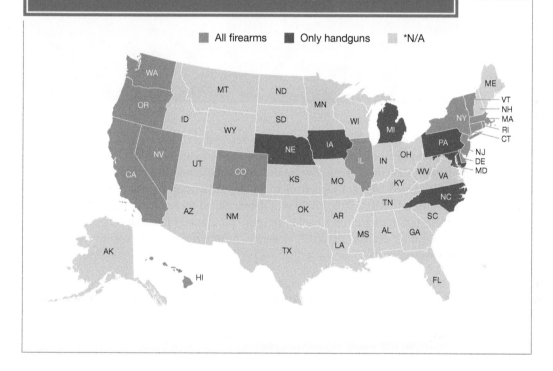

FIGURE 4.1

Gun Rights by State

Although state gun laws must conform to the Second Amendment as interpreted by the U.S. Supreme Court, laws concerning gun sales and ownership vary widely from state to state. It is much more difficult to buy a gun in, say, New York or California than in Texas or Kentucky. This map shows states that require criminal background checks for the sale of all firearms, only handguns, or none when purchasing firearms. While federal law requires background checks when purchasing a firearm from a licensed seller, only 21 states require them from unlicensed sellers as well.

*An answer of N/A indicates the state does not require criminal background checks for gun sales by unlicensed sellers.

SOURCE: Background Checks, Gun Law Navigator, www.everytownresearch.org/ (accessed 6/12/18).

■ All firearms ■ Only handguns ■ *N/A

is an entity of the federal government, and the Court did not indicate that its ruling applied to state firearms laws. However, in the 2010 case of *McDonald v. Chicago*, the Supreme Court applied the Second Amendment to the states, making this decision the first new incorporation decision by the Court in 40 years. The case concerned a Chicago ordinance that made it extremely difficult to own a gun within city limits, and the Court's ruling had the effect of overturning the law.[71]

Despite these rulings, the debate over gun control continues to loom large in American politics today. A recent series of tragic shootings (including the killing of 20 elementary school students in Newtown, Connecticut; 9 parishioners at a Charleston, South Carolina, church; 50 people at a nightclub in Orlando, Florida; 59 individuals at a concert in Las Vegas, Nevada; 27 worshipers at a church in Sutherland Springs, Texas; and 17 students and staff members at a high school in Parkland, Florida) has kept the issue of gun laws firmly on the national agenda. Proponents of gun control point to these shootings as evidence of the need to

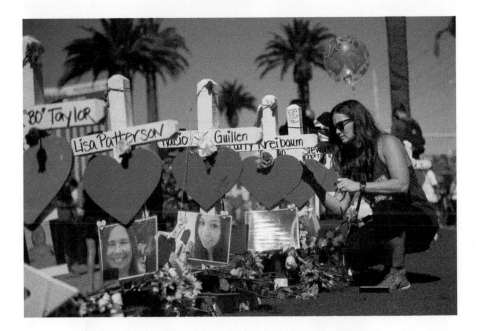

A string of mass shootings in the United States, including ones in which 59 people at a concert in Las Vegas and 17 students and staff members at a high school in Parkland, Florida, were killed, have prompted calls for legislation to limit the availability of guns.

restrict the availability of firearms while opponents of gun control say that shooting incidents demonstrate that Americans are not safe and should be free to carry arms for self protection. Interestingly, after each mass shooting opposition to gun control increased, perhaps suggesting that many Americans equate gun ownership with personal safety. In 2016, President Obama issued several executive orders designed to expand background checks for gun purchasers and licensure requirements for firearms dealers. In 2017, however, most of these orders were rescinded by President Trump.

Rights of the Criminally Accused

Explain the major rights that people have if they are accused of a crime

Except for the First Amendment, most of the battle to apply the Bill of Rights to the states has been fought over the various protections granted to individuals who are accused of a crime, who are suspects in the commission of a crime, or who are brought before the court as a witness to a crime (Table 4.4). The Fourth, Fifth, Sixth, and Eighth amendments, taken together, are the essence of the **due process of law**, even though these precise words for this fundamental concept do not appear until the end of the Fifth Amendment. In the next sections, we will look at specific cases that illuminate the dynamics of this important constitutional issue. The procedural safeguards that we will discuss may seem remote to most law-abiding citizens, but they help define the limits of government action against the personal liberty of every citizen. Many Americans believe that "legal technicalities" are responsible for setting many actual criminals free. In some cases, this is true. In fact, few convictions are actually lost because of excluded evidence. But one of America's traditional and most strongly held juridical values is that "it is far worse to convict an innocent man than to let a guilty man go free."[72] In civil suits, verdicts rest on "the preponderance of the evidence"; but in criminal cases, guilt has to be proven

due process of law the right of every individual against arbitrary action by national or state governments "beyond a reasonable doubt"—a far higher standard. The provisions for due process in the Bill of Rights were added in order to improve the probability that the standard of "reasonable doubt" would be respected.

THE FOURTH AMENDMENT AND SEARCHES AND SEIZURES

> The right of the people to be secure in their persons, houses, papers, and effects, against unreasonable searches and seizures, shall not be violated, and no Warrants shall issue, but upon probable cause, supported by Oath or affirmation, and particularly describing the place to be searched, and the persons or things to be seized.

The purpose of the Fourth Amendment is to guarantee the security of citizens against unreasonable (i.e., improper) searches and seizures. In 1990 the Supreme Court summarized its understanding of the Fourth Amendment brilliantly and succinctly: "A search compromises the individual interest in privacy; a seizure deprives the individual of dominion over his or her person or property."[73] But how are we to define what is reasonable and what is unreasonable?

The 1961 case of *Mapp v. Ohio* illustrates one of the most important of the principles that have grown out of the Fourth Amendment—the **exclusionary rule**, which prohibits evidence obtained during an illegal search from being introduced in a trial. Acting on a tip that Dollree (Dolly) Mapp was harboring a suspect in a bombing incident, several policemen forcibly entered Mapp's house, claiming they had a warrant to look for the bombing suspect. The police did not find the bombing suspect but, in an old trunk in the basement, did find some materials they declared to be obscene. Although no warrant was ever produced, the evidence that had been seized was admitted by a court, and Mapp was charged and convicted of illegal possession of obscene materials.

The question before the Court was whether any evidence produced under the circumstances of the search of her home was admissible. The Court's opinion affirmed the exclusionary rule: under the Fourth Amendment (applied to the states through the Fourteenth Amendment), "all evidence obtained by searches and seizures in violation of the Constitution . . . is inadmissible."[74] This means that even people who are clearly guilty of the crime of which they are accused must not be convicted if the only evidence for their conviction was obtained illegally.

The exclusionary rule is the most dramatic restraint imposed by the courts on police behavior because it rules out precisely the evidence that produces a conviction; it frees those people who are *known* to have committed the crime of which they have been accused. Thus, in recent years the Court has softened the application of the exclusionary rule, and federal courts have relied on its discretionary use,

TABLE 4.4

The Rights of the Accused from Arrest to Trial

No improper searches and seizures (Fourth Amendment)

No arrest without probable cause (Fourth Amendment)

Right to remain silent (Fifth Amendment)

No self-incrimination during arrest or trial (Fifth Amendment)

Right to be informed of charges (Sixth Amendment)

Right to counsel (Sixth Amendment)

No excessive bail (Eighth Amendment)

Right to grand jury (Fifth Amendment)

Right to open trial before a judge (Article I, Section 9)

Right to speedy and public trial before an impartial jury (Sixth Amendment)

Evidence obtained by illegal search not admissible during trial (Fourth Amendment)

Right to confront witnesses (Sixth Amendment)

No double jeopardy (Fifth Amendment)

No cruel and unusual punishment (Eighth Amendment)

exclusionary rule the ability of courts to exclude evidence obtained in violation of the Fourth Amendment

Under what circumstances can the police search an individual's car? The Fourth Amendment protects against "unreasonable searches and seizures," but the Supreme Court has had to interpret what is unreasonable.

whereby they make a judgment as to the "nature and quality of the intrusion."[75] In 2006, in the case of *United States v. Grubbs*, the Supreme Court ruled that the police could conduct searches using such "anticipatory warrants"—warrants issued when the police know that incriminating material is not yet present but have reason to believe that it will eventually arrive at a particular premises.[76] The warrants are held until the police are ready to conduct their search. In some instances, such as during an arrest, the authorities can conduct searches without obtaining any warrants at all.

The Fourth Amendment is also at issue in the controversy over mandatory drug testing. Such tests are most widely applied to public employees. In 1989 the Supreme Court upheld the U.S. Customs Service's drug-testing program for its employees[77] and drug and alcohol tests for railroad workers if they were involved in serious accidents.[78] Since then, more than 40 federal agencies have initiated mandatory employee drug tests, giving rise to public appeals against the general practice of "suspicionless testing" of employees, in violation of the Fourth Amendment. A 1995 case, in which the Court upheld a public school district's policy requiring all students participating in interscholastic sports to submit to random drug tests, surely contributed to the efforts of federal, state, and local agencies to initiate random and suspicionless drug and alcohol testing.[79]

The most recent cases suggest, however, that the Court is beginning to consider limits on the war against drugs. In a decisive 8–1 decision in 1997, the Court applied the Fourth Amendment as a shield against "state action that diminishes personal privacy" in cases that do not involve high-risk or safety-sensitive tasks.[80] And in 2013, the Court held that the use of a drug-sniffing dog on the front porch of a home constituted a search that violates the Fourth Amendment in the absence of consent of a warrant.[81]

Changes in technology have also had an impact on Fourth Amendment jurisprudence. In the 2012 case of *United States v. Jones,* the Court held that prosecutors violated Jones's rights when they attached a Global Positioning System (GPS) device to his Jeep and monitored his movements for 28 days.[82] On the other hand, in *Maryland v. King*, the Court upheld DNA testing of arrestees without the need for individualized suspicion. Writing for the majority, Justice Anthony Kennedy characterized DNA testing as an administrative tool for identifying the arrestee and thus legally indistinguishable from photographing and fingerprinting.[83] In the 2014 case of *Riley v. California*, the Court held that the police were constitutionally prohibited from seizing and searching the digital contents of a cell phone during an arrest. As new technologies develop, the Court will continue to face the question of what constitutes a reasonable search.[84] In 2016 the FBI sought to compel the Apple Corporation to unlock the cell phone used by Syed Farook, an alleged terrorist who, along with his wife Tashfeen Malik, had killed 14 people in San Bernardino, California. Apple asserted that creating new software to enable the FBI to unlock the phone would allow the agency to invade the privacy of millions of iPhone users. The case became moot when the FBI was able to unlock the phone without Apple's help.

Supporters of stop-and-frisk tactics argue that the practice reduces crime rates. However, since Mayor Bill de Blasio ended stop and frisk in New York City in 2014, crime rates have not increased or changed significantly. Here, plain clothes police officers stop and frisk Harlem residents.

Fourth Amendment issues have also been raised by aggressive police tactics, particularly the tactic known as "stop and frisk." This is a tactic in which the police confront an individual whom they believe to be acting "suspiciously," question the individual, and conduct a search for weapons. The practice was reviewed by the Supreme Court in the 1968 case of *Terry v. Ohio*, and the Court then held that if an officer had "probable cause" to believe the individual was armed, such a search was permitted.[85] In recent years, some police departments, most notably the New York City police, have made stop and frisk a routine practice, searching thousands and thousands of individuals whom they deemed to look suspicious. The police aver that this aggressive tactic has reduced crime rates. In August 2013 a federal judge, Shira Scheindlin, noted that most police stops occurred in minority communities and amounted to a form of racial profiling. The judge's order ending the practice, however, was stayed by a federal appeals court that removed Judge Scheindlin from the case and accused her of improper bias. In 2014 the City of New York dropped its appeal and agreed to engage in a process of mediation with community groups to curtail the practice. After his election in 2014, Mayor Bill de Blasio announced an end to aggressive stop-and-frisk tactics. Critics charged that the mayor's orders would lead to an increase in New York crime rates, though this has not occurred.

Finally, the Fourth Amendment places limits on government surveillance of individuals, an ongoing and controversial issue in the United States today. For example, a federal judge in Washington, D.C., recently ruled that an NSA program that collected millions of records of telephone calls was impermissible under the Fourth Amendment.[86]

THE FIFTH AMENDMENT

> No person shall be held to answer for a capital, or otherwise infamous crime, unless on a presentment or indictment of a Grand Jury, except in cases arising in the land or naval forces, or in the Militia, when in actual service in time of War or public danger; nor shall any person be subject for the same offence to be twice put in jeopardy of life or limb; nor shall be compelled in any criminal case to be a witness against himself, nor be deprived of life, liberty, or property, without due process of law; nor shall private property be taken for public use, without just compensation.

Grand Juries The first clause of the Fifth Amendment, the right to a **grand jury** to determine whether a trial is warranted, is considered "the oldest institution known to the Constitution."[87] A grand jury is a body of citizens that must agree that the

grand jury jury that determines whether sufficient evidence is available to justify a trial; grand juries do not rule on the accused's guilt or innocence prosecutor has sufficient evidence to bring criminal charges against a suspect. Grand juries play an important role in federal criminal cases. However, the provision for a grand jury is the one important civil liberties provision of the Bill of Rights that was not incorporated into the Fourteenth Amendment to apply to state criminal prosecutions. Thus, some states operate without grand juries. In such states, the prosecuting attorney simply files a "bill of information" affirming that there is sufficient evidence available to justify a trial. If the accused person is to be held in custody, the prosecutor must take the available information before a judge to determine that the evidence shows probable cause.

double jeopardy the Fifth Amendment right providing that a person cannot be tried twice for the same crime

Double Jeopardy "Nor shall any person be subject for the same offence to be twice put in jeopardy of life or limb" is the constitutional protection from **double jeopardy**, or being tried more than once for the same crime. The protection from double jeopardy was at the heart of the *Palko* case in 1937, which, as we saw earlier in this chapter, also established the principle of selective incorporation of the Bill of Rights. In the *Palko* case, the Supreme Court ruled that the Fifth Amendment's prohibition of double jeopardy did not apply to the states. However, in the 1969 case of *Benton v. Maryland*, the Court expressly overruled *Palko* and declared that the double jeopardy clause did, in fact, apply to the states.[88] In this case, the state of Maryland sought to try a defendant, John Benton, for larceny, even though he had previously been acquitted by a jury. Maryland's constitution did not prohibit such a proceeding, and at the second trial Benton was convicted. The Supreme Court, however, ruled that the second trial violated Benton's rights under the U.S. Constitution. Double jeopardy now joined those rights "incorporated" via the Fourteenth Amendment.

Self-Incrimination Perhaps the most significant liberty found in the Fifth Amendment, and the one most familiar to the many Americans who watch television crime shows, is the guarantee that no citizen "shall be compelled in any criminal case to be a witness against himself." The most famous case concerning self-incrimination is one of such importance that Chief Justice Earl Warren assessed its results as going "to the very root of our concepts of American criminal jurisprudence."[89] Twenty-three-year-old Ernesto Miranda was sentenced to between 20 and 30 years in prison for the kidnapping and rape of an 18-year-old woman. The woman had identified him in a police lineup, and after two hours of questioning, Miranda confessed, subsequently signing a statement that his confession had been made voluntarily, without threats or promises of immunity. These confessions were admitted into evidence and served as the basis for Miranda's conviction. After his conviction, Miranda argued that his confession had not been truly voluntary and that he had not been informed of his right to remain silent or his right to consult an attorney. The Supreme Court agreed and overturned the conviction. Following one of the most intensely and widely criticized decisions ever handed down by the Supreme Court, Ernesto Miranda's case produced the rules the police must follow before questioning an arrested criminal suspect. The reading of a person's "Miranda rights" became a standard scene in every police station and on virtually every dramatization of police action on television and in the movies. *Miranda* advanced the civil liberties of accused persons not only by expanding the scope of the Fifth Amendment clause covering coerced confessions and self-incrimination but also by confirming the right to counsel (discussed later). The Supreme Court under Burger and Rehnquist considerably softened the *Miranda*

```
DEFENDANT                          LOCATION


        SPECIFIC WARNING REGARDING INTERROGATIONS

   1. YOU HAVE THE RIGHT TO REMAIN SILENT.

   2. ANYTHING YOU SAY CAN AND WILL BE USED AGAINST YOU IN A COURT
      OF LAW.

   3. YOU HAVE THE RIGHT TO TALK TO A LAWYER AND HAVE HIM PRESENT
      WITH YOU WHILE YOU ARE BEING QUESTIONED.

   4. IF YOU CANNOT AFFORD TO HIRE A LAWYER ONE WILL BE APPOINTED
      TO REPRESENT YOU BEFORE ANY QUESTIONING, IF YOU WISH ONE.

   SIGNATURE OF DEFENDANT                      DATE


   WITNESS                                     TIME


   □ REFUSED SIGNATURE    SAN FRANCISCO POLICE DEPARTMENT    PR.9.1.4
```

The case of Ernesto Miranda resulted in the creation of Miranda rights, which must be read to those arrested to make them aware of their constitutional rights.

restrictions, but the **Miranda rule** still stands as a protection against egregious police abuses of arrested persons.

Eminent Domain The other fundamental clause of the Fifth Amendment is the "takings clause," which extends to each citizen a protection against the "taking" of private property "without just compensation." Although this part of the Fifth Amendment is not specifically concerned with protecting persons accused of crimes, it is nevertheless a fundamentally important instance where the government and the citizen are adversaries. The power of any government to take private property for public use—a power essential to the very concept of sovereignty—is called **eminent domain**. The Fifth Amendment puts limits on that inherent power through procedures that require a showing of a public purpose and the provision of fair payment for the taking of someone's property. This provision is now universally observed in all U.S. principalities, but it has not always been meticulously observed.

The first modern case confronting the issue of public use involved a mom-and-pop grocery store in a run-down neighborhood of the District of Columbia. In carrying out a vast urban redevelopment program, the city government took the property as one of a large number of privately owned lots to be cleared for new housing and business construction. The owner of the grocery store took the government to court on the grounds that it was an unconstitutional use of eminent domain to take property from one private owner and eventually to turn that property back, in altered form, to another private owner. In 1945 the store owner lost the case. The Supreme Court's argument was a curious but very important one: the "public interest" can mean virtually anything a legislature says it means. In other words, since the overall slum clearance and redevelopment project was in the public interest, according to the legislature, the eventual transfers of property were justified.[90] This principle was reaffirmed in the 2005 case of *Kelo v. City of New London*, where the Court held that the city could seize land from one private owner and transfer it to another as part of a redevelopment plan.[91]

Miranda rule the requirement, articulated by the Supreme Court in *Miranda v. Arizona*, that persons under arrest must be informed prior to police interrogation of their rights to remain silent and to have the benefit of legal counsel

eminent domain the right of government to take private property for public use

THE SIXTH AMENDMENT AND THE RIGHT TO COUNSEL

> In all criminal prosecutions, the accused shall enjoy the right to a speedy and public trial, by an impartial jury of the State and district wherein the crime shall have been committed, which district shall have been previously ascertained by law, and to be informed of the nature and cause of the accusation; to be confronted with the witnesses against him; to have compulsory process for obtaining witnesses in his favor, and to have the Assistance of Counsel for his defence.

Some provisions of the Sixth Amendment, such as the right to a speedy trial and the right to confront witnesses before an impartial jury, are not very controversial in nature. The "right to counsel" provision, like the exclusionary rule of the Fourth Amendment and the self-incrimination clause of the Fifth Amendment, is notable for sometimes freeing defendants who seem to be guilty as charged.

Gideon v. Wainwright (1963) is the perfect case study because it involved a disreputable person who seemed patently guilty of the crime of which he was convicted. In and out of jails for most of his 51 years, Clarence Earl Gideon received a five-year sentence for breaking and entering a poolroom in Panama City, Florida. While serving time in jail, Gideon became a fairly well-qualified "jailhouse lawyer," made his own appeal on a handwritten petition, and eventually won the landmark ruling on the right to counsel in all felony cases.[92]

The right to counsel has been expanded during the past few decades, even as the courts have become more conservative. For example, although at first the right to counsel was met by judges assigning lawyers from the community as a formal public obligation, now most states and cities have created an office of public defender; these state-employed professional defense lawyers typically provide poor defendants with much better legal representation. In addition, defendants have the right to appeal a conviction on the grounds that the counsel provided by the state was deficient. For example, in 2003 the Supreme Court overturned the death sentence of a Maryland death-row inmate, holding that the defense lawyer had failed to inform the jury fully of the defendant's history of "horrendous childhood abuse."[93] Moreover, the right to counsel extends beyond serious crimes to any trial, with or without a jury, that holds the possibility of imprisonment.[94]

THE EIGHTH AMENDMENT AND CRUEL AND UNUSUAL PUNISHMENT

> Excessive bail shall not be required, nor excessive fines imposed, nor cruel and unusual punishment inflicted.

Virtually all the debate over Eighth Amendment issues focuses on the last clause of the amendment: one of the greatest challenges in interpreting this provision consistently is that what is considered "cruel and unusual" varies from culture to culture and from generation to generation.

In 1972 the Supreme Court overturned several state death penalty laws, not because they were cruel and unusual but because they were being applied unevenly—that is, African Americans were much more likely than whites to be sentenced to death, the poor more likely than the rich, and men more likely than women.[95] Very soon after that decision, a majority of states revised their capital punishment provisions to meet the Court's standards, and the Court reaffirmed that the death penalty could be used if certain standards were met.[96] Since 1976, the Court has consistently upheld state laws providing for capital punishment, although the Court also continues to review death penalty appeals each year.

Between 1976 and April 2017, states executed 1,448 people. Most of those executions occurred in southern states, with Texas leading the way at 542. As of October 2018, 30 states had statutes providing for capital punishment for specified offenses, a policy supported by a majority of Americans, according to polls. On the other hand, 19 states bar the death penalty, and since the end of the 1990s, both the number of death sentences and the number of executions have declined annually.[97] In 2017, 23 people were executed in the United States, a slight increase over the 20 executed in 2016.

Despite the seeming popularity of the death penalty, the debate has become, if anything, more intense. Many death penalty supporters assert its deterrent effects on other would-be criminals. Although studies of capital crimes usually fail to demonstrate any direct deterrent effect, this failure may be due to the lengthy delays—typically years and even decades—between convictions and executions. A system that eliminates undue delays might enhance deterrence. And deterring even one murder or other heinous crime, proponents argue, is ample justification for such laws.

Death penalty opponents are quick to counter that the death penalty has not been proven to deter crime, either in the United States or abroad. In fact, America is the only Western nation that still executes criminals. If the government is to serve as an example of proper behavior, say foes of capital punishment, it has no business sanctioning killing when incarceration will similarly protect society. Furthermore, execution is time-consuming and expensive—more expensive than life imprisonment—precisely because the government must make every effort to ensure that it is not executing an innocent person. Curtailing legal appeals would make the possibility of a mistake too great. And although most Americans do support the death penalty, people also support life imprisonment without the possibility of parole as an alternative. Race also intrudes in death penalty cases: people of color are disproportionately more likely than whites charged with identical crimes to be given the ultimate punishment.

The Supreme Court has long struggled to establish principles to govern executions under the Eighth Amendment. In recent years, the Court has issued a number of death penalty opinions, declaring that death was too harsh a penalty for the crime of rape of a child,[98] prohibiting the execution of a defendant with an IQ under 70 and of a youthful defendant, and invalidating a death sentence for an African Americans defendant after the prosecutor improperly excluded African Americans from the jury.[99] In 2015 the Court upheld lethal injection as a mode of execution despite arguments that this form of execution was likely to cause considerable pain.[100]

The question of cruel and unusual punishment goes beyond the death penalty. Federal courts have on occasion held that overcrowding and other dangerous conditions within prisons, such as inadequate food, medical care, and sanitation, may constitute cruel and unusual punishment. Also, prison officials employing threats and beatings against inmates may be guilty of violating this Eighth Amendment right.[101] The Court has also been concerned with punishments meted out to the mentally disabled and to juveniles. In a recent case, the Court held that life imprisonment without parole for a juvenile, even one convicted of murder, constituted

Opponents argue that the death penalty constitutes cruel and unusual punishment. In recent years the use of lethal injection drugs including Midazolam has come under scrutiny after some troubling executions where the process was drawn out and painful. In 2015 the Supreme Court upheld the use of lethal injection.

cruel and unusual punishment.[102] The "Who Are Americans?" feature takes a look at the U.S. prison population.

The Right to Privacy

Assess whether people have a right to privacy under the Constitution

A **right to privacy** was not granted in the Bill of Rights, but a clause in the Fourth Amendment provides for "the right of the people to be secure in their persons, houses, papers, and effects, against unreasonable searches and seizures." In a 1928 case, Justice Louis Brandeis argued in a dissent that the Fourth Amendment should be extended to a more general principle of "privacy in the home."[103] Another step in this direction was taken when several Jehovah's Witnesses directed their children not to salute the flag or say the Pledge of Allegiance in school because the first of the Ten Commandments prohibits the worship of "graven images." They lost their case in 1940, but the Supreme Court, reversing itself in 1943, held that the 1940 case had been "wrongly decided" and recognized "a right to be left alone" as part of the free speech clause of the First Amendment.[104] Another small step was taken in 1958, when the Supreme Court recognized "privacy in one's association" in its decision that the state of Alabama could not use the membership list of the National Association for the Advancement of Colored People (NAACP) in state investigations.[105]

right to privacy the right to be left alone, which has been interpreted by the Supreme Court to entail individual access to birth control and abortions

BIRTH CONTROL

The sphere of privacy was formally recognized in 1965, when the Court ruled that a Connecticut statute forbidding the use of contraceptives violated the right of marital privacy. Estelle Griswold, the executive director of the Planned Parenthood League of Connecticut, was arrested by the state of Connecticut for providing information, instruction, and medical advice about contraception to married couples. She and her associates were found guilty as accessories to the crime and fined $100 each. The Supreme Court reversed the lower-court decisions and declared the Connecticut law unconstitutional because it violated "a right of privacy older than the Bill of Rights— older than our political parties, older than our school system."[106] Justice William O. Douglas, author of the majority decision in the *Griswold* case, argued that this right of privacy is also grounded in the Constitution because it fits into a "zone of privacy" created by a combination of the Third, Fourth, and Fifth amendments. A concurring opinion, written by Justice Arthur Goldberg, attempted to strengthen Douglas's argument by adding that "the concept of liberty...embraces the right of marital privacy though that right is not mentioned explicitly in the Constitution [and] is supported by numerous decisions of this Court...and *by the language and history of the Ninth Amendment* [emphasis added]."[107] The Ninth Amendment provides that "the enumeration in the Constitution, of certain rights, shall not be construed to deny or disparage others retained by the people." According to Justice Goldberg, this language means, in effect, that just because the Constitution does not specifically mention a particular right to privacy does not mean that the people do not retain that right. The language of the Ninth Amendment, when taken with the evidence provided by the First, Third, Fourth, and Fifth amendments, was sufficient for the Court to find that the Bill of Rights implies a constitutional right to privacy.

FOR CRITICAL ANALYSIS

Read the Third, Fourth, Fifth, and Ninth amendments in the appendix at the end of this book. In your opinion, do American citizens have a constitutional right to privacy?

Who Is in Prison?

Despite the many freedoms protected by the Bill of Rights, the United States imprisons more of its people than any other country. Although African Americans make up only about 13 percent of the total U.S. population, they make up 35.7 percent of the prison population. Incarceration rates by state range from a low of 189 per 100,000 residents in Maine to a high of 1,072 per 100,000 residents in Louisiana.*

OTHER
9.0%

WHITE
33.6%

HISPANIC
21.6%

BLACK
35.7%

FEMALE
7.0%

MALE
93.0%

PROPERTY
OFFENDERS
19.3%

VIOLENT
OFFENDERS
53.2%

PUBLIC-ORDER
OFFENDERS
11.0%

DRUG
OFFENDERS
15.7%

Violent offenses include murder, manslaughter, rape/sexual assault, robbery, and aggravated or simple assault. Property offenses include burglary, motor vehicle theft, and fraud. Drug offenses include trafficking and possession. Public order offenses include weapons, drunk driving, and indecency.

Incarceration Rates by State

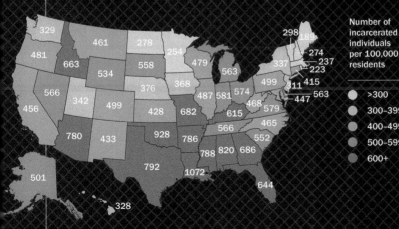

Number of
incarcerated
individuals
per 100,000
residents

- >300
- 300–399
- 400–499
- 500–599
- 600+

SOURCE: U.S. Department of Justice, "Prisoners in 2014," September 2015,
www.bjs.gov/index.cfm?ty=pbdetail&iid=5387 (accessed 2/18/16).

FOR CRITICAL ANALYSIS

1. Due process guarantees the same legal protections to anyone accused of a crime. However, studies have shown that African Americans and Hispanics are more likely to be jailed—and jailed for longer—than whites convicted of similar crimes. Is this a violation of civil liberties?

2. Some people have argued that prison terms for relatively minor drug offenses violate the Eighth Amendment's ban on cruel and unusual punisment. What do you think?

ABORTION

The right to privacy was confirmed and extended in 1973 in an important Supreme Court decision: *Roe v. Wade*. This decision established a woman's right to seek an abortion and prohibited states from making abortion a criminal act prior to the point at which the fetus becomes viable, which in 1973 was the twenty-seventh week.[108] The Burger Court's decision in *Roe* took a revolutionary step toward establishing the right to privacy. It is important to emphasize that the preference for privacy rights and for their extension to include the rights of women to control their own bodies was not something the Supreme Court invented in a vacuum. Most states did not regulate abortions in any fashion until the 1840s, at which time only six of the 26 existing states had any regulations governing abortion. In addition, many states had begun to ease their abortion restrictions well before the 1973 *Roe* decision, although in recent years a number of states have reinstated some restrictions on abortion including lowering the viability standard: 20 weeks (Texas), 12 weeks (Arkansas), and 6 weeks (North Dakota).

By extending the umbrella of privacy, this sweeping ruling dramatically changed abortion practices in America. In addition, it galvanized and nationalized the abortion debate. Groups opposed to abortion, such as the National Right to Life Committee, organized to fight the liberal new standard, while abortion rights groups have sought to maintain that protection. While the Supreme Court has continued to affirm a woman's right to seek an abortion, the Court has since qualified that right as the legal standard shifted against abortion rights supporters. In *Webster v. Reproductive Health Services* (1989), the Court narrowly upheld (by a 5–4 majority) the constitutionality of restrictions on the use of public medical facilities for abortion.[109] And in the 1992 case of *Planned Parenthood of Southeastern Pennsylvania v. Casey*, another 5–4 majority of the Court upheld *Roe* but narrowed its scope, refusing to invalidate a Pennsylvania law that significantly limits freedom of choice. The Court's decision defined the right to an abortion as a "limited or qualified" right subject to regulation by the states as long as the regulation does not constitute an "undue burden."[110] In the 2006 case of *Ayotte v. Planned Parenthood of Northern*

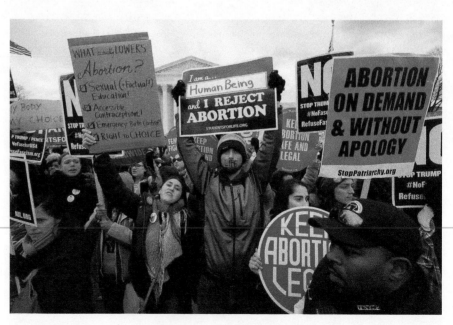

One of the most important cases related to the right to privacy was *Roe v. Wade*, which established a woman's right to seek an abortion. However, the decision has remained highly controversial, with opponents arguing that the Constitution does not guarantee this right.

New England, the Court held that a law requiring parental notification before a minor could obtain an abortion was not an undue burden.[111] And in the 2007 *Gonzales v. Carhart* decision, the Court effectively upheld the federal partial-birth abortion ban, which outlaws a particular type of abortion procedure.[112]

SEXUAL ORIENTATION

In the last three decades, the right to be left alone began to include the privacy rights of gay people. One morning in Atlanta, Georgia, in the mid-1980s, a police officer came to the home of Michael Hardwick to serve a warrant for Hardwick's arrest for failure to appear in court to answer charges of drinking in public. One of Hardwick's unknowing housemates invited the officer to look in Hardwick's room, where he found Hardwick and another man engaging in "consensual sexual behavior" and then proceeded to arrest him under Georgia's laws against heterosexual and homosexual sodomy. Hardwick filed a lawsuit against the state, challenging the constitutionality of the Georgia law, and won his case in the federal court of appeals. The state of Georgia, in an unusual move, appealed the court's decision to the Supreme Court. In 1986 the majority of the Court reversed the lower-court decision, holding against Hardwick on the grounds that "the federal Constitution confers [no] fundamental right upon homosexuals to engage in sodomy" and that therefore there was no basis to invalidate "the laws of the many states that still make such conduct illegal and have done so for a very long time."[113]

Seventeen years later, and to almost everyone's surprise, in *Lawrence v. Texas* (2003) the Court overturned *Bowers v. Hardwick* with a dramatic pronouncement that gays are "entitled to respect for their private lives"[114] as a matter of constitutional due process. Drawing from the tradition of negative liberty, the Court maintained, "In our tradition the State is not omnipresent in the home. And there are other spheres of our lives and existence outside the home, where the State should not be a dominant presence." Explicitly encompassing lesbians and gay men within the umbrella of privacy, the Court concluded that the "petitioners are entitled to respect for their private lives. The State cannot demean their existence or control their destiny by making their private sexual conduct a crime."[115] This decision added substance to the "right of privacy."[116] In 2015 the Court took another important step in the protection of gay rights by declaring that state bans on same-sex marriage were unconstitutional.[117] The Court said that the refusal to issue marriage licenses to same-sex couples constituted a violation of the Fourteenth Amendment's equal protection and due process clauses. See Chapter 5 for more on same-sex marriage.

THE RIGHT TO DIE

Another area ripe for litigation and public discourse is the so-called right to die. A number of highly publicized physician-assisted suicides in the 1990s focused attention on whether people have a right to choose their own death and to receive assistance in carrying it out. Can this become part of the privacy right? Or is it a new substantive right? The Supreme Court has not definitively answered this question. However, the Court refused to intervene in the well-publicized case of Terri Schiavo, a woman who suffered irreversible brain damage and was kept alive in a vegetative state via a feeding tube for 15 years. During this period, Schiavo's husband wanted to withdraw life support, citing his wife's wishes, while her

Civil Liberties around the World

Elections are only a small part of what makes a democracy a democracy. *Liberal democracies*—a term political scientists use to refer to countries they consider fully democratic—also have extensive civil rights and civil liberties.

Freedom House, an independent watchdog organization focusing on freedom and democracy around the world, collects data on political rights and civil liberties from each country. They measure freedom of expression and belief, respect for the "rule of law,"[a] the right to organize and form associations, and personal autonomy and individual rights to rank countries as free, partly free, and not free (shown below).

All countries vary in how they prioritize specific liberties. The United States is generally comparable to other democracies when it comes to the freedom of expression and belief and the right to organize and form associations, but the United States places exceptionally high emphasis on personal autonomy and individual rights. In comparison, Latvia is ranked slightly higher on the right to organize and form associations, but concerns regarding the treatment of women and minorities mean its individual rights score is lower.

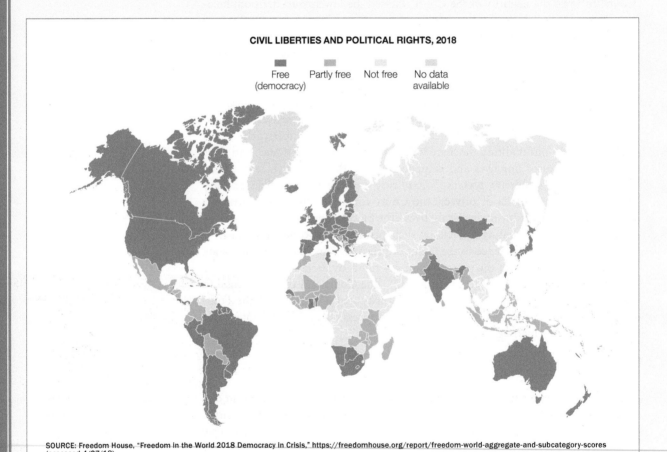

CIVIL LIBERTIES AND POLITICAL RIGHTS, 2018

Free (democracy)　Partly free　Not free　No data available

SOURCE: Freedom House, "Freedom in the World 2018 Democracy in Crisis," https://freedomhouse.org/report/freedom-world-aggregate-and-subcategory-scores (accessed 4/27/18).

[a] A legal principle that laws should govern a country—including its leaders—rather than having decisions made arbitrarily by individuals in the government.

parents wanted support continued indefinitely. The case was heard multiple times in the Florida state courts and the federal courts. In 2005, Schiavo's husband finally prevailed, and she was removed from life support and subsequently died.[118] In the 2006 case of *Gonzales v. Oregon*, the Supreme Court did intervene to uphold a law allowing doctors to use drugs to facilitate the deaths of terminally ill patients who requested such assistance.[119] Thus, although the Court has not ruled definitively on the right-to-die question, it does not seem hostile to the idea.

Civil Liberties
WHAT DO WE WANT?

The prominent place of civil liberties is one of the hallmarks of American government. The freedoms enshrined in the Constitution and its amendments help define the relationship between government and citizens by limiting what government can do to individuals.

But these freedoms also come with trade-offs. We saw in the chapter opener that the freedom afforded to the Slants rock band to reimagine an ethnic slur as a term of empowerment undermined Native Americans' efforts to end the use of an ethnic term they found offensive. Trade-offs are prominent in many areas of government. Surveillance is one where difficult trade-offs are particularly acute. Government eavesdropping on communications, travel, and personal conduct has become a fact of American life. Revelations in the summer of 2013 of extensive electronic surveillance by the NSA of Americans' phone and internet communications caused considerable consternation in Congress and in the news media. However, many Americans believe that they are the beneficiaries rather than the potential victims of government surveillance. Those who have nothing to hide, goes the saying, have nothing to fear. But as law professor Daniel Solove shows, surveillance can entrap even the most innocent individuals in a web of suspicions and allegations from which they may find it extremely difficult to extricate themselves.[120]

National Intelligence director James Clapper and other defense officials testified before Congress following revelations in 2013 of extensive government surveillance programs. Electronic monitoring allows the government to gather vast quantities of data from private communications.

The trade-off between individual privacy and government surveillance raises questions not just about security but also about political power. Popular government requires that citizens possess a good deal of knowledge about the actions of the state. In essence, citizens must undertake their own surveillance of the government and its officials as a precondition for exerting influence over them. At the same time, citizens' ability to exercise power also requires that they have considerable protection from the state's scrutiny. Those who disagree with government must be both free to organize and voice their opinions and free from government retaliation.

Thus, popular government requires a combination of government transparency and citizen privacy. Questions about privacy will continue to grow as surveillance technologies become more sophisticated and we, as citizens, will be challenged to adapt eighteenth-century constitutional protections to twenty-first-century issues. How have new technologies affected the government's ability to monitor its citizens? What are your expectations of privacy in your email conversations, your plane tickets, your reading habits?

These issues, along with questions about the right to bear arms, the use of the death penalty, and religious freedom (see the "**Who Participates?**" feature on the facing page) are unlikely to go away any time soon and will continue to challenge Americans in the years to come.

Religious Affiliation and Freedom of Religion

Percentage of American Adults in Each Religious Tradition

Under the First Amendment, Americans enjoy the freedom to practice (or not practice) the religion of their choice. Most Americans identify with and participate in some form of religion.

- Protestant **44%**
- Catholic **20%**
- Other Christian **3%**
- Jewish **2%**
- Muslim **1%**
- Buddhist **1%**
- Hindu **1%**
- Other faiths **1%**
- Nothing in particular **17%**
- Agnostic **3%**
- Atheist **3%**
- Don't know **4%**

SOURCE: Robert P. Jones and Daniel Cox, *America's Changing Religious Identity*, 2016, www.prri.org/ (accessed 11/4/17).

WHAT YOU CAN DO ★

Know Your First Amendment Rights

✓ Learn more about freedom of religion from a variety of legal scholars at **www.constitutioncenter.org**.

✓ Share your opinion about the First Amendment and religion on campus with your school newspaper. Find information about students' religious rights at **www.thefire.org**.

✓ Learn more about your other First Amendment rights, such as free speech on the internet, at **www.eff.org**.

Civil Liberties and the Constitution

Explain the origins and evolution of the civil liberties in the Bill of Rights as they apply to federal government and the states (pp. 117–22)

Although some of the framers believed that a bill of rights was unnecessary and potentially dangerous, the Federalists made a pledge to add one in order to secure support for the Constitution during the ratification process. Over the course of the first 100 years of American history, the Bill of Rights was interpreted to limit only the actions of the federal government. One by one, most of the important provisions of the first 10 amendments have been incorporated into the Fourteenth Amendment and applied to the states.

Key Terms

habeas corpus (p. 118)

Bill of Rights (p. 118)

civil liberties (p. 118)

selective incorporation (p. 120)

Practice Quiz

1. From 1791 until the end of the nineteenth century, the Bill of Rights was interpreted to put limits on
   a) the national government only.
   b) the state government only.
   c) both the national and state governments.
   d) neither the national nor the state government.
   e) political parties and interest groups.

2. Which of the following rights was *not* included in the original Constitution?
   a) prohibition of bills of attainder
   b) prohibition of ex post facto laws
   c) guarantee of habeas corpus
   d) guarantee of trial by jury in the state where the crime was committed
   e) None. They were all included in the original Constitution.

3. The process by which some of the liberties in the Bill of Rights were applied to the states is known as
   a) preemption.
   b) selective incorporation.
   c) judicial activism.
   d) civil liberties.
   e) establishment.

4. Which of the following provisions of the Bill of Rights was incorporated in the 1897 Supreme Court case *Chicago, Burlington, and Quincy R.R. v. Chicago*?
   a) the right to counsel in any criminal trial
   b) the right against self-incrimination
   c) freedom from unnecessary searches and seizures
   d) freedom to petition the government for redress of grievances
   e) protection against the "taking" of private property by state governments "without just compensation"

The First Amendment and Freedom of Religion

Describe how the First Amendment protects freedom of religion (pp. 123–27)

Two parts of the First Amendment touch on religious freedom: the establishment clause and the free exercise clause. The courts have been somewhat inconsistent in determining how solid the establishment clause's "wall of separation" between church and state actually is in practice. While the courts have been more consistent in protecting the free exercise of religious beliefs, they have taken pains to distinguish between religious beliefs and actions based on those beliefs.

Key Terms

establishment clause (p. 123)

Lemon test (p. 124)

free exercise clause (p. 125)

Practice Quiz

5. The Supreme Court's ruling in *Lemon v. Kurtzman*, which led to the *Lemon* test, concerned the issue of
   a) school desegregation.
   b) financial assistance to religious schools.
   c) cruel and unusual punishment.
   d) obscenity.
   e) prayer in school.

The First Amendment and Freedom of Speech and of the Press

Describe how the First Amendment protects free speech and freedom of the press (pp. 127–36)

Given the importance of freedom of speech and of the press to the functioning of democratic government, Americans are assumed to have the right to speak and broadcast their ideas unless there is some compelling reason to stop them. According to the courts, although virtually all speech is protected by the Constitution, some forms of speech are entitled to a greater degree of protection than others. Libel, slander, and speech that incites lawless action are examples of speech that can be limited by the government.

Key Terms

"clear and present danger" test (p. 128)

fighting words (p. 129)

"speech plus" (p. 133)

prior restraint (p. 133)

libel (p. 134)

slander (p. 134)

Practice Quiz

6. The judicial doctrine that places a heavy burden of proof on the government when it seeks to regulate or restrict speech is called
   a) judicial restraint.
   b) judicial activism.
   c) habeas corpus.
   d) prior restraint.
   e) strict scrutiny.

7. The standard articulated by the Supreme Court in *R.A.V. v. City of St. Paul* suggests that
   a) virtually all "hate speech" is not constitutionally protected by the First Amendment.
   b) virtually all "hate speech" is constitutionally protected by the First Amendment.
   c) "hate speech" is not constitutionally protected by the First Amendment when it is directed at religious groups.
   d) "hate speech" is not constitutionally protected by the First Amendment when it is directed at racial or ethnic minority groups.
   e) "hate speech" is not constitutionally protected by the First Amendment when it is expressed on college campuses.

8. Which of the following describes a written statement made in "reckless disregard of the truth" that is considered damaging to a victim because it is "malicious, scandalous, and defamatory"?
   a) slander
   b) libel
   c) speech plus
   d) fighting words
   e) expressive speech

The Second Amendment and the Right to Bear Arms

Explore whether the Second Amendment means people have a right to own guns (pp. 136–38)

The Second Amendment granted Americans the right "to keep and bear Arms" in order to provide for state militias. Prior to 2010, the Second Amendment was not incorporated. In *McDonald v. Chicago*, the Supreme Court asserted that the right to bear arms applies to both state governments and the federal government.

Practice Quiz

9. In *District of Columbia v. Heller*, the Supreme Court ruled that
   a) states can require citizens to own firearms.
   b) federal grants can be used to support the formation of state militias.
   c) felons cannot be prevented from purchasing assault rifles.
   d) the Second Amendment provides a constitutional right to keep a loaded handgun at home for self-defense.
   e) the Second Amendment applies only to the federal government and not to states.

Rights of the Criminally Accused

Explain the major rights that people have if they are accused of a crime (pp. 138–46)

The essence of the Constitution's due process of the law is found in the Fourth, Fifth, Sixth, and Eighth amendments. The Fourth Amendment protects individuals from unreasonable searches and seizures. The Fifth Amendment provides individuals with the right to a grand jury, protection from double jeopardy, and a guarantee against self-incrimination. The Sixth Amendment provides the right to legal counsel, the right to a speedy trial, and the right to confront witnesses before an impartial jury. The Eighth Amendment protects individuals against "cruel and unusual" punishment.

Key Terms

due process of law (p. 138)

exclusionary rule (p. 139)

grand jury (p. 141)

double jeopardy (p. 142)

Miranda rule (p. 143)

eminent domain (p. 143)

Practice Quiz

10. In *Mapp v. Ohio*, the Supreme Court ruled that
    a) evidence obtained from an illegal search could not be introduced in a trial.
    b) the government must provide legal counsel for defendants who are too poor to provide it for themselves.
    c) persons under arrest must be informed prior to police interrogation of their rights to remain silent and to have the benefits of legal counsel.
    d) the government has the right to take private property for public use if just compensation is provided.
    e) a person cannot be tried twice for the same crime.

11. Which of the following is called "the oldest institution known to the Constitution"?
    a) The Third Amendment's freedom from forced quartering of soldiers during peacetime.
    b) The Fourth Amendment's freedom from warrantless search and seizure.
    c) The Fifth Amendment's right to remain silent.
    d) The Fifth Amendment's right against self-incrimination and forced confessions.
    e) The Fifth Amendment's right to a grand jury in order to determine whether a trial is warranted.

12. Which famous case deals with the Sixth Amendment's guarantee of the right to counsel?
    a) *Roe v. Wade*
    b) *Mapp v. Ohio*
    c) *Gideon v. Wainwright*
    d) *Terry v. Ohio*
    e) *Miranda v. Arizona*

The Right to Privacy

Assess whether people have a right to privacy under the Constitution (pp. 146–51)

A right to privacy is never explicitly mentioned in the Constitution. In fact, it was not until 1965 that the Supreme Court interpreted the Third, Fourth, Fifth, and Ninth amendments to create a constitutional "zone of privacy." The right to privacy has since been used to strike down laws limiting access to birth control, outlawing abortion, and criminalizing gay and lesbian sexual activity. The Supreme Court has not yet definitively answered the question of whether the right to privacy also gives individuals a right to choose their own death and to receive assistance in carrying it out.

Key Term

right to privacy (p. 146)

Practice Quiz

13. In which case was a right to privacy related to the use of birth control first formally recognized by the Court?
    a) *Griswold v. Connecticut*
    b) *Roe v. Wade*
    c) *Lemon v. Kurtzman*
    d) *Planned Parenthood v. Casey*
    e) *Baker v. Carr*

14. In which case did the Supreme Court rule that state governments no longer had the authority to make private sexual behavior a crime?
    a) *Texas v. Johnson*
    b) *Webster v. Reproductive Health Services*
    c) *Gonzales v. Oregon*
    d) *Lawrence v. Texas*
    e) *Bowers v. Hardwick*

For Further Reading

Amar, Akhil Reed. *The Law of the Land: A Grand Tour of Our Constitutional Republic*. New York: Basic Books, 2015.

Ash, Timothy Garton. *Free Speech*. New Haven, CT: Yale University Press, 2017.

Barbas, Samantha. *Newsworthy: The Supreme Court Battle over Privacy and Press Freedom*. Stanford, CA: Stanford University Press, 2017.

Brandon, Mark. *The Constitution in Wartime*. Durham, NC: Duke University Press, 2005.

Friendly, Fred W. *Minnesota Rag: The Dramatic Story of the Landmark Supreme Court Case That Gave New Meaning to Freedom of the Press*. New York: Vintage, 1982.

Gray, David. *The Fourth Amendment in an Age of Surveillance*. New York: Cambridge University Press, 2017.

Lewis, Anthony. *Freedom for the Thought That We Hate: A Biography of the First Amendment*. New York: Basic Books, 2010.

Lewis, Anthony. *Gideon's Trumpet*. New York: Random House, 1964.

O'Brien, David M. *Constitutional Law and Politics: Civil Rights and Civil Liberties*. 10th ed. Vol. 2. New York: W. W. Norton, 2017.

Richards, Neil. *Intellectual Privacy: Rethinking Civil Liberties in the Digital Age*. New York: Oxford University Press, 2015.

Smith, Steven D. *The Rise and Decline of American Religious Freedom*. Cambridge, MA: Harvard University Press, 2014.

Solove, Daniel. *Nothing to Hide: The False Tradeoff between Privacy and Security*. New Haven, CT: Yale University Press, 2011.

Tebbe, Nelson. *Religious Freedom in an Egalitarian Age*. Cambridge, MA: Harvard University Press, 2017.

Waldron, Jeremy. *The Harm in Hate Speech*. Cambridge, MA: Harvard University Press, 2012.

Weinrib, Laura. *The Taming of Free Speech: America's Civil Liberties Compromise*. Cambridge, MA: Harvard University Press, 2016.

Winkler, Adam. *Gunfight: The Battle over the Right to Bear Arms in America*. New York: W. W. Norton, 2013.

Recommended Websites

The American Civil Liberties Union (ACLU)
www.aclu.org
> The ACLU is committed to protecting for all individuals the freedoms found in the Bill of Rights. This sometimes controversial organization constantly monitors the government for violations of liberty and encourages its members to take political action.

Electronic Privacy Information Center
http://epic.org/privacy
> For an extensive list of privacy issues, go to the web page for the Electronic Privacy Information Center. Here you will find civil liberties concerns as they relate to all forms of information technology, including the internet.

The Free Expression Network
www.freeexpression.org
> The Free Expression Network is an organization "dedicated to preserving the right to free expression." On its website you can find links to important First Amendment issues and organizations.

Freedom Forum
www.freedomforum.org
> Freedom of speech and freedom of the press are considered critical in any democracy; however, only some kinds of speech are fully protected against restrictions. Freedom Forum is a nonpartisan agency that investigates and analyzes such First Amendment restrictions.

National Abortion and Reproductive Rights Action League
www.naral.org

National Right to Life Committee
www.NRLC.org
> The National Abortion and Reproductive Rights Action League and the National Right to Life Committee are two of the nation's largest interest groups weighing in on the abortion issue. See what these opposing groups have to say about privacy rights.

Religious Freedom
http://guides.lib.virginia.edu/content.php?pid5147534&sid51255449
> The establishment clause of the U.S. Constitution has been interpreted to mean a "wall of separation" between government and religion. On the Religious Freedom Page you can find information on a variety of issues pertaining to religious freedom in the United States and around the world.

U.S. Supreme Court Media
www.oyez.org
> This website for U.S. Supreme Court media has a great search engine for finding information on cases affecting civil liberties, such as *Lemon v. Kurtzman*, *Miranda v. Arizona*, *Mapp v. Ohio*, and *New York Times v. Sullivan*, to name a few.

chapter 05

Civil Rights

WHAT GOVERNMENT DOES AND WHY IT MATTERS U.S. Naval Academy midshipman Regan Kibby always knew he wanted to join the military. "I felt if I could do it, I should. It felt like a duty." His father had served in the Navy, and Regan had enrolled in the Junior Reserve Officer Training Corps in high school. In the summer before senior year, he attended three service-oriented summer programs, at the U.S. Naval Academy, the U.S. Military Academy, and the U.S. Air Force Academy, ultimately choosing the naval academy for the next step in his career training.

During Kibby's "plebe summer" in 2015, the rigorous training program before freshman year, Defense Secretary Ashton Carter made an announcement: the Pentagon would allow transgender people to serve openly. Kibby, who had been born a girl but never felt that designation quite right, started coming out as transgender to his roommates, to members of Navy Spectrum, an organization for LGBTQ midshipmen, and to his company officer. In November 2016 the Navy issued a protocol for service members with gender dysphoria who wished to transition. Kibby's transition was later approved, and he was thrilled: he would no longer have to choose between the "fundamental parts of his identity." "I just thought I could fly under the radar,

Americans agree over the basic notion of civil rights but often clash over their application. The rights of transgender people have been a topic of heated debate. After facing several legal and political roadblocks, transgender Americans were allowed to both enlist and serve openly in the military, starting in 2018.

graduate, and serve my country like I always planned to." He knew it would be a challenge. An older transgender Naval Academy alum who had had to retire before transitioning and who had become an advocate for transgender service members had told him, "Make yourself indispensable. You're going to have to work twice as hard to get the respect you deserve." Kibby took on a double major and leadership positions. He also found a clinic that accepts the military's health insurance, Tricare, and that provides transgender services.[1]

Then in July 2017, President Donald Trump tweeted that transgender people would no longer be allowed to serve in the U.S. military. "It was devastating," said Kibby, who would not be allowed to graduate from the Naval Academy if the ban were to stand. "I'm very likely not going to be able to continue my education, the path that I planned for my life."[2] Trump released a presidential memorandum the following month requiring all transgender service members to be discharged starting in March 2018. When transgender members of the military sued, the issue went to court. After four federal courts ruled against the ban, the Trump administration announced in December 2017 that it would not take the issue to the Supreme Court, and openly transgender Americans were allowed to enlist beginning January 1, 2018.[3] Kibby's career was saved.

As we saw in the previous chapter, in the Bill of Rights, civil liberties are phrased as negatives—what government must *not* do. Civil rights, on the other hand, are positives—what the government *must* do to guarantee equal citizenship and protect citizens from discrimination. Civil liberties protect Americans from various forms of governmental abuse. Civil rights regulate *who* can participate in the political process and civil society and *how* they can participate: for example, who can vote, who can hold office, who can have a trial or serve on juries, and when and how citizens can petition the government to take action. Civil rights also define how people are treated in employment, education, and other aspects of American society.

As in the case of civil liberties, Americans agree with the basic principle of civil rights but quarrel frequently over their application. The question of who has the constitutional right to do what underlies some of the major controversies of American history. Fifty years ago, the African American struggle for equal rights took center stage. Many goals of the civil rights movement that once aroused bitter controversy are now widely accepted as part of the American commitment to equal rights. But even today the question of what is meant by "equal rights" is hardly settled. To what extent can states mandate racial preferences in college admissions? What rights do undocumented immigrants possess? Do transgender individuals have the right to use a public restroom based upon their gender identification rather than their physical characteristics, and can they serve in the military?

As we saw in Chapter 4, the evolution of civil liberties in the United States mainly, though not exclusively, involved the actions of the federal courts. Liberties are limits on government action, and the courts are the institution best situated to tell Congress, the president, and state governments what they may not do. Civil rights, though, involve the government's obligation to act, and the evolution of civil rights required much more action on the part of Congress and the president.

CHAPTER GOALS

★ **Trace the legal developments and social movements that expanded civil rights (pp. 161–79)**

★ **Describe how different groups have fought for and won protection of their civil rights (pp. 179–94)**

★ **Contrast arguments for and against affirmative action (pp. 195–97)**

The Struggle for Civil Rights

Trace the legal developments and social movements that expanded civil rights

In the United States the history of slavery and legalized racial **discrimination** against African Americans coexists uneasily with a strong tradition of individual liberty. Indeed, for much of our history Americans have struggled to reconcile such exclusionary racial practices with our notions of individual rights. With the adoption of the Fourteenth Amendment in 1868 **civil rights** became part of the Constitution, guaranteed to each citizen through "equal protection of the laws." This **equal protection clause** launched a century of political movements and legal efforts to press for racial equality.

For African Americans, the central fact of political life for most of American history has been a denial of full citizenship rights. By accepting the institution of slavery, the Founders embraced a system fundamentally at odds with the "Blessings of Liberty" promised in the Constitution. Their decision set the stage for two centuries of African American struggles to achieve full citizenship.

For women, electoral politics was a decidedly masculine world. Until 1920, not only were women barred from voting in national politics but electoral politics was closely tied to such male social institutions as lodges, bars, and clubs. Yet the exclusion of women from this political world did not prevent them from engaging in public life. Instead, women carved out a "separate sphere" for their public activities. Emphasizing female stewardship of the moral realm, women became important voices in social reform well before they won the right to vote.[4] Prior to the Civil War, women played leading roles in the abolitionist movement.

SLAVERY AND THE ABOLITIONIST MOVEMENT

No issue in the nation's history so deeply divided Americans as that of slavery. The importation and subjugation of Africans kidnapped from their native lands was a practice virtually as old as the country itself: the first slaves brought to what became

discrimination the use of any unreasonable and unjust criterion of exclusion

civil rights obligation imposed on government to take positive action to protect citizens from any illegal action of government agencies and of other private citizens

equal protection clause provision of the Fourteenth Amendment guaranteeing citizens "the equal protection of the laws." This clause has been the basis for the civil rights of African Americans, women, and other groups

Slavery tore the nation apart and ultimately led to the Civil War. The abolition movement organized in the North and pushed to end slavery. Harriet Tubman (far left in photograph) was an abolitionist and ex-slave who helped many slaves escape bondage through a system of safe houses called the "underground railroad."

the United States arrived in 1619, a year before the Plymouth colony was established in Massachusetts. White southerners built their agricultural economy (especially cotton production) on a large slave labor force. By 1840 nearly half of the populations of Alabama and Louisiana consisted of black slaves. Even so, only about one-quarter of southern white families owned slaves.

Slavery was so much a part of southern culture that efforts to restrict or abolish the institution were met with fierce resistance. Despite the manifest cruelties of the slave system, southerners referred to it merely as their "peculiar institution." This quaint label meant little to slavery's opponents, however; and an abolitionist movement grew and spread among northerners in the 1830s (although abolitionist sentiment could be traced back to the prerevolutionary era). The abolitionist movement spread primarily through local organizations in the North. Soon two political parties emerged: the staunchly antislavery Liberty Party and the more moderate Free Soil Party, which sought primarily to restrict slavery from spreading into new western territories. Some opponents of slavery took matters into their own hands, aiding in the escape of runaway slaves along the Underground Railroad. In the South, a similar, if contrary, fervor prompted mobs to break into post offices in order to seize and destroy antislavery literature.

In 1857 the Supreme Court inflamed this tense atmosphere with its infamous decision in *Dred Scott v. Sanford*. Dred Scott was a slave who had been taken by his owner to the free state of Illinois and the territory of Wisconsin, where slavery was forbidden. Scott sued for his freedom, arguing that his residence in a free territory meant he was a free man. The Court, however, disagreed, holding that slaves—indeed, all blacks—were not citizens of the United States. Scott had no due process rights because, as a slave, he was his master's permanent property, regardless of his master's having taken him to a free state or territory.[5] This decision split the country deeply over the issue of slavery; the emotional power of the slavery issue was such that it precipitated the nation's bloodiest conflict, the Civil War. From the ashes of the Civil War came the Thirteenth, Fourteenth, and Fifteenth amendments, which would redefine civil rights from that time on.

THE WOMEN'S RIGHTS MOVEMENT

The quiet upstate New York town of Seneca Falls played host to what would later come to be known as the starting point of the modern women's movement. Convened in July 1848 and organized by the activists Elizabeth Cady Stanton and Lucretia Mott, the Seneca Falls Convention drew 300 delegates to formulate plans for advancing the political and social rights of women.

The centerpiece of the convention was its Declaration of Sentiments and Resolutions. Patterned after the Declaration of Independence, the Seneca Falls document declared, "We hold these truths to be self-evident: that all men and women are created equal" and "The history of mankind is a history of repeated injuries and usurpations on the part of man toward woman, having in direct object the establishment of an absolute tyranny over her." The most controversial provision of the declaration, nearly rejected as too radical, was the call for the right to vote for women. Although most of the delegates were women, about 40 men participated, including the renowned abolitionist Frederick Douglass. The link to the antislavery movement was not new. Stanton and Mott had attended the World Anti-Slavery Convention in London in 1840 but had been denied delegate seats because of their sex. This rebuke helped precipitate the 1848 convention in Seneca Falls.

The convention and its participants were subjected to widespread ridicule, but similar conventions were organized in other states. And in the same year as the Seneca Falls Convention, New York State passed the Married Women's Property Act in order to restore the right of married women to own property.

THE CIVIL WAR AMENDMENTS TO THE CONSTITUTION

The hopes of African Americans for achieving full citizenship rights initially seemed fulfilled when three constitutional amendments were adopted after the Civil War: the **Thirteenth Amendment** abolished slavery, the **Fourteenth Amendment** guaranteed equal protection and due process under the law, and the **Fifteenth Amendment** guaranteed voting rights for blacks. Protected by the presence of federal troops, African American men were able to exercise their political rights immediately after the war. Between 1869 and 1877 blacks were elected to many political offices: two black senators were elected from Mississippi, and a total of 14 African Americans were elected to the House of Representatives. African Americans also held many state-level political offices. As voters and public officials, black citizens found a home in the Republican Party, which had secured the ratification of the three constitutional amendments guaranteeing black rights. After the war, the Republican Party continued to reach out to black voters as a means to build party strength in the South.[6]

This political equality was short-lived, however. The national government withdrew its troops from the South and turned its back on African Americans in 1877, when Reconstruction ended. In the Compromise of 1877, southern Democrats agreed to allow the Republican candidate, Rutherford B. Hayes, to become president after a disputed election. In exchange, northern Republicans dropped their support for the civil liberties and political participation of African Americans. After that, southern states erected a "Jim Crow" system of social, political, and economic inequality that made a mockery of the promises in the Constitution. The first **Jim Crow laws** were adopted in the 1870s, in each southern state, to criminalize intermarriage of the races and to segregate trains and depots. These were promptly followed by laws segregating all public accommodations, and within 10 years all southern states had adopted laws segregating the schools.

Immediately after the Civil War, when male ex-slaves won the franchise, some women pressed for the right to vote at the national level; but politicians in both parties rejected women's suffrage as disruptive and unrealistic. Women also started to press for the vote at the state level in 1867, when a referendum to give women the vote in Kansas failed. Frustration with the general failure to win reforms accelerated suffrage activism. In 1872, Susan B. Anthony and several other women were arrested in Rochester, New York, for illegally registering and voting in that year's national election. (The men who allowed the women to register and vote were also indicted. Anthony paid their expenses and eventually won presidential pardons for them.) At Anthony's trial, Judge Ward Hunt ordered the jury to find her guilty without deliberation. Yet Anthony was allowed to address the court, saying, "Your denial of my citizen's right to vote is the denial of my right of consent as one of the

THE FIRST CONVENTION

EVER CALLED TO DISCUSS THE

Civil and Political Rights of Women,

SENECA FALLS, N. Y., JULY 19, 20, 1848.

———

WOMAN'S RIGHTS CONVENTION.

———

A Convention to discuss the social, civil, and religious condition and rights of woman will be held in the Wesleyan Chapel, at Seneca Falls, N. Y., on Wednesday and Thursday, the 19th and 20th of July current; commencing at 10 o'clock A. M. During the first day the meeting will be exclusively for women, who are earnestly invited to attend. The public generally are invited to be present on the second day, when Lucretia Mott, of Philadelphia, and other ladies and gentlemen, will address the Convention.*

*This call was published in the *Seneca County Courier*, July 14, 1848, without any signatures. The movers of this Convention, who drafted the call, the declaration and resolutions were Elizabeth Cady Stanton, Lucretia Mott, Martha C. Wright, Mary Ann McClintock, and Jane C. Hunt.

Many see the Seneca Falls Convention of 1848 as the starting point of the modern women's rights movement. Its Declaration of Sentiments proclaiming equality for women is one of the movement's most important documents.

Thirteenth Amendment one of three Civil War amendments; it abolished slavery

Fourteenth Amendment one of three Civil War amendments; it guaranteed equal protection and due process

Fifteenth Amendment one of three Civil War amendments; it guaranteed voting rights for African American men

Jim Crow laws laws enacted by southern states following Reconstruction that discriminated against African Americans governed, the denial of my right of representation as one of the taxed, the denial of my right to a trial of my peers as an offender against the law."[7] Hunt assessed Anthony a fine of $100 but did not sentence her to jail. She refused to pay the fine.

CIVIL RIGHTS AND THE SUPREME COURT: "SEPARATE BUT EQUAL"

Resistance to equality for African Americans in the South led Congress to adopt the Civil Rights Act of 1875, which attempted to protect blacks from discrimination by proprietors of hotels, theaters, and other public accommodations. But the Court declared the legislation unconstitutional on the grounds that the act sought to protect blacks against discrimination by *private* businesses, whereas the Fourteenth Amendment, according to the Court's interpretation, was intended to protect individuals from discrimination only against actions by *public* officials of state and local governments.

In the infamous case of *Plessy v. Ferguson* (1896), the Court went still further by upholding a Louisiana statute that *required* segregation of the races on trolleys and other public carriers (and, by implication, in all public facilities, including schools). Homer Plessy, a man defined as "one-eighth black," sat in a trolley car reserved for whites and was found guilty of violating a Louisiana law that provided for "equal but separate accommodations" on trains and levied a $25 fine on any white passenger who sat in a car reserved for blacks or on any black passenger who sat in a car reserved for whites. The Supreme Court held that the Fourteenth Amendment's equal protection clause was not violated by racial distinction as long as the facilities were equal, thus establishing the **"separate but equal" rule** that prevailed through the mid-twentieth century. White people generally pretended that segregated accommodations were equal as long as some accommodation for blacks existed. The Court said that although "the object of the [Fourteenth] Amendment was undoubtedly to enforce the absolute equality of the two races before the law...it could not have

"separate but equal" rule doctrine that public accommodations could be segregated by race but still be considered equal

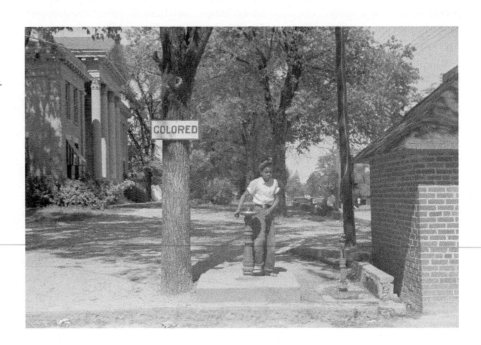

The 1896 Supreme Court case of *Plessy v. Ferguson* upheld legal segregation and created the "separate but equal" rule, which fostered national segregation. Overt discrimination in public accommodations was common.

intended to abolish distinctions based on color, or to enforce social, as distinguished from political, equality, or a commingling of the two races upon terms unsatisfactory to either."[8] What the Court was saying in effect was that the use of race as a criterion of exclusion in public matters was reasonable.

FOR CRITICAL ANALYSIS
What were the consequences of the "separate but equal" policy for southern society and for blacks' civil rights?

ORGANIZING FOR EQUALITY

The creation of a Jim Crow system in the southern states and the lack of a legal basis for "equal protection of the laws" prompted the beginning of a long process in which African Americans built organizations and devised strategies for asserting their constitutional rights.

The National Association for the Advancement of Colored People One such strategy sought to win political rights through political pressure and litigation. This approach was championed by the National Association for the Advancement of Colored People (NAACP), established in 1909 by a group of black and white reformers that included W. E. B. Du Bois, one of the twentieth century's most influential and creative thinkers on racial issues. Because the northern black vote was so small in the early 1900s, the NAACP relied primarily on the courts to press for black political rights. After the 1920s it built a strong membership base, with some strength in the South, which would be critical when the civil rights movement gained momentum in the 1950s.

Women's Organizations and the Right to Suffrage The 1886 unveiling in New York Harbor of the Statue of Liberty, depicting liberty as a woman, prompted women's rights advocates to call it "the greatest hypocrisy of the nineteenth century," in that "not one single woman throughout the length and breadth of the Land is as yet in possession of political Liberty."[9]

The climactic movement toward women's suffrage had been formally launched in 1878 with the introduction of a proposed constitutional amendment in Congress. Parallel efforts were made in the states. Many states granted women the right to vote before the national government did. Western states with less entrenched political systems opened politics to women earliest. When Wyoming became a state in 1890, it was the first state to grant full suffrage to women. Colorado, Utah, and Idaho all

Women fought for decades for the right to vote. The Nineteenth Amendment, ratified in 1920 over the opposition of President Wilson, guaranteed that right. Pictured here on the right are women voting for the first time after the passage of the amendment.

followed suit in the next several years. Suffrage organizations grew—the National American Woman Suffrage Association (NAWSA), formed in 1890, claimed 2 million members by 1917 and staged mass meetings, parades, petitions, and protests. NAWSA organized state-by-state efforts to win the right for women to vote. Members of a more militant group, the National Woman's Party, staged pickets and got arrested in front of the White House to protest President Wilson's opposition to a constitutional amendment granting women this right. When the Nineteenth Amendment was ratified in 1920, women were finally guaranteed the right to vote.

LITIGATING FOR EQUALITY AFTER WORLD WAR II

The shame of discrimination against black military personnel during World War II, plus revelations of Nazi racial atrocities, moved President Harry S. Truman finally to bring the problem of racial discrimination to the White House and national attention, with the appointment in 1946 of the President's Commission on Civil Rights. In 1948 the commission submitted its report, *To Secure These Rights*, which laid bare the extent of the problem and its consequences and revealed the success of experiments with racial integration in the armed forces during World War II. This was intended to demonstrate to southern society that it had nothing to fear. But the commission recognized that the national government had no clear constitutional authority to pass and implement civil rights legislation. It proposed tying such legislation to the commerce power described in Article I of the Constitution, which allows Congress to regulate interstate commerce, although it was clear that discrimination was not itself related to the flow of interstate commerce.[10] The committee even suggested using the treaty power as a source of constitutional authority for civil rights legislation.[11]

The Supreme Court had begun to change its position on racial discrimination before World War II by being stricter about the criterion of equal facilities in the "separate but equal" rule. In 1938, for example, the Court rejected Missouri's policy of paying the tuition of qualified blacks to out-of-state law schools rather than admitting them to the University of Missouri Law School.[12]

After the war, modest progress resumed. In 1950 the Court rejected Texas's claim that its new "law school for Negroes" afforded education equal to that of the all-white University of Texas Law School, anticipating its future civil rights rulings by opening the question of whether *any* segregated facilities could be truly equal.[13] But in ordering the admission of blacks to all-white state law schools, the Supreme Court did not directly confront the "separate but equal" rule. The most important pre-1954 decision was probably *Shelley v. Kraemer*, in which the Court ruled against the widespread practice of "restrictive covenants" whereby the seller of a home added a clause to the sales contract requiring the buyer to agree never to sell the home to any non-Caucasian, non-Christian, and so on. The Court ruled that such covenants could not be judicially enforced since the Fourteenth Amendment prohibits any organ of the state, including the courts, from denying equal protection of its laws.[14]

Although none of those pre-1954 cases confronted "separate but equal" and the principle of racial discrimination as such, they were extremely significant to black leaders in the 1940s and gave them encouragement to believe that at last they had an opportunity and enough legal precedent to change the constitutional framework itself. Much of this legal work was done by the Legal Defense and Educational Fund of the NAACP, which until the late 1940s had concentrated on winning small victories within the existing framework. In 1948 the Legal Defense Fund upgraded its approach by simultaneously filing suits in different federal districts and through each level of schooling. After nearly two years of these mostly successful equalization suits, the lawyers decided the time was ripe to confront the "separate but equal" rule head-on, but they felt they needed some heavier artillery to lead the attack. Their choice was the African American lawyer Thurgood Marshall, who had been fighting, and often winning, equalization suits since the early 1930s. Marshall was pessimistic about the readiness of the Supreme Court for a full confrontation with segregation itself and the constitutional principle sustaining it. But the unwillingness of Congress after the 1948 election to consider fair-employment legislation seems to have convinced Marshall that the courts were the only hope.

In the fall of 1952 the Court had on its docket cases from Delaware, Kansas, South Carolina, Virginia, and the District of Columbia challenging the constitutionality of school segregation. Of these, the case filed in Kansas became the one chosen by the NAACP. This case was further along in the process of adjudication in its district court, and it had the advantage of being located in a state outside the Deep South, a fact that would minimize any local opposition to a favorable decision.[15]

Oliver Brown, the father of three girls, lived "across the tracks" in a low-income, racially mixed Topeka neighborhood. Every school day, Linda Brown took the school bus to the Monroe Elementary School, for black children, about a mile away. In September 1950, Oliver Brown took Linda to the all-white Sumner School, which was closer to home, to enter her into the third grade, in defiance of state law and local segregation rules. When they were refused, Brown took his case to the NAACP, and soon thereafter, the case **Brown v. Board of Education** was born. In mid-1953 the Court announced that the several cases on their way up would be reargued within a set of questions having to do with the intent of the Fourteenth Amendment. Almost exactly a year later, the Court responded to those questions in one of the most important decisions in its history:

> Does segregation of children in public schools solely on the basis of race, even though the physical facilities and other "tangible" factors may be equal, deprive the children of the minority group of equal educational opportunities? We believe that it does.... We conclude that in the field of public education the doctrine of "separate but equal" has no place. Separate educational facilities are inherently unequal.[16]

The *Brown* decision altered the constitutional framework by indicating that racial discrimination violated the Constitution.

CIVIL RIGHTS AFTER *BROWN V. BOARD OF EDUCATION*

Brown v. Board of Education withdrew all constitutional authority to use race as a criterion of exclusion, and it signaled more clearly the Court's determination to use the **strict scrutiny** test in cases related to racial discrimination. This meant that the burden of proof would fall on the government to show that the law in question *was* constitutional—not on the challengers to show the law's *un*constitutionality.[17] Although the use of strict scrutiny would give an advantage to those attacking racial discrimination, the historic decision in *Brown v. Board of Education* was merely a small opening move. First, most states refused to cooperate until sued, and many ingenious schemes were employed to delay obedience (such as paying the tuition for white students to attend newly created "private" academies). Second, even as southern school boards began to cooperate by eliminating their legally enforced

Brown v. Board of Education
the 1954 Supreme Court decision that struck down the "separate but equal" doctrine as fundamentally unequal; this case eliminated state power to use race as a criterion of discrimination in law and provided the national government with the power to intervene by exercising strict regulatory policies against discriminatory actions

strict scrutiny a test used by the Supreme Court in racial discrimination cases and other cases involving civil liberties and civil rights that places the burden of proof on the government rather than on the challengers to show that the law in question is constitutional

"Massive resistance" among white southerners attempted to block the desegregation efforts of the national government. For example, at Little Rock Central High School in 1957, an angry mob of white students prevented black students from entering the school.

de jure literally, "by law"; refers to legally enforced practices, such as school segregation in the South before the 1960s

de facto literally, "by fact"; refers to practices that occur even when there is no legal enforcement, such as school segregation in much of the United States today

FOR CRITICAL ANALYSIS

Describe the changes in American society between the *Plessy v. Ferguson* and the *Brown v. Board of Education* decisions. How have changes in civil rights policy since the *Brown* case impacted society?

(**de jure**) school segregation, extensive actual (**de facto**) school segregation remained, in the North as well as in the South, as a consequence of racially segregated housing that could not be addressed by the 1954–55 *Brown* principles. Third, discrimination in employment, public accommodations, juries, voting, and other areas of social and economic activity was not directly touched by *Brown*.

School Desegregation, Phase One Although the District of Columbia and some of the school districts in the border states began to respond almost immediately to court-ordered desegregation, the states of the Deep South responded with a carefully planned delaying tactic commonly called "massive resistance." Southern politicians stood shoulder to shoulder to declare that the Supreme Court's decisions and orders were without effect. The legislatures in these states enacted statutes ordering school districts to maintain segregated schools and state superintendents to terminate state funding wherever there was racial mixing in the classroom. Some southern states violated their own long traditions of local school autonomy by centralizing public school authority under the governor or the state board of education, and they gave themselves the power to close the schools and to provide alternative private schooling wherever local school boards might be inclined to obey the Supreme Court.

Most of these plans of "massive resistance" were tested in the federal courts and struck down as unconstitutional.[18] But southern resistance was not confined to legislation. Perhaps the most serious incident occurred in Arkansas in 1957, when Governor Orval Faubus mobilized the Arkansas National Guard to intercede against enforcement of a federal court order to integrate Little Rock Central High School. President Eisenhower was compelled to deploy U.S. troops and place the city under martial law. This action by the federal government underlined that a right was at issue. The Supreme Court considered the Little Rock confrontation so historically important that the opinion it rendered in that case was not only agreed to unanimously but, unprecedentedly, signed personally by every one of the justices.[19]

The end of massive resistance, however, became simply the beginning of still another southern strategy. "Pupil placement" laws authorized school districts to place each pupil in a school according to a variety of academic, personal, and psychological considerations, never mentioning race at all. This put the burden of transferring to an all-white school on the nonwhite children and their parents, making it almost impossible for a single court order to cover a whole district, let alone a whole state, thereby delaying desegregation awhile longer.[20]

Social Protest after _Brown_ Ten years after _Brown_, fewer than 1 percent of black school-age children in the Deep South were attending schools with whites.[21] A decade of frustration made it fairly obvious to all observers that adjudication alone would not succeed. The goal of "equal protection" required positive, or affirmative, action by Congress and by administrative agencies. And given massive southern resistance and a generally negative national public opinion toward racial integration, progress would not be made through courts, Congress, or federal agencies without intense, well-organized support. Figure 5.1 shows the increase in the number of civil rights demonstrations for voting rights and public accommodations during the years following _Brown_.

The number of organized demonstrations began to mount slowly but surely after _Brown v. Board of Education_. Only a year after _Brown_, black citizens in Montgomery, Alabama, challenged the city's segregated bus system with a yearlong boycott. The boycott began with the arrest of Rosa Parks, who refused to give up her seat for a white man. A seamstress who worked with civil rights groups, Parks eventually became a civil rights icon, as did one of the ministers leading the boycott, Martin Luther King, Jr. After a year of private carpools and walking, Montgomery's bus system desegregated, but only after the Supreme Court ruled the system unconstitutional.

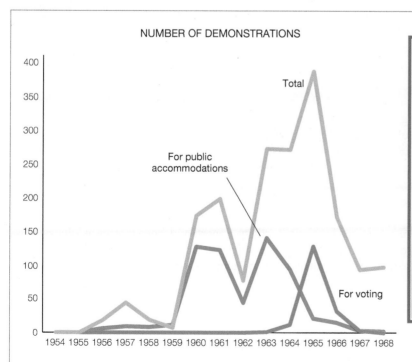

NUMBER OF DEMONSTRATIONS

FIGURE 5.1

Peaceful Civil Rights Demonstrations, 1954–68

Peaceful demonstrations were an important part of the civil rights movement. Why did the number of demonstrations grow after 1955? Why do you think the focus shifted from public accommodations to voting rights after 1964?

NOTE: The data are drawn from a search of the _New York Times_ index for all references to civil rights demonstrations.

SOURCE: Jonathan D. Casper, _The Politics of Civil Liberties_ (New York: Harper and Row, 1972), 90.

The struggle for African American civil rights has spanned decades. Among the key moments are Rosa Parks and the Montgomery Bus Boycott (1955–56), sit-ins at segregated lunch counters throughout the South, the March on Washington and Martin Luther King, Jr.'s famous "I Have a Dream" speech (1963), and the Black Lives Matter movement that persists today.

By the 1960s the many organizations that made up the civil rights movement had accumulated experience and built networks capable of launching large-scale direct action campaigns against southern segregationists. The Southern Christian Leadership Conference, the Student Nonviolent Coordinating Committee, and many other organizations had built a movement that stretched across the South, using the media to attract nationwide attention and support. The image of protesters being beaten, attacked by police dogs, and set upon with fire hoses did much to win broad sympathy for the cause of black civil rights and to discredit state and local governments in the South. In the massive March on Washington in 1963, the Reverend Martin Luther King, Jr., staked out the movement's moral claims in his famous "I Have a Dream" speech. Steadily, the movement created intense pressure for a reluctant federal government to take more assertive steps to defend black civil rights.

Protests against discriminatory practices toward African Americans did not end in the 1960s. In recent years, a variety of protests coalesced under the banner Black Lives Matter to focus attention on allegations of police misconduct directed at African Americans. The movement took off in Ferguson, Missouri, after the shooting of an unarmed black man by a white police officer and spread across the nation often via social media, which presented live photos and films taken by cell phone cameras, as the television news carried reports, photos, and videos of police violence against blacks in Chicago, South Carolina, Baltimore, New York, and many other cities. African Americans had long asserted that they were often victims of racial profiling and more likely than whites to be harassed, physically harmed, or arrested by the police. Police departments had often replied that blacks were more likely than whites to be engaged in criminal activity. Reports and video footage of killings, however, proved difficult for the police to justify and led many police departments to introduce new training methods and to adopt new rules governing police behavior.

THE CIVIL RIGHTS ACTS

It is important to observe here the mutual dependence of the courts and legislatures: the legislatures need constitutional authority to act, and the courts need legislative and administrative assistance to implement court orders and focus political

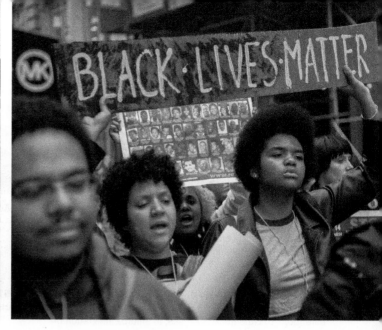

support. Consequently, even as the U.S. Congress finally moved into the field of school desegregation (and other areas of "equal protection"), the courts continued to exercise their powers, not only by placing court orders against recalcitrant school districts but also by extending and reinterpreting aspects of the equal protection clause to support legislative and administrative actions (see Table 5.1).

Three civil rights acts were passed during the first decade after the 1954 Supreme Court decision in *Brown v. Board of Education*. But these acts were of only marginal importance.

By far the most important piece of legislation passed by Congress concerning equal opportunity was the Civil Rights Act of 1964. It not only put some teeth in the voting rights provisions of the 1957 and 1960 acts but also went far beyond voting to attack discrimination in public accommodations, segregation in the schools, and, at long last, the discriminatory conduct of employers in hiring, promoting, and laying off their employees. Discrimination against women was also included, extending the important 1963 provisions. The 1964 act seemed bold at the time, but it was enacted fully 10 years after the Supreme Court had declared racial discrimination "inherently unequal" and long after blacks had demonstrated that discrimination was no longer acceptable. With the Civil Rights Act of 1964, Congress pointed to a different part of the Constitution as the primary source of its authority to ban racial discrimination in some businesses: the "commerce clause," which empowers Congress to "regulate commerce...among the several states." Over the previous twenty years, Congress and the courts had come to agree that this clause empowered Congress to regulate commercial activity broadly defined. And this time, when southern business owners challenged the law, the Supreme Court upheld it.

Public Accommodations After the passage of the 1964 Civil Rights Act, public accommodations quickly removed some of the most blatant forms of racial discrimination. Signs defining "colored" and "white" restrooms, water fountains, waiting rooms, and seating arrangements were removed; and a host of other practices that relegated black people to separate and inferior arrangements were ended. In addition, the federal government filed more than 400 antidiscrimination suits in federal courts against hotels, restaurants, taverns, gas stations, and other "public accommodations."

TABLE 5.1

Cause and Effect in the Civil Rights Movement

Political action and government action worked in tandem to produce dramatic changes in American civil rights policies.

JUDICIAL AND LEGAL ACTION	POLITICAL ACTION
1954 *Brown v. Board of Education*	**1955** Montgomery, Alabama, bus boycott
1956 Federal courts order school integration; of special note is one ordering Autherine Lucy admitted to the University of Alabama, with Governor Wallace officially protesting	
1957 Civil Rights Act creating Civil Rights Commission; President Eisenhower sends 101st Airborne Division paratroops to Little Rock, Arkansas, to enforce integration of Central High School	**1957** Southern Christian Leadership Conference formed, with Martin Luther King, Jr., as president
1960 First substantive Civil Rights Act, primarily voting rights	**1960** Student Nonviolent Coordinating Committee formed to organize protests, sit-ins, freedom rides
1961 Interstate Commerce Commission orders desegregation on all buses and trains and in terminals; President Kennedy (JFK) favors executive action over civil rights legislation	
1963 JFK shifts, supports strong civil rights law; JFK's assassination; President Johnson asserts strong support for civil rights	**1963** Nonviolent demonstrations in Birmingham, Alabama, lead to King's arrest and his "Letter from Birmingham Jail"; March on Washington
1964 Congress passes historic Civil Rights Act covering voting, employment, public accommodations, education	
1965 Voting Rights Act	**1965** King announces drive to register 3 million blacks in the South
1966 War on Poverty in full swing	**Late 1960s** Movement diverges: part toward litigation, part toward community action programs, part toward war protest, part toward more militant "Black Power" actions

Many aspects of legalized racial segregation—such as separate Bibles to swear in black and white witnesses in the courtroom—seem like ancient history today. But the issue of racial discrimination in public settings is by no means over. In 2014, for example, an African American customer at a Vancouver, Washington "Elmer's" restaurant noticed that he was being asked to prepay for his food while white customers were presented with their bills after they had finished their meals. The case was settled out of court for an undisclosed amount.[22] Other forms of racial discrimination in public accommodations are harder to challenge, however. For example, there is considerable evidence that taxicabs often refuse to pick up black passengers.[23] Such practices may be common, but they are difficult to prove and remedy through the law.

School Desegregation, Phase Two The 1964 Civil Rights Act also declared discrimination by private employers and state governments (school boards, etc.) illegal and then went further to provide for administrative agencies to help the courts implement these laws. Title IV of the act, for example, authorized the executive branch, through the Justice Department, to implement federal court orders to desegregate schools and to do so without having to wait for individual parents to bring complaints. Title VI of the act vastly strengthened the role of the executive branch and the credibility of court orders by providing that federal grants-in-aid to state and local governments for education must be withheld from any school system practicing racial segregation. Title VI became the most effective weapon for desegregating schools outside the South because the situation in northern communities was subtler and more difficult to address. In the South, the problem was segregation by law coupled with overt resistance to the national government's efforts to change the situation. In contrast, outside the South, segregated facilities were the outcome of hundreds of thousands of housing choices made by individuals and families. Once racial residential patterns emerged, racial homogeneity, property values, and neighborhood schools and churches were defended by real estate agents, neighborhood organizations, and the like. Thus, in order to eliminate discrimination nationwide, the 1964 Civil Rights Act gave (1) the president, through the Justice Department's Office for Civil Rights, the power to withhold federal education grants[24] and (2) the attorney general of the United States the power to initiate suits (rather than having to await complaints) wherever there was a "pattern or practice" of discrimination.[25]

In the decade following the 1964 Civil Rights Act, the Justice Department brought legal action against more than 500 school districts. During the same period, administrative agencies filed lawsuits against 600 school districts, threatening to suspend federal aid to education unless real desegregation steps were taken.

Busing One step taken toward desegregation was busing children from poor urban school districts to wealthier suburban ones. In 1971 the Supreme Court held that state-imposed desegregation could be brought about by busing children across

The 1964 Civil Rights Act made desegregation a legal requirement. The policy of busing from black neighborhoods to white schools bitterly divided the black and white communities in Boston. In 1976 a protester waved an American Flag threateningly at an innocent black bystander—a lawyer on his way to his office—as another white man sought to help him get out of the way.

school districts.[26] But the decision went beyond that, adding that under certain limited circumstances even racial quotas could be used as the "starting point in shaping a remedy to correct past constitutional violations" and that pairing or grouping schools and reorganizing school attendance zones would also be acceptable.

Three years later, however, this principle was severely restricted when the Supreme Court determined that only cities found guilty of deliberate and de jure racial segregation would have to desegregate their schools,[27] effectively exempting most northern states and cities from busing because school segregation in northern cities is generally the de facto result of segregated housing and thousands of acts of private discrimination against blacks and other minorities.

Boston provides a good illustration of the agonizing problem of making further progress in civil rights in the schools under the constitutional framework established by these decisions. Boston school authorities were found guilty of deliberately building school facilities and drawing school district boundaries "to increase racial segregation." After vain efforts by Boston school authorities to draw up an acceptable plan to remedy the segregation, in 1974 federal judge W. Arthur Garrity ordered an elaborate desegregation plan of his own, involving busing between the all-black neighborhood of Roxbury and the nearby white, working-class community of South Boston. The city's schools were so segregated and uncooperative that even the conservative administration of President Richard Nixon had already initiated a punitive cutoff of funds. But even many liberals criticized Judge Garrity's plan as being badly conceived for involving two neighboring communities with a history of tension and mutual resentment. The plan did work well at the elementary school level, but proved explosive at the high school level, generating a continuing crisis for the city of Boston and for the whole nation.[28]

The prospects for further school integration diminished with a 1991 Supreme Court decision holding that lower federal courts could end supervision of local school boards if they could show "good faith" compliance with court orders to desegregate and that "vestiges of past discrimination" had been eliminated "to the extent practicable."[29] It is not necessarily easy for a school board to prove that the new standard has been met, but this was the first time since *Brown* and the 1964 Civil Rights Act that the Court had opened the door at all to retreat.

In 2007 the Court's ruling in *Parents Involved in Community Schools v. Seattle School District No. 1* limited school integration measures still further.[30] By making race one factor in assigning students to schools, the cities of Seattle, Washington, and Louisville, Kentucky, had hoped to achieve greater racial balance across the public schools. The Court ruled that these plans were unconstitutional because there was no compelling government interest in using race as a criterion in assigning students to schools. Many observers described the decision as the end of the *Brown* era because it attacked one of the few public strategies left to promote racial integration.

Outlawing Discrimination in Employment Despite the agonizingly slow progress of school desegregation, some progress was made in other areas of civil rights during the 1960s and '70s. Voting rights were established and fairly quickly began to revolutionize southern politics. Service on juries was no longer denied to minorities. But progress in the right to participate in politics and government dramatized the relative lack of progress in the economic domain, where battles over civil rights were increasingly being fought.

The federal courts and the Justice Department entered this area through Title VII of the Civil Rights Act of 1964, which outlawed job discrimination by all private and public employers, including governmental agencies (such as fire and police departments) that employed more than 15 workers. Title VII makes it unlawful to discriminate in employment on the basis of color, religion, sex, or national origin, as well as race.

Title VII delegated some of the powers to enforce fair-employment practices to the Justice Department's Civil Rights Division and others to a new agency created in the 1964 act, the Equal Employment Opportunity Commission (EEOC). By executive order, these agencies had the power of the national government to revoke public contracts for goods and services and to refuse to engage in contracts with any private company that could not guarantee that its rules for hiring, promotion, and firing were nondiscriminatory. And in 1972, President Nixon and a Democratic Congress cooperated to strengthen the EEOC by giving it authority to initiate suits rather than wait for grievances.

But one problem with Title VII was that the accusing party had to show that deliberate discrimination was the cause of the failure to get a job or a training opportunity. The courts have since allowed aggrieved parties (the plaintiffs) to make their case if they can show that an employer's hiring practices had the *effect* of exclusion. A leading case in 1971 involved a "class action" by several black employees in North Carolina attempting to show with statistical evidence that blacks had been relegated to only one department in the Duke Power Company, which involved the least desirable manual-labor jobs, and that they had been kept out of contention for better jobs because the employer had added attainment of a high school education and the passing of specially prepared aptitude tests as qualifications for higher jobs. The Supreme Court held that although the statistical evidence did not prove intentional discrimination and although the requirements were race-neutral in appearance, their effects were sufficient to shift the burden of justification to the employer to show that the requirements were a "business necessity" that bore "a demonstrable relationship to successful performance."[31] The ruling in this case was subsequently applied to other hiring, promotion, and training programs.[32]

Voting Rights In the 1965 Voting Rights Act, Congress significantly strengthened legislation protecting voting rights by barring literacy and other tests as a condition for voting in six southern states,[33] by setting criminal penalties for interference with efforts to vote, and by providing for the replacement of local registrars with federally appointed registrars in counties designated by the attorney general as significantly resistant to registering eligible blacks to vote. The right to vote was further strengthened with ratification in 1964 of the Twenty-Fourth Amendment, which abolished the poll tax, and in 1975 with legislation permanently outlawing literacy tests in all 50 states and mandating bilingual ballots or oral assistance for Spanish, Chinese, Japanese, and Korean speakers; and Native Americans and Alaska natives.

In the long run, the laws extending and protecting voting rights could prove to be the most effective of all the great civil rights legislation because the progress in black political participation produced by these acts has altered the shape of American politics. In 1965, in the seven states of the Old Confederacy covered by the Voting Rights Act, 29.3 percent of the eligible black residents were registered to vote, compared with 73.4 percent of the white residents (see Table 5.2). By 1972 the gap between black and white registration in the seven states was only 11.2 points. At one time, white leaders in Mississippi had attempted to dilute the influence of this growing black vote by **gerrymandering** districts to ensure that no blacks would

gerrymandering the apportionment of voters in districts in such a way as to give unfair advantage to one racial or ethnic group or political party

TABLE 5.2

Registration by Race and State in Southern States Covered by the Voting Rights Act (VRA)

The VRA had a direct impact on the rate of black voter registration in the southern states, as measured by the gap between white and black voters in each state. Further insights can be gained by examining changes in white registration rates before and after passage of the VRA and by comparing the gaps between white and black registration. Why do you think registration rates for whites increased significantly in some states and dropped in others? What impact could the increase in black registration have had on public policy?

	BEFORE THE ACT*			AFTER THE ACT* 1971–72		
	WHITE %	BLACK %	GAP** %	WHITE %	BLACK %	GAP %
Alabama	69.2	19.3	49.9	80.7	57.1	23.6
Georgia	62.6	27.4	35.2	70.6	67.8	2.8
Louisiana	80.5	31.6	48.9	80.0	59.1	20.9
Mississippi	69.9	6.7	63.2	71.6	62.2	9.4
North Carolina	96.8	46.8	50.0	62.2	46.3	15.9
South Carolina	75.7	37.3	38.4	51.2	48.0	3.2
Virginia	61.1	38.3	22.8	61.2	54.0	7.2
TOTAL	73.4	29.3	44.1	67.8	56.6	11.2

*Available registration data as of March 1965 and 1971–72.

**The gap is the percentage-point difference between white and black registration rates.

SOURCE: U.S. Commission on Civil Rights, *Political Participation* (1968), Appendix VII: Voter Education Project, attachment to press release, October 3, 1972.

be elected to Congress. But the black voters changed Mississippi before Mississippi could change them. In 1988, 11 percent of all elected officials in Mississippi were black—still well below the percentage of blacks in the state's voting-age population, which was 32 percent in 1990, but progress nonetheless.[34]

Several provisions of the 1965 act were scheduled to expire in 2007. However, in 2006, responding to charges that black voters still faced discrimination at the polls, Congress renewed the act for another 25 years. Pressure for renewal of the act had been intense since the disputed 2000 presidential election. The U.S. Commission on Civil Rights conducted hearings on the election in Florida, at which black voters testified about being turned away from the polls and wrongly purged from the voting rolls and about the unreliable voting technology in their neighborhoods. On the basis of this testimony and after an analysis of the vote, the commission charged that there had been extensive racial discrimination.[35] Recently, Texas has come under fire for gerrymandering congressional districts that discriminate against Latino voters. Due to population growth, most of it among Latinos, Texas gained four new congressional seats after the 2010 census. The heavily Republican state legislature drew a map designed to ensure that three of the new seats would go to Republican candidates. However, a coalition of minority groups and the Justice Department contested the map in court, charging that it failed to create a sufficient number of majority-minority districts. After extensive legal wrangling, the new redistricting plan included three majority-minority districts.[36]

The 1965 Voting Rights Act had also required some state and local governments to obtain federal preclearance before making any changes to their voting laws or practices. The designation of which jurisdictions needed preclearance was based upon a formula that calculated each jurisdiction's history of past voting discrimination. In the 2013 case *Shelby County v. Holder*, the Supreme Court overturned the formula, saying it was based on data more than 40 years old.[37] The Obama administration was critical of the decision, but there seemed little possibility that Congress would take action to devise a new preclearance formula.

A new area of controversy in the realm of voting rights concerns is so-called voter ID laws. Some 34 states have enacted legislation requiring voters to show positive identification at the polls. As of 2018, 18 of these states required prospective voters to show an official photo ID before they would be allowed to cast ballots. Republicans generally support such laws, arguing that they deter voter fraud. Democrats generally oppose such laws, countering that they are particularly burdensome to poor and minority voters, who they say are less likely than others to possess such IDs. Cases challenging the laws on equal protection grounds have met mixed success. In 2008 the Supreme Court upheld the constitutionality of Indiana's voter ID law, affirming the states' "valid interest" in improving election procedures and deterring fraud.[38] On the other hand, in 2013 the Supreme Court struck down an Arizona law requiring that individuals produce proof of U.S. citizenship in order to register to vote. In 2016 voter ID laws were struck down or modified by courts in Kansas, North Carolina, North Dakota, Texas, and Wisconsin, indicating increased judicial suspicion of these statutes. Given the political controversy over voter ID laws, it seems likely that the Court will be asked to rule yet again on the question.

Housing The Civil Rights Act of 1964 did not address housing, but in 1968 Congress passed another civil rights act specifically to outlaw housing discrimination. Called the Fair Housing Act, the law prohibited discrimination in the sale or rental of most housing—eventually covering nearly all the nation's housing. Housing was among the most controversial of discrimination issues because of deeply entrenched patterns of residential segregation across the United States. Such segregation was not simply a product of individual choice. Local housing authorities deliberately segregated public housing, and federal guidelines had sanctioned discrimination in Federal Housing Administration mortgage lending, effectively preventing blacks from joining the exodus to the suburbs in the 1950s and '60s. Nonetheless, Congress had been reluctant to tackle housing discrimination, fearing the tremendous controversy it could arouse. But just as the housing legislation was being considered in April 1968, the civil rights leader Martin Luther King, Jr., was assassinated; this tragedy brought the measure unexpected support in Congress.

Although it pronounced sweeping goals, the Fair Housing Act had little effect on housing segregation because its enforcement mechanisms were so weak. Individuals who believed they had been discriminated against had to file suit themselves. The burden was on the individual to prove that housing discrimination had occurred, even though such discrimination is often subtle and difficult to document. Although local fair housing groups emerged to assist

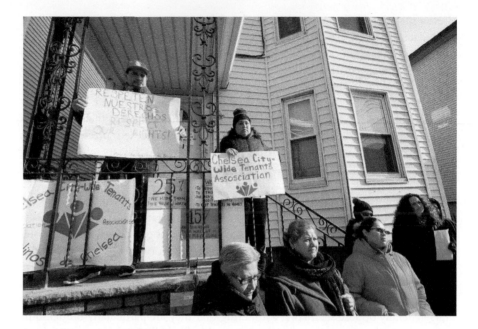

The mortgage crisis that led to foreclosures on many homes in 2008 and 2009 hit minority communities especially hard. Civil rights organizations argued that some lenders discriminated against African Americans and Latino home buyers, making it harder for them to get a fair deal on a mortgage.

redlining a practice in which banks refuse to make loans to people living in certain geographic locations

individuals in their court claims, the procedures for proving discrimination constituted a formidable barrier to effective change. These procedures were not altered until 1988, when Congress passed the Fair Housing Amendments Act. This new law put more teeth in the enforcement procedures and allowed the Department of Housing and Urban Development (HUD) to initiate legal action in cases of discrimination.[39]

Efforts to prohibit discrimination in lending have met some success. Several laws passed in the 1970s required banks to report information about their mortgage lending patterns, making it more difficult for them to engage in **redlining**, the practice of refusing to lend to entire neighborhoods. The 1977 Community Reinvestment Act required banks to lend in neighborhoods in which they do business. Through vigorous use of this act, many neighborhood organizations have reached agreements with banks that, as a result, have significantly increased investment in some poor neighborhoods.

Even so, racial discrimination in home mortgage lending remains a significant issue. In 2007 the issue of predatory lending—offering loans well above market rates, often with complex provisions that borrowers do not understand—attracted nationwide attention as the number of home foreclosures skyrocketed. In 2009 civil rights organizations, several states, and some cities filed charges against banks and other lenders claiming they had illegally discriminated against African American and Latino home buyers. Minority home buyers, the suits charged, had been offered subprime mortgage products with higher interest rates, in contrast to whites with similar income levels, who were offered loans at lower interest rates. By 2012 some of these lawsuits had resulted in the largest financial settlements ever issued for lending discrimination. In announcing one settlement, the Justice Department vowed to "vigorously pursue those who would take advantage of certain Americans because of their race, national origin, gender or disability," noting that such discrimination "betrays the promise of equal opportunity that is enshrined in our Constitution and our legal framework."[40]

Marriage The Civil Rights Act of 1964 was also silent on the question of interracial marriage, which 16 states continued to outlaw in 1967. In that year, the Supreme Court ruled in *Loving v. Virginia* that such state laws were unconstitutional. The case concerned a Virginia couple, a white man and a black woman, who married in Washington, D.C., where such unions were legal. When they moved back to Virginia, which outlawed interracial marriage, authorities charged the couple with violating Virginia law. The Lovings moved back to Washington, D.C., and challenged the Virginia law. Nine years later the Supreme Court struck down state laws banning marriage on the basis of racial classifications. In so doing, the Court declared marriage "one of the 'basic civil rights of man,' fundamental to our very existence and survival."[41]

The Supreme Court ruled in 1967 that state laws banning interracial marriage were unconstitutional. The case *Loving v. Virginia* was invoked numerous times in the Court's decision almost 50 years later, declaring marriage a fundamental right for same-sex couples.

Extending Civil Rights

> **Describe how different groups have fought for and won protection of their civil rights**

Even before equal employment laws began to have a positive effect on the economic situation of blacks, something equally dramatic began happening: the extension of civil rights to other groups. The right not to be discriminated against was being successfully claimed by the other groups listed in Title VII of the 1964 Civil Rights Act, those defined by sex, religion, or national origin, and eventually by still other groups defined by age or sexual orientation. This extension of civil rights has become the new frontier of the civil rights struggle.

Once racial discrimination began to be seen as an important civil rights issue, other groups rose to demand recognition and active protection of their civil rights. Under Title VII, any group or individual can try, and in fact is encouraged to try, to convert goals and grievances into questions of rights and of the deprivation of those rights. A plaintiff must establish only that his or her membership in a group is an unreasonable basis for discrimination. In the United States today, a large number of individuals and groups have and are claiming illegal discrimination.

LEVELS OF SCRUTINY UNDER THE EQUAL PROTECTION CLAUSE

Before we examine the civil rights movements of the past 60 years, it is useful to take a moment to describe how the courts have analyzed laws in cases where an individual or group has claimed discrimination. As has already been made clear, the courts have been a very important actor in the contest for rights protections. Recall that civil rights are the rules governing who may participate in the political process and regulating the ways in which the government may or may not treat its citizens. The equal protection clause of the Fourteenth Amendment does not require that everyone be treated equally. State and federal laws often create classifications allowing some, but not other, individuals to engage in activities or receive benefits. States, for example, allow only those with certain qualifications to engage in various occupations (such as medical professions) and set a minimum age for driving automobiles, voting, and consuming alcohol. Courts generally recognize the need for such systems of classification. Some systems of classification, on the other hand, such as those based on race, gender, or religion, raise serious constitutional questions. When dealing with challenges to state-imposed systems of classification, the courts employ a three-tiered approach, placing a greater burden of proof on the government to defend some types of classificatory schemes than others. The three tiers are often called "levels of scrutiny."

First Level The first and lowest level of scrutiny is applied by the courts to most state and federal regulatory schemes, such as motor vehicle and occupational licensing, as well as laws setting a minimum age for the purchase of alcohol and cigarettes. Here, the courts will generally apply the "rational basis test." Under this level of scrutiny, the burden of proof is on the plaintiff to show that there is no rational basis whatsoever for the government's rules. Such a showing is extremely difficult, and few plaintiffs succeed.

Second Level The next level of judicial review of state action under the equal protection clause is **intermediate scrutiny** (or exacting scrutiny). Here, there is a greater burden on the government to show that its classification scheme not only is rational but also serves an important interest. Courts generally apply intermediate scrutiny to laws that afford differential treatment to men and women or that discriminate against the inheritance and property rights of illegitimate children. In recent years, federal courts have generally applied intermediate scrutiny in cases involving gender orientation. For example, in the 2013 case of *Windsor v. United States* the Second Circuit Courts of Appeals employed intermediate scrutiny in holding that the federal Defense of Marriage Act, which applied the terms *marriage* and *spouse* only to heterosexual unions, served no legitimate state interest.[42] The U.S. Supreme Court affirmed the decision but did not indicate which level of scrutiny it had applied.

intermediate scrutiny a test used by the Supreme Court in gender discrimination cases that places the burden of proof partially on the government and partially on the challengers to show that the law in question is unconstitutional

Third Level The highest level of scrutiny employed by the courts, "strict scrutiny," places the burden of proof on the government to show that discrimination serves a "compelling interest," that the law is "narrowly tailored to achieve that goal," and that the government has used the "least restrictive means" for achieving its compelling interest. Strict scrutiny generally applies to laws that discriminate on the basis of race, religion, or national origin. These are termed *suspect classifications*. Strict scrutiny also applies to laws that hinder the exercise of fundamental rights, such as access to the courts or the right to vote. When a federal court employs strict scrutiny, the government is seldom able to meet its burden of proof. All race-based classifications are automatically subject to strict scrutiny.[43] In 2013 the Supreme Court also applied strict scrutiny to a case involving a claim of reverse discrimination. In the case of *Fisher v. University of Texas*, a white plaintiff charged that she had been rejected in favor of less qualified minority applicants.[44] The Supreme Court remanded the case for reconsideration by a lower federal court, which was instructed to apply strict scrutiny to the school's admissions process. The court of appeals still rejected Fisher's claim, and in 2016 the Supreme Court upheld the university's procedures.[45]

WOMEN AND GENDER DISCRIMINATION

Title VII provided a valuable tool for the growing women's movement in the 1960s and '70s. In fact, in many ways the law fostered the growth of the women's movement. The first major campaign of the National Organization for Women (NOW)

involved picketing the EEOC for its refusal to ban sex-segregated employment advertisements. NOW also sued the *New York Times* for continuing to publish such ads after the passage of Title VII. Another organization, the Women's Equity Action League (WEAL), pursued legal action on a wide range of gender-discrimination issues, filing lawsuits against law schools and medical schools for discriminatory admission policies, for example.

Building on these victories and the growth of the women's movement, feminist activists sought an "Equal Rights Amendment" (ERA) to the Constitution. The proposed amendment was short: its substantive passage stated that "equality of rights under the law shall not be denied or abridged by the United States or by any State on account of sex." The amendment's supporters believed that such a sweeping guarantee of equal rights was a necessary tool for ending all discrimination against women and for making gender roles more equal. Opponents charged that the amendment would be socially disruptive and would introduce changes (such as unisex restrooms) that most Americans did not want. The amendment easily passed Congress in 1972 and won quick approval in many state legislatures, but it fell three states short of the 38 needed to ratify it by the 1982 deadline.[46]

Despite the failure of the ERA, efforts to stop gender discrimination expanded dramatically as an area of civil rights law. In the 1970s the conservative Burger Court (under Chief Justice Warren Burger) helped establish gender discrimination as a major and highly visible civil rights issue. Although the Supreme Court refused to treat gender discrimination as the equivalent of racial discrimination,[47] it did make it easier for plaintiffs to file and win suits on the basis of gender discrimination by applying an "intermediate" level of review to these cases, as described earlier.[48]

In recent years, laws and court decisions designed to deal with discrimination against women have been used by groups representing transgender individuals to press for equal rights, especially in the realm of employment. For example, Title VII of the 1964 Civil Rights Act makes it unlawful to discriminate in employment on the basis of color, religion, sex, national origin, or race. The act is enforced by the EEOC. Pressed by groups representing transgender workers, in July 2015 President Obama issued an executive order prohibiting federal contractors from discriminating against workers based on their sexual orientation or gender identity. Two months later, the EEOC filed its first-ever lawsuits to protect transgender workers under Title VII. In late December, then–attorney general Eric Holder announced that, going forward, the Justice Department would consider discrimination against transgender people as covered by the Civil Rights Act's prohibition of sex discrimination.[49] Nonetheless, attempts have been made to pass legislation requiring transgender individuals to use public bathrooms that correspond to the gender designated on their birth certificates. In 2016, North Carolina enacted such a law, leading to boycotts and protests, with several corporations announcing plans to reduce their operations in the state. When the Department of Justice warned North Carolina that the law violated the Civil Rights Act, the state sued the federal government in order to defend its new law. In 2017, under pressure from the business community, North Carolina repealed its ordinance.

As discussed in this chapter's introduction, more recently, President Trump tweeted that transgender individuals would be barred from the armed forces, though there has been no plan to implement the president's tweet pending further clarification.

Gains for women in the area of civil rights have come, but slowly. Title IX of the 1972 Education Act has helped promote gender equality in education and helped increase women's participation in college sports, though women continue to be underrepresented in science, technology, engineering, and math. In 2009, President Obama signed the Lily Ledbetter Fair Pay Act to help combat pay discrimination. After serving in the military for decades, women were finally allowed to serve in combat in 2013. Despite these steps forward, gender inequity persists in American life.

FOR CRITICAL ANALYSIS

Has Title IX created equality in men's and women's college athletic programs? Should there be public efforts to encourage more female students to enter well-paid fields such as science and technology, or is that mainly a matter of individual choice?

Equality in Education Title IX of the 1972 Education Act forbade gender discrimination in education, but it initially sparked little litigation because of its weak enforcement provisions. In 1992 the Supreme Court ruled in *Franklin v. Gwinnett County Public Schools* that monetary damages could be awarded for gender discrimination, opening the door for more legal action in the area of education.[50] The greatest impact has been in the areas of sexual harassment (the subject of the *Franklin* case) and in equal treatment of women's athletic programs. The potential for monetary damages has made universities and public schools take the problem of sexual harassment more seriously. And in the two years after the *Franklin* case, complaints to the Education Department's Office for Civil Rights about unequal treatment of women's athletic programs nearly tripled. In several high-profile legal cases, some prominent universities were ordered to create more women's sports programs, prompting many other colleges and universities to follow suit in order to avoid potential litigation.[51] In 1997 the Supreme Court refused to hear a petition by Brown University challenging a lower-court order that the university establish strict sex equity in its athletic programs. The Court's decision meant that in colleges and universities across the country, varsity athletic positions for men and women must reflect the schools' overall enrollment numbers.[52] Though the ruling has a major impact on college athletic programs, advocates for gender equality note that many differences between male and female students continue to exist. They point to gender barriers in important fields such as science, technology, engineering, and math, which female students are much less likely to enter.[53]

In 1996 the Supreme Court made another important decision about gender and education by putting an end to all-male schools supported by public funds. It ruled that the Virginia Military Institute's (VMI) policy of not admitting women was unconstitutional.[54] Along with the Citadel, an all-male military college in South Carolina, VMI had never admitted women in its 157-year history. VMI argued that the unique educational experience it offered (including intense physical training and the harsh treatment of freshmen) would be destroyed if women were admitted. The Court, however, ruled that the male-only policy denied "substantial equality" to women. Two days after the ruling, the Citadel announced that it would accept women. Even without formal barriers to entry, the experience of the new female cadets at these schools was not easy. Of the four women admitted to the Citadel immediately after the Supreme Court decision, two quit within months. They charged harassment from male students, including attempts to set the female cadets on fire.[55] Women persevered, and today women constitute nearly 10 percent of the Citadel's corps of cadets.[56]

Sexual Harassment Courts began to find sexual harassment to be a form of sex discrimination during the late 1970s. Most such law has been developed by courts through interpretation of Title VII of the 1964 Civil Rights Act. In 1986 the Supreme Court recognized two forms of sexual harassment. One type is "quid pro quo" harassment, which involves an explicit or strongly implied threat that submission is a condition of continued employment. The second is harassment that creates offensive or intimidating employment conditions amounting to a "hostile environment."[57] Employers and many employees have complained that "hostile environment" sexual harassment is too ambiguous. When can an employee bring charges? When is the employer liable? In 1986 the Court said that sexual harassment may be legally actionable even if the employee did not suffer tangible economic or job-related losses in relation to it and in 1993 added that tangible psychological costs did not have to be a result either to warrant legal action.[58] In two 1998 cases, the Court further strengthened the law when it said that whether or not sexual harassment results in economic harm to the employee, an employer is liable for the harassment if it was committed by someone with authority over the employee—by a supervisor, for example. But the Court also said that an employer may defend itself by showing that it had a sexual harassment prevention and grievance policy in effect.[59]

In 2011 the Department of Education's Office of Civil Rights (OCR) issued a "Dear Colleague" letter to the more than 7,000 colleges and universities receiving federal money, advising them, under the authority of Title IX, to adopt stringent procedures to adjudicate charges of sexual assault and harassment on campus. OCR told colleges to shift the burden of proof from the accuser toward the accused in such cases, to allow accusers to appeal not-guilty findings (double jeopardy contrary to the language of the Fifth Amendment) and to refrain from allowing accused persons from cross-examining their accusers (contrary to the Sixth Amendment). These procedures have led to a furor on many campuses and a flurry of charges of false accusations and unfair proceedings.[60]

Sexual harassment remains an issue today. Recently, a number of cases of sexual harassment of female members of the U.S. military have come to light. These cases have led to several courts-martial of both officers and noncommissioned officers. Some observers argue that the problem is systemic, however, and have urged the military to enact reforms that would hopefully have the effect of stemming the abuse of women in the military.

Equality in Employment Women have also pressed for civil rights in employment. In particular, women have fought against pay discrimination—when a male employee is paid more than a female employee of equal qualifications in the same job. After the Equal Pay Act of 1963 made such discrimination illegal, women's pay slowly moved toward the level of men's pay. In 2007 this movement received a setback when the Supreme Court ruled against a claim of pay discrimination. The case, *Ledbetter v. Goodyear Tire and Rubber Co.*, involved a female supervisor named Lily Ledbetter, who learned late in her career that she was being paid up to 40 percent less than male supervisors, including those with less seniority. Ledbetter filed a grievance with the EEOC, charging sex discrimination.[61] The Supreme Court denied her claim, ruling that, according to the law, workers must file their grievance 180 days after the discrimination occurs. Many observers found the ruling unfair because workers often do not know about pay differentials until well after the initial decision to discriminate has been made. Justice Ruth Bader Ginsburg, the only female member of the Court at the time, marked her disagreement by reading her dissent aloud, a rare occurrence. In January 2009 the Lily Ledbetter Fair Pay Act became the first bill that President Obama signed into law. The new law gave workers expanded rights to sue in cases, such as Ledbetter's, when an employee learns of discriminatory treatment well after it has started. Despite such cases, women continue to earn about 20 percent less than men in the U.S. workforce.[62]

The fight against gender discrimination as an important part of the civil rights struggle has coincided with the rise of women's politics as a discrete movement in American politics. As with the struggle for racial equality, the relationship between changes in government policies and political action suggests that, to a great degree, changes in government policies produce political action. The inclusion of gender as a protected class in the 1964 Civil Rights Act prompted women to take steps to press for their rights where they were denied in education and employment. The "Who Are Americans?" feature on page 185 considers the progress on women's rights.

LATINOS

The labels *Latino* and *Hispanic* encompass a wide range of groups with diverse national origins, distinctive cultural identities, and particular experiences. As a result, civil rights issues for them have varied considerably by group and by place. For example, the early political experiences of Mexican Americans were shaped by race and by region. In 1848, under the Treaty of Guadalupe Hidalgo, Mexico ceded to the United States territory that now comprises Arizona, California, New Mexico, and parts of Colorado, Nevada, and Utah, as well as extended the Texas border to the Rio Grande. Although the treaty guaranteed full civil rights to the residents of these territories, Mexican Americans in fact experienced ongoing discrimination, which they sought to remedy through the courts. In 1898 the courts reconfirmed Mexican Americans' formal political rights, including the right to vote. In many places, however, and especially in Texas, Mexican Americans were segregated and

Have Women Achieved Equal Rights?

Title VII of the 1964 Civil Rights Act prohibits gender discrimination, and the Supreme Court has consistently upheld the principle that women should have the same rights as men. Since 1960 the United States has made great strides toward gender equality in some areas but, as the data show, still has a long way to go in other areas.

Education

Percentage of college students who are women

Year	%
1960	39%
1970	39%
1980	42%
1990	45%
2000	48%
2010	56%
2017	56%

Politics

Percentage of members of Congress who are women

Percentage of state legislators who are women

Year	Congress	State legislators
1960		4%
1970		2%
1980	11%	2%
1990	17%	6%
2000	23%	13%
2010	25%	17%
2017	19%	25%

Median Weekly Earnings by Race and Gender

In 2016 women who were full-time wage and salary workers had median usual weekly earnings that were 82 percent of those of male full-time wage and salary workers.

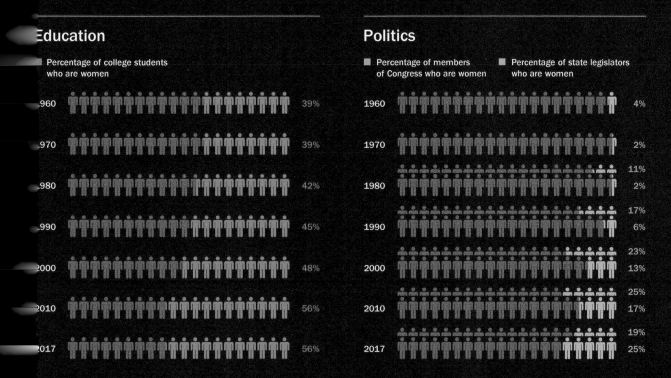

White		African American		Latino		Asian American	
Men	Women	Men	Women	Men	Women	Men	Women
$942	$766	$718	$641	$663	$586	$1,151	$902

FOR CRITICAL ANALYSIS

1. How much does each of these factors—education, political office, and income—say about gender equality in the United States?

2. While most Americans support the principle of equal opportunity for all groups, there is disagreement over how much the government should do to ensure equal outcomes. Discuss the difference between equal opportunity and equal outcomes in the context of women's rights.

SOURCES: National Center for Education Statistics, www.nces.ed.gov (accessed 11/4/17); Congressional Research Service, www.fas.org; National Conference of State Legislators, www.ncsl.org; Bureau of Labor Statistics, www.bls.gov (accessed 11/4/17).

Immigration is one of today's most controversial issues. President Trump campaigned on a promise to build a protective wall on the U.S.–Mexico border. Supporters of stricter immigration policies believe they will help protect jobs for American citizens. Others support the rights of undocumented people—especially young people brought to the United States by their parents—and believe that they should have a path to American citizenship.

prevented from voting through such means as the white primary and the poll tax.[63] Texas established separate schools for Mexicans, a practice also common in southern California. In the housing markets, Mexicans were often banned by restrictive covenants from buying or renting houses in many neighborhoods.

The earliest Mexican American independent political organizations included the League of United Latin American Citizens (LULAC), founded in 1929, and the GI Forum, created in 1948. Both groups worked to stem discrimination against Mexican Americans. LULAC pursued a legal strategy like the NAACP's to eliminate the segregation of Mexican American students. One of its earliest victories came in 1930, when it successfully challenged a Texas school district's decision to establish separate schools for Anglos and Mexicans.[64] LULAC also litigated the 1946–47 *Mendez v. Westminster* case, which overturned school segregation in Orange County, California.[65] This case was an important precursor to *Brown v. Board of Education*, and many of the same actors were involved.

In the 1960s a new kind of Mexican American political movement was born. By the late 1950s the first Mexican American was elected to Congress, and four others followed in the 1960s. A central inspiration for political mobilization emerged from the United Farm Workers union and its charismatic leader, César Chávez. In an era of unprecedented economic prosperity, California's farmworkers, mainly Mexican migrants, remained poorly paid and lacked basic rights for fair treatment on the job. Employing novel tactics such as the national grape boycott, the union drew Americans' attention to the plight of farmworkers and the injustices that confronted Mexican migrants and Mexican Americans in the fields. Chávez, whose hunger strikes and inspirational speeches kept the movement in the public eye, came to symbolize the quest for Mexican American civil rights more broadly.[66] The fields were not the only focus of conflict. In the late 1960s, Mexican American students, inspired by the black civil rights movement, launched boycotts of high school classes in East Los Angeles, Denver, and San Antonio, demanding bilingual education, an end to discrimination, and more cultural recognition. They were soon joined by students in colleges and universities across California.

Since that time, Latino political strategy has developed along two tracks. One is a traditional ethnic group path of voter registration and voting along ethnic lines. The other is a legal strategy using the various civil rights laws designed to ensure fair access to the political system. The Mexican American Legal Defense and Education Fund (MALDEF), founded in 1968, has played a key role in designing and pursuing the latter strategy.

Immigrants and Civil Rights Since the 1960s, rights for Latinos have been intertwined with immigrant rights. For much of American history, legal immigrants were treated much the same as citizens. But continuing immigration and mounting economic insecurity have undermined this sense of equality. Groups of voters across the country now strongly support drawing a sharper line between immigrants and citizens. The Supreme Court has ruled that unauthorized immigrants are eligible for education and emergency medical care but can be denied other social benefits. The movement to deny benefits to noncitizens gathered steam in California, which experienced sharp economic distress in the early 1990s and has the highest levels of immigration of any state. In 1994 an ultimately unsuccessful movement in California sought to deny unauthorized immigrants all services except emergency medical care in an attempt to discourage unauthorized immigration and to pressure those already in the country to leave.

Unauthorized immigration has continued to be a hot-button political issue. One priority for advocacy groups has been the issue of undocumented immigrants who came to the United States as young children, were raised in the United States, and have no real ties to the nation in which they were born. One proposed piece of legislation to benefit such individuals is the Development, Relief, and Education Act for Alien Minors, known as the DREAM Act. This proposal would provide a route to permanent residency for such individuals via military service or college attendance. The DREAM Act was introduced in Congress in 2001 but has been defeated every year on the grounds that it would encourage illegal immigration. Absent legislation, the Department of Homeland Security has instituted its own policy, Deferred Action for Childhood Arrivals (DACA), instructing immigration officials to take no action to deport law-abiding individuals who entered the United States illegally as children. In 2014, President Obama issued executive memoranda granting quasi-legal status and work permits to some 5 million individuals who entered the United States illegally as children or who have children who are American citizens. The president's orders were challenged in the federal courts, and in 2016 a 4–4 tie in the Supreme Court left in place a lower-court decision disallowing the president's plan.[67] In 2018 the Supreme Court declined to hear the Trump administration's appeal from a lower-court ruling requiring continuation of the DACA program. However, DACA cases before several U.S. district courts at the end of 2018 may result in competing rulings that could force the Supreme Court to address the question.

Efforts to curb illegal immigration have led to civil rights violations of legal immigrants. Latino organizations opposed the Immigration Reform and Control Act of 1986 because it imposed sanctions on employers who hire undocumented workers. Such sanctions, they feared, would lead employers to discriminate against Latinos. These suspicions were confirmed in a 1990 report by the General Accounting Office, which found employer sanctions had created a "widespread pattern of discrimination" against Latinos and others who appear foreign.[68]

Another ongoing issue is federal cooperation with local and state law-enforcement agencies to enforce federal immigration laws. Programs initiated by the Department of Homeland Security in the final years of the George W. Bush administration led to immigrant "sweeps," which rounded up Latinos, many of whom were legal immigrants or even American citizens. A broad coalition of civil rights organizations opposed the program for engaging in racial profiling and violating civil rights, and the congressional Hispanic Caucus called on the next president to end it. Yet, the Obama administration's Secure Communities program, which initially sought to focus on major drug offenders, violent criminals, and those already in prison, came under fire for illegally detaining citizens and legal immigrants. The Secure Communities Program was terminated in 2014 in favor of an effort to refocus law enforcement attention on serious criminals.

In 2017, however, President Trump ordered stricter immigration enforcement and began to expand the ranks of Immigration and Customs Enforcement (ICE) agents. Many thousands of immigrants who had not committed serious crimes were slated for deportation, and immigration enforcement at the border was stepped up as well. Several cities and a handful of states declared themselves "sanctuaries" and declined to cooperate with ICE agents. The administration responded by threatening to cut off federal funding from local governments that failed to help federal authorities.

Finally, as we saw in Chapter 3, while some local governments declared themselves to be sanctuaries, a number of states, including Arizona, Utah, South Carolina, Indiana, Georgia, and Alabama, passed very strict immigration laws within the past few years. Civil rights groups have contested the laws in court, and the federal Justice Department has instituted its own legal challenges. Arizona's 2010 law provided the inspiration for these far-reaching state measures. Arizona's law required immigrants to carry identity documents with them at all times, made it a crime for an undocumented immigrant to apply for a job, gave the police greater powers to stop anyone they suspected of being an unauthorized immigrant, and required them to check the immigration status of a person they detain if they suspect that person is an unauthorized immigrant. The Justice Department challenged the law on the grounds that the federal government was responsible for making immigration law, not the states. The Supreme Court's 2012 decision was a partial victory for the federal government. The Court struck down three parts of the Arizona law on the grounds that they intruded upon federal responsibility. These included the provision that immigrants carry identity papers, that undocumented immigrants cannot apply for jobs, and that police can stop persons they suspect of being undocumented immigrants. The Court let stand the provision that required local police to check the immigration status of an individual detained for other reasons if they had grounds

Soon after taking office, President Trump instituted a "travel ban" on people from some predominantly Muslim countries. He claimed that the move would cut down on foreign terrorism in the United States. Opponents protested this ban on the grounds that it was singling out certain religious groups and not others. The matter moved quickly to the U.S. Supreme Court, which ruled that a modified version of the ban could remain in place.

to suspect that the person was in the country illegally. Opponents of the police checks vowed to challenge that part of the law on the grounds that it led to illegal racial profiling.[69]

Immigration was, of course, a very divisive topic during the 2016 presidential election. During the campaign for the Republican nomination, Donald Trump asserted that he would build a wall along the U.S. border with Mexico, institute a temporary ban on Muslims seeking to travel to the United States, and end the Obama administration's program to accept several thousand Syrian refugees every year. When Trump took office, he lost little time in seeking to implement these campaign promises pertaining to immigration, though not all have come to fruition. As of 2018, while the fence on the U.S.-Mexico border had been extended in some places, no wall had been built.

However, in January 2017, Trump issued executive orders barring entry into the United States for travelers from six predominantly Muslim countries and blocking the admission of all refugees seeking admission to the United States for 120 days. Critics charged Trump, who had frequently stated his concerns that Muslim immigrants might include terrorists, with religious discrimination, and in particular with violating the 1965 Immigration Act, which states that people should not experience preferences or discrimination on account of their "race, sex, nationality, place of birth or place of residence." At least one federal appeals court agreed with this argument, though other immigration laws seem to give the president broad discretion in the matter. In a 5–4 decision, the U.S. Supreme Court upheld the ban, though the dissenting opinion argued the ban infringed on the right to religious liberty.

ASIAN AMERICANS

Like the term *Latino*, the label *Asian American* encompasses a wide range of people from very different national backgrounds who came to the United States at different moments in history. As a consequence, Asian Americans have had very diverse experiences.

The early Asian experience in the United States was shaped by a series of naturalization laws dating back to 1790, the first of which declared that only white aliens were eligible for citizenship. Chinese immigrants began arriving in California in the 1850s, drawn by the boom of the gold rush, but they were immediately met with virulent antagonism. In 1870, Congress declared Chinese immigrants ineligible for citizenship; in 1882 the first Chinese Exclusion Act suspended the entry of Chinese laborers.

At the time of the Exclusion Act, the Chinese community was composed predominantly of single male laborers, with few women and children. The few Chinese children in San Francisco were initially denied entry to the public schools; only after parents of American-born Chinese children pressed legal action were the children allowed to attend public school. Even then, however, they were segregated into a separate Chinese school. American-born Chinese children could not be denied citizenship, however; this right was confirmed by the Supreme Court in 1898, when it ruled in *United States v. Wong Kim Ark* that anyone born in the United States was entitled to full citizenship.[70] Still, new Chinese immigrants were barred from the United States until 1943, after China had become a key wartime ally and Congress repealed the Chinese Exclusion Act and permitted Chinese residents to become citizens.

The earliest Japanese immigrants, who came to California in the 1880s, at the height of the anti-Chinese movement, faced similar discrimination. Like Chinese immigrants, Japanese immigrants were ineligible to become citizens because of their race. During the first part of the twentieth century, California and several other western states enacted laws that denied Japanese immigrants the right to own property. The denial of basic civil rights to Japanese Americans culminated in the decision to forcibly remove Americans of Japanese descent as well as Japanese noncitizen residents from their homes and confine them in internment camps during World War II. After the Japanese government launched its attack on Pearl Harbor, America's Japanese residents and citizens were suspected of disloyalty. Some 120,000 individuals of Japanese descent or heritage, including 90,000 American citizens, were forcibly relocated from their homes to 10 internment camps located in California, Idaho, Utah, Arizona, Wyoming, Colorado, and Arkansas. Conditions in the camps were poor and characterized by overcrowding, food rationing, and primitive sanitary facilities. Despite a vigorous legal challenge, the Supreme Court ruled that the internment was constitutional on the grounds of military necessity.[71] In 1944, President Roosevelt rescinded the order that began the internment process and closed the camps. Many of the internees, however, had suffered property losses and health problems during the period of internment and would never recover from its effects. Not until the Civil Liberties Act of 1988 did the federal government formally acknowledge this denial of civil rights as a "grave injustice" that had been "motivated largely by racial prejudice, wartime hysteria, and a failure of political leadership."[72]

Asian immigration increased rapidly after the 1965 Immigration Act, which lifted discriminatory quotas. In spite of this and other developments, societal discrimination coupled with limited English proficiency barred many new Asian American (in addition to Latino) immigrants from full participation in American life. Two developments in the 1970s, however, established rights for language minorities. In 1974 the Supreme Court ruled in *Lau v. Nichols*, a suit filed on behalf of Chinese students in San Francisco, that school districts have to provide education for students whose English is limited.[73] It did not mandate bilingual education, but it established a duty to provide instruction that the students could understand. As we saw earlier, the 1970 amendments to the Voting Rights Act permanently outlawed literacy tests in all 50 states and mandated bilingual ballots or oral assistance for those who speak Chinese, Japanese, Korean, Spanish, or Native American or Alaskan languages.

NATIVE AMERICANS

The political status of Native Americans was left unclear in the Constitution. But by the early 1800s the courts had defined each of the Indian tribes as a nation. As members of Indian nations, Native Americans were thus declared noncitizens of the United States. The political status of Native Americans changed in 1924, when congressional legislation granted citizenship to all persons born in the United States. A variety of changes in federal policy toward Native Americans during the 1930s paved the way for a later resurgence of their political power. Most important was the federal decision to encourage Native Americans on reservations to establish local self-government.[74] Since the 1920s and '30s, Native American tribes have sued the federal government for illegal land seizures; both monetary reparations and land have been awarded as damages but only in small amounts. Native American tribes have been more successful at winning federal recognition of their sovereignty.

The Native American political movement gathered force in the 1960s as Native Americans began to use protest, litigation, and assertion of tribal rights to improve their situation. The federal government responded to the rise in Native American activism with the Indian Self-Determination and Education Assistance Act, which began to give Native Americans more control over their own land.[75]

As a language minority, Native Americans also benefited from the 1975 amendments to the Voting Rights Act and the *Lau* decision, which established the right of Native Americans to be taught in their own languages. This marked quite a change from the boarding schools run by the Bureau of Indian Affairs, where members of Native American tribes were forbidden to speak their own languages until reforms began in the 1930s. In addition to these language-related issues, Native Americans have sought to expand their rights on the basis of their sovereign status. Most significant in economic terms was a 1987 Supreme Court decision that freed Native American tribes from most state regulations prohibiting gambling. The establishment of casino gambling on Native American lands has brought a substantial flow of new income to desperately poor reservations.

DISABLED AMERICANS

The concept of rights for the disabled began to emerge in the 1970s as the civil rights model spread to other groups. The seed was planted in a little-noticed provision of the 1973 Rehabilitation Act, which outlawed discrimination against individuals on the basis of disabilities. As in many other cases, the law itself helped give rise to the movement demanding rights for the disabled.[76] Inspired by the NAACP's use of a legal defense fund, the disability movement founded the Disability Rights Education and Defense Fund to press its legal claims. The movement achieved its greatest success with the passage of the Americans with Disabilities Act (ADA) of 1990, which guarantees equal employment rights and access to public businesses for the disabled and prohibits discrimination in employment, housing, and health care. Claims of discrimination in violation of this act are considered by the EEOC.

The impact of the law has been far-reaching as businesses and public facilities have installed ramps, elevators, and other devices to meet the act's requirements.[77]

LGBTQ AMERICANS

In less than 50 years, the lesbian, gay, bisexual, transgender, and queer (LGBTQ) movement has become one of the largest civil rights movements in contemporary America. For much of the country's history, any sexual orientation other than heterosexuality was considered "deviant," and many states criminalized sexual acts considered to be "unnatural." Gay people were often afraid to reveal their sexual orientation for fear of reprisals, including being fired from their jobs; and the police in many cities raided bars and other establishments where it was believed that gay people gathered. While no formal restrictions existed on their political participation, gay people faced the possibility of ostracization, discrimination, and even prosecution.[78]

The contemporary gay rights movement began in earnest in the 1960s. In 1962, Illinois became the first state to repeal its sodomy laws. The movement drew national attention in 1969, when patrons at the Stonewall Inn, a popular gay bar in Greenwich Village, New York, rioted when police attempted to raid the establishment. The first gay pride parade was held in New York City the following year to commemorate the anniversary of the Stonewall riots, and gay pride parades now take place in dozens of cities across the country.

Gay rights drew national attention again in 1993, when President Bill Clinton confronted the question of whether gays should be allowed to serve in the military. As a candidate, Clinton had said he favored lifting the ban on gay people in the military. The issue set off a huge controversy in the first months of Clinton's presidency. After nearly a year of deliberation, the administration enunciated a compromise: its "Don't Ask, Don't Tell" policy allowed gay men and lesbians to serve in the military as long as they did not openly proclaim their sexual orientation or engage in homosexual activity. Many gay rights advocates expressed disappointment, charging the president with reneging on his campaign promise. After nearly 20 years of challenges, President Obama signed an executive order in 2010 repealing "Don't Ask, Don't Tell," allowing gay men and lesbians to serve openly in the military.

No Supreme Court ruling or national legislation explicitly protected gay men and lesbians from discrimination until 1996. In its first gay rights case, *Bowers v. Hardwick*, the Court ruled against a right to privacy that would protect consensual homosexual activity.[79] After the *Bowers* decision, the gay rights movement sought suitable legal cases to test the constitutionality of discrimination against gay men and lesbians, much as the African American civil rights movement had done in the late 1940s and '50s. Test cases stemmed from local ordinances restricting gay rights (including the right to marry), allowing job discrimination, and affecting family law issues such as adoption and parental rights. In 1996 the Supreme Court, in *Romer v. Evans*, explicitly extended fundamental civil rights protections to gay men and lesbians by declaring unconstitutional a 1992 amendment to the Colorado state constitution that prohibited local governments from passing ordinances to protect gay rights.[80] In its decision, the Court highlighted the connection between gay rights and civil rights.

It was not until 2003, in *Lawrence v. Texas*, that the Court overturned *Bowers* and struck down a Texas statute criminalizing certain intimate sexual conduct between consenting partners of the same sex.[81] This significant victory for gay men and lesbians extends the right to privacy to sexual minorities.

However, this decision did not undo the various exclusions that deprive gay men and lesbians of full civil rights, including the right to marry. In 1993, Hawaii's supreme court declared the state's ban on same-sex marriage discriminatory, raising the possibility that such marriages could become legal. In Washington, D.C., the Republican congressional majority responded with the Defense of Marriage Act, which defined marriage as the union of a man and a woman for purposes of federal law and benefits, such as Social Security.

More than a decade later, in 2015, the Supreme Court clarified the law concerning same-sex marriage. In the case of *Obergefell v. Hodges*, the Court ruled that the Constitution's equal protection clause and the Fourteenth Amendment's due process clause guarantee same-sex couples the right to marry in all states and require states to recognize same-sex marriages performed in other jurisdictions (see Chapter 2).[82] Some local officials briefly refused to issue marriage licenses to same-sex couples, but opposition soon melted away. Though the Court was closely divided in the case, the Court's opinion appeared to reflect a shift in public opinion on same-sex unions, with a majority of Americans favoring the right of same-sex couples to wed.[83]

In 2015 the Supreme Court legalized same-sex marriage nationwide with its decision in *Obergefell v. Hodges*. The Obama administration showed its support by illuminating the White House in rainbow light.

Gay rights advocates won a significant victory of a different kind in national politics in 2009 when new legislation extended the definition of hate crimes to include crimes against gay and transgender people. Such legislation had been sought since the 1998 murder of Matthew Shepard, a Wyoming college student who was brutally slain because of his sexual orientation. The new law allowed for tougher penalties when a crime is designated a hate crime. In another win in 2013, the Senate approved a law that bans discrimination in the workplace based on sexual orientation and gender identity (discussed earlier), with a vote of 64 to 32 in which 10 Republicans joined 54 Democrats. The House did not take up the bill, however, so it has not yet become law. Like other minorities fighting for civil rights, the LGBTQ community is organized politically to support such measures. The Human Rights Campaign is the primary national political action committee focused on gay rights; it provides campaign financing and volunteers to work for political candidates endorsed by the group. The movement has also formed legal rights organizations, including the Lambda Legal Defense and Education Fund.

FOR CRITICAL ANALYSIS

Political conflicts over gay rights have been carried out in the courts, in state legislatures, in Congress, and in elections. What are some of the decisions that have been reached in each of these different decision-making arenas? Where should decisions about gay rights be made?

DO THE POOR HAVE CIVIL RIGHTS?

One category often omitted from discussions of rights is the poor. Yet America's poor have also struggled for recognition as a group with rights that should be protected. From the colonial period until the early nineteenth century, state income and property restrictions excluded poor people from voting and officeholding. In modern times, advocates have argued that the poor have a right to education, health care, and other social benefits. Such rights are guaranteed in many European constitutions. And, in the United States, various social policies appear to recognize such rights.

Women's Rights

Every year, the World Economic Forum (a nonprofit based in Switzerland) ranks countries based on how close they are to achieving gender equality. In 2017 the United States was ranked 49th out of 144 countries, comparable to countries such as Peru and Zimbabwe.[a] One of the interesting findings in this report is that the United States has reached full gender parity in regards to educational attainment, yet lags regarding women's economic participation and opportunity, health and survival, and political empowerment.

When we compare the United States to other democracies, we notice that the United States lacks key legislation that impacts how women interact in the workforce. While most wealthy democracies mandate employers provide *paid* maternity and paternity leave, the United States has no legislation that guarantees even *unpaid* leave. As a result, it is more difficult for women in the United States to balance motherhood and pursuing a career. Largely thanks to various court decisions, U.S. law protects women from gender-based discrimination in hiring and, increasingly, from sexual harassment in the workplace, yet lacks sufficient protections guaranteeing equal pay for equal work.

	CONSTITUTION CONTAINS A NON-DISCRIMINATION CLAUSE BASED ON GENDER	ABORTION PERMITTED UPON REQUEST	GENDER PARITY REACHED IN LITERACY AND IN PRIMARY, SECONDARY, AND TERTIARY EDUCATION	LAW MANDATES NON-DISCRIMINATION BASED ON GENDER IN HIRING	LAW MANDATES EQUAL PAY FOR EQUAL WORK	LAW MANDATES MATERNITY LEAVE (PAID OR UNPAID)
Australia		✓	✓	✓	✓	
Brazil	✓		✓	✓		✓
Canada	✓	✓	✓		✓	✓
France		✓	✓	✓	✓	✓
Germany		✓		✓		✓
India	✓			✓		✓
Japan	✓			✓		✓
Mexico	✓	✓		✓		✓
South Africa	✓	✓		✓	✓	✓
United States		✓	✓	✓		

SOURCES: World Bank, "Gender Data Portal," 2018, www.datatopics.worldbank.org (accessed 7/2/18); Pew Research Center, "Worldwide Abortion Politics," October 5, 2015, www.pewresearch.org (accessed 7/2/18); World Economic Forum, "Global Gender Gap Report," 2017, www.reports.webforum.org (accessed 7/2/18).

[a] World Economic Forum, "Global Gender Gap Report," 2017, www.reports.weforum.org/global-gender-gap-report-2017/dataexplorer/ (accessed 5/28/18).

Affirmative Action

Contrast arguments for and against affirmative action

Over the past half-century or so, the relatively narrow goal of equalizing opportunity by eliminating discriminatory barriers evolved into the broader goal of **affirmative action**, compensatory action to overcome the consequences of past discrimination and encourage greater diversity. Affirmative action policies take race or some other status into account in order to provide greater opportunities to groups that have previously been at a disadvantage due to discrimination.

In 1965, President Lyndon Johnson issued executive orders promoting minority employment in the federal civil service and in companies doing business with the government. But affirmative action did not become a prominent goal of the national government until the 1970s.

Affirmative action also took the form of efforts by the agencies in the Department of Health, Education, and Welfare to shift their focus from "desegregation" to "integration."[84] Federal agencies, sometimes with court orders and sometimes without them, required school districts to present plans for busing children across district lines, for closing certain schools, and for redistributing faculties as well as students or face the loss of grants-in-aid from the federal government. These efforts dramatically increased the number of black children attending integrated classes.

affirmative action government policies or programs that seek to redress past injustices against specified groups by making special efforts to provide members of those groups with access to educational and employment opportunities

THE SUPREME COURT AND THE BURDEN OF PROOF

Efforts by the executive, legislative, and judicial branches to shape the meaning of affirmative action today tend to center on one key issue: What is the appropriate level of review in affirmative action cases—that is, on whom should the burden of proof be placed: the plaintiff, to show that discrimination has not occurred, or the defendant, to show that discrimination has occurred? The reason this question is difficult is because the cases in which the Court critically scrutinized and struck down racially discriminatory laws—cases like *Brown* and *Loving*—all involved historically disadvantaged racial minority groups. The Court struck down those laws partly because it concluded they were motivated by racial hostility—which is not a valid government purpose—and partly because the Court concluded that disadvantaged minority groups were effectively unable to use the political process to challenge laws that harmed them. The new cases, however, did not fit this pattern. Instead of being motivated by racial hostility, they were enacted with the objective of assisting victims of past injustice. And instead of harming minority groups, they disadvantaged members of the dominant majority racial group. Yet critics argued that discriminating against *any* individual because of their race violated the Equal Protection clause.

This question was addressed directly by the Supreme Court in the case of Allan Bakke (see Table 5.3). Bakke, a white male, brought suit against the University of California at Davis Medical School on the grounds that, in denying him admission, the school had discriminated against him on the basis of his race. (That year, the school had reserved 16 of 100 available slots for minority applicants.) Bakke argued that his grades and test scores ranked him well above many students who were accepted and that he had been rejected because he was white, whereas those others accepted were black or Latino. In 1978, Bakke won his case before the Supreme Court and was admitted to the medical school, but the Court stopped short of

TABLE 5.3

Supreme Court Rulings on Affirmative Action

CASE	COURT RULING
Regents of the University of California v. Bakke, 438 U.S. 265 (1978)	Affirmative action upheld, but quotas and separate admission for minorities rejected; burden of proof on defendant
Wards Cove Packing Co., Inc. v. Atonio, 490 U.S. 642 (1989)	All affirmative action programs put in doubt: burden of proof shifted from defendant to plaintiff (victim), then burden of proof shifted back to employers (defendants)
St. Mary's Honor Center v. Hicks, 509 U.S. 502 (1993)	Required victim to prove discrimination was intentional
Adarand Constructors Inc. v. Peña, 515 U.S. 200 (1995)	All race-conscious policies must survive "strict scrutiny," with burden of proof on government to show the program serves "compelling interest" to redress past discrimination
Hopwood v. Texas, 78 F.3d 932 (5th Cir., 1996)	Race can *never* be used as a factor in admission, even to promote diversity (Supreme Court refusal to review limited application to the Fifth Circuit— Texas, Louisiana, Mississippi)
Gratz v. Bollinger, 539 U.S. 244 (2003)	Rejection of a "mechanical" point system favoring minority applicants to University of Michigan as tantamount to a quota; *Bakke* reaffirmed
Grutter v. Bollinger, 539 U.S. 306 (2003)	Upheld race-conscious admission to Michigan Law School, passing strict scrutiny with diversity as a "compelling" state interest, as long as admission was "highly individualized" and not "mechanical," as in *Gratz*
Fisher v. University of Texas, 570 U.S. __ (2013)	Held that strict scrutiny should be applied to college admissions policies that used race as a factor even if the intent was to favor black applicants

declaring affirmative action unconstitutional. The Court rejected the procedures at the University of California because its medical school had used both a quota *and* a separate admissions system for minorities. The Court accepted the argument that achieving "a diverse student body" was a "compelling public purpose" but found that the method of a rigid quota of student slots assigned on the basis of race was incompatible with the Fourteenth Amendment's equal protection clause. Thus, the Court permitted universities (and presumably other schools, training programs, and hiring authorities) to continue to consider minority status but limited the use of quotas to situations (1) in which previous discrimination had been shown and (2) where quotas served more as a guideline for social diversity than as a mathematically defined ratio.[85]

For nearly a decade after *Bakke*, the Court was tentative and permissive about efforts by universities, corporations, and governments to experiment with affirmative action programs.[86]

But in 1995 another Supreme Court ruling further weakened affirmative action. This decision stated that race-based policies, such as preferences given by the government to minority contractors, must survive strict scrutiny, placing the burden on the government to show that such affirmative action programs serve a compelling government interest and address identifiable past discrimination.[87]

This ambiguous status of affirmative action was how things stood in 2003, when the Supreme Court took two cases against the University of Michigan. The first suit alleged that by automatically awarding 20 points (out of 150) to African American, Latino, and Native American applicants, the university discriminated unconstitutionally against white students of otherwise equal or superior academic qualifications. The Supreme Court agreed, arguing that something tantamount to a quota was involved because undergraduate admissions lacked the necessary "individualized consideration" and had employed instead a "mechanical one," based too much on the favorable minority points.[88]

The second case, *Grutter v. Bollinger*, broke new ground. Barbara Grutter sued the law school on the grounds that it had discriminated in a race-conscious way against white applicants with equal or superior grades and law boards. A 5–4 decision for the first time aligned the majority of the Supreme Court with Justice Powell's lone plurality opinion in *Bakke*. Powell had argued that (1) diversity in education is a compelling state interest and (2) race could be constitutionally considered as a plus factor in admissions decisions. In *Grutter*, the Court reiterated Powell's holding and, applying strict scrutiny to the law school's policy, found that the law school's admissions process was tailored to the school's compelling state interest in diversity because it gave a "highly individualized, holistic review of each applicant's file" in which race counted but was not used in a "mechanical" way.[89] The Court's ruling that racial categories can be deployed to serve a compelling state interest put affirmative action on stronger ground. The Court reaffirmed the *Grutter* decision in 2013 when it decided *Fisher v. University of Texas*, in which a white student challenged the use of race as one factor among many in the admissions decision. In a 7–1 decision, the Court sent the case back to the district court with instructions to apply "strict scrutiny" to the school's policy, as articulated in *Grutter*.[90] As noted earlier, the Court eventually accepted the university's plan.

Civil Rights
WHAT DO WE WANT?

The debate about civil rights and affirmative action is ongoing because Americans hold fundamentally different views about whether and how the government should recognize racial distinctions. At the risk of gross oversimplification, we can divide those with differing views into two groups and label them *liberals* and *conservatives*.[91] Conservatives argue, first, that rights in the American tradition are *individual* rights and that affirmative action violates this concept by concerning itself with "group rights," an idea said to be alien to the American tradition. Second, conservatives argue that the Constitution is "color-blind" and that any discrimination, even if it is called positive or benign, must inevitably rely on quotas and thus ultimately violate the equal protection clause.

Liberals agree that rights ultimately come down to individuals but argue that since the essence of discrimination is the unreasonable and unjust exclusion of *an entire group* from something valuable the society has to offer, discrimination itself has to be attacked on a group basis. Despite progress toward racial equality, liberals argue that race still matters. They can also cite Supreme Court history because the first definitive interpretation of the Fourteenth Amendment by the Court, in 1873, stated that

> the existence of laws in the state where the newly emancipated Negroes resided, which discriminated with gross injustice and hardship against them *as a class*, was the evil to be remedied by this clause [emphasis added].[92]

As to the conservative argument concerning quotas, the liberal response is that the Supreme Court has already accepted ratios (a form of quota) that are admitted as evidence to prove a "pattern or practice of discrimination" sufficient to reverse the burden of proof—to obligate the employer to show that there was *not* an intent to discriminate. Further, benign quotas have often been used by Americans both to compensate for some bad action in the past and to provide some desired distribution of social characteristics—that is, diversity. For example, a long-respected policy in the United States is the "veterans' preference" by which the government automatically gives extra consideration in hiring to persons who have served in the country's armed forces. And the goal of social diversity has long justified "positive discrimination," especially in higher education. For example, many private colleges and universities regularly reserve admissions places for the children of loyal alumni and of their own faculty, even when, in a pure competition based solely on test scores and high school records, many of those same students would not have been admitted. These practices underscore the liberal argument that affirmative or compensatory action for minorities is not alien to American experience. Because our nation has a history of slavery and legalized racial discrimination and because discrimination continues to exist (although it has declined), the issue of racial justice, more than any other, highlights the difficulty of reconciling our values to our practice.

The civil rights revolution, a revolution that began with African Americans, has broadened to include women and Latinos and to address such matters as sexual orientation, sexual identification, and immigration status. The "**Who Participates?**" feature on the facing page shows a time line of groups that have fought for their rights throughout American history. As our nation becomes more and more diverse, equal protection of the laws will become more and more important. If we are to succeed and prosper as a nation, we must be inclusive. The tumultuous history of civil rights in America demonstrates that exclusion is a recipe for national calamity. It also demonstrates that struggles for civil rights often take a long time, beginning with political action by a small group of committed individuals and often ending with legislation and legal decisions from the highest court in the country. What civil rights battles now appear on the country's horizon? What can and should be done to remedy past wrongs that have current consequences, such as when past discrimination results in an economic underclass for a racial or ethnic minority? And, most fundamentally, how does a country based on the democratic principle of majority rule ensure that the civil rights of minorities are protected? In 2017 the Department of Justice declared that it was planning to investigate discrimination against whites. Some said it was high time for such an investigation, while others lamented what they saw as a step backward for the nation. Civil rights continue to be contested terrain in America.

Who Has Fought for Their Rights?

Time Line of Major Civil Rights Movements

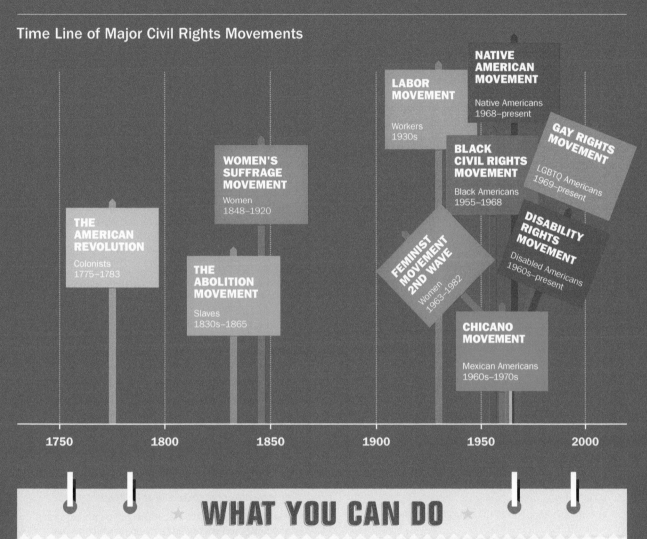

NATIVE AMERICAN MOVEMENT

Native Americans
1968–present

LABOR MOVEMENT

Workers
1930s

GAY RIGHTS MOVEMENT

LGBTQ Americans
1969–present

WOMEN'S SUFFRAGE MOVEMENT

Women
1848–1920

BLACK CIVIL RIGHTS MOVEMENT

Black Americans
1955–1968

DISABILITY RIGHTS MOVEMENT

Disabled Americans
1960s–present

THE AMERICAN REVOLUTION

Colonists
1775–1783

THE ABOLITION MOVEMENT

Slaves
1830s–1865

FEMINIST MOVEMENT 2ND WAVE

Women
1963–1982

CHICANO MOVEMENT

Mexican Americans
1960s–1970s

1750   1800   1850   1900   1950   2000

★ WHAT YOU CAN DO ★

Advocate Your Position on Civil Rights

☑ To learn more about your civil rights, explore the Civil Rights page of the U.S. Department of Health and Human Services at **www.hhs.gov/ocr**.

☑ Do you think the government should do more to protect civil rights in your community? Speak out about civil rights on social media. Post to your Facebook page or Tumblr, launch a hashtag campaign on Twitter, or start an online petition at **www.change.org**.

☑ Make a phone call to voice your opinion on civil rights. Call the White House (**202-456-1111**) or your members of Congress (**202-224-3121**). You can also contact the White House online (**www.whitehouse.gov/contact**) or email your members of Congress (**www.congress.gov/members**).

The Struggle for Civil Rights

Discrimination against individuals on the basis of their race and gender was tolerated and even enforced by government policy through much of American history. With the adoption of the Fourteenth Amendment in 1868, civil rights became a part of the Constitution. The political struggles of African Americans and women have narrowed the gap between Americans' belief in equality and the reality of life in the United States, but they have not eliminated it.

Key Terms

discrimination (p. 161)

civil rights (p. 161)

equal protection clause (p. 161)

Thirteenth Amendment (p. 163)

Fourteenth Amendment (p. 163)

Fifteenth Amendment (p. 163)

Jim Crow laws (p. 163)

"separate but equal" rule (p. 164)

Brown v. Board of Education (p. 167)

strict scrutiny (p. 167)

de jure (p. 168)

de facto (p. 168)

gerrymandering (p. 175)

redlining (p. 178)

Practice Quiz

1. When did civil rights first become part of the Constitution?
   a) in 1789 at the Founding
   b) with the adoption of the Fourteenth Amendment in 1868
   c) in 2008 when Barack Obama was elected president
   d) with the adoption of the Nineteenth Amendment in 1920
   e) in the 1954 *Brown v. Board of Education* decision

2. Which of the following could be described as a Jim Crow law?
   a) a law forcing blacks and whites to ride on separate trains
   b) a law criminalizing interracial marriage
   c) a law requiring blacks and whites to attend different schools
   d) a law segregating all public accommodations, such as hotels, restaurants, and theaters
   e) All of the above are examples of Jim Crow laws.

3. Which civil rights case established the "separate but equal" rule?
   a) *Plessy v. Ferguson*
   b) *Grutter v. Bollinger*
   c) *Brown v. Board of Education*
   d) *Regents of the University of California v. Bakke*
   e) *Adarand Constructors Inc. v. Peña*

4. Which of the following organizations established a legal defense fund to challenge segregation?
   a) the Association of American Trial Lawyers
   b) the National Association of Evangelicals
   c) the National Association for the Advancement of Colored People
   d) the Student Nonviolent Coordinating Committee
   e) the Southern Christian Leadership Council

5. *Massive resistance* refers to efforts by southern states during the late 1950s and early 1960s to
   a) build public housing for poor blacks.
   b) defy federal mandates to desegregate public schools.
   c) give women the right to have an abortion.
   d) bus black students to white schools.
   e) stage large-scale protests against Jim Crow laws.

6. Which of the following outlawed discrimination by employers in hiring, promoting, and laying off their employees and state governments illegal?
   a) the Fourteenth Amendment
   b) the Fifteenth Amendment
   c) *Brown v. Board of Education*
   d) the 1964 Civil Rights Act
   e) *Regents of the University of California v. Bakke*

7. The Voting Rights Act of 1965 significantly extended and protected voting rights by doing which of the following?
   a) barring literacy tests as a condition for voting in six southern states
   b) requiring all voters to register two weeks before any federal election
   c) eliminating all federal-level registration requirements
   d) allowing voters to sue election officials for monetary damages in civil court
   e) requiring that all voters show a valid government-issued photo ID

Extending Civil Rights

Describe how different groups have fought for and won protection of their civil rights (pp. 179–94)

In the 1970s the civil rights model created by African Americans began to spread beyond racial and ethnic groups to include groups defined by sex, religion, national origin, age, disabilities, and sexual orientation. For many of these groups, government policies played an important role in giving rise to movements that demanded equal treatment.

Key Term

intermediate scrutiny (p. 180)

Practice Quiz

8. The judicial test that places the burden of proof on government to show that a race-based policy serves a "compelling interest," is "narrowly tailored," and uses the "least restrictive means" for achieving its compelling interest is called
   a) strict scrutiny.
   b) intermediate scrutiny.
   c) limited scrutiny.
   d) de facto segregation.
   e) de jure segregation.

9. Which of the following declared that "equality of rights under the law shall not be denied or abridged by the United States or by any State on account of sex"?
   a) the Lily Ledbetter Fair Pay Act
   b) Title IV of the 1964 Civil Rights Act
   c) the DREAM Act
   d) the Equal Rights Amendment
   e) *Obergefell v. Hodges*

10. The Supreme Court's decision in *Mendez v. Westminster* was significant because it
    a) served as a precursor for *Brown v. Board of Education* by ruling that the segregation of Anglos and Mexican Americans into separate schools was unconstitutional.
    b) determined that anyone born in the United States was entitled to full citizenship.
    c) allowed school districts to achieve racial integration through busing.
    d) held that public accommodations could be segregated by race but still be equal.
    e) eliminated state power to use race as a criterion for discrimination in law.

11. In *United States v. Wong Kim Ark,* the Supreme Court ruled that
    a) school districts must provide bilingual education for students whose English is limited.
    b) the internment of Japanese Americans during World War II was constitutional on the grounds of military necessity.
    c) the 1882 Chinese Exclusion Act was an unconstitutional form of racial discrimination.
    d) anyone born in the United States was entitled to full citizenship.
    e) Chinese immigrants were ineligible for citizenship in the United States.

12. Which two Supreme Court decisions reached opposite conclusions about the constitutionality of state laws criminalizing intimate sexual conduct between consenting partners of the same sex?
    a) *Bowers v. Hardwick* and *Lawrence v. Texas*
    b) *Lau v. Nichols* and *Korematsu v. United States*
    c) *Romer v. Evans* and *Obergefell v. Hodges*
    d) *Grutter v. Bollinger* and *Gratz v. Bollinger*
    e) *Lawrence v. Texas* and *Texas v. Johnson*

Affirmative Action

Contrast arguments for and against affirmative action (pp. 195–97)

Affirmative action policies take race or some other status into account in order to provide greater educational and employment opportunities to groups that have been discriminated against. The Supreme Court has ruled that the government must show evidence that affirmative action programs serve a compelling government interest and are narrowly tailored to address identifiable past discrimination in order to be ruled constitutional. In recent years, challenges to affirmative action have also emerged at the state and local levels.

Key Term

affirmative action (p. 195)

13. In *Regents of the University of California v. Bakke*, the Supreme Court ruled that
    a) race can never be used as a factor in university admissions, even to promote diversity.
    b) achieving "a diverse student body" was a "compelling public purpose," and the method of a rigid quota of student slots assigned on the basis of race was consistent with the Fourteenth Amendment's equal protection clause.
    c) achieving "a diverse student body" was a "compelling public purpose," but the method of a rigid quota of student slots assigned on the basis of race was incompatible with the Fourteenth Amendment's equal protection clause.
    d) achieving "a diverse student body" was a "compelling public purpose," but affirmative action policies can only be used to give preferences to African Americans.
    e) achieving "a diverse student body" was a "compelling public purpose," but affirmative action policies can only be used to give preferences to Asian Americans.

14. In which case did the Supreme Court rule that that the burden of proof is on the government to show that race-based policies, such as preferences given by the government to minority contractors, serve a compelling government interest and address identifiable past discrimination?
    a) *Wards Cove Packing Co., Inc. v. Atonio*
    b) *St. Mary's Honor Center v. Hicks*
    c) *Adarand Constructors v. Peña*
    d) *Gratz v. Bollinger*
    e) *Fisher v. University of Texas*

For Further Reading

Ackerman, Bruce. *We the People*. Vol. 3, *The Civil Rights Revolution*. Cambridge, MA: Harvard University Press, 2014.

Ancheta, Angelo. *Race, Rights and the Asian American Experience*. New Brunswick, NJ: Rutgers University Press, 2006.

Chen, Anthony S. *The Fifth Freedom: Jobs, Politics, and Civil Rights in the United States, 1941–1972*. Princeton, NJ: Princeton University Press, 2009.

Chermerinsky, Erwin. *Closing the Courthouse Door: How Your Constitutional Rights Became Unenforceable*. New Haven, CT: Yale University Press, 2017.

Davis, Lennard J. *Enabling Acts: The Hidden Story of How the Americans with Disabilities Act Gave the Largest US Minority Its Rights*. Boston: Beacon Press, 2015.

Faderman, Lillian. *The Gay Revolution: The Story of the Struggle*. New York: Simon & Schuster, 2015.

Garrow, David J. *Bearing the Cross: Martin Luther King, Jr., and the Southern Christian Leadership Conference: A Personal Portrait*. New York: Morrow, 1986.

Gonzales, Roberto. *Lives in Limbo: Undocumented and Coming of Age in America*. Los Angeles: University of California Press, 2015.

Greenberg, Jack. *Crusaders in the Courts: How a Dedicated Band of Lawyers Fought for the Civil Rights Revolution*. New York: Basic Books, 1994.

Katznelson, Ira. *When Affirmative Action Was White: The Untold Story of Racial Inequality in Twentieth-Century America*. New York: W. W. Norton, 2006.

Lee, Sonia Song-Ha. *Building a Latino Civil Rights Movement*. Chapel Hill: University of North Carolina Press, 2014.

Nichols, Walter J. *The DREAMers: How the Undocumented Youth Movement Transformed the Immigrant Rights Debate*. Stanford, CA: Stanford University Press, 2013.

Rosenberg, Gerald N. *The Hollow Hope: Can Courts Bring about Social Change?* Chicago: University of Chicago Press, 2008.

Stone, Geoffrey. *Sex and the Constitution: Sex, Religion and Law From America's Origins to the Twenty-First Century*. New York: Liveright, 2017.

Taylor, Jami Kathleen, and Donald P. Halder-Markel, eds. *Transgender Rights and Politics*. Ann Arbor: University of Michigan Press, 2015.

Waldman, Michael. *The Fight to Vote*. New York: Simon & Schuster, 2016.

Recommended Websites

ADA Home Page
www.ada.gov

The Americans with Disabilities Act (ADA), enacted in 1990, guarantees equal employment rights and access to public businesses for the physically disabled. The U.S. Department of Justice maintains this website, which offers general information on ADA standards, changes in regulation, and policy enforcement.

Equal Employment Opportunity Commission
www.eeoc.gov

This website provides information on the federal agency and current employment laws. At this site you can even find out how someone might file a harassment or discrimination charge against an employer.

Equality Now
www.equalitynow.org

This is an organization dedicated to ending gender discrimination around the world. Read about how this group is fighting for the rights of women in Africa or campaigning against female genital mutilation and sex trafficking.

Federal Bureau of Investigation
www.fbi.gov/hq/cid/civilrights/hate.htm

Civil rights violations fall under the jurisdiction of the Federal Bureau of Investigation (FBI). Find out what steps the FBI is taking to combat the problem of hate crimes, and view some comprehensive statistical data.

Feminist Majority Foundation
www.feminist.org

This organization seeks to promote the legal, social, and political equality of women. They develop public policy, participate in grassroots organizing, and train leaders to promote their cause.

Gay and Lesbian Alliance against Defamation
www.glaad.org

Human Rights Campaign
www.hrc.org

These two prominent interest groups are dedicated to equal rights for lesbians and gay men and ending gender discrimination.

League of United Latin American Citizens
www.lulac.org

The League of United Latin American Citizens has worked to stem discrimination against Mexican Americans since World War II and is now the largest and oldest Latino organization in the United States.

See what this group is doing to guarantee racial equality based on the Fourteenth Amendment's equal protection clause.

The Martin Luther King, Jr., Research and Education Institute
http://mlk-kpp01.stanford.edu

Dr. Martin Luther King, Jr., was a key leader in the fight for civil rights and desegregation. At this website you can find Dr. King's important speeches and papers, as well as other information about social injustice.

Mexican American Legal Defense and Education Fund
www.maldef.org

The Mexican American Legal Defense and Education Fund (MALDEF) is the leading nonprofit Latino litigation, advocacy, and educational outreach institution in the United States. At this site, you will learn about litigation and other activities that MALDEF has initiated related to the rights of Latinos and of immigrants more generally.

NAACP
www.naacp.org

The NAACP is one of the oldest and largest civil rights organizations that is dedicated to equal rights and putting an end to racial discrimination. This group was particularly influential in the landmark case *Brown v. Board of Education*, which led to the desegregation of public schools.

National Organization for Women
www.now.org

This leading women's rights group continues to fight for gender equality and equal rights.

U.S. Commission on Civil Rights
www.usccr.gov

The U.S. Commission on Civil Rights was created by Congress in the late 1950s and continues to investigate complaints of discrimination in American society.

U.S. Supreme Court Media
www.oyez.org

This website has a good search engine for finding information on such landmark civil rights cases as *Plessy v. Ferguson, Brown v. Board of Education, Lawrence v. Texas,* and *United States v. Wong Kim Ark,* to name only a few.

Public Opinion

WHAT GOVERNMENT DOES AND WHY IT MATTERS Americans can have quite different opinions on important issues, even citizens who have had similarly vivid, harrowing experiences. In 1991, Suzanna Hupp was eating lunch in a Texas restaurant when a man drove his truck through the window and began shooting people. Hupp had often carried a handgun in her purse, but had recently taken it out because Texas did not allow concealed carry at the time, and she was afraid she would lose her license as a chiropractor if caught. "Could I have hit the guy? He was fifteen feet from me. . . . Could I have missed? Yeah, it's possible. But the one thing

nobody can argue with is that it would have changed the odds." The gunman killed 23 people, including her parents. She has become a strong proponent of gun rights since then. "One of my bugaboos is gun laws. Anytime we list a place where you can't carry guns, to me, that's like a shopping list for a madman. . . . If you think about nearly every one of these mass shootings, they have occurred at places where guns weren't allowed. That's frustrating to me, particularly when you talk about schools. Where do these madmen go? They go to schools and slaughter people."[1]

Fifteen-year-old Justin Gruber also survived a terrible shooting incident, in a school: the shooting

Suzanna Hupp (left) and Justin Gruber (right) were both present during episodes of gun violence. These events pushed Hupp to advocate for more gun rights, and Gruber to speak out for more restrictive gun laws. How do political opinions form? And how do government officials respond to shifts in public opinion?

at the Marjory Stoneman Douglas High School in Parkland, Florida, in February 2018. The incident left 17 students and teachers dead. But Gruber and many of his schoolmates reached the opposite view of Suzanna Hupp, arguing for greater gun control such as assault weapon bans and increased age limits for purchase. Objecting to one suggestion raised after the shooting, Gruber said that arming teachers is a "terrible idea." "Adding guns to solve a gun problem will increase the possible negative outcomes," he said. "Teachers shouldn't have to be trained to carry weapons. They are supposed to mold the minds of the next generation."[2] Some students formed a group, Never Again MSD, known by the hashtag #NeverAgain, to advocate for tighter gun control.

After mass shootings, support for stronger gun control measures tends to increase among the general public. The percentage of Americans telling the Gallup Organization that they wanted stricter laws covering the sale of firearms increased 5 points after the October 2017 mass shooting in Las Vegas and 7 more points after the Parkland shooting five months later, to 67 percent overall.[3] At the same time, gun sales typically increase after mass shootings as gun supporters fear tighter controls (although this pattern is more muted under Trump than it was under Obama).[4] Soon after, however, public outcry tends to fade—after the 2012 Sandy Hook Elementry School shooting in Connecticut, support for more gun control spiked then subsided—and elected politicians seem to take no action. In these cases, are politicians following public opinion or are they ignoring it?

The "consent of the governed," which is demanded in the Declaration of Independence, is critical for the functioning of a democracy. We expect government to pay attention to the people. But whose opinion gets represented in public policy, particularly on issues, such as gun rights and gun control, where there are strong divides among the public? What is the role of public opinion compared to that of other political actors, such as organized interests? How well informed are people, and by what channels can individuals have their voices heard? As we will see in this chapter, research shows that public opinion does indeed have a significant impact on public policy. But there are debates among scholars about whether the public is sufficiently informed about politics, as well as whether elected officials represent the interests of all Americans or only some Americans.

CHAPTER GOALS

★ **Define public opinion, and identify broad types of values and beliefs Americans have about politics (pp. 207–15)**

★ **Explain the major factors that shape specific individual opinions (pp. 216–25)**

★ **Explore when and why public opinion changes and what role political knowledge plays (pp. 225–32)**

★ **Describe the major forces that shape public opinion (pp. 232–34)**

★ **Analyze how public opinion shapes government policy and influences elected officials (pp. 234–37)**

★ **Describe basic survey methods and other techniques researchers use to measure public opinion (pp. 237–47)**

Defining Public Opinion

Define public opinion, and identify broad types of values and beliefs Americans have about politics

The term **public opinion** refers to the attitudes that people have about policy issues, events, elected officials, and politics. It is useful to distinguish between values and beliefs, on the one hand, and attitudes and opinions, on the other. **Values (or beliefs)** constitute a person's basic orientation to politics and include guiding principles. Values are not limited to the political arena, but they include deep-rooted morals, ethics, aspirations, and ideals that shape an individual's perceptions of society, government, and the economy. Liberty (i.e. freedom), democracy, and equality of opportunity, for example, are basic political values held by most Americans.

Another useful term for understanding public opinion is *ideology*. **Political ideology** refers to a set of beliefs and values that, as a whole, form a general philosophy about government. For example, many Americans believe that governmental solutions to problems are inherently inferior to solutions offered by the private sector and free markets. Such a philosophy about government may predispose individuals to form negative views of specific government programs, even before they know much about the policy.

An **attitude (or opinion)** is a view about a particular issue, person, or event. An individual may have an attitude toward American policy in the Middle East or an opinion about economic inequality in America. The attitude may have emerged from a broad belief about military intervention or about the role of government in the economy, but the opinion itself is very specific. Some attitudes may be short-lived and can change based on changing circumstances or new information; others may change over a few years and still others may not change over a lifetime.

To measure public opinion on an issue, one must study the individual opinions of thousands or millions of people aggregated together; it is a way to gauge what Americans think about politics and policy. When we think of public opinion, we often think in terms of differences of opinion. The media are fond of reporting political differences between Republicans and Democrats, blacks and whites, women and men, the young and the old, and so on. Certainly, Americans differ on many issues, and often these differences are associated with partisanship, economic status, or social and demographic characteristics such as race and ethnicity, gender, income, education, age, religion, and region. For example, individuals whose incomes differ substantially have varying views on many important economic and social programs, including government health care. In general, the poor, who are the chief beneficiaries of these programs, support them more strongly than do those who are wealthier and pay more of the taxes that fund the programs.

Political attitudes are increasingly influenced by partisanship (Republicans versus Democrats) and ideology (conservatives versus liberals). For example, shortly after taking office in January 2017 President Trump signed a controversial executive order immediately halting the U.S. refugee program and banning immigration to the United States from a half dozen predominantly Muslim countries, including Syria. In 2018 the Supreme Court upheld the travel ban as constitutional, despite legal challenges. Opinion polls show that while 63 percent of Republicans say refugees from the Middle East are a threat, only 30 percent of Democrats say the same.[5]

public opinion citizens' attitudes about political issues, leaders, institutions, and events

values (or beliefs) basic principles that shape a person's opinions about political issues and events

political ideology a cohesive set of beliefs that forms a general philosophy about the role of government

attitude (or opinion) a specific preference on a particular issue

Traditionally, there was an assumption that political attitudes were rooted in rational factors, such as self-interest. Now political scientists understand that opinions about issues and politics have emotional underpinnings as well.[6] Emotional responses to candidates, events, or policies run the gamut from strongly positive to strongly negative. These emotions are usually measured by survey questions asking if a candidate (or another individual, event, or issue) makes the respondent feel angry, fearful, anxious, or enthusiastic. Donald Trump's 2016 presidential campaign, for example, benefited from high enthusiasm from his supporters. Similarly high positive emotions may have given Barack Obama an advantage as the first African American president in 2008, overcoming racial resentment among some citizens.[7] Contrary to the idea that public opinion is purely rational, feelings are complicated and often irrational; once individuals become emotionally attached to particular beliefs, they tend to hold on to them even in the face of contradictory information. Using emotions as a guide, individuals form opinions quickly in response to current events. An important study called this "affective [meaning emotional] intelligence."[8]

Research has shown that individuals usually monitor political news by responding to familiar political figures or issues in a habitual and unthinking manner. However, when we encounter a new political actor, event, or issue, we tend to form a new evaluation. Anxiety triggered by a change in the political environment, such as a foreign enemy (e.g., Russia, North Korea, or ISIS) or an opposing party's candidate can trigger increased interest, attention, and information seeking, which in some cases prompts a change of opinion. These findings suggest that even individuals with strong opinions might abandon their political habits if they have feelings of anxiety and feel threatened.

For example, the mass shooting at Marjory Stoneman Douglas High School in Parkland, Florida, described in the beginning of this chapter, caused strong emotional responses, including fear and outrage among students and parents, and reopened a national debate about gun regulation. One month after the shooting, on March 14, 2018, thousands of students and teachers walked out of school to protest the government's lack of response to gun violence in the United States. In response

Dramatic events, and the emotions they stir, can alter public opinion. In the aftermath of the violence erupting at a 2017 white nationalist rally in Charlottesville, Virginia, seemingly everyone had an opinion on the state of race relations in America.

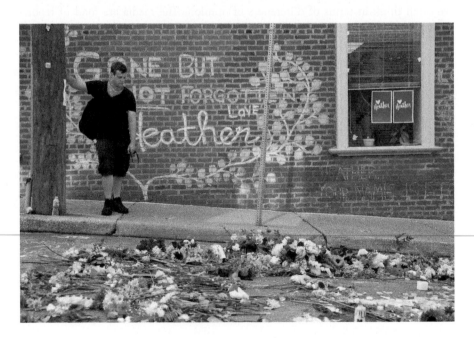

to the shooting and reactions to it, the Republican-controlled Florida state legislature passed a law raising the minimum age to purchase a gun from 18 to 21, despite opposition from the National Rifle Association. Alternatively, President Trump has suggested arming some teachers with handguns. Though most U.S. adults (55 percent) would oppose allowing teachers to carry guns in K–12 schools, a sizable minority (45 percent) said they favored such a measure. Among Republicans, the number was even larger, with about 7 in 10 Republicans and independents who lean Republican (69 percent) in support of this proposal.[9]

Emotions play a major role in public opinion about gun ownership and school violence; anxiety triggered by an event such as a mass shooting often leads to increased interest and attention around an issue, as well as motivation to fight for change in government policy.

POLITICAL VALUES

Despite their differences, most Americans share a common set of values, including a belief in the principles, if not always the actual practice, of liberty, equality, and democracy. The United States was founded on the principle of individual **liberty**, or freedom. Americans have always voiced strong support for the idea of liberty and typically support the notion that governmental interference with individuals' lives and property should be kept to a minimum. Liberty is, after all, tied inextricably to the birth of our nation—Puritans fled to America to escape persecution in England for their religious beliefs—and it remains as important in contemporary politics as it was during the Founding era when the colonists fought for their freedom from Britain during the Revolutionary War. Americans have stronger views about the importance of liberty and freedom of expression than do citizens in other democratic countries. One example is the growing concern with civil liberties related to privacy and security of personal information online. Three in four Americans don't see a need to sacrifice liberty (privacy and freedom) to be safe from terrorism.[10] Support for freedom of speech, a free internet, and a free press is higher in the United States than in most other countries in the world: 71 percent of Americans believe it is very important that "people can say what they want without state or government censorship," compared to a global average of 56 percent.[11] These data underscore the fact that government surveillance is of increasing concern to most Americans and that the value of liberty matters.

liberty freedom from governmental control

Similarly, **equality of opportunity** has always been an important theme in American society. Most Americans believe that all individuals should be allowed to seek personal and economic success. Moreover, most people generally believe that such success should be the result of individual effort and ability, rather than family connections or other forms of special privilege. Quality public education is one of the most important mechanisms for obtaining equality of opportunity in that it allows individuals, regardless of personal or family wealth, a chance to get ahead. Education is one of the most important pathways to a high paying job, but rising tuition limits access to a college degree for many people. Student loan debt has skyrocketed in the United States; Americans owed more than $1.3 trillion in loans in 2017.[12] Today 17 states offer free college for eligible students, reflecting the principle of equality of opportunity.

equality of opportunity a widely shared American ideal that all people should have the freedom to use whatever talents and wealth they have to reach their fullest potential

Most Americans also believe in democracy and the rule of law. They believe that every citizen should have the opportunity to take part in the nation's governmental and policy-making processes and to have some say in determining how they are

FIGURE 6.1

Americans Agree on Many Core Democratic Values

SOURCE: Pew Research Center, "Broad Public Agreement on Importance of Many Aspects of a Strong Democracy," March 2, 2017, www.people-press.org (accessed 1/23/18).

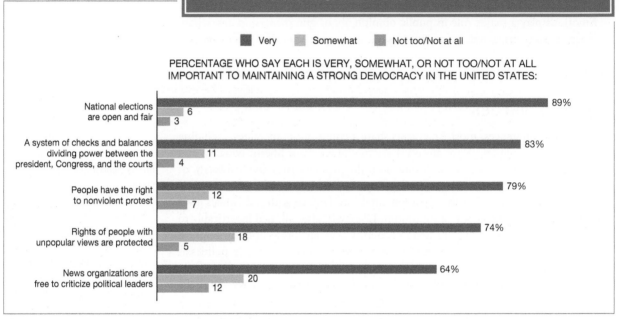

■ Very   ■ Somewhat   ■ Not too/Not at all

PERCENTAGE WHO SAY EACH IS VERY, SOMEWHAT, OR NOT TOO/NOT AT ALL IMPORTANT TO MAINTAINING A STRONG DEMOCRACY IN THE UNITED STATES:

National elections are open and fair — 89% / 6 / 3

A system of checks and balances dividing power between the president, Congress, and the courts — 83% / 11 / 4

People have the right to nonviolent protest — 79% / 12 / 7

Rights of people with unpopular views are protected — 74% / 18 / 5

News organizations are free to criticize political leaders — 64% / 20 / 12

governed, including the right to vote in elections.[13] (See Chapter 8 for a discussion of rules affecting voting in elections.) Figure 6.1 shows there is consensus among Americans on fundamental values: for instance, nearly 90 percent of Americans believe free and fair elections are essential to U.S. democracy, while 83 percent say checks and balances with power divided between the president, Congress, and the courts is also very important for democracy. Eighty percent believe people should be able to make statements that criticize the government, including nonviolent protest, and 74 percent believe democracy requires protecting the rights of people with unpopular views. But there are emerging partisan divisions, even over core values. For example, Republicans and Democrats differ significantly on the importance of the freedom of the press. Roughly half (49 percent) of Republicans say a free press is very important to maintaining a strong democracy, compared to 76 percent of Democrats.[14]

Threats to Political Values and the Rule of Law Nearly 90 percent of Americans believe a strong democracy in America depends on open and fair elections. In 2016, America's free and fair elections were threatened by Russia's leader Vladimir Putin, who orchestrated cyberattacks intended to sway the 2016 presidential election to favor Donald Trump and undermine his opponent, Hillary Clinton. The Central Intelligence Agency and the FBI confirmed the Russians hacked the Democratic National Committee (DNC) and the campaign of Hillary Clinton, releasing large amounts of data in an effort to undermine her campaign. The hacks produced a stream of leaked emails resulting in negative news about Clinton's campaign in the run-up to the election. In June 2017 the Department of Homeland Security confirmed that the computerized election systems of 21 states had been hacked by the Russians, although they could not confirm vote tallies had been changed. The National Security Administration (NSA) found Russian intelligence agents tried to hack the U.S. company that maintains and verifies voter rolls in multiple states. In Illinois, for example, Russian actors stole driver's license and social security numbers from 90,000 voter records.

In response to these events, most Americans believe Russia interfered with the 2016 U.S. presidential election. Eighty-eight percent of U.S. adults had heard about allegations that Russia was involved in hacking the Democratic National Committee and Hillary Clinton's campaign, and roughly 3 in 4 Americans believe Russia was definitely or probably behind the cyberattacks, according to a Pew survey. Today 73 percent of Americans see Russia as a serious problem or an adversary, more than any other foreign nation.[15] Historically Republicans have been more concerned with Russia than Democrats. But 39 percent of Democrats name Russia as the country representing the greatest danger to the United States, ahead of North Korea, countries in the Middle East, or China. Pew reports this is the highest percentage naming Russia in nearly three decades. In contrast, only 21 percent of Republicans say Russia represents the greatest threat to the United States.[16]

FOR CRITICAL ANALYSIS

The news often focuses on issues on which public opinion is sharply divided, but in fact there are many issues on which Americans largely agree. What other issues do you think have strong consensus among Americans?

Obviously, the political values that Americans espouse have not always been put into practice. For 200 years, Americans embraced the principles of equality of opportunity and individual liberty while denying them in practice to generations of African Americans. Ultimately, proponents of slavery and, later, of segregation were defeated in the arena of public opinion because their practices differed so sharply from the fundamental principles accepted by most Americans.

Yet even when there is broad agreement over principles, practical *interpretations* of principles can differ. For example, in contemporary politics Americans' fundamental commitment to equality of opportunity has led to divisions over affirmative action programs, with both proponents and opponents citing their belief in equality of opportunity as the justification for their position (see Figure 6.2). Proponents of these programs see them as necessary to ensure equality of opportunity, whereas opponents believe that affirmative action is a form of preferential treatment that violates basic American values (see Chapter 5).[17] We form our individual preferences and interpretation of values through interaction with family members, friends, teachers, coaches, mentors, and others in our social groups and networks in a process called *socialization*. This process of socialization is discussed in more detail later, under family and social networks.

POLITICAL IDEOLOGY

Americans share many fundamental political values, but the application of these values to specific policies varies. The set of underlying ideas and beliefs through which we come to understand and interpret politics is called a *political ideology*.

In the United States the definitions of the two most common political ideologies—liberalism and conservatism—have changed over time. To some extent, contemporary

FIGURE 6.2

Americans' Support for Fundamental Values

Americans support equality of opportunity, liberty, and democracy in principle; but do they always support these values in practice? What limits, if any, do you think Americans favor when it comes to equality, liberty, and democracy?

SOURCES: Pew Research Center for the People and the Press Values Survey, www.pewresearch.com (accessed 2/5/14); Jacob Poushter and Dionna Givens, "Where the World Sees Limits to Free Speech," Pew Research Center, November 18, 2015, www.pewresearch.com (accessed 11/18/15); First Amendment Center, www.firstamendmentcenter.org (accessed 11/18/15).

Equality of opportunity

86% completely or mostly agree

Our society should do what is necessary to make sure that everyone has an equal opportunity to succeed. Do you completely agree, mostly agree, mostly disagree, or completely disagree?

Liberty

95% agree

People should be able to make statements that criticize the government's policies.

Democracy

69% agree

Any group should be allowed to hold a rally for a cause.

liberalism and conservatism can be seen as differences in emphasis with regard to the fundamental American political values of liberty and equality. For liberals, equality is the most important of the core values. Liberals encourage government action in such areas as the economy and progressive taxation, health care and workers' rights, financial aid for college, environmental protection, and business practices to enhance race, class, and gender equality of opportunity. For conservatives, on the other hand, liberty is the core value. Conservatives oppose many efforts of the government, however well intentioned, to interfere in private life and free markets, including government regulations.

Liberalism In classical political theory, a liberal was someone who favored individual initiative and was suspicious of the motives of government and of its ability to manage economic and social affairs—a definition akin to that of today's libertarian. The proponents of a larger and more active government called themselves progressives. In the early twentieth century, many liberals and progressives coalesced around the doctrine of "social liberalism," which held that government action (laws and policy) might be needed to preserve individual liberty. Today's liberals are social liberals rather than classical liberals.

In contemporary politics being a **liberal** has come to mean supporting government policies to create a fairer economic system and opportunity for upward mobility, including raising taxes on the wealthy; the expansion of federal social services and health care; government spending on roads, infrastructure, science, technology, and alternative energy; more vigorous efforts on behalf of the poor and minorities; and greater concern for protecting the environment. For example, Senator Elizabeth Warren (D-Mass.) is a leading liberal politician. Warren is an

liberal today this term refers to those who generally support social and political reform, governmental intervention in the economy, more economic equality, expansion of federal social services, and greater concern for consumers and the environment

Profile of a Liberal: Senator Elizabeth Warren

★ Supports stricter environmental protections

★ Favors expanded health coverage for all Americans

★ Advocates increased funding for education

★ Supports same-sex marriage

★ Supports abortion rights and birth control

★ Supports an increase in the minimum wage

★ Supports more equitable tax policy that benefits middle-class Americans and imposes higher taxes on corporations

active consumer protection advocate whose work led to the establishment of the U.S. Consumer Financial Protection Bureau, which protects individuals from bankruptcy and banks selling high-interest loans. Liberals generally support reproductive rights for women, rights for gays and lesbians, and are concerned with protecting the rights of people accused of crimes, refugees, and immigrants. In international affairs, liberals often support foreign aid to poor nations, arms control, and international organizations that promote peace such as the United Nations and the European Union. Many liberals are opposed to military wars, but under President Obama some liberals tolerated military interventions in other countries. Liberals are also divided on issues of international trade, with some liberals seeking to support local businesses and locally sourced products.

Conservatism By contrast, **conservatives** believe strongly that a large government poses a threat to the freedom of individual citizens and to free markets and democracy. Ironically, today's conservatives support the views of classical liberalism. Today, conservatives generally oppose the expansion of governmental activity, asserting that solutions to many social and economic problems can and should be developed in the private sector, local communities, or by religious organizations. Conservatives support cutting taxes and reducing government spending. Conservatives generally oppose efforts to impose government regulation on business, maintaining that regulation frequently leads to economic inefficiency, is costly, and can lower the entire nation's standard of living by making U.S. manufactured products more expensive and less competitive. Former Speaker of the House Paul Ryan (R-Wisc.) is a leading conservative politician who is known to support cutting taxes and reducing regulations on businesses, among other conservative positions. In terms of social policy, many conservatives support traditional family values and generally oppose

conservative today this term refers to those who generally support the social and economic status quo and are suspicious of efforts to introduce new political formulas and economic arrangements; conservatives believe that a large and powerful government poses a threat to citizens' freedom

Profile of a Conservative: Former House Speaker Paul Ryan

★ Wants to trim the size of the federal government

★ Wants to reduce government regulation of business

★ Supports capital punishment for certain crimes

★ Opposes restrictions on the right to bear arms

★ Supports using traditional energy sources and opposes climate change action that reduces manufacturing jobs

★ Opposes many affirmative action programs

★ Favors tax cuts

abortion and same-sex marriage. They often oppose environmental protections that interfere with private business. Many conservatives prefer stricter criminal justice laws, oppose drug legalization, and seek to reduce immigration to the United States. Conservatives today are deeply divided on issues such as immigration, international trade, and the fairness of the U.S. economic system. In international affairs, conservatism has come to mean support for military intervention and the maintenance of American military power. There is a split among conservatives in terms of immigration, with pro-business conservatives often accepting immigration and social conservatives strongly opposing immigration to the United States.

Libertarianism Other political ideologies also influence American politics. **Libertarians**, for example, argue that government interferes with freedom of expression, free markets, and society, and thus should be limited to as few spheres of activity as possible (public education being a notable exception for many libertarians). In 2016, Republican Senator and libertarian Rand Paul ran for president based on his opposition to foreign wars and his commitment to civil liberties and smaller government.

Socialism and the Green Party While libertarians believe in less government intervention in economic and social realms, **socialists** argue that more government is necessary to promote justice and to reduce economic and social inequality. In 2016, Democratic presidential candidate Bernie Sanders called himself a "democratic socialist," gaining widespread support from Democrats, especially millennials. Like the Social Democratic parties in Europe, Sanders supports free markets and private enterprise but wants government to ensure more equality of opportunity for citizens such as free public college, single payer health care, and increased taxation on the very affluent. He also supports government policies to protect workers' rights and unions. Socialists are more to the ideological left than the

libertarian someone who emphasizes freedom and believes in voluntary association with small government

socialist someone who generally believes in social ownership, strong government, free markets, and reducing economic inequality mainstream Democratic Party although they share many policy issues. MoveOn.org, a massive online organization with millions of members, advocates a policy agenda consistent with social democrats, as does 2016 Green Party candidate Jill Stein and 2020 presidential candidate Tom Steyer.

Americans' Ideologies Today Although many Americans subscribe to libertarianism, socialism, or other ideologies in part, most describe themselves as either liberals, conservatives, or moderates. Figure 6.3 shows that the percentage of Americans who consider themselves moderates, liberals, or conservatives has remained relatively constant for the past 15 years. Gallup surveys indicate that as of 2017, 35 percent of Americans considered themselves conservatives, 35 percent moderates, and 26 percent liberals. But among young people aged 18-33, trends are different: just 15 percent identify as conservative, while 41 percent identify as liberals and 44 percent as moderates (and independent from the political parties).[18]

Within each ideological group, individual beliefs often vary. Many conservatives support at least some government social programs. Republican president George W. Bush called himself a "compassionate conservative," to indicate that he favored programs that assist the poor and needy. In contrast, staunch conservatives hold much more critical views of government's role in the economy and society. Many joined the rising Tea Party movement in 2009 to protest President Obama's efforts to expand the role of the federal government, especially in health care.

And while President Obama supported health care reform and other social programs, he was criticized by those on the left for extending the tax policies of his Republican predecessor, George W. Bush, which benefited the affluent; for expanding U.S. military involvement overseas; and for deportations of undocumented immigrants. In short, some of Obama's domestic, economic, and foreign policies are associated with conservatives and some with liberals. The real political world is far too complex to be seen simply in terms of a struggle between liberals and conservatives.

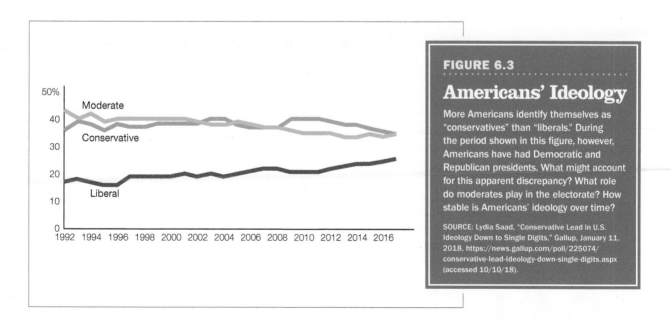

FIGURE 6.3

Americans' Ideology

More Americans identify themselves as "conservatives" than "liberals." During the period shown in this figure, however, Americans have had Democratic and Republican presidents. What might account for this apparent discrepancy? What role do moderates play in the electorate? How stable is Americans' ideology over time?

SOURCE: Lydia Saad, "Conservative Lead in U.S. Ideology Down to Single Digits," Gallup, January 11, 2018, https://news.gallup.com/poll/225074/conservative-lead-ideology-down-single-digits.aspx (accessed 10/10/18).

How We Form Political Opinions

As noted above, broad ideologies do not necessarily determine every political opinion a person holds. Though conservatives generally support small government, most also support some federal programs, such as the military, national parks, national security, and wish to see them—and hence the government—expanded. Some conservatives are not opposed to immigration and accept same-sex marriage. Though most liberals do not favor American military intervention abroad, many do favor military intervention for what they deem to be humanitarian purposes or to prevent terrorist attacks. How are political opinions like these formed?

POLITICAL SOCIALIZATION

political socialization the induction of individuals into the political culture; learning the underlying beliefs and values on which the political system is based

People's attitudes about political issues and elected officials tend to be shaped by their underlying political beliefs and values. For example, an individual who has negative feelings about government regulation of the economy would probably be predisposed to oppose the development of new health care programs. Similarly, someone who distrusts the military tends to be suspicious of the use of U.S. force for most foreign conflicts. The processes through which these underlying political beliefs and values are formed are collectively called **political socialization**.

agents of socialization social institutions, including families and schools, that help to shape individuals' basic political beliefs and values

Probably no nation, and certainly no democracy, could survive if its citizens did not share some fundamental beliefs. In contemporary America, the **agents of socialization** that foster differences in political opinions include the family and social networks, education, membership in social groups, religion, party affiliation, self-interest, and political environment. Other agents of socialization, such as public education, promote similarities.

Of course, no list of the agents of socialization can fully explain an individual's basic political beliefs. In addition to the factors that are important for everyone, experiences and influences that are unique to each individual play a role in shaping political orientation. An early encounter with an important mentor (for example, a teacher, coach, or religious leader), can have a lasting impact on an individual's views. A major political event, such as the terrorist attacks of September 11, 2001, or the 2016 presidential election, can leave an indelible mark on a person's political consciousness. And some deep-seated personality characteristic, such as paranoia or openness to new experiences, may strongly influence the formation of political beliefs. One recent experiment found that people who tend to be more fearful appear to support policies that protect the existing social structure from both external and internal threats.[19]

The family is one of the largest influences on a person's political views. Children raised in conservative or liberal families, usually, but not always, hold those same views later in life.

Some new research has found that political beliefs may have a genetic basis and thus be "hard-wired." Using data from a large sample of twins, scholars found that genes, in combination with environmental factors, may contribute to our ideology.[20] Individual backgrounds, experiences, and social factors also explain people's political attitudes. What follow are some of the most important agents of socialization that affect individuals' beliefs.

The Family and Social Networks Most people acquire their initial orientation to politics from their families. As might be expected, differences in family background tend to produce divergent political perspectives. Although relatively few parents spend significant time directly teaching their children about politics, political conversations occur in many households, and children tend to absorb the political views of parents and other caregivers, often without realizing it. Studies find, for example, that party preferences are initially acquired at home, even in households that don't explicitly talk about politics. Children raised in households in which both primary caregivers are Democrats or Republicans tend to become Democrats or Republicans respectively.[21] Of course, not all children absorb their parents' political views. Two of the late Republican president Ronald Reagan's three children, for instance, rejected their parents' conservative values and became active on behalf of Democratic candidates.

By sharing their personal stories with the #MeToo hashtag, woman and men were able to network and organize (online and offline) to draw attention to what they saw as pervasive sexual harassment in American life.

Nevertheless, family, friends, coworkers, and neighbors are an important source of political orientation for nearly everyone. Political scientist Betsy Sinclair argues that individuals are "social citizens" whose political opinions and behavior are significantly shaped by peer influence, including friends and family.[22] Sinclair shows that social networks can and do have the power to change an individual's opinion. When members of a social network express a particular political opinion or belief, Sinclair finds, others notice and conform, particularly if their conformity is likely to be highly visible. The conclusion is that basic political acts are surprisingly subject to social pressures.

Online social networks such as Facebook and Twitter may increase the role of peers in shaping public opinion. For example, the widely shared Facebook meme of an equal sign against a red background in 2013 communicated support for gay rights at the same time that the U.S. Supreme Court was deciding two controversial court cases affecting gay and lesbian marriage rights. This social media discussion was associated with upticks in public support for gay marriage nationally. Public opinion on this issue changed rapidly over a decade. In 2017, 62 percent of Americans believed marriages between same-sex couples should be recognized by law, an increase of over 20 percent from 2005 when only 36 percent of Americans felt this way.[23] Similarly, the #MeToo movement that emerged in 2017 to highlight and combat sexual harassment, used social media to organize online and offline.

Education After family, formal education can be an important source of differences in political perspectives. Governments use public education to try to teach all children a common set of civic values; it is mainly in school that Americans acquire their basic beliefs in liberty, equality, and democracy. In history classes, students are taught that the Founders fought for the principle of liberty (freedom). In the course of studying such topics as the Constitution, the Civil War, and the civil rights movement, students are taught the importance of equality. Research finds formal education is a strong predictor of tolerance for racial, ethnic, and religious minorities.[24]

At the same time, differences in formal education are strongly associated with differences in political opinions. In particular, those who attend college are often exposed to modes of thought that will distinguish them from their friends and neighbors who do not pursue college diplomas. Education is one of the most important factors in predicting who engages in behaviors that increase political knowledge, such as regularly following the news, voting, and participating in politics as well as higher earnings over a lifetime.[25]

SOCIAL GROUPS AND PUBLIC OPINION

The social groups to which individuals belong comprise another important source of political values. Social groups include those that individuals haven't chosen (national, religious, gender, and racial groups, for example) and those they join willingly (political parties, labor unions, the military, and environmental, educational, and occupational groups). Membership in a particular group can give individuals experiences and perspectives that shape their view of political and social life.

Race Race plays an important role in shaping political attitudes and opinions, among both minorities and whites. The experiences of blacks, whites, and Asian Americans, for example, can differ significantly. By 2045 the U.S. population is predicted to become majority minority, as the size of minority populations will outnumber white non-Hispanics, in large part due to youthful minorities.[26] Blacks are a minority and have been victims of persecution and discrimination throughout American history, while many Asians are relatively recent immigrants to the United States. Blacks and whites also have different occupational opportunities, often live in separate communities, and frequently attend separate schools. Such differences tend to produce distinctive political views. Many black Americans perceive other blacks as members of a group with a common identity and a shared political interest in overcoming persistent racial and economic inequality. Political scientists refer to this phenomenon as "linked fate": African Americans see their fate as linked to other members of the black community.[27] This linked fate acts as a sort of filter through which black Americans evaluate information and determine their own opinions and policy preferences.

That black and white Americans have different views is reflected in public perception of fair treatment across racial groups in the United States. Figure 6.4 shows that 84 percent of African Americans believe that blacks are treated less fairly than whites in dealing with the police, compared to 50 percent of whites. In a striking difference, 66 percent of blacks believe blacks are treated unfairly in applying for a loan or home mortgage compared to 25 percent of whites who share this perspective of racial discrimination, while 64 percent of blacks believe they are treated less fairly in the workplace compared to just 25 percent of whites. Blacks are over twenty percentage points more likely to believe blacks face racial discrimination in voting in elections compared to whites.[28]

Events and circumstances can cause opinions to change. In 2009, 80 percent of African Americans said blacks and other minorities do not get equal treatment under the law; the number of whites giving this response was just 40 percent.[29] In the past few years, however, widely publicized incidents of excessive use of police force against African Americans have begun to cause a shift in public opinion on this issue. The activist movement Black Lives Matter gained momentum in 2014 after the killing of Michael Brown, an unarmed, 18-year-old African American, by a white police officer in Ferguson, Missouri. Protests erupted across the nation when the officer, Daren Wilson, was not indicted. One month after that verdict, a white police officer in New York was not indicted despite video evidence that he had used a chokehold and other means of force on Eric Garner, an African American man, heard repeatedly saying that he could not breathe. By 2015, 90 percent of African Americans agreed that blacks and whites are not treated equally by police, and 54 percent of whites felt the same way (see Figure 6.4), showing that while there is still a racial divide on this issue, opinions on it have changed

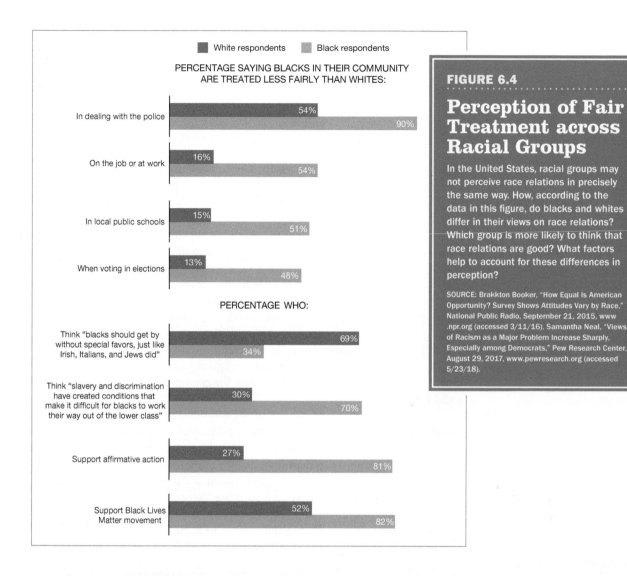

White respondents   Black respondents

PERCENTAGE SAYING BLACKS IN THEIR COMMUNITY ARE TREATED LESS FAIRLY THAN WHITES:

In dealing with the police
- 54%
- 90%

On the job or at work
- 16%
- 54%

In local public schools
- 15%
- 51%

When voting in elections
- 13%
- 48%

PERCENTAGE WHO:

Think "blacks should get by without special favors, just like Irish, Italians, and Jews did"
- 69%
- 34%

Think "slavery and discrimination have created conditions that make it difficult for blacks to work their way out of the lower class"
- 30%
- 70%

Support affirmative action
- 27%
- 81%

Support Black Lives Matter movement
- 52%
- 82%

FIGURE 6.4

Perception of Fair Treatment across Racial Groups

In the United States, racial groups may not perceive race relations in precisely the same way. How, according to the data in this figure, do blacks and whites differ in their views on race relations? Which group is more likely to think that race relations are good? What factors help to account for these differences in perception?

SOURCE: Brakkton Booker, "How Equal Is American Opportunity? Survey Shows Attitudes Vary by Race," National Public Radio, September 21, 2015, www.npr.org (accessed 3/11/16). Samantha Neal, "Views of Racism as a Major Problem Increase Sharply, Especially among Democrats," Pew Research Center, August 29, 2017, www.pewresearch.org (accessed 5/23/18).

significantly over the past few years.[30] Strikingly, half of all Americans now agree that racism is a big problem, compared to only 26 percent in 2009.[31]

Ethnicity Ethnicity also affects policy attitudes. Latinos are the fastest-growing minority population in the United States. While most Latinos are white in race, their shared Hispanic ethnicity contributes to a group consciousness that shapes opinions. The U.S. Latino population, which makes up 17 percent of the total population and 12 percent of the electorate, is diverse, comprising individuals of Central American, South American, and Caribbean descent, and thus their backgrounds and circumstances can be quite different.[32] In spite of the differences, however, the Latino population has a growing sense of "linked fate."

Unsurprisingly, immigration is one of the most important policy issues among Latinos, with significant majorities of Latinos concerned about restrictive immigration policies and the threat of deportation. The number of first-generation immigrants—or foreign-born citizens—living in the United States quadrupled from almost 10 million in 1970 to over 40 million today. Most immigrants legally reside in the United States.[33] Differences in opinion are found between Latinos and white non-Hispanics over immigration. Although most Americans (72 percent) support a path to legal status for undocumented immigrants, there are differences in opinion based on ethnicity. In 2015, 69 percent of white non-Hispanics said there should be a path to citizenship for immigrants compared to 86 percent of Latinos who shared this opinion.[34]

President Trump pushed for new immigration enforcement policies that expanded the pool of unauthorized immigrants who could be deported because of previous criminal charges, even for low-level offenses such as a parking ticket or drug possession. A 2017 Pew survey found 47 percent of Hispanic adults, regardless of their immigration status, say they worry "a lot" or "some" that they themselves, a family member, or a close friend could be deported. Among Hispanics that are lawful permanent residents but not U.S. citizens, 66 percent were very or somewhat concerned about deportation for themselves or their friends and family.[35]

With respect to ideology, Latinos typically are supportive of government laws to improve the lives of citizens and to reduce prevailing inequality, which includes favoring public funding for education, health, and welfare; Latinos generally see an active government as a good thing and favor liberal economic policies to create jobs and improve the economy. While Latinos tend to be fairly religious, Latino Decision surveys find they do not allow their religious beliefs to dictate their political decisions—they are thus less likely to vote for conservative politicians because of social issues.[36]

Gender Men and women have important differences of opinion as well. Reflecting differences in social roles and occupational patterns, women tend to oppose military intervention more than men do, are more likely than men to favor gun control, and are more supportive of government social programs. Perhaps because of these differences on issues, women are more likely than men to vote for Democratic candidates. In the 2016 presidential election, men were much more likely to favor Republican Donald Trump and women to favor Democrat Hillary Clinton. This tendency of men's and women's opinions to differ is known as the **gender gap**. Following the election, men are now much more likely than women to say they have "quite a lot" of confidence in the future of the United States then women; this represents a significant change from 2015 when men and women had similar levels of confidence. As of 2018, only 30 percent of women approved of the job Trump was doing as president, compared to 46 percent of men. This 16 percent gender gap in presidential approval is wider than for any other modern president.[37] (See Figure 6.5.)

Religion Religion is an important predictor of opinion on a wide range of issues. Religious individuals are usually defined in surveys regarding religious affiliation, frequency of church attendance, and the belief that religion and prayer are important in their lives. One of the fastest-growing groups in America are those without religious affiliation, rising from 5-6 percent of the population in the 1990s to almost 25 percent today.[38] Among religious groups, white evangelical Protestants tend to be even more conservative than Catholics. Just over 30 percent of evangelical Protestants believe abortion rights for women should always be permitted, compared to 75 percent of those without religious affiliation.

gender gap a distinctive pattern of voting behavior reflecting the differences in views between women and men

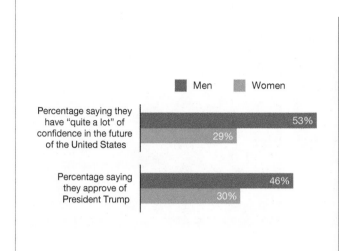

FIGURE 6.5

Differences in Public Opinion by Gender, 2018

Data reveal significant differences in men's and women's opinions about the political world. What might explain the differences we see in how optimistic men and women are about the future of the United States? What might explain the differences in how men and women view specific presidents?

SOURCE: Samantha Smith, "In Trump Era, Women's Views of Nation's Prospects Take a Negative Turn," Pew Research Center, May 15, 2017, www.pewresearch.org (accessed 5/23/18); "Trump Gets Negative Ratings for Many Personal Traits, but Most Say He Stands Up for His Beliefs," Pew Research Center, October 1, 2018, www.people-press.org/2018/10/01/trump-gets-negative-ratings-for-many-personal-traits-but-most-say-he-stands-up-for-his-beliefs/ (accessed 10/10/18).

Similarly sharp differences in opinion are also found in terms of attitudes about same-sex marriage: only 35 percent of evangelical Protestants support same-sex marriage compared to 76 percent of the nonreligious.[39] Religion also helps us understand opinions on teaching evolution in the public schools, environmental policy, immigration, partisanship, ideology, and other issues. White evangelicals and weekly churchgoers are much more likely to hold conservative views and be Republican, while the religiously unaffiliated are more likely to hold liberal views and favor the Democratic Party.

Party Affiliation Political party membership is one of the most important factors affecting political attitudes. We can think of partisanship as red- or blue-tinted glasses that color opinion on a vast array of issues. Self-identified partisans (individuals affiliating with the Republican or Democratic Party) tend to rely on party leaders and the media for cues on the appropriate positions to take on major political issues.[40]

In recent years, party polarization has become a defining feature of Congress and many state legislatures. As a result, the leadership of the Republican Party has become increasingly conservative, whereas that of the Democratic Party has become more liberal, a shift reflected in public opinion. Geographic sorting—where liberals choose to live in neighborhoods, cities, counties, and states that are more liberal, while conservatives move to areas with populations with more conservative views—also contributes to mass polarization. Large cities, such as New York City, Chicago, and Los Angeles, have predominantly Democratic populations, while Republicans are more numerous in rural and suburban areas.

According to recent studies, differences between Democratic and Republican partisans on a variety of political and policy questions are greater today than during any other period for which data are available. Across a wide range of issues, Democrats and Republicans strongly disagree. For example, 76 percent of Democrats strongly favor government policies to protect the environment compared to just

FOR CRITICAL ANALYSIS

Political scientists have observed "geographic sorting" in the United States, where liberals live in areas with other liberals and conservatives live in areas with other conservatives. Is the area where you live strongly liberal, conservative, or evenly mixed? What are the political consequences of geographic sorting?

The opinions of women and men diverge greatly on some, but by no means all, political issues. One of the biggest gender gaps appears around gun control. Many more women than men favor more restrictions on gun ownership.

30 percent of Republicans, and while 72 percent of Republicans oppose granting legal citizenship for immigrants with jobs in the United States, only 34 percent of Democrats do.[41] Figure 6.6 offers a more detailed look at Americans' attitudes toward immigration, broken down by party affiliation and by education. Wide differences in public opinion exist based on partisanship involving immigration, energy, income inequality, infrastructure, job creation, climate change and energy, national defense, budget deficit, taxes, terrorism, trade, and much more.

Despite the fact that the rift between the "red" (Republican-leaning) and "blue" (Democrat-leaning) states seems deeper than ever, political scientist Morris Fiorina and colleagues argue that most Americans hold moderate opinions.[40] While political elites and members of Congress may be highly polarized, there is general agreement among most Americans even on those issues thought to be most divisive. Thus, evidence of partisan polarization in public opinion is mixed: some see deep divisions while others see evidence of popular consensus.

Economic Class and Group Self-Interest Another way that membership in groups can affect political beliefs is through what might be called rational political interest. On many economic issues, for example, the interests of the rich and the poor differ significantly. Inevitably, these differences in interests will produce differences in political outlook.

The framers of the Constitution thought that the inherent gulf between the rich and the poor would always be the most important source of conflict in political life. Today significant numbers of Republicans and Democrats bemoan the chasm between the 99 percent of income earners and the top 1 percent. Donald Trump (on the right) and Bernie Sanders and Hillary Clinton (on the left) made income inequality a major piece of their 2016 campaigns. But while there might be agreement on the problem, there are huge disagreements about the solution. Republicans favor cutting taxes on business and wealthier Americans. In addition, President Trump favors creating jobs by promoting an isolationist foreign policy with reduced reliance on free-trade, tariffs on steel and aluminum, and limiting foreign immigration. Liberals tend to favor government policies to promote equality, such as raising the minimum wage to $15 an hour, free college education, and raising taxes on the wealthy, as well as incentives to encourage employee-owned

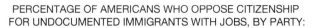

PERCENTAGE OF AMERICANS WHO OPPOSE CITIZENSHIP
FOR UNDOCUMENTED IMMIGRANTS WITH JOBS, BY PARTY:

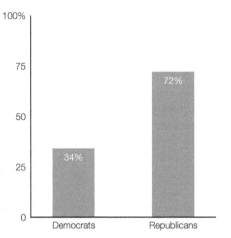

FIGURE 6.6

Social Group Influence on Public Opinion

Social groups have strong impacts on individuals' opinions. Party affiliation and level of education are two predictors of opinion on certain issues, like immigration.

*Highest level attained.

SOURCE: Brian Schaffner and Stephen Ansolabehere, "CCES Common Content, 2014," Harvard Dataverse, V2 http://dx.doi.org/10.7910/DVN/XFXJVY (accessed 5/4/16).

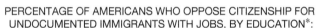

PERCENTAGE OF AMERICANS WHO OPPOSE CITIZENSHIP FOR
UNDOCUMENTED IMMIGRANTS WITH JOBS, BY EDUCATION*:

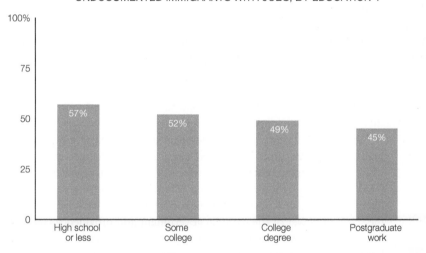

companies and strengthen employee unions. Wealthier individuals tend to favor the Republican solutions, including tax cuts, while the less wealthy tend to favor the liberal policies including government benefits.

However, some researchers have found that people don't necessarily translate broad concerns about inequality or their own economic self-interest into specific policy preferences.[43] For instance, two-thirds of Americans favored the 2001 and 2003 federal tax cuts supported by President George W. Bush, even though the tax reduction disproportionately benefited the very wealthy and therefore increased inequality. The poor, middle class, and affluent alike favored the tax cuts. Political scientist Larry Bartels concluded that the public is not always able to translate a concern for economic self-interest into policy preferences that would benefit average citizens because they lack necessary information about the effects of the tax cuts.[44]

Differences in interest also exist among the generations. Senior citizens and younger Americans have different views on such diverse issues as the war on drugs, Social Security, and criminal justice. The young, for example, are much more accepting of legalization of marijuana than are older citizens. The young are also more likely to favor same-sex marriage than are older age cohorts, and they are more concerned about the high cost of a college education, climate change, criminal justice issues, and privacy and security online (government surveillance). Older citizens are more concerned with protecting social security benefits than are the young. Some of these differences are rooted in where individuals learn about politics and media consumption; the young are significantly more likely to get their news online and are less likely to watch television news (see Chapter 7).

Nevertheless, group membership can never fully explain a given individual's political views. An individual's unique personality and life experiences may produce political views very different from those of the group to which one might nominally belong. Some African Americans are conservative Republicans, and some wealthy businesspeople are very liberal. Group membership is conducive to particular outlooks, but it is not determinative.

Political Environment A final set of factors that shape political attitudes and values are the conditions under which individuals become involved in political life. Although political beliefs are influenced by family background and group membership, the content and character of these views is, to a large extent, determined by political circumstances. For example, the baby-boom generation that came of age in the 1960s was exposed to the Vietnam War and the resulting widespread antiwar protests on college campuses and in urban areas throughout the nation. As a result, this generation has generally opposed foreign wars.

Similarly, the views held by members of a particular group can shift dramatically over time as political circumstances change. For example, white southerners were staunch members of the Democratic Party from the Civil War through the 1960s. As Democrats, they became key supporters of liberal New Deal and post–New Deal social programs that greatly expanded the size and power of the national government and provided social welfare programs. The 1960s mark the beginning of the South's move from the Democratic to the Republican camp—mainly because of white southerners' opposition to racial integration of schools and public facilities.

Since the 1960s a majority of southern whites have shifted to the Republican Party and away from the Democrats. Today Southern whites provide a solid base of support for efforts to scale back social programs and sharply reduce the size and power of the national government—hence the popularity of the Tea Party movement.[45] This major shift in partisanship in the South was the result of changes in the political environment and the policies promoted by the parties.

Another example of public opinion change can be seen in the evolving political environment in the West. California's Republican governor in the 1970s, Ronald Reagan, went on in the 1980s to become one of the most admired Republican presidents, ushering in major tax reform and scaling back the size and reach of the federal government. But since the 1990s, California, once a Republican stronghold, has become solidly

The terrorist attacks of September 11, 2001, certainly influenced public opinion in the months immediately following the attacks and likely also had a long-term effect on many Americans' basic political beliefs.

Democratic. Some argue that the shift began with a series of Republican-endorsed ballot measures targeting racial and ethnic minorities—including immigration, affirmative action, and bilingual education—which triggered a backlash especially among Latinos, who had previously participated in politics in very low numbers. In the 1990s, the number of Latino voters who favored more liberal public policy increased dramatically. With Latinos and blacks combined making up more than 50 percent of California's population, this demographic environmental change moved California to a solid Democratic state.[46] In this case, immigration and demographic change, two environmental factors, caused public opinion in the nation's largest state to change over time.

In sum, public opinion and orientations are shaped by the political circumstances in which individuals and groups find themselves, and those outlooks can change as circumstances change.

Political Knowledge and Changes in Public Opinion

> **Explore when and why public opinion changes and what role political knowledge plays**

The section above described what factors shape individuals' opinions, including political socialization, group identity, and political environment. These factors are relatively constant: one's level of education, for example, is generally set by early adulthood. However, these are not the only influences on public opinion. Individuals encounter new information from political leaders and the media throughout their lives. What role does political knowledge and information play in forming opinions? What causes people's opinions to change over time?

STABILITY AND CHANGE OF PUBLIC OPINION

One of the most important studies of how public opinion is formed is by political scientist John Zaller.[47] Zaller argues that individuals learn about politics by converting information from the news, elected officials, and other sources into opinions. His model of opinion formation works in three stages. In the "receive" stage, an individual receives information from a number of different sources. In the "accept" stage, the individual assesses this information through the lens of her own political views and accepts only those messages that are in line with previously held beliefs, meaning that some political information will be rejected. Finally, in the "sample" stage, the individual selects some of the accepted information—often the information that is most recent—and forms an opinion from it. So, according to this theory, if you receive information from various sources about a proposed tax cut, you will then assess the different messages based on your own previously held beliefs about tax cuts. If you believe tax cuts are generally good, you will likely reject information that suggests this particular cut is bad and accept only the messages suggesting that it is good.

The decision to accept or reject information is based on political knowledge. When asked about his opinion on a topic, the individual selects the most relevant or most recently acquired and accepted information from his "bucket" of information (the third stage above). Citizens with more political knowledge can differentiate between information that fits or does not fit with their beliefs—and then correctly accept or

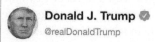

Donald J. Trump ✓
@realDonaldTrump

[Follow] ⌄

Excited to be heading home to see the House pass a GREAT Tax Bill with the middle class getting big TAX CUTS!

#MakeAmericaGreatAgain 🇺🇸

6:21 PM - 13 Nov 2017

After political opinions form, they remain relatively stable. The most knowledgeable people are generally able to discern whether new information fits or contradicts their previously held beliefs. Do you think the people in this protest (left) would change their opinions about tax cuts after seeing President Trump's tweet (right)?

reject it. For less-informed individuals, the media and political leaders may play a larger role in influencing public opinion. Low-informed individuals are more susceptible to fake news, partisan news, and political propaganda from elites than more-informed individuals. This reliance on politicians and the media, Zaller concludes, means that the public's opinions are often unstable and unreliable because these sources provide competing, changing information. As a result, public opinion is often a reflection of whatever recent campaign message (or media story) an individual has stored in her short-term memory. As we will see in Chapter 7, this effect is called *priming*.

Another way of understanding how individuals form political opinions is the online-processing model.[48] According to this model, an individual keeps a running tally of information and uses that tally to form an opinion on a policy issue or to decide which candidate to vote for. However, by the time an individual actually votes or voices an opinion on a specific issue, she may have forgotten some of the older information included in her decision-making process. This effect leads to the misconception that voters are uninformed, when in fact their opinion is informed but they have not retained all of the facts used to form that opinion. This model also implies a large role for political elites and the media but does not necessarily suggest that opinion is unstable. If public opinion is easily manipulated, the democratic process, which relies on citizens to play a significant part in the government, would be at risk. But other research has shown that individuals are quite stable in their policy attitudes.[49]

To take a closer look at whether and how public opinion changes, see Figure 6.7. The Pew Research Center tracks public opinion over time with annual surveys asking identical questions. Some opinions are relatively stable: support for abortion, for example, has remained virtually unchanged over the past decade, with over half of Americans saying abortion should be legal in all or most cases. Optimism about the economy and personal finances, however, experienced a gradual decline triggered by the financial crisis in 2008. In contrast, opinion on same-sex marriage has changed dramatically over the past two decades, with approval of marriage rights increasing by 25 percentage points. Notice that when public opinion has shifted, the shift has occurred fairly steadily in one direction; it doesn't simply jump around.[50]

The shift in public opinion on same-sex marriage has occurred partly in response to government policy. Political scientists call this "policy feedback." In 2009, Iowa was just the third U.S. state to allow same-sex marriages when the state Supreme Court issued a unanimous and at the time unpopular decision in the case *Varnum v. Brien*.[51] Changes in opinion immediately before and after the court decision were large. A survey of Iowans conducted immediately before and after the court legalized

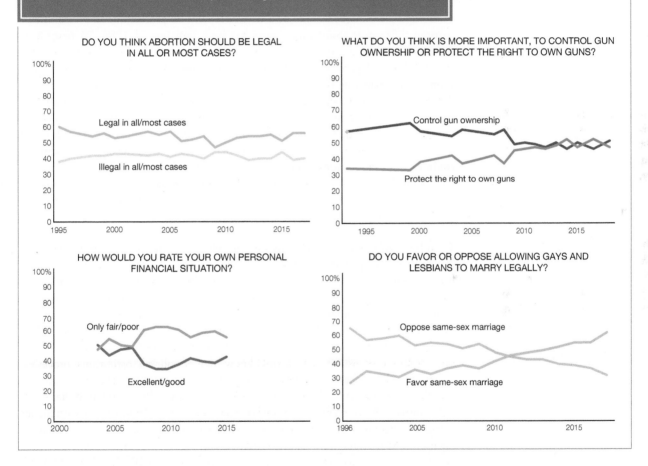

FIGURE 6.7

Stability and Change in Public Opinion

Public opinion on some issues has stayed stable in the last two decades, while opinion on other issues has shifted. What might explain why opinion on personal finance and same-sex marriage has changed, while opinion on abortion and the environment has stayed relatively constant?

NOTE: Personal finance data are from 2015.

SOURCES: "Changing Attitudes on Gay Marriage," Pew Research Center, June 26, 2017 www.pewforum.org (accessed 5/23/18); "Views on Abortion, 1995–2017," Pew Research Center, July 7, 2017 www.pewforum.org (accessed 5/23/18); "Public Views about Guns," Pew Research Center, June 22, 2017, www.people-press.org (accessed 5/23/18); "Economics and Personal Finances," Pew Research Center, www.pewresearch.org (accessed 12/23/15).

same-sex marriage showed that certain groups—Democrats, educated, young, non-religious, and people who have gay/lesbian family or friends—were the most likely to change their opinion in favor of same-sex marriage.[52] In 2015 the U.S. Supreme Court ruled in favor of legalizing same-sex marriage in all 50 states. Favorable public opinion may have helped pave the way for national policy change.[53]

Public opinion on environmental policy shows evidence of both stability and change. In June 2017 President Trump withdrew the United States from an international treaty signed by nearly 200 nations to protect the earth's environment. The political decision was widely criticized by global political leaders. The Paris Agreement sought to prevent rising temperatures and climate change by reducing reliance on fossil fuels such as coal, oil, and gas and develop alternative energy sources. Surveys reveal most Americans favor protecting the environment consistent with the terms of the Paris Agreement. In 2016 roughly three quarters (74 percent) of Americans believed "the country should do whatever it takes to protect the environment." Less than a quarter say "the country has gone too far in its efforts to protect the environment." Opinions on environmental protection go hand in hand with energy policy, as scientists find burning fossil fuels is linked to rising global temperatures. While Trump favors increasing coal production, most Americans (65 percent) favor developing alternative energy sources, such as wind and solar. This is a five percent increase from 2014. In some states, such as Iowa, 37 percent of energy is produced from wind power. Public opinion favoring alternative energy development may drive policy change.[54]

Though there might seem to be broad agreement on protecting the environment, partisan differences about these issues has been growing. In 1994, 74 percent of Republicans favored taking "any steps necessary" to protect the environment, but in 2016 only 52 percent agreed with this statement. Over the same time period support for protecting the environment increased among Democrats from 85 percent in 1994 to 90 percent in 2016. Today a 38 percent gap separates opinions on protecting the environment between Republicans and Democrats. Many Republicans are concerned that environmental laws and regulations hurt the economy and can cost jobs; today 6 in 10 Republicans are concerned with the economic costs of environmental regulations, up from 3 in 10 in 2007. In contrast, just 17 percent of Democrats believe environmental regulations hurt the economy.

POLITICAL KNOWLEDGE

What best explains whether citizens are generally consistent in their political views or inconsistent and open to the influence of others? In general, knowledgeable citizens are better able to evaluate new information and determine if it is relevant to and consistent with their beliefs and opinions; they are also more likely to be partisans and to have an ideology (such as liberal or conservative).[55] As a result, better-informed individuals can recognize their political interests and act consistently to further those interests.[56]

In an important recent study of political knowledge, researchers found that the average American exhibits little formal knowledge of political institutions, processes, leaders, or policy debates; many Americans could not name their member of Congress and did not know that U.S. senators serve six-year terms.[57] They also found that political knowledge is not evenly distributed throughout the population. Those with higher education, income, and occupational status and who are members of social or political organizations are more likely to know about and be active in politics. As a result, individuals with more income and education also have a disproportionate share of knowledge and influence and thus are better able to get what they want from government.

As mentioned above, political knowledge may protect individuals from exposure to misinformation that can distort public opinion. While social media have created new platforms for organizing and voter mobilizing, discussing politics, and creating networks (see Chapter 7), it has been associated with increased misinformation. Fake news on Facebook—with its billion users globally—was extensive in the 2016 election. A study found that the top 10 fake news stories circulated on Facebook were shared more widely than the top 10 authentic news stories about the election. The most viral story on Facebook was that the Pope had endorsed Trump for president. Russian Twitter "bot" accounts have been linked to breaking many of the fake news stories. Since the election, both Google and Facebook have implemented new protocols to block content from deceptive outlets, and Twitter, Reddit, and Instagram deleted thousands of fake accounts. Misinformation from elected officials and online news has encouraged more Americans to seek websites such as PolitiFact, FactCheck.org, and Snopes.com to verify the content of political information. It has also encouraged more Americans to turn to established media outlets, such as the *Washington Post*, *Wall Street Journal*, or *New York Times*, for news. Political knowledge and accurate political news is more important now than ever.

Shortcuts and Cues Because being informed politically requires a substantial investment of time and energy, most Americans seek to acquire political information and to make political decisions "on the cheap" by making use of shortcuts for political evaluation and decision making rather than engaging in a lengthy process of information-gathering. As noted above, researchers have found that individuals rely on cues from trusted party elites, interest groups, and the media to aid in attitude formation.[58] Today, tweets from elected officials are an increasingly important source of news; Donald Trump relies on Twitter more extensively than any other president, often tweeting multiple times a day. Other "inexpensive" ways to become informed involve taking cues from trusted friends, social networks and social media, relatives, colleagues, and perhaps religious leaders. Political scientists Richard Lau and David Redlawsk contend that by using informational shortcuts, average citizens can form political opinions that are, in most instances, consistent with their underlying preferences. They call this "voting correctly."[59] Even individuals with low levels of political knowledge are able to make relatively informed political choices by relying on these voter cues. It is generally accepted by scholars that people rely on shortcuts in forming public opinion on politics and public policy.[60] From this perspective, lower levels of political knowledge about politics, or instability of opinions, may not be a serious problem.

The public's reliance on elite cues has taken on new significance in today's era of party polarization. As elected officials have become increasingly polarized, has this change affected the way that citizens arrive at their opinions? Political scientists have found stark evidence that polarized political environments change how citizens make

People use cues from political elites and other trusted sources as a shortcut to forming opinions. Someone might not know the details about immigration and the DREAM act, but if they were a liberal or democrat, they might hear Senator Kamala Harris (D-Calif.) speaking on behalf of the bill and then feel they too supported it.

More and more people getting their news online, which seems to have altered reading habits. News articles have become shorter, and people are spending more time scanning headlines and less reading in-depth coverage.

decisions and form opinions. Notably, polarization between the parties means that party endorsements (of an issue or candidate) have a larger impact on public opinion formation than they used to. For example, if Republican leaders in Congress support a plan to impose higher taxes (tariffs) on foreign goods, citizens that identify as Republicans are more likely to support the plan as well. At the same time, polarization decreases the impact of other information on public opinion—that is, party polarization may actually reduce levels of political knowledge. Thus, elite polarization may have negative implications for public opinion formation.[61]

Skim and Scan Another factor affecting political knowledge is the *form* in which people consume information. The transformation of political information in the digital era has had a profound effect on the way the news is reported and how citizens learn about politics. Today more than three in four Americans read the news online or seek political information online.[62] Recent research also indicates a trend in journalism toward shorter articles and flashier headlines, and Twitter limits text to 280 characters. Americans today are likely to read the news by skimming and scanning multiple headlines online, in bits and bytes, rather than by reading long news articles.[63] There is a debate about whether the shift to digital media creates a more informed public, given the broader diversity of information sources and more personalized communication of the news via social media, or a public that is less informed because of a tendency to favor skimming and scanning over in-depth reading. However, as we've seen in this chapter, some research indicates that most individuals use simple cues and shortcuts to process political information. If this is correct, skimming and scanning headlines might provide a reasonable way to be informed about politics without extensive time or effort.

Costs to Democracy Political knowledge is necessary for effective citizenship. Those who lack political information cannot effectively defend their own political interests, rights, and freedoms and can easily become losers in political struggles and government policy. The presence of large numbers of politically ignorant individuals means that power can more easily be manipulated by political elites, the media, foreign governments and wealthy special interests that seek to shape public opinion. If knowledge is power, then a lack of knowledge can contribute to growing political and economic inequality. When individuals are unaware of their interests or how to pursue them, it is virtually certain that political outcomes will not favor them. The answer is to get informed and stay informed.

One of the most important areas of government policy is taxation. The United States has one of the largest gaps between the rich and the poor of any nation in the world. But rather than raise taxes, over the past several decades the United States has substantially reduced the rate of taxation levied on its wealthiest citizens. George W. Bush signed major tax cuts into law in 2001, providing a substantial tax break mainly for the top 1 percent of the nation's wage earners. Political scientist Larry Bartels has shown that, surprisingly, most Americans favored the 2001 tax cuts, including millions of middle- and lower-middle-class citizens who did not stand to benefit from the tax policy. Additionally, 40 percent of Americans had no opinion at all regarding the Bush tax cuts. The explanation for this odd state of affairs appears to be a lack of political knowledge. Millions of individuals who were unlikely to derive benefit from President Bush's tax policy thought they would. Since most Americans think they

Where Does Income Inequality Stem From?

> In your opinion, which generally has more to do with . . .

An individual's party identification, gender, and income may influence his or her opinions on specific issues. A recent study showed there are significant differences of opinion about the government's role in reducing the income gap between men and women and across income groups, but the most pronounced differences were between Democrats and Republicans.

SOURCE: Pew Research Center, "Why People Are Rich and Poor: Republicans and Democrats Have Very Different Views," www.pewresearch.org (accessed 11/19/17).

Why a person is rich

Worked harder ● Had advantages in life

Overall	By gender		By party	
45% 43%	49% 39%	41% 47%	66% 21%	29% 60%
	Men	Women	Republican	Democrats

By education		By income		
47% 41%	42% 47%	39% 49%	46% 44%	51% 37%
High school or less	College grad	Family income <$30K	Family income $30K–$74,999	Family income $75K+

Why a person is poor

Lack of effort ● Circumstances beyond control

Overall	By gender		By party	
34% 53%	42% 46%	26% 60%	56% 32%	19% 71%
	Men	Women	Republican	Democrats

By education		By income		
38% 49%	28% 59%	31% 56%	38% 51%	33% 57%
High school or less	College grad	Family income <$30K	Family income $30K–$74,999	Family income $75K+

FOR CRITICAL ANALYSIS

1. Do the findings in this study show that opinions are shaped by economic self-interest? Why or why not?

2. Which of these groups is most likely to support government action to address inequality? Are the other groups not concerned about inequality? Use the data to explain your answers.

pay too much in taxes, they favored the policy, even if the wealthy benefited much more than the middle class. (See the "Who Are Americans?" feature for public opinion on income inequality.) President Trump and the Republican-controlled Congress adopted even larger tax cuts for the affluent and corporations in 2017. Opinion polls showed a majority of Americans were opposed to the 2017 tax reform. Had political knowledge around taxes increased, or did the opposition reflect the low public opinion about President Trump and Congress at the time?

The Media, Government, and Public Opinion

Describe the major forces that shape public opinion

When individuals attempt to form opinions about particular political issues, events, and political leaders, they seldom do so in isolation. Typically, they are confronted with—sometimes bombarded by—the efforts of a host of individuals and groups seeking to persuade them to adopt a particular point of view. In the approach to the 2016 presidential election, someone trying to decide what to think about Hillary Clinton or Donald Trump could hardly avoid an avalanche of opinions expressed through the media, in meetings, or in conversations with friends. The **marketplace of ideas** is the interplay of opinions and views that takes place as competing forces attempt to persuade as many people as possible to accept a particular position on a particular issue. Given this constant exposure to the ideas of others, it is virtually impossible for most individuals to resist some modification of their own beliefs. Three forces that play important roles in shaping opinions in the marketplace are the government, private groups, and the news media.[64]

marketplace of ideas the public forum in which beliefs and ideas are exchanged and compete

POLITICAL LEADERS

All governments try to influence, manipulate, or manage their citizens' beliefs. But the extent to which public opinion is actually affected by governmental public relations can be limited. Often, governmental claims are disputed by the media, by interest groups, and increasingly by the opposing political party.

This hasn't stopped modern presidents from focusing a great deal of attention on shaping public opinion to boost support for their policy agendas. Franklin Delano Roosevelt promoted his policy agenda directly to the American people through his famous "fireside chat" radio broadcasts. A hallmark of the Clinton administration was the establishment of a political "war room" similar to the one that operated in his campaign headquarters, where staff met daily to discuss and coordinate the president's public-relations efforts.[65] The George W. Bush administration developed an extensive public-relations program to bolster popular support for the president's policies, including the war against terrorism.[66]

Like his predecessors, President Obama was effective in shaping public opinion. He built support for national health care reform by relying upon the power of his oratorical skills to build support for his administration's initiatives in domestic and foreign policy. Obama's White House was the first to use digital and social media to promote the president's policy agenda. Facebook posts promoted his policies and served to personalize the president. Obama was especially adept at using Twitter, with 70 million followers on that network. His use of multiple Twitter accounts to shape public opinion in favor of his policies allowed him to communicate directly with the people without having to be interviewed by the media.

Though Obama was the first president to use Twitter, Donald Trump is the nation's first Twitter president. Twitter was a key tool that helped Trump win the presidency; as president he uses it to promote his policy agenda and shape public opinion. Often tweeting in the early morning hours, Trump communicates his sentiments on politics like no other president in modern history. A website, the Trump Twitter Archives, lists thousands of Trump tweets searchable by topic. Former White House press secretary Sean Spicer said that although they often circumvent or contradict his own staff—and sometimes even himself—Trump's tweets will continue: "He has this direct pipeline to the American people, where he can talk back and forth." Trump uses Twitter for policy proposals, government announcements, attacking his enemies, defending himself and his campaign, building support for his party and his policies, and just plain venting. Laced with emotion and frequent typos, his tweets are authentic, if not always factually correct. He is known for Twitter rants, with multiple tweets on the same topic. For example, facing mounting criticism and a federal investigation into whether the Trump campaign coordinated with the Russians to sway the 2016 election, Trump tweeted in June 2017, "I am being investigated for firing the FBI Director by the man who told me to fire the FBI Director! Witch Hunt"[67] and "You are witnessing the single greatest WITCH HUNT in American political history - led by some very bad and conflicted people! #MAGA" ("Make America Great Again"—Trump's campaign slogan).[68] New scholarship argues political leaders like Trump prefer social media to traditional media since they can control the content unmitigated by the mainstream press.[69]

INTEREST GROUPS

The ideas that become prominent in political life are developed and spread not only by government officials and parties but also by important economic and political groups searching for issues that will advance their causes. One notable example is the abortion issue, which has inflamed American politics over the past 30 years. The notion of a fetal "right to life," whose proponents seek to outlaw abortion and overturn the Supreme Court's 1973 *Roe v. Wade* decision, was developed by conservative politicians who saw of abortion as a means of uniting Catholic and Protestant conservatives and linking both groups to the Republican Party.[70] To advance their cause, leaders of the right-to-life movement sponsored well-publicized

Interest groups focus much of their efforts on influencing public opinion. (Left) A member of the liberal group MoveOn.org hand delivers petitions in support of the Iran Nuclear agreement to New Jersey senators Cory Booker and Robert Menendez. (Right) Indivisible is another liberal group that formed after the 2016 elections to protest Donald Trump and Republican policies.

Senate hearings at which testimony, photographs, films (such as *The Silent Scream*), and other exhibits were presented to illustrate the movement's claim that abortion amounted to the murder of millions of unborn human beings. Finally, Catholic and Evangelical Protestant religious leaders were organized to denounce abortion from their church pulpits and, increasingly, from their electronic pulpits on the Christian Broadcasting Network and the various other television forums available for religious programming. Religious leaders have also organized demonstrations, pickets, and disruptions at abortion clinics throughout the nation.[71]

THE MASS MEDIA

FOR CRITICAL ANALYSIS

Does it matter what news sources an individual reads? How can the news influence public attitudes on issues of public policy?

The media are among the most powerful forces operating in the marketplace of ideas. As we shall see in Chapter 7, the mass media are not simply neutral messengers for ideas developed by others. Instead, the media are opinion makers and have an enormous impact on popular attitudes. For example, since the publication of the Pentagon Papers by the *New York Times* and the exposure of the Watergate scandal led by the *Washington Post* in the 1970s, the national news media have relentlessly investigated personal and official wrongdoing on the part of politicians and public officials. Today, the national media plays a similar role in exposing potential government corruption and Russian interference in the 2016 election, as discussed earlier. Media revelation of corruption in government has contributed to the cynicism and distrust of government that prevail in much of the general public.

At the same time, the ways in which media coverage interprets or "frames" specific events can have a major impact on popular responses and opinions about these events (see Chapter 7).[72] Given the critical importance of media framing to the way the public perceives the news, President George W. Bush went to great lengths to persuade broadcasters to follow his administration's lead in their coverage of both terrorism and America's response to terrorism in the months following the September 11, 2001, attacks. The media acquiesced, presenting the administration's military campaigns in Afghanistan and Iraq, as well as its domestic antiterrorist efforts, in a positive light. Even supposedly liberal newspapers such as the *New York Times* published articles supportive of the military invasion of Iraq in March 2003, when President Bush ordered the invasion. In 2002, Congress passed the Joint Resolution to Authorize the Use of United States Armed Forces Against Iraq. Public opinion in favor of invading Iraq remained above 50 percent between June and November of 2002, according to Gallup polls. By the time the invasion occurred, in March 2003, after months of presidential messages and media coverage focused on the threat of terrorism, public support had reached over 70 percent.[73]

Public Opinion and Government Policy

Analyze how public opinion shapes government policy and influences elected officials

In 1960 the authors of a book titled *The American Voter* argued that few Americans think about politics ideologically or consistently, so one would naturally expect public opinion to vary, as discussed earlier.[74] Given generally low levels of political knowledge among voters and the changing nature of public opinion, it's little wonder that politicians are sometimes unwilling to act solely on the basis of public opinion. But one could argue that consulting public opinion is a duty of elected officials in a democracy. Is government policy responsive to public opinion?

GOVERNMENT RESPONSIVENESS TO PUBLIC OPINION

Studies generally find that elected officials are influenced by the preferences of the public. Political scientists Benjamin Page and Robert Shapiro explored the relationship between broad changes in opinion toward various political issues and the policy outcomes that most closely correspond to the issues.[75] The results showed that shifts in public opinion on particular issues do in fact tend to lead to changes in public policy. This is especially true when there are wide swings in opinion regarding particularly high-profile issues that are relatively simple, such as legalization of same-sex marriage. Other studies have found similar evidence that government policy generally does track public opinion. Unsurprisingly, states where conservative opinions predominate tend to adopt more conservative laws and states with more liberal public opinion adopt more liberal policies.[76] Another example is in health care. A July 2009 Pew survey found that 65 percent of Americans favored a law "requiring all Americans to have health insurance, and government aid for those unable to afford it."[77] The federal government adopted the Affordable Health Care Act for America in 2010, which required health insurance for all citizens.

However, there is reason to question whether prevailing public opinion causes politicians to make policies that reflect the general will or whether government policy in fact causes changes in public opinion. The relationship between government policy and opinion may be dynamic, wherein policy responds to opinion but opinion also shifts based on new government policies.[78] Recent studies have found government policy to have an effect on opinion in various areas, such as the environment, health care, welfare reform, the death penalty, and smoking bans. For example, researchers found that in states that adopted smoking bans, public opinion then shifted to become more critical of cigarette smoking than in states without such bans.[79] Scholars have suggested a number of possible mechanisms to explain this process. New policy may expose the public to new ideas, causing opinion to change, or experience with a successful or unsuccessful policy may give the public new information. A policy might act as a "signal" of a moral or ethical view (such as a smoking ban acting as a "signal" that smoking should be stigmatized).

To what extent do political leaders listen to the opinions of their constituents? To what extent should they listen? Is Calvin's father right that leaders should do what they believe is right, not what the public wants?

Of course, sometimes public opinion and policy do not align, as the prior discussion of environmental policy and the Paris Agreement. Sometimes public officials act on their own preferences if they believe it will benefit government or society, and lawmakers typically do use their own judgment when making policy choices.[80] When elected officials pursue policies not aligned with public opinion, it is often because they view particular groups of the electorate as more important than others. Inevitably, loyal voting blocs or interest groups that regularly contribute to a candidate may have their interests more closely represented than the general public.[81]

DOES EVERYONE'S OPINION COUNT EQUALLY?

In a democracy, it is assumed that elected representatives will implement the policies favored by the majority of the people, and in a general sense this happens in the United States. But when policy issues are more complicated (such as taxation or foreign policy), the public is likely to have less of a voice. Further, citizens who are more affluent and more educated may have a disproportionate influence over politics and public policy decisions. This has been shown when comparing the responsiveness of elected officials to low- and high-income individuals, voters and nonvoters, and whites and minorities. The view that some groups in a society have more influence in politics is not new, but it is quite a departure from the traditional pluralist view of all citizens having equal access to the political sphere.

How do more affluent and educated citizens manage to wield outsize influence over policy makers? One way is obvious: they vote at higher rates, and they are more likely to contribute money to political campaigns. As we will discuss in Chapter 8, voters and individuals making political contributions tend to be more affluent and educated than nonvoters. Indeed, there is new evidence supporting the common, but generally untested, assumption that voters are better represented than nonvoters. In a comparative study of the roll-call votes of U.S. senators, political scientists John Griffin and Brian Newman demonstrated that elected officials are indeed responsive to the policy preferences of voters but not to those of nonvoters.[82]

In regard to income group, research has found that U.S. senators from both the Republican and Democratic parties are less likely to respond to the opinions of low-income constituents than to those of constituents with higher incomes.[83] Senate votes on such varied issues as the minimum wage, civil rights, and abortion are more likely to reflect the opinions of the rich. The influence of affluent Americans may explain government policies such as failure to increase the minimum wage and the 2017 tax reform that significantly reduced corporate taxes and reduced taxes paid by the wealthiest citizens, all of which contribute to growing income inequality.[84]

As an alternative to analyzing legislative votes, political scientist Martin Gilens has used survey results to confirm that those with higher incomes are more likely to have their policy preferences represented by actual policies.[85] He considered public opinion surveys on a wide variety of policy issues conducted over 20 years and compared the responses of upper- and lower-income groups with related federal policy outcomes. Gilens found a relationship between what the public wants and what the government actually does, albeit with a strong bias toward the status quo. But when Americans with different income levels differ in their policy preferences, policies strongly reflect the preferences of the most affluent and show little or no relationship to the preferences of poor or middle-income Americans.

Charles Koch, one of the wealthiest people in the world, is a major donor to Republican candidates and causes. Some say that the opinions of wealthier individuals have more influence on politicians and government policy, though this has been difficult to prove unequivocally.

Some argue that every American citizen has an equal right to voice opinions in the political arena, but others point out that some voices receive a very attentive listening, while others are hardly heard at all.[86]

Measuring Public Opinion

Describe basic survey methods and other techniques researchers use to measure public opinion

A century ago American political leaders gauged public opinion by the presence of crowds at meetings and their applause. This direct exposure to the people's views did not necessarily produce accurate knowledge of public opinion. It did, however, give political leaders confidence in their public support—and therefore confidence in their ability to govern by consent.

Today, public officials make extensive use of **public-opinion polls** to help them decide whether to run for office, what policies to support, how to vote on important legislation, and what types of appeals to make in their campaigns. All recent presidents and other major political figures have worked closely with polls and pollsters.

public-opinion polls scientific instruments for measuring public opinion

MEASURING PUBLIC OPINION FROM SURVEYS

It is not feasible to interview the more than 300 million Americans residing in the United States on their opinions of who should be the next president or what should be done about important policy issues such as how to improve the economy and create jobs. Instead, pollsters take a **sample** of the population and use it to make inferences (e.g., predictions and educated guesses) about the preferences of the population as a whole. For a political survey to be an accurate representation of the population, it must meet certain requirements, including an appropriate sampling method (i.e., randomization), a sufficient sample size, and the avoidance of selection bias.[87] While some are skeptical of sampling, random sample surveys, which are used extensively in business and marketing as well as politics, ensure that the samples are accurate and reliable predictions of the underlying population.

sample a small group selected by researchers to represent the most important characteristics of an entire population

Websites such as RealClearPolitics.com list the results of every political survey released each day; during elections, this can be dozens of different surveys daily. Every week, the opinions of Americans regarding candidates and public policies are measured, as well as opinions on a vast array of products (toothpaste), entertainment (movie star romances), and even college political science textbooks!

Representative Samples One way to obtain a representative sample is what statisticians call a **simple random sample (or probability sample)**. To take such a sample, one would need a complete list of all the people in the United States, and individuals would be randomly selected from that list. Imagine that everyone's name was entered into a lottery, with names then drawn blindly from an enormous box. If everyone had an equal chance of selection, the result is a random sample. Since we don't have a complete list of all Americans, pollsters use census data, lists of households (for in-person or telephone surveys), and telephone numbers to create lists, drawing samples from regions and then neighborhoods within regions. State voter registration files are often used in political surveys designed to predict the outcome of an election or public opinion. If respondents are chosen randomly and everyone has an equal chance of being selected, then their results can be used to predict

simple random sample (or probability sample) a method used by pollsters to select a representative sample in which every individual in the population has an equal probability of being selected as a respondent

Confidence in Democratic Institutions

Parliaments, political parties, and the press are three institutions that play an important role in making democracy work. Parliament is the branch of government that most directly represents the voters; it serves as a major forum for policy debate and prevents abuse of executive power. Political parties offer different ideological goals, thereby helping to organize government, mobilize voters, and ensure political competition and accountability. Finally, the press plays an important "watchdog" role in politics, informing voters and helping them hold their leaders accountable for their actions.

While these institutions are important to all democracies, we do notice that Americans tend to be much less confident in these institutions than are citizens in other democracies. This raises two important questions: Why are the U.S. scores so low, and what does it mean for politics when a large percentage of a population loses confidence in the institutions that keep its democracy functioning?

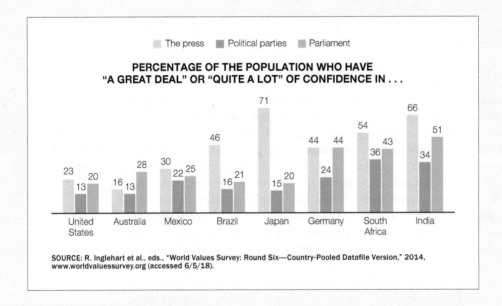

PERCENTAGE OF THE POPULATION WHO HAVE "A GREAT DEAL" OR "QUITE A LOT" OF CONFIDENCE IN . . .

Legend: The press · Political parties · Parliament

- United States: 23, 13, 20
- Australia: 16, 13, 28
- Mexico: 30, 22, 25
- Brazil: 46, 16, 21
- Japan: 71, 15, 20
- Germany: 44, 24, 44
- South Africa: 54, 36, 43
- India: 66, 34, 51

SOURCE: R. Inglehart et al., eds., "World Values Survey: Round Six—Country-Pooled Datafile Version," 2014, www.worldvaluessurvey.org (accessed 6/5/18).

behavior for the overall population. If randomization is not used or some people are excluded from the chance to be selected, then the sample will be biased and cannot be used to generalize to the population accurately.

Another method of drawing samples of the national population is a technique called **random digit dialing**. A computer random number generator is used to produce a list of 10-digit telephone numbers. Given that 95 percent of Americans have telephones (cell phones or landlines), this technique usually results in a random national sample because almost every citizen has a chance of being selected for the survey. Telephone surveys are fairly accurate, cost-effective, and flexible in the type of questions that can be asked; but many people refuse to answer political surveys, and response rates—the percent of those called who actually answer the survey—have been falling steadily, averaging less than 15 percent.[88]

Sample Size A sample must be large enough to provide an accurate representation of the population. Surprisingly, though, the size of the population being measured doesn't matter, only the size of the sample. A survey of 1,000 people is almost as effective for measuring the opinions of all Texans (28 million residents) as the opinions of all Americans (over 323 million residents).

Flipping a coin shows how this works. After tossing a coin 10 times, the number of heads and tails may not be close to 5 and 5. After 100 tosses of the coin, though, the percentage of heads should be close to 50 percent and after 1,000 tosses, very close to 50 percent. In fact, after 1,000 tosses, there is a 95 percent chance that the number of heads will be somewhere between 46.9 percent and 53.1 percent. This 3.1 percent variation from 50 percent is called the **sampling error (or margin of error)**: the chance that the sample used does not accurately represent the population from which it is drawn. In this case, 3.1 percent is the amount of uncertainty we can expect with a typical 1,000-person survey. If we conduct a national survey and find candidate A leads candidate B by 5 percent in the upcoming election and the uncertainty in the survey is 3 percent, it means candidate A leads candidate B by anywhere between 2 (5−3) and 8 (5 + 3) percentage points. Normally, samples of 1,000 people are considered sufficient for accurately measuring public opinion through the use of surveys.

Larger sample sizes can yield more accurate predictions of the opinions of a population, but there is a trade-off in terms of cost since it is also more expensive to survey more people. Why is a sample size of only 1,000 generally accepted as adequately representative of much larger populations? Consider the "diminishing returns" of sampling more and more people. The sample error from a sample of 500 people is 4.4 percent. With 1,000 respondents, it drops to 3.1 percent and with 1,500 to 2.5 percent. That is, the smaller and smaller gains in accuracy have to be weighed against the increasing costs of polling more people. The consensus among statisticians and pollsters is that the optimal trade-off point is 1,000—hence 1,000 is the "gold standard." But today many surveys conducted online include thousands of respondents, making their predictions potentially even more accurate.

When an election poll of 1,000 people indicates that 51 percent of voters surveyed favor the Republican candidate and 49 percent support the Democratic candidate, the outcome is considered too close to call because the difference, 2 percent, is within the margin of error of 3.1 percent. That is, a figure of 51 percent really means that between 48 percent and 54 percent of voters in the population *probably* favor the Republican, while a figure of 49 percent indicates that between 46 percent and 52 percent of all voters *probably* support the Democrat. Thus, in this

random digit dialing a polling method in which respondents are selected at random from a list of 10-digit telephone numbers, with every effort made to avoid bias in the construction of the sample

sampling error (or margin of error) polling error that arises based on the small size of the sample example, a 52-to-48 percent Democratic victory would still be consistent with polls predicting a 51-to-49 percent Republican triumph.

Survey Design and Question Wording Even with a good sample design, surveys may fail to reflect the true distribution of opinion within a target population. One frequent source of measurement error is the wording of survey questions. The words used in a question can have an enormous impact on the answers it elicits. The reliability of survey results can also be adversely affected by poor question format, the ordering of questions, poor vocabulary, ambiguity of questions, or questions with built-in biases.

Often, minor differences in the wording of a question can convey vastly different meanings to respondents and thus produce quite different response patterns (see Box 6.3). For example, for many years the University of Chicago's National Opinion Research Center has asked respondents whether they think the federal government is spending too much, too little, or about the right amount of money on "assistance for the poor." Answering the question posed this way, about two-thirds of all respondents seem to believe that the government is spending too little. However, the same survey also asks whether the government spends too much, too little, or about the right amount for welfare. When the word *welfare* is substituted for "assistance for the poor," about half of all respondents indicate that too much is being spent.[89]

Online Surveys Today, pollsters are increasingly turning to the use of online surveys, often using similar techniques to those of telephone surveys. Internet surveys can be more efficient, less costly, and more accurate than standard phone surveys; and they include much larger samples of young people and yield more accurate results within age cohorts. But many surveys you will find online do not use

---

BOX 6.3

It Depends on How You Ask

THE SITUATION

The public's desire for tax cuts can be hard to measure. In 2000, pollsters asked what should be done with the nation's budget surplus and got different results depending on the specifics of the question.

THE QUESTION

President [Bill] Clinton has proposed setting aside approximately two-thirds of an expected budget surplus to fix the Social Security system. What do you think the leaders in Washington should do with the remainder of the surplus?

VARIATION 1

Should the money be used for a tax cut, or should it be used to fund new government programs?

VARIATION 2

Should the money be used for a tax cut, or should it be spent on programs for education, the environment, health care, crime fighting, and military defense?

SOURCE: Pew Research Center, reported in the *New York Times*, January 30, 2000, WK 3.

probability sampling (random sampling) and thus are not representative of the American population. Instead, they reflect those willing to take a quiz online.

Knowledge Networks and YouGov are leaders in internet polling using sampling methods in which respondents complete surveys online instead of being interviewed on the phone. YouGov has a large population of respondents (hundreds of thousands of individuals) identified using probability sampling, so the sample is representative of the American population. Individuals without internet access are given free subscriptions or complete the surveys using the TV. If a client commissions a survey, YouGov randomly draws a sample of, say, 1,000 people from its population of online respondents. Because respondents have agreed to complete a number of surveys in exchange for free internet access, they are more likely to complete the surveys. YouGov has been more accurate in predicting the outcomes of recent presidential elections than other firms.[90]

Other polling companies use different methods for conducting internet surveys, often by using statistical weights to make the surveys generally representative of the American population.[91] Internet surveys such as the Cooperative Congressional Election Study can have very large samples, up to 50,000 people, and rolling panel survey designs, where the same respondents are interviewed repeatedly over months. In the future, internet surveys may be more representative of the American population than traditional telephone surveys and may replace telephone surveys entirely, especially given falling response rates and the growing number of households without landline phones but using cell phones exclusively.

Critics of internet surveys contend that the samples may still be biased by not including enough respondents from groups that are more likely to be offline, especially non-English speakers, Latinos, the elderly, and the poor. Online surveys may include more respondents who are interested in politics than the normal population. Proponents contend that minorities and the poor are increasingly online, even via mobile access, and that the samples are representative of the American population. Because online surveys from sites such as YouGov have proved to be more accurate in forecasting elections than many telephone surveys relying on cell phones and landlines, online surveys are likely here to stay.[92]

In contrast to online surveys, with more than 60 years' experience studying American public opinion, the American National Election Studies (ANES) is the premier broad general survey. The ANES traditionally has conducted surveys using face-to-face interviews, but because interviewing respondents in person is very costly, the ANES increasingly conducts online surveys as well. The ANES is considered the gold standard for political survey research because of its accuracy, design and question wording.

Telephone and online surveys increasingly embed experimental techniques within the design, in which one group of respondents is given a treatment, or unique question wording, and responses are compared with a control group of respondents that does not receive the treatment. The researcher is interested in the difference in responses between the treatment and control group. Experiments are one of the most rigorous methods for detecting causal relationships. During Obama's 2012 presidential campaign, for example, mobilizers found that if they asked individuals to list everything in their daily schedule, and state the time of day they planned to vote within that schedule, the individual was more likely to actually vote, compared to individuals who were simply asked to vote for the candidate. In another survey framing experiment, individuals in one group were exposed to a frame arguing that affirmative action is necessary to correct past discrimination, while those in a second group received a competing frame arguing that affirmative action gives African Americans special treatment. Not surprisingly, those in the first group showed greater support for affirmative action than did those in the second group for the same policies. By using a treatment and control group design, framing experiments provide more leverage in assessing cause and effect in measuring changes in public opinion. Framing experiments are an important way to understand how public opinion changes in response to political elites and the mass media.

WHEN POLLS ARE WRONG

The history of polling over the past century contains many instances of getting it wrong and learning valuable lessons in the process. As a result, polling techniques have grown more and more sophisticated, and pollsters have a more nuanced understanding of how public opinion is formed and how it is revealed. Polls are best understood as best guesses of a political outcome but not a prediction of fact. The 2016 election provides a recent example of inaccurate polling: the vast majority of opinion polls leading up to the election predicted that Hillary Clinton would win by a landslide.

social desirability effect the effect that results when respondents in a survey report what they expect the interviewer wishes to hear rather than what they believe

Social Desirability Effects Political scientists have found that survey results can be inaccurate when the surveys include questions about sensitive issues for which individuals do not wish to share their true preferences. For example, respondents tend to overreport voting in elections and the frequency of their church attendance because these activities are deemed socially appropriate. Political scientists call this the **social desirability effect**, whereby respondents report what they expect the interviewer wishes to hear or whatever they think is socially acceptable, rather than what they actually believe or know to be true.[93] On other topics, such as questions about income or alcohol and drug use, respondents may feel self-conscious and choose not to answer.

Given the failure of public opinion polls to predict the outcome of the 2016 election, many people question if polls systematically underreported support for Trump and his policies. Explanations for why Trump performed better at the ballot box than in the polls include that Trump did better in polls of voters (either registered or likely voters) than in polls of all adults, and he also performed better in polls conducted online or by automated script surveys with a live-telephone caller. This latter finding may be the result of the social desirability effect. Because Trump is a polarizing and controversial figure, some people may have been reluctant to tell an interviewer they support Trump or his policies; online surveys may allow respondents to reveal their true preferences without facing social pressure to conform.

Pew studied if telephone surveys were systematically underestimating public support for Trump. The researchers compared public support for the president's agenda using telephone surveys with live interviewers to online public support for his agenda using surveys. They expected the online surveys to show higher support for the president and his policies, because self-administered online surveys should reduce respondents' reluctance to reveal their true preferences. The study found little statistical difference in evaluations of Trump or his policies when varying the mode of the interview from online to telephone.[94] The fact that Clinton won 3 million more votes than Trump may be evidence that the 2016 election polls were partially right after all.

Questions that ask directly about race or gender are particularly problematic. Social desirability makes it difficult to learn voters' true opinions about touchy subjects such as racial attitudes because respondents hide their preferences from the interviewer for fear of social retribution (against what might be deemed "politically incorrect" opinions). For example, researchers have found respondents in surveys didn't want to admit that they opposed school integration and would not vote for the black candidate and, therefore, abstained from answering the question. Measuring public opinion can be a challenge; measuring opinions incorrectly can bias the findings. However, surveys using experiments can be designed to tap respondents' latent or hidden feelings about sensitive issues without directly asking them to express overt opinions.

Selection Bias The importance of accurate sampling was brought home early in the history of political polling. A 1936 *Literary Digest* poll predicted that the Republican candidate, Alf Landon, would defeat the Democratic incumbent, Franklin Roosevelt, in that year's presidential election. The actual election ended in a Roosevelt landslide. The main problem with the survey was what is called **selection bias** in drawing the sample. The pollsters had relied on telephone directories and automobile registration rosters to produce the survey sample. During the Great Depression, though, only wealthier Americans owned telephones and automobiles. Thus, the millions of working-class Americans who constituted Roosevelt's base of support were excluded from the sample.

Selection bias was also at play in preelection polls in the 2012 presidential election, when Gallup significantly overestimated Latino support for the Republican candidate, suggesting a close race between the Republican candidate, Mitt Romney, and the Democratic candidate, Barack Obama. The Gallup numbers were incorrect because of selection bias (that is, they had too few Latinos in their sample and therefore their predictions were inaccurate). Estimates based on aggregating information from many different statewide public opinion polls were more accurate.[95]

As discussed, in the 2016 presidential election, although most polls predicted the direction of the popular vote correctly in Hillary Clinton's favor, they failed

selection bias polling error that arises when the sample is not representative of the population being studied, which creates errors in overrepresenting or underrepresenting some opinions

Though public opinion is important, it is not always easy to interpret, and polls often fail to predict how Americans will vote. In 1948 election-night polls showed Thomas Dewey defeating Harry S. Truman for the presidency, which caused the *Chicago Daily Tribune* to incorrectly print a banner announcing Dewey's win. In 2016 polls considerably favored Hillary Clinton over Donald Trump, causing many to doubt the possibility of Trump winning the election.

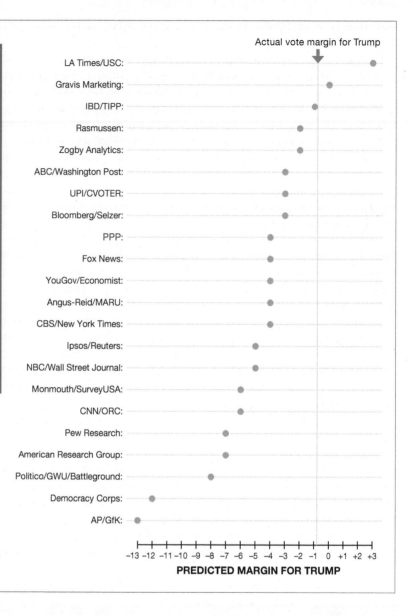

FIGURE 6.8

Accuracy of Final Preelection Polls, 2016

A large number of news organizations conducted polls to predict the outcome of the 2016 election. For how many of these polls was the actual result within their margin of error, assuming a sample size of 1,000 and a margin of error of plus or minus 3.1 percent? What might explain why some respected organizations, like Pew and Politico, were so far off the mark?

SOURCES: All poll data, except LA Times/USC, from HuffPost Pollster, www.elections.huffingtonpost.com/pollster (accessed 11/10/16). Poll results are from the most recent polls prior to election day in the database. USC/LATimes data from www.cesrusc.org/election/ (accessed 11/11/16). Popular vote margin data from "CNN 2016 Election Results," www.cnn.com/election/results (accessed 11/11/16).

to predict the size of the vote margin and the election outcome (see Figure 6.8). Other possible explanations for the polling inaccuracies included the use of "likely voter models," which left out some groups that ended up voting at higher-than-usual rates, such as rural, non-college educated, blue-collar voters who supported Trump in large numbers. Trump called these voters the "silent majority." Selection bias may have been at play in why the polls failed to predict the 2016 election outcome. Nonresponse bias may have also occurred, where Trump supporters were less likely to respond to surveys.

The *LA Times*/USC survey accurately predicted a Trump win, relying on a different methodology than the others. It used rolling panel surveys, where the same individuals were interviewed repeatedly over time. Panel surveys have a stronger internal research design, where the researcher can measure opinion change for the same sample of individuals. Scholars increasingly recognize that measuring change over time is the key to accurately measuring public opinion.

In recent years, the issue of selection bias has been complicated by the fact that growing numbers of individuals refuse to answer pollsters' questions, or they use voice mail or caller ID to screen unwanted callers. If pollsters could be certain that those who responded to their surveys simply reflected the views of those who refused to respond, there would be no problem. Some studies, however, suggest that the views of respondents and nonrespondents can differ, especially along social class lines. This can lead to incorrect inferences of public opinion.

Push Polling Push polls are not scientific polls and are not intended to yield accurate information about a population. Instead, they involve asking a respondent a loaded question about a political candidate designed to elicit the response sought by the pollster and, simultaneously, to shape the respondent's perception of the candidate in question. One of the most notorious uses of push polling occurred in the 2000 South Carolina Republican presidential primary, in which George W. Bush defeated John McCain and went on to win the presidency. Callers working for Bush supporters asked conservative white voters if they would be more or less likely to vote for McCain if they knew he had fathered an illegitimate black child (a false statement).

push poll a polling technique in which the questions are designed to shape the respondent's opinion

The Bandwagon Effect Public-opinion polls can influence political realities and elections. In fact, sometimes polling can even create its own reality. The so-called **bandwagon effect** occurs when polling results convince people to support a candidate marked as the probable victor. This is especially true in the presidential nomination process, where there may be multiple candidates within one party vying to be the party's nominee. Researchers found that the change in national media coverage received by a candidate before and after the Iowa caucuses, the first nominating event, was a major predictor of how well the candidate would do in the New Hampshire primary (the second nominating event) and in presidential primaries nationwide, controlling for other factors including money and standing in the polls.[96] A candidate who has "momentum"—that is, one leading in the polls—usually finds it considerably easier to raise campaign funds than a candidate whose poll standing is poor. Wanting to highlight the momentum he felt he had, Trump frequently cited his lead in the polls during the 2016 presidential primaries and general election to mobilize his base.

bandwagon effect a shift in electoral support to the candidate whom public opinion polls report as the front-runner

BIG DATA, POLLING AGGREGATORS, AND MEASURING PUBLIC OPINION

Computational data analysis and social media have opened new ways to measure mass opinion. Some of the most fundamental questions about politics and public opinion are now being measured not with surveys but in terms of actual behavior online, including Google searches. Big data refers to data sets that are so large and complex that they require advanced analytics, rather than traditional methods, to reveal insights on a massive scale. Journalist Sasha Issenberg shows how big data played a critical role in Obama's presidential election campaigns. By analyzing Netflix movie queues, for example, campaign consultants were able to investigate concern for global warming based on the titles a person puts into her rental queue, even if she does not actually end up watching the film. Opinions about a wide range of

FOR CRITICAL ANALYSIS

Is it important that public-opinion polls be accurate? How might polls fail to be accurate? What are the consequences if polls are systematically inaccurate?

policy issues could be gleaned from the aggregate preferences of millions of movie viewers. This type of analysis is called *data mining*.[97]

Twitter, the preferred medium of candidates and political elites, introduces another way to measure public opinion and agenda setting using text analysis. One study analyzed the number of Twitter followers for the 2016 presidential candidates and tracked changes over time, as well as tracked mentions of any of the candidates based on millions of tweets.[98] A candidate's lead in positive Twitter coverage may be more important to winning the White House than a lead in traditional public-opinion polls. Coding large amounts of Twitter data can also be valuable for measuring phenomena that are difficult or impossible to measure with standard telephone surveys, such as the use of racial slurs.

Rather than rely on surveys to measure the opinions of U.S. citizens, researchers are now using Google search data. An example is public response in Flint, Michigan, and the surrounding communities when the city's water supply was found to be contaminated by lead. The Flint drinking water disaster exposed roughly 100,000 residents to harmful contaminants, requiring residents to drink filtered or bottled water. Local residents used online search engines as way to follow the news and understand the health problems from drinking contaminated water. Pew Research Center analyzed 18 months of Google search data to track public interest in the Flint water contamination crisis. The study covered events including boiling-water advisories from bacteria, reports of elevated lead levels in children's blood and tap water samples, bottled-water distribution, emergency warnings, and criminal charges. The data based on 2,700 different search terms reveals that residents of Flint were searching for information about their water long before the government recognized the contamination and before the media drew national attention to the problem. Similarly, Google search data has been able to predict local flu outbreaks based on search terms of symptoms (fever, etc.) considerably earlier than the Centers for Disease Control (CDC) declares a flu outbreak in a local area.[99]

Beyond Twitter, big data are playing a role in election forecasting, predictive analytics, and measuring public opinion. For example, polling aggregators can be used to track public opinion more accurately. Blogger Nate Silver became an overnight sensation in 2008 by aggregating thousands of public-opinion polls conducted in each of the 50 states to predict the winner of the presidential election state by state more accurately than any single polling house—a feat he repeated in 2012 (though he was often incorrect in predicting the winner in the tumultuous 2016 primaries).[100]

Silver and FiveThirtyEight.com also use statistics to average thousands of public opinion polls overtime to create a more accurate estimate of presidential approval than any one single poll. The thousands of polls they draw from are weighted based on their sample size, methodological rigor, and past accuracy—polls that historically have been more accurate count more.[101] Five months after his victory in the 2016 election, Trump had the lowest approval ratings of any president in modern history during the first 150 days in office.

The Democratic Party and the Republican Party now use a database of 240 million Americans, including a wide range of data from voting history and party registration, social media, consumer purchasing patterns, and so on. Using big data and data mining, researchers can predict factors that make a person more likely to vote in the first place and whether he will cast a vote for the Republican or Democratic candidate. Data mining has been used for years in business, marketing, and economics but is growing in importance in campaigns, elections, and policy. The study of politics has been on the forefront of this big data revolution with sophisticated analyses of massive amounts of data including text scraping and text analysis of social media. These are just a few examples of how very large sample data—millions and millions of data points—are changing how we measure public opinion in the digital age.

Public Opinion and Democracy
WHAT DO WE WANT?

This chapter has focused on the role of public opinion in American politics. A major purpose of democratic government, with its participatory procedures and representative institutions, is to ensure that political leaders will heed the public will. And, indeed, a good deal of evidence suggests that they do. There are many instances in which public policy and public opinion do not coincide, but often the government's actions are consistent with citizens' preferences, at least in the most general sense.[102]

However, it is not always clear what the public will is. Mass shootings heighten the preferences of supporters of both gun control and gun rights. *Whose* preferences prevail when attitudes differ among groups? Or when they differ between the public and elites? Or between the affluent and the poor? Some political scientists argue that government policy is much less responsive to public opinion on the issues that really count and that when the interests of elites are at stake, government officials are much more likely to represent the opinions of the affluent than the poor.[103] People in lower income groups, moreover, are less likely to actively seek out ways to express their political opinions than are wealthier people (see the "**Who Participates?**" feature on p. 249).

New technology may be able to help. The migration of politics online has greatly expanded the amount of information available and the ease of becoming informed. And as we will see in Chapter 7, online media are more diverse than traditional media. Given this new media environment, we might expect public opinion to be more accurate, even about the nuances of public policy. Digital citizenship offers the promise of a more informed electorate, with citizens having multiple venues in which to translate their opinions into political action and demand improved representation from political leaders. The use of social media by students from the Marjory Stoneman Douglas High School to argue for greater gun regulations shows digital citizenship in action.

At the same time, the internet raises new concerns about the accuracy and consistency of public opinion and whether people hold opinions that depart from facts and the truth. As Chapter 7 will show, Americans may become trapped in a "filter bubble" in which they are exposed only to news consistent with their political preferences. There are internet vandals, or "bomb throwers," who defame other people and their opinions in ways that may negatively color public opinion. Misinformation—rumor masked as legitimate news—may be more common, especially in blogs or social media sites. Some research finds that the gap between the haves and the have-nots in terms of political knowledge actually increases with the availability of more information. The implications are significant, given the explosion of political coverage online. The research suggests that with more information, public opinion may actually be less consistent.[104]

Social media may be reshaping what is public opinion. The effects of new media—vast and still unfolding—include the wide dissemination of public-opinion polls and the rise of internet polling. Do new media make public opinion more or less important? Do they make elected officials more or less responsive to the citizens? Time will tell.

Who Expresses Their Political Opinions?

By income group

● < $20,000   ● $20,000–$39,999   ● $40,000–$74,999   ● $75,000+

Attended a town or city council meeting

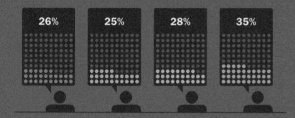

26% 25% 28% 35%

Signed a petition

19% 24% 24% 28%

Attended a protest march

4% 4% 4% 3%

Tried to contact a member of Congress

7% 9% 10% 15%

SOURCE: American National Election Study 2016 time series, www.electionstudies.org (accessed 11/4/17).

★ WHAT YOU CAN DO ★

Be an Informed Consumer of Opinion Polls

 When you encounter information from opinion polls, consider the source of the poll, the wording of the questions, and whether individuals were randomly selected to participate. Learn more at **www.umich.edu/~numbers/polls**.

 Go to **www.realclearpolitics.com** to see polls about the same issues from different sources. Note the margins of error, and notice how aggregating polls makes a difference.

 If asked, consider responding to an opinion poll—or take the initiative and express your views through one of the actions above.

★ STUDY GUIDE ★

Defining Public Opinion

Public opinion refers to the attitudes that people have about issues, events, elected officials, and public policy. Despite differences in opinion on many issues, most Americans share a common set of values, including a belief in the principles of liberty, equality, and democracy. Although many Americans subscribe to other ideologies, most describe themselves as either liberals, conservatives, or moderates. Contemporary liberalism and conservatism have different emphases with regard to the values of liberty and equality.

Key Terms

public opinion (p. 207)

values (or beliefs) (p. 207)

political ideology (p. 207)

attitude (or opinion) (p. 207)

liberty (p. 209)

equality of opportunity (p. 209)

liberal (p. 212)

conservative (p. 213)

libertarian (p. 214)

socialist (p. 214)

Practice Quiz

1. The term *public opinion* is used to describe
   a) the speeches and writings made by a president during his or her term in office.
   b) the analysis of events broadcast by news reporters during the evening news.
   c) the beliefs and attitudes that people have about issues, events, elected officials, and policies.
   d) decisions of the Supreme Court.
   e) any political statement that is made by a citizen outside of his or her home.

2. Today, the term _____ refers to someone who generally supports the social and economic status quo and is suspicious of efforts to introduce new political formulas and economic arrangements.
   a) libertarian
   b) liberal
   c) conservative
   d) democrat
   e) Whig

3. Socialism refers to
   a) a political ideology that emphasizes social ownership and strong government.
   b) a political ideology that emphasizes freedom and voluntary association with small government.
   c) a political ideology that argues for the need to place strict limitations on voting rights and civil liberties.
   d) a political ideology that argues a single ruler should have total control over every aspect of people's lives.
   e) a political ideology that argues governments are inherently repressive and should be abolished entirely.

How We Form Political Opinions

A number of factors, including the family, education, membership in social groups, self-interest, and the political environment, help form people's underlying political beliefs and values.

Key Terms

political socialization (p. 216)

agents of socialization (p. 216)

gender gap (p. 220)

Practice Quiz

4. The process by which Americans learn political beliefs and values is called
   a) brainwashing.
   b) propaganda.
   c) indoctrination.
   d) political socialization.
   e) political development.

5. The fact that women tend to oppose military intervention more than men do is an example of
   a) the rally around the flag effect.
   b) partisan polarization.
   c) the peace paradox.
   d) the bandwagon effect.
   e) the gender gap.

Political Knowledge and Changes in Public Opinion

Explore when and why public opinion changes and what role political knowledge plays (pp. 225–32)

As people encounter new information, it may (or may not) influence their opinions. Many people acquire political information and make political decisions by relying on cues from party elites, interest groups, trusted acquaintances, and the mass media. However, inadequate knowledge can prevent individuals from effectively defending their political interests.

Practice Quiz

6. Which of the following statements about political knowledge is not accurate?
   a) In general, citizens with high levels of political knowledge are more likely to be partisans (Democrats or Republicans).
   b) In general, citizens with high levels of political knowledge are more likely to have an ideology (liberal or conservative).
   c) In general, citizens with high levels of political knowledge are better able to evaluate new information and determine if it is consistent with their beliefs and opinions.
   d) In general, citizens with high levels of political knowledge are less likely to belong to political organizations and to be active in politics.
   e) In general, citizens with high levels of political knowledge are better able to recognize their political interests and to act to further those interests.

7. Three stages of John Zaller's model of opinion formation are
   a) "skim," "scan," and "sample."
   b) "skim," "scan," and "accept."
   c) "skim," "receive," and "accept."
   d) "scan," "receive," and "accept."
   e) "receive," "accept," and "sample."

The Media, Government, and Public Opinion

Describe the major forces that shape public opinion (pp. 232–34)

When individuals form opinions about specific issues, events, and politicians, they do not do so in isolation. They are bombarded by the efforts of many individuals and groups seeking to persuade them. Government officials and interest groups rely on messaging and a variety of media to get their messages across to citizens. The news media also serve as a powerful force in creating opinion and influencing popular attitudes.

Key Term

marketplace of ideas (p. 232)

Practice Quiz

8. Which of the following are the most important external influences on how political opinions are formed in the marketplace of ideas?
   a) the government, private groups, and the news media
   b) the unemployment rate, the Dow Jones industrial average, and the NASDAQ composite
   c) random digit dialing surveys, push polls, and framing experiments
   d) the Constitution, the Declaration of Independence, and the *Federalist Papers*
   e) the legislative branch, the executive branch, and the judicial branch

Public Opinion and Government Policy

Although there are many instances where government policy differs from the desires of the public, research has shown that there is generally a strong connection between what government does and what people want. Research has also shown, however, that more affluent and more educated citizens have disproportionately large influence over policy decisions.

Practice Quiz

9. Which statement best describes influence over politics and public policy decisions in the United States?
   a) All citizens exert an equal influence over politics and public policy decisions in the United States.
   b) Citizens who are less affluent and less educated have a disproportionately large influence over politics and public policy decisions in the United States.
   c) Citizens who are more affluent and more educated have a disproportionately large influence over politics and public policy decisions in the United States.
   d) Less affluent and less educated citizens only exert an influence over politics and public policy decisions when the Democratic Party controls the U.S. Congress.
   e) Less affluent and less educated citizens only exert an influence over politics and public policy decisions when the Republican Party controls the U.S. Congress.

Measuring Public Opinion

Surveys can provide a very accurate description of public opinion on an issue if they employ an appropriate sampling method, include a sufficient sample size, and avoid selection bias. In addition to the characteristics of the sample, the reliability of surveys is determined by the ordering and wording of the questions pollsters choose to ask.

Key Terms

public-opinion polls (p. 237)

sample (p. 237)

simple random sample (or probability sample) (p. 237)

random digit dialing (p. 239)

sampling error (or margin of error) (p. 239)

social desirability effect (p. 242)

selection bias (p. 243)

push poll (p. 245)

bandwagon effect (p. 245)

Practice Quiz

10. Which of the following is the term used in public-opinion polling to denote the small group representing the opinions of the whole population?
    a) control group
    b) sample
    c) micropopulation
    d) respondents
    e) median voters

11. A *push poll* is a poll in which
    a) the questions are designed to shape the respondent's opinion rather than measure the respondent's opinion.
    b) the questions are designed to measure the respondent's opinion rather than shape the respondent's opinion.
    c) the questions are designed to reduce measurement error.
    d) the sample is chosen to include only undecided or independent voters.
    e) the sample is not representative of the population it is drawn from.

12. A familiar polling problem is the *bandwagon effect*, which occurs when
    a) the same results are used over and over again.
    b) polling results influence people to support the candidate marked as the probable victor in a campaign.
    c) polling results influence people to support the candidate who is trailing in a campaign.
    d) background noise makes it difficult for a pollster and a respondent to communicate with each other.
    e) a large number of people refuse to answer a pollster's questions.

For Further Reading

Asher, Herbert. *Polling and the Public: What Every Citizen Should Know*. 8th ed. Washington, DC: CQ Press, 2011.

Barreto, Matt, and Gary M. Segura. *Latino America: How America's Most Dynamic Population Is Poised to Transform the Politics of the Nation*. New York: Public Affairs, 2014.

Bartels, Larry. *Unequal Democracy*. Princeton, NJ: Princeton University Press, 2008.

Berinsky, Adam. *Silent Voices: Public Opinion and Political Participation in America*. Princeton, NJ: Princeton University Press, 2005.

Clawson, Rosalee, and Zoe Oxley. *Public Opinion: Democratic Ideals and Democratic Practice*. Washington, DC: CQ Press, 2008.

Delli Carpini, Michael, and Scott Keeter. *What Americans Know about Politics and Why It Matters*. New Haven, CT: Yale University Press, 1997.

Erikson, Robert, Michael MacKuen, and James Simson. *The Macro Polity*. New York: Cambridge University Press, 2002.

Gallup, George. *The Pulse of Democracy*. New York: Simon and Schuster, 1940.

Gilens, Martin. *Affluence and Influence: Economic Inequality and Political Power in America*. Princeton, NJ: Princeton University Press, 2012.

Ginsberg, Benjamin. *The Captive Public: How Mass Opinion Promotes State Power*. New York: Basic Books, 1986.

Griffin, John, and Brian Newman. *Minority Report: Evaluating Political Equality in America*. New York: Cambridge University Press, 2008.

Hutchings, Vincent. *Public Opinion and Democratic Accountability: How Citizens Learn about Politics*. Princeton, NJ: Princeton University Press, 2005.

Lau, Richard, and David Redlawsk. *How Voters Decide: Information Processing in an Election Campaign*. New York: Cambridge University Press, 2006.

Lee, Taeku. *Mobilizing Public Opinion*. Chicago: University of Chicago Press, 2002.

Lippmann, Walter. *Public Opinion*. 1922. http://xroads.virginia.edu/,Hyper2/CDFinal/Lippman/cover.html.

Lodge, Milton, and Charles S. Taber. *The Rationalizing Voter*. New York: Cambridge University Press, 2013.

Marcus, George E., W. Russell Neuman, and Michael MacKuen. *Affective Intelligence and Political Judgment*. Chicago: University of Chicago Press, 2000.

Norrander, Barbara, and Clyde Wilcox. *Understanding Public Opinion*. Washington, DC: CQ Press, 2009.

Tesler, Michael, and David O. Sears. *Obama's Race: The 2008 Election and the Dream of a Post-Racial America*. Chicago: University of Chicago Press, 2010.

Wlezien, Christopher, and Stuart Soroka. *Degrees of Democracy: Politics, Public Opinion, and Policy*. New York: Cambridge University Press, 2010.

Zaller, John. *The Nature and Origins of Mass Opinion*. New York: Cambridge University Press, 1992.

Recommended Websites

American Association for Public Opinion Research
www.aapor.org
This website is one of the premier academic sites for public opinion data on a host of political and social topics.

FiveThirtyEight
www.fivethirtyeight.com/politics
FiveThirtyEight, named for the number of electors in the Electoral College, was founded as a polling aggregator site by political analyst Nate Silver. The blog now covers a broad range of topics, but it is still widely known for Silver's election forecasts.

Gallup
www.gallup.com
The Gallup Organization has been involved in the scientific study of public opinion for more than 70 years and is highly regarded. This website contains public-opinion data archives, video archives, and international polls.

Latino Decisions
www.latinodecisions.com
A leader in Latino opinion research, Latino Decisions presents data and analysis on Latino American political opinions, attitudes, and engagement.

Pew Religion and Public Life
www.pewforum.org
Pew Religion and Public Life conducts public opinion polling, demographic research, and content analyses of attitudes about religion and politics. Pew Research Center is an independent, nonpartisan think tank that also explores attitudes toward numerous other political issues.

Real Clear Politics
www.realclearpolitics.com
This website aggregates top news stories, analyses, editorials, videos, and polls with the goal of providing users with ideological diversity. The "Polls" section averages polling data for presidential and congressional races and has often been an effective predictor of election outcomes.

The Media

WHAT GOVERNMENT DOES AND WHY IT MATTERS When the chairman of the Federal Communications Commission, Ajit Pai, proposed to end "net neutrality" in 2017, teenagers across the country leapt into action. Many had lived their entire lives in an era of neutrality, aspects of which began in 2006 and were codified by President Barack Obama in 2015. Under net neutrality, internet service providers were regulated like a utility. They could not block websites, slow some data transmission while imposing fees for fast transmission, or charge consumers to connect to certain sites. Chairman Pai asserted that such rules overregulated the internet. But many

teenagers, who get the majority of their news and information from the internet, disagreed. They used social media to coordinate letter-writing, Twitter, and protest efforts.

Sixteen-year-old student Will Howes led a protest in front of a Verizon store in Sioux Falls, South Dakota, arguing, "They can throttle your Netflix, they can change your Google results. The right to access information online is threatened."[1] His fellow protesters worried that rural South Dakotans might get priced out of internet service, which was already limited there. Teen protesters in front of a Keene, New Hampshire, Verizon store had similar concerns

Net neutrality—the principle that all data and content on the web must be treated equally and not blocked or slowed for certain users—has been a hot-button issue. Anooha Dasari is just one of many young people who have spoken out and organized in support of net neutrality.

about the price and availability of high-speed internet, holding signs asking, "Hey Siri, how much does this sentence cost?" As high school senior Harrison Hicks said, "The internet is imperative to my education, and it's really hard to be a self-starter and to teach yourself the information you need without the internet, especially since we're the first generation who's grown up with the internet having been around our entire lives."[2] Anooha Dasari, a high school junior from Mundelein, Illinois, who sent classmates links for emailing the FCC, said, "For research, for news, to communicate with friends, the internet is a big part of my life. It has formulated my personality, opinions, and political ideology. If it is controlled, my generation of students could be inclined to be just on one part of the [political] spectrum. That's dangerous." In December 2017, Pai cast the deciding vote to end the neutrality rules. Dasari vowed to continue to fight: "I will tweet and email and call and stay in the process."[3]

The sharing of information, whether via traditional or digital media, is an essential component of American democracy. So central is information to citizen participation that the Constitution's First Amendment guarantees freedom of the press, and most Americans believe that a free press is an essential condition for both liberty and democratic politics. Today, as the means of communication has expanded, the media continue to play a central role in American politics, not only in setting the agenda of topics that Americans think about and discuss but also in shaping public opinion on political issues and politicians. The political implications of this media system are significant. Politics is increasingly defined by the individuals and groups who are best able to blend older and newer media—using, for example, both television and digital media to promote their message.

Discussing the right of press freedom, Thomas Jefferson wrote, "The basis of our government being the opinion of the people, the very first object should be to keep that right; and were it left to me to decide whether we should have a government without newspapers or newspapers without a government, I should not hesitate a moment to prefer the latter."[4] As the nature of media has evolved, its centrality to government and politics has never waned. In fact, in an era when politicians accuse each other and media members of promoting "fake news," and people fight for or against control of internet communications, a full understanding of America's dynamic media landscape may be more important than ever.

CHAPTER GOALS

★ Describe the key roles the media play in American political life (pp. 257–60)

★ Discuss how digital media have transformed how citizens learn about politics (pp. 261–77)

★ Analyze the ways the media can influence public opinion and politics (pp. 277–82)

★ Explain how politicians and others try to shape the news (pp. 283–85)

★ Trace the evolution of rules that govern broadcast media (pp. 285–87)

The Media in American Democracy

Describe the key roles the media play in American political life

Freedom of the press is protected under the First Amendment to the U.S. Constitution, along with the most cherished individual rights in American democracy, including freedom of speech and religion. Freedom of the press is the right to circulate opinions in print and digital media without censorship by the government. In the United States, citizens and private companies have the right to publish newspapers, magazines, and other forms of digital media with few government restrictions. In many authoritarian countries there is no freedom of the press and the government controls the news and political information through state-sponsored media.

Why would the Founders care so much about the rights of the media to report the news without interference from government? In the 1700s, when they were still under British control, freedom of speech did not exist in the American colonies. Criticizing the King of England was a crime punishable, in some cases, by death. When the colonists won their freedom from England they wanted to be able to freely express their political opinions without fear of retaliation. The first of 10 amendments to the U.S. Constitution adopted during the Founding period states, "Congress shall make no law respecting an establishment of religion, or prohibiting the free exercise thereof; or abridging the freedom of speech, or of the press; or the right of the people peaceably to assemble, and to petition the Government for a redress of grievances." Despite attacks from both Republicans and Democrats that claim major media outlets are biased, most Americans believe freedom of the press is very important for maintaining a strong democracy, and that "news organizations are free to criticize political leaders" (see Figure 6.1 in Chapter 6).

The **media** serve three important roles in American democracy: helping to inform the public about current political issues and events; providing a forum through which candidates, politicians, and even the public can debate policies and issues; and acting as a watchdog on the actions of politicians and other political actors. Part of the media's role of informing the public involves providing a variety of perspectives on current events and fact-checking sources to provide unbiased coverage of current events. The media serve as a type of public square where citizens become informed about their government, political leaders, societal problems, and possible solutions—a forum where information necessary for democracy is exchanged.

> **media** print and digital forms of communication, including television, newspapers, radio, and the internet, intended to convey information to large audiences

Without the work of journalists and the media, democracy and self-government would not be possible. The news media are how individuals learn about politics and current events, government policy, candidates, and political parties. The information presented by the media allows citizens to cast informed decisions in elections and to form opinions about policy issues. American philosopher John Dewey believed the media served to educate the public. A strong democracy, he said, was based not only on voting rights, but ensuring that public opinion on current issues is based on communication among citizens, experts, and elected officials. This communication ensures elected officials adopt policies consistent, for the most part, with the preferences of the citizens and serves as a counterweight to communication among elites, the wealthy, and corporations. In other words, the mass media help level the playing field between political elites and "the people," giving citizens a more potent voice in society. Without the media, citizens would not know the actions of political

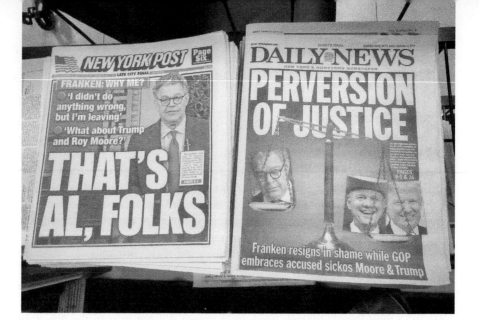

One of the media's role in American democracy is that of a watchdog, investigating and highlighting alleged and actual wrongdoing by public officials. Recently, the media have exposed episodes of alleged sexual misconduct by several politicians including Senator Al Franken (D-Minn.), senatorial candidate Roy Moore (R-Ala.), and Donald Trump.

leaders, corporations, or foreign governments and would be powerless to change the system. Journalists (people trained to report the news) give ordinary citizens information and knowledge, and this information is ultimately power.

Finally, the media serve as a watchdog for the public, scrutinizing the actions of elected officials on behalf of citizens—most of whom do not have the opportunity to closely follow the actions of politicians and government. Like an alarm system for a home, the media notify the public of actions taken by government that may harm them.

The watchdog role of the media is the most important for the study of politics. Political news is reported on page 1 of print newspapers or in news alerts on your cell phone. The media inform the public about what policy issues are at stake in terms of changes in government laws and regulations. The media seek to expose which individuals and groups are exerting power in politics and what are their tactics and strategies, and sheds light on the different perspectives being used by political actors (e.g., the arguments for and against building a wall between the United States and Mexico, a major federal tax cut or raise, or adopting a law to create free college tuition). The media often expose how financial interests are tied to political leaders and policy making, or scandalous behavior of politicians and other public figures, like allegations of sexual assault against Republican senatorial candidate Roy Moore or Democratic senator Al Franken (Minn.). By reporting the news in the public interest the media continuously monitor the actions of public officials in its surveillance mode and strives to protect the public from government overreach and corruption by serving as a check on political power.

Informing the public, creating a forum for debate, and keeping a watchful eye on government action are critical components to democracy. And it seems like a lot to ask of the media. Do the media meet these goals?

JOURNALISM

Most practicing journalists receive training in schools of journalism and mass communication. Journalists are guided by standards in reporting the news in the public interest, known as the principles of journalism. Above all the news media seek to report the truth via fact-checking, verification of sources, and investigative journalism (defined in more detail later). This includes reporting factual claims by relying on legitimate sources and citing people with credible positions, eyewitnesses and participants in events, and documents associated with recognizable and credible institutions. The traditional news media aim to balance coverage of current events by providing objective treatment of opposing sides, and it avoids including personal views of reporters or editors. While reporting the news without any bias—objectivity—is ultimately unattainable because all individuals have biases that influence how they understand events, objectivity is a method used by journalists to report both sides of a story.

THE PROFIT MOTIVE

The media are sometimes referred to as the fourth branch of government, providing a check on the power of government and political leaders. But who checks or controls the media? In the United States the media are not part of government and not subject to checks and balances like Congress, the presidency, and the courts. Instead most media in the United States are privately owned companies. Media companies, like technology companies such as Verizon, Amazon, or Apple, are for-profit corporations.

Public broadcasting refers to television, radio, and digital media that receive funding from the public through license fees, subsidies, or tax dollars. In most other democratic countries public broadcasting plays a major role in informing the public about politics and current events. In contrast, public broadcasting in the United States—such as National Public Radio or PBS—plays a very small role in the media system, at just 2 percent of market share, compared to 35 percent in France, 40 percent in Germany, and 65 percent in Denmark. What is unique about the media in the United States is that most are entirely privately owned and operated. There is evidence from cross-national surveys that U.S. citizens have lower levels of political knowledge than those in European democracies who consume more public broadcasting.[5]

Public media usually come with greater restrictions. Swiss law, for example, prohibits political campaign ads on radio and TV programs; they are only allowed in newspapers. In France, the media are prohibited from covering news about candidates running for public office the last few days before the election. American media face many fewer government regulations, as will be discussed later in this chapter.

U.S. media companies earn most of their revenue from advertising, rather than subscriptions, although revenue from subscriptions has been increasing. This means media actors—from journalists to editors to the owners of the media companies—are motivated by what audiences want, because higher ratings generate more advertising revenue. Because of the need to reach wide audiences to sell advertisements, the U.S. media are more focused on soft news, such as entertainment, sports, and celebrity news, than are European media, which provide more hard news coverage of politics and civic events. And when it comes to political news, American media tend to focus increasingly on more dramatic, highly conflictual events and issues. Sensational stories of scandals or candidate attacks often generate more interest—and thus

Because of the U.S. media's profit motive, they tend to focus on highly conflictual political events like presidential debates and less on the subtle details of changes in public policy.

revenue—than the stories of everyday governing and details of public policy. Nonetheless, objectivity is still the goal, and standard practice is that news, opinion, and ads should be separate and distinct; that is why the opinions of editors are reserved for the opinion pages.

The profit motive of the news industry may have contributed to Donald Trump's unexpected victory in the 2016 election. Due to the novelty of a television celebrity running for president, Trump's campaign was a financial boon for the media industry. His candidacy received double the media coverage of his Democratic opponent, Hillary Clinton, and his Republican challengers in the primaries. The head of CBS, Les Moonves, said the Trump phenomena "may not be good for America, but it's damn good for CBS..."[6] Throughout the election and Trump's first year in office, the cable news channels profited from higher ratings because of the public's fascination with Trump; CNN, for example, earned about $100 million in television and advertising revenue more than expected in 2016.[7] Newspapers and digital news outlets found that if the word *Trump* was mentioned in a title, it was more likely to be read and shared online.

MASS MEDIA OWNERSHIP

One noteworthy feature of the traditional media in the United States is the concentration of its ownership. A small number of giant corporations control a wide swath of media holdings, including television networks, movie studios, record companies, cable channels and local cable providers, book publishers, magazines, newspapers, and increasingly, online and digital media outlets. Large global corporations own much of the media offline and online.[8] **Media monopolies**, such as Disney, have prompted questions about whether enough competition exists among traditional media to produce a truly diverse set of views on political matters.[9] In 2019, for example, Disney purchased 21st Century Fox to become the third largest media company in the United States. As major newspapers, television stations, and radio networks fall into fewer hands, the risk increases that politicians and citizens who express less popular or minority viewpoints will have difficulty finding a public forum.

Despite the appearance of substantial numbers overall, the number of traditional news-gathering sources operating nationally is actually quite small—several wire services, four broadcast networks, a few elite print newspapers, and a smattering of other sources, such as a few large local papers and several small, independent radio networks. More than three-fourths of the daily print newspapers in the United States are owned by large media conglomerates such as the Hearst, McClatchy, and Gannett corporations. Much of the national news that is published by local newspapers is provided by one wire service, the Associated Press. More than 500 of the nation's television stations are affiliated with one of just four networks and carry that network's evening news programs.

The trend in concentration of traditional media ownership occurred in large part due to the relaxation of government regulations in the 1980s and '90s. The enactment of the 1996 Telecommunications Act opened the way for additional consolidation in the media industry, and a wave of mergers and consolidations has further reduced the field of independent media across the country. But as more digital-only news sources come online, these trends toward concentration in media ownership may reverse.

media monopoly the ownership and control of the media by a few large corporations

FOR CRITICAL ANALYSIS

In recent years, a number of major media corporations have acquired numerous newspapers, television stations, and radio properties. Is media concentration a serious problem? Why or why not?

The Media Today

The past three decades have resulted in a massive transformation of the U.S. news media. New competition from free digital sources has put pressure on traditional subscription-based news sources as Americans migrated to reading the news online. Today 93 percent of adults read the news online.[10] This picture is very different from the early 2000s, when most Americans said that after television, print newspapers were their main source for news and less than 20 percent read the news online (see Figure 7.1).[11] Though not replacing losses in subscription and traditional advertising revenue, digital advertising revenue continues to grow.[12]

Despite the digital transformation of the news media, much of what makes the media important in American politics remains the same. Major newspapers and TV networks—even if their content is increasingly delivered in digital form—remain popular and important sources of news. Political leaders are successful in making headline news and setting the news agenda. And journalists trained in professional schools create and develop much of what we consume as news, including original reporting.

But more and more, the media are online companies facing an environment where anyone with access to an internet connection can publish the news. It is still only a small number of organizations that have credibility and the largest audiences, however;[13] the leading newspapers in the United States, such as the *New York Times*, the *Wall Street Journal*, and the *Washington Post*, receive some of the highest traffic online. Nevertheless, the digital transformation of the media has created a reorganization of the media industry that impacts how the news is made and how consumers learn about politics.

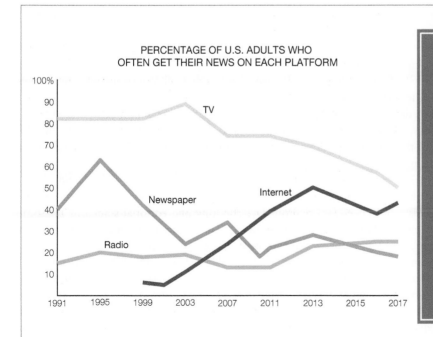

PERCENTAGE OF U.S. ADULTS WHO OFTEN GET THEIR NEWS ON EACH PLATFORM

FIGURE 7.1

Use of Online News Continues to Grow

The media landscape for news has seen remarkable shifts in a short period of time. Twenty years ago, more than 80 percent of Americans watched news on television and more than half read news in a newspaper. Today, fewer Americans watch news on TV and just over one-quarter read the newspaper. What media source has gained rather than lost its audience?

SOURCE: "Americans' Online News Use Is Closing in on TV News Use," Pew Research Center, September 5, 2017, www.pewresearch.org (accessed 5/23/18).

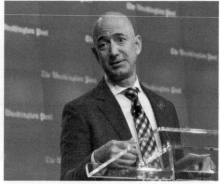

Two trends in media have been the consolidation of media outlets into large conglomerates and the growing influence of technology on media. Founded by Rupert Murdoch (left), News Corp is a media conglomerate that has owned Fox News and the *Wall Street Journal*, among other news outlets. Since he acquired the *Washington Post*, Amazon's Jeff Bezos (right) has deepened the paper's focus on investigative journalism, which some say has made the *Post* profitable again.

Before the internet, journalism organizations largely controlled the news, including original reporting, writing and production, packaging and delivery, and selecting editors. Over time, technology companies like Facebook, Apple, Google, and Amazon have become major players in the content and delivery of the news. These companies are partners in the business of journalism from the financial side to how the news is produced and delivered to consumers. They report the news using advanced technology, engineering, and market research to push specific news alerts to specific people, based on their interests and preferences. And it seems to be working: Facebook and Google, for example, generate the most digital advertising revenue for newspapers.[14]

The interdependence between technology and media companies continues to grow. In one of the latest trends, technology companies and their CEOs have been purchasing or developing major news media companies, such as the creation of the *Intercept* by Ebay founder Pierre Omidyar, or the purchase of the *Washington Post* by Amazon CEO Jeff Bezos. Both the *Intercept* and *Washington Post* have a reputation for forceful investigative journalism and original reporting. And Facebook editors control trending topics in the news on the global platform, a key editorial role in what makes the headline news.

Beyond making the news profitable again, these high-tech collaborations are changing how Americans learn about current events in the United States and globally.[15] This is evident in the growing number of Americans who read news by using social network platforms such as Twitter or Facebook—community forums designed to emphasize participation, networked communities, and transparency. How citizens read the news has changed in the digital age, but the role of the media in politics remains as important today as during the founding of our nation.

One of the costs of the transformation of the media to digital and citizen journalism—news produced by individuals and organizations beyond professional journalists—has been less rigorous fact-checking and editorial standards for some online news websites. Some digital-only news platforms, on both the ideological left and right, no longer follow the guiding principles of journalism.

Despite mass ownership of traditional news outlets, the American news media are among the world's freest and most diverse. Americans have thousands of available options in political reporting. These options include a wide variety of local and national newspapers, newsmagazines, broadcast media, radio, podcasts, and digital sources. The freedom to speak one's mind is one of the most cherished of American political values. Without the news media's investigations, citizens would be forced to rely entirely on information provided by politicians and the government, and would be deprived of information necessary to evaluate issues carefully and form reasoned opinions. Americans get their news from (1) newspapers and magazines; (2) broadcast media (radio and television); and increasingly, (3) digital media. Each of these three sources—newspapers, broadcast, and digital—has distinctive characteristics.

NEWSPAPERS

Newspapers are the oldest medium for the dissemination of the news, though most Americans read digital versions of print media today. Newspapers have an especially influential audience because they help set the political agenda for the nation. Their audience of political elites relies on the detailed coverage provided by professional journalists to inform their views about public matters.

The emergence of newspapers (and later radio and television networks) as mass-production businesses driven primarily for profit had major implications for the role of the media in politics in the late nineteenth and early twentieth centuries. The development of standardized reporting and writing practices emphasizing objectivity in political news coverage was due in large part to generate revenue for media organizations. The owners of large newspaper companies determined that the best way to make a profit was to appeal to as broad an audience as possible, which meant not alienating potential readers who held liberal or conservative political views. This, in turn, required methods to train and "discipline" reporters to produce a standardized, seemingly neutral news product. In contrast, some native digital news is less likely than like journalism from legacy media outlets to be value neutral.

These journalistic practices were successful in attracting audiences, and for a long time most cities and towns in the country had their own newspaper. However, for most traditional newspapers, recent decades have been financially challenging. Competition from broadcast media and free content online, combined with simultaneous declines in advertising revenue and circulation levels, have undermined the traditional business model of newspapers.[16] In 2018 there were roughly 39,210 working journalists, down from a high of 60,000 a decade before.[17] Estimates indicate daily newspaper print circulation has declined by over 30 percent over the past 20 years.[18] And lower circulation leads to lower advertising revenue.

Following the 2016 election, however, some major U.S. newspapers reported a sharp increase in digital subscriptions.[19] The *New York Times* added more than 500,000 digital subscriptions in 2016—a 47 percent increase from the previous year, while the *Wall Street Journal* had a 23 percent increase over the previous year, and the *Chicago Tribune* a 76 percent increase. The newspaper industry as a whole, however, continues to face declines in circulation and ad revenue. The *New York Times* saw a 9 percent decline in advertising revenue but a 3 percent rise in circulation revenue, for an overall revenue decline of 2 percent in 2016.[20]

The *Washington Post*, in contrast, may be a model for making the news media profitable. The *Post* is a private company owned by Amazon CEO Jeff Bezos. While revenues for most newspapers continued to decline (see Figure 7.2), the *Post* experienced double-digit revenue growth for three straight years. Along with a viable financial model, the *Post* has emerged as a leader in investigative reporting, data analytics, and marketing. Bezos rebuilt the *Post* into a media technology company,

The circulation and newsstand sales of traditional newspapers and news magazines have fallen in the last decade. However, because the remaining audience includes political elites and politically engages citizens, they remain important forums in the marketplace of ideas.

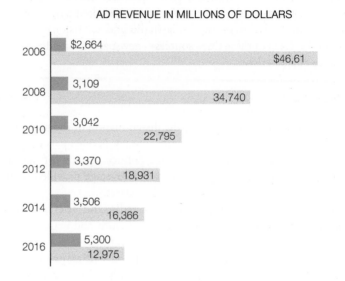

FIGURE 7.2

Advertising Revenue

Media is a business, not a branch of government, so media rely on subscription and advertising money to fund their services. As print newspapers' readership declined, their advertising revenue fell sharply. Some of this money shifted to online advertising, including ads for mobile devices.

SOURCE: Newspaper Association of America (2003–2013), Pew Research analysis of BIA/Kelsey data (2014), www.journalism.org/media-indicators/newspaper-print-and-online-ad-revenue/ (accessed 2/3/17).

AD REVENUE IN MILLIONS OF DOLLARS

Year		
2006	$2,664	$46,61
2008	3,109	34,740
2010	3,042	22,795
2012	3,370	18,931
2014	3,506	16,366
2016	5,300	12,975

producing 1,200 articles per day, an exploding readership, and dynamic digital content. The paper's content-distribution uses social media like Facebook and Twitter, offers discounts to Amazon Prime members, and the *Post* app is preinstalled on Amazon's Fire tablets. The *Post* now tracks how different headlines and story framings affect readership of each story. One of the three major newspapers in the United States, the 140-year-old *Washington Post* is known for investigative reporting and for breaking the story that revealed the Watergate scandal in 1970 that led to the impeachment and removal from office of President Nixon. Today the *Post* focuses on adversarial journalism of the Trump Administration and extensive reporting of Russian interference in U.S. elections.[21]

News organizations such as the *Washington Post*, the *New York Times*, and the *Economist* were among the first to charge customers for reading the news online. For most newspapers today, non-ad revenue comes mainly from digital subscriptions rather than print circulation. This model allows a certain number of free visits before requiring users to pay and appears to be a viable business model for the digital press. Elite newspapers have been able to create a viable business model whereby people will pay digital subscriptions to access content, and paid digital news is increasing revenue and improving content. Digital subscription models have not been as viable for many smaller or mid-sized local, regional, and even big-city papers, however.

Legacy newspapers face the greatest competition from digital-only news outlets, such as Politico, Bloomberg News, the Drudge Report, the National Review, and a host of others. And the pace of technological change in the news media shows no signs of slowing down.[22]

While the media were widely criticized during the 2016 presidential campaign for a lack of scrutiny and uneven coverage of candidates, the media's investigative reporting on the Trump campaign is noteworthy. During the election investigative articles in the *Washington Post*, for example, revealed the history around candidate Donald Trump's casino bankruptcies, failure to release his taxes, and ties between Russia and the Trump campaign, while others focused on the defunct and fraudulent Trump University.[23] Russia's involvement in the election was especially troubling, and public knowledge of possible foul play in what are normally free and fair elections would not be possible without the deep investigative reporting by the media.[24]

BROADCAST MEDIA

Television news reaches more Americans than any other single news source. It is estimated that over 95 percent of Americans have a television, and tens of millions of people watch national and local news programs every day. Pew reports that combined average viewership for the ABC, CBS, and NBC evening newscasts remained stable in 2016 at about 24 million.[25] Despite the rise of digital media, television news (local, national network, and cable) still commands truly massive audiences, much larger than other sources. Television news, however, generally covers relatively few topics and provides little depth of coverage. It serves the important function of alerting viewers to issues and events—headline news—via brief quotes and short characterizations of the day's events. Furthermore, **broadcast media** do very little of their own reporting, instead relying on leading newspapers or digital media to set their news agenda. Print and digital media, as written text, also provide more detailed and complete information than radio or television media, offering a better context for analysis.

broadcast media television, radio, or other media that transmit audio and/or video content to the public

Because they are aware of the character of television news coverage, politicians and others often seek to manipulate the news by providing the media with sound bites that will dominate news coverage. Sound bites can work for or against politicians. During the 2016 presidential election, calls for deporting undocumented immigrants were a frequent sound bite topic from candidates such as Donald Trump.

Twenty-four-hour cable news stations such as MSNBC, CNN, and Fox News offer more detail and commentary than the half-hour evening news shows found on the three broadcast news stations—ABC, NBC, and CBS. But even these channels offer more headlines and sound bites than newspapers, especially during their prime-time broadcasts.

Politicians generally consider local broadcast news a friendlier venue than the national news. National reporters are often inclined to criticize and question, whereas local and state reporters are more likely to accept the pronouncements of national leaders at face value. Local TV continues to be a major source of news, especially for older Americans, though its importance as a news source is decreasing among the younger generation in favor of social media such as Facebook (see Figure 7.3). Generally, however, Americans' reliance on television does not appear to be going away.

RADIO

Radio is another broadcast news source that has evolved with the popularity of podcasting. In the 1990s, talk radio became an important source of commentary as well as entertainment. Conservative radio hosts, such as Rush Limbaugh and Sean Hannity, have huge audiences and have helped to mobilize support for conservative political causes and candidates. In the political center or center left, National Public Radio (NPR) is a coveted source for in-depth political reporting. In recent years radio news listening has experienced significant growth; in 1990 there were 400 radio stations, a number that has grown to over 2,000 today.

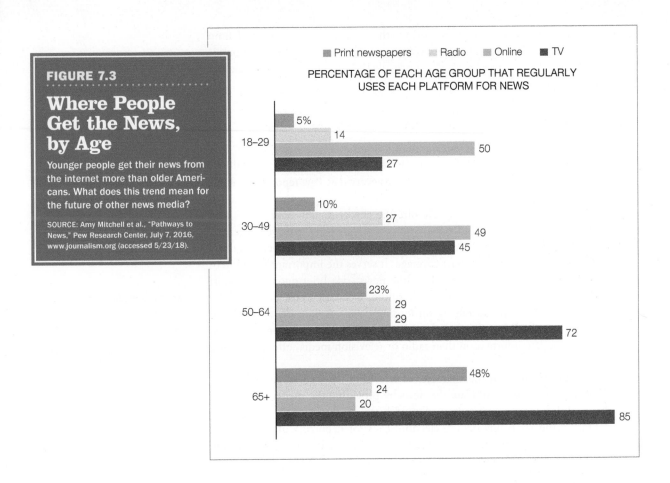

FIGURE 7.3

Where People Get the News, by Age

Younger people get their news from the internet more than older Americans. What does this trend mean for the future of other news media?

SOURCE: Amy Mitchell et al., "Pathways to News," Pew Research Center, July 7, 2016, www.journalism.org (accessed 5/23/18).

PERCENTAGE OF EACH AGE GROUP THAT REGULARLY USES EACH PLATFORM FOR NEWS

■ Print newspapers   ■ Radio   ■ Online   ■ TV

18–29
- 5%
- 14
- 50
- 27

30–49
- 10%
- 27
- 49
- 45

50–64
- 23%
- 29
- 29
- 72

65+
- 48%
- 24
- 20
- 85

Broadcast radio includes traditional AM/FM radio and digital formats such as online radio and podcasting. While AM/FM radio reaches almost all Americans and remains steady in its revenue, online radio and podcasting has expanded rapidly in the past decade, steadily growing to 64 percent of Americans who reported tuning in during the last month in 2018, up from 12 percent in 2007. While public broadcasting has a much smaller share of the total media market in the United States than in other countries, NPR is still popular and an important way for people to learn about politics each day. In 2017 there were 5.4 million unique downloads of NPR podcasts every week, a number that continues to grow.[26] Mobile devices, including satellite radios and cell phones, have triggered a growth in radio use as online radio listening can occur nearly anywhere. Listening to radio news while commuting is a primary way many Americans become informed about politics.[27]

Comedy Comedy talk shows with political content, such as *The Daily Show*, *The Late Show*, and *Saturday Night Live* attract millions of television viewers. These shows use humor, sarcasm, and social criticism to discuss serious topics, generally covering almost every major political event. Pew surveys have shown that these talk shows are important sources of political news, especially for young people and liberals, and that followers of comedic talk shows are well informed about politics.[28] It is also likely that more-informed viewers are self-selecting into watching comedy news. These shows combine political news and entertainment and are an important source of news for young people.

DIGITAL MEDIA

The twenty-first century has experienced a profound transformation of the media, as discussed in the introduction. The impact of the internet in mass communication parallels that of the printing press in nineteenth-century America, which saw the rise of the **penny press** and widespread literacy.[29] Today, even as the print newspaper business has consolidated, readership of online news has soared. Digital has become the medium of choice to consume entertainment, news, and information about politics for all age groups below 50. In 2000 just 35 percent of adult internet users said they looked for news or information about politics or the upcoming campaigns online. Today 94 percent of young people get news online from mobile devices, and even 67 percent of Americans over age 65 go online for news.[30] In 2017 online news closed in on TV as the major source for news; 43 percent of Americans primarily get news online, compared to 50 percent who rely on TV.[31]

Streaming videos is a growing substitute for television for some viewers, fundamentally altering broadcast news, as dedicated channels provide political analysis, commentary, full-length features, and comedy. Presidential addresses are now regularly streamed live, and millions of people tune in to hear the president in this format.[32] Similarly, podcasts are restructuring radio news by allowing listeners to tune in to the news at any time online.

While many traditional news sources, such as newspapers, now publish online, other digital-only outlets tend to be smaller and more specialized and have lower personnel and overhead costs than mainstream publishers. Besides digital-only news outlets, other digital news sources include news websites, citizen journalism such as blogs, social media such as Twitter and YouTube, podcasts, and nonprofit journalism. (See the "Who Are Americans?" feature on p. 279 for more information on where Americans get their news.) Do digital media ultimately help or hinder progress toward the ideal of a well-informed citizenry that can govern itself effectively? The following discussion helps to answer this question.

News aggregators such as Google News, Reddit, and RealClear Politics generally compile and repackage stories that were created by other sources, and then deliver them online to consumers in convenient formats. They serve as a platform that allows users to share and comment on the news. Some of this content is produced by digital-only news organizations, mainstream media, social movement organizations, ordinary users and other "amateurs," as well as powerful political groups, governments, candidates, nonprofits, corporations, and professional media organizations. News aggregators cover thousands of news stories each day, as well as the latest public-opinion polls and their own synthesis of the headline news. Mirroring the digital revolution, digital advertising has grown as a percentage of total media advertising across all platforms. The main benefactors of digital advertising continue to be social media and technology companies, such as Google and Facebook.[33]

Social media sites are particularly convenient for obtaining breaking news 24 hours a day, and formats for doing so are becoming more diverse and interactive. Fully 73 percent of Americans use YouTube, the most commonly used social media platform, followed by Facebook (68 percent).[34] Rather than merely providing a forum to connect with friends and family, social media are spaces for learning about politics and now a primary source for news—a dramatic change from just a few years ago. A majority of American adults—67 percent—gets news on social media. The trend in using social media for political information continues to grow at a rapid rate across all demographic groups.

penny press cheap, tabloid-style newspaper produced in the nineteenth century, when mass production of inexpensive newspapers first became possible due to the steam-powered printing press; a penny press newspaper cost one cent compared with other papers, which cost more than five cents

news aggregator an application or feed that collects web content such as news headlines, blogs, podcasts, online videos, and more in one location for easy viewing

The rise of digital media has made it easier for Americans to get political news, but one in five Americans still lacks home internet access. People without high-speed internet access at home often get free access in public libraries, but access is restricted to certain times.

digital citizen a daily internet user with broadband (high-speed) home internet access and the technology and literacy skills to go online for employment, news, politics, entertainment, commerce, and other activities

digital divide the gap in access to the internet among demographic groups based on education, income, age, geographic location, and race/ethnicity

social media web- and mobile-based technologies that are used to turn communication into interactive dialogue among organizations, communities, and individuals; social media technologies take on many different forms including text, blogs, podcasts, photographs, streaming video, Facebook, and Twitter

The rise of digital media has changed the way that people get information and share it, affecting everything from political activism, campaign advertising, and voter mobilization to public opinion. Online media are more diverse and have created a more participatory press, one in which citizens and nonprofit organizations now play a prominent role, and journalists regularly interact with readers via social media, especially Twitter. Readers can now post comments online, upload videos, and participate in a community, providing feedback on almost all online news articles. Digital media, by representing a wider range of political views than traditional media, have created more information and a more vibrant media environment.

The term *digital citizenship* refers to the ability to participate in culture and politics online. Today's internet has the potential to benefit society as a whole by facilitating political participation and social inclusion through greater access to political information and news.[35] The internet helps provide the information and skills needed for democratic engagement and economic opportunity. However, regular and effective use of the internet requires high-speed access and digital literacy to evaluate and use information online.[36] Individuals without the access or skills to use the internet may be increasingly uninformed and excluded from the world of politics online. In 2018, 73 percent of Americans were **digital citizens**, individuals with home high-speed access and the technology and literacy skills to use it.[37] Access to the internet is shaped by income and education. While only half of the working poor (those earning less than $20,000 a year) had home broadband, 85 percent of those earning more than $100,000 a year did. Sixty-three percent of high school graduates have home broadband compared with almost 90 percent of college graduates.[38] These data suggest that there are significant inequalities in access to digital media, what is called the **digital divide**.[39] Because digital media are essential to participation in society, some argue that government has a responsibility to provide affordable and universal access, as is provided by most other democratic countries.

Today, mobile internet on smartphones is increasingly important for news and participation in society, especially for the young, racial and ethnic minorities, and foreign-born populations. Similar inequalities based on demographic factors, such as income and education, are also found for mobile internet access. While many people see smartphone access as the bridge over the digital divide, others consider it an inferior form of access because many human capital–intensive activities—applying for a job, research for school, or work—require a computer and a broadband internet connection.[40] So while young people may think of smartphone access as a panacea, and the percentage of those reading the news on mobile phones has soared, it is definitely far from a perfect replacement for a computer and broadband.

Social Media and Filtering Social media, such as Facebook and Twitter, tend to be a secondary source for news after television for many Americans but are a primary source for the young. While television remains the main source of news for one in two Americans, young people ages 18–33 increasingly learn about politics and news online and are significantly less likely than older Americans to turn to local TV. Seventy-eight percent of people under age 50 get their news from social media.[41]

The high rate of exposure to political news via social media is notable since young Americans overall are less engaged in politics—just 46 percent of people age 18–29

As the Hispanic population continues to grow, Latino-oriented news outlets are increasingly influential. Jorge Ramos is a popular news anchor on the Spanish-language network Univision, which in recent years has beat out major networks ABC, CBS, Fox, and NBC for the number 1 primetime spot.

voted in the 2016 election compared to 59 percent for the 30–44 age group.[42] As the web becomes an increasingly important source for political news, young people may become more engaged in politics.[43]

Because they are more personalized and interactive than anonymous news organizations, social media allow Americans to learn about politics and political news from each other. Growing use of social media for news is evident across *all* demographic groups, including older people, women and men, and groups defined by race, education, and income. Figure 7.4 shows the percentage of adults who use each social networking site as well as the percentage who get news from that site. Worldwide, Facebook had over 2.2 billion users in 2018, with 214 million users in the United States. Two-thirds of Americans use social media.[44] As of 2018, roughly 68 percent use Facebook and 24 percent use Twitter, both of which have high rates of exposure to political news.[45] With President Trump tweeting multiple times per day, as well as the use of Twitter and Facebook by congressional leaders and other politicians, social media sites have become a news source in their own right, as well as forums to share news published in the mainstream media.

Facebook provides a more interactive forum for learning about politics than does Twitter, with users more likely to post and respond to news about government and politics, while Twitter's strength is in providing news coverage as it happens, focusing on live events. More than two-thirds of users of both sites say they have posted about news at least at some point. Compared to passively watching television or reading the news, this is a high rate of engagement with political news.[46]

Before social media, most people read a daily newspaper or tuned into a television program to keep up with the daily news. Social media, now a key way to disseminate the news, have changed how people access news and have also increased filtering of the news. Both Facebook and Twitter have contributed to political mobilization and information sharing by creating virtual social networks where groups of like-minded individuals can quickly and easily share information. While many news stories posted on social media are still produced by major newspapers and digital media organizations, they are consumed differently. Political scientists Jason Gainous and Kevin Wagner use the metaphor of social media as the new dinner table, in that discussions of politics and current events occur within digital social networks of friends and family. Their research shows people prefer news that is consistent with their pre-existing beliefs; social networks tend to be more homogeneous

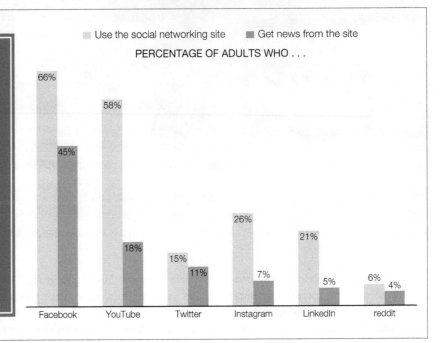

FIGURE 7.4

Social Media and the News

Many Americans who use social media use those sites as a way to obtain political news. This graph shows the percentage of American adults who use each social media site compared with the percentage who report getting news from that site. What are the advantages of getting news on social media, and what are some potential drawbacks?

SOURCE: Jeffrey Gottfried and Elisa Shearer, "News Use across Social Media Platforms 2017," Pew Research Center, September 7, 2017, www.journalism.org (accessed 5/23/18).

with people holding similar perspectives. This has contributed to growing party polarization in politics.[47]

Social media also provide a platform for citizens to be directly engaged with political candidates and elected officials, who have been quick to adopt Facebook and Twitter as means of communicating with their supporters and filtering the daily news for them. Gainous and Wagner, in their book *Tweeting to Power,* argue that social media is how citizens learn about politics: "Social media alters the political calculus in the United States by filtering who controls information, who consumes information, and how that information is distributed."[48] Because the networks operate outside of traditional media, and users pick their own friend networks and can avoid disagreeable ideas and information, parties, groups, and political candidates are able to directly dictate the content of these information networks. This study found individuals who are more active politically online and read the news using social media hold stronger partisan opinions. This means using social media for reading the news can exaggerate party polarization among the mass public.

Obama was the first American president to use social media extensively in his campaign and during his administration. Political candidates and organizations representing the ideological right, such as the Tea Party, and the left, such as MoveOn. org, have taken advantage of this power to filter the news for their audiences. But Donald Trump is the nation's first "Twitter President," directly communicating his opinions on issues and other politicians directly to the people, unmediated by the media or even his White House press staff. With more than 50 million Twitter followers, Trump has an enormous audience. His unconventional political strategy involves using social media and rallies to communicate directly with the American people and set the media agenda, while attacking the credibility of other sources that provide information countering his statements. On any given day, the president tweets multiple times, often calling out his opponents in his famous celebrity take-down mode he perfected from his experience as a reality TV host. Among his core supporters, the truth is what Trump says it is on Twitter or in emotional speeches before rally crowds. However, fact-checking websites such as PolitiFact have found 70 percent of Trump's statements are false or misleading and another 15 percent are only half true.[49]

While Trump effectively used Twitter to his advantage to filter the news for his supporters during the election and then set the media's agenda, his strategy of going public all the time may backfire. While most Americans believe Twitter does allow Trump to communicate directly to the people, few Americans think this is a good idea. A 2017 Gallup survey found a majority (52 percent) say his tweets are not an effective way for him to share his views on important issues, and 72 percent say the tweets do not send the right message to other world leaders. Seven in 10 Americans believe Trump's tweets are often in response to TV news the president has heard, and 71 percent say Twitter is a "risky way for a president to communicate," leading to misunderstandings.[50]

Social media used for news make citizens more informed and engaged in politics, and more likely to participate. On the down side, citizens may be more vulnerable to misinformation from political actors and candidates, especially if the candidate or organization is their only source of news. Are social media empowering or disempowering? The answer may lie somewhere in between.

CITIZEN JOURNALISM

Digital news is creating a new generation of whistle-blowers, enhancing the media's traditional role as a watchdog for the people against government corruption. A distinguishing feature of this phenomenon is the development of **citizen journalism**, which is interactive and participatory. Citizen journalism includes news reporting and political commentary by ordinary citizens and even crisis coverage from eye-witnesses on the scene, thus involving a wider range of voices in gathering news and interpreting political events. The near-universal availability of cameras on cell phones gives millions of Americans the capacity to photograph or record events, thus providing eye-witness accounts. At the same time, social media permit users to upload videos that can be viewed by hundreds of thousands of subscribers or relayed by the mainstream media for even wider dissemination.

citizen journalism news reported and distributed by citizens, rather than professional journalists and for-profit news organizations

In 2017 a global firestorm erupted over United Airlines' treatment of a passenger, an older Asian man, who was violently dragged off a boarded plane for refusing to voluntarily give up his seat. The video footage of the bloodied passenger was filmed by other passengers using smartphones and uploaded to social media. The video was viewed by millions of people globally, creating an outcry against mistreatment of airline passengers. In response the CEO of United Airlines apologized for the mis-treatment of the passenger and the airline changed its policies; this event also led to a congressional investigation of regulations on U.S. airlines.[51] The United example illustrates how the mechanism of social media and grassroots politics can fuel policy change as well as candidate campaigns.

Citizen journalism is enhanced by the ease of starting a blog. There are mil-lions of blogs, covering virtually every topic imaginable, and a large share of these include political news and commentary on local, national, and world events. Many blogs are citizen-run and more and more representative of the diversity of

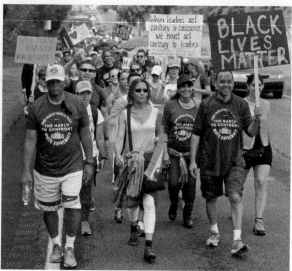

As we have seen with recent dramatic events like the Charlottesville white nationalist rally (left) and Black Lives Matter protests (right), social media and citizen journalism are transforming the news. Groups can mobilize and push out their messages quickly using social media, and citizen journalists can use mobile technology to capture and disseminate news without the filter of mainstream media outlets.

American views than traditional news, which generally reflects the priorities of political elites.

Citizen journalism supplements the work of professional journalists in many important ways. The diversity of online media has created new opinion leaders and new voices and has even, at times, improved information. In recent years, for example, bloggers have uncovered major factual errors in media reports and forced the networks and newspapers to issue corrections. Furthermore, because bloggers and social media posts do not have strict editorial boards, they can post a story within minutes. This ability to scoop the mainstream media means bloggers can frame stories about political candidates before those stories break in the mainstream media.[52] By sharply lowering the technological and financial barriers that previously prevented all but a few individuals from reaching mass audiences, blogs increase the ability of ordinary people to engage in effective political action.

The freewheeling nature of blogging and social media often means that there is less traditional quality control employed by professional journalists and institutional old media. Because they do not face the burden of fact-checking required for the mainstream media or some digital-only news outlets, even well-meaning bloggers can post false information. This is one reason why misinformation about some political issues is higher among blog readers than those reading online news from the mainstream press.[53]

NONPROFIT JOURNALISM

As traditional news organizations have cut budgets and investigative journalism, political information is increasingly emanating from universities, think tanks, nonprofits, and private foundations. Think tanks such as the Brookings Institution, the Cato Institute, and the Pew Research Center provide news and analysis on current events to influence public debate. While some are ideologically driven, these institutions often provide critical analysis of policy issues. Universities have expanded their public outreach, encouraging faculty to explain their findings for a general audience. Community-based nonprofit newspapers are supported by local foundations seeking to fill the void in local news as local papers close their doors. For example, the Bill and Melinda Gates Foundation, established by Microsoft founder Bill Gates, provides extensive funding to National Public Radio. Nonprofits can provide rigorous original reporting and critical analysis of current events.

BENEFITS OF ONLINE NEWS

As digital news media has become mainstream, it is worthwhile to reexamine why Americans appear to prefer online news. The reasons include (1) the convenience of getting news online, (2) the up-to-the-minute currency of the information available online, (3) the depth of the information available online, (4) the diversity of viewpoints, and (5) the low cost.[54] At the same time, changes to the media have raised some concerns, as we will see in the following sections.

Convenience Information online is convenient and always available for those with access to the internet on a computer or through mobile devices. Pew surveys show that nearly half of those who use online news and political information cite its convenience.[55] Because political knowledge is central to the formation of political attitudes, the convenience of online news may lead to a more informed and engaged citizenry. Use of digital media is associated with more interest in politics, greater knowledge of politics, and a greater likelihood of discussing politics with friends and family, as well as voting.[56]

Currency One of the fundamental changes ushered in by an era of online news is the speed with which local, national, and international events are covered, as well as the scope of coverage. Major news stories regularly break first online. Social media have accelerated even further the speed with which news travels around the globe. For example, news of President Trump firing FBI director James Comey in 2016 spread rapidly through messaging and social media even before it could be verified by traditional media.

Depth Online news provides more information than the 60-second sound bites found in television and radio news. By blending more detailed treatment of topics with the visual and emotive appeal of streaming videos, digital media shares qualities both of print media (promoting knowledge) and of the visual aspects of television (promoting interest and engagement).[57] The multimedia and even immersive (virtual reality) capacity of the digital media notwithstanding, most websites still rely heavily upon written text, and most political "web surfing" consists mainly of reading, which facilitates greater recall of information and, in turn, encourages the acquisition of political knowledge.[58]

Diversity Online sources are much more diverse than those found in the traditional media, and this diversity may lead to an increase in political knowledge and interest.[59] While major players online often include mainstream outlets,[60] the web remains populated by a wide range of information sources. By making foreign media such as the British Broadcasting Company (BBC) and Al Jazeera television easily available, digital media have reduced the importance of physical proximity and created more global news. Such a vast array of voices, of course, means that online sources also can provide misinformation or outright lies—just as can happen in mainstream media, campaign events, and even presidential debates.

CONCERNS ABOUT ONLINE NEWS

While online news holds significant promise for improving access to the political information citizens need, the shift toward online media has also given rise to several major concerns. These potential disadvantages include a decline in investigative journalism, uneven quality in news content, fake news, and negative effects on knowledge and tolerance.

Loss of Investigative Power In a democracy, the press is expected to be a watchdog for the people and to inform citizens about government abuses of power. The greatest challenge for journalism organizations is to generate enough revenue to finance original reporting and investigative journalism.[61] When readers paid subscription fees to read the news, circulation was high and advertising provided sufficient revenue to allow newspapers and broadcasters to cover both basic news (weather, sports, business) and political events. Revenue from publishing basic news subsidized political analysis and investigative journalism. The internet has made it harder for news outlets to draw advertising dollars, since ad firms are migrating online to deliver targeted ads directly to consumers via social media and search engines. Firms can now reach consumers without paying news organizations. By breaking apart mainstream news organizations, digital news may actually reduce the media's ability to engage in the kind of sustained, in-depth reporting that is critical to the media's watchdog role.

More Variation in the Quality of News As already noted, the growing diversity of digital news has led to substantial variation in the quality of available information. Multiple perspectives create a stronger marketplace of ideas, but the freewheeling nature of the internet also means that hate speech, unsubstantiated rumors, and factual errors can overwhelm thoughtful, original, and civic-oriented voices. This is especially so in anonymous online forums.

Fake News Political candidates and political leaders are particularly susceptible to attack when negative stories go viral and spread quickly without fact-checking

Without traditional media's commitment to fact-checking, digital media sometimes spread inaccurate information and rumors. In 2008, the false claim that President Obama was not a natural-born citizen spread rapidly online and remained a top story even after Obama released his official long-form certificate.

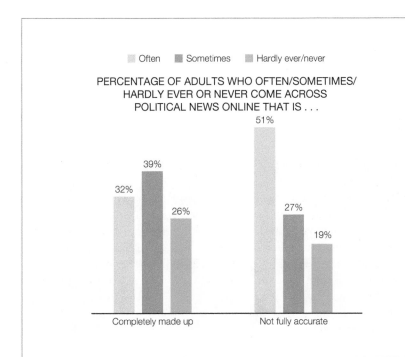

Often ▓ Sometimes ▓ Hardly ever/never

PERCENTAGE OF ADULTS WHO OFTEN/SOMETIMES/ HARDLY EVER OR NEVER COME ACROSS POLITICAL NEWS ONLINE THAT IS . . .

Completely made up	Not fully accurate
32%	51%
39%	27%
26%	19%

FIGURE 7.5

Who Sees Fake News?

Especially during and since the 2016 elections, much attention has been paid to "fake news." How prevalent is it? Are we likely to see more of it?

SOURCE: "Many Americans Believe Fake News Is Sowing Confusion," Pew Research Center, December 14, 2016, www.journalism.org (accessed 5/23/18).

or respect for the privacy of public figures. In contrast to legitimate new stories, *fake news* are false stories circulated to generate ad revenue or to benefit one political candidate or party over another. The most widely publicized fake news story in the 2016 election, for example, was that the Pope had endorsed Trump for president.[62] Circulation of the top 10 fake news stories on Facebook was more widespread than the top real news stories about the election (for more on who sees false news, see Figure 7.5). A study published by Stanford University found fake news stories on social media in the 2016 presidential election disproportionately favored Trump. The Russian government was involved in generating many of the fake news stories to discredit Clinton and her campaign.[63] To verify media reports found in both traditional and online media, there are websites such as FactCheck.org, Snopes.com, and PolitiFact.com devoted exclusively to checking the veracity of political claims.

Potential Effects on Knowledge and Tolerance Perhaps the greatest concern about politics in the digital age is that the very diversity of online news may actually *lower* tolerance for social, religious, and political diversity, leading to more partisan polarization and societal conflict. Digital media often do not abide by traditional media's principle of objective journalism. Instead, the specialization of information online and on cable television means that liberals and conservatives alike can self-select media that are consistent with their underlying assumptions and avoid exposure to information that might challenge their preconceived beliefs.[64] The natural tendency to select news that conforms with our own beliefs is exacerbated by the way search engines cater to our individual preferences—called the "filter bubble," or "self-selection bias"—which screens out exposure to information that might challenge or broaden our worldview.[65]

FOR CRITICAL ANALYSIS

Does digital news coverage differ from traditional print and television media? What impact does digital media have on American politics?

Though the media generally attempt to remain unbiased, a number of media figures and outlets are distinctly left- or right-leaning, such as Rachel Maddow of MSNBC and Tucker Carlson of Fox News. Consumers are increasingly turning to partisan media, reflecting a tendency to self-select information that already conforms with their beliefs, making it more difficult to evaluate information objectively.

In general, individuals who frequently consume political news are more likely to be interested in politics, to have political knowledge, and to vote in elections. But exposure to highly partisan news (Fox News for conservatives, MSNBC for liberals) or news on social media and blogs may lower political knowledge.

The media in all their varying forms—traditional and digital—lead to a more informed public, but also to growing gaps between the informed and uninformed.[66] And yet, despite the dramatic rise in political information and the diversity of the media, average levels of political knowledge in the population have remained constant for the last few decades, due to individuals "customizing" the political information they receive through their choice of news outlets, which, as discussed earlier, makes users less likely to encounter information that challenges their partisan viewpoints.[67]

If the new digital media are to create a more informed democratic process, citizens must have "information literacy" or the ability to find and evaluate information.[68] Greater access to information online makes education and critical thinking among citizens more important than ever before.

DO AMERICANS TRUST THE MEDIA TODAY?

One negative consequence of media concentration combined with party polarization may be a growing distrust of mainstream media. Political scientist Jonathan Ladd argues that fifty years ago the political parties were less polarized and were less likely to attack one another in the press, and newspaper editors also had less incentive to attack their competitors.[69] Ladd maintains that as competition increased in party politics and journalism, the public's distrust of the mass media grew, leading the public to reject the mainstream press's reporting and turn to alternative partisan media sources—those expressly favored by Republicans or Democrats. There are growing partisan divisions in confidence in the news media. Just 11 percent

FOR CRITICAL ANALYSIS

To what extent, do you think, are the media biased? As more news sources have become available, has this led to more or less bias in the media?

of Republicans have a lot of trust in national news media compared to 34 percent of Democrats, according to a 2017 Pew survey.[70]

Distrust in the mainstream media has increased with the Trump presidency. In response to the negative media coverage of his campaign and presidency, Trump has waged an unprecedented war on the American media, frequently referring to major newspapers and broadcast media as "fake news" to discredit them (though these mainstream sources are not producing fabricated news).

In February 2017, Trump upped the ante in a tweet where he called the press "the enemy of the American people." Conservative Republican senator John McCain publicly criticized Trump, warning that without a free and adversarial press, "That's how dictators get started . . . by suppressing free press. In other words, a consolidation of power when you look at history, the first thing that dictators do is shut down the press. And I'm not saying that President Trump is trying to be a dictator. I'm just saying we need to learn the lessons of history."[71]

In an age of digital media, it is more important than ever for citizens to find and evaluate information (see the "What You Can Do" section at the end of the chapter). Political fact-checking websites such as PolitiFact.com, Snopes.com, and FactCheck.org have grown in importance and popularity.

DEBUNKING FALSE STORIES

CNN Not Shutting Down

By Angelo Fichera

Posted on May 25, 2018

The internet has facilitated both diversity and specialization in the news media. Websites such as FactCheck.org exist solely for the purpose of evaluating statements made by U.S. politicians. The site corrects misinformation every day, such as the false story that CNN was shutting down because of poor ratings.

Media Influence

Analyze the ways the media can influence public opinion and politics

The content and character of news and public affairs programming— what the media choose to present and how they present it—can have far-reaching political consequences. The media can shape and modify, if not fully form, the public's perception of events, issues, and institutions. Media coverage can rally support for, or intensify opposition to, national policies on important matters such as health care, the economy, or international wars. Media disclosures can greatly enhance or fatally damage the careers of public figures, as discussed earlier. At the same time, the media are influenced by the individuals or groups who are subjects of the news. The president in particular has the power to set the news agenda through speeches and actions. All politicians, for that matter, seek to shape or manipulate their media images by cultivating good relations with reporters and through news leaks and staged news events.

In recent American political history, the media have played a central role in many major events. For example, the media were a critically important factor in the civil rights movement of the 1950s and '60s. Television images showing peaceful civil rights marchers attacked by club-swinging police helped to generate sympathy among northern whites for the civil rights struggle and greatly increased the pressure on Congress to bring an end to segregation.[72] To take another example, the media were also instrumental in compelling the Nixon administration to negotiate an end to American involvement in the Vietnam War by portraying the war as misguided and unwinnable.[73]

Conservatives have long charged that the liberal biases of reporters and journalists result in distorted news coverage.[74] Though some professional journalists

TABLE 7.1

Media and Viewers' Ideology

Percentage of each ideological group who report getting news about politics in the previous week from each source

SOURCE	CONSISTENTLY LIBERAL	MOSTLY LIBERAL	MIXED	MOSTLY CONSERVATIVE	CONSISTENTLY CONSERVATIVE
CNN	52	48	49	32	20
Fox News	10	24	39	61	84
ABC News	33	38	42	32	26
NBC News	37	44	40	29	21
CBS News	30	32	32	24	22
MSNBC	38	32	25	23	13
NPR	53	23	12	10	8

SOURCE: Pew Research Center, "Where News Audiences Fit on the Political Spectrum," www.journalism.org/interactives/media-polarization/table/consume/ (accessed 3/7/16).

do lean Democratic, they generally defend their professionalism, insisting that their personal political leanings do not affect the way they perform their jobs.[75] Today journalists represent liberals, conservatives, and moderates. Those who decry "the liberal media" seldom acknowledge the partisan or ideological leanings of media owners. Rupert Murdoch, for example, the chief executive officer of News Corporation and 21st Century Fox, is a politically active conservative. Sheldon Adelson is another wealthy media mogul with a clear conservative partisan and ideological agenda.

Many news sources are perceived as distinctly left- or right-leaning, and, as discussed earlier, people have a tendency to select news that conforms with their own ideology. Table 7.1 shows where different ideological groups get political news. With the exception of Fox News and, perhaps, MSNBC, there is not much credible empirical evidence for the idea that any particular mainstream news source is, as a whole, explicitly ideologically biased in one direction or another, at least in terms of the news coverage. Most have been found to be centrist.[76] Of course, many people perceive particular news stories to be biased. This perception may be what drives ideological self-selection of news sources.

HOW THE MEDIA INFLUENCE POLITICS

Traditional and digital media influence American politics in a number of important ways.[77] The power of all media collectively, both traditional and online, lies in their ability to shape what issues Americans think about (agenda setting) and what opinions Americans hold about those issues (framing and priming).

Where Do Americans Get Their News?

Percentage of each voter group who got news about politics and government in the previous week from …

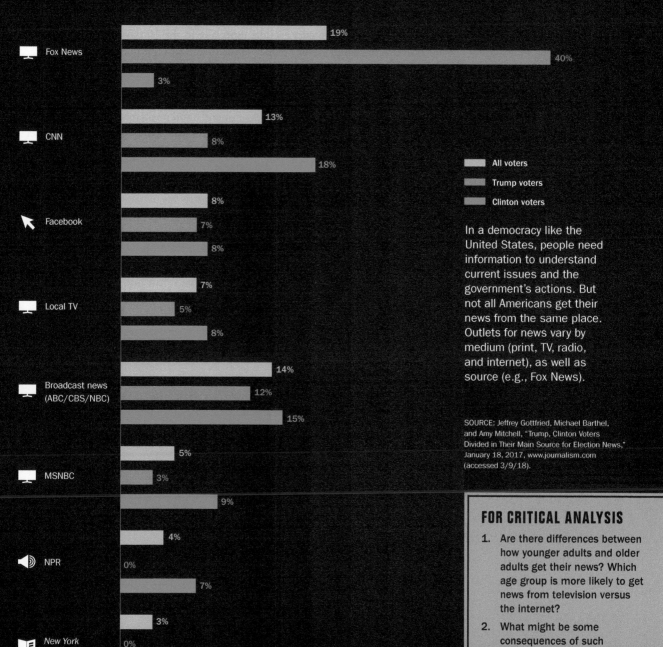

Legend:
- All voters
- Trump voters
- Clinton voters

Fox News
- 19%
- 40%
- 3%

CNN
- 13%
- 8%
- 18%

Facebook
- 8%
- 7%
- 8%

Local TV
- 7%
- 5%
- 8%

Broadcast news (ABC/CBS/NBC)
- 14%
- 12%
- 15%

MSNBC
- 5%
- 3%
- 9%

NPR
- 4%
- 0%
- 7%

New York Times
- 3%
- 0%
- 5%

In a democracy like the United States, people need information to understand current issues and the government's actions. But not all Americans get their news from the same place. Outlets for news vary by medium (print, TV, radio, and internet), as well as source (e.g., Fox News).

SOURCE: Jeffrey Gottfried, Michael Barthel, and Amy Mitchell, "Trump, Clinton Voters Divided in Their Main Source for Election News," January 18, 2017, www.journalism.com (accessed 3/9/18).

FOR CRITICAL ANALYSIS

1. Are there differences between how younger adults and older adults get their news? Which age group is more likely to get news from television versus the internet?

2. What might be some consequences of such differences?

agenda setting the power of the media to bring public attention to particular issues and problems

Agenda Setting and Selection Bias The first source of media power is **agenda setting**; that is, the media help to set the agenda for political discussion. Agenda setting involves identifying the issues that politicians will pay attention to: some things are deemed important while others are not. Groups and forces that wish to bring their ideas before the public in order to generate support for policy proposals or political candidacies must secure media coverage. If the media are persuaded that an idea is newsworthy, then they may declare it an "issue" that must be confronted or a "problem" to be solved, thus clearing the first hurdle in the policy-making process. If, on the other hand, an idea lacks or loses media appeal, its chance of resulting in new programs or policies is diminished.

In the lead-up to the 2016 election, for example, the mainstream media and Donald Trump focused extensively on Hillary Clinton's use of a private email server during her tenure as Secretary of State, and the risk of jeopardizing government secrets. Clinton's email use dominated the media agenda, especially in the 10 days before the election when FBI director James Comey reopened the investigation into her email server.

Some stories have such overwhelming significance—such as wars, natural disasters, and domestic and international acts of terrorism—that in these cases the main concern of political leaders is not whether a story will receive attention but whether political leaders themselves will figure prominently and positively in media accounts. At the same time, many important issues are *not* on the media's agenda, such as alternative energy sources to fossil fuels like solar and wind power. Likewise, these issues are often absent from major policy discussions.

Media attention plays a central role in whether or not officials act on a policy issue, but how policy issues make the news in the first place has remained a puzzle. Political scientist Amber Boydstun has shown that the media have two modes: an "alarm mode" for breaking stories and a "patrol mode" for covering them in greater depth.[78] The incentive to reach a wider audience (and generate ad revenue) often initiates "alarm mode" around a story, after which news outlets go into watchdog "patrol mode" to monitor policy implications until the next big media storm hits. This pattern results in skewed coverage of political issues, with a few issues receiving the majority of media

Through agenda setting, the media have the power to influence which issues the public pays attention to. After FBI director James Comey released a letter indicating the reopening of the investigation into Hillary Clinton's use of a private email server days before the 2016 election, the media's intense coverage of the investigation caused the Clinton campaign to respond to the letter publicly.

During the 1960s, civil rights protesters learned a variety of techniques designed to elicit sympathetic media coverage. Television images of police brutality in Alabama led directly to the enactment of the 1965 Civil Rights Act.

attention while others receive none at all. Today, Twitter often sets off "alarm mode" by breaking news and causing it to go viral, setting the agenda for mainstream news.

Political candidates need the media's agenda-setting role to win elections. Candidates who receive positive news coverage gain momentum, pick up political endorsements, attract campaign contributions, and win support from voters.[79] In the 2008 Democratic primaries for president, Barack Obama exceeded the media's expectations with his early win in the Iowa caucuses. Obama's unexpected victory earned him increased press attention and eventually led the first African American president to the White House.[80] In 2016, Donald Trump exceeded media expectations by coming in second in Iowa and winning New Hampshire. But candidates who disappoint media expectations, such as 2016 Republican candidate Jeb Bush, see their political endorsements, campaign contributions, and polling numbers dwindle. The influence of the media on political candidates is just one example of the media's vitally important role in American democracy.

Because the media are businesses and seek to attract the largest possible audiences, they naturally tend to cover stories with dramatic or entertainment value, giving less attention to important stories that they deem less compelling. News coverage often focuses on crimes and scandals, especially those involving prominent individuals. **Selection bias** means that the news media may provide less information about important political issues that the public depends upon. For example, there was a media frenzy in January 1998 when reports surfaced that Democratic president Clinton might have had an affair with a White House intern. In 2016, Donald Trump's sensationalist statements during the course of his campaign dominated headline news for months. Partisanship and ideology notwithstanding, the age-old journalistic instinct for sensational stories often trumps both the media's responsibility to inform the public about what really matters and the public's responsibility to demand that from the media.

What the mainstream media decide to report on and what they ignore has important implications. For example, the Bush tax cuts of 2001 and 2003, extended under Obama in 2010, had widespread effects, dramatically increasing the federal budget deficit and widening the income gap between the super-rich and most other Americans. But the media provided little coverage of these measures, the result being

selection bias (news) the tendency to focus news coverage on only one aspect of an event or issue, avoiding coverage of other aspects that 40 percent of Americans had no opinion on whether they favored the massive tax cuts in 2001.[81] In contrast, the media paid more attention to the Trump administration's 2017 tax reform plan, and most Americans had definitive opinions about it. While the bill only had a 36 percent approval rating according to a Pew Research survey, it was adopted by Congress anyway.[82]

Access to the print and broadcast media is such an important political resource that political forces that have less media access, such as Black Lives Matter, have only a very limited opportunity to influence the political process. The skewed coverage of traditional media, however, may be partially balanced out by the diversity of media sources online, especially the growing influence of social media.

Framing The language and context in which the media present the news, known as **framing**, can determine how the American people interpret political events. Robert Entman defines *framing* as the social construction of phenomena by the mass media, political or social movements, political leaders, or other political actors and organizations. Frames shape how individuals perceive meaning from words or phrases, photographs, or video.[83] Knowing this, politicians take care to choose language that presents their ideas in the most favorable light possible. For example, during the 2016 presidential campaign, Donald Trump framed Hillary Clinton as a criminal for her use of a private email server.

Because few citizens read legislation, when forming opinions about policy and politics, the public relies on media coverage. This means that arguments made by elected officials and other political actors—or frames—are critical in how the public interprets events and policy.

For example, Obama's health care initiative was framed differently by Democrats and Republicans. The Obama administration labeled the initiative the Patient Protection and Affordable Care Act, thus framing the proposal as a matter of compassionate responsibility and good economic sense. Early press coverage framed the bill as "health care reform." Sensing that Americans generally approve of the idea of "reform," Republican opponents of the legislation chose different language: the law's provisions for limiting excessive medical testing were labeled as "health care rationing," for example, and proposals to create committees to advise patients about end-of-life care were called "death panels."

Priming A third important way the media can shape political events is known as **priming**. Priming involves "calling attention to some matters while ignoring others" when evaluating political officials.[84] As a result, the public will be *primed* to use certain criteria when evaluating a politician or an issue and ignore other criteria. In the lead-up to the 2008 presidential election, for example, the serious economic recession took the media spotlight. As a result the economy—far more than other issues—became one of the most important lenses through which the public evaluated the 2008 presidential candidates.

In the case of political candidates, the media's focus on which candidate "has momentum" and "is winning the horse race" can prime the public to evaluate the candidates based on their likelihood to win the election rather than on their positions on policy issues. For example, when the media declared that Donald Trump had momentum after his unexpected victories and polling numbers exceeded expectations early in the primary season, he went on to win the Republican nomination. News media are not alone in agenda setting, framing, and priming; elected officials, interest groups, and other political players compete over all three in hopes of influencing public opinion.

framing the power of the media to influence how events and issues are interpreted

priming process of preparing the public to bring specific criteria to mind when evaluating a politician or issue

FOR CRITICAL ANALYSIS

How do the media distort political reality? How do politicians use the media for their own purposes? What are the consequences for American democracy when the electorate is informed through such a filter? How might the quality of political information in America be improved?

News Coverage

Explain how politicians and others try to shape the news

News coverage, or the content of the news, comes from numerous sources. Governments, politicians, corporations, interest groups, non-profit organizations, and others issue press releases to draw attention to an issue and tell their side of the story. The news media continues to be dominated by official government sources. Journalists also gain information through investigative journalism and media leaks.

MEDIA LEAKS

The media may report information that is leaked by government officials. A leak is the disclosure of confidential information to the news media. Leaks may emanate from a variety of sources, including "whistle-blowers," lower-level officials who hope to publicize what they view as their bosses' or the government's improper activities. In 1971, for example, Daniel Ellsberg, a minor Defense Department staffer, sought to discredit official justifications for America's military involvement in Vietnam by leaking top-secret documents to the press. The Pentagon Papers—the Defense Department's own secret history of the war—were published by the *New York Times* and the *Washington Post* after the U.S. Supreme Court ruled that the government could not block their release.[85] The Pentagon's credibility was severely damaged, hastening the erosion of public support for the war. Most leaks, though, originate not with low-level whistle-blowers but rather with senior government officials, prominent politicians, and political activists. Journalists are likely to regard high-level sources of confidential information as valuable assets whose favor must be retained.

Digital technology has taken the cat-and-mouse game of leaks to a new level. WikiLeaks, an international organization dedicated to publishing classified information, posts leaked government documents to its website and uses an anonymous system so that leakers cannot be identified. In recent years, WikiLeaks has released thousands of secret government documents involving instances of government corruption, war crimes in Afghanistan and Iraq, torture at U.S. military detention camps, and stolen emails from the Democratic National Committee in the 2016 election.

In 2013, Edward Snowden, a former employee of the Central Intelligence Agency (CIA) and contractor for the National Security Agency (NSA), disclosed thousands of classified digital documents to journalists and international media. The leaks revealed widespread global surveillance programs by the U.S. government working with telecommunication companies. The world learned the NSA was searching millions of emails and tapping cell phones, even of foreign political leaders. For revealing the mass surveillance programs, Snowden has been called a hero, a whistle-blower, a dissident, and a traitor. The leaks garnered intense media attention and sparked heated public debate over government surveillance and privacy of information for individuals. Critics of WikiLeaks and Snowden argue that governments must have some secrets and that the release of some government documents may jeopardize national security as well as American soldiers and their local allies by revealing their identities. Media leaks play a pivotal role in informing the public of government wrongdoings in terms of foreign policy and infringement of privacy and security in a digital age.

The United States charged Julian Assange, founder of WikiLeaks, for breaching national security by publishing classified documents. Since 2012, Assange has been living in exile.

The famous photograph of the aftermath of a napalm attack was one of many media images that shaped the American public's views on the Vietnam War. Media accounts critical of the war helped to turn public opinion against it and hastened the withdrawal of American troops.

ADVERSARIAL JOURNALISM

The political power of the news media vis-à-vis the government has greatly increased in recent years through the growing prominence of *adversarial journalism*, a form of reporting in which the media adopt a skeptical or even hostile posture toward the government and public officials.

Presidents were the first national officials to make use of the opportunities presented by this development. By communicating directly to the electorate through newspapers and magazines, Theodore Roosevelt and Woodrow Wilson established political constituencies for themselves, independent of party organizations, and thereby strengthened their own power relative to that of Congress. President Franklin Delano Roosevelt used the radio, most notably in his famous fireside chats, to reach out to voters throughout the nation and to make himself the center of American political life. Subsequent presidents all sought to use the media to enhance their popularity and power, and the media became a cornerstone of presidential power.

The Vietnam War shattered this amicable relationship between the press and the presidency. During the early stages of U.S. involvement, American officials in Vietnam who disapproved of the way the war was being conducted leaked to reporters information critical of administrative policy. Publication of this material infuriated the White House, which pressured publishers to block its release, but the national broadcast media and especially the two leading national newspapers, the *Washington Post* and the *New York Times*, refused to do so. As the Vietnam War dragged on, adverse media coverage fanned antiwar sentiment. In turn, these shifts in popular and congressional sentiment emboldened journalists and publishers to continue to present news reports critical of the war. The media were also central actors in the Watergate affair, the cluster of scandals that ultimately forced President Nixon to resign from office in disgrace just two years later. A relentless series of investigations launched by the *Washington Post*, the *New York Times*, and the television networks led to disclosures of the various crimes of which Nixon was guilty, leading to threats of impeachment and his subsequent resignation. Gradually, a generation of journalists developed a commitment to adversarial journalism.

Adversarial journalism intensified during Trump's first year in office as the president became embroiled by a federal investigation into possible collusion between his campaign for president and Russia. The national news media, led by the *New York Times* and *Washington Post*, reported almost daily on breaking news revealing how Russia used a sophisticated cyber campaign to interfere in the 2016 election. The media's reporting has revealed that Russian president Vladimir Putin tried to discredit Hillary Clinton and tip the outcome of the 2016 election in favor of Donald Trump. The media first reported that Russian operatives hacked the accounts of the Democratic Party and publically released 30,000 embarrassing emails related to Clinton's presidential campaign. They have also reported frequently on the federal investigation by Robert Mueller and his team regarding whether anyone close to Trump participated in the Russian interference in the election. Trump's former campaign chairman, Paul Manafort, surrendered to the FBI and pleaded guilty to charges that he laundered millions of dollars through overseas shell companies after reaching a deal with the Justice Department. Rick Gates, Manafort's longtime associate as well as a campaign adviser, also pleaded guilty to federal crimes.

FOR CRITICAL ANALYSIS

Richard Nixon, Bill Clinton, Donald Trump, and many other presidents have criticized the media. Why are many politicians hostile to media? Do you share their views?

Without the rigorous investigative and adversarial journalism of the news media on behalf of political leaders, the people would not have the means (and information) necessary to hold their elected representatives accountable to the people. Throughout this chapter we have discussed the watchdog role of the media. Adversarial journalism, where the news media seeks to expose political corruption through reporting that is skeptical of government and public officials, is a critical part of what makes democratic governments work.

Aggressive use of the techniques of investigation, publicity, and exposure has allowed the national media to enhance their autonomy and carve out a prominent place for themselves in American government and politics. Without aggressive media coverage, important questions about the conduct of American foreign and domestic policy, police violence, drone attacks, election interference by foreign governments, political corruption, and civil liberty violations may not ever be raised. It is easy to criticize the media for their aggressive tactics, but our democracy may not function effectively without the critical role of the press. Independent media are needed as the watchdogs of American politics.

Regulation of the Media

Trace the evolution of rules that govern broadcast media

In many countries, such as China, the government exercises strict control over traditional media content. In others, the government owns the broadcast media (for example, the BBC in Britain) but does not tell the media what to say.

In the United States, the print and online media are essentially free from government interference. The broadcast media, on the other hand, are subject to federal regulation. American radio and television are regulated by the Federal Communications Commission (FCC), an independent agency established in 1934. Radio and TV stations must have FCC licenses, which must be renewed every five years. Through regulations prohibiting obscenity, indecency, and profanity, the FCC has sought to prohibit radio and television stations from airing explicit sexual and excretory references between 6 A.M. and 10 P.M., the hours when the audience is most likely to include children. Generally speaking, FCC regulation applies only to the over-the-air broadcast media. It does not apply to cable television, the internet, or satellite radio.

In 1996, Congress passed the Telecommunications Act, a broad effort to end most regulations. The legislation loosened restrictions on media ownership and allowed telephone companies, cable television providers, and broadcasters to compete with one another to provide telecommunication services. Following the passage of this act, mergers between telephone and cable companies and different entertainment media produced a greater concentration of media ownership than had been possible since regulation of the industry began in 1934.

Though the act loosened many regulations, it did include an attempt to regulate the content of material transmitted over the internet. This law, known as the Communications Decency Act, made it illegal to make "indecent" sexual material on the internet accessible to those under age 18. The act was immediately denounced by civil libertarians, and in 1997 the Supreme Court ruled that the Communications Decency Act was an unconstitutional infringement of the right to freedom of speech guaranteed by the First Amendment (see Chapter 4).

FOR CRITICAL ANALYSIS

In wartime, can media criticism of government action aid the nation's enemies? Should there be limits on media criticism of the government during times of war? Or does criticism actually enhance the nation's strength?

Although the government's ability to regulate the content of the internet is limited, the FCC has used its licensing power to impose several regulations that can affect the political content of radio and TV broadcasts. The first of these is the **equal time rule**, under which broadcasters must provide to candidates for the same political office equal opportunities to communicate their messages to the public. Under the terms of the Telecommunications Act, during the 45 days before an election, broadcasters are required to make time available to candidates at the lowest rate charged for that time slot.

The second regulation affecting the content of broadcasts is the **right of rebuttal**, which requires that individuals be given the opportunity to respond to personal attacks. For many years, a third important federal regulation was the *fairness doctrine*. Under this rule, broadcasters that aired programs on controversial issues were required to provide time for opposing views. In addition, the fairness doctrine included a requirement that TV and radio stations cover controversial issues of public and social importance in their communities. In 1985, however, the FCC stopped enforcing the fairness doctrine on the grounds that there were so many radio and television stations—to say nothing of newspapers and newsmagazines—that in all likelihood many different viewpoints were already being presented without each station being required to try to present all sides of every argument. In 1987 the FCC officially revoked the fairness doctrine. Critics of this FCC decision charge that in many media markets the number of competing viewpoints is actually quite small.

The rise of online media challenges our thinking about regulation of the media as it is more difficult—some say impossible—to regulate political content online. In 2011 the United Nations declared that access to the internet is a human right.[86] While this declaration came in response to threats by authoritarian governments against internet access, it demonstrates the significance of information technology in modern life.[87]

The Internet and Global Democracy

The internet and social media play an increasing role in elections, as demonstrated in this chapter. Critics of this trend have raised concerns that a lack of "quality control" allows the spreading of fake news by unscrupulous groups.[a] A number of foreign and domestic actors have used the open nature of this media to manipulate campaign rhetoric for political gain. The British government opened investigations into the spread of false news during the "Brexit" vote on leaving the European Union,[b] and Russia used internal techniques to manipulate elections in the United States and Europe.[c]

Supporters, however, point out that the internet and social media have allowed voters to connect better with their political systems. Nonprofit groups like GotToVote.cc run social media campaigns to help African citizens register to vote and identify their polling stations. In Kenya, biometric voter registration has made it more difficult for people to cast multiple ballots, and real-time texting has improved oversight on election counts, helping to combat voter fraud.[d]

While internet and social media are certainly transforming politics, it is important to remember that not all global citizens are part of this trend. Internet access may be near-universal in wealthy countries, but there are still many countries where less than a third of the population ever go online. If the future of politics is online, then many poor and older people around the world may be increasingly left behind.

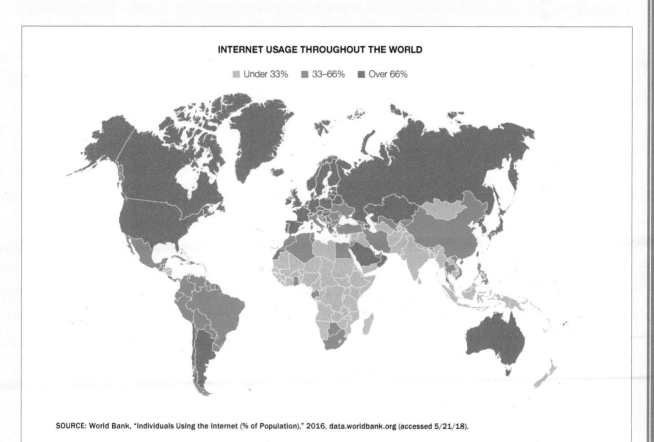

INTERNET USAGE THROUGHOUT THE WORLD

■ Under 33% ■ 33–66% ■ Over 66%

SOURCE: World Bank, "Individuals Using the Internet (% of Population)," 2016, data.worldbank.org (accessed 5/21/18).

[a] Thomas B. Edsall, "Opinion: Democracy, Disrupted," March 2, 2017, *New York Times*, www.nytimes.com/2017/03/02/opinion/how-the-internet-threatens-democracy.html (accessed 5/21/18).

[b] "What Are the Links between Cambridge Analytica and a Brexit Campaign Group?" Reuters, March 21, 2018, www.reuters.com/article/us-facebook-cambridge-analytica-leave-eu/what-are-the-links-between-cambridge-analytica-and-a-brexit-campaign-group-idUSKBN1GX2IO (accessed 5/21/18).

[c] Constanze Stelzenmüller, "Testimony: The Impact of Russian Interference on Germany's 2017 Election," June 28, 2017, www.brookings.edu/testimonies/the-impact-of-russian-interference-on-germanys-2017-elections/ (accessed 5/21/18).

[d] Loren Treisman, "How Kenyans Are Using Tech to Stop Election Fraud," August 3, 2017, *CNN*, www.cnn.com/2017/07/27/africa/kenya-elections-technology/index.html (accessed 5/21/18).

The Media and Democracy
WHAT DO WE WANT?

The freedom of the press is essential to democratic government. Ordinary citizens depend on the media to investigate wrongdoing, publicize and explain governmental policy, evaluate politicians, and bring to light matters that might otherwise be known to only a handful of governmental insiders. In short, without free and active media, democratic government would be virtually impossible. Citizens would have few means through which to know or assess the government's actions—other than the claims or pronouncements of the government itself. Moreover, without active (indeed, aggressive) media, citizens would be hard-pressed to make informed choices among competing candidates at the polls— one reason that the teenage defenders of net neutrality discussed at the beginning of the chapter hoped to keep the internet open as a source of information on public affairs.

Today's media are not only adversarial but also increasingly partisan. Blogs, digital-only news websites, social media, and others can be unabashedly partisan. To some extent, increasing ideological and partisan stridency is an inevitable result of the expansion and proliferation of news sources. When the news was dominated by three networks and a handful of national papers, each sought to appeal to the entire national audience. This required a moderate and balanced tone so that consumers would not be offended and transfer their attention to a rival network or newspaper. Today, there are so many news sources that few can aim for a broad-based national audience. Instead, many target a partisan or ideological niche and aim to develop a strong relationship with consumers in that audience segment by catering to their biases and predispositions.

The rise of digital media has fundamentally changed how political information is gathered and distributed. News today is participatory and involves citizens as well as professional journalists. Wikipedia, the free online encyclopedia founded by Jimmy Wales, has millions of pages compiled by legions of volunteers and provides relatively unbiased content on virtually every political topic imaginable. Social media, Wikipedia, and all Wiki-type sites involve people working collaboratively to write and create information and transmit knowledge. Social media also enable citizens to express their political opinions. (The **"Who Participates?"** feature on the facing page shows some of the ways Americans participate in politics via social media.) Is such a system the future of the news media? Or will the movement away from net neutrality push out smaller voices in favor of powerful media companies?

The media can make or break reputations, help to launch or destroy political careers, and build support for or rally opposition to programs and institutions.[88] Wherever there is so much power, at least the potential exists for its abuse or overly zealous use. All things considered, free media are so critically important to the maintenance of a democratic society that Americans must be prepared to take the risk that the media will occasionally abuse their power. Governmental controls that would prevent the media from misusing their power would also limit freedom. The ultimate beneficiaries of free and active media are the American people.

Civic Engagement in the Digital Age

In the last 12 months, did you send a message on Facebook or Twitter about political issues?

Percentage who said "yes" to this question

Age

- 42%
- 30%
- 43%
- 18%

- ● 18–29   ● 50–64
- ● 30–49   ● 65+

Income group

- 32%
- 35%
- 34%
- 34%

- ● <$20K   ● $40K – <$75K
- ● $20K – <$40K   ● $75K+

Partisanship

- 36%
- 33%
- 31%

- ● Democrats   ● Republicans
- ● Independents

Education

- 37%
- 25%
- 20%
- 18%

- ● < High school   ● College graduate
- ● Some college   ● Postgraduate

Sex

- 30%
- 36%

- ● Male   ● Female

Race / ethnicity

- 28%
- 25%
- 34%
- 32%

- ● White   ● Asian
- ● Black   ● Hispanic / Latino

SOURCE: American National Election Study 2016 time series, www.electionstudies.org (accessed 11/4/17).

★ WHAT YOU CAN DO ★

Be an Informed Consumer of Media

☑ Gather information from a variety of news sources rather than relying on just one. You can set up a news aggregator with a variety of free downloadable apps, including Flipboard (**www.flipboard.com**) and Feedly (**www.feedly.com**).

☑ Check media watchdog organizations such as the Columbia Journalism Review (**www.cjr.org**), Fairness & Accuracy in Reporting (**www.fair.org**), and Accuracy in Media (**www.aim.org**) for reports of media bias and censorship.

☑ For information on the factual accuracy of what is said by political players, go to **www.factcheck.org**. For investigative journalism in the public interest, go to **www.propublica.org**. For reporting on the accuracy of news rumors, go to **www.snopes.com**.

The Media in American Democracy

Describe the key roles the media play in American political life (pp. 257–60)

The First Amendment to the U.S. Constitution guarantees the right to publish newspapers, magazines, and other forms of digital media without censorship by the government. The media serve three central roles in American democracy: informing the public about current political developments; providing a forum for debating political issues; and acting as a watchdog on the actions of political leaders. Unlike many other democracies, public broadcasting is a relatively small part of the American media landscape and a few giant corporations control a wide swath of media holdings in the United States.

Key Terms

media (p. 257)

media monopoly (p. 260)

Practice Quiz

1. Public broadcasting outlets that receive government funding through license fees, subsidies, or tax dollars
   a) are prohibited by the Constitution from operating in the United States.
   b) account for less than 5 percent of media market share in the United States.
   c) account for nearly one-third of media market share in the United States.
   d) account for approximately half of media market share in the United States.
   e) account for more than two-thirds of media market share in the United States.

2. More than three-fourths of the daily print newspapers in the United States are owned by
   a) large media conglomerates.
   b) the national government.
   c) small local companies.
   d) private individuals.
   e) the employees who run them.

The Media Today

Discuss how digital media have transformed how citizens learn about politics (pp. 261–77)

The rise of the internet over the last three decades has produced a massive transformation in the U.S. news media. While newspapers, magazines, television programs, and radio broadcasts are still important sources of news, many Americans now rely on digital media to learn about politics. The convenience, currency, depth, and diversity of online news has led many Americans to prefer it to more traditional sources. Changes arising from the emergence of the internet have, however, also raised concerns that online news may produce a decline in investigative journalism, a decrease in the quality of news content, and a reduction in political knowledge and tolerance.

Key Terms

broadcast media (p. 265)

penny press (p. 267)

news aggregator (p. 267)

digital citizen (p. 268)

digital divide (p. 268)

social media (p. 268)

citizen journalism (p. 271)

Practice Quiz

3. Digital citizenship requires
   a) an online subscription to one or more online newspapers.
   b) high-speed internet access and the skills to use and evaluate online information.
   c) a social media account.
   d) maintaining a political blog.
   e) registering one's computer with the government.

4. News reporting devoted to a targeted portion of readers based on content or ideological presentation is called
   a) nonprofit journalism.
   b) for-profit journalism.
   c) niche journalism.
   d) citizen journalism.
   e) adversarial journalism.

5. Which of the following is *not* a reason that many Americans appear to prefer online news?
   a) the convenience of getting news online
   b) the up-to-the-minute currency of the information available online
   c) the depth of the information available online
   d) the diversity of online viewpoints
   e) the accuracy and objectivity compared to traditional media outlets

Media Influence

Analyze the ways the media can influence public opinion and politics (pp. 277–82)

The content and character of news programming can have far-reaching political consequences. In recent American political history, the media have played a central role in numerous major events, such as the civil rights movement of the 1950s and '60s, the Vietnam War, and the Watergate affair. The power of the media lies in their ability to shape what issues Americans think about (agenda setting) and what opinions Americans hold about those issues (framing and priming).

Key Terms

agenda setting (p. 280)
selection bias (news) (p. 281)
framing (p. 282)
priming (p. 282)

Practice Quiz

6. The media's powers to determine what becomes a part of political discussion is known as
   a) framing.
   b) priming.
   c) agenda setting.
   d) selection bias.
   e) niche journalism.

7. The fact that Democrats discussed the Patient Protection and Affordable Care Act as a matter of compassionate responsibility and good economic sense while Republicans discussed it as a matter of "health care rationing" is an example of
   a) framing.
   b) priming.
   c) agenda setting.
   d) selection bias.
   e) niche journalism.

News Coverage

Explain how politicians and others try to shape the news (pp. 283–85)

While many politicians, corporations, interest groups, and nonprofit organizations attempt to shape media coverage, the content of news is typically dominated by official government sources. In addition to government sources, however, reporters frequently gain information through leaks and practicing adversarial journalism. Leaks, which are confidential pieces of information disclosed to members of the media, have driven press coverage on issues ranging from foreign policy to government corruption. Also incorporated into daily news coverage are thousands of press releases authored by advocates of influential political interests. Adversarial journalism, a form of reporting in which the media adopt a skeptical or even hostile posture toward public officials, has increased the political power of the press in recent years.

Practice Quiz

8. Most leaks originate with
   a) low-level government whistle-blowers.
   b) senior government officials, prominent politicians, and political activists.
   c) members of the public who witness misbehavior.
   d) ambassadors from foreign countries.
   e) members of the media.

9. Which organization has used the internet to anonymously release thousands of secret U.S. government documents relating to corruption, war crimes, and torture in recent years?
   a) the Federal Communications Commission
   b) WikiLeaks
   c) the National Security Agency
   d) the Project for Excellence in Journalism
   e) the Freedom of Information Agency

10. *Adversarial journalism* refers to
    a) the recent shift in American society away from general-purpose sources of information and toward narrowly focused niche sources.
    b) an era in American history when political parties provided all of the financing for newspapers.
    c) a form of reporting in which the media adopt a skeptical or even hostile posture toward the opinions and behaviors of their audience.
    d) a form of reporting in which the media adopt an accepting and friendly posture toward the government and public officials.
    e) a form of reporting in which the media adopt a skeptical or even hostile posture toward the government and public officials.

11. Which event shattered the amicable relationship between the press and the presidency?
    a) September 11, 2001
    b) the Vietnam War
    c) Watergate
    d) World War II
    e) the Monica Lewinsky affair

Regulation of the Media

Trace the evolution of rules that govern broadcast media (pp. 285–87)

Although American print and online media are free from government interference, broadcast media are subject to significant federal regulation. Radio and television stations in the United States are licensed by the Federal Communications Commission (FCC). The FCC has used its licensing power to impose several regulations, such as the equal time rule, the right of rebuttal, and the fairness doctrine, that affect the political content of radio and television broadcasts.

Key Terms

equal time rule (p. 286)

right of rebuttal (p. 286)

Practice Quiz

12. In general, FCC regulations apply only to
    a) cable television.
    b) internet websites.
    c) over-the-air broadcast media.
    d) satellite radio.
    e) newspapers and magazines.

13. The now defunct requirement that broadcasters provide time for opposing views when they air programs on controversial issues was called
    a) the equal time rule.
    b) the free speech doctrine.
    c) the fairness doctrine.
    d) the right of rebuttal.
    e) the response rule.

For Further Reading

Boydstun, Amber E. *Making the News: Politics, the Media, and Agenda Setting.* Chicago: University of Chicago Press, 2013.

Carr, Nicholas. *The Shallows: What the Internet Is Doing to Our Brains.* New York: W. W. Norton, 2011.

Chadwick, Andrew. *The Hybrid Media System: Politics and Power.* New York: Oxford University Press, 2013.

Timothy E. Cook, "The News Media as a Political Institution: Looking Backward and Looking Forward," *Political Communication* 23, no. 2 (September 2006).

Fenton, Tom. *Bad News: The Decline of Reporting, the Business of News, and the Danger to Us All.* New York: Harper Collins, 2005.

Hamilton, James T. *All the News That's Fit to Sell.* Princeton, NJ: Princeton University Press, 2004.

Iyengar, Shanto. *Media Politics: A Citizen's Guide.* New York: W. W. Norton, 2015.

Iyengar, Shanto, and Donald Kinder. *News That Matters: Television and American Public Opinion.* Chicago: University of Chicago Press, 2010.

Jamieson, Kathleen, and Paul Waldman. *The Press Effect.* New York: Oxford University Press, 2004.

Jenkins, Henry. *Convergence Culture: Where Old and New Media Collide.* New York: New York University Press, 2008.

Jenkins, Henry, Sam Ford, and Joshua Green. *Spreadable Media: Creating Value and Meaning in a Networked Culture.* New York: New York University Press, 2013.

Mossberger, Karen, Caroline Tolbert, and Ramona McNeal. *Digital Citizenship: The Internet, Society, and Participation.* Cambridge, MA: MIT Press, 2008.

Pariser, Eli. *The Filter Bubble: What the Internet Is Hiding from You.* New York: Penguin, 2011.

Shirky, Clay. *Here Comes Everybody: The Power of Organizing without Organizations.* New York: Penguin, 2009.

West, Darrell. *The Next Wave: Using Digital Technology to Further Social and Political Innovation.* Washington, DC: Brookings Institution Press, 2011.

Recommended Websites

Accuracy in Media
www.aim.org
> This nonprofit watchdog group attempts to ensure accuracy in media reporting by identifying botched or slanted stories and then "setting the record straight."

Columbia Journalism Review
www.cjr.org
> The Columbia Journalism Review is an organization committed to analyzing and critiquing trends in the media and journalism industries.

G. R. Boynton's New Media and Politics
ir.uiowa.edu/polisci_nmp/
> This website contains a collection of research on new media trends such as microblogging, streaming video, and Twitter, with a focus on how these developments have shaped the way people share political information.

Journalism.org
www.journalism.org
> This nonprofit, nonpolitical site, sponsored by the Project for Excellence in Journalism, examines the overall performance of the press as providers of information. Its aim is to help both consumers and producers of the news.

National Telecommunication and Information Administration
www.ntia.doc.gov
> The National Telecommunication and Information Administration advises the president on telecommunications policies for the technological advancement of the nation. The "Broadband" section of the website includes "Digital Nation Reports" on internet usage in the United States.

Pew Internet, Science, and Tech
www.pewinternet.org
> Pew Internet, Science, and Tech conducts public opinion polling, demographic research, and content analyses of trends around internet, science, and technology. Pew Research Center is an independent, nonpartisan think tank that also explores attitudes toward numerous other political issues.

Shorenstein Center on Media, Politics, and Public Policy
www.shorensteincenter.org
> This research center based out of Harvard University explores the intersection of the press, politics, and public policy. The "News and Events" section includes a weekly roundup of "Must-Reads" on the media and politics.

Political Participation and Voting

WHAT GOVERNMENT DOES AND WHY IT MATTERS Who votes affects who is elected and what issues politicians put at the top of their agenda. Historically there's been a great deal of concern that young people turn out at lower rates than older Americans. But these days, although their turnout can still be low, the sheer number of Americans under age 35 means that they constitute a larger share of the electorate than baby boomers and older Americans.[1] And they are beginning to flex their electoral muscles, shaping election outcomes.

The 2017 Virginia race for governor is a case in point. Early polls showed Republican Ed Gillespie ahead of Democrat Ralph Northam. But in the end Northam won by nine percentage points. Much of Northam's margin came from Virginians under 30, whose turnout increased from just 18 percent in 2009 to 34 percent in 2017 and who supported Northam over Gillespie 69 to 30 percent.[2]

Groups on both the political right and left mobilized Virginia voters at double or triple the rates of the previous gubernatorial election. The National Rifle Association and Americans for Prosperity

WE ARE A POWERFUL, PISSED-OFF MOVEMENT OF YOUNG PEOPLE

#OneYearOut

MORE VIDEOS

For much of the country's history, large groups of Americans were denied the right to vote. Most restrictions on voting have been eliminated for Americans age 18 and older, but turnout remains relatively low, especially among young voters. Will changes in voting laws increase participation?

reached out to conservative voters. The Virginia League of Conservation Voters and BlackPAC knocked on Democrats' doors. NextGen America, a group founded by billionaire Tom Steyer to mobilize young voters, sponsored a petting zoo at Virginia Tech to pull students in with baby animals and tell them where to vote.[3]

As important as the youth vote was, 34 percent is a pretty low turnout rate. Turnout is generally higher in presidential elections, but even at the modern peak, the election of 2008, only 62 percent of Americans voted;[4] in 2016, the turnout rate was 59 percent.[5]

In most democratic countries, residents are automatically registered to vote in elections at adult age. In the United States, citizens must actively register to vote and, in most states, must do so in advance of the election—sometimes 30 days beforehand. Young people especially are less likely to register to vote than are older Americans.[6] In an effort to boost voter turnout, a number of states have begun to offer same-day registration, which means that people can both register and vote when they go to the polls on Election Day. As of 2018, 18 states plus Washington, D.C., had enacted same-day registration laws.

Of the 10 states with the highest average voting rates, 7 offer same-day registration.[7]

Voting is just one form of political participation, and voter-registration requirements are just one factor that affects who participates in American politics. As we will see in this chapter, who participates and how they participate matter a great deal—in elections and in influencing government policy.

CHAPTER GOALS

★ Describe the major forms of traditional and digital participation in politics (pp. 297–310)

★ Describe the patterns of participation among major demographic groups (pp. 310–19)

★ Explain the factors in the political environment that influence whether individuals vote or not (pp. 319–23)

★ Explain the effect of electoral laws on voting (pp. 323–27)

Forms of Political Participation

Describe the major forms of traditional and digital participation in politics

We can think of political participation as falling into two major categories. Traditional participation in politics includes not only voting but also attending campaign events, rallies, and fund-raisers, volunteering on behalf of candidates and political organizations, canvassing, displaying campaign signs, contacting elected officials, contributing money to candidates and parties, or even challenging a law in court. Protests, demonstrations, and strikes, too, are age-old forms of participatory politics.

In addition to traditional participation, the growing world of digital politics includes not only the exchange of information but also fund-raising and voter mobilization. Though most experts now agree that digital politics is just a new way of engaging in traditional politics, as digital politics becomes more common, it continues to change participation in important ways that may increase engagement in politics overall.

TRADITIONAL POLITICAL PARTICIPATION

Traditional political participation refers to a wide range of activities designed to influence government, politics, and policy. For most citizens today, voting in elections is the most common form of participation in politics. Yet ordinary people took part in politics long before the advent of the election or any other formal mechanism of popular involvement in political life. If there is any natural or spontaneous form of popular political participation, it is not the election but the protest or riot. In fact, for much of American history, fewer Americans exercised their right to vote than participated in urban riots and rural uprisings, as voting for a long time was limited to white, male, landowning citizens.

The vast majority of Americans reject rioting or violence for political ends, but peaceful **protest** is protected by the First Amendment and generally recognized as a legitimate and important form of political activity. During the height of the civil rights movement in the 1960s, hundreds of thousands of Americans took part in peaceful protests to demand social and political rights for African Americans. Peaceful marches and demonstrations have been employed by a host of groups across the ideological spectrum, such as the conservative Tea Party Movement against big government and 2011 Occupy Wall Street protests against growing income inequality. To take a more recent example, in March 2018 thousands of people participated nationwide in March for Our Lives protests against gun violence and lack of gun regulations in the wake of a string of school shootings.

Protests have erupted particularly in response to the Trump presidency and some of his controversial measures. The nationwide Women's March the day after Trump's inauguration day was the largest single-day protest in U.S. history, with half a million protesters. The Women's March advocated policies to protect human rights, women's rights, LGBTQ rights, reproductive rights, racial equality, freedom of religion, workers' rights, immigration reform, universal health care, and protecting the environment. That same month there were massive protests against Trump's controversial travel restrictions on immigrants from seven predominantly

traditional political participation activities designed to influence government, including voting, campaign contributions and face-to-face activities such as volunteering for a campaign or working on behalf of a candidate or political organization

protest participation that involves assembling crowds to confront a government or other official organization

One advantage of protest is visibility: through media attention, protesters can raise awareness, attract like-minded individuals, and put pressure on politicians. That was the goal of (left to right) the Women's March, NFL players kneeling during the national anthem to protest police brutality, and white nationalists in Charlottesville, Virginia, protesting the removal of a Confederate statue.

Muslim countries. In August 2017 violent clashes erupted in Charlottesville, Virginia, between white nationalists, rallying against the city's decision to remove a statue of Confederate general Robert E. Lee, and counterprotesters. President Trump further inflamed emotions when he refused to denounce the white supremacists. The fallout from the controversial Charlottesville marches, and Trump's comments, led the CEOs of leading U.S. corporations to resign in protest from two White House advisory councils of American business leaders. Protests often lead to action and remain a common form of political participation across the ideological spectrum.

Growing concern over police discrimination and excessive use of force against African Americans has led to hundreds of protests across the nation in the past five years, including NFL players, coaches, and owners kneeling in locked arms during the playing of the national anthem in silent protest of racial inequality.

People participate in public protests to attract media attention, raise public awareness, and send a message to politicians about the policies they enact. The Black Lives Matter movement and protests by NFL players, for example, have prompted a national discussion and political action around police violence and reform, including revamped training programs and calls to equip police officers with body cameras. Opinion polls suggest that both white and black Americans increasingly feel that racism is a problem in American society.[8]

Elections, of course, are the hallmark of political participation in a democracy. In addition to voting (discussed below), citizens can give money to candidates or political organizations, volunteer to work on campaigns, contact political officials, sign petitions, attend public meetings, join organizations, display campaign signs and pins, write letters to the editor, and attend rallies. They can also lobby their representatives in Congress, and they can even sue the government or run for elected office. Such activities can communicate much more detailed information to public officials than voting can. By volunteering for a political campaign, writing or emailing their member of Congress, or contributing money to a political organization, people can convey their specific opinions, making these other political activities often more satisfying than voting.[9] However, these other forms of political action generally require more time, effort, and/or money than voting. As a result, as Figure 8.1 shows, the percentage of the population that participates in ways other than voting is relatively low.

Participation through Voting For most Americans, voting is the single most important political act. Voting is the most common way that individuals interact with politics. The right to vote gives ordinary Americans an equal voice in politics as each vote has the same value. Voting is especially important because it selects the officials who make the laws that the American people must follow.

The right to vote, or **suffrage**, is a legal right. During early periods of American history, suffrage was restricted to white males over the age of 21. Many states further limited voting to those who owned property or paid more than a specified amount of annual tax. Until the early 1900s, state legislatures elected U.S. senators, and there were no direct elections for members of the Electoral College (who in turn elect the president). As a result, elections for the U.S. House as well as state and local offices were the primary venue for citizen participation in government.

suffrage the right to vote; also called *franchise*

During the nineteenth and early twentieth centuries, states often acted to restrict suffrage, initially through poll taxes (fees to vote) and literacy tests (reading tests) designed to curtail immigrant voting in northern cities. These laws were later imported to the southern states to prevent African Americans and poor whites from voting during the Jim Crow era, the period between the Civil War and the 1960s (see Chapter 5). Voter eligibility requirements often varied greatly from state to state. Some states openly prevented the right to vote on the basis of race; others did not. Some states required property ownership for voting; others had no such restrictions.[10]

Over the past two centuries of American history, a dominant trend has been federal statutes, court decisions, and constitutional amendments designed to override state voting laws and expand suffrage.[11] In the South, voting rights for

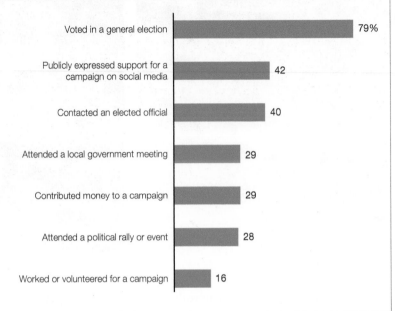

FIGURE 8.1

Political Participation

Political activities such as volunteering generally take more time and effort than voting. When asked about various forms of political participation, over 40 percent of respondents said they expressed support for a campaign on social media.

SOURCE: The ANES 2012 Time Series Study, www.electionstudies.org/studypages/anes_timesseries_2012/anes_timeseries_2012.htm (accessed 10/30/14). Based on a sample made up primarily of registered voters; "Political Engagement, Knowledge, and the Midterms," Pew Research Center, April 26, 2018, www.people-press.org/2018/04/26/10-political-engagement-knowledge-and-the-midterms/ (accessed 10/12/18).

PERCENTAGE OF PEOPLE WHO REPORT PARTICIPATING IN EACH ACTIVITY

Activity	%
Voted in a general election	79%
Publicly expressed support for a campaign on social media	42
Contacted an elected official	40
Attended a local government meeting	29
Contributed money to a campaign	29
Attended a political rally or event	28
Worked or volunteered for a campaign	16

African American men were established by the Fifteenth Amendment in 1870, which prohibited denying the right to vote on the basis of race. Despite the Fifteenth Amendment, the voting rights of African American men were effectively rescinded during the 1880s by the states of the former Confederacy with voting laws such as poll taxes and literacy tests, as discussed above. A goal of the civil rights movement in the 1950s and '60s was voting rights for African Americans. This goal was partially achieved with the enactment of the 1965 Voting Rights Act, which authorized the federal government to register voters in states that discriminated against minority citizens and allowed the government to challenge voting rules and practices that systematically disenfranchise minority voters. The result was the re-enfranchisement of southern blacks for the first time since the 1860s.

Women won the right to vote in 1920 through the adoption of the Nineteenth Amendment to the Constitution. This amendment resulted primarily from the activism of the women's suffrage movement, led by Elizabeth Cady Stanton, Susan B. Anthony, and Carrie Chapman Catt, among others, during the late nineteenth and early twentieth centuries. The suffragists held rallies, demonstrations, and protest marches for more than half a century before achieving their goal. Before the federal government granted women the right to vote, numerous states and territories adopted women's suffrage, paving the way for women to earn the right to vote nationally.

The most recent expansion of the right to vote in the United States, the Twenty-Sixth Amendment, lowered the voting age from 21 to 18. Ratified during the Vietnam War, in 1971, it was intended to channel the disruptive protest activities of students involved in the anti–Vietnam War movement into peaceful participation at the ballot box.

FOR CRITICAL ANALYSIS

Describe the expansion of suffrage in the United States since the Founding. Why might the government have denied participation to so many for so long? What forces influenced the expansion of voting rights?

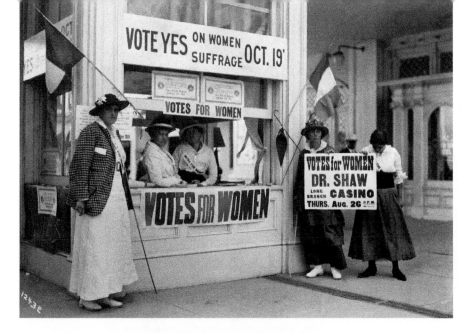

The campaign for women's suffrage gathered strength in the United States in the mid-eighteenth century. Activists fought for decades—with tactics ranging from protests to pickets to hunger strikes—before the Nineteenth Amendment to the Constitution granted all adult women the right to vote in 1920.

Current Trends in Voter Turnout Today, voting rights are granted to all American citizens aged 18 and above, although some states revoke this right from those who have committed a felony or are mentally impaired. Although eligibility to vote is now almost universal, America's overall rate of voting participation, or **turnout**, remains relatively low. The United States ranked 32nd in terms of voter turnout compared to other developed countries in 2016. Just over 58 percent voted in the 2012 and 2016 presidential elections. This pales in comparison to voting rates in the most recent national elections in other democracies: 87 percent in Belgium, 86 percent in Sweden, 71 percent in France, and 61 percent in the United Kingdom. Turnout in state and local elections, especially those that do not coincide with national contests or primaries, is typically much lower.[12]

> **turnout** the percentage of eligible individuals who actually vote

Not only does the United States have relatively low rates of participation in elections, but those who do not vote are more likely to lack a college education and have lower incomes. That education and income tracks so closely with voter turnout is unique to the United States among other Western democracies. Low voter turnout coupled with unequal participation rates can have negative outcomes, including the election of candidates who do not reflect the interests of most voters, government policies that benefit wealthy voters over the middle and lower classes, and lower trust in government and perceptions of government legitimacy.

Participation in U.S. presidential elections has declined over the past four decades from a high of 64 percent in 1960. In 1996 participation reached a modern low when only 52 percent of eligible voters went to the polls. Since then, however, overall trends have improved in presidential elections due to highly contested elections and major efforts to get out the vote. Turnout reached a modern high of 62 percent in 2008 when Barack Obama's campaign mobilized many new voters. Turnout in 2016 was the third highest in the modern period and broke a record in terms of votes cast at 137.5 million ballots or 59 percent of eligible

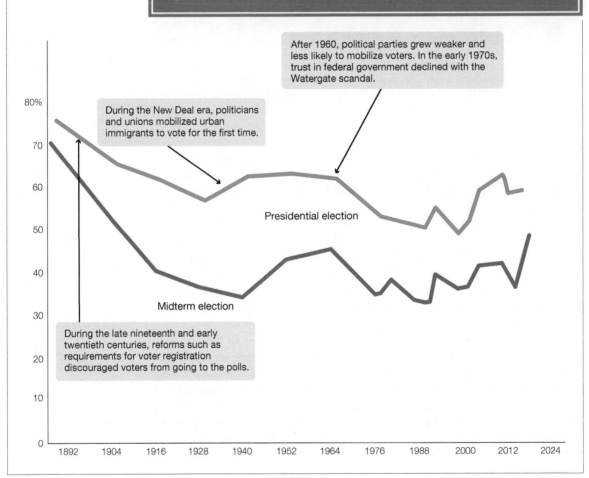

FIGURE 8.2

Voter Turnout* in Presidential and Midterm Elections, 1892–2018

Since the 1890s, participation in elections has declined substantially. One pattern is consistent across time: more Americans tend to vote in presidential election years than in years when only congressional and local elections are held. What are some of the reasons that participation rose and fell during the last century?

*Percentage of voting-eligible population

SOURCES: Erik Austin and Jerome Clubb, *Political Facts of the United States since 1789* (New York: Columbia University Press, 1986); United States Election Project, www.electproject.org (accessed 11/14/16); "2018 November General Election Turnout Rates," United States Election Project, November 7, 2018, www.electproject .org/2018g (accessed 11/9/18).

During the New Deal era, politicians and unions mobilized urban immigrants to vote for the first time.

After 1960, political parties grew weaker and less likely to mobilize voters. In the early 1970s, trust in federal government declined with the Watergate scandal.

Presidential election

Midterm election

During the late nineteenth and early twentieth centuries, reforms such as requirements for voter registration discouraged voters from going to the polls.

voters.[13] Midterm elections with only congressional elections at the national level tend to have much lower voter turnout. In 2014, 36 percent voted though in 2018 turnout rose to 49 percent, a record high seen in non-presidential elections since 1966 (see Figure 8.2). Despite these overall trends, there are significant differences in voter turnout rates across the states. We'll learn about why later in this chapter.

DIGITAL POLITICAL PARTICIPATION

Digital political participation is rapidly changing the way Americans experience politics. The internet and social media give citizens greater access to information about candidates and campaigns and a greater role in politics than ever before; digital politics is the new pulse of American democracy where political news frequently goes viral. Digital politics builds on traditional forms of participation but makes many of those activities easier and more immediate, giving citizens greater potential for community building and networked participation. The internet, and social media in particular, offers an active, two-way form of communication with feedback, rather than the more passive, one-way communication involved in reading printed newspapers, watching television, or listening to the radio. It allows for person-to-person communication as well as broadcast capability, especially through social media, where information can be widely shared.

Digital participation includes discussing issues or mobilizing supporters through social media, emailing and text messaging, reading blogs and online news stories, viewing YouTube videos and campaign ads, and sharing opinions on the internet, contributing money to candidates and political organizations, contacting political leaders and following them on Twitter, campaigning on social networking sites, working on behalf of candidates, and organizing face-to-face neighborhood meetings online. With 67 percent of Americans reading the news using social media, digital participation is the most common way average Americans participate in politics outside of voting.[14]

Why are digital media so effective for mobilization and political participation? Online mobilization works through emotional appeals, immediacy, personal networks, and social pressure. Political scientist Meredith Rolf argues that social connections are an essential component of political participation. Her work reveals that individual factors such as income and education are imperfect predictors of turnout, but one's social network *is* strongly predictive of political participation. When members of a social network indicate they have voted in an election or contributed to a candidate, for example, that can motivate others to do the same. Peer social pressure allows members of a social network to model and mimic actions of other members of their group.[15]

Social media in particular can efficiently coordinate the actions of millions of people required for political campaigns and winning elections. One in three social media users have encouraged others to vote, and roughly the same percentage have shared their own thoughts or comments on politics or government online.[16] Social media are characterized by tiny acts of political participation—sharing, following a candidate or organization, liking a post, commenting—that can scale up to dramatic changes, leading to real world political protests, voter mobilization drives, and the election of candidates and parties to government.[17] Small acts of political participation made possible by social media may give those uninterested in politics or who are rarely engaged a way of getting involved easily, which can than encourage them to do more.

Politicians, too, make much use of social media. In 2016 every serious presidential candidate had a Facebook page and Twitter account, with thousands or in some cases millions of fans who received daily updates from the candidates, political parties, and campaigns. These fans, in turn, signaled to their friends which candidates they supported for elected office, making politics a seamless part of everyday

digital political participation
activities designed to influence politics using the internet, including visiting a candidate's website, organizing events online, and signing an online petition

discussion. Donald Trump's supporters receive emails from his organization, follow him on Twitter and Facebook, and turn out for rallies and events. Based on a survey analysis of 65,000 registered voters and holding all other demographic factors constant, frequent social media users were more likely to vote for Trump than any other candidate in 2016.[18]

Unlike traditional social movements that gain momentum slowly over time, digital politics, and the use of social media especially, can create punctuated explosive bursts of collective action. For example, Bernie Sanders's supporters relied heavily on Reddit to organize rallies and rock concerts during the 2016 presidential primaries on behalf of the Vermont senator. Protests erupted after Trump won the 2016 election despite losing the popular vote by nearly 3 million votes. Over 700,000 people signed an online petition in a matter of days to eliminate the electoral college and elect the president based on actual votes cast.

Some have dismissed social media as *clicktivism*—forms of participation that require little effort and may or may not convert to offline acts of participation in politics. Others argue so-called clicktivism is the building block for sustained participation in politics. President Trump's extensive use of Twitter is evidence that audience-building on social media matters for political leadership and winning votes. The clicks of millions of Americans can and do add up.

Digital Politics Leads to Offline Participation An important question is whether online engagement in politics influences offline participation, especially voting. The discussion above suggests a number of mechanisms by which social networks and small acts of political participation lead to voting and offline engagement in politics. Many people use social media to facilitate organizing face-to-face neighborhood meetings or to get information about a local campaign event or where to vote. Digital politics encourages information-gathering and interaction among users and elected officials by combining the content of traditional media with interpersonal communication. The combination of information and interaction gives the internet the potential to promote interest in politics and increase participation. A growing body of research finds that online activities such as reading digital news, commenting on blogs, and using email or social media for politics increases the likelihood of voting and is associated with contributing to political campaigns, volunteering on behalf of candidates, and even contacting elected officials. Online participation is also linked with discussing politics with friends or family, developing an interest in politics in general, and being informed about politics.[19]

Additionally, the ease of making monetary contributions online has led to a dramatic increase in this form of political participation. The percentage of people who donated directly to candidates has doubled since 1992. Barack Obama was the first candidate to capitalize on online fundraising, raising much of the money needed to win the 2008 presidential election from small (less than $100) individual online donations. In fact, the 2008 presidential election and Obama's campaign ushered in the modern era of digital politics, building comprehensive online strategies to mobilize supporters, and citizens made unprecedented use of digital media to learn about candidates and to participate in campaigns.[20] In 2016, 12 percent of Americans said they contributed money to a candidate running for public office, up from 6 percent four years earlier. In large part because of online donations, 71 percent of Hillary Clinton's fundraising total[21] and 40 percent of Donald Trump's[22] in 2016 came from individual contributions.

Voter Turnout in Comparison

Over the past 20 years, voter turnout in U.S. national elections has hovered around 45 percent of the voting-age population. While the number is significantly higher in presidential elections than in midterm elections (though in the 2018 midterm election turnout was roughly 49 percent),[a] voting rates in the United States still lag behind those in many other democratic countries. Australia, despite seeing their lowest turnout since 1925, had 78.9 percent of their voting-age population participate in the 2016 parliamentary election.[b]

So why does voter turnout vary so much from country to country? Part of the explanation rests in how we calculate who is eligible to vote. In the United States, noncitizens and ex-felons are denied voting rights. If we exclude those populations when calculating voter percentages, U.S. turnout would be at least two percentage points higher in each election.[c]

Another explanation relates to the rules governing elections. Some countries have rules that make it easier or harder for citizens to vote, while others penalize those who do not vote. In many democracies, citizens are automatically registered to vote when they reach a certain age; in contrast, U.S. citizens generally must register themselves, reregister if they move, and, in many states, register a certain number of days before the election. Many countries hold their elections on a Sunday, send their ballots through the mail, or declare their election day a national holiday, meaning that fewer voters must choose between going to work or going to the polls. Voting is also compulsory in many countries. Australia, for instance, charges a $20 fine (about US$16) unless a citizen can provide a good excuse for why she did not vote.[d] Countries with frequent elections like the United States and Switzerland often see depressed turnout as well, despite laws that ease or hinder access to the polls.

TURNOUT IN NATIONAL ELECTIONS*

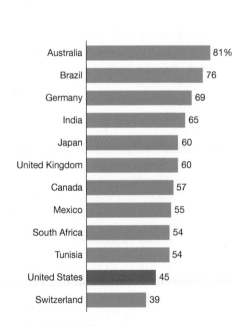

	Turnout	Compulsory voting	Weekend or holiday voting	Automatic or compulsory registration
Australia	81%	✓	✓	✓
Brazil	76	✓	✓	✓
Germany	69		✓	✓
India	65		✓	✓
Japan	60		✓	✓
United Kingdom	60			✓
Canada	57			
Mexico	55	✓	✓	✓
South Africa	54		✓	✓
Tunisia	54			
United States	45			
Switzerland	39		✓	✓

*Average 1990–2018.

SOURCES: International Institute for Democracy and Electoral Assistance (IDEA) voter turnout database, www.idea.int/vt/viewdata.cfm, and the ACE Electoral Knowledge Network, www.aceproject.org/epic-en/CDMap?question=VR008&f= (accessed 3/27/18).

[a]International Institute for Democracy and Electoral Assistance (IDEA), Voter Turnout Database, www.idea.int/vt/viewdata.cfm (accessed 4/12/18).

[b]Nicole Hasham, "Election 2016: Voter Turnout Lowest since Compulsory Voting Began in 1925," *Sydney Morning Herald*, August 8, 2016, www.smh.com.au/politics/federal/election-2016-voter-turnout-lowest-since-compulsory-voting-began-in-1925-20160808-gqnij2.html (accessed 4/12/18).

[c]Michael P. McDonald, "National General Election VEP Turnout Rates, 1789–Present," United States Election Project, June 11, 2014, www.electproject.org/national-1789-present (accessed 4/12/18).

[d]Hasham, "Election 2016."

Like the traditional "I Voted" stickers, political messages shared on social media may remind and encourage others to participate too. In recent elections, Facebook users could click an "I Voted" button to announce that they had cast a ballot.

Twitter has become an especially important tool for voter mobilization. The percentage of Americans following elected officials on Twitter continues to soar. Citizens like following political figures on social media because they feel more emotionally connected to the candidates.[23] Social media also allow users to avoid exposure to information that challenges their preexisting views—it's easier to follow people online whom you agree with. Elected officials and organizations on the ideological left and right have taken advantage of this dynamic to filter the news and current events. Recent research finds people who use social media for politics frequently hold stronger opinions and are more polarized by party. A benefit of Twitter for politics, however, is that it leads to more interest in politics and higher rates of participation and voter turnout.[24]

Researchers have suggested a number of possible reasons that digital politics may foster participation. First, information and political news are available 24 hours a day for those with internet access. Online news is often breaking news that can spread rapidly, and it is generally free. Digital politics may also engage individuals who otherwise would not be involved in politics. The internet creates a form of "accidental mobilization" for those who are greeted by political news on social media—sometimes politics finds the individual, rather than the other way around.[25] It is common for candidates to place political ads on social media sites and in Google searches, prompting the individuals exposed to these ads, who may be online for entirely separate reasons, to learn about politics. Donald Trump took advantage of online political ads in the 2016 campaign unlike any other modern candidate, spending millions of dollars on online ads. With two-thirds of Americans using social media, "Facebook was the 500-pound gorilla" that mobilized voters to support Trump. Facebook ads were more important than television ads in 2016.[26]

Further, digital media have unique characteristics that enhance participation. Streaming video online combines the qualities of print media that promote knowledge and in-depth reporting with the immediate and visual aspects of television that generate interest, engagement, and emotion.[27] Emotional responses to political candidates or issues learned from online media have been shown to trigger interest in politics and engagement.[28]And research has found that emotions are important in candidate evaluations and ultimately political behavior and participation. A recent study found Obama in 2008 and Trump in 2016 generated higher positive emotions from their supporters compared to other candidates. High emotional enthusiasm for these candidates was associated with their popularity, and ultimately their election victories.[29]

Finally, as we have discussed, online politics makes it easier for people to participate in politics because it requires less effort. By its very nature, digital politics occurs in ways that are less location-dependent than traditional politics: *community* takes on a very different meaning in an online social network compared with, say, a voter's actual neighborhood precinct. The internet facilitates participation that is potentially broad but with loose connections.[30] A large but more loosely knit online community may promote extensive organizing efforts and improve political knowledge, interest, and participation, but it also encourages forms of participation that can be low in intensity and sporadic—"clicktivism," as discussed above—possibly attracting individuals with only moderate political interest. Political scientist Bruce Bimber has shown that some interest groups are responding to this new political climate of sporadic participation by making it possible for individuals to support a specific issue or campaign without making a commitment to membership in the organization as a whole.[31] In this way, online politics widens the pool of political participation.

For all these reasons, digital media may foster a new kind of community building that has the potential to reverse the trends in declining political participation since the 1960s. Some analysts have cited reduced trust in government, unresponsive elected officials, and a diminishing stock of what Robert Putnam, author of *Bowling Alone*, calls social capital—community networks that motivate political participation—to explain low voter turnout in the United States.[32] By making political information, discussion, communication, and mobilization easier, the internet, and especially social media, may help Americans grow a new kind of digital social capital, one based on shared political experiences online.[33]

News about the Supreme Court's 2015 decision to legalize same-sex marriage spread rapidly, in part through viral activity on social media. Sites such as Twitter provided users with a highly visible platform to show support.

Expressive Politics Political scientist Russell Dalton has argued that participation in politics is becoming more expressive than ever before, largely aided by social media.[34] Today, individuals turn to social media to express their opinions on issues or candidates in many ways. This trend was exemplified by the response to the 2015 Supreme Court ruling that made same-sex marriage legal in all 50 states.

In the wake of the decision, digital politics created a media firestorm as responses to the decision took over the internet. The immediacy with which the news spread was remarkable. Traditional media and social media converged to celebrate or denounce the news that marriage for same-sex couples was the new law of the land. Social media enabled citizens to share their opinions in uniquely expressive ways. For example, the #LoveWins hashtag was used almost 5.5 million times in 24 hours, even by celebrities and President Obama, to recognize the Court's decision. Overall there were 10 million tweets about the Supreme Court decision in less than 12 hours.[35] And millions of people, too, used Facebook's tool to add a rainbow-colored background to their profile pictures or shared news stories and memes using rainbow images to show their support for marriage rights. Increased participation in digital politics, especially through social media, may force elected officials to better represent the people.[36]

Are There Drawbacks to Digital Participation? While social media can be effective in online political mobilization and activation, at the same time digital media create silos, echo chambers, and filter bubbles where individuals with shared views communicate to the exclusion of others, leading to increased ideological party polarization—and eventually hyper-partisanship. As mentioned earlier, people tend to surround themselves with news from like-minded sources. In such environments, people may uncritically believe news from outlets they trust while dismissing or ignoring information from sources they dislike. Social media algorithms can also create echo chambers that lead to extreme or biased views that get worse over time, creating a world of "alternative facts" where individuals cannot agree on basic principles.

There is evidence that social media—because of filter bubbles and polarized information environments—has exacerbated partisan conflict, social divisions, the culture wars, and intolerance based on race, ethnicity, gender, or religion. Anonymous social media discussion boards can have unintended consequences by allowing a forum for racism and hate speech, terrorist appeals, and sexual harassment—forums that have mobilized far right groups, including white nationalists. Some observers see a lack of civility in public discourse, or what is called a "coarsening of public discourse." Members of targeted groups—such as women and minorities—may opt out of participating in discussion of politics in what has been called the "disruption of the public square."[37]

THE DARK SIDE OF DIGITAL POLITICS: RUSSIAN VOTER SUPPRESSION AND MOBILIZATION

Free and fair elections are the foundation for democracies. But democratic elections may be increasingly vulnerable to manipulation by foreign governments and other extremists because of open networks and unregulated political advertising on social media. Donald Trump's campaign not only capitalized on social media and high enthusiasm from his supporters but also benefited from a Russian cyber campaign that used social media to discredit his opponent. Intelligence agencies have confirmed Russian interference in the election. Russian propaganda to disrupt the election was intended to mobilize Trump supporters to vote, demobilize Clinton supporters, promote third-party candidates to Bernie Sanders's supporters, and sow seeds of discord in the American public.

The first strategy focused on mobilizing voters to cast a ballot for Donald Trump. One notable ad featured a kneeling soldier and stated that the Constitution should be amended to take control of the army from Clinton should she be elected president. A similar ad had the false caption, "69 percent of veterans favor Trump" (in reality roughly 52 percent of veterans voted for Trump compared to 48 percent for Clinton—nearly a toss-up). As Senator Chris Coons (D-Del.) said, "This ad is nothing short of the Russian government directly interfering in our elections, lying to American citizens, duping folks who believe they are joining and supporting a group that is about veterans and based in Texas, when in fact it is paid for in rubles [Russian currency] by Russians."[38]

A second category of Russian propaganda worked to suppress votes for Clinton. These ads were targeted in sophisticated ways toward demographic and partisan groups in swing states such as Wisconsin, Michigan, and central Pennsylvania (three states Trump narrowly won over Clinton), but also nationwide. Fake news stories focused on Clinton's health and mental stability in the two weeks leading up to the election. The most troubling Russian propaganda ads encouraged people to cast a vote for Clinton by texting or tweeting their ballot, both of which are invalid forms of voting in the United States. Finally, to dissuade Bernie Sanders's supporters from turning out to vote for Clinton, the websites of Sanders supporters were found have extensive postings by fake eastern Europeans bot accounts.

The scope of Russian interference in the 2016 election and the foreign propaganda campaign was far greater than initially expected. Facebook and other social media platforms revealed thousands of false political ads appeared on their networks that were paid for by Russian operatives, with many of the ads focused on voter suppression. These ads are estimated to have reached 126 million people on Facebook alone, or 40 percent of the U.S. population. (To put this number in perspective, there were only 135 million votes cast in the 2016 election.) The information was shared hundreds of millions of times. Russian propaganda on Instagram during the election reached another 20 million people. Twitter found nearly 3,000 accounts controlled by Russian operatives and 36,000 more bot accounts that tweeted 1.4 million times during the election. A recent study from USC found that 1 in 5 tweets about the election were from bot accounts; the majority promoted stories damaging to Clinton.[39]

In addition to the aims described above, Russia's campaign on social media also sought more generally to divide the public over controversial issues such as race, immigration, abortion, gay rights, and gun ownership. Fake Facebook accounts linked to Russia included, for example, Infidels against Islam, Fed-up with Illegals, and Stop Killing White People.

Russian interference has exposed the outsized role played by platforms such as Facebook, Twitter, and Google in American politics and discourse—and that these companies don't always follow the same rules as government institutions. Russia's actions exposed the dark side of technology for democratic governance. Unlike traditional media (radio, television, print media) online political ads on Google and social media sites are not regulated. A foreign government was able to take advantage of the United States' open digital communication and media system to interfere in the election. In response Congress has enacted economic sanctions on Russia and is considering new regulations of online political advertising. The Honest Ads Act is aimed at preventing foreign influence on elections by subjecting political ads sold online to the same rules and transparency that apply to TV and radio.[40] The technology companies have also taken steps to crack down on fake accounts.

SUMMING UP DIGITAL PARTICIPATION

As we have seen, digital participation in politics has benefits and costs. It has the potential to foster innovation, free expression, social connections, information seeking, and political participation. But it may also foster misinformation, intolerance, a lack of civility, and breaches of privacy and even demobilization. A barrier to digital participation is the digital divide—defined as the gap between those with and those without home internet or mobile access. Growing inequalities online replicate existing societal inequalities based on race and economic class that threaten to widen gaps in who is informed about politics and who participates. Today, over 35 percent of Americans don't have home broadband, and those without access tend to be poorer, less educated, and older. The digital divide creates new inequalities as the world of politics moves online.

Perhaps the most transformative aspect of digital media is how they affect candidates and parties. Political candidates find campaigning online particularly attractive because it is cost-efficient and can reach a wide audience of prospective voters. Running for office can be enormously expensive, but social media may help level the playing field by reducing candidate reliance on money from corporations, special interests, and wealthy donors. Digital politics holds the promise of reinvigorating a more grassroots and participatory democracy. In 2016, Bernie Sanders largely rejected Super PAC funding for his campaign and relied heavily on digital media; Donald Trump did the same during the primaries. Grassroots funding in turn may allow political leaders to better connect to, and ultimately represent, the people.

Who Participates?

Describe the patterns of participation among major demographic groups

Individuals face a number of costs and benefits related to their decision to become involved in politics. Just as in any other activity in life, an individual is likely to vote in an election only if the benefits outweigh the costs.[41] One benefit associated with voting is the favorable policies that might result from having one's preferred candidate or party in office, which the potential voter weighs against the slim likelihood of her vote actually influencing the outcome of the election. Another benefit of voting is the sense of pride gained from fulfilling one's civic duty. The costs related to voting can include the time and resources needed to become informed and to cast a ballot, which may help explain why the poor and the less educated are less likely to vote and participate in politics in other ways.

To understand who votes, it helps to understand why some Americans don't vote. The U.S. Census indicates the top reason for not voting in the 2016 presidential election was "did not like the candidates or campaign issues." This reason was cited by almost 25 percent of nonvoters in 2016, compared to just 13 percent who gave this response in 2012. Fifteen percent of nonvoters said they were "not interested in politics"; 4 percent said they were "too busy or [had] conflicting schedules"; and almost 12 percent said they had an illness or disability that prevented them from voting. As we can see, even personal health can be a predictor of voting, with the healthier more likely to participate in politics.[42]

The factors that help us explain voting in elections can be grouped into three general categories: (1) a person's social and demographic characteristics and attitudes about politics; (2) the political environment in which elections take place, such as campaigns that seek to mobilize voters and whether an election is contested among two political candidates; and (3) the state electoral laws that shape the electoral process. We examine each in turn.

SOCIOECONOMIC STATUS

socioeconomic status status in society based on level of education, income, and occupational prestige

One of the most important and consistent findings from surveys about participation is that Americans with higher levels of education, more income, and higher-level occupations—collectively, what social scientists call higher socioeconomic status—participate much more in politics than do those with less education and less income.[43] Education is the single most important factor in predicting not only whether an individual will vote but also most kinds of participation. Unsurprisingly, income is another important factor when it comes to making contributions, as well as voting. People who are more affluent have the money, time, and capacity to participate effectively in the political system. Among people aged 45–64, for example, the 2016 Census found that 83 percent of individuals earning over $150,000 a year voted compared to 43 percent of those earning less than $20,000 per year.[44] These characteristics are also related to attitudes toward politics. Higher levels of political interest are associated with individuals higher on the socioeconomic scale.[45]

Figure 8.3 shows the differences in voter turnout linked to ethnic and racial groups, education level, employment status, and age. Just 52 percent of those with only a high school diploma voted in the recent presidential election, compared with 74 percent of college graduates.[46]

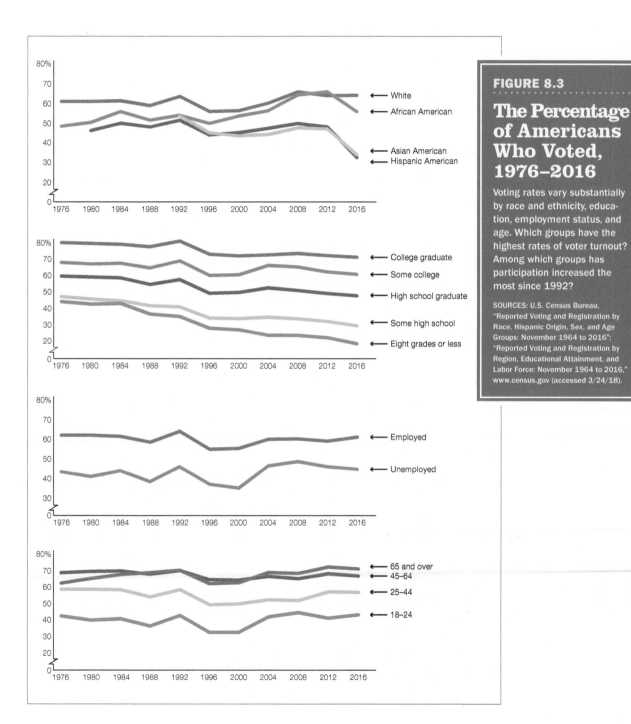

FIGURE 8.3

The Percentage of Americans Who Voted, 1976–2016

Voting rates vary substantially by race and ethnicity, education, employment status, and age. Which groups have the highest rates of voter turnout? Among which groups has participation increased the most since 1992?

SOURCES: U.S. Census Bureau, "Reported Voting and Registration by Race, Hispanic Origin, Sex, and Age Groups: November 1964 to 2016"; "Reported Voting and Registration by Region, Educational Attainment, and Labor Force: November 1964 to 2016," www.census.gov (accessed 3/24/18).

Education is one of the most important predictors of voting, and it is also associated with encouraging other people to vote or support an issue, as well making a donation to a candidate or cause.[47]

AGE AND PARTICIPATION

Older people have much higher rates of participation than do young people, in part because homeownership and property taxes, more common among older individuals, lead to a greater awareness of the importance of government. This pattern was evident in 2016 with citizens 65 years and older reporting the highest turnout (71 percent), followed by those age 45–66 (67 percent), 58 percent turnout for those age 30–44, and the lowest turnout for those age 18–29 (46 percent). Youth turnout remained lower than the average across all other age groups in 2016. In midterm elections without a presidential race, youth turnout has historically been extremely low. However, in 2018, youth voter turnout increased by 10 percent to 31 percent from 21 percent in 2014.[48]

Millennials (ages 18–35) are now the largest age cohort in the United States. According to Pew, 47 percent of millennials are Democrats or lean Democrat, compared to 34 percent who are Republicans or lean Republican. In 2018, 67 percent of young people supported Democratic candidates, compared to just 32 percent for Republican candidates, a larger gap than youth voting for Democrats in 2008 when President Barack Obama was first elected.[49]

A primary reason young people don't vote is that they lack an interest in politics or have not been mobilized to participate. Studies have found that if young people do vote, they tend to maintain this habit throughout their lifetime.[50] Another reason younger people vote less is that political campaigns often target older voters rather than young voters, because the former are more likely to vote. But this may be changing as more organizations channel energy and resources into getting younger people to vote. NextGen America (mentioned at the beginning of this chapter) for example, is an organization focusing on youth turnout that helped register 1 million voters in the 2016 election. NextGen supports candidates who favor addressing climate change, alternative energy, and reversing economic inequality.

Since the early 1990s, several campaigns have sought to increase the participation of young voters. Rock the Vote enlists musicians and actors to urge young people to vote. It has spawned other initiatives aimed at young voters, including Rap the Vote and Rock the Vote a lo Latino. The Obama campaign made young voters central to its electoral strategy in 2008 and 2012, winning a significantly higher percent of the youth vote than his opponents.[51] The Obama campaign posted videos on YouTube and used social media to reach out to young people rather than focusing primarily on television ads (which target older voters). In 2016, Democratic presidential candidate Bernie Sanders was also effective in inspiring youth participation in politics. Although Sanders failed to secure his party's nomination, election polls consistently showed over 80 percent of people aged 18 to

Even though much time and effort is spent mobilizing young voters, people who actually vote tend to be older than the average American.

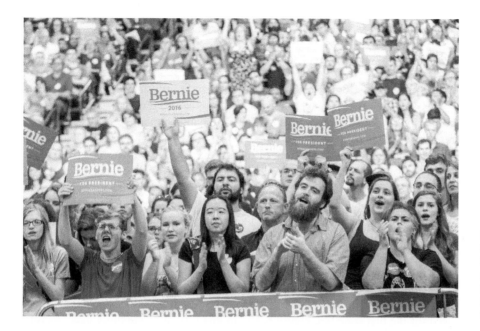

In the 2016 presidential primaries, Democratic candidate Bernie Sanders energized young people and swept the youth vote, despite trailing Hillary Clinton overall. Still, 18- to 24-year-olds turned out at lower rates than all other age groups.

29 preferred him to his opponent, Hillary Clinton. Sanders called for a political revolution and focused on ending a corrupt campaign finance system, combating economic inequality, and providing free college tuition. Young people were drawn to the candidate's reputation of honesty and authenticity.

Relatively low voter turnout by the young has implications for the policies addressed by government at the local, state, and federal levels. For example, young people share older Americans' concerns about the economy and national security, but they tend to be more concerned about economic inequality and student debt, and express support for stronger environmental laws, funding for public education and colleges, and more tolerance for personal freedoms than older people do. A recent survey of 13- to 25-year-olds showed the consequences of coming of age in an era of hyper-partisanship and scandal; most saw the political system as ineffective and broken, and 9 out of 10 would not consider running for office.[52] At the same time young people have a strong interest in community service, and nearly 20 percent are involved in community service projects, with numbers higher among those with college experience.[53] The distinctive attitudes of today's young people suggest that higher levels of political participation by this group could significantly alter government policy and politics.

FOR CRITICAL ANALYSIS

When the Twenty-Sixth Amendment changed the voting age from 21 to 18 in 1971, observers expected that the youth vote would add a significant new voice to American politics. Why has the youth vote turned out to be less important than was hoped? What changes would engage more young people in the political system?

AFRICAN AMERICANS

As we saw in Chapter 5, during much of the twentieth century in the South, the widespread use of the poll tax, literacy tests, and other measures such as the white primary deprived African Americans of the right to vote. This system of legal segregation meant that African Americans in the South had few avenues for participating in politics. Through a combination of protest, legal action, and political pressure, the civil rights movement compelled a reluctant federal government to enforce black civil and political rights.

The victories of the civil rights movement made blacks full citizens and stimulated a tremendous growth in voter turnout. The movement drew on an organizational base and network of communication rooted in black churches, the National Association for the Advancement of Colored People (NAACP), and historically black colleges and universities. Because they tended to vote as a cohesive bloc, African American voters began to wield considerable political power, and the number of African American elected officials grew significantly as blacks exercised their newfound political rights. Despite this progress, today, state laws requiring government voter identification have created a new impediment for black and other minority voters in some states.

Being represented by a member of one's group appears to have positive effects on participation levels. African Americans are more likely to vote when residing in states with increased representation in the state legislature, as measured by the percentage of black lawmakers.[54] African Americans represented by a black member of Congress are more likely to vote in elections, have a sense of efficacy—the belief that the government is responsive to them—and higher levels of political knowledge.[55]

With Barack Obama running in 2008 as the first black major-party candidate for president, African American interest in the election surged. The black–white voting gap went from 7 percent in 2004 to 1 percent in 2008 as many African Americans voted for the first time (see Figure 8.3).[56] In 2012, blacks were more likely to vote than whites.[57] Exit polls indicated that 95 percent of African Americans who voted cast ballots for Obama.

In the 2016 election, black turnout in the presidential election declined 7 percentage points compared to 2012. Possible explanations for this decrease include strict voter ID laws and a reduction in the days allowed for early voting in some states, the lack of an African American presidential candidate on the ballot, and a divisive presidential campaign including anti-minority rhetoric.[58]

Racial segregation remains a fact of life in the United States along with the persistence of black urban poverty.[59] These conditions, often called *concentrated poverty*, post barriers to African American political participation. As the previous section on socioeconomic status described, participation (for blacks as well as whites) is highly correlated with more income, higher education, and higher-level occupations. Nevertheless, comparing citizens of similar socioeconomic status, African Americans are somewhat more likely to vote than whites.[60]

This may be because African Americans are a minority group. African Americans who feel a shared sense of collective identity, a concept called *linked fate*, are more likely to vote and participate politically. Political scientist Michael Dawson argues that black linked fate is a major predictor of political behavior. Dawson uses the construct of *linked fate* to measure the degree to which African Americans believe that their own self-interests are linked to the interests of the race.[61] That is, the experiences of African Americans with race and racial discrimination in the United States, including a history of slavery, unify their personal interests in seeking a candidate and policies that benefit their racial group. Black civic, community, religious, and political organizations are also important in increasing political participation for this group.

LATINOS

For many years, analysts called the Latino vote "the sleeping giant" because Latinos, while accounting for a large portion of the population, as a group had relatively low levels of political participation. For instance, 48 percent of Latinos voted in the

Though their turnout was lower than in 2012, Latinos and African Americans strongly favored Clinton over Trump in 2016.

2016 presidential election compared to 65 percent of non-Hispanic whites and just under 60 percent of African Americans. Despite continuing growth of the Latino population in the United States, just 12.7 million Latinos cast a ballot in the presidential election out of roughly 26 million eligible.[62]

Political scientists Matt Barreto and Gary Segura explain why voting rates are lower for Latinos compared to whites and African Americans. As a group, more Latinos are recent immigrants to this country and thus have fewer opportunities, such as access to a quality education, than do other ethnic and racial groups; therefore, they are more likely to lack resources for participation in politics such as money, time, and language skills.[63]

Today, politicians, political parties, and scholars view Latinos, the largest and fastest-growing minority in the United States, as a political group of critical importance. Latinos make up 17 percent of the population and represent 1 in 10 voters. In large states such as California and Texas, Latinos are approaching 50 percent of the population.[64] Although Latino registration and turnout are lower than those of other racial groups, these numbers have been increasing. Rapid population growth, increased registration rates, and uncertain party attachment all magnify the importance of the Latino vote.

While Latinos have tended to favor the Democrats in national elections, particularly due to staunch Republican opposition to immigration, Latinos tend to be religious, which may be expected to make them more socially conservative. But national surveys of Latinos find that they often do not allow their religious beliefs to dictate their political decisions. In addition to favoring an easier path to citizenship for immigrants, Latinos also favor more liberal economic policies. In 2016, Latinos strongly favored Clinton over Trump. Trump made ending illegal immigration a major theme of his campaign, proposing to build a wall between the United States and Mexico. The issue of immigration has continued to widen the partisan divide between minorities and white non-Hispanics. While 55 percent of white non-Hispanics voted for Republicans in 2018, 76 percent of nonwhites voted for Democrats. In 2018, 69 percent of Latinos voted Democratic.[65]

Similar to African Americans, Latinos are also more likely to vote when residing in states with increased representation in the state legislature, as measured by the percentage of Latino lawmakers, or in a district with a Latino member of Congress.[66] This phenomenon is commonly referred to as *descriptive representation*—when individuals are represented in government by officials of their same race, ethnicity, or gender, allowing minority groups to have a greater ability to affect policy outcomes. Descriptive representation may also confer symbolic benefits, such as reducing levels of political alienation among racial and ethnic minorities.[67] As the Latino

FOR CRITICAL ANALYSIS

How significant a factor was the Latino vote in the 2016 election? Why does the percentage of eligible Latinos who vote still lag behind that of other groups?

population continues to grow, this group may influence more strongly who wins and who loses in U.S. elections.

ASIAN AMERICANS

Asian Americans are a smaller group than whites, Latinos, or African Americans, comprising roughly 6 percent of the population or 21 million citizens. In particular states, such as California, home to 33 percent of the nation's Asian American population, the group has become an important political presence. Asian Americans have education and income levels closer to those of whites than of Latinos or African Americans; but they are less likely to participate in politics than whites or African Americans.[68] Asian Americans have voter turnout rates similar to Latinos.[69]

No one national group dominates among the Asian American population, and this diversity has impeded the development of group-based political power. Asian Americans often have different political concerns from one another, stemming from their different national backgrounds and experiences in the United States. Historically, these groups have united most effectively around common issues of ethnic discrimination or anti-Asian violence, federal immigration policies, and discriminatory mortgage loan practices.

Asian American voter turnout rate increased to 49.3 percent in 2016, up from just under 47 percent in 2012 and surpassing Hispanics for the first time since 1996. But Asians constitute a much smaller share of the electorate than Latinos. In 2016, roughly 5 million Asians voted. Asian Americans have been moving, along with other minority groups, toward the Democratic Party in recent elections. Although a majority of Asian Americans voted Republican in the early 1990s, in the 2000s they have been voting increasingly Democratic; and 65 percent of Asian Americans voted for Hillary Clinton in 2016.[70]

The U.S. electorate in 2016 was the country's most racially and ethnically diverse ever; combined, African Americans, Latinos and Asians, and other racial or ethnic minorities accounted for nearly 27 percent of all voters almost an identical percentage as in 2012. However, since minority groups made up a larger share of the overall population in 2016 than 2012, this means many minorities chose not to vote in 2016. At the same time, turnout for non-Hispanic whites increased in 2016, in large part mobilized by Trump's campaign.

GENDER AND PARTICIPATION

gender gap a distinctive pattern of voting behavior reflecting the differences in views between women and men

Today, women register and vote at rates similar to or higher than those of men. The ongoing significance of gender issues in American politics is best exemplified by the **gender gap**—a distinctive pattern of male and female voting decisions—in electoral politics. Women tend to vote in higher numbers for Democratic candidates, whereas Republicans win more male votes. Behind these voting patterns are differing assessments of key policy issues. Women are more likely than men to oppose military activities, especially war, and to support gun control as well as social spending for health care, public education, and welfare. Though the gender gap generally runs around 10 points in presidential elections, the 2016 presidential election saw the first female major party candidate, Democrat Hillary Clinton, and the largest gender gap in history: surveys showed that 54 percent of women supported Clinton compared to 41 percent among men, a 13-point advantage.[71]

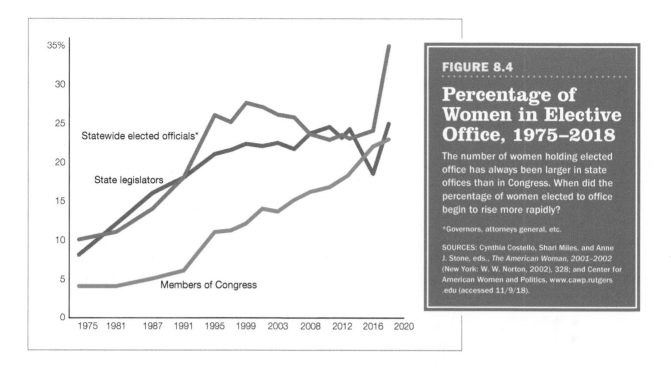

FIGURE 8.4

Percentage of Women in Elective Office, 1975–2018

The number of women holding elected office has always been larger in state offices than in Congress. When did the percentage of women elected to office begin to rise more rapidly?

*Governors, attorneys general, etc.

SOURCES: Cynthia Costello, Shari Miles, and Anne J. Stone, eds., *The American Woman, 2001–2002* (New York: W. W. Norton, 2002), 328; and Center for American Women and Politics, www.cawp.rutgers .edu (accessed 11/9/18).

One key development in gender politics in recent decades is the growing number of women in elective office (see Figure 8.4), an increasingly significant form of descriptive representation. A record number of women ran for office in 2018, and at least 125 women will serve in the 116th Congress, up from 107 in 2016. The numbers mark a new all-time high for the number of women in Congress. Over 100 women won House seats and at least 13 women won Senate seats, in addition to the 10 female senators who were not up for re-election this year.

Recent research has shown that one key to increasing the number of women in political office is to encourage more women to run for political office. Although women are just as likely as men to win an election, women are less likely to run for office, even if they are equally qualified. Because women are less likely than men to hold office, they also are less likely to benefit from the advantage of incumbency.[72] Organizations supporting female candidates have worked to encourage more women to run for office and have supported them financially. In addition to the bipartisan National Women's Political Caucus, the Women's Campaign Fund and EMILY's List provide prochoice Democratic women with early campaign financing, which is critical to establishing electoral momentum.

Why does the gender gap matter? Although women in public office by no means take uniform positions on policy issues, surveys show that, on the whole, female legislators are more supportive of women's rights, education, and health care spending and are also more attentive to children's and family issues. Nevertheless, partisanship matters more than gender in terms of representation of women's issues, especially in the current highly partisan political environment in Congress.[73] More women in Congress are Democrats, and Democratic lawmakers are much more likely to support these issues than Republican lawmakers regardless of gender.

RELIGIOUS IDENTITY

Religious identity plays an important role in American life. For many citizens, religious groups provide an organizational infrastructure for political participation. African American churches, for example, were instrumental in the civil rights movement, and African American religious leaders continue to play important roles in national and local politics. Jews have also been active as a group in politics but less through religious bodies than through a variety of social action agencies, including the American Jewish Congress and the Anti-Defamation League. In the United States churches are an important social institution that often fosters political participation. Through church activities many people learn civic skills that prepare them to participate in the political world. Today roughly one in four Americans are religiously unaffiliated and do not identify with any religion.

For most of American history, religious language, symbols, and values have been woven deeply into the fabric of public life. Until the mid-twentieth century, for example, public school students generally began the day with prayers or Bible readings. But a variety of court decisions greatly reduced this kind of overt religious influence on public life (see Chapter 4). These decisions helped to spawn a countermovement of religious activists seeking to restore the prominent role of religion in civic life and the mobilization of religious organizations has been one of the most significant political developments of the past half century. Some of the most divisive conflicts in politics today, such as those over abortion, birth control, and contraceptives, hinge on differences over religious beliefs. These divisions have become so salient that they now constitute what is called a "culture war," with repercussions throughout the political system and many policy areas.

One of the most significant drivers of this new politics was the mobilization of white evangelical Protestants into a cohesive political force. The Moral Majority, the first broad-based political organization of evangelical Christians, quickly rose to prominence in the 1980 election when it aligned with the Republican Party, eventually backing Ronald Reagan for president. Over the next few years, evangelicals strengthened their movement by registering voters and mobilizing them. Their success was evident in the 1984 election, when 8 in 10 evangelical Christian voters cast their ballots for Reagan. In 1988 the televangelist Pat Robertson ran for president. Although his candidacy was unsuccessful, his supporters gained control of some state Republican parties and won positions of power in others. President

Religious identity remains a significant factor in voting patterns. White evangelical Christians strongly support Republicans. Religious people of color tend to vote for Democrats, suggesting race may be a stronger predictor of voting behavior than religion.

George W. Bush was closely aligned with religious conservatives, and the religious right played an important role in electing him. In 2016 most evangelical Christians supported Trump in the general election.

Despite the influences of race and ethnicity, gender, age, religion, and socioeconomic status, these factors are not the only explanations for voter turnout or other forms of political participation. Our incomplete understanding of what motivates political participation is evident when we compare voting across countries. If more political resources lead to a greater likelihood of voting, why does the United States, one of the most prosperous countries in the world, have only moderate voting rates? And Americans have become more educated over the past century, with more people finishing high school and attending college. Given the well-documented links between educational attainment and voting, why has participation declined during this period?[74] These puzzles mean that we need to look beyond the socioeconomic characteristics of individuals and to the larger political environment in which participation occurs.

Political Environment and Voter Mobilization

Explain the factors in the political environment that influence whether individuals vote or not

Whether or not people feel engaged or are recruited to participate in politics depends on their political environment—that is, social setting, their friends and family, where they live, what associations they belong to. For example, citizens living in presidential battleground states (states with roughly equal numbers of Democrats and Republicans in the population) are exposed to a torrent of campaign ads, candidate visits, and grassroots mobilization efforts. These individuals are more knowledgeable about presidential elections, are more interested in the campaign, and have a higher probability of voting than residents of states that are "safe" for either the Republican Party, such as Texas, or the Democratic Party, such as New York or California.

MOBILIZATION

A critical aspect of political environments is whether people are mobilized—by parties, candidates, campaigns, interest groups, and social movements. A recent comprehensive study of the decline in political participation in the United States found that half of the drop-off could be accounted for by reduced **mobilization** efforts.[75] People become much more likely to participate when someone—especially someone they know—asks them to get involved.

A series of experiments conducted by the political scientists Donald Green and Alan Gerber demonstrate the importance of personal contact for mobilizing voters. Evaluating the results of several get-out-the-vote drives, the researchers showed that face-to-face interaction with a canvasser greatly increased the chances that the person contacted would go to the polls, boosting overall voter turnout by almost 10 percent. The impact of direct mail was much smaller, increasing turnout by just 0.5 percent.[76] "Robocalls" (prerecorded phone calls) from a phone bank had no measurable effect on voter turnout. Social media networks can mimic face-to-face communication. In a large study involving 61 million users on Facebook, political scientists found voter turnout in the 2010

mobilization the process by which large numbers of people are organized for a political activity midterm election increased by 340,000 additional people (who otherwise would not have voted). Users' closest friends on the network had the most influence in getting them to vote.[77] Thus, online and offline networks both played a role in mobilizing voters.[78]

In previous decades, political parties and social movements relied on personal contact to mobilize voters. As we will see in Chapter 9, during the nineteenth century, American political party machines employed hundreds of thousands of workers to bring voters to the polls. The result was a very high turnout rate, typically more than 90 percent of eligible voters.[79] But political party machines began to decline in strength at the beginning of the twentieth century. By the late twentieth century, political parties had become essentially fund-raising and advertising organizations rather than mobilizers of people. Without party workers to encourage them to go to the polls, many eligible voters will not participate.

Nevertheless, competitive presidential elections since 2000 have once again motivated both parties to build strong grassroots organizations to reach voters and turn them out on Election Day. In the 2004 elections, Republicans were more successful in their organizational efforts than Democrats, building an organization with more than 1.4 million volunteers who were trained to make calls, go door to door to register voters, write letters in favor of President Bush, post blogs online, and phone local radio call-in shows. In 2008, Barack Obama's campaign made mobilization a centerpiece of its strategy, organizing a base of volunteers to go door to door seeking support for their candidate. Many of Obama's crucial primary victories relied on direct voter mobilization. The campaign then created a nationwide organization, opening more than 700 field offices. Obama campaigned in all 50 states, rather than focusing on battleground states as his predecessors had done. By mobilizing support in places where Democrats had not seriously contended in the past, the Obama campaign expanded the electoral map. For the first time in decades, turnout rates were comparable to those in 1960.

FOR CRITICAL ANALYSIS

Why do efforts toward direct mobilization seem to be more successful than television advertising in promoting voter turnout? How is the internet becoming an important tool for increasing political participation?

People are more likely to turn out to vote if someone asks them face to face. Direct mail and impersonal phone calls are less likely to have an effect on turnout.

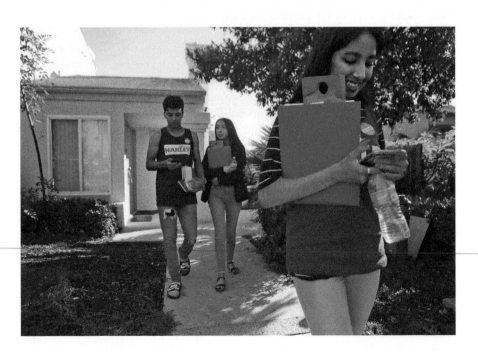

In 2016 political campaigns shifted to social media as a primary way to mobilize voters and directly provide their supporters with election updates. Three in 10 Americans received digital messages about news and the elections, with far more Americans turning to the candidates' social media posts rather than to their websites or emails.[80] The Trump campaign was especially effective in mobilizing voters via social media networks.

DATA ANALYTICS AND VOTER MOBILIZATION

Today's modern campaigns use massive computer databases and sophisticated data analytics to identify individuals and members of the electorate to mobilize turnout in elections. Digital politics creates digital footprints that can be used by candidate and issue campaigns for micro-targeting to mobilize voters in elections or shape their opinions about politics. In *Hacking the Electorate*, political scientist Eitan Hersh argues that most of what campaigns know about voters comes from a core set of public records based on the voter rolls from all fifty states with data on 240 million Americans. States vary in the kinds of records they collect from voters, however, and these variations in data by state make campaigns more or less effective at micro-targeting voters in different states. States with better record keeping and computerized public records allow better mobilization of voters in campaigns.[81]

In the past, social movements, such as the labor movement in the 1930s and the civil rights movement in the 1960s, played an important role in mobilizing people into politics. Though interest groups and political parties have generally reduced their efforts at direct mobilization since then, some have revived direct mobilization in recent years. The Tea Party movement in particular has engaged in widespread grassroots mobilization, as have organizations on the left such as MoveOn.org.[82]

ELECTORAL COMPETITION

To be motivated to vote, individuals must be interested in the election and knowledgeable about the candidates. An important factor, often overlooked in analyzing political participation, is whether elections are competitive; that is, whether there are at least two parties (and their candidates) actively contesting a position in government.[83] Competitive elections, and the campaign spending and mobilization efforts that go along with them, play a key role in turnout in the United States and cross-nationally.[84] Conversely, limited exposure to competitive elections may be one reason for the lower levels of turnout since the 1960s. In many congressional, statewide, and local races, a candidate (often the incumbent) runs unopposed or is expected to win by such a large margin that the challenger's chances are virtually nil. When congressional districts are drawn to favor one political party over another—what is termed *gerrymandering* (see Chapter 10)—election outcomes are thus often highly lopsided in favor of one candidate over another. Relatively uncompetitive elections are a primary reason why most members of Congress win by landslides.

Political scientist Todd Donovan uses a sports analogy to explain the importance of competitive elections in mobilizing turnout: "People watch a game to see their team win, or because of interest in an important game. Uncontroversial calls by the umpire and high scoring is meaningless if only one team takes the field, and attendance will suffer if two teams are playing that no one can cheer for."[85] When candidates and political parties spend more effort and money to compete for an elected office, more information becomes available to voters in the form of media ads, news coverage, door-to-door campaigns, online campaigns, and more. Electoral competition reduces the cost to individuals of becoming informed, leading to higher turnout. Conversely, if elections are uncompetitive (where the winner beats the loser by more than 5 percent) or uncontested (where only one name appears on the ballot), they generate little political information. Without active campaigns, individuals have few opportunities to be interested in an election and may not vote.[86]

Unique rules for presidential elections in the United States create variation in electoral competition across the 50 states. No other country uses an electoral college to mediate between a national or direct vote for presidential candidates and the actual winner. To win, a U.S. presidential candidate must receive a majority of the votes in the electoral college. Each state is given a set number of votes in the electoral college based on the size of its congressional delegation. (The electoral college is covered in more detail in Chapter 10.) Some citizens reside in competitive battleground states, such as Florida, Ohio, and Pennsylvania. These states are defined by high levels of competition between the parties. Most Americans, however, live in nonbattleground states (also called "safe" states) such as California, New York, and Texas, where one of the major parties is generally assured of victory in presidential elections. Hence, presidential elections are often decided by a relatively small number of voters in the United States' dozen or so battleground states. (For example, if Hillary Clinton had won just 110,000 more votes across Michigan, Pennsylvania, and Wisconsin, she would have won the 2016 election.) Every four years, residents of battleground states get smothered with attention from candidates and media, while citizens in states with few electoral votes or where one political party has a solid majority barely get noticed. One study found that voter turnout is higher in battleground states than in nonbattleground states and less skewed in terms of lower participation by the poor and young.[87]

Even the rules for nominating presidential candidates create variation across the states in electoral competition that effects voter turnout. Selecting presidential candidates involves a sequence of statewide primary elections and caucuses. The early phase of this process is dominated by a handful of small-population states. The privileged position of Iowa and New Hampshire, sites of the nation's first caucus and first primary respectively, can boost political participation in those states. Similarly, studies have shown that citizens residing in "Super Tuesday" states (the 12 states that hold primaries or caucuses on a single day about six weeks after the New Hampshire primary) are more likely to vote in presidential primaries and be interested in the election.[88] Usually the nomination contest is essentially over quickly, as one candidate secures a significant lead in early primaries, leaving many citizens with no role in selecting their party's nominee. Turnout in states with later primaries, include large states like California and Texas, naturally plummets.

BALLOT MEASURES

Beyond candidate races, ballot measures (initiatives and referenda) have been found to increase voter turnout, especially in lower-profile, midterm elections but also in presidential elections.[89] Elections that include controversial initiatives on the state ballot—in which citizens vote directly on policy questions such as the minimum wage, immigration, or taxation—have also been found to increase voter turnout, political interest, and contributions to interest groups.[90] In many states, ballot-measure campaigns are important for mobilizing voters and can have spillover effects on candidate races.[91] When citizens are asked to vote directly on controversial policy issues,

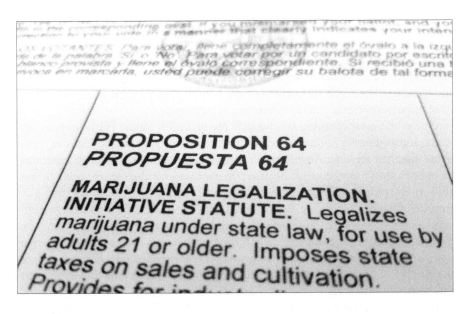

Voters often turn out in higher numbers when there are controversial initiatives on the ballot. In 2016 groups for and against Proposition 64 in California, which would legalize recreational marijuana, spent millions of dollars on media and mobilization campaigns.

public awareness of politics and policy debates increases. Initiatives often involve high campaign spending by proponents and opponents of the proposed laws, which generates mass media coverage. The *Los Angeles Times* estimated that $452 million was spent in California alone in 2016 on controversial ballot measures including legalizing the recreational use of marijuana and repealing the death penalty.[92] Additionally, simply being asked to vote on issues—salient or otherwise—can increase participation. This has been called the "educative effects" of direct democracy as voters are forced to make a yes-or-no choice on the policy issue.[93]

Only 24 of the 50 states have the initiative process that lets citizens draft legislation, circulate petitions, and place the issue on the ballot for a popular vote. This is another reason that what state one lives in can matter for how likely they are to participate in politics.

State Electoral Laws and Participation

Explain the effect of electoral laws on voting

As stipulated by the Constitution, the states, not the federal government, control voter registration and voting itself. This decentralized system continues to create wide variation in the laws governing elections and voting, which affect participation in politics.[94] Voter turnout in presidential elections in the last decade ranges from a high of over 70 percent of eligible voters in Maine to 42 percent in Hawaii. State electoral laws can facilitate or create barriers to voting that can reduce participation and help explain the differences in turnout across states.

REGISTRATION REQUIREMENTS

In most democratic countries, residents are automatically registered to vote in elections at adult age. In the United States, citizens must actively register to vote and, in most states, must do so in advance of the election—sometimes 30 days beforehand. An important factor reducing voter turnout is our nation's unique state-by-state patchwork of registration rules. In every American state but North Dakota, individuals who are eligible to vote must register with the state election board before they are actually allowed to vote, although a growing number of states allow same-day registration. At the turn of the nineteenth century, progressive reformers introduced registration requirements to limit political corruption and discourage immigrant and working-class voters from going to the polls so that political parties would be more responsive to middle-class voters and professionals.

One of the most common reasons that people in the United States give for not voting is that they are not registered. Young people especially are less likely to register to vote than are older Americans, in part because they tend to change residences more often than older people.[95] Registration requirements also reduce voting by less affluent individuals and those with lower levels of education because registering in advance of the election can be more difficult than the act of voting itself. Once individuals become interested in the election and learn about the candidates, it may be too late for them to register, especially if they live in states that require registration up to a month before the election. Registration requirements thus not only reduce the number of people who vote but also tend to create an electorate that is, on average, better educated, more affluent, older, and whiter than the citizenry as a whole.

In an effort to boost voter turnout, a number of states have begun to offer same-day registration, which means that people can both register and vote when they go to the polls on Election Day. As of 2018, 18 states plus Washington, D.C., had enacted same-day registration laws. Thirteen states and the District of Columbia have recently gone even further, adopting laws to automatically register their residents to vote in elections by information sharing between government agencies collecting similar information: the Department of Motor Vehicles and the secretary of state's office.[96] Though these states have adopted these laws, automatic voter registration was only in effect in Oregon for the 2016 election. Though turnout in Oregon did not increase in 2016 from 2012, some scholars believe automatic voter registration is more likely to have an impact on turnout in state and local elections, rather than in presidential elections when voters are better informed and don't need a reminder to vote.[97]

Although many U.S. citizens are strong advocates of universal suffrage and voter turnout, this reform triggers controversial debate and deep partisan conflict. Opponents contend that these laws make the states' voter rolls more vulnerable to fraud. Supporters say the new system may be more secure than traditional paper registration because rather than simply attesting to their eligibility with a signature, individuals have to submit proof of citizenship. Automatic voter registration is generally favored by Democrats, who want expanded access to the ballot box. Republicans, on the other hand, often don't want to add new voters who may be more likely to support the Democratic Party. It is important to note, however, that lawmakers are not always correct about which party will benefit from increased voter registration.

Voter Identification Requirements Another barrier to voting is the requirement that voters provide proof of identity. Despite near universal adult suffrage in the United States, recent adoption of voter ID laws in many states has reduced turnout rates, especially for the low-income, racial minorities, the elderly, and people with disabilities—all of whom disproportionately lack government ID. Thirty-four states have some identification requirements to cast a ballot at the polls, but 10 states had strict ID laws in 2018 that required voters to present a government-issued photo ID or nonphoto ID in order to cast a ballot.[98] Estimates indicate that 11 percent

Which States Make Voting Easier?

Convenience Voting, 2018

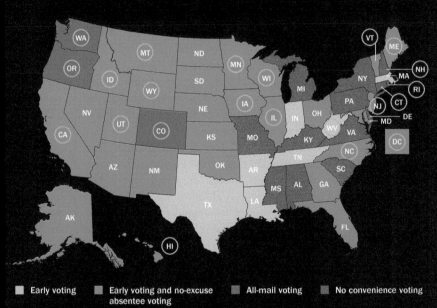

Legend:
- Early voting
- Early voting and no-excuse absentee voting
- All-mail voting
- No convenience voting
- ○ Same-day and/or automatic registration

States have increasingly passed laws to make voting easier, such as early voting, which allows voters to cast a ballot before Election Day; "no-excuse" absentee voting, which permits voters to request an absentee ballot without providing justification; all-mail voting, whereby voters fill in their ballot at home and mail it, eliminating polling places altogether; and same-day and automatic voter registration. At the same time, many states have passed voter identification requirements, which make voting harder for some people. The maps show these laws by state as of the 2018 election.

* Two additional states have adopted same-day registration to take effect in 2019.

Voter ID Requirements, 2018

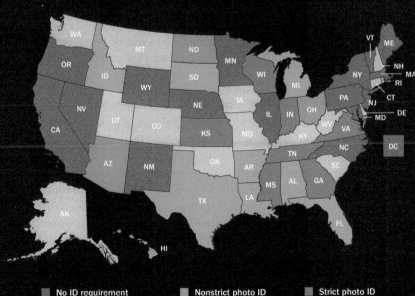

Legend:
- No ID requirement
- Nonstrict nonphoto ID
- Nonstrict photo ID
- Strict nonphoto ID
- Strict photo ID

SOURCES: National Conference of State Legislatures, www.ncsl.org/research/elections-and-campaigns/absentee-and-early-voting.aspx (accessed 11/4/17); National Conference of State Legislatures, www.ncsl.org/research/elections-and-campaigns/voter-id.aspx#Table1 (accessed 11/4/17).

FOR CRITICAL ANALYSIS

1. Find your state on the maps. Do you think your state's voting laws affected turnout in the 2018 election?

2. In which regions of the country do we find the most states with convenience voting? Why might this be the case?

of U.S. citizens, or 21 million Americans, do not have government-issued photo identification, including one in five African Americans. Government identification can be difficult to obtain even if an ID is available for free, because citizens must pay for a birth certificate to apply for a government-issued identification. Travel to the Department of Motor Vehicles can be difficult for the elderly, disabled, and those living in rural areas. While the true effect of these laws is still not known, some government reports estimate that strict voter ID laws reduce turnout by 2–3 percentage points, which can amount to millions of people who are prevented from voting nationwide. Voter ID laws may change election outcomes in swing states.[99]

For example, out of 2.8 million votes cast in Wisconsin, just 22,748 votes separated Trump's victory over Clinton in the 2016 presidential election, one of the closest competitions of any state. Wisconsin's new voter ID law requires a citizen to show government identification in order to cast a ballot. One study found that nearly 17,000 registered Wisconsin voters were prevented from voting in the 2016 presidential election by the state's new strict voter identification law.[100] The results suggest that enough voters could have been deterred from participating that it flipped the outcome of the presidential election in the state.

Photo identification is a partisan issue. In Wisconsin and elsewhere, Republicans argue that such laws protect against voter fraud and ensure that the vote is fair, regardless of party. Opponents of voter ID laws, mainly Democrats, counter that there have been almost no significant instances of voter fraud in the modern era and that these laws suppress the vote of segments of the population most likely to vote for Democrats but also least likely to have photo ID—racial minorities and the poor.[101] Studies have shown that illegal voting via impersonating someone else is very rare in the United States.

There is also wide variation in implementation of voter ID laws. In Texas a student identification card does not count to vote, but a gun owner's license does. A study by Caltech/MIT scholars found that minority voters are more frequently questioned to provide ID than white voters. The adoption of strict voter ID laws in 14 states appears to coincide with a decline in African American turnout in the 2016 election.

VOTING RIGHTS OF FELONS

A barrier to voting that has grown more important in recent years is the restriction on the voting rights of people who have committed a felony. Forty-eight states and the District of Columbia prohibit prison inmates who are serving a felony sentence from voting. In 21 states, felons on probation or parole are not permitted to vote, but voting rights are restored automatically after parole or probation is complete. In 13 states, felons lose their voting rights forever for some crimes. On the other end of the spectrum, felons never lose their right to vote in Maine and Vermont. With the sharp rise in incarceration rates over the past three decades, restrictions on voting for felons have had a significant impact on voting rights. By one estimate, 5.3 million people (2.4 percent of the voting-age population) have lost their voting rights as a result of these restrictions. Felon voting restrictions disproportionately affect minorities because 59 percent of the prison population is African American or Latino, though these groups make up only 30 percent of the population.[102] One in eight black men cannot vote because of a criminal record.[103] The impact of felon disenfranchisement has been especially strong in the South. Concern over the impact of these voting restrictions has led to campaigns to restore voting rights to people who have committed a felony.[104]

VOTING AND REGISTRATION REFORMS

Election reform efforts over the past century have focused on making voter registration and voting more accessible and convenient. As mentioned above, **same-day registration** (SDR) allows citizens to both register to vote and cast a ballot on the same day. Seventeen states plus the District of Columbia have SDR laws.[105] Concern over SDR focuses on fraud and noncitizens voting. As might be expected, in states that allow registration on the day of the election, not only is voter turnout higher than the national average but younger and less educated voters are also more likely to participate.[106] On average, SDR increases overall turnout by 5 percent.[107]

In 1998, Oregon was also the first state to create a system for voting exclusively by mail, thus eliminating polling places altogether. Individual voters fill in their ballot at home and place it in the mail or in drop boxes throughout the state. In Washington State, Colorado, California, and many other states, many citizens now cast votes using **permanent absentee ballots**, which are mailed. Twenty-seven states and the District of Columbia allow "no-excuse" absentee voting, which means any voter can request an absentee ballot without providing a justification. Not only does mail voting increase turnout, it also saves the government money by not having to staff polling stations throughout the state. But because the western states tend to have higher voter turnout than most other parts of the country, it's difficult to disentangle whether mail voting or regional political culture drives higher turnout.

Another reform that has been adopted by many states is **early voting**, which allows registered voters to cast a ballot at their regular polling place up to 40 days before the election. Thirty-three percent of votes cast in the 2016 election were cast early, either in person or via mail. As of 2018, 37 states allow early voting in which any qualified voter may cast a ballot in person during a designated period prior to Election Day.[108] Three of these states go so far as to mail a ballot to all registered voters. Some studies find that the effects of early voting laws on turnout and the demographic composition of who votes are not yet clear.[109] One study from Oregon found that voting by mail tends to advantage upper-class and older citizens, who are more likely to vote anyway.[110] But others contend that early voting increases turnout among groups that are traditionally less likely to vote, including minorities. For a political campaign, a vote cast early is like securing another dollar in the bank. (See inside the back cover of your textbook to find voter-registration requirements in your state.)

Overall, SDR has been found to have the greatest effect in boosting voting rates and making participation by different demographic groups more equal. Having the ability to vote at the last minute helps many people who otherwise may not vote, particularly young adults and individuals with a high school–level education or less.[111] An individual need not become aware of the registration process in order to register to vote; he merely needs to know the date of the election and the location of the polling place, where registering to vote and voting can happen at the same time.

same-day registration the option in some states to register on the day of the election, at the polling place, rather than in advance of the election

permanent absentee ballots the option in some states to have a ballot sent automatically to your home for each election, rather than having to request an absentee ballot each time

early voting the option in some states to cast a vote at a polling place or by mail before the election

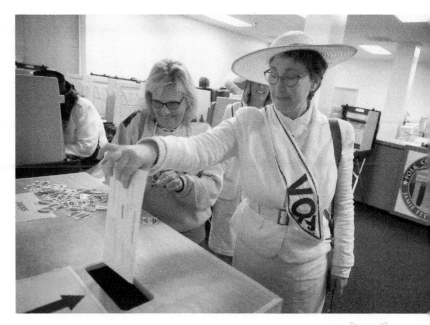

Convenience voting, such as early voting and voting by mail, removes the need to stand in a potentially long line to cast a vote and may result in increased voter turnout.

Political Participation
WHAT DO WE WANT

The American political community has expanded over the course of history, with new groups winning and asserting political rights. This expansion has brought American politics more closely into line with the fundamental values of liberty, equality, and democracy. But for much of the twentieth century, the electoral system in the United States failed to mobilize an active citizenry, giving rise to an uneven pattern of political participation that gives some people more of a voice in politics than others. Since 2000 a series of highly competitive presidential elections has spurred political campaigns to pay more attention to drawing greater numbers of voters into the political process; even so, many Americans still do not participate in politics. The "**Who Participates?**" feature on the facing page shows who participated in the 2016 presidential election.

Naturally enough, one of the most important factors in sustaining participation is a sense of political efficacy, the feeling that average citizens can help shape what government actually does. One important study found that elected officials respond more to the preferences of voters than nonvoters, confirming long-held assumptions that affluent, more educated, and older citizens have more voice in politics and public policy.[112] A study by the political scientist Larry Bartels showed that senators (both Republicans and Democrats) are much less responsive to the policy preferences of low-income citizens—who are also less likely to be active voters.[113] If the voices of only the more affluent are heard during election time, the issues that concern lower-income Americans may not find a place at the top of the political agenda.

What would it take to increase political engagement among citizens of all backgrounds? Several recent developments promise to give a greater number of people more of a voice in American government. Over the past few decades, innovative states have led the way by reforming and modernizing America's patchwork election system, with reforms ranging from automatic and same-day voter registration to early and mail voting. Some states, such as Iowa and California, use nonpartisan boards to draw legislative districts, which tends to boost competition in congressional and state legislative races. Increased competition, in turn, often results in a more informed and energized electorate, thus increasing turnout. What if every state adopted automatic voter registration? Would this increase turnout for young voters who are the most mobile and are now the largest age cohort? Would reforming America's elections allow most citizens to vote and elected representatives that adopt policies in the interests of the greatest number of people, not just wealthy elites? Would true universal suffrage make American great again?

For much of American history, formal barriers restricted the right to vote and created a pattern of unequal participation in politics. Today, most of those barriers have been eliminated, but voter turnout remains relatively low, especially among young voters.

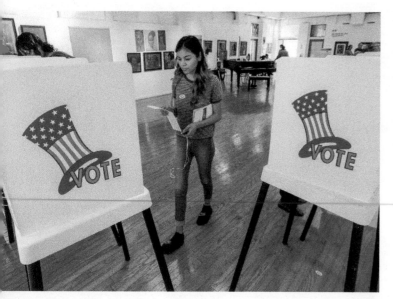

Who Participated in the 2016 Presidential Election?

Percentage of each age group who...

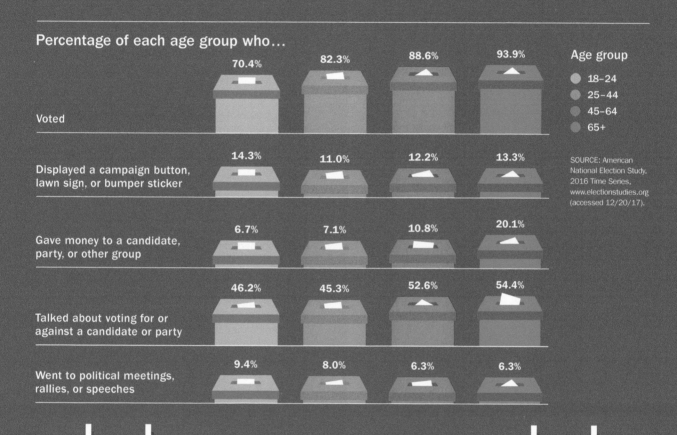

	18–24	25–44	45–64	65+
Voted	70.4%	82.3%	88.6%	93.9%
Displayed a campaign button, lawn sign, or bumper sticker	14.3%	11.0%	12.2%	13.3%
Gave money to a candidate, party, or other group	6.7%	7.1%	10.8%	20.1%
Talked about voting for or against a candidate or party	46.2%	45.3%	52.6%	54.4%
Went to political meetings, rallies, or speeches	9.4%	8.0%	6.3%	6.3%

Age group
- 18–24
- 25–44
- 45–64
- 65+

SOURCE: American National Election Study, 2016 Time Series, www.electionstudies.org (accessed 12/20/17).

★ WHAT YOU CAN DO ★

Register to Vote

✓ In most states you can register to vote using the National Mail Voter Registration Form found at **www.eac.gov**. The Election Assistance Commission website also includes various tips about registering and voting.

✓ Find out when you need to register in order to vote in the next election. Visit **www.usa.gov/register-to-vote** for a list of registration deadlines.

✓ Many states allow online registration. Go to **www.ncsl.org** and search "online voter registration" to find a list of these states with links to their websites.

✓ If you've moved to attend college or for another reason, you can register with your new address.

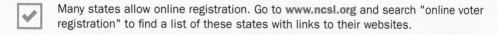

★ STUDY GUIDE ★

Forms of Political Participation

Describe the major forms of traditional and digital participation in politics (pp. 297–310)

Political participation refers to a wide range of activities designed to influence government, politics, and policy. These activities fall into two major categories: traditional political participation, which includes voting, engaging in protest, volunteering, and contributing to a candidate; and digital political participation, which refers to a newer set of activities carried out through the internet, such as reading online news stories, posting comments on social media, and visiting a political party's website. Voting is the most common form of traditional political participation, but voter turnout is relatively low overall in the United States. While digital political participation has the potential to encourage innovation, free expression, and higher levels of traditional political participation, it may also produce misinformation, intolerance, and a lack of civility in public discourse.

Key Terms

traditional political participation (p. 297)

protest (p. 297)

suffrage (p. 299)

turnout (p. 301)

digital political participation (p. 303)

Practice Quiz

1. Which of the following is *not* a form of traditional political participation?
   a) volunteering for a campaign
   b) attending an abortion rights rally
   c) displaying a yard sign for a Republican congressional candidate
   d) voting in an election
   e) signing an online petition

2. Which group won voting rights most recently?
   a) 18- to 20-year-olds
   b) Asian Americans
   c) white property owners
   d) women
   e) African Americans

3. The *digital divide* means
   a) some citizens watch television news and some do not.
   b) newspapers rarely publish the same stories on their websites that they do in their print editions.
   c) few politicians maintain websites once they are elected to office.
   d) not all citizens have equal access to the internet.
   e) people who learn about politics online are less informed than those who learn about politics through traditional media.

Who Participates?

Describe the patterns of participation among major demographic groups (pp. 310–19)

Socioeconomic status, race, gender, age, and religious affiliation are associated with different levels and types of political participation. Generally speaking, whites, older people, women, and those with higher levels of education and income vote most frequently. In recent elections, African Americans, Latinos, women, and young people have been more likely to support Democratic candidates than whites, males, and older people.

Key Terms

socioeconomic status (p. 310)

gender gap (p. 316)

Practice Quiz

4. Which of the following statements about young people's political attitudes is most accurate?
   a) Younger people are less supportive of strong environmental laws than older people.
   b) Younger people are less concerned about economic inequality than older people.
   c) Younger people express less tolerance for personal freedoms than older people.
   d) Younger people are less concerned about national security than older people.
   e) Younger people are more supportive of funding for public education and colleges than older people.

5. African Americans
   a) almost never participate in politics.
   b) consistently support the Republican Party in elections.
   c) vote at much higher rates than whites.
   d) have never voted as a cohesive bloc.
   e) are more likely to participate when they feel a shared sense of collective identity.

6. Which of the following statements about Latinos is *not* accurate?
   a) Latinos have tended to favor Democratic candidates in recent national elections.
   b) In some large states, such as California and Texas, Latinos are approaching 50 percent of the population.
   c) Latinos have tended to favor Republican candidates in recent national elections.

   d) Latinos make up approximately 17 percent of the population.
   e) Latino registration and turnout rates have been lower than those of whites and African Americans in recent elections.

7. One reason that there are fewer women than men in elected office is that
   a) there is a limit set by the Constitution on the number of women who can serve in the House of Representatives.
   b) fewer women are eligible to run for office under the rules created by state and local governments.
   c) women are less likely to vote in elections than men.
   d) women are less likely to run for office than men.
   e) women are less likely to win elections than men.

Political Environment and Voter Mobilization

Explain the factors in the political environment that influence whether individuals vote or not (pp. 319–23)

Three general factors in the political environment influence whether individuals vote or not: mobilization efforts, electoral competitiveness, and the presence or absence of state-level ballot initiatives. People who are mobilized by political parties, candidates, campaigns, interest groups, and social movements are more likely to participate than those who are not. In competitive elections, turnout is higher because there are more opportunities for individuals to become interested in and informed about the race as each side campaigns to get its message out. People also make the effort to vote when ballot measures address issues that are important to them.

Key Term

mobilization (p. 319)

Practice Quiz

8. Which of the following techniques is considered most effective in mobilizing voters?
   a) direct mailings
   b) "robocalls"
   c) phone calls made by volunteers
   d) face-to-face contact
   e) television advertisements

9. How many states currently have an initiative process that lets citizens draft legislation, circulate petitions, and place measures on the ballot for a popular vote?
   a) 0
   b) 12
   c) 24
   d) 36
   e) 50

State Electoral Laws and Participation

Explain the effect of electoral laws on voting (pp. 323–27)

As stated in the Constitution, states retain control of voter registration and voting. In practice, there is wide variation in the laws governing elections and voting from state to state. Voter-registration requirements and other barriers, such as felony disenfranchisement and ID requirements, may reduce participation. States have experimented with reforms, such as same-day registration, permanent absentee ballots, automatic registration, and early voting, to make it easier to vote.

Key Terms

same-day registration (p. 327)

permanent absentee ballots (p. 327)

early voting (p. 327)

Practice Quiz

10. Voter-registration requirements and processes are determined and controlled by
  a) local governments.
  b) the federal government.
  c) the U.S. Constitution.
  d) the states.
  e) an independent organization.

11. Which of the following factors is *not* currently an obstacle to voting in the United States?
  a) registration requirements
  b) that elections occur on Tuesdays
  c) the restriction of voting rights for people who have committed a felony
  d) literacy tests
  e) voter identification laws

12. States that allow for same-day registration
  a) have lower overall voter turnout rates than states that do not allow for same-day registration.
  b) have the same overall voter turnout rates as states that do not allow for same-day registration.
  c) have higher rates of voter turnout among younger and less educated voters than states that do not allow for same-day registration.
  d) have overall turnout rates that are very close to 100 percent.
  e) have lower rates of voter turnout among younger and less educated voters than states that do not allow for same-day registration.

For Further Reading

Barreto, Matt, and Gary Segura. *Latino America: How America's Most Dynamic Population Is Poised to Transform the Politics of the Nation*. New York: Public Affairs, 2014.

Bowler, Shaun, and Todd Donovan. *The Limits of Electoral Reform*. Oxford: Oxford University Press, 2013.

Cain, Bruce E., Todd Donovan, and Caroline J. Tolbert, eds. *Democracy in the States: Experiments in Election Reform*. Washington, DC: Brookings Institution Press, 2008.

Crenson, Matthew A., and Benjamin Ginsberg. *Downsizing Democracy: How America Sidelined Its Citizens and Privatized Its Public*. Baltimore: Johns Hopkins University Press, 2004.

Dalton, Russell J. *The Good Citizen: How a Younger Generation Is Reshaping American Politics*. Washington, DC: CQ Press, 2008.

Donovan, Todd, and Shawn Bowler. *Reforming the Republic: Democratic Institutions for the New America*. Upper Saddle River, NJ: Pearson/Prentice Hall, 2004.

Green, Donald P., and Alan S. Gerber. *Get Out the Vote! How to Increase Voter Turnout*. Washington, DC: Brookings Institution Press, 2004.

Griffin, John D., and Brian Newman. *Minority Report: Evaluating Political Equality in America*. Chicago: University of Chicago Press, 2008.

Hanmer, Michael J. *Discount Voting: Voter Registration Reforms and Their Effects*. New York: Cambridge University Press, 2009.

Karpf, David. *The MoveOn Effect: The Unexpected Transformation of American Political Advocacy*. New York: Oxford University Press, 2012.

Lewis-Beck, Michael S., William G. Jacoby, Helmut Norpoth, and Herbert F. Weisberg. *The American Voter Revisited*. Ann Arbor: University of Michigan Press, 2008.

Manza, Jeff, and Christopher Uggen. *Locked Out: Felon Disenfranchisement and American Democracy*. New York: Oxford University Press, 2006.

McDonald, Michael P., and John Samples, eds. *The Marketplace of Democracy: Electoral Competition and American Politics*. Washington, DC: Brookings Institution Press, 2006.

Mossberger, Karen, Caroline Tolbert, and Ramona McNeal. *Digital Citizenship: The Internet, Society and Participation*. Cambridge, MA: MIT Press, 2008.

Nicholson, Steven P. *Voting the Agenda: Candidates, Elections, and Ballot Propositions*. Princeton, NJ: Princeton University Press, 2005.

Piven, Frances Fox, and Richard Cloward. *Why Americans Don't Vote*. New York: Pantheon, 1988.

Putnam, Robert. *Bowling Alone: The Collapse and Revival of American Community*. New York: Simon & Schuster, 2000.

Rosenstone, Steven J., and John Mark Hansen. *Mobilization, Participation, and Democracy in America*. New York: Macmillan, 1993.

Schattschneider, E. E. *The Semisovereign People: A Realist's View of Democracy in America*. Boston: Wadsworth-Cengage Learning, 1975.

Sinclair, Betsy. *The Social Citizen: Peer Networks and Political Behavior*. Chicago: University of Chicago Press, 2010.

Smith, Daniel, and Caroline Tolbert. *Educated by Initiative: The Effects of Direct Democracy on Citizens and Political Organizations in the American States*. Ann Arbor: University of Michigan Press, 2004.

Springer, Melanie. *American Electoral Institutions and Voter Turnout, 1920–2000*. Chicago: University of Chicago Press, 2014.

Verba, Sidney, Kay Lehman Schlozman, and Henry Brady. *Voice and Equality: Civic Voluntarism in American Politics*. Cambridge, MA: Harvard University Press, 1995.

Recommended Websites

League of Women Voters
www.lwv.org

> Established in 1920 as part of the women's suffrage movement, the League of Women Voters encourages informed and active participation in government.

Open Secrets
www.opensecrets.org/elections/

> Campaign contributions are a form of political participation that is both necessary and controversial. This website uses data from the Federal Election Commission to publish the names of those who give elected officials campaign money and those who may be receiving preferential treatment.

Project Vote
www.projectvote.org

> Since 1982, Project Vote has worked to increase the participation of low-income, minority, youth, and other marginalized and underrepresented voters. The organization sponsors voter registration drives and get-out-the-vote programs and monitors election laws across the states. As a community organizer, Barack Obama worked for Project Vote, registering voters in Chicago.

Project Vote Smart
www.votesmart.org

> This nonpartisan site is dedicated to providing citizens with information on political candidates and elected officials. Here you can easily view candidates' biographical information, positions on issues, and voting records so that you can make an informed choice on Election Day.

United States Election Project
www.electproject.org

> Click on "Voter turnout data" for the best and most reliable source for voter turnout rates nationally and by state in presidential and midterm elections from 1980–2016.

U.S. Census Bureau: Voting and Registration
www.census.gov/population/www/socdemo/voting.html

> The U.S. Census Bureau collects statistics on voting and registration by various demographic and socioeconomic characteristics. See if you can find differences in voter turnout by race, age, gender, or socioeconomic status.

Political Parties

WHAT GOVERNMENT DOES AND WHY IT MATTERS Political parties play a variety of important roles in American democracy. They mobilize people to participate in the political arena and to vote. They convey information about what policies candidates support. And they are broader than interest groups, which generally seek narrow policy objectives. Political parties are capable of mobilizing many more voters to win control of government.

For all their important mobilizing and information-conveying functions, parties, like other aspects of government and politics, can seem far from ordinary people. But ordinary people can have a big impact in political parties. Early in 2009, before the term "Tea Party" was coined, Keli Carender was a conservative blogger in Seattle. She became concerned that the stimulus bill that Congress was considering to address the financial crisis and ensuing recession was simply more of "big government" trampling on her "freedom and liberty." After calls and emails to her congressional representative were ignored, she organized a "Porkulus Protest" in Seattle without support from any national organization. "I just got fed up and planned it....I had 120 people show up,

Individuals can have profound effects on political parties. Keli Carender took her belief in limited government and her anger over excessive government spending and started the Tea Party movement, which has strongly influenced the direction of the Republican Party.

which is amazing for the bluest of blue cities I live in, and on only four days' notice!! This was due to me spending the entire four days calling and email-ing every person, think tank, policy center, university professors (that were sympathetic), etc. in town, and not stopping until the day came." She also contacted conservative author Michelle Malkin, who publicized the rally on her blog. At a second rally later that month, twice as many people showed up, in part because Carender had collected email addresses at the first rally. Her advice to other would-be organiz-ers: "Number one: just get it done. Do you need a permit? Find out and then just get it. Do you want a guest speaker? Get on the phone and call anyone you can think of and get them there. You will need to alert the media, so just get that done. . . . Let people help you. Almost immediately I had two women email me and say, what can I do? And boom, I had two other organizers to start helping me with the next event."[1]

Carender's protests were among the first events in what became known as the Tea Party movement, which gained steam when CNBC business analyst Rick Santelli called for a "tea party" protest of the

Obama administration's plans for addressing the Great Recession. This conservative populist movement not only challenged Democratic policies but also the Republican party establishment. As political candidates associated with the Tea Party ran for office starting in the 2010 midterm elections, they sometimes won Republican Party endorsement but often ran against the mainstream party. Indeed, as a nontraditional Republican candidate, Donald Trump courted Tea Party supporters during his presidential campaign in 2016. As we will see in this chapter, parties play an important role in American democracy, mobilizing voters and organizing their choices. Revolts against the political parties by rank-and-file members occur very rarely in American history. But sometimes, parties are shaken up by grassroots activity like Keli Carender's. Her story, and others like it, show that individuals can make a difference, not just in political parties but also in the broader political arena. The key is to "just get it done."

CHAPTER GOALS

★ Define political parties and their functions in politics (pp. 337–40)

★ Explain the roles that parties play in elections (pp. 340–44)

★ Describe how the major American parties are structured at the national, state, and local levels (pp. 344–48)

★ Explain how parties organize legislative business and influence policy (pp. 348–52)

★ Identify the reasons for and sources of party identification (pp. 352–60)

★ Describe how the party system in the United States has changed over time and its main features today (pp. 360–71)

What Are Political Parties?

Political parties, like interest groups (see Chapter 11), are organizations that seek influence over government. They can generally be distinguished from interest groups on the basis of their mission. A party seeks to control the government by nominating candidates and electing its members to office. As we will see in Chapter 11, interest groups do not control the operation of government and its personnel but rather try to influence government policies, often through lobbying elected officials and contributing to campaigns.

Although the Founders did not envision the rise of political parties, they quickly became a core feature of the American political system. Parties and **partisanship** organize the political world and simplify complex policy debates for citizens and elected officials. Parties also play central roles in mobilizing citizens to vote, informing the public of government policy, and ensuring that the public voice is heard in policy debates.

Political parties have been the chief points of contact between government, on the one side, and individual citizens and interest groups, on the other. Through organized political parties, citizens and groups can influence government policies. As political scientist Walter Dean Burnham wrote, political parties "generate… collective power on behalf of the many [who are] individually powerless against the relatively few who are individually or organizationally powerful."[2] It may be difficult for ordinary citizens to have any real influence on government acting as individuals, but they can have an impact on what government does when they act collectively. Political parties also seek to organize and influence important groups in society to win elections and gain political power. They are instruments through which citizens and government attempt to influence each other.

In a landmark book written over a half-century ago, political scientist E. E. Schattschneider advocated for a political system run by party politics instead of interest groups.[3] To be an equal democracy where all groups are represented, there must be competitive and responsible political parties that provide real choices to the electorate so that the public can participate in the government's decision-making process. Parties, he believed, are able to mobilize more people than interest groups because they can expand the "scope of conflict" or the policy debate to include most or all of the electorate. While interest groups (see Chapter 11) benefit from focusing on specific policy issues, political parties broaden political conflict to the public arena and focus on a range of policy issues, from the economy to foreign policy, in order to win elections.

It is not enough, however, to simply have political parties: parties must be "competitive" and "responsible." When political parties compete with one another to win elections, Schattschneider contended, they have incentives to continually expand public debates to include nonvoting members of the electorate in order to gain a majority of voters and win the election. This strategy has been evident in the extremely competitive presidential elections since 2000, with widespread voter-mobilization campaigns on the part of the Democratic and Republican parties. Voter turnout in 2008, 2012, and 2016 was at the highest levels since 1960, largely because of the get-out-the-vote campaign drives organized by the political parties.

Political parties must also act "responsibly" by continually informing the people of current political issues that are in their best interests. And once in power, political parties must enact laws that represent their members' interests. In this idealized

political parties organized groups that attempt to influence the government by electing their members to important government offices

partisanship identification with or support of a particular party or cause view, competitive and responsible parties can help increase voter turnout, creating more equal representation for those in lower socioeconomic classes.

Some political scientists argue that Schattschneider's vision is far from reality. Today, we have large, powerful, and active political parties, but party candidates are often subsidized by big businesses and the wealthy. Political scientist Larry Bartels found that on economic issues both the Democratic and Republican parties are more responsive to the preferences of the upper and middle classes and ignore the policy wishes of the lower class. Bartels calls this "unequal democracy."[4] Stagnating wages for the middle class and rising income inequality help explain why many voters have grown increasingly frustrated by the Democratic and Republican parties; in the 2016 presidential election, many supported populist candidates, such as Republican Donald Trump and Independent Bernie Sanders, who sought to reform the political system.

Another criticism of parties stems from the idea that they are in fact controlled more by interest groups and wealthy campaign donors than by politicians and the public. This influence causes parties to be less likely to respond to voter preferences, and parties may even take advantage of the public's lack of attention to politics to promote their own agenda.[5]

Some observers believe that the problem in the United States today is that the two parties and political elites in Congress are too polarized along liberal and conservative lines, whereas the majority of Americans hold moderate opinions and values; thus, Congress and the parties do a poor job of representing the citizens.[6] Others argue that the rules governing our election system need reform so that there are more than two major political parties to better represent citizens' views.[7] Both of these topics are covered in more detail near the end of this chapter.

As long as political parties have existed, they have been criticized for introducing selfish, "partisan" concerns into public debates and national policy. Yet political parties are extremely important to the functioning of a democracy. Most Americans affiliate or lean toward one of the two major parties, Democrats or Republicans. As we will see, parties can increase participation in politics, provide a central cue for citizens to cast informed votes, and organize the business of legislatures and governing.

While both major parties often claim to be looking out for lower-income individuals (as did the Bernie Sanders and Trump campaigns in 2016), studies have shown that both Democrats and Republicans in Congress respond more to the interests of the affluent and middle-class Americans.

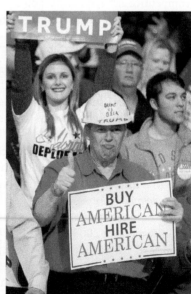

HOW DO POLITICAL PARTIES FORM AND CHANGE?

Historically, parties form in one of two ways. The first, which could be called *internal mobilization*, occurs when political conflicts prompt officials and competing factions within government to mobilize popular support. This is precisely what happened during the early years of the American Republic. Competition in Congress between northeastern merchants and southern farmers led each group to attempt to organize their supporters. The result was the foundation of America's first national parties: the Federalists, whose strength was greatest in the New England states and the Jeffersonians or Antifederalists, whose primary base was in the South.

The second way that parties form is called *external mobilization*, which takes place when a group of politicians outside of government organizes popular support to win governmental power. For example, during the 1850s a group of state politicians who opposed slavery, especially the expansion of slavery in U.S. territorial possessions, built what became the Republican Party by constructing party organizations and mobilizing popular support in the Northeast and West.

America's two major parties now are the Democrats and the Republicans. Both trace their roots back over 150 years, and both have evolved over time. Since they were formed, the two major parties have undergone significant changes in their policy positions and their membership. These changes have been prompted both by issues and events (economic change, the civil rights movement, immigration, etc.) and by demographic and social change in the United States. Today growing differences in the demographic profiles of Republicans and Democrats suggest more change in the party system is under way. Younger voters and racial and ethnic minorities increasingly affiliate with the Democratic Party, while white, older people are more likely to vote Republican. In the 2016 presidential campaign, a lack of trust in and frustration with the federal government mobilized many to support "outsider" populist candidates on both the ideological right and left. The success of outsider candidates may signal that change to the political parties is under way (see discussion in this chapter on the history of party systems and party realignments).

THE UNITED STATES' TWO-PARTY SYSTEM

Over the past 200 years, Americans' conception of political parties has changed considerably. In the early years of the Republic, parties were seen as threats to the social order and were referred to as "factions." In the *Federalist Papers*, both Alexander Hamilton and James Madison condemned factions that pursued narrow self-interest over the broader well-being of the nation as a whole.[8] In his 1796 Farewell Address, President George Washington warned his countrymen to shun partisan politics. Nonetheless, a **two-party system** emerged early in the new Republic. Beginning with the Federalists and the Jeffersonian Republicans in the late 1780s, two major parties have dominated national politics, although which two parties has changed with the times and issues. (See "Party Systems," which follows.)

two-party system a political system in which only two parties have a realistic opportunity to compete effectively for control

Most other countries in the world use a proportional representation system, in which seats in government (national legislature or parliament) are allocated to political parties based on their share of the total vote cast in the election. In contrast, the United States uses geographic single-member districts combined with winner-take-all elections. It doesn't matter, for example, if the contest for a U.S. House seat is won with 40 percent or 80 percent of the total vote; the candidate with the largest number of votes (a plurality) in that district wins the seat in Congress or a state legislature. That is why the system is "winner take all" or a plurality electoral system: unlike in proportional systems, runners-up do not gain seats in government (see Chapter 10 as well). The U.S. system is also called "first past the post" because the candidate with the most votes wins the election, even if she did not win a majority of the popular vote. In the United States, proportional voting rules are uncommon, especially above the local level, and are absent at the national level.

Election rules largely determine how many political parties there are in a country. Plurality voting rules in the United States create its two party–dominant system, and third parties have generally not won seats in Congress, state legislatures, or the presidency. Under U.S. election rules, voters have an incentive not to vote for small- or third-party candidates for fear of "wasting" their vote when only one party (usually one of the two largest parties) can win the election. Concern about wasting one's vote on third parties is called the spoiler effect or strategic voting. Proportional representation systems used in many other countries tend to result in multiple parties in government. If U.S. rules were to change, the number of political parties would likely change as well.

FOR CRITICAL ANALYSIS

What rules governing the American electoral process promote a two-party system? How might different rules impact the party system?

WHAT POLITICAL PARTIES DO

Without political parties, democracy as we know it would be difficult to achieve. In the United States, citizens take for granted that leaders will run for public office, that there will be competition among candidates, that they will have the opportunity to learn about candidates and policy issues from campaigns and cast their ballots in fair elections, and that once in office, political leaders will work together to make policy and govern. Each of these tasks is complex, however, and would be all the more so if political parties did not exist. Parties mobilize citizens in the electorate to vote, offer choices to voters in elections, and provide officeholders with organization for running government. As political scientist John Aldrich argues in *Why Parties*, parties solve three fundamental problems of democracy: how to regulate the number of people seeking public office, how to mobilize voters, and how to achieve and maintain the majorities needed to pass legislation once in office.[9]

Parties, Voter Mobilization, and Elections

Explain the roles that parties play in elections

Parties have always been central to the electoral process, and in recent years they have taken on a renewed role in recruiting candidates, coordinating campaigns, mobilizing voters, and raising money.[10] Just as companies seek to brand their products in the commercial marketplace using ad campaigns, branding and marketing now regularly happen in candidate campaigns. As campaigns become more candidate-centered, branding has become central. Barack Obama, for example, was especially effective in branding his campaign with the words "hope" and "change." In 2016, Donald Trump branded his campaign with the ubiquitous "Make American Great Again" red baseball caps. Parties succeed when they win elections; thus, we begin with parties and elections.

Two-Party and Multi-Party Systems

The American political system is dominated by two political parties, the Republican Party and the Democratic Party, but many other countries have more than two parties. The number varies depending on the electoral rules in place. Countries such as the United States, which use a first-past-the-post system (in which the candidate with the most votes wins the seat), tend to have two major parties that dominate the system. In contrast, the Netherlands uses a proportional representation system and has 13 parties in their current legislature, with 4 of the parties working together to form a coalition government.

In proportional representation systems like the Netherlands, voters select parties to represent them nationally rather than candidates to represent their region, and parties receive roughly the same percentage of votes in parliament as they received in the election. Thus, the legislature tends to more accurately resemble how the national electorate voted. The party representation in the 2017 Dutch parliament is almost identical to the 2017 national vote, whereas in the United States, the largest parties tend to be overrepresented while smaller parties lose out.

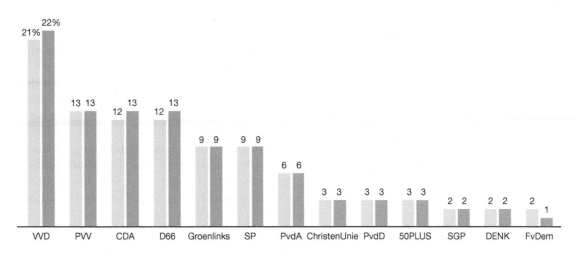

SOURCE: The U.S. Federal Election Commission, transition.fec.gov and the Kiesraad (Dutch Electoral Commission), www.kiesraad.nl (accessed 4/12/18).

RECRUITING CANDIDATES

One of the most important but least noticed party activities is the recruitment of candidates to run for office. As Schattschneider argued, "responsible parties" recruit candidates who are loyal to the party's philosophy and policy agenda, with the goal of controlling government and adopting laws that are consistent with the party's platform. Each election year, candidates run for thousands of state and local offices as well as congressional seats. When they do not have an incumbent running for re-election, party leaders attempt to identify strong candidates and encourage them to run for office in open-seat elections.

An ideal candidate will have a strong leadership record and the capacity to raise enough money to mount a serious campaign, especially if that candidate must challenge an incumbent or will face a well-funded opponent from the other party in the general election. Party leaders are usually not willing to provide financial backing to candidates who are unable to raise substantial funds on their own. For a U.S. House seat, this can mean several hundred thousand dollars; for a Senate seat, a serious candidate must be able to raise several million dollars. Presidential candidates raise hundreds of millions of dollars.

Often, party leaders have difficulty finding strong candidates and persuading them to run for office. Candidate recruitment is problematic in an era when politicians must assume that their personal lives will be intensely scrutinized on social media, in the press, and in negative campaign ads run by their opponents.[11] Other barriers to recruiting quality candidates include the extremely high cost of political campaigns, extensive time devoted to fundraising, and the numerous gerrymandered congressional and legislative districts (see Chapter 10), giving challengers a slim chance of success. There needs to be a decent chance of winning for quality challengers to run for office.

PARTY NOMINATIONS AND PRIMARIES

nomination the process by which political parties select their candidates for election to public office

primary elections elections held to select a party's candidate for the general election

caucus (political) a normally closed political party business meeting of citizens or lawmakers to select candidates, elect officers, plan strategy, or make decisions regarding legislative matters

Nomination is the process by which a party selects a single candidate to run for each elective office. Parties want only one candidate on the general-election ballot so that members of the same party do not split the vote, allowing the other party's candidate to win. Parties therefore undertake an internal process of nomination to settle on one candidate who will be on the ballot in the general election. The nomination process varies from state to state and office to office, but it usually involves a **primary election** or **caucus** among multiple candidates from the same party. Voters in the primary election select just one candidate to go on to the general election to represent each political party.

Scholars have found that although the nomination process appears democratic in that average citizens have a say, party elites play an outsized role in selecting the candidates who will compete to be the next president of the United States or member of Congress.[12] This is in part because of low turnout in primary elections, where generally only the most active members of the party vote. Political parties provide money and endorsements, which narrows the field of candidates who can win in the primaries. Without money and endorsements from one of the two major parties, most candidates cannot get out of the primary. Candidates' reliance on party money results in partisan voting blocs within government.[13] In 2016, however, the Republican Party insiders had less control over the process; reality-TV star Donald Trump, with no previous experience in public office, secured the nomination despite

With no incumbent running for New Hampshire's 1st Congressional District seat, Republican candidates debated one another in the primaries. Eddie Edwards, left, defeated four other Republican candidates to secure the party's nomination in the general election.

the fact that many members of the party emphatically spoke out against him. Only a handful of Republican members of Congress endorsed Trump for president.

GENERAL ELECTION AND MOBILIZING VOTERS

The general election begins after the nominations conclude. Throughout American history, the general election competition is a time of intense partisanship, when popular support for the parties is high. All the paraphernalia of party committees—from signs, bumper stickers, and buttons to social media slogans, hashtags, and YouTube ads—are on display, and party members are activated into local party workforces. One of the earliest activities of party workers is voter registration. Parties and candidate campaigns, along with nonprofit organizations, mail notices, call and email voters, organize voter-registration drives on college campuses, and knock on doors to ensure that citizens are registered. Confirming that citizens are registered to vote or helping them register, however, is only the first step.

The next step is turning out the vote. Convincing voters to actually show up to cast a ballot on Election Day is one of the hardest tasks that the parties face; it involves getting individuals to go to the polls, stand in line, and vote for the party's candidates on the ballot. If they are voting by mail—absentee ballots or mail voting is how one in three Americans now vote—each voter must fill out the ballot and return it. Some states, like Oregon and Washington, have all-mail elections, and all ballots are mailed to home addresses (see Chapter 8).

Voter mobilization, once an art, has now become a science. Campaigns now organize wide-scale voter-mobilization drives involving field offices with hundreds of thousands of volunteers and party workers contacting millions of voters. In recent years, the two major parties have developed an extensive database of over 240 million potential adult voters, combining state voter registration files, demographic data from the U.S. Census, and commercial behavior data, which allows the parties to more accurately seek out votes for their party candidates, contributions, and campaign volunteers. Using these vast computerized databases, modern

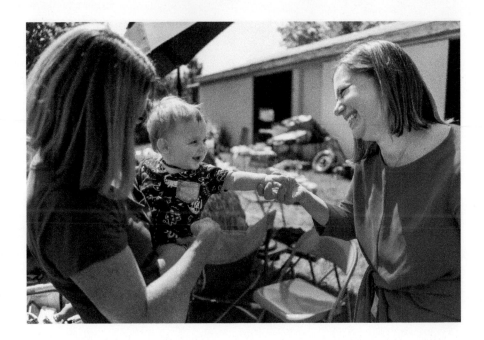

Research by political scientists and campaign organizations has shown that face-to-face, in-person contacts are much more effective than mailings, robocalls, or TV advertising in mobilizing voters.

micro-targeting when political campaigns tailor messages to individuals in small homogenous groups based on their group interests to support a candidate or policy issue

political campaigns can predict who you will vote for, and they are extremely effective at turning out the voters who are most likely to vote for their candidates. One way campaigns use these data is through **micro-targeting**, which involves tailoring campaign messages to individuals in small, homogeneous groups (e.g., suburban stay-at-home mothers or fans of NASCAR) and emphasizing specific, often heated issues, rather than a one-size-fits-all campaign message. This technique enables political parties to identify small groups based on specific characteristics—including geographic location—and to target candidates' strategies and messages to these groups.

Big data and targeted campaign messages have revolutionized how parties and candidates conduct voter-mobilization drives. It doesn't matter, after all, which party has more support if that party's voters stay home on Election Day. In 2008 the Obama campaign learned that face-to-face and in-person contacts are much more effective than mailings or robocalls at getting out the vote.[14] The lessons of 2008 were improved on in 2012 and 2016 as both parties built more accurate databases to use when developing their messages and turning out the vote. Facebook was especially important in turning out Republican voters for Trump in 2016.

Parties as Organizations

party organization the formal structure of a political party, including its leadership, election committees, active members, and paid staff

> Describe how the major American parties are structured at the national, state, and local levels

In the United States **party organizations** exist at virtually every level of government (see Figure 9.1). These organizations are usually committees made up of a number of active party members. State law and party rules dictate how such committees are created. Usually, committee members are elected at local party business meetings, called caucuses, or as part of the regular primary election. The best-known examples of these

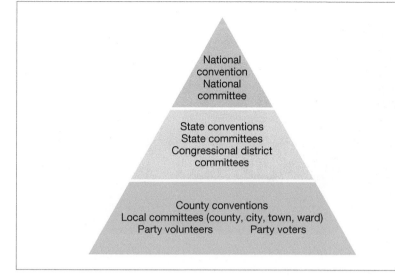

FIGURE 9.1

How American Parties Are Organized

National
convention
National
committee

State conventions
State committees
Congressional district
committees

County conventions
Local committees (county, city, town, ward)
Party volunteers   Party voters

committees are at the national level: the Democratic National Committee and the Republican National Committee.

NATIONAL CONVENTION

At the national level, the party's most important institution is the **national convention**. The convention, held every four years, is attended by delegates from each of the 50 states. The convention has three formal tasks, the most important of which is to nominate the party's presidential and vice-presidential candidates. Before World War II, presidential nominations occupied most of the time at the national convention, requiring days of negotiation and compromise. In recent years, however, presidential candidates have been chosen by winning enough delegates in state primary elections and caucuses to win the official nomination on the first ballot. Today, the convention serves as a media event to promote the party's candidates, not as a forum to decide which presidential candidate will represent the party.

The convention's other two formal tasks, determining the party's rules and its **platform**, are also important. Party rules can determine the influence of competing groups within the party, which may improve the party's chances for electoral success. In 1972, for example, the Democratic National Convention adopted a new set of rules favored by the party's liberal wing. State delegations to the Democratic Convention were required to include women and members of minority groups in rough proportion to those groups' representation among the party's membership in that state. The change also called for the use of the proportional voting rules. In the case of the Democratic Party, proportional representation increased the likelihood of women and minority delegates being elected, while in the Republican Party, which used proportional representation voting for the first time in 2012, it worked to increase representation of social conservatives and Tea Party members.

The convention also approves the party platform. Platforms are often dismissed as documents filled with promises that voters seldom read. To some extent this criticism is well founded: not one voter in a thousand so much as glances at the party platform, and even the news media pay little attention to the documents.

national convention convened by the Republican National Committee or the Democratic National Committee to nominate official candidates for president and vice president in the upcoming election, establish party rules, and adopt the party's platform

platform a party document, written at a national convention, that contains party philosophy, principles, and positions on issues

Today, the parties use their national conventions to provide more entertainment than substantive policy in order to attract media attention and promote their candidate.

Furthermore, the parties' presidential candidates make little use of the platforms in their campaigns and usually develop their own themes. Nonetheless, the platform is understood as a contract in which the various party groups attending the convention state their terms for supporting the ticket. Party platforms should be seen more as internal party documents than as public pledges.

NATIONAL COMMITTEES

Between conventions, each national political party is technically headed by its national committee. For the Democrats and Republicans, these are called the Democratic National Committee (DNC) and the Republican National Committee (RNC). Much of what these committees do is raise money for party candidates. The national committees also try to minimize disputes within the party and work to enhance the party's media image. The work of each national committee is overseen by its chairperson.

The DNC and RNC each used to raise tens of millions of dollars of so-called **soft money** every election cycle, which could be used to support party candidates throughout the nation. The 2002 Bipartisan Campaign Reform Act outlawed this practice. To circumvent the law and raise the large amounts of money needed for political campaigns, however, each party and most candidates establish Super PACs as sources of outside money. These Super PACs promote and publicize political issues, including airing negative campaign ads. As nonprofit political advocacy groups, Super PACs can claim tax-exempt status under Section 527 of the Internal Revenue Code (see Chapter 10); therefore the committees that comprise each Super PAC are called 527 committees. Super PACs can raise and spend unlimited amounts of money as long as their activities are not *coordinated* with those of the formal party organizations or the candidates, and if their aim is to inform the public and increase voter turnout. Many Super PACs are directed by former Republican and Democratic party officials and run shadow campaigns on behalf of the parties.[15] Super PACs can have outsized influence in elections because they run expensive television and media ads for and against candidates. Because wealthy funders, corporations, and even foreign donors can mask their identity by forming Super PACs, they have become synonymous with political corruption in some circles.

soft money money contributed directly to political parties and other organizations for political activities, such as voter mobilization drives, that is not regulated by federal campaign spending laws

CONGRESSIONAL, STATE, AND LOCAL CAMPAIGN COMMITTEES

Each party also forms House and Senate campaign committees, whose efforts may or may not be coordinated with the activities of the national committees (that is, the DNC and RNC). The congressional campaign committee is made up of members of each chamber that are expected to raise a certain sum of money, and doing so allows them to move up in the power structure. Congressional committees direct funds to the handful of very competitive House and Senate races each election. Presidential and congressional fundraising committees compete for dollars from the biggest donors, who are often corporations and billionaires. In recent years, both parties have attempted to better coordinate the fund-raising activities of all of their committees.

The Democrats and the Republicans also have a central committee in each state. The parties traditionally also have county committees and, in some instances, state Senate district committees, judicial district committees, and, in the case of larger cities, citywide party committees and local assembly district "ward" committees.

During the nineteenth and early twentieth centuries, many cities, counties, and occasionally even a few states had such well-organized parties that they were called **party machines**, whose leaders were called "bosses." The famous old machines of New York, Chicago, and Boston relied on "precinct captains" and a fairly tight group of party members around them. Precinct captains were usually leaders in neighborhood party clubhouses, which were important social centers and places for distributing favors (or bribes) to constituents.[16] Traditional party machines depended heavily on **patronage**, their power to control government jobs. With thousands of jobs to dispense, party bosses were able to recruit armies of political workers to turn out the vote. Voting for the party could mean the guarantee of a government job, such as a police officer, firefighter, or garbage collector. The party machines even distributed free turkeys on Thanksgiving, in exchange for support on Election Day.

Some of the major reform movements in American history, such as the Progressive movement in the early 1900s, were motivated by the excessive power, corruption, and abuses of these party machines and their bosses. Progressive reformers changed the rules of politics to reduce the power of parties and to give voters more voice in deciding who was elected to public office. A few of the many reforms to weaken the party machines included the direct election of U.S. senators; the secret ballot and long ballot, where the names of candidates running for both parties were listed; primary elections where voters, not parties, picked candidates; and voter registration, which reduced turnout and prevented party officials from casting false ballots for their candidate.

Few political machines are left today. With civil service and the merit system, party leaders no longer control many government jobs, which was a primary way the party rewarded loyal supporters. Nevertheless, state and local party organizations are very active in recruiting candidates and conducting voter-registration drives. In addition, under current federal law, state and local party organizations can spend unlimited amounts of money on "party-building" activities such as voter-registration and get-out-the-vote drives. National party organizations, which have enormous

party machines strong party organizations in late nineteenth- and early twentieth-century American cities; these machines were led by often corrupt "bosses" who controlled party nominations and patronage

patronage the resources available to higher officials, usually opportunities to make partisan appointments to offices and to confer grants, licenses, or special favors to supporters

Political parties used to be ruled by powerful local "bosses," who handed out jobs and favors in exchange for loyalty on Election Day. The cartoon shows "fat cat" New York boss Richard Croker controlling the Democratic Party organization (the donkey) with his pit bulls.

fund-raising abilities, transfer millions of dollars to the state and local party organizations. State and local parties, in turn, spend this soft money to promote national, state, and local political activities. Through the transfer of party campaign money, local organizations became linked financially to the national parties and American political parties became more integrated. State and local party organizations play an important role in elections despite the collapse of the old party machines.[17]

Parties in Government

> **Explain how parties organize legislative business and influence policy**

When the bumps, bruises, and dust of the campaign and election have settled, does it matter which party has won? It does. Especially when the parties are sharply divided ideologically, as they have been in recent years, the party that controls government can make significant changes to law and policy.

Beginning in the 1980s the Republican Party, led by Ronald Reagan, sought to expand its base by focusing on social issues that mattered to conservative religious voters. Ted Cruz (R-Tex.) announced his 2016 presidential campaign at Liberty University.

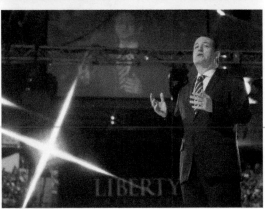

PARTIES AND POLICY

For decades, one of the most familiar complaints about American politics was that the two major parties try to be all things to all people and are therefore indistinguishable from each other. But since the 1980s fundamental differences have emerged between the positions of Democratic and Republican party leaders on a number of key issues. For example, the national leadership of the Republican Party supports limiting immigration to the United States, maintaining high levels of military spending, cuts in social programs including health care, tax relief for corporations and upper-income voters, protecting rights for gun owners, and a social agenda backed by members of conservative religious denominations, including opposition to abortion. The Republican Party opposes government regulation on businesses, including environmental laws. The Democratic Party, on the other hand, supports expanded funding for public education, social services and national health care, public spending for infrastructure such as roads, cuts in military spending, increased regulation of business to address climate change, raising taxes on the wealthy and corporations to combat growing income inequality, restrictions on gun ownership, and a variety of consumer protection programs. Democrats favor more lenient immigration policies and have been strong supporters of so-called DREAMers—undocumented immigrants brought to the United States as children.

Partisan conflict has intensified in recent years. More Americans believe there are stronger conflicts between Democrats and Republicans in U.S. society today than between blacks and whites, the rich and the poor, and other social groups (see Figure 9.2). In 2018, 86 percent of Americans said conflicts between Democrats and Republicans are either strong or very strong.[18]

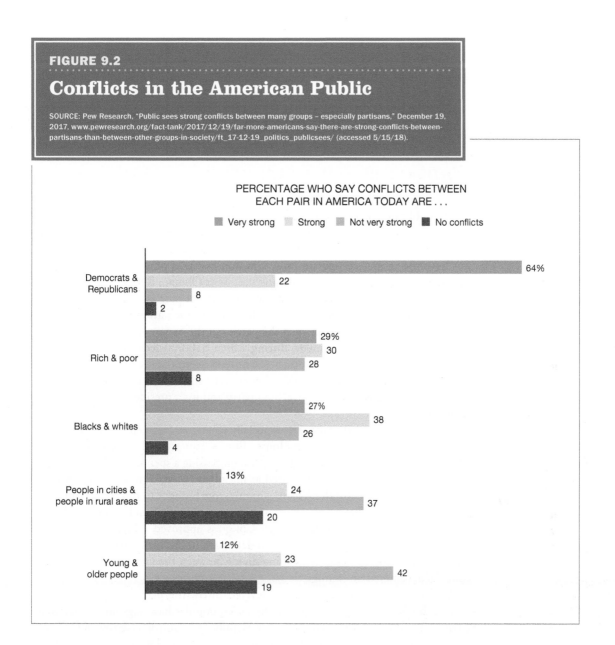

FIGURE 9.2

Conflicts in the American Public

SOURCE: Pew Research, "Public sees strong conflicts between many groups – especially partisans," December 19, 2017, www.pewresearch.org/fact-tank/2017/12/19/far-more-americans-say-there-are-strong-conflicts-between-partisans-than-between-other-groups-in-society/ft_17-12-19_politics_publicsees/ (accessed 5/15/18).

PERCENTAGE WHO SAY CONFLICTS BETWEEN
EACH PAIR IN AMERICA TODAY ARE . . .

■ Very strong   ■ Strong   ■ Not very strong   ■ No conflicts

Democrats & Republicans
- Very strong: 64%
- Strong: 22
- Not very strong: 8
- No conflicts: 2

Rich & poor
- Very strong: 29%
- Strong: 30
- Not very strong: 28
- No conflicts: 8

Blacks & whites
- Very strong: 27%
- Strong: 38
- Not very strong: 26
- No conflicts: 4

People in cities & people in rural areas
- Very strong: 13%
- Strong: 24
- Not very strong: 37
- No conflicts: 20

Young & older people
- Very strong: 12%
- Strong: 23
- Not very strong: 42
- No conflicts: 19

Party leaders often seek to develop issues they hope will add new groups to their party's constituent base. During the 1980s, for example, under the leadership of Ronald Reagan, the Republicans used social issues, including support for school prayer, opposition to abortion, and opposition to affirmative action, to gain the support of white southerners. This effort was successful at increasing Republican strength in the once solidly Democratic South. In 2008, Barack Obama campaigned on creating national health insurance for all Americans and ending the Iraq War; the effect was to build a coalition of working class and middle class voters. In the 2016 presidential election, Donald Trump proposed to build a wall between the southern U.S. border and Mexico to prevent illegal immigration, building a coalition of traditional conservatives and white working-class citizens who have faced economic hardship.

policy entrepreneur an individual who identifies a problem as a political issue and brings a policy proposal into the political agenda

As these examples suggest, party leaders can play the role of **policy entrepreneurs**, developing ideas and programs that will expand their party's base of support while eroding that of the opposition. Like their counterparts in the business world, party leaders seek to identify and develop programs and policies that will appeal to the public. The public, of course, has the ultimate voice. With its votes it decides whether or not to "buy" new policy offerings.

PARTISANSHIP AND GOVERNMENT SHUTDOWNS

Each year passing the federal budget requires cooperation between the Democratic and Republican parties, because the Senate must approve the spending bill for the nation with a supermajority vote (60 out of 100 votes)—and rarely does one party hold 60 seats. If these spending bills are not passed, the government does not have the money to operate fully, and non-essential offices and programs are shut down. In 2013, under Democratic president Obama, Republican lawmakers tried to delay or defund the Affordable Care Act in passing the federal budget. President Obama promised that he would veto any such attempt to end national health care. This stalemate between the parties in the Senate led to a 17-day shutdown of the federal government, during which 850,000 federal employees were furloughed (not paid), and another 1.3 million were required to work without knowing when they would be paid. Government shutdowns are costly, but there are also political costs, for the governing party and for a president unable to adopt their policy agenda.

Government shutdowns are rare, especially when one party controls both chambers of Congress and the White House. But in January 2018, Republicans and Democrats were again unable to reach a deal on passing a spending bill before funding for the federal government expired at midnight. At stake was protection from deportation for 700,000 DREAMers—immigrants brought to the country illegally as children but who have been allowed to live, work, and attend school legally for decades as green card holders. Though Congress approved a bipartisan compromise that protected the DREAMers from deportation, President Trump rejected the agreement, leaving the issue as a gaping divide between the parties as the stalemate continued, centered on immigration.

As the partisan politics reached a fevered pitch, the blame game heated up, with each side pointing the finger at the other. Popular hash tags on Twitter were #TrumpShutdown, clearly targeting the Republican-controlled government, and #SchumerShutdown, blaming the Senate leader of the Democratic Party who provided most of the votes for the shutdown. To end the stalemate a group of bipartisan moderate senators proposed a short-term stopgap spending bill to keep the government operating until early February. After five short-term spending bills, a final omnibus spending bill was passed in March 2018, but the fate of the DREAMers remains unclear.

FACTIONS WITHIN THE PARTIES

While party polarization, or the depth of divisions between Republicans and Democrats, is at an all-time high, the divisions *within* each political party may be nearly as important. Parties are broad coalitions of people and groups who agree on a common approach to address current challenges facing the nation, including foreign threats to security, economic growth, and social inequality. But political parties are also diverse and represent many people with competing interests for power and influence. For leaders in Congress and state legislatures, keeping these different groups working toward shared goals can be difficult. When cooperation among factions is not successful, a party's internal divisions can weaken the party itself.

The Republican Party today, for example, is divided in four ways. Pro-business conservatives, epitomized by Nebraska senator Benjamin Sasse, are traditional Republican conservatives, generally a relatively affluent group that favors small government and lower corporate taxes but also favors global free trade. Far-right or alt-right conservatives, such as President Trump, tend to be social conservatives, often with lower levels of education, and are opposed to immigration and U.S. involvement in the global economy and institutions like the United Nations. They favor tariffs on imports to the United States to protect American-made products. Social and religious conservatives, such as Texas senator Ted Cruz, are primarily driven by their socially conservative values, such as opposition to abortion and gay marriage. Finally, libertarians, such as Kentucky senator Rand Paul, believe in small government and reduced government regulations, and emphasize individual freedom. Libertarians are closer to traditional conservatives than to alt-right conservatives. These cleavages have presented severe challenges for governing. For example, far-right conservatives like Donald Trump favor very strict immigration policies in order to protect American workers, while pro-business conservatives see that immigration is important to maintain a healthy economy. These differences make it difficult to find common ground. Trump's electoral success in the 2016 Republican presidential primaries was due in part to a crowded field of candidates; no one candidate could secure a majority.

During his presidency, Donald Trump has waged a war, particularly through his use of Twitter, against many Republican leaders within his party, including Senate Majority Leader Mitch McConnell, former attorney general Jeff Sessions, former FBI director James Comey, the late Arizona senator John McCain, and Special Counsel Robert Mueller, among others.[19] Nonetheless, Republican lawmakers in Congress have generally rallied around the president even if they have personally been subject to his wrath on Twitter. Despite serious divisions within parties, when a job needs to get done, the parties often unify behind a shared goal.

The 2016 presidential election also revealed serious divides within the Democratic Party between its liberal wing (whose members favored Bernie Sanders) and traditional Democrats, who favored Hillary Clinton and who tend to be older and hold a mix of moderate and liberal values. Such divisions within the party may have contributed to the Democrats losing the White House and Congress in 2016, as many Sanders supporters refused to vote for Clinton in the general election. Today, however, the Democratic Party has renewed strength and has largely remained united in staunch opposition to President Trump. Within the Democratic Party, the coalitions all strongly favor social safety nets (national health care, etc.) but are divided in terms of government regulation of business.

PARTIES IN CONGRESS

Congress depends more on the party system than is generally recognized, as the parties form the basic organization for running Congress. The Speaker of the House is a party office. All the members of the House take part in the election of the Speaker, but the actual selection is made by the **majority party**—the party that holds a majority of seats in the House. (The other party is known as the **minority party.**)

majority party the party that holds the majority of legislative seats in either the House or the Senate

minority party the party that holds the minority of legislative seats in either the House or the Senate

When the majority party caucus presents a nominee for Speaker to the entire House, its choice is usually ratified in a straight vote along party lines. The committee system of both houses of Congress is also a product of the two-party system; the party with the most seats chairs the congressional committees, setting the policy agenda. Each party is also assigned a quota of members for each committee, depending on the percentage of total seats held by the party. As we shall see in Chapter 12, the assignment of individual members to committees is a party decision. Granting a member of Congress permission to transfer to another committee is also a party decision, as is advancement up the committee ladder toward serving as committee chair.

FOR CRITICAL ANALYSIS

How do parties attract the popular support they need to win elections?

Party Identification

Identify the reasons for and sources of party identification

One reason why parties are so important is that individual's tend to develop party identification with one of the major political parties. **Party identification** has been compared with wearing blue- or red-tinted glasses: they color voters' understanding of politics in general and are the most important cue in how to vote in elections. Party identification can create information bubbles and filters where citizens follow news media and candidates on social media that are of the same partisan leaning. Most Republicans vote for Republican party candidates, and most Democrats vote for Democrats. Slightly less than one-third of Americans are Republicans, while Democrats and Independents each make up slightly more than one-third of the population. However, most independents lean toward one of the major parties, and political scientists often consider independents who lean as identifying with that party. The number of people identifying as Democrats has outnumbered Republican identifiers for a long time (see Figure 9.3).

Although it is an emotional tie, party identification also has a rational component. Voters generally form attachments to the party that reflects their views and interests. Once those attachments are formed, usually in youth, they are likely to persist and even be handed down to children, unless some very strong factors convince individuals that their party is no longer serving their interests.

On any general-election ballot, there are a number of candidates about whom the average voter has little information. Without knowledge of local or judicial races, most voters fall back on their Republican or Democratic party identification or leaning. Some states allow a straight-ticket voting option, where individuals may check one box to cast a ballot for all the Republican or Democratic party candidates up and down the ballot, from local to national offices.

Party identification gives citizens a stake in election outcomes that goes beyond the particular race at hand. This is why strong party identifiers are more likely to go to the polls, to be contacted by political campaigns, and to support the party with which they identify. **Party activists** are drawn from rank and file members, but tend to be more ideologically extreme than the average person identifying with the party. Activists are those who not only vote but also contribute their time, money, and effort to party affairs, organization, and elections, thus giving them an outsize role in the party. No party could succeed without the thousands of

party identification an individual voter's psychological ties to one party or another

party activists partisans who contribute time, energy, and effort to support their party and its candidates

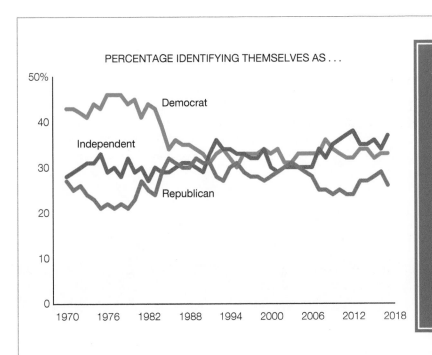

PERCENTAGE IDENTIFYING THEMSELVES AS . . .

FIGURE 9.3

Trends in Party Identification, 1970–2017

Over time, the Democrats have lost strength as more Americans identified themselves as Republicans and independents. Since 2004, however, the number of Democrats has held steady and the number of Republicans has declined, while the number of Americans identifying as independent of either party has increased to an all-time high. Why do you think this is?

SOURCE: Pew Research Center, "Party Identification," March 20, 2018, www.people-press.org/2018/03/20/party-identification-trends-1992-2017/ (accessed 5/15/18).

volunteers who undertake the tasks needed to keep the organization going. Many party activists devote their time to politics because they have strong beliefs on particular policy issues.

WHO ARE REPUBLICANS AND DEMOCRATS?

The Democratic and Republican parties are currently the only truly national parties in the United States. They are the only political organizations that draw support from every region of the country and from Americans of every racial, economic, religious, and ethnic group. The two parties do not draw equal support from members of every social and demographic stratum, however. In the United States today, several group characteristics are associated with each party. These include race and ethnicity, gender, religion, class (income and education), ideology, region, and age.

The parties have different philosophies and seek to appeal to different core constituencies. The Democratic Party at the national level seeks to unite organized labor, the poor and working class, college-educated middle-class professionals, members of racial and ethnic groups, the young, and government workers. The Republicans, by contrast, appeal to business, white non-Hispanics, white working-class voters, upper-class and affluent voters, military families, religious conservatives, and libertarian-leaning conservatives who want less government interference in all aspects of society and the economy. Rural and suburban areas provide more votes for the Republicans, while urban areas are dominated by Democrats.

Race and Ethnicity The United States' growing racial and ethnic diversity is reflected in changing partisanship and growing divisions among the Republican and Democratic parties. Since the 1930s and Franklin Delano Roosevelt's New Deal,

For many voters, race and ethnicity play a major role in party identification. Members of racial and ethnic minority groups tend to favor Democratic candidates. In 2016, Hillary Clinton gained strong support from African Americans, Asian Americans, and Latinos.

more African Americans have supported the Democratic Party than the Republican Party. Today more than 90 percent of African Americans describe themselves as Democrats and support Democratic candidates in national, state, and local elections. In 2016, 92 percent of African Americans voted for Democrat Hillary Clinton for president.[20]

Latino voters are less monolithic. Cuban Americans, for example, have generally leaned Republican whereas Mexican Americans have favored the Democrats. As a group, however, Latinos increasingly support the Democratic Party. A strong shift toward the Democratic Party occurred in 2008, when the exit polls showed that 67 percent of Latinos supported Obama. This trend has continued, with 65 percent voting for Hillary Clinton in 2016. Latino party affiliation is particularly important because it has the potential to alter the electoral map and change traditionally "red" states (states that reliably vote for the Republican presidential candidate) to "blue" states (states that reliably vote for the Democratic presidential candidate).[21]

Asian Americans have been divided in past elections but now solidly favor Democratic candidates. In 2016, 65 percent of Asian Americans voted for Hillary Clinton, and 29 percent voted for Donald Trump, according to exit polls. Asian Americans, like Latinos, are extremely diverse (see Chapter 8), reflecting cultural differences from their home countries, ranging from India, China, Korea, the Philippines, and more.

The affiliation of African Americans and Latinos with the Democratic Party can be traced to the party's historical policy positions. The Democrats were the party of the civil rights movement, desegregation, and affirmative action policies that solidified African American support. Similarly, Democrats tend to be more supportive than Republicans of policies that favor an easier path to citizenship for immigrants. Support for immigration is often critically important for Latino and Asian voters, especially in states like California, where 28 percent of the population are legal immigrants.

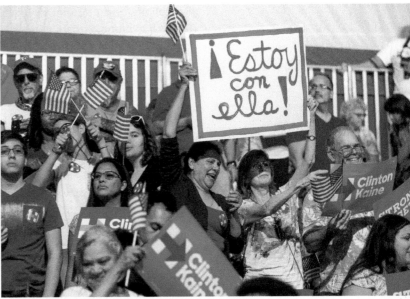

While to overgeneralize these groups is a disservice to the unique characteristics that make up these peoples, we also seek broad patterns to understand how Latinos, Asians, and African Americans are forming coalitions that may create the foundations for the Democratic Party.

Gender Women are somewhat more likely to support Democrats than Republicans, and men are somewhat more likely to support Republicans. This reflects the fact that women tend to prioritize health, education, and social services, issues favored by the Democratic Party, while men tend to prioritize fiscal and economic issues and national security, issues favored by the Republican Party. This difference is known as the **gender gap**. The gender gap has hovered at 10 percent since 1992.

The widest gender gap was in 2016, with the first female major-party presidential candidate. There was a 24 percentage-point gap between women and men in the 2016 election. The 2018 midterm elections, dubbed another year of the women, resulted in at least 125 women in Congress. Women voted for Democrats 59 to 40 percent; men split 47 to 51 percent. That 23-point gender gap is the biggest in a midterm election dating back to 1982. In 2016, 54 percent of women supported Democrat Hillary Clinton, compared to 41 percent of men.[22] Still, this is not much more than the Democratic advantage among women in 2012 and 2008. The advantage for Trump among men, however, was significantly larger than the 7-point advantage Romney had among men in 2012 and the one-point advantage Obama had over McCain in 2008. In 2016, 53 percent of men supported Trump compared to 41 percent for Clinton.[23]

Religion Just as racial and ethnic diversity continues to grow, so does religious diversity in the United States. Jews are among the Democratic Party's most loyal constituent groups and have been since the New Deal. Nearly 90 percent of Jewish Americans describe themselves as Democrats. Catholics were also once a strongly pro-Democratic group but have been shifting toward the Republican Party since the 1970s, when

gender gap a distinctive pattern of voting behavior reflecting the differences in views between women and men

Republicans began focusing on abortion and other social issues important to Catholics. White Protestants are more likely to identify with the Republican Party. Evangelical Protestants, in particular, have been drawn to the Republicans' conservative stands on social issues, such as marriage and abortion. Those who are unaffiliated with a religion—a growing segment of the population at roughly 25 percent—strongly favor the Democratic Party.[24] Today 56 percent of American adults believe it is not necessary to believe in God to be moral and have good values.[25]

The importance of religious conservatives to the Republican Party became more evident after 2000, when George W. Bush awarded federal grants and contracts to religious groups. By using so-called faith-based groups as federal contractors, Bush sought to ensure that these groups and churches would have a continuing stake in Republican success. Religious conservatives, particularly white born-again Christians, overwhelmingly supported Bush in 2004, accounting for one-third of his votes. In 2012 and 2016 white evangelical Protestants continued to vote overwhelmingly Republican.[26]

Class Rising income inequality is an important trend that has recently led to economic populism. The patterns of class voting that emerged from the New Deal of the 1930s were simple: upper-income Americans were considerably more likely to be Republican whereas lower-income Americans were far more likely to identify with the Democrats. This divide is reflected in the differences between the two parties on economic issues. In general, Republicans support cutting taxes, decreased regulation of business, and lower social spending—positions that reflect the interests of the wealthy. The Democrats, however, favor increasing social spending and in some cases raising taxes on the wealthy—a position consistent with the interests of less affluent Americans. But beginning in the 1970s, many white working-class voters turned to the Republican Party. When class is measured by education, white workers without a college degree have favored Republicans in recent elections. While both the Democratic and Republican parties appeal to working-class voters, working-class whites with low levels of education tend to vote Republican, while working-class minorities tend to vote Democratic.[27] This trend accelerated in the 2016 election, contributing to Republicans' electoral success. A wide gap in presidential preferences emerged between those with and without a college degree. College graduates backed Clinton by a 9-point margin (52 percent to 43 percent), while those without a college degree backed Trump (52 percent to 44 percent) in what is the widest gap in support among college graduates and non-college graduates in exit polls dating back to 1980.

Ideology Ideology and party identification are very closely linked. Most individuals who describe themselves as conservatives identify with the Republican Party, whereas most who call themselves liberals support the Democrats. This division has increased in recent years as the two parties have taken very different positions on social and economic issues.

The Pew Research Center's political typology finds that 36 percent of Americans are "ideological" and identify strongly with one of the two major parties. For most Americans, however, party and ideological identification are not so clear-cut: 54 percent of Americans are less partisan and less predictable as to which candidates they will support. These voters are only sporadically interested in politics, such as during an election cycle. Finally, the remaining 10 percent of Americans are completely on the sidelines of politics—this group tends to be young and diverse.[28] This varied political typography of our nation suggests that the categories of liberal and conservative may not capture the full picture.

Region After the 2000 election, red and blue maps appeared showing the regional distribution of the vote. Democrats, represented as "blue America," tend to be clustered on the coasts, the upper Midwest, across the northern states, and in most urban areas. Republicans, represented as "red America," tend to be concentrated in the Mountain West and the South, and in suburbs and rural areas.

The explanations for these regional variations are complex. Between the Civil War and the 1960s, the Democrats controlled the South. Today, the South is where Republicans gain strength, but this is changing in some states and urban areas. Southern Republicanism has come about because conservative white southerners associate the Democratic Party with liberal positions and policies that benefit urban and minority voters. Republican strength in the South is also related to the weakness of organized labor in this region and a dependence on military programs supported by the Republicans. Democratic strength in the Northeast and Midwest is a function of the continuing influence of organized labor in the large cities of these regions and of the regions' large populations of minority voters. The coastal West, especially California and the Pacific Northwest, shifted toward the Democrats in the 1990s, in part because of growing young/millennial populations, the importance of the Latino vote, concerns with the environment, and a growing population of the religiously unaffiliated.[29]

Many states that used to be solidly red or blue are now turning "purple" where Republicans and Democrats battle to win elections. These states include Texas, North Carolina, Virginia, Arizona and other states where Republicans used to dominate. For example, Democrat Hillary Clinton lost Texas by just 9 percent of the vote in 2016. On the other hand, Midwest states that used to be solidly Democratic favored Republicans in 2016, including Wisconsin, Michigan, Iowa, Ohio, and Pennsylvania. Demographic change and modern electoral campaigns that mobilize high turnout are blurring the lines between red and blue states (Figure 9.4).

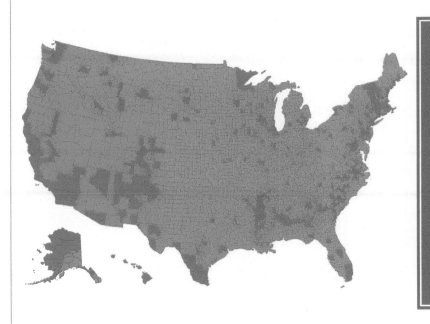

FIGURE 9.4

Presidential Vote by County, 2016

In 2016 the Republicans dominated in most counties in the center of the country. Though the map shows more "red" counties than "blue" covering a greater geographic area, Hillary Clinton and the Democrats won many of the most populous counties and several of the states with the most votes in the electoral college (see Chapter 10).

SOURCES: "Presidential Election Results: Donald Trump Wins," *New York Times*, www.nytimes.com/elections/results/president; Mark Newman, Maps of the 2016 U.S. presidential election results, www-personal.umich.edu/~mejn/election/2016/ (accessed 5/15/18).

Age Age is also associated with partisanship. Today young people are much more likely to be Democrats, while the oldest voters affiliate with the Republican Party. Why does age matter for partisanship? Individuals from the same age cohort are likely to have experienced a similar set of events during the period when their party loyalties were formed. Millennials, for example, who came of age during Bush's presidency and the Iraq War, also have a strong identification with the Democratic Party. The election of Barack Obama in 2008 saw a particularly striking shift among young voters toward the Democratic Party. In recent years, however, there has been a striking uptick in the percentage of young people who identify as independent, which may be a reflection of increasing frustration with government. Nonetheless, in 2016, 55 percent of people ages 18–29 voted for Hillary Clinton, compared to just 37 percent for Donald Trump.[30] As a group, young people have distinct policy preferences that overlap with those of the Democratic Party, including strong support for LGBTQ rights, legalization of marijuana, environmental protection, and greater economic equality.

RECENT TRENDS IN PARTY AFFILIATION

After the 1960s many analysts began to express concern that American parties had become too weak to play their vital role in converting popular political participation into effective government. These scholars noted a decline in partisan attachment within the electorate, the growth in the numbers of voters identifying as independent, and a rise in so-called split-ticket voting. This overall trend, sometimes termed **dealignment**, was seen as a product of growing social diversity and educational attainment, which made voters less reliant on parties to guide their political decision-making (see Figure 9.5). The growth of the mass media, particularly television, also seemed to reduce the role of parties in elections as television tends to focus on the personalities of individual candidates rather than the "institution" of the party.

dealignment a movement away from the major political parties; a decline in partisan attachment

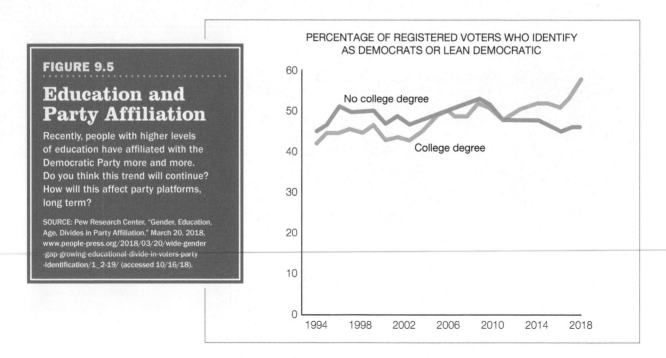

FIGURE 9.5

Education and Party Affiliation

Recently, people with higher levels of education have affiliated with the Democratic Party more and more. Do you think this trend will continue? How will this affect party platforms, long term?

SOURCE: Pew Research Center, "Gender, Education, Age, Divides in Party Affiliation," March 20, 2018, www.people-press.org/2018/03/20/wide-gender-gap-growing-educational-divide-in-voters-party-identification/1_2-19/ (accessed 10/16/18).

PERCENTAGE OF REGISTERED VOTERS WHO IDENTIFY AS DEMOCRATS OR LEAN DEMOCRATIC

Who Identifies with Which Party?

Gender		Republican	Democrat	Independent
	Men	31%	40%	28%
	Women	27%	34%	39%

Age				
	18–29	24%	41%	35%
	30–49	25%	41%	34%
	50–64	32%	34%	34%
	65+	29%	37%	34%

Race				
	White	35%	37%	28%
	Black	4%	23%	73%
	Hispanic	16%	39%	46%
	Asian	27%	39%	34%

Education				
	Postgraduate	24%	33%	44%
	College graduate	35%	34%	31%
	Some college	30%	39%	31%
	High school diploma or less	26%	39%	35%

Income				
	< $20K	20%	40%	40%
	$20–$40K	23%	39%	38%
	$40K–$75K	31%	37%	32%
	>$75K	34%	35%	32%

Party identification varies by income, race, and gender. For example, as these statistics from 2016 show, Americans with higher incomes are more supportive of the Republican Party than are Americans with lower incomes. Women are significantly more likely than men to identify with the Democratic Party, whereas more men identify as independents.

Republican Party

Democratic Party

Independent

FOR CRITICAL ANALYSIS

1. How do younger Americans differ from older Americans in their party identification? What is the best predictor of party identification?

2. Do you think of yourself as a Democrat, Republican, or independent? Are other Americans of your gender, age, race, and income level likely to share your references?

NOTES: Percentages do not add to 100 because the category "Other/don't know" is omitted. ANES does not include rural/urban/suburban data.

SOURCE: American National Election Study 2016 time series, www.electionstudies.org (accessed 11/4/17).

While they often lean toward one of the two parties and vote for the Republicans or Democrats in national elections, independents have unique views and are more supportive of third parties and election reform efforts that create opportunities for groups outside of government to have a voice in government.[31] With congressional approval ratings at an all-time low, the number of Americans identifying as independents has grown to roughly 40 percent.[32] In nine states, independent voters outnumber the two major political parties, including Alaska, which has 55 percent registered independents; Connecticut, with 41 percent; Colorado, 38 percent; and Iowa, 36 percent.[33]

Today, party loyalties in America are in a state of flux. On the one hand, the percentage of voters who declare no party loyalty remains at an all-time high.[34] On the other hand, party identification among a large number of the most active voters has grown stronger.[35] The "Who Are Americans?" feature indicates the relationship between party identification and a number of social criteria. Race and ethnicity, age, education, religion, region, and income seem to have the greatest influence on Americans' party affiliations.

Party Systems

> **Describe how the party system in the United States has changed over time and its main features today**

Historians often refer to the set of parties that are important at any given time as a nation's party system. The United States has usually had a two-party system, meaning that only two parties have a serious chance to win national elections. But the nation has not always had the same two parties and, as we shall see, minor parties often put forward candidates.

The term *party system*, however, refers to more than just the number of parties competing for power. It also includes the organization of the parties, the dominant form of campaigning, the main issue divisions between the parties, the balance of power between and within party coalitions, the parties' social and institutional bases, and the policies around which party competition is organized. Seen from this broader perspective, the character of a nation's party system can change even if the number of parties remains the same and even when the same two parties seem to be competing for power. Today's American party system is very different from the country's party system of 100 years ago, but the Democrats and Republicans continue to be the major competing forces. Over the course of American history, changes in political forces and alignments have produced six distinctive party systems.

THE FIRST PARTY SYSTEM: FEDERALISTS AND JEFFERSONIAN REPUBLICANS

The first party system emerged in the 1790s and pitted the Federalists, who favored a strong national government and president, against the Jeffersonian Republicans, or Antifederalists, who favored a weaker national government with the states retaining power protections for individuals from government interference. The Federalists were the establishment party at the time, and the Antifederalists were the outsiders. The Federalists represented mainly New England merchants and supported a program of protective tariffs to encourage manufacturing, forgiving states' Revolutionary

War debts, the creation of a national bank, and commercial ties with Britain. The Jeffersonians, led by southern agricultural interests, opposed these policies and instead favored free trade, the promotion of agricultural interests, and friendship with France. The Federalists sought, unsuccessfully, to use the force of law against the Jeffersonians by enacting the Alien and Sedition Acts to outlaw criticism of the government. These acts, however, proved virtually impossible to enforce, and the Jeffersonians gradually expanded their base from the South into the Middle Atlantic states. In the election of 1800, Thomas Jefferson defeated the incumbent Federalist president, John Adams, and led his party to power. Over the following years, the Federalists gradually weakened. The party disappeared after the pro-British sympathies of some Federalist leaders during the War of 1812 led to charges of treason against the party.

From the collapse of the Federalists until the 1830s, America had only one political party, the Jeffersonian Republicans, who gradually came to be known as the Democrats. This period of one-party politics was defined by an absence of party competition. Throughout this period, however, there was intense conflict within the Democratic Party, particularly between the supporters and opponents of General Andrew Jackson, America's great military hero of the War of 1812. Jackson was the first populist president with a wide base of mass support; he sought to give rank-and-file members more say in party politics. Jackson's opponents united to deny him the presidency in 1824, but Jackson won elections in 1828 and 1832. Jackson's support was in the South and West, and he generally espoused a program of free trade and policies that appealed to those regions.

THE SECOND PARTY SYSTEM: DEMOCRATS AND WHIGS

During the 1830s, groups opposing Jackson united to form a new political force, the Whig Party, giving rise to the second American party system. Both the Democrats and the Whigs built party organizations throughout the nation and sought to enlarge their bases of support by expanding the right to vote. They increased the number of eligible voters—still only white males—through the elimination of the requirement of property ownership in order to be able to vote. Support for the new Whig Party was stronger in the Northeast than in the South and West and among merchants than among small farmers. Hence, in some measure, the Whigs were the successors of the Federalists. Yet conflict between the two parties revolved more around personalities than policies. The Whigs were a diverse group united more by opposition to the Democrats than by agreement on programs. In 1840 the Whigs won their first presidential election under the leadership of General William Henry Harrison. The Whig campaign carefully avoided issues—since the party could agree on almost none—and emphasized the personal qualities and heroism of the candidate. They also invested heavily in campaign rallies and entertainment to win the hearts, if not exactly the minds, of the voters.

In the 1830s the Whig Party emerged as the Democrats' main rival. This drawing depicts a Whig rally and parade during the 1840 election.

During the late 1840s and early 1850s, conflicts over slavery produced sharp divisions within both the Whig and the Democratic parties. By 1856 the Whig Party had all but disintegrated under the strain, and many Whig politicians and voters, along with antislavery Democrats, joined the new Republican Party, which pledged to ban slavery from the western territories. In 1860 the new Republican Party nominated Abraham Lincoln for the presidency. Lincoln's victory in a four-way candidate race for president strengthened southern calls for secession from the Union and, soon thereafter, for all-out civil war.

THE CIVIL WAR AND POST–CIVIL WAR PARTY SYSTEM

During the course of the war, President Lincoln depended heavily on Republican governors and state legislatures to raise troops, provide funding, and maintain popular support for a long and bloody military conflict. The secession of the South had stripped the Democratic Party of many supporters, but the Democrats remained politically competitive throughout the war and nearly won the 1864 presidential election because of war weariness on the part of the northern public. With the defeat of the Confederacy in 1865, some Republicans sought to use Reconstruction to grant the right to vote to newly freed slaves, thus creating a large pro-Republican voting bloc. This Reconstruction program failed, in part because of violent resistance by southern whites via the Ku Klux Klan. With the end of Reconstruction, the former Confederate states regained full control of their internal affairs and party politics. Throughout the South, African Americans were deprived of political rights, including the right to vote, despite post–Civil War constitutional guarantees to the contrary. From the end of the Civil War to the 1890s, the Republican Party remained the party of the North, with strong business and middle-class support, while the Democrats were the party of the South, with support also from working-class and immigrant groups.

Following the Civil War, the Republican Party remained dominant in the North. This poster supporting Republican Benjamin Harrison in the 1888 election promises protective tariffs and other policies that appealed to the industrial states in the North.

THE SYSTEM OF 1896: POPULISM AND REPUBLICAN RESPONSES

During the 1890s, profound and rapid social and economic changes led to the emergence of a variety of protest parties, including the Populist Party, which won the support of hundreds of thousands of voters in the South and West. The Populists appealed mainly to small farmers but also attracted western mining interests and urban workers. In the 1892 presidential election, the Populist Party carried four states and elected governors in eight. In 1896 the Populist Party effectively merged with the Democrats, who nominated William Jennings Bryan, a Democratic senator with pronounced Populist sympathies, for the presidency. The Republicans nominated the conservative senator William McKinley. In the ensuing campaign, northern and midwestern businesses made an all-out effort to defeat what they saw as a radical threat from the Populist–Democratic alliance. When the dust settled, the Republicans had won a resounding victory. The GOP ("Grand Old Party"), or Republican Party, had carried the more heavily populated northern and midwestern states and confined the Democrats to their smaller bases of support in the South and far West. For the next 36 years, the Republicans were the nation's majority party, carrying seven of nine presidential elections and controlling both houses of Congress in 15 of 18 contests. The Republican Party was pro-business, advocating low taxes, high tariffs on imports, and a minimum of government regulation.

THE NEW DEAL PARTY SYSTEM: GOVERNMENT HELPS THE WORKING CLASS

Soon after the Republican presidential candidate Herbert Hoover won the 1928 presidential election, the nation's economy collapsed. The Great Depression, which produced unprecedented economic hardship, stemmed from a variety of causes; but from the perspective of millions of Americans, the Republican Party did not do enough to promote economic recovery when millions of Americans were starving and without jobs. In 1932, Americans elected Franklin Delano Roosevelt and a solidly Democratic Congress. Roosevelt developed a program for economic recovery that he dubbed the "New Deal." Under the auspices of the New Deal, the size of America's national government increased substantially. The federal government took responsibility for economic management and social welfare to an extent that was unprecedented in American history. For the first time, government took an active role in the individual lives of Americans, providing unemployment benefits, jobs, food, and more.

Roosevelt expanded the political base of the Democratic Party. He rebuilt and revitalized the party around unionized workers, upper-middle-class intellectuals and professionals, southern farmers, Jews, Catholics, and African Americans— the so-called New Deal coalition that made the Democrats the nation's majority party for the next 36 years. Groping for a response to the New Deal, Republicans often wound up supporting popular New Deal programs such as Social Security in what was sometimes derided as "me too" Republicanism. Even the relatively conservative administration of Dwight D. Eisenhower in the 1950s left the principal New Deal programs intact.

The New Deal coalition was severely strained during the 1960s by conflicts over civil rights and the Vietnam War. The struggle over civil rights initially divided northern Democrats, who supported the civil rights cause, from white southern Democrats, who defended the system of racial segregation. As the civil rights movement launched a northern campaign aimed at securing access to jobs and education and an end to racial discrimination in such realms as housing, northern Democrats also split, often along income lines. The struggle over the Vietnam War further divided the Democrats, with upper-income liberal Democrats strongly opposing the Johnson administration's decision to greatly expand the numbers of U.S. troops fighting in Southeast Asia. These divisions within the Democratic Party provided an opportunity for the GOP, which returned to power in 1968 under the leadership of Richard Nixon.

THE CONTEMPORARY AMERICAN PARTY SYSTEM

The Republican Party widened its appeal in the second half of the twentieth century. In 1964, for example, the Republican presidential candidate Barry Goldwater argued in favor of substantially reduced levels of taxation and spending, less government regulation of the economy, and the elimination of many federal social programs. Though Goldwater was defeated by Lyndon Johnson, his ideas continued to be major themes for the Republican Party. Richard Nixon's "southern strategy" gave GOP the votes it needed to end Democratic control of national politics. Nixon appealed to disaffected white southerners, and he sparked the shift that gave the party a strong position in all the states of the former Confederacy. The movement of white southerners to the Republican Party was spurred by opposition to desegregation of the South and to the civil rights movement supported by Democratic leaders, including President Kennedy. During the 1980s, under the leadership of President Ronald Reagan, Republicans added two additional important groups to their coalition. The first were religious conservatives, who were opposed to abortion and marriage equality and felt the Democrats were not protecting traditional family and religious values. The second were working-class whites, who were drawn to Reagan's tough approach to foreign policy and opposition to affirmative action. Many Republicans consider Reagan's tenure in office as a "golden era" that saw deregulation of many industries, reduced government intervention in the economy, and exhibited robust economic growth.

While Republicans built a political base around economic and social conservatives and white southerners, the Democratic Party maintained its support among a majority of unionized workers and upper-middle-class professionals. Democrats also appealed to racial and ethnic minorities. The 1965 Voting Rights Act had greatly increased black voter participation in the South and helped the Democratic Party retain some House and Senate seats in southern states. And whereas the Republicans appealed to social conservatives, the Democrats appealed to Americans concerned with economic fairness and inequality, women's rights, the environment and protections of public land, and other progressive social causes.

Republicans fared poorly at state and local levels until the 1990s, when conservative religious groups made a concerted effort to expand their influence within the

Richard Nixon's "southern strategy" helped broaden the Republican Party's base in the late 1960s and the 1970s by appealing to white southerners. Here, Nixon meets supporters in Georgia in 1973.

Republican Party. This effort led to conflict between members of the "religious right" and more traditional fiscal Republicans, whose major concerns were economic matters such as taxes and federal regulation of business. In 2000, George W. Bush united the party behind a program of tax cuts, education reform, military strength, and family values.

However, Republicans fared poorly again in the 2008 elections, campaigning during the worst financial crisis since the 1930s. Democrat Barack Obama, the nation's first African American president, was elected in 2008 and reelected for a second term in 2012. He united racial and ethnic minorities, youth, and other liberals with older white moderates in a powerful national coalition, winning large popular majorities in the 2008 and 2012 elections. Obama helped the nation recover from global economic recession; reformed national health care, the financial sector, and immigration; and promoted clean energy and environmental protections, labor policy, and LGBTQ rights. He was championed globally as a progressive leader with strong alliances in Europe. However, he became deeply unpopular with Republicans who objected to what they saw as overreach by the federal government. Republicans captured both houses of Congress in 2014, and in 2016, they retained both chambers and won the presidency in a tight race, signaling that sharp partisan differences and intense party conflict would continue to characterize American politics.

Transitions in the party systems over time are sometimes called **electoral realignments**. During these periods, the coalitions that support the parties and the balance of power between the parties change and are redefined. In historical terms, realignments occur when new issues, combined with economic or political crises, mobilize new voters and persuade large numbers of them to reexamine their traditional partisan loyalties and permanently shift their support from one party to another. Figure 9.6 charts the sequence of party systems and realignments in American history.

Although scholars dispute the timing of realignments, there is some agreement that five have occurred since the Founding. The first took place around 1790–1800, when the Jeffersonian Republicans defeated the Federalists and became the dominant force in American politics. The second realignment occurred in 1828, when the Jacksonian Democrats seized control of the White House and the Congress. In the third period of realignment, centered on the 1860 election, the newly founded Republican Party, led by Abraham Lincoln, won power, in the process destroying the Whig Party, which had been one of the nation's two major parties since the 1830s. Many northern voters who had supported the Whigs or the Democrats on the basis of their economic policies shifted their support to the Republicans as slavery replaced tariffs and economic concerns as the central issue on the nation's agenda. Many southern Whigs shifted their support to the Democrats. The new regional alignment of forces that emerged was solidified by the trauma of the Civil War and persisted almost to the end of the nineteenth century. In the fourth alignment, the election of 1896 saw Republican candidate William McKinley, emphasizing business, industry, and urban interests, defeat Democrat William Jennings Bryan, who spoke for populist economic interests, farmers, and miners. Republican dominance lasted until the fifth realignment, during the period 1932–36, when the Democrats, led by Franklin Delano Roosevelt, took control of the White House and Congress during the economic crisis of the Great Depression. Despite sporadic interruptions, the Democrats maintained control of both through the 1960s. Since that time, American party politics has been characterized by **divided government**, wherein the presidency is controlled by one party while the other party controls one or both houses of Congress.

Major party realignments are rare in America, occurring on average about once every 30 years. There are frequent false alarms, when pundits describe elections as realignments and they turn out not to be. In the 2016 presidential election, significant factions of the Republican Party were in disagreement over Donald Trump's candidacy, leading some observers to question whether the election was the beginning of a new party realignment. Many high-profile Republican politicians refused to support Trump, and some withdrew their support during the course of the campaign. However, during the first two years of the Trump administration, Republicans in Congress have generally supported the President's policy agenda.

PARTY POLARIZATION

A distinguishing feature of the contemporary party system is **party polarization**. The vast and growing gap between Democrats and Republicans has become a defining feature of American politics today, with more Democrats holding liberal positions

electoral realignment the point in history when a new party supplants the governing party, becoming in turn the dominant political force

divided government the condition in American government wherein the presidency is controlled by one party while the opposing party controls one or both houses of Congress

party polarization the division between the two major parties on most policy issues, with members of each party unified around their party's positions with little crossover

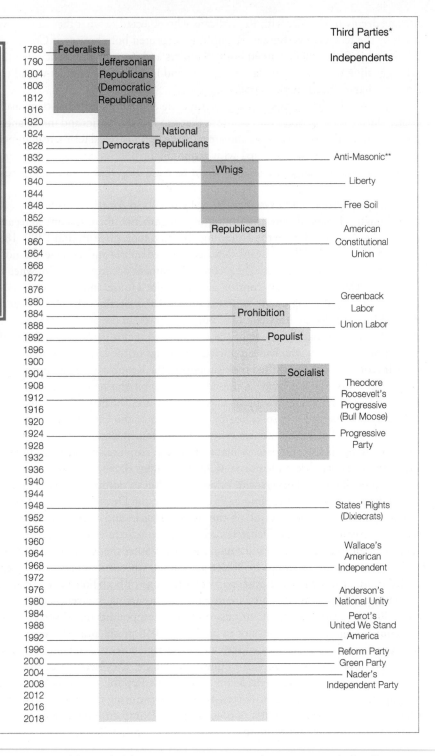

Third Parties*
and
Independents

Year	Major Parties	Third Parties
1788	Federalists	
1790	Jeffersonian	
1804	Republicans	
1808	(Democratic-	
1812	Republicans)	
1816		
1820		
1824	National	
1828	Democrats Republicans	
1832		Anti-Masonic**
1836	Whigs	
1840		Liberty
1844		
1848		Free Soil
1852		
1856	Republicans	American
1860		Constitutional
1864		Union
1868		
1872		
1876		Greenback
1880		Labor
1884	Prohibition	
1888		Union Labor
1892	Populist	
1896		
1900		
1904	Socialist	
1908		Theodore
1912		Roosevelt's
1916		Progressive
1920		(Bull Moose)
1924		Progressive
1928		Party
1932		
1936		
1940		
1944		
1948		States' Rights
1952		(Dixiecrats)
1956		
1960		Wallace's
1964		American
1968		Independent
1972		
1976		Anderson's
1980		National Unity
1984		Perot's
1988		United We Stand
1992		America
1996		Reform Party
2000		Green Party
2004		Nader's
2008		Independent Party
2012		
2016		
2018		

and more Republicans holding conservative views (see Figure 9.7). In Congress, polarization is measured by party unity in roll-call votes. Over 90 percent of the time, members of Congress vote in agreement with the majority of their party.[36] With this kind of party-line voting, legislation is often enacted by slim vote margins in Congress.

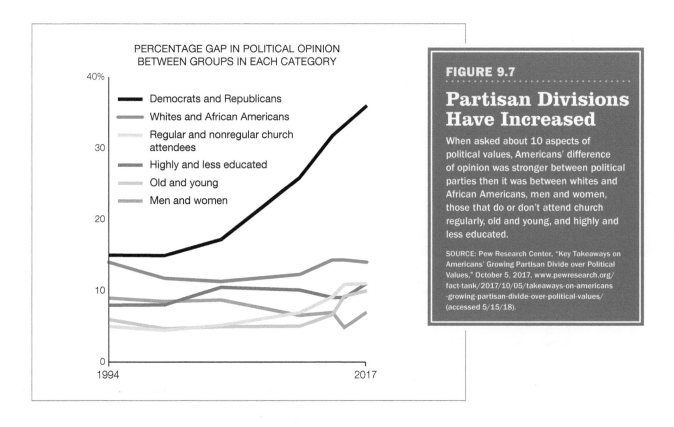

PERCENTAGE GAP IN POLITICAL OPINION
BETWEEN GROUPS IN EACH CATEGORY

- Democrats and Republicans
- Whites and African Americans
- Regular and nonregular church attendees
- Highly and less educated
- Old and young
- Men and women

FIGURE 9.7

Partisan Divisions Have Increased

When asked about 10 aspects of political values, Americans' difference of opinion was stronger between political parties then it was between whites and African Americans, men and women, those that do or don't attend church regularly, old and young, and highly and less educated.

SOURCE: Pew Research Center, "Key Takeaways on Americans' Growing Partisan Divide over Political Values," October 5, 2017, www.pewresearch.org/fact-tank/2017/10/05/takeaways-on-americans-growing-partisan-divide-over-political-values/ (accessed 5/15/18).

The extent of party polarization in Congress was exemplified by party-line voting in 2017 for the most significant overhaul of the U.S. tax code in three decades.[37] The bill reduced taxes temporarily to varying degrees for some Americans but, provided the most benefits to affluent citizens. The bill also provided a massive tax cut to corporations, lowering the rate from 35 to 21 percent. Through concessions, threats, and extended negotiations, Republican leaders secured votes of support from every Republican member of the House but 12 and every Senate Republican but one. Democrats in the House and Senate were in unanimous opposition to the tax bill.

While lawmakers in Congress are generally strong conservatives or strong liberals, Congress does not match the ideology of the American public; most Americans are moderates in terms of their opinions on major issues.[38] Party polarization in Congress may be the result of how congressional representatives are elected. Every 10 years, congressional district geographic boundaries are redrawn so that each district has roughly the same population. These districts are increasingly drawn to be "safe" for one political party or another so that the district has a clear majority of either Republicans or Democrats. Most lawmakers are elected from safe, homogeneous districts, where a majority of voters identify with their party, which means they have little chance of losing in the next election. Incumbents, on average, win 70 percent of the popular vote compared with challengers' 30 percent.[39] Uncompetitive elections in Congress and safe seats are associated with growing party polarization. Without facing competition from the other party during general elections, those elected to Congress are strong partisans. Today lawmakers face the greatest threats during their own party's primary elections, which can have the effect of moving candidates more to the ideological extremes of their party in order to win in the primary.

FOR CRITICAL ANALYSIS

What are the principal issues dividing the two major parties today? What are the chief areas of agreement between the two parties?

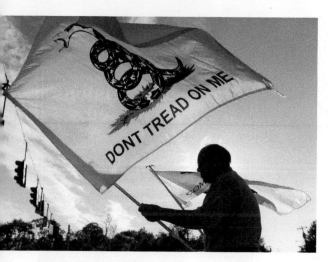

The Tea Party emerged after the election of Barack Obama in 2008. During the 2010 midterm elections, Tea Party activists around the country rallied to "reclaim the Capitol" and succeeded in electing a number of their candidates to office, which further increased party polarization in Congress.

Others argue that party polarization has occurred not because of how congressional districts are drawn but because individuals segregate themselves by choosing to live in liberal or conservative geographic areas or consume liberal or conservative news and social media. This is known as self-sorting. No matter what the cause, lawmakers elected from solidly safe districts have less incentive to compromise; thus, homogeneous Democratic and homogeneous Republican districts add to the polarization of the political parties.

A specific event that contributed to party polarization was the rise of the Tea Party movement (see the opening of this chapter). The Tea Party is an extremely conservative faction of the Republican Party, which has supported President Trump since the 2016 election. After the election of Barack Obama in 2008, a number of high-profile Tea Party candidates went on to win office in the 2010 midterm elections, defeating several incumbents and candidates endorsed by the Republican Party. In total, the Tea Party succeeded in electing about 32 percent of its candidates in 2010—a strong showing for a newly organized group—and its ideological influence in elections has continued through 2018.

As Congress has become more ideologically extreme, members have given more power to their party leaders, who have changed the rules in Congress so that the majority can control the legislative process more easily, further intensifying party polarization. The ability to debate legislation on the floor of the House has been restricted, and individual members exercise less personal choice in deciding how to vote. Even strong party leaders are not immune to the pressure from their most ideologically extreme members. In 2015, House Speaker John Boehner resigned in the middle of his term. The historic event occurred because of deep divisions within the Republican Party, especially the opposition of 40 of the most conservative House members—Tea Party activists—who wanted him to take a harder line against Obama and the Democrats.

THIRD PARTIES

third parties parties that organize to compete against the two major American political parties

Although the United States has a two party–dominant system, it has always had more than two parties. Typically, **third parties** in the United States have represented social and economic interests that for one reason or another were not given voice by the two major parties.[40] Such parties often influence elections. The Populists, a party centered in the rural areas of the West and Midwest, and the Progressives, spokespersons for the urban middle class in the late nineteenth and early twentieth centuries, are the most important examples in the previous century. The most successful recent third party candidate, H. Ross Perot, who ran in 1992 as an independent and in 1996 as the Reform Party's nominee, won the votes of almost one in five Americans in 1992.

Because third parties almost always lose at the national level, such parties exist mainly as a protest movement against the two parties or to promote specific issues. Third parties often are sources of new ideas and party realignment, and they can profoundly affect elections, taking votes from one of the major parties and enabling the other to win. In the extremely close 2000 presidential election, for example, third-party candidate Ralph Nader won just 3 percent of the popular vote, but that

Third-party candidates rarely win elections, but they can influence campaigns. In 2016, Jill Stein (left) and Gary Johnson and his vice-presidential running mate William Weld (right) ran as alternatives to the Democratic and Republican candidates. Enough votes went to Johnson and Stein that they denied Clinton and Trump from winning a majority.

split the Democratic vote enough to swing the election in favor of Republican George W. Bush. Leaders in both major political parties fear third-party challenges in presidential elections. In the controversial 2016 election, Republican Donald Trump won 46 percent of the popular vote compared to 48 percent for Democrat Hillary Clinton. Neither candidate won a majority because votes for third parties stole votes from the two major party candidates.

Table 9.1 lists the top candidates in the presidential election of 2016, including the top third-party and independent candidates who ran. Third-party candidates fared better in 2016 than in the last three presidential elections, leading some observers to suggest that third parties were one reason Clinton lost key battleground states and thus the election. Third-party and independent candidacies also arise at the state and local levels. The Libertarian and Green parties in particular run candidates in many state and local elections. In 2012 independent candidates won Senate races in Maine and Vermont and were re-elected in 2018.

Obstacles Facing Third Parties Americans usually assume that only candidates nominated by one of the two major parties have any chance of winning an election. As noted above, voters who would prefer a third-party candidate may feel compelled to vote for the major-party candidate whom they regard as the "lesser of two evils," to avoid wasting their votes in a futile gesture. This is called *strategic voting*.

Under federal election law, only parties that receive more than 5 percent of the national presidential vote are entitled to federal funds. The Reform Party qualified by winning 8.2 percent in 1996, but since then third parties have not won federal matching money. As discussed earlier, third-party candidates are also hampered by single-member district system for allocating seats. In many other nations, several individuals can be elected to represent each legislative district—a system of multiple-member districts, more favorable to third-party candidates. Some American states do have multiple-member districts for state legislature, but the vast majority do not. The plurality system of voting discussed earlier in this chapter also discourages many minor parties in the United States.[41] In the proportional system used in other countries, parties can earn seats in government with 15–20 percent of the popular vote.

The Influence of Third Parties Although the Republican Party was the only American third party to make itself permanent (by replacing the Whigs), other third parties have enjoyed an influence far beyond their electoral size. This is because

TABLE 9.1

Parties and Candidates in 2016

CANDIDATE	PARTY	VOTE TOTAL	PERCENTAGE OF VOTES	ELECTORAL COLLEGE VOTES*
Hillary Clinton	Democratic	65,147,421	48%	227
Donald Trump	Republican	62,634,907	46%	304
Gary Johnson	Libertarian	4,454,855	3%	0
Jill Stein	Green	1,426,922	1%	0
Other candidates		1,047,140	0.8%	0

*As was their right, seven members of the electoral college voted for other candidates despite Trump or Clinton carrying the state.

SOURCE: U.S. Election Atlas, "2016 Presidential General Election Results," www.uselectionatlas.org/RESULTS/national.php?year=2016&minper=0&f=0&off=0&elect=0 (accessed 12/1/16).

large parts of their programs were adopted by one or both of the major parties, which sought to appeal to the voters mobilized by the new party and thus expand their own electoral strength. The Democratic Party, for example, became a great deal more liberal when it adopted most of the Progressive Party reforms in the early twentieth century. Many socialists felt that President Franklin Roosevelt's New Deal had adopted most of their party's platform including unemployment compensation and laws guaranteeing workers the right to organize into unions. This kind of influence explains the short lives of third parties. Their causes are usually eliminated when the major parties adopt their policies and draw their supporters into the mainstream.

Election Reform and Third Parties In part because third parties have become increasingly common in American politics despite election rules favoring a two-party system, one-third of all winning presidential candidates since the Civil War have been elected with a plurality (simply more votes than any other candidate) but not a majority (more than 50 percent of all votes) of the national popular vote.[42] If the party that wins the presidency in one out of three elections is not favored by a majority of voters, that calls into question the legitimacy of our election system. Some scholars suggest that the failure to secure majorities may continue in the future with the rise of independent candidates and dissatisfaction with the two major political parties.[43]

Some proponents of election reform argue that two major parties are not sufficient to represent the varied interests of America's 320 million people and that more political parties would improve representation. Forms of proportional representation, multiple-member districts, or instant runoff voting would increase the probability of third-party representation in American politics. State ballot access laws are another major impediment for third parties. Third parties often fail to meet criteria to get on the ballot, such as registration fees or petition requirements in which a certain number of voters must sign a petition in order for the third-party or independent candidate to gain ballot access. Those who favor a stronger role for third parties argue that states should make it easier to get on the ballot. Supporters of the current system, on the other hand, contend that America's two-party system creates stability in governing and prevents the need for a coalition government, where multiple small parties work together to form a majority to govern.

Ranked Choice Voting An example of an election reform that may reduce party polarization and increase opportunities for third parties is ranked choice voting. Ranked choice voting is a form of instant runoff voting in that it guarantees that the winner of an election has support from a majority of those voting in the election, rather than a plurality. Ranked choice voting (or preference voting) is a ballot form used in countries around the world, notably Australia, that is growing in popularity in numerous American cities and some states. Rather than casting a single vote for one's most preferred choice, a voter ranks candidates from the most preferred to the least preferred (usually the top three) on the ballot. If a candidate wins a majority of first-place votes (50 percent plus one), the candidate is declared the winner and second- or third-place votes are not counted. But if the top candidate does not receive a majority of the votes cast, the candidate with the fewest first-choice votes is eliminated, and those voters' ballots are redistributed to their second-choice candidates. The ballots are recounted; if the leading candidate has a majority of votes cast, a winner is declared. The process is repeated until a majority winner is declared. This system eliminates the "spoiler" effect that occurs when votes for a third-party candidate are discarded.

Research suggests that ranked choice voting leads to more civility in political campaigns, fewer negative campaigns, and cooperation among candidates who seek to be a voter's second choice if they cannot be a first choice.[44] It is also associated with more grassroots mobilization of voters. Though ranked choice voting is used in many countries around the world, in the United States only the state of Maine uses it, as well as a handful of U.S. cities. Successful local experiments in election reform may open the doors to use of this process at the state or even national level.

Political Parties
WHAT DO WE WANT?

Parties provide an important opportunity for citizen participation in American politics. They make it easier for ordinary citizens to understand politics, evaluate candidates, participate in elections, and have a voice in government policy. They are also important to the health of the democracy. The presence of an opposition party is an important check on those in power. And competition among the political parties gives citizens an incentive to vote and politicians an incentive to get them to vote.[45] Voter mobilization is one of political parties' most important tasks, as voter turnout in the United States remains relatively low, especially in primaries and caucuses (see the **"Who Participates?"** feature on p. 373).

Parties in the United States are considered to be ground-up organizations, meaning that they get their power from the members of the mass public who support them at the local level. A century ago, political party bosses controlled the party platform, the party message, and often, through early money to candidates, who held elected office and who won the nomination for president. But changes to politics ranging from the advent of primary elections to the digital revolution more recently have altered many aspects of party politics. As Keli Carender's mobilizing efforts that helped kick off the Tea Party movement show, the internet has decentralized party power, opening up the possibilities for citizen influence. The four resources that political parties use to contest and win elections (time, money, expertise, and organization) no longer belong solely to party organizations. Now citizens can volunteer and give money to the party without ever being contacted by a party official. Online fund-raising allows millions of donors to give small contributions to parties, and social media allow the party to spread its message far and wide online. These changes are beneficial for parties because more people are involved, but at the same time there are more divergent opinions that must be recognized and appeased. No longer can party leaders craft their own message and relay it to the field; they must also listen to what their supporters want.

Questions remain, however, over what influence new groups and parties will have on politics given current U.S. election rules. Will party leaders pay more attention to the preferences of the mass public and party members? Is the two-party system ideal for American politics, or would electoral reforms encourage more parties to form and, hence, provide more choice for voters?

Who Votes in Primaries and Caucuses?

Turnout in 2016 Primaries
Percentage of voting-eligible population

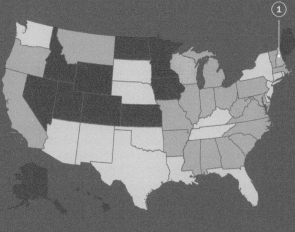

Turnout in 2016 Caucuses
Percentage of voting-eligible population

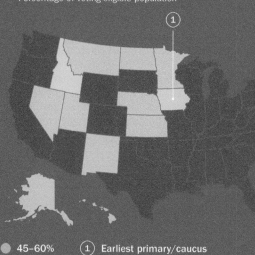

● 1–14%   ● 15–29%   ● 30–44%   ● 45–60%   ① Earliest primary/caucus

SOURCE: Michael P. McDonald, "2016 Presidential Nomination Contest Turnout Rates," United States Election Project, September 21, 2016, www.electproject.org/ (accessed 11/27/17).
NOTES:
Montana: Caucus data are for credentialed Republicans (only party leaders are allowed to vote). Both parties participated in the primary.
South Carolina: Data are for the Democratic primary only. No data are available for Republican primary.
Nevada: Data are for Republican caucus only. No data are available for Democratic caucus.
Alaska, Hawaii, Maine, North Dakota: Data are for Democratic caucuses only. No data are available for Republican caucuses.
Kentucky: Data are for the Democratic primary only. No data are available for the Republican caucus.
Nebraska, Washington: Data are for the Republican primary only. No data are available for the Democratic caucus.
Idaho: Data are for the Democratic caucus only. No data are available for the Republican primary.
Wyoming: Republican caucus was canceled. No data are available.
Colorado: No data are available.

★ WHAT YOU CAN DO ★

Get Involved with Your Preferred Party

☑ Participate in the next primary or caucus in your state. When you register to vote (see p. 329), you may be asked to indicate your party affiliation.

☑ If you're unsure which party best represents your views, visit **www.politicalcompass.org/tests/** to take a test to find out.

☑ Volunteer to help your preferred party with a political campaign by making phone calls, knocking on doors, distributing literature, and otherwise working to get out the vote. You can sign up with the Republican Party at **www.gop.com/get-involved** and with the Democratic Party at **www.democrats.org/volunteer**, and with other parties through their websites.

★ STUDY GUIDE ★

What Are Political Parties?

Define political parties and their functions in politics (pp. 337–40)

A political party is an organization that seeks influence over government by electing its members to office. Although some people are critical of political parties, they are extremely important to the functioning of a democracy because they increase participation in politics, provide a central cue for citizens to cast informed votes, and organize the business of Congress and governing. While the particular parties have changed over time, the United States has had a two-party system since the 1780s. Today, America's two major parties are the Democrats and the Republicans.

Key Terms

political parties (p. 337)

partisanship (p. 337)

two-party system (p. 339)

Practice Quiz

1. A political party is different from an interest group in that a political party
   a) seeks to control the government by nominating candidates and electing its members to office.
   b) is constitutionally exempt from taxation.
   c) is entirely nonprofit.
   d) has a much larger membership.
   e) has a much smaller membership.

2. The congressional election system in the United States is called "first past the post" because
   a) candidates must win both a primary election and a general election before taking office.
   b) seats in the House of Representatives and Senate are allocated to political parties based on their share of the total vote cast in the election.
   c) the candidate with the most votes wins even if she did not win a majority of the popular vote.
   d) a candidate can win an election only if he wins a majority of the popular vote.
   e) more Americans now vote by mail than at their local polling places.

Parties, Voter Mobilization, and Elections

Explain the roles that parties play in elections (pp. 340–44)

Because parties succeed when they win elections, parties have a large role in recruiting candidates, coordinating campaigns, mobilizing voters, and raising money.

Key Terms

nomination (p. 342)

primary election (p. 342)

caucus (political) (p. 342)

micro-targeting (p. 344)

3. The practice of tailoring campaign messages to individuals in small, homogeneous groups is referred to as
   a) indexing.
   b) micro-targeting.
   c) winnowing.
   d) external mobilization.
   e) internal mobilization.

Parties as Organizations

Describe how the major American parties are structured at the national, state, and local levels (pp. 344–48)

Party organizations exist at virtually every level of government in the United States, and they play an important role in structuring electoral competition. At the national level, for example, party organizations assemble conventions every four years that nominate the party's presidential and vice-presidential candidates, draft the party's campaign platform for the presidential race, and approve changes in the rules governing party procedures. Similarly, at the state and local levels, party organizations are active in recruiting candidates to run for office and in conducting voter registration and get-out-the-vote drives.

Key Terms

party organization (p. 344)

national convention (p. 345)

platform (p. 345)

soft money (p. 346)

party machines (p. 347)

patronage (p. 347)

Practice Quiz

4. Which of the following is *not* determined at a party's national convention?
   a) the party's candidate for president
   b) the party's candidate for vice president
   c) the party's campaign platform for the presidential race
   d) the congressional committees party representatives will be assigned to
   e) the rules and regulations governing party procedures

5. Super PACs
   a) were outlawed by the 2002 Bipartisan Campaign Reform Act.
   b) are ineligible for tax-exempt status under Section 527 of the Internal Revenue Code.
   c) are campaign fund-raising organizations legally affiliated with the Democratic National Committee.
   d) are prohibited from running advertisements during election campaigns.
   e) can raise and spend unlimited amounts of money as long as their activities are not coordinated with those of the formal party organizations or the candidates.

6. The strength of traditional party machines depended most heavily on
   a) patronage.
   b) primaries.
   c) hard money.
   d) soft money.
   e) dark money.

Parties in Government

Explain how parties organize legislative business and influence policy (pp. 348–52)

Political parties exert a great deal of influence over public policy, the structure of Congress, and the behavior of presidents. The sharp ideological divisions between Democrats and Republicans in recent years mean that election outcomes matter greatly for the kinds of laws that government enacts. The fact that political parties are broad coalitions of diverse interests means that party leaders must always work to overcome divisions between the different factions within their parties. Many of the most important organizational features of Congress, such as the role of the House Speaker, the committee system, and seniority, also depend on the party system.

Key Terms

policy entrepreneur (p. 350)

majority party (p. 351)

minority party (p. 351)

Practice Quiz

7. By identifying problems and proposing policies that will expand their party's base of support, party leaders can act as
   a) whips.
   b) convention delegates.
   c) patrons.
   d) policy entrepreneurs.
   e) party activists.

8. Which of the following features of the House of Representatives is determined by a vote of the whole membership rather than by decisions within each party?
   a) the assignments of individual members to particular committees.
   b) advancement up the committee ladder.
   c) the ability of individual members to transfer from one committee to another.
   d) the use of the seniority system for determining committee chairs.
   e) selection of the Speaker of the House.

Party Identification

> **Identify the reasons for and sources of party identification (pp. 352–60)**

Party identification refers to the psychological and emotional attachments people have to one of the political parties. In contemporary American politics, a wide variety of group characteristics, including race, ethnicity, gender, religion, class, ideology, region, and age, are associated with an individual's party identification. Party loyalties in the United States are currently in a state of flux, and more than one-third of Americans identify themselves as independents rather than as Democrats or Republicans.

Key Terms

party identification (p. 352)

party activists (p. 352)

gender gap (p. 355)

dealignment (p. 358)

Practice Quiz

9. The decline in partisan attachment in the electorate, the growth in the number of voters identifying as independent, and the rise in so-called split-ticket voting was referred to as
   a) partisan polarization.
   b) independentification.
   c) unalignment.
   d) realignment.
   e) dealignment.

Party Systems

> **Describe how the party system in the United States has changed over time and its main features today (pp. 360–71)**

A nation's party system refers to the organization of the parties within the country, the dominant form of campaigning, the main divisions between the parties, the balance of power between and within party coalitions, the parties' social and institutional bases, and the issues and policies around which party competition is organized. Over the course of American history, changes in political forces and alignments have produced six distinctive party systems. Although third parties have occasionally influenced election outcomes and placed new ideas on the political agenda, numerous factors limit their long-term success and they have rarely been able to win elections at the national level.

Key Terms

electoral realignment (p. 365)

divided government (p. 365)

party polarization (p. 365)

third parties (p. 368)

Practice Quiz

10. Which party was formed in the 1830s in opposition to Andrew Jackson's presidency?
    a) American Independent
    b) Federalist
    c) Jeffersonian Republican
    d) Democratic
    e) Whig

11. The so-called New Deal coalition was severely strained
    a) during the 1860s by conflicts over slavery and southern secession.
    b) during the 1890s by conflicts over the gold standard.
    c) during the 1930s by conflicts over the Great Depression and America's involvement in World War II.
    d) during the 1960s by conflicts over civil rights and the Vietnam War.
    e) during the 1990s by conflicts over abortion and affirmative action.

12. The periodic episodes in American history in which an "old" dominant political party is replaced by a "new" dominant political party are called
    a) constitutional revolutions.
    b) divided governments.
    c) unified governments.
    d) dealignments.
    e) electoral realignments.

13. Voters who prefer a third-party candidate but vote for the major-party candidate whom they regard as the "lesser of two evils" are engaging in
    a) strategic voting.
    b) split-ticket voting.
    c) straight-ticket voting.
    d) ranked choice voting.
    e) rational abstention.

For Further Reading

Aldrich, John H. *Why Parties? A Second Look*. Chicago: University of Chicago Press, 2011.

Bartels, Larry. *Presidential Primaries and the Dynamics of Public Choice*. Princeton, NJ: Princeton University Press, 1988.

Burnham, Walter Dean. *Critical Elections and the Mainsprings of American Politics*. New York: W. W. Norton, 1970.

Cohen, Marty, David Karol, Hans Noel, and John Zaller. *The Party Decides: Presidential Nominations before and after Reform*. Chicago: University of Chicago Press, 2008.

Donovan, Todd, and Shaun Bowler. *Reforming the Republic: Democratic Institutions for the New America*. Englewood Cliffs, NJ: Prentice Hall, 2003.

Green, Donald, Bradley Palmquist, and Eric Schickler. *Partisan Hearts and Minds: Political Parties and the Social Identities of Voters*. New Haven, CT: Yale University Press, 2002.

Maisel, L. Sandy. *Political Parties and Elections: A Very Short Introduction*. New York: Oxford University Press, 2007.

McCarty, Nolan, Keith Poole, and Howard Rosenthal. *Polarized America: The Dance of Ideology and Unequal Riches*. Cambridge, MA: MIT Press, 2006.

Polsby, Nelson W. *The Consequences of Party Reform*. New York: Oxford University Press, 1983.

Redlawsk, David P., Caroline J. Tolbert, and Todd Donovan. *Why Iowa? How Caucuses and Sequential Elections Improve the Presidential Nominating Process*. Chicago: University of Chicago Press, 2011.

Schattschneider, E. E. *The Semisovereign People: A Realist's View of Democracy in America*. New York: Holt, Rinehart and Winston, 1960.

Shefter, Martin. *Political Parties and the State: The American Historical Experience*. Princeton, NJ: Princeton University Press, 1994.

Recommended Websites

D.C.'s Political Report
www.dcpoliticalreport.com

Here you can find almost every organization that identifies itself as a political party, including such obscure groups as the American Beer Drinker's Party and the Scorched Earth Party.

Democratic Party
www.democrats.org

Republican Party
www.GOP.com, www.rnc.org

These are the official websites for the Democrats and Republicans. Compare the platforms of the two main U.S. parties and see whether there's "not a dime's worth of difference" between them.

Green Party
www.gp.org

Libertarian Party
www.lp.org

The Green Party and Libertarian Party are two of the largest and most successful third parties in recent years. Find out what these parties are trying to accomplish.

National Annenberg Election Survey
http://annenbergpublicpolicycenter.org

Individual voters tend to develop psychological ties to one party or another. The National Annenberg Election Survey uses survey data to track party identification by state every two years. Find out if your state has more Democratic or Republican identifiers.

Pew Research Center, Political Polarization
www.pewresearch.org/packages/political-polarization

This Pew Research Center series presents interactive graphics illustrating dramatic shifts in party polarization over time as it explores the current political landscape and the implications of party polarization for the American public.

Campaigns and Elections

WHAT GOVERNMENT DOES AND WHY IT MATTERS Elections are the core of any democracy. In a democratic system like the United States, citizens self-govern by choosing among candidates and electing leaders to represent them in government. The rules for elections affect who runs, how they run, who votes, and who wins.

The presidential election of 2016 was historic in several regards. It was a race between Democrat Hillary Clinton, who was the nation's first female major-party nominee, and Republican Donald Trump, who became the first person to win the presidency who had not previously served in elective office or in the military. Although their share of the electorate varies from one election to another, young people as always played an important role. Brian Bodine of the Texas Young Republican Federation explained his support for candidate Trump: "As the months went by, his vision resonated with me more and more....[His win sent] a powerful message to established politicians, struggling businesses, disenchanted blue-collar workers and tens of millions of people throughout the country. If he can accomplish even half of what he pledged to do during his campaign, it will be huge for the country and he will go down in history as a great President."[1] Jessica Valdes, a college student in Florida and naturalized citizen originally from Cuba, supported Clinton, who she viewed as wanting "to give (immigrants) the opportunity to achieve the American dream" and to make college more affordable.[2] Yet another student, Ethan Aliste, who attends community college in California, expressed frustration with some of his friends who were "apathetic about the political stakes or claimed registering to vote was too difficult."[3] Turnout among young voters remained lower than that of older age groups. Just over 46 percent of 18- to 29-year-olds voted in 2016, compared to 58.7 percent of 30- to 44-year-olds, 66.6 percent of 45- to 64-year-olds, and 70.9 percent of those aged 65 and older.[4] Clearly young people do not find the electoral arena as enticing as do their older counterparts, affecting whose voice gets heard in politics and government.

As a result of their low voter turnout, many young people miss out on one of the most remarkable features of democratic government: every few years, citizens are provided the means with which to change the government and select new leaders. In the United States, tens of thousands of political offices at the local, state, and national levels hold popular elections. Although most Americans do not often vote directly on specific policies and laws, they exert tremendous influence over political outcomes through the regular selection of their leaders. By allowing citizens to hold their elected representatives accountable for their actions, elections, like freedom of speech and a free press, are at the very heart of democracy. Without them, democratic self-government could not survive.

In this chapter, we will learn about how elections work in the United States and how electoral rules and other considerations influence campaign strategy. We will see how election laws, the candidates' campaigns, and voters' choices determined the outcome of the 2016 presidential and congressional elections, and thus determined who represents the American people in government.

CHAPTER GOALS

★ Describe the major rules and procedures of elections in the United States (pp. 381–93)

★ Explain how campaigns are typically conducted (pp. 393–400)

★ Describe how candidates raise the money they need to run (pp. 400–405)

★ Identify the major factors that influence voters' decisions (pp. 406–8)

★ Analyze the strategies, issues, and outcomes of the 2016 and 2018 elections (pp. 409–21)

Elections in America

Describe the major rules and procedures of elections in the United States

In the United States, elections are highly routinized events that occur on fixed dates and are subject to specific rules. National presidential elections take place every four years, on the first Tuesday after the first Monday in November. Congressional elections are held every two years, also on the first Tuesday after the first Monday in November. Congressional elections that do not coincide with a presidential election are often called **midterm elections**. Localities and states can choose when to hold their elections. Most Americans have the opportunity to vote in several elections each year. Voting in elections is the most common form of participation in American politics.

midterm elections congressional elections that do not coincide with a presidential election; also called *off-year elections*

THE BASIC RULES OF THE GAME FOR U.S. ELECTIONS

In the American federal system, the responsibility for running elections is decentralized, resting largely with state and local governments. Elections are administered by state, county, and city election boards that are responsible for establishing and staffing polling places, processing mail-in ballots, and verifying the eligibility of voters. State laws influence who may vote, how they vote, and where they vote. For example, states must choose whether to require photo identification to vote and whether or not to allow their residents to cast a ballot by mail, to vote early at an official polling place, and to register to vote and vote on the same day.

primary elections elections held to select a party's candidate for the general election

Election season begins with **primary elections**, which are held to select each party's candidates for the general election. Primary elections are used in races for offices at the national, state, and often local levels. They are used to select the best candidate to represent the political party in the general election. Thus, primary elections are races where Democrats compete against Democrats and Republicans against Republicans (except in states that have "top two primaries," in which candidates from

Elections are the most important way that Americans participate in politics. Some of the rules of elections have changed over time. (Left) African Americans vote for the first time in Wilcox County, Alabama, after the passage of the Voting Right Act in 1965. (Right) An 18-year-old woman registers to vote in Illinois after the Twenty-Sixth Amendment in 1971 lowered the nationwide voting age from 21 to 18.

all parties run against one another and the top two face each other in the general election; California and Washington State use this method). The winners of primary elections face one another as their parties' nominees in the **general election**, the decisive electoral contest. The winner of the general election is elected to office for a specified term.

The United States is one of the few nations in the world to hold primary elections. In most countries, nominations of candidates are controlled completely by party officials, as they once were in the United States. Primary elections were introduced at the turn of the twentieth century by reformers who hoped to weaken the power of party leaders; the introduction of primary elections for the first time enabled voters, rather than party elites, to pick the candidates to compete in the general election (see Chapter 9). In states with **closed primaries**, only registered members of a political party may vote in a primary election to select that party's candidates. States with **open primaries** allow all registered voters, including independents, to choose which party's primary they will participate in.

WHAT IT TAKES TO WIN—WINNER TAKE ALL

On the surface, the basic idea of how an election works may seem simple: voters select their preferred candidate on the ballot, votes are counted, and the candidate with the most votes wins the election. But there are actually many possible variations in how people vote and how the votes are counted.

While we take this system for granted in the United States, there are three different ways that ballots are counted and aggregated in countries using democratic elections. In some countries, a candidate must receive an absolute majority (50 percent plus 1) of all the votes cast in the relevant district in order to win the election. This type of electoral system is called a **majority system**. Majority systems usually include a provision for a **runoff election** between the two top candidates because if the initial race draws several candidates, there is little chance that any one will receive a majority.

In some other countries, including the United States, candidates for office need not win an absolute majority of the votes cast to win an election. Instead, victory is awarded to the candidate who receives the most votes, regardless of the actual percentage this represents. A candidate receiving 50 percent or even 30 percent of the popular vote can win if no other candidate receives more votes. This type of electoral system is called a **plurality system** and is used in most elections in the United States. The winning candidate needs to win a plurality (the most but not necessarily a majority) of the votes cast in the election. These voting rules are commonly referred to as "winner take all." In the 2016 Republican primaries, for example, Donald Trump was frequently referred to by the media as the winner, but in most states he only won around 35 percent of the vote because there were three or more candidates in the race. Trump also did not win a majority of the popular vote in the general election.

Most advanced democracies use a third type of electoral system, called **proportional representation**. Under proportional rules, competing political parties are awarded legislative seats in rough proportion to the percentage of popular votes that each party wins. A party that wins 30 percent of the popular vote will receive roughly 30 percent of the seats in the parliament or other representative body. Proportional representation benefits smaller groups and third parties, such as the Green Party, Libertarian Party, or even far-right populist parties, because it usually allows a party

general election a regularly scheduled election involving most districts in the nation or state, in which voters select officeholders; in the United States, general elections for national office and most state and local offices are held on the first Tuesday after the first Monday in November in even-numbered years (every four years for presidential elections)

closed primary a primary election in which voters can participate in the nomination of candidates but only of the party in which they are enrolled for a period of time prior to primary day

open primary a primary election in which the voter can wait until the day of the primary to choose which party to enroll in to select candidates for the general election

majority system a type of electoral system in which, to win a seat in the parliament or other representative body, a candidate must receive a majority of all the votes cast in the relevant district

runoff election a "second-round" election in which voters choose between the top two candidates from the first round

plurality system a type of electoral system in which, to win a seat in the parliament or other representative body, a candidate need only receive the most votes in the election, not necessarily a majority of the votes cast

proportional representation a multiple-member district system that allows each political party representation in proportion to its percentage of the total vote to win legislative seats with fewer votes than would be required under a majority or plurality system. A party that wins 10 percent of the national vote might win 10 percent of the parliamentary seats. In the United States, by contrast, a party that wins 10 percent of the vote would probably win no seats in Congress. Because they give small parties little chance of success, plurality and majority systems tend to reduce the number of political parties that can hold power. This is one of the reasons that the United States has only two significant political parties (see Chapter 9 for more on the two-party system in the United States).

THE BALLOT

Before the 1890s voters cast ballots according to political parties. Each party printed its own election ballots, listed only its own candidates for each office, and employed party workers to distribute the ballots at the polls. Because voters had to choose which party's ballot to use, it was very difficult for a voter to cast anything other than a **straight-ticket vote**, selecting candidates from the same political party for all offices on the ballot. The advent of a new, neutral ballot at the turn of the twentieth century brought a significant change to electoral procedure. The new ballot—called the Australian ballot or long-form ballot—was prepared and administered by the government rather than the political parties. Each ballot was identical and included the names of all candidates running for public office. This ballot reform made it possible for voters to make their choices on the merits of the individual candidates, rather than the overall party and to have their choice of candidates be private.

Because all candidates for the same office now appeared on the same ballot, voters were no longer forced to choose straight-ticket voting. This practice gave rise to the phenomenon of split-ticket voting, where voters may, for example, vote for a Democrat for Senate and a Republican for governor. If a voter supports candidates from more than one party in the same election, he is said to be casting a split-ticket vote. Split-ticket voting for national elections is far less common today than it was in the 1970s and 80s; today most people cast straight-ticket ballots or vote for candidates of the same political party for Congress and the president.[5]

In the United States, it is the states and county governments, not the federal government, that run elections and print the voting ballots. Some counties employ

straight-ticket voting selecting candidates from the same political party for all offices on the ballot

Ballots have changed dramatically over the years. In 2000 the configuration of the "butterfly" ballot (left) caused confusion in a key county in the swing state of Florida. This contested election led to the passage of the Help Americans Vote Act, which required states to upgrade their voting procedures. Many increased their use of computerized voting machines (right).

paper ballots, while most now use electronic or computerized voting systems. The controversial presidential election of 2000 led to a closer look at different ballot forms and voting systems used across the 3,000 counties in the United States. In 2000 the margin of victory for Republican George W. Bush over Democrat Al Gore in Florida was so small that the state ordered a recount. Careful examination of the results revealed that the punch card voting machines and butterfly ballot used in Florida had led to many voting and counting errors. The controversy made its way to the Supreme Court, which effectively reversed Florida's recount order, awarding the presidency to Bush. In the wake of the controversial election, Congress adopted the Help Americans Vote Act (HAVA) in 2003, requiring the states to use computerized voter registration databases. Critics of HAVA feared that such systems might be vulnerable to unauthorized use or hacking. In 2016, 21 states experienced intrusion by Russian hackers in their computerized state election systems, although to date there is no evidence that ballots were changed. In Illinois, for example, hackers viewed 300,000 active Illinois voter registration records (names, addresses, birthdates, voting history, etc.) but were unable to modify the data.[6] In the past, computerized voting machines have generally worked well and have significantly updated America's election system, but all computerized systems have vulnerabilities. Protecting state and county election systems from hackers is a new priority for reform.

LEGISLATIVE ELECTIONS AND ELECTORAL DISTRICTS

The boundaries for some elected offices are straightforward: all eligible U.S. citizens 18 years or older may vote for president; all eligible residents of each such state may vote for that state's governor and two U.S. Senators. Other political offices, such as members of the U.S. House of Representatives and state lawmakers, are elected from geographic legislative districts whose boundaries are drawn by state governments—either state legislatures or independent commissions or the courts. The boundaries for congressional and state legislative districts are redrawn every 10 years to reflect population changes, as determined by the U.S. Census. The process of redrawing district boundaries is called **redistricting**. The geographic shape of legislative district boundaries is influenced by several factors, including population size and existing government boundaries such as counties.

redistricting the process of redrawing election districts and redistributing legislative representatives; this happens every 10 years, to reflect shifts in population or in response to legal challenges in existing districts

Federal court decisions have played a major role in how legislative districts are drawn. In the 1962 landmark case *Baker v. Carr*, the Supreme Court ruled that federal courts can intervene on the issue of drawing legislative districts. In a series of decisions in 1963 and 1964, the Court held that legislative districts for Congress and state legislatures must include roughly equal populations so as to accord with the principle of "one person, one vote."[7] Prior to these decisions, many state legislative districts were simply county boundaries, with each county electing one representative, regardless of the population of the county. Drawing districts with roughly equal populations shifted power from rural areas to urban centers, where the population was higher. Today, average U.S. House districts have roughly 700,000 people (up from 30,000 people in 1800). State legislative districts vary from a few thousand people in some states to nearly a million (931,000) in the California Senate. During the 1980s the Supreme Court also declared that legislative districts should, insofar as possible, be contiguous, compact, and consistent with existing political subdivisions.[8]

The original gerrymander was a districting plan attributed to the Massachusetts governor Elbridge Gerry (1744–1814) that had the shape of a salamander. This practice continues today across the country, as seen here in the odd shape of Illinois's 4th Congressional District, which was drawn to create a majority Latino district.

Despite these legal requirements, state lawmakers who are responsible for drawing the district boundaries for Congress and state legislatures regularly seek to influence electoral outcomes to favor one political party over another (or incumbents over challengers). This strategy of drawing legislative districts to favor a political party is called **gerrymandering**. Gerrymandering is named for a nineteenth-century Massachusetts governor, Elbridge Gerry, who was alleged to have designed an odd-shaped district in the shape of a salamander to promote his party's interests.[9]

The principle behind gerrymandering is simple: different populations of voters residing in geographically defined districts can produce different electoral results. For example, by dispersing the members of a political party across two or more districts, state lawmakers can dilute that group's voting power and prevent it from electing a representative in any district. This technique is known as "cracking." Alternatively, by concentrating the members of a party in as few districts as possible, state lawmakers can try to ensure that their opponents will elect as few representatives as possible, a technique called "packing." The controversial but widespread practice of gerrymandering has created many "safe" districts in Congress, and state legislatures where incumbents rarely face a serious challenger. This contributes to the frequency with which members of Congress are re-elected in landslide elections. In 2018, 86 percent of Senators and 93 percent of House members won re-election, but a historic 56 members did not even run for re-election.[10] When candidates do not face serious challengers in elections there is concern that public officials will not represent the interests of the people but will instead make laws that benefit special interests. To address this problem, some states use nonpartisan redistricting boards or commissions where boundaries are drawn not to advantage one party over the other and the partisanship of voters in the district is not a consideration in drawing geographic boundaries.

Partisan gerrymandering—that is, drawing districts to advantage one party over another—has recently become highly controversial. Critics of this practice claim that these techniques go against the principle of "one person, one vote." Others believe that the process of legislative districting is by nature political, and parties strategically drawing districts to gain an advantage is part of the electoral game. They also contend there is no agreed-upon standard for too much partisan tilt in these

gerrymandering the apportionment of voters in districts in such a way as to give unfair advantage to one racial or ethnic group or political party

partisan gerrymandering occurs when politicians from one party intentionally manipulate the boundaries for legislative election districts to disadvantage their political opponents' chance of winning an election and advantage their own political party

majority-minority district an electoral district, such as a congressional district, in which the majority of the constituents belong to racial or ethnic minorities

decisions. This controversy has found its way into the courts. Legislative districts drawn by the Republican state legislature in Pennsylvania, for example, were ruled unconstitutional in 2018 because of gerrymandering. The U.S. Supreme Court took up the matter in *Gill v. Whitford,* in which Democratic voters of a Wisconsin district sued to overturn the allegedly gerrymandered state district map.[11] In June 2018 the Court unanimously agreed to send the case back to the district court, delaying Supreme Court action on partisan gerrymandering for at least another term.

The federal government has often supported congressional districts made up primarily of minority group members, a practice intended to increase the number of African Americans and Latinos elected to public office in accordance with the 1965 Voting Rights Act. Beginning with the 1993 case of *Shaw v. Reno,* however, the Supreme Court has generally opposed efforts to force the creation of **majority-minority districts.**[12] The Court has asserted that districting based exclusively on race/ethnicity is unlawful. However, most majority-minority districts in the United States occur naturally in states and geographic areas with large minority populations. Most African Americans in Congress, for example, are elected from districts with a majority of African American voters.

PRESIDENTIAL ELECTIONS

Presidential elections have special rules because they are the only public office in the U.S. elected by all American citizens (though the president is technically elected by the electoral college, not by direct popular vote of the citizens). Moreover, presidential candidates from the two major parties are officially nominated at the parties' national conventions, following a series of state-by-state primary elections and caucuses to select delegates to the conventions. While primary elections are also used to select candidates in congressional and other types of elections, the national convention delegate system for nominating candidates is unique to presidential elections.

Nominating Presidential Candidates: Primaries and Caucuses How do we pick presidential candidates in the United States? Before the presidential election every four years, the parties must select candidates to represent them in the general election. The process starts with primary elections and caucuses that are held by the major political parties to choose a candidate who will face the nominee from the other major party during the general election. Most states hold primary elections, but about one-third use caucuses instead.

Causes are essentially party business meetings. At the lowest level, precinct caucuses are meetings of registered voters within a local geographic area who are members of the same political party. There are hundreds of precinct caucuses in each state. The purpose of precinct caucuses is to elect delegates to county assemblies. The same process is repeated for county caucuses, which elect members to represent their preferences at the district caucuses, and finally for the state assembly. If members of a local precinct caucus prefer Bernie Sanders for president, for example, the delegates representing that precinct at the county, district, and state caucuses would continue to cast votes for Sanders. Thus citizens attending local caucuses end up electing delegates to statewide conventions, which is where delegates to the national party conventions are chosen. Compared to primary elections, caucuses give party leaders and activists a larger role in selecting candidates for public office.

Candidate strategies to win states holding primaries are very different than for states using caucuses. This is because voter turnout in caucuses tends to be much lower than in primary elections. Television and mass media campaigns typically are used to campaign in primary states, while face-to-face and retail politics are more common in caucus states.

The Iowa caucuses are especially famous, as the first state to select presidential candidates in the calendar year, as is the New Hampshire primary, as the second election in the presidential nomination process. Both the Iowa caucus and New Hampshire primary are characterized by **retail politics**, where presidential candidates spend a great deal of time in the state to meet with voters face to face. Like the general elections, early primaries and caucuses tend to be highly contested, with high levels of mass media coverage and intensive voter mobilization drives.

The primaries and caucuses traditionally begin in January of a presidential election year and end in June, with state elections roughly every two weeks. Iowa and New Hampshire's disproportionate role in picking presidential candidates is due to their being the first states to cast votes in the caucuses and primaries. These early voting states are important because they can help candidates gain momentum by securing national media attention, money in the form of campaign contributions, and higher ratings in public-opinion polls. Candidates that perform well in the Iowa caucuses and New Hampshire primary send signals to voters in states holding later primaries and caucuses that a candidate is viable (can win the nomination) and electable (can win the general election). A candidate who performs better than expected in Iowa and New Hampshire will usually be able to win public support and media coverage for subsequent races. A candidate who fares poorly in these two states may be written off as a loser and drop out of the race. In 2016, Donald Trump and Bernie Sanders beat expectations by both placing second in the Iowa caucuses and first in the New Hampshire primary. These early wins helped solidify Trump's nomination for the Republican party ticket, and indicated that Sanders would be a viable rival of Clinton throughout the Democratic party nomination. Today, the presidential nomination has become "front-loaded," with states vying to increase their political influence by holding their nominating processes earlier in the calendar year in order to receive more attention from candidates and the media.

retail politics a style of campaigning where candidates connect to voters at intimate gatherings and local events

Campaigning for early primaries and caucuses typically involves grassroots politics, with candidates attempting to connect directly with citizens. Here, 2016 presidential candidate Ted Cruz speaks to potential voters at a local diner in Keene, New Hampshire.

FOR CRITICAL ANALYSIS

Is it fair that two relatively small states (in terms of population) such as Iowa and New Hampshire should have such outsize influence in picking presidents?

delegate a representative who votes according to the preferences of his or her constituency

One study found that the change in mass media coverage that candidates receive before and after the Iowa caucuses predicts how well they will do in the New Hampshire primary and in presidential primaries nationwide measured by vote share.[13] This study suggests that it is not winning the Iowa caucuses that matters but doing better than expected by the national media. For example, if Barack Obama had not won the Iowa caucus in 2008, unexpectedly beating presumed Democratic front-runner Hillary Clinton, most commentators believe he would not have gone on to capture the Democratic nomination. Similarly, Republican candidate Donald Trump fared much better than expected by political elites and the mass media by placing second in the Iowa caucuses and first in the New Hampshire primary. In an era of viral digital social media, media coverage of early nominating events is even greater than before and may further increase the importance of states holding early primaries and caucuses.[14]

The result of the presidential primary or caucus determines how each state's **delegates** will vote at their party's national convention. As noted in Chapter 9, the Democratic Party requires that state presidential primaries allocate delegates on the basis of proportional representation; Democratic candidates win delegates in rough proportion to their percentage of the primary vote. The Republican Party does not require proportional representation, but many states now use the system. A few states use the winner-take-all system, by which the candidate with the most votes wins all the party's delegates in that state. When the primaries and caucuses are concluded, it is usually clear which candidates have won their parties' nominations.

Nominating Presidential Candidates: Party Conventions For more than 50 years after America's Founding, presidential nominations were controlled by each party's congressional caucus—all the party's members in the House and the Senate. Critics referred to this process as the "King Caucus" and charged that it did not fairly represent the views of party members throughout the nation. Thus, the King Caucus process was replaced by the system of national party conventions. As it developed over the next century, the convention became the decisive institution in the presidential nominating processes of the two major parties. Composed of delegates from each state who pledge loyalty to different presidential candidates, the convention was a deliberative body in which party elites argued, negotiated, and eventually chose a single candidate to support. The size of a state's delegation depended on the state's population, and each delegate was allowed one vote for the purpose of nominating the party's presidential and vice-presidential candidates. Between the 1830s and World War II, delegates to the national party conventions were selected by a state's party leaders. These individuals were public officials, political activists, and party notables from all regions of the state, representing most major party factions. Over time, reformers viewed the convention as a symbol of rule by party elites and the affluent. Around the turn of the twentieth century, many states adopted direct primary elections to choose presidential candidates, enabling average citizens to have a voice in picking their president. As we saw earlier in this chapter, today the nomination is determined in a series of primary elections and caucuses held in all 50 states during the months prior to the party's national convention. These elections determine how each state's convention delegates will vote. Candidates usually arrive at the convention knowing who has enough delegate support in hand to assure a victory in the first round of balloting. If one candidate does not win a majority of delegates, a second ballot is issued, and delegates can choose to vote for a different candidate.

Superdelegates are party elites who are not bound to the voting results in their state primaries and can vote as they wish. At the 2016 Democratic National Convention, most superdelegates backed Hillary Clinton, giving her a significant advantage over her opponent Bernie Sanders, despite Sanders's strong support among voters. The Republican Party does not use superdelegates, and the practice of reserving delegates for the party elite is increasingly controversial in the Democratic Party.

Even though the party convention no longer controls presidential nominations, it still has a number of important tasks. The convention makes the rules concerning delegate selection and future presidential primary elections. In 1972, for example, the Democratic Party adopted rules requiring convention delegates to be broadly representative of the party's membership in terms of race and gender. Another important task for the convention is the drafting of a **party platform**, a statement of principles and pledges around which the delegates can unite.

Most importantly, the convention is an opportunity for the party to showcase its candidate in anticipation of the upcoming general election. On a national stage with the television cameras rolling, the presidential and vice-presidential nominees deliver acceptance speeches. These speeches are opportunities for the nominees to begin their formal general-election campaigns and make a positive impression on the media. In her speech at the 2016 Democratic National Convention, for example, Hillary Clinton repeated three times the theme of her general-election campaign, "stronger together," insisting that the phrase was not just a slogan for the campaign, but "a guiding principle for the country we've always been and the future we're going to build."

Although the party's nominees for the president and vice president are officially announced at the party conventions, they are actually selected much earlier through caucuses and primary elections. In 2016, Hillary Clinton and Tim Kaine formally accepted the Democratic nomination at the national convention.

Picking Presidents: The Electoral College After they are officially nominated at the party convention, presidential candidates compete in the general election. As noted earlier, the presidential election differs from other elections in an important way: the voters do *not* directly elect the president. In the early history of popular voting, nations often made use of indirect elections. In these elections, voters would choose the members of an intermediate body. These members would, in turn, select public officials. The last vestige of this procedure in the United States is the **electoral college**, the group of electors who formally select the president and vice president of the United States.

When Americans go to the polls on Election Day, they are technically not voting directly for presidential candidates, even though they mark ballots as such; they are instead choosing among slates of electors selected by each party in the state and pledged, if elected, to support that party's presidential candidate. Electors are allocated to each state based on the size of the state's congressional delegation (Senators plus House members). Larger-population states thus have more votes in the electoral college. North Dakota, for example, has 3 votes in the electoral college (based on its 2 senators plus 1 representative), while California has 55 (2 senators plus 53 representatives).

The president of the United States is the winner of the electoral college—the candidate who wins at least 270 of the college's 538 votes—not necessarily the

party platform a party document, written at a national convention, that contains party philosophy, principles, and policy positions

electoral college the presidential electors from each state who meet after the general election to cast ballots for president and vice president candidate with the most votes from the people. This is in part because the electoral college and most elections in the United States are governed by plurality, winner-take-all rules. With only two exceptions, each state awards *all* of its electors to the candidate who receives the most votes in the state.[15] Thus, in 2016, Trump received all 29 of Florida's electoral votes, though he won only 49 percent of the votes in the state.

Since electoral votes are won on a state-by-state basis, it is mathematically possible for a candidate who receives the most popular votes nationwide to fail to carry states whose electoral votes would add up to a majority. Four times in the nation's history has the winner of the electoral college not won the popular vote (the most votes from the people). In 1876, Rutherford B. Hayes was the winner in the electoral college despite receiving fewer popular votes than his rival, Samuel Tilden. In 1888, Grover Cleveland received more popular votes than Benjamin Harrison but fewer electoral votes. The third instance was the election of 2000, discussed earlier, when the lengthy legal battle over recounting votes in Florida ultimately ended with the Supreme Court's decision in *Bush v. Gore* that handed George W. Bush the presidency, even though he had not won the popular vote.[16] Bush won a majority in the electoral college, but Democratic candidate Al Gore won 500,000 more votes from the people nationwide. And the fourth instance was in 2016 when Hillary Clinton won almost 3 million more votes than Donald Trump, but Trump won the majority in the electoral college. Because of these contentious cases where the popular vote winner has lost the election, calls for eliminating the electoral college and using a national popular vote for president are widespread. Public-opinion polls continue to show that most Americans prefer a direct election for the president.[17]

Replacing the electoral college with another system would require a constitutional amendment that most agree would be extremely difficult to pass. However, reform is still possible since the Constitution allows states to choose the method of selecting presidential electors. One example of a recent attempt to reform the electoral college is the National Popular Vote plan, which has been introduced and adopted in a number of state legislatures. Under the proposed rule change, a state's electoral college votes would go to the candidate who won the national popular vote, not the candidate with a plurality of votes in that specific state. States would enter a compact with other states making the same change, which would go into effect when a number of states representing a majority in the electoral college (270 electoral votes) approved it. The reform would effectively bypass the electoral college without the need for an amendment to the U.S. Constitution. As of 2018, 10 states plus Washington, D.C., for a total of 165 electoral college votes, have enacted the bill into law. The bill will take effect when enacted by states possessing an additional 105 electoral votes pass the law.

Another limitation of the electoral college system is that some presidents do not have widespread support. Few democracies in the world elect a president who does not win a majority of the popular vote. Since the Civil War, roughly one-third of American presidents have been elected with only a plurality (less than 50 percent) rather than a majority vote.[18] Notably, Abraham Lincoln won just 40 percent of the popular vote in a four-way election, Bill Clinton was elected with just 43 percent of the popular vote in 1992 and Trump with 46 percent in 2016.[19] This often happens when a third-party candidate receives a significant percentage of votes. If the third-party candidate is more closely aligned ideologically with the losing

Formation of an Exploratory Committee
Formed 18 to 24 months before the election, this committee begins fundraising and bringing the candidate's name to the attention of the media and influential groups.

Fundraising
Presidential candidates must develop fundraising strategies, hire expert fundraisers, and quickly build a substantial "war chest" early on to show they are serious contenders.

Campaigning
Months before the primaries, candidates begin meetings with local leaders, public appearances, ad campaigns, and other strategies.

Primaries and Caucuses
Candidates need to do well in early contests such as Iowa and New Hampshire in order to build momentum and win their party's nomination. Party debates give candidates an opportunity to impress large television audiences.

The Convention
The Democratic and Republican parties hold national conventions in September prior to the November general election. The parties' nominees for president and vice president are officially announced.

The General Election Campaign
In the months leading up to the November election, candidates focus on battleground or swing states as they aim to win at least 270 votes in the electoral college. They run television ads and use new media to reach voters. They must continue to raise money throughout this process.

The Debates
In October, the major-party candidates engage in several televised debates along with one vice-presidential debate.

The General Election
On the Tuesday following the first Monday in November, voters in each state cast ballots. In most states, the candidate who wins the most votes in the state wins all of the state's votes in the electoral college.

The Electoral College
The electors meet in their state capitals in December, and their votes are officially counted in January.

The Inauguration
The president is officially inaugurated on January 20.

FIGURE 10.1

Electing the President: Steps in the Process

major-party candidate, then a majority of voters may not support the winning presidential candidate.

DIRECT-DEMOCRACY ELECTIONS

ballot initiative a proposed law or policy change that is placed on the ballot by citizens or interest groups for a popular vote

Beyond presidential and congressional elections, 24 states also provide for the initiative process. **Ballot initiatives** allow citizens to circulate petitions to place policy change or proposed laws directly on the ballot for a popular vote. If a ballot initiative receives majority support, it becomes law (in Florida, a super majority is required to adopt constitutional initiatives). Controversial issues frequently appear on the ballots of states with the initiative process. In recent years, voters in several states have raised taxes, lowered taxes, prohibited social services for undocumented immigrants, provided universal health care, created nonpartisan redistricting, protected the environment, legalized marijuana, and much more. At the turn of the twentieth century, ballot initiatives were used to grant women the right to vote, prevent child labor, limit the workday to eight hours, and allow voters to elect U.S. senators directly (rather than having them chosen by state legislatures). All 50 states have the legislative **referendum**, in which the state legislature refers certain laws to the voters for a popular vote. Referendum votes are required for changes to state constitutions.

referendum the practice of referring a proposed law passed by a legislature to the vote of the electorate for approval or rejection

The initiative and the referendum, both referred to as *ballot measures,* are examples of direct democracy. They allow voters to govern directly and make laws without intervention by government officials or the political parties. Ballot measure campaigns often involve high spending by proponents and opponents, and mass media campaigns that can rival those of congressional and presidential candidates within a state. The validity of ballot measure results, however, is subject to judicial action. If a court finds that an initiative violates the state or national constitution, it can overturn the result. This happened in 2012 when the federal courts overturned California's Proposition 8, which banned same-sex marriage.[20]

Ballot initiatives not only change policy but also appear to affect political behavior. One study found that states with initiatives on the ballot have higher voter turnout over time. Citizens living in direct-democracy states report more interest in politics and are more likely to discuss politics. Why is this so? Ballot propositions offer voters the opportunity to directly make public policy and change government laws, which may have an "educative" effect on the people.[21] When they have more opportunities to act politically, citizens may learn to participate more and come to believe their participation has meaning.

Elections with policy choices on the ballot provide information to voters in the form of political campaigns and attention in the mass media. Ballot measures concerning controversial policy issues generate their own campaigns with television, newspaper, and digital media, and rely on volunteers for mobilization drives that contact potential voters.[22] Hundreds of initiatives and referenda appear on state election ballots every two years. In 2018 ballot measures included anti–sanctuary city initiatives in Missouri, Oklahoma, and Nevada, raising the minimum wage in Michigan, and paid family and medical leave in Massachusetts. An initiative in Maine in 2016 created a new system of voting called "ranked choice voting," discussed earlier, in which voters choose three candidates to rank in order of preference, rather than choosing only one. The new voting system applies to gubernatorial, congressional, and state legislative elections. Ballot initiatives are increasingly common: more initiatives and referenda have appeared on state ballots over the last 30 years than at any other time in American history, outside of the Progressive era at the turn of the twentieth century. In 2018, 157 ballot measures were certified for the ballot in 37 states.[23]

In addition, ballot measures can help shape both the national agenda and evaluations of candidates.[24] In 2006 coordinated ballot measures raising the minimum wage in multiple states may have influenced voters to focus on the economy, priming voters to cast ballots for Democrats in Congress and for Democratic governors. Placing issues on the ballot as part of an effort to influence candidate elections is an important strategy for political campaigns attempting to shape the political agenda.

Eighteen states also have legal provisions for **recall** elections, which allow voters to remove governors and other state officials from office prior to the expiration of their terms. In California, for example, if 12 percent of those who voted in the last general election sign petitions demanding a special recall election, one must be scheduled by the state board of elections. In 2003 many California voters blamed Governor Gray Davis for the state's $38-billion budget deficit; Davis became only the second governor in American history to be recalled by his state's electorate; the actor Arnold Schwarzenegger was elected in his place. In 2012, Wisconsin governor Scott Walker won a highly visible recall election, keeping his position. Federal officials, such as the president and members of Congress, are not subject to recall.

> **recall** a procedure to allow voters to remove state officials from office before their terms expire by circulating petitions to call a vote

Election Campaigns

> **Explain how campaigns are typically conducted**

A **campaign** is an effort by political candidates (and their political party) to win the backing of donors, elected officials, and voters in their quest for elected office. Campaigns precede every primary and general election. Because of the complexity of the campaign process and the amount of money that candidates must raise, presidential campaigns often begin almost two years before the November election; and congressional campaigns, 12 months in advance of the election. The campaign for any office consists of a number of steps. Candidates often form an exploratory committee consisting of supporters who will help them raise funds and bring their names to the attention of the media, potential donors, and voters. Money from corporations and affluent citizens is an important component of U.S. elections since public funding is limited. **Incumbents**, who already hold elected office, have an advantage over the candidates challenging them. Incumbents usually are already well known and have little difficulty attracting supporters and campaign contributors—unless, of course, they have been subject to damaging publicity while in office.

> **campaign** an effort by political candidates and their supporters to win the backing of donors, political activists, and voters in their quest for political office

> **incumbent** a candidate running for re-election to a position that he or she already holds

CAMPAIGN CONSULTANTS

A formal organization and professional campaign managers are critical for campaign success. For a local campaign, candidates generally need hundreds of volunteers and some paid professionals. State-level campaigns call for thousands of volunteers, and presidential campaigns require tens of thousands of volunteers and paid staff nationwide. Virtually all serious contenders for national and statewide office retain the services of professional campaign consultants. Most candidates need a professional campaign manager, media consultants, pollsters and a data analytics

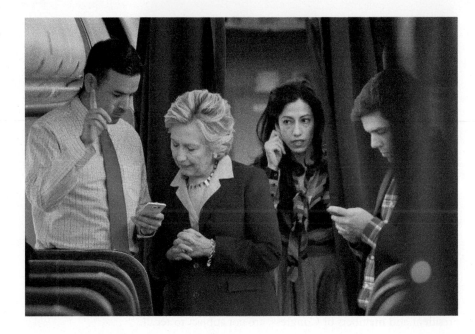

Candidates for national office rely on campaign advisers to guide their campaigns and direct volunteers. Here, Hillary Clinton collaborates with Huma Abedin, her longtime aide and her campaign's vice chairwoman; Brian Fallon (left), her national press secretary; and Nick Merrill (right), her traveling press secretary.

team, financial advisers, a press spokesperson, and staff directors to coordinate the activities of volunteer and paid workers. Consultants offer candidates the expertise necessary to craft appealing campaign messages, conduct accurate opinion polls, produce television and social media ads, organize direct-mail campaigns, open field offices, and leverage valuable information about their constituents from massive digital voter files or from surveys. Most consultants who direct campaigns specialize in politics, corporate advertising and strategic communication, public relations, communications, and computing. They may work with commercial clients in addition to politicians.

FUNDRAISING

Modern national political campaigns are fueled by enormous amounts of money, with more money necessary for highly competitive elections and federal offices. Candidates generally begin raising funds long before they face an election, and many politicians spend more time soliciting donations than engaging in any other campaign activity. Members of Congress spend a significant portion of their time fundraising; the Democratic leadership recommends that 40 to 50 percent of their time be spent on fundraising.[25] Serious fundraising efforts involve appealing to both small and large donors. To have a reasonable chance of winning a seat in the House of Representatives, a candidate may need to raise more than $1 million; in 2014 candidates in the most competitive House races spent $10 million or more. In the 2018 Senate races, candidates in the most competitive elections spent $31–94 million.[26]

Once elected to office, members of Congress find it much easier to raise campaign funds and are thus able to outspend their challengers (see Figure 10.2).[27] Incumbents can out-raise their opponent by significant amounts because most businesses and corporations, interest group contributions, and PAC money donations go to incumbents. These groups seek a voice in government from their investment in

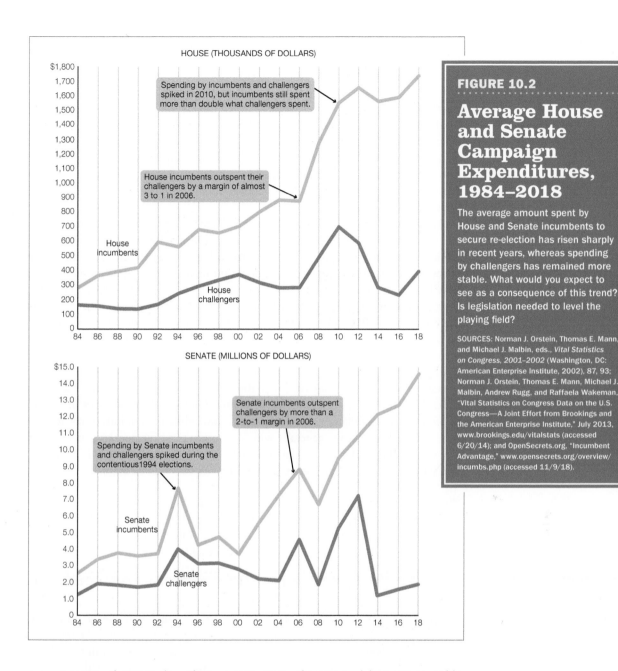

HOUSE (THOUSANDS OF DOLLARS)

Spending by incumbents and challengers spiked in 2010, but incumbents still spent more than double what challengers spent.

House incumbents outspent their challengers by a margin of almost 3 to 1 in 2006.

House incumbents

House challengers

SENATE (MILLIONS OF DOLLARS)

Senate incumbents outspent challengers by more than a 2-to-1 margin in 2006.

Spending by Senate incumbents and challengers spiked during the contentious 1994 elections.

Senate incumbents

Senate challengers

FIGURE 10.2

Average House and Senate Campaign Expenditures, 1984–2018

The average amount spent by House and Senate incumbents to secure re-election has risen sharply in recent years, whereas spending by challengers has remained more stable. What would you expect to see as a consequence of this trend? Is legislation needed to level the playing field?

SOURCES: Norman J. Orstein, Thomas E. Mann, and Michael J. Malbin, eds., *Vital Statistics on Congress, 2001–2002* (Washington, DC: American Enterprise Institute, 2002), 87, 93; Norman J. Orstein, Thomas E. Mann, Michael J. Malbin, Andrew Rugg, and Raffaela Wakeman, "Vital Statistics on Congress Data on the U.S. Congress—A Joint Effort from Brookings and the American Enterprise Institute," July 2013, www.brookings.edu/vitalstats (accessed 6/20/14); and OpenSecrets.org, "Incumbent Advantage," www.opensecrets.org/overview/incumbs.php (accessed 11/9/18).

campaign contributions; thus, these organizations—businesses, labor unions, public interest groups, and others—want to invest in the candidate most likely to win, and incumbents win a large percentage of the time. Members of the majority party in the House and Senate are particularly attractive to donors who want access to those in power.[28] In the "Money and Politics" section later in this chapter, we will discuss further the critical role that money plays in the electoral process.

CAMPAIGN STRATEGY

For those candidates who win the nomination process, the last hurdle is the general election. There are essentially two types of general election campaigns in the

grassroots campaigns political campaigns that operate at the local level, often using face-to-face communication to generate interest and momentum by citizens

United States today: **grassroots campaigns** and mass media campaigns. The first type is the organizationally driven, labor-intensive election. Candidates campaign in local elections and many congressional elections by recruiting large numbers of volunteers to knock on doors, hand out leaflets, and organize rallies. The candidates make public appearances in many places, including university campuses. Generally, local and congressional campaigns rely heavily on grassroots outreach and mobilization designed to make the candidate more visible than her opponent. Statewide campaigns, some congressional races, and the national presidential election fall into the second category: the media-driven, money-intensive electoral campaign. President Obama's campaigns in 2008 and 2012 were notable in combining both types of campaigns.

All campaigns must decide on a strategy: What will their main message be? How will they allocate their resources (television, social media, face-to-face mobilization)? Which voters will they target? The electoral college is one election rule that influences the campaign strategy of presidential candidates by forcing them to campaign heavily in a dozen battleground, or swing, states—those in which Democrats and Republicans are roughly even in the population—while often ignoring the rest of the country. In 2016, 94 percent of the presidential campaign events occurred in 12 battleground states, with the bulk in the populous swing states of Florida, Ohio, Pennsylvania, and Virginia.[29] Presidential candidates in the general election focus not on winning the most individual votes but rather on winning the electoral votes of states that are not considered safely Republican or safely Democratic. Residents of battleground states get smothered with attention from the candidates and media as presidential candidates vie for that state's votes, while the millions of residents of states where Republicans generally win (Texas, Utah) or Democrats generally win (New York, Illinois, California) are often ignored. Without electoral competition in safe states, the needs and concerns of the residents may well be ignored.

The Media Contemporary political campaigns rely on a number of communication tools to reach the voters they want to target for support, including social media, massive computerized databases, and micro-targeting. Digital communication strategy is especially important in mobilizing citizens to vote (see Chapter 7). Donald Trump used Facebook for mobilizing voters more effectively in 2016 than any previous U.S. president. Extensive use of the broadcast media, television in particular, is the hallmark of the modern political campaign. Airing television ads is the primary cost faced by presidential and congressional candidates. Two media techniques that became important in the 1990s are the talk show interview and the town hall meeting. The **town hall meeting** format allows candidates the opportunity to interact with ordinary citizens, thus showing the candidates' concern with the views and needs of the voters. Both talk show appearances and town hall meetings (when televised) allow candidates to deliver their messages to millions of Americans without the input of journalists or commentators who might criticize or question the candidates' assertions.

town hall meeting an informal public meeting in which candidates meet with ordinary citizens; allows candidates to deliver messages without the presence of journalists or commentators

Candidates spend millions of dollars for *paid media* time in the form of television and radio ads, as discussed in the previous section. Many of these ads consist of 15-, 30-, or 60-second spots (advertisements) that deliver a candidate's message to a target audience. One notable example was Lyndon Johnson's 1964 "daisy" ad, which suggested that Johnson's opponent, Barry Goldwater, would lead the United States into nuclear war. Television ads are used to establish candidate name recognition, create a favorable image of the candidate and a negative image of the opponent, link the candidate with desirable groups in the community, and communicate the candidate's stands on selected issues.

Often in the later stages of a campaign, candidates and the political advocacy groups that support them will "go negative," airing ads that criticize their opponents' policy positions, qualifications, or character. Though voters consistently say they reject so-called negative campaigning, political scientist John Geer found that negative campaign ads can benefit voters more than positive ads in some cases.[30] Negative ads are more likely to address important policy differences and provide supporting evidence, while positive ads tend to focus on candidates' personal characteristics. And even when negative ads are misleading or patently false, they are effective in that voters remember more from negative ads than from positive ads, possibly because negative ads are designed to elicit emotional responses, such as fear, anxiety, or anger.

In addition to ads sponsored by the candidates, a growing percentage of campaign ads are sponsored by the political parties and by political advocacy groups seeking to influence the outcome of the election. The 2010 *Citizens United* decision (discussed later in this chapter) allowed corporations, unions, and interest groups to spend unlimited amounts of their own money to advocate for political candidates. Corporations, unions, and interest groups can form Super PACs and run unlimited campaign ads for or against candidates, as long as the organizations are "independent" of the candidate's campaign. When viewers see attack ads against a candidate, it can be difficult to determine who sponsored the ad because a Super PAC with a generic name—Citizens for America, for example—paid for the ad. The effect of unlimited spending on television advertising remains unclear.

Candidates also benefit from *free media*, where the cost of airtime is borne by the media themselves when the media cover the candidates' statements and activities as news. In the 2016 presidential primaries, Donald Trump, largely due to his many controversial statements and tweets, benefited from free media coverage.[31] Critics claimed that the networks' tendency to focus on Trump, rather than provide balanced political coverage of all candidates, occurred because he drew the biggest audience.

Online media is free and has become a major weapon in modern political campaigns as more Americans turn to the internet and social media for news.

While voters often complain about the prevalence of negative advertising in campaigns, research shows that negative ads are more memorable, and sometimes contain more information about candidates' policy differences than positive ads.

APPROVED BY HILLARY CLINTON. PAID FOR BY HILLARY FOR AMERICA

Today, every presidential campaign and most campaigns for Congress and major state offices develop a social media strategy for fundraising, generating interest in the candidate, mobilizing supporters, and getting out the vote. (See Chapters 7 and 8 for a fuller discussion of political candidates' digital strategy.) One reason digital media are so effective at organizing presidential campaigns is cost: the internet enables inexpensive organization of volunteers and offers more opportunities for free advertising, such as on Twitter and YouTube. Online political videos may be more effective than television ads because viewers make a conscious choice to watch them, instead of having their television program interrupted by an unwanted ad.

Debates Public debates were a critical part of the democratic process of ancient Greece, where they were both a vital form of public entertainment and the principal means of what today would be called "voter education." Many successful American politicians, such as Abraham Lincoln and Barack Obama, came to prominence largely because of their skill as debaters. Today, both presidential and vice-presidential candidates hold debates, as do candidates for statewide and even local offices. Debates give voters the opportunity to see how the candidates fare in direct, face-to-face exchanges outside the "campaign bubble" of stage-managed public appearances and carefully scripted speeches. Candidates who can think on their feet may be seen as demonstrating the kind of on-the-spot decision-making that is more like actual governing than anything else they do in a campaign.

Televised presidential debates began with the famous 1960 Kennedy–Nixon clash. Kennedy's strong performance in the debate and the perception of many voters that the youthfully vigorous Kennedy "looked presidential" were major factors in bringing about his victory over the much better-known Richard Nixon. Indeed, candidates can make or break their campaigns with the strength of their debate performances, including high-profile gaffes during the debates and even unconscious gestures and the nuances of their facial expressions. Presidential debates usually involve civilized disagreement about substantive policy issues. The Republican primary debates in 2016, however, uncharacteristically included fierce arguments, harsh character attacks, and personal insults, many of which stemmed from the bombastic style of Donald Trump and his opponents' occasional attempts to match it. When Trump faced off against Democrat Hillary Clinton in the general election, the antagonistic tone continued, and their first televised debate broke viewership records as the most watched in U.S. history.[32]

Micro-Targeting and Polling The media and televised debates allow candidates to communicate their policy goals and promises to voters. While this method is efficient for campaigns, it is also blunt; different voters care about different issues, after all. As we saw in Chapter 9, the idea behind micro-targeting is to send different campaign ads or messages to different demographic groups of voters and potential voters. Suburban "soccer moms," for instance, would be targeted with ads different from those targeting rural "cowboy dads." Republican president George W. Bush is credited with successfully using micro-targeting in the 2000 and 2004 presidential elections. His campaign focused on wedge issues—issues where a voter's preferences diverge from those of his political party. By targeting such voters with messages focusing on Bush's position on the wedge issue, the campaign hoped to convince these voters to cast a ballot for Bush rather than for his opponent.[33]

Micro-targeting became more sophisticated during the 2008 presidential campaign as Democrats built an extensive organization to contact and turn out voters. The Obama campaign made use of an unprecedented volume of survey data, conducting thousands of short- and long-form random sample interviews each week to gauge voters' preferences. Statistical algorithms looked for patterns in these opinions and the many other data points the campaign had assembled for every voter based on massive state voter-registration files, consumer data warehouses, commercial data, and past campaign contacts. The campaign used this mountain of information to generate different, carefully targeted messages for different demographic, regional, and ideological groups to persuade them to turn out and vote for Obama.[34] It was the first time big data had been used to win a presidential election. Because of micro-targeting, millions of Americans heard from other Americans about issues that mattered the most to them. Virtually all campaigns for national and state-wide offices make extensive use of random sample opinion polling (see Chapter 6). To be competitive, a candidate must use random sample public-opinion polls to gauge public support. Polls of likely voters are conducted throughout most political campaigns. These polls provide the basic information that candidates and their staff use to craft campaign messages and strategies—that is, to select issues, assess the candidates' strengths and weaknesses and those of the opposition, and measure voter responses to the campaign.

Once campaigns have identified specific groups of voters, they reach out via face-to-face contacts, phone calls, mailings, and social media to their target audiences for fundraising and voter mobilization. Personal contact has been found to be the most effective at mobilizing voters to turn out but requires field offices and volunteers. Staffs of paid or volunteer telephone callers, using computer-assisted dialing systems and prepared scripts, also place calls to deliver their candidate's message. The targeted groups are often those identified by polls as either uncommitted or weakly committed, but strong supporters of the candidate are also contacted and encouraged to vote and donate money to the campaign. Since 2008 the presidential campaigns of both parties have also placed millions of automated "robocalls" urging voters to support their candidates.

Since John Kennedy and Richard Nixon debated on live television in 1960 (left), presidential debates have been one of the most closely watched events in election campaigns. The intense, bitter debates in 2016 between Donald Trump and Hillary Clinton (right) drew the largest audience for presidential debates in American history.

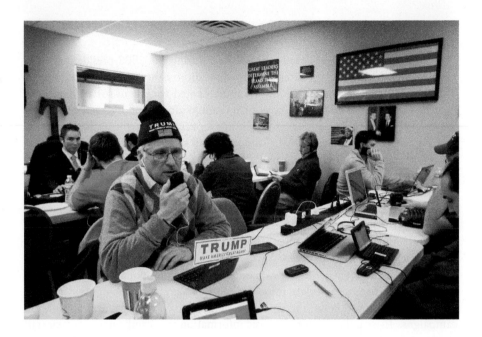

Contemporary presidential campaigns gather large amounts of data on potential voters in order to effectively tailor campaign messages to specific demographics. Armed with these data, volunteers for both the Trump and Clinton campaigns made thousands and thousands of phone calls to urge individuals to support their candidate on Election Day in 2016.

Direct mail is another vehicle for communicating with voters. After obtaining the appropriate mailing lists, candidates usually send pamphlets, letters, and brochures describing themselves and their views to voters believed to be sympathetic. Often, the letters sent to voters are personalized: the recipient is addressed by name in the text, and the letter appears actually to have been signed by the candidate. In addition to its use as a political advertising medium, direct mail is an important source of campaign funds. Computerized mailing lists permit campaign strategists to pinpoint individuals whose interests, background, and activities suggest that they may be potential donors to the campaign.

"People power" remains critical in modern political campaigns. Research suggests that direct mail and robocalls are less effective than in-person and phone contacts.[35] Candidates continue to use the political services of tens of thousands of volunteers, especially for grassroots get-out-the-vote drives. Still, even the recruitment of campaign volunteers has become a job for electronic technology. Employing a technique called "instant organization," paid staff use phone banks to contact not only potential voters but also potential campaign workers in areas targeted by a computer. Volunteer workers are recruited from among those called.

Money and Politics

FOR CRITICAL ANALYSIS

Do American political campaigns help voters make a decision? Or do they produce more confusion than enlightenment?

Describe how candidates raise the money they need to run

Although online fundraising has made raising money for campaigns more convenient, modern campaigns require a great deal of money. A 60-second spot on prime-time network television costs hundreds of thousands of dollars each time it is aired. Polling, social media campaigns, and data analytics can easily reach or exceed the six-figure mark. Campaign consultants can charge substantial fees.

In the nineteenth century, labor-intensive campaigns allowed parties whose chief support came from groups nearer the bottom of the socioeconomic scale to use their numerical superiority as a partial counterweight to the institutional and economic resources more readily available to the opposition. As many as 2.5 million individuals worked on political campaigns during the 1880s.[36] The money-intensive campaign of the modern era, by contrast, has given a major boost to the political fortunes of candidates whose supporters are able to furnish the large sums now needed to compete effectively.[37]

Candidates with the most campaign dollars often win. In 2008 and 2012, Barack Obama raised more than his Republican opponents. In 2016, though Hillary Clinton spent more than her opponent, Donald Trump, she did not win. Nonetheless, the 2016 election shattered previous records. Combined spending by candidates, parties, and interest groups on the congressional and presidential races was $6.5 billion in 2016 compared with $6.2 billion in 2012 and $5.3 billion in 2008. Of the $6.5 billion, $4.3 billion was spent on congressional races and $2.6 billion on the presidential race.[38]

THE COURTS AND CAMPAIGN SPENDING

The United States is rare among democracies in allowing candidates to raise unlimited sums of money to spend on their campaigns with no time restrictions of when the money can be spent. In most democratic countries, publicly financed campaigns are the norm; in such a system, candidates or parties are provided with a set amount of money to spend by the government. In the United States, candidates may raise ever-increasing amounts of money from private individuals, corporations, and interest groups. Reformers have long been concerned about the potential for corruption that exists when candidates are actively soliciting private interests for funding campaigns. In an attempt to limit the influence of money in politics, the federal government has adopted a number of laws to limit and regulate contributions to political campaigns. But two Supreme Court decisions adopted over a 40-year period have dismantled most of these restrictions on money in politics.

The first, *Buckley v. Valeo* (1976), was a landmark Supreme Court case that struck down several provisions of the Federal Election Campaign Act of 1974, including limits on candidate spending, use of personal funds, and independent expenditures. (Independent expenditures are sums of money spent to influence a campaign, but the donating organization is not allowed to coordinate with a candidate's official campaign.) The decision introduced the idea that money (in this case, campaign contributions) counts as "speech" under the First Amendment and that candidates could spend unlimited amounts of their own money on their own campaign. However, the Court left intact the provision of the law that sets limits on individuals' campaign contributions.[39]

In 2010 the U.S. Supreme Court ruled in *Citizens United v. Federal Election Commission* that the government could not restrict independent expenditures by corporations or unions in support of candidates.[40] The Court said restrictions on independent expenditures violated the First Amendment. With this decision, the United States entered a new era of campaign finance in which corporations and unions can spend unlimited sums. Following the *Citizens United* decision, *SpeechNow v. FEC* allowed wealthy individuals and organizations to form

Recently courts have ruled that campaign contributions are a form of speech and, for the most part, cannot be restricted. However, many people worry that these decisions reinforce the influence of the very affluent in American politics at the expense of everyone else.

committees, called Super PACs, which can raise unlimited amounts of money to run advertising for and against candidates so long as their efforts are not coordinated with those of the candidates.[41] These groups can spend unlimited amounts for or against candidates, but they cannot contribute directly to their campaign. This resulted in a significant increase in campaign spending in the 2010 midterm election and unprecedented spending in the 2012 and 2016 presidential elections.

As the Court struggles to balance free speech with preventing political corruption, the sum of these three court decisions tips the scale in favor of speech. Opponents raise concerns that unlimited spending by wealthy donors, corporations, and other organizations could worsen existing corruption in American politics. This concern is bolstered by a number of new studies finding that members of Congress make decisions that represent the interests of wealthy campaign donors, not average voters.[42]

FOR CRITICAL ANALYSIS

What purpose do limits on monetary contributions to political campaigns serve? Should there be limits? How do monetary contributions affect the outcomes of elections?

SOURCES OF CAMPAIGN FUNDS

Although restrictions remain on how money is raised and spent on elections, there is today a great deal of latitude on where money comes from and what it is used for. Campaigns have at least six potential sources of funds.

Individual Donors Politicians spend a great deal of time asking people for money. Money is solicited via direct mail, through the internet, over the phone, and in numerous face-to-face meetings. Under federal law, individuals may donate as much as $2,700 per candidate per election, $5,000 per federal PAC per calendar year,

Campaign Laws in Comparison

Electoral campaigns are more expensive in the United States than in any other country, with only India approaching the same amount of spending.[a] Both the United States and India are large federal countries, so spending is high partly because these countries have multiple levels of government to elect. India's population, however, is approximately four times the U.S. population, so the United States still spends significantly more per voter. Critics have argued that the amount of money in these campaigns creates an unfair advantage for certain candidates, increases the importance and influence of large campaign donors, and potentially undermines the quality of democracy.

Some countries have rules that limit campaign contributions or campaign spending. The United States has extensive rules regarding campaign contributions for candidates, but has few spending limits. The United Kingdom, in contrast, does not limit contributions but has strict rules on campaign spending. Some countries also allow qualified parties and/or candidates free or subsidized access to media, which reduces the need to raise huge sums.

However, a considerable amount of campaign spending is determined by the nature of the election. Norway bans political advertising on television and the radio and campaigns run for two weeks. Even though Norway sets no restrictions on campaign spending or fundraising, roughly 74.4 percent comes from public funds.[b]

	UNITED STATES	INDIA	UNITED KINGDOM	NORWAY
Campaign spending in a recent election (in U.S. dollars)	$6.5 billion (2016)	Roughly $5 billion (2014)	$55.7 million (2017)	Roughly $6.5 million (2013)
Length of national election	Unlimited	2+ weeks*	One month	2 weeks
Are public funds available?	Only for presidential candidates (federal funds)	No	Yes	Yes
Is media access free or subsidized?	No	Yes (for parties, not candidates)	Yes (for parties, not candidates)	No
Bans on television advertising?	No	No	No	Yes
Approximate spending per voter (in U.S. dollars)	$25.97	$6.35	$1.09	$1.76

*While the Electoral Commission of India lists the official campaign as only two weeks, (http://eci.nic.in/eci_main1/the_function.aspx#campaign) with all campaigning required to end the day before the election, polling took 5 weeks in 2014, as different regions of the country were scheduled to go to the polls on different days.

SOURCES: Campaign Laws from The International Institute for Democracy and Electoral Assistance Political Finance Database, www.idea.int (accessed 4/15/18); Christopher Ingraham, "Somebody Just Put a Price Tag on the 2016 Election. It's a Doozy," *Washington Post*, April 14, 2017, www.washingtonpost.com (accessed 4/15/18); The UK Electoral Commission, "Political Party Spending at Previous Elections," 2018, www.electoralcommission.org.uk (accessed 4/15/18); and "International Campaign Finance," CNN World, reporting of the 2013 election campaign contributions from Statistics Norway, www.ssb.no (accessed 4/30/16).

[a]Sruthi Gottipati and Rajesh Kumar Singh. "India Set to Challenge U.S. for Election-Spending Record," Reuters, March 9, 2014, www.reuters.com/article/2014/03/09/us-india-election-spending-idUSBREA280AR20140309#XxEPYA752ikcQRB5.97 (accessed 4/15/18).

[b]Office for Democratic Institutions and Human Rights, "Election Expert Team Report: Norway Parliamentary Elections 11 September 2017," p. 7, December 4, 2017. www.osce.org/odihr/elections/norway/360336?download=true (accessed 4/15/18).

$33,400 per national party committee per calendar year, and $10,000 to state and local committees per calendar year. (There is no limit to the number of candidates or PACs that an individual can give to, however—a result of the Supreme Court's decision in *McCutcheon et al. v. Federal Election Commission*.[43]) Bernie Sanders's 2016 presidential campaign raised an unprecedented $231 million in individual contributions, 58 percent of which was made up of small contributions under $200.[44] The "Who Participates?" feature at the end of this chapter looks at the characteristics of donors to political campaigns.

political action committee (PAC) a private group that raises and distributes funds for use in election campaigns

Political Action Committees Political Action Committees (PACs) are organizations established by corporations, labor unions, or interest or advocacy groups to channel the contributions of their members and employees into political campaigns. Under the terms of the 1971 Federal Election Campaign Act, which governs campaign finance in the United States, PACs are permitted to make larger contributions to any given candidate than individuals are allowed to make. Moreover, allied or related PACs often coordinate their campaign contributions, greatly increasing the amount of money a candidate actually receives from the same interest group. More than 4,600 PACs are registered with the Federal Election Commission, which oversees campaign finance practices in the United States. Nearly two-thirds of all PACs represent corporations, trade associations, and other business and professional groups. Many congressional and party leaders have established PACs, known as "leadership PACs," to provide funding for their political allies.

Soft Money Before 2002 most campaign dollars took the form of "soft money," unregulated contributions to the national parties nominally to assist in party building, voter registration efforts, and voter mobilization rather than for particular campaigns. Federal campaign finance legislation crafted by Senators John McCain and Russell Feingold and enacted in 2002 sought to ban soft money by prohibiting the national parties from receiving contributions from corporations, unions, or individuals and preventing them from directing such funds to their affiliated state parties. However, it did not reduce the overall importance of money in politics. Under federal rules, a national political party committee may make unlimited "independent expenditures" advocating support for its own presidential candidate or defeating an opposing party's candidate as long as these expenditures are not coordinated with the candidate's own campaign.

527 committee (Super PAC) a nonprofit independent political action committee that may raise unlimited sums of money from corporations, unions, and individuals but is not permitted to contribute to or coordinate directly with parties or candidates

501(c)(4) committees (dark money) politically active nonprofits; under federal law, these nonprofits can spend unlimited amounts on political campaigns and not disclose their donors as long as their activities are not coordinated with the candidate campaigns and political activities are not their primary purpose

Outside Spending: Super PACs and Dark Money 527 committees (Super PACs) and 501(c)(4) committees (dark money) are independent groups that are currently not covered by the campaign spending restrictions imposed in 2002 by the Bipartisan Campaign Reform Act, but now raise much of the money used for political campaigns. These groups, named for the sections of the tax code under which they are organized, can raise and spend unlimited amounts as long as their efforts are not coordinated with those of any candidate's campaign. As a result, each presidential campaign raises millions from sympathetic outside groups. A 527 is a group established specifically for the purpose of political advocacy and is required to report to the IRS. A 501(c)(4) is a nonprofit group that also engages in campaign advocacy but may not spend more than half its revenue for political purposes. Unlike a 527, a 501(c)(4) is not required to disclose where it gets its funds or exactly what it does with them—as a result, its funding has earned the name "dark money" and has raised growing concern that the lack of transparency in campaign funding threatens fair elections. Indeed, it has become a common practice for wealthy and corporate donors, as well as foreigners, to route campaign contributions through 501(c)(4)s to avoid the legal limits on contributions through other channels.

Outside spending via Super PACs and dark money (527s and 501(c)(4)s) played an unprecedented role in the 2012 and 2016 presidential races and 2018 midterm elections as outside groups ran extensive television and online ads. Super PACs on both sides relied on very large contributions. A growing concern is that elections in the United States can be bought with big money from corporations and wealthy donors, who will then hold significant influence when that candidate is elected. Political corruption and undue influence from Wall Street were recurring themes among the 2016 presidential candidates. But 2016 was characterized by lopsided campaign spending: Clinton raised and spent double that of the Trump campaign. By October 2016, Clinton had raised nearly $500 million, with an additional $189 million from outside money (Super PACs) compared to just $247 million raised by Trump, with another $59 million from outside money.

Public Funding The Federal Election Campaign Act also provides for public funding of presidential campaigns, as discussed earlier. Candidates running as a major party in the presidential primaries are eligible for public funds by raising at least $5,000 in individual contributions of $250 or less in each of 20 states. Candidates who reach this threshold may apply for federal funds to match, on a dollar-for-dollar basis, all contributions of $250 or less. But by accepting matching funds they agree to spend no more than $48.07 million in their presidential primary campaigns, including limits on using their personal funds and funds from private donors.

Under current law, no candidate is required to accept public funding for either the nominating races or the general presidential election. Candidates who do not accept public funding are not affected by any expenditure limits. In 2008, John McCain accepted public funding for the general election campaign, receiving $84 million, but Barack Obama declined, choosing to rely on his own fundraising prowess. Obama was ultimately able to outspend McCain by a wide margin. Neither major-party candidate accepted public financing in 2012 or 2016. As a result, many observers believed that the 2008 race was the last time that a major-party candidate would forgo personal fundraising in favor of public funding. The United States is unique from most other democratic countries, which rely on public funding for political campaigns to prevent corruption.

Unlimited Spending by Candidates of Their Own Money On the basis of the Supreme Court's 1976 decision in *Buckley v. Valeo*, the right of individuals to spend their *own* money to campaign for office is a constitutionally protected matter of free speech and is not subject to limitation.[45] Thus, extremely wealthy candidates often contribute millions of dollars to their own campaigns; Donald Trump, for example, spent millions of his own money on his 2016 campaign, as did Ross Perot in 1992 and 1996.

How Voters Decide

Identify the major factors that influence voters' decisions

Even if well-funded groups and powerful individuals influence the electoral process, it is the millions of individual decisions on Election Day that ultimately determine electoral outcomes. Sooner or later the choices of voters weigh more heavily than the schemes of campaign advisers or the leverage of interest groups. Three factors influence voters' decisions at the polls: partisan loyalty, issues and policy preferences, and candidate characteristics.

PARTISAN LOYALTY

Most voters feel a certain sense of identification or kinship with the Democratic Party or the Republican Party. This sense of identification is often handed down from parents to children and reinforced by social and cultural ties (see Chapter 9). Partisan identification predisposes voters to favor their party's candidates and oppose those of the other party (see Figure 10.3). At the level of the presidential contest, issues and candidate personalities may become very important. But partisanship is more likely to assert itself in the less visible races, where issues and the candidates are not as well known. State legislative races, for example, are often decided by voters' partisanship.

Once formed, voters' partisan loyalties seldom change. Individuals tend to keep their party affiliations unless some crisis causes them to reexamine the bases of their loyalties and to conclude that they have not given their support to the appropriate party. During these relatively infrequent periods of electoral change, millions of voters can change their party ties. For example, at the beginning of the New Deal era, between 1932 and 1936, millions of former Republicans transferred their allegiance to Franklin Roosevelt and the Democrats.

FIGURE 10.3

The Effect of Party Identification on the Vote, 2016

In 2016 around 90 percent of Democrats and Republicans supported their party's presidential candidate. Should candidates devote their resources to converting voters who identify with the opposition or to winning more support among independents? What factors might make it difficult for candidates to simultaneously pursue both courses of action?

Legend:
- Voted for Trump/Pence (R)
- Voted for Clinton/Kaine (D)
- Voted other

Democrats: 9, 89, 2
Republicans: 90, 7, 3
Independents: 48, 42, 10

ISSUES AND POLICY PREFERENCES

Policy preferences are a second factor influencing voters' choices at the polls. Voters may cast their ballots for the candidate whose position on economic issues they believe to be closest to their own or the candidate who has what they believe to be the best record on foreign policy or immigration. Though candidates for the presidency or Congress are often held accountable for the economy, other policy issues vary in importance depending on the election. In 2008, for example, Obama made ending the war in Iraq and providing national health care for all Americans his core issues. In 2016, Donald Trump made curbing immigration and building a wall along the U.S.–Mexico border a key issue in his campaign for the presidency. If candidates articulate and publicize very different positions on important policy issues, voters are more likely to be able to identify and act on whatever policy preferences they may have. The ability of voters to make choices on the basis of policy preferences is diminished, however, if voters are uninformed or misinformed about the issues and candidates. Voters' issue choices usually involve a mix of their judgments about the past behavior of competing parties and candidates and their hopes and fears about candidates' future behavior. Political scientists call choices that focus on future behavior **prospective voting**, whereas those based on past performance are called **retrospective voting**. Retrospective economic voting, in which voters evaluate candidates on the strength of the economy, has been found to be more important than prospective voting.

To some extent, whether prospective or retrospective evaluation is more important in a particular election depends on the strategies of competing candidates. Candidates always endeavor to define the issues of an election in terms that will serve their interests. Incumbents running during a period of prosperity will seek to take credit for the economy's strength and will define the election as revolving around their record of success. This strategy encourages voters to make retrospective judgments. By contrast, an insurgent running during a period of economic uncertainty will tell voters it is time for a change and ask them to make prospective judgments. Donald Trump focused on change in 2016 and "making America great again" and, through well-crafted media campaigns, was able to define voters' agenda of choices.

The Economy As we identify the strategies and tactics employed by opposing political candidates and parties, we should keep in mind that the best-laid plans of politicians often go awry. Election outcomes are affected by a variety of forces that candidates for office cannot fully control. Among the most important of these forces is the condition of the economy. If voters are satisfied with their economic conditions, they tend to support the party in power, while concern about the economy tends to favor the opposition. Thus, the 2008 financial crisis gave Barack Obama and the Democrats a significant advantage. Over the past quarter-century, the Consumer Confidence Index, calculated by the Conference Board, a business research group, has been a fairly accurate predictor of presidential outcomes. The index is based on surveys asking voters how optimistic they are about the future of the economy. It would appear that a generally rosy view, indicated by a score over 100, bodes well for the party in power. An index score under 100, indicating that voters are pessimistic about the economy's trend, suggests that incumbents should worry about their own job prospects (see Figure 10.4). In recent presidential elections personal economic conditions were an important factor in explaining voter decisions in the election.

prospective voting voting based on the imagined future performance of a candidate or political party

retrospective voting voting based on the past performance of a candidate or political party

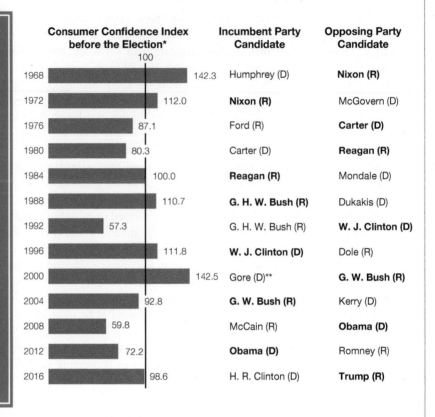

Year	Consumer Confidence Index before the Election*	Incumbent Party Candidate	Opposing Party Candidate
1968	142.3	Humphrey (D)	**Nixon (R)**
1972	112.0	**Nixon (R)**	McGovern (D)
1976	87.1	Ford (R)	**Carter (D)**
1980	80.3	Carter (D)	**Reagan (R)**
1984	100.0	**Reagan (R)**	Mondale (D)
1988	110.7	**G. H. W. Bush (R)**	Dukakis (D)
1992	57.3	G. H. W. Bush (R)	**W. J. Clinton (D)**
1996	111.8	**W. J. Clinton (D)**	Dole (R)
2000	142.5	Gore (D)**	**G. W. Bush (R)**
2004	92.8	**G. W. Bush (R)**	Kerry (D)
2008	59.8	McCain (R)	**Obama (D)**
2012	72.2	**Obama (D)**	Romney (R)
2016	98.6	H. R. Clinton (D)	**Trump (R)**

CANDIDATE CHARACTERISTICS

Candidates' personal attributes can influence voters' decisions. The more important candidate characteristics that affect voters' choices are race, ethnicity, religion, gender, geography, and socio-economic background. In general, voters may be proud to see someone of their gender or of their ethnic, religious, or geographic background in a position of leadership. They may presume that such candidates are likely to have views and perspectives close to their own. This is why politicians often seek to "balance the ticket," by making certain that their party's ticket included members of as many important groups as possible.

Just as candidates' personal characteristics may attract some voters, they may repel others. Some voters are prejudiced against candidates from certain ethnic, racial, or religious groups. And for many years, voters were reluctant to support the candidacies of women, although this is slowly changing. Indeed, the fact that the 2008 Democratic candidate was an African American man and the 2016 Democratic candidate a woman indicates the increasing diversity of candidates for public office.

Voters also pay attention to candidates' personality characteristics, such as "decisiveness," "honesty," and "vigor." In recent years, integrity has become a key election issue. In the 2016 presidential election many Americans questioned the trustworthiness of both Hillary Clinton and Donald Trump. Nonetheless, Trump supporters saw their candidate as unafraid to speak his mind. Clinton supporters, on the other hand, admired her ambition, toughness, and discipline.

FOR CRITICAL ANALYSIS

What factors influence voters' choices? What factors matter most to you when you decide how to cast your ballot?

The 2016 and 2018 Elections

Analyze the strategies, issues, and outcomes of the 2016 and 2018 elections

In 2016, Democrat Hillary Clinton faced Republican Donald Trump in a dramatic and bitterly fought presidential race. Despite media predictions of Democratic success, Trump won a surprise victory with a majority of votes in the electoral college, though Clinton won the popular vote, receiving 2.9 million more votes than Trump. The GOP also retained control of both houses of Congress. In the 2018 midterm elections, Democrats won control of the House of Representatives for the first time since 2010. Republicans, however, were able to expand their majority in the U.S. Senate.

In this section, we analyze how the 2016 and 2018 races unfolded and the major factors that contributed to the results. We conclude by considering what these elections might mean for the future of American government and politics.

THE 2016 PRESIDENTIAL NOMINATION

As we saw in Chapter 9, over the past 50 years America's two major political parties have experienced an ideological realignment that has made both parties more ideologically homogeneous. Today, the Republican Party is the party of conservatives, while the Democratic Party is the political home of those who view themselves as politically liberal. Within each party, though, there are some differences of political perspective. The Democratic camp includes different varieties of liberal opinion ranging from traditional social welfare liberalism, which traces its roots to the New Deal, to left-liberal progressivism, which envisions a substantially expanded role for the federal government. The Republican camp includes many shades of conservative opinion, ranging from business conservatives who support reducing government regulation and taxes, to social conservatives who oppose abortion and same-sex marriage. In 2016 each party's nomination was sharply contested by candidates representing different factions within the two parties as well as by "outsider" populist candidates.

The Democratic Primaries On the Democratic side, Hillary Clinton faced a serious challenge from Vermont senator Bernie Sanders, a left-liberal progressive and self-described Democratic Socialist. Though Clinton's experience, control of the party machinery, support in minority communities, and fund-raising prowess seemed to make her nomination a foregone conclusion, Sanders mounted an aggressive candidacy that gained momentum in large part through mobilizing young voters. Sanders's populist platform—which, to some, contained bold new ideas such as free college education—called for a political revolution to counter political corruption, corporate influence, and inequality. Though outmatched in money and organization, Sanders proved a tenacious competitor. He was widely seen as more trustworthy and "authentic" than Clinton, especially by young Americans. Ultimately, Sanders won 43 percent of the Democratic primary vote and carried 23 states and territories compared to Clinton's 34.

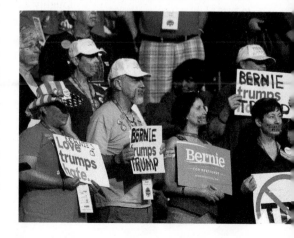

The 2016 Democratic National Convention exposed conflicts within the Democratic Party. While Hillary Clinton was ultimately nominated, Senator Bernie Sanders attracted many supporters.

The Republican Primaries On the Republican side, the 2016 presidential nomination battle also revealed deep divisions within the party. Seventeen candidates competed in the Republican primaries, including "establishment" candidates such as Jeb Bush and Marco Rubio, libertarian Rand Paul, and social conservatives like Ted Cruz. Real estate mogul and reality-TV star Donald Trump was an "outsider" populist candidate, claiming to represent the interests of ordinary Americans rather than elites. His platform included the enactment of harsher immigration laws, the repeal of Obamacare, the appointment of more conservative judges to the federal courts, an end to environmental and other regulations that increased manufacturing costs in the United States, and changes to international economic agreements to better serve American interests. With slogans like "Make America Great Again" and "America First," Trump's stances more closely mirrored those of European nationalist and radical right populist candidates than the views of mainstream conservatives in the United States.

In the early weeks of the Republican race, Donald Trump was not taken seriously as a presidential candidate by most pundits and party leaders. During the Republican primaries, however, Trump campaigned cleverly, making use of huge noisy rallies, social media (especially Twitter and Facebook), and the propensity of the broadcast media to focus on sound bites and sensationalism. At the first televised Republican presidential primary debate in August 2015, Trump sought to drive the agenda by insulting his rivals and making bold, outlandish, and even false political claims that served to make his opponents' carefully developed talking points seem pale and boring. Throughout the course of his campaign, Trump continued to command headlines with controversial and incendiary comments, including his assertions that he would build a wall along the U.S.–Mexico border and place a temporary ban on Muslim immigration to the United States. As Trump's provocative statements dominated the news media for much of the primary season, other Republican candidates dropped from the race.

THE GENERAL ELECTION

With their parties' nominations in hand, Clinton and Trump faced one another in the general election. Clinton seemed to possess several advantages, especially her experience in public office and the Democrats' seeming advantage in the electoral college. Based on voting patterns in recent elections, states with a total of roughly 217 electoral votes were considered "blue states," either safely Democratic or favorable to the Democrats. States with another 32 electoral votes leaned toward the Democrats, potentially putting the Democratic candidate within 21 of the 270 votes needed to win. The Republicans, by contrast, could generally only count on around 191 electoral votes from reliably "red" states.

Democratic candidates, moreover, usually receive support from the most rapidly growing segments of the electorate—namely, minority voters—along with women and young people. Republicans, on the other hand, rely primarily on the votes of white Americans, especially men, who represent a declining fraction of the electorate. As recently as 1976, 89 percent of the electorate was white, while in 2016 only about 69 percent was white non-Hispanic.[46] Clinton also entered

Donald Trump's provocative campaign rhetoric, including a promise to build a wall at the U.S.–Mexico border, helped energize supporters and generate media coverage.

the race with an enormous fund-raising edge over Trump. This ultimately allowed the former secretary of state to spend more than twice as much as her rival.

The Trump campaign was confident it could overcome the Democrats' advantages. Trump believed his appeal to blue-collar white voters, especially men, would make him competitive in Democratic strongholds in Midwestern states. He also calculated that he would increase Republican support among white voters sufficiently to offset the Democratic edge among nonwhite voters. Moreover, Trump hoped that his provocative style would continue to encourage extensive free media coverage, offsetting Clinton's fund-raising advantage and ability to spend freely on paid campaign ads.

Early in the general-election race, several trends emerged. First, Clinton and Trump were the two most disliked presidential nominees in modern American history. Both candidates had far lower favorability ratings than past presidential candidates, and as scandals raged on throughout the general-election campaign, many Americans reported that the election left them feeling "disgusted."[47]

Second, gender played a significant, though ultimately not decisive, role in 2016. Not only did this election see the first female presidential candidate representing a major party, but gender issues were also headline news throughout much of the election. Donald Trump made comments about women that many people deemed offensive and similar past comments of his were unearthed (discussed below). The Trump campaign countered that Clinton's husband had also treated women inappropriately. Nonetheless, by November, exit polls showed a gender gap of 13 percentage points, with 54 percent of women supporting Clinton compared with 41 percent of men.

Third, the media played an outsized role in 2016. Many observers, including President Obama, criticized the media for focusing excessively on Trump, with the goal of making headlines and viral news. In the general election, Trump received more than double Clinton's free media attention.[48] He excelled on the campaign trail, tweeting his daily campaign messages and effectively writing his own headline news. At the same time, some people, including Trump himself, believed that the news media's political bias favored Clinton. Trump began declaring that the mainstream media published and broadcast "fake news" and should be ignored.

And fourth, money mattered—and it didn't. Clinton raised and spent twice as much as the Trump campaign and had superior organization, with more field offices than Trump in almost every state. However, Trump's enormous free media coverage (estimated to be worth as much as $2 billion) more than offset Clinton's financial edge. Almost every morning, a new and ever more outrageous Trump tweet or Facebook post would dominate the news, leaving little space for Clinton to set the media agenda.

Personal Attacks, Scandal, and Campaign Strategy From the earliest years of the Republic, personal attacks have been an important weapon in the arsenals of competing political forces, but the 2016 campaign seemed to many observers to represent a new phase in aggressive mudslinging.

Leading up to the presidential election, Republicans in 2015 launched a congressional investigation of Hillary Clinton's role in the deaths of U.S. embassy officials in Benghazi, Libya, and another investigation of Clinton's use of a private email server to handle official State Department correspondence during her tenure as secretary of state. Democrats charged that the primary purpose of these investigations was to damage Clinton's reputation as the presumptive 2016 Democratic presidential nominee. While the investigations did not lead to formal charges against Clinton, they served to convince many Americans that the former secretary of state was dishonest and untrustworthy. During the course of the race, WikiLeaks made available a large quantity of Democratic National Committee emails and stolen emails from Clinton's campaign director, John Podesta. The emails revealed Clinton said different things in public and private, which, to some, showed she was disconnected from ordinary Americans. Democrats disputed the content of the leaks and suggested that WikiLeaks had been given its information by the Russian government, which had launched hacks as part of an effort to influence the American election—a claim later proved to be true.

For their part, Democratic opposition researchers had begun to develop a dossier on Trump as soon as he emerged as a potential GOP candidate. Democrats focused on his many controversial remarks—such as his comments about women and statements blaming undocumented immigrants for drugs, rape, and other crime—labeling them as offensive and Trump as xenophobic, racist, and sexist. On October 7, 2016, with one month before the November election, the *Washington Post* released a video from 2005 that contained audio of Trump making lewd comments about women and boasting about how his celebrity status gave him license to touch women inappropriately—comments that many people felt condoned sexual assault. The release of the tape was followed by allegations from more than a dozen women who reported having experienced unwanted sexual advances by Trump or who accused the candidate of sexual assault. Most of these accounts concerned events that had taken place some years in the past, and Trump contested their veracity. However, an increasingly unflattering image of Trump emerged. The recording, which Trump could not dispute, created explosive negative media coverage and a sharp drop in his polling numbers. Following these revelations, by mid-October most polls showed Clinton with a strong lead over Trump.

In October 2016 the *Washington Post* released a 2005 video in which Donald Trump was heard bragging that his fame gave him license to touch women inappropriately. After the video was released, multiple women—including Karena Virginia (right)—came forward to accuse Trump of sexual assault or unwanted sexual contact.

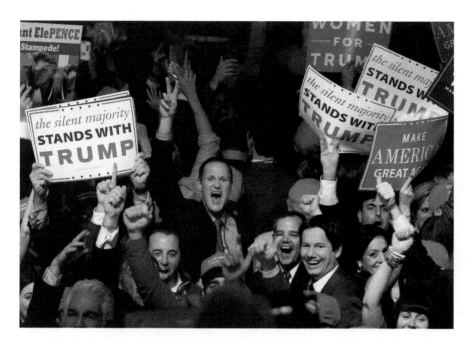

Two groups that were crucial to Trump's success were men and white working-class voters. White working-class voters in particular were unhappy with the economy and turned to Trump to bring factory jobs back to the United States. Here, Trump supporters celebrate his victory on election night.

Eleven days before the election, however, scandal and personal attacks turned back on Clinton. FBI director James Comey sent a letter to Congress saying his agency was investigating 650,000 newly discovered emails that could be pertinent to their earlier investigation of Clinton's use of a private email server during her time as secretary of state. The letter effectively reopened the investigation of Clinton's mishandling of email communications and the possibility of a national security breach, and the Trump campaign capitalized on the announcement as further proof of Clinton's alleged corruption. Two days before the election, Comey announced that the emails in fact did not support new charges; and as Americans went to the polls, most analysts gave Clinton a 70 to 80 percent chance of winning.

UNDERSTANDING THE 2016 RESULTS

In the end, the 2016 presidential election was a historic upset in which the national media and the polling forecasts were mistaken. On election night, the forecasts swung wildly, from the earlier predictions of a safe Clinton victory to reports indicating a Trump victory by wide margins. Many Americans who had been following the opinion polls and media analyses before the election were stunned by Trump's surprise win and by the Republicans' success in retaining control of both houses of Congress.

Trump swept every southern state and nearly all of the Midwest. He won most of the 15 battleground states that were considered competitive in the 2016 election, including the battleground states of Florida and Ohio. Trump's unexpected success in the northern industrial states of Michigan, Wisconsin, and Pennsylvania—all of which had gone to Obama in 2012—ultimately tipped the balance, leading to his victory in the electoral college (see Figure 10.5 and the "Who Are Americans?" feature). For only the fourth time in U.S. history the candidate who won a majority in the electoral college did not win the popular vote. Republicans also retained control of both houses of Congress as well as a majority of the state legislatures.

FOR CRITICAL ANALYSIS

In 2016 more Americans chose Hillary Clinton for president, but Donald Trump won the electoral college and thus the presidency. Should the electoral college system be replaced?

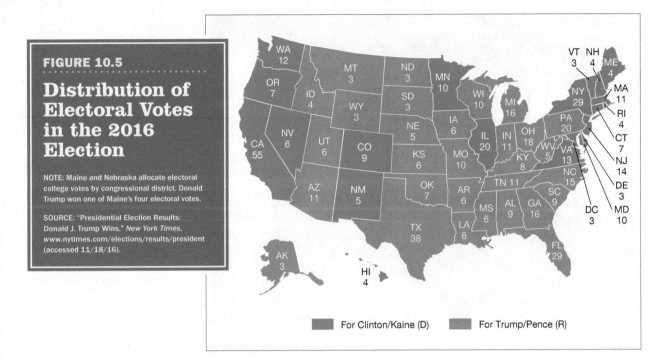

FIGURE 10.5

Distribution of Electoral Votes in the 2016 Election

NOTE: Maine and Nebraska allocate electoral college votes by congressional district. Donald Trump won one of Maine's four electoral votes.

SOURCE: "Presidential Election Results: Donald J. Trump Wins," *New York Times*, www.nytimes.com/elections/results/president (accessed 11/18/16).

■ For Clinton/Kaine (D)   ■ For Trump/Pence (R)

Voters' Choices Trump's popularity among working-class white Americans, especially white men, was crucial to his winning coalition. This demographic group had the most negative views of the economy and was generally opposed to the trade policies favored by the Democrats and mainstream conservatives. They looked to Trump to bring back factory jobs that had moved overseas and saw Clinton as representing Wall Street, government, and—as one Trump ad put it—"more of the same." According to exit polls, Trump won 67 percent of the votes among whites without a college degree compared to just 28 percent for Clinton—a 14 percentage point gain for Trump compared with the Republican vote from this group in 2012. This support enabled Trump to build a winning coalition that also included traditional Republican partisans. He won 90 percent of the votes among registered Republicans, 81 percent of the vote among ideological conservatives, and 81 percent among white born-again or evangelical Christians. The exit polls revealed that Trump also earned more of the votes among men, white voters in general, and voters over age 45. Among respondents who felt the country was "seriously off track," Trump won almost 70 percent of their votes.[49]

Among those who felt the country was generally going in the right direction, Hillary Clinton won 90 percent support. Clinton also received a majority of votes from women, African Americans, Latinos, Asian Americans, and college-educated voters, although blacks and Latinos voted at slightly lower rates for Clinton than they had for Obama four years earlier. She won 71 percent of the votes of minority college graduates and 75 percent among minorities without a college degree. Young voters favored Clinton (55 percent compared to only 37 percent for Trump), but high youth support for third-party candidates (10 percent, up from 3 percent in 2012) meant lower support for the Democratic candidate. In the swing states of

Who Supported Trump in 2016?

Donald Trump won enough votes in the electoral college to defeat Hillary Clinton in the 2016 presidential election, though he lost the popular vote. The map in Figure 10.5, to the left, shows who won each state; there, red clearly dominates. If we adjust the map to show each state in proportion to its population (below), red states still dominate, but there is more blue on the map, reflecting the fairly tight race.

Election Results by State's Population

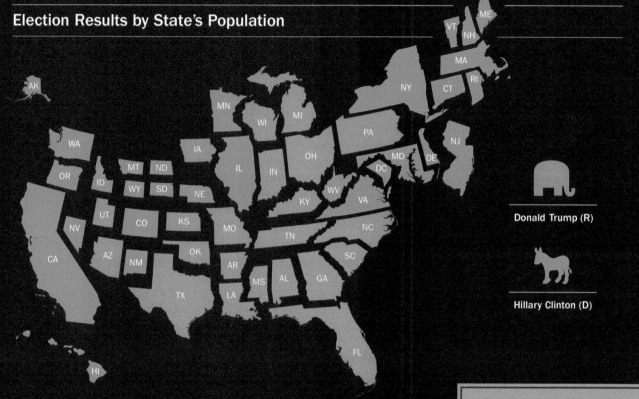

Donald Trump (R)

Hillary Clinton (D)

Votes in Electoral College

55	California
38	Texas
29	Florida
29	New York
20	Illinois
20	Pennsylvania
18	Ohio
16	Michigan
16	Georgia
15	North Carolina
14	New Jersey
13	Virginia
12	Washington
11	Massachusetts
11	Indiana
11	Arizona
11	Tennessee

10	Maryland
10	Minnesota
10	Wisconsin
10	Missouri
09	Colorado
09	Alabama
09	South Carolina
08	Louisiana
08	Kentucky
07	Connecticut
07	Oregon
07	Oklahoma
06	Iowa
06	Nevada
06	Arkansas
06	Kansas
06	Mississippi

06	Utah
05	New Mexico
05	Nebraska
05	West Virginia
04	Hawaii
03 / 01	Maine
04	New Hampshire
04	Rhode Island
04	Idaho
03	Delaware
03	District Of Columbia
03	Vermont
03	Alaska
03	Montana
03	North Dakota
03	South Dakota
03	Wyoming

FOR CRITICAL ANALYSIS

1. Clinton won three of the five states with the largest populations: California, New York, and Illinois. How are these states different from states with smaller populations? What do these differences tell us about the political differences between more densely populated areas (urban areas) and those with lower populations (rural areas)?

2. What do you think causes the differences between urban and rural America? Do you think these differences will continue long into the future?

Michigan, Pennsylvania, and Wisconsin, votes for third-party candidates may have cost Clinton those very close races. To many Americans Trump seemed authentic—a candidate with a bold vision he was not afraid to assert. He seemed to represent Americans who felt disenfranchised and left behind by the social and economic changes buffeting the nation.

Russian Interference Soon after the conclusion of the campaign, Democrats charged that Trump had been helped by Russian hacking of the Democratic National Committee and Clinton emails and "trolls" mounting a social media campaign aimed at defeating Clinton. Multiple reports from the national intelligence agencies confirmed the Russian government did seek to intervene in the 2016 election. For example, in October 2018, Twitter released millions of tweets from some 3,400 accounts linked to a Russian "troll farm" known as the Internet Research Agency run by the Kremlin.[50] At this agency, approximately 1,000 Russian agents, working 24 hours a day, spent more than a million dollars a week creating thousands of social media accounts impersonating Americans. These agents also purchased thousands of political ads promoting their posts on Facebook and other platforms. Russian groups also organized campaign rallies in the United States on behalf of Donald Trump and sought to discredit Hillary Clinton, portraying her as a criminal and untrustworthy.

Analysis of the tweets and Facebook posts emanating from Russian sources suggests that the Russian government's main goal was to sow discord in the United States by promoting an inflammatory discourse on such matters as race, religion, gun control, and police shootings of black men. Often troll farm agents would tweet on both sides of the issue to stir up trouble. Beginning in 2015 when it became clear that Hillary Clinton was the likely Democratic presidential candidate, Russian tweets and social media pages became uniformly hostile to Clinton. And once Trump became the official Republican nominee, Russia's propaganda campaign uniformly condemned Clinton and backed Trump. After the 2016 election, Russian interference returned to the familiar pattern of both praising and condemning Trump's actions in order to promote political conflict in the United States and to undermine popular confidence in the American electoral process. These activities continued during the 2018 election despite efforts by social media platforms to identify and delete fictitious Russian accounts as well as accounts traced to Iran and other foreign governments.

Both Republicans and Democrats recognized the gravity of foreign government interference with American elections. Former House Speaker Paul Ryan (R-Wisc.) said, "The Russians engaged in a sinister and systematic attack on our political system. It was a conspiracy to subvert the process, and take aim at democracy itself," while Senate Democratic Leader Chuck Schumer (D-N.Y.) said investigations had provided "proof that [Russian president] Vladimir Putin directed a campaign to interfere with our elections, with the goal of tipping the outcome."[51]

The fact that the Russians meddled in the 2016 election raised questions about whether the Trump campaign had knowledge of Russian efforts or in any way worked with the Russians. To answer these questions, a probe led by Special Counsel and former FBI director Robert Mueller was launched in May 2017. As a result of the Mueller probe, a half dozen Trump campaign officials have been indicted for various federal crimes and violations of campaign laws. President Trump has vehemently denied allegations of impropriety and denounced the Mueller probe as a "witch hunt" organized by his political foes. At the time of this writing the relationship between the Trump campaign and the Russian government remains unclear.

Immediately after the 2018 national elections, President Trump requested and received the resignation of Attorney General Jeff Sessions and named Sessions's chief of staff, Matthew Whitaker, acting attorney general. Whitaker had frequently criticized the Mueller probe and had suggested restricting its authority by cutting its budget to stop the investigation of the president. If Whitaker follows through on these ideas, the stage will be set for a tumultuous battle between the Trump administration and congressional Democrats.

THE 2018 ELECTION: A BLUE WAVE MEETS A RED WALL

Generally speaking, American national elections follow a pattern, sometimes called the cycle of surge and decline. In a presidential year like 2016, the party that captures the White House also gains seats in the House and Senate as many voters, drawn to the polls by the presidential contest, will also cast their ballots for other members of the president's party. In the ensuing off-year election, however, some of these "extra" seats are almost sure to be lost.

This normal cycle might already have given Democrats reason for confidence as they considered their tactics for 2018. But Democrats had even more reason to be optimistic. In office, President Trump continued his practice of making bombastic, misleading, and divisive statements that seemed inconsistent with the gravitas that Americans expect of a president. This behavior helped undermine Trump's public approval which, throughout his presidency, hovered near historically low levels. Trump, moreover, engaged in a number of bitter struggles with his opponents on such issues as immigration, environmental policy, and judicial appointments as he sought to implement programs based upon the promises presented in his campaign. These struggles helped energize Democrats to redouble their determination to take control of Congress and deal a setback to Trump's agenda.

Unique factors help decide the elections in each state and congressional district, but the 2018 election, more than most midterm contests, revolved around the president. Trump's outsized personality and frequent inflammatory rhetoric inspired anger on the part of some voters and fierce loyalty on the part of others. Between 2016 and 2018, across the nation, hundreds of thousands of Democrats who had never previously been much involved in politics, especially women and young people, entered the political arena to oppose Donald Trump. These Democrats engaged in political activity by signing petitions, attending rallies and protests, and contacting public officials. Republicans were also active, but according to a Kaiser Family Foundation survey, Democrats were almost twice as likely to be politically engaged as Republicans during this period.[52] In March 2018, for example, nearly 800,000 protestors in Washington, D.C., and a million more around the nation demonstrated in favor of gun control measures and against the president's failure to take action on the matter.[53] In addition, an unusually large number of women launched campaigns for national and state office, usually as Democrats. Some were veterans of the Bernie Sanders campaign, but many others were newcomers, drawn to politics as a result of the #MeToo movement. These women saw the GOP, and President Trump in particular, as insufficiently attentive to issues of sexual harassment. This view was underscored by Republican support for Brett Kavanaugh's nomination to the Supreme Court despite allegations of sexual assault made against him.

After Donald Trump's surprising win in 2016, Democrats across the country increased their efforts to organize and press for progress on key issues. In light of recent gun violence and what they saw as Trump administration inaction, in 2018 over 800,000 protestors in Washington, D.C., joined other protests around the country to push for stricter gun control regulation.

This grassroots enthusiasm gave Democratic candidates a sizable financial edge over the Republicans. Of course, major donors contributed hundreds of millions of dollars to both sides, but, in another sign of Democratic grass-roots enthusiasm, a record-shattering 5 million ordinary individuals contributed money to Democratic candidates through ActBlue and other Democratic fund-raising organizations. Sixty percent of these donors were first-time contributors and more than half were women.[54] All these developments led Democrats to hope that a "blue wave" would sweep the GOP from power in both Houses of Congress and even from many state governments as an expression of anger at Donald Trump and his fellow Republicans.

While Democrats mobilized their blue wave, the Republicans also planned their campaigns. The same issues that energized Democrats also invigorated Republicans. In particular, the battle over the Kavanaugh appointment convinced Republicans that they needed to fight hard to retain control of Congress. While Democrats had generally believed the charges against Kavanaugh, Republicans saw them as false and politically motivated. President Trump made the Kavanaugh fight along with such other hot-button issues as Trump's determination to stop a caravan of Central American immigrants from crossing the U.S. border major themes as he crisscrossed the country speaking to large and usually raucous Republican rallies in states and congressional districts that he had carried in 2016 and where incumbents were now threatened. At his rallies and in his tweets, Trump also pointed with pride to the strong economy, the renegotiation of U.S. trade deals, talks with North Korea, and to other achievements that pleased his political base. In 2016 many Republicans had been leery of too close an association with Trump. Now, most embraced him. In 2016, Trump had promised to build a wall on America's southern border to hold back immigrants. That wall was never built, but now President Trump was attempting to build a red wall around GOP strongholds to hold back the Democrats' blue wave.

The Outcome On November 6, 2018, the blue wave crashed against Trump's red wall with mixed results. Democrats won control of the U.S. House of Representatives for the first time since 2010, while Republicans expanded their majority in the Senate. Democrats won seven governor's races gained control of handful of state legislatures, and also won four new state attorney general offices.[55] The voter turnout in 2018 was 49 percent—the highest level since 1966 and a strong increase over recent midterm elections. Youth voter turnout, which is historically very hard to increase, soared by 10 percentage points to 31 percent of voters aged 18–29.

In House races, Democrats gained at least 38 seats for a 233-to-200 majority. (At the time of publication, two races were still undecided.) A number of close races were still to be decided in the days following the election with some recounts possible. Many of these "flipped" seats were in competitive states like Pennsylvania, Michigan, Wisconsin, and Iowa that had been carried by Trump in 2016. Women were critical to Democratic victories. Women made up more than half the 2018 electorate and supported Democratic candidates by margins of as much as 20 percentage points. The new 116th Congress will include over 100 women in the

House and more than 20 in the Senate, an all-time record. Two of the newly elected women, Democrats Rashida Tlaib of Michigan and Ilhan Omar of Minnesota, became the first Muslim women ever elected to the Congress. At the same time, Democrats Sharice Davids of Kansas and Debra Haaland of New Mexico were the first Native American women to win congressional elections.

In Senate races, Democrats began with a disadvantage. Of the 31 seats at stake in 2018, 23 were held by Democrats and only 8 by Republicans. This meant that the GOP had fewer seats to defend. Of the 23 Democratic seats, moreover, several were in "red" states where Republicans had the advantage. By the end of the night, Republicans had defeated Democratic incumbents in three red states—Indiana, Missouri, and North Dakota—while staving off a surprisingly strong Democratic challenge to Senator Ted Cruz in Texas. Two Senate seats previously held by Republicans went to the Democrats in Nevada and Arizona. These outcomes guaranteed GOP control of the Senate with at least 52 seats.

Democrats were generally successful in gubernatorial contests, taking seven seats, including Illinois, Kansas, Michigan, and Wisconsin, from the Republicans. Results in three other states, however, were disappointing to the Democratic Party. In the battleground state of Ohio, Republican Mike DeWine defeated Richard Cordray, former head of the Federal Consumer Financial Protection Bureau. Democrats had also hoped to elect African American governors in Florida and Georgia for the first time with Andrew Gillum and Stacey Abrams. Both had raised large sums of money and drawn tremendous media attention. In closely fought races, however, Gillum and Abrams were defeated. The margins were so close that recounts and court challenges seemed likely, though both candidates eventually conceded. Democrats did achieve a first in a gubernatorial race when Jared Polis won in Colorado to become the nation's first openly gay governor.

Democratic gubernatorial victories in Kansas, Michigan, and Wisconsin were especially important because in these states both houses of the legislature remained in Republican hands. Generally speaking, when one party controls both houses of

After the 2018 elections there will be a record number of female members of Congress, most of them Democrats. Here, Sharice Davids (left) celebrates after ousting Republican Kevin Yoder. With this victory, Davids became Kansas's first openly gay member of Congress and the first Native American woman elected to Congress. (She shares the latter distinction with New Mexico's Deb Haaland, another Native American Democrat elected to Congress in 2018.)

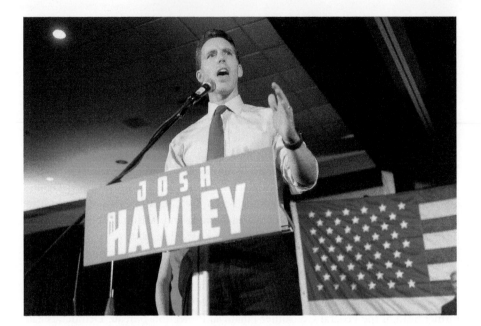

In 2018, Republicans increased their advantage in the Senate, winning critical races against vulnerable Democratic incumbents. Here, Republican Josh Hawley of Missouri celebrates his win over incumbent Democratic senator Claire McCaskill. This race was one of the most watched, and expensive, campaigns nationwide.

the state legislature and the governor's mansion it is likely to engage in partisan gerrymandering, drawing state legislative and congressional district boundaries that favor its own side. When control of a state government is divided, the two parties are often compelled to reach an agreement that protects incumbents on both sides of the aisle. New Democratic governors in Kansas, Michigan, and Wisconsin would likely prevent gerrymandering favorable to the Republicans after the 2020 census. At the same time, the Democrats won full control over state governments in Illinois, Maine, Nevada, and New Mexico and expected to be able to control post-census redistricting in all four states, to their own party's advantage. Overall, Republicans would have solid control of the governments in 21 states, Democrats in 14 states, and in 13 states control would be divided between the two parties.

Ballot Measures In a number of states, voters were also asked to decide ballot measures. Gerrymandering itself was on the ballot in some states. Voters in Colorado, Michigan, and Missouri overwhelmingly supported ballot initiatives creating independent commissions to draw district boundaries. Such commissions were established in Arizona in 2000 and California in 2010 and have long been practiced in Iowa. Supporters of the commission idea oppose gerrymandering— whether partisan or bipartisan—and favor a level electoral playing field.

Voters in Michigan and Missouri approved legalization of medical marijuana; voters in Arkansas and Missouri approved increases in the minimum wage; restrictions on abortion carried in Alabama and West Virginia. In Massachusetts, voters rejected a measure that would have repealed a 2016 law prohibiting discrimination in public places based on gender identity. In North Carolina and Arkansas, citizens approved state constitutional amendments requiring voters to present official photo IDs when casting ballots. A Florida referendum restored voting rights for most ex-felons.

Interestingly, voters in some solidly red states approved progressive ballot initiatives while voters in some solidly blue states approved initiatives generally associated with conservative forces. Voters in deeply red Idaho, Nebraska, and Utah approved referenda expanding Medicaid coverage, while voters in solidly blue Washington turned back a ballot measure imposing a fee on industries responsible for greenhouse gas emissions.[56] These results may appear peculiar, but ballot initiatives carry no party label. Stripped of party as a cue, voters often stray from their expected behavior. Whether, as a result, they become more or less rational is an open question.

THE 2018 ELECTION AND AMERICA'S FUTURE

The mixed results of the 2018 election were something of a disappointment to Democrats who thought they would hand President Trump a more crushing defeat. As Democrats had hoped, however, voter turnout increased sharply in 2018. Some 114 million Americans or 49 percent of the nation's eligible voters participated. In the last midterm election, 2014, voter turnout was only 36 percent. A majority of the nation's voters, according to exit polls, saw the election as a referendum on President Trump's performance in office. Given Trump's low levels of public approval, this should have helped the Democrats and, indeed, many more voters said they cast their votes to oppose Trump than voted to support him. On a national basis, Democrats received a clear majority of the votes cast in congressional elections, approximately 5 million more than were cast for Republicans.

The challenge, though, is that American elections are not national. They are a set of individual state by state and district by district contests. For the most part, the Democrats' blue wave meant that opposition to Trump increased sharply in states and urban and suburban districts where the president was already unpopular, without having much impact upon states and districts in America's small towns and rural areas, where the president drew his strongest support. Trump had spent the weeks before the election bolstering GOP enthusiasm in those areas, building a red wall to hold back the Democrats' blue wave.

Despite losses in the Senate, taking control of the House of Representatives was an important achievement. With control of the House, Democrats are in a position to block Trump's legislative efforts and to conduct investigations into the president's conduct as well as the activities of Trump appointees in the executive branch. Conceivably, House Democrats might work with the president in some areas, but the chance of any significant cooperation seems low. Democrats are unlikely to see any reason to help the president achieve anything for which he might claim credit in 2020. The president will almost certainly feel compelled to rely ever more heavily on executive orders and other forms of executive action that bypass the Congress. With the Senate firmly in Republican hands, Trump will continue to use his appointment powers to reshape the bureaucracy and the courts. The stage seems set for two more years of the partisan struggle that characterizes American democratic politics.

The 2018 elections also made clear that if the Republican Party is to remain competitive nationally it must develop a message that appeals to voters outside its current base of older white men in America's small towns and rural areas. The Democrats have built a coalition that includes women, minorities, and young people. It is no accident that the first Muslim and Native American women elected to Congress along with the first openly gay governor are all Democrats. The Democratic electorate is growing while the GOP's base represents a shrinking percentage of the national electorate and even of the electorate in rapidly growing red states like Texas where as formidable a Republican politician as Senator Ted Cruz had to scramble to avoid defeat. If the Republican Party cannot find a way to expand its constituency, 2018 may be the last time the red wall can hold back the blue wave.

FOR CRITICAL ANALYSIS

Given the factors that went into the 2018 elections, and the results, do you think Democrats or Republicans are more likely to control Congress going forward? Why?

Campaigns and Elections
WHAT DO WE WANT?

As politicians ponder the questions just discussed, individual Americans must think about what the 2016 and 2018 elections might mean for them. Will Republican economic policies create more jobs or leave Americans with less secure economic futures? What will Republican plans to eliminate Obamacare mean for Americans' access to medical services? Will Republican national security policies make us more or less safe? How will America's diverse communities be affected by potential GOP efforts to crack down on illegal immigration? Should we be more critical consumers of opinion polls and the political information circulated on social media?

Another question about elections concerns campaign finance and whose interests will be represented in government. Donald Trump was a unique candidate who was able to generate unprecedented free media coverage, but his campaign still raised and spent hundreds of millions of dollars, much of it collected as small donations from individuals. In a nation as large and diverse as the United States, to be sure, campaign contributors represent many different groups and, often, clashing interests. The fact remains, however, that those with more money will be able to give more and that, once in office, elected officials can be expected to represent the interests of those who supported them. The **"Who Participates?"** feature on the facing page shows who donated to the 2016 presidential campaign.

Two trends in campaign finance may play a role in how elections are funded in the future and, thus, who is elected to office and what policies are enacted. On the one hand, recent decisions by the Supreme Court have overturned federal laws that sought to set some limits on who could give and how much they could give. The laws existed in hopes of limiting the influence of affluent interests over the electoral process and government. But the Court has held that giving money is (in some circumstances) a form of political speech that is essential to the country's democratic process. Will moneyed interests continue to play a large role in the election process? What new laws may be needed to make the rules of the game fair? Will campaign spending increase to the point that the citizens of tomorrow enact reform for public financing or free media for all qualified candidates?

Who Donates to Political Campaigns?

Percentage of Adults Who Donated, 2016*

*To a political campaign, candidate, or organization

Income

11% | <$20k

15% | $20–$40k

21% | $40–$80k

30% | $80k+

Age

17% | 18–25

15% | 26–44

22% | 45–64

30% | 65+

Education**

**Highest level attained

12% | High school or less

23% | Some college

26% | College diploma

37% | Postgraduate degree

SOURCE: Cooperative Congressional Election Study (CCES) 2016. www.electproject.org/2016P (accessed 11/20/17).

★ WHAT YOU CAN DO ★

Your Views on Money in Politics

 Track campaign contributions at the federal level at **www.opensecrets.org** and at the state level at **www.followthemoney.org**.

 If you're concerned about the role of money in politics, voice your opinion on social media platforms such as Facebook and Twitter.

 You can also contact groups working to raise awareness of the role of money in politics, such as Common Cause (**www.commoncause.org**), Move to Amend (**www.movetoamend.org**), or Democracy Is for People (**www.democracyisforpeople.org**).

★ STUDY GUIDE ★

Elections in America

> **Describe the major rules and procedures of elections in the United States (pp. 381–93)**

American elections are subject to many specific rules. The responsibility for administering elections rests mainly with states and counties, and most elections in the United States today use the Australian ballot and operate under a plurality, rather than a majority or proportional representation, system. The United States is also one of the few nations in the world to hold primary elections in addition to a general election. Unlike members of the House of Representatives, who are elected through a direct vote from districts that are redrawn every 10 years, presidents are elected indirectly by the electoral college.

Key Terms

midterm elections (p. 381)

primary elections (p. 381)

general election (p. 382)

closed primary (p. 382)

open primary (p. 382)

majority system (p. 382)

runoff election (p. 382)

plurality system (p. 382)

proportional representation (p. 382)

straight-ticket voting (p. 383)

redistricting (p. 384)

gerrymandering (p. 385)

partisan gerrymandering (p. 385)

majority-minority district (p. 386)

retail politics (p. 387)

delegate (p. 388)

party platform (p. 389)

electoral college (p. 389)

ballot initiative (p. 392)

referendum (p. 392)

recall (p. 393)

Practice Quiz

1. An open primary is a primary election in which
   a) one's vote is made public.
   b) only registered members of the party may vote.
   c) all registered voters, including independents, are able to choose which party primary they will participate in.
   d) only two candidates are allowed to run.
   e) voting is conducted by mail.

2. To win under the plurality system used in most American elections a candidate must receive
   a) more than 50 percent of the popular vote.
   b) more than 50 percent in the runoff election.
   c) more than two-thirds of the popular vote.
   d) more than 75 percent of the popular vote.
   e) more votes than his or her opponents, regardless of the percentage.

3. If a voter supports candidates from more than one party in the same election, she is said to be engaging in
   a) retrospective voting.
   b) two-way voting.
   c) prospective voting.
   d) straight-ticket voting.
   e) split-ticket voting.

4. If a state has 10 members in the U.S. House of Representatives, how many votes in the electoral college does that state have?
   a) 2
   b) 10
   c) 12
   d) 20
   e) The number of votes cannot be determined from this information.

Election Campaigns

Explain how campaigns are typically conducted (pp. 393–400)

In order to successfully run for national or statewide office, candidates must create formal campaign organizations that employ a campaign manager, a media consultant, a pollster, a financial adviser, a press spokesperson, and a staff director. Modern national political campaigns are expensive to run, and candidates must start raising money well before the election. Campaigns must decide on a message and a strategy for communicating that message to the voters they want to target.

Key Terms

campaign (p. 393)

incumbent (p. 393)

grassroots campaigns (p. 396)

town hall meeting (p. 396)

Practice Quiz

5. An incumbent is a candidate who
   a) does not currently hold office.
   b) has the support of both major parties.
   c) already holds the office he or she is running for.
   d) has won his or her party's primary election.
   e) has been nominated at the party convention.

6. In nearly every election since 1980, the average amount of money spent by House incumbents to secure re-election has
   a) been about the same as the average amount of money spent by challengers.
   b) been greater than the average amount of money spent by challengers.
   c) been less than the average amount of money spent by challengers.
   d) been $0 due to federal laws that provide campaign funds for incumbents.
   e) been $1 million due to federal laws that provide campaign funds for incumbents.

Money and Politics

Describe how candidates raise the money they need to run (pp. 400–405)

Modern political campaigns in the United States are enormously expensive, and candidates with the most money often win. Supreme Court cases since the mid-1970s have removed many restrictions on campaign finance. Candidates finance their campaigns with money from individual donors, political action committees, political parties, and the candidates' own bank accounts. Election spending by Super PACs, 527s, 501(c)(4)s, and nonprofit groups must be independent of candidates' campaigns. The Federal Elections Campaign Act also provides for public funding of presidential campaigns.

Key Terms

political action committee (PAC) (p. 404)

527 committee (Super PAC) (p. 404)

501(c)(4) committees (dark money) (p. 404)

Practice Quiz

7. In *Buckley v. Valeo*, the Supreme Court ruled that
   a) PAC donations to campaigns are constitutionally protected.
   b) candidates cannot spend any of their own money to run for office.
   c) the right of individuals to spend their own money to campaign is constitutionally protected.
   d) there is no limit to the number of candidates to whom an individual can contribute.
   e) the Bipartisan Campaign Reform Act is unconstitutional.

8. The main difference between a 527 committee and a 501(c)(4) committee is that
   a) a 527 is not legally required to disclose where it gets its money while a 501(c)(4) is legally required to do so.
   b) a 501(c)(4) is not legally required to disclose where it gets its money while a 527 is legally required to do so.
   c) a 527 can only contribute to one campaign while a 501(c)(4) can contribute to many.
   d) a 501(c)(4) can only contribute to one campaign while a 527 can contribute to many.
   e) a 527 can legally coordinate its spending with a candidate's campaign while a 501(c)(4) cannot.

9. Public funding of presidential campaigns was
   a) outlawed by the Federal Election Campaign Act.
   b) declared unconstitutional by the Supreme Court in *McCutcheon et al. v. Federal Election Commission*.
   c) accepted by both major-party presidential candidates in 2016.
   d) rejected by all four major-party presidential candidates in 2012 and 2016.
   e) limited to only $25 million in 2008, 2012, and 2016.

How Voters Decide

Identify the major factors that influence voters' decisions (pp. 406–8)

Three factors influence the decisions that voters make at the polls: partisan loyalty, issues and policy preferences, and candidate characteristics. Partisan attachments do not change frequently and are an important influence on which candidates a voter chooses to support. Voters may also consider the past and future behavior of competing parties and candidates. A candidate's race, ethnicity, religion, gender, and social background are also weighed by voters on Election Day.

Key Terms

prospective voting (p. 407)
retrospective voting (p. 407)

Practice Quiz

10. When a voter decides which candidate to vote for based on imagined future performance, the voter is engaged in
    a) prospective voting.
    b) retrospective voting.
    c) introspective voting.
    d) straight-ticket voting.
    e) split-ticket voting.

11. The Consumer Confidence Index
    a) measures how business leaders rate the federal government's regulation of the economy during election years.
    b) was a federal government program designed to increase economic growth during the Reagan administration.
    c) has been an inaccurate predictor of presidential outcomes.
    d) has been a fairly accurate predictor of presidential outcomes.
    e) is based on government reports of objective economic indicators.

The 2016 and 2018 Elections

Analyze the strategies, issues, and outcomes of the 2016 and 2018 elections (pp. 409–21)

In a stunning upset, Donald Trump was elected president in 2016 over Hillary Clinton. After the elections, the Democrats regrouped and organized effectively to energize voters and win back the House of Representatives in 2018, though the Republicans retained control of the Senate. Voter turnout was the highest in decades, and the incoming Congress will have more women members than ever.

Practice Quiz

12. In the 2016 general election, voters who said they felt the country and the economy were headed in the wrong direction were most likely to vote for
    a) Hillary Clinton
    b) Donald Trump
    c) Jill Stein
    d) Gary Johnson
    e) Jeb Bush

13. In 2016, Trump and the Republicans received a majority of votes from
    a) whites and Asian Americans
    b) whites, Latinos, and women
    c) whites and men
    d) African Americans and more affluent voters
    e) Latinos and young voters

14. Which of the following states flipped from Democratic to Republican in the 2016 election?
    a) Florida, Ohio, and Pennsylvania
    b) California, New York, and Massachusetts
    c) Texas, Alabama, and Kentucky
    d) West Virginia, Missouri, and Kansas
    e) Oregon, Washington, and Delaware

15. Which of the following statements is true about the 2018 elections?
    a) Youth turnout increased significantly.
    b) Democrats won control of the Senate.
    c) Overall turnout was down from the 2014 midterm elections.
    d) After 2018 most incoming female members of Congress were Republicans.
    e) Republicans raised more money than Democrats in the 2018 election cycle.

16. In 2018 the Republicans won Senate seats in which of the following states:
    a) Arizona and Nevada
    b) Indiana, Missouri, and North Dakota
    c) Ohio and Pennsylvania
    d) California and New York
    e) New Mexico, Virginia, and West Virginia

For Further Reading

Abramson, Paul, John Aldrich, and David Rohde. *Change and Continuity in the 2008 Elections*. Washington, DC: CQ Press, 2009.

Ackerman, Bruce, and Ian Avres. *Voting with Dollars*. New Haven, CT: Yale University Press, 2004.

Browning, Graeme. *Electronic Democracy*. New York: Cyberage, 2002.

Ginsberg, Benjamin, and Martin Shefter. *Politics by Other Means: Institutional Conflict and the Declining Significance of Elections in America*. New York: W. W. Norton, 1999.

Heilemann, John, and Mark Halperin. *Game Change: Obama and the Clintons, McCain and Palin, and the Race of a Lifetime*. New York: Harper, 2010.

Maass, Matthias. *The World Views of the 2008 U.S. Presidential Election*. New York: Palgrave, 2009.

Nelson, Michael, ed. *The Elections of 2008*. Washington, DC: CQ Press, 2009.

Polsby, Nelson, Aaron Wildavsky, and David Hopkins. *Presidential Elections*. 12th ed. New York: Rowman and Littlefield, 2007.

Raymond, Allen, and Ian Spiegelman. *How to Rig an Election*. New York: Simon & Schuster, 2008.

Schier, Steven. *You Call This an Election?* Washington, DC: Georgetown University Press, 2003.

Wayne, Stephen. *Is This Any Way to Run a Democratic Election?* 3rd ed. Washington, DC: CQ Press, 2007.

Recommended Websites

Dark Money
www.opensecrets.org/dark-money/

Dark money refers to politically active organizations whose finances do not need to be disclosed. Learn more about how dark money spending works and its growing influence on election campaigns.

ElectionMail.com
www.electionmail.com

Are you thinking about running for office? Whether you aspire to be student government president or president of the United States, here you can find links to affordable political printing, including political brochures, campaign literature, and campaign signs.

FairVote
www.fairvote.org

FairVote is dedicated to open access to voting, equal representation, and a voice for all Americans. Read about some of their electoral reform proposals such as runoff elections, proportional representation, and alternatives to the electoral college.

Federal Election Commission
www.fec.gov

The Federal Election Commission (FEC) is an independent government agency that was created in 1975 to administer and enforce the Federal Election Campaign Act. At the official FEC website you can read about the rules and regulations that govern the financing of federal elections and other topics of interest.

JibJab.com
www.jibjab.com

This website became famous for its political video clips during the 2004 presidential campaign. For a good laugh check out some of the political jokes or rummage through the video archives to find one of the original Bush or Kerry clips.

National Archives and Records Administration
www.archives.gov/federal-register/electoral-college/index.html

The National Archives and Records Administration's U.S. Electoral College page is a great resource on presidential elections. Find answers to frequently asked questions about our electoral system, read about how electors vote, or try predicting who will win the next presidential election with the electoral college calculator.

OpenSecrets.org
www.opensecrets.org

Campaign funds come from a variety of sources, including individual donors, political action committees, self-contributions, independent spending, parties, and public funding. At this site you can research funding for all federal officials, including your own members of Congress.

Pew Research Center, Election 2016
www.pewresearch.org/topics/2016-election/

Pew Research Center's resource for the 2016 presidential election includes survey data, facts, figures, and public opinion.

Project Vote Smart
www.votesmart.org

Project Vote Smart is a nonpartisan site dedicated to providing citizens with information on political candidates and elected officials. Here you can easily view a candidate's biographical information, position on issues, and voting record so that you can make an informed choice on Election Day.

Voter Information Services
www.vis.org

Voter Information Services is a nonpartisan, nonprofit organization dedicated to helping interested citizens learn about their elected members of Congress. Here you can obtain a congressional report card for your members of Congress and find out where they stand on the issues.

Groups and Interests

WHAT GOVERNMENT DOES AND WHY IT MATTERS After graduating from college with a degree in physics, 25-year-old Ben Brown was working in New York City in the energy business when he read a newspaper article quoting former senator Alan Simpson, Republican of Wyoming. Simpson asserted that young people would lack political power until a young person "could walk into his office and say, 'I'm from the American Association of Young People. We have 30 million members, and we're watching you, Simpson.'"[1] He was referencing the political clout of AARP, formerly known as the American Association of Retired Persons, the largest membership organization in the country. AARP is known for its formidable defense of Social Security, Medicare, and other issues of interest to older Americans.

In contrast, young Americans have not had a broad-based membership group representing their interests, and in 2016 Brown decided to found one. Individuals can join the Association of Young Americans (AYA) for $20 per year and enjoy discounts on transportation and movies, much as AARP members have long enjoyed travel and insurance services. While those benefits are intended to entice members, the real purpose of AYA is to lobby on issues such as preserving net neutrality, stopping

Interest groups have a strong influence in American political life, but whose interests do these groups serve? Young people have struggled to have a strong voice in politics, but Ben Brown founded the Association for Young Americans to change that.

unpaid internships, and protecting student debt repayment programs. The organization has a weekly newsletter and provides a "Contact Our Reps" tool to "make it easy for anyone to connect with their elected officials" and make their preferences known. "We work to insert the voices of the 80 million Americans ages 18 to 35 into everyday politics," the group's website says.[2] Since 2016, AYA has grown to include 8,000 members. AYA demonstrates interest groups in action.

Tens of thousands of organized groups have formed in the United States, ranging from civic associations to huge nationwide organizations such as the National Rifle Association (NRA), whose chief cause is opposition to restrictions on gun ownership, and Common Cause, a public interest group that advocates for such issues as limits on campaign spending. Indeed, Alexis de Tocqueville, a famous nineteenth-century French writer, once wrote that America was "a nation of joiners."[3] This defining characteristic of American political life has not changed since Tocqueville made his observation. Americans are much more likely to join political and social organizations than people in other countries, and America has more organized interest groups than other nations.

Many believe this unique trend has a positive impact on democracy. But others worry that the power and money wielded by these groups can dominate Congress, the president, and the political process—such as elections—at the expense of average citizens and the public welfare. Another concern is that despite the array of interest groups in American politics, not all interests—like those of young people—are represented equally, and the results of competition among various interests are not always consistent with the common good. In this chapter we will examine the nature and consequences of interest group politics in the United States.

Despite the array of interest groups in American politics, however, not all interests—like those of young people—are represented equally, and the results of competition among various interests are not always consistent with the common good. In this chapter we will examine the nature and consequences of interest group politics in the United States.

CHAPTER GOAL

★ **Describe the major types of interest groups and whom they represent (pp. 431–39)**

★ **Describe how interest groups and social groups organize (pp. 439–45)**

★ **Analyze why the number of interest and advocacy groups has grown in recent decades (pp. 446–47)**

★ **Explain how interest groups try to influence government and policy (pp. 447–59)**

Defining Interest Groups

Describe the major types of interest groups and whom they represent

The framers of the U.S. Constitution feared the power that could be wielded by organized interests. Yet they believed that interest groups thrived because of liberty—the freedom that all Americans have to organize and to express their views. In the eighteenth and nineteenth centuries, organized groups were called "associations." The Federalists and the anti-Federalists themselves were organized groups of political elites that had different views about how to create America's new democracy. Both the Federalists and anti-Federalists agreed that if the government were given the power to regulate or in any way to forbid efforts by organized interests to participate in the political process, it would in effect have the power to suppress individual liberty. The solution to this dilemma was presented by James Madison in the *Federalist Papers* no. 10:

> Take in a greater variety of parties and interests [and] you make it less probable that a majority of the whole will have a common motive to invade the rights of other citizens.... [Hence the advantage] enjoyed by a large over a small republic.[4]

According to Madison, a good government encourages multitudes of interests so that no single interest, which he called a "faction," can ever consistently dominate the others. The basic assumption is that all the competing interests will regulate one another, producing balance.[5]

Today, this Madisonian principle is called **pluralism**. Pluralism is a theory of democracy based on the balancing of interests in society via groups that compete for policy outcomes from government. While an interest group may lose on one issue, it may win on the next; and overall the vast majority of society will be represented in government. According to pluralist theory, all interests are and should be free to compete for influence in government and politics. Moreover, according to the theory of pluralism, the outcome of this competition is compromise and moderation since no group is likely to be able to achieve any of its goals without accommodating itself to some of the views of its many competitors.[6]

pluralism the theory that all interests are and should be free to compete for influence in the government; the outcome of this competition is compromise and moderation

Pluralism was long the dominant view of the U.S. political system, but critics point out that not all interests are equally represented in the competition for political influence. Some interests speak with loud voices (i.e., affluent corporations), while others can barely make themselves heard (i.e., Midwest farmers). Pluralism does not guarantee political equality. Indeed, important research indicates that, through group politics, economic elites have considerably more influence than mass-based forces in the American political process.[7] This version of pluralism is called elite pluralism and more accurately describes American politics.

An **interest group** is an organized group of people that lobbies government to change public policy. This definition includes membership organizations (citizen groups) as well as businesses, corporations, universities, labor unions, and other institutions that restrict membership to particular occupational groups or other categories of persons. Individuals form groups to increase the chance that their views will be heard and their interests treated favorably by the government. Interest groups are sometimes negatively referred to as "lobbies," "special interests," or "pressure groups," or positively discussed as advocacy organizations or citizen groups. They are

interest group individuals who organize to influence the government's programs and policies

Although public school teachers are a minority of the total population, they are an influential interest group in many states because they are highly informed and act as a group in support of issues related to their profession, including teachers' salaries.

also sometimes confused with political action committees (PACs), which are groups that raise and distribute money for use in election campaigns (see Chapter 10). Many interest groups create PACs in their name to be the money-giving arm of the interest group. For example, the NRA Political Victory Fund donates money to political candidates and officeholders on behalf of the NRA, which represents the interests of gun owners.

One final distinction is that interest groups are also different from political parties: interest groups tend to focus on the *policies* of government, while parties tend to concern themselves with the *personnel* of government. Parties organize to win elected office and interest groups do not, although interest groups are increasingly engaged in political campaigns and seek to help candidates favorable to their policy goals win elections.

The number of interest groups in the United States is enormous, and millions of Americans are members of one or more groups, at least to the extent of paying dues, attending an occasional meeting, following a group on social media, reading news from the group, or being on an email list. By representing the interests of such large numbers of people and encouraging political participation, organized groups can and do enhance American democracy. Organized groups educate their members on policy issues and mobilize their members for elections and grassroots lobbying efforts using sophisticated social media campaigns, email listservs, letters and news reports, media campaigns, and more. Groups lobby members of Congress and the executive, engage in litigation, and generally represent their members' interests in the political arena. Interest groups also monitor government programs to make certain that these programs do not adversely affect their members. In all these ways, organized interest groups help promote democratic politics.

Because not all interests are represented equally in society, interest group politics works to the advantage of some and the disadvantage of others. Homeless people are generally not organized, for example, while the National Realtors Association spends more than most organized lobbyists in Washington, D.C. Furthermore, not all organized interests are successful. Organized interest groups in the United States are predominantly economic groups. Groups working on behalf of businesses and industry far outweigh citizen groups in terms of their number of registered lobbyists in Washington, D.C., and in state capitals, and of their financial resources to influence government and elections. The ability of economic groups to mobilize resources for elections often results in legislative victories when lawmakers win office and support policies that benefit their industry. Examples of such groups include the oil and gas industries (who supported recent legislation that opened up drilling in Alaska), telecommunication firms (who supported repealing of "net neutrality" regulations), and pharmaceutical companies (who seek fewer government regulations of drugs).

COMMON TYPES OF INTEREST GROUPS

Economic and Corporate Groups Interest groups come in as many shapes and sizes as the interests they represent. The most obvious are groups with a direct economic interest in governmental policy. Businesses and corporations make up over a third of the groups with lobbying offices in Washington, with trade associations comprising another 23 percent and labor unions just 2 percent of groups registered to lobby.[8] Trade associations are generally supported by groups of producers or manufacturers in a particular economic sector, such as the National Association of Manufacturers or the American Fuel and Petrochemical Manufacturers. Trade associations care about broad industrywide issues, and they lobby and make financial contributions to gain access to elected officials. In addition to these broadly representative groups, specific companies may be active in Washington on certain issues that are of particular concern to them. Combined, over 6 in 10 groups lobbying in Washington represent businesses, corporations, or trade associations.

Trade associations spent more than $716 million to lobby the federal government and Congress in 2017.[9] Some of the biggest spenders included the U.S. Chamber of Commerce, Blue Cross Blue Shield, the American Medical Association, Boeing, and The National Association of Realtors.

Which industry spends the most money on lobbying activities? Table 11.1 lists the top spenders from 1998–18. At the top of the list are financial groups, insurance, the real estate industry, and the pharmaceutical industry, which has spent more than $4 billion lobbying lawmakers in an effort to maintain high drug prices and patent protection for their products.[10]

Labor Groups Labor organizations are also active in lobbying government. The AFL-CIO, the United Mine Workers, and the Teamsters all lobby on behalf of organized labor. American Federation of State, County and Municipal Employees (AFSCME), represents 1.4 million members who work in public service and health care. AFSCME represents its members on thousands of issues, from improving unemployment benefits to raising the minimum wage. Labor unions represent all sectors of the American workforce, but according to one study, labor

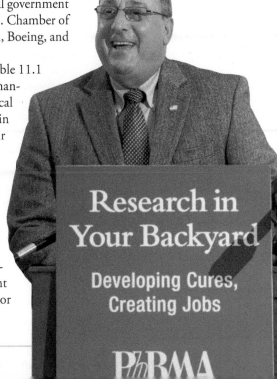

Wealthy corporate interest groups usually find it easier to gain attention from elected officials than do other types of groups. Here, Maine governor Paul LePage speaks at a news conference to discuss a report from the Pharmaceutical Research and Manufacturers of America (PhRMA), an interest group representing biopharmaceutical companies and researchers.

Research in Your Backyard

Developing Cures, Creating Jobs

PhRMA

TABLE 11.1

Top Spending on Lobbying by Industry, 1998–2018

INDUSTRY	TOTAL
Pharmaceuticals and health products	$4,001,631,064
Insurance	$2,751,743,572
Electric utilities	$2,384,646,037
Electronics manufacturing and equipment	$2,265,674,175
Business associations	$2,254,317,913
Oil and gas	$2,130,959,766
Miscellaneous manufacturing and distributing	$1,711,453,232
Education	$1,651,855,249
Hospitals and nursing homes	$1,628,529,677
Securities and investment	$1,571,585,579
Real estate	$1,560,196,283
Telecom services	$1,559,003,678
Health professionals	$1,473,898,726
Civil servants and public officials	$1,455,196,910
Air transport	$1,415,833,437
Health services and HMOs	$1,116,511,600
Defense aerospace	$1,114,819,742
Automotive	$1,109,408,742
Miscellaneous issues	$1,069,275,817
Television, movies, and music	$1,049,917,835

SOURCE: Center for Responsive Politics, "Top Spenders," www.opensecrets.org/lobby/top.php?indexType=i&showYear=a (accessed 11/8/18).

unions represent just 2 percent of the total number of interest groups registered to lobby in Washington.[11]

Despite being out-lobbied, labor unions continue to exercise influence in Washington. Union members vote, and organized labor can have a significant impact upon elections. Few members of Congress can ignore labor's power at the polls.

Professional Associations Professional lobbies such as the American Bar Association and the American Medical Association have been particularly successful at furthering their members' interests in state and federal legislatures. Trial lawyers are represented by the American Association for Justice. Accountants, real estate agents, dentists, teachers and even college faculty have professional associations. Professional associations comprise just over 10 percent of the total number of groups lobbying in Washington. Financial institutions, represented by organizations such as the American Bankers Association and the National Savings and Loan League, although often less visible than other lobbies, also play an important role in shaping legislative policy.

Public Interest Groups Recent years have witnessed the growth of a powerful "public interest" lobby, purporting to represent the general good rather than its own economic interests. **Public interest groups,** or citizen groups, have been most visible in the consumer protection and environmental policy areas, although public interest groups cover a broad range of issues. Citizen groups comprise only 20 percent of the groups with lobbying offices in Washington. However, a survey of 315 lobbyists and government officials, about 98 randomly selected policy issues, found that citizen groups were more likely to be mentioned as being influential in the debate than any other type of group.[12]

The Natural Resources Defense Council, the Sierra Club, the National Civic League, and Common Cause are all examples of public interest groups. Claims to represent *only* the public interest should be viewed with caution, however. It is not uncommon to find decidedly private interests seeking to hide behind the term *public interest*. For example, the benign-sounding Partnership to Protect Consumer Credit is a coalition of credit card companies fighting for less federal regulation of credit abuses, and Project Protect is a coalition of logging interests promoting increased timber cutting.[13] Economic interests often mask their financial interests by organizing public interest groups.

Ideological Groups and Advocacy Groups Closely related to and overlapping with public interest groups are ideological groups, organized in support of a particular political or philosophical perspective. The National Right to Life and the Christian Coalition, for example, promote conservative values and social goals, such as opposing abortion. The National Taxpayers Union and the Center for American Progress campaign to reduce the size of the federal government and cut taxes. Liberal-leaning groups, including EMILY's List and MoveOn.org, support causes such as protecting national parks and public lands, climate action, free college, and increasing the minimum wage.

Public-Sector Groups The perceived need for representation on Capitol Hill has generated a public-sector lobby in the past several years, including the National League of Cities, the National Conference of State Legislatures, and the "research" lobby. The latter group comprises think tanks and universities that have an interest in obtaining government funds for research and support, and it includes such institutions as Harvard University, the Brookings Institution, and the American

public interest groups groups that claim they serve the general good rather than only their own particular interests

Civil Society around the World

Political scientists who study democracy around the world emphasize the important role society may play in shaping democracy. Interest groups are part of what is known more broadly as civil society: organizations outside the state that help people define and promote their interests. These groups play an important role in maintaining the overall health of democracy. Countries with an active civil society may be more likely to transition to democracy. South Africa's strong civil society played a major role in protesting for democracy against a repressive Apartheid regime. In contrast, civil society membership was heavily co-opted by authoritarian regimes in Germany and Japan; rebuilding the independence and engagement of these groups remains a major democratic challenge to this day. So, while de Tocqueville may have been writing about the United States as a "nation of joiners," many other democracies have also joined this club.

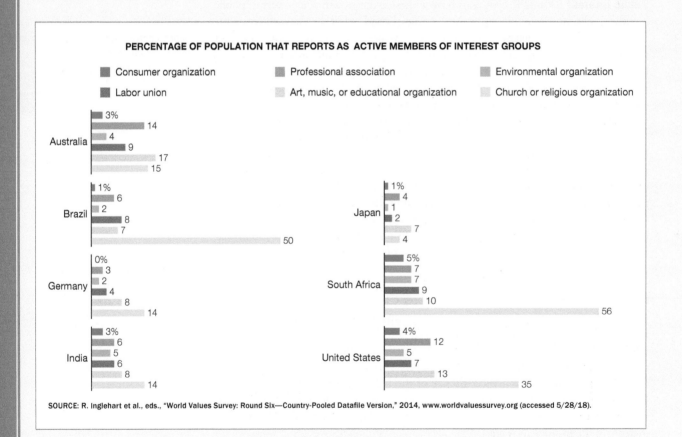

PERCENTAGE OF POPULATION THAT REPORTS AS ACTIVE MEMBERS OF INTEREST GROUPS

- Consumer organization
- Labor union
- Professional association
- Art, music, or educational organization
- Environmental organization
- Church or religious organization

Australia
- Consumer organization: 3%
- Professional association: 14
- Environmental organization: 4
- Labor union: 9
- Art, music, or educational organization: 17
- Church or religious organization: 15

Brazil
- Consumer organization: 1%
- Professional association: 6
- Environmental organization: 2
- Labor union: 8
- Art, music, or educational organization: 7
- Church or religious organization: 50

Germany
- Consumer organization: 0%
- Professional association: 3
- Environmental organization: 2
- Labor union: 4
- Art, music, or educational organization: 8
- Church or religious organization: 14

India
- Consumer organization: 3%
- Professional association: 6
- Environmental organization: 5
- Labor union: 6
- Art, music, or educational organization: 8
- Church or religious organization: 14

Japan
- Consumer organization: 1%
- Professional association: 4
- Environmental organization: 1
- Labor union: 2
- Art, music, or educational organization: 7
- Church or religious organization: 4

South Africa
- Consumer organization: 5%
- Professional association: 7
- Environmental organization: 7
- Labor union: 9
- Art, music, or educational organization: 10
- Church or religious organization: 56

United States
- Consumer organization: 4%
- Professional association: 12
- Environmental organization: 5
- Labor union: 7
- Art, music, or educational organization: 13
- Church or religious organization: 35

SOURCE: R. Inglehart et al., eds., "World Values Survey: Round Six—Country-Pooled Datafile Version," 2014, www.worldvaluessurvey.org (accessed 5/28/18).

Enterprise Institute. These groups represent roughly 10 percent of the total number of groups lobbying in Washington.

WHAT INTERESTS ARE NOT REPRESENTED?

It is difficult to categorize unrepresented interests precisely because they are not organized and are not able to demonstrate to government their identity and their demands. The political scientist David Truman referred to these interests as "potential interest groups."[14] He is undoubtedly correct that at any time, as long as there is freedom, it is possible that any interest shared by a lot of people can develop through "voluntary association" into a genuine interest group that can demand, usually successfully. But the fact remains that many widely shared interests are not represented by organized groups. Two such "potential" groups are the homeless and the poor. Both groups have shared interests in policy outcomes, such as job programs and affordable housing. But the groups lack organization through which to push for government policy to address these concerns.[15]

Unequal Representation and the Upper-Class Bias of Group Membership
Despite the benefits of interest groups in terms of mobilizing and educating the public and the arguments in favor of pluralism, there are concerns about the influence of special interests in the United States. One long-standing critic is E. E. Schattschneider, who argued in a famous quote, "The flaw in the pluralist heaven is that the heavenly chorus sings with a strong upper-class accent."[16] Critics contend that pressure politics, or interest group politics, is heavily skewed in favor of corporate, business, and upper-class groups, leaving those with lower socioeconomic status less able to participate in and influence politics.

Economic and upper class groups were strongly in favor of reducing corporate taxes and funded the election campaigns of Republican lawmakers who shared their interest in major tax reform. In December 2017 President Trump signed the Tax Cuts and Jobs Act that reduced corporate tax rates from 35 to 21 percent and reduced the top individual tax rate from nearly 40 to 37 percent, a sweeping tax cut

In a demonstration of the upper-class bias of interest group politics, Congress worked swiftly to relieve flight delays caused by budget cuts in 2013, prioritizing the issue over concerns about funding for public health and education affecting lower-income Americans.

Though interest groups are prevalent in America, certain people do not have a strong voice in government. These include the homeless, the unemployed, and students. Often these groups have little financial backing to help them organize.

for the wealthiest Americans and corporations. The total cost to taxpayers of the tax bill is $448 billion in lost revenue that will result in cuts to programs that benefit primarily lower and middle-class Americans.[17]

People with higher incomes, more education, and management or professional occupations are much more likely to become members of groups than are those who occupy the lower rungs on the socioeconomic ladder.[18] Well-educated, upper-income business and professional people are more likely to have the time, money, and skills needed to play a role in a group or association or contribute financially to an organized interest. Moreover, for business and professional people, group membership may provide personal contacts, access to information that can help advance their careers, travel perks, discounted insurance, and many other financial benefits. At the same time, of course, corporate entities—businesses and the like—usually have ample resources to form or participate in groups that seek to advance their interests.

The result is that interest group politics in the United States tends to have a pronounced upper-class bias. Certainly, many interest groups and political associations have a working- or lower-class membership—labor organizations or welfare rights organizations, for example—but the vast majority of interest groups and their members are drawn from the middle and upper-middle classes. Even when interest groups take opposing positions on issues and policies, the conflicting positions they take on policy issues usually reflect divisions among upper-income strata rather than conflicts between the upper and lower classes. Many policy issues critical to working and middle class people—quality public education, efficient transportation, affordable housing, safe neighborhoods—are often ignored by government. Thus, when the political system is run by interest groups, democracy will be unequal and many issues important to average Americans will be ignored.

Schattschneider believed that in order to have equal representation in government America needs strong competitive, responsible political parties willing and able to mobilize the lower classes and nonvoters. Interest groups are not enough. That is, citizens from the bottom rungs of the socioeconomic ladder must be organized on the massive scale associated with political parties. Competitive political parties provide alternative choices so that the public can participate in the

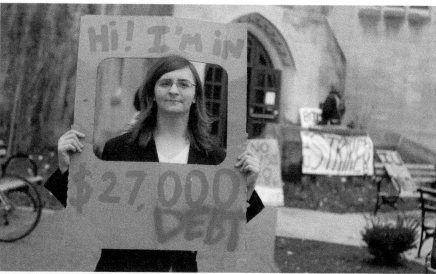

government's decision-making process. Interest groups benefit from a limited scope, When political parties compete with one another to win elections, they have incentives to continually expand political discussion to nonvoting members of the electorate to gain a majority of voters. Finally, political parties must also act "responsibly" by informing the public of salient issues in the public interest, not narrow economic interests.

By representing broad public interests, competitive parties could create more equal representation in American politics. Thus, the relative importance of political parties and interest groups in politics has far-ranging implications for the distribution of political power in the United States and for how well the interests of the lower and middle classes are represented. (It should be noted that some public interest and political advocacy groups discussed later seek to educate and inform the public and bring in new members, much like political parties.)

How Groups Organize

Describe how interest groups and social groups organize

Although interest groups are many and varied, most share certain key organizational components. These include leadership, money, an agency or office, and members.

Leadership and decision-making structure are critical for group organization. For some groups, this structure is very simple. For others, it can be quite elaborate and involve hundreds of local chapters that are melded into a national apparatus. Political entrepreneurs initially organize interest groups with a strong commitment to a particular set of goals. Such entrepreneurs see the formation of a group as a means both for achieving those goals and for enhancing their own influence in the political process. And just as is true in the business world, successful groups often become bureaucratized; a paid professional staff replaces the initial entrepreneurial leadership.

For example, MoveOn.org initially formed in 1998 as an email group by software entrepreneurs Joan Blades and Wes Boyd to push for the censure, but not

MoveOn.org is one of America's most influential liberal interest groups. They have claim millions of members and have 250 local chapters across the country. Here, MoveOn holds a rally encouraging Congress to reject President Trump's nomination of Mike Pompeo for Secretary of State.

impeachment, of President Bill Clinton so the country could "move on" to important national issues. Beginning as a ragtag band of liberal activists, MoveOn.org in the past two decades has raised millions of dollars for candidates and progressive policy issues such as legislation protecting consumers, the environment, immigrants, and the working class. Today MoveOn.org has millions of members and 250 local chapters in every state. It is a significant player in the network of progressive organized interest groups in the United States.

Today every group needs a social media strategy. Both progressive and conservative online advocacy groups often have a streamlined staff structure with little bureaucracy. As computer scientist Clay Shirky explains in *Here Comes Everybody*, the internet has given rise to a proliferation of online organizations without formal organizing structures.[19] An example is Wikipedia, whose content is provided by volunteers from around the world. But the real impact of the digital media revolution is the advent of new forms of organization. Leadership remains a priority for online organizations. Entrepreneurship and leadership are important for all interest groups but especially so for those with little staff and formal organization as the leader holds the organization together.

The second key organizational component of interest groups is a financial structure capable of sustaining the organization and funding the group's activities. Because the cost of maintaining groups with a significant online presence is lower than for traditional lobbying groups, more and varied types of organized interests have been able to form and succeed. These groups often raise money via targeted email campaigns for voluntary contributions rather than regular annual membership dues. Many groups also sell some ancillary services to members, such as insurance and vacation tours. In addition, many groups establish an agency that actually carries out the group's tasks, which may be a research organization, a public relations office, or a lobbying office in Washington or a state capital.

Finally, almost all interest groups must attract and keep members, whether membership is defined formally or informally. Groups must persuade individuals to invest the money, time, energy, or effort required to take part in the group's activities. Members play a larger role in some groups than in others. In **membership associations**,

membership association an organized group in which members play a substantial role, sitting on committees and engaging in group projects group members actually serve on committees and engage in projects. In the case of labor unions, members pay significant dues and attend rallies or march in picket lines. In the case of political or ideological groups, members may participate in demonstrations and protests. In another set of groups, **staff organizations**, a professional staff conducts most of the group's activities while members are called on only to make contributions. Among the well-known public interest groups, some, such as the National Organization for Women, are membership groups; others, such as the Children's Defense Fund, are staff organizations. Many online organized interests do not require membership beyond signing up for an online newsletter or signing an online petition.

staff organization a type of membership group in which a professional staff conducts most of the group's activities

THE "FREE-RIDER" PROBLEM

Whether they need individuals to volunteer or merely to write checks, groups need to recruit and retain members. Yet many groups find this task difficult, even when it comes to recruiting members who agree strongly with the group's goals. Why? As the economist Mancur Olson explains, the benefits of a group's success are often broadly available and cannot be denied to nonmembers.[20] Such benefits are called **collective goods**. This term is usually associated with certain government benefits, but it can also be applied to beneficial outcomes of interest group activity.

collective goods benefits sought by groups that are broadly available and cannot be denied to nonmembers

Olson offers this example: suppose a number of private property owners live near a mosquito-infested swamp. Each owner wants this swamp cleared. But if one or a few of the owners were to clear the swamp alone, their actions would benefit all the other owners as well, without any effort on the part of those other owners. Each of the inactive owners would be a **free rider** on the efforts of the ones who cleared the swamp. Thus, there is a disincentive for any of the owners to undertake the job alone. Since the number of concerned owners is small in this particular case, they might eventually be able to organize themselves to share the costs as well as to enjoy the benefits of clearing the swamp.

free riders those who enjoy the benefits of collective goods but did not participate in acquiring or providing them

But suppose the number of interested people is increased. Suppose the common concern is not the neighborhood swamp but polluted air or groundwater involving thousands or even millions of residents. National defense is the most obvious collective good whose benefits are shared by all residents, regardless of the taxes they pay or the support they provide. As the number of involved persons increases or as the size of the group increases, the free-rider phenomenon becomes more of a problem. The group would no doubt be more influential if all concerned individuals were active members—if there were no free riders. This collective action problem is one of the major reasons why many groups do not form.

WHY JOIN GROUPS?

Individuals do not have much incentive to become active members of a group that is already working more or less on their behalf. To overcome this free-rider problem, groups offer members "selective benefits" available only to group members. These benefits can be informational, material, solidary, purposive, or a combination of benefits. A community association, for example, can offer its members a sense of belonging (solidary benefit), involvement in community decision-making (purposive benefit), and reduced rates on homeowners' insurance (material benefit) or a community swimming pool (material benefit). Table 11.2 gives some examples of the range of benefits in each of these categories.

TABLE 11.2

Selective Benefits of Interest Group Membership

CATEGORY	BENEFITS
Informational benefits	Conferences
	Professional contacts
	Publications
	Coordination among organizations
	Research
	Legal help
	Professional codes
	Collective bargaining
Material benefits	Travel packages
	Insurance
	Discounts on consumer goods
Solidary benefits	Friendship
	Networking opportunities
Purposive benefits	Advocacy
	Representation before government
	Participation in public affairs

SOURCE: Adapted from Jack Walker, Jr., *Mobilizing Interest Groups in America: Patrons, Professions, and Social Movements* (Ann Arbor: University of Michigan Press, 1991), 86.

informational benefits special newsletters, periodicals, training programs, conferences, and other information provided to members of groups to entice others to join

material benefits special goods, services, or money provided to members of groups to entice others to join

solidary benefits selective benefits of group membership that emphasize friendship, networking, and consciousness-raising

purposive benefits selective benefits of group membership that emphasize the purpose and accomplishments of the group

Informational benefits are the most widespread and important category of selective benefits offered to group members. Information is provided through online communication such as email, conferences, training programs, and newsletters and other periodicals sent automatically to those who have paid membership dues. **Material benefits** include anything that can be measured monetarily, such as gifts, discount purchasing, shared advertising, and, perhaps most valuable of all, health and retirement insurance. **Solidary benefits** include the friendship and networking opportunities that membership provides. Extremely important to many of the newer citizen groups is "consciousness-raising," including the satisfaction of working toward a common goal with like-minded individuals. One example of this can be seen in the claims of many women's organizations that active participation conveys to each member an enhanced sense of her own value and a stronger ability to advance individual as well as collective rights. Members of associations based on ethnicity, race, or religion also derive solidary benefits from interacting with individuals they perceive as sharing their own backgrounds, values, and perspectives.

A fourth type of benefit involves the appeal of the purpose of an interest group. An example of these **purposive benefits** is businesses joining trade associations to further their economic interests. Similarly, individuals join consumer, environmental, or other civic groups to pursue goals important to them. Many of the most successful interest groups of the past 20 years have been citizen groups or public interest groups organized largely around shared ideological goals, including government reform, civil rights, economic equality, "family values," and even opposition to government itself.

DIGITAL COMMUNICATION AND INTEREST GROUPS

Digital communication is changing how interest groups encourage participation in politics and sustained collective action by citizens. Political scientist and former vice president of the Sierra Club David Karpf has argued that digital media and social media have created a new kind of interest group politics in America that has revolutionized political advocacy. For example, liberal-leaning MoveOn.org and conservative-leaning Americans for Prosperity have arisen over the past two decades to play an increasingly important role in citizen participation in politics. These grassroots online activist organizations have redefined membership and fund-raising practices via innovative methods for communicating with their members, measuring the opinions of their members, and moving their members into action—in terms of influencing public opinion, contributing money to campaigns, and working on behalf of the organization.[21]

Traditional interest groups are expensive to organize (one reason why group membership has an upper-class bias), and they rely on professional advocates and direct mail. They are also slow to change. By contrast, many of today's advocacy groups are relatively inexpensive to organize and quick to adapt to an ever-changing world of politics. Rather than requiring an annual membership fee to join, membership is free and defined by receiving communication from the group or working on behalf of the group. Targeted fund-raising drives—over local, state, or federal government legislation; over a salient event, such as raising money for victims of Hurricane Maria in Puerto Rico; or over an election—is how the organization raises funds to maintain itself. While most traditional interest groups are focused on a single issue—for instance, the Sierra Club seeks protection of the environment while AARP advocates on behalf of older Americans—online advocacy groups are often issue generalists that have a wide umbrella of issues for which they lobby.

Advocacy groups with a significant online structure are less expensive to organize because they have a streamlined staff structure with fewer staff who often work from virtual offices. In contrast, traditional interest groups must maintain offices in Washington, D.C., and other regional locations. The modified staff structure engages in different work routines that prioritize communication with members through email, Twitter, and other digital platforms rather than mailing expensive glossy newsletters or engaging in direct lobbying of members of Congress.

Today's advocacy groups employ grassroots strategies to pressure elected officials. These strategies may include the use of social media to organize rallies, generate news headlines, and promote fund-raising events, letter-writing campaigns, boycotts, and protests. Online advocacy groups may improve representation for citizens, counteracting the disproportionate influence of business and corporate interests in Washington. Liberal and conservative groups, as well as economic interest groups, have been better able to organize and affect government policy in the past decade with the help of the internet and social media.

APPROACHES TO INTEREST GROUP MEMBERSHIP: TWO CASE STUDIES

Online advocacy organizations may also differ from traditional groups in the types of benefits they offer members, as the cases of MoveOn and AARP illustrate.

MoveOn Rather than offering members material selective incentives to join the group, online activist groups like MoveOn offer informational selective benefits to members via daily or weekly news updates and solidary benefits of volunteering or donating money on behalf of the organization. Unlike mainstream news organizations, online advocacy groups are decidedly partisan in the information they provide members. In addition, the group offers their members purposive benefits—the knowledge that one is contributing to a dearly held cause. Purposive benefits may be the most important of all in maintaining the new online citizen advocacy groups.

AARP One group that has been extremely successful in recruiting members and mobilizing them for political action is AARP. The organization was founded as the American Association of Retired Persons in 1958 as a result of the efforts of a retired California high school principal, Ethel Percy Andrus, to find affordable health insurance for herself and the thousands of members of the National Retired Teachers Association. For the insurer, it provided an expanded market; for Andrus, it was a way to serve the ever-growing elderly population, whose problems and needs were expanding along with their numbers and their life

MoveOn.org pioneered a new model of interest group membership and operations. Founded in 1998 and claiming 2 million members, MoveOn seeks to leverage technology to lower the barriers to political participation. In 2018, MoveOn, along with pro-choice groups like NARAL, helped organize online to protest the confirmation of Supreme Court nominee Brett Kavanaugh.

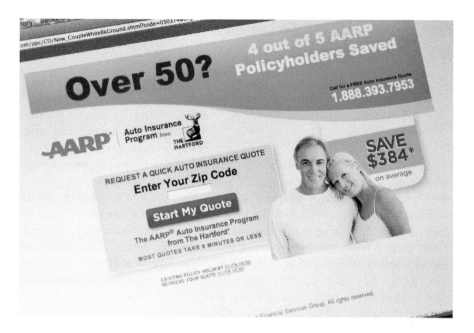

AARP is one of the largest interest groups in the country. One way that AARP attracts members is through selective benefits, such as hotel discounts, credit and identity theft prevention, free health tests, and all types of affordable insurance coverage.

expectancy. Today, AARP is a large and powerful organization with 38 million members and an annual income of $900 million.[22]

How did this large organization overcome the free-rider problem and recruit 38 million older people as members? First, no other organization has ever more successfully provided the selective benefits necessary to overcome the free-rider problem. It helps that AARP began as an organization to provide affordable health insurance for aging members rather than as an organization to influence public policy. But that fact only strengthens the argument that members need short-term individual benefits if they are to invest effort in a longer-term and less concrete set of benefits. As AARP evolved into a political interest group, its leadership added more selective benefits for individual members. It provided guidance against consumer fraud, offered low-interest credit cards, evaluated and endorsed products that were deemed valuable to members, and provided auto insurance and a discounted mail-order pharmacy.

The resources of AARP are so extensive that its leadership has been able to mobilize itself on issues of importance to the group. One of its most successful methods of mobilization for political action is a "telephone tree," with which AARP leaders can quickly mobilize thousands of members for and against proposals that affect Social Security, Medicare, and other questions of security for the aging. A "telephone tree" in each state enables the state AARP chair to phone all of the AARP district directors, who then can phone the presidents of the dozens of local chapters, who can call their local officers and individual members. Within 24 hours, thousands of individual AARP members can be contacting local, state, and national officials to express their opposition to proposed legislation. Other organizations have borrowed strategy from AARP, creating digital versions of the telephone tree using social media and email to allow members to contact their elective representatives over important policy issues.

The Growth of Interest and Advocacy Groups

Analyze why the number of interest and advocacy groups has grown in recent decades

Interest groups and concerns about them are not new. As long as there is government, as long as government makes policies that add value or impose costs, and as long as there is freedom to organize, interest groups will abound. If government expands, so will interest groups. There was, for example, a spurt of growth in the national government during the 1880s and '90s, arising largely from the first government efforts at economic intervention to fight large monopolies and to regulate some aspects of interstate commerce. In response, a parallel spurt of growth occurred in national interest groups. Many groups organized around specific agricultural products as well. This period also marked the beginning of the expansion of trade unions as interest groups. Later, in the 1930s, interest groups with headquarters in Washington began to grow significantly, concurrent with that decade's historic and sustained expansion of the national government (see Chapter 3).

Over the past half-century there has been an even greater increase both in the number of interest groups seeking to play a role in the American political process and in their ability to influence that process. Interest and advocacy groups have become much more numerous, more active, and more influential in American politics, with lobby groups and Super PACs playing major roles in Congress and in electoral politics. This explosion of interest group activity has two basic origins: first, the expansion of the role of government during this period and, second, the coming-of-age of a new and dynamic set of political forces in the United States—forces that have relied heavily on "public interest" groups to advance their causes.

THE EXPANSION OF GOVERNMENT

Modern governments' extensive economic and social programs have powerful politicizing effects, often sparking the organization of new groups and interests. Interest group activity is often a consequence of government. Government involvement in any area can be a powerful stimulus for political organization and action by those whose interests are affected.

For example, during the 1970s expanded federal regulation of the automobile, oil, gas, education, and health care industries compelled each of these industries to increase substantially its efforts to influence the government's laws and regulations. These efforts, in turn, spurred the organization of other groups to counter the activities of the first.[23] Similarly, federal social programs have sparked political organization. For example, federal programs and court decisions in such areas as abortion and school prayer were one factor leading to the rise of fundamentalist religious groups. Thus, the expansion of government in recent decades has also stimulated increased group activity and organization.

Like the federal government, the states too have expanded their scope of government and have likewise witnessed a growth in the number and diversity of interest groups. But interest group activity isn't uniform across the states. One study, for example, found that large-population, affluent states with higher per capita income and higher government expenditures have more trade associations than other states. These large-population, affluent states legislate on more policy areas, and thus activate the business community to lobby to protect their economic interests. Economists call this "rent seeking."[24]

GROWTH OF PUBLIC INTEREST GROUPS IN THE 1960S AND '70S

The second factor accounting for the explosion of interest group activity was the emergence of a new set of forces in American politics that can collectively be called the "New Politics movement," which began in the 1960s and '70s. For this cohort of upper-middle-class professionals, the civil rights and antiwar movements were formative political experiences. They formed groups to crusade against racial discrimination and the Vietnam War, and this experience taught them the political efficacy of organized group activity to affect politics. In more recent years, these citizens have focused attention on issues such as environmental protection, social and economic inequality, women's rights, and rights for the LGBTQ community. Members of this movement founded or strengthened public interest groups such as Common Cause, the Sierra Club, the Environmental Defense Fund, and NOW. Such groups were able to influence the media, Congress, and even the judiciary, and enjoyed a remarkable degree of success during the late 1960s and early '70s in securing the enactment of environmental, consumer, and occupational health and safety legislation.

A host of advocacy organizations also exist for the ideological right and have been equally successful. Founded in 1964, the American Conservative Union was one of the first public interest groups to form to advocate for conservative issues. Their primary concerns are liberty, personal responsibility rather than government welfare programs, traditional values, and national defense. Other examples include the American Family Association, one of the leading national Christian advocacy organizations concerned with the moral foundations of American culture, which lobbies for policies that strengthen traditional families; and Citizens United, which uses a combination of education, advocacy, and grassroots organization to seek to restore traditional American values of limited government, free markets, strong families, and national security. These organizations are also active in electoral campaigns, running ads to advantage Republican candidates and against Democratic candidates for public office.

Public interest groups often advocate for interests that are not addressed by traditional lobbies. For example, in addition to many other activities, the Public Interest Research Group (PIRG) publishes an annual toy safety report to help protect consumers and to encourage policy makers to address problems in this area.

Interest Group Strategies

Explain how interest groups try to influence government and policy

Interest groups work to improve the likelihood that their policy interests will be heard and treated favorably by the government. The quest for political influence or power takes many forms. Insider strategies include access to key decision makers, lobbying, and litigating cases in courts. Outsider strategies include going public and using electoral politics. These strategies do not exhaust all the possibilities, but they paint a broad picture of ways that groups use their resources in the fierce competition for power (see Figure 11.1).

Many groups employ a mix of insider and outsider strategies. For example, environmental groups such as the Sierra Club lobby members of Congress and key congressional staff members, participate in bureaucratic rule making by offering comments and suggestions to agencies on new environmental rules, and bring lawsuits under various environmental acts such as the Endangered Species Act, which authorizes groups and citizens to come to court if they believe the act is being violated. At the same time, the Sierra Club attempts to influence public opinion through media campaigns and to influence electoral politics by supporting candidates who it believes share its environmental views and by opposing candidates it views as foes of environmentalism. While most groups win sometimes and lose sometimes when advocating for their policy goals, in general groups that are well organized and have resources, including citizen groups, are more effective.

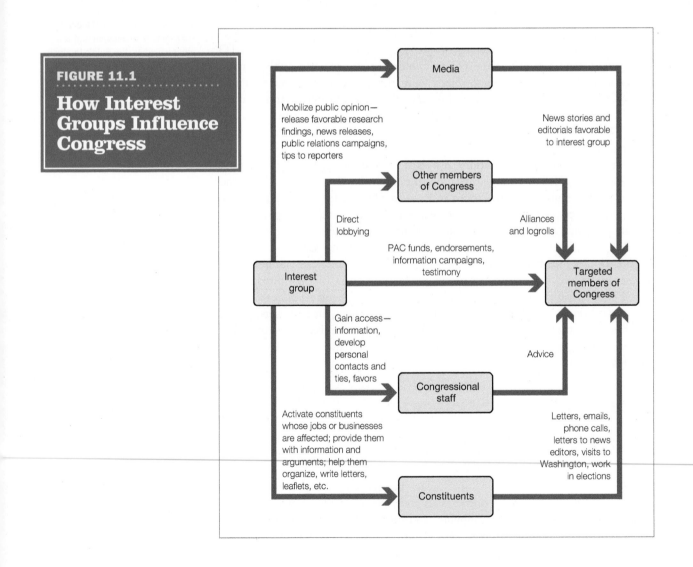

FIGURE 11.1

How Interest Groups Influence Congress

DIRECT LOBBYING

Lobbying is an attempt by a group to influence the policy process through persuasion of government officials. Most Americans tend to believe that interest groups exert their influence through direct contact with members of Congress, but lobbying encompasses a broad range of activities that groups engage in with all sorts of government officials and the public as a whole.

The 1946 Federal Regulation of Lobbying Act defines a lobbyist as "any person who shall engage himself for pay or any consideration for the purpose of attempting to influence the passage or defeat of any legislation of the Congress of the United States." The 1995 Lobbying Disclosure Act requires all organizations employing lobbyists to register with Congress and to disclose whom they represent, whom they lobby, what they are looking for, and how much they are paid. Approximately 9,443 lobbyists are currently registered, down from a height of over 14,000 in 2007.[25]

Lobbying involves a great deal of activity on the part of someone speaking for an interest, and lobbyists attempt to influence the policy process in a variety of ways.[26] Lobbyists first and foremost provide information to lawmakers, administrators, and committee staff about their interests and the legislation at hand. They often testify on behalf of their clients at congressional committee and agency hearings. Lobbyists talk to reporters, place ads in newspapers, and organize letter-writing, phone call, and email campaigns. Many lobbying efforts occur in private meetings with lawmakers and campaign leaders, and behind closed doors. They also play an important role in fund-raising, helping to direct clients' contributions to certain members of Congress and presidential candidates.

Lobbying Congress Traditionally, the term *lobbyist* referred mainly to individuals who sought to influence the passage of legislation in Congress. The First Amendment to the Constitution provides for the right to "petition the Government for a redress of grievances." But as early as the 1870s, *lobbying* became the common term for petitioning. And since petitioning cannot take place on the floor of the House or Senate, petitioners must confront members of Congress in the lobbies of the legislative chamber—hence the term *lobbying*.

Sophisticated lobbyists win influence by providing information about policies to busy members of Congress. Although interest groups do not necessarily buy votes, they do buy time, expertise, and influence. Studies have found that those interest groups providing the most money to representatives are more likely to be consulted by that representative and asked to provide information and expertise in discussing a bill pertaining to that group's area of interest. This, in essence, gives interest groups a voice in shaping how legislation is written; and while it cannot ensure votes for laws preferred by the group, by participating in the policy process, organized interests are influencing policy.

The influence of lobbyists, in many instances, is based on personal relationships and the behind-the-scenes services they are able to perform for lawmakers. Many of Washington's top lobbyists have close ties to important members of Congress or were themselves important political figures, thus virtually guaranteeing that their clients will have direct access to congressional leaders. Some important lobbyists have more than a business relationship to lawmakers: quite a few, in fact, are married to prominent political figures.

Through their lobbyists, interest groups also have substantial influence in setting the legislative agenda. They help to craft specific language in legislation and build coalitions and comprehensive campaigns around particular policy issues.[27]

lobbying a strategy by which organized interests seek to influence the passage of legislation by exerting direct pressure on government officials

Like many of their colleagues, John Boehner (R-Ohio, left) and Mary Landrieu (D-La., right) worked as lobbyists after leaving Congress. Members of Congress have knowledge and contacts that make them particularly attractive to lobbying firms.

These coalitions do not rise from the grassroots but instead are put together by Washington lobbyists who launch comprehensive campaigns that combine simulated grassroots activity with information and campaign funding for members of Congress.

What happens to interests that do not engage in extensive lobbying? They often find themselves "Microsofted"; that is, marginalized in the political process. In 1998 the software giant was facing antitrust action from the Justice Department and had few friends in Congress. One member of the House, Representative Billy Tauzin (R-La.), told Microsoft's chair, Bill Gates, that without an extensive investment in lobbying, the corporation would continue to be "demonized." Gates responded by quadrupling Microsoft's lobbying expenditures and hiring lobbyists with strong ties to Congress. The result was congressional pressure on the Justice Department that led to a settlement of the Microsoft suit on terms favorable to the company.[28] Today massive companies like Amazon and Facebook may be in a situation similar to Microsoft's in the '90s in that they need to increase lobbying efforts. President Trump and other leaders publically criticized Amazon for becoming too large in terms of market share and Facebook for not protecting the privacy of its members' information.

Lobbying the President So many individuals and groups clamor for the president's time and attention that only the most skilled and best-connected members of the lobbying community can hope to influence presidential decisions. Typically, a president's key political advisers and fund-raisers will include individuals with ties to the lobbying industry who can help their friends gain access to the White House.

Lobbying the president took an odd twist in 2018 when Donald Trump's personal lawyer, Michael Cohen, was widely criticized for accepting millions of dollars from corporations including AT&T and international drug companies for "insights" on the president's decision making, although Cohen is not registered as a lobbyist. Cohen is under investigation by the federal prosecutor for bank fraud, wire fraud, and campaign finance violations; crimes to which he plead guilty in August 2018.

Lobbying the Executive Branch Even when an interest group is successful at getting its bill passed by Congress and signed by the president, the prospect of full and faithful implementation of that law is not guaranteed. Often a group and its allies do not pack up and go home as soon as the president turns the new law they

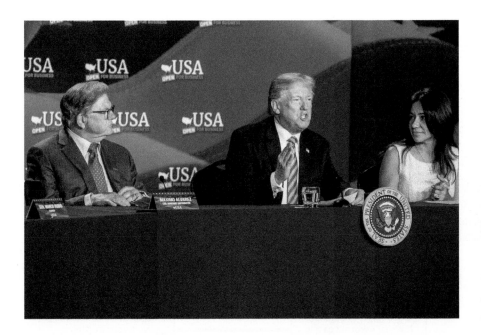

Business leaders are often able to gain special access to elected officials. Here, Maximo Alvarez, president of Sunshine Gasoline Distributors (left), and Irina Vilarino, owner of Las Vegas Cuban Cuisine (right), meet with President Trump to discuss tax cuts for small businesses.

lobbied for over to the appropriate agency. In some respects, interest group access to the executive branch is facilitated by federal law. The Administrative Procedure Act, first enacted in 1946 and frequently amended in subsequent years, requires most federal agencies to provide notice and an opportunity for comment before implementing proposed new rules and regulations. This "notice and comment rule making" is designed to allow interests an opportunity to make their views known and to participate in the implementation of federal legislation that affects them. Congress enacted the Negotiated Rulemaking Act in 1990 to encourage administrative agencies to engage in direct and open negotiations with affected interests when developing new regulations. These two pieces of legislation have played an important role in opening the bureaucratic process to interest group influence. Today, few federal agencies would consider attempting to implement a new rule without consulting affected interests, known in Washington as "stakeholders."[29]

How Interest Groups Make Policy; Iron Triangles and Issue Networks The development of government policy is the product of the so-called **iron triangle**, which has one angle in an executive branch program (bureaucratic agency), another angle in a Senate or House committee or subcommittee, and a third angle in some highly stable and well-organized interest group. In policy areas such as farming and agriculture policy or energy policy, interest groups, government agencies, and congressional committees routinely work together for mutual benefit. The interest group provides campaign contributions for members of Congress, lobbies for larger budgets for the agency, and provides policy expertise to lawmakers. The agency, in turn, provides government contracts for the interest group and constituency services for friendly members of Congress. The congressional committee or subcommittee, meanwhile, supports the agency's budgetary requests and the programs the interest group favors. Together the three actors that make up the angles in the triangle create a mutually supportive relationship that can last over a long period of time, especially if a committee member has considerable seniority in Congress. An interest cannot feel

iron triangle the stable, cooperative relationship that often develops among a congressional committee, an administrative agency, and one or more supportive interest groups; not all of these relationships are triangular, but the iron triangle is the most typical

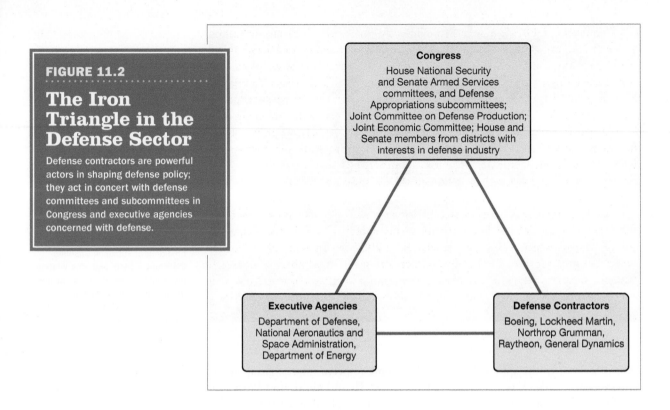

FIGURE 11.2

The Iron Triangle in the Defense Sector

Defense contractors are powerful actors in shaping defense policy; they act in concert with defense committees and subcommittees in Congress and executive agencies concerned with defense.

Congress

House National Security and Senate Armed Services committees, and Defense Appropriations subcommittees; Joint Committee on Defense Production; Joint Economic Committee; House and Senate members from districts with interests in defense industry

Executive Agencies

Department of Defense, National Aeronautics and Space Administration, Department of Energy

Defense Contractors

Boeing, Lockheed Martin, Northrop Grumman, Raytheon, General Dynamics

comfortable about its access to Congress until it has one or more of its "own" people with 10 or more years of continuous service on the relevant committee or subcommittee. Figure 11.2 illustrates an important iron triangle in recent American political history: that of the defense industry.

A number of important policy domains, such as the environment, tax policy, and immigration policy, are controlled not by highly structured and unified iron triangles but by broader **issue networks**. These networks consist of like-minded politicians, consultants, public officials, activists, and interest groups that care about the issue in question. Activists and interest groups recognized as being involved in the issue (the stakeholders) are customarily invited to testify before congressional committees or give their views to government agencies considering action in their domain. Issue networks and iron triangles may be overlapping and may coexist.

issue network a loose network of elected leaders, public officials, activists, and interest groups drawn together by a specific policy issue

REGULATING LOBBYING

Sometimes the actions of lobbyists are outside of the law. In 2005 a prominent Washington lobbyist, Jack Abramoff, was indicted on numerous charges of fraud and violations of federal lobbying laws. During the investigation of his activities, it was revealed that Abramoff, along with his associate Michael Scanlon, had collected tens of millions of dollars from several American Indian tribes that operated lucrative gambling casinos. (Indian gambling is currently a $30 billion industry in the United States.) What Abramoff provided in exchange was access to key Republican members of Congress, who helped his clients shut down rival casino operators. Abramoff was closely associated with several House members, including the former House majority leader Tom DeLay. Millions of tribal dollars found their way into the campaign war chests of Abramoff's friends in Congress. Thus, through a well-connected lobbyist, money had effectively purchased access and influence. Abramoff and several of his associates subsequently pleaded guilty to federal bribery and fraud charges, and Abramoff was sentenced to more than five years in prison.

Because lobbyists are so influential in Washington, D.C., Congress has tried to limit their role by adopting stricter guidelines. However, the effectiveness of the new rules is unclear. For example, businesses may no longer deduct lobbying costs as a business expense. Trade associations must report to members the proportion of their dues that goes toward lobbying, and that proportion of the dues may not be reported as a business expense. The most important new regulation was the 1995 Lobbying Disclosure Act, which expanded the definition of the organization and individuals that must register to lobby.

In 1996, Congress passed legislation limiting the size of gifts to its own members and banned the practice of honoraria for giving speeches, which special interests had used to supplement congressional salaries. In 2007 new rules prohibited lobbyists from paying for most meals, trips, parties, and gifts for members of Congress. Lobbyists were also required to disclose the amounts and sources of small campaign contributions they collected from clients and "bundled" into large contributions. And interest groups were required to disclose the funds they used to rally voters to support or oppose legislative proposals. According to the *Washington Post*, however, within a few weeks, lobbyists had learned how to circumvent many of the new rules, and lobbying firms were as busy as ever.[30]

USING THE COURTS

Interest groups sometimes turn to litigation when they lack access or when they feel they have insufficient influence to change a policy. Interest groups can use the courts to affect public policy in at least three ways: (1) by bringing suit directly on behalf of the group itself, (2) by financing suits brought by individuals, or (3) by filing a companion brief as an *amicus curiae* (literally "friend of the court") to an existing court case (see Chapter 15 for a discussion of amicus briefs).

Among the best-known illustrations of using the courts for political influence is found in the history of the National Association for the Advancement of Colored People (NAACP). In *Brown v. Board of Education of Topeka, Kansas*, the U.S. Supreme Court held that legal segregation of the schools was unconstitutional.[31] Later, extensive litigation accompanied the women's rights movement in the 1960s and the movement for rights for gays and lesbians in the 1990s. In 2015 the case of *Obergefell v. Hodges* illustrated the success of this litigation strategy as the Supreme Court declared that the Fourteenth Amendment prohibited states from refusing to issue marriage licenses to same-sex couples.[32]

The 1973 Supreme Court case of *Roe v. Wade*, which took away a state's power to ban abortions, sparked a controversy that organized conservatives nationwide.[33] Since 1973, conservative groups have made extensive use of the courts to whittle away at the scope of the privacy doctrine initially defined by the Supreme Court in *Roe v. Wade*. They obtained rulings, for example, that prohibit the use of federal funds to pay for voluntary abortions. And in 1989 right-to-life groups were able to use the case of *Webster v. Reproductive Health Services* to restore the right of states to place restrictions on abortion, thus undermining the

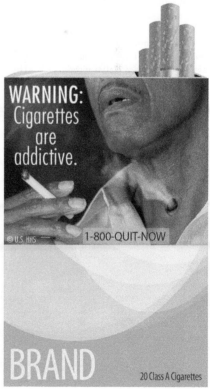

When the Food and Drug Administration (FDA) required cigarette packages to carry new warning labels such as the one below, a coalition of tobacco companies sued the government, claiming the labels violated First Amendment rights. The companies won their suit. In response, anticigarette groups such as the Campaign for Tobacco-Free kids are urging the FDA to develop new warnings.

Roe v. Wade decision (see Chapter 4).[34] The *Webster* case brought more than 300 interest groups on both sides of the abortion issue to the Supreme Court's door. On the other side of the political spectrum, the American Civil Liberties Union (ACLU) regularly uses litigation to challenge state and federal laws that restrict the rights of individuals and groups. This includes recent successful challenges to laws ending affirmative action in the states.

Litigation involving large businesses is voluminous in such areas as taxation, antitrust, interstate transportation, patents, and product quality and standardization. Often a business is brought to litigation against its will by virtue of initiatives taken against it by other businesses or by government agencies. But many individual businesses bring suit themselves to influence government policy, and business groups also frequently use the courts because of the number of government programs applied to them. Major corporations and their trade associations pay tremendous amounts of money each year in fees to the most prestigious Washington law firms. Much of this money is used to keep the best and most experienced lawyers prepared to represent the corporations in court or before administrative agencies when necessary.

MOBILIZING PUBLIC OPINION

Going public is a strategy to mobilize the widest and most favorable public opinion for an issue or societal problem, and a favored strategy of citizen groups, membership groups, and online advocacy groups. Many groups consider it imperative to maintain this climate at all times. As early as the 1930s, political analysts were distinguishing between the "old lobby" of direct group representation before Congress and the "new lobby" of public-relations professionals addressing the public at large as a way to ultimately reach Congress.[35]

One of the best-known ways of going public is the use of **institutional advertising**. A casual scanning of websites, newspapers, and television ads will provide numerous examples of expensive and well-designed ads by the major oil and gas companies, automobile and steel companies, other large corporations, and trade associations. The ads attempt to show how much these organizations are doing for the country. Their purpose is to create and maintain a positive association between an organization

institutional advertising
advertising designed to create a positive image of an organization

Throughout American history, groups have staged mass protests to bring greater attention to their causes. These have included (from left) the Selma to Montgomery march for civil rights, organized by Martin Luther King, Jr., and others in 1965; Tea Party rallies for lower taxes and smaller government, which erupted in 2009; the Occupy Wall Street movement of 2011, which protested income inequality; and the Black Lives Matter movement, which began in 2013 in response to the killing of Trayvon Martin by George Zimmerman.

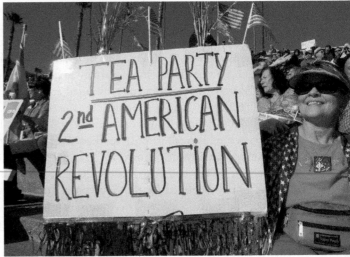

and the community at large in the hope of drawing on these favorable feelings as needed for specific political campaigns later on.

As discussed earlier, citizen groups and advocacy groups rely heavily on mobilizing the public opinion of their members via social media, such as Twitter campaigns and targeted email messages. On any given day a new viral media story may become headline news, and in most cases an interest group is behind the story. Such groups span the ideological spectrum from liberal to conservative and can wield significant pressure on elected officials to act.

Protests and Demonstrations Many groups resort to going public because they lack the resources, the contacts, or the experience to use other political strategies. The sponsorship of boycotts, sit-ins, mass rallies, and marches by Martin Luther King, Jr.'s, Southern Christian Leadership Conference and related organizations during the 1950s and '60s is one of the most significant and successful cases of going public to create a more favorable climate of opinion by calling attention to abuses. The success of these events inspired similar efforts by women's groups.

The 2010 Republican takeover of the House of Representatives began with the spontaneous self-organization of the Tea Party movement in 2009 as an angry response to the Obama administration's health care initiatives. In 2011 the Occupy Wall Street movement sparked demonstrations across America and around the world, giving voice to those who are outraged by economic inequality. In 2013 the Black Lives Matter movement took off after the shooting of an unarmed black teenager by a member of the local neighborhood watch and quickly spread across the nation. Shootings of black people by police and vigilantes across the country have led to major demonstrations protesting institutionalized racism, and calling in particular for the elimination of racial inequality in the criminal justice system.

Grassroots Mobilization Another form of going public is **grassroots mobilization**, in which a lobby group mobilizes its members and their families throughout the country to call or email their elected representatives in support of the group's position. Among the most effective users of the grassroots effort in contemporary American politics is the religious right. Networks of evangelical churches have the capacity to generate hundreds of thousands of letters, phone calls, and emails to Congress and

grassroots mobilization a lobbying campaign in which a group mobilizes its membership to contact government officials in support of the group's position the White House. Similarly, the NRA maintains a powerful grassroots lobbying effort, spending more on mobilization of its members than on professional lobbyists. The NRA's 5 million dues-paying members can be mobilized to flood congressional offices with letters and phone calls, and few members of Congress are eager to pick a fight with the group.[36] The interests of the NRA were seriously challenged in 2018 when, in the aftermath of a mass shooting at a high school in Parkland, Florida, in February 2018, students there used social media to mobilize Americans across the nation in support of stronger gun laws. Under the label "March for Our Lives," these students successfully coordinated a mass rally in Washington, D.C., as well as rallies around the country. Largely as a result of their efforts, and those of supporters they attracted, several states enacted tougher gun laws. Grassroots campaigns have been so effective in recent years that a number of Washington consulting firms have begun to specialize in this area.[37]

Sometimes, what initially appears to be an upswelling of grassroots mobilization is not in fact a genuine grassroots campaign but instead represents "Astroturf lobbying" (a play on the name of the artificial grass used on many sports fields). Such campaigns, often using email, have increased in frequency in recent years, yet members of Congress often continue to respond more to lobbyists than to public demonstrations of support for specific policy issues.

USING ELECTORAL POLITICS

In addition to attempting to influence members of Congress and other government officials, interest groups seek to use the electoral process to elect the right legislators in the first place and to ensure that those who are elected will owe them a debt of gratitude for their support. If we view matters in perspective, groups invest more resources in lobbying than in electoral politics. Nevertheless, financial support and campaign activism can be important tools for organized interests. The NRA, for example, dramatically increased its spending in the 2016 election, spending $30 million to support Trump.[38]

Political Action Committees and Super PACs By far the most common electoral strategy employed by interest groups is that of giving financial support to political parties or specific candidates running for office. But such support can easily cross the threshold into outright bribery. Therefore, Congress has occasionally attempted to regulate this strategy, but with limited success. The Federal Election Campaign Act of 1971 (amended in 1974) requires that each candidate or campaign committee itemize the full name and address, occupation, and principal business of each person who contributes more than $100. These provisions create an open record of which organizations and individuals fund the campaigns of candidates for public office.

The 1972 Watergate scandal was triggered by the illegal entry of a group of clandestine agents employed by the president's re-election committee into the office of the Democratic National Committee in the Watergate apartment and hotel complex. An investigation quickly revealed numerous violations of campaign finance laws, involving millions of dollars in unregistered cash from corporate executives to President Nixon's re-election committee. Reaction to Watergate produced further legislation on campaign finance in 1974 and 1976, but the effect was to restrict individuals rather than interest group campaign activity. In the 2017–18 election cycle, individuals could contribute no more than $2,700 to any candidate for federal office in any

Who Is Represented by PACs?

the 2016 election cycle, political action committees (PACs) spent a grand total of $1.7 billion to elect and defeat olitical candidates. PACs representing the financial sector spent the most, followed closely by agribusiness. For many ectors, the amount donated to Republican candidates exceeded that donated to Democratic candidates.

AC Contributions to Federal Candidates, 2016

Democratic candidates ▪ Republican candidates

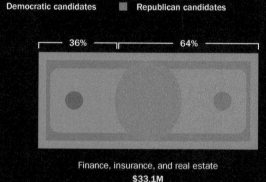

36%   64%

Finance, insurance, and real estate
$33.1M

26%   74%

Agribusiness
$26.1M

46%   53%

Ideology/single issue
$19.4M

39%   61%

Health
$18.3M

76%   24%

Labor
$17.6M

34%   65%

Miscellaneous business
$15.2M

24%   76%

Energy/natural resources
$11.0M

43%   56%

Communications/electronics
$10.3M

33%   67%

Transportation
$9.3M

35% 64%

Defense
$7.5M

22% 78%

Construction
$5.2M

52% 48%

Lawyers/lobbyists
$4.7M

FOR CRITICAL ANALYSIS

1. Business PACs are the biggest spenders. What effect might this have on which candidates get elected and what policies they pass?

2. Why do you think PACs are more likely to donate to Republican candidates than to Democratic candidates?

JRCE: Center for Responsive Politics, www.opensecrets.org/pacs/ (accessed 11/21/17).

primary or general election. A **political action committee (PAC)**, however, can contribute $5,000, provided it contributes to at least five different federal candidates each year. (Campaign finance regulations are discussed in more detail in Chapter 10.) The laws permit corporations, unions, and other interest groups to form PACs. PACs represent interest groups in electoral politics. The option to form a PAC was made available by law in the early 1970s. Before then it was difficult, if not downright illegal, for corporations, including unions, to get directly involved in elections by supporting parties and candidates.

The flurry of reform legislation in the 1970s attempted to reduce the influence that interest groups have over elections, but the effect has been almost the exact opposite. Electoral spending by interest groups has been increasing dramatically.

Given the enormous costs of running political campaigns, most politicians are eager to receive contributions and at least willing to give a friendly hearing to the needs and interests of contributors. While most politicians do not "sell out" to the interests that fund their campaigns, there is evidence that interest groups' campaign contributions do influence the overall pattern of political behavior in Congress and in the state legislatures, and that lawmakers represent affluent individuals and groups more than the middle class.[39] (See the "Who Are Americans?" feature for one depiction of who is represented by PACs.)

Concern about PACs grew through the 1980s and '90s, creating a constant drumbeat for reform of federal election laws. Proposals to abolish PACs were introduced in Congress on many occasions, with perhaps the most celebrated being the "McCain-Feingold bill" (the Bipartisan Campaign Reform Act of 2002). When originally proposed in 1996, McCain-Feingold was aimed at reducing or eliminating PACs. But in a stunning about-face, when the act was adopted in 2002, it did not restrict PACs in any significant way.

One consequence of this reform, was the creation of new organizations, to fund candidates: **Super PACs** and **527 committees**. As we saw above, a PAC has a maximum contribution limit of $5,000 per candidate in each election cycle. Super PACs, on the other hand, cannot donate to candidates or parties directly, but they can spend unlimited sums of money on campaigns to influence an election in favor of candidates or parties as long as their activity (for example, campaign ads or mobilization efforts) is not coordinated with the candidates or parties. Because there are no limits on the amount of money Super PACs may raise from corporations, unions, and interest groups, they have become more important than PACs and have had the effect of strengthening interest groups. As long as a group's campaign expenditures are not coordinated with those of a candidate's campaign, the group is free to spend as much money as it wishes. Such expenditures are viewed as "issue advocacy" and are protected by the First Amendment. The Supreme Court's landmark decision *Citizens United v. Federal Election Commission* (2010) dramatically increased the flow of money from interest groups, 527s, and Super PACs into politics and electoral campaigns. *Citizens United* removed restrictions on corporate and union political spending.[40]

In the 2016 presidential election, independent expenditures (commonly referred to as outside spending) totaled about $1.3 billion, of which $594 million came from Super PACs. Candidates Hillary Clinton and Donald Trump raised $1.5 billion total, and the Super PACs supporting them raised $618 million, according to the Center for Responsive Government.[41] Super PAC financing of U.S. elections represents a significant amount of all dollars spent on electoral campaigns. In 2016, Super PACs spent more than $1.1 billion on House and Senate races.[42] In the 2018 election there were 2,224 Super PACs, which together spent $815 million.[43]

Campaign Activism Financial support is not the only way that organized groups seek influence through electoral politics. Sometimes activism can be even more important than campaign contributions. Campaign activism on the part of conservative groups played a very important role in bringing about the Republican capture of both houses of Congress in 1994. For example, Christian Coalition activists played a role in many races, including those in which Republican candidates were not strongly identified with the religious right. One postelection study suggested that more than 60 percent of the more than 600 candidates supported by the Christian right were successful in state, local, and congressional races in 1994, especially in the South.[44] In many congressional districts, Christian Coalition efforts were augmented by grassroots campaigns launched by the NRA, which had been outraged by Democratic support for gun control legislation. Both groups are well organized at the local level and were able to mobilize their members across the country to participate in congressional races. In the 2012 presidential elections, prochoice groups mobilized their supporters to turn out and vote for Democratic candidate Obama via telephone get-out-the-vote drives.

The amount of money spent by organized interests on elections has increased dramatically in the last decade. This cartoon raises the concern that influence in government is for sale and only the extremely wealthy can buy it.

Ballot Initiatives Another political tactic that interest groups use is sponsorship of ballot initiatives at the state level. The initiative, available in half the states allows proposed laws to be placed on the general election ballot and submitted directly to the voters, bypassing the state legislature and the governor. The initiative was originally promoted by late-nineteenth-century Populists and Progressives as a mechanism that would allow the people to govern directly—an antidote to interest group influence in the legislative process.

Some studies have suggested that, ironically, many initiative campaigns today are actually sponsored by interest groups seeking to circumvent legislative opposition to their goals. In recent years, for example, initiative campaigns have been sponsored by the insurance industry, the automobile industry, trial lawyers' associations, and tobacco companies.[45] The success of business groups promoting successful tax limitation ballot measures in the 1970s and 1980s has led liberal activists to develop their own issue campaigns. Liberal activists established the Ballot Initiative Strategy Center to provide national coordination for these efforts, which led to successful statewide ballot measures to raise the minimum wage, protect the environment in Colorado, and increase taxes for corporations and high-income wage earners in Oregon and California. Both corporate and grassroots groups have had success with ballot initiatives over the past two decades.

But while businesses may sponsor ballot initiatives, such measures are much more likely to be rejected by voters on Election Day than initiatives sponsored by citizen groups. In an important study, political scientist Elisabeth Gerber finds that citizen groups and unions are the most effective at sponsoring ballot measures, whereas businesses, trade associations, and professional associations are more effective at lobbying state legislatures. The implication is that mechanisms of direct democracy, like the initiative process, favor citizen interests while lobbying favors economic interests.[46]

Interest Groups
WHAT DO WE WANT?

We would like to think that government policies are products of legislators representing the public interest. The truth of the matter is that few programs and policies ever reach the public agenda without the vigorous efforts of important national interest groups. In the realm of economic policy, social policy, and international trade policy, the activity of interest groups is of critical importance.

James Madison wrote that "liberty is to faction as air is to fire."[47] By this he meant that the organization and proliferation of interests are inevitable in a free society. As long as competition among different interests was free, open, and vigorous—that is, as long as pluralism thrived—there would be some balance of power among them, and no one interest would be able to dominate the political or governmental process.

Indeed, there is considerable competition among organized groups in the United States. Prochoice and antiabortion forces, for example, continue to be locked in a bitter struggle, as are the NRA and gun control groups. Nevertheless, interest group politics is not as balanced as Madison's theory and pluralism might suggest. Although the weak and poor do occasionally become organized to assert their interests, interest group politics is generally a form of political competition best suited to the wealthy and powerful.

Moreover, although groups sometimes organize to promote broad public concerns, they more often represent relatively narrow, selfish interests. Small groups seeking narrow interests can be organized much more easily than large and diffuse collectives. The members of relatively small groups—say, bankers or hunting enthusiasts—are usually able to recognize their shared interests and the need to pursue them in the political arena. Members of large and diffuse groups—say, consumers or the unemployed—often find it difficult to recognize their shared interests or the need to engage in collective action to achieve them.[48] Whether Ben Brown's new Association of Young Americans can grow and achieve legislative success remains to be seen, as younger Americans' activism may be undercut by the diverse array of interests they have and by the many immediate concerns that dominate their time (school, work, and family, among others).

Organized interest groups sometimes seem to have a greater impact than voters on the government's policies and programs, especially through lobbying and financial contributions to political candidates. (The "**Who Participates?**" feature on the facing page shows how much major groups spend on lobbying activities). Yet, before we decide that we should do away with interest groups, we should think carefully: If there were no organized interests, would the government pay more attention to ordinary voters? Would young people be better or worse off if there were no interest groups in the United States? Or would the government simply pay less attention to everyone? In his work *Democracy in America*, Alexis de Tocqueville argued that the proliferation of groups promoted democracy by encouraging governmental responsiveness. Does group politics foster democracy or impede democracy? It does both.

How Much Do Major Groups Spend?

Lobbying Expenditures, 2016 (top spenders)

 = $1,000,000

$103,950,000
U.S. Chamber of Commerce

$64,821,111
National Association of Realtors

$25,006,109
Blue Cross/Blue Shield

$22,006,109
American Hospital
Association

$19,730,000
Pharmaceutical Research
& Manufacturers of America

$19,410,000
American Medical
Association

$17,020,000
Boeing Co.

$16,438.000
National Association
of Broadcasters

$16,370,000
AT&T Inc.

$15,700,000
Business Roundtable

$15,430,000
Alphabet Inc.

$14,330,000
Comcast Corp.

$13,900,000
Southern Co.

$13,635,982
Dow Chemical

$13,615,811
Lockheed Martin

$13,420,000
The Internet & Television
Association (NCTA)

$12,541,000
FedEx Corp.

12,050,000
Northrop Grumman

$11,840,000
ExxonMobil

$11,354,000
Amazon.com

SOURCE: Center for Responsive Politics, www.opensecrets.org/lobby (accessed 11/21/17).

★ **WHAT YOU CAN DO** ★

Get Involved with Interest Groups and Lobbying

 Find an interest group that appeals to you at **votesmart.org/interest-groups**, then follow that group on Facebook or Twitter.

 Find out which groups give the most money to your representatives in Congress by clicking "Congress" at **www.opensecrets.org/politicians**. You can look up your representatives by zip code.

 Contact your Center for Campus Life to find out if groups you're interested in have chapters on your campus. Many groups will gladly help students start campus chapters.

★ STUDY GUIDE ★

Defining Interest Groups

> **Describe the major types of interest groups and whom they represent (pp. 431–39)**

An interest group is an organized group of people that makes policy-related appeals to government. Common types of interest groups include economic and corporate groups, labor groups, and citizen (or public interest) groups. Well-educated, upper-income, professional people are more likely to have the time, money, and skills to participate in interest groups. As a result, interest groups tend to skew in favor of corporate, business, and upper-class interests, leaving those with lower socioeconomic status less able to participate in and influence politics.

Key Terms

pluralism (p. 431)

interest group (p. 431)

public interest groups (p. 435)

Practice Quiz

1. The theory that competition among organized interests will produce balance and compromise, with all the interests regulating one another, is
   a) pluralism.
   b) elite power politics.
   c) democracy.
   d) socialism.
   e) libertarianism.

2. The Natural Resources Defense Council, the Sierra Club, the National Civic League, and Common Cause are all examples of
   a) membership associations.
   b) public interest groups.
   c) professional associations.
   d) ideological groups.
   e) public-sector groups.

How Groups Organize

> **Describe how interest groups and social groups organize (pp. 439–45)**

Almost all interest groups share a similar set of organizational components, including leadership, money, an office, and members. In order to overcome the free-rider problem, interest groups attempt to provide their potential members with informational, material, solidary, and purposive benefits. Online advocacy groups have established new approaches to organization and membership.

Key Terms

membership association (p. 440)

staff organization (p. 441)

collective goods (p. 441)

free riders (p. 441)

informational benefits (p. 442)

material benefits (p. 442)

solidary benefits (p. 442)

purposive benefits (p. 442)

Practice Quiz

3. Benefits sought by groups that are broadly available and cannot be denied to nonmembers are called
   a) purposive benefits.
   b) informational benefits.
   c) solidary benefits.
   d) material benefits.
   e) collective goods.

4. Friendship and networking are examples of
   a) purposive benefits.
   b) informational benefits.
   c) solidary benefits.
   d) material benefits.
   e) collective goods.

5. Discount purchasing and health insurance are examples of
   a) purposive benefits.
   b) informational benefits.
   c) solidary benefits.
   d) material benefits.
   e) collective goods.

The Growth of Interest and Advocacy Groups

Analyze why the number of interest and advocacy groups has grown in recent decades (pp. 446–47)

In recent decades there has been a significant growth in the number of interest groups seeking to influence the American political process. One reason for this change has been the dramatic expansion of the role of American government over the last four decades. Another reason for this change has been the emergence of a new set of political forces in the United States called the "New Politics" movement.

Practice Quiz

6. Which of the following is an important reason for the enormous increase in the number of groups seeking to influence the American political system?
   a) the decrease in the size and activity of government during the last few decades
   b) the increase in the size and activity of government during the last few decades
   c) the increase in the amount of soft money in election campaigns in recent decades
   d) the increase in legal protection provided to interest groups as a result of the Supreme Court's evolving interpretation of the First Amendment
   e) the increase in the number of people identifying themselves as independent in recent decades

Interest Group Strategies

Explain how interest groups try to influence government and policy (pp. 447–59)

Interest groups take action to improve the probability that their policy interests will be treated favorably by all branches and all levels of government. These actions often take many different forms. Insider strategies include direct lobbying, cultivating access to decision makers, and using the court system. Outsider strategies include mobilizing public opinion and using electoral politics.

Key Terms

lobbying (p. 449)
iron triangle (p. 451)
issue network (p. 452)
institutional advertising (p. 454)
grassroots mobilization (p. 455)
political action committee (PAC) (p. 458)
527 committee (Super PAC) (p. 458)

Practice Quiz

7. Which of the following best describes the federal government's laws regarding lobbying?
   a) Federal law allows lobbying but only on issues related to taxation.
   b) Federal law allows lobbying but only if the lobbyists receive no monetary compensation for their lobbying.
   c) Federal law strictly prohibits any form of lobbying.
   d) Federal law requires all organizations employing lobbyists to register with Congress and to disclose whom they represent, whom they lobby, what they are looking for, and how much they are paid.
   e) There are no laws regulating lobbying because the federal government has never passed any legislation on the legality of the activity.

8. A loose network of elected leaders, public officials, activists, and interest groups drawn together by a public policy issue is referred to as
   a) an issue network.
   b) a public interest group.
   c) a political action committee.
   d) pluralism.
   e) an iron triangle.

9. Which of the following is a way that interest groups use the courts to influence public policy?
   a) supplying judges with solidary benefits
   b) joining an issue network
   c) creating an iron triangle
   d) forming a political action committee
   e) filing amicus curiae briefs

10. Which of the following are examples of the "going public" strategy?
   a) free riding, pluralism, and issue networking
   b) donating money to political parties, endorsing candidates, and sponsoring ballot initiatives
   c) institutional advertising, grassroots advertising, and protests and demonstrations
   d) providing informational benefits, providing solidary benefits, and providing material benefits
   e) filing an amicus brief, bringing a lawsuit, and financing those who are filing a lawsuit

11. Which of the following is *not* an activity in which interest groups frequently engage?
   a) starting their own political party
   b) litigation
   c) sponsoring ballot initiatives at the state level
   d) lobbying
   e) contributing to campaigns

12. One of the major differences between PACs and Super PACs is that
   a) a PAC has a maximum contribution limit of $500 per candidate in each election cycle while a Super PAC has a maximum contribution limit of $1,000.
   b) a PAC has a maximum contribution limit of $1,000 per candidate in each election cycle while a Super PAC has a maximum contribution limit of $5,000.
   c) a PAC has a maximum contribution limit of $5,000 per candidate in each election cycle while a Super PAC has a maximum contribution limit of $10,000.
   d) a PAC has a maximum contribution limit of $5,000 per candidate in each election cycle while a Super PAC cannot donate to candidates directly.
   e) a Super PAC has a maximum contribution limit of $5,000 per candidate in each election cycle while a PAC cannot donate to candidates directly.

For Further Reading

Alexander, Robert, ed. *The Classics of Interest Group Behavior*. New York: Wadsworth, 2005.

Baumgartner, Frank, Jeffrey M. Berry, Beth L. Leech, David C. Kimball, and Marie Hojnacki. *Lobbying and Policy Change: Who Wins, Who Loses, and Why*. Chicago: University of Chicago Press, 2009.

Berry, Jeffrey. *Interest Group Society*. 5th ed. New York: Longman, 2008.

Cigler, Allan J., and Burdett A. Loomis, eds. *Interest Group Politics*. 9th ed. Washington, DC: CQ Press, 2015.

Drutman, Lee. *The Business of America Is Lobbying: How Corporations Became Politicized and Politics Became More Corporate*. New York: Oxford University Press, 2015.

Goldstein, Kenneth. *Interest Groups, Lobbying, and Participation in America*. New York: Cambridge University Press, 2008.

Herrnson, Paul, and Christopher Deering. *Interest Groups Unleashed*. Washington, DC: CQ Press, 2012.

Holyoke, Thomas. *Interest Groups and Lobbying: Pursuing Political Interests in America*. Boulder, CO: Westview, 2014.

Kaiser, Robert. *So Damn Much Money: The Triumph of Lobbying and the Corrosion of American Government*. New York: Vintage, 2010.

Karpf, David. *The MoveOn Effect: The Unexpected Transformation of American Political Advocacy*. New York: Oxford University Press, 2012.

Lessig, Lawrence. *Republic, Lost: How Money Corrupts Congress—and a Plan to Stop It*. New York: Twelve/Hachette Book Group, 2011.

Lowi, Theodore J. *The End of Liberalism: The Second Republic of the United States*. 2nd ed. New York: W. W. Norton, 1979.

Moe, Terry M. *The Organization of Interests: Incentives and the Internal Dynamics of Political Interest Groups*. Chicago: University of Chicago Press, 1980.

Nownes, Anthony. *Total Lobbying: What Lobbyists Want and How They Try to Get It*. New York: Cambridge University Press, 2006.

Olson, Mancur, Jr. *The Logic of Collective Action: Public Goods and the Theory of Groups*. Cambridge, MA: Harvard University Press, 1965.

Shirky, Clay. *Here Comes Everybody: The Power of Organizing without Organizations*. New York: Penguin Press, 2008.

Strolovitch, Dara. *Affirmative Advocacy: Race, Class, and Gender in Interest Group Politics*. Chicago: University of Chicago Press, 2007.

Recommended Websites

AARP

www.aarp.org

AARP (formerly the American Association of Retired Persons) is one of the largest and most significant interest groups in the United States. Read about the history of this organization, its group benefits, and how it is affecting political issues and elections.

AFL-CIO Legislative Alerts

www.aflcio.org/Legislation-and-Politics/Legislative-Alerts

Created in 1955, the AFL-CIO represents more than 10 million working men and women. See how this influential labor group is active and involved in political issues.

American Civil Liberties Union

www.aclu.org

American Conservative Union

www.conservative.org

The American Civil Liberties Union and the American Conservative Union are two of the nation's largest and most influential ideological interest groups. See what these opposing groups have to say about our government and current political issues.

American Israel Public Affairs Committee

www.aipac.org

Due to globalization, interest groups cannot limit their activities to one country. Decisions made in Washington, D.C., can affect countries around the world. The American Israel Public Affairs Committee works with Republicans and Democrats to maintain a strong relationship between the United States and Israel.

MoveOn

www.moveon.org

This progressive interest group is dedicated to bringing ordinary citizens back into the political process and electing liberal members of government. See how this group uses electoral politics, via political action committees and campaign activism, to achieve its agenda.

National Rifle Association

www.nra.org

Coalition to Stop Gun Violence

www.csgv.org

Brady Campaign to Prevent Gun Violence

www.bradycampaign.org

Lobbying is an attempt by a group to influence the policy process by persuading government officials. These three groups employ a variety of lobbying techniques on the issue of gun control.

U.S. Public Interest Research Group

www.uspirg.org

This public interest group stands up for ordinary citizens. Its special emphasis is on consumer rights and the environment. U.S. Public Interest Research Group (U.S. PIRG) mobilizes public opinion via institutional advertising, social movements, and grassroots efforts. U.S. PIRG chapters can be found in most states and at many colleges and universities.

World Wildlife Fund

www.wwf.org

The World Wildlife Fund is dedicated to protecting nature. It provides information to policy makers about conservation and advocates for policies to help preserve the natural environment.

Congress

WHAT GOVERNMENT DOES AND WHY IT MATTERS As the nation's chief legislative body, Congress affects Americans every day with its decisions. Guy Berkebile, founder of the Guy Chemical company of Somerset, Pennsylvania, was thrilled with the Tax Cut and Jobs Act passed by Congress in late 2017. The bill lowers taxes for both large corporations and small businesses like Guy Chemical, which manufacturers silicone and epoxy adhesives. Berkebile noted that high business taxes had presented a challenge for him as a small business owner. "I did not draw a salary from my company for five years when I started it because the survival of my business in paying my employees was always more important than how much I was making at the time," noted Berkebile, who mortgaged his house seven times to help finance the business. He will face a lower tax rate under the new law.[1]

Congressional *inaction* affects Americans as well. Hazel Hoffman is a 5-year-old Illinois girl who suffers from a severe form of epilepsy which frequently sends her to the hospital with powerful seizures and which requires expensive medications. Adding Hoffman to her mother's health insurance at work would cost $6,000 per year and would only cover half her health care costs. Instead, Hoffman is

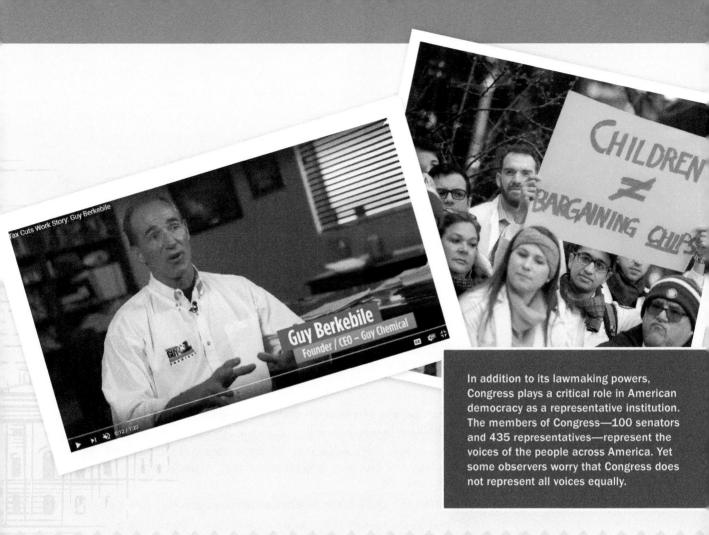

enrolled in the Children's Health Insurance Program (CHIP), created in 1997 to cover children in families with incomes too high for Medicaid but who can't afford private coverage. It has widely been viewed as a success, insuring nearly 9 million children for $13.6 billion in 2016[2] (In contrast, Medicare for older people and the permanently disabled insures 57 million people for $588 billion—6 times the people for 43 times the cost).[3] CHIP was due for renewal in September 2017, but Congress declined to take action for months, unable to agree on a spending bill and contemplating a federal government shutdown. With CHIP money running out, officials in a number of states were forced to draft letters to families terminating their coverage. Finally, in January 2018 Congress broke its logjam and reauthorized CHIP for six years, but not before sending families into a panic about what they would do for health insurance if CHIP collapsed.

Congress has vast authority over many aspects of American life. Laws related to federal spending, taxing, regulation, and federal judicial appointments all pass through Congress. While the debates over these laws may seem hard to follow because they are often complex and technical or because heated, partisan struggles distract from the substance of the issue, it is important for the American people to learn about what Congress is doing. As the example of the near government shutdown indicates, actions taken—or not taken—in Congress affect the everyday experiences we take for granted. With its power to spend and tax, Congress also affects the choices that people face and the opportunities they can expect in life. With so much information about Congress available on the internet, it is not hard to get beyond the heated rhetoric and simplistic headlines and ask your own questions about a proposed law. How will it affect my life and the lives of people I care about? What is the impact on my country? Making laws is a complex and often messy process. Even so, it is vital for citizens to monitor what Congress does because the laws it passes are so central to their lives.

CHAPTER GOALS

★ Describe who serves in Congress and how they represent their constituents (pp. 469–82)

★ Explain how party leadership, the committee system, the staff system, and caucuses help structure congressional business (pp. 482–89)

★ Outline the steps in the process of passing a law (pp. 489–94)

★ Analyze the factors that influence which laws Congress passes (pp. 494–502)

★ Describe Congress's influence over other branches of government (pp. 502–5)

Congress: Representing the American People

> **Describe who serves in Congress and how they represent their constituents**

Congress is the most important representative institution in American government. Each member's primary responsibility in theory is to the district, to his or her **constituency**, not to the congressional leadership, a party, or even Congress itself. Yet the task of representation is not a simple one. Views about what constitutes fair and effective representation differ, and constituents may have very different expectations of their representatives. Members of Congress must consider these diverse views and expectations as they represent their districts.

constituency the residents in the area from which an official is elected

HOUSE AND SENATE: DIFFERENCES IN REPRESENTATION

The framers of the Constitution provided for a **bicameral** legislature—that is, a legislative body consisting of two chambers. As we saw in Chapter 2, the framers intended each of these chambers, the House of Representatives and the Senate, to serve a different constituency. Members of the Senate, appointed by state legislatures for six-year terms, were to represent society's elite. Today, members of both the House and the Senate are elected directly by the people. The 435 members of the House are elected from districts apportioned according to population; the 100 members of the Senate are elected in a statewide vote, with two senators from each state. Senators continue to have much longer terms in office and usually represent much larger and more diverse constituencies than do their counterparts in the House (see Table 12.1).

bicameral having a legislative assembly composed of two chambers or houses, distinguished from *unicameral*

The House and Senate play different roles in the legislative process. In essence, the Senate is the more deliberative of the two bodies—the forum in which any and all ideas that senators raise can receive a thorough public airing. The House is the

TABLE 12.1

Differences between the House and the Senate

	HOUSE	SENATE
Minimum age of member	25 years	30 years
U.S. citizenship	At least 7 years	At least 9 years
Length of term	2 years	6 years
Number representing each state	1-53 per state (depends on population)	2 per state
Constituency	Local	Statewide

For its first 128 years, Congress was a decidedly masculine world. In 1917, Jeanette Rankin (R-Mont.; pictured back row, far right) became the first woman to serve in the House or Senate. As of 2016, a total of 297 women had served as U.S. representatives or senators, while 11,804 men have served.

more centralized and organized of the two bodies—better equipped to play a routine role in the governmental process. In part, this difference stems from the different rules governing the two bodies. These rules give House leaders more control over the legislative process and allow House members to specialize in certain legislative areas. The rules of the much smaller Senate give its leadership relatively little power and discourage specialization.

Both formal and informal factors contribute to differences between the two chambers of Congress. Differences in the length of terms and requirements for holding office, specified by the Constitution, generate differences in how members of each body develop their constituencies and exercise their powers of office. For the House, the small size and relative homogeneity of their constituencies and the frequency with which they must seek re-election—every two years—make members more attuned to the legislative needs of local interest groups. The result is that members of the House most effectively and frequently serve as the agents of well-organized local interests with specific legislative agendas—for instance, used-car dealers seeking relief from regulation, labor unions seeking more favorable legislation, or farmers looking for higher subsidies. Because House members seek re-election every two years, they are interested in doing what their constituents want right *now*.

Senators, on the other hand, serve larger and more heterogeneous constituencies. As a result, they are somewhat better able than members of the House to act as the agents for groups and interests organized on a statewide or national basis. Moreover, with longer terms in office (six years), senators have more time to consider "new ideas" or to bring together new coalitions of interests rather than simply serving existing ones.

TRUSTEE VERSUS DELEGATE REPRESENTATION

delegate a representative who votes according to the preferences of his or her constituency

trustee a representative who votes based on what he or she thinks is best for his or her constituency

For the Founders, Congress was the national institution that best embodied the ideals of representative democracy. But what is the role of a representative? A member of Congress can interpret her job as representative in two different ways: as a **delegate**, acting on the express preferences of her constituents, or as a **trustee**, more loosely tied to constituents and empowered to make the decisions she thinks best. The delegate role appears to be the more democratic because it forces representatives to heed the desires of their constituents. But this requires the representative to be in constant touch with constituents; it also requires constituents to follow each policy issue very closely. The problem with this form of representation is that most people do not follow every issue so carefully; instead, they focus only on the issue or issues of particular interest to them. Many people are too busy to get the information necessary to make informed judgments even on issues they care about. Thus, adhering to the delegate form of representation runs the risk that the voices of only a few active and informed constituents get heard. Although it seems more democratic at first glance, the delegate form of representation may actually open Congress up to even more influence by special interests.

When congressional members act as trustees, on the other hand, they may not pay sufficient attention to the wishes of their constituents. In this scenario, the only way the public can exercise influence is by voting every two years for representatives and every six years for senators. In fact, most members of Congress take this electoral check very seriously. They try to anticipate the wishes of their constituents even when they don't know exactly what those wishes are because they know that unpopular decisions can be used against them in the coming election.

SOCIOLOGICAL VERSUS AGENCY REPRESENTATION

We have become so accustomed to the idea of representative government that we tend to forget what a peculiar concept representation really is. A representative claims to act or speak for some other person or group. But how can one person be trusted to speak for another? How do we know that those who call themselves our representatives are actually speaking on our behalf, rather than simply pursuing their own interests?

There are two circumstances under which one person reasonably might be trusted to speak for another. The first occurs if the two individuals are so similar in background, character, interests, and perspectives that anything said by one would very likely reflect the views of the other as well. This principle is at the heart of what is sometimes called **sociological representation**—the sort of representation that takes place when representatives have the same racial, gender, ethnic, religious, or educational backgrounds as their constituents. The assumption is that sociological similarity helps to promote good representation; thus, the composition of a properly constituted representative assembly should mirror the composition of society.

The second circumstance under which one person might be trusted to speak for another occurs if the two are formally bound together so that the representative is in some way accountable to those he is supposed to represent. If representatives can somehow be punished for failing to speak properly for their constituents, then we know they have an incentive to provide good representation even if their own personal backgrounds, views, and interests differ from the backgrounds of those they represent. This principle is called **agency representation**—the sort of representation that takes place when constituents have the power to hire and fire their representatives.

Both sociological and agency representation play a role in the relationship between members of Congress and their constituencies, but in many ways, members of Congress do not reflect the American population (see the "Who Are Americans?" feature on p. 473).

The Social Composition of the U.S. Congress The extent to which the U.S. Congress is representative of the American people in a sociological sense can be seen by examining social characteristics of the House and Senate today. For example, the religious affiliations of members of both the House and Senate are overwhelmingly Protestant—the distribution is very close to the proportion in the population at large. Catholics are the second-largest category of religious affiliation and Jews a much smaller, third category.[4] Religious affiliations directly affect congressional debate on a limited range of issues where different moral views are at stake, such as abortion.

African Americans, women, Latinos, and Asian Americans have increased their congressional representation in the past two decades (see Figure 12.1), but the representation of minorities in Congress is still not comparable to their proportions in the general population. After the 2018 elections, Congress was 9 percent African American, 7 percent Latino, and 3 percent Asian American. By contrast, the American population was far more diverse, with 13.3 percent African Americans, 17.6 percent Latinos, and 5.6 percent Asian Americans.[5] As the United States has

sociological representation a type of representation in which representatives have the same racial, gender, ethnic, religious, or educational backgrounds as their constituents; it is based on the principle that if two individuals are similar in background, character, interests, and perspectives, then one can correctly represent the other's views

agency representation a type of representation in which a representative is held accountable to a constituency if he or she fails to represent that constituency properly; this is incentive for the representative to provide good representation when his or her personal backgrounds, views, and interests differ from those of his or her constituency

FOR CRITICAL ANALYSIS

Why is sociological representation important? If congressional representatives have racial, religious, or educational backgrounds similar to those of their constituents, are they better representatives? Why or why not?

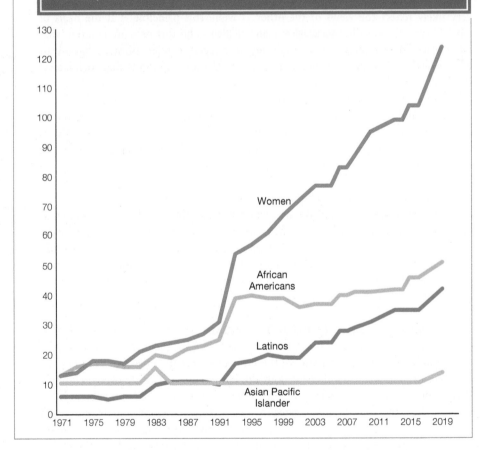

FIGURE 12.1

Number of Women, African Americans, and Latinos in the U.S. Congress, 1971–2019

Congress has become much more socially diverse since the 1970s. After a gradual increase from 1971 to 1990, the number of female and African American members grew quickly during the first half of the 1990s. Do you think these numbers will rise in the future? Why or why not?

SOURCES: Harold W. Stanley and Richard G. Niemi, eds., *Vital Statistics on American Politics 2003-2004* (Washington, DC: CQ Press, 2003), 207, Table 5-2; Jennifer E. Manning, *Membership of the 113th Congress: A Profile*, Congressional Research Service 7-5700, January 13, 2014, www.fas.org/sgp/crs/misc/R42964.pdf (accessed 2/24/14); Jennifer E. Manning, *Membership of the 114th Congress: A Profile*, Congressional Research Service, 7-5700 September 17, 2015, www.fas.org/sgp/crs/misc/R43869.pdf (accessed 9/28/15); R. Eric Petersen, *Representatives and Senators: Trends in Member Characteristics since 1945*, Congressional Research Service 7-5700, February 17, 2012, www.fas.org/sgp/crs/misc/R42365.pdf (accessed 9/28/15); 2019 racial data were calculated by the authors.

become more diverse, Congress has lagged behind in sociological representation. Similarly, the number of women in Congress continues to trail far behind their proportion of the population. In 2006, Nancy Pelosi (D-Calif.) became the first female Speaker of the House. Following the 2018 elections, the 116th Congress (2019–21) included at least 102 women in the House and 23 women in the Senate, an all-time high. Since many important contemporary issues cut along racial and

Who Are the Members of Congress?

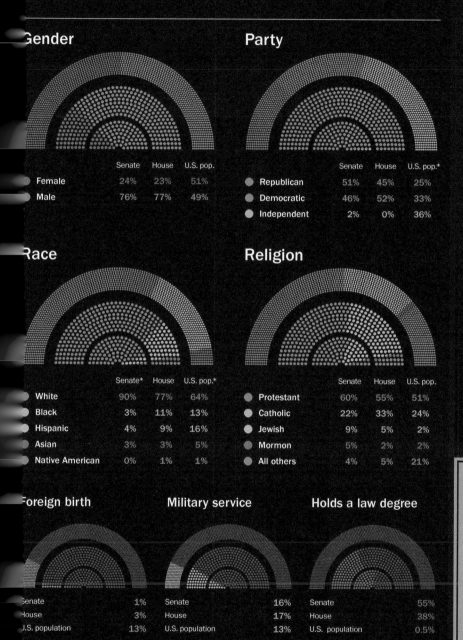

Gender

	Senate	House	U.S. pop.
Female	24%	23%	51%
Male	76%	77%	49%

Party

	Senate	House	U.S. pop.*
Republican	51%	45%	25%
Democratic	46%	52%	33%
Independent	2%	0%	36%

Key

U.S. population

Senate

House of Representatives

Although the number of women, African Americans, and Latinos in Congress has increased in recent decades, Congress is still much less diverse than the American population. Members of Congress are predominantly male, white, Protestant, and a large percentage hold a law degree. These data compare the 116th Congress, which took office in 2019, with the U.S. population as a whole.

Race

	Senate*	House	U.S. pop.*
White	90%	77%	64%
Black	3%	11%	13%
Hispanic	4%	9%	16%
Asian	3%	3%	5%
Native American	0%	1%	1%

Religion

	Senate	House	U.S. pop.
Protestant	60%	55%	51%
Catholic	22%	33%	24%
Jewish	9%	5%	2%
Mormon	5%	2%	2%
All others	4%	5%	21%

Foreign birth

Senate	1%
House	3%
U.S. population	13%

Military service

Senate	16%
House	17%
U.S. population	13%

Holds a law degree

Senate	55%
House	38%
U.S. population	0.5%

Average age

Senate 61   House 57   U.S. population 37

NOTES: As of November 13, 2018, 10 House races and 2 Senate races remain undecided.
Data for religion are from the 115th Congress.
Percentages do not sum to 100 because some Americans identify with other categories.
SOURCES: Jennifer E. Manning, "Membership of the 115th Congress: A Profile," Congressional Research Service,
www.fas.org/sgp/crs/misc/R43869.pdf (accessed 11/12/18); U.S. Census Bureau, www.census.gov/population/age/-
data/2012comp.html (accessed 3/19/14); and author's updates.

FOR CRITICAL ANALYSIS

1. Does it matter if the backgrounds of members of Congress reflect the population as a whole? Can members still represent their constituents effectively if they do not come from similar backgrounds?

2. Visit www.house.gov and www.senate.gov to identify your representatives in Congress and visit their web pages. How similar are their backgrounds to yours? How closely do their policy positions, as expressed on their web pages, match your own?

To more effectively promote a legislative agenda addressing issues that disproportionately affect racial and ethnic minority groups, members of Congress from those groups have formed caucuses. Here, Rep. Michelle Lujan Grisham (D-N. Mex.), former chair of the Congressional Hispanic Caucus, speaks out about Donald Trump's proposed changes to immigration policies.

gender lines, pressure for reform in the representative process is likely to continue until all groups are fully represented.

The occupational backgrounds of members of Congress have always been a matter of interest because many issues split along economic lines that are relevant to occupations and industries. The legal profession is the dominant career of most members of Congress prior to their election, and public service or politics is also a significant background. In addition, many members of Congress have important ties to business and industry.[6] Moreover, members of Congress are much more highly educated than most Americans. More than 9 in 10 members hold university degrees, and more than one-third of them have law degrees.[7] This is not a portrait of the U.S. population; Congress is not a sociological microcosm of American society.

Can Congress still legislate fairly or take account of a diversity of views and interests if it is not a sociologically representative assembly? There is reason to believe it can. Representatives, as we shall see shortly, can serve as the agents of their constituents even if they do not precisely mirror their sociological attributes. Yet sociological representation is a matter of some importance. At the least, the social composition of a representative assembly is important for symbolic purposes: to demonstrate to groups in the population that the government takes them seriously. If Congress is not representative symbolically, then its own authority, and indeed that of the entire government, is reduced.[8]

Representatives as Agents A good deal of evidence indicates that whether or not members of Congress share their constituents' sociological characteristics, they *do* work very hard to speak for their constituents' views and to serve their constituents' interests. The idea of representative as agent is similar to the relationship of lawyer and client. True, the relationship between the House member and an average of 710,767 "clients" in the district, or the senator and millions of "clients" in the state, is very different from that of the lawyer and client. But the criteria of performance are comparable. One expects at the very least that each representative will constantly seek to discover the interests of the constituency and take those interests into account as she governs. Whether members of Congress always represent the interests of their constituents is another matter, as we will see later in this chapter.[9]

There is constant communication between constituents and congressional offices, and the volume of email from constituents and advocacy groups has grown so large so quickly that congressional offices have struggled to find effective ways to respond in a timely manner.[10] At the same time, members of Congress have found new ways to communicate with constituents. They have created websites describing their achievements, established a presence on social networking sites, and issued e-newsletters that alert constituents to current issues. Many also have set up blogs and Twitter accounts to establish a more informal style of communication with constituents.

The seriousness with which members of the House attempt to behave as representatives can be seen in the amount of time they spend on behalf of their constituents. One way to measure the amount of time members of Congress devote to constituency service (called "casework") is to look at the percentage of personal House and Senate staff (personal staff being non-committee member staff) assigned to district and state offices. In 1972, 22.5 percent of House members' personal staff were located in district offices; by 2016 the number had grown to 47.3 percent. For the Senate, the staff in state offices grew from 12.5 percent in 1972 to 43.2 percent in 2016.[11] The service that these offices provide is not merely a matter of handling correspondence. It includes talking to constituents; providing them with minor services; presenting special bills for them; attempting to influence decisions by regulatory commissions on their behalf; helping them apply for federal benefits such as Social Security and Small Business Administration loans; and assisting them with immigration cases. For example, during his fight for re-election in 2014, Senate Minority Leader Mitch McConnell (R-Ky.) ran a campaign ad featuring Noelle Hunter, a Kentucky resident whose ex-husband abducted their daughter and took her to Africa. According to Hunter, McConnell "took up my cause personally" and worked with the State Department to bring her daughter back home. Senator Pat Roberts (R-Kans.) struck a similar tone when touting his success in helping Kate Forristall, a Kansan whose daughter was taken hostage while teaching English in Ethiopia. Roberts says in the ad, "We got the call. Top priority. We went to work."[12]

In many districts, there are two or three issues that are top priorities for constituents and, therefore, for the representatives. For example, representatives from districts that grow wheat, cotton, or tobacco will likely give legislation on these subjects great attention. In oil-rich states such as Oklahoma and Texas, senators and members of the House are likely to be leading advocates of oil interests. For one thing, representatives are probably fearful of voting against their district interests; for another, the districts are unlikely to have elected representatives who would *want* to vote against them. On the other hand, on many issues, constituents do not have very strong views, and representatives are free to act as they think best. Foreign policy issues often fall into this category.

The influence of constituencies is so pervasive that both parties generally agree that nothing should be done to endanger the re-election chances of any member. Party leaders obey this rule fairly consistently by not asking any member to vote in a way that might conflict with a district interest.

THE ELECTORAL CONNECTION

The sociological composition of Congress and the activities of representatives once they are in office are very much influenced by electoral considerations. Three factors related to the U.S. electoral system affect who gets elected and what they do once in office. The first factor concerns who decides to run for office and which candidates have an edge over others. The second issue is that of incumbency advantage. Finally, the way congressional district lines are drawn can greatly affect the outcome of an election. Let us examine more closely the impact that these considerations have on representation.

Who Runs for Congress Voters' choices are restricted from the start by who decides to run for office. In the past, decisions about who would run for a particular elected office were made by local party officials. A person who had a record of service to the party, who was owed a favor, or whose "turn" had come up might be nominated by party leaders. Today, few party organizations have the power to slate candidates in this way. Instead, parties try to ensure that well-qualified candidates run for Congress. During the 1990s the Republican Party developed "farm teams" of local officials who were groomed to run for Congress. Their success led Democrats to attempt a similar strategy. Even so, the decision to run for Congress is a personal one, and one of the most important factors determining who runs for office is an individual candidate's ambition.[13] A potential candidate may also assess whether he can attract enough money to mount a credible campaign. The ability to raise money depends on connections with other politicians, interest groups, and national party organizations.

Features distinctive to each congressional district also affect the field of candidates. For example, the way the congressional district overlaps with state legislative boundaries may affect a candidate's decision to run. A state-level legislator who is considering running for the U.S. Congress is more likely to assess her prospects favorably if her state district coincides with the congressional district (because the voters will already know her).

Incumbency Incumbency plays a very important role in the American electoral system and in the kind of representation citizens get in Washington. Once in office, members of Congress gain access to an array of tools they can use to stack the deck in favor of their re-election. Their success in winning re-election is evident in the high rates of re-election for congressional incumbents: as high as 98 percent for House members and 90 percent for members of the Senate in recent years (see Figure 12.2). It is also evident in what is called "sophomore surge"—the tendency for candidates to win a higher percentage of the vote when seeking subsequent terms in office. In 2018 approximately 93 percent of incumbents in the House and 86 percent in the Senate were re-elected.[14] Furthermore, incumbents often win by large margins: in 2018 only 76 of the 435 House races were decided by a margin of less than 10 percent.[15]

Incumbency can help a candidate by scaring off potential challengers. In many races, potential candidates may decide not to run because they fear that the incumbent simply has too much money or is too well liked or too well known or that a district's partisan leanings are too unfavorable. The efforts of incumbents to raise funds to ward off potential challengers start early. In addition to incumbents' own efforts, each political party makes a special effort to reelect incumbents viewed as especially vulnerable. The Democratic Congressional Campaign Committee (DCCC) places vulnerable incumbents in its "Frontline" program to receive extra funding, choice committee assignments, and high-profile speaking engagements. For the 2018 midterm elections, the DCCC placed 19 incumbents on its Frontline list, many of whom had won in 2016 in districts carried by Trump. For its part, the Republican Congressional Campaign Committee (RCCC) named 10 members to its own incumbent protection program.[16]

The advantage of incumbency thus tends to preserve the status quo in Congress. This fact has implications for the social composition of Congress. For example,

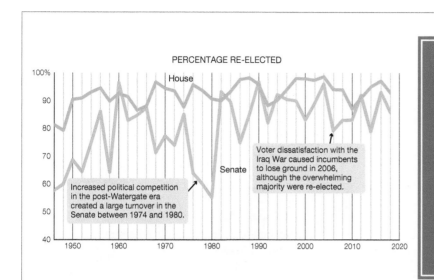

PERCENTAGE RE-ELECTED

House

Senate

Increased political competition in the post-Watergate era created a large turnover in the Senate between 1974 and 1980.

Voter dissatisfaction with the Iraq War caused incumbents to lose ground in 2006, although the overwhelming majority were re-elected.

FIGURE 12.2

The Power of Incumbency

Members of Congress who run for re-election have a very good chance of winning. Has the incumbency advantage generally been greater in the House or in the Senate? What are the consequences of the incumbency advantage for who serves in Congress?

SOURCES: Norman J. Ornstein et al., eds., *Vital Statistics on Congress, 1999-2000* (Washington, DC: AEI Press, 2000), 57-8; "Reelection Rates over the Years," opensecrets.org; and authors' update.

incumbency advantage makes it harder for women to increase their numbers in Congress because most incumbents are men. Women who run for open seats—that is, seats for which there are no incumbents—are just as likely to win as male candidates.[17] Supporters of **term limits** argue that such limits are the only way to get new faces into Congress. They believe that incumbency advantage and the tendency of many legislators to view politics as a career mean that very little turnover will occur in Congress unless limits are imposed on the number of terms a legislator may serve.

Yet the percentage of incumbents who are returned to Congress after each election also depends on how many members decide to run again. Because each year some members decide to retire, turnover in Congress is greater than the re-election rates of incumbents suggest. On average, 10 percent of the House and Senate decide to retire each election.

The precarious economy and the backlash against the party in power made 2008 and 2010 difficult election years for some incumbents, particularly Democrats, given that their party controlled the presidency and both houses of Congress in a year when economic woes contributed to strong anti-incumbent sentiment.[18] Incumbents have fared better in recent elections. In 2016, Trump's surprise victory in the presidential race benefited Republican incumbents, who appeared to be in danger of losing their seats. In 2018, 5 incumbents in the Senate and over 20 incumbents in the House lost their seats.

Apportionment and Redistricting The final factor affecting who wins a seat in the House is the way congressional districts are drawn. Every 10 years, state legislatures must redraw congressional districts to reflect population changes. Because the number of congressional seats has been fixed at 435 since 1929, redistricting is a zero-sum process: in order for one state to gain a seat, another must lose one. The process of allocating congressional seats among the 50 states is called **apportionment**. States with population growth gain additional seats; states with a population decline or with less population growth lose seats. Over the past several decades, the shift of the American population to the South and the West has greatly increased the size of the congressional delegations from those regions. This trend continued after the 2010 census and

term limits legally prescribed limits on the number of terms an elected official can serve

apportionment the process, occurring after every decennial census, that allocates congressional seats among the 50 states

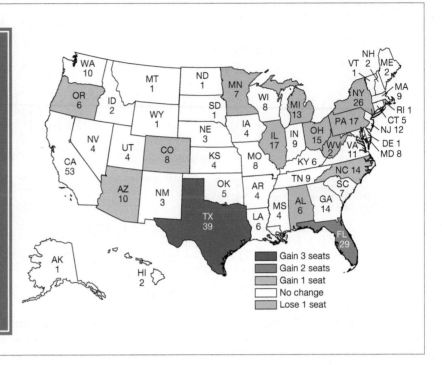

Legend:
- Gain 3 seats
- Gain 2 seats
- Gain 1 seat
- No change
- Lose 1 seat

redistricting the process of redrawing election districts and redistributing legislative representatives; this happens every 10 years to reflect shifts in population or in response to legal challenges to existing districts

gerrymandering the apportionment of voters in districts in such a way as to give unfair advantage to one racial or ethnic group or political party

will likely continue after 2020 (see Figure 12.3). Texas is likely to gain three seats (after gaining four after 2010), and Florida will likely gain two. States in the Northeast and "rust belt" are likely to lose seats. Latino voters are nearly three times as prevalent in states that gained seats than in states that lost seats, suggesting that the growth of the Latino population is a major factor in the American political landscape.[19]

States that gain or lose seats must then redraw their congressional district borders. Not surprisingly, **redistricting** is a highly political process: districts are shaped to create an advantage for the party with a majority in the state legislature, which controls the redistricting process in most states. In this complex process, those charged with drawing districts use sophisticated computer technologies to come up with the most favorable district boundaries. Redistricting can create open seats and may pit incumbents of the same party against one another, ensuring that one of them will lose. Redistricting can also give an advantage to one party by clustering voters with some ideological or sociological characteristics in a single district or by separating those voters into two or more districts. The manipulation of electoral districts to serve the interests of a particular group is known as **gerrymandering** (see Chapter 10).

Some analysts claim that Republicans have benefited from partisan gerrymandering since the 2010 redistricting cycle because they controlled the majority of state legislatures at the time. To support this argument, they point to the 2012 congressional election, in which the Republican Party maintained its majority in the House despite winning 1.4 million fewer votes than Democratic House candidates.[20] But others question whether districting that favors Republicans is a product of deliberate gerrymandering. They argue that these districts may reflect the natural clustering of Democrats in urban areas, not deliberate bias.[21] Even so, concern about partisan gerrymandering has led some states to take redistricting power away from state legislatures and give it to independent commissions. In the 2010 redistricting cycle,

Redrawing legislative districts is a difficult task because it has implications for who will be elected. Here, the attorney for Arizona's Independent Redistricting Commission discusses a possible layout with a city council member from Casa Grande. Arizona gained one congressional seat following the 2010 census.

six states—California, Arizona, Idaho, New Jersey, Washington, and Montana—required district lines to be drawn by commissions.[22] In 2015 a challenge to the use of commissions failed when the Supreme Court upheld the legality of relying on commissions to draw congressional district lines.[23] In 2018 the Supreme Court declined to rule on cases arising from charges of partisan gerrymandering in Wisconsin and Maryland. In the Wisconsin case, challengers had asked the Court to rule that the legislative districting of the state as a whole was designed to give Republicans a lopsided majority of congressional seats. The case was sent back to lower courts for further review.[24] The Supreme Court is, however, expected to rule on a North Carolina case where the Republican state official who led the state's recent redistricting efforts announced that the congressional map was drawn to give the GOP a large majority of the state's congressional seats.

As we saw in Chapter 10, since the passage of the 1982 amendments to the Voting Rights Act of 1965, race has become a major, and controversial, consideration in drawing voting districts. These amendments, which encouraged the creation of districts in which members of racial minorities have decisive majorities, have greatly increased the number of minority representatives in Congress. After the 1990 redistricting cycle, the number of predominantly minority districts doubled, rising from 26 to 52. Among the most fervent supporters of the new minority districts were white Republicans, who used the opportunity to create more districts dominated by white Republican voters. These developments raise thorny questions about representation. Some analysts argue that the system may grant minorities greater sociological representation but has made it more difficult for minorities to win substantive policy goals, while others dispute this argument.[25]

In the case of *Miller v. Johnson* (1995), the Supreme Court limited racial redistricting by ruling that race could not be the predominant factor in creating electoral districts.[26] The distinction between race being the "predominant" factor and its being one factor among many is hazy. As a result, concerns about redistricting and representation have not disappeared.[27] Questions about minority representation emerged in 2011 in Texas, which gained four new seats as a result of reapportionment. The Republican legislature drew a map that advantaged Republicans in three of those

FOR CRITICAL ANALYSIS

How does redistricting alter the balance of power in Congress? Why do political parties care so much about the redistricting process?

districts. But the plan drew a legal challenge on the grounds that it underrepresented Hispanic voters, who accounted for most of the state's population growth. Although federal judges drew a map more favorable to minorities (and Democrats), the Supreme Court ruled that the state did not have to use the map drawn by judges. The state ultimately agreed to a map that added two Latino-dominated districts. However, federal courts ruled that this map also weakened Latino and African American political power by creating too few minority districts.

The future of race in redistricting became more uncertain after the 2013 Supreme Court decision in *Shelby County v. Holder*. That decision invalidated a section of the Voting Rights Act requiring that the Justice Department approve the redistricting plans of jurisdictions with a history of racial discrimination.[28] Many Democrats expressed disappointment with the decision, fearing that the previously covered states, several of which are controlled by Republican majorities, might try to redraw district lines to partisan ends and further bias districts toward Republicans.[29] In 2015, Alabama's black legislators challenged that state's redistricting under the Voting Rights Act. They charged that the Republican legislature had diluted the vote of African Americans by packing black voters into districts that already had strong minority representation, thus enhancing the chances of white Republican candidates in the remaining districts. The legislature claimed, on the contrary, that it was acting in accordance with the Voting Rights Act by concentrating black voters. Although the Supreme Court did not declare the districting unconstitutional, it ruled that the lower court had erred in approving the districts.[30] The ruling signaled that state legislatures would not be able to use the Voting Rights Act to justify packing minority voters into districts. Because the drawing of district boundaries affects incumbents as well as the field of candidates who decide to run for office, it continues to be a key battleground on which political parties fight about the meaning of representation.

DIRECT PATRONAGE

As agents of their constituents, members of Congress have numerous opportunities to provide direct benefits, or **patronage**, for their districts. The most important such opportunity for direct patronage is in so-called **pork-barrel** legislation, which specifies a project to be funded within a particular district. Many observers of Congress argue that pork-barrel bills are the only ones that some members are serious about moving toward actual passage because they are seen as so important to members' re-election bids.

A common form of pork-barreling is the "earmark," by which members of Congress insert into bills language that provides special benefits for their own constituents. When the Democrats took over Congress in 2007, they vowed to limit the use of earmarks, which had grown from 1,439 per year in 1995 to 15,268 in 2006. More troubling, earmarks were connected to congressional scandals. For example, the Republican House member Randy "Duke" Cunningham (R-Calif.) was sent to jail in 2005 for accepting bribes by companies hoping to receive earmarks in return.[31] The House passed a new rule requiring that those representatives supporting each earmark identify themselves and guarantee that they have no personal financial stake in the requested project. A new ethics law applied similar provisions to the Senate. Though the new requirements appear to have had some impact, nonetheless, in the midst of the sharp economic downturn in 2009, Congress passed an economic stimulus bill that contained more than 8,000 earmarks. In his 2010 State of the Union address, President Obama called for Congress to publish a list of all earmark requests on a single website. Congress not only failed to enact such legislation but in 2010 set

patronage the resources available to higher officials, usually opportunities to make partisan appointments to offices and to confer grants, licenses, or special favors to supporters

pork barrel (or pork) appropriations made by legislative bodies for local projects that are often not needed but that are created so that local representatives can win re-election in their home districts a new record by passing 11,320 earmarks worth $32 billion. Still, in 2011 the House and the Senate agreed to a two-year moratorium on earmarks in spending bills and renewed the ban for the 113th, 114th, and 115th Congresses.[32] In 2018, President Trump suggested to Congress that it should consider restoring earmarks as a way of enhancing congressional power vis à vis the bureaucracy and to help "grease" the legislative wheels by giving members an incentive to support legislative programs. Trump's comments were greeted favorably by many congressional leaders.[33]

Some analysts claim that the lack of earmarks contributes to congressional gridlock. They argue that earmarks provide congressional leaders with incentives to promote compromise among members. Supporters of this position contend that earmarks are not inherently an abuse of power and note that they often support legitimate district projects, such as transportation and parks.[34]

There are a few other types of direct patronage (see Figure 12.4). One important form of constituency service is intervention with federal administrative agencies on behalf of constituents. Members of the House and Senate and their staff spend a great deal of time on the telephone and in administrative offices seeking to secure favorable treatment for constituents and supporters. For example, members of Congress can assist senior citizens who are having Social Security or Medicare benefit eligibility problems. Most members of Congress have a "constituent services" section on their websites, providing information about what they can and cannot do to assist their constituents.

A different form of patronage is the **private bill**. Unlike a public bill, which is supposed to deal with general rules and categories of behavior, people, and institutions, a private bill proposes to grant some kind of relief, special privilege, or exemption to the person named in the bill. As many as 75 percent of all private bills introduced (and one-third of those that pass) are concerned with obtaining citizenship for

FOR CRITICAL ANALYSIS

Would Congress work more effectively if it brought back earmarks? Why are earmarks so difficult to eliminate?

private bill a proposal in Congress to provide a specific person with some kind of relief, such as a special exemption from immigration quotas

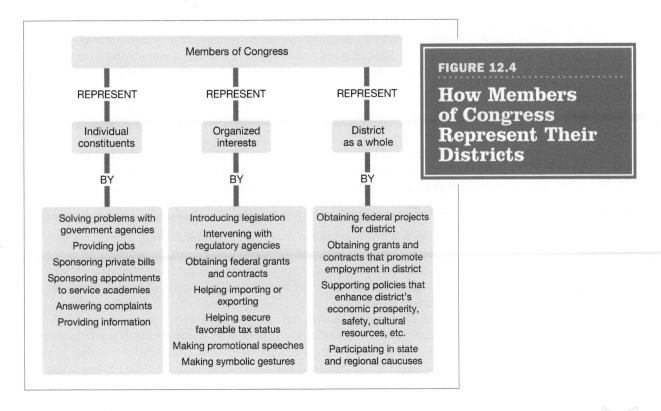

FIGURE 12.4

How Members of Congress Represent Their Districts

foreign nationals who do not have resident status in the United States. Other private bills address a diverse set of issues involving a claim against the federal government, such as problems with veterans' benefits or taxation. Private legislation is a congressional privilege that can be abused, but it is impossible to imagine members of Congress completely giving up one of the easiest, cheapest, and most effective forms of patronage available to them. It can be defended as an indispensable part of the process by which members of Congress seek to fulfill their role as representatives. And obviously they like the privilege because it helps them win re-election.

The Organization of Congress

> Explain how party leadership, the committee system, the staff system, and caucuses help structure congressional business

The U.S. Congress is not only a representative assembly but also a legislative body. To exercise its power to make laws, Congress must first bring about something close to an organizational miracle. The building blocks of congressional organization include the political parties, the committee system, congressional staff, the caucuses, and the parliamentary rules of the House and Senate. Each of these factors plays a key role in the organization of Congress and in the process through which Congress formulates and enacts laws.

PARTY LEADERSHIP IN THE HOUSE

conference a gathering of House Republicans every two years to elect their House leaders; Democrats call their gathering the "caucus"

caucus (political) a normally closed political party business meeting of citizens or lawmakers to select candidates, elect officers, plan strategy, or make decisions regarding legislative matters

Speaker of the House the chief presiding officer of the House of Representatives; the Speaker is the most important party and House leader and can influence the legislative agenda, the fate of individual pieces of legislation, and members' positions within the House

majority leader the elected leader of the majority party in the House of Representatives or in the Senate; in the House, the majority leader is subordinate in the party hierarchy to the Speaker of the House

minority leader the elected leader of the minority party in the House or Senate

whip a party member in the House or Senate responsible for coordinating the party's legislative strategy, building support for key issues, and counting votes

Every two years, at the beginning of a new Congress, the members of each party gather to elect their House leaders. House Republicans call their gathering the **conference**. House Democrats call theirs the **caucus**. The elected leader of the majority party is later proposed to the whole House and is automatically elected to the position of **Speaker of the House**, with voting along straight party lines. The House majority conference or caucus then also elects a **majority leader**. The minority party goes through the same process and selects a **minority leader**. Each party also elects a **whip** to line up party members on important votes and to relay voting information to the leaders.

Next in order of importance for each party after the Speaker and majority or minority leader is what Democrats call the Steering and Policy Committee—Republicans have a separate steering committee and a separate policy committee—whose tasks are to assign new legislators to committees and to deal with the requests of incumbent members for transfers from one committee to another. At one time, party leaders strictly controlled committee assignments, using them to enforce party discipline. Today, in principle, representatives receive the assignments they want. But often several individuals seek assignments to the most important committees, which gives the leadership an opportunity to cement alliances when it resolves conflicting requests.

Generally, representatives seek assignments that will allow them to influence decisions of special importance to their districts. Representatives from farm districts, for example, may request seats on the Agriculture Committee.[35] Seats on powerful committees such as Ways and Means, which is responsible for tax legislation, and Appropriations are especially popular.

PARTY LEADERSHIP IN THE SENATE

Within the Senate, the majority party usually designates a member with the greatest seniority to serve as president pro tempore, a position of primarily ceremonial leadership. Real power is in the hands of the majority leader and minority leader, each elected by party conference. Together they control the Senate's calendar, or agenda for legislation. Each party also elects a policy committee, which advises the leadership on legislative priorities. The structure of majority party leadership in the House and the Senate is shown in Figures 12.5 and 12.6.

THE COMMITTEE SYSTEM

The committee system is central to the operation of Congress. At each stage of the legislative process, Congress relies on committees and subcommittees to do the hard work of sorting through alternatives and writing legislation. There are several different kinds of congressional committees: standing committees, select committees, joint committees, and conference committees.

Standing Committees The most important arenas of congressional policy making are **standing committees**. These committees remain in existence from one session of Congress to the next; they have the power to propose and write legislation. The jurisdiction of each standing committee covers a particular subject matter, which in most cases parallels a major department or agency in the executive branch (see Table 12.2). Among the most important standing committees are those in charge of finances. The House Ways and Means Committee and the Senate Finance Committee are powerful because of their jurisdiction over taxes, trade, and expensive entitlement programs such as Social Security and Medicare. The Senate and House Appropriations committees also play important ongoing roles because they decide how much funding various programs will actually receive; they also determine exactly how the money will be spent. A seat on an appropriations committee allows a member the opportunity to direct funds to a favored program—perhaps one in his home district.

standing committee a permanent committee with the power to propose and write legislation that covers a particular subject, such as finance or agriculture

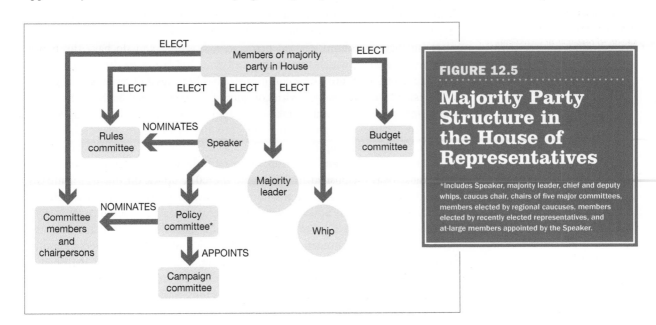

FIGURE 12.5

Majority Party Structure in the House of Representatives

*Includes Speaker, majority leader, chief and deputy whips, caucus chair, chairs of five major committees, members elected by regional caucuses, members elected by recently elected representatives, and at-large members appointed by the Speaker.

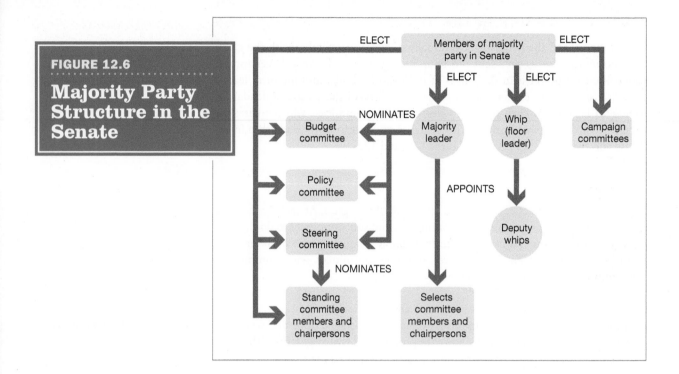

FIGURE 12.6

Majority Party Structure in the Senate

ELECT — Members of majority party in Senate — ELECT

ELECT — ELECT

Budget committee ← NOMINATES — Majority leader

Whip (floor leader)

Campaign committees

Policy committee

Steering committee

APPOINTS

Deputy whips

NOMINATES

Standing committee members and chairpersons

Selects committee members and chairpersons

Except for the House Rules Committee, all standing committees receive proposals for legislation and process them into official bills. The House Rules Committee decides the order in which bills come up for a vote on the House floor and determines the specific rules that govern the length of debate and opportunity for amendments. The Senate, which has less formal organization and fewer rules, does not have a rules committee.

Select Committees Select committees are usually not permanent and usually do not have the power to present legislation to the full Congress. (The House and Senate Select Intelligence committees are permanent, however, and do have the power to report legislation, which means they can send legislation to the full House or Senate for consideration.) These committees hold hearings and serve as focal points for the issues they are charged with considering. Congressional leaders form select committees when they want to take up issues that fall outside the jurisdictions of existing committees, to highlight an issue, or to investigate a particular problem. For example, the Senate set up the Senate Watergate Committee in 1973 to investigate the Watergate break-in and cover-up. More recently, the House Select Committee on Benghazi was established to investigate the 2012 attack on the U.S. Embassy in Benghazi, Libya. In 2015 the committee held hearings to investigate Hillary Clinton's use of a private email server during her tenure as secretary of state.

Select committees set up to highlight ongoing issues have included the House Select Committee on Hunger, established in 1984, and the House Select Committee on Energy Independence and Global Warming, created in 2007 but abolished in 2011, when Republicans assumed control of the House. In 2003 an important select committee, the House Select Committee on Homeland Security, was created to oversee the new Department of Homeland Security. Unlike most select committees,

select committees (usually) temporary legislative committees set up to highlight or investigate a particular issue or address an issue not within the jurisdiction of existing committees

TABLE 12.2
Permanent Committees of Congress

HOUSE COMMITTEES

Agriculture	Financial Services	Oversight and Government Reform
Appropriations	Foreign Affairs	Rules
Armed Services	Homeland Security	Science, Space, and Technology
Budget	House Administration	Small Business
Education and the Workforce	Intelligence	Transportation and Infrastructure
Energy and Commerce	Judiciary	Veterans' Affairs
Ethics	Natural Resources	Ways and Means

SENATE COMMITTEES

Agriculture, Nutrition, and Forestry	Energy and Natural Resources	Intelligence
Appropriations	Environment and Public Works	Judiciary
Armed Services	Finance	Rules and Administration
Banking, Housing, and Urban Affairs	Foreign Relations	Small Business and Entrepreneurship
Budget	Health, Education, Labor, and Pensions	Veterans' Affairs
Commerce, Science, and Transportation	Homeland Security and Governmental Affairs	

this one had the ability to present legislation. Initially the committee had only temporary status. It was made a regular permanent committee in 2005.

Joint Committees Joint committees involve members from both the Senate and the House. There are four such committees: economic, taxation, library, and printing. These joint committees are permanent, but they do not have the power to present legislation. The Joint Economic Committee and the Joint Taxation Committee have often played important roles in collecting information and holding hearings on economic and financial issues.

joint committees legislative committees formed of members of both the House and Senate

Conference Committees Finally, **conference committees** are temporary committees whose members are appointed by the Speaker of the House and the presiding officer of the Senate. These committees are charged with reaching a compromise on legislation once it has been passed by the House and the Senate. Conference committees play an extremely important role in determining the laws that are actually passed

conference committees joint committees created to work out a compromise on House and Senate versions of a piece of legislation

Committees hold hearings to gather information for legislation or investigate the activities of government agencies. Here, President Trump's first attorney general, Jeff Sessions, testifies in front of the House Judiciary Committee.

because they must reconcile any differences in the legislation passed by the House and Senate.

When control of Congress is divided between two parties, each is guaranteed significant representation in conference committees. When a single party controls both houses, the majority party is not obligated to offer such representation to the minority party. In 2003, Democrats complained that Republicans took this power to the extreme by excluding them and adding new provisions to legislation at the conference committee stage. Democrats even prevented several conference committees from convening to protest their near exclusion from conference committees on major energy, health care, and transportation laws. After they returned to power in 2007, the Democrats also largely bypassed the conference committees; when their early efforts to reach compromises in committee were derailed by partisan differences, the Democrats began making closed-door agreements between top leaders in the House and the Senate. Although the process facilitated compromises across the two chambers, it meant that important changes to bills were made in private, without the transparency that would have been part of the conference committee process. After 2010, Congress continued to avoid conference committees. Instead, the Republican House and Democratic Senate exchanged amendments as they sought to reach agreement on the final version of a bill, a practice known informally as "ping-pong."[36]

Politics and the Organization of Committees Within each committee, hierarchy has usually been based on **seniority**, determined by years of continuous service on that particular committee. In general, each committee is chaired by the most senior member of the majority party. But the principle of seniority is not absolute. When the Republicans took over the House in 1995, they violated the principle of seniority in the selection of key committee chairs. House Speaker Newt Gingrich defended the new practice, saying, "You've got to carry the moral responsibility of fielding the team that can win or you cheat the whole conference."[37] Since then, Republicans have continued to depart from the seniority principle, often choosing committee chairs on the basis of loyalty or fund-raising abilities rather than seniority. In 2007, Democrats returned to the seniority principle for choosing committee chairs but altered traditional practices in other ways by offering freshmen Democrats choice committee assignments to increase their chances of re-election.[38]

seniority the ranking given to an individual on the basis of length of continuous service on a committee in Congress

Over the years, Congress has reformed its organizational structure and operating procedures. Most changes have been made to improve efficiency, but some reforms have also been a response to political considerations. For example, the Republican leadership of the 104th Congress (1995–97), seeking to concentrate more authority in the party leadership, reduced the number of subcommittees and limited the time committee chairs could serve to three terms. They made good on this in 2001, when they replaced 13 committee chairs.

As a consequence of these changes, committees no longer have the central role they once held in policy making. Furthermore, sharp partisan divisions have made it difficult for committees to deliberate and bring bipartisan expertise to bear on policy making as in the past. With committees less able to engage in effective decision making, they typically do not deliberate for very long or call witnesses, and it has become more common in recent years for party-driven legislation to go directly to the floor, bypassing committees altogether.[39] Nonetheless, committees continue to play a role in the legislative process, especially on issues that are not sharply partisan.[40]

THE STAFF SYSTEM: STAFFERS AND AGENCIES

The congressional institution second in importance only to the committee system is the staff system. Every member of Congress employs many staff members whose tasks include handling constituent requests and, to a large extent, dealing with legislative details and the activities of administrative agencies. Staffers often bear the primary responsibility for formulating and drafting proposals, organizing hearings, dealing with administrative agencies, and negotiating with lobbyists. Indeed, legislators typically deal with one another through staff, rather than through direct personal contact. Staffers even develop policy ideas, draft legislation, and, in some instances, have a good deal of influence over the legislative process. Representatives and senators together employ roughly 11,500 staffers in their Washington and home offices. In addition, Congress employs more than 2,000 committee staffers.[41] These individuals make up the permanent staff that stays attached to every House and Senate committee regardless of turnover in Congress and that is responsible for organizing and administering the committee's work, including doing research, scheduling, organizing hearings, and drafting legislation. Committee staffers can play key roles in the legislative process.

Not only does Congress employ personal and committee staff, but it has also established **staff agencies** designed to provide the legislative branch with resources and expertise independent of the executive branch. These agencies enhance Congress's capacity to oversee administrative agencies and to evaluate presidential programs and proposals. They include the Congressional Research Service, which performs research for legislators who wish to know the facts and competing arguments relevant to policy proposals or other legislative business; the Government Accountability Office, through which Congress can investigate the financial and administrative affairs of any government agency or program; and the Congressional Budget Office, which assesses the economic implications and likely costs of proposed federal programs.

staff agencies legislative support agencies responsible for policy analysis

Members of Congress rely heavily on their personal staffs and on committee staffs, who often play an important role in the legislative process.

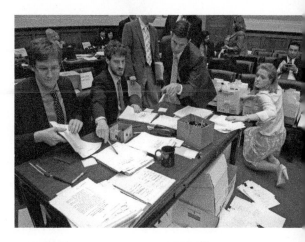

Women's Parliamentary Representation Worldwide

In April 2018 a special election in Arizona propelled Republican Debbie Lesko into the House, raising the number of women in Congress to 107.[a] This marked the first time in U.S. history that women comprised 20 percent of Congress, with 19.3 percent of the House and 23 percent of the Senate being women. While this may seem an impressive achievement, when we look around the world we find that the United States lags behind many countries in gender representation in government. As of 2018, the Inter-Parliamentary Union ranked the United States as 102 (out of 188) in women's parliamentary representation. Examining the lower house of parliament only (since not all countries have an upper house) reveals that the United States ranks between Saudi Arabia (19.9 percent) and Kyrgyzstan (19.2 percent).

Past research on women's global representation offers a few suggestions for why the U.S. percentage is so low, with the main explanations focusing on election rules and party systems.[b] Women candidates benefit from gender quotas and may be at a disadvantage in "winner-take-all" elections like those in the United States. In Rwanda, women comprise 61 percent of parliament, and there is both a gender quota (30 percent of the legislature is required to be women) and proportional representation (election rules where parties receive seats based on the percentage of the vote they received). Party recruitment also plays a major role, as cross-country research has found that "new left" parties (parties that favor environmental and social justice issues) also more actively recruit women into running for public office.

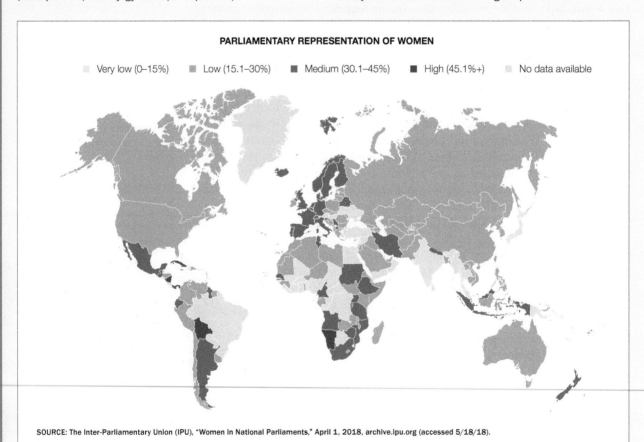

PARLIAMENTARY REPRESENTATION OF WOMEN

Very low (0–15%)　　Low (15.1–30%)　　Medium (30.1–45%)　　High (45.1%+)　　No data available

SOURCE: The Inter-Parliamentary Union (IPU), "Women in National Parliaments," April 1, 2018, archive.ipu.org (accessed 5/18/18).

[a] The Center for American Women and Politics (CAWP), "With Election of Debbie Lesko (AZ-08), Record Number of Women in Congress," April 24, 2018, cawp.rutgers.edu/sites/default/files/resources/18.4.24_pr_lesko_az08.pdf (accessed 5/18/18).

[b] Lena Wängnerud, "Women in Parliaments: Descriptive and Substantive Representation," *Annual Review of Political Science*, 12 (2009): 51–69.

INFORMAL ORGANIZATION: THE CAUCUSES

In addition to the official organization of Congress, an unofficial organizational structure also exists: the caucuses. **Caucuses** are groups of senators or representatives who share certain opinions, interests, or social characteristics. A large number of caucuses are composed of legislators representing particular economic or policy interests, such as the Travel and Tourism Caucus, the Steel Caucus, and Concerned Senators for the Arts. Legislators who share common backgrounds have organized caucuses such as the Congressional Black Caucus, the Congressional Caucus for Women's Issues, and the Congressional Hispanic Caucus. All these caucuses seek to advance the interests of the groups they represent by promoting legislation, encouraging Congress to hold hearings, and pressing administrative agencies for favorable treatment. In recent years, some caucuses have evolved into powerful lobbying organizations, well funded by interest groups. For example, the Sportsmen's Caucus receives funds from a nonprofit foundation that itself benefits from donations from the National Rifle Association, sports equipment manufacturers, and firearms manufacturers. In 2010 conservative Republicans in the House and Senate formed the Tea Party Caucus (now called the Freedom Caucus) to advance antispending policies.

> **caucuses (congressional)** associations of members of Congress based on party, interest, or social group, such as gender or race

Rules of Lawmaking: How a Bill Becomes a Law

> **Outline the steps in the process of passing a law**

The institutional structure of Congress is a key factor in shaping the legislative process. A second and equally important set of factors is the rules of congressional procedure. These rules govern everything from the introduction of a **bill** through its submission to the president for signing (see Figure 12.7). Not only do these regulations influence the fate of every bill, but they also help determine the distribution of power in the Congress.

> **bill** a proposed law that has been sponsored by a member of Congress and submitted to the clerk of the House or Senate

COMMITTEE DELIBERATION

The first step in getting a law passed is drafting legislation. Members of Congress, the White House, and federal agencies all take roles in developing and drafting initial legislation. Bills can originate in the House or the Senate, but only the House can introduce "money bills," those that spend or raise revenues. The framers inserted this provision in the Constitution because they believed that the chamber closest to the people should exercise greater authority over taxing and spending. The bill is then officially submitted by a senator or representative to the clerk of the House or Senate and referred to the appropriate committee for deliberation. During the course of its deliberations, the committee typically refers the bill to one of its subcommittees, which may hold hearings, listen to expert testimony, and amend the proposed legislation before referring it to the full committee for consideration. The full committee may then accept the recommendation of the subcommittee or hold its own hearings and prepare its own amendments.

The next steps in the process are the **committee markup** sessions, in which committees rewrite bills to reflect changes discussed during the hearings. In the

> **committee markup** the session in which a congressional committee rewrites legislation to incorporate changes discussed during hearings on a bill

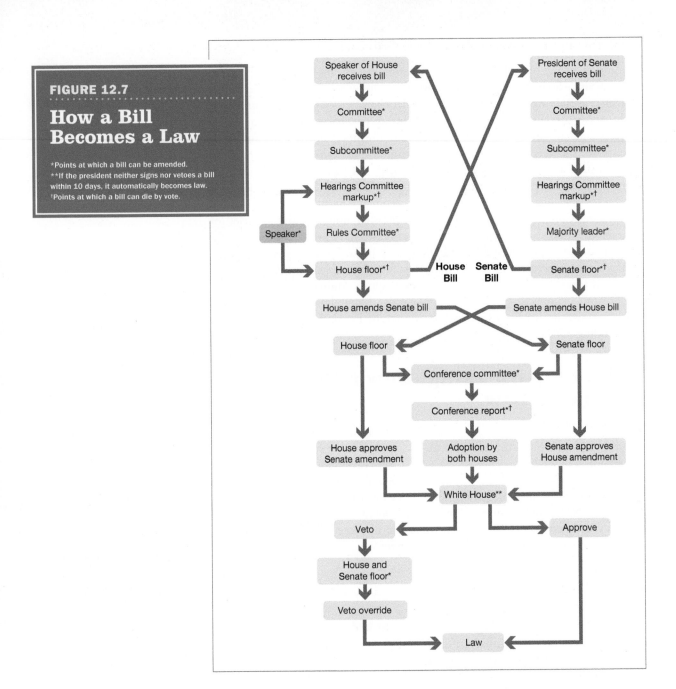

FIGURE 12.7

How a Bill Becomes a Law

*Points at which a bill can be amended.
**If the president neither signs nor vetoes a bill within 10 days, it automatically becomes law.
†Points at which a bill can die by vote.

Speaker of House receives bill → **Committee*** → **Subcommittee*** → **Hearings Committee markup*†** → **Rules Committee*** → **House floor*†**

Speaker*

President of Senate receives bill → **Committee*** → **Subcommittee*** → **Hearings Committee markup*†** → **Majority leader*** → **Senate floor*†**

House Bill **Senate Bill**

House amends Senate bill **Senate amends House bill**

House floor **Senate floor**

Conference committee*

Conference report*†

House approves Senate amendment **Adoption by both houses** **Senate approves House amendment**

White House**

Veto **Approve**

House and Senate floor*

Veto override

Law

partisan fighting that has characterized Congress in recent years, the minority party has charged that its members are often not given enough time to study proposed legislation before markup. In 2003 conflict over this issue drew the Capitol police to the House and almost resulted in a fistfight among representatives when Democrats protested their treatment by the House Ways and Means Committee. Charging that they had been given a complex pension bill only 10 hours before markup, House Democrats walked out. The ensuing commotion, with Republicans calling the police and a Democratic congressperson threatening a Republican, presented a sorry spectacle for the evening news. Though the committee chair apologized,

Democrats lost a resolution to censure the committee for its actions. At every stage of the legislative process, members protest that they are not given enough time to read proposals. In March 2018, members were handed a 2,200-page omnibus appropriations bill which would come to a vote in just 52 hours. Not allowing much time for readings of committee markups or bills themselves is usually a leadership tactic designed to push legislation forward before members can find items with which to disagree.

Frequently, the committee and subcommittee do little or nothing with a bill that has been submitted to them. Many bills are simply allowed to "die in committee" without serious consideration. Often, members of Congress introduce legislation that they neither expect nor even desire to see enacted into law but present mainly to please a constituency group by taking a stand. Many such bills are of narrow interest or stand little chance of passing given the political climate. For example, Representative Barbara Lee (D-Calif.) introduced the Department of Peacebuilding Act of 2015 to establish a "Department of Peacebuilding" in the executive branch, dedicated to promoting peace in international affairs.

As with most bills that are not reported out of committee, Lee's bill attracted little serious interest and only 26 cosponsors.[42] These bills die a quick and painless death. Other pieces of legislation have ardent supporters and die in committee only after a long battle. But in either case, most bills are never reported out of the committees to which they are assigned. In a typical congressional session, 80 to 90 percent of the more than 10,000 bills introduced die in committee.[43]

In the House, the relative handful of bills that are presented out of committee must pass one last hurdle within the committee system—the Rules Committee, which determines the rules that will govern action on the bill on the House floor. In particular, the Rules Committee allots the time for debate and decides to what extent amendments to the bill can be proposed from the floor. A bill's supporters generally prefer a **closed rule**, which puts severe limits on floor debate and amendments. Opponents of a bill usually prefer an **open rule**, which permits potentially damaging floor debate and makes it easier to add amendments that may cripple the bill or weaken its chances for passage. Thus, the outcome of the Rules Committee's deliberations can be extremely important, and the committee's hearings can be an occasion for sharp conflict. In recent years, the Rules Committee has become less powerful because the House leadership exercises so much influence over its decisions.

DEBATE

The next step in getting a law passed is debate on the floor of the House and Senate. Party control of the agenda is reinforced by the rule giving the Speaker of the House and the president of the Senate the power of recognition during debate on a bill. Usually the chair knows the purpose for which a member intends to speak well in advance of the occasion. Spontaneous efforts to gain recognition are often foiled. For example, the Speaker may ask, "For what purpose does the member rise?" before deciding whether to grant recognition.

In the House, virtually all the time allotted by the Rules Committee for debate on a given bill is controlled by the bill's sponsor and by its leading opponent. In almost every case, these two people are the committee chair and the ranking minority member of the committee that processed the bill—or those they designate. These two participants are, by rule and tradition, granted the power to allocate most of the debate time in small amounts to members who are seeking to speak for or against

closed rule a provision by the House Rules Committee limiting or prohibiting the introduction of amendments during debate

open rule a provision by the House Rules Committee that permits floor debate and the addition of new amendments to a bill

Once a senator is granted the floor, Senate rules permit him to speak for as long as he wishes. Although "talking filibusters" are rare today, in May 2015 Senator Rand Paul (R-Ky.) spoke continuously for 10½ hours, challenging the legality of government surveillance in his opposition to renew the Patriot Act.

filibuster a tactic used by members of the Senate to prevent action on legislation they oppose by continuously holding the floor and speaking until the majority backs down; once given the floor, senators have unlimited time to speak, and it requires a vote of three-fifths of the Senate to end a filibuster

cloture a rule or process in a legislative body aimed at ending debate on a given bill; in the U.S. Senate, 60 senators (three-fifths) must agree in order to impose a time limit and end debate

the measure. Preference in the allocation of time goes to the members of the committee whose jurisdiction covers the bill.

Filibuster In the Senate, the leadership has much less control over floor debate. Indeed, the Senate is unique among the world's legislative bodies for its commitment to unlimited debate. Once given the floor, a senator may speak as long as she wishes. On a number of memorable occasions, senators have used this opportunity to prevent action on legislation that they opposed. Through this tactic, called the **filibuster**, small minorities or even one individual in the Senate can force the majority to give in. Filibusters can be ended by a Senate vote to cut off debate, called **cloture**. From 1917 to 1975, it took two-thirds of the Senate or 67 votes to end a filibuster. In 1975 the Senate changed the rules to three-fifths of the Senate or 60 votes needed for cloture. The threat of a filibuster ensures that, in crafting legislation and proposing judicial appointments, the majority takes into account the viewpoint of the political minority.

For much of American history, senators only rarely used the filibuster, though during the 1950s and '60s, opponents of civil rights legislation often used filibusters to block its passage. In the last 20 years, the filibuster has become so common that observers routinely note that it takes 60 votes to get anything passed in the Senate. The 113th Congress (2013–15) broke the record with 218 cloture votes.[44] The 115th Congress held 192 cloture votes as of November 1, 2018.

In 2013 the Democratic Senate leader Harry Reid (Nev.) mobilized his party to alter the filibuster rules for the first time in many decades. Frustrated by the repeated failure of the Senate to vote on many of the president's nominees to fill positions in the executive branch, as well as judgeships to important federal courts, Reid invoked what senators had come to call "the nuclear option," a change to the filibuster rules. Under the new rules, nominees for positions in the executive branch and the federal courts—except the Supreme Court—could not be filibustered. This means that they can be approved by a simple majority vote. Not surprisingly, the two parties had different views on the decision. Reid defended it as necessary, due to what he called "unbelievable, unprecedented obstruction." Republicans denounced the new rule, stating, in the words of Pat Roberts (R-Kans.), "We have weakened this body permanently."[45] After winning control of both houses of Congress and the White House in 2016, however, Republicans expanded Reid's rule to include Supreme Court justices and so were able to secure the appointment of Justice Neil Gorsuch, who would undoubtedly have been blocked by Senate Democrats under the old rules. Legislation is still subject to filibuster, though some Republicans, along with President Trump, have declared that it is time to bring an end to the filibuster altogether.

Amendments and Holds The filibuster is not the only technique used to block Senate debate. Under Senate rules, members have virtually unlimited ability to propose amendments to a pending bill. Each amendment must be voted on before the bill can come to a final vote. The introduction of new amendments can be stopped only by unanimous consent. This, in effect, can permit a determined minority to filibuster by amendment, indefinitely delaying the passage of a bill. Senators can also place "holds," or stalling devices, on bills to delay debate. Senators place holds on bills when they fear that openly opposing them will be unpopular. Because holds are kept secret, the senators placing the holds do not have to take public responsibility for their actions. There have been several efforts to eliminate holds. In 2007 reformers succeeded in passing the Honest Leadership and Open Government

Act. Although the new law did not eliminate holds, it contained provisions requiring senators who imposed a hold to identify themselves in the *Congressional Record* after six days and state the reasons for the hold.[46] Even with this provision, senators continued to impose holds on legislation and especially on presidential appointees. Senator Lindsey Graham (R-S.C.) aroused the ire of the White House in 2013 for threatening to use holds on all of President Obama's nominees unless the administration made survivors of the 2012 terrorist attack on the U.S. mission in Benghazi, Libya, available to Congress for questioning.[47]

FOR CRITICAL ANALYSIS

Two of Congress's chief responsibilities are representation and lawmaking. How do these responsibilities support and reinforce each other? How might they also conflict with each other?

Voting Once a bill is debated on the floor of the House and the Senate, the leaders schedule it for a vote on the floor of each chamber. Leaders do not bring legislation to the floor unless they are fairly certain it is going to pass. On rare occasions, the last moments of the floor vote can be very dramatic as each party's leadership puts its whip organization into action to make sure that wavering members vote with the party. In 2015 the House of Representatives failed to pass a spending bill to fund the Department of Homeland Security hours before the agency was to run out of money and begin to shut down. Despite having a majority in the chamber and an early vote that suggested that the bill would pass easily, House Republican Party leaders failed to prevent the most conservative members of the party from suddenly abandoning the bill over objections that it left out provisions to block President Obama's executive actions on immigration. As midnight approached, the House agreed on a one-week extension to keep the department open.[48] Leaders later secured sufficient support to enact longer-term funding for Homeland Security. The importance of being able to attract wavering members with "pork" for their districts is one reason President Trump urged Congress in 2018 to restore earmarks, which have been banned since 2011.

CONFERENCE COMMITTEE: RECONCILING HOUSE AND SENATE VERSIONS OF LEGISLATION

Getting a bill out of committee and through both houses of Congress is no guarantee that the bill will be enacted into law; it must be considered by a conference committee. Frequently, bills that begin with similar provisions in both chambers emerge with little resemblance to each other. Alternatively, a bill may be passed by one chamber but undergo substantial revision in the other chamber. In such cases, a conference committee composed of the senior members of the committees or subcommittees that initiated the bill may be required to iron out differences between the two now dissimilar pieces of legislation. Sometimes members or leaders will let objectionable provisions pass on the floor, knowing that they will get the chance to make changes in conference. Usually, conference committees meet behind closed doors. Agreement requires a majority of each of the two delegations. Legislation that emerges successfully from a conference committee is more often a compromise than a clear victory for one side. In recent years, as we have seen, polarization in Congress has led to much less reliance on conference committees. Instead, leaders exchange amendments in the hope of reaching agreement.

When a bill comes out of conference, it faces one more hurdle. Before it can be sent to the president for signing, the House-Senate conference committee's version of the bill must be approved on the floor of each chamber. Usually such approval is given quickly. Occasionally, however, a bill's opponents use this round of approval as one last opportunity to defeat a piece of legislation.

PRESIDENTIAL ACTION

veto the president's constitutional power to turn down acts of Congress; a presidential veto may be overridden by a two-thirds vote of each house of Congress

pocket veto a presidential veto that is automatically triggered if the president does not act on a given piece of legislation passed during the final 10 days of a legislative session

The final step in passing a law is presidential approval. Once adopted by the House and Senate, a bill goes to the president, who may choose to sign the bill into law or veto it. If the president does not sign the bill or veto it within 10 days and Congress is in session, the bill automatically becomes law. The **veto** is the president's constitutional power to reject a piece of legislation. To veto a bill, the president returns it unsigned within 10 days to the house of Congress in which it originated. If Congress adjourns during the 10-day period and the president has taken no action, the bill is also considered to be vetoed. This latter method is known as the **pocket veto**. The possibility of a presidential veto affects how willing members of Congress are to push for different pieces of legislation at different times. If they think a proposal is likely to be vetoed, they might shelve it until a later time.

A presidential veto may be overridden by a two-thirds vote in both the House and Senate. A veto override says much about the support that a president can expect from Congress, and it can deliver a stinging blow to the executive branch. Presidents will often back down from a veto threat if they believe that Congress will override the veto.

How Congress Decides

> **Analyze the factors that influence which laws Congress passes**

What determines the kinds of legislation that Congress ultimately produces? According to the simplest theories of representation, members of Congress respond to the views of their constituents. In fact, the process of creating a legislative agenda, drawing up a list of possible measures, and deciding among them is a very complex one, in which a variety of influences from inside and outside government play important roles. External influences include a legislator's constituency and various interest groups. Influences from inside government include party leadership, congressional colleagues, and the president. Let us examine each of these influences individually and then consider how they interact to produce congressional policy decisions.

Representatives spend a lot of time meeting with constituents in their districts to explain how they have helped their district and learn what issues their constituents care about. Such meetings are often informal events at local restaurants or fairs, or town halls where constituents can ask questions. Here, Senator Chuck Grassley (R-Iowa) meets with constituents.

CONSTITUENCY

Because members of Congress, for the most part, want to be re-elected, we would expect the views of their constituents to be a primary influence on the decisions that they make. Yet constituency influence is not so straightforward. In fact, most constituents pay little attention to politics and often do not even know what policies their representatives support. Nonetheless, members of Congress spend a lot of time worrying about what their constituents think because they realize that the choices they make may be scrutinized in a future election and used as ammunition by an opposing candidate. Because of this possibility, members of Congress do try to anticipate their constituents' policy views, especially if they think that voters will take them into account during elections.[49] In this way, constituents may affect congressional policy choices even when there is little direct evidence of their influence. In October 1998, for example, 31

House Democrats broke party ranks and voted in favor of an impeachment inquiry against President Clinton because they believed a "no" vote could cost them re-election that November. In 2017, despite a personal effort by President Trump to persuade dissident Republicans, the House GOP leadership could not muster enough Republican votes to pass a measure that would have repealed Obamacare. Some Republicans from swing districts feared upsetting constituents who favored Obamacare, while more conservative Republicans thought the bill did not go far enough in dismantling government-sponsored health insurance. Then-White House press secretary Sean Spicer said, "This isn't a dictatorship and we've got to expect members to ultimately vote how they will according to what they think."[50]

INTEREST GROUPS

Interest groups are another important external influence on congressional policies. Members of Congress pay close attention to interest groups for a number of reasons: interest groups can mobilize constituents, serve as watchdogs on congressional action, and supply candidates with money. When members of Congress are making voting decisions, those interest groups that have some connection to constituents in particular districts are most likely to be influential, and those groups with the ability to mobilize followers in many congressional districts may be especially influential. In recent years, Washington-based interest groups with little grassroots strength have recognized the importance of locally generated activity. Accordingly, they have sought to simulate grassroots pressure with so-called Astroturf lobbying (see Chapter 11). Such campaigns encourage constituents to sign form letters, postcards, or emails, which are then sent to congressional representatives. Lobbying campaigns set up toll-free telephone numbers for a system in which simply reporting your name and address to the listening computer will generate a letter to your congressional representative. One Senate office estimated that such organized campaigns to demonstrate "grassroots" support account for two-thirds of the mail the office received. As such campaigns increase, however, they become less influential because members of Congress are aware of how rare real constituent interest actually is.[51]

Many interest groups also use legislative "scorecards" that rate how members of Congress vote on issues of importance to that group. A high or low rating by an important interest group may provide a potent weapon in the next election. Interest groups can increase their influence over a particular piece of legislation by signaling their intention to include it in their scoring. Among the most influential groups that use scorecards, often posting them on their websites for members and the public to see, are the National Federation of Independent Business, the American Federation of Labor-Congress of Industrial Organizations (AFL-CIO), National Right to Life, the League of Conservation Voters, and the National Rifle Association.

Interest groups also have substantial influence in setting the legislative agenda and in helping to craft specific language in legislation. Today, sophisticated lobbyists win influence by providing information about policies, as well as campaign contributions, to busy members of Congress. The $1.1 trillion end-of-year spending bill passed at the end of 2014 included an amendment exempting many financial transactions from federal regulation under the Dodd-Frank Act. The amendment language was taken from a bill originally written by Citigroup lobbyists, with 70 of 85 lines of the bill directly copying Citigroup's language.[52] After further lobbying by the banking industry, legislation enacted in 2018 loosened a number of Dodd-Frank rules and exempted regional banks from a number of remaining rules. In recent years, interest groups have also begun to build broader coalitions and comprehensive campaigns around particular policy issues. These coalitions do not rise from the grass roots but instead are put together by Washington lobbyists, who launch comprehensive lobbying campaigns that combine simulated grassroots activity with information and campaign funding for members of Congress.

Close financial ties between members of Congress and interest group lobbyists often raise eyebrows because they suggest that interest groups get special treatment in exchange for political donations. Concerns about the influence of lobbyists in Congress mounted in the early 2000s when Republicans launched the K Street Project, named after the street in Washington where many high-powered lobbyists have offices. The K Street Project placed former Republican staffers in key lobbying positions and ensured a large and steady flow of corporate cash into Republican coffers. Congressional relationships to lobbyists came under close scrutiny when the lobbyist Jack Abramoff, a self-proclaimed big supporter of the K Street Project, pleaded guilty in early 2006 to charges of conspiracy, mail fraud, and tax evasion.

Concern over such corruption led Congress to enact new ethics legislation in 2007. Now lobbyists are required to disclose the names of the individual contributors to these political donations. Although the new law provides additional transparency, revealing more about the relationship between lobbyists and members of Congress, it is widely viewed as lacking sufficient authority to go after those who are suspected of ethics violations. Moreover, the large sums of cash raised by "Super PACs" (political action committees)—discussed in Chapter 10—have introduced a whole new set of questions about the role of special interests in politics, especially because donors to Super PACs can remain anonymous. Although they cannot openly coordinate with candidates, Super PACs can endorse candidates by name and are often run by people close to the candidates they support. In 2016, Super PACs poured unprecedented sums of money into the race for president, but they also targeted key congressional contests in an effort to affect the balance of power between the parties in Congress. In 2018, 10 individuals—5 Democrats and 5 Republicans—collectively contributed several hundred million dollars to Super PACs supporting congressional candidates all across the country as the two parties fought for control of Congress.[53]

FOR CRITICAL ANALYSIS

How does congressional ethics legislation address concerns about corruption? Why is it important that lawmakers identify the earmarks they add to legislation?

PARTY

In both the House and Senate, party leaders have a good deal of influence over the behavior of their party members. This influence, sometimes called "party discipline," was once so powerful that it dominated the lawmaking process. In the late 1800s, party leaders could often command the allegiance of more than 90 percent of their members. A vote in which half or more of the members of one party take one position while at least half of the members of the other party take the opposing position is called a **party unity vote**. At the beginning of the twentieth century, nearly half of all **roll-call votes** in the House of Representatives were party votes. For much of the twentieth century, the number of party votes declined as bipartisan legislation became more common. The 1990s witnessed a return to strong party discipline as partisan polarization drew sharper lines between Democrats and Republicans, and congressional party leaders aggressively used their powers to promote party discipline. By 2015 party discipline has been at an all-time high.

Typically, party unity is greater in the House than in the Senate. House rules grant greater procedural control of business to the majority party leaders, which

party unity vote a roll-call vote in the House or Senate in which at least 50 percent of the members of one party take a particular position and are opposed by at least 50 percent of the members of the other party

roll-call vote a vote in which each legislator's yes or no vote is recorded as the clerk calls the names of the members alphabetically gives them more influence over House members. In the Senate, however, the leadership has few sanctions over its members. The former Senate minority leader Tom Daschle once observed that a Senate leader seeking to influence other senators has as incentives "a bushel full of carrots and a few twigs."[54]

Though it has not reached nineteenth-century levels, party unity has been on the rise in recent years because the divisions between the parties have deepened on many high-profile issues such as abortion, health care, and financial reform (see Figure 12.8). Party unity scores rise when congressional leaders try to put a partisan stamp on legislation. For example, in 1995 then-Speaker Newt Gingrich sought to enact a Republican "Contract with America" that few Democrats supported. The result was more party unity in the House than in any year since 1954. Since then, the polarization of political parties has resulted in very high party unity scores. In 2016, House Democrats voted with the majority 96 percent of the time, marking an all-time high, at least in modern times. That year Senate Democrats voted with their caucus 92 percent of the time, seven points below the record set in 2014. Republicans were also very united. In 2016, House Republicans voted with their party 96 percent of the time, an all-time record high; Senate Republicans voted with their party 86 percent of the time, only five points below the record set in 2015.[55]

To some extent, party unity is based on ideology and background. Republican members of the House are more likely than Democrats to have been elected by rural or suburban districts. Democrats are likely to be more liberal on economic and social questions than their Republican colleagues in both houses. These differences certainly help to explain roll-call divisions between the two parties. Ideology and background, however, are only part of the explanation for party unity. The other part has to do with party organization and leadership. Among the resources that

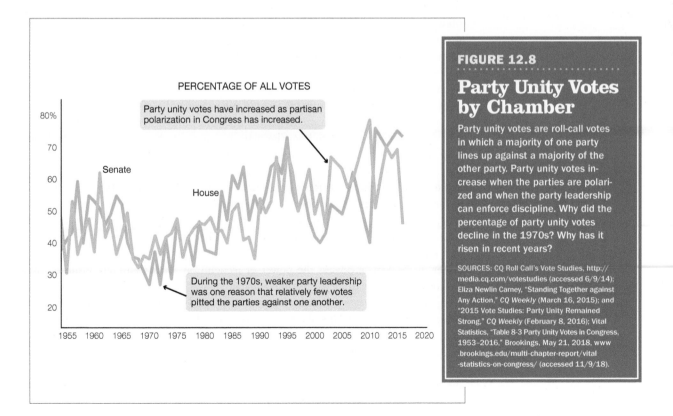

PERCENTAGE OF ALL VOTES

Party unity votes have increased as partisan polarization in Congress has increased.

Senate

House

During the 1970s, weaker party leadership was one reason that relatively few votes pitted the parties against one another.

FIGURE 12.8

Party Unity Votes by Chamber

Party unity votes are roll-call votes in which a majority of one party lines up against a majority of the other party. Party unity votes increase when the parties are polarized and when the party leadership can enforce discipline. Why did the percentage of party unity votes decline in the 1970s? Why has it risen in recent years?

SOURCES: CQ Roll Call's Vote Studies, http://media.cq.com/votestudies (accessed 6/9/14); Eliza Newlin Carney, "Standing Together against Any Action," CQ Weekly (March 16, 2015); and "2015 Vote Studies: Party Unity Remained Strong," CQ Weekly (February 8, 2016); Vital Statistics, "Table 8-3 Party Unity Votes in Congress, 1953–2016," Brookings, May 21, 2018, www.brookings.edu/multi-chapter-report/vital-statistics-on-congress/ (accessed 11/9/18).

party leaders have at their disposal to reward loyal members who vote with the party are (1) leadership PACs, (2) committee assignments, (3) access to the floor, (4) the whip system, (5) logrolling, and (6) the presidency.

Leadership PACs Leaders have increased their influence over members in recent years with aggressive use of leadership PACs. Leadership PACs are organizations that members of Congress use to raise funds that they then distribute to other members of their party running for election. Republican congressional leaders pioneered the aggressive use of leadership PACs to win their congressional majority in 1995, and the practice has spread widely since that time. The former House majority leader Tom DeLay was especially aggressive in raising funds, creating several important PACs, including Americans for a Republican Majority (ARMPAC), Retain Our Majority Program (ROMP), and the Republican Majority Issues Committee. In recent years, Democrats have also formed well-funded leadership PACs. Money from leadership PACs can be directed to the most vulnerable candidates or to candidates who are having trouble raising money. For example, Kirsten Gillibrand, the junior Democratic senator from New York, has used her leadership PAC to promote Democratic women candidates running for Congress. In 2016 the PAC, which she named Off the Sidelines, supplied funds to 61 candidates running for seats in the House and 10 for the Senate, all of them women.[56]

Committee Assignments Party leaders can create debts among members by helping them get favorable committee assignments. These assignments are made early in the congressional careers of most members and cannot be taken from them if they later balk at party discipline. Nevertheless, if the leadership goes out of its way to get the right assignment for a member, this effort is likely to create a bond of obligation that can be called on without any other payments or favors. This is one reason the Republican leadership gave freshmen favorable assignments when the Republicans took over Congress in 1995. When Nancy Pelosi assumed the position of Speaker in 2007, she sought to spread power more widely by limiting the number of committees that any one member could chair. She also gave freshmen representatives access to key committees that would raise their political stature.[57] By offering attractive committee assignments to members in competitive races, especially to new members, she sought to boost her party's chances in the next elections. And she engendered loyalty to the party among its new members.

Access to the Floor The most important everyday resource available to the parties is control over access to the floor. With thousands of bills awaiting passage and most members clamoring for access in order to influence a bill or publicize themselves, floor time is precious. Floor time is allocated in both houses of Congress by the majority and minority leaders. More important, the Speaker of the House and the majority leader in the Senate possess the power of recognition. This seemingly insubstantial authority is, in fact, quite formidable and can be used to stymie a piece of legislation completely or frustrate a member's attempts to speak on a particular issue. Because the power is significant, members of Congress usually attempt to stay on good terms with the Speaker and the majority leader to ensure they will continue to be recognized.

As House Speaker, Nancy Pelosi was particularly generous in offering freshmen Democrats and other especially vulnerable Democrats an opportunity to speak on the floor. When Republicans assumed control of the House in 2010, they likewise ensured that the voices of freshmen Republicans were heard on the House floor.[58] As we saw above, each party makes an effort to protect potentially vulnerable members, and freshmen are often high on that list.

The Whip System Some influence accrues to party leaders through the whip system, which is primarily a communications network for conveying the leaders' wishes and plans to the members. Between 12 and 20 assistant and regional whips are selected to operate at the direction of the majority or minority leader and the whip. They poll all the members to learn their intentions on specific bills, enabling the leaders to know if they have enough support to allow a vote as well as whether the vote is so close that they will need to put pressure on undecided members. In those instances, the Speaker or a lieutenant will go to a few party members who have indicated they will switch if their vote is essential—an expedient that the leaders try to limit to a few times per session.

The whip system helps maintain party unity in both houses of Congress, but it is particularly critical in the House of Representatives because of the large number of legislators whose positions and votes must be accounted for. The majority and minority whips and their assistants must be adept at inducing compromise among legislators who hold widely differing viewpoints. In 2015 a group of conservative Republicans, organized into the House Freedom Caucus, regularly disputed the positions of the party leadership. Frustrated with the lack of discipline, House majority whip Steve Scalise (R-La.) expelled several members from his whip team for failing to support party positions.[59] Indeed, conflict with these same rebellious Republicans prompted Speaker John Boehner to make the stunning announcement in September 2015 of his retirement from the speakership and from the House.

logrolling a legislative practice whereby agreements are made between legislators in voting for or against a bill; vote trading

When John Boehner became Speaker of the House in 2010, he was overwhelmingly backed by House Republicans. By 2015, the most conservative factions of the party, frustrated that Boehner hadn't been more effective against the Obama administration, pressured him to resign.

Logrolling An agreement between two or more members of Congress who have nothing in common except the need for support is called **logrolling**. The agreement states, in effect, "You support me on bill X, and I'll support you on another bill of your choice." Since party leaders are the center of the communications networks in the two chambers, they can help members create large logrolling coalitions. Hundreds of logrolling deals are made each year, and although there are no official record-keeping books, it would be a poor party leader whose whips did not know who owed what to whom. In some instances, logrolling produces strange alliances. A most unlikely alliance emerged in Congress in October 1991, an alliance that one commentator dubbed "the corn for porn plot."[60] The alliance joined Senate supporters of the National Endowment for the Arts (NEA) with senators seeking limits on the cost of grazing rights on federal lands. The NEA, which provides federal funding to the arts, had been under fire from the conservative senator Jesse Helms (R-N.C.) for funding some controversial artists whose work Helms believed to be indecent. In an effort to block federal support for such works, Helms attached a provision to the NEA's funding that would have prohibited the agency from awarding grants to any work that in a "patently offensive way" depicted "sexual or excretory activities or organs." Supporters of the NEA condemned such restrictions as a violation of free speech and pointed out that many famous works of art could not have been funded under such restrictions. When it appeared that the amendment would pass, NEA supporters offered western senators a deal. In exchange for voting down the Helms amendment, they would eliminate a planned increase in grazing fees. Republican senators from 16 western states switched their votes and defeated the Helms amendment. Although Helms called his defeat

After Democrats took control of the House of Representatives in November 2018, former House minority leader Nancy Pelosi (D-Calif.) was poised to take over the role of Speaker of the House from retiring Speaker Paul Ryan (R-Wisc.). She had previously served in the same position from 2007–11.

the product of "back-room deals and parliamentary flimflam," his amendment was simply the victim of the time-honored congressional practice of logrolling.[61]

The Presidency Of all the influences that maintain the clarity of party lines in Congress, the influence of the presidency is probably the most important. Indeed, the office is a touchstone of party discipline in Congress. Since the late 1940s, under President Harry Truman, presidents each year have identified a number of bills that they want to be considered part of their administration's program. By the mid-1950s both parties in Congress began to look to the president for these proposals, which became the most significant part of Congress's agenda. The president's support is a criterion for party loyalty, and party leaders are able to use it to rally some members. Though President Trump was personally unpopular with many members of Congress, legislators still looked to him to set the agenda and most of the major legislative initiatives of 2017 and 2018, including border security, immigration, the repeal of Obamacare, and tax reform originated in the White House.

WHEN CONGRESS CAN'T DECIDE

We've considered the major factors that influence congressional decisions, but what happens if Congress as a whole can't decide and fails to act? Some recent congresses have been notable for their inability to pass laws. The 114th Congress (2015–17), 113th Congress (2013–15), and the 112th Congress (2011–13) were the three least productive Congresses in modern history.[62]

As the end of its second session neared, the 115th Congress seemed likely to become the least productive Congress in modern history in terms of number of new laws enacted. A number of those new laws, however, were important. These included a sanctions law targeting Russia, Iran, and North Korea; the enactment of a major revision of the tax code; a budget bill that averted a government shutdown; and bills overturning a number of Obama-era regulations.[63] The Republican-controlled Senate also approved the appointment of two conservatives, Neil Gorsuch and Brett Kavanaugh, to the Supreme Court. These appointments are likely to affect Supreme Court decisions for years to come.

In 2018, President Trump and congressional leaders agreed on a spending bill that provided for increased defense and domestic social spending. Though the bill was opposed by Republican "deficit hawks," and by some Democrats who demanded legislation to protect undocumented immigrants, a majority of Republicans and more than 73 House Democrats supported the legislation. In the Senate, Rand Paul (R-Ky.) briefly filibustered the bill, but it was ultimately passed by a large majority and signed into law. By increasing overall spending levels, Trump and congressional leaders provided funding for programs that each party supported. The GOP got more money for the military, and the Democrats won more money for domestic programs.[64] It was the sort of classic logroll hated by ideological purists but necessary in a democratic legislature.

Congressional Polarization Congress's frequent inability to decide reflects the deep ideological differences that separate the two parties. Efforts to measure the ideological distance between the two parties show that since the mid-1970s

Republicans and Democrats have been diverging sharply and are now more polarized than at any time in the last century. Democrats have become more liberal and Republicans have become more conservative on issues related to the economy and the role of government.[65] But as Figure 12.9 shows, the Republican Party has experienced the greatest ideological shift, becoming sharply more conservative. Moreover, because congressional districts are increasingly homogeneous in their ideology—in part due to gerrymandering but mainly because of natural clustering of the population—most members of Congress are in safe seats. Their constituents will not punish them for failing to compromise. Moreover, active mobilization by organizations on the right, such as the Club for Growth, means that Republican members of Congress who support compromises might be punished. These outside organizations have financed alternative candidates to challenge members who vote against

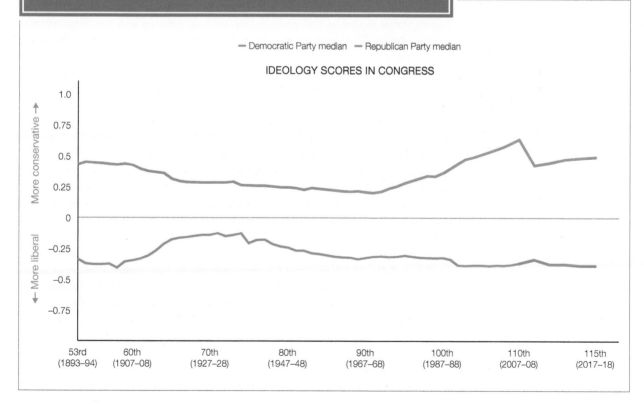

FIGURE 12.9

Polarization in Congress

In recent decades Democrats and Republicans in Congress are increasingly polarized as Democrats have become more liberal and Republicans more conservative. One way of measuring polarization is to estimate the ideology of members of Congress based on their roll-call votes and then graph the ideologies of each party's members. As the graph shows, polarization was lower in the 1940s and 1950s, with some Democrats and some Republicans even overlapping in their ideologies.

SOURCE: Voteview, http://voteview.com/dwnl.htm (accessed 10/15/18).

— Democratic Party median — Republican Party median

IDEOLOGY SCORES IN CONGRESS

FOR CRITICAL ANALYSIS

How does polarization contribute to congressional gridlock? How has the use of congressional procedures made it more difficult to enact legislation in recent years?

the organizations' positions. Despite rebukes by Republican congressional leadership, groups such as the Club for Growth actively worked to recruit and support candidates in the 2016 election.[66]

However, congressional polarization is here to stay so long as voters elect representatives with sharply different views about what government should and shouldn't do. Until there is more agreement about the role of government and the best way to manage the budgetary challenges that face the country, congressional stand-offs on major legislation will remain a regular feature of American politics.

Beyond Legislation: Other Congressional Powers

> Describe Congress's influence over other branches of government

In addition to the power to make the law, Congress has at its disposal an array of other instruments through which to influence the process of government. The Constitution gives the Senate the power to approve treaties and appointments. And Congress has a number of other powers through which it can share with the other branches the capacity to administer the laws.

OVERSIGHT

oversight the effort by Congress, through hearings, investigations, and other techniques, to exercise control over the activities of executive agencies

appropriations the amounts of money approved by Congress in statutes (bills) that each unit or agency of government can spend

Oversight, as applied to Congress, refers to the effort to oversee or to supervise how the executive branch carries out legislation. Oversight is carried out by committees or subcommittees of the Senate or the House, which conduct hearings and investigations to analyze and evaluate bureaucratic agencies and the effectiveness of their programs. Their purpose may be to locate inefficiencies or abuses of power, to explore the relationship between what an agency does and what a law intends, or to change or abolish a program. Most programs and agencies are subject to some oversight every year during the course of hearings on **appropriations**, the funding of agencies and government programs.

Committees or subcommittees have the power to subpoena witnesses, administer oaths, cross-examine, compel testimony, and bring criminal charges for contempt (refusing to cooperate) and perjury (lying under oath). Hearings and investigations are similar in many ways, but they differ on one fundamental point. A hearing is usually held on a specific bill, and the questions asked are usually intended to build a record with regard to that bill. In an investigation, the committee or subcommittee does not begin with a particular bill but examines a broad area or problem and then concludes its investigation with one or more proposed bills.

In recent years, congressional oversight power has increasingly been used as a tool of partisan politics. The Republican Congress aggressively investigated President Clinton but failed to scrutinize seriously the actions of the George W. Bush administration during Bush's first six years in office. The investigation into the abuse of prisoners in Iraq's Abu Ghraib prison, for example, entailed only 12 hours of sworn testimony.

When the Democrats took control of Congress in 2007, congressional oversight increased dramatically. To highlight the importance of oversight, Democrats renamed the House Government Reform Committee, calling it the Committee on Oversight and Government Reform, and added four new subcommittees dedicated to oversight. They also hired more than 200 new investigative staffers.[67] Armed with these resources, the Democratic Congress held 942 oversight hearings during its first six months in power, compared with 579 for the same period when Republicans controlled Congress in 2005.[68] Congressional leaders are quite aware of oversight hearings as political tools. After 2010 the Republican House used the oversight power to highlight the politically weak points in President Obama's record, holding extensive hearings on the Affordable Care Act and on the militant attack of the American consulate in Benghazi, Libya, that resulted in American deaths.[69] First convened in 2014, the Select Committee on Benghazi became enmeshed in partisan contention after Hillary Clinton, secretary of state during the attacks, announced that she would run for president. In 2015, as revelations emerged that Clinton had used a private email server during her tenure as secretary of state, the committee began to investigate whether appropriate procedures had been followed and whether national security was compromised.[70] When the FBI undertook an investigation into the matter in 2016, FBI director James Comey recommended no criminal charges against Clinton but also questioned her judgment and called her actions "extremely careless."

Almost as soon as Donald Trump took office in 2017, Democrats called for investigations into allegations the Trump administration had colluded with Russian operatives to help Trump win the 2016 election. House and Senate committees, chaired by Republicans, failed to find evidence of presidential wrongdoing. Democrats, however, demanded the appointment of a special counsel after President Trump's firing of FBI director James Comey. Over the course of the investigation, the special counsel indicted several close Trump aides for improper contacts with Russian officials. As of October 2018, four former Trump aides—George Papadopoulos, Paul Manafort, Rick Gates, and Michael Flynn—had pleaded guilty to a variety of crimes related to the investigation.

ADVICE AND CONSENT: SPECIAL SENATE POWERS

The Constitution has given the Senate another special power, one that is not based on lawmaking. The president has the power to make treaties and to appoint top executive officers, ambassadors, and federal judges—but only "with the Advice and Consent of the Senate" (Article II, Section 2). For treaties, two-thirds of those present must concur; for appointments, a simple majority is required.

The power to approve or reject presidential requests includes the power to set conditions. In fact, the Senate only occasionally exercises its power to reject treaties and appointments, and despite recent debate surrounding judicial nominees, only a small number of judicial nominees have been rejected by the Senate or withdrawn by the president to avoid rejection during the past century, whereas hundreds have been approved. However, the recent increase in use of the filibuster to block judicial nominees led the Democratic Senate to bar the filibuster in deliberations about judicial and executive branch appointments.

Most presidents make every effort to take potential Senate opposition into account in treaty negotiations with foreign powers. Instead of treaties, presidents frequently resort to **executive agreements** that do not need Senate approval. The Supreme Court has held that such agreements are equivalent to treaties.[71] In the past, presidents sometimes concluded secret agreements without informing Congress of the agreements' contents or even their existence. For example, American involvement in the Vietnam War grew in part out of a series of secret arrangements made between American presidents and the South Vietnamese during the 1950s and '60s. Congress did not even learn of the existence of these agreements until 1969. In 1972,

executive agreement an agreement, made between the president and another country, that has the force of a treaty but does not require the Senate's "advice and consent"

The Constitution provides the Senate with the power to confirm executive branch appointments such as Supreme Court nominee Neil Gorsuch (left). Congress also has the power to approve or reject treaties made by the President. Secretary of State John Kerry (bottom right) and other members of President Obama's cabinet testified before the Senate Foreign Relations Committee on behalf of a nuclear weapons agreement with Iran.

impeachment the formal charge by the House of Representatives that a government official has committed "Treason, Bribery, or other high Crimes and Misdemeanors"

Congress passed the Case Act, which requires that the president inform Congress of any executive agreement within 60 days of its having been reached. This provides Congress with the opportunity to cancel agreements it opposes. In addition, Congress can limit the president's ability to conduct foreign policy through executive agreement by refusing to appropriate the funds needed to implement an agreement. In this way, for example, Congress can modify or even cancel executive agreements to provide American economic or military assistance to foreign governments.

IMPEACHMENT

The Constitution also grants Congress the power of impeachment over the president, vice president, and other executive officials. **Impeachment** means to charge a government official (president or otherwise) with "Treason, Bribery, or other high Crimes and Misdemeanors" and bring him before Congress to determine guilt. Impeachment is thus like a criminal indictment in which the House of Representatives acts like a grand jury, voting (by simple majority) on whether the accused ought to be impeached. If a majority of the House votes to impeach, the impeachment trial moves to the Senate, which acts like a trial jury by voting whether to convict and forcibly remove the person from office (which requires a two-thirds majority of the Senate). The impeachment power is a considerable one; its very existence in the hands of Congress is a highly effective safeguard against the executive tyranny so greatly feared by the framers of the Constitution. The House has initiated impeachment proceedings more than 60 times in U.S. history. Fewer than 20 officials were ultimately impeached, and only eight—all federal judges—were convicted by the Senate and removed from office.[72]

Controversy over Congress's impeachment power has arisen over the grounds for impeachment, especially the meaning of "high Crimes and Misdemeanors." A strict reading of the Constitution suggests that the only impeachable offense is an actual crime. But a more common working definition is that "an impeachable offense is whatever the majority of the House of Representatives considers it to be at a given moment in history."[73] In other words, impeachment, especially impeachment of a president, is a political decision.

The political nature of impeachment was very clear in the two instances of presidential impeachment that have occurred in American history. In the first, in 1867, President Andrew Johnson, a southern Democrat who had battled a congressional Republican majority over Reconstruction, was impeached by the House but saved

FOR CRITICAL ANALYSIS

Under what circumstances should Congress exercise its power of impeachment? Why has impeachment been used so rarely in U.S. history?

The Senate possesses the power to impeach federal officials. In American history, 16 federal officials have been impeached, including two presidents. Andrew Johnson was impeached in 1868 for improperly removing the Secretary of War. In 1998 the House impeached President Bill Clinton for lying under oath about his affair with White House intern Monica Lewinsky.

from conviction by one vote in the Senate. In 1998 the House impeached President Bill Clinton on two counts, for lying under oath and obstructing justice during the investigation into his sexual affair with the White House intern Monica Lewinsky. The vote was highly partisan, with only five Democrats voting for impeachment on each charge. In the Senate, where a two-thirds majority was needed to convict the president, only 45 senators voted to convict on the first count of lying and 50 voted to convict on the second charge of obstructing justice. As in the House, the vote for impeachment was highly partisan, with all Democrats and only five Republicans supporting the president's ultimate acquittal.

Congress
WHAT DO WE WANT?

Much of this chapter has described the major institutional components of Congress and has shown how they work as Congress makes policy. But what do these institutional features mean for how Congress represents the American public? As we saw with Guy Berkebile and Hazel Hoffman at the beginning of the chapter, congressional actions—and inaction—have profound effects on Americans' lives. Does the organization of Congress promote the equal representation of all Americans? Or are there institutional features of Congress that allow some interests more access and influence than others? What can we learn from a tax cut that passes congress and a CHIP reauthorization that almost fails?

As we noted at the beginning of this chapter, Congress instituted a number of reforms in the 1970s to make itself more accessible and to distribute power more widely within the institution. These reforms sought to respond to public views that

Congress had become a stodgy institution ruled by a powerful elite that made decisions in private. We have seen that these reforms increased the number of subcommittees, prohibited most secret hearings, and increased the staff support for Congress. These reforms spread power more evenly throughout the institution and opened new avenues for the public to contact and influence Congress.

But the opening of Congress ultimately did not benefit the broad American public as reformers had envisioned. In fact, the congressional reforms enacted during the 1970s actually made Congress less effective and, ironically, more permeable to special interests. Open committee meetings made it possible for sophisticated interest groups to monitor and influence every aspect of developing legislation. The unanticipated, negative consequences of these reforms highlighted the trade-off between representation and effectiveness in Congress.[74] Efforts to improve representation by opening Congress up made it difficult for Congress to be effective.

When Congress is ineffective, American democracy suffers. As we have seen in this chapter, prolonged stalemates in Congress have led to a reduction in America's credit rating and a costly government shutdown. Moreover, Americans have lost confidence in Congress as it has lurched from crisis to crisis. Is it time for some major changes to make Congress work better? Disillusionment with congressional gridlock has led some to say that the United States should become a parliamentary system, where the winning party can enact the legislation it promised in its party platform. Such a system is more accountable to voters and less prone to stalemate. But Americans would have to jettison the presidency and become a unicameral body to operate as a true parliamentary system, like that of Britain.

Changes in the way Congress conducts its business could also promote more bipartisan decision making. For example, former House Speaker John Boehner decided that he would only bring legislation to the floor if a majority of Republicans supported it. Speaker Paul Ryan also followed the same practice. The "Hastert rule," as this practice is called, could easily be abandoned, allowing bipartisan majorities to enact legislation. Another significant change—eliminating the filibuster in the Senate—would heighten partisan differences but ease gridlock. As we have seen, the Senate voted to eliminate the filibuster for executive branch appointments and judicial candidates in 2013 and for the Supreme Court in 2017. Abandoning the filibuster altogether would allow legislation to move more smoothly through the Senate. Will any of these changes—or other measures—be adopted? Each carries risks to political parties and to politicians. Yet, gridlock also carries political risks, as the public grows frustrated with congressional inaction on important policy areas. What areas of public policy might suffer if Congress continues its inability to decide? How politicians weigh these different choices will shape how—and whether—Congress fills its central position in American democracy.

Gridlock and bitter disagreements in Congress turn some Americans off to politics. However, as the core representative institution of government, Congress is supposed to represent all Americans. As the "**Who Participates?**" feature on the facing page shows, the electorate that turns out to vote for Congress is on average older, whiter, and more affluent than the average American.

Who Elects Congress?

2018 Voters as Compared with U.S. Population

← U.S. population

↑
Electorate

*Numbers may not add up to 100 percent due to rounding.

SOURCES: CNN House Exit Polls, www.cnn.com/election/2018/exit-polls (accessed 11/12/18); U.S. Census Bureau, 2014 American Community Survey, www.census.gov/programs-surveys/acs/data.html (accessed 10/22/15).

Gender	U.S. pop.	Electorate
Women	51%	52%
Men	49%	48%

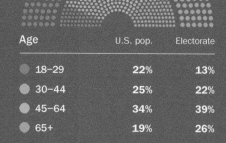

Age	U.S. pop.	Electorate
18–29	22%	13%
30–44	25%	22%
45–64	34%	39%
65+	19%	26%

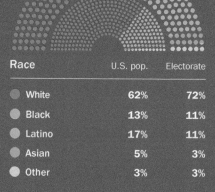

Race	U.S. pop.	Electorate
White	62%	72%
Black	13%	11%
Latino	17%	11%
Asian	5%	3%
Other	3%	3%

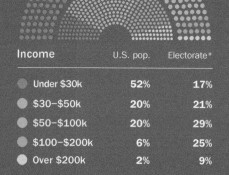

Income	U.S. pop.	Electorate*
Under $30k	52%	17%
$30–$50k	20%	21%
$50–$100k	20%	29%
$100–$200k	6%	25%
Over $200k	2%	9%

★ WHAT YOU CAN DO ★

Know Your Members of Congress

 Vote in the next congressional election. If you haven't registered, see page 329 for instructions on how to do so.

 Discover what bills are currently under consideration in Congress by visiting **www.congress.gov**.

 Contact your member of Congress to state your opinion. Go to **www.house.gov** and enter your ZIP code to find your representative. Go to **www.senate.gov** and find your state in the drop-down menu to find your two U.S. senators.

★ STUDY GUIDE ★

Congress: Representing the American People

Describe who serves in Congress and how they represent their constituents (pp. 469–82)

A member of Congress's primary responsibility is to his or her constituency. While the number of African Americans, women, Latinos, and Asian Americans in Congress has increased over the last two decades, these groups are still significantly underrepresented relative to their proportions in the general population. Regardless of whether members of Congress share their constituents' sociological characteristics, however, representatives do work hard to speak for their constituents' views and to serve their constituents' interests. Generally speaking, there are three factors related to the U.S. electoral system that affect who gets elected and what they do once in office: who decides to run for Congress, the incumbency advantage, and the way congressional districts are drawn.

Key Terms

constituency (p. 469)

bicameral (p. 469)

delegate (p. 470)

trustee (p.470)

sociological representation (p. 471)

agency representation (p. 471)

incumbency (p. 476)

term limits (p. 477)

apportionment (p. 477)

redistricting (p. 478)

gerrymandering (p. 478)

patronage (p. 480)

pork-barrel (or pork) (p. 480)

private bill (p. 481)

Practice Quiz

1. Which of the following is a way in which the House and the Senate are different?
   a) The House is a more deliberative legislative body than the Senate.
   b) The House is more centralized and organized than the Senate.
   c) Senators serve smaller and more homogeneous constituencies than members of the House.
   d) Senators are often more attuned to the legislative needs of local interest groups than members of the House.
   e) There are no important differences between the House and the Senate.

2. What type of representation is described when constituents have the power to hire and fire their representative?
   a) agency representation
   b) sociological representation
   c) philosophical representation
   d) ideological representation
   e) economic representation

3. Which of the following statements best describes the social composition of the U.S. Congress?
   a) The majority of representatives do not have university degrees.
   b) Men and women are equally represented in Congress.
   c) Most members of Congress do not affiliate with any specific religion.
   d) The legal profession is the dominant career of most members of Congress prior to their election.
   e) The number of African American, Latino, and Asian American representatives has decreased over the last 20 years.

4. The Supreme Court has ruled that
   a) only the House of Representatives has the constitutional authority to redraw congressional district lines.
   b) race can be the predominant factor in drawing congressional districts.
   c) race cannot be the predominant factor in drawing congressional districts.
   d) states cannot use unelected, nonpartisan committees to draw congressional districts.
   e) only the Senate has the constitutional authority to redraw congressional district lines.

5. An *earmark* is
   a) a rule in the House of Representatives that limits who can be heard during legislative debates.
   b) a congressional district drawn to advantage candidates from a certain racial or ethnic group.
   c) a law that grants some special privilege or exemption to a single individual.
   d) language inserted into a bill by a member of Congress that provides special benefits for the member of Congress's constituents.
   e) a weekly, informal meeting between members of Congress and their constituents.

The Organization of Congress

Explain how party leadership, the committee system, the staff system, and caucuses help structure congressional business (pp. 482–89)

Congress is not only a representative body but also a lawmaking institution. The political parties, the committee system, congressional staff, the caucuses, and the parliamentary rules of the House and Senate play key roles in the process by which Congress formulates and enacts law. The committee system is particularly important because Congress relies on committees and subcommittees to do the difficult work of sorting through alternatives and writing bills.

Key Terms

conference (p. 482)

caucus (political) (p. 482)

Speaker of the House (p. 482)

majority leader (p. 482)

minority leader (p. 482)

whip (p. 482)

standing committee (p. 483)

select committees (p. 484)

joint committees (p. 485)

conference committees (p. 485)

seniority (p. 486)

staff agencies (p. 487)

caucuses (congressional) (p. 489)

Practice Quiz

6. Which of the following types of committees include members of both the House and the Senate?
   a) standing committee
   b) select committee
   c) conference committee
   d) rules committee
   e) No committees include both House members and senators.

7. A series of reforms instituted by Congress in the 1970s, including an increase in the number of subcommittees and greater autonomy for subcommittee chairs, had the effect of
   a) reducing the power of committee chairs.
   b) increasing the power of committee chairs.
   c) eliminating the incumbency advantage in congressional elections.
   d) ending the filibuster.
   e) expanding the number of joint committees in Congress.

Rules of Lawmaking: How a Bill Becomes a Law

Outline the steps in the process of passing a law (pp. 489–94)

The rules of congressional procedure influence the fate of every bill and determine the distribution of power in Congress. Debate over bills is much less restricted in the Senate than in the House, and the filibuster gives tremendous power to individual senators. The president's veto power also exerts an important influence on Congress's lawmaking because the possibility of a presidential veto affects how willing members of Congress are to push for different pieces of legislation.

Key Terms

bill (p. 489)

committee markup (p. 489)

closed rule (p. 491)

open rule (p. 491)

filibuster (p. 492)

cloture (p. 492)

veto (p. 494)

pocket veto (p. 494)

Practice Quiz

8. What is the difference between a closed rule and an open rule in the House?
   a) A closed rule puts severe limits on floor debate and amendments, whereas an open rule permits floor debate and makes amendments easier.
   b) An open rule puts severe limits on floor debate and amendments, whereas a closed rule permits floor debate and makes amendments easier.
   c) A closed rule allows journalists and members of the public to listen to debates about a bill, whereas an open rule prevents journalists and members of the public from listening to debates about the bill.
   d) An open rule allows journalists and members of the public to listen to debates about a bill, whereas a closed rule prevents journalists and members of the public from listening to debates about the bill.
   e) A closed rule prevents the federal judiciary from declaring a bill unconstitutional once passed, whereas an open rule allows the federal judiciary to declare a bill unconstitutional.

9. Which of the following statements about the filibuster is most accurate?
   a) The filibuster was first used in 1975.
   b) The votes of 67 senators are currently required to end a filibuster.
   c) The filibuster was used far more frequently in the 1930s and 1940s than it has been in the last two decades.
   d) Nominees for positions in the executive branch and the federal courts cannot currently be filibustered.
   e) Filibusters were declared unconstitutional by the Supreme Court in 2013.

How Congress Decides

Analyze the factors that influence which laws Congress passes (pp. 494–502)

A variety of influences from inside and outside government play a role in congressional decision making. External influences include the policy preferences of the legislator's constituency and the lobbying of various interest groups. Party leaders within Congress use many methods, including leadership PACs, logrolling, and the president's support, to influence how representatives behave. The growing polarization of Democrats and Republicans has significantly hindered the legislative productivity of Congress in recent years.

Key Terms

party unity vote (p. 496)
roll-call vote (p. 496)
logrolling (p. 499)

Practice Quiz

10. Members of Congress take their constituents' views into account because
    a) the Supreme Court can invalidate laws passed without majority support in the public.
    b) interest groups are forbidden from lobbying during legislative votes.
    c) most constituents pay close attention to what's going on in Congress at all times.
    d) they worry that their voting record will be scrutinized at election time.
    e) they can be impeached if they go against their constituents' policy preferences.

11. Which of the following is *not* a resource that party leaders in Congress use to create party discipline?
    a) leadership PACs
    b) committee assignments
    c) access to the floor
    d) the whip system
    e) party unity votes

12. An agreement between members of Congress to trade support for each other's bills is known as
    a) oversight.
    b) filibuster.
    c) logrolling.
    d) patronage.
    e) cloture.

Beyond Legislation: Other Congressional Powers

Describe Congress's influence over other branches of government (pp. 502–5)

Congress has many other powers than simply lawmaking. Using hearings, investigations, and other techniques, Congress exercises control over the agencies of the executive branch. Under the Constitution, the president can only make treaties and appoint top executive officers, ambassadors, and federal judges "with the Advice and Consent of the Senate." The Constitution also grants Congress the power of impeachment over the president, vice president, and other executive officials.

Key Terms

oversight (p. 502)
appropriations (p. 502)
executive agreement (p. 503)
impeachment (p. 504)

Practice Quiz

13. When Congress conducts an investigation to explore the relationship between what a law intended and what an executive agency has done, it is engaged in
    a) oversight.
    b) advice and consent.
    c) appropriations.

d) executive agreement.

e) direct patronage.

14. Which of the following statements about impeachment is *not* true?

a) The president is the only official who can be impeached by Congress.

b) Impeachment means to charge a government official with "Treason, Bribery, or other high Crimes and Misdemeanors."

c) The House of Representatives decides by simple majority vote whether the accused ought to be impeached.

d) The Senate decides whether to convict and remove the person from office.

e) There have only been two instances of presidential impeachment in American history.

For Further Reading

Adler, E. Scott, and John D. Wilkerson. *Congress and the Politics of Problem Solving.* New York: Cambridge University Press. 2013.

Chafetz, Josh. *Congress's Constitution: Legislative Authority and the Separation of Powers.* New Haven, CT: Yale University Press, 2017.

Connelly, William F., John J. Pitney, and Gary Schmitt, eds. *Is Congress Broken? The Virtues and Defects of Partisanship and Gridlock.* Washington, DC: Brookings Institution Press, 2017.

Dodd, Lawrence C., and Bruce I. Oppenheimer, eds. *Congress Reconsidered.* 10th ed. Washington, DC: CQ Press, 2012.

Dodson, Debra L. *The Impact of Women in Congress.* New York: Oxford University Press, 2006.

Fenno, Richard F. *Homestyle: House Members in Their Districts.* Boston: Little, Brown, 1978.

Fiorina, Morris. *Congress: Keystone of the Washington Establishment.* 2nd ed. New Haven, CT: Yale University Press, 1989.

Koger, Gregory. *Filibustering: A Political History of Obstruction in the House and Senate.* Chicago: University of Chicago Press, 2010.

Lee, Frances E. *Beyond Ideology: Politics, Principles, and Partisanship in the U.S. Senate.* Chicago: University of Chicago Press, 2009.

Mann, Thomas E., and Norman J. Ornstein. *It's Even Worse Than It Looks: How the American Constitutional System Collided with the New Politics of Extremism.* New York: Basic Books, 2012.

Mayhew, David R. *Congress: The Electoral Connection.* New Haven, CT: Yale University Press, 1974.

Palmer, Barbara, and Denise Simon. *Breaking the Political Glass Ceiling: Women and Congressional Elections.* 2nd ed. New York: Routledge, 2008.

Schickler, Eric, and Frances E. Lee. *The Oxford Handbook of the American Congress.* New York: Oxford University Press, 2011.

Tate, Katherine. *Concordance: Black Lawmaking in the U.S. Congress from Carter to Obama.* Ann Arbor: University of Michigan Press, 2014.

Wawro, Gregory J., and Eric Schickler. *Filibuster: Obstruction and Lawmaking in the U.S. Senate.* Princeton, NJ: Princeton University Press, 2006.

Recommended Websites

Cook Political Report
www.cookpolitical.com

The Cook Political Report, by Charlie Cook, is a nonpartisan analysis of electoral politics. Check out current House and Senate races for an in-depth analysis of past elections and previews of future congressional elections.

Roll Call
www.rollcall.com

Roll Call, the newspaper of Capitol Hill, provides daily coverage on the members, legislation, and events taking place in and around the U.S. legislature.

The Sunlight Foundation and Taxpayers for Common Sense Open Congress
www.opencongress.org

Informative and very user-friendly means to explore legislation passed and proposed, compare legislators, and keep up with recent action on bills.

U.S. House of Representatives
www.house.gov

U.S. Senate
www.senate.gov

These are the official websites for the U.S. House of Representatives and the U.S. Senate. Here you can find information on your members of Congress, key congressional leaders, bills currently under consideration, and legislative committees.

The Presidency

WHAT GOVERNMENT DOES AND WHY IT MATTERS Kevin Hartley of Tennessee was 21 years old in April 2017 when he collapsed and died from cardiac arrest after using methylene chloride to strip paint from a bathtub during a renovation job. Although the chemical was associated with dozens of deaths dating back to the 1940s, the Environmental Protection Agency, established in 1970, had lacked the regulatory teeth to remove such widely available products from the market. Wendy Cleland-Hamnett, the EPA's top official overseeing pesticides and toxic chemicals, lamented, "How is it possible that you can go to a home improvement store and buy a paint remover that can kill you?"[1]

In summer 2016, Congress passed and President Obama signed a reform of the Toxic Substances Control Act of 1976, giving the EPA more power to regulate toxic chemicals. Passed with bipartisan support, the new law required the EPA to evaluate both new and existing chemicals, including the 10 most toxic chemicals in wide use. In the last days of the Obama administration in January 2017, after 10 years of research, the EPA proposed banning certain uses of methylene chloride,

While presidents inherit policies and regulations implemented during previous administrations, they are empowered to reverse or alter them according to their beliefs. As a former businessman, President Trump rejected the regulations put in place by the Obama administration that could put restraints on some businesses.

especially by ordinary consumers and non-industrial businesses.

But as presidential administrations switched from Obama to Trump, these new rules remained mere proposals. As a candidate Donald Trump said that he wanted to eliminate two regulations for every one that his agencies enacted. And when the Trump Administration took office in January 2017, it froze rules and proposed regulations across government, including those at the EPA. Kevin Hartley died three months later.

The Trump EPA did release new rules about toxic chemicals in summer 2017. They were written by Nancy Beck, a toxicologist who, between stints at the EPA under Presidents George W. Bush and Trump, had worked for the American Chemistry Council, contesting EPA regulations over what she called "phantom risks." The new rules reflected changes that had been requested by the chemical industry and did not include a ban on methylene chloride. The new leadership at the EPA also overturned Cleland-Hamnett's recommendation to ban the use of the pesticide chlorpyrifos, associated with development disabilities in children, and undermined tracking of the health effects of a chemical once used in nonstick pans associated with birth defects and kidney cancer. Recognizing that the agency's leadership was going in a different direction, Cleland-Hamnett, who had worked for the EPA since 1979, under presidents of both parties, announced her retirement. "It's time for me to go." In the face of continued public concern over toxic paint strippers, then-EPA head Scott Pruitt indicated in May 2018 that the agency would implement the methylene chloride ban. But months of inaction passed, and in October 2018 a coalition of consumer groups threatened to sue the EPA for delaying the ban after four more people died.

In this chapter, we examine the foundations of the American presidency and assess the origins and character of presidential power. Presidents are empowered by democratic political processes and, increasingly, by their ability to control and expand the institutional resources of the office. They sit atop the executive branch, a large bureaucracy of departments and agencies such as the EPA. They influence policy with their appointments to the Cabinet, the White House staff, and to the Executive Office of the President, choosing officials who are sympathetic to their policy goals and using regulatory review as with the EPA and executive orders to make policy. They set the tone for government as well, as the sole elected official representing the entire country. But, as we will see, presidential power is not without limit, nor should it be. The U.S. Constitution emphasizes checks and balances among the branches of government, not unlimited power. The framers thought a powerful and energetic president would make the U.S. government more effective but knew that presidential power needed to be subject to constraints to prevent it from becoming a threat to citizens' liberties.

CHAPTER GOALS

★ Understand the expressed, implied, delegated, and inherent powers of the presidency (pp. 515–29)

★ Identify the institutional resources presidents have to help them exercise their powers (pp. 529–33)

★ Explain how modern presidents have become even more powerful (pp. 533–43)

The Constitutional Powers of the Presidency

Understand the expressed, implied, delegated, and inherent powers of the presidency

The presidency was established by Article II of the Constitution, which begins by asserting that "The executive power shall be vested in a President of the United States of America." This language is known as the Constitution's "vesting clause." The president's executive power is underscored in Section 3 of Article II, the "take care clause," which confers upon the president the duty to "take care that the laws be faithfully executed. The president's oath of office at the end of Section 1, moreover, obligates—and thus empowers—the chief executive to "preserve, protect and defend the Constitution of the United States." This language seems to require the president to take action, without specifying any limits to that action, if constitutional government is threatened. President Abraham Lincoln cited his oath of office as justification for suspending the writ of habeas corpus in 1861. He declared that his oath would be broken if the government was overthrown. Suspension of the writ, he said, was necessary to prevent that calamity from taking place. By vesting the executive power in the president, Article II also implies that the president serves as America's head of state and is, therefore, entitled to special deference and respect. In Europe, the chief executives and heads of state were monarchs. While presidents are not monarchs, as the holders of executive power, they might appear to be entitled to the kingly respect due a head of state. On the basis of Article II, presidents make use of three types of powers. These are called the expressed powers of the office, implied powers, and delegated powers. A fourth type of power claimed by presidents does not appear in Article II. This is called the inherent power of the office.

Abraham Lincoln, like many other presidents, cited the presidential oath of office as providing the president the authority to take all the necessary actions to protect the nation.

EXPRESSED POWERS

expressed powers specific powers granted by the Constitution to Congress (Article I, Section 8) and to the president (Article II)

The **expressed powers** of the presidency are those specifically established by the language of the Constitution. These fall into several categories:

1. *Military.* Article II, Section 2, provides for the power as "Commander in Chief of the Army and Navy of the United States, and of the Militia of the several States, when called in to the actual Service of the United States."

2. *Judicial.* Article II, Section 2, also provides the power to "grant Reprieves and Pardons for Offences against the United States, except in Cases of Impeachment."

3. *Diplomatic.* Article II, Section 2, further provides the power "by and with the Advice and Consent of the Senate to make Treaties." Article II, Section 3, provides the power to "receive Ambassadors and other public Ministers."

4. *Executive.* Article II, Section 3, also authorizes the president to see to it that all the laws are faithfully executed; Section 2 gives the chief executive power to appoint, remove, and supervise all executive officers and to appoint all federal judges.

5. *Legislative.* Article I, Section 7, and Article II, Section 3, give the president the power to participate authoritatively in the legislative process.

commander in chief the role of the president as commander of the national military and the state National Guard units (when called into service)

Military Power The president's military powers are among the most important exercised by the chief executive. The position of **commander in chief** makes the president the highest military authority in the United States, with control of the entire defense establishment. The president is also head of the nation's intelligence network, which includes not only the Central Intelligence Agency (CIA) but also the National Security Council (NSC), the National Security Agency (NSA), the Federal Bureau of Investigation (FBI), and a host of less well-known but very powerful international and domestic security agencies.

Military Sources of Domestic Power The president's military powers extend into the domestic sphere. Article IV, Section 4, provides that the "United States shall [protect] every State...against...Invasion...and...domestic Violence." Congress has made this an explicit presidential power through statutes directing the president as commander in chief to discharge these obligations.[2] The Constitution restrains the president's use of domestic force by providing that a state legislature (or governor when the legislature is not in session) must request federal troops before the president can send them into the state to provide public order. Yet this proviso is not absolute. First, presidents are not obligated to deploy national troops merely because the state legislature or governor makes such a request. More important, the president may deploy troops in a state or city without a specific request from the state legislature or governor if the president considers it necessary to maintain an essential national service during an emergency, enforce a federal judicial order, or protect federally guaranteed civil rights.[3]

One historic example of the unilateral use of presidential emergency power, even when the states don't request it, is the decision by President Dwight D. Eisenhower in 1957 to send troops into Little Rock, Arkansas, against the wishes of the state of Arkansas, to enforce court orders to integrate Little Rock's Central High School. The governor of Arkansas, Orval Faubus, had posted the Arkansas National Guard at the entrance to Central High School to prevent the court-ordered admission of nine black students. After an effort to negotiate with Governor Faubus failed, President Eisenhower reluctantly sent 1,000 paratroopers from the U.S. Army's 101st Airborne Division to Little Rock; they stood watch while the black students took their places in the all-white classrooms.

In most instances of domestic disorder, whether from human or from natural causes, presidents tend to exercise unilateral power by declaring a "state of emergency," as President Trump did in response to the three hurricanes striking America in 2017, thereby making available federal grants, insurance, and direct aid.

One of the president's responsibilities is the maintenance of public order in times of crisis. In 1951, President Eisenhower used this to justify sending the troops to Little Rock to enforce racial integration of public schools (left). President Trump sent troops to Puerto Rico to assist in the aftermath of Hurricane Maria in 2017.

Judicial Power The presidential power to grant reprieves, pardons, and amnesty involves power over all individuals who may be a threat to the security of the United States. Presidents may use this power on behalf of a particular individual, as did Gerald Ford when he pardoned Richard Nixon in 1974 "for all offenses against the United States which he…has committed or may have committed." Or they may use it on a large scale, as did President Andrew Johnson in 1868, when he gave full amnesty to all southerners who had participated in the "Late Rebellion." Presidents' use of the pardon power can be very controversial. President Trump was criticized for pardoning former Arizona sheriff Joe Arpaio after Arpaio was found guilty of criminal contempt for ignoring a court order that directed his office to halt illegal racial profiling practices. The pardon was criticized because Trump did not first consult with the Justice Department's office of pardons and it was issued before Arpaio had been sentenced.

Diplomatic Power The president is America's "head of state," its chief representative in dealings with other nations, having the power to make treaties for the United States (with the advice and consent of the Senate) as well as the power to "recognize" other countries. Diplomatic recognition means that the United States acknowledges a government's legitimacy and territorial claims. In 2015, President Obama restored American diplomatic ties with Cuba, which had been severed by President Eisenhower in 1961 after the United States' relations with the Castro regime deteriorated. In 2017, after several staffers at the U.S. embassy in Cuba demonstrated neurological symptoms after being exposed to strange sounds, some blamed these "sonic attacks" on the Cuban government, which prompted President Trump to revisit newly restored American ties with Cuba. In 2018, President Trump met with North

As the head of state, the president is America's chief representative in dealings with other countries. Here, President Trump meets with North Korea's Supreme Leader Kim Jong-un in 2018 to discuss nuclear disarmament on the Korean Peninsula.

executive agreement an agreement, made between the president and another country, that has the force of a treaty but does not require the Senate's "advice and consent"

Korean leader, Kim Jong-un in an effort to defuse tensions on the Korean Peninsula. Earlier in the year, North Korea and America had exchanged threats in the wake of North Korean nuclear missile tests.

In recent years, presidents have expanded the practice of using executive agreements instead of treaties to establish relations with other countries.[4] An **executive agreement** is exactly like a treaty because it is a contract between two countries, but it does not require Senate approval. There are actually two types of executive agreements. One is the *executive–congressional agreement*. For this type of agreement, the president will submit the proposed arrangement to Congress for a simple majority vote in both houses, usually easier for presidents to win than the two-thirds approval of the Senate that is required for a treaty. The United States' 2015 accord with Iran is a recent example of an executive–congressional agreement. The other type of executive agreement is the *sole executive agreement*, which is simply an understanding between the president and a foreign state and is not submitted to Congress for approval. In the past, sole executive agreements were used to flesh out commitments already made in treaties or to arrange for matters well below the level of policy. Since the 1930s, however, presidents have entered into sole executive agreements on important issues when they were uncertain about their prospects for securing congressional approval. For example, the General Agreement on Tariffs and Trade (GATT), one of the cornerstones of U.S. international economic policy in the post–World War II era, was based on an executive agreement. The courts have held that executive agreements have the force of law, as though they were formal treaties.

Executive Power The Constitution focuses executive power and legal responsibility on the president. The most important basis of the president's power as chief executive is found in Article II, Section 3, of the Constitution, which stipulates that the president must see that all the laws are faithfully executed, and Section 2, which provides that the president will appoint and supervise all executive officers and appoint all federal judges (with Senate approval; after some early controversy, presidents' sole power to remove executive branch officials was accepted). The power to appoint the principal executive officers and to require each of them to report to the president on subjects relating to the duties of their departments makes the president the true chief executive officer (CEO) of the nation. The president is subject to some limitations because the appointment of all such officers, including ambassadors, ministers, and federal judges, is subject to a majority approval by the Senate. But these appointments are at the discretion of the president, and the loyalty and the responsibility of each appointee are presumed to be directed toward the president.

Another component of the president's power as chief executive is **executive privilege**, the claim that confidential communications between a president and close advisers should not be revealed without presidential consent. Presidents have made this claim ever since George Washington refused a request from the House of Representatives to deliver documents concerning negotiations of an important treaty. Washington refused (successfully) on the grounds that, first, the House was not constitutionally part of the treaty-making process and, second, diplomatic negotiations required secrecy.

Although many presidents have claimed executive privilege, the concept was not tested in the courts until the 1971 "Watergate" affair, when President Richard Nixon refused congressional demands that he turn over secret White House tapes that congressional investigators suspected would establish his complicity in illegal activities. In *United States v. Nixon* (1974), the Supreme Court ordered Nixon to turn over the tapes.[5] The president complied with the order and was forced to resign from office. The *United States v. Nixon* case is often seen as a blow to presidential power, but in actuality, the Court's ruling recognized for the first time the legal validity of executive privilege, though holding that it did not apply in this particular instance. Subsequent presidents have cited *United States v. Nixon* in support of their claims of executive privilege. The Obama administration invoked executive privilege once, in response to congressional demands for records from Attorney General Eric Holder relating to Operation Fast and Furious, an arms-trafficking sting operation that went awry, with federal agents losing track of hundreds of guns they sold to suspected gun smugglers.

Legislative Power The president plays a role not only in the administration of government but also in the legislative process. Two constitutional provisions are the primary sources of the president's power in the legislative arena. The first of these is the portion of Article II, Section 3, providing that the president "shall from time to time give to the Congress Information of the State of the Union, and recommend to their Consideration such Measures as he shall judge necessary and expedient." Delivering a "State of the Union" address may at first appear to be little more than the president's obligation to make recommendations for Congress's consideration. But as political and social conditions began to favor an increasingly prominent presidential role, each president, especially since FDR, began to rely on this provision in order to become the primary initiator of proposals for legislative action in Congress and the most important single participant in legislative decision making, as well as the principal source for public awareness of national issues.[6]

The second of the president's legislative powers is the veto power assigned by Article I, Section 7.[7] The **veto** is the president's constitutional power to reject acts of Congress (see Figure 13.1), making the president the most important single legislative leader.[8] No bill vetoed by the president can become law unless both the

The Supreme Court's decision in *United States v. Nixon* is often seen as a blow to presidential power because Nixon was required to turn over secret tapes related to the Watergate scandal, despite his claims of executive privilege. Here, Nixon points to transcripts of the tapes that he is turning over to House impeachment investigators.

executive privilege the claim that confidential communications between a president and close advisers should not be revealed without the consent of the president

veto the president's constitutional power to turn down acts of Congress; a presidential veto may be overridden by a two-thirds vote of each house of Congress

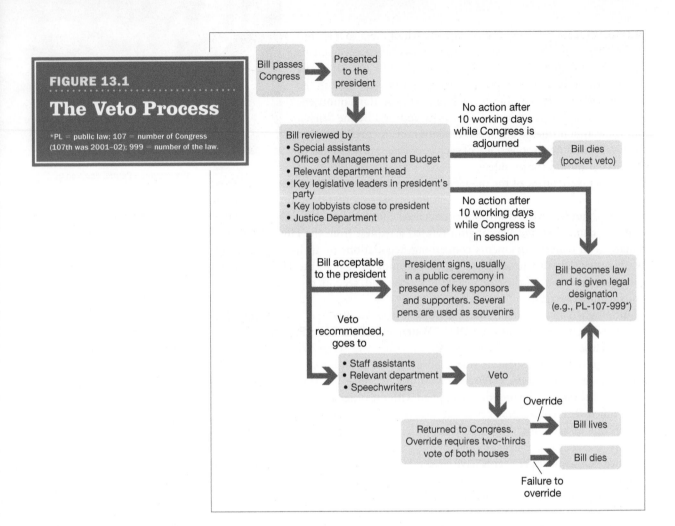

Bill passes Congress → Presented to the president

Bill reviewed by
- Special assistants
- Office of Management and Budget
- Relevant department head
- Key legislative leaders in president's party
- Key lobbyists close to president
- Justice Department

No action after 10 working days while Congress is adjourned → Bill dies (pocket veto)

No action after 10 working days while Congress is in session

Bill acceptable to the president → President signs, usually in a public ceremony in presence of key sponsors and supporters. Several pens are used as souvenirs → Bill becomes law and is given legal designation (e.g., PL-107-999*)

Veto recommended, goes to
- Staff assistants
- Relevant department
- Speechwriters
→ Veto → Returned to Congress. Override requires two-thirds vote of both houses

Override → Bill lives

Failure to override → Bill dies

---

pocket veto a presidential veto that is automatically triggered if the president does not act on a given piece of legislation passed during the final 10 days of a legislative session

House and Senate override the veto by a two-thirds vote. In the case of a **pocket veto**, Congress does not have the option of overriding the veto but must reintroduce the bill in the next session. Usually, if a president is presented with a bill and does not sign it within 10 days, it automatically becomes law. But this is true only while Congress is in session. If a president chooses not to sign a bill presented within the last 10 days of a legislative session and Congress is out of session when the 10-day limit expires, instead of becoming law, the bill is vetoed.

Use of the veto varies according to the political situation each president confronts. During his last two years in office, when Democrats had control of both houses of Congress, Republican president George W. Bush vetoed 10 bills, including legislation designed to prohibit the use of harsh interrogation tactics, saying it "would take away one of the most valuable tools in the war on terror."[9] Similarly, 10 of President Obama's 12 vetoes occurred during his last two years in office, when Republicans held the majority in both Houses. Among Obama's most significant vetoes was his 2015 decision to veto a bill authorizing construction of the Keystone XL oil pipeline that would have carried oil from Canada to U.S. refineries. The bill had been opposed by environmentalists and other interests. An attempt to override

In his 2018 State of the Union address, President Trump emphasized the need to tighten immigration laws and highlighted the importance of recently passed tax-overhaul legislation.

the president's veto failed to obtain the necessary two-thirds majority of both houses of Congress. Since the time of George Washington, presidents have used their veto power over 3,000 times, and on only 111 occasions has Congress overridden them. As of November 2018, despite several threats to use his veto power, President Trump had not vetoed a single bill.

Though not explicitly, the Constitution provides the president with the power of **legislative initiative**—the implied power to bring a legislative agenda before Congress. The framers of the Constitution clearly saw legislative initiative as one of the keys to executive power. *Initiative* implies the ability to formulate proposals for important policies, and the president, as an individual with a great deal of staff assistance, is able to initiate decisive action more frequently than Congress, with its large assemblies that have to deliberate and debate before taking action. With some important exceptions, Congress depends on the president to set the agenda of public policy. For example, under the terms of the 1921 Budget and Accounting Act, the president is required to submit a budget to the Congress. In the case of the budget and other matters, initiative confers the power of being able to set the terms of discourse in the making of public policy.

For example, during the weeks immediately following September 11, George W. Bush took many presidential initiatives to Congress, and each was given almost unanimous support. President Obama made health care his chief domestic priority and engaged in sharp battles with congressional Republicans to bring about the enactment of the Affordable Care Act, informally known as "Obamacare." President Trump sought to lead Congress in the elimination of Obamacare and in a massive tax reform effort but found it difficult to unite the fractious Republicans behind his agenda. Congress was unable to muster a majority for the repeal of Obamacare but did enact a sweeping reform of the tax system and a major new budget that substantially lifted spending on military and domestic programs.

legislative initiative the president's inherent power to bring a legislative agenda before Congress

FOR CRITICAL ANALYSIS

Although Congress passes laws, the president has influence too. What is the president's role in the legislative process?

IMPLIED POWERS

implied powers powers derived from the necessary and proper clause of Article I, Section 8, of the Constitution; such powers are not specifically expressed but are implied through the expansive interpretation of delegated powers

The list of expressed presidential powers is brief, but each expressed power has become the foundation of a second set of presidential powers, the so-called **implied powers** of the office. An implied power is one that can be said to be necessary to allow presidents to exercise their expressed power. For example, the Constitution expressly gives the president the power to appoint "all other officers of the United States...which shall be established by law." Article II does not, however, expressly grant the president the power to remove such officials from office. There is no reason to assume *a priori* that the power to appoint necessarily indicates the power to remove an official. The president of France appoints the prime minister but only the national legislature can remove that official from office. From the earliest years of the Republic, though, presidents claimed that the removal power was implied by the appointment power. This claim was generally accepted until 1867 when, during its struggles with President Andrew Johnson, Congress enacted the *Tenure of Office Act* (repealed in 1887) requiring the president to obtain senatorial approval to remove officials whose appointments had required Senate confirmation. Johnson's refusal to comply with this Act led to the president's 1868 impeachment and trial. Johnson escaped his own removal from office by a one-vote margin. Fifty years later, the U.S. Supreme Court held in the case of *Myers* v. *United States* that the removal power was, indeed, implied by the appointment power.[10]

Presidents have also made much of the very first sentence of Article II, which declares, "The executive power shall be vested in a President of the United States of America." This grant of power, along with the subsequent admonition to presidents to see to it that the laws are faithfully executed, as well as the president's oath of office, have been cited by successive White Houses as justifications for actions not expressly sanctioned by the Constitution. In recent years, the vesting clause has been said by presidents and their advisers to support what has come to be known as the "theory of the unitary executive."[11]

Unitary executive theory holds that all executive power inheres in the president except as explicitly limited by the Constitution.[12] Thus, according to this view, the president is a sovereign subject to some restraints, such as Congress's control of revenues, its impeachment power, and its power to override presidential vetoes. Some proponents of unitary executive theory also maintain that presidents have their own power to interpret the Constitution as it applies to the executive branch and need not necessarily defer to the judiciary. This claim was advanced by President George W. Bush when he signed a Defense Appropriation Bill that included language on the treatment of terrorist suspects—the so-called anti-torture provision introduced by Senator John McCain—that the president had opposed. In his signing statement, Bush declared that he would construe the portion of the act relating to the treatment of detainees, "in a manner consistent with the constitutional authority of the President to supervise the unitary executive branch and as Commander in Chief and consistent with the constitutional limitations on the judicial power."[13] The president was claiming, in other words, that particularly in the military realm, he possessed the authority to execute acts of Congress according to his own understanding of the law and the nation's interests. He also seemed to be claiming that the authority of the courts to interfere with his actions was limited.

Unitary executive theory particularly holds that the president controls all policy making by the executive branch with Congress wielding only limited, if any, direct power over executive agencies. Only presidents, say unitary executive theorists, may exercise discretionary authority over the actions of these agencies. This idea has been the basis for such presidential programs as "regulatory review," to be discussed below, which has been used by every president since Ronald Reagan to guide rule making by the various federal agencies, sometimes using this process to write authoritative rules when they could not persuade Congress to enact laws they sought.[14]

The president is, of course, a unitary chief executive. But the principle of constitutional checks and balances would appear to provide Congress with powers over the many important agencies of the executive branch through what has come to be called "congressional oversight" of the executive. Article I of the Constitution gives Congress a number of powers, including the power to appropriate funds, to raise and support armies and navies, to regulate interstate commerce, and to impeach officials of the executive branch. Article I also gives Congress the authority "to make all laws which shall be necessary and proper for carrying into execution the foregoing powers." Congressional oversight, which includes legislative hearings, investigations, studies, and reports, is arguably implied by this language. If Congress is to carry out its constitutional responsibilities, it must possess the ability to obtain information regarding the activities of executive branch agencies and officials. Thus, the stage is set for conflict between the implied powers of Congress and those of the president.

DELEGATED POWERS

Many of the powers exercised by the president and the executive branch are not found in the Constitution but are **delegated powers**, the products of congressional statutes and resolutions. Over the past century, Congress has voluntarily delegated a great deal of its own legislative authority to the executive branch. To some extent, this delegation of power has been an almost inescapable consequence of the expansion of government activity in the United States since the New Deal. Given the vast range of the federal government's responsibilities, Congress cannot execute and administer all of the programs it creates and the laws it enacts. Inevitably, Congress must turn to the hundreds of departments and agencies in the executive branch or, when necessary, create new agencies to implement its goals. Thus, for example, in 2002, when Congress sought to protect America from terrorist attacks, it established the Department of Homeland Security, with broad powers in the realms of law enforcement, public health, and immigration.

As they implement congressional legislation, federal agencies collectively develop thousands of rules and regulations and issue thousands of orders and findings every year. Agencies interpret Congress's intent, promulgate rules aimed at implementing that intent, and issue orders to individuals, firms, and organizations to impel them to conform to the law. When it establishes an agency, Congress sometimes grants it only limited discretionary authority, providing very specific guidelines and standards that must be followed by the administrators charged with the program's implementation. Take the Internal Revenue Service (IRS), for example. Most Americans view the IRS as a powerful agency whose dictates can have an immediate and sometimes unpleasant impact on their lives. In fact, congressional tax legislation is very specific and detailed, leaving little to the discretion of IRS administrators.[15] The agency certainly develops numerous rules and procedures to enhance tax collection. It is Congress, however, that establishes the structure of the tax liabilities, tax exemptions, and tax deductions that determine each taxpayer's burdens and responsibilities.

delegated powers constitutional powers that are assigned to one governmental agency but that are exercised by another agency with the express permission of the first

Executive Branches in Comparison

All democracies have an executive branch, but the specific form it takes varies. In presidential systems, such as the United States, the position of the head of state (the symbolic leader of a country) and the head of government (the leader in charge of the day-to-day running of the government) is combined into one position—the president. In parliamentary systems, these roles are often held by different people, with the head of government being the more powerful position. For example, in Germany, the head of government is the prime minister (called the chancellor), while the head of state is the president, who plays a largely ceremonial role similar to the United Kingdom's queen.

Most democracies use parliamentary executive systems, though presidential systems are common in the Americas, in part due to the historical influence of the United States. Political scientists have long debated which system is "best," contrasting parliamentary and presidential systems on their effectiveness, stability, and representativeness. In presidential systems, for example, the separation of powers may protect against the "tyranny of the majority," in which a majority pursues its interests without regard to those of minority groups (see Chapter 2), but it can also lead to deadlock, policy inefficiencies, and polarization.

A small but growing group of countries uses a hybrid "semipresidential" system. France, for instance, divides the executive between a powerful head of state (the president) and the head of government (the prime minister) who have different but (theoretically) equal powers. While this arrangement is intended to combine the best of both systems, conflict can emerge in semi-presidential systems between the prime minister and president over differences in legislation or constitutional authority. In most semi-presidential systems, the president holds the majority of the power, including the power to appoint and dismiss the prime minister. Occasionally, presidents in these systems can use their power advantage to undermine the legislature and threaten democracy.

	PRESIDENTIAL	PARLIAMENTARY
Examples	United States, Mexico, Brazil, Chile, Ghana, South Korea	United Kingdom, India, Germany, Japan, Canada, Austria, Norway
Executive title	President	Prime Minister, Chancellor, etc.
Is the executive the . . . Head of state? Head of government?	Yes Yes	No Yes
Executive elected by . . .	Voters*	Parliament
Term in office	Fixed by law	Subject to support of the parliament
Separation of powers	Yes	No; the Prime Minister is a member of the parliament
Executive role in legislating	Veto power	Initiates most bills

*In the United States, the president is elected by the Electoral College, not by the voters directly. Other presidential systems have the voters directly elect the president.

In most instances, though, congressional legislation is not very detailed. Often, Congress defines a broad goal or objective and delegates enormous discretionary power to administrators to determine how that goal is to be achieved. Agency administrators have the power to draft rules and regulations that have the effect of law. Indeed, the courts treat these administrative rules like congressional statutes. For all intents and purposes, when Congress creates an agency such as the Department of Homeland Security, giving it a broad mandate to achieve some desirable outcome, it transfers its own legislative power to the executive branch.

At least since the New Deal, Congress has tended to give executive agencies broad mandates and to draft legislation that offers few clear standards or guidelines for implementation by the executive. For example, the 1933 National Industrial Recovery Act gave the president the authority to set rules to bring about fair competition in key sectors of the economy without ever defining what the term meant or how it was to be achieved.[16] This pattern of broad delegation became typical in the ensuing decades. The 1972 Consumer Product Safety Act, for example, authorizes the Consumer Product Safety Commission to reduce unreasonable risk of injury from household products but offers no suggestions to guide the commission's determination of what constitutes reasonable and unreasonable risks or how these are to be reduced.[17] This means the executive branch, under the president's direction, has wide discretion to make rules that impact American citizens and businesses. A recent example of the executive branch's role is the 2010 Affordable Care Act. After the law passed, several members of Congress admitted that they did not fully understand how the act would work and were depending upon the Department of Health and Human Services, the agency with primary administrative responsibility for the act, to explain it to them. The case of the Affordable Care Act is fairly typical. As administrative scholar Jerry L. Nashaw has observed, "Most public law is legislative in origin but administrative in content."[18]

In the nineteenth century there were relatively well-defined congressional guidelines for administrators. During much of the nineteenth century, the federal government had relatively few domestic responsibilities, and Congress could pay close attention to details. Today, the operation of an enormous executive establishment and literally thousands of programs under varied and changing circumstances requires that administrators be allowed some considerable measure of discretion to carry out their jobs. Nevertheless, the end result is to shift power from Congress to the executive branch.

The influence of the president and the executive branch is widespread as the executive is responsible for the implementation of many laws that Congress passes. For example, after Congress passed the Affordable Care Act, it was up to the executive branch to orchestrate the health insurance enrollment process for millions of Americans.

INHERENT POWERS

Presidents have also claimed a fourth source of power. These are powers not specified in the Constitution but said to stem from "the rights, duties and obligations of the presidency." These are referred to as **inherent powers** and are most often asserted by presidents in time of war or national emergency. President Lincoln relied upon a claim of inherent power to raise an army after the fall of Fort Sumter. Similarly, Presidents Roosevelt (World War II), Truman (Korean War), and both Presidents Bush (Persian Gulf and Middle East wars) claimed inherent powers to defend the nation. Since the Korean War, presidents have used their claim of inherent powers along with their constitutional power as Commander in Chief to bypass the constitutional provision giving Congress the power to declare war. Congress declared war after the Japanese attack on Pearl Harbor on December 7, 1941. Since that time, American forces have been sent to fight foreign wars on more than one hundred occasions but not once was Congress asked for a Declaration of War. In 1973, Congress passed the War

inherent powers powers claimed by a president that are not expressed in the Constitution but are inferred from it

Powers Resolution designed to restore its role in military policy. Presidents, however, have regarded the resolution as an improper limitation on the inherent powers of the presidency and have studiously ignored the provisions of the War Powers Resolution.

The difference between inherent and implied powers is often subtle and the two are frequently jointly claimed in support of presidential action. Implied powers can be traced to the powers expressed in the actual language of the Constitution.[19] Inherent powers, on the other hand, derive from national sovereignty. Under international law and custom, sovereign states possess a number of inherent rights and powers. The most important of these are the right to engage in relations with other nations, the right of self-defense against attacks from other states, and the right to curb internal violence and unrest. Who is actually to act to give effect to the nation's various rights and powers? The executive power is vested by the Constitution in the president, who is acknowledged to have the power to "make" if not "declare" war, to negotiate treaties with other nations and to see to it that the laws are faithfully executed. Thus, it might be said to be constitutionally implied that it is the president who possesses the inherent power to act to defend the nation, to conduct its foreign relations, and to safeguard law and order.

Most presidents believe that they and only they are constitutionally authorized to manage the nation's relations with foreign states. If challenged, presidents and their aides will cite the words of John Marshall's 1800 speech to the House of Representatives where the future Chief Justice called the president, "the sole organ of the nation in its external relations, and its sole representative with foreign nations."[20] According to constitutional scholar Louis Fisher, Marshall meant that the president was the sole organ in implementing, not making, foreign policy.[21] Yet, the Supreme Court took the more expansive view in its famous *Curtiss-Wright* decision, which cites Marshall in support of the idea that the president possesses broad inherent power in the making of foreign policy.[22]

A number of presidents have claimed that the presidency also possessed inherent powers in military affairs and in dealing with domestic emergencies—powers that were not necessarily spelled out in the Constitution or sanctioned by law.[23] In 1861, Abraham Lincoln suspended the writ of habeas corpus, ordered martial law in a number of areas, called out the state militias, withdrew funds from the Treasury, and ordered a naval blockade of Southern ports, all without congressional authorization.

No president has acted so frequently on the basis of inherent powers as President George W. Bush. He claimed that the inherent powers of the presidency gave him the authority to create military commissions, designate U.S. citizens as enemy combatants, engage in "extraordinary renditions" of captured suspects who would be moved to unknown facilities in unnamed countries for interrogation, and authorize the National Security Agency (NSA) to monitor phone conversations between the United States and other nations.[24] When challenged, some but not all of these actions were overturned by the courts. We will examine these decisions in some detail in Chapter 15. It is worth noting, however, that the decisions hardly put to rest the idea of inherent power. Indeed, Bush's successor, President Barack Obama, continued to rely on the concept of inherent power in ordering drone strikes against suspected terrorists and ordering American air strikes in Libya. Testifying before Congress in 2014, Attorney General Eric Holder defended the president's unilateral actions, saying, "Given what the president's responsibility is in running the executive branch, I think there is an inherent power there for him to act in the way that he has."[25] In 2017, President Trump's order banning travelers from several Muslim

Who Are America's Presidents?

American presidents have all been men. Until the election of Barack Obama in 2008, they had all been white. As the data show, a majority of presidents have come from the eastern United States, with Virginia producing the most American presidents, especially in the nation's first decades.

Gender

++++++++++++++++++++++++
++++++++++++++++++++++++

Male **44**   Female **0**

Race

White **43**   African American **1**

Age

Number of presidents (y-axis: 1, 2, 3, 4, 5)

Age of president when first elected (x-axis: 40, 45, 50, 55, 60, 65, 70)

Party*

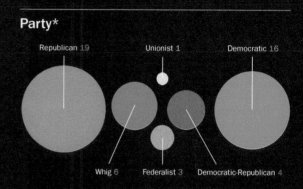

Republican 19 · Unionist 1 · Democratic 16 · Whig 6 · Federalist 3 · Democratic-Republican 4

Top Occupations**

Number of presidents (y-axis: 5, 10, 15, 20, 25)

Occupation before elected president: Lawyer · Military · Teacher · Farmer · Business/merchant

Region†

Presidents
- 0
- 1
- 2
- 4
- 5
- 7
- 8

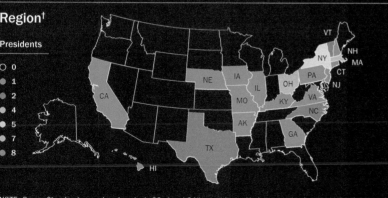

(Map labels: VT, NY, NH, MA, PA, CT, NJ, IA, OH, NE, IL, KY, VA, CA, MO, NC, AK, GA, TX, HI)

FOR CRITICAL ANALYSIS

1. Why do you think all presidents have been men and all but one have been white? Do you think this is likely to change in coming years?

2. Why do you think so many presidents have come from the South and the East? What electoral or historical factors may have produced this trend?

NOTE: Grover Cleveland served as America's 22nd and 24th presidents. He is counted only once in the demographic data here, thus the total number of people who have served as U.S. president is 44.

*Some presidents switched parties during their political careers, thus the numbers sum to more than 44.

**This chart reflects the top nonpolitical careers of U.S. presidents. (All presidents except George Washington and Donald Trump had previous political and/or public service experience.) Presidents may have had more than one occupation, and some occupations do not appear on this list, thus the numbers do not sum to 44.

† Andrew Jackson was born in the Waxhaw area, on the North Carolina–South Carolina border.

SOURCES: Roper Center, www.ropercenter.uconn.edu/elections/common/pop_vote.html; David Leip, http://uselectionatlas.org/RESULTS/; the American Presidency Project, www.presidency.ucsb.edu/showelection.php?year=1840; Miller Center, University of Virginia.

Governors must ask the federal government for help in an emergency, as Governor Greg Abbott did in the face of Hurricane Harvey. However, some say decisions whether or not to provide support are largely driven by politics.

countries was based mainly on a claim that the president had the inherent power to bar any class of immigrants whom he thought to be a threat to the United States.

Congress has endeavored to place some limits on powers that presidents claim to be inherent. One example is the case of emergency powers. Presidents believe they have the inherent power to deal with emergencies. But Congress has, by statute, sought to circumscribe and guide the use of these powers. Under the 1976 National Emergencies Act, which was built upon prior enactments, the president is authorized to declare a national emergency in the event of major threats to America's national security or economy.[26] An emergency declaration relating to foreign threats allows the president to embargo trade, seize foreign assets, and prohibit transactions with whatever foreign nations are involved. During a state of emergency, constitutional rights, including the right of habeas corpus, may be suspended. An emergency declaration, however, does not remain in force indefinitely. Such a declaration remains in force for only one year unless it is renewed by the president. Several declarations have been renewed annually for quite some time. President Carter's 1979 declaration of an emergency during the Iranian hostage crisis has been renewed every year, as has been President Bush's 2001 emergency declaration following the September 11 terror attacks. These declarations have provided a basis for various trade embargoes, asset freezes, and restrictions on money transfers ordered by successive presidents.[27] Congress may, by a joint resolution of the two houses, terminate a state of emergency.

A closely related area in which Congress has sought to regulate matters that presidents tend to view as involving their own inherent power is the nation's response to natural disasters. Under the 1988 Stafford Act, the governor of a state affected by a disastrous flood, hurricane, earthquake, or other calamitous event must ask the Federal Emergency Management Agency (FEMA) for a determination that the scope of the disaster is beyond the abilities of state and local authorities to handle. The president may then declare a disaster and make the state eligible for federal funds and relief. The purpose of the Stafford Act was to ensure that presidential disaster declarations were governed by statutory criteria. In recent years, however, critics have charged that presidential determinations and funding authorizations seemed, nevertheless, to be driven by political motivations.[28]

The Presidency as an Institution

> **Identify the institutional resources presidents have to help them exercise their powers**

After considering and rejecting the idea of a three-person executive or a multi-headed executive council, the framers of the Constitution created a unitary, or one-person, executive because they thought this would make the presidency a more energetic institution, better able to deal efficiently with the nation's concerns. Nevertheless, since the ratification of the Constitution, the president has been joined by thousands of officials and staffers who work for, assist, or advise the chief executive (see Figure 13.2). Collectively, these individuals could be said to make up the institutional presidency and to give the president a capacity for action that no single individual, however energetic, could duplicate. The first component of the institutional presidency is the president's Cabinet.

FIGURE 13.2
The Institutional Presidency

THE WHITE HOUSE STAFF

Includes:
- Chief of Staff
- Press Secretary
- Senior Advisers
- Special Assistants

INDEPENDENT AGENCIES AND GOVERNMENT CORPORATIONS

Includes:
- Central Intelligence Agency
- Environmental Protection Agency
- Federal Labor Relations Authority
- General Services Administration

THE PRESIDENT

THE CABINET

Department of Agriculture
Department of Commerce
Department of Defense
Department of Education
Department of Energy
Department of Health and Human Services
Department of Homeland Security
Department of Housing and Urban Development
Department of the Interior
Department of Justice
Department of Labor
Department of State
Department of Transportation
Department of the Treasury
Department of Veterans Affairs

EXECUTIVE OFFICE OF THE PRESIDENT

Council of Economic Advisers
Council on Environmental Quality
National Security Council
Office of Administration
Office of Management and Budget
Office of National Drug Control Policy
Office of Science and Technology Policy
Office of the United States Trade Representative
President's Intelligence Advisory Board and Intelligence Oversight Board
White House Military Office
White House Office

THE CABINET

Cabinet the secretaries, or chief administrators, of the major departments of the federal government; Cabinet secretaries are appointed by the president with the consent of the Senate

In the American system of government, the **Cabinet** is the traditional but informal designation for the heads of all the major federal government departments. The Cabinet has no constitutional status. Unlike in Great Britain and many other parliamentary countries, where the cabinet *is* the government, the American Cabinet is not a collective body. It meets but makes no decisions as a group. Each appointment must be approved by the Senate, but Cabinet members are not responsible to the Senate or to Congress at large. However, cabinet secretaries and their deputies frequently testify before congressional committees to justify budgets and policy objectives, or explain policies or recent major events or issues.

All U.S. Cabinet departments, and about half the other agencies, were created by acts of Congress. The remaining agencies were created by executive order, the orders of department secretaries, or through the reorganization of existing agencies.[29] Major agencies created by executive order include the Environmental Protection Agency (EPA), the Federal Emergency Management Agency (FEMA), and the Drug Enforcement Administration (DEA). Presidents have claimed the power to create agencies and Congress has acquiesced by providing funding.

Each of the 15 government departments is led by a secretary who is a member of the president's Cabinet. Reporting to the secretary is a deputy secretary, while individual offices and activities are led by undersecretaries and assistant secretaries. The major independent agencies, such as the Social Security Administration, are usually headed by a senior official whose title might be commissioner, administrator, or director and who is in turn supported by deputies and assistant deputies. Government departments range in size from the tiny Department of Education, which employs only about 4,200 individuals, to the massive Department of Defense (DoD), which oversees some 700,000 civilian employees and 1.3 million military personnel. The DoD is also responsible for maintaining the military readiness of 1.1 million reserve and National Guard troops.

The independent agencies also vary in size. The Social Security Administration employs about 60,000 individuals, while some of the smaller agencies are staffed by only a few dozen individuals.

THE WHITE HOUSE STAFF

White House staff analysts and advisers to the president, each of whom is often given the title "special assistant"

The White House staff is composed mainly of analysts and advisers.[30] Although many of the top **White House staff** members hold such titles as "adviser to the president," "assistant to the president," "deputy assistant," and "special assistant" for a particular task or sector, the judgments and advice they are supposed to provide are a good deal broader and more generally political than those coming from the Executive Office of the President or from the Cabinet departments. The members of the White House staff also tend to be more closely associated with the president than are other presidentially appointed officials. This is especially true in the Trump White House, where the president's daughter Ivanka is an assistant to the president, and her husband, Jared Kushner, is a senior adviser to the president.

THE EXECUTIVE OFFICE OF THE PRESIDENT

Executive Office of the President (EOP) the permanent agencies that perform defined management tasks for the president; created in 1939, the EOP includes the OMB, the CEA, the NSC, and other agencies

Created in 1939, the **Executive Office of the President (EOP)** is a major part of the institutional presidency. Somewhere between 1,500 and 2,000 highly specialized people work for EOP agencies.[31] The importance of each agency in the EOP varies according to the personal orientation of each president. The most important and the largest EOP agency is the Office of Management and Budget (OMB). Its roles in preparing the national budget, designing the president's program, reporting on agency activities, and overseeing regulatory proposals connect the OMB to every conceivable presidential responsibility. The status and power of the OMB have grown in importance with each successive president, and the director of the OMB is now one of the most powerful officials in Washington. At one time the process of budgeting was a "bottom-up" procedure, with expenditure and program requests passing from the lowest bureaus through the departments to "clearance" in the OMB and thence to Congress, where each agency could be called in to explain what its "original request" was before the OMB revised it. Now the budgeting process is "top-down": the OMB sets the terms of discourse for agencies as well as for Congress.

The staff of the Council of Economic Advisers (CEA) constantly analyzes the economy and economic trends in order to help the president anticipate events rather than waiting and reacting to them. The Council on Environmental Quality was designed to do for environmental issues what the CEA does for economic issues. The **National Security Council (NSC)** is composed of designated Cabinet officials who meet regularly with the president to give advice on the large national security picture. The staff of the NSC assimilates and analyzes data from all intelligence-gathering agencies (CIA, etc.). In some administrations, the head of the NSC, the president's national security adviser, has held the president's confidence and been a more important figure in the making of American foreign and military policy than the cabinet secretaries in these domains. Henry Kissinger, President Nixon's national security adviser, was such an individual. Other national security advisers have been disappointments to the presidents who appointed them. For example, General Michael Flynn, President Trump's first national security adviser, was forced to resign amid charges of improper relations with Russian officials.

National Security Council (NSC) a presidential foreign policy advisory council composed of the president, the vice president, the secretary of state, the secretary of defense, and other officials invited by the president

THE VICE PRESIDENCY

The vice presidency is a constitutional anomaly, even though the office was created along with the presidency by the Constitution. The vice president exists for two purposes only: to succeed the president in case of death, resignation, or incapacity, and to preside over the Senate, casting a tie-breaking vote when necessary.[32]

The main value of the vice president as a political resource for the president is electoral. Traditionally, presidential candidates choose running mates who can win the support of at least one state (preferably a large one) that may not otherwise support the ticket. It is very doubtful that John Kennedy would have won in 1960 without his vice-presidential candidate, Lyndon Johnson, and the contribution Johnson made to winning in Texas. Another traditional guideline holds that the vice-presidential nominee should provide some regional balance and, wherever possible, ideological or ethnic balance as well. In 2016, Donald Trump chose Governor Mike Pence of Indiana as his running mate for a number of reasons. First, Pence, a former host of conservative radio and television talk shows, was well known among conservatives. Second, Pence served in Congress for 12 years. He worked to reassure skeptical party leaders that Trump was a qualified candidate. Third and most important, Pence is a devout Christian who is very well regarded by social conservatives. As vice president, Pence is often the person Trump relies on to smooth relations with Republican members of Congress.

The vice president is also important because, in the event of the death or incapacity of the president, he or she will succeed to the nation's highest office. During

Mike Pence, who served as a member of Congress and then governor of Indiana, is devoutly Christian and socially conservative. He helped improve Donald Trump's electoral appeal among social conservatives and establishment Republicans.

the course of American history, eight vice presidents have had to replace presidents who died in office. One vice president, Gerald Ford, found himself at the head of the nation when President Richard Nixon was forced to resign as a result of the Watergate scandal.

Until the ratification of the Twenty-Fifth Amendment in 1965, the succession of the vice president to the presidency was a tradition, launched by John Tyler when he assumed the presidency after William Henry Harrison's death, rather than a constitutional or statutory requirement. The Twenty-Fifth Amendment codified this tradition by providing that the vice president would assume the presidency in the event of the chief executive's death or incapacity and setting forth the procedures that would be followed. The Twenty-Fifth Amendment also provides that if the vice presidency becomes vacant, the president will nominate an individual who must be confirmed by a majority vote of both houses of Congress. Thus, in 1973 when Vice President Spiro Agnew was forced to resign, President Nixon nominated Gerald Ford, who was confirmed. Later, when Nixon was forced to resign, Ford became president. In the event that both the president and vice president are killed, the Presidential Succession Act of 1947 establishes an order of succession, beginning with the Speaker of the House and continuing with the president pro tempore of the Senate and the Cabinet secretaries. This piece of legislation, adopted during the Cold War and prompted by fear of a nuclear attack, has taken on new importance in an age of global terrorism.

THE FIRST SPOUSE

The president serves as both chief executive and chief of state—the equivalent of Great Britain's prime minister and monarch rolled into one, simultaneously leading the government and representing the nation at official ceremonies and functions.

Because they are generally associated exclusively with the head-of-state aspect of America's presidency, presidential spouses are usually not subject to the same sort of media scrutiny or partisan attack as that aimed at the president. Traditionally,

First Lady Melania Trump is an immigrant from Slovenia and a former model. During the 2016 presidential campaign, Mrs. Trump campaigned for her husband, speaking at the Republican National Convention and occasionally at rallies.

most first ladies have limited their activities to the ceremonial portion of the presidency: greeting foreign dignitaries, visiting other countries, and attending important national ceremonies.

Some first spouses, however, have had considerable influence over policy. Franklin Roosevelt's wife, Eleanor, was widely popular but also widely criticized for her active role in many elements of her husband's presidency. During the 1992 campaign, Bill Clinton often implied that his wife would be active in the administration; he joked that voters would get "two for the price of one." And indeed, after the election, Hillary Clinton took a leading role in many policy areas, most notably heading the administration's health care reform effort. She also became the first first lady to seek public office on her own, winning a seat in the U.S. Senate in 2000 and then running for president in 2008 and 2016, having served in between as President Obama's secretary of state.

Melania Trump is the first foreign-born first lady in almost 200 years. With no political or public affairs experience, Mrs. Trump said that she would be a traditional first lady. Given the current expectation that the first spouse should assume some public responsibility, however, Mrs. Trump may become a visible advocate for an important social cause. Thus far, she has spoken out against online bullying.

The Contemporary Bases of Presidential Power

> **Explain how modern presidents have become even more powerful**

During the nineteenth century, Congress was America's dominant institution of government, and members of Congress sometimes treated the president with disdain. Today, however, no one would assert that the presidency is unimportant. Presidents seek to dominate the policy-making process and claim the power to lead the nation in time of war. The expansion of presidential power over the course of the past century has come about not by accident but as the result of an ongoing effort by successive presidents to enlarge the powers of the office.

Generally, presidents can expand their power in two primary ways: through popular mobilization and through the administration. First, presidents may use popular appeals to create a mass base of support that will allow them to dominate their political foes, a tactic called "going public."[33] Second, presidents may seek to bolster their control of established executive agencies or to create new administrative institutions and procedures that will reduce their dependence on Congress and give them a more independent governing and policy-making capability. Perhaps the most obvious example of this is the use of executive orders to achieve policy goals in lieu of seeking to persuade Congress to enact legislation.

Presidents do have a third, less reliable tool: their political party. Most presidents have relied on their own party to implement their legislative agenda. For example, in 2009–10, President Obama relied on congressional Democrats to pass the Affordable Care Act ("Obamacare") in the face of virtually unanimous Republican opposition. However, the president does not control his party; party members have considerable autonomy. President Trump was unable to rally enough Republican legislators to repeal Obamacare, although he was able to bring about the enactment of tax reform. Consequently, although the party is valuable to chief executives, it has not been a fully reliable presidential tool.

Moreover, in America's system of separated powers, the president's party may be in the minority in Congress and unable to do much for the chief executive's programs. As a result, contemporary presidents are more likely to use the two other methods, popular mobilization and executive administration, to achieve their political goals.

GOING PUBLIC

In the nineteenth century, it was considered inappropriate for presidents to engage in personal campaigning on their own behalf or in support of programs and policies. When Andrew Johnson broke this unwritten rule and made a series of speeches vehemently seeking public support for his Reconstruction program, even some of his supporters were shocked at what they saw as his lack of decorum and dignity. The president's opponents cited his "inflammatory" speeches in one of the articles of impeachment drafted by the Congress.[34]

In the twentieth century, though, popular mobilization became a favored weapon in the political arsenals of most presidents. The first to make systematic use of appeals to the public were Theodore Roosevelt and Woodrow Wilson, but the president who used public appeals most effectively was Franklin Delano Roosevelt. FDR was "firmly persuaded of the need to form a direct link between the executive office and the public."[35] He developed a number of tactics for forging such a link. He often embarked on speaking trips around the nation to promote his programs. On one such tour, he told a crowd, "I regain strength just by meeting the American people."[36] In addition, FDR made effective use of a new electronic medium, the radio, to reach millions of Americans. In his famous "fireside chats," the president's voice could be heard in every living room in the country, discussing programs and policies and generally assuring Americans that Franklin Delano Roosevelt was aware of their difficulties and working diligently toward solutions.

Roosevelt was also an innovator in the realm of what now might be called press relations. When he entered the White House, FDR faced a mainly hostile press, typically controlled by conservative members of the business establishment.[37] To circumvent the editors and publishers who were generally unsympathetic to his goals, the president worked to cultivate the reporters who covered the White House. FDR made himself available for biweekly press conferences, where he offered candid answers to reporters' questions and made certain to make important policy announcements that would provide the reporters with significant stories for their papers.[38] Franklin Roosevelt's press secretary, Stephen Early, was charged with organizing press conferences and making certain that reporters observed the informal rules distinguishing those presidential comments that could be attributed directly to the president from those that were off the record.

Every president since FDR has sought to craft a public-relations strategy that would emphasize the incumbent's strengths and maximize his popular appeal. For John F. Kennedy, who was handsome and quick-witted, the televised press conference was an excellent public-relations vehicle. Both Bill Clinton and Barack Obama held televised town meetings—carefully staged events that gave these presidents opportunities to appear to consult with rank-and-file citizens about their goals and policies without having to face the sorts of pointed questions preferred by reporters.

Bill Clinton introduced an innovation that continued to be used by Bush, Obama, and Trump. This was to make the White House Communications Office an important institution within the EOP. The Communications Office became responsible not only for responding to reporters' queries but also for developing and implementing a coordinated communications strategy—promoting the president's policy goals, developing responses to adverse news stories, and making certain that a favorable image of the president would, insofar as possible, dominate the news.

We must not let #CrookedHillary take her CRIMINAL SCHEME into the Oval Office. #DrainTheSwamp

12:20 PM - 28 Oct 2016 from Manchester, NH

Over the last century, presidents and candidates have made more and more used of direct appeals to the American people. President Franklin Roosevelt made effective use of radio to build public support for his programs (top). Donald Trump (bottom) has likewise used Twitter to promote his message, both as a candidate and as president.

Going Public Online President Obama was the first chief executive to make full use of another new communication medium—the internet. Drawing on the interactive tools of the web, Obama's 2008 and 2012 campaigns changed the way politicians organize supporters, advertise to voters, defend against attacks, and communicate with their constituents.[39] In the 2016 presidential campaign, candidates Hillary Clinton and especially Donald Trump made particular use of Twitter to communicate with millions of voters, bypassing traditional media. Trump usually tweeted many times a day, often making outrageous claims that guaranteed that he would dominate media coverage as reporters rushed to analyze and criticize Trump's assertions. Trump did not care if the media criticized him or refuted his claims—his goal was to dominate coverage. During the course of the campaign, Trump received a quantity of free coverage that would have cost several billion dollars if he had purchased advertising time. The Clinton campaign spent much more money than Trump, but Trump's clever use of Twitter and his manipulation of the media gave him an enormous air-time advantage.

The internet has changed not only the way modern presidents campaign but also how they govern. The Whitehouse.gov website keeps the president's constituents abreast of his policy agenda with a weekly streaming video address by the president, press briefings, speeches and remarks, a daily blog, photos of the president, the White House schedule, and other information. Virtually everything the president does is recorded online. YouTube aired Obama's press conferences and public appearances on a daily basis. Every presidential address is now streamed live online. Obama also created a website that allowed citizens to submit petitions to the White House. Any petition receiving 100,000 signatures was slated for review by the administration and a response issued. For example, in 2015 the president issued extensive comments on the death of Michael Brown, a black man shot by a white police officer in Ferguson, Missouri, in response to citizen petitions demanding a federal investigation of the incident.

Circumventing television and other traditional media, the internet allows the president to broadcast his policy ideas directly to the citizens. Every Trump legislative initiative and policy direction is preceded by a flurry of tweets repeated by the broadcast and print media. And, Trump's language seems tailored to the twitter age. Calling North Korean leader Kim Jong-un "Little Rocket Man" in his tweets allowed Trump to boil down his sense of contempt and harsh posture toward North Korea into a tweet-sized threat to use force.

FOR CRITICAL ANALYSIS

What are the advantages and disadvantages of presidents governing via digital media? How do these pros and cons compare with "going public" in the age of television?

The Limits of Going Public Some presidents have been able to make effective use of popular appeals to overcome congressional opposition. Popular support, though, has not been a firm foundation for presidential power: President George W. Bush maintained an approval rating of over 70 percent for more than a year following the September 11 terrorist attacks. By the end of 2005, however, Bush's approval rating had dropped to 39 percent as a result of the growing unpopularity of the Iraq War, the administration's inept handling of hurricane relief, and a number of White House scandals, including the conviction of Vice President Cheney's chief of staff on charges of lying to a federal grand jury. Between the time President Obama took office in January 2009 and May 2016, his public approval ranged from a high of 76 percent in January 2009 to a low of 36 percent in the fall of 2014.[40] Such declines in popular approval during a president's term in office are nearly inevitable and follow a predictable pattern.[41] Both before and after they are elected, presidents generate popular support by promising to undertake important programs that will contribute directly to the well-being of large numbers of Americans. Almost without exception, presidential performance falls short of promises and popular expectations, leading to a decline in public support and the ensuing weakening of presidential influence.[42] It is a rare American president, such as Bill Clinton, who exits the White House more popular than when he went in. Donald Trump's approval rating had risen to 45 percent by June 2018, after hitting a low of 35 percent in 2017.[43]

THE ADMINISTRATIVE STRATEGY

Contemporary presidents have increased the administrative capabilities of their office in three ways. First, they have enhanced the reach and power of the EOP. Second, they have sought to increase White House control over the federal bureaucracy. Third, they have expanded the role of executive orders and other instruments of direct presidential governance. Taken together, these three components of what might be called the White House "administrative strategy" have given presidents a capacity to achieve their programmatic and policy goals even when they are unable to secure congressional approval. Indeed, some recent presidents have been able to accomplish a great deal with remarkably little congressional, partisan, or even public support.

The Growth of the EOP The EOP has grown from six administrative assistants in 1939 to several hundred employees working directly for the president in the White House office, along with some 2,500 individuals staffing the several divisions of the

Executive Office. The creation and growth of the White House staff have given the president an enormously enhanced capacity to gather information, plan programs and strategies, communicate with constituencies, and exercise supervision over the executive branch. The staff multiplies the president's eyes, ears, and arms, becoming a critical instrument of presidential power.[44]

In particular, the OMB, an agency within the EOP, serves as a potential instrument of presidential control over federal spending and hence a mechanism through which the White House has greatly expanded its power. The OMB has the capacity to analyze and approve all legislative proposals, not only budgetary requests, emanating from all federal agencies before being submitted to Congress. This procedure, now a matter of routine, greatly enhances the president's control over the entire executive branch. All legislation originating in the White House as well as all executive orders also go through the OMB.[45] Thus, through one White House agency, the president has the means to exert major influence over the flow of money and the shape and content of national legislation.

Regulatory Review A second instrument that presidents have used to increase their power and reach is an agency within OMB called the Office of Information and Regulatory Affairs (OIRA), which supervises the process of regulatory review through which presidents have sought to seize control of rule-making by the agencies of the executive branch. Whenever Congress enacts a statute, its actual implementation requires the promulgation of hundreds of rules by the agency charged with administering the law and giving effect to the will of Congress. For example, if Congress wishes to improve air quality, it must delegate to an agency—say the Environmental Protection Agency (EPA)—the power to establish numerous rules and regulations that will govern the actions of the government agencies, firms, and individuals whose conduct may have an impact upon the atmosphere. The agency rule-making process is, itself, governed by a number of statutory requirements concerning public notice (most importantly publication in the *Federal Register*), hearings, and appeals, but once completed and published in the massive *Code of Federal Regulations*, administrative rules have the effect of law and will be enforced by the federal courts.

The discretion Congress delegates to administrative agencies has provided recent presidents with an important avenue for expanding their own power. Beginning with little fanfare during the Nixon administration, presidents—through regulatory review—gradually have endeavored to take control of the rule-making process and to use it as a quasi-legislative mechanism through which they can engage in law-making without the interference of the legislature.

For example, during the course of his presidency, Clinton issued 107 directives to administrators, ordering them to propose specific rules and regulations and, pursuant to the requirements of the Administrative Procedures Act, to publish them in the *Federal Register* for public commentary. Clinton's presidential rule-making directives covered a wide variety of topics. For example, Clinton ordered the Food and Drug Administration (FDA) to develop rules designed to restrict the marketing of tobacco products to children.[46] President George W. Bush continued the Clinton-era practice of issuing presidential directives to agencies to spur them to issue new rules and regulations. The Obama administration not only issued a number of major regulatory directives to federal agencies but also launched a "look back" program. Under this program, the administration sought to eliminate several hundred existing rules it deemed obsolete.[47] In 2015, Obama sought new regulations governing power plant emissions, overtime pay for workers, the educational practices of career (for-profit) colleges, and a host of other matters. President Trump moved aggressively to reverse these and other directives by issuing new rules or repealing existing ones to roll back environmental regulations, reduce banking regulations, eliminate workplace safety regulations, and remove protections for transgender workers, among others. Most notably, in the first year of his presidency, Trump eliminated nearly 70 environmental regulations.[48]

Governing by Decree: Executive Orders and Memoranda A third mechanism through which contemporary presidents have sought to enhance their power to govern unilaterally is through the use of executive orders and other forms of presidential decrees, including executive agreements, national security findings and directives, proclamations, reorganization plans, and memoranda.

executive order a rule or regulation issued by the president that has the effect and formal status of legislation

An **executive order** is a direct presidential directive to the bureaucracy to undertake some action, bypassing Congress and the legislative process. Executive orders have a long history in the United States and have been the instruments for a number of important policies, including the purchase of Louisiana, the annexation of Texas, the emancipation of the slaves, the wartime internment of Japanese Americans, the desegregation of the military, the initiation of affirmative action, and the creation of a number of federal agencies including the Environmental Protection Agency, the Food and Drug Administration, and the Peace Corps.[49]

Historically, executive orders were most often used during times of war or national emergency. President Lincoln relied heavily on executive orders in the early months of the Civil War to mobilize troops, purchase warships, and obtain funds from the U.S. Treasury.[50] During World War II, President Roosevelt issued 286 executive orders, establishing wartime agencies and authorizing the government to take control of factories and property for wartime needs.[51] In recent years, though, executive orders have become routine instruments of presidential governance rather than emergency wartime measures (Figure 13.3).

President George W. Bush issued more than 300 executive orders, many relating to the war on terrorism but others pertaining to domestic policy matters, such as his ban on the use of federal funds to support international family planning groups and his prohibition of the use of embryonic stem cells in federally funded research projects. President Obama issued an executive action halting the deportation of undocumented immigrants who had come to the United States as children, prohibiting federal agencies and contractors from discriminating against transgender employees, and declaring more than 700,000 square miles of the central Pacific Ocean off-limits to fishing. President Trump rescinded most of Obama's orders on immigration and opened the way for the deportation of those who had been protected by the previous president's orders. Trump also issued a number of orders, including a controversial "travel ban" decree seeking to prevent travelers from several majority-Muslim countries from entering the United States. Trump's orders led to a number of lawsuits, but the Supreme Court ultimately upheld the ban.

Presidential use of executive orders is constrained by law. When presidents issue executive orders, in principle they do so pursuant to the powers granted to them by the Constitution or delegated to them by Congress. When presidents issue orders they generally must state the constitutional or statutory basis for their actions. For example, when President Johnson ordered U.S. government contractors to initiate programs of affirmative action in hiring, he said the order was designed to implement the 1964 Civil Rights Act, which prohibited employment discrimination.

FIGURE 13.3

Presidential Executive Orders*

Executive orders are a tool presidents have for influencing policy. Their use has varied considerably over time. Each bar in the graph shows the average number of executive orders each president issued per year in office. Which presidents issued the most executive orders? What events in U.S. history were occurring when those presidents were in office?

*Does not include memoranda or other forms of executive action
**As of October 2018.

SOURCE: Gerhard Peters, www.presidency.ucsb.edu/data/orders.php (accessed 10/1/18).

Trump (77)**
Obama (33)
G. W. Bush (36)
Clinton (46)
G. H. W. Bush (42)
Reagan (48)
Carter (80)
Ford (48)
Nixon (31)
Johnson (46)
Kennedy (71)
Eisenhower (61)
Truman (60)
F. D. Roosevelt (282)
Hoover (242)
Coolidge (219)
Harding (209)
Wilson (225)
Taft (181)
T. Roosevelt (135)
McKinley (46)
Cleveland (35)
Harrison (36)
Cleveland (28)
Arthur (27)
Garfield (12)
Hayes (23)
Grant (27)
Johnson (20)
Lincoln (12)
Buchanan (4)
Pierce (9)
Fillmore (6)
Taylor (3)
Polk (5)
Tyler (4)
Harrison (0)
van Buren (3)
Jackson (2)
J. Q. Adams (0.75)
Monroe (0.125)
Madison (0.125)
Jefferson (0.5)
J. Adams (0.25)
Washington (1)

Where the courts have found no constitutional or statutory basis for a presidential order they have invalidated it. Such cases, however, are rare. Generally, the judiciary has accepted executive orders as the law of the land.

Executive orders are one form of presidential decree. Others include administrative orders, national security directives, presidential memoranda, presidential proclamations, and presidential findings.[52] Like executive orders, the other instruments establish policy and have the force of law, and presidents often use them interchangeably. Generally speaking, though, administrative orders apply to matters of administrative procedure and organization; directives seem most often associated with national or homeland security; memoranda are used to clarify or modify presidential positions and orders; and proclamations are usually used to give emphasis to an especially important presidential decree, such as Lincoln's proclamation emancipating all slaves.

Congress is not entirely without power vis-à-vis executive decrees. Legislators can overturn presidential orders that were based on the president's legislative authority (as opposed to constitutional authority) via legislation declaring that the order "shall not have legal effect," or actually repeal the statute upon which the order was based. In 1993, for example, Congress revoked an order by President George H. W. Bush to the secretary of Health and Human Services to establish a human fetal tissue bank for research purposes. Congress directed that "the provisions of Executive Order 12806 shall not have any legal effect."[53] Efforts to overturn the orders of sitting presidents are, however, hindered by the fact that any such legislation can be vetoed by the president. Thus, two-thirds of the members of both houses of Congress would have to agree to the move. One study indicates that only about 4 percent of all presidential orders have ever been rescinded by legislation.[54] Even these were almost always orders issued by presidents no longer in office.[55] Usually, the best Congress can do is inhibit the implementation of an executive order by preventing funds from being spent to implement the order. This, too, is relatively unusual.[56] Failure by Congress to act, moreover, strengthens the legal validity of a presidential order. The Supreme Court has held that congressional inaction tends to validate an order by indicating congressional "acquiescence" to the president's decision.[57] This idea begs an important question. Many presidential orders take the form of secret national security directives and findings of which Congress is unaware. Can Congress be said to acquiesce in presidential decisions made without its knowledge?

signing statements
announcements made by the president when signing bills into law, often presenting the president's interpretation of the law

Signing Statements To negate congressional actions to which they objected, recent presidents have made frequent and calculated use of presidential **signing statements** when signing bills into law.[58] The signing statement is an announcement made by the president, at the time of signing a congressional enactment into law, that offers the president's interpretation of the law and usually innocuous remarks predicting the many benefits the new law will bring to the nation. Occasionally, presidents have used signing statements to point to sections of the law they have deemed improper or even unconstitutional, and to instruct executive branch agencies how to execute the law.[59] In 2013, for example, President Obama signed a bill containing a provision requiring the president to notify Congress before transferring any prisoner from Guantánamo Bay. In his signing statement Obama declared that the provision was unconstitutional and ignored the legislation.

Presidential Nonenforcement of Laws A final instrument of direct presidential governance is nonenforcement of statutes. Congress may make the law, but

In 2017, President Trump signed an Executive Order on health care. The administration claimed this order would provide patients expanded options for health insurance, though many felt it would undermine the stability of Obamacare.

presidents implement and enforce it. If the president decides that a particular law is not to his liking and refuses to enforce it, Congress may find that its intent is stymied. President Obama, for example, suspended enforcement of portions of the Affordable Care Act when the rollout of "Obamacare" produced public confusion and inefficient implementation. President Trump, in an effort to undercut the ACA, has effectively ordered the IRS to not enforce a provision of the Affordable Care Act requiring taxpayers to indicate on their tax returns that they had health insurance—a major blow to the law's mandate. Since the president is the nation's chief law enforcer, refusal to enforce a law can become a unilateral negation of its effects.

The Advantages of the Administrative Strategy Through the course of American history, party leadership and popular appeals have played important roles in presidential efforts to overcome political opposition, and both continue to be instruments of presidential power. Yet, as we have seen, in the modern era presidents have not always been able to rely upon support from their own parties, and the effects of popular appeals have often proven evanescent. The limitations of the alternatives have increasingly impelled presidents to try to expand the administrative capabilities of the office and their own capacity for unilateral action as means of achieving their policy goals. In recent decades, the expansion of the Executive Office, the development of regulatory review, and the use of executive orders and signing statements have given presidents a substantial capacity to achieve significant policy results despite congressional opposition to their legislative agendas.

In principle, perhaps, Congress could respond more vigorously to unilateral policy making by the president than it has. Certainly, a Congress willing to impeach a president should have the mettle to overturn the chief executive's administrative directives. But the president has significant advantages in such struggles with Congress. In battles over presidential directives and orders, Congress is on the defensive, reacting to presidential initiatives. The framers of the Constitution saw "energy," or the ability to take the initiative, as a key feature of executive power.[60] When the president takes action by issuing an order or an administrative directive, Congress must respond through the cumbersome and time-consuming lawmaking process, overcome internal divisions, and enact legislation that the president may ultimately veto. Moreover, as the political scientist Terry Moe has argued, in such battles Congress faces a significant collective action problem: members are likely to be more sensitive to the substance of a president's actions and its short-term effects on their constituents than to the more general long-term implications of presidential power for the vitality of their institution.[61]

THE LIMITS OF PRESIDENTIAL POWER: CHECKS AND BALANCES

From the Constitution, presidents derive expressed, implied, and delegated powers. Claims of inherent powers are derived from the basic principles of national sovereignty coupled with the constitutional grant of executive power. But while the framers sought an energetic executive, they were also concerned that executive power could be abused and might stifle citizens' liberties. To guard against this possibility, the framers contrived a number of checks on executive power. The president's term is limited to four years, though with the possibility of reappointment. The Congress is empowered to impeach and remove the president, to reject presidential appointments and refuse to ratify treaties, to refuse to enact laws requested by the president, to deny funding for the president's programs, and to override presidential vetoes of congressional enactments.

The framers viewed the threat of impeachment as an important check upon executive power. The Constitution provides that a president may be impeached for "high crimes and misdemeanors." Such offenses are to be charged by the House and tried in the Senate, with the Chief Justice presiding and a two-thirds vote needed for conviction. During the course of American history, only two presidents, Andrew Johnson and Bill Clinton, have been impeached though neither was convicted. Johnson's impeachment was, as noted earlier, triggered by his veto of the Tenure in Office Act; and Clinton's by charges of sexual improprieties and lying under oath about them. A third president, Richard Nixon, would almost certainly have been impeached for his misdeeds in the Watergate affair, but Nixon chose to resign to avoid the impeachment process.

The requirement that the Senate concur in treaties and presidential appointments was seen by the framers as another important check on executive power. However in recent years severe partisan disagreements often have led presidents to resort to "recess appointments." These are authorized by Article II, Section 2, which states, "The President shall have power to fill up all Vacancies that may happen during the Recess of the Senate, by granting Commissions which shall expire at the End of their next Session." Until recent years, recess appointments were made only between Senate sessions or when the Senate was adjourned for lengthy periods. However, recess appointments have become more frequent and the Senate has resorted to a strategy similar to the one employed to prevent pocket vetoes. One senator is assigned the task of calling the chamber to order for a few moments every day for a pro forma session during periods of recess so that the president cannot claim the Senate was closed for business. Presidents have viewed this procedure as nothing more than a subterfuge since the Senate is incapable of actually conducting business during these periods.

And, of course, under the Constitution, only the Congress would have the power to enact legislation or to levy taxes or to appropriate funds. Indeed, so many were the constitutional checks on executive power that some delegates to the Constitutional Convention feared that the executive would be too weak and the potential energy of executive power lost. As we can see, however, from the many actions of presidents in recent years, presidential power has grown significantly beyond the framers' vision.

Presidential Power
WHAT DO WE WANT?

The framers of the Constitution created a system of government in which the Congress and the executive branch were to share power. At least since the New Deal, however, the powers of Congress have waned, whereas those of the presidency have expanded dramatically. There is no doubt that Congress continues to be able to confront presidents and even, on occasion, hand the White House a sharp rebuff.

In the larger view, however, presidents' occasional defeats, however dramatic, have to be seen as temporary setbacks in a gradual but decisive shift toward increased presidential power. Louis Fisher, a leading authority on the separation of powers, recently observed that in what are arguably the two most important policy arenas, national defense and the federal budget, the powers of Congress have been in decline for at least the past 50 years.[62]

What might the growth of executive power mean to students reading this book today? It might mean, on the one hand, that policies they favor can more easily become the law of the land. Congress works slowly while the president can work quickly, making law by the stroke of a pen or an instruction to the federal bureaucracy. Presidential strength works both ways, however: for those who oppose a particular policy or have qualms about some aspect of it, the stroke of the presidential pen might seem hasty and autocratic. The consequences can even be deadly, as we saw in the chapter opener, when a ban on a toxic chemical is at stake.

Today's students should also consider one of the chief concerns about presidential power expressed by the framers of the Constitution. The framers feared that executives were often too ready to go to war. Legislatures, they thought, were more likely to consider the costs and sacrifices entailed by war. Accordingly, the war power was given to Congress to "leash the dogs of war."[63] The framers possessed a good deal of practical experience, and their views merit consideration. Does presidential unilateralism or congressional deliberation offer better protection from the dogs of war so feared by the framers? In an era of significant international tension and trouble spots, including Iran, North Korea, Iraq, Syria, Libya, and Ukraine, the ease with which the country's leaders enter armed conflict may be a real concern.

A powerful presidency, a weak Congress, and a partially apathetic electorate make for a dangerous mix. Who we vote into the office of the president matters, as the example of EPA policy on toxic chemicals demonstrates. (The **"Who Participates?"** feature on the facing page shows who voted for Donald Trump in 2016.)

Presidents have increasingly asserted the right to govern unilaterally. Presidential power, to be sure, can be a force for good. To cite one example from the not-so-distant past, it was President Lyndon Johnson, more than Congress or the judiciary, who faced up to the task of smashing America's racial apartheid system. Yet, as the framers knew, unchecked power—whether executive or legislative—is always dangerous. The framers of the Constitution believed that liberty required checks and balances. However useful presidential power may seem, we should always be mindful of the framers' concern.

Who Voted for Donald Trump in 2016?

Age

37% 55%	42% 50%	53% 44%	53% 45%
18–29	30–44	45–64	65+

Race

58% 37%	8% 88%	29% 65%	29% 65%	37% 56%
White	African American	Hispanic	Asian American	Other

Income

41% 52%	50% 46%	48% 47%
<$50,000	$50,000–$99,999	$100,000+

Legend:
- Trump
- Clinton
- Other candidates

Sex

53% 41%	42% 54%
Men	Women

SOURCE: "2016 Election Exit Polls," *Washington Post*, November 10, 2016, www.washingtonpost.com/graphics/politics/2016-election/exit-polls/ (accessed 11/10/16).

WHAT YOU CAN DO

Contact the White House

☑ After he or she is elected, the president is expected to represent all Americans. Ask a question or share your view on a policy with the president and White House staff via **www.whitehouse.gov/contact**.

☑ Create a petition at **http://petitions.whitehouse.gov** regarding an issue you care about, and try to get as many signatures as possible.

☑ Watch a few recent presidential speeches, including this year's State of the Union address, on YouTube. Share your views with your fellow students, friends, and family.

★ STUDY GUIDE ★

The Constitutional Powers of the Presidency

Presidents have four kinds of powers: expressed, implied, delegated, and inherent. The president's expressed powers, as defined by Article II of the Constitution, include military, judicial, diplomatic, executive, and legislative powers. The expressed powers also entail a set of implied powers, which can be considered necessary in order to carry out the expressed powers. The president's delegated powers are not found in the Constitution but are, instead, the product of congressional statutes and resolutions. The president's inherent powers grow from "the rights, duties and obligations of the presidency" that presidents often assert during times of war and national crisis.

Key Terms

expressed powers (p. 516)

commander in chief (p. 516)

executive agreement (p. 518)

executive privilege (p. 519)

veto (p. 519)

pocket veto (p. 520)

legislative initiative (p. 521)

implied powers (p. 522)

delegated powers (p. 523)

inherent powers (p. 525)

Practice Quiz

1. Which of the following does *not* require the Senate's approval?
   a) a sole executive agreement
   b) a treaty
   c) an appointment of an ambassador
   d) a Supreme Court nomination
   e) an appointment of an executive officer

2. What did the Supreme Court rule in *United States v. Nixon*?
   a) Nixon had to turn his secret White House tapes over to congressional investigators because presidents do not have the power of executive privilege.
   b) Nixon did not have to turn his secret White House tapes over to congressional investigators because, in general, presidents have the power of executive privilege.
   c) Nixon had to turn his secret White House tapes over to congressional investigators but, in general, presidents have the power of executive privilege.

d) Nixon did not have to turn his secret White House tapes over to congressional investigators but, in general, presidents do not have the power of executive privilege.
   e) All presidents are immune from criminal investigations and cannot, therefore, be tried in any court of law.

3. What are the requirements for overriding a presidential veto?
   a) 50 percent plus one vote in both houses of Congress
   b) two-thirds vote in both houses of Congress
   c) two-thirds vote in the Senate only
   d) three-fourths vote in both houses of Congress
   e) A presidential veto cannot be overridden by Congress.

4. The Supreme Court has ruled that
   a) the power to remove executive appointees belongs exclusively to the Senate.
   b) the power to remove executive appointees belongs exclusively to the House of Representatives.
   c) the power to remove executive appointees belongs exclusively to the president.
   d) the power to remove executive appointees belongs exclusively to the federal judiciary.
   e) executive appointees can only be removed from office through formal impeachment hearings in both houses of Congress.

5. The "theory of the unitary executive" argues that
   a) Congress should control all policy making by the executive branch and the president should wield only limited power over executive agencies.
   b) the president should control all policy making by the executive branch and Congress should wield only limited power over executive agencies.
   c) all executive agencies should be independent from the influence of both the president and Congress.
   d) presidents should be limited to serving only a single term in office.
   e) the presidency should be replaced by a three-person executive council.

6. A system in which the positions of head of state and head of government are held by a single individual is referred to as
   a) a presidential system.
   b) a parliamentary system.
   c) a semi-parliamentary system.
   d) a semi-presidential system.
   e) a plural executive system.

7. President Harry S. Truman justified his attempt to seize the nation's steel mills during the Korean War on the basis of
   a) the president's expressed powers to deal with national emergencies.
   b) the president's inherent powers to deal with national emergencies.
   c) the president's delegated powers to deal with national emergencies.
   d) the president's implied powers to deal with national emergencies.
   e) the president's imperial powers to deal with national emergencies.

8. Which of the following statements about presidential declarations of national emergency is *not* accurate?
   a) Presidents can only declare a state of national emergency in response to foreign threats with the approval of Congress.
   b) Once the president has declared a state of national emergency, constitutional rights, including the right of habeas corpus, may be temporarily suspended.
   c) A declaration of national emergency in response to foreign threats allows the president to embargo trade, seize foreign assets, and prohibit transactions with whatever foreign nations are involved.
   d) Declarations of national emergency remain in force for only one year unless they are renewed by the president.
   e) Congress may, by a joint resolution of the two houses, terminate a declaration of national emergency.

The Presidency as an Institution

Identify the institutional resources presidents have to help them exercise their powers (pp. 529–33)

The institutionalized presidency is made up of the cabinet, the White House staff, the Executive Office of the President, the vice presidency, and the first spouse. Through their advice and assistance, these thousands of individuals give the president a capacity for action that he could never have by himself. When coupled with the president's formal powers, the institutionalized presidency makes the chief executive an important player in the country's policy-making process.

Key Terms

Cabinet (p. 530)

White House staff (p. 530)

Executive Office of the President (EOP) (p. 530)

National Security Council (NSC) (p. 531)

Practice Quiz

9. The EOP agency responsible for preparing the national budget, designing the president's program, and overseeing regulatory proposals is called
   a) the Office of Management and Budget.
   b) the National Security Council.
   c) the Council of Economic Advisers.
   d) the Congressional Budget Office.
   e) the Bureau of Economic Analysis.

10. Approximately how many people work for agencies within the Executive Office of the President?
    a) 25 to 50
    b) 700 to 1,000
    c) 1,500 to 2,000
    d) 4,500 to 5,000
    e) 25,000 to 30,000

11. Which of the following statements about vice presidents is *not* true?
    a) The vice president succeeds the president in case of death, resignation, or incapacitation.
    b) The vice president casts the tie-breaking vote in the Senate when necessary.
    c) The vice president serves as an honorary member of the Supreme Court.
    d) Eight vice presidents have had to replace American presidents who died in office.
    e) Presidential candidates often select a vice-presidential candidate who is likely to bring the support of a state that would not otherwise support the ticket.

The Contemporary Bases of Presidential Power

> Explain how modern presidents have become even more powerful (pp. 533–43)

Although Congress was the dominant institution in the American political system throughout the nineteenth century, modern presidents have expanded the policy-making power of their office in a number of ways. While some presidents have relied primarily on the support of party members to advance their legislative goals, contemporary presidents more commonly turn to popular mobilization and executive administration in pursuing policy change.

Key Terms

executive order (p. 538)

signing statements (p. 540)

Practice Quiz

12. What are two primary ways that presidents can expand their power?
    a) avoiding popular appeals and loosening their control of executive agencies
    b) using popular appeals and bolstering their control of executive agencies
    c) using popular appeals and loosening their control of executive agencies
    d) avoiding popular appeals and bolstering their control of executive agencies
    e) weakening national partisan institutions and bolstering their control of executive agencies

13. The Environmental Protection Agency and the Food and Drug Administration were created through the use of
    a) a pocket veto.
    b) an executive-congressional agreement.
    c) a sole executive agreement.
    d) an executive order.
    e) executive privilege.

14. When the president makes an announcement about his interpretation of a congressional enactment that he is signing into law, it is called
    a) a signing statement.
    b) a line-item veto.
    c) an executive order.
    d) legislative initiative.
    e) regulatory review.

For Further Reading

Edwards, George. *Why the Electoral College Is Bad for America.* New Haven, CT: Yale University Press, 2004.

Fisher, Louis. *Constitutional Conflicts between President and Congress*, 6th ed. Lawrence: University Press of Kansas, 2014.

Gellman, Barton. *Angler: The Cheney Vice Presidency.* New York: Penguin, 2008.

Gerhardt, Michael J. *The Forgotten Presidents: Their Untold Constitutional Legacy.* New York: Oxford University Press, 2013.

Ginsberg, Benjamin. *Presidential Government.* New Haven, CT: Yale University Press, 2016.

Griffin, Stephen. *Long Wars and the Constitution.* Cambridge, MA: Harvard University Press, 2013.

Hendrickson, Ryan. *Obama at War.* Lexington: University Press of Kentucky, 2015.

Kumar, Martha J. *Managing the President's Message: The White House Communications Operation.* Baltimore: Johns Hopkins University Press, 2010.

Milkis, Sidney. *The American Presidency: Origins and Development.* Washington, DC: CQ Press, 2011.

Nelson, Michael. *The Presidency and the Political System.* Washington, DC: CQ Press, 2013.

Neustadt, Richard E. *Presidential Power: The Politics of Leadership from Roosevelt to Reagan.* Rev. ed. New York: Free Press, 1990.

Ragsdale, Lyn. *Vital Statistics on the Presidency.* Washington, DC: CQ Press, 2014.

Schlesinger, Arthur. *The Imperial Presidency.* Reprint, New York: Mariner, 2004.

Skowronek, Stephen. *The Politics Presidents Make: Leadership from John Adams to Bill Clinton.* Cambridge, MA: Belknap Press of Harvard University Press, 1997.

Suri, Jeremy. *The Impossible Presidency.* New York: Basic Books, 2017.

Tulis, Jeffrey K. *The Rhetorical Presidency.* Princeton, NJ: Princeton University Press, 2017.

John Yoo. *The Powers of War and Peace: The Constitution and Foreign Affairs after 9/11.* Chicago: University of Chicago Press, 2006.

Recommended Websites

The American Presidency Project
www.americanpresidency.org
> Directed by Gerhard Peters and John T. Woolley at the University of California Santa Barbara, this site contains over 88,000 documents related to the study of the presidency, including party platforms, candidates' remarks, statements of administration policy, documents released by the Office of the Press Secretary, and election debates. This site is also an excellent resource for data related to the study of the presidency.

Dave Leip's Atlas of U.S. Presidential Elections
www.uselectionatlas.org
> For information on upcoming and past presidential elections, refer to this website. Experiment with the electoral college calculator to see how your state could affect the electoral outcome.

The National Archives: Executive Branch
www.archives.gov/executive
> Research official executive branch documents at the Executive Branch website, provided by the U.S. National Archives and Records Administration.

The White House
www.whitehouse.gov
> This is the official website of the White House. Here you can read about current presidential news, the president's Cabinet, executive orders, and presidential appointments.

White House Historical Association
www.whitehousehistory.org
> The White House Historical Association is dedicated to the understanding, appreciation, and preservation of the White House. At its website you can find historical facts and take a detailed online tour of the numerous rooms and the property.

The White House: Past First Ladies
www.whitehouse.gov/history/firstladies/
> The first lady is an important resource for the president in his role as head of state. Read about the current and past first ladies on this website.

Bureaucracy in a Democracy

WHAT GOVERNMENT DOES AND WHY IT MATTERS Lee Ann Walters couldn't figure out what was wrong with her 4-year-old twins. They had just moved to a new house in Flint, Michigan, and had rashes all over their bodies. One doctor thought it was contact dermatitis, another eczema. The prescribed creams had no effect. Yet another doctor suspected scabies, but tests were negative. Then Walters had an epiphany: every time her sons swam in the kiddie pool in the yard, or took a bath, the rash flared up. She told her family to stop drinking the tap water, which was orange-brown even after running through a filter she had installed.

That was December 2014. Eight months earlier, the cash-strapped city of Flint, under a state-appointed emergency manager, had switched its water supply to save money. Rather than draw water from the Detroit system, the city switched to the Flint River, which had been an industrial dumping ground for years. Soon, the local General Motors engine plant stopped using the river water, which was corroding the auto parts. Walters had the city test her tap water: the lead count was 104 parts per billion (ppb); the legal limit is 15. A follow-up test a week later: 397 parts per billion. Flint's utility administrator told her not to use the water. A researcher from Virginia Tech began testing water around the city: one-third of the samples had elevated lead levels, one as high as 13,200 ppb. A local pediatrician announced a spike

Government bureaucracies affect ordinary Americans in countless ways. The Flint water crisis, exposed by Lee Ann Walters, demonstrates how the failures of bureaucracy on every level of government can affect citizens' lives directly.

in lead levels among young children. Lead exposure can cause developmental delays and disability in children. The damage is permanent.

Walters tracked down an EPA drinking water expert who discovered that in switching to the Flint River, city officials had failed to add anti-corrosive chemicals to the water (despite a federal regulation requiring corrosion control). Running through old pipes, the untreated river water was leaching lead into the drinking supply. An official from Michigan's Department of Environmental Quality assured the EPA that there was corrosion control in place. Meanwhile, the city had been testing for lead but telling residents to flush their water before collecting

their samples and retesting in houses where the initial lead levels were low, not high.[1]

Finally, in January 2016, in the face of growing outcry from city residents, researchers, and advocates such as the ACLU, the EPA declared a state of emergency in Flint and took over lead testing in the city. In March 2016 the Flint Water Advisory Task Force, appointed by Michigan governor Rick Snyder to examine the crisis, issued its final report. The report cited a "series of government failures" at all levels: the local water department rushed to switch the water supply without corrosion control; the state Departments of Environmental Quality and Health and Human Services ignored mounting evidence of unsafe water; the federal EPA delayed enforcement of the Safe Water Drinking Act and Lead and Copper Rule; and the governor's office failed to reverse the poor decisions of the emergency manager and state agencies despite the urgings of senior staff members.[2]

The Flint water crisis is a dramatic example of bureaucratic failure. Americans depend on public bureaucracies for providing services they use every day and in emergencies. On a typical day, a college student might check the weather forecast, drive on an interstate highway, mail the rent check, drink from a public water fountain, check the calories on the side of a yogurt container, attend a class, go online, and meet a relative at the airport. Each of these activities is possible because of the work of a government bureaucracy: the U.S. Weather Service, the U.S. Department of Transportation, the U.S. Postal Service, the Environmental Protection Agency, the Food and Drug Administration, the student loan programs of the U.S. Department of Education, the Advanced Research Projects Agency (which developed the internet in the 1960s), and the Federal Aviation Administration. Without the ongoing work of these agencies, many of these common activities would be impossible, unreliable, or more expensive. When bureaucracies work well, we barely notice.

But when they fail, the results can be truly alarming, like the Flint crisis, or the September 11 terror attacks, widely viewed as a failure of the national security bureaucracy.[3] Such failures play into Americans' ambivalence about the role of government. Some disasters prompt politicians to promise that they will slash the bureaucracy, especially at the federal level. Yet others result in an increase in the bureaucracy, like the creation of the federal Department of Homeland Security after September 11. Each instance raises a number of questions: should the bureaucracy be smaller or larger? How can it become more efficient and effective? How can the bureaucracy be made more responsive to the needs of the American people?

CHAPTER GOALS

- ★ Define bureaucracy, and describe the basic features of the executive branch (pp. 553–62)
- ★ Describe the major goals we expect federal agencies to promote (pp. 563–73)
- ★ Evaluate some of the ways politicians have tried to make the bureaucracy more efficient (pp. 573–79)
- ★ Explain why it is often difficult to control the bureaucracy (pp. 579–83)

Bureaucracy and Bureaucrats

Define bureaucracy, and describe the basic features of the executive branch

Although Congress, the president, and the courts may garner more attention in the American system as they make policy, the **bureaucracy** plays a crucial role in administering public policy on the ground. Bureaucrats carry out the normal work of government, implementing the policies that Congress and the president have passed and that the court system may have adjudicated. The teachers you had in elementary school, the Social Security officer who approved your grandmother's retirement pension, the air traffic controller who guided the plane on your last vacation, the engineers who designed the roads that carried you to class, and the inspector who approved the meat in this morning's breakfast sausage are all bureaucrats.

At its best, bureaucracy ensures fair, accountable administration performed by expert professionals. To provide services, government bureaucracies employ specialists such as meteorologists, doctors, and scientists. To do their jobs effectively, these specialists require resources and tools (ranging from paper to complex computer software). They must coordinate their work with others (for example, traffic engineers must communicate with construction engineers). And they must effectively reach out to the public (for example, doctors must be made aware of health warnings). Bureaucracy is a means of coordinating the many different parts that must work together for the government to provide useful services.

When bureaucracy runs well, it can be virtually invisible. When it fails, the results can be spectacularly public, as when Hurricane Katrina breached levies built by the Army Corps of Engineers and the Federal Emergency Management Agency reacted ineffectually, or when the Department of Veterans Affairs was criticized in 2014 for long waiting lists for veterans seeking medical care and even blamed for veteran deaths in Phoenix.[4] How bureaucrats carry out their responsibilities shapes individuals' experiences of government in profound ways.

bureaucracy the complex structure of offices, tasks, rules, and principles of organization that is employed by all large-scale institutions to coordinate the work of their personnel

WHAT BUREAUCRATS DO

Bureaucrats execute and implement laws, determining who is eligible for Medicare, studying whether a new medicine is safe and effective. They deliver mail, tell national park campers that they can build a fire *here* but not *there*, calculate how long it would take a spacecraft to reach the edge of the solar system. They gather data and conduct research. Some, like customs officials, are "street-level bureaucrats" who regularly interact with the public. Yet others, like researchers at the National Institutes of Health, work in specialized facilities with other experts. As they carry out their responsibilities, implementing and enforcing laws, making rules, and innovating, they exercise discretion and help define how public policy gets expressed.

Bureaucrats Implement Laws Congress is responsible for making the laws, but in most cases legislation only sets the broad parameters for government action. Bureaucracies are responsible for filling in the blanks by determining how the laws should be implemented. This requires bureaucracies to draw up detailed rules that guide the process of **implementation** and to play a key role in enforcing the laws. Congress needs the bureaucracy to engage in rule making and implementation for several

implementation the efforts of departments and agencies to translate laws into specific bureaucratic rules and actions reasons. One is that bureaucracies employ people who have much more specialized expertise in specific policy areas than do members of Congress. Decisions about how to achieve many policy goals—from managing the national parks to regulating air quality to ensuring a sound economy—rest on the judgment of specialized experts. A second reason that Congress needs bureaucracy is that because updating legislation can take many years, bureaucratic flexibility can ensure that laws are administered in ways that take new conditions into account. Finally, members of Congress often prefer to delegate politically difficult decision-making to bureaucrats.

Bureaucrats Make Rules One of the most important activities that government agencies do is issue rules that provide more detailed and specific indications of what a given congressional policy will actually mean. For example, the Clean Air Act empowers the Environmental Protection Agency (EPA) to assess whether current or projected levels of air pollutants pose a threat to public health, determine whether motor vehicle emissions are contributing to such pollution, and create rules designed to regulate these emissions. After the Supreme Court ruled in 2007 that the EPA had the authority to regulate auto emissions, the agency in the Obama administration imposed new emission standards for automobiles, which would raise the average fuel economy for new vehicles to 35.5 miles per gallon starting in 2016, a standard later boosted to 54.4 miles per gallon by 2025.[5] In 2014 the EPA extended its reach to regulate factories and power plants that emit greenhouse gases. Especially controversial was the Clean Power Plan, requiring power plants to reduce greenhouse gas emissions by 32 percent by 2030. The plan never went into effect due to lawsuits filed by a number of states, and in 2017 the head of the EPA in the Trump administration repealed the plan.[6]

The rule-making process is thus a highly political one. Once a new law is passed, the relevant agency studies the legislation and proposes a set of rules to guide implementation. These proposed rules are then open to comment by anyone who wishes to weigh in. Representatives for the regulated industries and advocates of all sorts commonly submit comments. But anyone who wishes to can go to the website www.regulations.gov to read proposed rules, enter comments, and view the comments of others. Once rules are approved, they are published in the *Federal Register* and have the force of law. That said, the Trump administration's repeal of the Obama EPA's Clean Power Plan demonstrates the fragility of government by bureaucratic rule-making, compared to government by congressional legislation.[7] If Congress passes a new law, changing it usually requires another congressional action, while rules made by the bureaucracy in one administration can be easily reversed by the next.

During the 1970s and '80s, the length of time required to develop an administrative rule from a proposal to actual publication in the *Federal Register* (when it takes on full legal status) grew from an average of 15 months to an average of 35 to 40 months. Inefficiency? No. Most of the increased time is attributable to new procedures requiring more public notice, more public hearings in Washington and elsewhere, more cost-benefit analysis, and stronger legal obligations to prepare "environmental impact statements" demonstrating that the proposed rule or agency action will not have an unacceptably large negative impact on the human or physical environment.[8] Thus, a great deal of what is popularly decried as the lower efficiency of public agencies can be attributed to the political, judicial, legal, and public-opinion restraints and extraordinarily high expectations imposed on public bureaucrats. If a private company such as Apple were required to open up all its decision processes and management practices to full view by the media, its

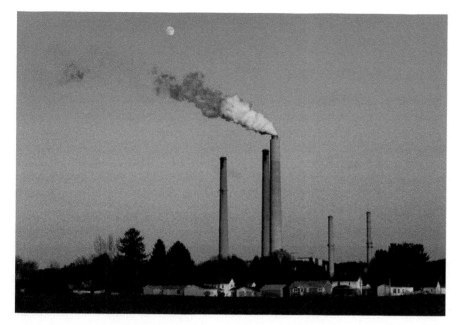

An example of bureaucratic rules that affect Americans both positively and negatively are the regulations set forth by the Environmental Protection Agency (EPA). When President Obama extended the EPA's authority to regulate greenhouse gas emissions in 2014, many people applauded the benefits to the environment, but at the same time, thousands lost jobs because of the new rules.

competitors, and all interested citizens, Apple—despite its profit motive and the pressure of competition—would likely appear far less efficient, perhaps no more efficient than public bureaucracies.

Bureaucrats Enforce Laws In addition to rule making, bureaucracies play an essential role in enforcing the laws, thus exercising considerable power over private actors. In 2015 the EPA charged Volkswagen with cheating on emissions tests of its diesel vehicles. For over seven years, the company had installed software that showed emissions at legal levels during testing conditions, but once the cars were on the road emissions were actually 10 to 40 percent higher. After the EPA threatened to bar the company from selling some of its 2016 cars in the United States, Volkswagen admitted that it had cheated. The financial repercussions for the company will be long-lasting. In 2016 the company agreed to a $15.8-billion settlement that required it to buy back the faulty vehicles and compensate owners. As part of the settlement, Volkswagen also agreed to fund several clean air programs. Even with these payments, Volkswagen faced additional lawsuits from states and investors.[9]

Bureaucrats Innovate A good case study of the important role agencies can play is the story of how ordinary federal bureaucrats created the internet. Yes, it's true: what became the internet was developed largely by the U.S. Department of Defense, and defense considerations still shape the basic structure of the internet. In 1957, immediately following the profound American embarrassment over the Soviet Union's launching of *Sputnik*, the first satellite to orbit the Earth, Congress authorized the establishment of the Advanced Research Projects Agency (ARPA) to develop, among other things, a means of maintaining communications in the event of a strategic attack on the existing telecommunications network (the telephone system). Since the telephone network was highly centralized and therefore could have been completely disabled by a single attack, ARPA developed a decentralized, highly redundant network with an improved probability of functioning after an attack. The full design, called *ARPANET*, took almost a decade to create. By 1971 around

20 universities were connected to the ARPANET. The forerunner to the internet was born.[10]

WHO ARE BUREAUCRATS?

merit system a product of civil service reform, in which appointees to positions in public bureaucracies must objectively be deemed qualified for those positions

Bureaucrats are considered members of the "civil service" and work under the **merit system** created by the Civil Service Act of 1883. With this act, the federal government attempted to imitate business by requiring appointees to public office be qualified for the job to which they were appointed. The goal was to end political appointments under the "spoils system," which awarded jobs based on political connections, and to create a system of competitive examinations through which the very best candidates were to be hired for every job. As a further safeguard against political interference, merit-system employees were given legal protection against being fired without a show of cause. Reasonable people may disagree about the value of such job security and how far it should extend in the civil service, but the justifiable objective of this job protection, cleansing bureaucracy of political interference while upgrading performance, cannot be disputed. At the higher levels of government agencies, including such posts as cabinet secretaries and assistant secretaries, many jobs are filled with political appointees and are not part of the merit system.

The State Department's foreign service officer corps represents U.S. interests abroad. To become a foreign service officer, you must take both a written and an oral exam. Approximately 75 percent of the 20,000 or so applicants who take the exam each year do not pass.

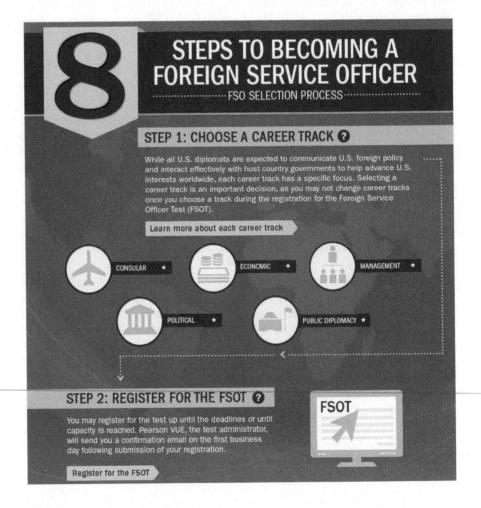

8 STEPS TO BECOMING A FOREIGN SERVICE OFFICER
·········· FSO SELECTION PROCESS ··········

STEP 1: CHOOSE A CAREER TRACK ?

While all U.S. diplomats are expected to communicate U.S. foreign policy and interact effectively with host country governments to help advance U.S. interests worldwide, each career track has a specific focus. Selecting a career track is an important decision, as you may not change career tracks once you choose a track during the registration for the Foreign Service Officer Test (FSOT).

Learn more about each career track

CONSULAR ★   ECONOMIC ★   MANAGEMENT ★
POLITICAL ★   PUBLIC DIPLOMACY ★

STEP 2: REGISTER FOR THE FSOT ?

You may register for the test up until the deadlines or until capacity is reached. Pearson VUE, the test administrator, will send you a confirmation email on the first business day following submission of your registration.

Register for the FSOT

FSOT

Who Are "Bureaucrats"?

Bureaucrats are often stereotyped as being more concerned with procedure and forms than with helping people. But the reality is that the millions of executive branch employees that work in agencies in D.C. and around the country are essential to keeping America running smoothly. Bureaucrats manage everything from national security and veterans services to providing help for needy families and ensuring that Americans have clean and safe drinking water. But who are bureaucrats? How is the bureaucracy similar to the American population? How is it different?

Executive Branch Employees, 2017

Sex

● Female ● Male

55% | 45%
Executive branch employees

51% | 49%
U.S. population

Race / ethnicity

● White ● Black ● Latino ● Asian

73% | 18% | 6% | 3%
Executive branch employees

64% | 12% | 16% | 4%
U.S. population

Education

● Less than high school ● High school degree ● Some college ● College degree ● Postgraduate degree

Executive branch employees: 1% | 6% | 12% | 50% | 30%

U.S. population: 13% | 28% | 21% | 27% | 12%

Military service

● Yes ● No

Executive branch employees: 29% | 71%

U.S. population: 8% | 92%

Location, 2017

434,710
21% WASHINGTON, D.C., AREA

1,635,337
79% — OTHER

FOR CRITICAL ANALYSIS

1. How do the demographics of the United States compare to the demographics of the bureaucracy? What do you think explains the differences?

2. With 2 million people working for the executive branch, mostly outside of the Washington, D.C., area, how can Congress and the president be sure that they are serving the public's interests?

NOTE: Numbers may not add up to 100 percent due to rounding. The category of "other" has been omitted.
SOURCES: American Community Survey 5-year Estimates, www.factfinder.census.gov (accessed 3/9/18); Gallup, news.gallup.com (accessed 3/9/18).

Today's federal bureaucrats are distributed around the country—nearly 4 out of 5 federal employees work outside of Washington, D.C. For example, California has over 141,000 federal workers, and Texas has more than 114,000.[11] Compared to private sector workers, members of the full-time civilian federal workforce are more educated—more hold college and advanced degrees—and are more likely to hold professional occupations in science, engineering, diplomacy, and other advanced fields.[12] Federal workers are more diverse than the private workforce: as of 2017, 36.7 percent were minority group members, 18.2 percent black, 8.8 percent Hispanic, 6 percent Asian, 2.2 percent Native Hawaiian/Pacific Islander/American Indian/Alaska Native, and 1.5 percent non-Hispanic multiracial. Federal workers are more likely to be male than private sector workers (57 percent compared to 54 percent in the private sector),[13] and nearly one-third of federal workers are veterans.[14]

The size of the federal service has been a subject of political contention for decades. Particularly in the post–Watergate era of low trust in government, politicians from both parties, from Reagan to Clinton, have asserted that the federal government is too big. President Barack Obama struck a different note in his first inaugural address, saying, "The question we ask today is not whether our government is too big or too small, but whether it works."[15] President Trump's first budget proposed major decreases in federal departments outside of Defense and Homeland Security. Despite fears of bureaucratic growth getting out of hand, however, the federal service has hardly grown at all during the past 35 years; it reached its peak postwar level in 1968, with 3.0 million civilian employees plus an additional 3.6 million military personnel (a figure swollen by the war in Vietnam). The number of civilian federal employees has since fallen to fewer than 2.7 million in 2017; the number of military personnel totals 1.29 million.[16]

The growth of the federal service over the past 50 years is even less imposing when placed in the context of the total workforce and when compared with the size of state and local public employment. Figure 14.1 indicates that since 1950 the ratio of federal employment to the total workforce has in fact *declined* slightly in the past 60 years. Figure 14.2 shows that although the dollar increase in federal spending shown by the bars is impressive, the trend line indicating the relation of federal spending to the gross domestic product remained close to what it had been in 1960 (that is, the size of the federal government as a proportion of the total economy has been flat). Meanwhile, state and local employment has grown: in 1950 there were 4.3 million state and local civil service employees (about 6.5 percent of the country's workforce). In 2015 there were roughly 19.3 million state and local employees (nearly 14 percent of the nation's employed workforce).[17] Federal employment, in contrast, exceeded 6 percent of the workforce only during World War II, and almost all of that temporary growth was military. That said, the number of federal contractors has grown considerably, as we shall see below.

In sum, the national government is indeed "very large," but it has not been growing any faster than the economy or society. Bureaucracy keeps pace with society, despite people's seeming dislike of it, because the airport control towers, the prisons, the Social Security system, and other essential elements of modern-day society cannot be operated without bureaucracy. Indeed, the recent growth of government spending does not reflect a growth in the federal bureaucracy or even growth in federal contractors but rather an increase in payments to individuals for valued social programs such as Social Security and Medicare (which provides health care for people over age 65).

FOR CRITICAL ANALYSIS

How has the size of the federal service changed over the past six decades? How are calls for smaller government related to the size of the federal service?

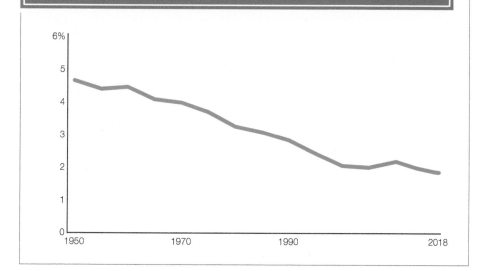

FIGURE 14.1

Employees in the Federal Service as a Percentage of the National Workforce, 1950–2018

Since 1950, the ratio of federal employment to the total workforce has gradually declined. Today, federal employees make up less than 2 percent of the total workforce in the United States. Even at its height, federal employees made up less than 6 percent. What do these numbers suggest about the size of the federal government today?

NOTE: Employment numbers are for December of each year; 2018 numbers are from September.

SOURCE: Bureau of Labor Statistics, Current Employment Statistics, "Employment, Hours, and Earnings from the Current Employment Statistics Survey (National)," https://data.bls.gov/timeseries/CES9091000001 (accessed 10/13/18).

THE ORGANIZATION OF THE EXECUTIVE BRANCH

Cabinet **departments**, agencies, and bureaus are the operating parts of the bureaucratic whole. At the top is the head of the department, who in the United States is called the "secretary" of the department.[18] Below the secretary and the deputy secretary is a second tier of "undersecretaries," who have management responsibilities for one or more operating agencies. Those operating agencies are the third tier of the department, yet they are the highest level of responsibility for the actual programs around which the entire department is organized. This third tier is generally called the "bureau level." Each bureau-level agency usually operates under a statute, enacted by Congress, that set up the agency and gave it its authority and jurisdiction. The names of these bureau-level agencies are often quite well known to the public—the Forest Service and the Food Safety and Inspection Service, for example. These are the so-called line agencies, those that deal directly with the public. Sometimes these agencies are officially called "bureaus," such as the Federal Bureau of Investigation (FBI), which is part of the third tier of the Department of Justice. But *bureau* is also the conventional

department the largest subunit of the executive branch; the secretaries of the 15 departments form the Cabinet

FIGURE 14.2

Annual Federal Outlays, 1950–2018*

As the bars in the figure indicate, when measured in dollars, federal government spending has gone up over time, from $423 billion in 1950 to over $3 trillion in 2017. (The amounts here are measured in constant 2009 dollars, which means the numbers have been adjusted for inflation.) But as the red line shows, federal spending as a percentage of gross domestic product (GDP) has moved up and down just slightly over time. Thus, while government spending has grown, it has basically kept pace with the growing size of the U.S. economy.

*Data for 2017–18 are estimated.

SOURCE: Office of Management and Budget, "Table 1.3—Summary of Receipts, Outlays, and Surpluses or Deficits in Current Dollars, Constant (FY 2009) Dollars, and as Percentages of GDP: 1940–2023," www.whitehouse.gov/omb/budget/historicals (accessed 10/13/18).

term for this level of administrative agency, even though many agencies or their supporters have preferred over the years to adopt a more politically palatable designation, such as "service" or "administration." Each bureau is, of course, even further subdivided into divisions, offices, or units—all are parts of the bureaucratic hierarchy.

Not all government agencies are part of Cabinet departments. Some **independent agencies** are set up by Congress outside the departmental structure altogether, even

independent agency agency that is not part of a Cabinet department

The National Aeronautics and Space Administration (NASA), an independent agency of the federal government, was established by President Eisenhower in 1958. Its mission is "To reach for new heights and reveal the unknown so that what we do and learn will benefit all humankind." Here, NASA public affairs officer Dwayne Brown announces the presence of water on Mars.

though the president appoints and directs the heads of these agencies. Independent agencies usually have broad powers to provide public services that are either too expensive or too important to be left to private initiatives. Some examples of independent agencies are the National Aeronautics and Space Administration (NASA), the Central Intelligence Agency (CIA), and the EPA. **Government corporations** are a third type of government agency but are more like private businesses in performing and charging for a market service, such as transporting railroad passengers (Amtrak).

Yet a fourth type of agency is the independent regulatory commission, given broad discretion to make rules. The first regulatory agencies established by Congress, beginning with the Interstate Commerce Commission in 1887, were set up as independent regulatory commissions because Congress recognized that regulatory agencies are "mini-legislatures," whose rules are exactly the same as legislation but require the kind of expertise and full-time attention that is beyond the capacity of Congress. Until the 1960s most of the regulatory agencies set up by Congress, such as the Federal Trade Commission (1914) and the Federal Communications Commission (1934), were independent regulatory commissions. But beginning in the late 1960s and the early 1970s, all new regulatory programs, with two or three exceptions (such as the Federal Election Commission), were placed within existing departments and made directly responsible to the president. After the financial crisis that began in 2008, Congress passed legislation to improve regulation of banks and other nonbank financial institutions. The legislation also created an important new regulatory agency, the Consumer Financial Protection Bureau. The bureau enforces consumer protection laws, for example, regulating bank practices that affect credit cards and mortgages. The agency aims to eliminate deceptive practices and act as the voice of consumers. Its website (www.consumerfinance.gov) also takes complaints from consumers and provides easy-to-understand information on many topics, including student debt repayment.

government corporation
government agency that performs a market-oriented public service and raises revenues to fund its activities

Bureaucracy in Comparison

As one of the world's largest and most populous countries, the United States has a vast bureaucracy to run government programs and services. However, as a percentage of the labor force, the number of government employees in the United States is not especially high. As the first graph below shows, the size of government bureaucracies, relative to each country's work force, varies widely. For example, the Norwegian government employs nearly 30 percent of the labor force, whereas only around 8 percent of Japanese workers work for the government.

We can also see differences in whether most government employees work at the national level or the subnational level in each country. In the United States, most government employees work at the state or local level, rather than the national level. In other countries, such as Turkey, most bureaucrats work for the national government. What do you think accounts for these differences? How does federalism influence American bureaucracy, and what differences do we see in countries like Turkey or Ireland that do not have federalism?

TOTAL GOVERNMENT EMPLOYMENT AS A PERCENTAGE OF THE LABOR FORCE MARKET

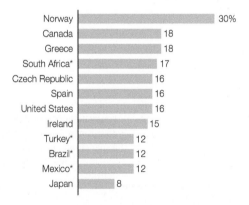

Country	Percentage
Norway	30%
Canada	18
Greece	18
South Africa*	17
Czech Republic	16
Spain	16
United States	16
Ireland	15
Turkey*	12
Brazil*	12
Mexico*	12
Japan	8

NOTE: Includes national and sub-national government employees.
*Brazil, Mexico, South Africa, and Turkey data are from 2014.

GOVERNMENT EMPLOYMENT BY LEVEL OF GOVERNMENT

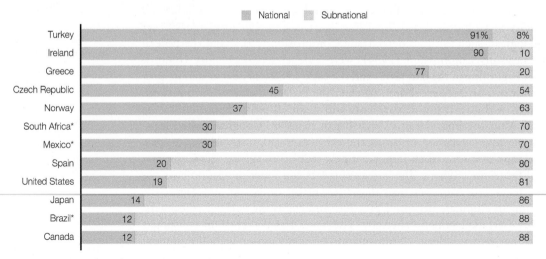

■ National   ■ Subnational

Country	National	Subnational
Turkey	91%	8%
Ireland	90	10
Greece	77	20
Czech Republic	45	54
Norway	37	63
South Africa*	30	70
Mexico*	30	70
Spain	20	80
United States	19	81
Japan	14	86
Brazil*	12	88
Canada	12	88

*Brazil, Mexico, and South Africa data are from 2013.

SOURCE: OECD, "Public employment and Pay," Government at a Glance, 2017, www.stats.oecd.org (accessed 4/16/18).

Goals of the Federal Bureaucracy

Describe the major goals we expect federal agencies to promote

The different agencies of the executive branch can be classified into three main groups by the services they provide to the American public. The first category of agencies provides services and products that seek to promote the public welfare. The second group of agencies works to promote national security. The third group provides services that help maintain a strong economy. Let us look more closely at what each set of agencies offers to the American public.

PROMOTING PUBLIC WELL-BEING

One of the most important activities of the federal bureaucracy is to promote the public good by providing services, building infrastructure, and enforcing regulations that serve citizen needs. Departments that have important responsibilities for promoting public well-being include the Departments of Housing and Urban Development, Health and Human Services, Veterans Affairs, the Interior, Education, and Labor. Ensuring the public welfare is also the main activity of agencies in other departments, such as the Department of Agriculture's Food and Nutrition Service, which administers the federal school lunch program and the Supplemental Nutrition Assistance Program (SNAP, formerly known as food stamps). In addition, multiple independent regulatory agencies enforce regulations that aim to safeguard the public health and welfare.

The Department of Health and Human Services (HHS) administers the cash assistance program Temporary Assistance for Needy Families (TANF). Yet this program is one of the smallest activities of the department. HHS also oversees the National Institutes of Health (NIH), which is responsible for cutting-edge biomedical research, and the two major health programs of the federal government: Medicaid, which provides health care for low-income families and for many elderly and disabled people; and Medicare, which is the health insurance available to most elderly people in the United States.

A different notion of public well-being, but one highly valued by most Americans, is provided by the National Park Service, under the Department of the Interior. First created in 1916, the National Park Service is responsible for the care and upkeep of national parks. Since the nineteenth century, Americans have seen protection of the natural environment as an important public goal and have looked to federal agencies to implement laws and administer programs that preserve natural areas and keep them open to the public.

The federal bureaucracy also promotes the public good through the watchdog activities of many **regulatory agencies**. These include the Food and Drug Administration (FDA), within the HHS; the Occupational Safety and Health Administration (OSHA), in the Department of Labor; as well as numerous independent regulatory commissions, such as the Consumer Product Safety Commission, the Federal Communications Commission, and the EPA.

regulatory agency department, bureau, or independent agency whose primary mission is to impose limits, restrictions, or other obligations on the conduct of individuals or companies in the private sector

The National Institutes of Health (NIH) is an example of a federal bureaucracy that promotes the public welfare by conducting cutting-edge biomedical research. NIH research has helped doctors to treat diabetes and cardiovascular disease, among many other illnesses. This scientist is studying pancreatic beta cells, which play a role in diabetes.

An agency or commission is regulatory if Congress delegates to it relatively broad powers over a sector of the economy or a type of commercial activity and authorizes it to make rules within that jurisdiction. Rules made by regulatory agencies have the force and effect of law.

Bureaucracies, Clienteles, and the Public Some of the public agencies that provide services are tied to a specific group or segment of American society that is often thought of as the main clientele of that agency. For example, the Department of Agriculture was established in 1862 to promote the interests of farmers. Likewise, the Department of Veterans Affairs has strong links to veterans' organizations such as the American Legion and the Veterans of Foreign Wars. The Department of Education relies on teachers' organizations for support. Figure 14.3 is a representation of this type of politics. This configuration is known as an iron triangle, a pattern of stable relationships among an agency in the executive branch, a congressional committee or subcommittee, and one or more organized groups of agency clientele. (Iron triangles are discussed in detail in Chapter 11.)

These relationships with particular clienteles are often important in preserving agencies from political attack. During his 1980 campaign, Ronald Reagan promised to dismantle the Department of Education as part of his commitment to get government "off people's backs." After his election, Reagan even appointed a secretary of

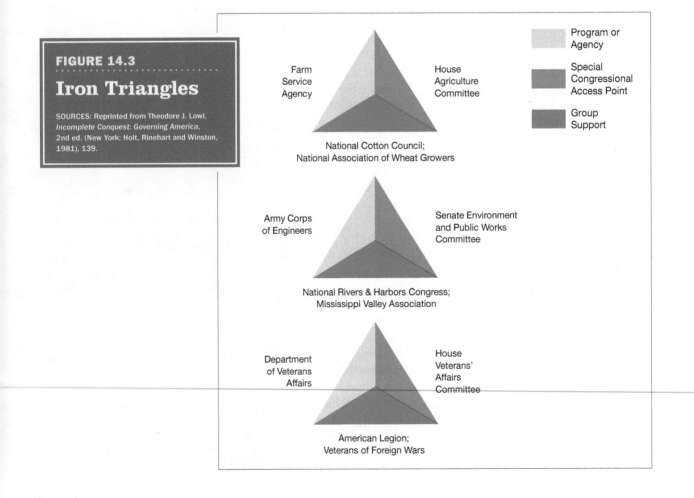

FIGURE 14.3

Iron Triangles

SOURCES: Reprinted from Theodore J. Lowi, *Incomplete Conquest: Governing America*, 2nd ed. (New York: Holt, Rinehart and Winston, 1981), 139.

Program or Agency

Special Congressional Access Point

Group Support

Farm Service Agency

House Agriculture Committee

National Cotton Council; National Association of Wheat Growers

Army Corps of Engineers

Senate Environment and Public Works Committee

National Rivers & Harbors Congress; Mississippi Valley Association

Department of Veterans Affairs

House Veterans' Affairs Committee

American Legion; Veterans of Foreign Wars

the department who was publicly committed to eliminating it. Yet by the end of his administration, the Department of Education was still standing and barely touched. In 1995 the Republican Congress vowed to eliminate the Department of Education, along with two other departments; but it, too, failed. The educational constituency of the department (its clientele) mobilized to save it each time. Teachers' unions and educational administrators formed a powerful alliance to defend the department. Trump administration Education Secretary Betsy DeVos has not proposed eliminating the department but has clashed with teacher unions over her promotion of charter schools and private school choice initiatives.[19]

Indeed, the ability of clientele groups to get their way is not automatic, as agencies have to balance limited resources, competing interests, and political pressures. For example, the Department of Veterans Affairs long resisted the efforts of Vietnam veterans to be compensated for exposure to Agent Orange, a chemical defoliant used extensively during the Vietnam War. Veterans charged that exposure to Agent Orange had left them with a variety of diseases ranging from cancer to severe birth defects in their children. Only after decades of lobbying, lawsuits, and federally sponsored studies did the Department of Veterans Affairs provide assistance to affected veterans.

FOR CRITICAL ANALYSIS

What is the impact of iron triangles on government services in the United States? Do the ties among agencies, congressional committees, and organized groups promote the efficient provision of government services?

PROVIDING NATIONAL SECURITY

One of the remarkable features of American federalism is that the most vital agencies for providing security for the American people (namely, the police) are located in state and local governments. But some agencies vital to maintaining national security are located in the national government, and they can be grouped into two categories: agencies to confront threats to internal national security and agencies to defend American security from external threats. The departments of greatest influence in these areas are Homeland Security, Justice, Defense, and State.

Agencies for Internal Security The task of maintaining domestic security changed dramatically after the terrorist attacks of September 11, 2001. The creation of the

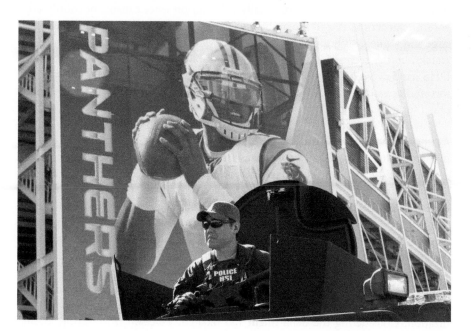

The Department of Homeland Security (DHS) is tasked with the broad goal of keeping America safe. Its 240,000 employees work in jobs as diverse as aviation security, emergency response, and chemical facility inspection. The DHS also provides security for the Super Bowl.

Department of Homeland Security in late 2002 signaled the high priority that domestic security would now have. The orientation of domestic agencies also shifted as agencies geared up to prevent terrorism, a very different task from their former charge of investigating crime. With this shift in responsibility came broad new powers, many of them controversial, including the power to detain terrorist suspects and to engage in extensive domestic intelligence gathering about possible terrorists.

Before September 11, most of the effort put into maintaining internal national security took the form of legal work related to prosecuting federal crimes. The largest and most important unit of the Justice Department is the Criminal Division. Lawyers in the Criminal Division represent the U.S. government when it is the plaintiff enforcing federal criminal laws, except for those cases (about 25 percent) specifically assigned to other divisions or agencies. Criminal litigation is handled by U.S. attorneys, who are appointed by the president. There is one U.S. attorney in each of the 94 federal judicial districts; he or she supervises the work of a number of assistant U.S. attorneys.

The Civil Division of the Justice Department deals with litigation in which the United States is the defendant being sued for injury and damages allegedly inflicted by a government official or agency. The missions of the other divisions of the Justice Department—Antitrust, Civil Rights, Environment and Natural Resources, and Tax—are described by their names.

In 2002 the new Department of Homeland Security joined the Justice Department as the major bureaucracy charged with domestic security. The department took over some of the security-oriented agencies previously controlled by other departments. (See Table 14.1 for a look inside the Department of Homeland Security.) Growing pains were evident in Homeland Security's first years. Different bureaucratic cultures, now part of a single operation, quickly became embroiled in turf battles with one another and with the FBI (which remained in the Justice Department) as the two departments attempted to sort out their respective responsibilities. These early problems signaled deeper challenges that the Department of Homeland Security has continued to face throughout its existence. DHS has been unable to establish itself as a strong institutionally coherent presence capable of coordinating government action. Part of the problem is that its portfolio of responsibilities is both large and vague. It is responsible for all kinds of internal security including terrorist attacks, border security, natural disasters, and food safety. Under President Trump DHS has new visibility in implementing the president's travel bans on certain visitors and arresting undocumented immigrants, and his first two budget proposals called for increased funding for the department.[20]

FOR CRITICAL ANALYSIS

Why was the Department of Homeland Security created? What problems has the new department faced?

Agencies for External National Security Two departments occupy center stage in maintaining external national security: the Departments of State and Defense.

The State Department's primary mission is diplomacy. As the most visible public representative of American diplomacy, the secretary of state works to promote American perspectives and interests in the world. For example, President Trump's first Secretary of State Rex Tillerson traveled to Moscow in 2017 in a bid to weaken Russia's support for Syrian President Bashar al-Assad amid concerns about his use of chemical weapons.[21] Although diplomacy is the primary task of the State Department, diplomatic missions are only one of its organizational dimensions. As of 2016 the State Department comprised several dozen bureau-level units, each under the direction of an undersecretary, although Tillerson proposed a departmental reorganization. Considering the department too bloated, Tillerson froze hiring, pushed

TABLE 14.1

Department of Homeland Security

SELECTED OFFICES	FUNCTION	2018 BUDGET, IN BILLION $	ESTIMATED NUMBER OF EMPLOYEES
U.S. Customs and Border Protection	Responsible for securing America's borders to protect the United States against terrorist threats and prevent the illegal entry of inadmissible persons and contraband, while facilitating lawful travel, trade, and immigration	14	59,753
U.S. Immigration and Customs Enforcement	The principal investigative arm of the Department of Homeland Security	7.1	21,289
Transportation Security Administration	Provides security for the nation's transportation system	7.9	52,956
Coast Guard	Safeguards our nation's maritime interests and natural resources on our rivers, in U.S. ports, on the high seas, and in the maritime domain around the world	12.1	14,117
U.S. Secret Service	Protects national leaders and safeguards the nation's financial infrastructure and payment systems	1.99	
National Protection and Programs Directorate	Combats cyber-attacks and foreign espionage by enhancing infrastructure and preventing hacking	1.9	
Federal Emergency Management Agency	Manages and coordinates the federal response to and recovery from major domestic disasters and emergencies of all types	7.9	

SOURCE: U.S. House Appropriations Committee, "FY 2018 Omnibus: Homeland Security," March 21, 2018, https://appropriations.house.gov (accessed 3/29/18); House Appropriations Committee, "Fiscal Year 2018 Homeland Security Bill," March 21, 2018, https://appropriations.house.gov (accessed 3/29/18).

out top career officials, and limited promotions, steps that earned criticism from some in Congress.[22] Secretary of State Mike Pompeo lifted Tillerson's hiring freeze, although many positions remain unfilled.

These bureaus support the responsibilities of the elite foreign-service officers, who staff U.S. embassies around the world and who hold almost all of the most powerful positions in the department below the rank of ambassador.[23] The ambassadorial positions, especially the plum positions in the major capitals of the world, are filled by presidential appointees, many of whom get their posts by having been important donors to victorious political campaigns.

Despite the importance of the State Department in foreign affairs, fewer than 20 percent of all U.S. government employees working abroad are directly under its authority. By far the largest number of career government professionals working abroad are under the authority of the Defense Department.

The Defense Department is charged with providing the military forces needed to deter war and protect the nation. Headquartered in the Pentagon, across the Potomac River from Washington, D.C., the Department of Defense (DoD) is one of the largest bureaucracies in the world, composed of 2 million people across five sets of institutions.[24] The president, as commander-in-chief, appoints the Secretary

The Departments of Defense and State are the most important parts of the federal bureaucracy focused on national security. Secretary of Defense James Mattis (left) is the civilian head of the military (reporting to the president as commander in chief). Secretary of State Mike Pompeo (center right) is the United States' chief diplomat. He is pictured meeting with Qatari foreign minister Sheikh Mohammed bin Abdulrahman Al Thani in 2018. The State Department runs embassies around the world. U.S. embassy to Grenada principal officer Stephen Frahm (right) speaks with U.S. citizens in Grenada about how to access government services in case of emergency.

of Defense, whose Office of the Secretary of Defense (OSD) plans and carries out the nation's security policies as directed by the secretary and president. The OSD provides civilian oversight of the military. The second institution is the Joint Chiefs of Staff, consisting of the Chairman of the Joint Chiefs of Staff, who is the president's principal military adviser, and the five military service chiefs (Army, Navy, Air Force, Marine Corps, and National Guard; the Coast Guard is in the Department of Homeland Security except in wartime). Third, there are three military departments, each with its own civilian secretary and military secretary (Army, Navy, Air Force; the Marine Corps is part of the Department of the Navy). The military departments train and equip military forces. Fourth, the Unified Combatant Commands (COCOMs) are the entities that execute military operations. There are six regional COCOMs (Africa Command; European Command; Central Command; Northern Command; Southern Command; and Pacific Command) and three functional COCOMS (Strategic Command; Special Operations Command; and Transportation Command). Finally there are the defense agencies that perform supply or service activities that are common to more than one military department. There are currently 20 such defense agencies. [25]

The Department of Defense is an enormously complex organization, and has been reformed several times to increase efficiency and effectiveness. The contemporary DoD was created in 1947, after concerns arose during World War II that the Departments of War and Navy, then separate entities, were insufficiently integrated to fight effectively. Another major reorganization came in 1986, when the Goldwater-Nichols Defense Reform Act made the Chairman of the Joint Chiefs of Staff the president's main military adviser, rather than the service chiefs. Also, operational control was moved from the service chiefs to the unified commands, permitting those commanders to use all military assets available on an integrated basis. More recently, the Budget Control Act of 2011 (see "sequestration," discussed later in this chapter) reduced annual defense appropriations (outside of current military operations) by 5 percent from 2013 on, prompting further efforts to prioritize DoD's many tasks.[26] However, the 2018 federal spending bill signed by President Trump in

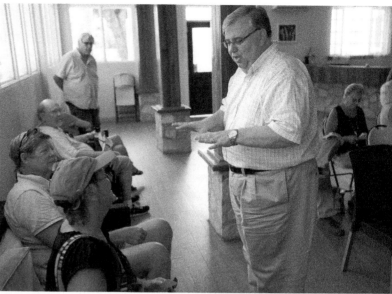

March 2017 raised the sequestration caps and increased both defense and domestic spending.

National Security and Democracy Of all the agencies in the federal bureaucracy, those charged with providing national security most often come into conflict with the norms and expectations of American democracy. Two issues in particular arise as these agencies work to ensure national security: (1) the trade-offs between respecting the personal rights of individuals versus protecting the general public, and (2) the need for secrecy in matters of national security versus the public's right to know what the government is doing. Needless to say, Americans often disagree about what activities the government should be able to pursue to defend U.S. national security.

When national security is at stake, federal agencies have taken actions that are normally considered incompatible with individual rights. For example, during World War II President Franklin Roosevelt ordered thousands of American citizens of Japanese descent to be relocated to internment camps due to national security concerns. Although the Supreme Court approved this action, the federal government has since acknowledged that it constituted unjustified discrimination and has offered reparations to those who were interned.

Protecting national security often requires the government to conduct its activities in secret. Yet, as Americans have come to expect a more open government, many believe that federal agencies charged with national security keep too many secrets from the American public. The effort to make information related to national security more available began in 1966 with the passage of the Freedom of Information Act (FOIA). Strengthened in 1974 after Watergate, the act allows any person to request classified information from any federal agency. The information obtained often reveals unflattering or unsuccessful aspects of national security activities. One private organization, the National Security Archive, makes extensive use of FOIA requests to obtain information about the activities of national security agencies; it has published many of these documents on its website and maintains an archive in Washington, D.C., that is open to the public. The website's "The Torture Archive,"

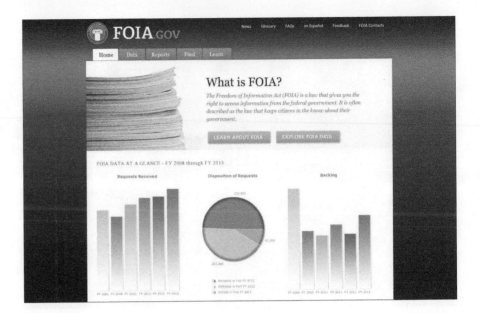

The U.S. media have used Freedom of Information Act requests to obtain important information, such as federal drug safety reports and conditions at local jails. Americans are likely to always debate just how much secrecy their government is entitled to.

for example, is a searchable database of documents related to the authorized use of torture by the American government.

With the advent of the war on terrorism, the government gained unprecedented powers to detain foreign suspects, carry out wiretaps and searches, conduct secret military tribunals, and build an integrated law-enforcement and intelligence system. Congress hastily enacted many of these sweeping provisions of the USA PATRIOT Act several weeks after the terrorist attacks, with little debate.

The threat of terrorism also dramatically sharpened the tension between secrecy and democracy. After the September 11 attacks, access under the FOIA was curtailed, and the range of information deemed sensitive greatly expanded. Some analysts worried that secrecy would prevent Congress from carrying out its basic oversight responsibilities. They also claimed that much of the secrecy had nothing to do with national security. President Obama ordered federal agencies to administer the FOIA law more liberally and signed an executive order to speed declassification of secret documents. However, Obama's campaign to make government more transparent was challenged by national security contract worker Edward Snowden's leak of sensitive national security documents in 2013. The Snowden documents exposed the extent, and potential illegality, of the National Security Agency's (NSA) global surveillance operations. Following the revelation that the NSA was collecting private data on millions of Americans and foreign nationals—tracking not only phone calls but also email messages, web browser histories, and personal contacts—concern mounted among the American public, government watchdog groups, and representatives in Congress, while foreign allies threatened to suspend cooperation on global antiterrorism efforts.[27] A panel of intelligence experts appointed by President Obama to assess the NSA's activities concluded that its massive data collection "made only a modest contribution to the nation's security." They recommended, among dozens of other reforms, that the government stop the collection program and relinquish the files to a third party.[28] Congress barred the bulk collection of telephone data and instituted other limits on government surveillance in the 2015 USA Freedom Act. The restrictions in the new legislation sought to ensure security without jeopardizing privacy, although critics remain concerned about the scope of government surveillance.[29]

MAINTAINING A STRONG ECONOMY

In our capitalist economic system, the government does not directly run the economy. Yet many federal government activities are critical to maintaining a strong economy. Foremost among these are the agencies responsible for fiscal and monetary policy. Other agencies, such as the Internal Revenue Service (IRS), collect private resources into use for public purposes. Tax policy may also strengthen the economy through decisions about whom to tax, how much, and when. Finally, the federal government, through such agencies as the Department of Transportation, the Commerce Department, and the Energy Department, may directly provide services or goods that bolster the economy.

Fiscal and Monetary Agencies Fiscal policy can refer to any government policy having to do with public finance. However, Americans often reserve *fiscal* for taxing and spending policies and use *monetary* for policies having to do with banks, credit, and currency.

While the responsibility for making fiscal policy lies with Congress, the administration of fiscal policy occurs primarily in the Treasury Department. In addition to collecting income, corporate, and other taxes, the Treasury manages the national debt: $21 trillion in 2018.[30] The Treasury Department is also responsible for printing U.S. currency, but currency is only a tiny proportion of the entire money economy. Most of the trillions of dollars used in the transactions of the private and public sectors of the U.S. economy exist virtually—in computerized accounts rather than as actual currency. The Treasury Department also performs tax and economic policy analysis, as does the Council of Economic Advisors, located within the Executive Office of the President.

A key monetary agency is the **Federal Reserve System** (called simply the Fed), which is headed by the Federal Reserve Board. The Fed has authority over the interest rates and lending activities of the nation's most important banks. Congress established the Fed in 1913 as a clearinghouse responsible for adjusting the supply of money and credit to the needs of commerce and industry in different regions of the country. The Fed is also responsible for ensuring that banks do not overextend themselves, a policy that guards against bank failures during a sudden economic scare, such as occurred in 1929. The Treasury and the Federal Reserve took center stage when a string of bank failures threatened economic catastrophe in 2008. These agencies designed a $700-billion bailout package and convinced Congress that a rapid response was needed to avert a worldwide depression. Although the Treasury and the Federal Reserve sprang into action when economic calamity loomed, critics charged that the crisis could have been prevented if these agencies had exercised more regulatory oversight over the financial sector during the previous decade. In 2010, Congress and the president created the Financial Stability Oversight Council to identify systemwide risks to the financial sector. As part of its duties, the council devised a rule to identify "systemically important" nonbank financial companies that would pose a grave threat to U.S. financial stability in the event that they failed and to prompt stiffer regulatory oversight of those companies.[31]

Revenue Agencies One of the first actions Congress took under President George Washington was to create the Department of the Treasury, and probably its oldest function is the collection of taxes on imports, called tariffs. Now part of the Department of Homeland Security, federal customs agents are located at every U.S. seaport

fiscal policy the government's use of taxing, monetary, and spending powers to manipulate the economy

Federal Reserve System a system of 12 Federal Reserve banks that facilitates exchanges of cash, checks, and credit; regulates member banks; and uses monetary policies to fight inflation and deflation

Several government agencies are focused on maintaining a strong economy. These include the Federal Reserve, headed by Jerome Powell (left), which regulates interest rates and lending activity. The Treasury Department (which oversees the IRS and thus collects taxes) is headed by Secretary Steven Mnuchin (center). The federal government also provides small business loans and other incentives for economic development in large and small sectors of the economy. In 2015 the Obama administration announced more money for research to protect bee habitats (right).

revenue agency an agency responsible for collecting taxes. Examples include the Internal Revenue Service for income taxes; the U.S. Customs Service for tariffs and other taxes on imported goods; and the Bureau of Alcohol, Tobacco, Firearms and Explosives for collection of taxes on the sale of those particular products

and international airport to oversee the collection of tariffs. But far and away the most important of the **revenue agencies** is the Internal Revenue Service, a bureau within the Treasury Department.

The IRS is the government agency that Americans love to hate. As one expert put it, "probably no organization in the country, public or private, creates as much clientele *dis*favor as the Internal Revenue Service. The very nature of its work brings it into an adversarial relationship with vast numbers of Americans every year [emphasis added]."[32] Taxpayers complain about the IRS's needless complexity, its lack of sensitivity and responsiveness to individual taxpayers, and its overall lack of efficiency. Such complaints led Congress to pass the IRS Restructuring and Reform Act of 1998, which instituted a number of new protections for taxpayers. Yet Congress continued to cut the IRS budget—$900 million over eight years through 2018—despite Treasury Secretary Steven Mnuchin's request for a larger budget and more staff to allow the agency to enhance enforcement, bring in more tax revenue, fend off hackers, and restore customer service.[33]

Economic Development Agencies Federal agencies also conduct programs designed to strengthen particular segments of the economy or to provide specific services aimed at strengthening the entire economy. Created in 1889, the Department of Agriculture is the fourth-oldest Cabinet department. Its initial mission, to strengthen American agriculture by providing information about effective farming practices, reflected the enormous importance of farming in the American economy. Through its Agricultural Extension Service, the Department of Agriculture established a significant presence in rural areas throughout the country. It also built strong support for its activities among the nation's farmers and at the many land-grant colleges, where agricultural research has been conducted for over 100 years.

At first glance, the Department of Transportation, which oversees the nation's highway and air traffic systems, may seem to have little to do with economic development. But effective transportation is the backbone of a strong economy. The interstate highway system, for example, is widely acknowledged as a key factor in promoting economic growth in the decades after World War II. The Small Business Administration, in the Department of Commerce, provides loans and technical assistance to small businesses across the country.

Can the Bureaucracy Be Reformed?

Evaluate some of the ways politicians have tried to make the bureaucracy more efficient

When citizens complain that government is too bureaucratic, what they often mean is that government bureaucracies seem inefficient, waste money, and perform poorly. The botched roll-out of healthcare.gov, the federal government's online health insurance marketplace, handicapped the implementation of the Affordable Care Act when it opened and subsequently crashed in October 2013. A report by the Inspector General of the Department of Health and Human Services concluded afterward that the Centers for Medicare and Medicaid Services, tasked with overseeing the website, lacked the necessary managerial and technical capacity and ignored warnings that the enormous software project was headed for trouble.[34] In the waiting list scandal that rocked the Veterans Health Administration in 2014, some VHA hospitals that had not met the target of getting appointments for veterans within 14 days had created unofficial lists to make their waiting times look better. A VA audit and FBI investigation found that over 120,000 veterans were left waiting or never got appointments. Congress passed and President Obama signed new legislation in late 2014 that added funding, allowed some veterans to get private health care at government expense, and gave the VA Secretary increased authority to fire poorly performing managers.[35] When citizens have negative personal experience with the federal government—mountains of forms to fill out, lengthy waits, and unsympathetic service—they wonder why government can't do better.

The government has often sought to find ways to make the federal bureaucracy more efficient. In 1993, President Bill Clinton launched the National Performance Review—part of his promise to "reinvent government"—to make the federal bureaucracy more efficient, accountable, and effective. The National Performance Review sought to prompt federal agencies to adopt flexible, goal-driven practices. Clinton promised that the result would be a government that would "work better and cost less." Virtually all observers agreed that the review made substantial progress. Its original goal was to save more than $100 billion over five years, in large part by cutting the federal workforce by 12 percent (more than 270,000 jobs) by the end of 1999. In fact, by 2000, $136 billion in savings were already assured through legislative or administrative action, and the federal workforce had been cut by 426,200.[36]

In 2015, President Obama created a Social and Behavioral Sciences team to help departments incorporate insights from behavioral science—how people make decisions and act on them—to make government processes more efficient. The team launched a number of experiments to improve services, such as an effort to boost military service members' enrollment in the government retirement savings plan, which was lower than that of other federal employees. By requiring service members to make a choice as part of their orientation upon arrival at a new military base, the experiment increased enrollment by over 8 percent.[37]

Beyond these efforts seeking greater efficiency and effectiveness, government reorganization is a recurrent theme. Presidents Nixon, Carter, Clinton, and Obama each ordered a reorganization of the executive branch. Nixon, for example, sought to retain the Departments of State, Defense, Treasury, and Justice but streamline other departments by function (Natural Resources, Human Resources, Community Development, and Economic Development). However, Congress objected, as executive branch structures reflect committee and subcommittee jurisdictions in Congress, which are important to lawmakers who wish to address constituent concerns and who therefore resist consolidation.[38] At the beginning of his term, President Trump too issued an executive order asking each department to file reorganization plans, but after his administration's first year, only a few departments had done so.[39]

In recent decades there have been several attempts to "reinvent government." In 1993, President Bill Clinton and Vice President Al Gore established the National Performance Review for this purpose. Gore promoted this on David Letterman's show, where he railed against the government's procurement requirements, which even specified the number of pieces into which a government ashtray may shatter.

Although streamlining efforts like Clinton's did help make government work more effectively, it did not institute the more sweeping approach to reform demanded by some political leaders. Reform has instead been pursued through efforts to terminate, devolve, or contract out government functions. In general, Democratic administrations have aimed to make the existing bureaucracy work more effectively, whereas Republican administrations have sought to sideline the bureaucracy, especially by contracting out government work to private companies.

ELIMINATING PROGRAMS AND AGENCIES

The only certain way to reduce the size of the bureaucracy is to eliminate programs through termination, a rare occurrence. Even in the 12 years of the Reagan and George H. W. Bush administrations, both of which proclaimed a strong commitment to the reduction of the national government, not a single national government agency or program was terminated. In the 1990s, Republicans did succeed in eliminating two small agencies. The 2018 spending bill, passed by a Republican-led Congress, not only increased federal spending but also prohibited agencies from eliminating programs or offices without congressional authorization.[40]

The overall difficulty in terminating bureaucracy is a reflection of Americans' love–hate relationship with the national government. As antagonistic as Americans may be toward bureaucracy in general, they benefit from the services being rendered and the protections being offered by particular bureaucratic agencies. They fiercely defend their favorite agencies while perceiving no inconsistency in their hostility toward the bureaucracy in general. A good case in point is the agonizing problem of closing military bases in the wake of the end of the Cold War with the former Soviet Union, when the United States no longer needed so many bases. Since every base was in some congressional member's district, it proved impossible for Congress to decide to close any of them. Consequently, beginning in 1988, Congress established the Defense Base Closure and Realignment Commission (BRAC) to decide on base closings, allowing Congress only an up or down vote on the commission's proposals.[41] Five different BRAC reports, the most recent in 2005, formed the basis for closing bases and modifying the operations in the remaining bases. When the Pentagon proposed another round of base closings in 2014, it met with resistance from members of Congress, few of whom wanted to run the risk that a base in their district could close.[42]

Elected leaders have come to rely on a more incremental approach to downsizing the bureaucracy. Much has been done by budgetary means. In 2011, due to concerns among House Republicans about the size of the national debt, Congress failed to raise the nation's debt ceiling—the amount of national debt that can be issued by the Treasury—usually an uncontroversial step to keep government in operation. The Treasury Department came within days of being unable to pay bondholders and other creditors. The resolution to the crisis was the Budget Control Act of 2011, which required Congress to pass a deficit-cutting budget in exchange for raising the debt ceiling or else trigger sequestration, across-the-board cuts to both domestic and defense spending. Congress failed to pass a budget, triggering cuts.[43] As a result, a number of agencies made personnel reductions at that time. President Trump imposed a federal hiring freeze upon taking office, but did not issue a formal

Americans may desire smaller government in the abstract, but they defend the agencies that affect them. Closing military bases in the United States has proved particularly controversial. Citizens mobilized across the country to urge the Base Closure and Realignment Commission not to close military bases in their areas.

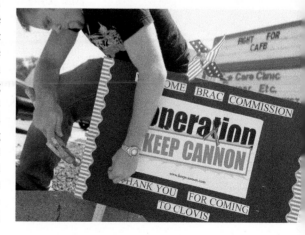

plan. Some agencies operated as if under a freeze, and some, like the Social Security Administration, made early buyout offers to their workforce in summer 2017, but the size of the federal workforce remained largely unchanged.[44]

DEVOLUTION

devolution a policy to remove a program from one level of government by delegating it or passing it down to a lower level of government, such as from the national government to the state and local governments

The next most effective approach to reducing the size of the federal bureaucracy is **devolution**, downsizing the federal bureaucracy by delegating the implementation of programs to state and local governments (also see Chapter 3, Federalism). Devolution often alters the pattern of who benefits most from government programs. Opponents of devolution in social policy, for example, charge that it reduces the ability of the government to remedy inequality. They argue that state governments, which cannot run deficits as the federal government does and which have more limited taxing capabilities, will inevitably cut spending on programs that serve low-income residents. They point to the State Children's Health Insurance Program (SCHIP), which was created in 1997 to extend health insurance to low-income children. When the economy was booming, states added children to the rolls and some states even extended benefits to the children's parents. But during the recession of the early 2000s, as states faced significant budget crises, many cut back on SCHIP. And during the Great Recession that began in 2008, Arizona closed SCHIP to new enrollments altogether and did not reopen the program until late 2016, long after the recession was over.[45] States, with their tight fiscal circumstances, can have difficulty keeping pace with economic need.

Often the central aim of devolution is to provide more efficient and flexible government services. Yet, by its very nature, devolution entails variation across the states. In some states, government services may improve as a consequence of devolution. In other states, services may deteriorate as the states use devolution as an opportunity to cut spending and reduce services. This has been the pattern in the implementation of the welfare reform passed in 1996, the most significant devolution of federal government social programs in many decades. Some states, such as Oregon, have used the flexibility of the reform to design innovative programs that respond to clients' needs; other states, such as Idaho, have virtually dismantled their welfare programs. The recession that began in 2008 provided the first real evidence about what increased state flexibility meant for low-income Americans. Studies showed that the number of people on public assistance rose by 14 percent even as the unemployment rate increased by 88 percent between 2007 and 2010.[46] Moreover, states varied widely in how they responded: for example, although the unemployment rate rose by 146 percent in Arizona—increasing from 4 percent at the end of 2007 to almost 10 percent in 2010—public-assistance rolls actually fell by 48 percent. In Oregon, by contrast, public-assistance cases rose by 70 percent, although unemployment grew by only 41 percent. The overall lack of growth and state variation in welfare contrast sharply with the rise in food stamp recipients during 2008–09, a program run by the federal government. Recipients of food stamps (now called the Supplemental Nutrition Assistance Program) grew by 45 percent between 2009 and 2010 and pulled an estimated 8 percent of Americans out of poverty in 2009.[47] Critics argued that devolution gave the states too much flexibility in designing their own welfare programs and that the result has been a program unable to assist the poor when they need it most.

FOR CRITICAL ANALYSIS

Dissatisfied citizens have supported a range of bureaucratic reforms, including termination of agencies, devolution of responsibility to lower levels of government, and privatization. Are such reforms likely to make the bureaucracy more responsive to public wishes?

This is the dilemma that devolution poses. Up to a point, variation can be considered one of the virtues of federalism. But in a democracy, it is inherently dangerous to have large variations in the provisions of services and benefits.

PRIVATIZATION AND CONTRACTING OUT

Most of what is called "privatization" is the provision of government goods and services by private contractors under direct government supervision. Except for top-secret strategic materials, virtually all military hardware, from boats to bullets, is produced on a privatized basis by private contractors. Research services worth billions of dollars are bought under contract by governments from universities and from ordinary industrial corporations and private "think tanks." **Privatization** simply means that a formerly public activity is picked up under contract by a private company or companies. But such programs are still very much government programs—paid for by government and supervised by government. Privatization downsizes the government only in that the workers providing the service are no longer counted as part of the government bureaucracy. Privatization may not mean less government but rather a different role for government, as managerial expertise is needed to write contracts and oversee private companies carrying out government work.[48]

privatization a formerly public service that is now provided by a private company but paid for by the government

The central aim of privatization is to reduce the cost of government. When private contractors can perform a task as well as government can but for less money, taxpayers win. President George W. Bush made privatization a central component of his effort to reform the federal bureaucracy. He introduced new procedures that would subject more than 800,000 federal jobs, nearly half the federal civilian workforce, to competitive outsourcing. If it were determined that a company could do the job more efficiently, the work would be contracted out. Under Bush, government outsourcing grew dramatically as the government sought to staff the new Department

One strategy to carry out the tasks of government is privatization. The U.S. military and Department of Defense contract many services to companies such as Booz Allen Hamilton, which provides systems for personnel management, program support, and assessment, among other services.

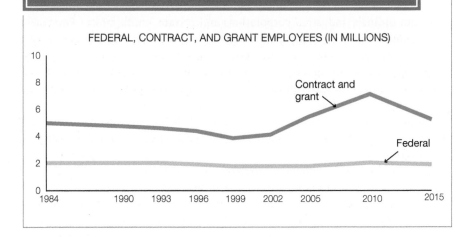

FIGURE 14.4

Outsourcing the Government

The number of contractors employed by the federal government has increased, especially after September 11, 2001. Does contracting out government jobs save money, or does it create problems of oversight and accountability? Or both?

NOTE: Includes both new contracts and payments against existing contracts.

SOURCES: Paul Light, "The True Size of Government," *The Volcker Alliance,* October 2017, www .volckeralliance.org (accessed 4/4/18).

FEDERAL, CONTRACT, AND GRANT EMPLOYEES (IN MILLIONS)

Contract and grant

Federal

of Homeland Security and pursue wars in Afghanistan and Iraq without increasing the numbers of federal employees. Payments for federal contracts grew from $209 billion in 2000 to $537 billion in 2011.[49] Although military contracts account for much of the growth, contracting is common throughout the federal bureaucracy. In fact, contracting has become so widespread that it has been called a "virtual fourth branch of government"[50] (Figure 14.4).

Depending on how it is conducted, competitive outsourcing may not lead to extensive privatization; instead, competition may improve government performance by forcing federal agencies to reexamine how they can do their work more efficiently. But when public bureaucracies are *not* granted a fair chance to bid in the contracting competition and, too, if there is little competition among private firms, private firms have a monopoly on service provision and often end up being less efficient and more costly than government. In 2015 close to 60 percent of all contracts were awarded competitively. But that year was an exception: from 2000 to 2011, less than half of existing contracts were subject to open competition. In fact, there is no good evidence that privatization saves the government money.

In most aspects of government activity, contract employees work side by side with government employees in what has been called a "blended workforce."[51] Many agencies that rely on technical expertise, such as the National Oceanographic and Atmospheric Administration, routinely rely on contractors. Although federal regulations forbid the outsourcing of "inherently governmental work," no clear line separates governmental and nongovernmental work.[52]

Concerns about adequate government oversight, accountability, and performance of private contractors escalated when the scale of contracting dramatically increased. In 2008, Congress responded to the concerns about contractors by creating a "Commission on Wartime Contracting." Its final report sharply criticized the use of private contractors, estimating that the practice had wasted between $31 and $60 billion during the wars in Afghanistan and Iraq. It made numerous recommendations for reform but noted that successful reforms would require congressional action and funding for new oversight capabilities.[53] Congress created databases to record contractor performance and to keep track of legal or contractual violations.[54] However, both the Government Accountability Office (GAO) and government transparency groups found the databases poorly documented and of little use in agency decision-making or congressional oversight.[55]

Some members of Congress have sought far-reaching regulations on contractors, including forbidding contractors from performing sensitive functions in war settings such as interrogations, security, and intelligence activities. Proposals for such major reforms, however, are difficult to enact given the political connections of many federal contractors.

The Obama administration sought to address the concerns about contracting in several ways. In July 2009 the White House Office of Management and Budget (OMB) took steps to reduce the government's reliance on outside contractors. Departments and agencies were told to cut contract spending by 7 percent over the next two years.[56] By 2011 the administration announced that for the first time in 13 years, spending on outside contractors had declined.[57] In 2016 the Obama Department of Justice decided to end the use of private prisons for federal inmates after an audit found more safety and security problems than in government-run facilities.[58]

In 2013 the national security leaks by Edward Snowden and a mass shooting at the Washington Navy Yard, a U.S. military base—both by government contractors—raised fresh concerns about the outsourcing of government and prompted Congress to pass legislation calling for a review of contractors' security clearances.[59] The White House also drafted an executive order requiring government contractors to disclose their political donations, though Congress blocked those efforts by passing a federal spending bill in 2014 that prohibits any funding to require contractors to disclose campaign donations.[60] In addition, in 2015 Obama set new requirements for federal contractors in a very different area, compelling contractors to pay a $10.10 minimum wage and to provide paid sick leave for their employees (even if he had failed to win congressional approval for measures to assist workers in general).[61] In March 2017, President Trump signed legislation rolling back several Obama regulations, including a rule barring companies from receiving a federal contract if they had violated labor, wage, or workplace safety rules.[62]

FOR CRITICAL ANALYSIS

Private firms play a significant role in providing government services, including both internal and external security. What are the advantages and disadvantages of relying on private firms to provide essential services? Can government provide adequate oversight of these private companies?

Managing the Bureaucracy

Explain why it is often difficult to control the bureaucracy

By their very nature, bureaucracies pose challenges to democratic governance. Although bureaucracies provide the expertise needed to implement the public will, they can also become entrenched organizations that serve their own interests. The public's task is neither to retreat from bureaucracy nor to attack it but to take advantage of its strengths while making it more accountable to the demands of democratic politics and representative government.

THE PRESIDENT AS CHIEF EXECUTIVE

In 1937, President Franklin Roosevelt's Committee on Administrative Management officially addressed a plea that had been growing increasingly urgent: "The president needs help." The national government had grown rapidly during the preceding 25 years, but the structures and procedures necessary to manage the burgeoning executive branch had not yet been established. The response to the call for "help" for the president initially took the form of three management policies: (1) all communications and decisions that related to executive policy decisions must pass through the Executive Office of the President (EOP); (2) in order to cope with such a flow, the EOP must have an adequate staff of specialists in research, analysis, legislative and legal writing, and public affairs; and (3) the EOP must have additional staff to ensure that presidential decisions are made, communicated to Congress, and carried out by the appropriate agency.

Making the Managerial Presidency The story of the modern presidency can be told largely as a series of responses to the plea for managerial help as the scope of the federal government—and presidential power—has grown.[63]

The president heads the federal government, which is the largest employer in the country and the largest purchaser of goods and services in the world.[64] As the CEO of this enormous organization, the president may have goals associated with management (striving for efficiency) and control (shaping policy outcomes). Presidents have several tools at their disposal. They have appointment power over the top layer of the executive branch, the political appointees who sit on top of the career civil service. They can issue executive orders, making policy and shaping the executive branch unilaterally. They can also alter an agency's budget or organizational scheme. Indeed, the presidency has been marked by waves of executive branch reorganization by presidents seeking to exert administrative and political control.[65]

After Roosevelt's reforms, perhaps the most important were those under President Jimmy Carter, whose reorganization of the civil service will long be recognized as one of the most significant contributions of his presidency. The Civil Service Reform Act of 1978 was the first major revamping of the federal civil service since its creation in 1883. The 1978 act created the Merit Systems Protection Board to defend competitive merit recruitment and promotion from political encroachment. The separate Federal Labor Relations Authority was set up to administer collective bargaining and to address individual personnel grievances. The third new agency, the Office of Personnel Management, was created to manage recruiting, testing, training, and the retirement system. The Senior Executive Service, a top management rank for civil servants, was also created to recognize and foster "public management" as a profession and to facilitate the movement of "super-grade" career officials across agencies and departments.[66]

President Bill Clinton was often criticized for the way he managed his administration—his loose approach to administration included all-night "bull sessions," complete with pizza—yet, as we have seen, he inaugurated one of the most systematic efforts "to change the way government does business" in his National Performance Review. Heavily influenced by the theories of management consultants who prized decentralization, customer responsiveness, and employee initiative, Clinton sought to infuse these new practices into government.[67]

Subsequent presidents have made their own mark. George W. Bush was the first president with a degree in business. He followed the standard business school dictum to select skilled subordinates and then delegate responsibility to them. Critics contended, however, that his administration's distrust of the bureaucracy led it to exercise inappropriate political control over agency experts. Obama's approach to the managerial presidency featured a deep belief in the importance of scientific expertise, which was reflected in his appointments to key regulatory agencies such as the FDA, OSHA, and the EPA. But he had his own critics, who complained about micromanagement and centralization.[68]

President Trump called for deep budget cuts and reorganization in a number of executive branch departments and agencies. His presidency has also raised the specter of a "deep state" of bureaucrats who exert power independent of political control. Political scientist Michael Glennon has used the term "the double state" to describe a phenomenon in which, for example, Bush-era national security policies such as covert drone strikes and use of the Guantánamo Bay prison continued under President Obama, even though Obama as a candidate had criticized them. Glennon raises the possibility of a "double government" of bureaucrats that continues to pursue policies of its preference outside of political or democratic control.[69] Episodes such as EPA employees informing the media about a report on climate change they feared would be suppressed seemed to confirm Trump supporters' fears of the limits of presidential control over the bureaucracy.[70] There is little evidence of the truly rogue bureaucracy that figures in the most extreme versions of conspiracy theories, but questions of who controls the bureaucracy and how much autonomy bureaucrats should have have occupied political scientists and government leaders for decades.

CONGRESSIONAL OVERSIGHT

Another lever of control over the bureaucracy is Congress. Congress passes legislation, which the bureaucracy must then implement. Such delegation derives from the constitutionally mandated roles for each branch of government; the president must "faithfully execute" the laws Congress passes. But because Congress cannot possibly stipulate every detail of every law, the bureaucracy must interpret legislative intent.[71] The delegation of implementation introduces the principal-agent problem: does the bureaucracy (the agent) implement laws in the manner Congress (the principal) intended?

One way Congress can hold the bureaucracy accountable is **oversight**. Congressional committees and subcommittees have jurisdictions roughly parallel to one or more departments and agencies in the executive branch, and members of Congress who sit on these committees can develop expertise equal to that of the bureaucrats. The most visible indication of Congress's oversight efforts is the use of public hearings, before which bureaucrats and other witnesses are summoned to discuss and defend agency budgets and past decisions.

Studies show that congressional committee and subcommittee hearings and meetings grew quite dramatically in the late 1960s and 1970s, as Congress tried to keep pace with the expansion of the executive branch; this growth was especially pronounced in the House, which conducts more total days of oversight hearings than the Senate.[72] However, concern has grown in recent years about failures of oversight.[73] There appears to be less **"police patrol" oversight**—regular or even preemptive

oversight the effort by Congress, through hearings, investigations, and other techniques, to exercise control over the activities of executive agencies

"police patrol" oversight regular or even preemptive congressional hearings on bureaucratic agency operations hearings on agency operations—and more **"fire alarm" oversight** prompted by media attention or advocacy group complaints. For example, consumer outrage prompted the House Oversight and Government Reform Committee's 2016 inquiry into a 500-percent price hike on EpiPens used to treat severe allergic reactions.[74] There are also more oversight hearings under divided government, when the executive branch and at least one chamber of Congress are controlled by different parties.[75] For example, the House select committee on Benghazi, the eighth committee in the Republican-led Congress to investigate the attack on the American mission in Benghazi, Libya, called former secretary of state Hillary Clinton to appear for a second time in 2015. Republican members of the committee questioned the former secretary for more than eight hours, while Democrats charged that the hearing was designed to harm Clinton's presidential campaign.[76] Some observers worry that the extreme partisan polarization of recent years has politicized oversight, with the hearings that do occur dismissed as partisan while other issues are ignored.[77]

Individual members of Congress can also carry out oversight inquiries. Such standard congressional "casework" can address significant questions of public

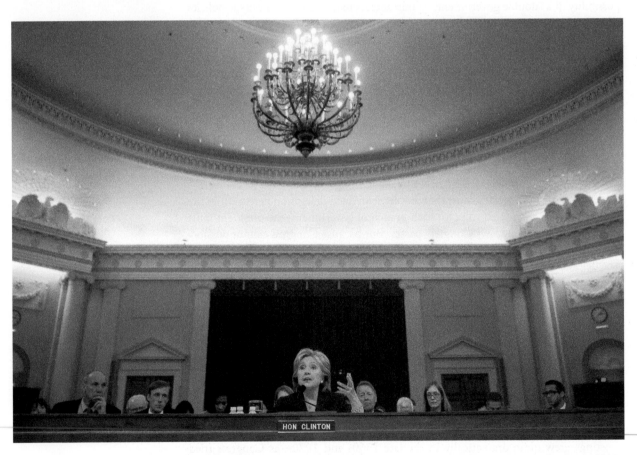

The most visible aspect of congressional oversight is the use of public hearings. Following the 2012 attack on the U.S. embassy in Benghazi, Libya, Congress held multiple highly publicized—and highly politicized—hearings to investigate the matter, focusing on the activities of former secretary of state Hillary Clinton.

responsibility even when they are motivated only by the demands of an individual constituent. Oversight also encompasses the communications between congressional staff and agency staff. In addition, Congress has created for itself three large agencies whose obligations are to engage in constant research on matters related to the executive branch. These are the General Accounting Office (GAO), the Congressional Research Service, and the Congressional Budget Office, each designed to give Congress information independent of the information it can get directly from the executive branch through hearings and other communications.[78] Another source of information for oversight is directly from citizens through the FOIA, which, as we have seen, gives ordinary citizens the right to gain access to agency files and agency data. Nevertheless, the information citizens gain through the FOIA can be made effective only through the institutionalized channels of congressional committees and, though rarely, through public interest litigation in the federal courts.

FOR CRITICAL ANALYSIS

Through elected officials (the president and Congress), the public can achieve some control over the bureaucracy. What are the relative advantages and disadvantages of presidential and congressional control of the bureaucracy?

Bureaucracy
WHAT DO WE WANT?

Americans' views about the federal government bureaucracy present something of a paradox. On the one hand, the public expresses dislike for "big government," exemplified by bureaucracy. From this perspective, the federal government is too large, inherently wasteful, and at odds with individual freedom. On the other hand, Americans support many government programs and have high expectations for government. Indeed, high expectations lead many Americans to blame bureaucrats when the country faces problems, such as the prolonged economic downturn of recent years. One consequence of these divergent views is that public discussion about bureaucracy is often high on emotion and short on facts. Another consequence can be that bureaucracies try to maximize one value but undermine others. As we saw in the chapter opener, the decision to switch the Flint water supply was made to save money, but it endangered the health of Flint residents.

Arguments contending that the federal government is too large ignore the fact that the number of government employees has not grown disproportionately large when compared with the size of the American workforce. Charges that government wastes the taxpayers' money must also be put into perspective. As we have seen in this chapter, outsourcing government activities to private contractors does not offer a remedy for wasteful spending. In fact, private firms may be more wasteful than the public sector unless there is strong government oversight of private activities. Finally, it is true that bureaucratic rules often limit the freedom of individuals and corporations. But the laws that bureaucracies implement were enacted by our elected representatives in Congress. They are, in fact, the product of our democratic political system. As these considerations suggest, building a bureaucracy that reflects American values is not a simple task. Adequate congressional oversight is one important part of the solution because a bureaucracy that is shielded from the public eye may wind up pursuing its own interests rather than those of the public. Even so, an administration whose every move is subject to intense public scrutiny may be hamstrung in its efforts to carry out the public interest. (The "**Who Participates?**" feature on the facing page shows the bureaucracy's response to public concerns about health care accessibility for veterans.) Finding the right balance between bureaucratic autonomy and public scrutiny is a central task of creating an effective government; it requires both presidential and congressional vigilance to build an effective and responsive bureaucracy.

The emergence of "big data" is likely to change the way bureaucracies operate in the future. The term *big data* refers to very large data sets that compile information on a wide range of topics including climate, traffic, and health, and the NSA's huge database of phone calls and use of social media. Big data have the potential to improve government performance by linking sources of information that were previously unconnected. They also will allow the government to analyze information that was stored as text or went uncollected. Advances in government's ability to implement programs in public health, food safety, and transportation are only the beginning of what big data promise. At the same time, however, big data pose a threat to individual privacy, as the revelations about the NSA's data suggest. As bureaucracies tap into the promise of big data to create more effective programs, a close public eye on the implications for the right to privacy will be needed. How might big data improve the government's delivery of services in the future? What additional safeguards might be needed to protect individuals' privacy?

Waiting for a Veterans Affairs Health Care Appointment

After media reports about excessive waits endured by veterans seeking health care appointments, and widespread fraud in reporting those wait times, Congress passed the 2014 Veterans Choice Act, which allows veterans to go to private doctors if they would otherwise have to wait more than 30 days to see a Veterans Affairs provider. This act was supplemented in 2017 by the website, Access to Care (accesstocare.va.gov), which reports wait times at veterans clinics around the country. The vast majority of veterans seeking health care appointments are now able to schedule one at their local VA within 30 days.

93%
195,604,902 total

Total appointments requested in 2017:
208,065,313

4%
7,306,571 total

1.4%
2,835,626 total

0.3%
545,582 total

Scheduled Within 30 days

Scheduled Within 31–60 days

Scheduled Within 61–90 days

Scheduled Within 90+ days

Note: Numbers may not add up to 100 percent due to rounding.

SOURCES: "Attempted Fix for VA Health Delays Creates New Bureaucracy," npr.org; Patient Access Data, www.va.gov (accessed 3/9/18).

★ WHAT YOU CAN DO ★

Ask Questions about Federal Agencies

☑ Find out how veterans access their benefits and more about the U.S. Department of Veterans Affairs by visiting **www.va.gov**. For more information on veterans access to health care, visit **www.accestocare.va.gov**.

☑ To find more information on how the bureaucracy affects your life, visit **www.usa.gov/federal-agencies** and search by agency.

☑ Ask a question about how federal agencies can help you. Most agencies have FAQ and contact pages on their websites.

★ STUDY GUIDE ★

Bureaucracy and Bureaucrats

Bureaucracy is defined as the complex structure of offices, tasks, and rules that private and public organizations use to coordinate the work of their personnel. The federal executive branch is composed of cabinet departments, independent agencies, government corporations, and independent regulatory commissions. Through their implementation, innovation, rule making, and enforcement decisions, the federal service touches on many important aspects of daily life.

Key Terms

bureaucracy (p. 553)

implementation (p. 553)

merit system (p. 556)

department (p. 559)

independent agency (p. 560)

government corporation (p. 561)

Practice Quiz

1. Which of the following statements about Congress and the bureaucracy is *not* true?
   a) Bureaucracies employ people who have much more specialized expertise in specific policy areas than do members of Congress.
   b) Members of Congress often prefer to delegate politically difficult decision-making to bureaucrats.
   c) While Congress is responsible for making laws, the bureaucracy is responsible for filling in the blanks by determining how the laws should be implemented.
   d) Congress banned rule making by the federal bureaucracy in 1995.
   e) Congress relies heavily on bureaucratic flexibility in implementing laws because updating legislation can take many years and bureaucrats can ensure that laws are administered in ways that take new conditions into account.

2. The Civil Service Act of 1883 required that appointees to positions within the federal bureaucracy
   a) pledge an oath of loyalty to the United States.
   b) register as independents rather than as members of an organized political party.
   c) be qualified for the job to which they were appointed.
   d) serve for no more than 10 years.
   e) serve for no fewer than 10 years.

3. Federal bureaucrats
   a) all work in Washington, D.C.
   b) are more likely to be female than private sector workers.
   c) are more racially and ethnically diverse than the private sector workforce.
   d) are less educated than the private sector workforce.
   e) are less likely to hold professional occupations in science, engineering, diplomacy, and other advanced fields than the private sector workforce.

4. Which of the following best describes the size of the federal service?
   a) The size of the federal service has grown exponentially over the last 35 years.
   b) The size of the federal service has changed very little over the last 35 years.
   c) The size of the federal service reached its peak in 1955 and has been dramatically declining ever since.
   d) The federal service has employed at least 15 percent of the American workforce every year since 1950.
   e) The federal service was eliminated during the 1990s in order to hire more state government employees.

5. Which of the following is an example of a government corporation?
   a) National Aeronautics and Space Administration
   b) Amtrak
   c) Federal Bureau of Investigation
   d) Environmental Protection Agency
   e) Department of Justice

Goals of the Federal Bureaucracy

Describe the major goals we expect federal agencies to promote (pp. 563–73)

The federal bureaucracy promotes public well-being through a diverse set of services, products, and regulations. Some federal agencies, such as the Department of Defense, the Department of Justice, and the Department of Homeland Security, protect the country against internal and external security threats. Other federal agencies, such as the Federal Reserve System and the Internal Revenue Service, promote the public's welfare by helping maintain a strong economy.

Key Terms

regulatory agency (p. 563)

fiscal policy (p. 571)

Federal Reserve System (p. 571)

revenue agency (p. 572)

Practice Quiz

6. A stable relationship between a bureaucratic agency, a clientele group, and a legislative committee is called
   a) a standing committee.
   b) a conference committee.
   c) a cabinet.
   d) an issue network.
   e) an iron triangle.

7. Americans refer to government policy about banks, credit, and currency as
   a) interstate commerce policy.
   b) deficit policy.
   c) fiscal policy.
   d) monetary policy.
   e) regulatory policy.

Can the Bureaucracy Be Reformed?

Evaluate some of the ways politicians have tried to make the bureaucracy more efficient (pp. 573–79)

Many Americans express frustration with the performance of the federal bureaucracy. As a result, politicians have frequently explored various methods of making the federal bureaucracy more efficient. In general, politicians have attempted to promote bureaucratic reform through reorganization, termination of programs, devolution, and privatization.

Key Terms

devolution (p. 576)

privatization (p. 577)

Practice Quiz

8. Which president instituted the bureaucratic reform of the National Performance Review?
   a) Richard Nixon
   b) Lyndon Johnson
   c) Jimmy Carter
   d) Bill Clinton
   e) George W. Bush

9. *Devolution* refers to
   a) the gradual decline in efficiency that always comes when government begins to implement a new program.
   b) moving all or part of a program from the public sector to the private sector.
   c) a policy of reducing or eliminating regulatory restraints on the conduct of individuals or private institutions.
   d) a policy to remove a program from one level of government by passing it down to a lower level of government.
   e) reducing the overall number of regulatory agencies in the federal bureaucracy.

10. Which of the following statements best describes termination of government programs?
    a) In the 12 years of the Reagan and George H. W. Bush administrations over 50 national government programs were terminated.
    b) In the 12 years of the Reagan and George H. W. Bush administrations over 100 national government programs were terminated.
    c) In the 12 years of the Reagan and George H. W. Bush administrations over 1,000 national government programs were terminated.
    d) The Supreme Court has ruled that government programs can only be terminated through a constitutional amendment.
    e) Terminating government programs is a difficult process that rarely occurs at the federal level.

11. Which of the following has been referred to as the "virtual fourth branch of government"?
    a) independent regulatory commissions
    b) government contracting
    c) the Government Accountability Office
    d) the Defense Base Closure and Realignment Commission
    e) the White House Office of Management and Budget

Managing the Bureaucracy

The federal bureaucracy provides the expertise that is needed to implement the law. However, parts of the bureaucracy can also become entrenched organizations that serve their own interests rather than the public will. Presidents have several powerful tools at their disposal to exert administrative and political control over the federal bureaucracy, including high-level appointments and executive orders. Congress can also exert influence over bureaucratic behavior by enacting specific legislation and engaging in vigorous oversight.

Key Term

oversight (p. 581)

"police patrol" oversight (p. 581)

"fire alarm" oversight (p. 582)

Practice Quiz

12. The concept of *oversight* refers to the effort made by
    a) Congress to make executive agencies accountable for their actions.
    b) the president to make executive agencies accountable for their actions.
    c) the president to make Congress accountable for its actions.
    d) the courts to make executive agencies responsible for their actions.
    e) the states to make the executive branch accountable for its actions.

13. "Police patrol" oversight refers to
    a) hearings conducted by the FBI to investigate lawbreaking by members of Congress.
    b) any congressional hearings related to state or local law enforcement agencies.
    c) episodic, as-needed congressional hearings on bureaucratic agency operations, usually prompted by media attention or advocacy group complaints.
    d) regular or even preemptive congressional hearings on bureaucratic agency operations.
    e) any congressional hearings related to federal law enforcement agencies.

14. Which of the following agencies were created to give Congress independent information about matters related to the executive branch?
    a) Government Accountability Office, Congressional Research Service, Congressional Budget Office
    b) Department of Justice, Department of the Interior, Department of the Treasury
    c) Congressional Oversight Organization, Bureau of Government Performance, National Performance Review Association
    d) Office of Management and Budget, Council of Economic Advisers, Oversight and Government Reform
    e) Government Accountability Office, National Performance Review, Troubled Asset Relief Program

For Further Reading

Aberbach, Joel D., and Mark A. Peterson, eds. *Institutions of American Democracy: The Executive Branch*. Institutions of American Democracy Series. New York: Oxford University Press, 2006.

Arnold, Peri E. *Making the Managerial Presidency: Comprehensive Organization Planning*. Princeton, NJ: Princeton University Press, 1986.

Dilulio, John J., Jr. *Bring Back the Bureaucrats: Why More Federal Workers Will Lead to Better (and Smaller!) Government*. West Conshohocken, PA: Templeton Press, 2014.

Glennon, Michael J. *National Security and Double Government*. New York: Oxford University Press, 2015.

Gormley, William, and Stephen Balla. *Bureaucracy and Democracy: Accountability and Performance*. 3rd ed. Washington, DC: CQ Press, 2012.

Kettl, Donald F. *System under Stress: The Challenge to 21st Century Government*. 3rd ed. Los Angeles: Sage/CQ Press, 2014.

Kettl, Donald F., and James W. Fesler. *The Politics of the Administrative Process*. 4th ed. Washington, DC: CQ Press, 2008.

Light, Paul C. *A Government Ill Executed: The Decline of the Federal Service and How to Reverse It*. Cambridge, MA: Harvard University Press, 2008.

Moffitt, Susan. *Making Public Policy: Participatory Bureaucracy in American Democracy*. New York: Cambridge University Press, 2014.

Wilson, James Q. *Bureaucracy: What Government Agencies Do and Why They Do It*. New York: Basic Books, 1989.

Zegart, Amy B. *Spying Blind: The CIA, The FBI, and the Origins of 9/11*. Princeton, NJ: Princeton University Press, 2009.

Recommended Websites

Central Intelligence Agency
www.cia.gov

The Central Intelligence Agency (CIA) is one of several bureaucracies responsible for providing national security. A major problem facing this clandestine agency is how to provide security and meet the public's right to know what the government is doing. At the official website for the CIA, see what questions are often asked.

Department of Homeland Security
www.dhs.gov

The Department of Homeland Security was created after September 11 to promote bureaucratic communication and domestic security. See what the department is doing to protect America from foreign threats.

Federal Emergency Management Agency
www.fema.gov

In the aftermath of Hurricane Katrina, the Federal Emergency Management Agency (FEMA) became infamous for its role in the disaster relief efforts. View the disaster history of your state, and see what FEMA is currently doing to prevent disasters and assist Americans in need.

Office of Personnel Management
www.opm.gov/

OPM manages the federal government's civil service, listing federal jobs, conducting background and security checks, upholding the merit system, managing health and retirement benefits, and providing training and development programs for federal employees.

Official U.S. Executive Branch Websites
www.loc.gov/rr/news/fedgov.html

This resource page at the Library of Congress website provides links to every federal department, independent agency, and regulatory commission in the federal bureaucracy.

Project on Government Oversight
www.pogo.org

The Project on Government Oversight is an independent, nonprofit organization that seeks to make government more accountable by investigating corruption and misconduct. Originally set up to focus on the military, this organization now examines all types of government bureaucracies.

Reason Foundation
reason.org

The Reason Foundation is dedicated to promoting libertarian principles and limited government. Its website includes studies and opinion pieces on a range of policy issues, including many related to the size and effectiveness of the federal bureaucracy.

USAFacts
www.usafacts.org/

A project of former Microsoft CEO Steve Ballmer and Seattle design studio Artefact, USAFacts assembles and presents data from a variety of U.S. government jurisdictions in an accessible interface.

U.S. Agency for International Development
www.usaid.gov

In 1961 Congress created the U.S. Agency for International Development (USAID) to provide economic and social development assistance to foreign countries. Often criticized for promoting American values and foreign policy objectives, USAID is currently involved in numerous global issues.

The Federal Courts

WHAT GOVERNMENT DOES AND WHY IT MATTERS Mark Janus works for the Illinois Department of Healthcare and Family Services as a child support specialist. He is not a member of the union representing many public sector workers in the state, the American Federation of State, County, and Municipal Employees (AFSCME). Nonetheless, he is required to pay a "fair-share" fee to the union on the grounds that nonmembers benefit from the union's bargaining activities over issues such as pay and benefits. Nonmembers do not have to contribute to the union's political activities, such as endorsements of political candidates.[1]

Janus argues, however, that *all* activity that public sector unions engage in is inherently political. In particular, he disagrees with the union's bargaining for increased benefits when Illinois was facing a budget crisis due in part to mismanagement of the state pension program. "The union's fight is not my fight," he says. "For years it supported politicians who put the state into its current budget and pension crises....That's not public service." He believes that being forced to pay a fee that supports the union's activities violates his First Amendment rights.

His case went to the Supreme Court, which heard oral arguments in February 2018. Janus's

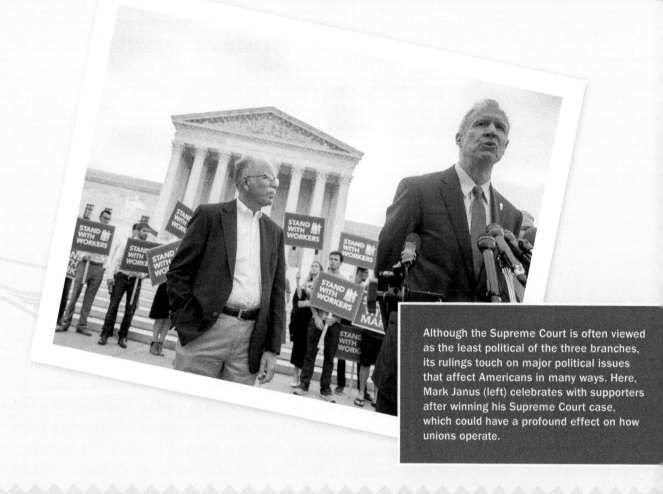

Although the Supreme Court is often viewed as the least political of the three branches, its rulings touch on major political issues that affect Americans in many ways. Here, Mark Janus (left) celebrates with supporters after winning his Supreme Court case, which could have a profound effect on how unions operate.

lawsuit challenged a 1977 case, *Abood v. Detroit Board of Education*, in which the Court allowed state and local governments to require public employees to pay union fees, a practice in 22 states. The Court almost overturned *Abood* in 2015 in a case in which a California teacher sued the local teachers' union over such fees. But after Justice Antonin Scalia died in February 2016, the Court split 4–4 in the California case.[2]

After taking office in 2017, Trump nominated conservative appeals court judge Neil Gorsuch to the vacant seat. With the Gorsuch appointment, conservatives once again enjoyed a 5–4 Supreme

Court majority. Perhaps not surprisingly, the Gorsuch appointment resulted in a conservative decision in *Janus v. AFSCME*, and Janus's First Amendment rights would be upheld. But union supporters say the decision will have devastating effects on public-sector unions' ability to protect workers, including female, African American, and Hispanic employees, who face a smaller gap in pay in union jobs compared to nonunion jobs, according to the Economic Policy Institute and the National Women's Law Center.[3]

For both Democrats and Republicans, the importance of the Supreme Court's 5–4 decision underscored the significance of President Trump's Supreme

Court appointments. Had Obama nominee Merrick Garland, rather than Trump nominee Neil Gorsuch, been seated on the High Court, the mandatory-dues requirement would likely have been upheld. With the *Janus* decision in mind, Democrats and Republicans prepared to redouble their efforts to win subsequent battles over judicial appointments, as President Trump announced the nomination of Brett Kavanaugh, another conservative judge, to take the place of Justice Anthony Kennedy, who announced his retirement in July 2018. After a divisive political battle, Kavanaugh was confirmed by the Senate and joined the Court in October.

Every year, nearly 25 million cases are tried in American courts. Cases can arise from disputes between citizens, from efforts by government agencies to punish wrongdoing, from citizens' efforts to prove that their rights have been infringed on as a result of government action—or inaction—and from efforts by interest groups to promote their agendas. Many critics of the U.S. legal system assert that Americans have become too litigious (ready to use the courts for all purposes). But the heavy use that Americans make of the courts is also an indication of the extent of conflict in American society. And given the existence of social conflict, it is far better that Americans seek to settle their differences through the courts than resort to violence or otherwise take matters into their own hands. The framers of the Constitution called the Supreme Court the "least dangerous branch" of American government. Today, though, it is not unusual to hear the Court described as an all-powerful "imperial judiciary." But before we can understand this transformation and its consequences, we must look in some detail at America's judicial process.

CHAPTER GOALS

★ Identify the general types of cases and types of courts in our legal system (pp. 593–97)

★ Describe the different levels of federal courts and their functions (pp. 598–603)

★ Explain how the Supreme Court exercises the power of judicial review (pp. 604–10)

★ Describe the process the Supreme Court follows in the exercise of its power of judicial review (pp. 610–18)

★ Consider the personal and political influences on judges and the courts (pp. 618–24)

The Legal System

Identify the general types of cases and types of courts in our legal system

Originally, a "court" was the place where a sovereign ruled—where the king or queen governed. Settling disputes between citizens was part of governing. In modern democracies, courts and judges have taken over the power to settle conflicts by hearing the facts on both sides and deciding which side possesses the greater merit. But since judges are not kings and queens, they must have a basis for their authority. That basis in the United States is the Constitution and the law. Courts decide cases by hearing the facts on both sides of a quarrel and applying the relevant law or principle to the facts. This can be a sensitive matter because courts have been given the authority to settle disputes not only between citizens but also between citizens and the government itself, where the courts are obliged to maintain the same neutrality and impartiality as they do in disputes involving two citizens. This is the essence of the "rule of law": that "the state" and its officials must be judged by the same laws as the citizenry.

CASES AND THE LAW

Court cases in the United States proceed under two broad categories of law: criminal law and civil law, each with myriad subdivisions.

Cases of **criminal law** are those in which the government charges an individual with violating a statute that has been enacted to protect public health, safety, morals, or welfare. In criminal cases, the government is always the **plaintiff** (the party that brings charges) and alleges that a criminal violation has been committed by a named **defendant.** Most criminal cases arise in state and municipal courts and involve matters ranging from traffic offenses to robbery and murder. Although the great bulk of criminal law is still a state matter, a large and growing body of federal criminal law deals with matters ranging from tax evasion and mail fraud to acts of terrorism and

criminal law the branch of law that regulates the conduct of individuals, defines crimes, and specifies punishment for proscribed conduct

plaintiff the individual or organization that brings a complaint in court

defendant the one against whom a complaint is brought in a criminal or civil case

In criminal cases, the government charges an individual with violating a statute protecting health, safety, morals, or welfare. Most such cases arise in state and municipal courts. Here, an Illinois county court hears testimony in a murder case.

the sale of narcotics. Defendants found guilty of criminal violations may be fined or sent to jail or prison.

Cases of **civil law** involve disputes among individuals, groups, corporations, and other private entities or between such litigants and the government, in which no criminal violation is charged. Unlike in criminal cases, the losers in civil cases cannot be fined or incarcerated, although they may be required to pay monetary damages for their actions. The two most common types of civil cases involve contracts and torts. In a typical contract case, an individual or corporation charges that it has suffered because of another's violation of a specific agreement between the two. For example, the Smith Manufacturing Corporation may charge that Jones Distributors failed to honor an agreement to deliver raw materials at a specified time, causing Smith to lose business. Smith asks the court to order Jones to compensate it for the damage it allegedly suffered. In a typical tort case, one individual charges that he has been injured by another's negligence or malfeasance. Medical malpractice suits are one example of tort cases. Another important area of civil law is administrative law, which involves disputes over the jurisdiction, procedures, or authority of administrative agencies. A plaintiff may assert, for example, that an agency did not follow proper procedures when issuing new rules and regulations. A court will then examine the agency's conduct in light of the Administrative Procedure Act, the legislation that governs agency rule making.

In deciding cases, courts apply statutes (laws) and legal **precedents** (prior decisions). State and federal statutes, for example, often govern the conditions under which contracts are and are not legally binding. Jones Distributors might argue that it was not obliged to fulfill its contract with the Smith Manufacturing Corporation because actions by Smith, such as the failure to make promised payments, constituted fraud under state law. Precedents established in previous cases also guide courts' decisions in new cases. Attorneys for a physician being sued for malpractice might search for prior instances in which courts ruled that actions similar to those of their client did not constitute negligence. Such precedents are applied under the doctrine of **stare decisis**, a Latin phrase meaning "let the decision stand."

If a case involves the actions of the federal government or a state government, a court may also be asked to examine whether the government's conduct was consistent with the Constitution. In a criminal case, for example, defendants might assert that their constitutional rights were violated when the police searched their property. Similarly, in a civil case involving federal or state restrictions on land development, plaintiffs might assert that government actions violated the Fifth Amendment's prohibition against taking private property without just compensation. Thus, both civil and criminal cases may raise questions of constitutional law.

TYPES OF COURTS

In the United States, systems of courts have been established both by the federal government and by the governments of the individual states. Both systems have several levels, as shown in Figure 15.1. More than 97 percent of all court cases in the United States are heard in state courts. The overwhelming majority of criminal cases, for example, involve violations of state laws prohibiting such actions as murder, robbery, fraud, theft, and assault. If such a case is brought to trial, it will be heard at a state **trial court**, in front of a judge and sometimes a jury, who will determine whether the defendant violated state law. If the defendant is convicted, she may appeal the conviction to a higher court, such as a state **court of appeals**, and from there to a court

civil law the branch of law that deals with disputes that do not involve criminal penalties

precedent prior case whose principles are used by judges as the basis for their decision in a present case

stare decisis literally, "let the decision stand"; the doctrine that a previous decision by a court applies as a precedent in similar cases until that decision is overruled

trial court the first court to hear a criminal or civil case

court of appeals a court that hears appeals of trial court decisions

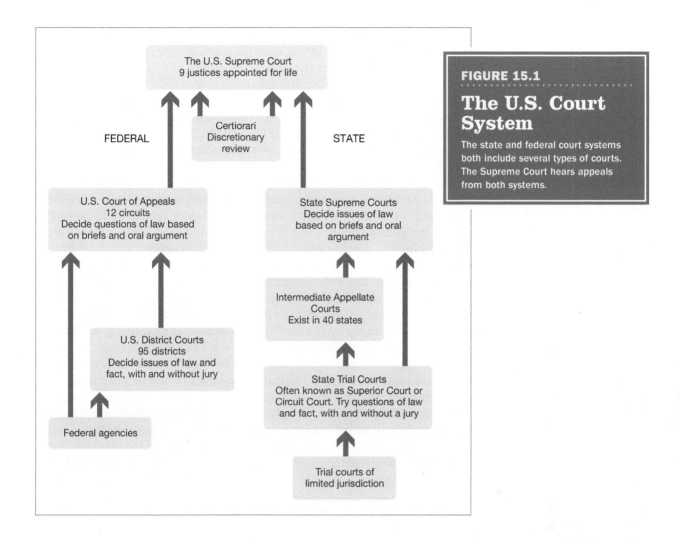

FIGURE 15.1

The U.S. Court System

The state and federal court systems both include several types of courts. The Supreme Court hears appeals from both systems.

The U.S. Supreme Court
9 justices appointed for life

FEDERAL

Certiorari Discretionary review

STATE

U.S. Court of Appeals
12 circuits
Decide questions of law based on briefs and oral argument

State Supreme Courts
Decide issues of law based on briefs and oral argument

Intermediate Appellate Courts
Exist in 40 states

U.S. District Courts
95 districts
Decide issues of law and fact, with and without jury

State Trial Courts
Often known as Superior Court or Circuit Court. Try questions of law and fact, with and without a jury

Federal agencies

Trial courts of limited jurisdiction

---

of last resort, usually called the state's **supreme court**. The government is not entitled to appeal if the defendant is found not guilty in a criminal case.

The party filing an appeal, known as an *appellant*, usually must show that the trial court made a legal error in deciding the case. Appeals courts do not hear witnesses or examine additional evidence and will consider new facts only under unusual circumstances. Thus, for example, a physician who loses a malpractice case might appeal on the basis that the trial court misapplied the relevant law or incorrectly instructed the jury. It should be noted that in both criminal and civil matters most cases are settled before trial through negotiated agreements between the parties. In criminal cases these agreements are called **plea bargains**.

Cases are heard in the federal courts if they involve federal laws, treaties with other nations, or the U.S. Constitution; these areas are the official **jurisdiction** of the federal courts. In addition, any case in which the U.S. government is a party is heard in the federal courts. If, for example, an individual is charged with violating a federal criminal statute, such as evading the payment of income taxes, charges are brought before a federal judge by a federal prosecutor. Civil cases involving the citizens of more than one state and in which more than $75,000 is at stake may be heard in either the federal or the state courts, usually depending on the preference of the plaintiff.

supreme court the highest court in a particular state or in the United States; this court primarily serves an appellate function

plea bargain a negotiated agreement in a criminal case in which a defendant agrees to plead guilty in return for the state's agreement to reduce the severity of the criminal charge or prison sentence the defendant is facing

jurisdiction the sphere of a court's power and authority

But even if a matter belongs in federal court, how do we know which federal court should exercise jurisdiction over the case? For the most part, Congress has assigned jurisdictions on the basis of geography. The nation is currently, by statute, divided into 94 judicial districts. Each of the 94 U.S. district courts, including one court for each of three U.S. territories, exercises jurisdiction over federal cases arising within its district. The judicial districts are, in turn, organized into 11 regional circuits and the D.C. circuit (see Figure 15.2). Each circuit court exercises appellate jurisdiction over cases heard by the district courts within its region.

original jurisdiction the authority to initially consider a case; distinguished from appellate jurisdiction, which is the authority to hear appeals from a lower court's decision

Article III of the Constitution gives the Supreme Court **original jurisdiction** in a limited variety of classes, including (1) cases between the United States and one of the 50 states, (2) cases between two or more states, (3) cases involving foreign ambassadors or other ministers, and (4) cases brought by one state against citizens of another state or against a foreign country. Article III assigns original jurisdiction in all other federal cases to the lower courts that Congress was authorized to establish. Importantly, the Constitution gives the Supreme Court appellate jurisdiction in all federal cases, and almost all cases heard by the Supreme Court today are under its appellate jurisdiction. Courts of original jurisdiction are the courts that are responsible for discovering the facts in a controversy and creating the record on which a judgment is based. In courts that have appellate jurisdiction, judges receive cases after the factual record is established by the trial court. Ordinarily, new facts cannot be presented before appellate courts.

Geography, however, is not the only basis for federal court jurisdiction. Congress has also established several specialized courts that have nationwide original jurisdiction in certain types of cases. These include the U.S. Court of International Trade, created to deal with trade and customs issues; and the U.S. Court of Federal Claims,

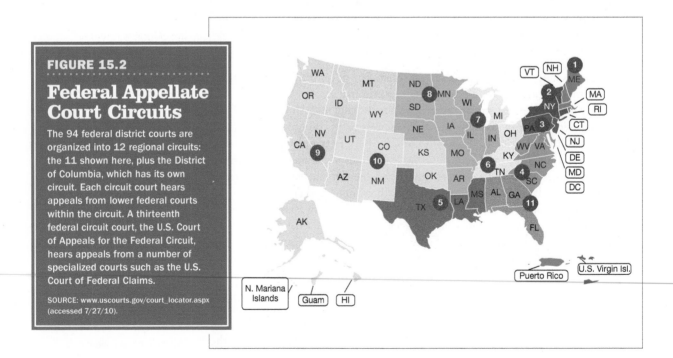

FIGURE 15.2

Federal Appellate Court Circuits

The 94 federal district courts are organized into 12 regional circuits: the 11 shown here, plus the District of Columbia, which has its own circuit. Each circuit court hears appeals from lower federal courts within the circuit. A thirteenth federal circuit court, the U.S. Court of Appeals for the Federal Circuit, hears appeals from a number of specialized courts such as the U.S. Court of Federal Claims.

SOURCE: www.uscourts.gov/court_locator.aspx (accessed 7/27/10).

which handles damage suits against the United States. Congress has also established a court with nationwide appellate jurisdiction, the U.S. Court of Appeals for the Federal Circuit, which hears appeals involving patent law and those arising from the decisions of the trade and claims courts. Other federal courts assigned specialized jurisdictions by Congress include the U.S. Court of Appeals for Veterans Claims, which exercises exclusive jurisdiction over cases involving veterans' claims, and the U.S. Court of Military Appeals, which deals with questions of law arising from trials by court-martial.

With the exception of the claims court and the Court of Appeals for the Federal Circuit, these specialized courts were created by Congress on the basis of the powers the legislature exercises under Article I, rather than Article III, of the Constitution. Article III is designed to protect judges from political pressure by granting them life tenure and prohibiting reduction of their salaries while they serve. The judges of Article I courts, by contrast, are appointed by the president for fixed terms of 15 years and are not protected by the Constitution from salary reduction. As a result, these "legislative courts" are generally viewed as less independent than the courts established under Article III of the Constitution. The three territorial courts (for Guam, the U.S. Virgin Islands, and the Northern Mariana Islands) were also established under the provisions in Article I, and their judges are appointed for 10-year terms.

The appellate jurisdiction of the federal courts extends to cases originating in the state courts. In both civil and criminal cases, a decision of the highest state court can be appealed to the U.S. Supreme Court by raising a federal issue. A defendant who appeals a lower-court decision in federal court might assert, for example, that he or she was denied the right to counsel or was otherwise deprived of the **due process of law** guaranteed by the federal Constitution or that important issues of federal law were at stake in the case. The U.S. Supreme Court is not obligated to accept such appeals and will do so only if it believes that the matter has considerable national significance. In addition, in criminal cases, defendants who have been convicted in a state court may request a **writ of habeas corpus** from a federal district court. Sometimes known as the "Great Writ," habeas corpus is a court order to the authorities to show cause for a prisoner's incarceration. The court will then evaluate the sufficiency of the cause and may order the release of a prisoner deemed to be held in violation of her legal rights. In 1867 its distrust of southern courts led Congress to authorize federal district judges to issue such writs to prisoners who they believed had been deprived of constitutional rights in state court. Generally speaking, state defendants seeking a federal writ of habeas corpus must show that they have exhausted all available state remedies and must raise issues not previously raised in their state appeals. Federal courts of appeals and, ultimately, the U.S. Supreme Court have appellate jurisdiction for federal district court habeas decisions.

Although the federal courts hear only a small fraction of all the civil and criminal cases decided each year in the United States, their decisions are extremely important. It is in the federal courts that the Constitution and federal laws that govern all Americans are interpreted and their meaning and significance established. Moreover, it is in the federal courts that the powers and limitations of the increasingly powerful national government are tested. Finally, through their power to review the decisions of the state courts, it is ultimately the federal courts that dominate the American judicial system.

due process of law the right of every individual against arbitrary action by national or state governments

writ of habeas corpus a court order that the individual in custody be brought into court and shown the cause for detention; habeas corpus is guaranteed by the Constitution and can be suspended only in cases of rebellion or invasion

Federal Courts

During the year ending in March 2017, federal district courts (the lowest federal level) received 362,628 cases. Though large, this number is less than 1 percent of the number of cases heard by state courts (see Figure 15.3). The federal courts of appeal listened to 58,951 cases during the same period. Generally, about 15 percent of the verdicts rendered by the lower courts are appealed to the U.S. Supreme Court. Most of the 9,000 or so cases filed with the Supreme Court each year are dismissed without a ruling on their merits. The Court has broad latitude to decide what cases it will hear and generally listens to

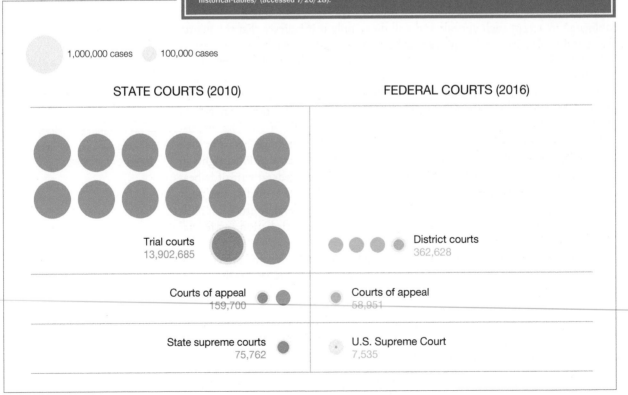

FIGURE 15.3

Caseloads of American Courts

This figure shows the total incoming caseloads of U.S. courts in 2016 (the most recent year for which complete state court data are available is 2010). More than 97 percent of the cases heard in American courts every year are heard in state courts. At both the federal and the state levels, lower-court decisions can be appealed to the appropriate court of appeals. Why do you think a larger percentage of federal district court decisions are appealed compared with state trial court decisions?

SOURCES: Court Statistics Project, National Center for State Courts, www.courtstatistics.org/; Supreme Court, 2017 Year-End Report on the Federal Judiciary, www.supremecourt.gov/publicinfo/year-end/2017year-endreport.pdf White House Office of Management and Budget, Historical Tables, Table 3.1, https://www.whitehouse.gov/omb/historical-tables/ (accessed 7/20/18).

1,000,000 cases   100,000 cases

STATE COURTS (2010)

FEDERAL COURTS (2016)

Trial courts
13,902,685

District courts
362,628

Courts of appeal
159,700

Courts of appeal
58,951

State supreme courts
75,762

U.S. Supreme Court
7,535

only those cases it deems raise the most important issues. In recent years, fewer than 80 cases per year have received full-dress Supreme Court reviews.[4]

FEDERAL TRIAL COURTS

Most of the cases of original federal jurisdiction are handled by the federal district courts. Although the Constitution gives the Supreme Court original jurisdiction in several types of cases, such as those affecting ambassadors and those in which a state is one of the parties, most original jurisdiction goes to the lowest courts—the trial courts.

Congress has authorized the appointment of 678 federal district judges to staff the 94 federal district courts. At any given time, some of these positions may be vacant and awaiting the appointment of new judges. District judges are assigned to district courts according to the workload; the busiest of these courts may have as many as 28 judges. Only one judge is assigned to each case, except where statutes provide for three-judge courts to deal with special issues. The routines and procedures of the federal district courts are essentially the same as those of the state trial courts except that federal procedural requirements tend to be stricter. States, for example, do not have to provide a grand jury, a 12-member trial jury, or a unanimous jury verdict. Federal courts must follow all these procedures.

FEDERAL APPELLATE COURTS

Roughly 20 percent of all lower-court cases, along with appeals from some federal agency decisions, are subsequently reviewed by federal appeals courts. As noted earlier, the country is divided geographically into 11 regional circuits and the D.C. circuit, each of which has a U.S. Court of Appeals. A thirteenth appellate court, the U.S. Court of Appeals for the Federal Circuit, has a subject matter, rather than a geographical, jurisdiction. Congress has authorized the appointment of 179 court of appeals judges, though, as in the case of the district courts, some spots may be vacant at any given point in time.

Except for cases selected for review by the Supreme Court, decisions made by the appeals courts are final. Because of this finality, certain safeguards have been built into the system. The most important is the provision of more than one judge for every appeals case. Each court of appeals has from 6 to 28 permanent judgeships, depending on the workload of the circuit. Although normally three judges hear appealed cases, in some instances a larger number of judges sit together en banc.

Another safeguard is provided by the assignment of a Supreme Court justice as the circuit justice for each of the 12 circuits. The circuit justice deals with requests for special action by the Supreme Court. The most frequent and best-known action of circuit justices is that of reviewing requests for stays of execution when the full Court is unable to do so—primarily during the summer, when the Court is in recess.

THE SUPREME COURT

The Supreme Court is America's highest court. Article III of the Constitution vests "the judicial power of the United States" in the Supreme Court, and this court is supreme in fact as well as form. The Supreme Court is the only federal court established by the Constitution. The lower federal courts are created by statute and can be restructured or, presumably, even abolished by the Congress. The Supreme Court

chief justice justice on the
Supreme Court who presides over
the Court's public sessions and
whose official title is "chief justice
of the United States"

is made up of the chief justice of the United States and eight associate justices. The **chief justice** presides over the Court's public sessions and conferences and is always the first to speak and vote when the justices deliberate; voting then proceeds in order of seniority. In the Court's actual deliberations and decisions, the chief justice has no more authority than his colleagues. Each justice casts one vote. In addition, if the chief justice has voted with the majority, she decides which of the justices will write the formal opinion for the Court. The character of the opinion can be an important means of influencing the evolution of the law beyond the mere affirmation or denial of the appeal on hand. To some extent, the influence of the chief justice is a function of her own leadership ability. Some chief justices, such as the late Earl Warren, have been able to lead the Court in a new direction. In other instances, forceful associate justices, such as the late Felix Frankfurter or William Brennan, are the dominant figures on the Court.

The Constitution does not specify the number of justices who should sit on the Supreme Court; Congress has the authority to change the Court's size. In the early nineteenth century, there were six Supreme Court justices; later there were seven. Congress set the number of justices at nine in 1869, and the Court has remained that size ever since.

HOW JUDGES ARE APPOINTED

Federal judges are nominated by the president and confirmed by the Senate. They are generally selected from among the more prominent or politically active members of the legal profession. Many federal judges previously served as state court judges or state or local prosecutors.

There are no formal qualifications for service as a federal judge. In general, presidents endeavor to appoint judges who possess legal experience and good character and whose partisan and ideological views are similar to their own. Once the president has formally nominated an individual, the nominee must be considered by the Senate Judiciary Committee and confirmed by a majority vote in the full Senate. In recent years, a good deal of partisan conflict has surrounded judicial appointments. Senate Democrats have sought to prevent Republican presidents from appointing conservative judges, while Senate Republicans have worked to prevent Democratic presidents from appointing liberal judges. During the early months of the Obama administration, Republicans were able to slow the judicial appointment process through filibusters and other procedural maneuvers so that only 3 of the president's 23 nominations for federal judgeships were confirmed by the Senate.[5] Some of Obama's allies urged the president to take a more aggressive stance or risk allowing Republicans to block what had been considered a key Democratic priority. In November 2013 the Senate voted 52 to 48 to end the use of the filibuster against all executive branch and judicial nominees except those to the Supreme Court, allowing President Obama to quickly secure the appointment of more than 300 new district court judges and 55 new appeals court judges.

In 2017, as we saw earlier, Republicans turned the tables and extended these rule changes to include Supreme Court nominees, thus blocking Democratic efforts to prevent President Trump from appointing Neil Gorsuch to the High Court. In July 2018, Justice Anthony Kennedy, who had been a swing vote on the Court, announced his resignation. President Trump nominated Judge Brett Kavanaugh to replace Kennedy. Kavanaugh was generally seen as a conservative in the Gorsuch mold. Liberal groups promised an all-out fight to block the nomination but, with Republican control of the Senate and the elimination of filibusters on judicial appointments, there was little chance Democrats could derail the Kavanaugh appointment.

Supreme Court Appointments While political factors play an important role in the selection of district and appellate court judges, they are decisive when it comes to Supreme Court appointments. Because the high court has so much influence over American law and politics, virtually all presidents have made an effort to select justices who share their political philosophies.

Five of the nine current justices, as of October 2018, were appointed by Republican presidents (Table 15.1). With the exception of the months between the passing of Antonin Scalia in February 2016 and the confirmation of Neil Gorsuch in April 2017, the Court has had a conservative majority for 46 years, most recently consisting of Chief Justice Roberts and justices Alito, Thomas, Gorsuch, and Kavanaugh. As we saw in earlier chapters, this majority propelled the Court in a more conservative direction in a variety of areas, including civil rights (Chapter 5) and election law (Chapter 10).

In recent decades, Supreme Court nominations have come to involve intense partisan struggle. Typically, after the president has named a nominee, interest

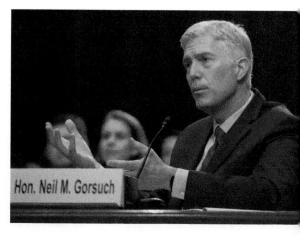

Hon. Neil M. Gorsuch

Senate Republicans' strategy to not take up Obama's nomination of Merrick Garland, and to eliminate filibusters on Supreme Court nominations, paid off when President Trump nominated Neil Gorsuch in 2017. Gorsuch was confirmed in a 54-to-45 vote, with several Senate Democrats voting for the Republican nominee.

TABLE 15.1

Supreme Court Justices, 2019* (in Order of Seniority)

NAME	YEAR OF BIRTH	LAW SCHOOL ATTENDED	PRIOR EXPERIENCE	APPOINTED BY	YEAR OF APPOINTMENT
Clarence Thomas	1948	Yale	Federal judge	G. H. W. Bush	1991
Ruth Bader Ginsburg	1933	Columbia	Federal judge	Clinton	1993
Stephen Breyer	1938	Harvard	Federal judge	Clinton	1994
John Roberts, Jr. (Chief Justice)	1955	Harvard	Federal judge	G. W. Bush	2005
Samuel Alito	1950	Yale	Federal judge	G. W. Bush	2006
Sonia Sotomayor	1954	Yale	Federal judge	Obama	2009
Elena Kagan	1960	Harvard	Solicitor general	Obama	2010
Neil Gorsuch	1967	Harvard	Federal judge	Trump	2017
Brett Kavanaugh	1965	Yale	Federal judge	Trump	2018

*As of October 2018

After Justice Anthony Kennedy announced his retirement in 2018, Trump nominated Brett Kavanaugh to the Supreme Court. After a contentious confirmation process, Kavanaugh took his seat on the Court. Many feel that Kavanaugh will shift the Court in a more conservative direction.

groups opposed to the nomination mobilize opposition in the media, among the public, and in the Senate. One bitter struggle occurred in 1987 when President Ronald Reagan nominated Robert Bork to the Supreme Court. Bork had been a Yale law professor, a federal judge, and Solicitor General of the United States. Despite this distinguished record, liberal political forces were very concerned about Bork's conservative views and angrily recalled that it was Bork who, as Solicitor General, had done Richard Nixon's bidding and fired the Watergate special prosecutor in what went down in history as the "Saturday Night Massacre." Senate Democrats subjected Bork to a relentless grilling, using excerpts from his speeches, writings, and judicial opinions to paint him as a right-wing extremist. The Bork nomination was defeated, and this type of attack came to be known as "borking" a nominee.

The next year, when President George H. W. Bush proposed the conservative judge Clarence Thomas for the Court, liberal groups launched a campaign to discredit Thomas, promising to bork him as well. After extensive research into his background, opponents of the nomination were able to produce evidence suggesting that Thomas had sexually harassed a former subordinate, Anita Hill. Thomas denied the charge. After contentious Senate Judiciary Committee hearings, highlighted by testimony from both Thomas and Hill, Thomas narrowly won confirmation.

Republicans severely criticized Obama's nomination of Sonia Sotomayor in 2009 and Elena Kagan in 2010, though both were ultimately confirmed by the Senate. In 2016, however, the death of conservative justice Antonin Scalia gave President Obama an opportunity to replace Scalia with a more liberal jurist, and Obama named Judge Merrick Garland. Republicans held a majority in the Senate and, as we saw earlier, refused to act on Garland. In 2017 newly elected President Trump secured the appointment of a conservative jurist, Neil Gorsuch.

Senate Democrats vowed to filibuster the Gorsuch appointment. Republicans, however, used their Senate majority to change the rules and prevent such a filibuster. In so doing, the GOP followed and extended a playbook that had been developed by the Democrats when they held a Senate majority. In 2018, President Trump nominated Judge Brett Kavanaugh to replace retiring Justice Anthony Kennedy. Kavanaugh promised to push the Court a bit further to the political right.

The Kavanaugh nomination touched off one of the most intense political struggles in recent American history. Days before the Senate was to vote, Christine Blasey Ford, who had known Kavanaugh in high school, came forward to assert that the judge had attempted to sexually assault her 36 years ago when he was 17 and she was 15. Kavanaugh vehemently denied the accusation as well as accusations of sexual impropriety by two other women who had known him in college. Televised testimony before the Senate Judiciary Committee by Kavanaugh and Ford divided the Senate and the nation, primarily along partisan lines. Democrats argued that Kavanaugh was unfit to serve on the Court while Republicans asserted that the charges against Kavanaugh had been invented for political reasons. An FBI investigation failed to shed light on the allegations, and Kavanaugh was confirmed, receiving the votes of all but one Republican and only one Democrat.[6]

Who Are Federal Judges?

ne factor among many that presidents may take into account when selecting judicial nominees is diversity. The number
f Supreme Court justices is relatively small, so it is easy to count the number of African Americans who have served as
upreme Court justices (2), female justices (4), and Hispanic justices (1). How diverse is the rest of the federal judiciary?
he first section below shows the racial, ethnic, and gender composition of the lower federal courts.

ederal Judges in 2018,* by Race and Gender *As of March 2018

 = 10 federal judges

ite men 781

African American men 90

Hispanic men 62

Asian American men 17

ite women 259

African American women 48

Hispanic women 27

Asian American women 10

ppointments to Federal Courts, by Administration

- White men
- White women
- African American men
- African American women
- Hispanic men
- Hispanic women
- Asian American men
- Asian American women

CARTER   REAGAN   G.H.W. BUSH   CLINTON   G.W. BUSH   OBAMA   TRUMP

171 — 310 — 138 — 195, 83 — 215, 50, 16 — 119, 89, 34, 26, 23, 13, 11 — 21

33
30
15
6 27
1 1 13
2 1

5 2 31
5 9
3

5 15
4 18
1

8 18
3 12
1

9

2 5

1

FOR CRITICAL ANALYSIS

1. Would you describe the federal judiciary as diverse? Does racial, ethnic, and gender diversity of federal judges matter? Why or why not?

2. What similarities and differences do you notice among the judicial appointments of the presidents shown? What might account for the differences in terms of the diversity of their appointees?

The Power of the Supreme Court: Judicial Review

judicial review the power of the courts to review and, if necessary, declare actions of the legislative and executive branches invalid or unconstitutional; the Supreme Court asserted this power in *Marbury v. Madison* (1803)

> **Explain how the Supreme Court exercises the power of judicial review**

The term **judicial review** refers to the power of the judiciary to examine and, if necessary, invalidate actions undertaken by the legislative and executive branches if it finds them unconstitutional. The term is sometimes also used to describe the scrutiny that appellate courts give to the actions of trial courts, but, strictly speaking, this is an improper use. A higher court's examination of a lower court's decisions might be called "appellate review," but it is not judicial review.

JUDICIAL REVIEW OF ACTS OF CONGRESS

Because the Constitution does not give the Supreme Court the power of judicial review over congressional enactments, the Court's exercise of it seems like something of a usurpation. Judicial review was discussed at the Constitutional Convention. Some delegates expected the courts to exercise this power, while many others were "departmentalists," believing that each branch of the new government would interpret the Constitution as it applied to its own actions, with the judiciary mainly ensuring that individuals did not suffer injustices.

Ambiguity over the framers' intentions was settled in 1803 in the case of *Marbury v. Madison*.[7] This case arose after Thomas Jefferson replaced John Adams in the White House. Jefferson's secretary of state, James Madison, refused to deliver an official commission to William Marbury, who had been appointed to a minor office by Adams and approved by the Senate just before Adams left the presidency. Marbury petitioned the Supreme Court to order Madison to deliver the commission. Jefferson and his followers did not believe that the Court had the power to undertake such an action and might have resisted the order. Chief Justice John Marshall was determined to assert the power of the judiciary but knew he must avoid a direct confrontation with the president. Accordingly, Marshall turned down Marbury's petition but gave as his reason the unconstitutionality of the legislation upon which Marbury had based his claim. Thus, Marshall asserted the power of judicial review but did so in a way that would not provoke a battle with Jefferson. The Supreme Court's decision in this case established the power of judicial review:

> It is emphatically the province and duty of the Judicial Department [the judicial branch] to say what the law is. Those who apply the rule to particular cases must, of necessity, expound and interpret that rule. If two laws conflict with each other, the Courts must decide on the operation of each.... So, if a law [e.g., a statute or treaty] be in opposition to the Constitution, if both the law and the Constitution apply to a particular case, so that the Court must either decide that case conformably to the law, disregarding the Constitution, or conformably to the Constitution, disregarding the law, the Court must determine which of these conflicting rules governs the case. This is of the very essence of judicial duty.

The Court's legal power to review acts of Congress has not been seriously questioned since 1803. One reason for that is that the Supreme Court makes a self-conscious effort to give acts of Congress an interpretation that will make them constitutional.

For example, in its 2012 decision upholding the constitutionality of the Affordable Care Act, the Court agreed with the many legal scholars who had argued that the Congress had no power under the Constitution's commerce clause to order Americans to purchase health insurance. But, rather than invalidate the act, the Court declared that the law's requirement that all Americans purchase insurance was actually a tax and, thus, represented a constitutionally acceptable use of Congress's power to levy taxes.[8]

In more than two centuries, the Court has concluded that fewer than 160 acts of Congress directly violated the Constitution.[9] These cases are often highly controversial. For example, in 2007 and 2014, the high court struck down key portions of the Bipartisan Campaign Reform Act, through which Congress had sought to regulate spending in political campaigns.[10] The Court found that provisions of the act limiting political advertising violated the First Amendment. And as we saw in Chapter 4 with the 2017 case of *Matal v. Tam*, the Court also cited free speech concerns in striking down a federal law that prohibited trademarks that disparaged people or groups. The decision was cheered by fans of the Washington Redskins football team. These cases are important but unusual in that the Court rarely overturns acts of Congress.

JUDICIAL REVIEW OF STATE ACTIONS

The power of the Supreme Court to review state legislation or other state action and to determine its constitutionality is neither granted by the Constitution nor inherent in the federal system. But the logic of the **supremacy clause** of Article VI of the Constitution, which declares the Constitution itself and laws made under its authority to be the supreme law of the land, is very strong. Furthermore, in the Judiciary Act of 1789, Congress conferred on the Supreme Court the power to reverse state constitutions and laws whenever they are clearly in conflict with the U.S. Constitution, federal laws, or treaties.[11] This power gives the Supreme Court appellate jurisdiction over all the millions of cases that American courts handle each year.

The supremacy clause of the Constitution not only established the federal Constitution, statutes, and treaties as the "supreme Law of the Land" but also provided that "the Judges in every State shall be bound thereby, any Thing in the Constitution or Laws of the State to the Contrary notwithstanding." Under this authority, the Supreme Court has frequently overturned state constitutional provisions or statutes, state court decisions, and local ordinances it deems to contravene rights or privileges guaranteed under the federal Constitution or federal statutes.

The civil rights arena abounds with examples of state laws that the Supreme Court has overturned because the statutes violated guarantees of due process and equal protection contained in the Fourteenth Amendment to the Constitution. For example, in the 1954 case of *Brown v. Board of Education*, the Court overturned statutes from Kansas, South Carolina, Virginia, and Delaware that either required or permitted segregated public schools, ruling that such statutes denied black schoolchildren equal protection under the law.[12] In 2003 the Court ruled that Texas's law criminalizing sodomy violated the right to liberty protected by the due process clause.[13] In the 2017 case of *Pavan v. Smith*, the Court overturned an Arkansas law that denied same-sex couples the right to include a spouse's name on a birth certificate—a right granted to other couples. The Court said the statute denied same-sex couples equal protection of the law.[14]

supremacy clause Article VI of the Constitution, which states that laws passed by the national government and all treaties are the supreme law of the land and superior to all laws adopted by any state or any subdivision

Term Limits for High Court Justices

Once appointed, Supreme Court justices "shall hold their Offices during good Behaviour,"[a] which has effectively meant they serve for life. Only once (in 1804) has the Senate started impeachment proceedings against a Supreme Court justice, and this judge was ultimately acquitted.[b]

While the founding fathers may have created life terms with the intention of preserving judicial independence and isolating justices from partisan pressures, the life term limits may have created other political problems. Scholars point out that the extreme partisan nature and tensions that emerge during Supreme Court appointment hearings (as described in this chapter) may be due to the life term rule.[c] After all, appointing a justice favorable to your partisan position is considered a major political coup given that the average Supreme Court justice serves over 25 years.

Constitutional courts (courts with the power of judicial review) aim to preserve judicial independence as they play an important role in guaranteeing democracy by checking executive overreach. Other countries, however, have sought to balance this with the need of also having a more dynamic and changing court. Canada, for instance, sets a mandatory retirement age of 75 for their Supreme Court justices. Other countries have set term limits so that justices serve one long, non-renewable term. This system insulates justices from political pressures yet still promotes judicial turnover. If the United States used the same rules as Germany (see below), only 3 of the 9 current justices—Sotomayor, Kagan, and the recently appointed Gorsuch—would still be on the court.

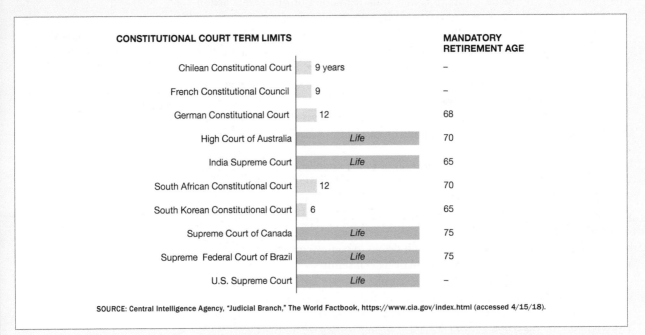

CONSTITUTIONAL COURT TERM LIMITS		MANDATORY RETIREMENT AGE
Chilean Constitutional Court	9 years	–
French Constitutional Council	9	–
German Constitutional Court	12	68
High Court of Australia	Life	70
India Supreme Court	Life	65
South African Constitutional Court	12	70
South Korean Constitutional Court	6	65
Supreme Court of Canada	Life	75
Supreme Federal Court of Brazil	Life	75
U.S. Supreme Court	Life	–

SOURCE: Central Intelligence Agency, "Judicial Branch," The World Factbook, https://www.cia.gov/index.html (accessed 4/15/18).

[a] U.S. Constitution, Article III, Section 1.
[b] U.S. Senate, "Senate Prepares for Impeachment Trial," www.senate.gov/artandhistory/history/minute/Senate_Tries_Justice.htm (accessed 4/15/18).
[c] Steven G. Calabresi and James Lindgren, "Term Limits for the Supreme Court: Life Tenure Reconsidered," *Harvard Journal of Law & Public Policy*, 29, no. 3 (2005): 769–878.

State statutes in other areas of law are equally subject to challenge. Many of the Supreme Court's recent decisions overturning state law have come in cases concerning election law. In 2015, for example, the Court ruled against an Alabama legislative districting plan that opponents charged was designed to reduce the influence of black voters.[15] During the same year the Court ruled against an effort by the Arizona legislature to invalidate a districting plan drawn up by an independent commission created by a voter referendum.[16] In the 2017 case of *Cooper v. Harris*, the Court invalidated a North Carolina legislative districting plan that moved tens of thousands of black voters into congressional districts that already had large black majorities.[17] This tactic is known as "packing," and is designed to reduce the number of seats that might be affected by some group of voters by packing them all into as few districts as possible.

One realm in which the Court constantly monitors state conduct is that of law enforcement. As we saw in Chapter 4, over the years, the Supreme Court has developed a number of principles regulating police conduct to ensure that the police do not violate constitutional liberties. These principles, however, must often be updated to keep pace with changes in technology. In a 2012 decision, the Supreme Court found that police use of a GPS tracker—a device invented more than two centuries after the adoption of the Bill of Rights—constituted a "search" as defined by the Fourth Amendment.[18] And in the 2014 case of *Riley v. California*, the Court held that the police could not undertake a warrantless search of the digital contents of a cell phone—another device hardly imagined by the framers.[19]

The Supreme Court has the power to review state action. In *Pavan v. Smith*, the Supreme Court overturned Arkansas's law that disallowed same-sex parents to have both of their names listed on their children's birth certificates. Here, Marisa Pavan, the plaintiff in the case, holds her daughter and her birth certificate showing both parents' names.

JUDICIAL REVIEW OF FEDERAL AGENCY ACTIONS

Although Congress makes the law, as we saw in Chapters 12 and 14, it can hardly administer the thousands of programs it has enacted and must therefore delegate power to the president and to a huge bureaucracy to achieve its purposes. For example, if Congress wishes to improve air quality, it cannot possibly anticipate all the conditions and circumstances that may arise with respect to that general goal. Inevitably, Congress must delegate to the executive substantial discretionary power to make judgments about the best ways to bring about improved air quality in the face of changing circumstances. Thus, over the years, almost any congressional program will result in thousands upon thousands of pages of administrative regulations developed by executive agencies nominally seeking to implement the will of the Congress.

Delegation of power to the executive poses a number of problems for Congress and the federal courts. If Congress delegates broad authority to the president, it risks seeing its goals subordinated to and subverted by those of the executive branch.[20] If Congress attempts to limit executive discretion by enacting precise rules and standards to govern the conduct of the president and the executive branch, it risks writing laws that do not conform to real-world conditions and that are too rigid to be adapted to changing circumstances.[21]

Over the past two centuries, the issue of delegation of power has led to a number of court decisions regarding the scope of the delegation. Courts have also been called on to decide whether the regulations adopted by federal agencies are consistent with Congress's express or implied intent.

As presidential power expanded during the New Deal era, one indication of increased congressional subordination to the executive was the enactment of laws that contained few, if any, principles limiting executive discretion. Congress enacted legislation, often at the president's behest, that gave the executive virtually unfettered authority to address a particular concern. For example, the Emergency Price Control Act of 1942 authorized the executive to set "fair and equitable" prices without spelling out what those terms might mean.[22] Although the Court initially challenged these delegations of power to the president during the New Deal, it retreated from its position when faced with a confrontation with President Franklin Delano Roosevelt. Perhaps as a result, no congressional delegation of power to the president since then has been struck down as impermissibly broad. Particularly in recent years, the Supreme Court has found that so long as federal agencies developed rules and regulations "based upon a permissible construction" or "reasonable interpretation" of Congress's statute, the judiciary would accept the views of the executive branch. Generally, the courts also give considerable deference to administrative agencies as long as those agencies engage in a formal rule-making process as prescribed by the various statutes governing agency rule making.

JUDICIAL REVIEW AND PRESIDENTIAL POWER

The federal courts are also called on to review the actions of the president. On many occasions, members of Congress as well as individuals and groups have challenged presidential orders and actions in the federal courts. In recent years, the federal bench has, more often than not, upheld assertions of presidential power in such realms as foreign policy, war and emergency powers, legislative power, and administrative authority. In June 2004, however, the Supreme Court ruled on three cases involving President George W. Bush's antiterrorism initiatives and claims of executive power and in two of the three cases appeared to place some limits on presidential authority.

One important case was *Hamdi v. Rumsfeld*.[23] Yaser Esam Hamdi, apparently a Taliban soldier, was captured by American forces in Afghanistan and brought to the United States, where he was incarcerated at the Norfolk Naval Station. Hamdi was classified as an enemy combatant and denied civil rights, including the right to counsel, despite the fact that he had been born in Louisiana and held American citizenship. In June 2004 the Supreme Court ruled that Hamdi was entitled to a lawyer and "a fair opportunity to rebut the government's factual assertions." Thus the Supreme Court did assert that presidential actions were subject to judicial scrutiny and that the Court could place some constraints on the president's power. But at the same time the Court affirmed the president's single most important claim: the unilateral power to declare individuals, including U.S. citizens, "enemy combatants," who could be detained by federal authorities under adverse legal circumstances. Several of the justices intimated that once designated an enemy combatant, a U.S. citizen might be tried before a military tribunal, without the normal presumption of innocence.

In the 2006 case of *Hamdan v. Rumsfeld*,[24] Salim Hamdan, a Taliban fighter, was captured in Afghanistan and held at the Guantánamo Bay naval base. The Bush administration planned to try Hamdan before a military commission authorized by a 2002 presidential order. The Supreme Court ruled that the commissions created by the president planned to use procedures that would violate federal law and U.S. treaty obligations. President Bush responded by demanding that Congress rewrite the law. Congress quickly obliged and enacted the Military Commissions

The courts may be called on to review the actions of the president. After President Trump's "travel ban" was implemented in early 2017, many court cases challenged this decision, and eventually one case was tried before the Supreme Court. In a 5–4 decision, the Court upheld the travel ban, sparking outrage from Democratic lawmakers.

Act, which gave the president statutory authority for his actions. In Section 7 of the act, Congress declared that Guantánamo prisoners could not bring habeas corpus petitions to federal courts to seek their release. In the 2008 case of *Boumediene v. Bush,* however, the Supreme Court struck down Section 7 and declared habeas corpus to be a fundamental right.[25] Judicial review of presidential actions is not limited to presidential war powers and the realm of terrorism. In 2013 the Fourth U.S. Circuit Court of Appeals ruled that President Obama violated the Constitution when he made so-called recess appointments to the National Labor Relations Board in order to avoid the need to secure Senate confirmation. Recess appointments are customarily used only when the Senate adjourns at the end of the year, but the president made the appointments in question when the Senate was on a short break. In June 2014 the Supreme Court ruled that a Senate recess of less than 10 days was "presumptively too short" to justify a recess appointment. In this case, the Senate had recessed for only 3 days.[26]

In its 2018 decision in the case of *Trump v. Hawaii,* however, the Court upheld the use of presidential power.[27] Through an executive order, President Trump had prohibited travel into the United States by people from several Muslim-majority countries. In a 5–4 decision, the Court held that the president had broad authority, given by statute, to determine that certain travelers might impose a risk to the security of the United States.

JUDICIAL REVIEW AND LAWMAKING

Much of the work of the courts involves the application of statutes to the particular case at hand. Over the centuries, judges have also developed a body of rules and principles of interpretation that are not grounded in specific statutes. This body of judge-made law is called **common law.** For example, **tort case,** which determines whether one person is liable for causing harm to another, is based more upon cases and precedents than statute.

FOR CRITICAL ANALYSIS

During his 2005 confirmation hearings, senators asked Chief Justice Roberts why the Supreme Court was more willing to declare acts of Congress unconstitutional than it was to confront the president on the constitutionality of his actions. What reasons might you identify?

common law law made through court precedent rather than legislative enactments

tort case a lawsuit by one individual (the plaintiff) demanding compensation for harm allegedly caused by the actions of another (the defendant)

The appellate courts, however, are in another realm. Their rulings can be considered laws, but they govern the behavior only of the judiciary. The written opinion of an appellate court is about halfway between common law and statutory law. As in common law, the opinion is judge-made and draws heavily on the precedents of previous cases. But, as in statutory law, it tries to articulate the rule of law controlling the case in question and future cases like it. It differs from a statute in that a statute addresses itself to the future conduct of citizens, whereas a written opinion addresses itself mainly to the future willingness or ability of courts to take cases and render favorable opinions. Decisions by appellate courts affect citizens by opening or closing access to the courts.

The Supreme Court in Action

Describe the process the Supreme Court follows in the exercise of its power of judicial review

Given the millions of disputes that arise every year, the job of the Supreme Court would be impossible if it were not able to control the flow of cases and its own caseload. Over the years, the courts have developed specific rules that govern which cases within their jurisdiction they will and will not hear. In order to be heard by the courts, cases must meet certain criteria that are initially applied by the trial court but may be reconsidered by appellate courts. These rules of access can be broken down into three major categories: case or controversy, standing, and mootness.

Article III of the Constitution and Supreme Court decisions define judicial power as extending only to "cases and controversies." This means that the case before a court must be an actual controversy, not a hypothetical one, with two truly adversarial parties. The courts have interpreted this language to mean that they do not have the power to render advisory opinions to legislatures or agencies about the constitutionality of proposed laws or regulations. Furthermore, even after a law is enacted, the courts will generally refuse to consider its constitutionality until it is actually applied.

standing the right of an individual or organization to initiate a court case, on the basis of having a substantial stake in the outcome

Parties to a case must also have **standing**—that is, they must show that they have a substantial stake in the outcome of the case. The traditional requirement for standing has been to show injury to oneself; that injury can be personal, economic, or even aesthetic, such as a neighbor's building a high fence that blocks one's view of the ocean. In order for a group or class of people to have standing (as in class-action suits), each member must show specific injury. This means that a general interest in the environment, for instance, does not provide a group with sufficient basis for standing.

mootness a criterion used by courts to screen cases that no longer require resolution

The Supreme Court also uses a third criterion in determining whether it will hear a case: that of **mootness**. In theory, this requirement disqualifies cases that are brought too late—after the relevant facts have changed or the problem has been resolved by other means. The criterion of mootness, however, is subject to the discretion of the courts, which have begun to relax the rules of mootness, particularly in cases where a situation that has been resolved is likely to come up again. In the abortion case *Roe v. Wade*, for example, the Supreme Court rejected the lower court's argument that because the pregnancy in question had already come to term, the case was moot. The Court agreed to hear the case because no pregnancy was likely to outlast the lengthy appeals process.[28] Related to mootness but less frequently cited is the idea of *ripeness*, which means the readiness of a case for litigation. The courts try to avoid becoming entangled in issues that remain hypothetical or events that may never occur.

Putting aside the formal criteria, the Supreme Court is most likely to accept cases that involve conflicting decisions by the federal circuit courts, cases that present important questions of civil rights or civil liberties, and cases in which the federal government is the appellant. Ultimately, however, the question of which cases to accept can come down to the preferences and priorities of the justices. If a group of justices believes that the Court should intervene in a particular area of policy or politics, they are likely to look for a case or cases that will serve as vehicles for judicial intervention. For many years, the Court was not interested in considering challenges to affirmative action or other programs designed to provide particular benefits to minorities. In recent years, however, several of the Court's more conservative justices have been eager to push back the limits of affirmative action and racial preference and have therefore accepted a number of cases that would allow them to do so. In the 2014 case *Schuette v. Coalition to Defend Affirmative Action*, for example, the Court ruled that a Michigan ballot initiative that resulted in a ban on racial preferences in college admissions was constitutional.[29] The decision paved the way for other states to prohibit the use of race as a factor in college admissions. In the 2016 case of *Fisher v. University of Texas*, however, the Court ruled that race could be one of the factors taken into account in college admissions if the school so desired.[30]

Writs Most cases reach the Supreme Court through a **writ of certiorari**. Certiorari is an order to a lower court to deliver the records of a particular case to be reviewed for legal errors. The term *certiorari* is sometimes shortened to *cert*, and cases deemed to merit certiorari are referred to as "certworthy." An individual who loses in a lower federal court or state court and wants the Supreme Court to review the decision has 90 days to file a petition for a writ of certiorari with the clerk of the U.S. Supreme Court. Petitions for thousands of cases are filed with the Court every year (see Figure 15.4).

Since 1972 most of the justices have participated in a "certiorari pool" in which their law clerks work together to evaluate the petitions. Each petition is reviewed by one clerk, who writes a memo for all the justices participating in the pool, summarizing the facts and issues and making a recommendation. Clerks for the other justices add their comments to the memo. After the justices have reviewed the memos, any one of them may place any case on the "discuss list," which is circulated by the chief justice. If a case is not placed on the discuss list, it is automatically denied certiorari. Cases placed on the discuss list are considered and voted on during the justices' closed-door conference.

For certiorari to be granted, four justices must be convinced that the case satisfies rule 10 of the Rules of the Supreme Court of the United States. Rule 10 states that certiorari is not a matter of right but is to be granted only when there are special and compelling reasons. These include conflicting decisions by two or more circuit courts, conflicts between circuit courts and state courts of last resort, conflicting decisions by two or more state courts of last resort, decisions by circuit courts on matters of federal law that should be settled by the Supreme Court, and a circuit court decision on an important question that conflicts with Supreme Court decisions. It should be clear from this list that the Court will usually take action under only the most compelling circumstances—when there are conflicts among the lower courts about what the law should be, when an important legal question has been raised in the lower courts but not definitively answered, or when a lower court

writ of certiorari a decision of at least four of the nine Supreme Court justices to review a decision of a lower court; *certiorari* is Latin, meaning "to make more certain"

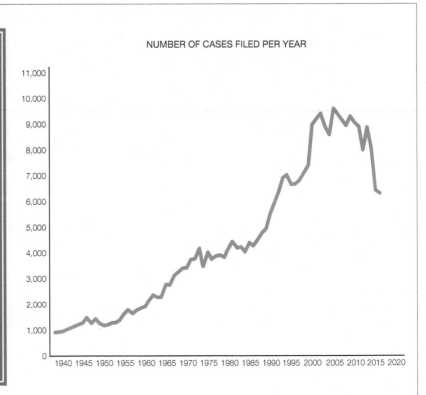

FIGURE 15.4

Cases Filed in the U.S. Supreme Court, 1938–2017 Terms*

*Number of cases filed in term starting in year indicated.

SOURCES: Years 1938–69, 1970–83, 1984–99: reprinted with permission from *The United States Law Week* (Washington, DC: Bureau of National Affairs), vol. 56, no. 3102; vol. 59, no. 3064; vol. 61, no. 3098; vol. 63, no. 3134; vol. 65, no. 3100; vol. 67, no. 3167; vol. 69, no. 3134 (copyright © Bureau of National Affairs Inc.); 2000–05 U.S. Bureau of the Census, *Statistical Abstract of the United States*; 2006–07: Office of the Clerk, Supreme Court of the United States; and Supreme Court of the United States, Cases on Docket, www.uscourts. gov/statistics-reports/caseload-statistics-data-tables; Supreme Court, 2017 Year-End Report on the Federal Judiciary, www.supremecourt. gov/publicinfo/year-end/2017year-endreport. pdf (accessed 4/5/18).

NUMBER OF CASES FILED PER YEAR

solicitor general the top government lawyer in all cases before the Supreme Court where the government is a party

Mr. Noel J. Francisco

Before becoming solicitor general in the Trump administration, Noel Francisco has had experience in the Justice Department and in private practice, where he argued several cases in front of the Supreme Court.

deviates from the principles and precedents established by the high court. Few cases are able to gain the support of four justices needed for certiorari. In recent sessions, although thousands of petitions were filed, the Court has granted certiorari to barely more than 80 petitioners each year—about 1 percent of those seeking a Supreme Court review.

A handful of cases reach the Supreme Court through avenues other than certiorari. One of these is the writ of certification, which can be used when a U.S. court of appeals asks the Supreme Court for instructions on a point of law that has never been decided. A second alternative avenue is the writ of appeal, which is used to appeal the decision of a three-judge district court.

CONTROLLING THE FLOW OF CASES

In addition to the judges, other actors play important roles in shaping the flow of cases through the federal courts: the solicitor general and federal law clerks.

The Solicitor General If any single person has greater influence than individual judges over the federal courts, it is the **solicitor general** of the United States. The solicitor general is the third-ranking official in the Justice Department (below the attorney general and the deputy attorney general) but the top government lawyer in virtually all cases before the Supreme Court in which the government is a party. The solicitor general has the greatest control over the flow of cases; his or her actions are not reviewed by any higher authority in the executive branch. More than half the Supreme Court's total workload consists of cases under the direct charge of the solicitor general.

The solicitor general exercises especially strong influence by screening cases before any agency of the federal government can appeal them to the Supreme Court.[31] Agency heads may lobby the president or otherwise try to circumvent the solicitor general, and a few of the independent agencies have a statutory right to make direct appeals; but without the solicitor general's support, these requests are seldom reviewed by the Court. Congress has given only a few agencies, including the Federal Communications Commission, the Federal Maritime Commission, and in some cases the Department of Agriculture (even though it is not an independent agency), the right to appeal directly to the Supreme Court without going through the solicitor general.

The solicitor general can enter a case even when the federal government is not a direct litigant by writing an **amicus curiae** ("friend of the court") brief. A friend of the court is not a direct party to a case but has a vital interest in its outcome. Thus, when the government has such an interest, the solicitor general can file an amicus brief or a federal court can invite such a brief because it wants an opinion in writing. Other interested parties may file briefs as well.

> **amicus curiae** literally, "friend of the court"; individuals or groups who are not parties to a lawsuit but who seek to assist the Supreme Court in reaching a decision by presenting additional briefs

In addition to exercising substantial control over the flow of cases, the solicitor general can shape the arguments used before the federal courts. Indeed, the Supreme Court tends to give special attention to the way the solicitor general characterizes the issues. The solicitor general is the person who appears most frequently before the Court and, theoretically at least, is the most disinterested. The credibility of the solicitor general is not hurt when several times each year he comes to the Court to withdraw a case with the admission that the government has made an error.

Law Clerks Every federal judge employs law clerks to research legal issues and assist with the preparation of opinions. Each Supreme Court justice is assigned four clerks, almost always honors graduates of the nation's most prestigious law schools. A clerkship with a Supreme Court justice is a great honor and generally indicates

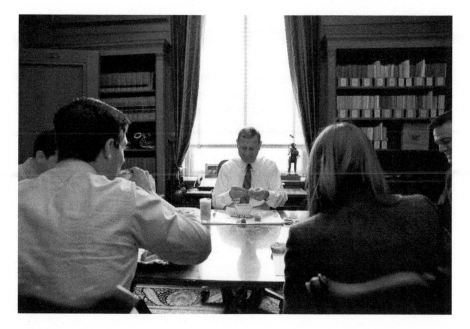

Federal judges, including Supreme Court justices, rely on their clerks for research and help in preparing opinions. Serving as a law clerk to a Supreme Court justice is a prestigious position. Four current justices—Roberts, Breyer, Kagan, and Gorsuch (pictured here)—clerked for a Supreme Court justice early in their careers.

that the fortunate individual is likely to reach the very top of the legal profession. The work of the Supreme Court clerks is a closely guarded secret, but it is likely that some justices rely heavily on their clerks for advice in writing opinions and in deciding whether the Court should hear specific cases. In a recent book, a former law clerk to the late justice Harry Blackmun charged that Supreme Court justices yielded "excessive power to immature, ideologically driven clerks, who in turn use that power to manipulate their bosses."[32]

LOBBYING FOR ACCESS: INTERESTS AND THE COURT

At the same time that the Court exercises discretion over which cases it will review, groups and forces in society often seek to persuade the justices to listen to their problems. Lawyers representing interest groups try to choose the proper client and the proper case so that the issues in question are most dramatically and appropriately portrayed. When possible, they also pick a district or jurisdiction with a sympathetic judge in which to bring the case. Sometimes they even have to wait for an appropriate political climate. They must also attempt to develop a proper record at the trial court level, one that includes some constitutional arguments and even, when possible, errors on the part of the trial court.

One of the most effective strategies that litigants use in getting cases accepted for review by the appellate courts is to bring the same type of suit in more than one circuit (that is, to develop a "pattern of cases") in the hope that inconsistent treatment by two different courts will improve the chance of a Supreme Court review. The two most notable users of the pattern-of-cases strategy in recent years have been the National Association for the Advancement of Colored People (NAACP) and the American Civil Liberties Union (ACLU). For many years, the NAACP (and its Defense Fund—now a separate group) has worked through local chapters and with many individuals to encourage litigation on issues of racial discrimination and segregation. Sometimes it distributes petitions to be signed by parents and filed with local school boards and courts, deliberately sowing the seeds of future litigation. The NAACP and the ACLU often encourage private parties to bring suit and then join the suit as amici curiae.

In many states, it is considered unethical and illegal for attorneys to engage in "fomenting and soliciting legal business in which they are not parties and have no pecuniary right or liability." The NAACP was sued by the state of Virginia in the late 1950s in an attempt to restrict or eliminate its efforts to influence the pattern of cases. The Supreme Court reviewed the case in 1963, recognized that the strategy was being used, and held that the NAACP strategy was protected by the First and Fourteenth amendments, just as other forms of speech and petition are protected.[33]

Thus, many pathbreaking cases are eventually granted certiorari because repeated refusal to review one or more of them would amount to a rule of law just as much as if the courts had handed down a written opinion. In this sense, the flow of cases, especially the pattern of significant cases, influences the behavior of the appellate judiciary.

THE SUPREME COURT'S PROCEDURES

The Supreme Court's decision to accept a case is the beginning of what can be a lengthy and complex process (see Figure 15.5). After a petition is filed and certiorari is granted, the Court considers the reasoning on both sides as presented in

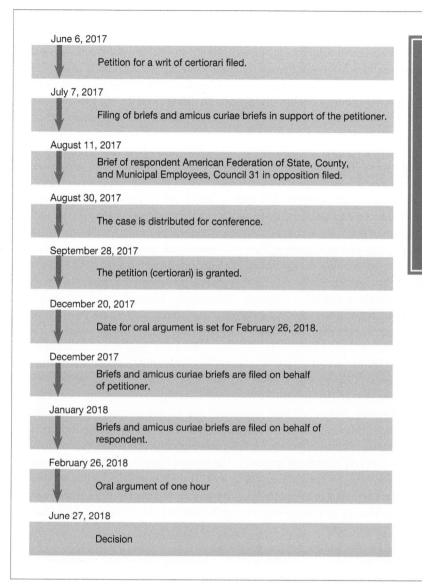

FIGURE 15.5

Time Line of a Supreme Court Case

This calendar of events in the case of *Janus v. American Federation of State, County, and Municipal Employees* illustrates the steps of the process a case goes through as it moves through the Supreme Court. The total time from petition to the Supreme Court to the decision is just over one year, although the initial case was filed years ago in a lower court.

June 6, 2017
Petition for a writ of certiorari filed.

July 7, 2017
Filing of briefs and amicus curiae briefs in support of the petitioner.

August 11, 2017
Brief of respondent American Federation of State, County, and Municipal Employees, Council 31 in opposition filed.

August 30, 2017
The case is distributed for conference.

September 28, 2017
The petition (certiorari) is granted.

December 20, 2017
Date for oral argument is set for February 26, 2018.

December 2017
Briefs and amicus curiae briefs are filed on behalf of petitioner.

January 2018
Briefs and amicus curiae briefs are filed on behalf of respondent.

February 26, 2018
Oral argument of one hour

June 27, 2018
Decision

briefs and oral argument, the justices discuss the case in conference, and opinions are carefully drafted.

Briefs First, the attorneys on both sides must prepare **briefs**, written documents in which the attorneys explain why the Court should rule in favor of their client. Briefs are filled with referrals to precedents specifically chosen to show that other courts have frequently ruled in the same way the attorneys are requesting that the Supreme Court rule. The attorneys for both sides muster the most compelling precedents they can in support of their arguments.

As the attorneys prepare their briefs, they often ask sympathetic interest groups for their help. These groups are asked to file amicus curiae briefs that support the claims of one or the other litigant. In a case involving separation of church and

briefs written documents in which attorneys explain, using case precedents, why the court should find in favor of their client state, for example, liberal groups such as the ACLU and People for the American Way are likely to be asked to file amicus briefs in support of strict separation, whereas conservative religious groups are likely to file amicus briefs advocating increased public accommodation of religious ideas. Often, dozens of briefs will be filed on each side of a major case. Amicus filings are one of the primary methods used by interest groups to lobby the Court. By filing these briefs, groups indicate to the Court where they stand and signal to the justices that they believe the case to be an important one.

Oral Argument The next stage of a case is **oral argument**, in which attorneys for both sides appear before the Court to present their positions and answer the justices' questions. Each attorney has only a half hour to present a case, and this time includes interruptions for questions. Certain members of the Court, such as the late Justice Antonin Scalia, are known to interrupt attorneys dozens of times. Others, such as Justice Clarence Thomas, seldom ask questions. For an attorney, the opportunity to argue a case before the Supreme Court is a singular honor and a mark of professional distinction. It can also be a harrowing experience, as when justices interrupt a carefully prepared presentation. Nevertheless, oral argument can be very important to the outcome of a case. It allows justices to understand better the heart of the case and to raise questions that might not have been addressed in the opposing sides' briefs. It is not uncommon for justices to go beyond the strictly legal issues and ask opposing counsel to discuss the implications of the case for the Court and the nation at large.

The Conference Following oral argument, the Court discusses the case in its Wednesday or Friday conference, a strictly private meeting that no outsiders are permitted to attend. The chief justice presides over the conference and speaks first; the other justices follow in order of seniority. The justices discuss the case and eventually reach a decision on the basis of a majority vote. If the Court is divided, a number of votes may be taken before a final decision is reached. As the case is discussed, justices may try to influence or change one another's opinions. At times, this may result in compromise decisions.

Opinion Writing After a decision has been reached, one of the members of the majority is assigned to write the **opinion**. This assignment is made by the chief justice or by the most senior justice in the majority if the chief justice is on the losing side. The assignment of the opinion can make a significant difference to the interpretation of a decision. Every opinion of the Supreme Court sets a major precedent for future cases throughout the judicial system. Lawyers and judges in the lower courts will examine the opinion carefully to ascertain the Supreme Court's intent. Differences in wording and emphasis can have important implications for future litigation. Thus, in assigning an opinion, the justices must give serious thought to the impression the case will make on lawyers and on the public and to the probability that one justice's opinion will be more widely accepted than another's.

One of the more dramatic instances of this tactical consideration occurred in 1944, when Chief Justice Harlan F. Stone chose Justice Felix Frankfurter to write the opinion in the "white primary" case *Smith v. Allwright*.[34] The chief justice believed that this sensitive case, which overturned the southern practice of prohibiting black participation in nominating primaries, required the efforts of the most brilliant and

oral argument the stage in the Supreme Court procedure in which attorneys for both sides appear before the Court to present their positions and answer questions posed by justices

opinion the written explanation of the Supreme Court's decision in a particular case

The Supreme Court allocates just one hour to hear oral arguments, even in difficult and contentious cases. Attorneys for both sides must make their arguments succinctly and respond to questions from the nine justices, which are often very pointed.

scholarly jurist on the Court. But the day after Stone made the assignment, Justice Robert H. Jackson wrote a letter to Stone urging a change of assignment and arguing that Frankfurter, a foreign-born Jew from New England, would not win the South with his opinion, regardless of its brilliance. Stone accepted the advice and substituted Justice Stanley Reed, an American-born Protestant from Kentucky and a southern Democrat in good standing.

Once the majority opinion is drafted, it is circulated to the other justices. Some members of the majority may agree with both the outcome and the rationale but wish to emphasize or highlight a particular point. For that purpose, they draft a concurring opinion, called a *regular concurrence*. In other instances, one or more justices may agree with the majority decision but disagree with the rationale presented in the majority opinion. These justices may draft *special concurrences*, explaining their own rationale for the decision and how it differs from the majority's rationale.

Dissent Justices who disagree with the majority decision of the Court may choose to publicize the character of their disagreement in the form of a **dissenting opinion**. The dissenting opinion is generally assigned by the senior justice among the dissenters. Dissents can be used to express irritation with an outcome or to signal to defeated political forces in the nation that their position is supported by at least some members of the Court. Ironically, the most dependable way an individual justice can exercise a direct and clear influence on the Court is to write a dissent. Because there is no need to please a majority, dissenting opinions can be more eloquent and less guarded than majority opinions. The current Supreme Court often produces 5–4 decisions, with dissenters writing long and detailed opinions that, they hope, will help them persuade a swing justice to join their side on the next round of cases dealing with a similar topic. During the Court's 2006–07 term, Justice Ruth Bader Ginsburg was so unhappy about the majority's decisions in a number of cases that she began to read forceful dissents from the bench, a practice she has continued

dissenting opinion a decision written by a justice in the minority in a particular case in which the justice wishes to express his or her reasoning in the case

Supreme Court justices can use a dissenting opinion to express their opposing viewpoint with the hope of influencing future cases on similar questions. Justice Ruth Bader Ginsburg is known for her forceful dissents such as in the 2014 Hobby Lobby case, which allowed a corporation to claim religious grounds for refusing to provide contraceptive coverage in its health insurance program.

to underscore her disagreements with several recent decisions and point the way toward other possibilities.

Dissent plays a special role in the work and impact of the Court because it amounts to an appeal to lawyers all over the country to keep bringing similar cases. Therefore, an effective dissent influences the flow of cases through the Court and the arguments that lawyers will use in later cases. Even more important, dissent points out that although the Court speaks with a single opinion, it is the opinion only of the majority—and one day the majority might go the other way.

Often, the division between the majority and the dissenting justices in major cases reflects deep divisions in American society. Take the 2015 same-sex marriage case of *Obergefell v. Hodges* in which the majority opinion, written by Justice Anthony Kennedy, asserted that state same-sex marriage bans violated the Fourteenth Amendment by arbitrarily intruding upon personal choices, "central to individual dignity and autonomy," and thus denying such persons due process and equal protection of the laws.[35] The dissenters, Chief Justice Roberts and Justices Alito, Scalia, and Thomas, declared that the Fourteenth Amendment had never been intended or interpreted as providing a right to same-sex marriage, and they criticized the majority opinion as little more than an effort by jurists to write their own views into the Constitution. In its split decision, the Court mirrored a division in American society between those who see gay rights as a natural extension of civil rights and those offended, often for religious reasons, by open expressions of same-sex partnership. The dissenting justices hope to encourage further litigation in this realm, but generally speaking, once a right is granted it is seldom subject to revocation.

Explaining Supreme Court Decisions

> **Consider the personal and political influences on judges and the courts**

The Supreme Court makes its mark on American politics and society through the decisions it hands down. But judicial decision-making does not take place in a vacuum, of course. Like other actors in government, justices are influenced by institutional concerns, prior experience, and personal philosophy. In addition, the Court as a whole is affected by the overarching political system in which it plays a role. Over time, that role has shifted as a result of political developments both inside and outside the Court.

INFLUENCES ON SUPREME COURT DECISION-MAKING

The Supreme Court explains its decisions in terms of law and precedent. But it is the Court itself that decides what the laws actually mean and what importance the precedent will actually have. Throughout its history, the Court has shaped and reshaped the law. In the late nineteenth and early twentieth centuries, for example, the Supreme Court held that the Constitution, law, and precedent permitted racial segregation in the United States. Beginning in the 1950s, however, the Court found that the Constitution prohibited segregation on the basis of race and indicated that the use of racial categories in legislation was always suspect. By the 1970s and '80s the Court once again held that the Constitution permitted the use of racial categories—when such categories were needed to help members of minority groups achieve full participation in American society. Since the 1990s the Court has retreated from this position, too, indicating that governmental efforts to provide extra help to racial minorities could represent an unconstitutional infringement on the rights of the majority.

Institutional Interests The Supreme Court's justices are acutely aware of the Court's place in history, and they care about protecting the Court's power and reputation. This desire to protect the institutional integrity of the Court can sometimes influence judicial thinking. During the 1930s, for example, the Supreme Court became embroiled in a political struggle with President Franklin Roosevelt over his "New Deal" programs. During the 1935–36 term, the Court struck down several of the president's initiatives in a series of 5–4 votes. Furious, the president responded by proposing a Court-reform plan that would have increased the size of the Court to as many as 15 justices. Roosevelt hoped to pack the Court with his own appointees and, thus, win future cases over New Deal programs. Justice Owen Roberts, who had been one of the five justices voting against the president's initiatives, made a sudden reversal, voting in favor of an important New Deal policy he had been expected to oppose. The media dubbed Roberts's shift "The switch in time that saved nine."

Such institutional concerns are not isolated incidents, however. More recently, Chief Justice John Roberts seemed to have institutional concerns in mind when he surprised fellow conservatives by casting the deciding vote in favor of the constitutionality of the Affordable Care Act in 2012. The Court's conservative majority had come under increasing political fire for its positions on such matters as campaign finance and affirmative action. Roberts, according to one commentator, saw himself as "uniquely entrusted with the custodianship of the Court's legitimacy, reputation, and stature" and was determined to show that the Court stood above mere political ideology.[36] As we saw above, Roberts repeated his support of the Affordable Care Act in 2015 in the case of *King v. Burwell*.

Activism and Restraint Judicial philosophy also plays a role in the decisions of all judges, including those on the Supreme Court. One element of judicial philosophy is the issue of activism versus restraint. Over the years, some justices have believed that courts should interpret the Constitution according to the stated intentions of its framers and defer to the views of Congress when interpreting federal statutes. Justice Felix Frankfurter, for example, advocated judicial deference to legislative bodies and avoidance of the "political thicket" in which the Court would entangle itself by deciding questions that were essentially political rather than legal in character. Some, but not all, advocates of **judicial restraint** are also called "strict constructionists" because they look strictly to the words of the Constitution in interpreting its meaning. The late Justice Scalia, along with Justice Thomas, Justice Gorsuch, and Justice Kavanaugh advocate originalism in interpreting the Constitution and textualism in interpreting statutes.

The alternative to restraint is **judicial activism**. Activist judges such as Chief Justice Earl Warren believed that the Court should go beyond the words of the Constitution or a statute to consider the broader societal implications of its decisions. Activist judges sometimes strike out in new directions, promulgating new interpretations or inventing new legal and constitutional concepts when they

judicial restraint judicial philosophy whose adherents refuse to go beyond the clear words of the Constitution in interpreting the document's meaning

judicial activism judicial philosophy that posits that the Court should go beyond the words of the Constitution or a statute to consider the broader societal implications of its decisions believe these to be socially desirable. For example, Justice Harry Blackmun's opinion in *Roe v. Wade* was based on a constitutional right to privacy that is not found in the words of the Constitution but was, rather, from the Court's prior decision in *Griswold v. Connecticut*.[37] Blackmun and the other members of the majority in the *Roe* case argued that the right to privacy was implied by other constitutional provisions. In this instance of judicial activism, the Court knew the result it wanted to achieve and was not afraid to make the law conform to the desired outcome.

Activism and restraint can overlap with but are not always the same as liberalism and conservatism. For example, conservative politicians often castigate "liberal activist" judges and call for the appointment of conservative jurists who will refrain from reinterpreting the law. But the Rehnquist Court, dominated by conservatives, was among the most activist courts in American history, particularly in such areas as federalism and election law. The Roberts Court is continuing along the same route. For example, in the 2014 case of *McCutcheon v. Federal Election Commission*, the Court struck down one of the major remaining elements of Congress's efforts to regulate campaign finance. The Court's five more conservative justices said that limits on how much individuals could contribute in any given election were a restraint on free speech.[38] This decision could be described as "activist" because it broadens the interpretation of "speech" and overturns congressional legislation that has significant public support. As the examples of these conservative courts illustrate, a judge may be philosophically conservative and believe in strict construction of the Constitution but also be jurisprudentially activist and believe that the courts must play an active and energetic role in policy making, if necessary striking down acts of Congress to ensure that the intent of the framers is fulfilled.

Political Ideology and Partisanship The philosophy of activism versus restraint is sometimes a smokescreen for political ideology, and indeed, the liberal or conservative attitudes or partisan leanings of justices play an important role in their decisions.[39] In the past, liberal judges have often been activists, willing to use the law to achieve social and political change, whereas conservatives have been associated with judicial restraint. Interestingly, however, in recent years some conservative justices who have long called for restraint have actually become activists in seeking to undo some of the work of liberal jurists.

From the 1950s to the 1980s the Supreme Court took an activist role in such areas as civil rights, civil liberties, abortion, voting rights, and police procedures. For example, the Supreme Court was more responsible than any other governmental institution for breaking down America's system of racial segregation. In the following decades, however, the conservative justices appointed by presidents Ronald Reagan, George H. W. Bush, and George W. Bush became the dominant bloc on the Court and, as we saw earlier, moved the Court to the right on a number of issues, including affirmative action and abortion.

The political struggles of recent years amply illustrate the importance of judicial ideology. Is abortion a fundamental right or a criminal activity? How much separation must there be between church and state? Does application of the Voting Rights Act to increase minority representation constitute a violation of the rights of whites? The answers to these and many other questions cannot be found in the words of the Constitution. They must be located, instead, in the hearts and minds of the judges who interpret that text.

Judicial philosophy, ideology, and institutional interest all influence the thinking of justices. In the end, however, the Supreme Court is a court of law and must pay heed to statutes and legal precedent. A decision that cannot be justified by law and precedent cannot be issued. To ignore the law would be to undermine the rule of law and to destroy the constitutional structure in which the Supreme Court occupies such a prominent place.

JUDICIAL POWER AND POLITICS

One of the most important institutional changes to occur in the United States during the past half-century has been the striking transformation of the role and power of the federal courts, and of the Supreme Court in particular. Understanding how this transformation came about is the key to understanding the contemporary role of the courts in America.

Traditional Limitations on the Federal Courts For much of American history, the power of the federal courts was subject to a number of limitations.[40] First, unlike other governmental institutions, courts cannot exercise power on their own initiative. Judges must wait until a case is brought to them before they can make authoritative decisions. Traditionally, moreover, courts were constrained by judicial rules of standing that limited access to the bench. Claimants who simply disagreed with governmental action or inaction could not obtain access to the courts, which was limited to individuals who could show that they were specifically affected by the government's behavior in some area. This limitation on access diminished the judiciary's capacity to forge links with important political and social forces.

Second, courts were traditionally limited in the character of the relief they could provide. In general, courts acted only to offer relief or assistance to individuals and not to broad social classes, again inhibiting the formation of alliances between the courts and important social forces.

Third, courts lacked enforcement powers of their own and were compelled to rely on executive or state agencies to ensure compliance with their edicts. If the executive or state agencies were unwilling to assist the courts, judicial enactments could go unheeded, as when President Andrew Jackson declined to enforce Chief Justice John Marshall's 1832 order to the state of Georgia to release two missionaries it had arrested on Cherokee lands. Marshall asserted that the state had no right to enter the lands without the Cherokees' assent.[41] Jackson is reputed to have said, "John Marshall has made his decision, now let him enforce it."

Fourth, federal judges are, of course, appointed by the president (with the consent of the Senate). As a result, the president and Congress can shape the composition of the federal courts and ultimately, perhaps, the character of judicial decisions. Finally, Congress has the power to change both the size and jurisdiction of the Supreme Court and other federal courts. In many areas, federal courts obtain their jurisdiction not from the Constitution but from congressional statutes. On a number of occasions, Congress has threatened to take matters out of the courts' hands when it was unhappy with the courts' policies.[42] For example, in 1996, Congress enacted several pieces of legislation designed to curb the jurisdiction of the federal courts. One of these laws was the Prison Litigation Reform Act, which limits the ability of federal judges to issue "consent decrees," under which the judges could take control of state prison systems. As to the size of the Court, on one memorable occasion that

Are the federal courts "imperial,"
or are they subordinate to the
elected branches of government?
In what respect does the federal
judiciary still play a "checks and
balances" role?

we mentioned earlier, presidential and congressional threats to expand the size of the Supreme Court—Franklin Delano Roosevelt's "Court packing" plan—encouraged the justices to drop their opposition to New Deal programs.

As a result of these limitations on judicial power, through much of their history the chief function of the federal courts was to provide judicial support for executive agencies and to legitimize acts of Congress by declaring them to be consistent with constitutional principles. Only on rare occasions have the federal courts dared to challenge Congress or the executive branch.[43]

Two Judicial Revolutions Since the Second World War, however, the role of the federal judiciary has been strengthened and expanded. There have been two judicial revolutions in the United States since then. The first and more visible of these was the substantive revolution in judicial policy. As we saw earlier in this chapter and in Chapters 4 and 5, in many policy areas, including school desegregation, legislative apportionment, and criminal procedure, and in obscenity, abortion, and voting rights, the Supreme Court was at the forefront of a series of sweeping changes in the role of the U.S. government and, ultimately, the character of American society.[44]

At the same time that the courts were introducing important policy innovations, they were also bringing about a second, less visible revolution. During the 1960s and '70s the Supreme Court and other federal courts instituted a series of changes in judicial procedures that fundamentally expanded the power of the courts in the United States.

First, the federal courts liberalized the concept of standing to permit almost any group that seeks to challenge the actions of an administrative agency to bring its case before the federal bench. In 1971, for example, the Supreme Court ruled that public interest groups could use the National Environmental Policy Act to challenge the actions of federal agencies by claiming that the agencies' activities might have adverse environmental consequences.[45]

Congress helped to make it even easier for groups dissatisfied with government policies to bring their cases to the courts by adopting Section 1983 of the U.S. Code, which permits the practice of "fee shifting"—that is, allowing citizens who successfully bring a suit against a public official for violating their constitutional rights to collect their attorneys' fees and costs from the government. Thus, Section 1983 encourages individuals and groups to bring their problems to the courts rather than to Congress or the executive branch. These changes have given the courts a far greater role in the administrative process than ever before. Many federal judges are concerned that federal legislation in areas such as health care reform will create new rights and entitlements that give rise to a deluge of court cases. "Any time you create a new right, you create a host of disputes and claims," warned Barbara Rothstein, chief judge of the federal district court in Seattle, Washington.[46]

Second, the federal courts broadened the scope of relief to permit themselves to act on behalf of broad categories or classes of persons in "class-action" cases, rather than just on behalf of individuals.[47] A **class-action suit** is a procedural device that permits large numbers of persons with common interests to join together under a representative party to bring or defend a lawsuit. One example of a class-action suit is the case of *In re Agent Orange Product Liability Litigation*, in which a federal judge in New York certified Vietnam War veterans as a class with standing to sue

class-action suit a legal action by which a group or class of individuals with common interests can file a suit on behalf of everyone who shares that interest a manufacturer of herbicides for damages allegedly incurred from exposure to the defendant's product while in Vietnam.[48] The class potentially numbered in the tens of thousands.

Third, the federal courts began to employ so-called structural remedies, in effect retaining jurisdiction of cases until the court's mandate had actually been implemented to its satisfaction.[49] The best known of these instances was the effort of federal judge W. Arthur Garrity, Jr., to operate the Boston school system from his bench in order to ensure its desegregation. Between 1974 and 1985, Judge Garrity issued 14 decisions relating to different aspects of the Boston school desegregation plan that had been developed under his authority and put into effect under his supervision.[50] In 1985, as a result of a suit brought by the NAACP five years earlier, federal judge Leonard B. Sand imposed fines that would have forced the city of Yonkers, New York, into bankruptcy if it had refused to accept his plan to build public housing in white neighborhoods. Twenty-two years and $1.6 million in fines later, the city finally gave in to the judge's ruling in 2007.

Through these three judicial mechanisms, the federal courts paved the way for an unprecedented expansion of national judicial power. In essence, liberalization of the rules of standing and expansion of the scope of judicial relief drew the federal courts into linkages with important social interests and classes, while the introduction of structural remedies enhanced the courts' ability to serve these constituencies. Thus, during the 1960s and '70s, the power of the federal courts expanded in the same way the power of the executive expanded during the 1930s: through links with

Today, the Supreme Court is frequently at the center of major political issues. In a historic decision in 2015, the Court declared same-sex marriage a fundamental right protected by the due process and equal protection clauses of the Fourteenth Amendment to the Constitution.

FOR CRITICAL ANALYSIS

In what ways are courts, judges, and justices shielded from politics and political pressure? In what ways are they vulnerable to political pressure? Are the courts an appropriate place for politics?

constituencies, such as civil rights, consumer, environmental, and feminist groups, that staunchly defended the Supreme Court in its battles with Congress, the executive, and other interest groups.

The Federal Judiciary
WHAT DO WE WANT?

In the original conception of the framers, the judiciary was to be the institution that would protect individual liberty from the government. As we saw in Chapter 2, the framers believed that in a democracy the great danger was what they termed "tyranny of the majority"—the possibility that a popular majority, "united or actuated by some common impulse or passion," would "trample on the rules of justice."[51] The framers hoped that the courts would protect liberty from the potential excesses of democracy. And for most of American history, the federal courts' most important decisions were those that protected the freedoms—to speak, worship, publish, vote, and attend school—of groups and individuals whose political views, religious beliefs, or racial or ethnic backgrounds made them unpopular.

Today, Americans of all political persuasions seem to view the courts as useful instruments through which to pursue their goals rather than as protectors of individual rights. Conservatives want to ban abortion and help business maintain its profitability, whereas liberals want to promote school integration and help enhance the power of workers in the workplace. (The "Who Participates?" feature on the facing page looks at efforts to influence the Supreme Court through amicus briefs.) These may all be noble goals, but they present a basic dilemma for students of American government. If the courts are simply one more set of policy-making institutions, who is left to protect the liberty of individuals?

The decisions made by the Supreme Court today will have important consequences for our lives and futures. The Court's campaign-finance decisions will have consequences for who will govern the nation you inherit. The Court's decisions on health care will influence the type of care you receive and its cost. The Court's decisions in the realm of immigration will affect who will and will not be able to call themselves Americans. The Court's decision in Mark Janus's case against public-sector unions could influence your future job and taxes. The Supreme Court is not an abstract entity in far-off Washington. It reaches directly into your life.

Influencing the Supreme Court?

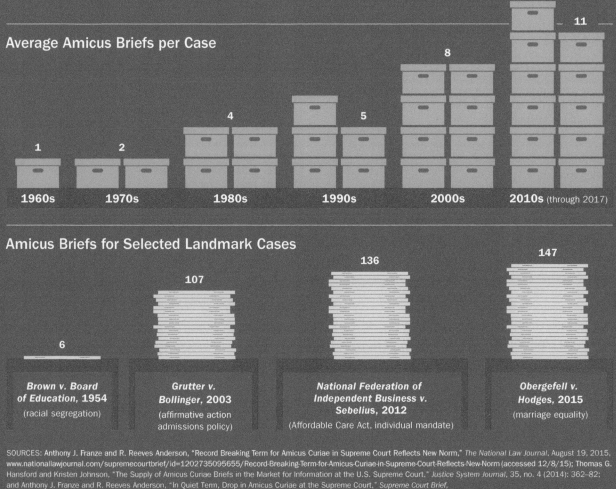

Average Amicus Briefs per Case

1 — 1960s

2 — 1970s

4 — 1980s

5 — 1990s

8 — 2000s

11 — 2010s (through 2017)

Amicus Briefs for Selected Landmark Cases

6 — *Brown v. Board of Education, 1954* (racial segregation)

107 — *Grutter v. Bollinger, 2003* (affirmative action admissions policy)

136 — *National Federation of Independent Business v. Sebelius, 2012* (Affordable Care Act, individual mandate)

147 — *Obergefell v. Hodges, 2015* (marriage equality)

SOURCES: Anthony J. Franze and R. Reeves Anderson, "Record Breaking Term for Amicus Curiae in Supreme Court Reflects New Norm," *The National Law Journal*, August 19, 2015, www.nationallawjournal.com/supremecourtbrief/id=1202735095655/Record-Breaking-Term-for-Amicus-Curiae-in-Supreme-Court-Reflects-New-Norm (accessed 12/8/15); Thomas G. Hansford and Kristen Johnson, "The Supply of Amicus Curiae Briefs in the Market for Information at the U.S. Supreme Court," *Justice System Journal*, 35, no. 4 (2014): 362–82; and Anthony J. Franze and R. Reeves Anderson, "In Quiet Term, Drop in Amicus Curiae at the Supreme Court," *Supreme Court Brief*, September 6, 2017, www.law.com (accessed 12/23/17).

★ WHAT YOU CAN DO ★

Look inside the Federal Courts

- [✓] Find which groups filed amicus briefs for U.S. Supreme Court cases at **www.scotusblog.com**, and read a few of the briefs.

- [✓] Click on the "Court Locator" tab at **www.uscourts.gov** to find which federal courts are near you and to view their calendar of oral arguments. Court dockets and some case files are available at **www.pacer.gov**.

- [✓] Watch videos of cases from the Cameras in Courts pilot project at **www.uscourts.gov/about-federal-courts/cameras-courts**.

The Legal System

American court cases proceed under two broad categories
of law: criminal law and civil law. There are court systems at
both the federal and state levels in the United States. While
state courts hear only cases involving questions of state
law, the federal courts decide cases addressing federal
laws, treaties with other nations, and the Constitution.

Key Terms

criminal law (p. 593)

plaintiff (p. 593)

defendant (p. 593)

civil law (p. 594)

precedent (p. 594)

stare decisis (p. 594)

trial court (p. 594)

court of appeals (p. 594)

supreme court (p. 595)

plea bargain (p. 595)

jurisdiction (p. 595)

original jurisdiction (p. 596)

due process of law (p. 597)

writ of habeas corpus (p. 597)

Practice Quiz

1. What is the name for the body of law that involves
   disputes between private entities such as individuals,
   groups, and corporations?
   a) civil law
   b) privacy law
   c) criminal law
   d) household law
   e) common law

2. The doctrine that previous court decisions should apply
   as precedents in similar cases is known as
   a) habeas corpus.
   b) a writ of certiorari.
   c) stare decisis.
   d) rule of four.
   e) senatorial courtesy.

3. Where do most trials in America take place?
   a) U.S. Court of Federal
   b) claims
   c) federal district courts
   d) federal circuit courts
   e) the Supreme Court of the United States

4. Which of the following is not included in the original
   jurisdiction of the Supreme Court?
   a) cases between the United States and one of
      the 50 states
   b) cases brought by one state against citizens of
      another state or against a foreign country
   c) cases involving challenges to the constitutionality
      of state laws
   d) cases between two or more states
   e) cases involving foreign ambassadors or other ministers

5. The term *writ of habeas corpus* refers to
   a) a short, unsigned decision by an appellate court,
      usually rejecting a petition to review the decision of
      a lower court.
   b) a criterion used by courts to screen cases that no
      longer require resolution.
   c) a decision of at least four of the nine Supreme
      Court justices to review a decision of a lower court.
   d) a court order that an individual in custody be brought
      into court and shown the cause for his or her detention.
   e) a brief filed by the solicitor general when the federal
      government is not a direct litigant in a Supreme
      Court case.

Federal Courts

The federal judiciary is composed of 94 district courts, 12
circuit courts, several specialized courts that have nationwide
original jurisdiction in certain types of cases, and the U.S.

Supreme Court. The federal courts hear a very small percentage
of the cases decided in the United States each year. Presidents typically nominate judges for the federal judiciary who
are prominent members of the legal profession and who share
their partisan and ideological views. The importance of appointments to the federal judiciary has made the confirmation
process in the Senate increasingly contentious in recent years.

6. The size of the Supreme Court is determined by
   a) the president.
   b) the chief justice.
   c) the Department of Justice.
   d) Congress.
   e) the Constitution.

7. The formal requirements for service as a federal judge include
   a) experience as a state-level judge.
   b) a minimum age of 30.
   c) a minimum of 10 years' legal experience.
   d) a neutral political background.
   e) There are no formal requirements for service as a federal judge.

The Power of the Supreme Court: Judicial Review

Explain how the Supreme Court exercises the power of judicial review (pp. 604–10)

The U.S. Supreme Court has the power to review the constitutionality of acts of Congress and the federal executive branch, as well as state actions. Although this power is not explicitly provided for in the Constitution, the Supreme Court asserted the power of judicial review in its 1803 *Marbury v. Madison* decision; and this power has generally been accepted since then.

Key Terms

judicial review (p. 604)

supremacy clause (p. 605)

common law (p. 609)

tort case (p. 609)

Practice Quiz

8. The Supreme Court's decision in *Marbury v. Madison* was important because
   a) it invalidated state laws prohibiting interracial marriage.
   b) it ruled that the recitation of prayers in public schools is unconstitutional under the establishment clause of the First Amendment.
   c) it established that arrested people have the right to remain silent, the right to be informed that anything they say can be held against them, and the right to counsel before and during police interrogation.
   d) it provided an expansive definition of *commerce* under the interstate commerce clause.
   e) it established the power of judicial review.

9. The U.S. Supreme Court's power to review state actions comes from
   a) tort law.
   b) *Hamdi v. Rumsfeld* and *Hamdan v. Rumsfeld*.
   c) the supremacy clause of the Constitution and the Judiciary Act of 1789.
   d) certiorari and amicus curiae.
   e) The Supreme Court does not have the power to review state actions.

The Supreme Court in Action

Describe the process the Supreme Court follows in the exercise of its power of judicial review (pp. 610–18)

Most cases reach the Supreme Court by a writ of certiorari. The Supreme Court is most likely to grant a writ of certiorari to cases that involve conflicting decisions by the federal circuit courts, cases that present important questions of civil rights or civil liberties, and cases in which the federal government is the appellant. Much of the Supreme Court's power in the American political system comes from its power to invalidate actions taken by the legislative and executive branches of government if these actions violate the Constitution.

Key Terms

standing (p. 610)

mootness (p. 610)

writ of certiorari (p. 611)

solicitor general (p. 612)

amicus curiae (p. 613)

briefs (p. 615)

oral argument (p. 616)

opinion (p. 616)

dissenting opinion (p. 617)

10. Which of the following is *not* included as a "special and compelling" reason to hear a case under Rule 10 of the Rules of the Supreme Court of the United States?
    a) the president of the United States authors an amicus curiae brief on the issue in question
    b) a circuit court decision on the issue in question conflicts with previous Supreme Court decisions
    c) there are conflicting decisions by two or more state courts of last resort on the issue in question
    d) there are conflicting decisions between circuit courts and state courts of last resort on the issue in question
    e) there are conflicting decisions by two or more circuit courts on the issue in question

11. Which of the following play an important role in shaping the flow of cases heard by the Supreme Court?
    a) the attorney general and the secretary of state
    b) the solicitor general and federal law clerks
    c) the president and Congress
    d) state legislatures
    e) the federal district and circuit courts

12. Which of the following is a brief submitted to the Supreme Court by someone other than one of the parties in the case?
    a) amicus curiae brief
    b) writ of habeas corpus
    c) writ of certiorari
    d) dissenting opinion
    e) de jure brief

Explaining Supreme Court Decisions

Consider the personal and political influences on judges and the courts (pp. 618–24)

Through most of American history, the federal courts avoided confrontations with the other branches of government and worked primarily to provide support for executive actions and congressional laws by declaring them to be consistent with constitutional principles. During the 1960s and '70s the federal courts liberalized the concept of standing, broadened the scope of relief courts could provide, and began to employ structural remedies. As a result of these changes, the power of the federal court system expanded dramatically.

Key Terms

judicial restraint (p. 619)
judicial activism (p. 619)
class-action suit (p. 622)

Practice Quiz

13. If a justice refuses to go beyond the clear words of the Constitution in interpreting the document's meaning, he or she would be considered an advocate of which judicial philosophy?
    a) judicial restraint
    b) judicial activism
    c) stare decisis
    d) judicial liberalism
    e) judicial conservatism

14. Which of the following procedures adopted by the federal courts after 1960 fundamentally expanded the power of the judiciary in the United States?
    a) banning the practice of "fee shifting"
    b) prohibiting the courts from acting on behalf of broad categories of persons in "class-action" cases
    c) expanding the concept of standing to permit almost any group that seeks to challenge the actions of an administrative agency to bring its case before the federal bench
    d) creating a "Department of Judicial Enforcement" to independently implement the federal judiciary's decisions
    e) granting federal courts the ability to exercise power on their own initiative through the issuance of "mootness" rulings

For Further Reading

Baum, Lawrence. *Ideology in the Supreme Court*. Princeton, NJ: Princeton University Press, 2017.

Baum, Lawrence. *The Supreme Court*. 12th ed. Washington, DC: CQ Press, 2015.

Block, Frederick. *Disrobed: An Inside Look at the Life and Work of a Federal Trial Judge*. New York: Westlaw, 2012.

Breyer, Stephen. *The Court and the World: American Law and the New Global Realities*. New York: Knopf, 2015.

Chermerinsky, Erwin. *Closing the Courthouse Door: How Your Constitutional Rights Became Unenforceable*. New Haven, CT: Yale University Press, 2017.

Cross, Frank. *Decision Making in the U.S. Courts of Appeals*. Stanford, CA: Stanford University Press, 2007.

Greenhouse, Linda. *The U.S. Supreme Court: A Very Short Introduction*. New York: Oxford University Press, 2012.

Hirshman, Linda. *Sisters in Law: How Sandra Day O'Connor and Ruth Bader Ginsburg Went to the Supreme Court and Changed the World*. New York: Harper, 2015.

Peppers, Todd, and Artemus Ward. *In Chambers: Stories of Supreme Court Law Clerks and Their Justices*. Charlottesville: University of Virginia Press, 2012.

Posner, Richard. *Reflections on Judging*. Cambridge, MA: Harvard University Press, 2013.

Posner, Richard A. *The Federal Judiciary: Strengths and Weaknesses*. Cambridge, MA: Harvard University Press, 2017.

Raskin, Jamin B. *We the Students: Supreme Court Decisions for and about Students*. Washington, DC: CQ Press, 2003.

Rosenberg, Gerald. *The Hollow Hope: Can Courts Bring about Social Change?* 2nd ed. Chicago: University of Chicago Press, 2008.

Rossum, Ralph. *Antonin Scalia's Jurisprudence*. Lawrence: University Press of Kansas, 2006.

Stevens, John Paul. *Five Chiefs: A Supreme Court Memoir*. Boston: Little, Brown, 2011.

Sunstein, Cass. *Are Judges Political?* Washington, DC: Brookings Institution Press, 2006.

Toobin, Jeffrey. *The Nine: Inside the Secret World of the Supreme Court*. New York: Anchor Books, 2008.

Toobin, Jeffrey. *The Oath: The Obama White House and the Supreme Court*. New York: Anchor Books, 2013.

Trachtman, Michael. *The Supreme Court's Greatest Hits: The 44 Supreme Court Cases That Most Directly Affect Your Life*. 3rd ed. New York: Sterling, 2016.

Tribe, Lawrence. *Uncertain Justice: The Roberts Court and the Constitution*. New York: Picador, 2015.

Urofsky, Melvin. *Dissent and the Supreme Court: Its Role in the Court's History and the Nation's Constitutional Dialogue*. New York: Pantheon, 2015.

Whittington, Keith. *Political Foundations of Judicial Supremacy: The President, the Supreme Court, and Constitutional Leadership in U.S. History*. Princeton, NJ: Princeton University Press, 2008.

Recommended Websites

Concourts
www.concourts.net
The U.S. Supreme Court has the responsibility for examining and interpreting the Constitution. The Concourts website assumes a comparative perspective and looks at systems of constitutional review in over 150 countries.

FindLaw
www.findlaw.com
FindLaw's website provides answers to most legal questions and helps individuals find legal counsel.

Justice Talking
www.justicetalking.org
Justice Talking is a public radio program that examines current legal issues and important court cases.

Legal Information Institute
www.law.cornell.edu
The Legal Information Institute at Cornell University is a wonderful website for conducting legal research.

Office of the Solicitor General
www.usdoj.gov/osg
The solicitor general conducts litigation on behalf of the U.S. Supreme Court and has a tremendous amount of control over the cases that it hears. See what cases are currently being considered by this powerful official of the Justice Department.

U.S. Courts
www.uscourts.gov
The U.S. court system consists of trial, appellate, and supreme courts. The U.S. Courts website provides a look at the different types of courts in the federal judiciary.

U.S. Supreme Court
www.supremecourtus.gov
The website for the U.S. Supreme Court provides information on recent decisions. Take a moment to read some oral arguments, briefs, or court opinions.

U.S. Supreme Court Media
www.oyez.org
The website for U.S. Supreme Court Media has a great search engine for finding information on such landmark cases as *Marbury v. Madison*, *Miranda v. Arizona*, and *Roe v. Wade*.

Government and the Economy

WHAT GOVERNMENT DOES AND WHY IT MATTERS Imagine that the beer from your craft brewery was declared one of the best in the world by a prominent consumer website. Also imagine that demand is so great that liquor stores in your home state have to impose a six-bottle ration per purchase. You would want to expand production, right? But for Three Floyds Brewing Co. of Munster, Indiana, that's not so easy. A 1935 alcohol distribution law, passed just as Prohibition was ending, created a middleman—distributors—between alcohol makers and retailers (most states have similar laws). The law was intended to be a "brake in the system, to avoid the unregulated flow of cheap and easily

available alcohol," according to the head of the Indiana Beverage Alliance, which represents the state's 25 wholesale beer distributors. It does advantage the state—and the distributors—by centralizing distribution and tax collection. But the problem for small brewers is that once they produce more than 30,000 barrels per year they can no longer self-distribute and must give up the tasting rooms and restaurants they say are necessary to compete with the big national brands. At Three Floyds, brewmaster Chris Boggess calls such production caps "stupid" and "arbitrary" and a hindrance to the brewery's growth.[1]

Just getting started as a craft brewer is an uphill climb, due to many barriers to entry. Prospective

Debates about economic policy center around how the government should raise and spend money to promote growth and fairness in the economy. Regulations, like the ones faced by Chris Boggess and Three Floyds Brewing Company, are just one way that the government tries to shape economic outcomes.

brewers must obtain a Brewer's Notice from the Alcohol and Tobacco Tax and Trade Bureau (TTB) of the U.S. Department of Treasury, which requires background checks, equipment inspections, and legal analyses. Beer formulas, brewing methods, and even beer labels have to meet regulations from the TTB, Food and Drug Administration, and, in the case of organic beer, the U.S. Department of Agriculture. Most states impose a parallel set of regulations. At the local level the prospective brewer must deal with zoning, incorporation rules, and tax compliance. There are fees and wait times associated with many of these steps. And compliance with all of these regulations comes on top of the "entry costs" that any

new business faces, such as developing a business plan and obtaining financing.[2]

Government can make matters complicated for both entrepreneurs and existing firms. However, without government, conducting business would be impossible. Government creates property rights and enforces contracts, writes regulations to ensure fair competition, issues insurance that encourages investment, provides subsidies, and at times hires private firms to perform government work on a contractual basis. Government helps educate workers and builds the roads, ports, and airports that facilitate commerce.

Thinking about the economy at large, government leaders have a wide variety of tools they can use to boost economic performance, including public spending, tax cuts, and interest rate changes. Since the 1930s in particular, Americans have counted on the federal government to ensure a prosperous economy. And in 2008 and 2009, the government intervened to combat economic instability and to prevent the collapse of the financial, insurance, and auto sectors during the Great Recession. Hence government is deeply involved both in individual businesses like Three Floyds Brewing and in the broader economy.

As in many policy areas, there are fundamental questions about the role of the government in the economy. On one side of the spectrum are those who believe that the government should have a minimal role. Government's main purpose should be to set and enforce rules that ensure economic stability. At the other end of the spectrum are those who want to see the state actively engaged in shaping economic outcomes. Not only should the government promote economic growth, according to this perspective, but it should also step in to protect individuals from economic harm. The government's role in the economy should be active, to shape the kind of society we want. Each of these sentiments has prevailed at one time or another. American economic policy has historically reflected the belief that individual liberty is the key to a thriving economy. On the other hand, Americans have periodically demanded restrictions on market freedoms to protect consumers and the environment. Although Americans are often uneasy with the idea of government intervention into the market, on balance they show little support for unraveling existing regulations.

What is government's role in the economy? Who are the key players in shaping economic policy and what are their goals? What are the rules and institutions that facilitate the economy's operation? These questions cut to the heart of what Americans want prosperity and economic opportunity to look like.

CHAPTER GOALS

★ Identify the broad reasons government gets involved in the economy (pp. 633–41)

★ Explore why economic policy is often controversial (pp. 641–49)

★ Describe how the government uses monetary, fiscal, and regulatory policies to influence the economy (pp. 649–63)

★ Explain why the government tries to balance economic prosperity with policies that protect the environment (pp. 663–67)

The Goals of Economic Policy

Identify the broad reasons government gets involved in the economy

The job of this and the next chapter is to step beyond the politics and the institutions to look at the goals of government: the public policies. **Public policy** can be defined simply as an officially expressed purpose or goal backed by a sanction (a reward or a punishment). Public policy can be embodied in a law, a rule, a regulation, or an order. This chapter will focus on policies aimed at the economy.

At the most basic level, government makes it possible for the economy to function efficiently by setting the rules for economic exchange and punishing those who violate those rules. Among the most important rules for the economy are those that define property rights, contracts, and standards for goods. This kind of government rule making allows markets to expand by making it easier for people who do not know each other to engage in economic transactions: they do not have to rely only on personal trust to do business. Likewise, government helps markets expand by creating money and standing behind its value. Money allows diverse goods to be traded and greatly simplifies economic transactions. Without government involvement in providing and standardizing a national currency, it would be very difficult to purchase such basic items as groceries: imagine a world in which different stores used different currencies or in which you needed to trade something you made yourself for your groceries. This would be a major impediment to economic exchange!

Government involvement in the economy now extends far beyond these basic market-creating functions. Government has become involved in many aspects of the economy in order to promote the public well-being. Of course, there is often vigorous disagreement about the extent to which government should intervene in the economy. Further, beliefs about which forms of government intervention in the economy are most necessary and most effective have changed over time. Although the policies have changed, government intervention in the economy has, for nearly a century, sought to achieve four fundamental goals: (1) to promote economic stability, (2) to stimulate economic growth, (3) to promote business development, and (4) to protect employees and consumers.

public policy a law, rule, statute, or edict that expresses the government's goals and provides for rewards and punishments to promote those goals' attainment

PROMOTING STABLE MARKETS

One of the central reasons for government involvement in the economy is to protect the welfare and property of individuals and businesses. Maintaining law and order is one of the most important ways government can protect welfare and property. The federal government has also enacted laws designed to protect individuals and businesses in economic transactions. Federal racketeering laws, for example, aim to end criminal efforts to control businesses through such illegal means as extortion and kickbacks.

Another reason that Congress began to adopt national business regulatory policies was that companies felt burdened by the inconsistent regulations across the various states. Companies often preferred a single, national regulatory authority, no matter how

At the most basic level, government's role in the economy is to make it easier for markets to function. The government sets rules for doing business, creates money, and backs its value—functions that influence even the simplest economic transactions, such as buying groceries at a typical farmer's market.

The interstate highway system is an important public good provided by the government to support the economy. While almost everyone benefits from the highway system, no single participant could afford to provide it alone.

public goods goods or services that are provided by the government because they either are not supplied by the market or are not supplied in sufficient quantities

gross domestic product (GDP) the total value of goods and services produced within a country

burdensome, because it would ensure consistency throughout the United States; the companies could thereby treat the nation as a single market.[3]

The government also promotes economic stability by providing **public goods**. This term refers to facilities the state provides because no single participant can afford to provide those facilities. The provision of public goods may entail supplying the physical marketplace itself—such as the commons in New England towns or an interstate highway system to stimulate the trucking industry. The provision of public goods is essential to market operation, and the manner in which the government provides these goods will affect the market's character.

PROMOTING ECONOMIC PROSPERITY

In addition to setting the basic conditions that allow markets to function, governments may actively intervene in the economy to promote economic growth. Although the idea that government should stimulate economic growth can be traced back to Alexander Hamilton's views about promoting industry, it was not until the twentieth century that the federal government assumed such a role.

Measuring Economic Growth Since the 1930s the federal government has carefully tracked national economic growth by measuring it in several different ways. The two most important measures are the gross national product, which is the market value of the goods and services produced in the economy, and the **gross domestic product (GDP)**, the same measure but excluding income from foreign investments. In the late 1990s the American economy grew at a rate of over 4 percent a year, considered high by modern standards (see Figure 16.1). Growth was slower during the first decade of the 2000s, averaging 1.9 percent annually. This was largely the result of two recessions: one early after the turn of the century and one that began in 2008. In the middle part of the decade (2003–7), the economy grew at a strong 2.8 percent annually.[4] As Figure 16.1 shows, the recession that began in 2008 led to negative economic growth in 2008 and 2009. Although the economy began to grow again after 2010, it remained below the high levels of growth experienced in the 1990s.

The engine of American economic growth has shifted over the centuries. In the 1800s the nation's rich endowment of natural resources was especially important in propelling growth. Manufacturing industries became the driving force of economic growth during the late nineteenth century as mass production made it possible to manufacture goods at a pace that was once unimaginable. In more recent times, the high-technology boom fostered unanticipated and vigorous economic growth that made the United States the envy of the world. Despite these very different economic engines, the basic prerequisites of growth were similar in each case: strong investment, technological innovation, and a productive workforce. Throughout the nation's history, the federal government has adopted policies to promote each of these conditions needed to sustain economic growth.

The most fundamental way that government affects investment is by promoting business as well as investor and consumer confidence. When businesses fear political instability, unpredictable government action, or widespread disregard of the law, they are unlikely to invest. When consumers are insecure about the future, they are unlikely to spend.

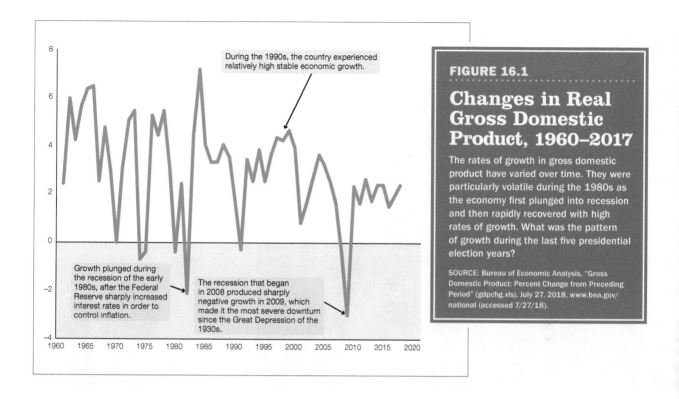

FIGURE 16.1

Changes in Real Gross Domestic Product, 1960–2017

The rates of growth in gross domestic product have varied over time. They were particularly volatile during the 1980s as the economy first plunged into recession and then rapidly recovered with high rates of growth. What was the pattern of growth during the last five presidential election years?

SOURCE: Bureau of Economic Analysis, "Gross Domestic Product: Percent Change from Preceding Period" (gdpchg.xls), July 27, 2018, www.bea.gov/national (accessed 7/27/18).

During the 1990s, the country experienced relatively high stable economic growth.

Growth plunged during the recession of the early 1980s, after the Federal Reserve sharply increased interest rates in order to control inflation.

The recession that began in 2008 produced sharply negative growth in 2009, which made it the most severe downturn since the Great Depression of the 1930s.

The federal government also promotes investment through its regulation of financial markets. The most important federal agency in this regard is the Securities and Exchange Commission (SEC), created after the stock market crash of 1929. The SEC requires companies to disclose information about the stocks and bonds they are selling, inform buyers of the investment risks, and protect investors against fraud. In this way the SEC helps maintain investor confidence and a strong supply of capital for American business. The SEC received harsh criticism during the financial crisis in 2008. Analysts pointed to weak SEC oversight and regulation as an important factor in the near collapse of the financial sector. Major financial reforms, including the Dodd-Frank Act of 2010, substantially beefed up the SEC's enforcement capabilities and required the agency to take the lead in implementing many of the key regulations.[5] However, a May 2018 law passed by Congress and signed by President Trump eliminated some of the new regulations, especially for smaller banks.[6]

Public investment is another important source of growth in the American economy. In the 1930s and again in the late 1970s the federal government promoted public investment as a means to spark economic growth. Some kinds of public investment promote growth as a by-product of other, more central objectives. One of the most important of these is spending on the nation's defense. Many analysts credited the rise in military spending associated with the war in Iraq with helping to spur economic growth in 2003.

The second important condition for economic growth is innovation. The federal government has sought to support innovation in a variety of ways. One of the most important is through the National Science Foundation. Created in 1950, the National Science Foundation supports basic research across a range of fields in order to advance fundamental knowledge that may be broadly useful.[7] Federal

As a way of promoting economic prosperity, the government subsidizes scientific and technological research. The precursor to the internet, ARPAnet (left), was funded by the U.S. military. The National Institute of Health (right) has recently focused its attention on fighting bioterrorism and infectious diseases like Zika.

government sponsorship of health research began in the late 1800s. Today, the National Institutes of Health (NIH) conducts basic and applied research in biomedicine. The Human Genome Project—the effort to map the basic genetic structure of human life—was initiated by government researchers and only later taken up by private corporations. Recently, the NIH has taken the lead in basic research to counter bioterrorism. Its efforts to understand the biology of various infectious agents and to develop vaccines are expected to produce important new knowledge about the human immune system. Research sponsored by the military has long been an important source of innovation for the American economy. Such key twentieth-century innovations as radar and nuclear power stemmed from military research. And as we saw in Chapter 14, military research also created the technology for the twenty-first century with ARPANET, the precursor to the internet.

A third fundamental condition for economic growth is a sufficient and productive workforce. Federal immigration policy has played a key role in ensuring an adequate supply of labor throughout American history. Immigration laws routinely give special priority to workers who have skills that are in demand among American employers. Immigrants with nursing degrees, for example, have long received special priority.

Today, a productive workforce is a highly educated workforce. Education, as we will see in Chapter 17, is primarily the responsibility of state and local governments. The federal government, however, supports the development of a productive workforce with a variety of programs to promote higher education, such as educational grants, tax breaks, and loans. The federal government also sponsors a limited array of job-training programs that focus primarily on low-skilled workers. Some analysts argue that the federal government must do much more to support the development of a highly skilled workforce if the United States is to sustain economic growth in the future.

Full Employment Before the 1930s neither the federal government nor the state governments sought to promote full employment. Unemployment was widely viewed as an unfortunate occurrence that government could do little to alter. The New Deal response to the prolonged and massive unemployment of the Great Depression changed that view. The federal government put millions of people back to work on public projects sponsored by such programs as the Works Progress Administration. The bridges, parks, and buildings they constructed can still be seen across the United States today. The federal government viewed these programs as temporary measures, however. As the buildup for World War II boosted the economy and unemployment melted away, the employment programs were dismantled.

The New Deal and government wartime spending, however, showed that government could help ensure full employment. Public expectations changed as well: after the war, Americans looked to the federal government to reduce unemployment. Moreover, economic theory now supported their expectations. John Maynard Keynes's theories that government could boost employment by stimulating demand had become very influential.

Federal policy placed the most emphasis on achieving full employment during the 1960s. Keynesian economists—who believe that putting money in the hands of consumers creates a strong economy—in the Council of Economic Advisers persuaded President Kennedy to enact the first tax cut designed to stimulate the economy and promote full employment.[8] The policy was widely seen as a success, and unemployment declined to a low of 3.4 percent in 1968. Favorable economic conditions in the 1990s reduced unemployment to record lows once again.

The worldwide economic recession of 2008 led to the loss of over 8 million American jobs. The Obama administration and Congress responded by passing a sweeping stimulus package called the American Recovery and Reinvestment Act in 2009, to help encourage economic growth, save existing jobs, and make longer-term investments that would encourage job creation, such as in weatherization projects and clean-technology construction. Despite these actions, it was not until 2016 that the unemployment rates dipped below 5 percent.

Low Inflation During the 1970s and early 1980s **inflation**, a consistent increase in the general level of prices, was one of America's most vexing problems. Rising prices harm consumers, especially those on a fixed income such as the elderly. Inflation also undermines the entire economy because it creates uncertainty about future prices, making investors cautious. Inflation was finally reduced from its historic highs of nearly 20 percent down toward 2 and 3 percent a year by the mid-1980s. Since that time, inflation has remained low. Even so, economic policy makers watch prices closely for any sign of increasing inflation.

PROMOTING BUSINESS DEVELOPMENT

During the nineteenth century, the national government promoted the development of important markets that eventually contributed significantly to the U.S. GDP. National roads and canals were built to tie states and regions together. National tariff policies promoted domestic markets by restricting imported goods; a tax on an import raised its price and weakened its ability to compete with similar

inflation a consistent increase in the general level of prices

One reason unemployment rose after 2008 was that numerous companies went out of business. Chrysler laid off thousands of employees before filing for bankruptcy in 2009, when the U.S. government paid $4 billion to bail the company out.

RICH FARMING LANDS!
ON THE LINE OF THE
Union Pacific Railroad!

Located in the GREAT CENTRAL BELT of POPU-
LATION, COMMERCE and WEALTH, and
adjoining the WORLD'S HIGHWAY
from OCEAN to OCEAN.

12,000,000 ACRES!

3,000,000 Acres in Central and
Eastern Nebraska, in the Platte Valley, now for sale!

We invite the attention of all parties seeking
a HOME, to the LANDS offered for sale by this Company.

O. F. DAVIS,
Land Commissioner, U. P. R. R.

Since the early nineteenth century, the government has been an important promoter of business development in the United States. Then, governments gave railroad companies land to development rail service. More recently, the government has incentivized businesses to develop "green" technologies such electric or fuel-efficient automobiles.

domestic products. The national government also heavily subsidized the railroad system. Until the 1840s railroads were thought to be of limited commercial value. But between 1850 and 1872, Congress granted more than 100 million acres of public-domain land to railroad interests, and state and local governments pitched in an estimated $280 million in cash and credit. Before the end of the century, 35,000 miles of track existed, almost half the world's total at the time.

Railroads were not the only clients of federal support for the private markets. Many sectors of agriculture began receiving federal subsidies during the nineteenth century. Agriculture remains highly subsidized to this day. In 2017, 46 percent of farms in the United States received subsidies totaling $13.2 billion.[9] One of the many criticisms of the farm subsidy program is that it disproportionately supports large-scale farmers rather than small family farmers. The list of farm subsidy recipients includes many large corporations.

categorical grants congressional grants given to states and localities on the condition that expenditures be limited to a problem or group specified by the law

The national government also promotes business development indirectly through **categorical grants** (see Chapter 3), by which the federal government offers grants to states on condition that the state (or local) government undertake a particular activity. Thus, in order to use motor transportation to improve national markets, a 900,000-mile national highway system was built during the 1930s, based on a formula whereby the national government would pay 50 percent of the cost if the state provided the other 50 percent. Over 20 years, beginning in the late 1950s, the federal government constructed an additional 45,000 miles of interstate highways. In this program, the national government agreed to pay 90 percent of the construction costs on the condition that each state provide 10 percent of the costs of any portion of a highway built within its boundaries.[10] The tremendous growth of highways was a major boon to the automobile and trucking industries.

The federal government supports specific business sectors with direct subsidies, loans, and tax breaks. In 1953 the Small Business Administration was created to offer loans, loan guarantees, and disaster assistance to small businesses. Recognizing that such businesses often find it harder to obtain financing and to recover from unexpected events such as fires, the federal government has provided assistance where the market would not. Today the Small Business Administration provides more than $44 billion in such assistance to small businesses.[11]

Among the many contemporary examples of policies promoting private industry, Sematech may be the most instructive. Sematech is a nonprofit research and development consortium of major U.S. computer microchip manufacturers, set up in 1987 to work with government and academic institutions to reestablish U.S. leadership in semiconductor manufacturing. (The United States appeared to be in danger of losing out to the Japanese in this area during the 1980s.) The results of its research were distributed among the consortium members.[12] For nine years, industry and government together spent $1.7 billion to make the American microchip industry the leader in the world. The government contributed about half of the total expenditures. In 1997 federal funding was phased out. Industry leaders, convinced they no longer needed federal support, initiated the break with government. At a critical moment, the federal government had stepped in to save the chip industry; it stepped out once that goal had been achieved.

Since September 11, 2001, the federal government has taken on a major role in promoting technological innovation related to national security. Even before the September 11 terrorist attacks, the CIA had set up its own venture capital firm, In-Q-Tel (the Q stands for a character in the James Bond movies), to invest in high-tech start-ups whose work could enhance intelligence efforts. More recently, the federal government has aimed to support the alternative energy industry. The Energy Policy Act of 2005 greatly increased the number and cost of tax credits and loan programs for renewable and efficient energy technologies. As the recession hit, Washington stepped up its efforts to support the alternative energy industry, seeing it as a way to expand economic growth in an emerging sector. The Emergency Economic Stabilization Act of 2008 and the American Recovery and Reinvestment Act of 2009 expanded subsidies and created a new program allowing companies to receive a one-time cash grant in lieu of tax credits. Between 2015 and 2019 the federal government was projected to spend $46.5 billion in tax-related support for the production of renewable energy, as well as an additional $3.1 billion to support energy efficiency.[13] The Trump administration's fiscal year 2018 budget proposal sought a 70 percent cut in funding for the Department of Energy's Office of Energy Efficiency and Renewable Energy, but Congress pushed back by fully funding the office in the FY 2018 spending bill it passed in March 2018.[14]

PROTECTING EMPLOYEES AND CONSUMERS

Stable relations between business and labor are important elements of a productive economy. During the latter half of the nineteenth century, strikes over low wages or working conditions became a standard feature of American economic life. In fact, the United States has one of the most violent histories of labor relations in the world. Yet for most of American history, the federal government did little to regulate relations between business and labor. Local governments and courts often weighed in on the side of business by prohibiting strikes and arresting strikers.

In the wake of the Great Recession, President Obama established the Consumer Financial Protection Bureau to help protect consumers from unfair practices by banks and other financial companies. The CFPB was originally headed by Elizabeth Warren (left).

As the economic depression enveloped the United States in the 1930s, plummeting wages and massive strikes for union recognition prompted Congress to pass the 1935 National Labor Relations Act, which set up a new framework for industrial relations. The new law created a permanent agency, the National Labor Relations Board, charged with overseeing union elections and collective bargaining between labor and industry. The federal government weighed in further on the side of organized labor in 1938, when it passed the Fair Labor Standards Act, which created the minimum wage. Because it is not indexed to inflation, the value of the minimum wage declines if it is not raised periodically. Since 1938 conflicts over increasing the minimum wage have been a regular feature of American politics. The federal minimum wage reached its highest value in 1968. It was last raised in 2009 but since then has lost nearly 10 percent of its value to inflation.[15]

During the 1950s and '60s the federal government played an active role in industrial relations. The Department of Labor and occasionally even the president directly intervened in labor–management disputes to ensure peaceful industrial relations. Although Democrats were generally seen as more supportive of labor, both parties sought to achieve a balance between business and labor that would promote a strong, stable economy.

President Reagan made a decisive break with this tradition of compromise in 1981, when he fired striking air traffic controllers (who were federal employees) and hired permanent replacements to take their jobs, effectively ceding more power to employers. Politicians are now much less likely to intervene in labor relations.

Economic policies also protect consumers. The idea that the federal government should protect consumers emerged in the first decade of the 1900s. Upton Sinclair's graphic exposé of the meatpacking industry, *The Jungle* (1906), galvanized public concern about unsanitary food processing. These concerns prompted the U.S. Department of Agriculture to inspect packing plants and the meat they produced, stamping approved meats with the now-familiar "USDA" certification. Similar concern about the safety of food, drugs, and cosmetics led to the creation of the Food and Drug Administration in 1927.

Federal agencies help ensure safe products. Recently, hoverboard manufactures have come under scrutiny by the Consumer Product Safety Commission when it was reported that some hoverboards were catching fire while charging.

The movement for consumer protection took off again in the 1960s. The consumer advocate Ralph Nader's 1965 book *Unsafe at Any Speed* helped spark new demands for federal action. Nader's book showed that design flaws in the Corvair, a popular car model, had caused deaths that could have been prevented. Nader's book not only led to the demise of the Corvair but also mobilized calls for more federal action to protect consumers. The first response was the 1966 National Traffic and Motor Vehicle Safety Act, which gave the Department of Transportation responsibility for ensuring vehicle safety. Federal responsibility for consumer safety expanded in 1972, when Congress created the Consumer Product Safety Commission, an independent agency that informs consumers about hazards associated with products and works with industry to set product standards. In cases where safety concerns are severe, the commission will see that such products are recalled. Through the Consumer Product Safety Commission, the Department of Transportation, and the Food and Drug Administration, the federal government continues to play an active role in protecting the public from unsafe products.

Federal agencies are active in ensuring safe products. In 2016 the Consumer Product Safety Commission sent a letter to hoverboard manufacturers, importers, and retailers noting 52 reported fires, including the destruction of two homes and an automobile. The CPSC warned that self-balancing scooters whose batteries do not meet test requirements could be subject to recall or seizure.[16] A number of retailers decided to stop selling hoverboards as a result, although the voluntary nature of the safety rules means that potentially dangerous hoverboards are still available for purchase.

FOR CRITICAL ANALYSIS

What does the American government do to ensure that the products Americans buy are safe? What challenges does it face in making certain that products are safe?

The Politics of Economic Policy Making

Explore why economic policy is often controversial

All politicians want a healthy economy, but they often differ in their views about how to attain it. Addressing economic challenges and maintaining a strong economy are extremely important to political leaders. As presidents from Herbert Hoover (who presided over the beginning of the Great Depression of the 1930s) to Jimmy Carter (who faced double-digit inflation) discovered, voters will punish politicians for poor economic performance. In the 50 years that followed the Great Depression and the federal government's first big steps into the economy, politicians from both parties agreed that the government played an important role in ensuring a strong economy, though they often disagreed about what priorities should guide economic policy. Democrats generally expressed more concern about unemployment than did Republicans, who focused more on reducing budget deficits. In the 1980s, however, the differences between the parties on economic policy became much more fundamental. While Democrats and Republicans alike embraced a smaller role for the government in the economy, growing numbers of Republicans began to reject the idea that government should intervene in the economy at all. Instead, they argued that a free market was the best way to ensure economic prosperity. Democrats continued to believe that economic prosperity required government action. Once in power, however, parties acted very differently. Budget deficits have soared under Republican presidents since the 1980s, and Democrats have often taken limited action for fear of upsetting the markets.

HOW MUCH SHOULD THE GOVERNMENT INTERVENE IN THE ECONOMY?

Until 1929 most Americans believed that government had little to do with actively managing the economy. The world was guided by the theory—called *laissez-faire economics*—that the economy, if left to its own devices, would produce full employment and maximum production. This traditional view of the relationship between government and the economy crumbled in 1929 before the stark reality of the Great Depression of 1929–39. Some misfortune befell nearly everyone. Around 20 percent of the workforce became unemployed, and few of these individuals had any monetary resources or the old family farm to fall back on. Banks failed, wiping out the savings of millions who had been prudent enough or fortunate enough to have any. Thousands of businesses closed, throwing middle-class Americans onto the bread lines alongside unemployed laborers and dispossessed farmers. The Great Depression proved to Americans that the economic system was not, in fact, perfectly self-regulating, as had been generally believed.

Demands grew for the federal government to act. In Congress, some Democrats proposed that the federal government finance public works to aid the economy and put people back to work. Other members introduced legislation to provide federal grants to the states to assist their relief efforts.

When President Franklin Delano Roosevelt took office in 1933, he energetically threw the federal government into the business of fighting the Depression. He proposed a variety of temporary measures to provide federal relief and work programs. Most of the programs he proposed were to be financed by the federal government but administered by the states. In addition to these temporary measures, Roosevelt presided over the creation of several important federal programs designed to provide future economic security for Americans. Since that time, the public has held the government, and the president in particular, responsible for ensuring a healthy economy.

After World War II, Republicans and Democrats broadly agreed that Keynesian ideas, such as running deficits during periods of recession to stimulate demand, could best guide economic policy. By the 1960s **Keynesians** believed that economic policy did not need to provoke political controversy because they could ensure ongoing prosperity by "fine-tuning" the economy. Democrats and Republicans often disagreed about how much the government should do to alleviate unemployment or inflation, but they shared a pragmatic view that government intervention could solve economic problems. The question about whether and how government should intervene in the economy appeared settled.

Partisan Divisions over the Government Role in the Economy By the 1980s the broad consensus about the role of the government in the economy had evaporated. Growing numbers of Republicans began to reject the idea that government could help ensure economic prosperity. Instead, they argued that freeing markets from government intervention would produce the best economic results. As Ronald Reagan put it in his first inaugural address, "Government is not the solution to our problem, government is the problem."[17]

Thus, the ideas of **laissez-faire capitalism** began to make a comeback in American politics. These arguments were first elaborated in the late 1700s by the great Scottish economist Adam Smith. Smith believed that most government involvement in the economy (such as the government-authorized monopolies that dominated trade in

Keynesians followers of the economic theories of John Maynard Keynes, who argued that the government can stimulate the economy by increasing public spending or by cutting taxes

laissez-faire capitalism an economic system in which the means of production and distribution are privately owned and operated for profit with minimal or no government interference his day) suppressed economic growth. Instead, he argued that competition among free enterprises would unleash economic energy, fostering growth and innovation. In his view, the self-seeking behavior of individuals, when subject to the discipline of market competition, would create products that consumers wanted at the best possible price. Smith praised "the invisible hand" of the market, by which he meant that millions of individual economic transactions together create a greater good—far better than the government could create. Smith believed that the government role should be restricted to national defense, establishing law and order (including the protection of private property), and providing basic public goods (such as roads) that facilitate commerce.

Although only a few politicians would entirely remove government from the economy, Republicans today draw on the ideas of laissez-faire economics as they argue for significant reductions in nonmilitary spending. Many Democrats, on the other hand, stress the important role of government in promoting a strong economy. This fundamental disagreement between the parties over the appropriate role of government underlies the fierce contemporary political debates over the government role in taxes, spending, and economic regulation.

Taxes Today some of the most intense conflicts between Democrats and Republicans concern taxes. As Republicans embraced the idea that reducing the role of government in the economy would promote investment and spur economic growth, they made tax cuts their highest priority. Rejecting Keynesian ideas, they adopted the idea of **supply-side economics.** This approach maintains that lower tax rates create incentives for more productive and efficient use of resources. When individuals know they can keep more of their earnings, they are more likely to be productive workers and creative investors. In this perspective, low taxes are not just a temporary measure to stimulate the economy; taxes should remain low at all times to ensure a growing economy.

Because no one really likes to pay taxes, Republican support for tax cuts creates a political dilemma for Democrats. How can they defend taxes? Polls show that most of the time—although less often after the Bush tax cuts of 2001 and 2003—a majority of Americans think that their taxes are too high.[18] Aware of the political damage that might come from opposing tax cuts, many Democratic members of Congress have supported tax cuts. But because most Democrats favor higher levels of public spending than do Republicans, they ultimately need taxes to fund government programs. To resolve this political problem, Democrats have sought to increase taxes on the wealthy. One reliable finding in public opinion polls is that the majority of Americans agree that neither corporations nor upper-income people pay their fair share of taxes.[19] However, the Tax Cuts and Jobs Act passed by the Republican-led Congress and signed by President Trump in 2017 cut corporate taxes and lowered taxes for individuals, with the largest reductions going to high earners.[20]

Spending Government spending is another area where the two parties have locked horns. Contending

supply-side economics an economic theory that posits that reducing the marginal rate of taxation will create a productive economy by promoting levels of work and investment that would otherwise be discouraged by higher taxes

"Supply-siders" argue that reducing tax rates will spur economic growth as people are able to spend and invest more of their money. In the 1980s, President Ronald Reagan—shown here holding an oversize tax form—sought to simplify the tax laws and reduce taxes.

that the federal government has become too big, Republicans argue for reduced government spending. In their view, big government is not only wasteful but also a drag on the economy. Moreover, fiscal conservatives argue, excessive spending creates deficits, which can harm the economy. It is not hard to convince Americans that government spending is wasteful or that government is too big or that deficits are bad. When asked, a majority of Americans regularly say they would prefer a smaller government with fewer services (although in 2017 slightly more said they would prefer a bigger government with more services—48 percent, compared to 45 percent preferring smaller government).[21]

Yet, polls reveal little support for cutting specific government programs.[22] In fact, the public shows the strongest support for the most expensive government programs. Social Security, which provides pensions to the elderly, and Medicare, which supplies health insurance for the elderly, are both politically popular. Only the most ardent spending foes among Republicans have argued for cutting these programs. Indeed, in 2003 Republicans agreed to a major expansion in Medicare spending by adding a prescription drug benefit to the program. And recent proposals from Republican Paul Ryan to cut Medicare spending by transforming it into a voucher program went nowhere. The popularity of these programs reflects the fact that government provides real benefits to real people. Democrats support government spending on education, infrastructure, health care, and other public programs. They believe that taking away these programs will deny economic opportunities to Americans and hurt the national economy.

Because neither party wishes to cut big, expensive, popular programs and because tax increases have been so difficult to enact, budget deficits have grown periodically over the past three decades. Democratic critics and most economists point to rising deficits as proof that supply-side economics does not work; they argue that the economy would be better off without tax cuts. Some go further, arguing that Republicans deliberately reduced taxes in order to win support for spending cuts. This strategy, called "starving the beast," suggests that spending cuts would become more popular in the face of rising deficits.[23]

Because it is politically difficult to raise taxes or reduce big-spending programs, most cuts have fallen on smaller programs, often those administered by the states. This is what happened in 2013 after a Republican and Democratic standoff over the deficit led to a set of cuts applied to smaller programs. Unusually, in 2013 these spending reductions also applied to military spending. The 2015 budget deal, a complex compromise between Republicans and Democrats, avoided cutting small programs by raising spending and making targeted cuts in entitlements. Even so, spending for small programs has fallen quite significantly since 2010. Non-defense discretionary spending includes everything the government does outside of defense and mandatory programs such as Social Security and Medicare; for 2018 such spending was 16 percent below the 2010 level in inflation-adjusted terms, the lowest level as a share of the economy ever recorded, with data going back to 1962.[24]

Economic Regulation The federal government regulates business to achieve a broad range of objectives, including economic stability, workplace safety, wages and hours, consumer satisfaction, and environmental goals. Economic regulation often attracts intense political conflict as businesses seek to limit the government role and other interests press for stronger government action. Democrats have usually been more favorable toward government regulation than have Republicans. Each party can point to public-opinion polls to support its position. Public views about regulation shift over time, but on the whole, Americans agree with the statement that government regulation of business does more harm than good.[25] However, as is the case for spending, Americans tend to express strong support for maintaining or even strengthening current regulations. Only a small percentage of Americans want to roll back existing regulations.

One area of regulation that sharply divides the parties is the minimum wage. As we have seen, the minimum wage was first enacted in 1938 as part of the Fair Labor Standards Act. Because it is not indexed to rise with inflation (see Figure 16.2), it has become a regular target of political conflict as supporters aim to raise it to keep pace with inflation. Most Americans strongly support an increase in the minimum wage, with 59 percent of Americans supporting a boost in the minimum wage in 2017.[26] Respondents who identify as Democrats are far more likely to back an increased minimum wage, but about half of Republicans polled also express support.[27]

FIGURE 16.2

The Minimum Wage, 1968–2018

The federal government and most U.S. states have minimum-wage laws. The minimum wage has increased over time across the United States. However, near-constant inflation during this time period has reduced the real value of these wages, so the purchasing power of the minimum wage has declined. How do the data in this graph relate to arguments for or against a higher federal minimum wage?

SOURCES: Department of Labor, Wage and Hour Division, "History of Federal Minimum Wage Rates under the Fair Labor Standards Act, 1968–2009," www.dol.gov/whd/minwage/chart.htm#.UNuMXXeDmSo (accessed 11/1/17).

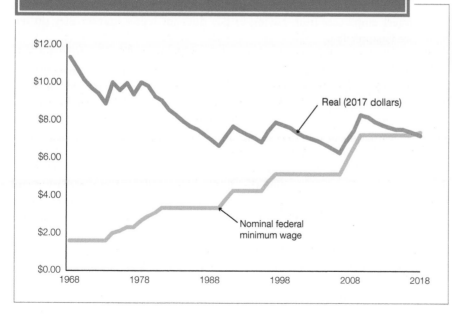

In 2014, President Obama signed an executive order increasing the minimum wage for federal contractors to $10.10 an hour and urged Congress similarly to raise the federal minimum wage from $7.25 to $10.10 an hour. Twenty-nine states and nearly two dozen cities and counties enacted minimum wages higher than the federal wage.[28] Although a $15 an hour minimum wage became a rallying cry for the Bernie Sanders presidential campaign in 2016, Republican opposition has prevented Congress from considering the issue. An August 2016 poll found that 52 percent of Americans, but just 21 percent of Donald Trump's supporters, favored a $15 an hour minimum wage.[29]

ORGANIZED INTERESTS AND THE POLITICS OF ECONOMIC POLICY

The groups that influence decisions about economic policy are as wide-ranging as the objectives of policy. Consumer groups, environmentalists, businesses, and labor all work to shape economic policy. Of these groups, organized labor and business are the most consistent actors that weigh in across the spectrum of policies. In the past, organized labor was much more important in influencing economic policy than it is today. At the height of their strength in the 1950s, unions represented some 35 percent of the labor force. Today, labor unions, representing 11.1 percent of the labor force, are much less powerful in influencing economic policy.[30] Democratic presidents continue to court labor because unions control resources and votes important to Democratic politicians. On particular issues, organized labor can still exercise significant influence. Unions launched a "Fight for Fifteen" campaign in 2012 that helped lead to some of the state and local government minimum wage increases mentioned earlier. However, labor's overall power has waned. Twenty-eight states now have "right to work" provisions that guarantee that a worker does not have to belong to a union or pay union dues as a condition of employment. Unions and other opponents of such laws say they make it more difficult for unions to collect dues, which they use to fund collective bargaining efforts for all workers. Business groups and other supporters say right-to-work laws protect employees from having to pay dues for representation they do not want (see Chapter 15).[31]

Business organizations are the most consistently powerful actors in economic policy. Business groups are most united around the goal of reducing government regulation. Organizations, such as the U.S. Chamber of Commerce, which represents small business, and the Business Roundtable and the National Association of Manufacturers, which represent big business, actively worked to roll back government regulation in the 1970s and '80s. These organizations have been vocal supporters of Republican efforts to limit government involvement in the economy. For example, the National Restaurant Association has denounced efforts to raise the minimum wage, warning that higher wages will lead to automation and fewer jobs. Yet when business groups representing particular sectors of the economy weigh in on issues that are of special concern to them, they often embrace government action. The high-tech industry regularly argues in favor of granting more visas to allow skilled foreign workers into the country. Other industry groups, particularly in agriculture, lobby to retain subsidies that they have enjoyed for decades.

Who Earns the Minimum Wage?

In recent years, many states have passed laws raising the minimum wage, and Congress has debated taking action at the federal level. Most Americans support raising the minimum wage, but there are differences in who earns the minimum wage based on age, gender, and race.

Percentage of Minimum Wage Earners

Age

16–24	45%
25–34	24%
35–44	11%
45–54	10%
55–64	6%
65+	3%

Gender

Women	64%
Men	36%

Race / ethnicity

White 74%

Black 18%

Asian 5%

Hispanic 17%

Percentage of all American workers (age 16+) who earn the minimum wage

2.7%

FOR CRITICAL ANALYSIS

1. Based on these data, which of these groups are more likely to support raising the minimum wage?

2. Women make up about 47 percent of the workforce. How does this compare to the percentage of minimum wage workers who are women?

SOURCE: U.S. Bureau of Labor Statistics, "Characteristics of Minimum Wage Workers, 2016," April 2017, www.bls.gov (accessed 1/11/18).

POLITICS AND THE GREAT RECESSION OF 2008

The severe economic downturn that began in 2008, often called the "Great Recession," provoked unprecedented government intervention into the economy. As the near-collapse of the financial sector in 2008 reverberated throughout the United States (and the world) economy, thousands of Americans lost their homes, banks refused to lend, and unemployment rose. The federal government, first under George W. Bush and then under Barack Obama, initiated large-scale interventions in the hope of staving off the downward economic spiral. These included emergency measures to bail out failing companies, short-term stimulus to get the economy moving again, and proposals for regulations that would prevent similar financial meltdowns in the future. However, support for these measures wavered as fear of rising deficits, exploding long-term debt, and, more abstractly, "big government" grew.

Propping up the financial sector presented an economic challenge for federal officials. President Bush found he could not count on support from congressional Republicans when he sought to enact a major bailout for the financial sector. A bipartisan group in Congress ultimately approved a $700-billion emergency "bailout" in October 2008 (known as the Troubled Asset Relief Program, or TARP), which the Treasury Department drew on to infuse major financial institutions with capital. It was not just major banking institutions that faced ruin. Auto companies, teetering on the edge of bankruptcy, also received major infusions of cash from the federal government.[32] By late 2010 the economy had stabilized sufficiently that many of the financial institutions that had received funds under TARP were able to pay the federal government back. The CBO estimated that TARP would end up costing taxpayers $34 billion, far less than the initial $700 billion.[33]

Congress also passed a sweeping package in 2009 to help stimulate the economy, save jobs (particularly in the public sector), and make longer-term investments that would help stimulate economic growth. The $787-billion American Recovery and Reinvestment Act (more commonly known as the "stimulus" bill of 2009) contained a number of measures to stimulate growth in the short term and prevent drastic cuts to public services. Among the most important measures in the act were reductions in individual and business taxes by $288 billion in order to generate more spending and job hiring. The measure also spent $195.5 billion on aid, health insurance subsidies, and job training for low-income and unemployed workers and $44.5 billion designed to limit teacher layoffs and cutbacks in local school districts. The rest of the investments aimed not only to create new jobs in the short term but also to be long-term investments in infrastructure and education that would help future growth. The act reflected Keynesian logic that called for public investment during periods of economic downturn.

Although only some Republicans and Democrats had balked at supporting the financial bailout package in 2008, by early 2009 a sharp partisan rift had become evident. No Republicans in the House and only three in the Senate voted to support the 2009 stimulus package. Republicans denounced the House measure as overly tilted toward spending rather than tax cuts. But even when Senate Democrats added significant new tax cuts to the bill, most Republicans still opposed it. While Democrats defended the measure as an infusion of funds needed to prevent a depression, Republicans denounced it as wasteful spending and made their opposition a defining stance toward the Obama administration. Mounting unemployment complicated the political judgments about the stimulus; despite the injection of public funds into the economy, national unemployment rose to a seasonally adjusted

The American Recovery and Reinvestment Act provided $787 billion to support economic growth following the recession that began in 2008. Among other provisions, the act included funding for projects that would help keep Americans employed during the downturn.

rate of 9.6 percent by September 2010, with rates much higher in some states.[34] The nonpartisan CBO estimated that at its height in 2010, the American Recovery and Reinvestment Act increased the number of full-time jobs by as many as 3.6 million.[35] Yet because unemployment remained high, the act did not get much credit from the public for helping the economy, and it attracted considerable criticism for contributing to the budget deficit. When Congress considered a second stimulus bill focused on job creation, it succeeded in enacting a relatively small job-creation package worth $15 billion, most of which consisted of tax credits for businesses that hired new employees.[36]

The Tools of Economic Policy

Describe how the government uses monetary, fiscal, and regulatory policies to influence the economy

The U.S. economy is no accident; it is the result of specific policies that have expanded American markets and sustained massive economic growth. The Constitution provides that Congress shall have the power "To lay and collect Taxes...to pay the Debts and provide for the common Defence and general Welfare...To borrow Money... To coin Money [and] regulate the Value thereof." These clauses of Article I, Section 8, are the constitutional sources of the fiscal and monetary policies of the national government. The Constitution says nothing, however, about *how* these powers can be used. As it works to meet the multiple goals of economic policy, the federal government relies on a broad set of tools that has evolved over time. As we will see, decisions about which tools to use are not simply technical; they are highly political and reflect conflicts over whether the government should act at all and, if so, how.

MONETARY POLICIES

Monetary policies manipulate the growth of the entire economy by controlling the availability of money to banks. With very few exceptions, banks in the United States are privately owned and locally operated. Until well into the twentieth century, banks were regulated, if at all, by state legislatures. Each bank was granted a charter, which gave it permission to make loans, hold deposits, and make investments within

monetary policies efforts to regulate the economy through the manipulation of the supply of money and credit; America's most powerful institution in this area of monetary policy is the Federal Reserve Board that state. Although thousands of banks continue to be chartered by the states, they are less important in the overall financial picture than they used to be, as the most important banks now are members of the federal banking system.

Federal Reserve System Banks did not become the core of American capitalism without intense political controversy. The Federalist majority in Congress, led by Alexander Hamilton, did in fact establish a Bank of the United States, in 1791; but it was vigorously opposed by agrarian interests, led by Thomas Jefferson, who feared that the interests of urban, industrial capitalism would dominate such a bank. The Bank of the United States was terminated during the administration of Andrew Jackson, but the fear of a central, public bank lingered eight decades later, when, in 1913, Congress established an institution, the **Federal Reserve System**, to integrate private banks into a single national system. The Federal Reserve System is composed of 12 Federal Reserve banks, each located in a major commercial city. The Federal Reserve banks are not ordinary banks; they are bankers' banks that make loans to other banks, clear checks, and supply the economy with currency and coins. They also play a regulatory role over the member banks. Every national bank must be a member of the Federal Reserve System and must follow national banking rules. State banks and savings and loan associations may also join if they accept national rules. At the top of the system is the Federal Reserve Board—"the Fed"—comprising seven members appointed by the president (with Senate confirmation) for 14-year terms. The chair of the Fed is selected by the president from among the seven members of the board for a four-year term. In all other concerns, however, the Fed is an independent agency (see Chapter 14) inasmuch as its members cannot be removed during their terms except "for cause," and the president's executive power does not extend to them or their policies. Nonetheless, observers charged the longtime Federal Reserve chair, Alan Greenspan, with being attentive to politics, for example, in his endorsement of President George W. Bush's tax cuts. In his 2017 confirmation hearings to head the Fed, nominee Jerome Powell told Congress he was "strongly committed to an independent Federal Reserve."[37]

The major advantage that a bank gains from being in the Federal Reserve System is that it can borrow from the system. This enables banks to expand their loan operations continually, as long as there is demand for loans in the economy. On the other hand, it is this very access of member banks to the Federal Reserve System that gives the Fed its power: the ability to expand and contract the amount of credit available in the United States.

The Fed can affect the total amount of credit through the interest (called the **federal funds rate**) that member banks charge one another for loans. If the Fed significantly decreases the federal funds rate, making it cheaper to borrow money, this can give a boost to a sagging economy. In the steep recession that began in 2008, the Fed acted aggressively. By December 2008 it had cut rates nine times from a high in September 2007 of 4.75 percent to a historically low percentage rate close to zero. Moreover, the Federal Reserve kept interest rates at that same low level well into 2015, in an attempt to encourage lending again and thus economic growth.[38] If the Fed raises the federal funds rate, it can put a brake on the economy because the higher rates make it more expensive to borrow money. This makes it more difficult for new businesses to get loans, for instance.

Although the Federal Reserve is responsible for ensuring high employment as well as price stability, it has been particularly important in fighting inflation. During the late 1970s and early 1980s, with inflation at record high levels, Federal Reserve chair Paul

Federal Reserve System a system of 12 Federal Reserve banks that facilitates exchanges of cash, checks, and credit; regulates member banks; and uses monetary policies to fight inflation and deflation

federal funds rate the interest rate on loans between banks that the Federal Reserve Board influences by affecting the supply of money available

Financial markets closely watch the statements of the Federal Reserve. Here, Fed Chair Jerome Powell speaks about the necessity of raising interest rates to fight inflation.

Volcker aggressively raised interest rates in order to dampen inflation. Although his actions provoked a sharp recession, they raised the stature of the Fed, demonstrating its ability to manage the economy. Because the Fed is so closely associated with inflation fighting, Senate Democrats pressed Ben Bernanke, President George W. Bush's nominee to head the Fed, to indicate at his nomination hearings that he would view maximum employment as a goal of equal importance to that of fighting inflation. In 2018, Jerome Powell, the new head of the Fed, noted that unemployment was low and vowed to keep raising benchmark interest rates slowly to stay ahead of inflation.[39]

Fostering Investment The federal government also provides insurance to foster credit and encourage private capital investment. The Federal Deposit Insurance Corporation insures bank deposits up to $250,000. Another important promoter of investment is the federal insurance of home mortgages through the Department of Housing and Urban Development. By guaranteeing mortgages, the government can reduce the risks that banks run in making such loans, thus allowing banks to lower their interest rates and making such loans more affordable to middle- and lower-income families. Such programs have enabled millions of families that could not otherwise have afforded it to finance the purchase of a home.

FOR CRITICAL ANALYSIS

Why is the Federal Reserve so important to economic policy?

This system began to unravel in the first decade of the 2000s, with the growth of the subprime market for lending. This market made home loans available to people who could not otherwise have afforded to buy a home. At the same time, however, it created new instabilities in the market by offering risky loans that would become more costly due to adjustable interest rates. The slowing housing market in 2007 set off a wave of foreclosures as many homeowners discovered that they could not pay back their loans. During the height of the crisis, between 2007 and 2013, more than 14 million homes were lost to foreclosure.[40]

The foreclosure crisis in turn sent shock waves through the financial system as investment banks found themselves holding worthless loans. One casualty of the home loan meltdown was the Wall Street investment bank Bear Stearns, which faced bankruptcy early in March 2008. Seeking to limit the harm to the broader economy that such a bankruptcy would cause, Fed chair Bernanke arranged for Bear Stearns to be bought, at bargain-basement prices, by JPMorgan Chase, another investment bank. In making this move, Bernanke was exercising powers of the Federal Reserve Act that had not been used since the 1930s.[41] After the firm Lehman Brothers collapsed in 2008 and several other investment banks and insurance companies moved closer to insolvency, the Federal Reserve also provided billions of dollars to banks so that they could continue to lend money for student loans, auto loans, and residential mortgages. In all, the Fed gave nearly $1.5 trillion in emergency loans to financial institutions.[42]

Although many were impressed by the swift action undertaken by the Fed, critics charged that its supervision of the banking system prior to the crisis had been too lax. This led to an unusually contentious set of Senate confirmation hearings for Bernanke, whom President Obama had renominated in 2009. Most Democrats prefer that the Federal Reserve take a strong stand in regulating banks and in prioritizing the problem of unemployment. Republicans, on the other hand, fear that excessive regulation will limit economic growth. Republicans are more likely to see unemployment as a problem of workers who lack appropriate job skills, rather than a problem that requires more stimulus of the economy.

FISCAL POLICIES

fiscal policy the government's use of taxing, monetary, and spending powers to manipulate the economy

Fiscal policy includes the government's taxing and spending powers. Personal and corporate income taxes, which raise the majority of the U.S. government's revenues, are the most prominent examples. Although the direct purpose of an income tax is to raise revenue, each tax has a different impact on the economy, and government can attempt to plan for that impact.

tariff a tax on imported goods

Taxation During the nineteenth century, the federal government received most of its revenue from a single tax, the **tariff**. It also relied on excise taxes, which are taxes levied on specific products, such as tobacco and alcohol. As federal activities expanded in the 1900s, the federal government added new sources of tax revenue. The most important was the income tax, proposed by Congress in 1909, ratified by the states, and added to the Constitution in 1913 as the Sixteenth Amendment. The income tax is levied on individuals and corporations. With the creation of the Social Security system in 1935, social insurance taxes became an additional source of federal revenue.

Before World War II, individual income taxes accounted for only 14 percent of federal revenues.[43] The need to raise revenue for World War II made the income tax much more important. Congress expanded the base of the income tax so that most Americans paid income taxes after World War II. Figure 16.3 shows several notable shifts that have occurred in taxes since 1966. Social insurance taxes now compose a much greater share of federal revenues, rising from 19.5 percent of revenues in 1966 to an estimated 35 percent in 2018. The share of the federal individual income tax has remained fairly stable; it was 42.4 percent in 1966 and estimated at 49.7 percent in 2018. Receipts from corporate income taxes declined over the same period, dropping from 23 percent of receipts in 1966 to 6.5 percent in 2018.

progressive taxation taxation that hits upper-income brackets more heavily

regressive taxation taxation that hits lower-income brackets more heavily

One of the most important features of the American income tax is that it is a "progressive," or "graduated," tax, with the heaviest burden carried by those most able to pay. A tax is called **progressive** if the rate of taxation goes up with each higher income bracket. A tax is called **regressive** if people in lower-income brackets pay a higher proportion of their income toward the tax than people in higher-income brackets. For example, a sales tax is deemed regressive because everybody pays at the

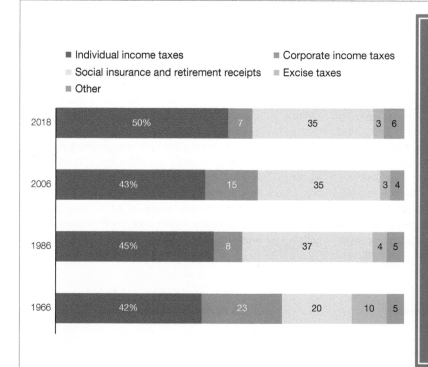

■ Individual income taxes   ■ Corporate income taxes
■ Social insurance and retirement receipts   ■ Excise taxes
■ Other

Year	Individual income taxes	Corporate income taxes	Social insurance and retirement receipts	Excise taxes	Other
2018	50%	7	35	3	6
2006	43%	15	35	3	4
1986	45%	8	37	4	5
1966	42%	23	20	10	5

FIGURE 16.3

Federal Revenues by Type of Tax

The federal government collects revenue from a variety of different taxes. Most important is the individual income tax, which has accounted for approximately 50 percent of federal revenue over the past 50 years. Revenues from corporate income tax have fallen considerably over this time period, from 23 percent in 1966 to 7 percent in 2018. In the same period, taxes for social insurance and retirement have grown substantially. Does the federal government draw more of its revenue from progressive taxes or regressive taxes?

NOTE: Data for 2018 are estimated.

SOURCE: Office of Management and Budget, "Table 2.3—Receipts by Source as Percentages of GDP: 1934–2022." 2—Percentage Composition of Receipts by Source: 1934–2021." www.whitehouse.gov/omb/budget/Historicals (accessed 11/1/17).

same rate so that people who make less money end up paying a greater share of their income in sales taxes than do people who make more money. The Social Security tax is another example of a regressive tax. In 2018, Social Security law applied a tax of 6.2 percent on the first $128,400 of income for the retirement program.[44] This means that a person earning $128,400 pays $7,960 and a person making twice as much, $256,800, pays the same $7,960, a rate of 3.1 percent. And a CEO earning $5 million in income also pays the same $7,960, for a rate of 0.16 percent. In contrast, the income tax is progressive; in 2018, a single person pays no tax on the first $12,000 of earned income due to the standard deduction (they may have additional deductions from taxable income such as retirement savings (see "tax expenditures" in Chapter 17). Income above that amount is taxed in a graduated way: the next $9,525 is taxed at 10 percent, the next $29,175 is taxed at 12 percent, and so on through brackets at 22, 24, 32, and 35 percent, up to the top bracket, which taxes income above $500,000 at the highest marginal income tax rate, 37 percent.

Although the primary purpose of the graduated income tax is, of course, to raise revenue, an important second objective is to collect revenue in such a way as to reduce the disparities of wealth between the lowest and the highest income brackets. We call this a policy of **redistribution**. Another policy objective of the income tax is the encouragement of the capitalist economy by rewarding investment. The tax laws allow individuals or companies to deduct from their taxable income any money they can justify as an investment or a "business expense"; this gives an incentive to individuals and companies to spend money to expand their production, advertising, or staff and reduces the income taxes that businesses have to pay. These kinds of deductions are called incentives by those who support them; others call them **loopholes**. The tax reforms of the 1980s closed a number of

redistribution a policy whose objective is to tax or spend in such a way as to reduce the disparities of wealth between the lowest and the highest income brackets

loophole incentive to individuals and businesses to reduce their tax liabilities by investing their money in areas the government designates

Tax Rates around the World

Do Americans pay more or less in taxes compared to citizens in other wealthy democracies? Taxation can be difficult to compare across countries. Regarding income tax, some countries set different rates for married people and those with children (see the left-side graph). The United States also has fewer cash transfer programs (such as social security and unemployment insurance) than other democracies, which further reduces individual tax burdens. When these factors are taken into account, the United States income tax rate is close to average.[a]

However, taxes on personal income are not the only taxes governments collect. They also collect sales tax, property tax, and social security contributions. If we look at the total tax revenue as a share of a country's economy (GDP), we see that the U.S. tax burden is significantly less than that of many other wealthy countries (see the right-side graph). Europeans in particular pay more in sales and other taxes, leading to a higher tax burden. There is a trade-off between higher taxes and government services: Europeans receive a number of benefits that Americans have to pay for out of their personal incomes, including cheaper health care, lower (or free) college tuition, and subsidized child and senior care.[b]

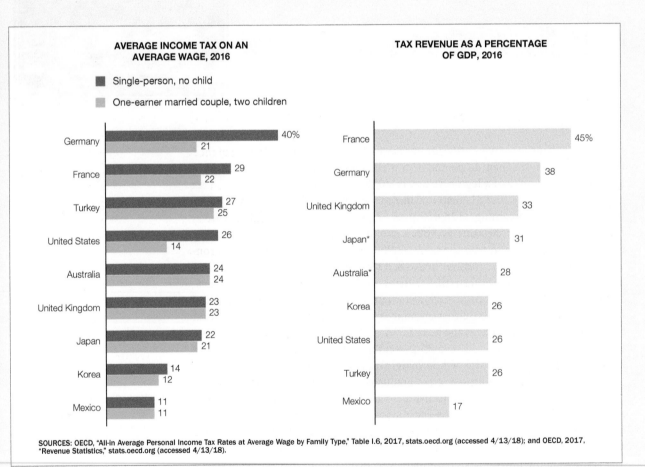

AVERAGE INCOME TAX ON AN AVERAGE WAGE, 2016

- Single-person, no child
- One-earner married couple, two children

Country	Single-person, no child	One-earner married couple, two children
Germany	40%	21
France	29	22
Turkey	27	25
United States	26	14
Australia	24	24
United Kingdom	23	23
Japan	22	21
Korea	14	12
Mexico	11	11

TAX REVENUE AS A PERCENTAGE OF GDP, 2016

Country	Percentage
France	45%
Germany	38
United Kingdom	33
Japan*	31
Australia*	28
Korea	26
United States	26
Turkey	26
Mexico	17

SOURCES: OECD, "All-in Average Personal Income Tax Rates at Average Wage by Family Type," Table I.6, 2017, stats.oecd.org (accessed 4/13/18); and OECD, 2017, "Revenue Statistics," stats.oecd.org (accessed 4/13/18).

[a] When compared to the average of the members of the Organization for Economic Co-Operation and Development (OECD), an international organization of upper- and middle-income democracies.

[b] Steven Hill, "The Myth of Low-Tax America: Why Americans Aren't Getting Their Money's Worth," *The Atlantic*, April 15, 2013, www.theatlantic.com/business/archive/2013/04/the-myth-of-low-tax-america-why-americans-arent-getting-their-moneys-worth/274945/ (accessed 4/13/18).

important loopholes in U.S. tax laws. But others still exist—on employer-provided health insurance and on business expenses, for example—and others returned because there is a strong consensus among members of Congress, both Democrats and Republicans, that businesses often need such incentives. The differences between the two parties focus largely on which incentives are justifiable.[45] The tax reform passed by Congress and signed by President Trump in 2017 both lowered corporate tax rates and left many special tax provisions for business in place.[46] The tax reform also tried to reduce the incentives for corporations to limit their taxes by merging with foreign firms in lower tax countries—a practice known as "corporate inversion"—by introducing new tax preferences: allowing firms to bring home foreign earnings at a one-time lower tax rate and eliminating the taxation of dividends that U.S.-based multinational corporations bring home from their foreign subsidiaries.[47]

The tax reform laws of 1981, 1986, and 2001–03 significantly reduced the progressiveness of the federal income tax by reducing tax rates and the number of brackets. In the 1960s the highest tax bracket applied a 91 percent tax to income over $200,000 (which is the equivalent of $1.5 million in today's dollars).[48] By the late 1970s there were 25 different tax brackets, with a top rate of 70 percent. Under Ronald Reagan, the Economic Recovery Tax Act of 1981 first indexed brackets to inflation, and then, dramatically, the Tax Reform Act of 1986 established just two tax brackets at 15 percent and 28 percent, beginning in the 1988 tax year.

During the administrations of George H. W. Bush and Bill Clinton, the number of tax brackets expanded again and the top rate rose to 39.6 percent. In 2001 and 2003, the George W. Bush administration and Republican-led Congress passed major cuts to taxes on income, dividends and capital gains, and estates. Due to procedural rules, these tax cuts were scheduled to expire at the end of 2010. The tax cuts reduced federal revenues by an estimated $1.3 trillion over 10 years.[49] The argument for the tax cuts was that they would make for a prosperous economy. Opponents charge that it made no sense to cut taxes since the benefits of the tax cuts went primarily to the wealthy. Critics also charge that the tax cuts caused the federal budget, which was in surplus when Bush took office, to fall into deficit.[50]

Upon taking office in 2009, President Obama and the Democratic leadership proposed extending the tax cuts for everyone with annual incomes under $250,000; those making more would have their income taxes revert back to the rates in the 1990s. Republicans preferred to extend the tax cuts for everyone. With the economy weak due to the Great Recession, all tax cuts were extended until a complex series of negotiations in late 2012 increased income taxes on high earners from 35 percent (Bush level) to 39.6 percent (Clinton level) and restored the estate tax (although with a very high exemption, so that only 0.2 percent of estates are taxed each year).

In 2017 the Tax Cuts and Jobs Act (TCJA) under President Trump reduced the top rate again to 37 percent, changed tax rate thresholds, and doubled the exemption for the estate tax to $22 million per couple. It also lowered the top corporate tax rate from 35 to 21 percent and allowed small businesses ("pass-throughs") to be taxed at 21 percent rather than at the relevant individual tax rate. (See Table 16.1 for the tax brackets in 2018. The brackets go up every year to keep pace with inflation, although the TCJA changed the measure of inflation used, which will push taxpayers into higher tax brackets more quickly than did the previous measure.)

Spending and Budgeting The federal government's power to spend is one of the most important tools of economic policy. Decisions about how much to spend

TABLE 16.1

Taxable Income Brackets and Rates, 2018

This table shows the federal tax rates that Americans pay on their income. The United States has a progressive tax system in that the tax rate goes up on Americans with more income.

TAX RATE (%)	INDIVIDUALS	MARRIED COUPLES FILING JOINTLY	HEAD OF HOUSEHOLD FILERS
10	$0 to $9,525	$0 to $19,050	$0 to $13,600
12	$9,525 to $38,700	$19,050 to $77,400	$13,600 to $51,800
22	$38,700 to $82,500	$77,400 to $165,000	$51,800 to $82,500
24	$82,500 to $157,500	$165,000 to $315,000	$82,500 to $157,500
32	$157,500 to $200,000	$315,000 to $400,000	$157,500 to $200,000
35	$200,000 to $500,000	$400,000 to $600,000	$200,000 to $500,000
37	$500,000+	$600,000+	$500,000+

SOURCE: Tax Foundation, "2018 Tax Brackets (Updated)," January 2018, https://files.taxfoundation.org/20180207142513/TaxFoundation-FF567-Updated.pdf (accessed 3/29/18).

FOR CRITICAL ANALYSIS

Think about a specific instance of government intervention in the American economy since the New Deal. What economic policy tool was used? What other tools might have been used? In your opinion, when is government action in the economy necessary?

affect the overall health of the economy. They also affect every aspect of American life, from the distribution of income to the availability of different modes of transportation to the level of education in society.

The president and Congress have each created institutions to assert control over the budget process. The Office of Management and Budget (OMB) in the Executive Office of the President is responsible for preparing the president's budget. This budget contains the president's spending priorities and the estimated costs of the president's policy proposals. It is viewed as the starting point for the annual debate over the budget. When different parties control the presidency and Congress, the president's budget may have little influence on the budget that is ultimately adopted. Members of the president's own party also may have different priorities.

Congress has its own budget institutions. Congress created the Congressional Budget Office (CBO) in 1974 so that it could have reliable information about the costs and economic impact of the policies it considers. At the same time, it set up a budget process designed to establish spending priorities and to consider individual expenditures in light of the entire budget. A key element of the process is the annual budget resolution, which designates broad targets for spending. By estimating the costs of policy proposals, Congress hoped to control spending and reduce deficits. When the congressional budget process proved unable to hold down deficits in the 1980s, Congress established stricter measures to control spending, including "spending caps" that limit spending on some types of programs.

Not surprisingly, the fight for control over spending is one of the most contentious in Washington as interest groups and politicians strive to determine the priorities and appropriate levels of spending. Decisions about spending are made as part of the annual budget process. During the 1990s, when the federal **budget deficit** first became a major political issue and parties were deeply split on spending, the budget process became the focal point of the entire policy-making process. With the rapid swing from budget surpluses in 2000 to record deficits by 2003, deficits once again emerged as a political issue (Figure 16.4). This time, however, Republican leaders, who had made deficits the focal point of politics in the mid-1990s, largely dismissed their importance. As House majority leader Tom DeLay put it, "The Soviet Union had a balanced budget. Well, you can raise taxes until you balance it, but the economy will go into the toilet."[51]

The deficit once again drove the economic policy agenda between 2010 and 2013, when Republicans in the House of Representatives and Democrats in the Senate and White House engaged in a contentious series of battles over the federal deficit and President Obama's economic policies.[52] The impasse stemmed from Republicans' insistence that the deficit, which had grown substantially in the aftermath of the Great Recession, be reduced primarily through spending cuts, while Democrats pushed for deficit reduction through a mix of spending cuts and tax increases for the wealthiest Americans. The resolution to the standoff, the Budget Control Act of 2011, achieved $1 trillion in deficit reduction over 10 years, all through spending cuts, but also scheduled additional, automatic across-the-board "sequestration" cuts beginning in 2013 if a bipartisan "super-committee" failed to reach a deal securing an additional $1.2 trillion in deficit reduction. To the frustration of all, the super-committee failed to agree on a new deficit-reduction plan, and in March 2013 the sequestration cuts finally came into effect. A period of high-stakes back-and-forth negotiation over the debt finally came to an end in October 2013 when another failure to agree on the terms of raising the debt

budget deficit amount by which government spending exceeds government revenue in a fiscal year

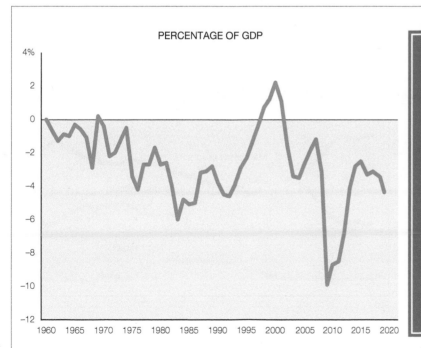

PERCENTAGE OF GDP

FIGURE 16.4

U.S. Budget Deficits and Surpluses, 1960–2018*

The federal deficit grew substantially during the 1980s under President Reagan. During the 1990s, the budget deficit declined significantly but then grew dramatically after 2001. When was the last time that the federal budget showed a surplus? Why did the budget deficit grow so much after 2001?

*Data for 2018 are estimated.

SOURCE: Office of Management and Budget, "Historical Tables Table 1.2—Summary of Receipts, Outlays, and Surpluses or Deficits (–) as Percentages of GDP: 1930–2023," www.whitehouse.gov/omb/budget/Historicals (accessed 7/28/18).

ceiling—with Republicans demanding a one-year delay in the implementation of the Affordable Care Act, further spending cuts on social programs, and negotiations on entitlements reform; and Democrats insisting on a clean, no-strings-attached increase in the debt limit—led to a shutdown of the federal government for the first time in almost two decades.[53] The government reopened after 16 days with a resolution cleanly raising the debt limit and funding the government for another two years. In 2015 it appeared that the government once again would shut down as conservative Republicans threatened to withhold their approval. But after the resignation of John Boehner as Speaker and several months of negotiation, Congress was able to enact a budget.

A very large and growing proportion of the annual federal budget is **mandatory spending**, expenditures that are, in the words of the OMB, "relatively uncontrollable." Interest payments on the national debt, for example, are determined by the actual size of the national debt. Legislation has mandated payment rates for such programs as retirement under Social Security, retirement for federal employees, unemployment assistance, Medicare, and farm price supports (see Figure 16.5). These payments increase with the cost of living; they increase as the average age of the population goes up; they increase as national and world agricultural surpluses go up. In 1965, 26.9 percent of the total federal budget was made up of such mandatory spending, rising to 45.5 percent in 1975 and 62 percent by 2018. This means that the national government now can do very little **discretionary spending** that will allow it to counteract fluctuations in the business cycle (the rise and fall of economic growth). (Figure 16.6 shows discretionary spending in 2018.)

Government spending as a fiscal policy works fairly well when deliberate deficit spending is used to stop a recession and to speed up the recovery period, but it does not work very well in fighting inflation because elected politicians are often politically unable to make the drastic expenditure cuts and tax hikes necessary to balance the budget, much less to produce a budgetary surplus.

mandatory spending federal spending that is made up of budget items that cannot be controlled through the regular budget process, such as interest on the national debt, Social Security and Medicare benefits, and certain programs in the Departments of Agriculture and Veterans Affairs, among others

discretionary spending federal spending on programs that are controlled through the regular budget process

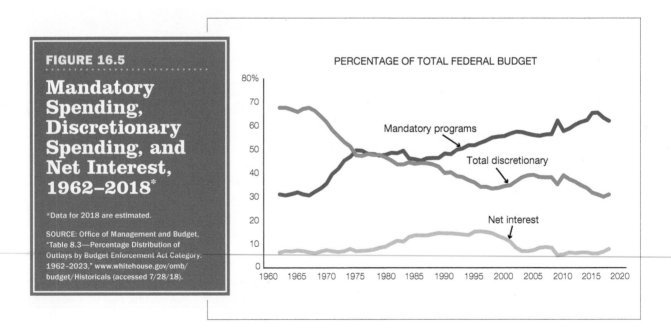

FIGURE 16.5

Mandatory Spending, Discretionary Spending, and Net Interest, 1962–2018*

*Data for 2018 are estimated.

SOURCE: Office of Management and Budget, "Table 8.3—Percentage Distribution of Outlays by Budget Enforcement Act Category: 1962–2023," www.whitehouse.gov/omb/budget/Historicals (accessed 7/28/18).

PERCENTAGE OF TOTAL FEDERAL BUDGET

Mandatory programs

Total discretionary

Net interest

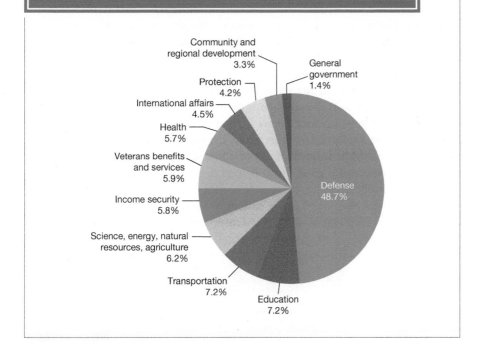

Discretionary Spending, 2018*

The biggest items in the federal budget are mandatory programs, including Social Security and Medicare. These programs are supported by contributory taxes and enjoy broad support. It is easier to cut discretionary spending because appropriations must be approved each year. With rising budget deficits and congressional unwillingness to raise taxes, discretionary spending—including defense but especially domestic programs—is often a target for cuts.

*Estimate.

NOTE: Health includes discretionary spending on Medicare.

SOURCE: Office of Management and Budget, "Table 8.7—Outlays for Discretionary Programs, 1962–2023." www.whitehouse.gov/omb/budget/Historicals (accessed 7/28/18).

Community and regional development 3.3%
General government 1.4%
Protection 4.2%
International affairs 4.5%
Health 5.7%
Veterans benefits and services 5.9%
Income security 5.8%
Science, energy, natural resources, agriculture 6.2%
Transportation 7.2%
Education 7.2%
Defense 48.7%

REGULATION AND ANTITRUST POLICY

In addition to monetary and fiscal policy, another tool of economic policymaking is regulation and antitrust policy. Federal economic regulation aims to protect the public against potential abuses by concentrated economic power in two ways. First, the federal government can establish conditions that govern the operation of big businesses to ensure fair competition. For example, it can require a business to make information about its activities and account books available to the public. Second, the federal government can force a large business to break up into smaller companies if it finds that the business has established a **monopoly.** This is called **antitrust policy.** In addition to economic regulation, the federal government engages in social regulation. Social regulation establishes conditions on businesses in order to protect workers, the environment, and consumers.

monopoly a single firm in a market that controls all the goods and services of that market; absence of competition

antitrust policy government regulation of large businesses that have established monopolies

Federal regulatory policy has evolved, in part, as a reaction to public demands. As the American economy prospered throughout the nineteenth century, some companies grew so large that they were recognized as possessing "market power." This meant that they were powerful enough to eliminate competitors and to impose conditions on consumers rather than catering to consumer demand. The growth of billion-dollar corporations led to collusion among companies to control prices, much to the dismay of smaller businesses and ordinary consumers. Small businesses, laborers, farmers, and consumers all began to clamor for protective regulation. Although the states had been regulating businesses in one way or another all along, interest groups turned to Washington as economic problems appeared to be beyond the reach of the individual state governments. If markets were national, there would have to be national regulation.[54]

The first national regulatory policy was the Interstate Commerce Act of 1887, which created the first national independent regulatory commission, the Interstate Commerce Commission, designed to control the monopolistic practices of the railroads. Three years later, the Sherman Antitrust Act extended regulatory power to cover all monopolistic practices. The Interstate Commerce Commission and the Sherman Antitrust Act were strengthened in 1914 with the enactment of the Federal Trade Commission Act (creating the Federal Trade Commission) and the Clayton Antitrust Act. At the same time, public demands to protect consumers led the federal government to enact a more limited number of social regulations. As we have seen, Upton Sinclair's best-seller about the meatpacking industry, *The Jungle*, led to the Federal Meat Inspection Act of 1906. Two decades later, the Food and Drug Administration was given broad powers to test and regulate products viewed as essential to public health.

The modern era of comprehensive national regulation began in the 1930s. Most of the regulatory programs of the 1930s were established to regulate the conduct of

Regulatory policies to protect consumers first emerged in the early twentieth century. The publication of Upton Sinclair's *The Jungle* in 1906 exposed the unsanitary practices of the meatpacking industry, spurring concerns about food safety that led to the Federal Meat Inspection Act that same year.

companies within specifically designated sectors of American industry. For example, the jurisdiction of one agency was the securities industry; the jurisdiction of another was the radio (and eventually television) industry. Others included banking, coal mining, and agriculture. At this time, Congress also set the basic framework of American labor regulation, including the rules for collective bargaining and the minimum wage. Regulation increased in the 1970s, with increased scope for agencies such as the Occupational Safety and Health Administration, the Consumer Product Safety Commission, and the Environmental Protection Agency (EPA).

Despite occasional high-profile regulatory cases such as the one against Microsoft in the 1990s, the trend since the late 1970s has been against regulation. Over the years, businesses complained about the burden of the new regulations they confronted, and many economists began to argue that excessive regulation was hurting the economy. In the 1980s, Congress and the president responded with a wave of **deregulation.** For example, President Reagan went about the task of changing the direction of regulation by way of "presidential oversight." Shortly after taking office, he gave the OMB authority to review all executive branch proposals for new regulations. By this means, Reagan reduced the total number of regulations issued by federal agencies, dropping the number of pages in the *Federal Register* from 74,000 in 1980 to 49,600 in 1987.[55]

> **deregulation** a policy of reducing or eliminating regulatory restraints on the conduct of individuals or private institutions

The financial crisis that began in 2008 put regulation on the agenda once again. As the economic emergency subsided, Congress began to consider long-term reform of the financial industry. A central question was how to create regulations that would prevent excessive risk-taking by investors, seen as the principal cause of the recession. The complex reform that Congress enacted in 2010 (the Dodd-Frank Wall Street Reform and Consumer Protection Act) included a range of new regulations on the financial industry. It created the Consumer Financial Protection Bureau (CFPB), placed under the auspices of the Federal Reserve but independent of it. The new agency has a broad mandate to regulate consumer financial products, such as mortgages and credit cards, to ensure that they are fair and competitive. President Trump sought to restrict the CFPB's powers, replacing the Obama-era head with his budget chief, Mick Mulvaney, reducing the agency's enforcement mission, and reconsidering rules for payday- and other lenders.[56]

SUBSIDIES AND CONTRACTING

Subsidies and contracting are the carrots of economic policy. Their purpose is to encourage people to do something they might otherwise not do or to get people to do more of what they are already doing. Sometimes the purpose is merely to compensate people for something done in the past.

Subsidies Subsidies are simply government grants of cash or other valuable commodities, such as land. Although subsidies are often denounced as "giveaways," they have played a fundamental role in the history of government in the United States. Subsidies were the dominant form of public policy of the national government and the state and local governments throughout the nineteenth century. They continue to be an important category of public policy at all levels of government.

> **subsidies** government grants of cash or other valuable commodities, such as land, to an individual or an organization; used to promote activities desired by the government, reward political support, or buy off political opposition

Economic sectors receiving substantial subsidies include agriculture, energy, transportation, health, and national defense. Policies using the subsidy technique continued to be plentiful in the twentieth century and into the twenty-first, even after the 1990s, when there was widespread public and official hostility toward

American farmers have long benefited from government subsidies. Agricultural subsidies are designed to help farmers stay in business even when the markets for their crops are less favorable so that the country can rely on a steady food supply.

subsidies. In 2017 the annual value of corporate subsidies was estimated at more than $100 billion.[57] Politicians have always favored subsidies because subsidies can be treated as "benefits" that can be spread widely in response to many demands that might otherwise produce profound political conflict. Subsidies can, in other words, be used to buy off the opposition.

Contracting Like any corporation, a government agency must purchase goods and services by contract. The law requires open bidding for a substantial proportion of these contracts because government contracts are extremely valuable to businesses in the private sector and because the opportunities and incentives for abuse surrounding contracting are very great. But contracting is more than a method of buying goods and services. It is also an important technique of policy because government agencies are often authorized to use their **contracting power** as a means of encouraging corporations to improve themselves, helping to build up whole sectors of the economy, and encouraging certain desirable goals or behavior, such as equal employment opportunity. For example, the infant airline industry of the 1930s was nurtured by the national government's lucrative contracts to carry airmail. A more recent example is the use of government contracting to encourage industries, universities, and other organizations to engage in research and development on a wide range of issues in basic and applied science.

Military contracting has long been a major element in government spending. So tight was the connection between defense contractors and the federal government during the Cold War that as he was leaving office President Eisenhower warned the nation to beware of the powerful "military–industrial complex." After the Cold War, as military spending and production declined, major defense contractors began to look for alternative business activities to supplement the reduced demand for weapons. For example, Lockheed Martin, the nation's largest defense contractor, began to bid on contracts related to welfare reform. Since the terrorist attacks of 2001, however, the military budget has been awash in new funds, and military contractors are

contracting power the power of government to set conditions on companies seeking to sell goods or services to government agencies

Military contracting has been a major component of government spending for decades. In the wars in Afghanistan and Iraq, George W. Bush relied heavily on defense contractors to provide services from intelligence analysis to security.

flooded with business. President Bush increased the Pentagon budget by more than 7 percent a year, requesting so many weapons systems that one observer called the budget a "weapons smorgasbord."[58] Military contractors geared up to produce not only weapons for foreign warfare but also surveillance systems to enhance domestic security.

The Environment and the Economy

> **Explain why the government tries to balance economic prosperity with policies that protect the environment**

One of the most important reasons that the government intervenes in the economy is to protect the environment. Although federal interest in environmental conservation stretches back to the beginning of the twentieth century, federal regulation of industry grew more extensive with the rise of the modern environmental movement in the 1970s. By then the consequences of economic growth that paid little attention to environmental impact were evident all over America. Cleveland's Cuyahoga River, long a dumping ground for industrial waste, caught fire in 1969, and the burning river became an especially vivid symbol of environmental neglect. The first "Earth Day," in 1970, highlighted the new ecological concerns, which became a major feature of American politics in subsequent decades.[59]

A wave of new laws wrote environmental goals into policy. The 1969 National Environmental Policy Act (NEPA), the Clean Air Act amendments of 1970, the 1972 Clean Water Act, and the 1974 Safe Drinking Water Act together established a new set of goals and procedures for protecting the environment. These acts are properly considered part of economic policy because they affect virtually every aspect of the economy. NEPA, for example, requires federal agencies to prepare an environmental impact statement for every major development project they propose. In this

> **FOR CRITICAL ANALYSIS**
>
> What are some of the policies that can be used to address climate change? Which policies have the best chance of being enacted?

way, environmental impacts routinely become factored into considerations about whether a particular project is feasible or desirable.

Environmental disasters have often drawn attention to new environmental hazards and have prompted greater federal regulation. For example, the explosion and sinking of the Deepwater Horizon oil rig in the Gulf of Mexico in 2010 resulted in 11 deaths and the largest oil spill in the history of marine drilling, devastating Gulf economies and wildlife. The Department of the Interior issued new regulations on well casings and "blowout preventers" and increased monitoring of drilling and spill containment as a result.[60] Yet government action and corporate liability are often bitterly contested issues in this area. Protecting the environment presents policy makers with difficult trade-offs. Compliance with environmental regulations can be very costly. Moreover, critics maintain that federal standards are sometimes too high. How clean should the air be? What is the difference between pure drinking water and safe drinking water? Who should bear the costs of protecting the environment? Not only do citizens, consumers, and businesses take different perspectives on these questions but the goals themselves often present a moving target. As new scientific evidence shows new or suspected environmental hazards, conflicts emerge over the proper role of government.

THE DEBATE ON CLIMATE CHANGE

Nowhere have these conflicts been more acute than in the debate over climate change. A large and growing body of scientific evidence suggests that greenhouse gas emissions from cars, power plants, and other human-made sources are causing temperatures on Earth to rise.[61] The projected environmental consequences are dire: melting polar ice caps, extreme weather, droughts, fire, rising sea levels, and disease. All would have profound economic consequences. Yet these projections come with considerable uncertainty. How likely are the most catastrophic scenarios? Should we prepare for the most damaging outcomes or only the most likely outcomes of climate change?[62] These questions are important because the costs of transforming the world's carbon-based technologies through lower energy use and newer green technologies are enormous. These questions are especially salient for the United States, which has the world's largest economy and is responsible for 14 percent of the world's greenhouse gas emissions but has only 4 percent of the world's population.[63] And because the United States relies so heavily on fossil fuels for its energy sources, the effort to reduce carbon emission requires a major shift in how we obtain and use energy.

As scientists have learned more about the effects of human activity on the climate, the issue of climate change has risen on the national agenda. But it has become embroiled in partisan politics, with many Republicans challenging the argument that human activity causes global warming. A growing share of Americans say the Earth is warming, 74 percent in 2017, up from 57 percent in 2010. However, public opinion remains divided. Some 92 percent of Democrats and 52 percent of Republicans believe the Earth is warming, but the large majority of Democrats say the cause is human activity, compared to about half of Republicans. Three-quarters of Democrats but only one-third of Republicans say that "stricter environmental laws and regulations are worth the cost."[64] Despite Republican opposition and public ambivalence, the Obama administration made climate change an important focus of attention and encouraged federal agencies to move aggressively on this issue. In 2009 the EPA began to set standards so that it could, for the first time ever, regulate

Low-lying coastal areas are particularly vulnerable to the effects of climate change. Here, residents of Spring, Texas, wait to be rescued from rising floodwaters due to Hurricane Harvey.

greenhouse gas emissions under the Clean Air Act. In 2014 the EPA moved to regulate factories and power plants that emit greenhouse gases. Especially controversial was a rule that required coal plants to reduce greenhouse gas emissions by 30 percent by 2030. This Clean Power Plan never went into effect due to lawsuits filed by opposing states, and in October 2017 the head of the EPA in the Trump administration signed a measure to repeal the plan.[65] In addition, President Trump announced in June 2017 that the United States would leave the Paris Climate Accord, which President Obama had helped negotiate in 2015 and which was aimed at lowering the Earth's temperature.[66]

ENVIRONMENTAL POLICIES

Policy makers charged with devising approaches to climate change have identified three basic policy approaches. The first is mitigation, or reduction, of greenhouse gas emissions. The second is large-scale research and development to promote alternative technologies. The third consists of measures that allow us to adapt to a warmer climate. Each of these strategies entails potentially gargantuan costs in the form of higher energy prices, subsidies to industry, infrastructure projects, and relocation decisions. When specific policy proposals are discussed and these costs become apparent, the consensus for addressing climate change breaks down.

Mitigation: Reducing Emissions The mitigation approach, which seeks to reduce greenhouse gas emissions, has garnered the most attention from policy makers. Two proposed policies that aim to achieve this goal, both controversial, are tougher standards for auto fuel mileage and higher taxes on gasoline. Although the public strongly supports higher gas-mileage standards, auto companies resisted such standards for nearly 30 years after they were first put in place in the early 1970s. In 2009 the EPA announced that it would set standards for greenhouse gas emissions for automobiles under the Clean Air Act, raising the fuel economy standards for new vehicles to 35.5 miles per gallon beginning in

One approach to addressing climate change is reducing emissions from factories, power plants, and cars. Capping emissions can be controversial if doing so imposes costs on businesses and ultimately on consumers, but recent cap-and-trade proposals may offer a more efficient way to reduce pollution.

2016, a standard later boosted to 54.5 miles per gallon by 2025.[67] In August 2017 the EPA and Transportation Department under President Trump announced a potential relaxation of these rules.[68] As for proposals to increase gasoline taxes, public-opinion polls routinely show that a majority of Americans oppose a tax on gasoline as a way to reduce emissions, and few politicians want to sponsor such an unpopular policy.[69]

Proponents of reducing carbon emissions pinned their hopes on a "cap-and-trade" system as the most politically feasible strategy to achieve their goal. This approach sets a target for carbon emissions for each industry but allows companies to trade "carbon credits" with one another. This market-based system is attractive to political leaders because it achieves its goals by creating incentives for private actors and allows them flexibility as they seek to reduce emissions. More than 23 large firms, including leading automakers, joined environmentalists in a coalition called the U.S. Climate Action Partnership to press for a cap-and-trade system to reduce carbon emissions.[70] In 2009 the House of Representatives passed a landmark cap-and-trade bill aimed at reducing greenhouse gas emissions. However, opposition from some Democrats and most Republicans in the Senate blocked further movement on cap-and-trade legislation.

Promoting Alternative Technologies Many analysts and politicians prefer a second strategy for addressing the problems associated with fossil fuels, one that centers on increased research and development to promote alternative technologies. President Obama came out strongly in favor of a comprehensive energy and climate change bill that would, among other things, provide funding and large tax incentives for the production and adoption of clean-energy technologies. He also warned that the United States was falling behind other countries, including China, in the production of clean-energy products, arguing that this industry would be a vital source of millions of new jobs over the next few decades.[71] The 2009 Recovery Act allocated nearly $30 billion to support alternative energy technology investment and to improve energy efficiency. President Trump, through executive orders and budget proposals, has reduced support for such initiatives.

Green technologies may prove to be a boon for the American economy. Indeed, in 2015 more than 80 companies, including Apple, Coca-Cola, McDonald's, and Google, signed an "American Business Act on Climate Pledge" aimed at making low-carbon investments and reducing emissions in their operations.[72] Because highly skilled labor is required to produce most such technologies, America has a competitive advantage over many other countries. Furthermore, a move toward green technologies could significantly improve American national security. Indeed, some argue that reducing the use of fossil fuels and adopting more fuel-efficient technologies would take money away from regimes that support terrorism against the United States.

One strategy for curtailing the effects of climate change is to reduce the use of fossil fuels in favor of "clean-energy" or "green" technologies. In 2016 the Nellis Air Force Base in Las Vegas opened its array of solar panels, which provides 42 percent of the base's electricity requirements. Military leaders have deemed climate change a national security "threat multiplier" that both affects military operations and drives political instability abroad. (*Data from U.S. Department of Defense, "2014 Climate Change Adaptation Roadmap," http://ppec.asme.org/wp-content/uploads/2014/10/CCARprint.pdf [accessed 11/28/17].*)

Adaptation Policies A final approach to climate change is adaptation to a warmer climate. Adaptation would entail a diverse set of policies, including establishment of green corridors, pest and disease control, water conservation to deal with drought, and new infrastructure such as seawalls to cope with rising sea levels.[73] Many scientists believe that deliberate adaptation has to be part of any approach to climate change because even if we take major steps to mitigate carbon emissions and pour resources into developing new technologies, climate change has already arrived.

Many aspects of a deliberate adaptation strategy would be difficult to implement in the market-oriented, decentralized context of the United States. Although some European countries, such as the low-lying Netherlands, are relocating people as part of their adaptation strategy, American politicians have little stomach for initiating such controversial measures. Moreover, the combination of conservation and new infrastructure requires considerable public resources and broad coordination across multiple public agencies. Both are hard to achieve in the context of American politics. For example, the environmentally sensitive Sacramento delta is extremely vulnerable to rising sea levels. The delta, a swath of land that lies below sea level, is economically important because it supplies much of Northern California, including California agribusiness, with water. Yet decisions about what happens in the delta involve more than 200 government agencies.[74]

Global climate change poses a difficult economic challenge for the United States. It presents the opportunity for American industry to take the lead in developing green technologies, placing the nation's economic prosperity on a fundamentally new base. Yet it also calls for government to enforce the reduction of carbon emissions and adapt current practices to a changing world. Many industries have expressed support for action to address climate change, but such a major economic transformation creates winners and losers. Firms, such as the auto companies, whose profits are jeopardized and workers whose jobs are threatened by change have successfully blocked bold action in the past. The diffuse long-term harms that climate change poses are hard to pit against the specific concentrated costs that industries face today. Nonetheless, growing recognition that climate change is real and poses potentially catastrophic consequences ensures that economic policy and environmental policy will be ever more closely intertwined in the future.

Economic Policy
WHAT DO WE WANT?

Economic policy brings up issues that cut to the core of how Americans set priorities about their livelihoods and who has access to the American Dream. Just as Chris Boggess is frustrated by the regulations that affect his craft brewery, you may have frustrations with government economic policies that affect your life in areas such as college funding, wages, taxes, and transportation. In myriad ways government policy affects your future job opportunities, what kinds of further education or training you can access, and where you may live. Changing policy in any of these areas means tough decisions: If more government funding is provided for, say, college financial aid, where does the money come from? Cuts to other programs? If so, which ones? Higher taxes, but on whom? Economic policy spotlights these kinds of trade-offs.

The sharp partisan divide that has driven the politics of economic policy the last three decades makes public debate about such issues more complicated than ever. Most Republicans have pressed for freer markets and less government, while most Democrats have defended the need for market regulation and more government intervention in the economy. The partisan divisions have made it difficult for policy makers to come to terms with an economy that has changed radically since the debate over more or less government commenced during the Reagan years. The American economy is now far more open to the rest of the world, and many American firms do most of their production in China and other developing economies, not in the United States. At the same time, the distribution of economic gains in the United States has shifted upward. As the debate about more or less government has led to a series of policy stalemates among politicians, the income of the American middle class has stagnated while the gains going to the top 1 percent have soared.[75] Some Americans think the government should do more to address income inequality through tax policy, for example, by taxing the wealthy at higher rates, while others disagree. The "**Who Participates?**" feature on the facing page shows taxes as a percentage of income at both the federal and state and local levels.

Everyone agrees that economic policy should address the needs of the next generation. This focus on the future requires shifting the debate over economic policy from "more or less government" to "what kind of government." And as the federal government has stalled over these issues, much action has shifted to states and localities. We saw that some states and localities have raised their minimum wages. Some, including Tennessee, Minnesota, Oregon, Rhode Island, and New York, have passed laws to make community college free. These and other state models offer important guideposts that can inform federal policy and perhaps ultimately help to break the stalemate over government's role in the economy.

Who Pays Taxes?

Taxes as a Percentage of Income, 2017

● Federal taxes   ● State and local taxes

Income group	Lowest 20%	Second 20%	Middle 20%	Fourth 20%	Next 10%	Next 5%	Next 4%	Top 1%
Federal taxes	7%	12%	16%	20%	22%	23%	23%	25%
State and local taxes	12%	12%	11%	11%	11%	11%	10%	9%
Average tax cut due to 2017 tax bill	$100	$410	$800	$1,400	$2,770	$2,770	$12,470	$55,190

Household income: $15,000

● Federal taxes: 7%
● State and local taxes: 12%

Income after taxes: $12,150

Household income: $310,000

● Federal taxes: 23%
● State and local taxes: 11%

Income after taxes: $204,600

SOURCES: Institute on Taxation and Economic Policy, "Who Pays Taxes in America in 2018?," April 2017, itep.org; "The Final Trump-GOP Tax Plan," December 2017, itep.org (accessed 1/11/18).

WHAT YOU CAN DO

Compare Tax Rates

☑ Learn more about how tax rates vary by income, state, and local area at **www.taxfoundation.org**. Contact your representatives at the state or federal level to express your opinion.

☑ Compare tax rates in the United States to those paid in countries around the world at **www.businessinsider.com/america-taxes-charts-2013-1**.

☑ Learn more about your rights as a taxpayer, how to get help with your taxes, and how to avoid tax scams from the Internal Revenue Service (**www.irs.gov**).

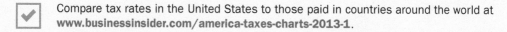

★ STUDY GUIDE ★

The Goals of Economic Policy

Identify the broad reasons government gets involved in the economy (pp. 633–41)

Public policies, which are officially expressed goals backed by rewards or punishments, can be embodied in laws, rules, regulations, or orders. In contemporary societies, government makes it possible for the economy to function efficiently by setting the rules for economic exchange and punishing those who violate the rules. Through a variety of different policies, the U.S. government has pursued four economic goals over the last century: to promote economic stability, to stimulate economic growth, to promote business development, and to protect employees and consumers.

Key Terms

public policy (p. 633)

public goods (p. 634)

gross domestic product (GDP) (p. 634)

inflation (p. 637)

categorical grants (p. 638)

Practice Quiz

1. Which of the following is *not* one of the goals of government intervention in the economy?
   a) to guarantee economic equality
   b) to promote economic stability
   c) to stimulate economic growth
   d) to promote business development
   e) to protect employees and consumers

2. The total value of goods and services produced within a country is referred to as
   a) the gross national product.
   b) the gross domestic product.
   c) the Dow Jones Industrial Average.
   d) the federal funds rate.
   e) the Gini coefficient.

3. *Inflation* refers to
   a) a lack of change in the general level of prices.
   b) a tax on imported goods.
   c) a consistent increase in the general level of prices.
   d) a consistent decrease in the general level of prices.
   e) an increase in the interest rate on loans between banks.

The Politics of Economic Policy Making

Explore why economic policy is often controversial (pp. 641–49)

Although all politicians want a healthy economy, they often have different views about how to attain it and what the priorities of economic policy should be. The three schools of economic thought that have been most influential with American policy makers, interest groups, and members of the public are Keynesianism, laissez-faire capitalism, and supply-side economics. Government spending is controversial, but there is usually little public support for cutting specific programs. Consumer groups, environmentalists, businesses, and labor all work to shape economic policy.

Key Terms

Keynesians (p. 642)

laissez-faire capitalism (p. 642)

supply-side economics (p. 643)

Practice Quiz

4. The argument for laissez-faire capitalism was first elaborated by
   a) Ben Bernanke.
   b) Milton Friedman.
   c) Alan Greenspan.
   d) James Madison.
   e) Adam Smith.

5. Which of the following economic perspectives argues that government can stimulate economic growth by increasing public spending or by cutting taxes?
   a) Keynesianism
   b) laissez-faire
   c) libertarianism
   d) monetarism
   e) fiscalism

6. Supply-side economics is
   a) an economic theory that argues government regulation of the economy should be limited to environmental protection.
   b) an economic theory that argues for government ownership of the means of production and distribution.
   c) an economic theory that argues tax reductions will spur economic growth because people will be able to spend and invest more of their money.
   d) an economic theory that argues every taxpayer should pay exactly the same tax rate.
   e) an economic theory that argues all taxes should be paid by the consumers of goods and services rather than the suppliers of goods and services.

The Tools of Economic Policy

Describe how the government uses monetary, fiscal, and regulatory policies to influence the economy (pp. 649–63)

The sustained growth of the American economy is the result of specific policies enacted by the U.S. government. The Constitution gives the federal government the power to set monetary and fiscal policies. Monetary policy in the United States is determined primarily by the Federal Reserve Board. Most of the U.S. government's revenues come from personal and corporate income taxes, and most of the federal government's budget is now made up of mandatory, rather than discretionary, spending.

Key Terms

monetary policies (p. 649)
Federal Reserve System (p. 650)
federal funds rate (p. 650)
fiscal policy (p. 652)
tariff (p. 652)
progressive taxation (p. 652)
regressive taxation (p. 652)
redistribution (p. 653)
loophole (p. 653)
budget deficit (p. 657)
mandatory spending (p. 658)
discretionary spending (p. 658)
monopoly (p. 659)
antitrust policy (p. 659)
deregulation (p. 661)
subsidies (p. 661)
contracting power (p. 662)

Practice Quiz

7. Monetary policy seeks to influence the economy through
   a) taxing and spending.
   b) privatizing and nationalizing selected industries.
   c) controlling the availability of money and credit to banks.
   d) foreign exchange of currency.
   e) administrative regulation.

8. Monetary policy is determined primarily by
   a) state governments.
   b) the Department of the Treasury.
   c) the federal judiciary.
   d) the Federal Reserve Board.
   e) the president.

9. Government attempts to affect the economy by using its taxing and spending powers are called
   a) antitrust policies.
   b) expropriation policies.
   c) monetary policies.
   d) fiscal policies.
   e) redistributive policies.

10. A tax that places a greater burden on those who are better able to afford it is called
    a) regressive.
    b) progressive.
    c) inflationary.
    d) a flat tax.
    e) voodoo economics.

11. A policy whose objective is to tax or spend in such a way as to reduce the disparities of wealth between the highest and lowest income brackets is called
    a) antitrust policy.
    b) deregulation.
    c) discretionary spending.
    d) equalization.
    e) redistribution.

12. Which of the following statements best describes the U.S. budget deficit?
    a) The budget deficit grew substantially in the 1980s and declined substantially in the 1990s before rising sharply again in the 2000s.
    b) The budget deficit declined substantially in the 1980s and grew substantially in the late 1990s into the 2000s.
    c) The budget deficit grew consistently between 1980 and the present.

d) The budget deficit declined consistently between 1980 and the present.

e) The budget deficit has remained exactly the same since 1980.

13. Which of the following statements best describes spending in the federal budget?

a) Mandatory and discretionary spending now make up approximately equal parts of the total budget.

b) Mandatory spending has been outlawed, and the total budget is now made up of discretionary spending.

c) Mandatory spending is now a much larger percentage of the total budget than discretionary spending.

d) Discretionary spending has been outlawed, and the total budget is now made up of mandatory spending.

e) Discretionary spending is now a much larger percentage of the total budget than mandatory spending.

The Environment and the Economy

Explain why the government tries to balance economic prosperity with policies that protect the environment (pp. 663–67)

The federal government frequently regulates industry in order to protect the environment. One of the most important environmental issues currently facing the U.S. government is climate change. Policy makers charged with devising approaches to the problem of climate change have identified three basic approaches: mitigation of greenhouse emissions, promotion of alternative energy technologies, and adaptation to a warmer climate.

Practice Quiz

14. A cap-and-trade system is an example of which kind of policy approach to global warming?

a) adaptation to a warmer climate

b) not in my backyard (NIMBY)

c) supply-side economics

d) mitigation of greenhouse gas emissions

e) promotion of alternative energy technologies

Further Reading

Baldwin, Robert, Martin Cave, and Martin Lodge. *Understanding Regulation*. New York: Oxford University Press, 2012.

Bernanke, Ben S. *The Federal Reserve and the Financial Crisis*. Princeton, NJ: Princeton University Press, 2013.

Blanchard, Olivier, Paul Romer, Michael Spence, and Joseph Stiglitz. *In the Wake of the Crisis: Leading Economists Reassess Economic Policy*. Cambridge, MA: MIT Press, 2012.

Frank, Robert H. *Falling Behind: How Rising Inequality Harms the Middle Class*. Berkeley: University of California Press, 2007.

Friedman, Milton, and Walter Heller. *Monetary versus Fiscal Policy*. New York: W. W. Norton, 1969.

Hacker, Jacob S., and Paul Pierson. *Winner-Take-All Politics: How Washington Made the Rich Richer—and Turned Its Back on the Middle Class*. New York: Simon and Schuster, 2010.

Harris, Richard A., and Sidney M. Milkis. *The Politics of Regulatory Change*. 2nd ed. New York: Oxford University Press, 1996.

Jacobs, Lawrence, and Theda Skocpol, eds. *Inequality and American Democracy: What We Know and What We Need to Learn*. New York: Russell Sage Foundation, 2005.

McCarty, Nolan, Keith T. Poole, and Howard Rosenthal. *Political Bubbles: Financial Crises and the Failure of American Democracy*. Princeton, NJ: Princeton University Press, 2013.

Page, Benjamin I., and Lawrence R. Jacobs. *Class War: What Americans Really Think about Economic Inequality*. Chicago: University of Chicago Press, 2009.

Schick, Allen. *The Federal Budget: Politics, Policy, Process*. 3rd ed. Washington, DC: Brookings Institution Press, 2007.

Stein, Robert M., and Kenneth N. Bickers. *Perpetuating the Pork Barrel: Policy Subsystems and American Democracy*. New York: Cambridge University Press, 1995.

Stiglitz, Joseph E. *Rewriting the Rules of the American Economy: An Agenda for Growth and Shared Prosperity*. New York: W. W. Norton, 2015.

Waterhouse, Benjamin C. *Lobbying America: The Politics of Business from Nixon to NAFTA*. Princeton, NJ: Princeton University Press, 2014.

Wells, David. *The Federal Reserve System*. Jefferson, NC: McFarland, 2004.

Recommended Websites

Board of Governors of the Federal Reserve System
www.federalreserve.gov

The Federal Reserve System consists of 12 banks that use monetary policy to fight inflation and deflation. Visit the Fed's official website to see how it is working to maintain a strong economy.

Citizens for Tax Justice
www.ctj.org

Review federal, state, and local tax laws at the website of Citizens for Tax Justice. This nonprofit organization is dedicated to educating ordinary citizens about tax laws and reducing the tax burden on low- and middle-income Americans.

National Bureau of Economic Research
www.nber.org

The National Bureau of Economic Research is a non-profit, nonpartisan organization dedicated to creating a better understanding of the economy. Take a minute to review some of its free research publications.

Tax Foundation
www.taxfoundation.org

The Tax Foundation is a respected organization that has been providing Americans with information about tax policy for more than 50 years. Click on your state to learn about current tax and spending policies.

Treasury Direct
www.treasurydirect.gov/govt/govt.htm

Treasury Direct, part of the U.S. Department of the Treasury, provides a statistical look at federal, state, and public debt.

U.S. Department of Commerce
www.commerce.gov

The U.S. Department of Commerce promotes domestic and international commerce to foster economic progress. Review the initiatives and programs designed to encourage economic development.

U.S. Department of Labor
www.dol.gov

The U.S. Department of Labor seeks to promote the well-being of wage earners, retired workers, and people looking for work. Look under "popular topics" to see some of the ways that the department aims to improve the conditions of workers.

Foreign Policy and Democracy

WHAT GOVERNMENT DOES AND WHY IT MATTERS Foreign policy may seem like a distant or abstract matter, but it carries tremendous consequences for ordinary people. In January 2017, President Trump signed an executive order banning travel to the United States for people from Iran, Iraq, Libya, Somalia, Sudan, Syria, and Yemen. The president's purpose was to protect U.S. borders and prohibit entry from countries with lax security standards. As with any public policy, views on the travel ban varied. Amanda Patrick of Georgia, a 38-year-old tax associate with a young son, supported the ban, saying, "The biggest thing for me, especially with having a child now, is the safety factor. Just people coming in that we aren't properly vetting." Susan Richardson, a 74-year-old artist and entrepreneur from Florida and an immigrant from England, believes countries have a right to defend their borders: "When I came to this country, if you didn't have the right visa, if you didn't have somebody who sponsored you, you were turned back at the airport."[1]

For yet others, the travel ban has meant personal turmoil. Mohamed Iye, an American citizen born in Somalia, was about to be reunited with his Somali wife and two American daughters after a two-year separation when the travel ban was issued, stranding

America's foreign policy can have profound effects on the lives of individuals here and abroad. President Trump's decision to ban immigration from certain countries put many lives in limbo, like that of Mohamed Iye (pictured here). Iye was reunited with his family after being stranded in Kenya when the ban was declared. Supporters of the ban maintain it is necessary to protect America from foreign threats.

his family in Nairobi. He and many others joined lawsuits against the ban. "It was never my intention to go against the president of the United States. I was just following the law and doing everything the way it's in the books. And it came to this." Ali Asaei, a 27-year-old originally from Iran who holds a master's degree and works at a psychiatric research institute in New York, also joined a lawsuit against the travel ban. He hadn't seen his family in four years, and their visa applications to visit him were rejected after the travel ban went into effect. He said that in Iran, "There is no freedom of speech, no freedom of press...One of the reasons I came here was

because I thought, here we're going to have the freedom of speech and religion and all these. But if I don't have those freedoms, then what would be the point of staying here?"[2]

The Trump administration's travel ban was challenged in the federal courts and was finally upheld by the U.S. Supreme Court in the 2018 case of *Trump v. Hawaii*.[3] The issue illustrates just one of the complexities of foreign policy. A government's first duty is to protect its citizens, but should protection mean the exclusion of citizens of foreign countries from America's shores? What about foreign trade? America's interests and those of foreign countries are so closely intertwined that the Trump administration's tariffs against foreign auto companies, and subsequent retaliation from America's trading partners, hurt workers in South Carolina where BMWs (a German car) are assembled and then shipped all over the world. In the realm of security interests, when dealing with America's rivals such as Russia, China, and North Korea, what is the proper mix of such foreign policy tools as diplomacy, economic pressure, and the threat of force? To make matters even more complicated, some threats require international rather than national responses, but achieving international cooperation is sometimes problematic. President Trump has demanded that America's NATO allies pay a larger share of the collective cost of defense, though his demands threaten to undermine the NATO alliance. The United States, like other nations, struggles to strike the right balance between competition and cooperation in the international arena.

CHAPTER GOALS

★ Explain how foreign policy is designed to promote security, prosperity, and humanitarian goals (pp. 717–22)

★ Identify the major players in foreign policy making, and describe their roles (pp. 722–33)

★ Describe the means the United States uses to carry out foreign policy today (pp. 733–41)

★ Analyze the foreign policy problems facing American policy makers today (pp. 741–45)

The Goals of Foreign Policy

Explain how foreign policy is designed to promote security, prosperity, and humanitarian goals

The term *foreign policy* refers to the programs and policies that determine America's relations with other nations and foreign entities. Foreign policy includes diplomacy, military and security policy, international human rights policies, and various forms of economic policy, such as trade policy and international energy policy. Of course, foreign policy and domestic policy are not completely separate categories but are instead closely intertwined. As we will see, domestic politics affects foreign policy and foreign policy certainly affects domestic politics. Take security policy, for example. Defending the nation requires the design and manufacture of tens of billions of dollars' worth of military hardware. The manufacture and procurement of this military equipment might provide jobs in American communities where the equipment is built, while paying for it involves raising taxes or choosing not to fund other types of programs. Various domestic interests, including corporations and communities, battle constantly to win defense contracts.

In this section we will examine the goals of American foreign policy. Although U.S. foreign policy has a number of purposes, two main goals stand out: security and prosperity. Some Americans also favor a third goal—improving the quality of life for all the world's people. Others say the United States should remain focused on its own challenges and not get involved in solving the world's problems. These foreign policy goals overlap with one another, and none can be pursued fully in isolation.

SECURITY

To many Americans, the chief goal of the nation's foreign policy is protection of U.S. security in an often hostile world. Traditionally, the United States has been concerned about threats that might emanate from other countries, such as Nazi Germany during the 1940s and then Soviet Russia until the Soviet Union's collapse in the late 1980s. Today, American security policy is concerned not only with the actions of other nations but also with the activities of terrorist groups and other hostile **non-state actors**.[4] To protect the nation's security from foreign threats, the United States has built an enormous military apparatus and a complex array of intelligence-gathering institutions, such as the Central Intelligence Agency (CIA), charged with evaluating and anticipating challenges from abroad.[5]

Security is, of course, a broad term. Policy makers must be concerned with Americans' physical security. The September 11, 2001, terrorist attacks killed and injured thousands of Americans, and the government constantly fears that new attacks could be even more catastrophic. Policy makers must also be concerned with such matters as the security of America's food supplies, transportation infrastructure, and energy supplies. Many American efforts in the Middle East, for example, are aimed at ensuring continuing American access to vital oil fields. In recent years, cyberspace has become a new security concern. The nation's dependence on computers means that the government must be alert to efforts by hostile governments, groups, or even individual "hackers" to damage computer networks or access sensitive or proprietary information. The U.S. government has often charged Chinese and Russian government and military agencies with stealing American secrets through cyber espionage.

non-state actors groups other than nation-states that attempt to play a role in the international system; terrorist groups are one type of non-state actor

In 2017 it appeared that a popular antivirus software marketed by a Russian company was being used by the Russian government to spy on American corporations and government agencies.

During the eighteenth and nineteenth centuries, American security was based mainly on the geographic isolation of the United States. Separated by two oceans from European and Asian powers, many Americans thought that the country's security would be best preserved by our remaining aloof from international power struggles. This policy was known as **isolationism**. In his 1796 Farewell Address, President George Washington warned Americans to avoid permanent alliances with foreign powers; and in 1823, President James Monroe warned foreign powers not to meddle in the Western Hemisphere. Washington's warning and what came to be called the Monroe Doctrine were the cornerstones of the U.S. foreign policy of isolationism until the end of the nineteenth century. The United States saw itself as the dominant power in the Western Hemisphere and, indeed, believed that its "manifest destiny" was to expand from sea to sea. The rest of the world, however, should remain at arm's length.

In the twentieth century, technology made oceans less of a barrier to foreign threats, and the world's growing economic interdependence meant that the nation could no longer ignore events abroad. Early in the twentieth century, the United States entered World War I on the side of Great Britain and France when the Wilson administration concluded that a German victory would adversely affect the economic and security interests of the United States. In 1941 the United States was drawn into World War II when Japan, hoping to become the dominant power in the Pacific, attacked the U.S. Pacific fleet anchored at Pearl Harbor, Hawaii. Even before the attack, the Roosevelt administration had concluded that the United States must act to prevent a victory by the German–Japanese–Italian Axis alliance. Until the Japanese attack, however, Roosevelt had been unable to overcome proponents of American isolationism, who declared that our security was best served by leaving foreigners to their own devices. With their attack, the Japanese proved that the Pacific Ocean could not protect the United States from foreign foes and effectively discredited isolationism as a security policy.

Following World War II, the United States developed a new security policy known as **containment** to check or "contain" the growing power of the Soviet Union, which, by the end of the 1940s, had built a huge empire, enormous military forces, and nuclear weapons and bombers capable of attacking the United States. The United States was committed to maintaining its own military might as a means of deterrence, to discourage the Soviets from attacking the United States or its allies. Some Americans wanted a more aggressive policy and argued that we should attack the Soviets before it was too late, a policy known as **preventive war**. Others said that we should show our peaceful intentions and attempt to placate the Soviets. This policy is called **appeasement**. Before World War II, the British had sought to prevent war by appeasing Nazi Germany. The disastrous results of this British effort left most Americans with little confidence in appeasement as a policy.

The policies that the United States actually adopted, **deterrence** and containment, could be seen as midway between preventive war and appeasement. A nation pursuing a policy of deterrence, on the one hand, signals its peaceful intentions but, on the other hand, indicates its willingness and ability to fight if attacked. Thus, during the era of confrontation with the Soviet Union, known as the **Cold War**, the United States frequently asserted that it had no intention of attacking the Soviet Union but also built a huge military force, including a vast

isolationism avoidance of involvement in the affairs of other nations

containment a policy designed to curtail the political and military expansion of a hostile power

preventive war policy of striking first when a nation fears that a foreign foe is contemplating hostile action

appeasement the effort to forestall war by giving in to the demands of a hostile power

deterrence An effort to prevent hostile action by promising to retaliate forcefully against an attacker

Cold War the period of struggle between the United States and the former Soviet Union lasting from the late 1940s to about 1990

arsenal of over 1,500 nuclear warheads, and frequently asserted that, in the event of a Soviet attack, it had the ability and will to respond with overwhelming force. The Soviet Union, which had also built powerful nuclear and conventional military forces, announced that its nuclear weapons were also intended for deterrent purposes. Eventually, the two sides possessed such enormous arsenals of nuclear missiles that each potentially had the ability to destroy the other in the event of war. This heavily armed standoff came to be called a posture of "mutually assured destruction," which discouraged either side from attacking the other. Eventually, this situation led to a period of "détente," in which a number of arms control agreements were signed and the threat of war was reduced.

A policy of deterrence requires not only the possession of large military forces but also that the nation pursuing such a policy convince potential adversaries that it is willing to fight. Thus, as part of its policy of deterrence, the United States engaged in wars in Korea and Vietnam, where it had no particular interests, because American policy makers believed that if the United States did not fight in these areas, the Soviets would be emboldened to pursue an expansionist policy elsewhere, thinking that the Americans would not respond. The Soviet Union collapsed in 1991, and the new Russia, though still a formidable power, at the time seemed to pose less of a threat to the United States.

A policy of deterrence assumes certainty and rationality. *Certainty* means that a potential adversary must know for sure that the United States will reply with force if attacked. *Rationality* means that, to be deterred, a potential adversary must be capable of rationally assessing the risks and costs of aggression against the United States. These two assumptions may not be valid in the context of some contemporary security threats. The September 11 terrorist attacks, for example, demonstrated the threat that non-state actors and so-called rogue states might acquire significant military capabilities, including nuclear weapons, and would not be affected by America's deterrent capabilities. Unlike **nation-states**, which are countries with governments and fixed borders, terrorist groups are non-state actors having no fixed geographic location that can be attacked. Terrorists may believe they can attack and melt away, leaving the United States with no one against whom to retaliate. Hence, the threat of massive retaliation does not deter them. Rogue states are nations with often unstable and erratic leaders who seem to pursue policies driven by ideological or religious fervor rather than careful consideration of economic or human costs. The United States considers North Korea and Iran to be rogue states, though most academic analysts see both nations' leaders as behaving belligerently but not necessarily irrationally.

To counter these new security threats, the George W. Bush administration shifted from a policy of deterrence to one of preventive war—the willingness to strike first in order to prevent an attack, particularly by enemies that might be armed with weapons of mass destruction. The United States declared that, if necessary, it would take action to disable terrorist groups and rogue states before they could develop the capacity to harm the United States.[6] The Bush administration's "global war on terror" was an expression of prevention, as was the U.S. invasion of Iraq. The United States also refused to rule out the possibility

During the Cold War, the United States and the Soviet Union engaged in an arms race, each acquiring nuclear weapons to deter the other from attacking.

nation-states political entities consisting of a people with some common cultural experience (nation) who also share a common political authority (state), recognized by other sovereignties (nation-states)

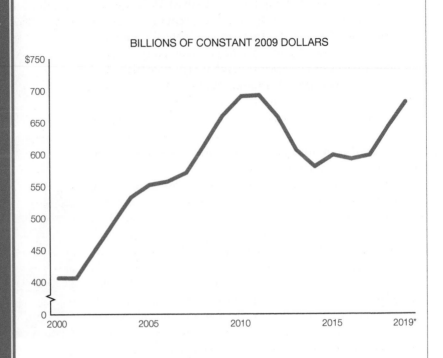

FIGURE 18.1

U.S. Spending on National Defense since 2000*

During the 1990s the budget for national defense declined as the country enjoyed a "peace dividend" following the conclusion of the Cold War. After the attacks of September 11 and the commencement of the war on terrorism, however, national defense spending rose steadily; in a decade, spending increased by 70 percent. Since that time, defense spending has fallen, partly as a result of sequestration (see Chapter 16). Defense spending rose somewhat in 2019 as a result of the lifting of spending caps in the 2018 budget agreement.

*Data for 2018 and 2019 are estimated.

SOURCE: Office of Management and Budget, "Table 3.1—Outlays by Superfunction and Function: 1940–2023," www.whitehouse.gov/omb/historical-tables/ (accessed 7/23/18).

BILLIONS OF CONSTANT 2009 DOLLARS

that it would attack North Korea or Iran if it deemed those nations' nuclear programs to be imminent threats to American security interests. Accompanying this shift in military doctrines was an enormous increase in overall U.S. military spending (see Figure 18.1).

President Obama took a less aggressive line, saying that the United States would rely on diplomacy and economic sanctions. President Trump, however, said that the United States was prepared to use overwhelming force against its adversaries. Trump called North Korean leader Kim Jong-un "little rocket man" and declared that only force would thwart Kim's ambitions. Nevertheless, in April 2018, Trump agreed to a meeting with Kim to discuss ways of reducing tensions on the Korean Peninsula. After the two leaders met, Trump declared that progress had been made toward a more peaceful resolution of the Korean conflict. In July 2018, Trump met with Russian president Vladimir Putin. Trump called the meeting a great success but critics charged that the president had not been sufficiently aggressive in demanding an accounting for Russian attempts to influence the 2016 American election.

ECONOMIC PROSPERITY

A second major goal of U.S. foreign policy is promoting American prosperity. America's international economic policies are intended to expand employment opportunities in the United States, to maintain access to foreign energy supplies at a reasonable cost, to promote foreign investment in the United States, and to lower the prices Americans pay for goods and services.

Among the key elements of U.S. international economic policy is trade policy, which seeks to promote American goods and services abroad. The United States is the world's largest importer and exporter of goods and services. In 2017 the United States exported more than $2.3 trillion in goods and services while importing $2.9 trillion in goods and services. Roughly 40 million jobs in the United States are directly or indirectly tied to international trade. Accordingly, America has a vital interest in maintaining international trade and monetary practices that promote American prosperity. This effort involves a complex arrangement of treaties, tariffs, and other mechanisms of policy formation. Trade policy is always complicated because most Americans benefit from a policy of free trade, which tends to reduce the cost of goods and services. Consumer electronics such as televisions, smartphones, and other gadgets would be far more expensive except for the fact that they are imported from all over the world, which drives down their prices. However, many American industries and their employees are hurt by free trade if it results in factories and jobs moving abroad. Hence, trade policy always produces huge political battles between those who stand to benefit and those who stand to lose from particular policies. In 2016 one of Donald Trump's main campaign pledges was to end free trade policies that he deemed harmful to American workers. In 2018 the president imposed a series of tariffs on foreign imports that sparked retaliation from U.S. trading partners. Some American manufacturers benefited from the tariffs while others were hurt by foreign retaliation against U.S. goods.

The most important international organization for promoting trade is the **World Trade Organization (WTO)**, established in 1995. The WTO grew out of the **General Agreement on Tariffs and Trade (GATT)**. Since World War II, GATT had brought together a wide range of nations for regular negotiations designed to reduce barriers to trade. Such barriers, many believed, had contributed to the breakdown of the world economy in the 1930s and had helped cause World War II. The WTO has 151 members worldwide, including the United States. Similar policy goals are pursued in regional arrangements, such as the **United States–Mexico–Canada Agreement (USMCA)**, formerly known as NAFTA, a trade treaty among the United States, Canada, and Mexico that the Trump administration renegotiated in 2018.

HUMAN RIGHTS

Many Americans believe that the United States has an obligation to protect human rights and to provide assistance to needy groups throughout the world. Other Americans say we should spend our resources at home and let other nations look after their own people. Still a third group of Americans view human rights and humanitarian policies as a form of "soft power," serving American interests and winning friends by demonstrating our concern for the less fortunate throughout the world. This third group has generally been dominant within the American foreign policy community.

The United States has a long-standing commitment to human rights and is a party to most major international human rights agreements. Although the United States is committed to promoting human rights, this commitment has a lower priority in American foreign policy than the nation's security concerns and economic interests. Thus, the United States is likely to overlook human rights violations by its major trading partners, such as China, and remain silent in the face of human rights violations by such allies as Saudi Arabia. Nevertheless, human

World Trade Organization (WTO) international organization promoting free trade that grew out of the General Agreement on Tariffs and Trade

General Agreement on Tariffs and Trade (GATT) international trade organization, in existence from 1947 to 1995, that set many of the rules governing international trade

United States–Mexico–Canada Agreement (USMCA) trade treaty between the United States, Canada, and Mexico to lower and eliminate tariffs among the three countries rights concerns do play a role in American foreign policy. For example, beginning in 2007 the United States has annually made available several million dollars in small grants to pay medical and legal expenses incurred by individuals who have been the victims of retaliation in their own countries for working against their governments' repressive practices. In this small way, the United States is backing its often-asserted principles.

FOR CRITICAL ANALYSIS

Why does the United States pursue international humanitarian policy? Should the United States pay more attention to the human rights records of its trading partners, like China, or allies, like Saudi Arabia?

U.S. foreign policy also includes support for international peacekeeping efforts. At any time, border wars, civil wars, and guerrilla conflicts flare somewhere in the world—usually in its poorer regions—and can generate humanitarian crises in the form of casualties, disease, and refugees. In cooperation with international agencies and other nations, the United States funds efforts to keep the peace in volatile regions and to address the health care and refugee problems associated with conflict. In 2015 the United States provided nearly $2 billion in humanitarian assistance to help Syrian refugees displaced by the civil war in that nation and by the end of 2016 had donated over $7 billion to the cause.[7]

As the world's wealthiest nation, the United States also recognizes an obligation to render assistance to nations facing emergencies. In 2011, for example, the United States provided support to Japan when a tsunami devastated a portion of the Japanese coast and damaged a nuclear reactor. In addition, between 2010 and 2017 the U.S. provided more than $5 billion in assistance to Haiti after a huge earthquake devastated the island nation.[8]

Who Makes American Foreign Policy?

Identify the major players in foreign policy making, and describe their roles

As we have seen, domestic policies are made by governmental institutions and influenced by a variety of interest groups, political movements, and even the mass media. The same is true in the realm of foreign policy. The president and the chief advisers are the principal architects of U.S. foreign policy. However, Congress, the bureaucracy, the courts, political parties, interest groups, and trade associations also play important roles in this realm. Often, the president and Congress are at odds over foreign policy.

PRESIDENTS AND THE EXECUTIVE BRANCH

The president is the leading figure in the conduct of American foreign policy. The president's foreign policy powers today, particularly in the military realm, are far greater than the Constitution's framers had thought wise. The framers gave the power to declare war to Congress and made the president the nation's top military commander if and when Congress chose to go to war. Today, presidents both command the troops and decide when to go to war.

Most American presidents have been domestic politicians whose chief interests were in the realm of domestic policy. Among America's 14 presidents during the past century only four—Hoover, Eisenhower, Nixon, and George H. W. Bush—had any extensive foreign policy experience before taking office. The others were forced to learn on the job.[9]

Building Influence through International Connections

Since World War II, the United States has been considered the leading global hegemon: an international actor so powerful that it can spread its influence across continents. When thinking of U.S. hegemony, most people focus on the dominant military power of the United States. However, the military is only one tool for expanding a country's interest, and we might consider a country's level of globalization to be another measure of influence. Globalization is the process of increasing interactions across country borders and between societies and economies; countries that are more globalized have built multiple connections and influence.

Comparing the United States to two main international challengers, Russia and China, we can see how highly integrated the United States is into the global system. While all three countries are close on political globalization, the United States has a clear lead in social and economic globalization. This means that in terms of international negotiations, the United States has more tools at their disposal than any other country.

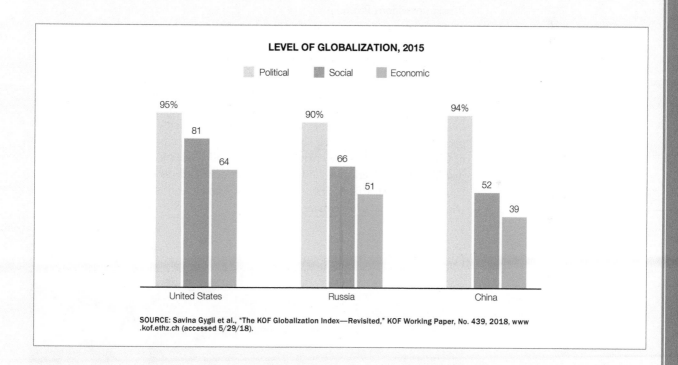

LEVEL OF GLOBALIZATION, 2015

Political   Social   Economic

United States: 95%, 81, 64
Russia: 90%, 66, 51
China: 94%, 52, 39

SOURCE: Savina Gygli et al., "The KOF Globalization Index—Revisited," KOF Working Paper, No. 439, 2018, www.kof.ethz.ch (accessed 5/29/18).

All four recent presidents, like most of their predecessors, were nevertheless faced with momentous challenges to American security and to America's international interests. George W. Bush, in particular, was compelled to develop a response to the September 11 terror attacks. By 2002 foreign policy had become the centerpiece of the Bush administration's agenda. In a June 1, 2002, speech at West Point, the president announced a policy of unilateral action and preemptive war—what came to be called the **"Bush Doctrine."** Bush said, "our security will require all Americans...to be ready for preemptive action when necessary to defend our liberty and to defend our lives." In his 2014 West Point speech, President Obama appeared to articulate a different policy when he said the United States must reduce its reliance on military force and make more use of diplomacy. But even though Obama expressed reservations about unilateral preemption, during the Obama years the United States continued to launch many attacks against suspected terrorists before they were able to strike. President Trump rattled America's allies by declaring an "America first" foreign policy and adopting a confrontational posture toward North Korea and Iran. In terms of actions, however, as of July 2018, Trump seemed to have given diplomacy a greater emphasis as evidenced by his meetings with North Korea's leader and Russian president Putin.

As the dominant figure in the realm of American foreign and military policy, the president exercises substantial control over the nation's diplomatic and military institutions and, as a result, is in a position to decide with whom, when, and how the United States will interact in the international arena. Since World War II, American military forces have fought in many parts of the world. In every instance, the decision to commit troops to battle was made by the president, often without much consultation with the Congress. When President Obama ordered special operations soldiers to attack Osama bin Laden's compound in Pakistan, members of Congress learned of the operation and bin Laden's death from news broadcasts— just like other Americans. And it is the president and his emissaries who conduct negotiations with Russia, Iran, North Korea—and a host of other nations—to deal with international problems and crises.

Bush Doctrine foreign policy based on the idea that the United States should take preemptive action against threats to its national security

The president is the key actor in American foreign policy and often acts without the approval or input from Congress. Here, President Obama and his national security team watch as the military performs a raid on Osama bin Laden's compound in Afghanistan. Bin Laden was killed in the raid.

Presidents can also make use of **executive agreements** to partially bypass congressional power in the realm of foreign relations. Executive agreements are presidential orders enforceable by the courts that do not require Senate ratification. Since presidents seem free to use executive agreements as they see fit, the importance of the Senate's constitutional treaty power has sharply diminished. Since 1947 the United States has entered into more than 17,000 different agreements with other nations and international entities. Of these, only 6 percent were submitted to the Senate for approval.[10]

Beyond the president, several government agencies within the executive branch play important roles in shaping and executing American foreign policy.

executive agreement an agreement, made between the president and another country, that has the force of a treaty but does not require the Senate's "advice and consent"

The National Security Council The National Security Council (NSC) was created in 1947 as an entity within the Executive Office of the President (EOP) to oversee the foreign policy establishment, synthesize information coming from the bureaucracy, and help the president develop foreign policy.[11] The NSC is a "subcabinet" made up of the president, the vice president, the secretaries of defense and state plus other presidential appointees, including the heads of the CIA, Homeland Security, and the Director of National Intelligence. The heart of the NSC is its staff, consisting of about 200 foreign policy experts capable of evaluating political, economic, and military issues throughout the world. The head of the NSC staff is the president's national security adviser (NSA).[12] Some NSAs have been close presidential confidants and have exercised considerable power because they had the president's ear and trust. In March 2018, President Trump named John Bolton as his NSA.

The State Department Routine matters of international diplomacy come under the purview of the Department of State. The State Department was the first federal agency created by the first Congress in 1789. The State Department is headed by the Secretary of State, a member of the president's cabinet and, nominally, the most important foreign policy official after the president. The secretary's actual importance varies with his or her relationship to the president. Some presidents rely very little on their secretaries, while for other presidents, the secretary becomes their chief foreign policy adviser. Franklin D. Roosevelt, for example, was barely aware that Cordell Hull existed, relegating the secretary to an observer of the diplomatic scene. On the other end of the spectrum, George W. Bush worked very closely with Condoleezza Rice, who served as his chief foreign policy adviser. In some instances, presidents use their secretaries as roving ambassadors more than as advisers like John Kerry in the Obama administration. Donald Trump relied occasionally on Rex Tillerson but severely criticized the secretary for his belief that diplomacy could reduce the nuclear threat from North Korea. Trump asserted that only force could end the threat. In 2018, Trump fired Tillerson and designated CIA director Mike Pompeo as his new Secretary of State. Having faulted Tillerson for promoting a diplomatic solution to the Korea problem, Trump changed course and launched his own diplomatic initiative, meeting with Korean leader Kim Jong-un. Both sides pledged to work toward denuclearization of the Korean Peninsula and more peaceful relations, but whether these goals will be met remains to be seen.

The State Department oversees more than 300 U.S. embassies, consulates, and diplomatic missions around the world. Embassies are headed by ambassadors. While most embassy staff members are officers of the U.S. Foreign Service, the State Department's professional diplomatic corps, a number of ambassadors have no diplomatic expertise and are, instead, political appointees rewarded with an ambassadorial title for their campaign contributions to the president. Most of America's Western European embassies, then, are actually run by their number 2 person, the Deputy Chief of Mission, a foreign service professional.

The United States "recognizes" and maintains diplomatic relations with 195 countries. The United States does not officially recognize Iran or North Korea. Recognition means that the United States accepts the nation's government as lawful, will engage in routine trade and diplomatic exchanges with it, and will accept its citizens' passports for travel into America. At the various embassies and missions, State Department officials monitor American treaty and trade relations with the host country, provide assistance for American business interests and tourists, and deal with foreign nationals attempting to emigrate to or visit the United States. Diplomatic officials are responsible for reporting on political and economic developments at their posts that might have implications for American policy. Some staff may officially or unofficially work for the Central Intelligence Agency (CIA) or other American intelligence services. Embassy staff is also tasked with developing good relations with prominent citizens of other nations in order to disseminate positive views of the United States and to secure information that might be useful to American interests. At the same time, the State Department monitors the conduct of foreign nationals. Though preventing outright foreign espionage is the responsibility of the FBI, the State Department is expected to keep an eye on the activities of foreign diplomats assigned to the United States.

The president also makes ceremonial visits to America's allies and other important states to demonstrate America's friendship and, in turn, hosts foreign dignitaries at the White House. Serious negotiations with other nations are usually handled by professional State Department diplomats deemed to have subject matter expertise as well as a good understanding of the priorities and sensibilities of their negotiating partners. Only in the case of the most important talks is the president likely to become involved personally. Usually, talks begin at a lower level among professional diplomats. If progress is made, more influential officials are summoned and

The president meets with many foreign leaders, often after key agreements have been hammered out by the president's staff. In a highly controversial move, President Trump met alone with Russian president Vladimir Putin in July 2018, leaving many staffers and observers wondering what the two said.

the president called to meet with his counterpart to formally "seal the deal." Thus, in the aftermath of the Russian annexation of Crimea, professional American and Russian diplomats were assigned to open talks, followed by meetings between U.S. Secretary of State John Kerry and Russian Foreign Minister Sergei Lavrov. When an agreement had been hammered out, President Obama met with President Putin and shook hands, though soon enough each side again accused the other of engaging in provocative acts. President Trump generally does not follow this well-established set of procedures. Trump prefers to begin with a face-to-face meeting with a foreign leader and leave it to staff to fill in details later. In the case of Trump's July 2018 meeting with Russian president Putin, the two leaders met alone, without staff. State Department and other staff were left trying to determine exactly what had been said during the meeting.

Department of Defense Since its creation in 1947, the Defense Department (DoD) has played a major role in the making of American foreign policy. The United States Department of Defense employs more than two million military and civilian personnel and is a huge and complex bureaucratic entity.[13] Reporting to the Secretary of Defense are 27 assistant secretaries, undersecretaries, and directors, each commanding hundreds of staffers and charged with such responsibilities as health affairs, budgets, acquisitions, testing and evaluation of equipment, and legal affairs. Working for these functionaries are 31 agencies, such as the National Security Agency, employing tens of thousands of individuals. These and numerous other entities help to plan and sustain America's military efforts and allow America to put tens of thousands of combat troops into the field.

This set of structures does not even include the actual military services. Each of the three services possesses its own civilian and military bureaucracies to administer and support its combat forces. For example, a U.S. Army division will include, in addition to its combat troops, large numbers of military personnel, and civilian employees and contractors organized into units whose functions include supply, transportation, finance, life support, signal infrastructure, public information, and more. In the modern U.S. Army, approximately three noncombat personnel are devoted to the support of each combat soldier.[14] American combat forces are, themselves, exemplars of organizational complexity. A U.S. Army division, for instance, typically deploying between ten and seventeen thousand troops, is usually composed of four brigades that are divided into battalions that, in turn, are composed of combat companies, each consisting of three platoons. Along with its combat companies the division will include a host of logistical, administrative, and service units to provide the food, fuel, ammunition, and other supplies and services needed to support the division's activities.[15]

This entire military structure is supported by the vast industrial contracting system that produces the aircraft, missiles, electronics, transport systems, and other materiel and supplies upon which the military depends. Many nominally civilian entities, such as Boeing, are heavily dependent on military contracts and are functionally integrated into the military bureaucracies. Military planning and research is undertaken by another set of private and quasi-private firms, which are technically Federally Funded Research and Development Centers (FFRDCs), independent nonprofit corporations working for the federal government.[16]

DoD implements American military policy by deploying troops anywhere in the world at the president's command. Increasingly, DoD has assumed a leading nonmilitary foreign policy role as well. To a significant extent, American foreign policy is driven by military and antiterrorism concerns, and the agencies deemed capable of addressing these concerns are coming to play a larger role in American foreign policy. In recent years, American ambassadors have complained that they have been relegated to secondary status as the White House has looked to military commanders for information, advice, and policy implementation. For every region of the world, the U.S. military has assigned a "combatant commander," always a senior general or admiral, to take charge of operations in that area. In many instances, these combatant commanders, who control troops, equipment, and intelligence capabilities, have become the real eyes, ears, and voices for American foreign policy in their designated regions. The combatant commanders report to the Joint Chiefs of Staff, who report to the Secretary of Defense, who reports to the president.

Treasury and Commerce The Treasury Department and Commerce Department coordinate the United States' international economic and monetary policies and, along with the Office of the U.S. Trade Representative (USTR), work to implement America's international trade policies. The United States works to discourage other nations from erecting tariff barriers to American goods and to maintain exchange rates between the dollar and other currencies that do not price American goods out of foreign markets or flood the American market with foreign goods. The United States is also alert to efforts by other nations to drive American manufacturers out of business by underpricing exports, a practice known as "dumping," or stealing American technology through reverse engineering or outright piracy. Treasury, Commerce, and the U.S. Trade Representative are constantly engaged in negotiations with America's trading partners while overall policy is generally set by executive agreements negotiated between the White House and other nations.

Intelligence Agencies The CIA is the United States' chief civilian intelligence agency, collecting information throughout the world, preparing analyses, and launching covert operations if the president wishes to use force but is unwilling to publicly acknowledge America's involvement. CIA operators also pilot many of the drones used to attack and kill suspected terrorists.

The CIA and DoD were created by the same piece of legislation, but the CIA Director and Secretary of Defense have generally viewed one another as rivals in the intelligence field. The Secretary of Defense controls substantial intelligence assets including the Defense Intelligence Agency that dwarf those of the CIA. In 2005, Congress created the position of Director of National Intelligence (DNI) to coordinate intelligence activities and prepare the president's daily intelligence summary—a responsibility previously held by the CIA's director. This change came about because Congress believed that the intelligence community's failure to anticipate the September 11, 2001, attacks was the result of a lack of coordination among the various agencies. Both the CIA and DoD resented the creation of the DNI and put aside their mutual suspicions to join forces against the new position. Both agencies generally refuse to share information with the DNI who, having no operational capabilities, has been left in the dark on many intelligence matters. National intelligence agencies seem generally to regard one another as rivals, which, for budgetary purposes, they are.[16]

Two other important executive agencies in the intelligence field are the FBI and the Department of Homeland Security (DHS). The FBI is generally responsible for the collection and analysis of intelligence data in the Western Hemisphere, as the CIA is barred by law from operating inside the United States. DHS was established after September 11, 2001, through a merger of 22 existing agencies. One agency within DHS is Immigration and Customs Enforcement (ICE), which is charged with maintaining border security and enforcing America's immigration policies.

The National Security Agency The National Security Agency (NSA) is a highly influential, and controversial, intelligence agency. Though housed within DoD, the NSA effectively reports directly to the president and provides the chief executive with the results of its worldwide electronic surveillance efforts. Surveillance of electronic communication has a long history in the United States, going back to a World War I government effort to read suspicious telegrams.[18] During the 1970s, however, Congress became concerned about a variety of secret White House surveillance efforts and, in 1978, enacted the Foreign Intelligence Surveillance Act (FISA) designed to regulate electronic surveillance by government agencies.

FISA stipulated that in order to undertake electronic surveillance of Americans, the government would be required to apply for a warrant from a special court created by the statute. FISA stipulated that the court would issue a warrant only if it found probable cause to believe that the target of the surveillance was acting in concert with a foreign power or agent. The 1978 act defined foreign power as a nation-state, but this was subsequently amended to include non-state actors such as terrorist groups. The act also allowed the president to authorize surveillance within the United States without a warrant if the Attorney General certified to the FISA Court that the target was a foreign intelligence agent and there was little chance that the privacy of any American citizen would be violated.

In June 2013 an NSA contractor named Edward Snowden leaked classified documents describing NSA's theretofore top-secret PRISM surveillance program that had operated since 2007. Snowden's disclosures were published in the *Guardian* and the *Washington Post* and revealed that through PRISM and several other programs, NSA had been collecting data on its own as well as collaborating with virtually all major telecommunications companies to intercept, examine, and store the electronic communications of millions of Americans. These included email, social network posts,

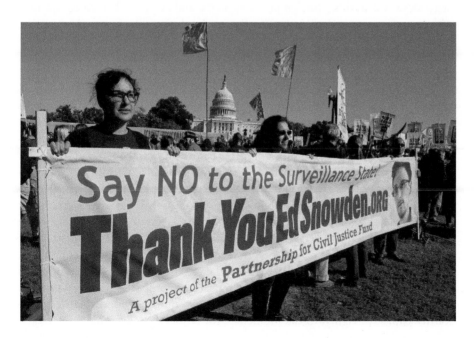

The National Security Agency has come under scrutiny in recent years after reports that it had been collecting, storing, and examining the electronic data of millions of Americans. These actions have sparked intense debate about the trade-offs between personal liberty and national security.

internet searches, and even local telephone calls. In essence, NSA appeared to have the capacity to monitor and store all forms of electronic communication.

The NSA and its intelligence collection activities raise major questions about the trade-off between national security and liberty. Government agencies monitor communications to protect the nation against foreign threats. But doesn't government eavesdropping also pose its own threat to the nation's liberties? President Richard Nixon, for example, used surveillance and eavesdropping to harass his political foes. Do we wish to purchase security by paying with liberty?

CONGRESS

Through its general legislative powers, Congress can exercise broad influence over foreign policy. Congress may, for example, refuse to appropriate funds for presidential actions it deems to be unwise or inappropriate. This power of the purse also extends to military action. Not only does Congress have the constitutional power to declare war, but under its general legislative powers it must appropriate the funds needed to support military activities. In *Federalist 69*, Hamilton argues that Congress's power of the purse provides it with an ultimate check on the president's power as commander-in-chief.[19]

Presidents, as we saw, control several enormous bureaucracies through which to develop and implement foreign and security policies. These include the State and Defense departments and a host of other agencies. Congress has far less bureaucratic capacity of its own, but it has committees that can influence the nation's international and military programs. Chief among these are the House and Senate committees charged with overseeing foreign policy, military affairs, and the collection and analysis of intelligence.

Key Congressional Committees in the Foreign Policy Realm On the Senate side, the first, oldest, and most influential committee dealing with foreign policy is the U.S. Senate Committee on Foreign Relations. The Committee oversees the State Department, other foreign policy agencies, and executive branch compliance with several statutes including the War Powers Resolution. The Committee consists of 18 members and was established in 1816 as one of the original ten standing committees of the Senate. Each of its seven subcommittees has jurisdiction over a specific region or subject matter.

Throughout its history, the Foreign Relations Committee has viewed its role as the guardian of congressional power in the foreign policy realm. The power of the Foreign Relations Committee stems from its responsibility to confirm State Department officials and the fact that treaties proposed by the executive branch must be reviewed by the Committee before they can be referred to the full Senate for a vote on ratification. In recent years, the Committee's efforts to influence presidential foreign policy initiatives have been somewhat less successful as presidents, as we noted above, have made use of executive agreements rather than treaties that would require senatorial approval. For example, while members of the Committee were sharply critical of the Obama administration's negotiations with Iran in 2015, the president generally ignored their comments. Nevertheless, the Committee occasionally flexes its muscles. One example is its refusal for a number of years to report the proposed Law of the Sea Treaty, which codifies international maritime law, on the grounds that it would restrict U.S. sovereignty, to the full Senate for ratification. Eventually the treaty,

The Senate Foreign Relations Committee helps shape American foreign policy. One key way is in approving presidential nominees. Here, the committee questions Rex Tillerson, President Trump's first nominee for Secretary of State. Despite a contentious hearing process, the Senate approved Tillerson for the post.

appropriately known as LOST, was reported to the Senate but lacked the two-thirds vote needed for ratification.

In addition to its role in the treaty process, the Foreign Relations Committee also considers presidential nominees for important foreign policy posts, including the position of Secretary of State. In 2017 the Committee held contentious hearings on President Trump's nomination of Exxon executive Rex Tillerson for the post. Senate Democrats charged that Tillerson's business ties, especially with Russia, would represent conflicts of interest—a charge denied by the nominee. Eventually, Tillerson received the Committee's endorsement and was confirmed by the full Senate (though Trump later fired Tillerson, who reportedly disagreed with Trump on a number of matters).

Paralleling the jurisdiction of the Senate Foreign Relations Committee is the House Committee on Foreign Affairs. The House committee is considerably less influential than its Senate counterpart because it is neither involved in appointments nor in the ratification of treaties. For the most part, the House committee's hearings focus on symbolic questions. In 2015, for example, after holding hearings, the House committee adopted a nonbinding resolution condemning the mass killings of Armenian civilians by Turkish forces in 1915. The committee had adopted similar resolutions in the past, but none had ever reached the House floor. In the face of Turkish lobbying, the 2015 resolution was not brought before the full House.

In both houses of Congress, standing subcommittees of the appropriations committees are responsible for funding the State Department, foreign aid programs, and other matters in the foreign policy realm. Through these subcommittees as well as through the Foreign Relations and Foreign Affairs Committees, the Senate and House can indicate their displeasure with presidential programs by cutting or withholding funds. In 2012, for example, Rep. Kay Granger of Texas, who then chaired the House appropriations subcommittee dealing with foreign aid, used her position to block $450 million in aid to Egypt that had been requested by the Obama administration.[20]

Armed Services and Intelligence A number of standing committees of the House and Senate deal with defense matters. The House and Senate Armed Services Committees oversee the Department of Defense and the Department of Energy (which houses America's nuclear weapons programs). In both houses of Congress, other standing committees are responsible for such matters as veterans' affairs. Defense appropriations are the domains of the House and Senate Defense Appropriations subcommittees.

Generally, the House and Senate Armed Services committees are friendly to the military and to the legions of defense contractors who provide support and equipment for America's military services. The two committees, however, do not always limit themselves to supporting the military brass. Sometimes they will make use of their staff resources and contacts in the military community to advocate for military programs not currently in the Pentagon's plans. In 2015, for example, both committees released reports calling for the armed services to focus on the growing threat of cyberattacks against U.S. weapons and communications software, and authorized the expenditure of $200 million for this purpose.[21]

While the two armed services committees have cozy relations with their bureaucratic counterparts, the same is not true of the House and Senate Intelligence committees. These were established during the 1970s to oversee America's growing intelligence bureaucracies and to review their activities at home and abroad. These

Interest groups play a key role in foreign policy. Amnesty International (left) pushes for human rights around the world. Cuban Americans have strong voices in Congress in Senator Marco Rubio (R-Fla., center) among others. AIPAC (right) is a powerful advocate for pro-Israel policies.

committees have focused on such matters as American intelligence failures, including the failure to predict and prevent the September 11 terrorist attacks, the use of private military contractors in missions organized by the CIA, clandestine CIA missions in other nations, and the use of drones to carry out military and intelligence missions in other nations. Both committees also have been sharply critical of intelligence collection efforts that impinged on the privacy rights of American citizens.

INTEREST GROUPS

Although the president, the executive branch bureaucracy, and Congress are the true makers of foreign policy, the "foreign policy establishment" is a much larger arena, including significant shapers of foreign policy. These unofficial players possess varying degrees of influence depending on their prestige, reputation, socioeconomic standing, and, most important, the party and ideology that are dominant at a given moment.

The most important nonofficial players are the interest groups. Economic interest groups are reputed to wield the most influence, yet myths about their influence far outweigh the realities. In fact, the influence of organized economic interest groups in foreign policy varies enormously from issue to issue and year to year. On many broader and more sustained policy issues—such as the USMCA, the TPP, and the general question of U.S. involvement in international trade—the larger interest groups, or peak associations, have difficulty getting their many members to speak with a single voice. Some business groups represent export industries, and others represent firms threatened by imports. Hence, "business" has more than one view on trade policy. More successful in influencing foreign policy are the single-issue groups that are most active when their particular issue is on the agenda. These include interest groups representing the tobacco industry, which have prevented heavy restrictions on international trade in and advertising of tobacco products, and those representing computer hardware and software industries, which have hardened the United States' attitude toward Chinese piracy of intellectual property rights.

Another type of interest group with significant foreign policy influence comprises people who strongly identify with a particular country. For example, many Jewish

Americans and evangelical Protestants possess strong emotional ties to Israel. In 2015 many, albeit not all, Jewish and evangelical groups lobbied heavily but ultimately unsuccessfully against the Obama administration's agreement with Iran, which they argued posed a threat to both the United States and Israel. Similarly, Cuban Americans, most recently represented by two powerful senators, Marco Rubio and Ted Cruz, have long been a strong voice in support of maintaining sanctions against the Castro regime in Cuba, which helps explain why relations with Cuba were not normalized until 2015 and remain tenuous today.

A third type of interest group, more prominent in recent decades, is devoted to human rights or other global causes such as protection of the environment. An example is Amnesty International, whose exposés of human rights abuses have altered the practices of some regimes. Groups devoted to protecting the environment often depend more on demonstrations than on lobbying and electoral politics. Demonstrations in strategically located areas can have significant influence on American foreign policy. In recent years environmental activists have staged major protests, such as at the 2009 London and 2010 Toronto international economic summits, and at the 2015 Paris environmental summit that led to the signing of a series of international accords aimed at limiting the production of greenhouse gases.

The Instruments of Modern American Foreign Policy

Describe the means the United States uses to carry out foreign policy today

Any government possesses a variety of instruments, or tools, to use in implementing its foreign policy. There have been many instruments of American foreign policy, and we examine those instruments most important today: diplomacy, the United Nations, the international monetary structure, economic aid and sanctions, collective security, military force, soft power, and arbitration.

The Secretary of State is America's chief diplomat. Here, Secretary of State Mike Pompeo meets with North Korean leader Kim Jong-un.

DIPLOMACY

diplomacy the representation of a government to other governments

Diplomacy is the representation of a government to other foreign governments. Its purpose is to promote national values or interests by peaceful means. As mentioned earlier, the United States maintains diplomatic missions throughout the world. American ambassadors are tasked with maintaining good relations with foreign governments, promoting a positive view of the United States abroad, and securing information about foreign governments that might be helpful to the United States in its international dealings. When it comes to major diplomatic initiatives, however, such as new international agreements, presidents or their personal representatives usually take charge. The United States' nuclear weapons agreement with Iran, for example, was negotiated by Secretary of State John Kerry acting on instructions from President Obama. In 2018, President Trump launched personal diplomatic initiatives with Russian and North Korean leaders.

THE UNITED NATIONS

United Nations (UN) an organization of nations founded in 1945 to be a channel for negotiation and a means of settling international disputes peaceably; the UN has had frequent successes in providing a forum for negotiation and, on some occasions, a means of preventing international conflicts from spreading; on a number of occasions, the UN has been a convenient cover for U.S. foreign policy goals

The **United Nations (UN)** is a very large and unwieldy institution with few powers and no standing armed forces of its own to implement its rules and resolutions. It has little organization that can make it an effective decision-making body, with only six standing committees, few tight rules of procedure, and no political parties to provide priorities and discipline. However, the utility of the UN to the United States as an instrument of foreign policy can be too easily underestimated. Its defenders are quick to add that although it lacks armed forces, it relies on the power of world opinion—and this is not to be taken lightly.

The United Nations' supreme body is the UN General Assembly, comprising one representative of each of the 192 member-states; each member representative has one vote, regardless of the size of the country. Important issues require a two-thirds majority vote, and the annual session of the General Assembly runs only from September to December (although it can call extra sessions). The powers of the UN devolve mainly to the organization's "executive committee," the UN Security Council, which alone has the real power to make decisions and rulings that member states are obligated by the UN Charter to implement. The

While the United Nations may not have a military, its opinion does influence foreign policy around the world. Here, U.S. ambassador to the UN Nikki Haley speaks to the UN General Assembly on Israel-Palestine relations in June 2018.

Security Council may be called into session at any time, and each member (or a designated alternate) must be present at UN headquarters in New York at all times. The Security Council is composed of 15 members: 5 are permanent (the victors of World War II), and 10 are elected by the General Assembly for unrepeatable two-year terms. The 5 permanent members are China, France, Russia, the United Kingdom, and the United States. Each of the 15 members has only one vote, and a 9-vote majority of the 15 is required on all substantive matters. But each of the 5 permanent members also has a negative vote, a "veto"; and one veto is sufficient to reject any substantive proposal.

The UN can serve as a useful forum for international discussions and as an instrument for multilateral action. Most peacekeeping efforts to which the United States contributes, for example, are undertaken under UN auspices.

THE INTERNATIONAL MONETARY STRUCTURE

Fear of a repeat of the economic devastation that followed World War I brought the United States together with its allies (except the USSR) to Bretton Woods, New Hampshire, in 1944 to create a new international economic structure for the postwar world. One major goal of this structure was to prevent economic instability that might, in turn, lead to political instability and war. Participants in the Bretton Woods conference were mindful of the economic collapse in Germany that had opened the way for Nazism. At the same time, the structure would give the United States and its allies greater leverage in the economic and political affairs of developing countries.

The Bretton Woods conference resulted in two institutions: the International Bank for Reconstruction and Development (commonly called the World Bank) and the International Monetary Fund. The World Bank's chief mission is development aid to poor countries through long-term capital investments. A second institution, the **International Monetary Fund (IMF)**, was set up to provide for the short-term flow of money. After the war, the U.S. dollar replaced gold as the chief means by which the

International Monetary Fund (IMF) an institution established in 1944 that provides loans and facilitates international monetary exchange

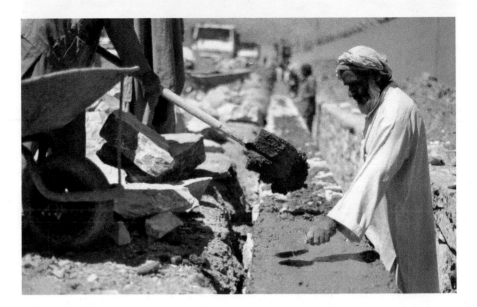

The United States is the most influential member of the World Bank, which provides loans and other assistance to developing countries. Here, workers in Afghanistan work to improve roads. The World Bank has provided hundreds of millions of dollars to help rebuild Afghanistan over the past decade.

currency of one country would be "changed into" the currency of another country for purposes of making international transactions. To permit debtor countries with no international balances to make purchases and investments, the IMF was prepared to lend dollars or other appropriate currencies to such needy member countries to help them overcome temporary trade deficits.

During the 1990s the importance of the IMF increased through its efforts to reform some of the largest debtor nations and formerly communist countries, to bring them more fully into the global capitalist economy. For example, in the early 1990s Russia and 13 other former Soviet republics were invited to join the IMF and the World Bank, with the expectation that they would receive $10.5 billion from these two agencies, primarily for a currency stabilization fund. Each republic was to get a permanent IMF representative, and the IMF increased its staff by at least 10 percent to provide the expertise necessary to cope with the problems of these emerging capitalist economies.[22]

The IMF, with tens of billions of dollars contributed by its members, has more money to lend poor countries than does the United States, Europe, or Japan (the three leading IMF shareholders) individually. It makes its policy decisions in ways that are generally consistent with the interests of the leading shareholders.[23] Two weeks after September 11, 2001, the IMF approved a $135-million loan to economically troubled Pakistan, a key player in the war against the Taliban government of Afghanistan because of its strategic location.[24]

ECONOMIC AID AND SANCTIONS

Every year, the United States provides nearly $30 billion in economic assistance to other nations. Some aid has a humanitarian purpose, such as helping to provide health care, shelter for refugees, or famine relief. A good deal of American aid, however, is designed to promote American security interests or economic concerns. For example, the United States provides military assistance to a number of its allies in the form of advanced weapons or loans to help them purchase such weapons. These loans generally stipulate that the recipient must purchase the designated weapons from American firms. In this way, the United States hopes to bolster its security and economic interests with one grant. The two largest recipients of American military assistance are Israel and Egypt, American allies that fought two wars against each other. The United States believes that its military assistance allows both countries to feel sufficiently secure to remain at peace with each other.

Aid is an economic carrot. Sanctions are an economic stick. Economic sanctions that the United States employs against other nations include trade embargoes, bans on investment, and efforts to prevent the World Bank or other international institutions from extending credit to a nation against which the United States has a grievance. Sanctions are most often employed when the United States seeks to weaken what it considers a hostile regime or when it is attempting to compel some particular action by another regime. In 2017, for example, the United States tightened its already existing economic sanctions against North Korea in response to that nation's missile tests. The United States also uses economic sanctions to advance its international humanitarian policy goals. The United States currently has sanctions in place against a number of governments with records of serious violations of civil and political rights.[25]

Unilateral sanctions by the United States usually have little effect since the target can usually trade elsewhere, sometimes even with foreign affiliates of U.S. firms. If, however, the United States is able to persuade its allies to cooperate, sanctions have a better chance of success. International sanctions against Iran, for example, influenced that regime's decision to enter into negotiations with the United States, culminating in the nuclear weapons deal of 2015. Economic sanctions against North Korea have been less effective since that regime is able to trade with China and several other nations.

FOR CRITICAL ANALYSIS

There has been a good deal of debate about whether economic sanctions can convince North Korea to halt its nuclear weapons programs. What factors might help to determine the effectiveness of economic sanctions?

COLLECTIVE SECURITY

Collective security refers to the development of alliances and agreements among a group of nations that pledge to aid one another in fending off or confronting security threats. In the aftermath of World War II, the United States' first collective security agreement was the Rio Treaty, which created the Organization of American States. This was the model treaty, anticipating all succeeding collective security treaties by providing that an armed attack against any of its members "shall be considered as an attack against all the American States," including the United States. This model was followed by the North Atlantic Treaty (signed in April 1949), which created the North Atlantic Treaty Organization (NATO). The Australian, New Zealand, United States Security (ANZUS) Treaty, which tied Australia and New Zealand to the United States, was signed in September 1951. Three years later, the Southeast Asia Treaty created the Southeast Asia Treaty Organization (SEATO).

In a 1998 expansion, NATO took its first steps toward including former Warsaw Pact members, extending membership to the Czech Republic, Hungary, and Poland. Most of Washington embraced this expansion as the true and fitting end of the Cold War, and the U.S. Senate echoed this with a resounding 80–19 vote to induct these three former Soviet satellites into NATO. After the collapse of the Soviet Union, the importance of NATO as a military alliance seemed to wane. However, since 2014 the resurgence of Russia as a military power has forced NATO members once again to look to one another for support. In 2014, Russia seized the Crimean Peninsula from the Ukraine and appeared to pose a threat to the Baltic states and other portions of the old Soviet empire. Russia has also sent military forces to support the Assad regime in Syria. Facing an aggressive new Russia, NATO's period of relative quiet seemed to be coming to a close.

The September 11 attacks marked the first time in its more than 50-year history that Article 5 of the North Atlantic Treaty was invoked; it provides that an attack on one country is an attack on all the member countries. In fighting "the war on terror," the Bush administration recognized that no matter how preponderant American power was, some aspects of U.S. foreign policy could not be achieved without multilateral cooperation. On the other hand, the United States did not want to be constrained by its alliances. The global coalition initially forged after September 11, 2001, numbered more than 170 countries. Not all joined the war effort in Afghanistan, but most provided some form of support for some aspect of "the war on terror," such as economic sanctions and intelligence.

MILITARY FORCE

The most visible instrument of foreign policy is, of course, military force. The United States has built the world's most imposing military, with army, navy, marine, and air force units stationed in virtually every corner of the globe. The United States is responsible for one-third of the world's total military expenditures. The Prussian military strategist Carl von Clausewitz famously called war "politics by other means." By this he meant that nations used force not simply to demonstrate their capacity for violence. Rather, force or the threat of force is a tool nations must sometimes use to achieve their foreign policy goals. Military force may be needed to protect a nation's security interests and economic concerns. Ironically, force may also be needed to achieve humanitarian goals. For example, in 2014 and 2015, international military force was required to protect tens of thousands of Yazidi refugees

Often, military efforts abroad do not turn out as the government or the public expected. Though most Americans were in favor of U.S. involvement in Afghanistan following September 11, 2001, public opinion on the issue has shifted.

Who Serves in the U.S. Military?

The Department of Defense and the military are often responsible for implementing foreign policy that relates to security. Who are the men and women in the armed forces? The military has a far greater proportion of men to women than the general population, but in terms of race and ethnicity, the military is fairly similar to the United States as a whole. Residents of southern states are significantly more likely to enlist than those from other regions.

Gender

U.S. military
15% Female
85% Male

85%

U.S. population
47% Female
53% Male

53%

Race/Ethnicity

U.S. military
70% White   4% Asian
20% Black   6% Other
14% Hispanic

70%

U.S. population
77% White
14% Black
20% Hispanic
6% Asian
2% Other

77%

Education

New enlistees, 2015

U.S. military
99% High school graduates

99%

U.S. population
85% High school graduates

85%

NOTE: Civilian comparison groups are 17- to 55-year-olds for gender and race/ethnicity, 18- to 44-year-olds for education, and 18- to 24-year-old noninstitutional civilians for geographic origin. Percentages under race/ethnicity sum to more than 100 because some people identify as more than one race.

SOURCE: CNA Analysis & Solutions, "Population Representation in the Military Services 2015," www.cna.org, appendix B (accessed 12/26/17).

Geographic Origin

U.S. military new enlistees, 2015

13%
24%   19%
44%

Northeast 13%   Midwest 19%
South   44%   West   24%

U.S. population

18%
24%   21%
37%

Northeast 18%   Midwest 21%
South   37%   West   24%

FOR CRITICAL ANALYSIS

1. The move to an all-volunteer military in the United States in 1973 resulted in a more educated and professionalized force. However, the United States has used the draft in the past, and some countries require military service of all citizens. Can you think of some arguments for and against each approach?

2. Does it matter if some groups are more heavily represented in the armed forces than others?

threatened by ISIS forces in Iraq. Without the use of military force, humanitarian assistance to the Yazidis would have been irrelevant.[26]

Military force is generally considered a last resort and avoided if possible because its use may be problematic. First, the use of military force is extremely costly in both human and financial terms. Over the past 50 years, tens of thousands of Americans have been killed and hundreds of billions of dollars spent in America's military operations. Before they employ military force to achieve national goals, policy makers must be certain that achieving those goals is essential and that other means are unlikely to succeed.

Second, the use of military force is inherently fraught with risk. However carefully policy makers and generals plan for military operations, results can seldom be fully anticipated. Variables ranging from the weather to unexpected weapons and tactics deployed by opponents may turn calculated military operations into costly disasters, or convert maneuvers that were expected to be quick and decisive into long, drawn-out, expensive struggles. In 2003, American policy makers expected to defeat the Iraqi army quickly and easily—and they did. Policy makers did not anticipate, however, that American forces would still be struggling years later to defeat the insurgency that arose in the war's aftermath.

Finally, in a democracy, any government that chooses to address policy problems through military means is almost certain to encounter political difficulties. Generally speaking, the American public will support relatively short and decisive military engagements. If, however, a conflict drags on, producing casualties and expenses with no clear outcome, the public loses patience and opposition politicians point to the government's lies and ineptitude. The wars in Korea, Vietnam, and Iraq are all examples of protracted conflicts whose domestic political repercussions became serious liabilities for the governments that initially decided to make use of military force.

Thus, military force remains a major foreign policy tool, and the United States currently possesses a more powerful and effective set of military forces than any other nation. Nevertheless, even for the United States, the use of military force is fraught with risk and is not to be undertaken lightly.

SOFT POWER

The term *soft power* refers to efforts by one nation to influence the people and governments of other nations by persuasion rather than coercion. The instruments of soft power include development aid, cultural diplomacy, student exchange programs, and other mechanisms designed to shape perceptions. Cultural programs that send American actors, athletes, and musicians around the world are thought to offer a positive view of the United States that will encourage foreign governments and their citizens to see America as the "good guy" in international disputes. Exchange programs that bring foreign students to the United States serve a similar purpose. The effects of soft power are diffuse and difficult to measure, but the United States makes an effort to promote its "brand" of freedom and democracy throughout the world. Other nations do the same. Chinese development projects in Africa, for example, are partly intended to promote a favorable image of China on the continent.[27]

ARBITRATION

The final foreign policy tool to be considered is dispute arbitration. *Arbitration* means referring an international disagreement to a neutral third party for resolution. Arbitration is itself sometimes seen as a form of soft power, as distinguished from military force, economic sanctions, and other coercive foreign policy instruments. The United States will occasionally turn to international tribunals to resolve disputes with other countries—in February 2008 the U.S. government asked the International Court of Justice to resolve a long-standing dispute with Italy over American property confiscated by the Italian government more than 40 years earlier. To take another example, in 1981 the United States and Iran established an arbitral tribunal to deal with claims arising from Iran's seizure of the U.S. embassy in Tehran in 1979; the tribunal resulted in a settlement.

More important, the United States relies heavily on the work of arbitral panels to maintain the flow of international trade on which the U.S. economy depends. U.S. firms would be reluctant to do business abroad if they could not be certain that their property and contractual rights would be honored by other nations. Arbitration helps produce that certainty. Almost every international contract contains an arbitration clause requiring that disputes between the parties will be resolved not by foreign governments but by impartial arbitral panels accepted by both sides. By the terms of the New York Convention, virtually every nation in the world has agreed to accept and enforce arbitral verdicts. The United States has incorporated the terms of the New York Convention into federal law, and U.S. courts vigorously enforce arbitral judgments. The United States may not be happy with the outcome of every arbitral proceeding, but the arbitral system is essential to America's economic interests.

Current Foreign Policy Issues Facing the United States

> **Analyze the foreign policy problems facing American policy makers today**

The United States currently faces many foreign policy problems, but this section will examine a few major foreign policy issues that stand out: relations with Russia; relations with Iran and North Korea; what to do about the global environment; and international trade policy. Each reveals how the key players in foreign policy use the tools at their disposal to achieve their policy goals.

A POWERFUL CHINA AND A RESURGENT RUSSIA

After the United States, China and Russia are the world's greatest military powers. China is an economic power as well, with an economy that in some respects already outpaces America's and continues to grow. China seems determined to expand its military capabilities and to replace the United States as the dominant power in Asia. The United States has no desire to engage in a military conflict with China but, at the same time, would prefer to blunt Chinese ambitions. This situation is what Graham Allison has called "Thucydides's Trap."[28] According to Allison, the ancient Greek historian Thucydides explained that the great war between Athens and Sparta came about because the growth of Athenian power caused fear in Sparta and pushed the Spartans toward a war both cities would have preferred to avoid. The relationship between the United States and China is not at such a point of crisis but represents a growing concern for American policy makers who have sought to strengthen U.S. alliances with other Asian nations, including India, Japan, and Vietnam, in order to increase American power in the region and prevent the rise of China.

While relations with China are a long-term problem, the interactions of the United States with Russia present a more immediate set of issues. Once a global superpower and America's chief rival in the world, Russia remains heavily armed but economically weak. Under its current leader, Vladimir Putin, Russia has challenged the United States in Europe and in the Middle East, and has even meddled in American politics.[29]

The first in this series of direct Russian challenges to the United States came in 2014, when Russian forces seized control of the Crimean Peninsula, an area that had been part of the Ukraine, though many of the peninsula's inhabitants were ethnic Russians. Russian president Vladimir Putin said Russia's actions were necessary to prevent disorder and bloodshed and to reassert Russia's historical rights to the region. Russian troops next massed along other portions of the Ukrainian border. The Obama administration urged the Russians to withdraw, announced a program of economic sanctions, and sought through diplomacy to encourage NATO allies to impose sanctions as well. The result illustrated the difficulties inherent in collective action and the use of sanctions. Many of the United States' European allies depend on Russian energy supplies and engage in a good deal of trade with the Russians. As a result, while all agreed in principle that Russia should withdraw from Crimea, none were prepared to follow the American lead of imposing sanctions, and it seemed that nothing would be done to dislodge the Russians from the area. That same year Russia formally annexed Crimea, though the action was not officially recognized by the United States. Subsequently, Russian forces supported separatist groups in several other parts of the Ukraine.

In 2015, Russia challenged the United States in another part of the world when Russian forces entered the Syrian civil war in support of the Assad regime, which the United States had sought to oust. Russia claimed that its military actions were aimed at the Islamic State of Iraq and Syria (ISIS) and other terrorist groups, but in reality Russian attacks seemed to be directed at anti-Assad rebels. With American military advisers fighting alongside some of these same rebel groups, there was danger of a direct clash between Russia and the United States. President Obama called for Russian withdrawal and for negotiations to prevent an accidental confrontation between Russian and American military forces. In 2016, Russia claimed to have

From the beginning of the Syrian civil war in 2011, the United States has backed rebels against the Bashar al-Assad regime but has increased its involvement in recent years with the aim of targeting ISIS. The United States first deployed Special Operations forces on the ground in Syria in late 2015.

withdrawn its forces, but it was unclear whether this action had, in fact, occurred. During the course of the year, the United States and Russia continued to negotiate—and violate—new agreements as the fighting continued.

To counter Russia's actions, the United States has worked to strengthen and enlarge NATO to include Eastern European nations that feel threatened by Russia, including Poland, Lithuania, Albania, Bulgaria, and Slovenia. Russia, for its part, views NATO's expansion into its former satellite empire as a provocative action and has sought to enhance its own military capabilities in the region.

In 2016, Russia also sought to intrude into American presidential politics. Russian agents purchased ads on Facebook and other social media designed to cause dissention in the United States, and to exploit ethnic and economic tensions. For the most part, Russian efforts seemed to favor Donald Trump and oppose Hillary Clinton. Whether these had any effect or not is open to question.[30]

Both the Chinese and the Russians have made use of extensive electronic "hacking" to break into the computer systems of American government agencies and American firms. Both countries deny these allegations—as does the United States when accused of hacking into Russian and Chinese systems.[31]

NUCLEAR PROLIFERATION IN IRAN AND NORTH KOREA

Unlike China and Russia, Iran and North Korea are not great powers, but both present challenges to the United States, especially in the realm of nuclear proliferation. Though it is a nuclear power, the United States has generally seen nuclear proliferation as leading to a more dangerous world and has done what it can to prevent more countries—especially those it sees as opposed to the interests of the United States and its allies—from developing nuclear weapons.

Iran and the United States have been adversaries since 1979, when Iranians overthrew an unpopular U.S.-backed leader, Shah Reza Pahlavi. For years the United States has worried that Iran is working toward obtaining nuclear weapons with which it could threaten Saudi Arabia and Israel—both close U.S. allies—and bring Middle Eastern oil fields under its control. To prevent Iran from obtaining nuclear weapons, U.S. presidents have used a mix of carrots (in the form of diplomacy) and sticks (in the form of sanctions). Sanctions made it more difficult for Iran to sell its oil, its major export, hurting its economy. In this case, U.S. allies mostly cooperated with the sanctions. In 2015 the United States and Iran signed an agreement; the Iranians pledged not to build nuclear weapons in exchange for a lifting of the economic sanctions. Critics of the agreement expressed fears that it would not deter the Iranians from continuing with their nuclear program, and during his presidential campaign Donald Trump promised to abrogate the agreement. At the same time, the United States has had considerable success in encouraging Israel, Egypt, Saudi Arabia, and the smaller Persian Gulf states to develop closer relations with one another and, possibly, work toward an anti-Iran alliance.

With North Korea, U.S. diplomacy has thus far been fraught with difficulty, because North Korea's major backer and trading partner—China—will not cooperate with efforts by the United States to undermine the North Korean regime. China regards North Korea as a useful pawn on the geopolitical chessboard, preventing the United States and two of its allies, Japan and South Korea, from dominating the Sea of Japan. As a result, the North Koreans have continued to build nuclear warheads and to test missiles capable of carrying them. The current North Korean leader, Kim Jong-un, angered the Chinese by arresting and killing several members of

North Korea's leadership, including members of Kim's own family, whom he deemed too closely associated with China. With his actions, Kim reduced Chinese influence over North Korea's policies, leaving the country's Chinese patrons unsure of how to proceed. President Trump met with North Korean leader Kim Jong-un in June 2018 seeking to improve America's relations with North Korea and, perhaps, to move that nation out of the Chinese orbit.

TRADE POLICY

Trade is one of the most contentious issues in contemporary international relations. Figure 18.2 shows that the United States persistently imports more than it exports, producing a substantial trade deficit with the rest of the world. The United States has accused China and other nations of unfair trade practices that limit the sale of goods in their markets while they export billions of dollars in goods to the United States. Trade also affects job growth in the United States, which has been low for several years. Populist politicians like Donald Trump charge that this is the result of trade policies that allowed American jobs to be exported to Asia and Mexico where labor is cheaper. Trade, as we saw above, supports many millions of jobs in the United States. However, U.S. workers whose jobs were lost when industries moved abroad call for tariffs and other remedies they hope might bring their jobs back to the United States.

Many workers voted for Donald Trump, who criticized U.S. trade policies during his campaign and promised to bring these jobs back. One of Trump's first acts in office was to withdraw from the Trans-Pacific Partnership (TPP), a free-trade agreement between the United States and 11 Pacific Rim nations. Trump said the TPP would allow foreign countries to profit at America's expense.

Trade disputes have especially complicated America's relationship with China. In 2010 the United States accused China of manipulating trade rules to its own

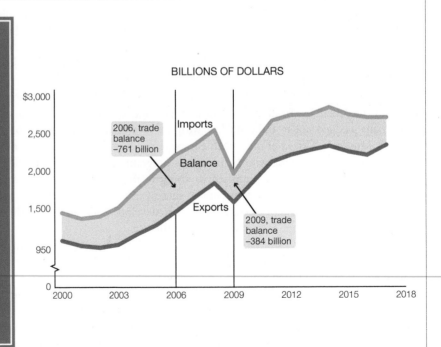

FIGURE 18.2

U.S. International Trade in Goods and Services

The United States has a "trade deficit" with the rest of the world, which means it imports more goods and services from abroad than it exports. Economists argue about whether this is a problem for the U.S. economy. Some assert that a deficit means the United States is a debtor nation, living beyond its means. Others assert that the trade deficit reflects investment in American productive capabilities. Still others argue that imports as well as exports are good for the American economy.

SOURCE: U.S. Census Bureau, Foreign Trade Statistics, www.census.gov/foreign-trade/statistics/historical/index.html (accessed 7/20/18).

advantage, and China, in return, accused the United States of mismanaging its own economy. In 2012, China announced that it would reduce its purchases of U.S. government securities in order to become less vulnerable to fluctuations in the value of the dollar. The United States pointed out that this might result in a reduction of its imports of Chinese goods. President Trump has declared that the Chinese trade unfairly and has promised to change the rules in America's favor—a move sure to increase Chinese enmity toward the United States. In 2018, President Trump announced the imposition of $50 billion in tariffs on Chinese steel, aluminum and electronic goods sold to the U.S. China quickly announced that it would retaliate with tariffs on U.S. farm products, sea foods, and autos sold in China. These moves raised the prospect of an all-out trade war between the world's two largest economies.

GLOBAL ENVIRONMENTAL POLICY

A final trouble spot for American policy makers is international environmental policy. The environment is a global matter. Pollutants produced in one country affect all others. Generally speaking, the United States supports various international efforts to protect the environment. These include the United Nations Framework Convention on Climate Change, an international agreement to study and ameliorate harmful changes in the global environment, and the Montreal Protocol, an agreement signed by over 150 countries to limit the production of substances potentially harmful to the world's ozone layer. Other nations have criticized the United States for withdrawing from the 1997 Kyoto Protocol, an agreement setting limits on industrial countries' emissions of greenhouse gases. The United States asserted that the Kyoto Protocol would harm American economic interests. The Kyoto Protocol expired in 2012, but 37 of the original signatories signed the Doha Amendment to renew their commitment to reduce greenhouse gas emissions. The United States refrained from signing this new agreement as well.

In 2015, however, the United States did agree to the Paris Agreement to reduce greenhouse gas emissions. Each country agreed to reduce emissions but would set its own contribution to the effort. Many Republicans, including Donald Trump, opposed the agreement, and as president, Trump ended U.S. participation in the Paris accord, stating that strict environmental controls would undermine American manufacturing interests and cause more jobs to leave the United States in favor of developing nations without such standards. America's western European allies, on the other hand, remain committed to the Paris accord and view the American administration as uninformed and reckless.[32]

Foreign Policy
WHAT DO WE WANT?

The five policy areas discussed above are only a few of the problems facing America in the world. How should we respond to these and other problems facing our nation? The nineteenth-century British statesman Lord Palmerston famously said, "Nations have no permanent friends or allies; they only have permanent interests." Palmerston's comment illustrates what is sometimes known as the "realist" view of foreign policy. The realist school holds that foreign policies should be guided by the national interest (mainly security and economic interests) and that policy makers should steel themselves to the necessity of making decisions that might be viewed from the outside as cold and ruthless if they serve the nation's interests. Although many public officials have denounced such views in public—especially if they are running for office—many became realists once in power. Every one of America's post–World War II presidents, Democrats and Republicans alike, has been willing to order young Americans into battle and to visit death and destruction on the citizens of foreign states if he believed the national interest required it.

The harsh rationality of foreign policy often clashes with America's history and ideals. U.S. democratic and liberal traditions lead Americans to hope for a world in which ideals rather than naked interests govern foreign policy and in which U.S. leaders pay heed to ideals. The ideals that Americans historically have espoused (though not always lived by) assert that U.S. foreign policies should have a higher purpose than the pursuit of self-interest and that the United States is to use force only as a last resort. Since the realities of U.S. foreign policy often clash with these historical ideals, American policy makers often struggle to explain their actions and avoid admitting to motivations that don't embody those ideals.

"Simply stated, there is no doubt that Saddam Hussein now has weapons of mass destruction," said Vice President Dick Cheney in 2002. When it turned out that these weapons did not exist, Assistant Defense Secretary Paul Wolfowitz explained, "For bureaucratic reasons, we settled on one issue, weapons of mass destruction [as justification for invading Iraq], because it was the one reason everyone could agree on."[33] As a candidate for the presidency, Barack Obama was praised for denouncing the Bush administration's treatment of enemy combatants. Obama was especially critical of the Guantánamo detention facility, where some alleged enemy combatants were incarcerated. Once in office, however, Obama did not rush to close the Guantánamo facility—though he continued to plan for its eventual closure. Donald Trump, for his part, did not bother to hide his support for interests over principles. His motto was "America first."

Must the United States always choose between its ideals and its interests? American ideals are what attracted many of those affected by the 2017 travel ban (and generations of immigrants before them) to the United States in the first place. The Founders of the Republic believed that America would be different from other nations. They believed that its ideals would be its source of power, that its ideals would allow it to inspire and lead others as a "shining beacon." But international events can make it difficult to always pursue those ideals. The forces of globalization mean that it is easier than ever for small groups of extremists with violent intentions to travel to American shores and carry out their plans. (The "Who Participates?" feature on the facing page shows public opinion on security issues and reflects strong concern about international terrorism among all age groups.) On the other hand, those same forces of globalization have been the source of many positive outcomes. Greater trade reduces the price of many products for American consumers as well as those abroad. Furthermore, many scholars believe that the increasing global economic interdependence is a force for peace: it is difficult to go to war with one's major trading partners because the harm domestically would be too great. What can U.S. leaders do in the future to make sure that globalization is a positive force that promotes U.S. security and prosperity? If, in the pursuit of national power and security, our political leaders always choose narrow interests over transcendent ideals, might they be robbing the United States of its true source of international power and global security?

Public Opinion on Security Issues

Percentage who think each is a major threat to the well-being of the United States

Iran's nuclear program
- 🐴 Democrats 45%
- 🐘 Republicans 63%

Global climate change
- 🐴 83%
- 🐘 28%

North Korea's nuclear program
- 🐴 75%
- 🐘 74%

China's power & influence
- 🐴 43%
- 🐘 48%

Russia's power & influence
- 🐴 63%
- 🐘 38%

Cyberattacks from other countries
- 🐴 75%
- 🐘 70%

ISIS
- 🐴 64%
- 🐘 74%

🐴 Democrats
🐘 Republicans

As we learned in this chapter, public opinion can influence foreign policy. However, many Americans are not engaged with or knowledgeable about foreign policy. Moreover, public opinion varies by political party. These figures show what percentage of members of each major political party think each issue is a major threat to the United States.

SOURCE: Pew Research Center, "Partisans Have Starkly Different Opinions about How the World Views the U.S.," pewresearch.org (accessed 1/11/18).

★ **WHAT YOU CAN DO** ★

Stay Informed about International News

☑ Learn more about the issues above and others through coverage in major U.S. newspapers such as the *New York Times* (**www.nytimes.com**) and the *Wall Street Journal* (**www.wsj.com**).

☑ Check out foreign news sites for different perspectives on U.S. foreign policies and activities such as Al Jazeera English (**www.aljazeera.com**) and the BBC (**www.bbc.com**).

☑ For in-depth conversations about world affairs, watch videos at the World Affairs Council (**www.worldaffairs.org**) or the Council on Foreign Relations (**www.cfr.org**).

☑ Consider working with an interest group on a foreign policy issue you care about, such as Amnesty International (human rights), Move America Forward (supporting American troops), or Just Foreign Policy (equality and justice from a nonpartisan perspective).

The Goals of Foreign Policy

> **Explain how foreign policy is designed to promote security, prosperity, and humanitarian goals (pp. 717–22)**

The programs and policies that determine U.S. relations with other nations and foreign entities are referred to as *American foreign policy*. The two main goals of American foreign policy are security and prosperity. America's security policy is focused on terrorist groups, hostile non-state actors, and foreign countries. America's international economic policies are concentrated on expanding employment opportunities, maintaining access to foreign energy supplies, promoting foreign investment in the United States, and lowering the prices Americans pay for goods and services. Although many Americans are also committed to promoting human rights, this commitment has a lower priority in American foreign policy than the nation's security concerns and economic interests.

Key Terms

non-state actors (p. 717)

isolationism (p. 718)

containment (p. 718)

preventive war (p. 718)

appeasement (p. 718)

deterrence (p. 718)

Cold War (p. 718)

nation-states (p. 719)

World Trade Organization (WTO) (p. 721)

General Agreement on Tariffs and Trade (GATT) (p. 721)

United States–Mexico–Canada Agreement (USMCA) (p. 721)

Practice Quiz

1. Which of the following terms best describes the American posture toward the world prior to the twentieth century?
   a) interventionist
   b) isolationist
   c) appeasement
   d) humanitarian
   e) internationalist

2. Which of the following terms describes an effort to forestall war by giving in to the demands of a hostile power?
   a) appeasement
   b) détente
   c) deterrence
   d) containment
   e) preventive war

3. The World Trade Organization is
   a) an agency in the federal executive branch that analyzes trade deficits.
   b) an American interest group that lobbies Congress for the passage of agricultural and manufacturing tariffs.
   c) an American interest group that lobbies Congress for the passage of so-called "Fair Trade" laws.
   d) an international organization composed of Western European countries that oppose free trade.
   e) an international organization promoting free trade that grew out of the General Agreement on Tariffs and Trade.

Who Makes American Foreign Policy?

> **Identify the major players in foreign policy making, and describe their roles (pp. 722–33)**

While the president and the chief advisers are the principal architects of U.S. foreign policy, many other actors in the American political system play an important role in determining how the United States interacts with other nations. Specifically, Congress, the executive branch, bureaucracy, and interest groups all exert some influence over American foreign policy. Often, the president and Congress are at odds over foreign policy.

Key Terms

Bush Doctrine (p. 724)

executive agreement (p. 725)

Practice Quiz

4. The "Bush Doctrine" refers to
   a) the idea that the United States should not allow foreign powers to meddle in the Western Hemisphere.
   b) the idea that the United States should avoid future wars by giving in to the demands of hostile foreign powers.

c) the idea that the United States should take preemptive action against threats to its national security.

d) the idea that the United States should never take preemptive action against threats to its national security.

e) the idea that the United States should always secure international approval before taking any military action.

5. The Foreign Intelligence Surveillance Act (FISA)

a) prohibited the government from collecting intelligence data in countries outside of the Western Hemisphere.

b) required that the government receive a warrant from a special court before undertaking electronic surveillance of American citizens.

c) prevented the United States from officially recognizing the North Korean government under Kim Jong-il.

d) established the National Security Agency.

e) eliminated the Department of Homeland Security.

6. Which of the following statements about the U.S. Senate Committee on Foreign Relations is *not* accurate?

a) The Committee consists of 18 members from the Senate.

b) The Committee was established in 1816 as one of the original ten standing committees of the Senate.

c) The Committee oversees the State Department.

d) The Committee must unanimously approve all treaties before they are enacted.

e) The Committee includes seven subcommittees, each with a regional or subject-matter jurisdiction.

7. The Constitution assigns the power to declare war to

a) the National Security Council.

b) the president.

c) Congress.

d) the secretary of defense.

e) the chief justice of the United States.

The Instruments of Modern American Foreign Policy

Describe the means the United States uses to carry out foreign policy today (pp. 733–41)

The most important tools for the United States in implementing its foreign policy in the modern era have been diplomacy, the United Nations, the international monetary structure, economic aid and sanctions, collective security, military force, soft power, and arbitration. Many of the international organizations that influence contemporary American foreign policy, such as the United Nations, the International Monetary Fund, the World Bank, NATO, and the International Court of Justice, were formed in the years immediately following World War II. As a result of the fact that the United States possesses a more powerful and effective military than any other nation, military force is a particularly important tool for American foreign policy.

Key Terms

diplomacy (p. 734)

United Nations (UN) (p. 734)

International Monetary Fund (IMF) (p. 735)

Practice Quiz

8. Which of the following statements about the United Nations is *not* true?

a) It gives every country one vote in the General Assembly.

b) It has a powerful army to implement its decisions.

c) The five permanent members of the UN Security Council are China, France, Russia, the United Kingdom, and the United States.

d) It was designed to be a channel for negotiation and a means of settling international disputes peaceably.

e) Important issues require a two-thirds majority vote in the General Assembly.

9. Which of the following were founded during the 1940s in order to create a new international economic structure for the postwar world?

a) the Federal Reserve System and the Council of Economic Advisers

b) the North Atlantic Treaty Organization and the Southeast Asia Treaty Organization

c) the International Monetary Fund and the World Bank

d) the International Court of Justice and the Warsaw Pact

e) the Office of Management and Budget and the General Agreement on Tariffs and Trade

10. The North Atlantic Treaty Organization was formed by the United States,

a) Canada, and most of Eastern Europe.

b) Canada, and the Soviet Union.

c) Canada, and Mexico.

d) Canada, and most of Western Europe.

e) Canada, and the United Kingdom.

11. Cultural programs that send American actors, athletes, and musicians around the world in order to promote a positive view of the United States are examples of the United States' use of

a) soft power.

b) star power.

c) arbitration.

d) "Thucydides's Trap."

e) hard power.

Current Foreign Policy Issues Facing the United States

Analyze the foreign policy problems facing American policy makers today (pp. 741–45)

The United States is currently facing a number of important short- and long-term foreign policy problems: threats from China and Russia; nuclear proliferation in Iran and North Korea; international trade disputes; and global environmental degradation. The Trump administration has maintained the policies of previous presidents on some of these problems and shifted directions on others.

Practice Quiz

12. The United States
    a) exports more goods and services to other countries than it imports.
    b) imports more goods and services from other countries than it exports.
    c) exports the same number of goods and services from other countries than it imports.
    d) does not import goods and services from other countries.
    e) does not export goods and services to other countries.

13. In 2015 the United States entered into an international agreement to reduce greenhouse gas emissions called the
    a) Kyoto Protocol.
    b) Doha amendment.
    c) Trans-Pacific Partnership.
    d) Montreal Protocol.
    e) Paris Agreement.

For Further Reading

Allison, Graham. *Destined for War: Can America and China Escape Thucydides's Trap?* New York: Houghton Mifflin Harcourt, 2017.

Art, Robert. *The Use of Force: Military Power and International Politics*. New York: Rowman and Littlefield, 2009.

Bacevich, Andrew. *The Limits of Power: The End of American Exceptionalism*. New York: Metropolitan Books, 2008.

Dorman, Andrew, and Joyce Kaufman, eds. *Providing for National Security*. Palo Alto, CA: Stanford University Press, 2014.

Drezner, Daniel. "The Realist Tradition in American Public Opinion." *Perspectives on Politics* 6, no. 1 (March 2008): 51–70.

Gaddis, John L. *The Cold War: A New History*. New York: Penguin Press, 2005.

Ginsberg, Benjamin. *The Worth of War*. New York: Prometheus, 2014.

Haass, Richard. *A World in Disarray: Foreign Policy and the Crisis of the Old Order*. New York: Penguin, 2017.

Herring, George C. *From Colony to Superpower: U.S. Foreign Relations since 1776*. New York: Oxford University Press, 2011.

Hook, Steven. *U.S. Foreign Policy: The Paradox of World Power*. Washington, DC: CQ Press, 2010.

Ikenberry, John. *American Foreign Policy*. New York: Wadsworth, 2010.

Irwin, Douglas. *Clashing Over Commerce: A History of US Trade Policy*. Chicago: University of Chicago Press, 2017.

Kagan, Robert. *Dangerous Nation*. New York: Knopf, 2006.

Kaufman, Joyce. *A Concise History of U.S. Foreign Policy*. New York: Rowman and Littlefield, 2010.

Kennan, George F. *Around the Cragged Hill: A Personal and Political Philosophy*. New York: W. W. Norton, 1993.

Nasr, Vali. *The Dispensable Nation: American Foreign Policy in Retreat*. New York: Anchor, 2014.

Pillar, Paul. *Intelligence and U.S. Foreign Policy*. New York: Columbia University Press, 2011.

Satter, David. *The Less You Know, the Better You Sleep: Russia's Road to Terror and Dictatorship under Yeltsin and Putin*. New Haven, CT: Yale University Press, 2016.

Stiglitz, Joseph. *Globalization and Its Discontents*. New York: W. W. Norton, 2017.

Recommended Websites

American Israel Public Affairs Committee
www.aipac.org

Interest groups are some of the main shapers of foreign policy. One of the top lobbies in the nation, the American Israel Public Affairs Committee works to strengthen the U.S.–Israeli relationship.

Foreign Policy Association
www.fpa.org

This nonprofit organization tries to generate interest in and draw attention to global issues and policies.

International Monetary Fund
www.imf.org

World Trade Organization
www.wto.org

The International Monetary Fund (IMF) and the World Trade Organization (WTO) have been considered instruments of modern American foreign policy. Read about how these organizations are trying to promote capitalism, free trade, and economic development.

National Security Council
www.whitehouse.gov/nsc/

The National Security Council was formed in 1947 and consists of senior advisers and Cabinet officials who keep the president informed on all matters of national security and foreign policy.

Peterson Institute for International Economics
www.piie.com

The Peterson Institute for International Economics is dedicated to analyzing international economic policy. Take a minute to review some of the studies that have influenced the policies of such international organizations as NAFTA, the WTO, and the IMF.

United Nations
www.un.org

Founded in 1945, the United Nations (UN) promotes international peace and security. Visit the UN website for information on the General Assembly, the Security Council, economic and social development, and humanitarian issues.

U.S. Department of State
www.state.gov

The U.S. Department of State is the primary bureaucratic department for American diplomacy and national security.

U.S. Senate: Treaties
www.senate.gov/legislative/treaties.htm

The most important foreign policy task of the Senate is reviewing and approving treaties. Learn more about the Senate's treaty-making powers, and find information about treaty action at this U.S. Senate website.

Appendix

The Declaration of Independence

In Congress, July 4, 1776

The unanimous Declaration of the thirteen united States of America,

When in the Course of human events, it becomes necessary for one people to dissolve the political bands which have connected them with another, and to assume among the powers of the earth, the separate and equal station to which the Laws of Nature and of Nature's God entitle them, a decent respect to the opinions of mankind requires that they should declare the causes which impel them to the separation.

We hold these truths to be self-evident, that all men are created equal, that they are endowed by their Creator with certain unalienable Rights, that among these are Life, Liberty and the pursuit of Happiness.—That to secure these rights, Governments are instituted among Men, deriving their just powers from the consent of the governed.—That whenever any Form of Government becomes destructive of these ends, it is the Right of the People to alter or to abolish it, and to institute new Government, laying its foundation on such principles and organizing its powers in such form, as to them shall seem most likely to effect their Safety and Happiness. Prudence, indeed, will dictate that Governments long established should not be changed for light and transient causes; and accordingly all experience hath shewn, that mankind are more disposed to suffer, while evils are sufferable, than to right themselves by abolishing the forms to which they are accustomed. But when a long train of abuses and usurpations, pursuing invariably the same Object evinces a design to reduce them under absolute Despotism, it is their right, it is their duty, to throw off such Government, and to provide new Guards for their future security.—Such has been the patient sufferance of these Colonies; and such is now the necessity which constrains them to alter their former Systems of Government. The history of the present King of Great Britain is a history of repeated injuries and usurpations, all having in direct object the establishment of an absolute Tyranny over these States. To prove this, let Facts be submitted to a candid world.

He has refused his Assent to Laws, the most wholesome and necessary for the public good.

He has forbidden his Governors to pass Laws of immediate and pressing importance, unless suspended in their operation till his Assent should be obtained; and when so suspended, he has utterly neglected to attend to them.

He has refused to pass other Laws for the accommodation of large districts of people, unless those people would relinquish the right of Representation in the Legislature, a right inestimable to them and formidable to tyrants only.

He has called together legislative bodies at places unusual, uncomfortable, and distant from the depository of their public Records, for the sole purpose of fatiguing them into compliance with his measures.

He has dissolved Representative Houses repeatedly, for opposing with manly firmness his invasions on the rights of the people.

He has refused for a long time, after such dissolutions, to cause others to be elected; whereby the Legislative powers, incapable of Annihilation, have returned to the People at large for their exercise; the State remaining in the mean time exposed to all the dangers of invasion from without, and convulsions within.

He has endeavoured to prevent the population of these States; for that purpose obstructing the Laws for Naturalization of Foreigners; refusing to pass others to encourage their migrations hither, and raising the conditions of new Appropriations of Lands.

He has obstructed the Administration of Justice, by refusing his Assent to Laws for establishing Judiciary powers.

He has made Judges dependent on his Will alone, for the tenure of their offices, and the amount and payment of their salaries.

He has erected a multitude of New Offices, and sent hither swarms of Officers to harrass our people, and eat out their substance.

He has kept among us, in times of peace, Standing Armies without the Consent of our legislatures.

He has affected to render the Military independent of and superior to the Civil power.

He has combined with others to subject us to a jurisdiction foreign to our constitution, and unacknowledged by our laws; giving his Assent to their Acts of pretended Legislation:

For Quartering large bodies of armed troops among us:

For protecting them, by a mock Trial, from punishment for any Murders which they should commit on the Inhabitants of these States:

For cutting off our Trade with all parts of the world:

For imposing Taxes on us without our Consent:

For depriving us in many cases, of the benefits of Trial by Jury:

For transporting us beyond Seas to be tried for pretended offences:

For abolishing the free System of English Laws in a neighboring Province, establishing therein an Arbitrary government, and enlarging its Boundaries so as to render it at once an example and fit instrument for introducing the same absolute rule into these Colonies:

For taking away our Charters, abolishing our most valuable Laws, and altering fundamentally the Forms of our Governments:

For suspending our own Legislatures, and declaring themselves invested with power to legislate for us in all cases whatsoever.

He has abdicated Government here, by declaring us out of his Protection and waging War against us.

He has plundered our seas, ravaged our Coasts, burnt our towns, and destroyed the lives of our people.

He is at this time transporting large Armies of foreign Mercenaries to compleat the works of death, desolation and tyranny, already begun with circumstances of Cruelty & perfidy scarcely paralleled in the most barbarous ages, and totally unworthy the Head of a civilized nation.

He has constrained our fellow Citizens taken Captive on the high Seas to bear Arms against their Country, to become the executioners of their friends and Brethren, or to fall themselves by their Hands.

He has excited domestic insurrections amongst us, and has endeavoured to bring on the inhabitants of our frontiers, the merciless Indian Savages, whose known rule of warfare, is an undistinguished destruction of all ages, sexes and conditions.

In every stage of these Oppressions We have Petitioned for Redress in the most humble terms: Our repeated Petitions have been answered only by repeated injury. A Prince whose character is thus marked by every act which may define a Tyrant, is unfit to be the ruler of a free people.

Nor have We been wanting in attentions to our Brittish brethren. We have warned them from time to time of attempts by their legislature to extend an unwarrantable jurisdiction over us. We have reminded them of the circumstances of our emigration and settlement here. We have appealed to their native justice and magnanimity, and we have conjured them by the ties of our common kindred to disavow these usurpations, which, would inevitably interrupt our connections and correspondence. They too have been deaf to the voice of justice and of consanguinity. We must, therefore, acquiesce in the necessity, which denounces our Separation, and hold them, as we hold the rest of mankind, Enemies in War, in Peace Friends.

We, Therefore, the Representatives of the United States of America, in General Congress, Assembled, appealing to the Supreme Judge of the world for the rectitude of our intentions, do, in the Name, and by Authority of the good People of these Colonies, solemnly publish and declare, That these United Colonies are, and of Right ought to be Free and Independent States; that they are Absolved from all Allegiance to the British Crown, and that all political connection between them and the State of Great Britain, is and ought to be totally dissolved; and that as Free and Independent States, they have full Power to levy War, conclude Peace, contract Alliances, establish Commerce, and to do all other Acts and Things which Independent States may of right do. And for the support of this Declaration, with a firm reliance on the protection of divine Providence, we mutually pledge to each other our Lives, our Fortunes and our sacred Honor.

The foregoing Declaration was, by order of Congress, engrossed, and signed by the following members:

John Hancock

NEW HAMPSHIRE
Josiah Bartlett
William Whipple
Matthew Thornton

MASSACHUSETTS BAY
Samuel Adams
John Adams
Robert Treat Paine
Elbridge Gerry

RHODE ISLAND
Stephen Hopkins
William Ellery

CONNECTICUT
Roger Sherman
Samuel Huntington
William Williams
Oliver Wolcott

NEW YORK
William Floyd
Philip Livingston
Francis Lewis
Lewis Morris

NEW JERSEY
Richard Stockton
John Witherspoon
Francis Hopkinson
John Hart
Abraham Clark

PENNSYLVANIA
Robert Morris
Benjamin Rush
Benjamin Franklin
John Morton
George Clymer
James Smith
George Taylor
James Wilson
George Ross

DELAWARE
Caesar Rodney
George Read
Thomas M'Kean

MARYLAND
Samuel Chase
William Paca
Thomas Stone
Charles Carroll,
   of Carrollton

VIRGINIA
George Wythe
Richard Henry Lee
Thomas Jefferson
Benjamin Harrison
Thomas Nelson, Jr.
Francis Lightfoot Lee
Carter Braxton

NORTH CAROLINA
William Hooper
Joseph Hewes
John Penn

SOUTH CAROLINA
Edward Rutledge
Thomas Heyward, Jr.
Thomas Lynch, Jr.
Arthur Middleton

GEORGIA
Button Gwinnett
Lyman Hall
George Walton

Resolved, That copies of the Declaration be sent to the several assemblies, conventions, and committees, or councils of safety, and to the several commanding officers of the continental troops; that it be proclaimed in each of the United States, at the head of the army.

The Articles of Confederation

Agreed to by Congress November 15, 1777;
ratified and in force March 1, 1781

To all whom these Presents shall come, we the undersigned Delegates of the States affixed to our Names, send greeting. Whereas the Delegates of the United States of America, in Congress assembled, did, on the fifteenth day of November, in the Year of Our Lord One thousand Seven Hundred and Seventy seven, and in the Second Year of the Independence of America, agree to certain articles of Confederation and perpetual Union between the States of Newhampshire, Massachusettsbay, Rhodeisland and Providence Plantations, Connecticut, New-York, New-Jersey, Pennsylvania, Delaware, Maryland, Virginia, North-Carolina, South-Carolina and Georgia in the words following, viz. "Articles of Confederation and perpetual Union between the states of Newhampshire, Massachusettsbay, Rhodeisland and Providence Plantations, Connecticut, New-York, New-Jersey, Pennsylvania, Delaware, Maryland, Virginia, North-Carolina, South-Carolina and Georgia.

Art. I. The Stile of this confederacy shall be "The United States of America."

Art. II. Each state retains its sovereignty, freedom and independence, and every Power, Jurisdiction and right, which is not by this confederation expressly delegated to the United States, in Congress assembled.

Art. III. The said states hereby severally enter into a firm league of friendship with each other, for their common defence, the security of their Liberties, and their mutual and general welfare, binding themselves to assist each other, against all force offered to, or attacks made upon them, or any of them, on account of religion, sovereignty, trade, or any other pretence whatever.

Art. IV. The better to secure and perpetuate mutual friendship and intercourse among the people of the different states in this union, the free inhabitants of each of these states, paupers, vagabonds and fugitives from Justice excepted, shall be entitled to all privileges and immunities of free citizens in the several states; and the people of each state shall have free ingress and regress to and from any other state, and shall enjoy therein all the privileges of trade and commerce, subject to the same duties, impositions and restrictions as the inhabitants thereof respectively, provided that such restriction shall not extend so far as to prevent the removal of property imported into any state, to any other state, of which the Owner is an inhabitant; provided also that no imposition, duties or restriction shall be laid by any state, on the property of the united states, or either of them.

If any Person guilty of, or charged with treason, felony, or other high misdemeanor in any state, shall flee from Justice, and be found in any of the united states, he shall, upon demand of the Governor or executive power, of the state from which he fled, be delivered up and removed to the state having jurisdiction of his offence.

Full faith and credit shall be given in each of these states to the records, acts and judicial proceedings of the courts and magistrates of every other state.

Art. V. For the more convenient management of the general interests of the united states, delegates shall be annually appointed in such manner as the legislature of each state shall direct, to meet in Congress on the first Monday in November, in every year, with a power reserved to each state, to recall its delegates, or any of them, at any time within the year, and to send others in their stead, for the remainder of the Year.

No state shall be represented in Congress by less than two, nor by more than seven Members; and no person shall be capable of being a delegate for more than three years in any term of six years; nor shall any person, being a delegate, be capable of holding any office under the united states, for which he, or another for his benefit receives any salary, fees or emolument of any kind.

Each state shall maintain its own delegates in a meeting of the states, and while they act as members of the committee of the states.

In determining questions in the united states, in Congress assembled, each state shall have one vote.

Freedom of speech and debate in Congress shall not be impeached or questioned in any Court, or place out of Congress, and the members of congress shall be protected in their persons from arrests and imprisonments, during the time of their going to and from, and attendance on congress, except for treason, felony, or breach of the peace.

Art. VI. No state without the Consent of the united states in congress assembled, shall send any embassy to, or receive any embassy from, or enter into any conference, agreement, or alliance or treaty with any King, prince or state; nor shall any person holding any office or profit or trust under the united states, or any of them, accept of any present, emolument, office or title of any kind whatever from any king, prince or foreign state; nor shall the united states in congress assembled, or any of them, grant any title of nobility.

No two or more states shall enter into any treaty, confederation or alliance whatever between them, without the consent of the united states in congress assembled, specifying accurately the purposes for which the same is to be entered into, and how long it shall continue.

No state shall lay any imposts or duties, which may interfere with any stipulations in treaties, entered into by the united states in congress assembled, with any king, prince or state, in pursuance of any treaties already proposed by congress, to the courts of France and Spain.

No vessels of war shall be kept up in time of peace by any state, except such number only, as shall be deemed necessary by the united states in congress assembled, for the defence of such state, or its trade; nor shall any body of forces be kept up by any state, in time of peace, except such number only, as in the judgment of the united states, in congress assembled, shall be deemed requisite to garrison the forts necessary for the defence of such state; but every state shall always keep up a well regulated and disciplined militia, sufficiently armed and accoutred, and shall provide and constantly have ready for use, in public stores, a due number of field pieces and tents, and a proper quantity of arms, ammunition and camp equipage.

No state shall engage in any war without the consent of the united states in congress assembled, unless such state be actually invaded by enemies, or shall have received certain advice of a resolution being formed by some nation of Indians to invade such state, and the danger is so imminent as not to admit of a delay, till the united states in congress asssembled can be consulted; nor shall any state grant commissions to any ships or vessels of war, nor letters of marque or reprisal, except it be after a declaration of war by the united states in congress assembled, and then only against the kingdom or state and the subjects thereof, against which war has been so declared, and under such regulations as shall be established by the united states in congress assembled, unless such state be infested by pirates; in which case vessels of war may be fitted out for that occasion, and kept so long as the danger shall continue, or until the united states in congress assembled shall determine otherwise.

Art. VII. When land-forces are raised by any state for the common defence, all officers of or under the rank of colonel, shall be appointed by the legislature of each state respectively, by whom such forces shall be raised, or in such manner as such state shall direct, and all vacancies shall be filled up by the state which first made the appointment.

Art. VIII. All charges of war, and all other expences that shall be incurred for the common defence or general welfare, and allowed by the united states in congress assembled, shall be defrayed out of a common treasury, which shall be supplied by the several states in proportion to the value of all land within each state, granted to or surveyed for any Person, as such land and the buildings and improvements thereon shall be estimated according to such mode as the united states in congress assembled, shall from time to time direct and appoint.

The taxes for paying that proportion shall be laid and levied by the authority and direction of the legislatures of the several states within the time agreed upon by the united states in congress assembled.

Art. IX. The united states in congress assembled, shall have the sole and exclusive right and power of determining on peace and war, except in the cases mentioned in the sixth article—of sending and receiving ambassadors—entering into treaties and alliances, provided that no treaty of commerce shall be made whereby the legislative power of the respective states shall be restrained from imposing such imposts and duties on foreigners, as their own people are subjected to, or from prohibiting the exportation of any species of goods or commodities whatsoever—of establishing rules for deciding in all cases, what captures on land or water shall be legal, and in what manner prizes taken by land or naval forces in the service of the united states shall be divided or appropriated—of granting letters of marque and reprisal in times of peace—appointing courts for the trial of piracies and felonies committed on the high seas and establishing courts for receiving and determining finally appeals in all cases of captures, provided that no member of congress shall be appointed a judge of any of the said courts.

The united states in congress assembled shall also be the last resort on appeal in all disputes and differences now subsisting or that hereafter may arise between two or more states concerning boundary, jurisdiction or any other cause whatever; which authority shall always be exercised in the manner following. Whenever the legislative or executive authority or lawful agent of any state in controversy with another shall present a petition to congress stating the matter in question and praying for a hearing, notice thereof shall be given by order of congress to the legislative or executive authority of the other state in controversy, and a day assigned for the appearance of the parties by their lawful agents, who shall then be directed to appoint by joint consent, commissioners or judges to constitute a court for hearing and determining the matter in question: but if they cannot agree, congress shall name three persons out of each of the united states, and from the list of such persons each party shall alternately strike out one, the petitioners beginning, until the number shall be reduced to thirteen; and from that number not less than seven, nor more than nine names as congress shall direct, shall in the presence of congress be drawn out by lot, and the persons whose names shall be so drawn or any five of them, shall be commissioners or judges, to hear and finally determine the controversy, so always as a major part of the judges who shall hear the cause shall agree in the determination: and if either party shall neglect to attend at the day appointed, without shewing reasons, which congress shall judge sufficient, or being present shall refuse to strike, the congress shall proceed to nominate three persons out of each state, and the secretary of congress shall strike in behalf of such party absent or refusing; and the judgment and sentence of the court to be appointed, in the manner before prescribed, shall be final and conclusive; and if any of the parties shall refuse to submit to the authority of such court, or to appear to defend their claim or cause, the court shall nevertheless proceed to pronounce sentence, or judgment, which shall in like manner be final and decisive, the judgment or sentence and other proceedings being in either case transmitted to congress, and lodged among the acts of congress for the security of the parties concerned: provided that every commissioner, before he sits in judgment, shall take an oath to be administered by one of the judges of the supreme or superior court of the state, where the cause shall be tried, "well and truly to hear and determine the matter in question, according to the best of his judgment, without favour, affection or hope of reward:" provided also, that no state shall be deprived of territory for the benefit of the united states.

All controversies concerning the private right of soil claimed under different grants of two or more states, whose jurisdictions as they may respect such lands, and the states which passed such grants are adjusted, the said grants or either of them being at the same time claimed to have originated antecedent to such settlement of jurisdiction, shall on the petition of either party to the congress of the united states, be finally determined as near as may be in the same manner as is before prescribed for deciding disputes respecting territorial jurisdiction between different states.

The united states in congress assembled shall also have the sole and exclusive right and power of regulating the alloy and value of coin struck by their own authority, or by that of the respective states—fixing the standard of weights and measures throughout the united states—regulating the trade and managing all affairs with the Indians, not members of any of the states, provided that the legislative right of any state within its own limits be not infringed or violated—establishing and regulating post-offices from one state to another, throughout all the united states, and exacting such postage on the papers passing thro' the same as may be requisite to defray the expences of the said office—appointing all officers of the land forces, in the service of the united states, excepting regimental officers—appointing all the officers of the naval forces, and commissioning all officers whatever in the service of the united states—making rules for the government and regulation of the said land and naval forces, and directing their operations.

The united states in congress assembled shall have authority to appoint a committee, to sit in the recess of congress, to be denominated "A Committee of the States," and to consist of one delegate from each state; and to appoint such other committees and civil officers as may be necessary for managing the general affairs of the united states under their direction—to appoint one of their number to preside, provided that no person be allowed to serve in the office of president more than one year in any term of three years; to ascertain the necessary sums of Money to be raised for the service of the united states, and to appropriate and apply the same for defraying the public expenses—to borrow money, or emit bills on the credit of the united states, transmitting every half year to the respective states an account of the sums of money so borrowed or emitted,—to build and equip a navy—to agree upon the number of land forces, and to make requisitions from each state for its quota, in proportion to the number of white inhabitants in such state; which requisition shall be binding, and thereupon the legislature of each state shall appoint the regimental officers, raise the men and cloath, arm and equip them in a soldier like manner, at the expense of the united states; and the officers and men so cloathed, armed and equipped shall march to the place appointed, and within the time agreed on by the united states in congress assembled: But if the united states in congress assembled shall, on consideration of circumstances judge proper that any state should not raise men, or should raise a smaller number than its quota, and that any other state should raise a greater number of men than the quota thereof, such extra number shall be raised, officered, cloathed, armed and equipped in the same manner as the quota of such state, unless the legislature of such state shall judge that such extra number cannot be safely spared out of the same, in which case they shall raise officer, cloath, arm and equip as many of such extra number as they judge can be safely spared. And the officers and men so cloathed, armed and equipped, shall march to the place appointed, and within the time agreed on by the united states in congress assembled.

The united states in congress assembled shall never engage in a war, nor grant letters of marque and reprisal in time of peace, nor enter into any treaties or alliances, nor coin money, nor regulate the value thereof, nor ascertain the sums and expenses necessary for the defence and welfare of the united states, or any of them, nor emit bills, nor borrow money on the credit of the united states, nor appropriate money, nor agree upon the number of vessels of war, to be built or purchased, or the number of land or sea forces to be raised, nor appoint a commander in chief of the army or navy, unless nine states assent to the same: nor shall a question on any other point, except for adjourning from day to day be determined, unless by the votes of a majority of the united states in congress assembled.

The congress of the united states shall have power to adjourn to any time within the year, and to any place within the united states, so that no period of adjournment be for a longer duration than the space of six Months, and shall publish the Journal of their proceedings monthly, except such parts thereof relating to treaties, alliances or military operations, as in their judgment require secrecy; and the yeas and nays of the delegates of each state on any question shall be entered on the Journal, when it is desired by any delegate; and the delegates of a state, or any of them, at his or their request shall be furnished with a transcript of the said Journal, except such parts as are above excepted, to lay before the legislatures of the several states.

Art. X. The committee of the states, or any nine of them, shall be authorised to execute, in the recess of congress, such of the powers of congress as the united states in congress assembled, by the consent of nine states, shall from time to time think expedient to vest them with; provided that no power be delegated to the said committee, for the exercise of which, by the articles of confederation, the voice of nine states in the congress of the united states assembled is requisite.

Art. XI. Canada acceding to this confederation, and joining in the measures of the united states, shall be admitted into, and entitled to all the advantages of this union: but no other colony shall be admitted into the same, unless such admission be agreed to by nine states.

Art. XII. All bills of credit emitted, monies borrowed and debts contracted by, or under the authority of congress, before the assembling of the united states, in pursuance of the present confederation, shall be deemed and considered as a charge against the united states, for payment and satisfaction whereof the said united states and the public faith are hereby solemnly pledged.

Art. XIII. Every state shall abide by the determinations of the united states in congress assembled, on all questions which by this confederation are submitted to them. And the Articles of this confederation shall be inviolably observed by every state, and the union shall be perpetual; nor shall any alteration at any time hereafter be made in any of them; unless such alteration be agreed to in a congress of the united states, and be afterwards confirmed by the legislatures of every state.

And Whereas it hath pleased the Great Governor of the World to incline the hearts of the legislatures we respectively represent in congress, to approve of, and to authorize us to ratify the said articles of confederation and perpetual union. Know Ye that we the undersigned delegates, by virtue of the power and authority to us given for that purpose, do by these presents, in the name and in behalf of our respective constituents, fully and entirely ratify and confirm each and every of the said articles of confederation and perpetual union, and all and singular the matters and things therein contained: And we do further solemnly plight and engage the faith of our respective constituents, that they shall abide by the determinations of the united states in congress assembled, on all questions, which by the said confederation are submitted to them. And that the articles thereof shall be inviolably observed by the states we respectively represent, and that the union shall be perpetual. In Witness whereof we have hereunto set our hands in Congress. Done at Philadelphia in the state of Pennsylvania the ninth day of July, in the Year of our Lord one Thousand seven Hundred and Seventy-eight, and in the third year of the independence of America.

The Constitution of the United States of America

We the People of the United States, in Order to form a more perfect Union, establish Justice, insure domestic Tranquility, provide for the common defence, promote the general Welfare, and secure the Blessings of Liberty to ourselves and our Posterity, do ordain and establish this Constitution for the United States of America.

ARTICLE I

SECTION 1
[LEGISLATIVE POWERS]

All legislative Powers herein granted shall be vested in a Congress of the United States, which shall consist of a Senate and House of Representatives.

SECTION 2
[HOUSE OF REPRESENTATIVES, HOW CONSTITUTED, POWER OF IMPEACHMENT]

The House of Representatives shall be composed of Members chosen every second Year by the People of the several States, and the Electors in each State shall have the Qualifications requisite for Electors of the most numerous Branch of the State Legislature.

No Person shall be a Representative who shall not have attained to the Age of twenty five Years, and been seven Years a Citizen of the United States, and who shall not, when elected, be an Inhabitant of that State in which he shall be chosen.

Representatives and *direct Taxes*[1] shall be apportioned among the several States which may be included within this Union, according to their respective Numbers, *which shall be determined by adding to the whole Number of free Persons, including those bound to Service for a Term of Years, and excluding Indians not taxed, three fifths of all other Persons.*[2] The actual Enumeration shall be made within three Years after the first Meeting of the Congress of the United States, and within every subsequent Term of ten Years, in such Manner as they shall by Law direct. The Number of Representatives shall not exceed one for every thirty Thousand, but each State shall have at Least one Representative; *and until such enumeration shall be made, the State of New Hampshire shall be entitled to chuse three, Massachusetts eight, Rhode-Island and Providence Plantations one, Connecticut five, New-York six, New Jersey four, Pennsylvania eight, Delaware one, Maryland six, Virginia ten, North Carolina five, South Carolina five, and Georgia three.*[3]

When vacancies happen in the Representation from any State, the Executive Authority thereof shall issue Writs of Election to fill such Vacancies.

The House of Representatives shall chuse their Speaker and other Officers; and shall have the sole Power of Impeachment.

SECTION 3
[THE SENATE, HOW CONSTITUTED, IMPEACHMENT TRIALS]

The Senate of the United States shall be composed of two Senators from each State, *chosen by the Legislature thereof,*[4] for six Years; and each Senator shall have one Vote.

Immediately after they shall be assembled in Consequence of the first Election, they shall be divided as equally as may be into three Classes. The Seats of the Senators of the first Class shall be vacated at the Expiration of the second Year, of the second Class at the Expiration of the fourth Year, and of the third Class at the Expiration of the sixth Year, so that one third may be chosen every second Year; *and if Vacancies happen by Resignation, or otherwise, during the Recess of the Legislature of any State, the Executive thereof may make temporary Appointments until the next Meeting of the Legislature, which shall then fill such Vacancies.*[5]

No Person shall be a Senator who shall not have attained to the Age of thirty Years, and been nine Years a Citizen of the United States, and who shall not, when elected, be an Inhabitant of that State for which he shall be chosen.

The Vice President of the United States shall be President of the Senate, but shall have no Vote, unless they be equally divided.

The Senate shall chuse their other Officers, and also a President pro tempore, in the Absence of the Vice President, or when he shall exercise the Office of President of the United States.

---

[1]Modified by Sixteenth Amendment.

[2]Modified by Fourteenth Amendment.

[3]Temporary provision.

[4]Modified by Seventeenth Amendment.

[5]Modified by Seventeenth Amendment.

The Senate shall have the sole Power to try all Impeachments. When sitting for that Purpose, they shall be on Oath or Affirmation. When the President of the United States is tried, the Chief Justice shall preside: And no Person shall be convicted without the Concurrence of two thirds of the Members present.

Judgment in Cases of Impeachment shall not extend further than to removal from Office, and disqualification to hold and enjoy any Office of honor, Trust or Profit under the United States: but the Party convicted shall nevertheless be liable and subject to Indictment, Trial, Judgment and Punishment, according to Law.

SECTION 4
[ELECTION OF SENATORS AND REPRESENTATIVES]

The Times, Places and Manner of holding Elections for Senators and Representatives, shall be prescribed in each State by the Legislature thereof; but the Congress may at any time by Law make or alter such Regulations, except as to the Places of chusing Senators.

The Congress shall assemble at least once in every Year, and such Meeting shall be on the first Monday in December, unless they shall by Law appoint a different Day.[6]

SECTION 5
[QUORUM, JOURNALS, MEETINGS, ADJOURNMENTS]

Each House shall be the Judge of the Elections, Returns and Qualifications of its own Members, and a Majority of each shall constitute a Quorum to do Business; but a smaller Number may adjourn from day to day, and may be authorized to compel the Attendance of absent Members, in such Manner, and under such Penalties as each House may provide.

Each House may determine the Rules of its Proceedings, punish its Members for disorderly Behaviour, and, with the Concurrence of two thirds, expel a Member.

Each House shall keep a Journal of its Proceedings, and from time to time publish the same, excepting such Parts as may in their Judgment require Secrecy; and the Yeas and Nays of the Members of either House on any questions shall, at the Desire of one fifth of those Present, be entered on the Journal.

Neither House, during the Session of Congress, shall, without the Consent of the other, adjourn for more than three days, nor to any other Place than that in which the two Houses shall be sitting.

SECTION 6
[COMPENSATION, PRIVILEGES, DISABILITIES]

The Senators and Representatives shall receive a Compensation for their Services, to be ascertained by Law, and paid out of the Treasury of the United States. They shall in all Cases, except Treason, Felony and Breach of the Peace, be privileged from Arrest during their Attendance at the Session of their respective Houses, and in going to and returning from the same; and for any Speech or Debate in either House, they shall not be questioned in any other Place.

No Senator or Representative shall, during the Time for which he was elected, be appointed to any civil Office under the Authority of the United States, which shall have been created, or the Emoluments whereof shall have been encreased during such time; and no Person holding any Office under the United States, shall be a Member of either House during his Continuance in Office.

SECTION 7
[PROCEDURE IN PASSING BILLS AND RESOLUTIONS]

All Bills for raising Revenue shall originate in the House of Representatives; but the Senate may propose or concur with Amendments as on other Bills.

Every Bill which shall have passed the House of Representatives and the Senate, shall, before it become a Law, be presented to the President of the United States: If he approve he shall sign it, but if not he shall return it, with his Objections to that House in which it shall have originated, who shall enter the Objections at large on their Journal, and proceed to reconsider it. If after such Reconsideration two thirds of that House shall agree to pass the Bill, it shall be sent, together with the Objections, to the other House, by which it shall likewise be reconsidered, and if approved by two thirds of that House, it shall become a Law. But in all such Cases the Votes of both Houses shall be determined by yeas and Nays, and the Names of the Persons voting for and against the Bill shall be entered on the Journal of each House respectively. If any Bill shall not be returned by the President within ten Days (Sundays excepted) after it shall have been presented to him, the Same shall be a Law, in like Manner as if he had signed it, unless the Congress by their Adjournment prevent its Return, in which Case it shall not be a Law.

Every Order, Resolution, or Vote to which the Concurrence of the Senate and House of Representatives may be necessary (except on a question of Adjournment) shall be presented to the President of the United States; and before the Same shall take Effect, shall be approved by him, or being disapproved by him, shall be repassed by two thirds of the Senate and House of Representatives, according to the Rules and Limitations prescribed in the Case of a Bill.

SECTION 8
[POWERS OF CONGRESS]

The Congress shall have Power

To lay and collect Taxes, Duties, Imposts and Excises, to pay the Debts and provide for the common Defence and general Welfare of the United States; but all Duties, Imposts and Excises shall be uniform throughout the United States;

To borrow Money on the credit of the United States;

---

[6]Modified by Twentieth Amendment.

To regulate Commerce with foreign Nations, and among the several States, and with the Indian Tribes;

To establish an uniform Rule of Naturalization, and uniform Laws on the subject of Bankruptcies throughout the United States;

To coin Money, regulate the Value thereof, and of foreign Coin, and fix the Standard of Weights and Measures;

To provide for the Punishment of counterfeiting the Securities and current Coin of the United States;

To establish Post Offices and post Roads;

To promote the Progress of Science and useful Arts, by securing for limited Times to Authors and Inventors the exclusive Right to their respective Writings and Discoveries;

To constitute Tribunals inferior to the supreme Court;

To define and punish Piracies and Felonies committed on the high Seas, and Offences against the Law of Nations;

To declare War, grant Letters of Marque and Reprisal, and make Rules concerning Captures on Land and Water;

To raise and support Armies, but no Appropriation of Money to that Use shall be for a longer Term than two Years;

To provide and maintain a Navy;

To make Rules for the Government and Regulation of the land and naval Forces;

To provide for calling forth the Militia to execute the Laws of the Union, suppress Insurrections and repel Invasions;

To provide for organizing, arming, and disciplining, the Militia, and for governing such Part of them as may be employed in the Service of the United States, reserving to the States respectively, the Appointment of the Officers, and the Authority of training the Militia according to the discipline prescribed by Congress;

To exercise exclusive Legislation in all Cases whatsoever, over such District (not exceeding ten Miles square) as may, by Cession of particular States, and the Acceptance of Congress, become the Seat of the Government of the United States, and to exercise like Authority over all Places purchased by the Consent of the Legislature of the State in which the Same shall be, for the Erection of Forts, Magazines, Arsenals, dock-Yards, and other needful Buildings;—And

To make all Laws which shall be necessary and proper for carrying into Execution the foregoing Powers, and all other Powers vested by this Constitution in the Government of the United States, or in any Department or Officer thereof.

SECTION 9
[SOME RESTRICTIONS ON FEDERAL POWER]

The Migration or Importation of such Persons as any of the States now existing shall think proper to admit, shall not be prohibited by the Congress prior to the Year one thousand eight hundred and eight, but a Tax or duty may be imposed on such Importation, not exceeding ten dollars for each Person.[7]

The Privilege of the Writ of Habeas Corpus shall not be suspended, unless when in Cases of Rebellion or Invasion the public Safety may require it.

No Bill of Attainder or ex post facto Law shall be passed.

No Capitation, or other direct, Tax shall be laid, unless in Proportion to the Census or Enumeration herein before directed to be taken.[8]

No Tax or Duty shall be laid on Articles exported from any State.

No Preference shall be given by any Regulation of Commerce or Revenue to the Ports of one State over those of another; nor shall Vessels bound to, or from, one State, be obliged to enter, clear, or pay Duties in another.

No Money shall be drawn from the Treasury, but in Consequence of Appropriations made by Law; and a regular Statement and Account of the Receipts and Expenditures of all public Money shall be published from time to time.

No Title of Nobility shall be granted by the United States: And no Person holding any Office of Profit or Trust under them, shall, without the Consent of the Congress, accept of any present, Emolument, Office, or Title, of any kind whatever, from any King, Prince, or foreign State.

SECTION 10
[RESTRICTIONS UPON POWERS OF STATES]

No State shall enter into any Treaty, Alliance, or Confederation; grant Letters of Marque and Reprisal; coin Money; emit Bills of Credit; make any Thing but gold and silver Coin a Tender in Payment of Debts; pass any Bill of Attainder, ex post facto Law, or Law impairing the Obligation of Contracts, or grant any Title of Nobility.

No State shall, without the Consent of the Congress, lay any Imposts or Duties on Imports or Exports, except what may be absolutely necessary for executing its inspection Laws: and the net Produce of all Duties and Imposts, laid by any State on Imports or Exports, shall be for the Use of the Treasury of the United States; and all such Laws shall be subject to the Revision and Control of the Congress.

No State shall, without the Consent of Congress, lay any Duty of Tonnage, keep Troops, or Ships of War in time of Peace, enter into any Agreement or Compact with another State, or with a foreign Power, or engage in War, unless actually invaded, or in such imminent Danger as will not admit of delay.

ARTICLE II
SECTION 1
[EXECUTIVE POWER, ELECTION, QUALIFICATIONS OF THE PRESIDENT]

The executive Power shall be vested in a President of the United States of America. *He shall hold his Office during the Term of*

---

[7]Temporary provision.

[8]Modified by Sixteenth Amendment.

four Years, and, together with the Vice President, chosen for the same Term, be elected, as follows[9]

Each State shall appoint, in such Manner as the Legislature thereof may direct, a Number of Electors, equal to the whole Number of Senators and Representatives to which the State may be entitled in the Congress: but no Senator or Representative, or Person holding an Office of Trust or Profit under the United States, shall be appointed an Elector.

The electors shall meet in their respective States, and vote by ballot for two Persons, of whom one at least shall not be an Inhabitant of the same State with themselves. And they shall make a List of all the Persons voted for, and of the Number of Votes for each; which List they shall sign and certify, and transmit sealed to the Seat of the Government of the United States, directed to the President of the Senate. The President of the Senate shall, in the Presence of the Senate and House of Representatives, open all the Certificates, and the Votes shall then be counted. The Person having the greatest Number of Votes shall be the President, if such Number be a Majority of the whole Number of Electors appointed; and if there be more than one who have such Majority, and have an equal Number of Votes, then the House of Representatives shall immediately chuse by Ballot one of them for President; and if no Person have a Majority, then from the five highest on the List the said House shall in like Manner chuse the President. But in chusing the President, the Votes shall be taken by States, the Representation from each State having one Vote; A quorum for this Purpose shall consist of a Member or Members from two thirds of the States, and a Majority of all the States shall be necessary to a Choice. In every Case, after the Choice of the President, the person having the greatest Number of Votes of the Electors shall be the Vice President. But if there should remain two or more who have equal Votes, the Senate shall chuse from them by Ballot the Vice President.[10]

The Congress may determine the Time of chusing the Electors, and the Day on which they shall give their Votes; which Day shall be the same throughout the United States.

No Person except a natural born Citizen, or a Citizen of the United States, at the time of the Adoption of this Constitution, shall be eligible to the Office of President; neither shall any Person be eligible to that Office who shall not have attained to the Age of thirty five Years, and been fourteen Years a Resident within the United States.

In Case of the Removal of the President from Office, or his Death, Resignation, or Inability to discharge the Powers and Duties of the said Office, the Same shall devolve on the Vice President, and the Congress may by Law provide for the Case of Removal, Death, Resignation or Inability, both of the President and Vice President, declaring what Officer shall then act as President, and such Officer shall act accordingly, until the Disability be removed, or a President shall be elected.

---

[9]Number of terms limited to two by Twenty-Second Amendment.

[10]Modified by Twelfth and Twentieth Amendments.

The President shall, at stated Times, receive for his Services, a Compensation, which shall neither be increased nor diminished during the Period for which he shall have been elected, and he shall not receive within that Period any other Emolument from the United States, or any of them.

Before he enter on the Execution of his Office, he shall take the following Oath or Affirmation:—"I do solemnly swear (or affirm) that I will faithfully execute the Office of President of the United States, and will to the best of my Ability, preserve, protect and defend the Constitution of the United States."

SECTION 2
[POWERS OF THE PRESIDENT]

The President shall be Commander in Chief of the Army and Navy of the United States, and of the Militia of the several States, when called into the actual Service of the United States; he may require the Opinion, in writing, of the principal Officer in each of the executive Departments, upon any Subject relating to the Duties of their respective Offices, and he shall have Power to grant Reprieves and Pardons for Offences against the United States, except in Cases of Impeachment.

He shall have Power, by and with the Advice and Consent of the Senate, to make Treaties, provided two thirds of the Senators present concur; and he shall nominate, and by and with the Advice and Consent of the Senate, shall appoint Ambassadors, other public Ministers and Consuls, Judges of the supreme Court, and all other Officers of the United States, whose Appointments are not herein otherwise provided for, and which shall be established by Law: but the Congress may by Law vest the Appointment of such inferior Officers, as they think proper, in the President alone, in the Courts of Law, or in the Heads of Departments.

The President shall have Power to fill up all Vacancies that may happen during the Recess of the Senate, by granting Commissions which shall expire at the End of their next Session.

SECTION 3
[POWERS AND DUTIES OF THE PRESIDENT]

He shall from time to time give to the Congress Information of the State of the Union, and recommend to their Consideration such Measures as he shall judge necessary and expedient; he may, on extraordinary Occasions, convene both Houses, or either of them, and in Case of Disagreement between them, with Respect to the Time of Adjournment, he may adjourn them to such Time as he shall think proper; he shall receive Ambassadors and other public Ministers; he shall take Care that the Laws be faithfully executed, and shall Commission all the Officers of the United States.

SECTION 4
[IMPEACHMENT]

The President, Vice President and all civil Officers of the United States, shall be removed from Office on Impeachment for, and Conviction of, Treason, Bribery, or other high Crimes and Misdemeanors.

ARTICLE III

SECTION 1
[JUDICIAL POWER, TENURE OF OFFICE]

The judicial Power of the United States, shall be vested in one supreme Court, and in such inferior Courts as the Congress may from time to time ordain and establish. The Judges, both of the supreme and inferior Courts, shall hold their Offices during good Behaviour, and shall, at stated Times, receive for their Services, a Compensation, which shall not be diminished during their Continuance in Office.

SECTION 2
[JURISDICTION]

The judicial Power shall extend to all Cases, in Law and Equity, arising under this Constitution, the Laws of the United States, and Treaties made, or which shall be made, under their Authority;—to all Cases affecting Ambassadors, other public Ministers and Consuls;—to all Cases of admiralty and maritime Jurisdiction;—to Controversies to which the United States shall be a Party;—to Controversies between two or more States;—*between a State and Citizens of another State;*—between Citizens of different States,—between Citizens of the same State claiming Lands under Grants of different States, *and between a State,* or the Citizens thereof, *and foreign States, Citizens or Subjects.*[11]

In all Cases affecting Ambassadors, other public Ministers and Consuls, and those in which a State shall be Party, the supreme Court shall have original Jurisdiction. In all the other Cases before mentioned, the supreme Court shall have appellate Jurisdiction, both as to Law and Fact, with such Exceptions, and under such Regulations as the Congress shall make.

The Trial of all Crimes, except in Cases of Impeachment, shall be by Jury; and such Trial shall be held in the State where the said Crimes shall have been committed; but when not committed within any State, the Trial shall be at such Place or Places as the Congress may by Law have directed.

SECTION 3
[TREASON, PROOF, AND PUNISHMENT]

Treason against the United States, shall consist only in levying War against them, or in adhering to their Enemies, giving them Aid and Comfort. No Person shall be convicted of Treason unless on the Testimony of two Witnesses to the same overt Act, or on Confession in open Court.

The Congress shall have Power to declare the Punishment of Treason, but no Attainder of Treason shall work Corruption of Blood, or Forfeiture except during the Life of the Person attainted.

ARTICLE IV

SECTION 1
[FAITH AND CREDIT AMONG STATES]

Full Faith and Credit shall be given in each State to the public Acts, Records, and judicial Proceedings of every other State. And the Congress may by general Laws prescribe the Manner in which such Acts, Records and Proceedings shall be proved, and the Effect thereof.

SECTION 2
[PRIVILEGES AND IMMUNITIES, FUGITIVES]

The Citizens of each State shall be entitled to all Privileges and Immunities of Citizens in the several States.

A Person charged in any State with Treason, Felony or other Crime, who shall flee from Justice, and be found in another State, shall on Demand of the executive Authority of the State from which he fled, be delivered up, to be removed to the State having Jurisdiction of the Crime.

No person held to Service or Labour in one State, under the Laws thereof, escaping into another, shall, in Consequence of any Law or Regulation therein, be discharged from such Service or Labour, but shall be delivered up on Claim of the Party to whom such Service or Labour may be due.[12]

SECTION 3
[ADMISSION OF NEW STATES]

New States may be admitted by the Congress into this Union; but no new State shall be formed or erected within the Jurisdiction of any other State; nor any State be formed by the Junction of two or more States, or Parts of States, without the Consent of the Legislatures of the States concerned as well as of the Congress.

The Congress shall have Power to dispose of and make all needful Rules and Regulations respecting the Territory or other Property belonging to the United States; and nothing in this Constitution shall be so construed as to Prejudice any Claims of the United States, or of any particular State.

SECTION 4
[GUARANTEE OF REPUBLICAN GOVERNMENT]

The United States shall guarantee to every State in this Union a Republican Form of Government, and shall protect each of them against Invasion; and on Application of the Legislature, or of the Executive (when the Legislature cannot be convened), against domestic Violence.

ARTICLE V
[AMENDMENT OF THE CONSTITUTION]

The Congress, whenever two thirds of both Houses shall deem it necessary, shall propose Amendments to this Constitution, or, on the Application of the Legislatures of two thirds of the

---

[11]Modified by Eleventh Amendment.

[12]Repealed by the Thirteenth Amendment.

several States, shall call a Convention for proposing Amendments, which, in either Case, shall be valid to all Intents and Purposes, as Part of this Constitution, when ratified by the Legislatures of three fourths of the several States, or by Conventions in three fourths thereof, as the one or the other Mode of Ratification may be proposed by the Congress; *Provided that no Amendment which may be made prior to the Year One thousand eight hundred and eight shall in any Manner affect the first and fourth Clauses in the Ninth Section of the first Article;*[13] and that no State, without its Consent, shall be deprived of its equal Suffrage in the Senate.

ARTICLE VI
[DEBTS, SUPREMACY, OATH]

All Debts contracted and Engagements entered into, before the Adoption of this Constitution, shall be as valid against the United States under this Constitution, as under the Confederation.

This Constitution, and the Laws of the United States which shall be made in Pursuance thereof; and all Treaties made, or which shall be made, under the Authority of the United States, shall be the supreme Law of the Land; and the Judges in every State shall be bound thereby, any Thing in the Constitution or Laws of any State to the Contrary notwithstanding.

The Senators and Representatives before mentioned, and the Members of the several State Legislatures, and all executive and judicial Officers, both of the United States and of the several States, shall be bound by Oath or Affirmation, to support this Constitution; but no religious Test shall be required as a Qualification to any Office or public Trust under the United States.

ARTICLE VII
[RATIFICATION AND ESTABLISHMENT]

The Ratification of the Conventions of nine States, shall be sufficient for the Establishment of this Constitution between the States so ratifying the Same.[14]

Done in Convention by the Unanimous Consent of the States present the Seventeenth Day of September in the Year of our Lord one thousand seven hundred and Eighty seven and of the Independence of the United States of America the Twelfth. *In Witness* whereof We have hereunto subscribed our Names,

---

[13]Temporary provision.

[14]The Constitution was submitted on September 17, 1787, by the Constitutional Convention, was ratified by the conventions of several states at various dates up to May 29, 1790, and became effective on March 4, 1789.

G:⁰ WASHINGTON—
Presidt. and deputy from Virginia

NEW HAMPSHIRE
John Langdon
Nicholas Gilman

MASSACHUSETTS
Nathaniel Gorham
Rufus King

CONNECTICUT
Wm. Saml. Johnson
Roger Sherman

NEW YORK
Alexander Hamilton

NEW JERSEY
Wil: Livingston
David Brearley
Wm. Paterson
Jona: Dayton

PENNSYLVANIA
B Franklin
Thomas Mifflin
Robt. Morris
Geo. Clymer
Thos. FitzSimons
Jared Ingersoll
James Wilson
Gouv Morris

DELAWARE
Geo: Read
Gunning Bedford jun
John Dickinson
Richard Bassett
Jaco: Broom

MARYLAND
James McHenry
Dan of St Thos. Jenifer
Danl. Carroll

VIRGINIA
John Blair—
James Madison Jr.

NORTH CAROLINA
Wm. Blount
Richd. Dobbs Spaight
Hu Williamson

SOUTH CAROLINA
J. Rutledge
Charles Cotesworth Pinckney
Charles Pinckney
Pierce Butler

GEORGIA
William Few
Abr Baldwin

Amendments to the Constitution

Proposed by Congress and Ratified by the Legislatures of the Several States, Pursuant to Article V of the Original Constitution.

Amendments I–X, known as the Bill of Rights, were proposed by Congress on September 25, 1789, and ratified on December 15, 1791.

AMENDMENT I
[FREEDOM OF RELIGION, OF SPEECH, AND OF THE PRESS]

Congress shall make no law respecting an establishment of religion, or prohibiting the free exercise thereof; or abridging the freedom of speech, or of the press; or the right of the people peaceably to assemble, and to petition the Government for a redress of grievances.

AMENDMENT II
[RIGHT TO KEEP AND BEAR ARMS]

A well regulated Militia, being necessary to the security of a free State, the right of the people to keep and bear Arms, shall not be infringed.

AMENDMENT III
[QUARTERING OF SOLDIERS]

No Soldier shall, in time of peace be quartered in any house, without the consent of the Owner, nor in time of war, but in a manner to be prescribed by law.

AMENDMENT IV
[SECURITY FROM UNWARRANTABLE SEARCH AND SEIZURE]

The right of the people to be secure in their persons, houses, papers, and effects, against unreasonable searches and seizures, shall not be violated, and no Warrants shall issue, but upon probable cause, supported by Oath or affirmation, and particularly describing the place to be searched, and the persons or things to be seized.

AMENDMENT V
[RIGHTS OF ACCUSED PERSONS IN CRIMINAL PROCEEDINGS]

No person shall be held to answer for a capital, or otherwise infamous crime, unless on a presentment or indictment of a Grand Jury, except in cases arising in the land or naval forces, or in the Militia, when in actual service in time of War or in public danger; nor shall any person be subject for the same offence to be twice put in jeopardy of life or limb; nor shall be compelled in any criminal case to be a witness against himself, nor be deprived of life, liberty, or property, without due process of law; nor shall private property be taken for public use, without just compensation.

AMENDMENT VI
[RIGHT TO SPEEDY TRIAL, WITNESSES, ETC.]

In all criminal prosecutions, the accused shall enjoy the right to a speedy and public trial, by an impartial jury of the State and district wherein the crime shall have been committed, which district shall have been previously ascertained by law, and to be informed of the nature and cause of the accusation; to be confronted with the witnesses against him; to have compulsory process for obtaining witnesses in his favor, and to have the Assistance of Counsel for his defence.

AMENDMENT VII
[TRIAL BY JURY IN CIVIL CASES]

In suits at common law, where the value in controversy shall exceed twenty dollars, the right of trial by jury shall be preserved, and no fact tried by a jury, shall be otherwise reexamined in any Court of the United States, than according to the rules of the common law.

AMENDMENT VIII
[BAILS, FINES, PUNISHMENTS]

Excessive bail shall not be required, nor excessive fines imposed, nor cruel and unusual punishments inflicted.

AMENDMENT IX
[RESERVATION OF RIGHTS OF PEOPLE]

The enumeration in the Constitution, of certain rights, shall not be construed to deny or disparage others retained by the people.

AMENDMENT X
[POWERS RESERVED TO STATES OR PEOPLE]

The powers not delegated to the United States by the Constitution, nor prohibited by it to the States, are reserved to the States respectively, or to the people.

AMENDMENT XI

[Proposed by Congress on March 4, 1794;
declared ratified on January 8, 1798.]
[RESTRICTION OF JUDICIAL POWER]

The Judicial power of the United States shall not be construed to extend to any suit in law or equity, commenced or prosecuted against one of the United States by Citizens of another State, or by Citizens or Subjects of any Foreign State.

AMENDMENT XII

[Proposed by Congress on December 9, 1803;
declared ratified on September 25, 1804.]
[ELECTION OF PRESIDENT AND VICE PRESIDENT]

The Electors shall meet in their respective states and vote by ballot for President and Vice-President, one of whom, at least, shall not be an inhabitant of the same state with themselves; they shall name in their ballots the person voted for as President, and in distinct ballots the person voted for as Vice-President, and they shall make distinct lists of all persons voted for as President, and of all persons voted for as Vice-President, and of the number of votes for each, which lists they shall sign and certify, and transmit sealed to the seat of the government of the United States, directed to the President of the Senate;—the President of the Senate shall, in presence of the Senate and House of Representatives, open all the certificates and the votes shall then be counted;—The person having the greatest number of votes for President, shall be the President, if such number be a majority of the whole number of Electors appointed; and if no person have such majority, then from the persons having the highest numbers not exceeding three on the list of those voted for as President, the House of Representatives shall choose immediately, by ballot, the President. But in choosing the President, the votes shall be taken by states, the representation from each state having one vote; a quorum for this purpose shall consist of a member or members from two-thirds of the states, and a majority of all the states shall be necessary to a choice. And if the House of Representatives shall not choose a President whenever the right of choice shall devolve upon them, before the fourth day of March next following, then the Vice-President shall act as President, as in the case of the death or other constitutional disability of the President.—The person having the greatest number of votes as Vice-President, shall be the Vice-President, if such number be a majority of the whole number of Electors appointed, and if no person have a majority, then from the two highest numbers on the list, the Senate shall choose the Vice-President; a quorum for the purpose shall consist of two-thirds of the whole number of Senators, and a majority of the whole number shall be necessary to a choice. But no person constitutionally ineligible to the office of President shall be eligible to that of Vice-President of the United States.

AMENDMENT XIII

[Proposed by Congress on January 31, 1865;
declared ratified on December 18, 1865.]

SECTION 1
[ABOLITION OF SLAVERY]

Neither slavery nor involuntary servitude, except as a punishment for crime whereof the party shall have been duly convicted, shall exist within the United States, or any place subject to their jurisdiction.

SECTION 2
[POWER TO ENFORCE THIS ARTICLE]

Congress shall have power to enforce this article by appropriate legislation.

AMENDMENT XIV

[Proposed by Congress on June 13, 1866;
declared ratified on July 28, 1868.]

SECTION 1
[CITIZENSHIP RIGHTS NOT TO BE ABRIDGED BY STATES]

All persons born or naturalized in the United States, and subject to the jurisdiction thereof, are citizens of the United States and of the State wherein they reside. No State shall make or enforce any law which shall abridge the privileges or immunities of citizens of the United States; nor shall any State deprive any person of life, liberty, or property, without due process of law; nor deny to any person within its jurisdiction the equal protection of the laws.

SECTION 2
[APPORTIONMENT OF REPRESENTATIVES IN CONGRESS]

Representatives shall be apportioned among the several States according to their respective numbers, counting the whole number of persons in each State, excluding Indians not taxed. But when the right to vote at any election for the choice of electors for President and Vice-President of the United States, Representatives in Congress, the Executive and Judicial officers of a State, or the members of the Legislature thereof, is denied to any of the male inhabitants of such State, being twenty-one years of age, and citizens of the United States, or in any way abridged, except for participation in rebellion, or other crime, the basis of representation therein shall be reduced in the proportion which the number of such male citizens shall bear to the whole number of male citizens twenty-one years of age in such State.

SECTION 3
[PERSONS DISQUALIFIED FROM HOLDING OFFICE]

No person shall be a Senator or Representative in Congress, or elector of President and Vice-President, or hold any office, civil or military, under the United States, or under any State, who, having previously taken an oath, as a member of Congress, or as an officer of the United States, or as a member of any State legislature, or as an executive or judicial officer of any State, to support the Constitution of the United States, shall have engaged in insurrection or rebellion against the same, or given aid or comfort to the enemies thereof. But Congress may by a vote of two-thirds of each House, remove such disability.

SECTION 4
[WHAT PUBLIC DEBTS ARE VALID]

The validity of the public debt of the United States, authorized by law, including debts incurred for payment of pensions and bounties for services in suppressing insurrection or rebellion, shall not be questioned. But neither the United States nor any State shall assume or pay any debt or obligation incurred in aid of insurrection or rebellion against the United States, or any claim for the loss or emancipation of any slave; but all such debts, obligations and claims shall be held illegal and void.

SECTION 5
[POWER TO ENFORCE THIS ARTICLE]

The Congress shall have power to enforce, by appropriate legislation, the provisions of this article.

AMENDMENT XV
[Proposed by Congress on February 26, 1869; declared ratified on March 30, 1870.]

SECTION 1
[NEGRO SUFFRAGE]

The right of citizens of the United States to vote shall not be denied or abridged by the United States or by any State on account of race, color, or previous condition of servitude.

SECTION 2
[POWER TO ENFORCE THIS ARTICLE]

The Congress shall have power to enforce this article by appropriate legislation.

AMENDMENT XVI
[Proposed by Congress on July 2, 1909; declared ratified on February 25, 1913.]
[AUTHORIZING INCOME TAXES]

The Congress shall have power to lay and collect taxes on incomes, from whatever source derived, without apportionment among the several States, and without regard to any census or enumeration.

AMENDMENT XVII
[Proposed by Congress on May 13, 1912; declared ratified on May 31, 1913.]
[POPULAR ELECTION OF SENATORS]

The Senate of the United States shall be composed of two Senators from each State, elected by the people thereof, for six years; and each Senator shall have one vote. The electors in each State shall have the qualifications requisite for electors of the most numerous branch of the State legislatures.

When vacancies happen in the representation of any State in the Senate, the executive authority of such State shall issue writs of election to fill such vacancies: *Provided,* That the legislature of any State may empower the executive thereof to make temporary appointments until the people fill the vacancies by election as the legislature may direct.

This amendment shall not be so construed as to affect the election or term of any Senator chosen before it becomes valid as part of the Constitution.

AMENDMENT XVIII
[Proposed by Congress December 18, 1917; declared ratified on January 29, 1919.]

SECTION 1
[NATIONAL LIQUOR PROHIBITION]

After one year from the ratification of this article the manufacture, sale, or transportation of intoxicating liquors within, the importation thereof into, or the exportation thereof from the United States and all territory subject to the jurisdiction thereof for beverage purposes is hereby prohibited.

SECTION 2
[POWER TO ENFORCE THIS ARTICLE]

The Congress and the several States shall have concurrent power to enforce this article by appropriate legislation.

SECTION 3
[RATIFICATION WITHIN SEVEN YEARS]

This article shall be inoperative unless it shall have been ratified as an amendment to the Constitution by the legislatures of the several States, as provided in the Constitution, within seven years from the date of the submission hereof to the States by the Congress.[1]

AMENDMENT XIX
[Proposed by Congress on June 4, 1919; declared ratified on August 26, 1920.]
[WOMAN SUFFRAGE]

The right of citizens of the United States to vote shall not be denied or abridged by the United States or by any State on account of sex.

Congress shall have power to enforce this article by appropriate legislation.

---

[1]Repealed by the Twenty-First Amendment.

AMENDMENT XX

[*Proposed by Congress on March 2, 1932;
declared ratified on February 6, 1933.*]

SECTION 1
[TERMS OF OFFICE]

The terms of the President and Vice President shall end at noon on the 20th day of January, and the terms of Senators and Representatives at noon on the 3d day of January, of the years in which such terms would have ended if this article had not been ratified; and the terms of their successors shall then begin.

SECTION 2
[TIME OF CONVENING CONGRESS]

The Congress shall assemble at least once in every year, and such meeting shall begin at noon on the 3d day of January, unless they shall by law appoint a different day.

SECTION 3
[DEATH OF PRESIDENT-ELECT]

If, at the time fixed for the beginning of the term of the President, the President elect shall have died, the Vice President elect shall become President. If a President shall not have been chosen before the time fixed for the beginning of his term, or if the President elect shall have failed to qualify, then the Vice President elect shall act as President until a President shall have qualified; and the Congress may by law provide for the case wherein neither a President elect nor a Vice President elect shall have qualified, declaring who shall then act as President, or the manner in which one who is to act shall be selected, and such person shall act accordingly until a President or Vice President shall have qualified.

SECTION 4
[ELECTION OF THE PRESIDENT]

The Congress may by law provide for the case of the death of any of the persons from whom the House of Representatives may choose a President whenever the right of choice shall have devolved upon them, and for the case of the death of any of the persons from whom the Senate may choose a Vice President whenever the right of choice shall have devolved upon them.

SECTION 5
[AMENDMENT TAKES EFFECT]

Sections 1 and 2 shall take effect on the 15th day of October following the ratification of this article.

SECTION 6
[RATIFICATION WITHIN SEVEN YEARS]

This article shall be inoperative unless it shall have been ratified as an amendment to the Constitution by the legislatures of three-fourths of the several States within seven years from the date of its submission.

AMENDMENT XXI

[*Proposed by Congress on February 20, 1933;
declared ratified on December 5, 1933.*]

SECTION 1
[NATIONAL LIQUOR PROHIBITION REPEALED]

The eighteenth article of amendment to the Constitution of the United States is hereby repealed.

SECTION 2
[TRANSPORTATION OF LIQUOR INTO "DRY" STATES]

The transportation or importation into any State, Territory, or Possession of the United States for delivery or use therein of intoxicating liquors, in violation of the laws thereof, is hereby prohibited.

SECTION 3
[RATIFICATION WITHIN SEVEN YEARS]

This article shall be inoperative unless it shall have been ratified as an amendment to the Constitution by conventions in the several States, as provided in the Constitution, within seven years from the date of the submission hereof to the States by the Congress.

AMENDMENT XXII

[*Proposed by Congress on March 21, 1947;
declared ratified on February 27, 1951.*]

SECTION 1
[TENURE OF PRESIDENT LIMITED]

No person shall be elected to the office of President more than twice, and no person who has held the office of President or acted as President, for more than two years of a term to which some other person was elected President shall be elected to the office of the President more than once. But this Article shall not apply to any person holding the office of President when this Article was proposed by the Congress, and shall not prevent any person who may be holding the office of President, or acting as President, during the term within which this Article becomes operative from holding the office of President or acting as President during the remainder of such term.

SECTION 2
[RATIFICATION WITHIN SEVEN YEARS]

This article shall be inoperative unless it shall have been ratified as an amendment to the Constitution by the legislatures of three-fourths of the several States within seven years from the date of its submission to the States by the Congress.

AMENDMENT XXIII

[*Proposed by Congress on June 16, 1960;
declared ratified on March 29, 1961.*]

SECTION 1
[ELECTORAL COLLEGE VOTES FOR THE DISTRICT
OF COLUMBIA]

The District constituting the seat of Government of the United States shall appoint in such manner as the Congress may direct:

A number of electors of President and Vice President equal to the whole number of Senators and Representatives in Congress to which the District would be entitled if it were a State, but in no event more than the least populous State; they shall be in addition to those appointed by the States, but they shall be considered, for the purposes of the election of President and Vice President, to be electors appointed by a State; and they shall meet in the District and perform such duties as provided by the twelfth article of amendment.

SECTION 2
[POWER TO ENFORCE THIS ARTICLE]

The Congress shall have power to enforce this article by appropriate legislation.

AMENDMENT XXIV

[*Proposed by Congress on August 27, 1962;
declared ratified on January 23, 1964.*]

SECTION 1
[ANTI-POLL TAX]

The right of citizens of the United States to vote in any primary or other election for President or Vice President, for electors for President or Vice President, or for Senator or Representative of Congress, shall not be denied or abridged by the United States or any State by reason of failure to pay any poll tax or other tax.

SECTION 2
[POWER TO ENFORCE THIS ARTICLE]

The Congress shall have power to enforce this article by appropriate legislation.

AMENDMENT XXV

[*Proposed by Congress on July 6, 1965;
declared ratified on February 10, 1967.*]

SECTION 1
[VICE PRESIDENT TO BECOME PRESIDENT]

In case of the removal of the President from office or his death or resignation, the Vice President shall become President.

SECTION 2
[CHOICE OF A NEW VICE PRESIDENT]

Whenever there is a vacancy in the office of the Vice President, the President shall nominate a Vice President who shall take the office upon confirmation by a majority vote of both houses of Congress.

SECTION 3
[PRESIDENT MAY DECLARE OWN DISABILITY]

Whenever the President transmits to the President pro tempore of the Senate and the Speaker of the House of Representatives his written declaration that he is unable to discharge the powers and duties of his office, and until he transmits to them a written declaration to the contrary, such powers and duties shall be discharged by the Vice President as Acting President.

SECTION 4
[ALTERNATE PROCEDURES TO DECLARE AND
TO END PRESIDENTIAL DISABILITY]

Whenever the Vice President and a majority of either the principal officers of the executive departments, or of such other body as Congress may by law provide, transmit to the President pro tempore of the Senate and the Speaker of the House of Representatives their written declaration that the President is unable to discharge the powers and duties of his office, the Vice President shall immediately assume the powers and duties of the office as Acting President.

Thereafter, when the President transmits to the President pro tempore of the Senate and the Speaker of the House of Representatives his written declaration that no inability exists, he shall resume the powers and duties of his office unless the Vice President and a majority of either the principal officers of the executive department, or of such other body as Congress may by law provide, transmit within four days to the President pro tempore of the Senate and the Speaker of the House of Representatives their written declaration that the President is unable to discharge the powers and duties of his office. Thereupon Congress shall decide the issue, assembling within forty eight hours for that purpose if not in session. If the Congress, within twenty one days after receipt of the latter written declaration, or, if Congress is not in session, within twenty one days after Congress is required to assemble, determines by two-thirds vote of both Houses that the President is unable to discharge the powers and duties of his office, the Vice President shall continue to discharge the same as Acting President; otherwise, the President shall resume the powers and duties of his office.

AMENDMENT XXVI

[Proposed by Congress on March 23, 1971; declared ratified on July 1, 1971.]

SECTION 1
[EIGHTEEN-YEAR-OLD VOTE]

The right of citizens of the United States, who are eighteen years of age or older, to vote shall not be denied or abridged by the United States or by any State on account of age.

SECTION 2
[POWER TO ENFORCE THIS ARTICLE]

The Congress shall have power to enforce this article by appropriate legislation.

AMENDMENT XXVII

[Proposed by Congress on September 25, 1789; declared ratified on May 8, 1992.]
[CONGRESS CANNOT RAISE ITS OWN PAY]

No law varying the compensation for the services of the Senators and Representatives, shall take effect, until an election of representatives shall have intervened.

The Federalist Papers

NO. 10: MADISON

Among the numerous advantages promised by a well constructed Union, none deserves to be more accurately developed than its tendency to break and control the violence of faction. The friend of popular governments never finds himself so much alarmed for their character and fate, as when he contemplates their propensity to this dangerous vice. He will not fail therefore to set a due value on any plan which, without violating the principles to which he is attached, provides a proper cure for it. The instability, injustice, and confusion introduced into the public councils have, in truth, been the mortal diseases under which popular governments have everywhere perished, as they continue to be the favorite and fruitful topics from which the adversaries to liberty derive their most specious declamations. The valuable improvements made by the American constitutions on the popular models, both ancient and modern, cannot certainly be too much admired; but it would be an unwarrantable partiality to contend that they have as effectually obviated the danger on this side, as was wished and expected. Complaints are everywhere heard from our most considerate and virtuous citizens, equally the friends of public and private faith and of public and personal liberty, that our governments are too unstable, that the public good is disregarded in the conflicts of rival parties, and that measures are too often decided, not according to the rules of justice and the rights of the minor party, but by the superior force of an interested and overbearing majority. However anxiously we may wish that these complaints had no foundation, the evidence of known facts will not permit us to deny that they are in some degree true. It will be found, indeed, on a candid review of our situation, that some of the distresses under which we labor have been erroneously charged on the operation of our governments; but it will be found, at the same time, that other causes will not alone account for many of our heaviest misfortunes; and, particularly, for that prevailing and increasing distrust of public engagements and alarm for private rights which are echoed from one end of the continent to the other. These must be chiefly, if not wholly, effects of the unsteadiness and injustice with which a factious spirit has tainted our public administration.

By a faction I understand a number of citizens, whether amounting to a majority or minority of the whole, who are united and actuated by some common impulse of passion, or of interest, adverse to the rights of other citizens, or to the permanent and aggregate interests of the community.

There are two methods of curing the mischiefs of faction: the one, by removing its causes; the other, by controlling its effects.

There are again two methods of removing the causes of faction: the one, by destroying the liberty which is essential to its existence; the other, by giving to every citizen the same opinions, the same passions, and the same interests.

It could never be more truly said than of the first remedy, that it is worse than the disease. Liberty is to faction what air is to fire, an aliment without which it instantly expires. But it could not be a less folly to abolish liberty, which is essential to political life, because it nourishes faction, than it would be to wish the annihilation of air, which is essential to animal life, because it imparts to fire its destructive agency.

The second expedient is as impracticable, as the first would be unwise. As long as the reason of man continues fallible, and he is at liberty to exercise it, different opinions will be formed. As long as the connection subsists between his reason and his self-love, his opinions and his passions will have a reciprocal influence on each other; and the former will be objects to which the latter will attach themselves. The diversity in the faculties of men, from which the rights of property originate, is not less an insuperable obstacle to a uniformity of interests. The protection of these faculties is the first object of Government. From the protection of different and unequal faculties of acquiring property, the possession of different degrees and kinds of property immediately results; and from the influence of these on the sentiments and views of the respective proprietors, ensues a division of the society into different interests and parties.

The latent causes of faction are thus sown in the nature of man; and we see them everywhere brought into different degrees of activity, according to the different circumstances of civil society. A zeal for different opinions concerning religion, concerning Government, and many other points, as well of speculation as of practice; an attachment to different leaders ambitiously contending for pre-eminence and power; or to persons of other descriptions whose fortunes have been interesting to the human passions, have in turn divided mankind into parties, inflamed them with mutual animosity, and rendered them much more disposed to vex and oppress each other, than to co-operate for their common good. So strong is this propensity of mankind to fall into mutual animosities, that where no substantial occasion presents itself, the most frivolous and fanciful distinctions have been sufficient to kindle their unfriendly passions, and excite their most violent conflicts. But the most common and durable source of factions has been the various and unequal distribution of property. Those who hold and those who are without property have ever formed distinct interests in society. Those who are creditors, and those who are debtors, fall under a like discrimination. A landed interest, a manufacturing interest, a mercantile interest, a moneyed interest, with many lesser interests, grow up of necessity in civilized nations, and divide them into different classes, actuated by different sentiments and views. The regulation of these various and interfering interests forms the principal task of modern Legislation, and involves the spirit of party and faction in the necessary and ordinary operations of Government.

No man is allowed to be judge in his own cause, because his interest would certainly bias his judgment and, not improbably, corrupt his integrity. With equal, nay with greater reason, a body of men are unfit to be both judges and parties at the same time; yet what are many of the most important acts of legislation but so many judicial determinations, not indeed concerning the rights of single persons, but concerning the rights of large bodies of citizens; and what are the different classes of legislators but advocates and parties to the causes which they determine? Is a law proposed concerning private debts? It is a question to which the creditors are parties on one side and the debtors on the other. Justice ought to hold the balance between them. Yet the parties are, and must be, themselves the judges; and the most numerous party, or in other words, the most powerful faction must be expected to prevail. Shall domestic manufacturers be encouraged, and in what degree, by restrictions on foreign manufacturers? are questions which would be differently decided by the landed and the manufacturing classes, and probably by neither with a sole regard to justice and the public good. The apportionment of taxes on the various descriptions of property is an act which seems to require the most exact impartiality; yet there is, perhaps, no legislative act in which greater opportunity and temptation are given to a predominant party to trample on the rules of justice. Every shilling with which they overburden the inferior number is a shilling saved to their own pockets.

It is in vain to say that enlightened statesmen will be able to adjust these clashing interests and render them all subservient to the public good. Enlightened statesmen will not always be at the helm. Nor, in many cases, can such an adjustment be made at all without taking into view indirect and remote considerations, which will rarely prevail over the immediate interest which one party may find in disregarding the rights of another or the good of the whole.

The inference to which we are brought is that the *causes* of faction cannot be removed and that relief is only to be sought in the means of controlling its *effects*.

If a faction consists of less than a majority, relief is supplied by the republican principle, which enables the majority to defeat its sinister views by regular vote. It may clog the administration, it may convulse the society; but it will be unable to execute and mask its violence under the forms of the Constitution. When a majority is included in a faction, the form of popular government, on the other hand, enables it to sacrifice to its ruling passion or interest both the public good and the rights of other citizens. To secure the public good and private rights against the danger of such a faction, and at the same time to preserve the spirit and the form of popular government, is then the great object to which our enquiries are directed. Let me add that it is the great desideratum by which alone this form of government can be rescued from the opprobrium under which it has so long labored and be recommended to the esteem and adoption of mankind.

By what means is this object attainable? Evidently by one of two only. Either the existence of the same passion or interest in a majority at the same time must be prevented, or the majority, having such co-existent passion or interest, must be rendered, by their number and local situation, unable to concert and carry into effect schemes of oppression. If the impulse and the opportunity be suffered to coincide, we well know that neither moral nor religious motives can be relied on as an adequate control. They are not found to be such on the injustice and violence of individuals, and lose their efficacy in proportion to the number combined together, that is, in proportion as their efficacy becomes needful.

From this view of the subject it may be concluded that a pure Democracy, by which I mean a Society consisting of a small number of citizens, who assemble and administer the Government in person, can admit of no cure for the mischiefs of faction. A common passion or interest will, in almost every case, be felt by a majority of the whole; a communication and concert results from the form of Government itself; and there is nothing to check the inducements to sacrifice the weaker party or an obnoxious individual. Hence it is that such Democracies have ever been spectacles of turbulence and contention; have ever been found incompatible with personal security or the rights of property; and have in general been as short in their lives as they have been violent in their deaths. Theoretic politicians, who have patronized this species of Government, have erroneously supposed that by reducing mankind to a perfect equality in their political rights, they would at the same time be perfectly equalized and assimilated in their possessions, their opinions, and their passions.

A Republic, by which I mean a Government in which the scheme of representation takes place, opens a different prospect and promises the cure for which we are seeking. Let us examine the points in which it varies from pure Democracy, and we shall comprehend both the nature of the cure and the efficacy which it must derive from the Union.

The two great points of difference between a Democracy and a Republic are: first, the delegation of the Government, in the latter, to a small number of citizens elected by the rest; secondly, the greater number of citizens and greater sphere of country over which the latter may be extended.

The effect of the first difference is, on the one hand, to refine and enlarge the public views by passing them through the medium of a chosen body of citizens, whose wisdom may best discern the true interest of their country and whose patriotism and love of justice will be least likely to sacrifice it to temporary or partial considerations. Under such a regulation it may well happen that the public voice, pronounced by the representatives of the people, will be more consonant to the public good than if pronounced by the people themselves, convened for the purpose. On the other hand, the effect may be inverted. Men of factious tempers, of local prejudices, or of sinister designs, may, by intrigue, by corruption, or by other means, first obtain the suffrages, and then betray the interests of the people. The question resulting is, whether small or extensive Republics are most favorable to the election of proper guardians of the public weal; and it is clearly decided in favor of the latter by two obvious considerations.

In the first place it is to be remarked that however small the Republic may be, the Representatives must be raised to a certain number in order to guard against the cabals of a few; and that however large it may be they must be limited to a certain number in order to guard against the confusion of a multitude. Hence, the number of Representatives in the two cases not being in proportion to that of the Constituents, and being proportionally greatest in the small Republic, it follows that if the proportion of fit characters be not less in the large than in the small Republic, the former will present a greater option, and consequently a greater probability of a fit choice.

In the next place, as each Representative will be chosen by a greater number of citizens in the large than in the small Republic, it will be more difficult for unworthy candidates to practise with success the vicious arts by which elections are too often carried; and the suffrages of the people being more free, will be more likely to centre on men who possess the most attractive merit and the most diffusive and established characters.

It must be confessed that in this, as in most other cases, there is a mean, on both sides of which inconveniencies will be found to lie. By enlarging too much the number of electors, you render the representative too little acquainted with all their local circumstances and lesser interests; as by reducing it too much, you render him unduly attached to these, and too little fit to comprehend and pursue great and national objects. The Federal Constitution forms a happy combination in this

respect; the great and aggregate interests being referred to the national, the local and particular to the State legislatures.

The other point of difference is the greater number of citizens and extent of territory which may be brought within the compass of Republican than of Democratic Government; and it is this circumstance principally which renders factious combinations less to be dreaded in the former than in the latter. The smaller the society, the fewer probably will be the distinct parties and interests composing it; the fewer the distinct parties and interests, the more frequently will a majority be found of the same party; and the smaller the number of individuals composing a majority, and the smaller the compass within which they are placed, the more easily will they concert and execute their plans of oppression. Extend the sphere and you take in a greater variety of parties and interests; you make it less probable that a majority of the whole will have a common motive to invade the rights of other citizens; or if such a common motive exists, it will be more difficult for all who feel it to discover their own strength and to act in unison with each other. Besides other impediments, it may be remarked, that where there is a consciousness of unjust or dishonorable purposes, communication is always checked by distrust in proportion to the number whose concurrence is necessary.

Hence, it clearly appears that the same advantage which a Republic has over a Democracy in controlling the effects of faction is enjoyed by a large over a small republic—is enjoyed by the Union over the States composing it. Does this advantage consist in the substitution of representatives whose enlightened views and virtuous sentiments render them superior to local prejudices and to schemes of injustice? It will not be denied that the representation of the Union will be most likely to possess these requisite endowments. Does it consist in the greater security afforded by a greater variety of parties, against the event of any one party being able to outnumber and oppress the rest? In an equal degree does the increased variety of parties comprised within the Union increase this security? Does it, in fine, consist in the greater obstacles opposed to the concert and accomplishment of the secret wishes of an unjust and interested majority? Here again the extent of the Union gives it the most palpable advantage.

The influence of factious leaders may kindle a flame within their particular States but will be unable to spread a general conflagration through the other States: a religious sect may degenerate into a political faction in a part of the Confederacy; but the variety of sects dispersed over the entire face of it must secure the national Councils against any danger from that source: a rage for paper money, for an abolition of debts, for an equal division of property, or for any other improper or wicked project, will be less apt to pervade the whole body of the Union than a particular member of it; in the same proportion as such a malady is more likely to taint a particular county or district than an entire State.

In the extent and proper structure of the Union, therefore, we behold a republican remedy for the diseases most incident to Republican Government. And according to the degree of pleasure and pride we feel in being republicans ought to be our zeal in cherishing the spirit and supporting the character of federalist.

PUBLIUS
November 22, 1787

NO. 51: MADISON

To what expedient, then, shall we finally resort, for maintaining in practice the necessary partition of power among the several departments as laid down in the constitution? The only answer that can be given is that as all these exterior provisions are found to be inadequate the defect must be supplied, by so contriving the interior structure of the government as that its several constituent parts may, by their mutual relations, be the means of keeping each other in their proper places. Without presuming to undertake a full development of this important idea I will hazard a few general observations which may perhaps place it in a clearer light, and enable us to form a more correct judgment of the principles and structure of the government planned by the convention.

In order to lay a due foundation for that separate and distinct exercise of the different powers of government, which to a certain extent is admitted on all hands to be essential to the preservation of liberty, it is evident that each department should have a will of its own; and consequently should be so constituted that the members of each should have as little agency as possible in the appointment of the members of the others. Were this principle rigorously adhered to, it would require that all the appointments for the supreme executive, legislative, and judiciary magistracies should be drawn from the same fountain of authority, the people, through channels having no communication whatever with one another. Perhaps such a plan of constructing the several departments would be less difficult in practice than it may in contemplation appear. Some difficulties, however, and some additional expense would attend the execution of it. Some deviations, therefore, from the principle must be admitted. In the constitution of the judiciary department in particular, it might be inexpedient to insist rigorously on the principle: first, because peculiar qualifications being essential in the members, the primary consideration ought to be to select that mode of choice which best secures these qualifications; second, because the permanent tenure by which the appointments are held in that department must soon destroy all sense of dependence on the authority conferring them.

It is equally evident that the members of each department should be as little dependent as possible on those of the others for the emoluments annexed to their offices. Were the executive magistrate, or the judges, not independent of the legislature in this particular, their independence in every other would be merely nominal.

But the great security against a gradual concentration of the several powers in the same department consists in giving to those who administer each department the necessary constitutional means and personal motives to resist encroachments of the others. The provision for defence must in this, as in all other cases, be made commensurate to the danger of attack. Ambition must be made to counteract ambition. The interest of the man must be connected with the constitutional rights of the place. It may be a reflection on human nature that such devices should be necessary to control the abuses of government. But what is government itself but the greatest of all reflections on human nature? If men were angels, no government would be necessary. If angels were to govern men, neither external nor internal controls on government would be necessary. In framing a government which is to be administered by men over men, the great difficulty lies in this: You must first enable the government to control the governed; and in the next place oblige it to control itself. A dependence on the people is, no doubt, the primary control on the government; but experience has taught mankind the necessity of auxiliary precautions.

This policy of supplying, by opposite and rival interests, the defect of better motives, might be traced through the whole system of human affairs, private as well as public. We see it particularly displayed in all the subordinate distributions of power, where the constant aim is to divide and arrange the several offices in such a manner as that each may be a check on the other; that the private interest of every individual may be a sentinel over the public rights. These inventions of prudence cannot be less requisite in the distribution of the supreme powers of the State.

But it is not possible to give to each department an equal power of self-defense. In republican government, the legislative authority necessarily predominates. The remedy for this inconveniency is to divide the legislature into different branches; and to render them, by different modes of election and different principles of action, as little connected with each other as the nature of their common functions and their common dependence on the society will admit. It may even be necessary to guard against dangerous encroachments by still further precautions. As the weight of the legislative authority requires that it should be thus divided, the weakness of the executive may require, on the other hand, that it should be fortified. An absolute negative on the legislature appears, at first view, to be the natural defense with which the executive magistrate should be armed. But perhaps it would be neither altogether safe nor alone sufficient. On ordinary occasions it might not be exerted with the requisite firmness, and on extraordinary occasions it might be perfidiously abused. May not this defect of an absolute negative be supplied by some qualified connection between this weaker branch of the stronger department, by which the latter may be led to support the constitutional rights of the former, without being too much detached from the rights of its own department?

If the principles on which these observations are founded be just, as I persuade myself they are, and they be applied as a criterion to the several State constitutions, and to the federal Constitution, it will be found that if the latter does not perfectly correspond with them, the former are infinitely less able to bear such a test.

There are, moreover, two considerations particularly applicable to the federal system of America, which place that system in a very interesting point of view.

First. In a single republic, all the power surrendered by the people is submitted to the administration of a single government; and usurpations are guarded against by a division of the government into distinct and separate departments. In the compound republic of America, the power surrendered by the people is first divided between two distinct governments, and then the portion allotted to each subdivided among distinct and separate departments. Hence a double security arises to the rights of the people. The different governments will control each other, at the same time that each will be controlled by itself.

Second. It is of great importance in a republic not only to guard the society against the oppression of its rulers, but to guard one part of the society against the injustice of the other part. Different interests necessarily exist in different classes of citizens. If a majority be united by a common interest, the rights of the minority will be insecure. There are but two methods of providing against this evil: The one by creating a will in the community independent of the majority—that is, of the society itself; the other, by comprehending in the society so many separate descriptions of citizens as will render an unjust combination of a majority of the whole very improbable, if not impracticable. The first method prevails in all governments possessing an hereditary or self-appointed authority. This, at best, is but a precarious security; because a power independent of the society may as well espouse the unjust views of the major as the rightful interests of the minor party, and may possibly be turned against both parties. The second method will be exemplified in the federal republic of the United States. Whilst all authority in it will be derived from and dependent on the society, the society itself will be broken into so many parts, interests and classes of citizens, that the rights of individuals, or of the minority, will be in little danger from interested combinations of the majority. In a free government the security for civil rights must be the same as that for religious rights. It consists in the one case in the multiplicity of interests, and in the other in the multiplicity of sects. The degree of security in both cases will depend on the number of interests and sects; and this may be presumed to depend on the extent of country and number of people comprehended under the same government. This view of the subject must particularly recommend a proper federal system to all the sincere and considerate friends of republican government: Since it shows that in exact proportion as the territory of the Union may be formed into more circumscribed Confederacies, or States, oppressive combinations of a majority will be facilitated; the best security, under the republican form, for the rights of every class of citizens, will be diminished; and consequently the stability and independence of some member of the government, the only other security, must be proportionally increased. Justice is the end of government. It is the end of civil society. It ever has been and ever will be pursued until it be obtained, or until liberty be lost in the pursuit. In a society under the forms of which the stronger faction can readily unite and oppress the weaker, anarchy may as truly be said to reign as in a state of nature, where the weaker individual is not secured against the violence of the stronger: And as, in the latter state, even the stronger individuals are prompted, by the uncertainty of their condition, to submit to a government which may protect the weak as well as themselves: So, in the former state, will the more powerful factions or parties be gradually induced, by a like motive, to wish for a government which will protect all parties, the weaker as well as the more powerful. It can be little doubted that if the State of Rhode Island was separated from the Confederacy and left to itself, the insecurity of rights under the popular form of government within such narrow limits would be displayed by such reiterated oppressions of factious majorities that some power altogether independent of the people would soon be called for by the voice of the very factions whose misrule had proved the necessity of it. In the extended republic of the United States, and among the great variety of interests, parties, and sects which it embraces, a coalition of a majority of the whole society could seldom take place on any other principles than those of justice and the general good; and there being thus less danger to a minor from the will of the major party, there must be less pretext, also, to provide for the security of the former, by introducing into the government a will not dependent on the latter, or, in other words, a will independent of the society itself. It is no less certain than it is important, notwithstanding the contrary opinions which have been entertained, that the larger the society, provided it lie within a practicable sphere, the more duly capable it will be of self-government. And happily for the *republican cause*, the practicable sphere may be carried to a very great extent by a judicious modification and mixture of the *federal principle*.

PUBLIUS
February 6, 1788

The Anti-Federalist Papers

Essay by Brutus in the *New York Journal*

When the public is called to investigate and decide upon a question in which not only the present members of the community are deeply interested, but upon which the happiness and misery of generations yet unborn is in great measure suspended, the benevolent mind cannot help feeling itself peculiarly interested in the result.

In this situation, I trust the feeble efforts of an individual, to lead the minds of the people to a wise and prudent determination, cannot fail of being acceptable to the candid and dispassionate part of the community. Encouraged by this consideration, I have been induced to offer my thoughts upon the present important crisis of our public affairs.

Perhaps this country never saw so critical a period in their political concerns. We have felt the feebleness of the ties by which these United-States are held together, and the want of sufficient energy in our present confederation, to manage, in some instances, our general concerns. Various expedients have been proposed to remedy these evils, but none have succeeded. At length a Convention of the states has been assembled, they have formed a constitution which will now, probably, be submitted to the people to ratify or reject, who are the fountain of all power, to whom alone it of right belongs to make or unmake constitutions, or forms of government, at their pleasure. The most important question that was ever proposed to your decision, or to the decision of any people under heaven, is before you, and you are to decide upon it by men of your own election, chosen specially for this purpose. If the constitution, offered to your acceptance, be a wise one, calculated to preserve the invaluable blessings of liberty, to secure the inestimable rights of mankind, and promote human happiness, then, if you accept it, you will lay a lasting foundation of happiness for millions yet unborn; generations to come will rise up and call you blessed. You may rejoice in the prospects of this vast extended continent becoming filled with freemen, who will assert the dignity of human nature. You may solace yourselves with the idea, that society, in this favoured land, will fast advance to the highest point of perfection; the human mind will expand in knowledge and virtue, and the golden age be, in some measure, realised. But if, on the other hand, this form of government contains principles that will lead to the subversion of liberty—if it tends to establish a despotism, or, what is worse, a tyrannic aristocracy; then, if you adopt it, this only remaining assylum for liberty will be shut up, and posterity will execrate your memory.

Momentous then is the question you have to determine, and you are called upon by every motive which should influence a noble and virtuous mind, to examine it well, and to make up a wise judgment. It is insisted, indeed, that this constitution must be received, be it ever so imperfect. If it has its defects, it is said, they can be best amended when they are experienced. But remember, when the people once part with power, they can seldom or never resume it again but by force. Many instances can be produced in which the people have voluntarily increased the powers of their rulers; but few, if any, in which rulers have willingly abridged their authority. This is a sufficient reason to induce you to be careful, in the first instance, how you deposit the powers of government.

With these few introductory remarks, I shall proceed to a consideration of this constitution:

The first question that presents itself on the subject is, whether a confederated government be the best for the United States or not? Or in other words, whether the thirteen United States should be reduced to one great republic, governed by one legislature, and under the direction of one executive and judicial; or whether they should continue thirteen confederated republics, under the direction and controul of a supreme federal head for certain defined national purposes only?

This enquiry is important, because, although the government reported by the convention does not go to a perfect and entire consolidation, yet it approaches so near to it, that it must, if executed, certainly and infallibly terminate in it.

This government is to possess absolute and uncontroulable power, legislative, executive and judicial, with respect to every object to which it extends, for by the last clause of section 8th, article 1st, it is declared "that the Congress shall have power to make all laws which shall be necessary and proper for carrying into execution the foregoing powers, and all other powers vested by this constitution, in the government of the United States; or in any department or office thereof." And by the 6th article, it is declared "that this constitution, and the laws of the United States, which shall be made in pursuance thereof, and the treaties made, or which shall be made, under the authority of the United States, shall be the supreme law of the land; and the judges in every state shall be bound thereby, any thing in the constitution, or law of any state to the contrary notwithstanding." It appears from these articles that there is no need of any intervention of the state governments, between the Congress and the people, to execute any one power vested in the general government, and that the constitution and laws of every state are nullified and declared void, so far as they are or shall be inconsistent with this constitution, or the laws made in pursuance of it, or with treaties made under the authority of the United States.—The government then, so far as it extends, is a complete one, and not a confederation. It is as much one complete government as that of New York or Massachusetts, has as absolute and perfect powers to make and execute all laws, to appoint officers, institute courts, declare offences, and annex penalties, with respect to every object to which it extends, as any other in the world. So far therefore as its powers reach, all ideas of confederation are given up and lost. It is true this government is limited to certain objects, or to speak more properly, some small degree of power is still left to the states, but a little attention to the powers vested in the general government, will convince every candid man, that if it is capable of being executed, all that is reserved for the individual states must very soon be annihilated, except so far as they are barely necessary to the organization of the general government. The powers of the general legislature extend to every case that is of the least importance—there is nothing valuable to human nature, nothing dear to freemen, but what is within its power. It has authority to make laws which will affect the lives, the liberty, and property of every man in the United States; nor can the constitution or laws of any state, in any way prevent or impede the full and complete execution of every power given. The legislative power is competent to lay taxes, duties, imposts, and excises;—there is no limitation to this power, unless it be said that the clause which directs the use to which those taxes, and duties shall be applied, may be said to be a limitation: but this is no restriction of the power at all, for by this clause they are to be applied to pay the debts and provide for the common defence and general welfare of the United States; but the legislature have authority to contract debts at their discretion; they are the sole judges of what is necessary to provide for the common defence, and they only are to determine what is for the general welfare; this power therefore is neither more nor less, than a power to lay and collect taxes, imposts, and excises, at their pleasure; not only [is] the power to lay taxes unlimited, as to the amount they may require, but it is perfect and absolute to raise them in any mode they please. No state legislature, or any power in the state governments, have any more to do in carrying this into effect, than the authority of one state has to do with that of another. In the business therefore of laying and collecting taxes, the idea of confederation is totally lost, and that of one entire republic is embraced. It is proper here to remark, that the authority to lay and collect taxes is the most important of any power that can be granted; it connects with it

almost all other powers, or at least will in process of time draw all other after it; it is the great mean of protection, security, and defence, in a good government, and the great engine of oppression and tyranny in a bad one. This cannot fail of being the case, if we consider the contracted limits which are set by this constitution, to the late [state?] governments, on this article of raising money. No state can emit paper money—lay any duties, or imposts, on imports, or exports, but by consent of the Congress; and then the net produce shall be for the benefit of the United States: the only mean therefore left, for any state to support its government and discharge its debts, is by direct taxation; and the United States have also power to lay and collect taxes, in any way they please. Every one who has thought on the subject, must be convinced that but small sums of money can be collected in any country, by direct taxe[s], when the foederal government begins to exercise the right of taxation in all its parts, the legislatures of the several states will find it impossible to raise monies to support their governments. Without money they cannot be supported, and they must dwindle away, and, as before observed, their powers absorbed in that of the general government.

It might be here shewn, that the power in the federal legislative, to raise and support armies at pleasure, as well in peace as in war, and their controul over the militia, tend, not only to a consolidation of the government, but the destruction of liberty.—I shall not, however, dwell upon these, as a few observations upon the judicial power of this government, in addition to the preceding, will fully evince the truth of the position.

The judicial power of the United States is to be vested in a supreme court, and in such inferior courts as Congress may from time to time ordain and establish. The powers of these courts are very extensive; their jurisdiction comprehends all civil causes, except such as arise between citizens of the same state; and it extends to all cases in law and equity arising under the constitution. One inferior court must be established, I presume, in each state, at least, with the necessary executive officers appendant thereto. It is easy to see, that in the common course of things, these courts will eclipse the dignity, and take away from the respectability, of the state courts. These courts will be, in themselves, totally independent of the states, deriving their authority from the United States, and receiving from them fixed salaries; and in the course of human events it is to be expected, that they will swallow up all the powers of the courts in the respective states.

How far the clause in the 8th section of the 1st article may operate to do away all idea of confederated states, and to effect an entire consolidation of the whole into one general government, it is impossible to say. The powers given by this article are very general and comprehensive, and it may receive a construction to justify the passing almost any law. A power to make all laws, which shall be *necessary and proper*, for carrying into execution, all powers vested by the constitution in the government of the United States, or any department or officer thereof, is a power very comprehensive and definite [indefinite?], and may, for ought I know, be exercised in a such manner as entirely to abolish the state legislatures. Suppose the legislature of a state should pass a law to raise money to support their government and pay the state debt, may the Congress repeal this law, because it may prevent the collection of a tax which they may think proper and necessary to lay, to provide for the general welfare of the United States? For all laws made, in pursuance of this constitution, are the supreme law of the land, and the judges in every state shall be bound thereby, any thing in the constitution or laws of the different states to the contrary notwithstanding.—By such a law, the government of a particular state might be overturned at one stroke, and thereby be deprived of every means of its support.

It is not meant, by stating this case, to insinuate that the constitution would warrant a law of this kind; or unnecessarily to alarm the fears of the people, by suggesting, that the federal legislature would be more likely to pass the limits assigned them by the constitution, than that of an individual state, further than they are less responsible to the people. But what is meant is, that the legislature of the United States are vested with the great and uncontroulable powers, of laying and collecting taxes, duties, imposts, and excises; of regulating trade, raising and supporting armies, organizing, arming, and disciplining the militia, instituting courts, and other general powers. And are by this clause invested with the power of making all laws, *proper and necessary*, for carrying all these into execution; and they may so exercise this power as entirely to annihilate all the state governments, and reduce this country to one single government. And if they may do it, it is pretty certain they will; for it will be found that the power retained by individual states, small as it is, will be a clog upon the wheels of the government of the United States; the latter therefore will be naturally inclined to remove it out of the way. Besides, it is a truth confirmed by the unerring experience of ages, that every man, and every body of men, invested with power, are ever disposed to increase it, and to acquire a superiority over every thing that stands in their way. This disposition, which is implanted in human nature, will operate in the federal legislature to lessen and ultimately to subvert the state authority, and having such advantages, will most certainly succeed, if the federal government succeeds at all. It must be very evident then, that what this constitution wants of being a complete consolidation of the several parts of the union into one complete government, possessed of perfect legislative, judicial, and executive powers, to all intents and purposes, it will necessarily acquire in its exercise and operation.

Let us now proceed to enquire, as I at first proposed, whether it be best the thirteen United States should be reduced to one great republic, or not? It is here taken for granted, that all agree in this, that whatever government we adopt, it ought to be a free one; that it should be so framed as to secure the liberty of the citizens of America, and such an one as to admit of a full, fair, and equal representation of the people. The question then will be, whether a government thus constituted, and founded on such principles, is practicable, and can be exercised over the whole United States, reduced into one state?

If respect is to be paid to the opinion of the greatest and wisest men who have ever thought or wrote on the science of government, we shall be constrained to conclude, that a free republic cannot succeed over a country of such immense extent, containing such a number of inhabitants, and these encreasing in such rapid progression as that of the whole United States. Among the many illustrious authorities which might be produced to this point, I shall content myself with quoting only two. The one is the baron de Montesquieu, spirit of laws, chap. xvi. vol. I [book VIII]. "It is natural to a republic to have only a small territory, otherwise it cannot long subsist. In a large republic there are men of large fortunes, and consequently of less moderation; there are trusts too great to be placed in any single subject; he has interest of his own; he soon begins to think that he may be happy, great and glorious, by oppressing his fellow citizens; and that he may raise himself to grandeur on the ruins of his country. In a large republic, the public good is sacrificed to a thousand views; it is subordinate to exceptions, and depends on accidents. In a small one, the interest of the public is easier perceived, better understood, and more within the reach of every citizen; abuses are of less extent, and of course are less protected." Of the same opinion is the marquis Beccarari.

History furnishes no example of a free republic, any thing like the extent of the United States. The Grecian republics were of small extent; so also was that of the Romans. Both of these, it is true, in process of time, extended their conquests over large territories of country; and the consequence was, that their governments were changed from that of free governments to those of the most tyrannical that ever existed in the world.

Not only the opinion of the greatest men, and the experience of mankind, are against the idea of an extensive republic, but a variety of reasons may be drawn from the reason and nature of things, against it. In every government, the will of the sovereign is the law. In despotic governments, the supreme authority being lodged in one, his will is law, and can be as easily expressed to a large extensive territory as to a small one. In a pure democracy the people are the sovereign, and their will is declared by themselves; for this purpose they must all come together to deliberate, and decide. This kind of government cannot be exercised, therefore, over a country of any considerable extent; it must be confined to a single city, or at least limited to such bounds as that the people can conveniently assemble, be able to debate, understand the subject submitted to them, and declare their opinion concerning it.

In a free republic, although all laws are derived from the consent of the people, yet the people do not declare their consent by themselves in person, but by representatives, chosen by them, who are supposed to know the minds of their constituents, and to be possessed of integrity to declare this mind.

In every free government, the people must give their assent to the laws by which they are governed. This is the true criterion between a free government and an arbitrary one. The former are ruled by the will of the whole, expressed in any manner they may agree upon; the latter by the will of one, or a few. If the people are to give their assent to the laws, by persons chosen and appointed by them, the manner of the choice and the number chosen, must be such, as to possess, be disposed, and consequently qualified to declare the sentiments of the people; for if they do not know, or are not disposed to speak the sentiments of the people, the people do not govern, but the sovereignty is in a few. Now, in a large extended country, it is impossible to have a representation, possessing the sentiments, and of integrity, to declare the minds of the people, without having it so numerous and unwieldly, as to be subject in great measure to the inconveniency of a democratic government.

The territory of the United States is of vast extent; it now contains near three millions of souls, and is capable of containing much more than ten times that number. Is it practicable for a country, so large and so numerous as they will soon become, to elect a representation, that will speak their sentiments, without their becoming so numerous as to be incapable of transacting public business? It certainly is not.

In a republic, the manners, sentiments, and interests of the people should be similar. If this be not the case, there will be a constant clashing of opinions; and the representatives of one part will be continually striving against those of the other. This will retard the operations of government, and prevent such conclusions as will promote the public good. If we apply this remark to the condition of the United States, we shall be convinced that it forbids that we should be one government. The United States includes a variety of climates. The productions of the different parts of the union are very variant, and their interests, of consequence, diverse. Their manners and habits differ as much as their climates and productions; and their sentiments are by no means coincident. The laws and customs of the several states are, in many respects, very diverse, and in some opposite; each would be in favor of its own interests and customs, and, of consequence, a legislature, formed of representatives from the respective parts, would not only be too numerous to act with any care or decision, but would be composed of such heterogenous and discordant principles, as would constantly be contending with each other.

The laws cannot be executed in a republic, of an extent equal to that of the United States, with promptitude.

The magistrates in every government must be supported in the execution of the laws, either by an armed force, maintained at the public expence for that purpose; or by the people turning out to aid the magistrate upon his command, in case of resistance.

In despotic governments, as well as in all the monarchies of Europe, standing armies are kept up to execute the commands of the prince or the magistrate, and are employed for this purpose when occasion requires: But they have always proved the destruction of liberty, and [are] abhorrent to the spirit of a free republic. In England, where they depend upon the parliament for their annual support, they have always been complained of as oppressive and unconstitutional, and are seldom employed in executing of the laws; never except on extraordinary occasions, and then under the direction of a civil magistrate.

A free republic will never keep a standing army to execute its laws. It must depend upon the support of its citizens. But when a government is to receive its support from the aid of the citizens, it must be so constructed as to have the confidence, respect, and affection of the people. Men who, upon the call of the magistrate, offer themselves to execute the laws, are influenced to do it either by affection to the government, or from fear; where a standing army is at hand to punish offenders, every man is actuated by the latter principle, and therefore, when the magistrate calls, will obey: but, where this is not the case, the government must rest for its support upon the confidence and respect which the people have for their government and laws. The body of the people being attached, the government will always be sufficient to support and execute its laws, and to operate upon the fears of any faction which may be opposed to it, not only to prevent an opposition to the execution of the laws themselves, but also to compel the most of them to aid the magistrate; but the people will not be likely to have such confidence in their rulers, in a republic so extensive as the United States, as necessary for these purposes. The confidence which the people have in their rulers, in a free republic, arises from their knowing them, from their being responsible to them for their conduct, and from the power they have of displacing them when they misbehave: but in a republic of the extent of this continent, the people in general would be acquainted with very few of their rulers: the people at large would know little of their proceedings, and it would be extremely difficult to change them. The people in Georgia and New-Hampshire would not know one another's mind, and therefore could not act in concert to enable them to effect a general change of representatives. The different parts of so extensive a country could not possibly be made acquainted with the conduct of their representatives, nor be informed of the reasons upon which measures were founded. The consequence will be, they will have no confidence in their legislature, suspect them of ambitious views, be jealous of every measure they adopt, and will not support the laws they pass. Hence the government will be nerveless and inefficient, and no way will be left to render it otherwise, but by establishing an armed force to execute the laws at the point of the bayonet—a government of all others the most to be dreaded.

In a republic of such vast extent as the United-States, the legislature cannot attend to the various concerns and wants of its different parts. It cannot be sufficiently numerous to be acquainted with the local condition and wants of the different districts, and if it could, it is impossible it should have sufficient time to attend to and provide for all the variety of cases of this nature, that would be continually arising.

In so extensive a republic, the great officers of government would soon become above the controul of the people, and abuse their power to the purpose of aggrandizing themselves, and oppressing them. The trust committed to the executive offices, in a country of the extent of the United-States, must be various and of magnitude. The command of all the troops and navy of the republic, the appointment of officers, the power of pardoning offences, the collecting of all the public revenues, and the power of expending them, with a number of other powers, must be lodged and exercised in every state, in the hands of a few. When these are attended with great honor and emolument, as they always will be in large states, so as greatly to interest men to pursue them, and to be proper objects for ambitious and designing men, such men will be ever restless in their pursuit after them. They will use the power, when they have acquired it, to the purposes of gratifying their own interest and ambition, and it is scarcely possible, in a very large republic, to call them to account for their misconduct, or to prevent their abuse of power.

These are some of the reasons by which it appears, that a free republic cannot long subsist over a country of the great extent of these states. If then this new constitution is calculated to consolidate the thirteen states into one, as it evidently is, it ought not to be adopted.

Though I am of opinion, that it is a sufficient objection to this government, to reject it, that it creates the whole union into one government, under the form of a republic, yet if this objection was obviated, there are exceptions to it, which are so material and fundamental, that they ought to determine every man, who is a friend to the liberty and happiness of mankind, not to adopt it. I beg the candid and dispassionate attention of my countrymen while I state these objections— they are such as have obtruded themselves upon my mind upon a careful attention to the matter, and such as I sincerely believe are well founded. There are many objections, of small moment, of which I shall take no notice—perfection is not to be expected in any thing that is the production of man—and if I did not in my conscience believe that this scheme was defective in the fundamental principles—in the foundation upon which a free and equal government must rest—I would hold my peace.

BRUTUS
October 18, 1787

Presidents and Vice Presidents

	PRESIDENT	VICE PRESIDENT		PRESIDENT	VICE PRESIDENT
1	George Washington *(Federalist 1789)*	John Adams *(Federalist 1789)*	12	Zachary Taylor *(Whig 1849)*	Millard Fillmore *(Whig 1849)*
2	John Adams *(Federalist 1797)*	Thomas Jefferson *(Dem.-Rep. 1797)*	13	Millard Fillmore *(Whig 1850)*	
3	Thomas Jefferson *(Dem.-Rep. 1801)*	Aaron Burr *(Dem.-Rep. 1801)*	14	Franklin Pierce *(Democratic 1853)*	William R. D. King *(Democratic 1853)*
		George Clinton *(Dem.-Rep. 1805)*	15	James Buchanan *(Democratic 1857)*	John C. Breckinridge *(Democratic 1857)*
4	James Madison *(Dem.-Rep. 1809)*	George Clinton *(Dem.-Rep. 1809)*	16	Abraham Lincoln *(Republican 1861)*	Hannibal Hamlin *(Republican 1861)*
		Elbridge Gerry *(Dem.-Rep. 1813)*			Andrew Johnson *(Unionist 1865)*
5	James Monroe *(Dem.-Rep. 1817)*	Daniel D. Tompkins *(Dem.-Rep. 1817)*	17	Andrew Johnson *(Unionist 1865)*	
6	John Quincy Adams *(Dem.-Rep. 1825)*	John C. Calhoun *(Dem.-Rep. 1825)*	18	Ulysses S. Grant *(Republican 1869)*	Schuyler Colfax *(Republican 1869)*
7	Andrew Jackson *(Democratic 1829)*	John C. Calhoun *(Democratic 1829)*			Henry Wilson *(Republican 1873)*
		Martin Van Buren *(Democratic 1833)*	19	Rutherford B. Hayes *(Republican 1877)*	William A. Wheeler *(Republican 1877)*
8	Martin Van Buren *(Democratic 1837)*	Richard M. Johnson *(Democratic 1837)*	20	James A. Garfield *(Republican 1881)*	Chester A. Arthur *(Republican 1881)*
9	William H. Harrison *(Whig 1841)*	John Tyler *(Whig 1841)*	21	Chester A. Arthur *(Republican 1881)*	
10	John Tyler *(Whig and Democratic 1841)*		22	Grover Cleveland *(Democratic 1885)*	Thomas A. Hendricks *(Democratic 1885)*
11	James K. Polk *(Democratic 1845)*	George M. Dallas *(Democratic 1845)*	23	Benjamin Harrison *(Republican 1889)*	Levi P. Morton *(Republican 1889)*

PRESIDENT	VICE PRESIDENT	PRESIDENT	VICE PRESIDENT
24 Grover Cleveland *(Democratic 1893)*	Adlai E. Stevenson *(Democratic 1893)*	34 Dwight D. Eisenhower *(Republican 1953)*	Richard M. Nixon *(Republican 1953)*
25 William McKinley *(Republican 1897)*	Garret A. Hobart *(Republican 1897)*	35 John F. Kennedy *(Democratic 1961)*	Lyndon B. Johnson *(Democratic 1961)*
	Theodore Roosevelt *(Republican 1901)*	36 Lyndon B. Johnson *(Democratic 1963)*	Hubert H. Humphrey *(Democratic 1965)*
26 Theodore Roosevelt *(Republican 1901)*	Charles W. Fairbanks *(Republican 1905)*	37 Richard M. Nixon *(Republican 1969)*	Spiro T. Agnew *(Republican 1969)*
27 William H. Taft *(Republican 1909)*	James S. Sherman *(Republican 1909)*		Gerald R. Ford *(Republican 1973)*
28 Woodrow Wilson *(Democratic 1913)*	Thomas R. Marshall *(Democratic 1913)*	38 Gerald R. Ford *(Republican 1974)*	Nelson Rockefeller *(Republican 1974)*
29 Warren G. Harding *(Republican 1921)*	Calvin Coolidge *(Republican 1921)*	39 James E. Carter *(Democratic 1977)*	Walter Mondale *(Democratic 1977)*
30 Calvin Coolidge *(Republican 1923)*	Charles G. Dawes *(Republican 1925)*	40 Ronald Reagan *(Republican 1981)*	George H. W. Bush *(Republican 1981)*
31 Herbert Hoover *(Republican 1929)*	Charles Curtis *(Republican 1929)*	41 George H. W. Bush *(Republican 1989)*	J. Danforth Quayle *(Republican 1989)*
32 Franklin D. Roosevelt *(Democratic 1933)*	John Nance Garner *(Democratic 1933)*	42 William J. Clinton *(Democratic 1993)*	Albert Gore, Jr. *(Democratic 1993)*
	Henry A. Wallace *(Democratic 1941)*	43 George W. Bush *(Republican 2001)*	Richard Cheney *(Republican 2001)*
	Harry S. Truman *(Democratic 1945)*	44 Barack H. Obama *(Democratic 2009)*	Joseph R. Biden, Jr. *(Democratic 2009)*
33 Harry S. Truman *(Democratic 1945)*	Alben W. Barkley *(Democratic 1949)*	45 Donald J. Trump *(Republican 2017)*	Michael R. Pence *(Republican 2017)*

Endnotes

CHAPTER 1

1. Lindsey Bever, "Meet Saira Blair, 18, Soon to Be the Nation's Youngest Lawmaker," *Washington Post,* November 7, 2014, www.washingtonpost.com/news/morning-mix/wp/2014/11/07/meet-saira-blair-18-soon-to-be-the-nations-youngest-lawmaker/?utm_term=.708303648d03 (accessed 1/16/18); Lucy McCalmont, "Conservative, Lawmaker, Student," *Politico,* November 5, 2014, www.politico.com/story/2014/11/saira-blair-west-virginia-112602 (accessed 11/16/18); Jae Jones, "This Texas City Just Elected the Youngest City Council Member in the State," *The Nation,* June 1, 2017, www.thenation.com/article/texas-city-just-elected-youngest-person-hold-office-state/ (accessed 1/16/18); City of Prairie View, TX, "Kendric Jones—Position #3," www.prairieviewtexas.gov/departments/kendric_jones_-_pos_3.php (accessed 1/16/18).

2. Arch Puddington and Tyler Roylance, Freedom in the World, 2016, freedomhouse.org/sites/default/files/FH_FITW_Report_2016.pdf (accessed 4/10/16).

3. Eugen Weber, *Peasants into Frenchmen: The Modernization of Rural France, 1870–1914* (Stanford, CA: Stanford University Press, 1976), chap. 5.

4. V. O. Key, *Politics, Parties, and Pressure Groups* (New York: Crowell, 1964), 201.

5. Harold Lasswell, *Politics: Who Gets What, When, How* (New York: Meridian Books, 1958).

6. Abby Goodnough, "Maine Voters Approve Medicaid Expansion, a Rebuke of Gov. LePage," *New York Times,* November 7, 2017, www.nytimes.com/2017/11/07/us/maine-medicaid-healthcare.html (accessed 12/27/17); "2018 Ballot Measures," Ballotpedia, https://ballotpedia.org/2018_ballot_measures (accessed 10/10/18).

7. This definition is taken from Norman H. Nie, Jane Junn, and Kenneth Stehlik-Barry, *Education and Democratic Citizenship in America* (Chicago: University of Chicago Press, 1996).

8. Kyle Dropp and Brendan Nyhan, "One-Third Don't Know Obamacare and Affordable Care Act Are The Same," *New York Times,* The Upshot, February 7, 2017, www.nytimes.com/2017/02/07/upshot/one-third-dont-know-obamacare-and-affordable-care-act-are-the-same.html?_r=0 (accessed 12/28/17).

9. John B. Horrigon and Lee Rainie, "Americans' Views on Open Government Data," Pew Research Center, April 21, 2015, www.pewinternet.org/2015/04/21/open-government-data/ (accessed 7/22/15).

10. Pew Research Center, "Beyond Distrust," November 23, 2015, http://assets.pewresearch.org/wp-content/uploads/sites/5/2015/11/11-23-2015-Governance-release.pdf (accessed 4/15/18).

11. Pew Research Center, "Beyond Distrust."

12. U.S. Census Bureau, Population Clock, April 15, 2018, www.census.gov/popclock/ (accessed 4/15/18).

13. Susan B. Carter, Scott Sigmund Gartner, Michael R. Haines, Alan L. Olmstead, Richard Sutch, and Gavin Wright, eds., *Historical Statistics of the United States: Millennial Edition Online* (New York: Cambridge University Press, 2006), Table Aa145-184, Population, by Sex and Race: 1790–1990, 23. Data from 2016 available at U.S. Census Bureau, "2016 American Community Survey 1-Year Estimates: Selected Characteristics of the Native and Foreign-Born Populations," https://factfinder.census.gov/faces/tableservices/jsf/pages/productview.xhtml?pid=ACS_16_1YR_S0501&prodType=table (accessed 12/26/17).

14. Carter et al., *Historical Statistics of the United States*, Table Aa145-184, Population, by Sex and Race: 1790–1990, 23.

15. Carter et al., *Historical Statistics of the United States*, Table Aa145-184, Population, by Sex and Race: 1790–1990, 23; Table Aa2189-2215, Hispanic Population Estimates.

16. Campbell J. Gibson and Emily Lennon, "Historical Census Statistics on the Foreign-Born Population of the United States: 1850–1990," February 1999, www.census.gov/population/www/documentation/twps0029/twps0029.html (accessed 4/10/16).

17. Carter et al., *Historical Statistics of the United States*, Table Aa22-35, Selected Population Characteristics.

18. Michael B. Katz and Mark J. Stern, *One Nation Divisible: What America Was and What It Is Becoming* (New York: Russell Sage Foundation, 2006), 16.

19. Carter et al., *Historical Statistics of the United States*, Table Aa145-184, Population, by Sex and Race: 1790–1990, 23. Karen R. Humes, Nicholas A. Jones, and Roberto R. Ramirez, "Overview of Race and Hispanic Origin: 2010. *2010 Census Briefs*," no. C2010BR-02 (Washington, DC: U.S. Census Bureau, March 2011), 4, www.census.gov/prod/cen2010/briefs/c2010br-02.pdf (accessed 10/14/2011).

20. U.S. Census Bureau, "2016 American Community Survey 1-Year Estimates: Selected Characteristics of the Native and Foreign-Born Populations."

21. U.S. Census Bureau, "2016 American Community Survey 1-Year Estimates: Selected Characteristics of the Native and Foreign-Born Populations."

22. U.S. Census Bureau, "2016 American Community Survey 1-Year Estimates: Selected Characteristics of the Foreign-Born Population by Region of Birth: Latin America," https://factfinder.census.gov/faces/tableservices/jsf/pages/productview.xhtml?pid=ACS_16_1YR_S0506&prodType=table (accessed 12/26/17).

23. U.S. Census Bureau, "2016 American Community Survey 1-Year Estimates: Selected Characteristics of the Foreign-Born Population by Region of Birth: Asia," https://factfinder.census.gov/faces/tableservices/jsf/pages/productview.xhtml?pid=ACS_16_1YR_S0505&prodType=table (accessed 12/2/17).

24. U.S. Census Bureau, "2016 American Community Survey 1-Year Estimates: Selected Characteristics of the Foreign-Born Population by Region of Birth: Europe," https://factfinder.census.gov/faces/tableservices/jsf/pages/productview.xhtml?pid=ACS_16_1YR_S0503&prodType=table (accessed 12/26/17).

25. Bryan Baker and Nancy Rytina, "Estimates of the Unauthorized Immigrant Population Residing in the United States: January 2012," *Population Estimates*, Office of Immigration Statistics, Department of Homeland Security, March 2013, www.dhs.gov/sites/default/files/publications/Unauthorized%20Immigrant%20Population%20Estimates%20in%20the%20US%20January%202012_0.pdf (accessed 12/26/17).

26. Anthony Faiola, "States' Immigrant Policies Diverge," *Washington Post*, October 15, 2007, A1.

27. *Plyler v. Doe*, 457 U.S. 202 (1982).

28. Robert P. Jones and Daniel Cox, "America's Changing Religious Identity, 2016," Public Religion Research Institute, September 6, 2017, www.prri.org/wp-content/uploads/2017/09/PRRI-Religion-Report.pdf (accessed 11/4/17).

29. Jones and Cox, "America's Changing Religious Identity."

30. U.S. Census Bureau, "Demographic Trends in the 20th Century, Table 5: Population by Age and Sex for the United States: 1900 to 2000," www.census.gov/prod/2002pubs/censr-4.pdf (accessed 4/11/16); U.S.

31. World Bank, "Population Ages 65 and Above (% of Total)," March 1, 2018, http://data.worldbank.org/indicator/SP.POP.65UP.TO.ZS (accessed 4/15/18).

32. U.S. Census Bureau, "2010 Census Urban Area Facts," www.census.gov/geo/reference/ua/uafacts.html (accessed 4/11/16); Central Intelligence Agency, "World Factbook: Urbanization," 2017, www.cia.gov/library/publications/the-world-factbook/fields/2212.html (accessed 4/15/18).

33. Thomas Piketty and Emmanuel Saez, "Income Inequality in the United States, 1913–1998," *Quarterly Journal of Economics* 118, no. 1 (2003) (Tables and Figures Updated to 2015), http://eml.berkeley.edu/~saez/TabFig2015prel.xls (accessed 12/26/17).

34. U.S. Census Bureau, "Income: Historical Income Data. Tables F-2, F-3, and F-6." www.census.gov/hhes/www/income/data/historical/index.html (accessed 4/12/16).

35. U.S. Census Bureau, "Historical Poverty Tables, Table 2: Poverty Status of People by Family Relationship, Race, and Hispanic origin: 1959 to 2016," www.census.gov/data/tables/time-series/demo/income-poverty/historical-poverty-people.html (accessed 4/15/18).

36. U.S. Census Bureau, "Historical Poverty Tables, Table 2: Poverty Status of People by Family Relationship, Race, and Hispanic Origin: 1959 to 2014," www.census.gov/hhes/www/poverty/data/historical/hstpov2.xls (accessed 4/11/16).

37. Jesse Sussell and James A. Thomson, "Are Changing Constituencies Driving Rising Polarization in the U.S. House of Representatives?" RAND Corporation Research Report RR-396-RC, 2015, www.rand.org/pubs/research_reports/RR896.html (accessed 1/15/18).

38. See Judith N. Shklar, *American Citizenship: The Quest for Inclusion* (Cambridge, MA: Harvard University Press, 1991).

39. Herbert McClosky and John Zaller, *The American Ethos: Public Attitudes toward Capitalism and Democracy* (Cambridge, MA: Harvard University Press, 1984), 19.

40. *Burwell v. Hobby Lobby Stores, Inc.*, 573 U.S. __ (2014).

41. Kevin McCoy and Kevin Johnson, "U.S. Demands Apple Unlock Phone in Drug Case," April 10, 2016, www.usatoday.com/story/news/2016/04/08/justice-moving-forward-separate-apple-case/82788824 (accessed 4/10/16).

42. J. R. Pole, *The Pursuit of Equality in American History* (Berkeley: University of California Press, 1978), 3.

43. *Plessy v. Ferguson*, 163 U.S. 537 (1896).

44. *Brown v. Board of Education*, 347 U.S. 483 (1954).

45. See Rogers M. Smith, *Liberalism and American Constitutional Law* (Cambridge, MA: Harvard University Press, 1985), chap. 6.

46. The case was *San Antonio Independent School District v. Rodriguez*, 411 U.S. 1 (1973). See the discussion in Smith, *Liberalism and American Constitutional Law*, 163–4;

see also Alana Semuels, "Good School, Rich School; Bad School, Poor School," *The Atlantic*, August 25, 2016, www.theatlantic.com/business/archive/2016/08/property-taxes-and-unequal-schools/497333/ (accessed 12/26/17).

47. Janell Fetterolf, "Many Around the World Say Women's Equality Is Very Important," Pew Research Center, January 19, 2017, www.pewresearch.org/fact-tank/2017/01/19/many-around-the-world-say-womens-equality-is-very-important/ (accessed 2/16/18); John Gramlich, "10 Things We Learned about Gender Issues in the U.S. in 2017," Pew Research Center, December 28, 2017, www.pewresearch.org/fact-tank/2017/12/28/10-things-we-learned-about-gender-issues-in-the-u-s-in-2017/ (accessed 2/16/18); "The Partisan Divide on Political Values Grows Even Wider," Pew Research Center, October 5, 2017, www.people-press.org/2017/10/05/1-partisan-divides-over-political-values-widen/ (accessed 2/16/18); Pew Research Center, "Support for Same-Sex Marriage Grows, Even among Groups That Had Been Skeptical," June 26, 2017, www.people-press.org/2017/06/26/support-for-same-sex-marriage-grows-even-among-groups-that-had-been-skeptical/ (accessed 2/16/18); Pew Research Center, "Trends in American Values, 1987–2012," June 4, 2012; Pew Research Center for the People and the Press and for the Public, "For the Public, It's Not about Class Warfare, but Fairness," March 2, 2012, www.peoplepress.org/2012/03/02/for-the-public-its-not-about-class-warfare-but-fairness (accessed 2/16/18).

48. See the discussion in Eileen McDonagh, "Gender Political Change," in *New Perspectives on American Politics*, ed. Lawrence C. Dodd and Calvin C. Jillson (Washington, DC: CQ Press, 1994), 58–73. The argument for moving women's issues into the public sphere is made by Jean Bethke Elshtain, *Public Man, Private Woman* (Princeton, NJ: Princeton University Press, 1981).

49. Roger Lowenstein, "The Way We Live Now: The Inequality Conundrum," *New York Times Magazine*, June 10, 2007, 11.

50. New York Times/CBS News Poll, "Americans' Views on Income Inequality and Workers' Rights," www.nytimes.com/interactive/2015/06/03/business/income-inequality-workers-rights-international-trade-poll.html (accessed 12/27/17); Frank Newport, "Majority Say Wealthy Americans, Corporations Taxed Too Little," April 18, 2017, news.gallup.com/poll/208685/majority-say-wealthy-americans-corporations-taxed-little.aspx (accessed 12/27/17).

51. Kevin Phillips, *Arrogant Capital: Washington, Wall Street, and the Frustration of American Politics* (Boston: Little, Brown, 1994); Richard L. Hasen, *Plutocrats United: Campaign Money, the Supreme Court, and the Distortion of American Elections* (New Haven, CT: Yale University Press, 2016).

52. FairVote, "Voter Turnout," www.fairvote.org/voter_turnout#voter_turnout_101 (accessed 4/10/16).

53. Center for the Study of the American Electorate, "2008 Turnout Report: African-Americans, Anger, Fear and Youth Propel Turnout to Highest Level since 1960," December 17, 2008, www.american.edu/research/news/loader.cfm?csModule5security/getfile&pageid523907 (accessed 2/19/16).

54. Lydia Saad, "Conservatives Lead in U.S. Ideology Down to Single Digits," Gallup News, January 11, 2018, http://news.gallup.com/poll/225074/conservative-lead-ideology-down-single-digits.aspx?g_source=IDEOLOGY&g_medium=topic&g_campaign=tiles (accessed 1/15/18).

55. Art Swift, "Majority in U.S. Say Federal Government Has Too Much Power," Gallup News, October 5, 2017, news.gallup.com/poll/220199/majority-say-federal-government-power.aspx (accessed 1/15/18); Pew Research Center, "Summer 2017 Political Landscape Survey," Final Toplines, October 24, 2017, http://assets.pewresearch.org/wp-content/uploads/sites/5/2017/10/04163936/10-05-2017-Political-landscape-toplines-for-release.pdf (accessed 4/3/18).

56. Pew Research Center, "How Republicans and Democrats View Federal Spending," April 24, 2017, www.people-press.org/2017/04/24/how-republicans-and-democrats-view-federal-spending/ (accessed 1/15/18).

57. Benjamin I. Page and Lawrence R. Jacobs, *Class War? What Americans Really Think about Economic Inequality* (Chicago: University of Chicago Press, 2009).

58. Pew Research Center, "Public Trust in Government, 1958–2017," www.people-press.org/2017/05/03/public-trust-in-government-1958-2017/ (accessed 12/27/17).

59. Pew Research Center, "Public Trust in Government, 1958–2017."

60. Joseph S. Nye, Jr., "Introduction: The Decline of Confidence in Government," in *Why People Don't Trust Government*, ed. Joseph S. Nye, Jr., Philip D. Zelikow, and David C. King (Cambridge, MA: Harvard University Press, 1997), 4.

CHAPTER 2

1. "Jim Obergefell," *Biography*, www.biography.com/people/jim-obergefell (accessed 3/4/18).

2. Jim Obergefell, "Gay Activist Jim Obergefell: Love, Loss and Steadfast Commitment Lead a Nation Forward," *Variety*, June 29, 2015, http://variety.com/2015/biz/news/gay-activist-jim-obergefell-love-loss-commitment-lead-nation-forward-1201529672/ (accessed 3/4/18).

3. *Obergefell v. Hodges*, 576 U.S. __ (2015).

4. Obergefell, "Love, Loss and Steadfast Commitment."

5. Richard E. Neustadt, *Presidential Power and the Modern Presidents: The Politics of Leadership from Roosevelt to Reagan* (New York: Simon & Schuster, 1991), 29.

6. The social makeup of colonial America and some of the social conflicts that divided colonial society are discussed in Jackson Turner Main, *The Social Structure of*

Revolutionary America (Princeton, NJ: Princeton University Press, 1965).

7. George B. Tindall and David E. Shi, *America: A Narrative History*, 8th ed. (New York: W. W. Norton, 2010), 202.

8. For a discussion of events leading up to the Revolution, see Charles M. Andrews, *The Colonial Background of the American Revolution* (New Haven, CT: Yale University Press, 1924).

9. See Carl Becker, *The Declaration of Independence* (New York: Knopf, 1942).

10. An excellent and readable account of the development from the Articles of Confederation to the Constitution will be found in Alfred H. Kelly, Winfred A. Harbison, and Herman Belz, *The American Constitution: Its Origins and Development*, 7th ed., vol. 1 (New York: W. W. Norton, 1991), chap. 5.

11. Reported in Samuel E. Morrison, Henry Steele Commager, and William Leuchtenburg, *The Growth of the American Republic*, vol. 1 (New York: Oxford University Press, 1969), 244.

12. Quoted in Morrison, Commager, and Leuchtenburg, *Growth of the American Republic*, 242.

13. Charles A. Beard, *An Economic Interpretation of the Constitution of the United States* (New York: Macmillan, 1913).

14. Max Farrand, ed., *The Records of the Federal Convention of 1787*, vol. 1 (New Haven, CT: Yale University Press, 1966).

15. Madison's notes, along with the somewhat less complete records kept by several other participants in the convention, are available in a four-volume set. See Max Farrand, ed., *The Records of the Federal Convention of 1787*, 4 vols., rev. ed. (New Haven, CT: Yale University Press, 1966).

16. Farrand, *Records of the Federal Convention of 1787*, 476.

17. Alexander Hamilton, James Madison, and John Jay, *The Federalist Papers*, ed. Clinton L. Rossiter (New York: New American Library, 1961), no. 71.

18. *Federalist Papers*, no. 70.

19. Max Farrand, *The Framing of the Constitution of the United States* (New Haven, CT: Yale University Press, 1962), 49.

20. Melancton Smith, quoted in Herbert J. Storing, *What the Anti-Federalists Were For* (Chicago: University of Chicago Press, 1981), 17.

21. "Essays of Brutus," no. 1, in *The Complete Anti-Federalist*, ed. Herbert Storing (Chicago: University of Chicago Press, 1981).

22. *Federalist Papers*, no. 57.

23. "Essays of Brutus," no. 15, in Storing, *Complete Anti-Federalist*.

24. *Federalist Papers*, no. 10.

25. "Essays of Brutus," no. 7, in Storing, *Complete Anti-Federalist*.

26. "Essays of Brutus," no. 6, in Storing, *Complete Anti-Federalist*.

27. Storing, *What the Anti-Federalists Were For*, 28.

28. *Federalist Papers*, no. 51.

29. Quoted in Storing, *What the Anti-Federalists Were For*, 30.

30. *Federalist Papers*, no. 10.

CHAPTER 3

1. Steph Sherer, "Medical Marijuana Users Caught in State-Federal Conflict," CNN.com, November 10, 2014, www.cnn.com/2014/09/05/opinion/sherer-medical-marijuana-prosecutions/index.html (accessed 7/31/17).

2. "33 Legal Medical Marijuana States and DC," November 7, 2018, https://medicalmarijuana.procon.org/view.resource.php?resourceID=000881 (accessed 11/7/18).

3. Sherer, "Medical Marijuana Users."

4. Brady Dennis, "Obama Administration Will Not Block State Marijuana Laws, If Distribution Is Regulated," *Washington Post*, August 29, 2013, http://articles.washingtonpost.com/2013-08-29/national/41566270_1_marijuana-legalization-attorney-general-bob-ferguson-obama-administration (accessed 11/17/13).

5. John Hudak, "The Disorienting Effect of Marijuana on the Trump Administration," Brookings Institution, April 20, 2017, www.brookings.edu/blog/fixgov/2017/04/20/disorienting-effects-of-marijuana-on-the-trump-administration/ (accessed 7/31/17).

6. The public policy exception stems from developments in case law tracing back to the 1930s. In Section 283 of the Restatement (Second) of Conflict of Laws (1971) a group of judges and academics codified existing case law related to marriage: "A marriage which satisfies the requirements of the state where the marriage was contracted will everywhere be recognized as valid unless it violates the strong public policy of another state which had the most significant relationship to the spouses and the marriage at the time of the marriage." However, in *Baker v. General Motors Corp*, 522 U.S. 222 (1998), the Supreme Court explicitly stated that its decision "creates no general exception to the full faith and credit command."

7. Adam Liptak, "Bans on Interracial Unions Offer Perspective on Gay Ones," *New York Times*, March 17, 2004, A22.

8. *Loving v. Virginia*, 388 U.S. 1 (1967). The Lovings were charged with violating Virginia's miscegenation laws and were sentenced to one year in jail, which would be suspended if they left the state for 25 years. Five years later, with the assistance of the American Civil Liberties Union, the Lovings filed a motion to vacate their conviction. The Supreme Court heard the case and overturned the Lovings' conviction, finding Virginia's miscegenation law unconstitutional under the due process clause and equal protection clause of the Fourteenth Amendment.

9. Ken I. Kersch, "Full Faith and Credit for Same-Sex Marriages?" *Political Science Quarterly* 112 (Spring 1997):

117–36; Joan Biskupic, "Once Unthinkable, Now under Debate," *Washington Post*, September 3, 1996, A1.

10. *United States v. Windsor*, 570 U.S. __ (2013).

11. *Obergefell v. Hodges,* 576 U.S. __ (2015).

12. Elliot C. McLaughlin, "Most States to Abide by Supreme Court's Same-Sex Marriage Ruling, but . . . ," CNN, June 30, 2015, www.cnn.com/2015/06/29/us/same-sex-marriage-state-by-state/ (accessed 8/16/15).

13. *Hicklin v. Orbeck*, 437 U.S. 518 (1978).

14. *Sweeny v. Woodall*, 344 U.S. 86 (1952).

15. Council of State Governments, "Interstate Compacts Toolkit—Backgrounder," www.csg.org/knowledgecenter/docs/ToolKit05InterstateCompacts.pdf (accessed 6/5/18).

16. A good discussion of the constitutional position of local governments is in Richard Briffault, "Our Localism: Part I, the Structure of Local Government Law," *Columbia Law Review* 90, no. 1 (January 1990): 1–115. For more on the structure and theory of federalism, see Larry N. Gerston, *American Federalism: A Concise Introduction* (Armonk, NY: M. E. Sharpe, 2007), and Martha Derthick, "Up-to-Date in Kansas City: Reflections on American Federalism" (1992 John Gaus Lecture), *PS: Political Science and Politics* 25 (December 1992): 671–75.

17. *McCulloch v. Maryland*, 4 Wheaton 316 (1819).

18. *Gibbons v. Ogden*, 9 Wheaton 1 (1824).

19. The Sherman Antitrust Act, adopted in 1890, for example, was enacted not to restrict commerce but rather to protect it from monopolies, or trusts, in order to prevent unfair trade practices and to enable the market again to become self-regulating. Moreover, the Supreme Court sought to uphold liberty of contract to protect businesses. For example, in *Lochner v. New York*, 198 U.S. 45 (1905), the Court invalidated a New York law regulating the sanitary conditions and hours of labor of bakers on the grounds that the law interfered with liberty of contract.

20. The key case in this process of expanding the power of the national government is generally considered to be *NLRB v. Jones & Laughlin Steel Corporation*, 301 U.S. 1 (1937), in which the Supreme Court approved federal regulation of the workplace and thereby virtually eliminated interstate commerce as a limit on the national government's power.

21. Kenneth T. Palmer, "The Evolution of Grant Policies," in *The Changing Politics of Federal Grants*, ed. Lawrence D. Brown, James W. Fossett, and Kenneth T. Palmer (Washington, DC: Brookings Institution Press, 1984), 15.

22. Palmer, "Evolution of Grant Policies," 6.

23. Morton Grodzins, *The American System*, ed. Daniel J. Elazar (Chicago: Rand McNally, 1966).

24. See Terry Sanford, *Storm over the States* (New York: McGraw-Hill, 1967).

25. James L. Sundquist, *Making Federalism Work*, with David W. Davis (Washington, DC: Brookings Institution Press, 1969), 271. George Wallace was mistrusted by the architects of the War on Poverty because he was a strong proponent of racial segregation and "states' rights."

26. See Donald F. Kettl, *The Regulation of American Federalism* (Baton Rouge: Louisiana State University Press, 1983).

27. Cindy Skrzycki, "Trial Lawyers on the Offensive in Fight against Preemptive Rules," *Washington Post*, September 11, 2007, D2.

28. *Gonazales v. Oregon*, 546 U.S. 243 (2006).

29. *Wyeth v. Levine*, 555 U.S. 555 (2009).

30. Philip Rucker, "Obama Curtails Bush's Policy of 'Preemption,'" *Washington Post*, May 22, 2009, A3.

31. Evan Halper, "Trump and California Are Set to Collide Head-On over Fuel Standards," *Los Angeles Times*, April 27, 2018, www.latimes.com/politics/la-na-pol-mileage-20180427-story.html (accessed 5/1/18).

32. The phrase "laboratories of democracy" was coined by Supreme Court Justice Louis Brandeis in his dissenting opinion in *New State Ice Co. v. Liebmann*, 285 U.S. 262 (1932).

33. *United States v. Darby Lumber Co.*, 312 U.S. 100 (1941).

34. W. John Moore, "Pleading the 10th," *National Journal*, July 29, 1996.

35. *United States v. Lopez*, 14 U.S. 549 (1995).

36. *Printz v. United States*, 521 U.S. 98 (1997).

37. Timothy Conlan, *New Federalism: Intergovernmental Reform from Nixon to Reagan* (Washington, DC: Brookings Institution Press, 1988); U.S. Advisory Commission on Intergovernmental Relations, *Federal Regulation of State and Local Governments*.

38. For an assessment of the achievements of the 104th and 105th Congresses, see Timothy Conlan, *From New Federalism to Devolution: Twenty-Five Years of Intergovernmental Reform* (Washington, DC: Brookings Institution Press, 1998).

39. Robert Frank, "Proposed Block Grants Seen Unlikely to Cure Management Problems," *Wall Street Journal*, May 1, 1995, 1.

40. Sarah Kershaw, "U.S. Rule Limits Emergency Care for Immigrants," *New York Times*, September 22, 2007, A1.

41. Education Commission of the States, "50-State Comparison: Charter School Policies," January 2018, www.ecs.org/charter-school-policies/ (accessed 6/5/18).

42. Zach Winn, "A List of States That Allow Concealed Guns on Campus," *Campus Safety Magazine*, August 30, 2017, www.campussafetymagazine.com/university/list-of-states-that-allow-concealed-carry-guns-on-campus/ (accessed 10/12/18).

43. National Council of State Legislatures, "NCSL Fiscal Brief: State Balanced Budget Requirements," October 2010, www.ncsl.org/documents/fiscal/StateBalancedBudgetProvisions2010.pdf (accessed 7/26/17).

44. Robert Jay Dilger and Richard S. Beth, "Unfunded Mandates Reform Act: History, Impact, and Issues" (Washington, DC: Congressional Research Service, April 19, 2011), 40, http://digital.library.unt.edu/ark:/67531/metadc40084/m1/1/high_res_d/R40957_2011Apr19.pdf (accessed 11/16/13).

45. See U.S. Advisory Commission on Intergovernmental Relations, *Federal Regulation of State and Local Governments: The Mixed Record of the 1980s* (Washington, DC: Advisory Commission on Intergovernmental Relations, July 1993).

46. Congressional Budget Office, "A Review of CBO's Activities in 2014 under the Unfunded Mandates Reform Act," March 31, 2015, www.cbo.gov/sites/default/files/114th-congress-2015-2016/reports/50051-UMRA2_0.pdf (see Appendix B, p. 39) (accessed 8/16/15).

47. Adam Liptak, "Justices to Hear Health Care Case as Race Heats Up," *New York Times*, November 15, 2011, A1.

48. Kaiser Family Foundation, "Status of State Medicaid Expansion Decisions," May 31, 2018, www.kff.org/health-reform/slide/current-status-of-the-medicaid-expansion-decision/ (accessed 6/5/18); Ballotopedia, "2018 Ballot Measure Election Results," https://ballotpedia.org/2018_ballot_measure_election_results (accessed 11/7/18).

49. U.S. Committee on Federalism and National Purpose, *To Form a More Perfect Union* (Washington, DC: National Conference on Social Welfare, 1985). See also the discussion in Paul E. Peterson, *The Price of Federalism* (Washington, DC: Brookings Institution Press, 1995), esp. chap. 8.

50. Malcolm Gladwell, "Remaking Welfare: In States' Experiments, a Cutting Contest," *Washington Post*, March 10, 1995, 6.

51. Ashley Burnside and Ife Floyd, "TANF Benefits Remain Low Despite Recent Increases in Some States," Center on Budget and Policy Priorities, October 12, 2018, www.cbpp.org/sites/default/files/atoms/files/10-30-14tanf.pdf (accessed 10/12/18).

52. Cohen, Elissa, Sarah Minton, Megan Thompson, Elizabeth Crowe, and Linda Giannarelli, "Welfare Rules Databook: State TANF Policies as of July 2015," OPRE Report 2016-67 (Washington, DC: Office of Planning, Research and Evaluation, Administration for Children and Families, U.S. Department of Health and Human Services, 2016), http://wrd.urban.org/wrd/data/databooks/2015%20Welfare%20Rules%20Databook%20(Final%2009%2026%2016).pdf (accessed 7/30/17); and Mary Jo Pitzi, "Arizona Limits Poverty Aid to 1 Year; Strictest in U.S." azcentral.com, July 1, 2016, www.azcentral.com/story/news/politics/arizona/2016/07/01/arizona-limits-poverty-aid-1-year-strictest-us/86499262/ (accessed 7/30/17).

53. Andrea Louise Campbell, *Trapped in America's Safety Net: One Family's Struggle* (Chicago: University of Chicago Press, 2014), 82.

54. Frank J. Thompson, *Medicaid Politics: Federalism, Policy Durability, and Health Reform* (Washington, DC: Georgetown University Press, 2012).

55. Insurance Institute for Highway Safety, "Motor Vehicle Fatalities in 1996 Were 12 Percent Higher on Interstates, Freeways in 12 States That Raised Speed Limits," press release, October 10, 1997.

56. *Gonzales v. Raich*, 545 U.S. 1 (2005). For more, see William Yardley, "New Federal Crackdown Confounds States That Allow Medical Marijuana," *New York Times*, May 8, 2011, A13.

57. *Gonzales v. Oregon*, 546 U.S. 243 (2006).

58. Josh Sanburn, "Colorado Approves a 'Right to Die' for Terminally Ill Patients," *Time*, November 9, 2016, time.com/4563632/colorado-right-to-die-approved/ (accessed 11/10/16).

59. National Conference of State Legislatures, "Collecting E-Commerce Taxes," www.ncsl.org/research/fiscal-policy/collecting-ecommerce-taxes-an-interactive-map.aspx (accessed 11/17/13).

60. Richard Rubin, "States Set Up Fight over Web Sales Tax," *Wall Street Journal*, February 23, 2016, www.wsj.com/articles/states-seek-new-ways-to-tax-online-sales-1456262265 (accessed 4/11/16).

61. *United States v. Texas*, 579 U.S. __ (2016).

62. Alexander Bolton, "GOP Looks for Plan B after Failure of Immigration Measures," The Hill, February 16, 2018, thehill.com/homenews/senate/374143-gop-looks-for-plan-b-after-failure-of-immigration-measures (accessed 2/18/18).

63. Kate Linthicum, "Obama Ends Secure Communities Program as Part of Immigration Action," *Los Angeles Times*, November 21, 2014, www.latimes.com/local/california/la-me-1121-immigration-justice-20141121-story.html (accessed 8/16/15).

64. "Enhancing Public Safety in the Interior of the United States," Executive Order 13768, January 25, 2017, www.federalregister.gov/documents/2017/01/30/2017-02102/enhancing-public-safety-in-the-interior-of-the-united-states (accessed 7/27/17).

65. Camila Domonoske, "Judge Blocks Trump Administration from Punishing 'Sanctuary Cities,'" NPR, November 21, 2017, www.npr.org/sections/thetwo-way/2017/11/21/565678707/enter-title (accessed 2/18/18).

66. Nicole Rodriguez, "Trump Administration Wants to Arrest Mayors of 'Sanctuary Cities,'" *Newsweek,* January 16, 2018, www.newsweek.com/trump-administration-wants-arrest-mayors-sanctuary-cities-783010 (accessed 2/18/18).

67. *NFIB v. Sebelius,* 567 U.S. 519 (2012).

68. Adam Liptak, "In Health Law, Asking Where U.S. Power Stops," *New York Times*, November 14, 2011, A1.

69. Robert Barnes, "Affordable Care Act Survives Supreme Court Challenge," *Washington Post*, June 25, 2015, www.washingtonpost.com/politics/courts_law/obamacare-survives-supreme-court-challenge/2015/06/25/af87608e-188a-11e5-93b7-5eddc056ad8a_story.html (accessed 8/16/15).

70. National League of Cities, "City Rights in an Era of Preemption: A State-by-State Analysis," 2017, http://nlc.org/preemption (accessed 7/27/17).

71. Emma G. Ellis, "Guess How Much That Anti-LGBTQ Law Is Costing North Carolina," *Wired*, September 18, 2016, www.wired.com/2016/09/guess-much-anti-lgbtq-law-costing-north-carolina/ (accessed 7/27/17).

72. Celeste Bott, "St. Louis $10 Minimum Wage to Revert Back to $7.70 in August, Greitens Announces," *St. Louis Post-Dispatch,* July 1, 2017, www.stltoday.com/news/local/govt-and-politics/st-louis-minimum-wage-will-revert-back-to-in-august/article_0428b488-d4e2-5778-895b-f44ad92cc65a.html (accessed 7/27/17); Celeste Bott, "More Than 100 St. Louis Businesses Opt to Keep $10 Minimum Wage, Despite New State Law," *St. Louis Post-Dispatch,* August 7, 2017, www.stltoday.com/news/local/metro/more-than-st-louis-businesses-opt-to-keep-minimum-wage/article_920788cd-47b2-5a39-b494-8ee7e6c0f676.html (accessed 2/18/18); CBS St. Louis, "McDonalds 'Save the Raise' Protest Happening Today," August 17, 2017, stlouis.cbslocal.com/2017/08/17/mcdonalds-save-the-raise-protest-happening-today/ (accessed 2/18/18).

73. Melia Robinson, "Here's Where You Can Legally Smoke Weed in 2018," *Business Insider,* January 23, 2018, www.businessinsider.com/where-can-you-can-legally-smoke-weed-2018-1/#alaska-1 (accessed 2/13/18); "33 Legal Medical Marijuana States and DC," November 7, 2018, https://medicalmarijuana.procon.org/view.resource.php?resourceID=000881 (accessed 11/7/18).

CHAPTER 4

1. This account taken from April Baer, "The Slants: Trading in Stereotypes," NPR, June 11, 2008, www.npr.org/templates/story/story.php?storyId=90278746; Katy Steinmetz, "'The Slants' Suit: Asian-American Band Goes to Court over Name," *Time,* October 23, 2013, http://entertainment.time.com/2013/10/23/the-slants-suit-asian-american-band-goes-to-court-over-name/; Kat Chow, "The Slants: Fighting for the Right to Rock a Racial Slur," NPR, January 19, 2017, www.npr.org/sections/codeswitch/2017/01/19/510467679/the-slants-fighting-for-the-right-to-rock-a-racial-slur; *Matal v. Tam,* 582 U.S. __ (2017); Ian Shapira and Ann E. Marimow, "Washington Redskins Win Trademark Fight over the Team's Name," *Washington Post,* June 29, 2017, www.washingtonpost.com/local/public-safety/2017/06/29/a26f52f0-5cf6-11e7-9fc6-c7ef4bc58d13_story.html?utm_term=.22ed3bf39917 (accessed 2/4/18).

2. Alexander Hamilton, James Madison, and John Jay, *The Federalist Papers,* ed. Clinton Rossiter (New York: New American Library, 1961), no. 84, 513.

3. *Federalist Papers,* no. 84, 513.

4. Clinton Rossiter, *1787: The Grand Convention* (New York: W. W. Norton, 1987), 302.

5. Rossiter, *1787,* 303. Rossiter also reports that "in 1941 the States of Connecticut, Massachusetts, and Georgia celebrated the sesquicentennial of the Bill of Rights by giving their hitherto withheld and unneeded assent."

6. *Barron v. Baltimore,* 7 Peters 243, 246 (1833).

7. The Fourteenth Amendment also seems designed to introduce civil rights. The final clause of the all-important Section 1 provides that no state can "deny to any person within its jurisdiction the equal protection of the laws." It is not unreasonable to conclude that the purpose of this provision was to obligate the state governments as well as the national government to take positive actions to protect citizens from arbitrary and discriminatory actions, at least those based on race. Civil rights will be explored in Chapter 5.

8. For example, *The Slaughterhouse Cases,* 16 Wallace 36 (1883).

9. *Chicago, Burlington and Quincy Railroad Company v. Chicago,* 166 U.S. 226 (1897).

10. *Gitlow v. New York,* 268 U.S. 652 (1925).

11. *Near v. Minnesota,* 283 U.S. 697 (1931); *Hague v. C.I.O.,* 307 U.S. 496 (1939).

12. *Palko v. Connecticut,* 302 U.S. 319 (1937).

13. All of these were implicitly included in the *Palko* case as "not incorporated" into the Fourteenth Amendment as limitations on the powers of the states.

14. There is one interesting exception, which involves the Sixth Amendment right to public trial. In the 1948 case *In re Oliver,* 33 U.S. 257, the right to a public trial was, in effect, incorporated as part of the Fourteenth Amendment. However, the issue in that case was put more generally as "due process," and public trial itself was not actually mentioned in so many words. Later opinions, such as *Duncan v. Louisiana,* 391 U.S. 145 (1968), cited the *Oliver* case as the precedent for more explicit incorporation of public trials as part of the Fourteenth Amendment.

15. *Abington School District v. Schempp,* 374 U.S. 203 (1963).

16. *Engel v. Vitale,* 370 U.S. 421 (1962).

17. *Wallace v. Jaffree,* 472 U.S. 38 (1985).

18. *Lemon v. Kurtzman,* 403 U.S. 602 (1971). The *Lemon* test is still good law, but as recently as the 1994 Court term, four justices have urged that the test be abandoned. Here is a settled area of law that may soon become unsettled.

19. *Rosenberger v. Rector and Visitors of the University of Virginia,* 515 U.S. 819 (1995).

20. *Elk Grove United School District v. Newdow,* 542 U.S. 1 (2004).

21. *Van Orden v. Perry,* 545 U.S. 677 (2005).

22. *McCreary County v. American Civil Liberties Union of Kentucky,* 545 U.S. 844 (2005).

23. *West Virginia State Board of Education v. Barnette,* 319 U.S. 624 (1943). The case it reversed was *Minersville School District v. Gobitus,* 310 U.S. 586 (1940).

24. *Cantwell v. Connecticut,* 310 U.S. 296 (1940).

25. *Holt v. Hobbs,* 574 U.S. __ (2015).

26. *Equal Employment Opportunity Commission v. Abercrombie & Fitch Stores, Inc.,* 575 U.S. __ (2015).

27. *Burwell v. Hobby Lobby Stores,* 573 U.S. __ (2014).

28. *Abrams v. United States,* 250 U.S. 616 (1919).

29. *United States v. Carolene Products Company,* 304 U.S. 144 (1938), n4. This footnote is one of the Court's most important doctrines. See Alfred H. Kelly, Winfred A. Harbison, and Herman Belz, *The American Constitution: Its Origins and Development,* 7th ed. (New York: W. W. Norton, 1991), 2:519–23.

30. *Schenck v. United States*, 249 U.S. 47 (1919).

31. *Brandenburg v. Ohio*, 395 U.S. 444 (1969).

32. *Buckley v. Valeo*, 424 U.S. 1 (1976).

33. *McConnell v. Federal Election Commission*, 540 U.S. 93 (2003).

34. *Federal Election Commission v. Wisconsin Right to Life*, 551 U.S. 449 (2007).

35. *Citizens United v. Federal Election Commission*, 558 U.S. 310 (2010).

36. *McCutcheon v. Federal Election Commission*, 572 U.S. __ (2014).

37. Arthur Delaney, "Supreme Court Rolls Back Campaign Finance Restrictions," Huffington Post, March 23, 2010, updated May 25, 2011, www.huffingtonpost.com/2010/01/21/supreme-court-rolls-back_n_431227.html (accessed 7/9/12).

38. *Chaplinsky v. State of New Hampshire*, 315 U.S. 568 (1942).

39. *Dennis v. United States*, 341 U.S. 494 (1951), which upheld the infamous Smith Act of 1940 that provided criminal penalties for those who "willfully and knowingly conspire to teach and advocate the forceful and violent overthrow and destruction of the government."

40. Laura Kipness, *Unwanted Advances* (New York: Harper, 2017).

41. *Capitol Broadcasting Company v. Acting Attorney General*, 405 U.S. 1000 (1972).

42. *R.A.V. v. City of St. Paul*, 505 U.S. 377 (1992).

43. *United States v. Schwimmer*, 279 U.S. 644 (1929).

44. *Bethel School District No. 403 v. Fraser*, 478 U.S. 675 (1986).

45. *Hazelwood School District v. Kuhlmeier*, 484 U.S. 260 (1988).

46. *Morse v. Frederick*, 551 U.S. 393 (2007).

47. *City Council v. Taxpayers for Vincent*, 466 U.S. 789 (1984).

48. Louis Fisher, *American Constitutional Law* (New York: McGraw-Hill, 1990), 546.

49. *Bigelow v. Virginia*, 421 U.S. 809 (1975).

50. *Virginia State Board of Pharmacy v. Virginia Citizens Consumer Council*, 425 U.S. 748 (1976). Later cases restored the rights of lawyers to advertise their services.

51. *Lorillard Tobacco v. Reilly*, 533 U.S. 525 (2001).

52. *Hague v. Committee for Industrial Organization*, 307 U.S. 496 (1939).

53. *Texas v. Johnson*, 491 U.S. 397 (1989).

54. Charles Babington, "Senate Rejects Flag Desecration Amendment," *Washington Post*, June 28, 2006, www.washingtonpost.com/wp-dyn/content/article/2006/06/27/AR2006062701056.html (accessed 11/13/13).

55. *Snyder v. Phelps*, 562 U.S. __ (2011).

56. For a good general discussion of speech plus, see Fisher, *American Constitutional Law*, 544–46. The case upholding the buffer zone against the abortion protesters is *Madsen v. Women's Health Center*, 512 U.S. 753 (1994).

57. *Near v. Minnesota*, 283 U.S. 697 (1931).

58. *New York Times Co. v. United States*, 403 U.S. 713 (1971).

59. *Branzburg v. Hayes*, 408 U.S. 665 (1972).

60. *New York Times Co. v. Sullivan*, 376 U.S. 254 (1964).

61. Shannon Hutzler, "Protecting Informed Public Participation," *Valparaiso University Law Review* 41, no. 3 (Spring 2007): 1235–84.

62. See *Zeran v. America Online*, 129 F3d 327 (4th Cir. 1997).

63. *Roth v. United States*, 354 U.S. 476 (1957).

64. Concurring opinion in *Jacobellis v. Ohio*, 378 U.S. 184 (1964).

65. *Miller v. California*, 413 U.S. 15 (1973).

66. *Reno v. American Civil Liberties Union*, 521 U.S. 844 (1997).

67. *United States v. Williams*, 553 U.S. 285 (2008).

68. *United States v. Playboy Entertainment Group*, 529 U.S. 803 (2000).

69. *Brown v. Entertainment Merchants Association*, 564 U.S. __ (2011).

70. *District of Columbia v. Heller*, 554 U.S. 570 (2008).

71. *McDonald v. Chicago*, 561 U.S. 742 (2010).

72. *In re Winship*, 397 U.S. 358 (1970). An outstanding treatment of due process in issues involving the Fourth through Seventh amendments will be found in Fisher, *American Constitutional Law*, chap. 13.

73. *Horton v. California*, 496 U.S. 128 (1990).

74. *Mapp v. Ohio*, 367 U.S. 643 (1961). Although Mapp went free in this case, she was later convicted in New York on narcotics trafficking charges and served 9 years of a 20-year sentence.

75. For a good discussion of the issue, see Fisher, *American Constitutional Law*, pp. 884–9.

76. *United States v. Grubbs*, 547 U.S. 90 (2006).

77. *National Treasury Employees Union v. Von Raab*, 489 U.S. 656 (1989).

78. *Skinner v. Railway Labor Executives' Association*, 489 U.S. 602 (1989).

79. *Vernonia School District 47J v. Acton*, 515 U.S. 646 (1995).

80. *Chandler v. Miller*, 520 U.S. 305 (1997).

81. *Florida v. Jardines*, 569 U.S. __ (2013).

82. *United States v. Jones*, 132 S. 565 U.S. __ (2012).

83. *Maryland v. King*. 569 U.S. __ (2013).

84. *Riley v. California*, 573 U.S. __ (2014).

85. *Terry v. Ohio*, 392 U.S. 1 (1968).

86. Marjorie Cohn, "NSA Metadata Collection: Fourth Amendment Violation," JURIST, January 15, 2014, http://jurist.org/forum/2014/01/marjorie-cohn-nsa-metadata.php (accessed 4/19/16).

87. Edwin S. Corwin and J. W. Peltason, *Understanding the Constitution* (New York: Holt, 1967), 286.

88. *Benton v. Maryland*, 395 U.S. 784 (1969).

89. *Miranda v. Arizona*, 348 U.S. 436 (1966).

90. *Berman v. Parker*, 348 U.S. 26 (1954). For a thorough analysis of the case, see Benjamin Ginsberg, "*Berman v. Parker*: Congress, the Court, and the Public Purpose," *Polity* 4 (1971): 48–75. For a later application of the case that suggests that "just compensation"—defined as something approximating market value—is about all a

property owner can hope for protection against a public taking of property, see Theodore Lowi et al., *Poliscide: Big Government, Big Science, Lilliputian Politics*, 2nd ed. (Lanham, MD: University Press of America, 1990), 267–70.

91. *Kelo v. City of New London*, 545 U.S. 469 (2005).
92. *Gideon v. Wainwright*, 372 U.S. 335 (1963).
93. *Wiggins v. Smith*, 539 U.S. 510 (2003).
94. For further discussion of these issues, see Corwin and Peltason, *Understanding the Constitution*, 319–23.
95. *Furman v. Georgia*, 408 U.S. 238 (1972).
96. *Gregg v. Georgia*, 428 U.S. 153 (1976).
97. Death Penalty Information Center, "Facts about the Death Penalty," October 11, 2018, https://deathpenalty info.org/documents/FactSheet.pdf (accessed 10/12/18).
98. *Kennedy v. Louisiana*, 554 U.S. 407 (2008).
99. *Snyder v. Louisiana*, 552 U.S. 472 (2008).
100. *Glossip v. Gross,* 576 U.S. __ (2015).
101. *Hudson v. McMillan*, 503 U.S. 1 (1992).
102. *Miller v. Alabama*, 567 U.S. __ (2012).
103. *Olmstead v. United States*, 277 U.S. 438 (1928). See also David M. O'Brien, *Constitutional Law and Politics*, vol. 1, 6th ed. (New York: W. W. Norton, 2005), 76–84.
104. *West Virginia State Board of Education v. Barnette* 319 U.S. 624 (1943).
105. *NAACP v. Alabama ex rel. Patterson*, 357 U.S. 449 (1958).
106. *Griswold v. Connecticut*, 381 U.S. 479 (1965).
107. *Griswold*, concurring opinion. In 1972 the Court extended the privacy right to unmarried women: *Eisenstadt v. Baird*, 405 U.S. 438 (1972).
108. *Roe v. Wade*, 410 U.S. 113 (1973).
109. *Webster v. Reproductive Health Services*, 492 U.S. 490 (1989), which upheld a Missouri law that restricted the use of public medical facilities for abortion. The decision opened the way for other states to limit the availability of abortion.
110. *Planned Parenthood of Southeastern Pennsylvania v. Casey*, 505 U.S. 833 (1992).
111. *Ayotte v. Planned Parenthood*, 546 U.S. 320 (2006).
112. *Gonzales v. Carhart*, 550 U.S. 124 (2007).
113. *Bowers v. Hardwick*, 478 U.S. 186 (1986).
114. *Lawrence v. Texas*, 539 U.S. 558 (2003).
115. *Lawrence* (2003).
116. It is worth recalling here the provision of the Ninth Amendment: "The enumeration in the Constitution, of certain rights, shall not be construed to deny or disparage others retained by the people."
117. *Obergefell v. Hodges*, 576 U.S. __ (2015).
118. Arthur L. Caplan, ed., *The Case of Terri Schiavo: Ethics at the End of Life* (Amherst, NY: Prometheus Books, 2016).
119. *Gonzales v. Oregon*, 546 U.S. 243 (2006).
120. Daniel J. Solove, *Nothing to Hide: The False Tradeoff between Privacy and Security* (New Haven, CT: Yale University Press, 2011).

CHAPTER 5

1. Maia Silber, "A Trailblazing Transgender Midshipman Navigates an Uncertain Path in the Wake of Trump's Tweet." *Washington Post*, July 29, 2017, www.washingtonpost.com/lifestyle/style/a-trailblazing-transgender-midshipman-navigates-an-uncertain-path-in-the-wake-of-trumps-tweet/2017/07/29/bf92a6c6-73c5-11e7-9eac-d56bd5568db8_story.html?utm_term=.34e163b1fd55 (accessed 2/3/18).
2. Silber, "Trailblazing Transgender Midshipman." See also "A Transgender Midshipman Fights Trump's Ban," CNN, November 21, 2017, www.cnn.com/2017/11/21/politics/trump-transgender-military-ban-second-order/index.html (accessed 2/3/18).
3. Mark Joseph Stern, "Trump Administration Relents, for Now: Trans Americans May Enlist in the Military Starting Monday," Slate, December 30, 2017, slate.com/news-and-politics/2017/12/trump-administration-wont-appeal-trans-troops-ban-to-the-supreme-court.html (accessed 2/3/18).
4. Paula Baker, "The Domestication of Politics: Women and American Political Society, 1780–1920," *American Historical Review* 89 (June 1984): 620–47.
5. *Dred Scott v. Sandford*, 60 U.S. 393 (1857).
6. August Meier and Elliott Rudwick, *From Plantation to Ghetto* (New York: Hill and Wang, 1976), 184–88.
7. Jill Dupont, "Susan B. Anthony," New York Notes (Albany: New York State Commission on the Bicentennial of the U.S. Constitution, 1988), 3.
8. *Plessy v. Ferguson*, 163 U.S. 537 (1896).
9. Dupont, "Susan B. Anthony," 4.
10. The prospect of a "fair employment practices" law tied to the commerce power produced the Dixiecrat break with the Democratic Party in 1948. The Democratic Party organization of the States of the Old Confederacy seceded from the national party and nominated its own candidate, the then-Democratic governor of South Carolina, Strom Thurmond, who later became a Republican senator. This almost cost President Truman the election.
11. This was based on the provision in Article VI of the Constitution that "all treaties made…under the Authority of the United States" shall be the "supreme Law of the Land." The commission recognized that if the U.S. Senate ratified what became the Universal Declaration of Human Rights (a treaty), then that power could be used as the constitutional umbrella for effective civil rights legislation. The Supreme Court had recognized in *Missouri v. Holland*, 252 U.S. 416 (1920), that a treaty could enlarge federal power at the expense of the states.
12. *Missouri ex rel. Gaines v. Canada*, 305 U.S. 337 (1938).
13. *Sweatt v. Painter*, 339 U.S. 629 (1950).
14. *Shelley v. Kraemer*, 334 U.S. 1 (1948).
15. The District of Columbia case came up, too; but since the District of Columbia is not a state, this case did not

directly involve the Fourteenth Amendment and its equal protection clause. The plaintiffs confronted the Court on the same grounds, however—that segregation is inherently unequal. Their victory in effect was "incorporation in reverse," with equal protection moving from the Fourteenth Amendment to become part of the Bill of Rights. See *Bolling v. Sharpe*, 347 U.S. 497 (1954).

16. *Brown v. Board of Education of Topeka, Kansas*, 347 U.S. 483 (1954).

17. The Supreme Court first declared that race was a suspect classification requiring strict scrutiny in the decision *Korematsu v. United States*, 323 U.S. 214 (1944). In this case, the Court upheld President Roosevelt's executive order of 1941 allowing the military to exclude persons of Japanese ancestry from the West Coast and to place them in internment camps. It is one of the few cases in which classification based on race survived strict scrutiny.

18. The two most important cases were *Cooper v. Aaron*, 358 U.S. 1 (1958), which required Little Rock, Arkansas, to desegregate, and *Griffin v. Prince Edward County School Board*, 377 U.S. 218 (1964), which forced all the schools of that Virginia county to reopen after five years of closing to avoid desegregation.

19. In *Cooper v. Aaron*, the Supreme Court ordered immediate compliance with the lower court's desegregation order and went beyond that with a stern warning that it is "emphatically the province and duty of the judicial department to say what the law is."

20. *Shuttlesworth v. Birmingham Board of Education of Jefferson City* 358 U.S. 101 (1958) upheld a "pupil placement" plan purporting to assign pupils on various bases, with no mention of race. This case interpreted *Brown* to mean that school districts had to stop explicit racial discrimination but were under no obligation to take positive steps to desegregate. For a while black parents were doomed to a case-by-case approach.

21. For good treatments of this long stretch of the struggle of the federal courts to integrate the schools, see Paul Brest and Sanford Levinson, *Processes of Constitutional Decision-Making: Cases and Materials*, 2nd ed. (Boston: Little, Brown, 1983), 471–80; and Alfred H. Kelly, Winfred A. Harbison, and Herman Belz, *The American Constitution: Its Origins and Development*, 6th ed. (New York: W. W. Norton, 1983), 610–16.

22. Aimee Green, "Elmer's Restaurant Says It Made Black Man Prepay Because He Sat in a Bar, Ordered Alcohol," *Oregon Live*, October 29, 2015, www.oregonlive.com/clark-county/index.ssf/2015/10/elmers_told_state_investigator.html (accessed 8/2/18).

23. See Hamil Harris, "For Blacks, Cabs Can Be Hard to Get," *Washington Post*, July 21, 1994, J1.

24. For a thorough analysis of the Office for Civil Rights, see Jeremy Rabkin, "Office for Civil Rights," in *The Politics of Regulation*, ed. James Q. Wilson (New York: Basic Books, 1980).

25. This was an accepted way of using quotas or ratios to determine statistically that blacks or other minorities were being excluded from schools or jobs and then, on the basis of that statistical evidence, to authorize the Justice Department to bring suits in individual cases and class-action suits. In most segregated situations outside the South, it is virtually impossible to identify and document an intent to discriminate.

26. *Swann v. Charlotte-Mecklenberg Board of Education*, 402 U.S. 1 (1971).

27. *Milliken v. Bradley*, 418 U.S. 717 (1974).

28. For a good evaluation of the Boston effort, see Gary Orfield, *Must We Bus? Segregated Schools and National Policy* (Washington, DC: Brookings Institution, 1978), 144–6. See also Bob Woodward and Scott Armstrong, *The Brethren: Inside the Supreme Court* (New York: Simon and Schuster, 1979), 426–27; and J. Anthony Lukas, *Common Ground* (New York: Random House, 1986).

29. *Board of Education v. Dowell*, 498 U.S. 237 (1991).

30. *Parents Involved in Community Schools v. Seattle School District No. 1*, 551 U.S. 701 (2007).

31. *Griggs v. Duke Power Company*, 401 U.S. 424 (1971). See also Allan Sindler, *Bakke, DeFunis, and Minority Admissions* (New York: Longman, 1978), 180–89.

32. For a good treatment of these issues, see Charles O. Gregory and Harold A. Katz, *Labor and the Law* (New York: W. W. Norton, 1979), chap. 17.

33. In 1970 this act was amended to outlaw for five years literacy tests as a condition for voting in all states.

34. Joint Center for Political Studies, *Black Elected Officials: A National Roster—1988* (Washington, DC: Joint Center for Political Studies Press, 1988), 9–10. For a comprehensive analysis and evaluation of the Voting Rights Act, see Bernard Grofman and Chandler Davidson, eds., *Controversies in Minority Voting: The Voting Rights Act in Perspective* (Washington, DC: Brookings Institution, Press, 1992).

35. Ford Fessenden, "Ballots Cast by Blacks and Older Voters Were Tossed in Far Greater Numbers," *New York Times*, November 12, 2001, A17.

36. Aaron Blake, "Texas Redistricting Case: Five Things You Need to Know," *Washington Post*, December 13, 2011, www.washingtonpost.com/blogs/the-fix/post/texas-redistricting-case-five-things-you-need-to-know/2011/12/13/gIQAdowHsO_blog.html; Manny Fernandez, "Federal Judges Approve Final Texas Redistricting Maps," *New York Times*, February 28, 2012, www.nytimes.com/2012/02/29/us/final-texas-redistricting-maps-approved.html (accessed 6/22/12).

37. *Shelby County v. Holder*, 570 U.S. __ (2013).

38. *Crawford v. Marion County Election Board*, 553 U.S. 181 (2008). See also David Stout, "Supreme Court Upholds Voter Identification Law in Indiana," *New York Times*, April 29, 2008, www.nytimes.com/2008/04/29/washington/28cnd-scotus.html (accessed 1/13/14).

39. See Douglas S. Massey and Nancy A. Denton, *American Apartheid: Segregation and the Making of the Underclass* (Cambridge, MA: Harvard University Press, 1993), chap. 7.

40. Michael Powell, "Bank Accused of Pushing Mortgage Deals on Blacks," *New York Times*, June 6, 2009, www.nytimes.com/2009/06/07/us/07baltimore.html; Charlie Savage, "Countrywide Will Settle a Bias Suit," *New York Times*, December 22, 2011, B1.

41. *Loving v. Virginia*, 388 U.S. 1 (1967).

42. *Windsor v. United States*, 699 F.3d 169 2nd Cir. (2012).

43. *Adarand Constructors Inc. v. Pena*, 515 U.S. 200 (1995).

44. *Fisher v. University of Texas*, 570 U.S. __ (2013).

45. *Fisher v. University of Texas*, 579 U. S. __ (2016).

46. See Jane J. Mansbridge, *Why We Lost the ERA* (Chicago: University of Chicago Press, 1986); and Gilbert Steiner, *Constitutional Inequality* (Washington, DC: Brookings Institution Press, 1985).

47. See *Frontiero v. Richardson*, 411 U.S. 677 (1973).

48. See *Craig v. Boren*, 429 U.S. 190 (1976).

49. Claire Zillman, "Barnes & Noble Is Latest Retailer to Face Transgender Discrimination Lawsuit," *Fortune*, May 7, 2015, http://fortune.com/2015/05/07/barnes-noble-transgender-lawsuit/ (accessed 12/23/15).

50. *Franklin v. Gwinnett County Public Schools*, 503 U.S. 60 (1992).

51. Jennifer Halperin, "Women Step Up to Bat," *Illinois Issues* 21 (September 1995): 11–14.

52. Joan Biskupic and David Nakamura, "Court Won't Review Sports Equity Ruling," *Washington Post*, April 22, 1997, A1.

53. Debra DeMeis and Rosanna Hertz, "Sex, Sports, and Title IX on Campus: The Triumphs and Travails," *Daily Beast*, June 22, 2012, www.dailybeast.com/articles/2012/06/22/sex-sports-and-title-ix-on-campus-the-triumphs-and-travails.html (accessed 6/22/12).

54. *United States v. Virginia*, 518 U.S. 515 (1996).

55. Judith Havemann, "Two Women Quit Citadel over Alleged Harassment," *Washington Post*, January 13, 1997, A1.

56. Petula Dvorak, "The Citadel Didn't Want to Admit Women. but Once This Woman Got In, She Was Unstoppable," *Washington Post*, October 27, 2016, www.citadel.edu/root/the-citadel-didnt-want-to-admit-women-but-once-this-woman-got-in-she-was-unstoppable (accessed 10/9/18).

57. *Meritor Savings Bank v. Vinson*, 477 U.S. 57 (1986). See also Gwendolyn Mink, *Hostile Environment: The Political Betrayal of Sexually Harassed Women* (Ithaca, NY: Cornell University Press, 2000), 28–32.

58. *Harris v. Forklift Systems, Inc.*, 510 U.S. 17 (1993).

59. *Burlington Industries v. Ellerth*, 524 U.S. 742 (1998); *Faragher v. City of Boca Raton*, 524 U.S. 775 (1998).

60. Laura Kipness, *Unwanted Advances: Sexual Paranoia Comes to Campus* (New York: Harper, 2017).

61. *Ledbetter v. Goodyear Tire and Rubber Co.*, 550 U.S. 618 (2007).

62. Sarah Kliff, "A Stunning Chart Shows the True Cause of the Gender Wage Gap," Vox, February 19, 2018, www.vox.com/2018/2/19/17018380/gender-wage-gap-childcare-penalty (accessed 10/9/18).

63. New Mexico had a different history because not many Anglos settled there initially. (*Anglo* is the term for a non-Hispanic white, generally of European background.) Mexican Americans had considerable power in territorial legislatures between 1865 and 1912. See Lawrence H. Fuchs, *The American Kaleidoscope* (Hanover, NH: University Press of New England, 1990), 239–40.

64. *Salvatierra v. Del Rio Independent School District*, 33 S.W.2d 790 (Tex. Civ. App. 1930).

65. *Mendez v. Westminster*, 64 F. Supp. 544 (S.D. Cal. 1946), aff'd, 161 F.2d 774 (9th Cir. 1947) (en banc).

66. On the United Farm Workers and César Chávez, see Marshall Ganz, *Why David Sometimes Wins: Leadership, Organization, and Strategy in the California Farm Worker Movement* (New York: Oxford University Press, 2009); Miriam Pawel, *The Union of Their Dreams: Power, Hope and Struggle in Cesar Chavez's Farm Worker Movement* (New York: Bloomsbury Press, 2010); and Jacques E. Levy, *Cesar Chavez: Autobiography of La Causa* (Minneapolis: University of Minnesota Press, 2007).

67. *United States v. Texas*, 579 U.S. __ (2016).

68. Dick Kirschten, "Not Black and White," *National Journal*, March 2, 1991, 497.

69. *Arizona v. United States*, 567 U.S. __ (2012); Robert Barnes, "Supreme Court Rejects Much of Arizona Immigration Law," *Washington Post*, June 25, 2012, www.washingtonpost.com/politics/supreme-court-rules-on-arizona-immigration-law/2012/06/25/gJQA0Nrm1V_story.html?hpid5zl (accessed 6/25/12).

70. *United States v. Wong Kim Ark*, 169 U.S. 649 (1898).

71. *Korematsu v. United States*, 323 U.S. 214 (1944).

72. Children of the Camps, "Historical Documents: Civil Liberties Act of 1988," http://pbs.org/childofcamp/history/civilact.html (accessed 2/17/08).

73. *Lau v. Nichols*, 414 U.S. 563 (1974).

74. Not all Native American tribes agreed with this, including the Navajos. See Ronald Takaki, *A Different Mirror: A History of Multicultural America* (Boston: Little, Brown, 1993), 238–45.

75. On the resurgence of Native American political activity, see Stephen Cornell, *The Return of the Native: American Indian Political Resurgence* (New York: Oxford University Press, 1990); and Dee Brown, *Bury My Heart at Wounded Knee* (New York: Holt, Rinehart, 1971).

76. See the discussion in Robert A. Katzmann, *Institutional Disability: The Saga of Transportation Policy for the Disabled* (Washington, DC: Brookings Institution Press, 1986).

77. For example, after pressure from the Justice Department, one of the nation's largest rental-car companies agreed to make special hand controls available to any customer requesting them. See "Avis Agrees to Equip Cars for Disabled," *Los Angeles Times*, September 2, 1994, D1.

78. For more, see Dale Carpenter, *Flagrant Conduct: The Story of Lawrence v. Texas* (New York: W. W. Norton, 2013).

79. *Bowers v. Hardwick*, 478 U.S. 186 (1986).

80. *Romer v. Evans*, 517 U.S. 620 (1996).

81. *Lawrence v. Texas*, 539 U.S. 558 (2003).

82. *Obergefell v. Hodges*, 576 U.S. __ (2015).

83. Pew Research Center, "Changing Attitudes on Gay Marriage," June 26, 2017, www.pewforum.org/fact-sheet/changing-attitudes-on-gay-marriage/ (accessed 10/9/18).

84. The Department of Health, Education, and Welfare (HEW) was the cabinet department charged with administering most federal social programs. In 1980, when education programs were transferred to the newly created Department of Education, HEW was renamed the Department of Health and Human Services.

85. *Regents of the University of California v. Bakke*, 438 U.S. 265 (1978).

86. See, for example, *United Steelworkers v. Weber*, 443 U.S. 193 (1979); and *Fullilove v. Klutznick*, 448 U.S. 448 (1980).

87. *Adarand Constructors Inc. v. Peña*.

88. *Gratz v. Bollinger*, 539 U.S. 244 (2003).

89. *Grutter v. Bollinger*, 539 U.S. 306 (2003).

90. *Fisher v. University of Texas*.

91. There are still many genuine racists in America, but with the exception of a lunatic fringe, made up of neo-Nazis and members of the Ku Klux Klan, most racists are too ashamed or embarrassed to take part in normal political discourse. They are not included in either category here.

92. *Slaughterhouse Cases*, 83 U.S. 36 (1873).

CHAPTER 6

1. Suzanna Hupp, "In Their Own Words: The Gun Rights Advocate," *Texas Monthly,* March 23, 2016, www.texasmonthly.com/list/in-their-own-words/the-gun-rights-advocate/ (accessed 3/3/18).

2. Brianna Sacks, "After Florida School Shooting, Several Survivors and Victims' Parents Pan Trump's Idea to Arm Teachers," BuzzFeed News, February 24, 2018, www.buzzfeed.com/briannasacks/students-and-parents-react-to-armed-teacher-proposal?utm_term=.rtNPqM580#.xrVbnry1A (accessed 3/3/8).

3. Jeffrey M. Jones, "U.S. Preference for Stricter Gun Laws Highest since 1993," Gallup Social & Policy Issues, March 14, 2018, http://news.gallup.com/poll/229562/preference-stricter-gun-laws-highest-1993.aspx (accessed 5/30/18).

4. Alvin Chang, "Gun Sales Usually Skyrocket after Mass Shootings. But Not This Time," Vox, March 7, 2018, www.vox.com/2018/3/7/17066352/gun-sales-mass-shooting-data (accessed 5/30/18).

5. Samantha Smith, "Young People Less Likely to View Iraqi, Syrian Refugees as Major Threat to U.S.," Pew Research Center, February 3, 2017, www.pewresearch.org/fact-tank/2017/02/03/young-people-less-likely-to-view-iraqi-syrian-refugees-as-major-threat-to-u-s/ (accessed 4/3/18).

6. Milton Lodge and Charles Taber, "Three Steps toward a Theory of Motivated Political Reasoning," in *Elements of Reason: Cognition, Choice, and the Bounds of Rationality*, ed. Arthur Lupia, Mathew D. McCubbins, and Samuel L. Popkin (London: Cambridge University Press, 2000); David Redlawsk, "Hot Cognition or Cool Consideration? Testing the Effects of Motivated Reasoning on Political Decision Making," *Journal of Politics* 64 (2002): 1021–44; David Redlawsk, Andrew Civettini, and Karen Emmerson, "The Affective Tipping Point: Do Motivated Reasoners Ever 'Get It'?" *Political Psychology* 31, no. 4 (2010): 563–93.

7. Caroline J. Tolbert, David P. Redlawsk,, and Kellen J. Gracey, "Racial Attitudes and Emotional Responses to the 2016 Republican Candidates," *Journal of Elections, Public Opinion and Parties* 28, no. 2 (2018): 245–62.

8. George E. Marcus, W. Russell Neuman, and Michael MacKuen, *Affective Intelligence and Political Judgment* (Chicago: University of Chicago Press, 2000).

9. Juliana Menasce Horowitz, "In 2017, Americans Narrowly Opposed Allowing Teachers and School Officials to Carry Guns," Pew Research Center, Fact Tank, February 23, 2018, www.pewresearch.org/fact-tank/2018/02/23/in-2017-americans-narrowly-opposed-allowing-teachers-and-school-officials-to-carry-guns/ (accessed 3/17/18).

10. Pew Research Center, "Beyond Red vs. Blue: The Political Typology. Section 6: Foreign Affairs, Terrorism and Privacy," June 26, 2014, www.people-press.org/2014/06/26/section-6-foreign-affairs-terrorism-and-privacy/ (accessed 3/11/16).

11. Richard Wike and Katie Simmons, "Global Support for Principle of Free Expression, but Opposition to Some Forms of Speech: Americans Especially Likely to Embrace Individual Liberties," Pew Research Center, November 18, 2015, www.pewglobal.org/2015/11/18/global-support-for-principle-of-free-expression-but-opposition-to-some-forms-of-speech/ (accessed 11/18/15).

12. Anthony Cilluffo, "5 Facts about Student Loans," Pew Research Center, Fact Tank, August 24, 2017, www.pewresearch.org/fact-tank/2017/08/24/5-facts-about-student-loans/ (accessed 3/17/18).

13. Paul R. Abramson, *Political Attitudes in America* (San Francisco: Freeman, 1983).

14. Pew Research Center, "Large Majorities See Checks and Balances, Right to Protest as Essential for Democracy," March 2, 2017, www.people-press.org/2017/03/02/large-majorities-see-checks-and-balances-right-to-protest-as-essential-for-democracy/ (accessed 3/2/18).

15. Jocelyn Kiley, "U.S. Public Sees Russian Role in Campaign Hacking, But Is Divided Over New Sanctions." Pew Research Center, January 10, 2017, www.pewresearch.org/fact-tank/2017/01/10/u-s-public-says-russia-hacked-campaign/ (accessed 3/17/18).

16. Rob Suls, "Share of Democrats Calling Russia 'Greatest Danger' to U.S. Is at Its Highest since End of Cold War."

Pew Research Center, April 20, 2017, www.pewresearch.org/fact-tank/2017/04/20/share-of-democrats-calling-russia-greatest-danger-to-u-s-at-its-highest-since-end-of-cold-war/ (accessed 4/3/18).

17. See Paul M. Sniderman and Edward G. Carmines, *Reaching beyond Race* (Cambridge, MA: Harvard University Press, 1997).

18. Lydia Saad, "Conservative Lead in U.S. Ideology Is Down to Single Digits," Gallup, January 11, 2018, http://news.gallup.com/poll/225074/conservative-lead-ideology-down-single-digits.aspx (accessed 3/17/18).

19. Douglas R. Oxley et al., "Political Attitudes Vary with Physiological Traits," *Science* 321, no. 5896 (September 19, 2008): 1667–70. See also Jeffrey Mondak, *Personality and the Foundation of Political Behavior* (Cambridge: Cambridge University Press, 2010).

20. John Alford, Carolyn Funk, and John Hibbing, "Are Political Orientations Genetically Transmitted?" *American Political Science Review* 99, no. 2 (2005): 153–67; Rich Morin, "Study on Twins Suggests Our Political Beliefs May Be Hard-Wired," Pew Research Center, Fact Tank, December 9, 2013, www.pewresearch.org/fact-tank/2013/12/09/study-on-twins-suggests-our-political-beliefs-may-be-hard-wired/ (accessed 1/20/14).

21. See Angus Campbell et al., *The American Voter* (New York: Wiley, 1960), 147.

22. Betsy Sinclair, *The Social Citizen: Peer Networks and Political Behavior* (Chicago: University of Chicago Press, 2012).

23. Pew Research Center, "Support for Same-Sex Marriage Grows, Even among Groups That Had Been Skeptical," June 26, 2017, www.people-press.org/2017/06/26/support-for-same-sex-marriage-grows-even-among-groups-that-had-been-skeptical/ (accessed 5/21/18).

24. Jennifer A. Heerwig and Brian J. McCabe, "Education and Social Desirability Bias: The Case of a Black Presidential Candidate," *Social Science Quarterly* 90, no. 3 (2009): 674–86.

25. Raymond E. Wolfinger and Steven J. Rosenstone, *Who Votes?* (New Haven, CT: Yale University Press, 1980). See also Steven J. Rosenstone and John Mark Hansen, *Mobilization, Participation, and Democracy in America* (New York: Macmillan, 1993).

26. Frey, William. "The U.S. Will Become Minority White in 2045, Census Predicts: Youthful Minorities Are Engines Future Growth." Brookings Institution, March 14, 2018, www.brookings.edu/blog/the-avenue/2018/03/14/the-us-will-become-minority-white-in-2045-census-projects/?utm_campaign=Brookings%20Brief&utm_source=hs_email&utm_medium=email&utm_content=61375295 (accessed 3/17/18).

27. Katherine Tate, *Black Faces in the Mirror* (Princeton, NJ: Princeton University Press, 1993).

28. Pew Research Center. "On Views of Race and Inequality, Blacks and Whites Are Worlds Apart: About Four-in-Ten Blacks Are Doubtful That the U.S. Will Ever Achieve Racial Equality," June 27, 2016, www.pewsocialtrends.org/2016/06/27/on-views-of-race-and-inequality-blacks-and-whites-are-worlds-apart/ (accessed 4/3/18).

29. Tate, *Black Faces*.

30. Brakkton Booker, "How Equal Is American Opportunity? Survey Shows Attitudes Vary by Race," National Public Radio, September 21, 2015, www.npr.org/sections/thetwo-way/2015/09/21/442068004/how-equal-is-american-opportunity-survey-shows-attitudes-vary-by-race (accessed 3/11/16).

31. Pew Research Center, "Across Racial Lines, More Say Nation Needs to Make Changes to Achieve Racial Equality," August 5, 2015, www.people-press.org/2015/08/05/across-racial-lines-more-say-nation-needs-to-make-changes-to-achieve-racial-equality/8-4-2015_02a/ (accessed 2/24/16).

32. Jens Manuel Krogstad, "Key Facts about the Latino Vote in 2016," October 14, 2016; and Flores, Antonio, "Facts on U.S. Latinos, 2015. Statistical Portrait of Hispanics in the United States," September 18, 2017, Pew Research Center, www.pewresearch.org/fact-tank/2016/10/14/key-facts-about-the-latino-vote-in-2016/ and www.pewhispanic.org/2016/04/19/statistical-portrait-of-hispanics-in-the-united-states-key-charts/ (accessed 3/17/18).

33. Anna Brown and Renee Stepler, "Statistical Portrait of the Foreign-Born Population in the United States, 1960–2013," Pew Research Center, September 28, 2015, www.pewhispanic.org/2015/09/28/statistical-portrait-of-the-foreign-born-population-in-the-united-states-1960-2013-key-charts/#2013-fb-origin (accessed 12/22/15).

34. Author analysis of 2014 Cooperative Election Study, Harvard University, released February 2015, http://projects.iq.harvard.edu/cces/home (accessed 3/4/16); Pew Research Center, "Broad Public Support for Legal Status for Undocumented Immigrants, Other Attitudes About Immigration More Mixed, June 4, 2015," www.people-press.org/2015/06/04/broad-public-support-for-legal-status-for-undocumented-immigrants/ (accessed 3/17/18).

35. Pew Research Center, "Latinos and the New Trump Administration," February 23, 2017, www.pewhispanic.org/2017/02/23/latinos-and-the-new-trump-administration/ (accessed 4/3/17).

36. Matt Barreto and Gary M. Segura, *Latino America: How America's Most Dynamic Population Is Poised to Transform the Politics of the Nation* (New York: Public Affairs, 2014).

37. "Trump Gets Negative Ratings for Many Personal Traits, but Most Say He Stands Up for His Beliefs," Pew Research Center, October 1, 2018, www.people-press.org/2018/10/01/trump-gets-negative-ratings-for-many-personal-traits-but-most-say-he-stands-up-for-his-beliefs/ (accessed 10/10/18).

38. Michael Lipka, "Religious 'Nones' Are Not Only Growing, They're Becoming More Secular," *Pew Research Center, Fact Tank*, November 11, 2015, www.pewresearch.org/fact-tank/2015/11/11/religious-nones-are-not-only-growing-theyre-becoming-more-secular/ (accessed 11/11/15).

39. 2014 Cooperative Comparative Election Study.

40. See Richard Lau and David Redlawsk, *How Voters Decide: Information Processing during an Election Campaign* (New York: Cambridge University Press, 2006).

41. Brian Schaffner and Stephen Ansolabehere, "CCES Common Content, 2014," Harvard Dataverse, V2, http://dx.doi.org/10.7910/DVN/XFXJVY (accessed 5/4/16).

42. Morris Fiorina, Samuel Abrams, and Jeremy Pope, *Culture War? The Myth of a Polarized America* (New York: Longman, 2004).

43. Nathan J. Kelly and Peter K. Enns, "Inequality and the Dynamics of Public Opinion: The Self-Reinforcing Link between Economic Inequality and Mass Preferences," *American Journal of Political Science* 54, no. 4 (2010): 855–70; Jacob S. Hacker and Paul Pierson, *Winner-Take-All Politics: How Washington Made the Rich Richer—and Turned Its Back on the Middle Class* (New York: Simon and Schuster, 2010).

44. Larry M. Bartels, "Homer Gets a Tax Cut: Inequality and Public Policy in the American Mind," *Perspectives on Politics* 3, no. 1 (2005): 15–31; Larry Bartels, *Unequal Democracy: The Political Economy of the New Gilded Age* (Princeton, NJ: Princeton University Press, 2008).

45. Thomas E. Mann and Norman J. Ornstein, *It's Even Worse Than It Looks: How the American Constitutional System Collided with the New Politics of Extremism* (New York: Basic Books, 2012).

46. Shaun Bowler, Gary Segura, and Stephen Nicholson, "Earthquakes and Aftershocks: Race, Direct Democracy, and Partisan Change," *American Journal of Political Science* 50 (2006): 146–59. For a more general discussion of the spillover effects of ballot measures on public opinion, see Stephen Nicholson, *Voting the Agenda: Candidates, Elections, and Ballot Propositions* (Princeton, NJ: Princeton University Press, 2005).

47. John R. Zaller, *The Nature and Origins of Mass Opinion* (New York: Cambridge University Press, 1992).

48. Milton Lodge, Kathleen McGraw, and Patrick Stroh, "An Impression-Driven Model of Candidate Evaluation," *American Political Science Review* 83, no. 2 (1989): 399–419.

49. Benjamin I. Page and Robert Y. Shapiro, *The Rational Public: Fifty Years of Trends in Americans' Policy Preferences* (Chicago: University of Chicago Press, 1995); Eugene Wittkopf, *Faces of Internationalism: Public Opinion and Foreign Policy* (Durham, NC: Duke University Press, 1990).

50. Pew Research Center, "In Gay Marriage Debate, Both Supporters and Opponents See Legal Recognition as 'Inevitable,'" June 6, 2013, www.people-press.org/2013/06/06/in-gay-marriage-debate-both-supporters-and-opponents-see-legal-recognition-as-inevitable (accessed 3/19/14).

51. *Varnum v. Brien*, 763 N.W.2d 862 (Iowa 2009).

52. Rebecca J. Kreitzer, Allison J. Hamilton, and Caroline J. Tolbert, "Does Policy Adoption Change Opinions on Minority Rights? The Effects of Legalizing Same-Sex Marriage," *Political Research Quarterly* 67, no. 4 (July 10, 2014): 795–808.

53. *Obergefell v. Hodges*, 576 U.S. __ (2015).

54. Monica Anderson, "For Earth Day, Here's How Americans View Environmental Issues," Pew Research Center, April 20, 2017, www.pewresearch.org/fact-tank/2017/04/20/for-earth-day-heres-how-americans-view-environmental-issues/ (accessed 3/17/18); Brian Kennedy, "Two-Thirds of Americans Give Priority to Developing Alternative Energy over Fossil Fuels," Pew Research Center, January 23, 2017, www.pewresearch.org/fact-tank/2017/01/23/two-thirds-of-americans-give-priority-to-developing-alternative-energy-over-fossil-fuels/ (accessed 3/17/18); Michael Shea, "Trump Will Withdraw U.S. from Paris Climate Agreement," *New York Times*, June 1, 2017, www.nytimes.com/2017/06/01/climate/trump-paris-climate-agreement.html (accessed 3/17/18).

55. Zaller, *Nature and Origins*.

56. Carroll Glynn et al., *Public Opinion*, 2nd ed. (Boulder, CO: Westview, 2004), 293. See also Michael X. Delli Carpini and Scott Keeter, *What Americans Know about Politics and Why It Matters* (New Haven, CT: Yale University Press, 1996).

57. Delli Carpini and Keeter, *What Americans Know*.

58. Adam J. Berinsky, "Assuming the Costs of War: Events, Elites and American Support for Military Conflict," *Journal of Politics* 69, no. 4 (2007): 975–97; Zaller, *Nature and Origins*.

59. Richard R. Lau and David P. Redlawsk, "Advantages and Disadvantages of Cognitive Heuristics in Political Decision Making," *American Journal of Political Science* 45 (October 2001): 951–71; Lau and Redlawsk, *How Voters Decide*.

60. For a discussion of the role of information in politics, see Arthur Lupia and Matthew D. McCubbins, *The Democratic Dilemma: Can Citizens Learn What They Need to Know?* (New York: Cambridge University Press, 1998). See also Shaun Bowler and Todd Donovan, *Demanding Choices: Opinion and Voting in Direct Democracy* (Ann Arbor: University of Michigan Press, 1998). See also Samuel Popkin, *The Reasoning Voter: Communication and Persuasion in Presidential Campaigns* (Chicago: University of Chicago Press, 1991); Arthur Lupia, "Shortcuts versus Encyclopedias: Information and Voting Behavior in California Insurance Reform Elections," *American Political Science Review* 88 (1994): 63–76; and Wendy Rahn, "The Role of Partisan Stereotypes in Information Processing about Political Candidates," *American Journal of Political Science* 37 (1993): 472–96.

61. James Druckman, Erik Petersen, and Rune Slothuus, "How Elite Partisan Polarization Affects Public Opinion Formation," *American Political Science Review* 107, no. 1 (February 2013): 57–79.

62. Lee Rainie et al., "Social Media and Political Engagement," Pew Research Center, October 19, 2012, www.pewinternet.org/2012/10/19/social-media-and-political-engagement (accessed 8/14/14).

63. Tony Dokoupil, "Is the Internet Making Us Crazy? What the New Research Says," *Newsweek*, July 9, 2012, http://mag.newsweek.com/2012/07/08/is-the-internet-making-us-crazy-what-the-new-research-says.html (accessed 3/19/14); Nicholas Carr, *The Shallows: What the Internet Is Doing to Our Brains* (New York: W. W. Norton, 2011).

64. Benjamin Ginsberg, *The American Lie: Government by the People and Other Political Fables* (Boulder, CO: Paradigm, 2007).

65. Gerald F. Seib and Michael K. Frisby, "Selling Sacrifice," *Wall Street Journal*, February 5, 1993, 1.

66. Peter Marks, "Adept in Politics and Advertising, 4 Women Shape a Campaign," *New York Times*, November 11, 2001, B6.

67. Donald J. Trump (@realDonaldTrump), "I am being investigated for firing the FBI director by the man who told me to fire the FBI director! Witch Hunt" Twitter, June 16, 2017, 6:07 a.m., https://twitter.com/realdonaldtrump/status/875701471999864833?lang=en (accessed 4/3/18).

68. Donald J. Trump (@realDonaldTrump), "You are witnessing the single greatest WITCH HUNT in American political history - led by some very bad and conflicted people! #MAGA" Twitter, June 15, 2017, 4:57 a.m., https://twitter.com/realdonaldtrump/status/875321478849363968?lang=en (accessed 4/3/18).

69. Jason Gainous and Kevin Wagner, *Tweeting to Power: The Social Media Revolution in American Politics* (New York: Oxford University Press, 2013).

70. *Roe v. Wade*, 410 U.S. 113 (1973).

71. See Gillian Peele, *Revival and Reaction* (Oxford: Clarendon, 1985). See also Connie Paige, *The Right-to-Lifers* (New York: Summit, 1983).

72. See Shanto Iyengar, *Is Anyone Responsible? How Television Frames Political Issues* (Chicago: University of Chicago Press, 1991); and Shanto Iyengar, *Do the Media Govern?* (Thousand Oaks, CA: Sage, 1997).

73. David W. Moore, "Support for Invasion of Iraq Remains Contingent on U.N. Approval," Gallup, November 12, 2002, www.gallup.com/poll/7195/support-invasion-iraq-remains-contigent-un-approval.aspx (accessed 3/2/18); Pew Research Center, "Public Attitudes toward the War in Iraq: 2003–2008," March 19, 2008, www.pewresearch.org/2008/03/19/public-attitudes-toward-the-war-in-iraq-20032008 (accessed 2/19/14).

74. Campbell et al., *The American Voter*.

75. Benjamin I. Page and Robert Y. Shapiro, "The Rational Public: Fifty Years of Trends in Americans' Policy Preferences," (Chicago: University of Chicago Press, 1992).

76. Gerald C. Wright, Rober S. Erikson, and John P. McIver, "Public Opinion and Policy Liberalism in the American States," *American Journal of Political Science* 31, no. 4 (November 1987): 980–1001.

77. Pew Research Center, "Mixed Views of Economic Policies and Health Care Reform Persist: Support for Health Care Principles, Opposition to Package," October 8, 2009, www.people-press.org/2009/10/08/mixed-views-of-economic-policies-and-health-care-reform-persist/ (accessed 2/15/14).

78. Christopher Wlezien, "The Public as Thermostat: Dynamics of Preferences for Spending," *American Journal of Political Science* 39, no. 4 (1995): 981–1000.

79. See Julianna Pacheco, "Attitudinal Policy Feedback and Public Opinion: The Impact of Smoking Bans on Attitudes toward Smokers, Secondhand Smoke, and Anti-Smoking Policies," *Political Research Quarterly* 77, no. 3 (2013): 714–34; Barbara Norrander, "The Multi-Layered Impact of Public Opinion on Capital Punishment Implementation in the American States," *Political Research Quarterly* 53, no. 4 (2000): 771–93; Suzanne Mettler and Joe Soss, "The Consequences of Public Policy for Democratic Citizenship: Bridging Policy Studies and Mass Politics," *Perspectives on Politics* 2, no. 1 (2004): 55–73; Andrea Hetling and Monika L. McDermott, "Judging a Book by Its Cover: Did Perceptions of the 1996 U.S. Welfare Reforms Affect Public Support for Spending on the Poor?" *Journal of Social Policy* 37, no. 3 (2008): 471–87; Joe Soss, "Lessons of Welfare: Policy Design, Political Learning, and Political Action," *American Political Science Review* 93, no. 2 (1999): 363–80; Joe Soss and Sanford F. Schram, "A Public Transformed? Welfare Reform as Policy Feedback," *American Political Science Review* 101, no. 1 (2007): 111.

80. Malcolm E. Jewell, *Representation in State Legislatures* (Lexington: University Press of Kentucky, 1982).

81. Lawrence R. Jacobs and Robert Y. Shapiro, *Politicians Don't Pander: Political Manipulation and the Loss of Democratic Responsiveness* (Chicago: University of Chicago Press, 2000).

82. John Griffin and Brian Newman, "Are Voters Better Represented?" *Journal of Politics* 67 (2005): 1206–27.

83. Bartels, *Unequal Democracy*.

84. Other authors have endorsed Bartels's view that government policy exacerbates income inequality. See, for example, Hacker and Pierson, *Winner-Take-All Politics*.

85. Martin Gilens, "Inequality and Democratic Responsiveness," *Public Opinion Quarterly* 69, no. 5 (2005): 778–96; and Martin Gilens, "Preference Gaps and Inequality in Representation," *PS: Political Science and Politics* 42, no. 2 (2009): 335–41.

86. Robert Dahl, *A Preface to Democratic Theory* (Chicago: University of Chicago Press, 1956).

87. Herbert Asher, *Polling and the Public* (Washington, DC: CQ Press, 2001), 64.

88. Drew DeSilver and Scott Keeter, "The Challenges of Polling When Fewer People Are Available to be Polled," July 21, 2015, www.pewresearch.org/fact-tank/2015/07/21/the-challenges-of-polling-when-fewer-people-are-available-to-be-polled/ (accessed 3/1/16).

89. Michael Kagay and Janet Elder, "Numbers Are No Problem for Pollsters, Words Are," *New York Times*, August 9, 1992, E6.

90. Adam J. Berinsky, "The Two Faces of Public Opinion," *American Journal of Political Science* 43, no. 4 (1999): 1209–30.

91. Lynn Vavreck and Douglas Rivers, "The 2006 Cooperative Congressional Election Study," *Journal of Elections, Public Opinion and Parties* 18, no. 4 (2008): 355–66. See also Simon Jackman and Lynn Vavreck, "Primary Politics: Race, Gender, and Age in the 2008 Democratic Primary," *Journal of Elections, Public Opinion and Parties* 20, no. 2 (2010): 153–86.

92. Nate Silver, "FiveThirtyEight's Pollster Ratings," August 5, 2016, *FiveThirtyEight* (blog), http://projects.fivethirtyeight.com/pollster-ratings/ (accessed 10/16/16).

93. Berinsky, "Two Faces of Public Opinion." See also Adam Berinsky, "Political Context and the Survey Response: The Dynamics of Racial Policy Opinion," *Journal of Politics* 64, no. 2 (2002): 567–84.

94. Pew Research Center. "Are Telephone Polls Understating Support for Trump?" March 31, 2017, www.pewresearch.org/2017/03/31/are-telephone-polls-understating-support-for-trump/ (accessed 3/17/18)

95. Nate Silver, "Which Polls Fared Best (and Worst) in the 2012 Presidential Race," *FiveThirtyEight* (blog), November 10, 2012, http://fivethirtyeight.blogs.nytimes.com/2012/11/10/which-polls-fared-best-and-worst-in-the-2012-presidential-race/ (accessed 2/24/16).

96. Redlawsk, Tolbert, and Donovan, *Why Iowa?*

97. Sasha Issenberg, *The Victory Lab: The Secret Science of Winning Campaigns* (New York: Broadway Books, 2012); Sasha Issenberg, "A More Perfect Union: How President Obama's Campaign Used Big Data to Rally Individual Voters," *MIT Technology Review*, December 19, 2012, www.technologyreview.com/featuredstory/509026/how-obamas-team-used-big-data-to-rally-voters/ (accessed 11/25/15).

98. Nanette Byrnes, "Twitter May Have Predicted the Election," *Technology Review*, December 2, 2016, www.technologyreview.com/s/603010/twitter-may-have-predicted-the-election/ (accessed 8/2/18).

99. Katerina Eva Matsa, Amy Mitchell, and Galen Stocking, "Searching for News: The Flint Water Crisis," April 27, 2017, www.journalism.org/essay/searching-for-news/ (accessed 3/17/18).

100. Chris Taylor, "Triumph of the Nerds: Nate Silver Wins in 50 States," November 7, 2012, http://mashable.com/2012/11/07/nate-silver-wins/#6aWvyWVGcaqq (accessed 2/24/16).

101. "How Popular/Unpopular Is Donald Trump? An Updating Calculation of the President's Approval Rating, Accounting for Each Poll's Quality, Recency, Sample Size and Partisan Lean" *FiveThirtyEight* (blog), June 23, 2017, www.fivethirtyeight.com/features/how-were-tracking-donald-trumps-approval-ratings/ (accessed 3/17/18).

102. Christopher Wlezien and Stuart Soroka, "The Relationship between Public Opinion and Policy," in *Oxford Handbook of Political Behavior*, ed. Russell Dalton and Hans-Dieter Klingemann (New York: Oxford University Press, 2009), 799–817.

103. Gilens, "Inequality and Democratic Responsiveness"; Bartels, *Unequal Democracy*.

104. Ryan Claassen and Benjamin Highton, "Does Policy Debate Reduce Information Effects in Public Opinion? Analyzing the Evolution of Public Opinion on Health Care," *Journal of Politics* 68, no. 2 (2006): 410–20.

CHAPTER 7

1. Patrick Anderson, "Net Neutrality Protest Reaches Sioux Falls, Lincoln Student Takes on the FCC," *Argus Leader*, December 7, 2017, www.argusleader.com/story/news/business-journal/2017/12/07/net-neutrality-protest-sioux-falls-fcc/930819001/ (accessed 3/26/18).

2. Meg McIntyre, "Local High School Students Protest Proposed Rollback of Net Neutrality Rules," *Keene Sentinel*, December 8, 2017, www.sentinelsource.com/news/local/local-high-school-students-protest-proposed-rollback-of-net-neutrality/article_204cec19-3104-58f4-930a-404c65d84e65.html (accessed 3/26/18).

3. Cecilia Kang, "In Protests of Net Neutrality Repeal, Teenage Voices Stood Out," *New York Times*, December 20, 2017, www.nytimes.com/2017/12/20/technology/net-neutrality-repeal-teens.html (accessed 3/26/18).

4. Julian P. Boyd et al., eds., *The Papers of Thomas Jefferson* (Princeton, NJ: Princeton University Press), http://press-pubs.uchicago.edu/founders/documents/amendI_speechs8.html (accessed 5/30/14).

5. Shanto Iyengar, *Media Politics* (New York: W.W. Norton & Company, 2015).

6. Quoted in Rodney Tiffen, "Journalism in the Trump Era," Inside Story, February 24, 2017, http://insidestory.org.au/journalism-in-the-trump-era (accessed 4/4/18).

7. David Folkenflik, "AT&T Deal for Time Warner Casts Renewed Attention on CNN," *NPR*, October 25, 2016, www.npr.org/2016/10/25/499299869/at-t-deal-for-time-warner-casts-renewed-attention-on-cnn (accessed 5/21/18).

8. Columbia Journalism Review, "Resources," https://archives.cjr.org/resources/index.php (accessed 8/2/18).

9. For a criticism of the increasing consolidation of the media, see the essays in Patricia Aufderheide et al., *Conglomerates and the Media* (New York: New Press, 1997).

10. Pew Research Center, "2017 Pew Research Center's American Trends Panel," March 27, 2017,

http://assets.pewresearch.org/wp-content/uploads/sites/13/2017/05/09125944/PJ_2017.05.10_Media-Attitudes_TOPLINE.pdf (accessed 1/22/18).

11. Pew Research Center, "Amid Criticism, Support for Media's 'Watchdog' Role Stands Out," August 8, 2013, www.people-press.org/2013/08/08/amid-criticism-support-for-medias-watchdog-role-stands-out (accessed 4/27/14).

12. Pew Research Center, "Digital News Fact Sheet" August 7, 2017, www.journalism.org/fact-sheet/digital-news/ (accessed 1/22/18).

13. Clay Shirky, *Here Comes Everybody: The Power of Organizing without Organizations* (New York: Penguin Books, 2008).

14. Amy Mitchell, Jesse Holcomb, and Rachel Weisel, "State of the News Media 2016," Pew Research Center, June 15, 2016, www.journalism.org/2016/06/15/state-of-the-news-media-2016/?utm_content=buffer6871f&utm_medium=social&utm_source=twitter.com&utm_campaign=buffer (accessed 3/19/18).

15. Shirky, *Here Comes Everybody*; Mitchell, Holcomb, and Weisel, "State of the News Media 2016."

16. Robert McChesney and John Nichols, *The Death and Life of American Journalism: The Media Revolution That Will Begin the World Again* (New York: Nation Books, 2010).

17. "Newspapers Fact Sheet," Pew Research Center, June 13, 2018, www.journalism.org/fact-sheet/newspapers/ (accessed 10/10/18).

18. Darrell West, *The Next Wave: Using Digital Technology to Further Social and Political Innovation* (Washington, DC: Brookings Institution Press, 2011).

19. Laura Wamsley, "Big Newspapers Are Booming: 'Washington Post' to Add 60 Newsroom Jobs," NPR, December 27, 2016, www.npr.org/sections/thetwo-way/2016/12/27/507140760/big-newspapers-are-booming-washington-post-to-add-sixty-newsroom-jobs (accessed 1/22/18).

20. Michael Barthel, "Circulation and Revenue Fall for Industry Overall," Pew Research Center, June 1, 2017, www.pewresearch.org/fact-tank/2017/06/01/circulation-and-revenue-fall-for-newspaper-industry/(accessed 1/22/18).

21. Eugene Kim, "Jeff Bezos Reinvented the *Washington Post*," *Business Insider,* May, 15 2016, www.businessinsider.com/how-the-washington-post-changed-after-jeff-bezos-acquisition-2016-5/#because-of-its-affiliation-with-bezos-the-post-says-its-now-finding-it-a-lot-easier-to-recruit-engineers-bezos-has-also-instilled-a-much-stronger-culture-of-customer-obsession-post-execs-often-receive-reader-complaint-emails-forwarded-by-bezos-12 (accessed 1/22/18).

22. Mitchell, Holcomb, and Weisel, "State of the News Media 2016."

23. Robert O'Harrow, Jr., "Trump's Bad Bet: How Too Much Debt Drove His Biggest Casino Aground," *Washington Post*, January 18, 2016, www.washingtonpost.com/investigations/trumps-bad-bet-how-too-much-debt-drove-his-biggest-casino-aground/2016/01/18/f67cedc2-9ac8-11e5-8917-653b65c809eb_story.html (accessed 3/9/16); Robert O'Harrow, Jr., "Trump Swam in Mob-Infested Waters in Early Years as an NYC Developer," *Washington Post*, October 16, 2015, www.washingtonpost.com/investigations/trump-swam-in-mob-infested-waters-in-early-years-as-an-nyc-developer/2015/10/16/3c75b918-60a3-11e5-b38e-06883aacba64_story.html (accessed 3/9/16).

24. Tim Hains, "Donald Trump Jr.'s Emails Are Not A 'Smoking Gun' of Anything," RealClear Politics, July 14, 2017, www.realclearpolitics.com/video/2017/07/14/greenwald_donald_trump_jrs_emails_are_not_a_smoking_gun_for_anything_not_evidence_of_any_crime.html (accessed 1/22/18).

25. Mitchell, Holcomb, and Weisel, "State of the News Media 2016."

26. Pew Research Center, "Audio and Podcasting Fact Sheet," July 12, 2018, www.journalism.org/fact-sheet/audio-and-podcasting/ (accessed 9/22/18).

27. Mitchell, Holcomb, and Weisel, "State of the News Media 2016."

28. Pew Research Center, "The Internet's Broader Role in Campaign 2008," January 11, 2008, www.people-press.org/2008/01/11/internets-broader-role-in-campaign-2008/; and "Journalism, Satire or Just Laughs? '*The Daily Show* with Jon Stewart' Examined," May 8, 2008, www.journalism.org/2008/05/08/journalism-satire-or-just-laughs-the-daily-show-with-jon-stewart-examined/ (accessed 9/7/12).

29. West, *The Next Wave*; Edward Glaeser, *Triumph of the City: How Our Greatest Invention Makes Us Richer, Smarter, Greener, Healthier, and Happier* (New York: Penguin Press, 2011).

30. Kristin Lu, "Growth in Mobile News Use Driven by Older Adults." Pew Research Center, June 12, 2017, www.pewresearch.org/fact-tank/2017/06/12/growth-in-mobile-news-use-driven-by-older-adults/ (accessed 3/20/18).

31. Jeffrey Gottfriend and Elisa Shearer, "Americans' Online News Use Is Closing in on TV News Use," Pew Research Center, September 7, 2017, www.pewresearch.org/fact-tank/2017/09/07/americans-online-news-use-vs-tv-news-use/ (accessed 3/20/18); Kristin Bialik and Katerina Eva Matsa, "Key Trends in Social and Digital Media Use," Pew Research Center, October 4, 2017, www.pewresearch.org/fact-tank/2017/10/04/key-trends-in-social-and-digital-news-media/ (accessed 3/20/18).

32. Aaron Smith and Maeve Duggan, "Online Political Videos and Campaign 2012," Pew Research Center, November 2, 2012, www.pewinternet.org/2012/11/02/online-political-videos-and-campaign-2012 (accessed 4/29/14).

33. Pew Research Center, "State of the News Media: Digital News Fact Sheet," August 7, 2017, www.journalism.org/fact-sheet/digital-news/ (accessed 5/21/18).

34. Aaron Smith and Monica Anderson, "Social Media Use in 2018," Pew Research Center, March 1, 2018, www.pewinternet.org/2018/03/01/social-media-use-in-2018/ (accessed 3/19/18).

35. Antony Wilhelm, *Digital Nation: Toward an Inclusive Information Society* (Cambridge, MA: MIT Press, 2006); Paul DiMaggio et al., "Social Implications of the Internet," *Annual Review of Sociology* 27, no. 1 (2001): 307–36.

36. Karen Mossberger, Caroline J. Tolbert, and Mary Stansbury, *Virtual Inequality: Beyond the Digital Divide* (Washington, DC: Georgetown University Press, 2003); Pippa Norris, *Digital Divide: Civic Engagement, Information Poverty, and the Internet Worldwide* (New York: Cambridge University Press, 2001).

37. Karen Mossberger, Caroline Tolbert and Ramona McNeal, "Digital Citizenship," MIT Press, Internet Broadband Fact Sheet, 2008; Pew Research Center, February 5, 2018, www.pewinternet.org/fact-sheet/internet-broadband/ (accessed 3/19/18).

38. U.S. Census Bureau, "Nearly 8 in 10 Americans Have Access to High-Speed Internet," American Community Survey, November 13, 2014, www.census.gov/newsroom/press-releases/2014/cb14-202.html (accessed 3/2/16).

39. Mossberger, Tolbert, and Stansbury, *Virtual Inequality*.

40. Karen Mossberger, Caroline J. Tolbert, and William W. Franko, *Digital Cities: The Internet and the Geography of Opportunity* (New York: Oxford University Press, 2013).

41. Elisa Shearer and Jeffrey Gottfried, "News Use across Social Media Platforms 2017," Pew Research Center, September 7, 2017, www.journalism.org/2017/09/07/news-use-across-social-media-platforms-2017/ (accessed 8/1/18).

42. Thom File, "Voting in America: A Look at the 2016 Presidential Election," *Census Blogs*, May 20, 2017, www.census.gov/newsroom/blogs/random-samplings/2017/05/voting_in_america.html (accessed 3/19/18).

43. Amy Mitchell, Jeffrey Gottfried, and Katerina Eva Matsa, "Political Interest and Awareness Lower among Millennials," Pew Research Center, June 1, 2015, www.journalism.org/2015/06/01/political-interest-and-awareness-lower-among-millennials/ (accessed 12/7/15).

44. Smith and Anderson, "Social Media Use 2018."

45. Elisa Shearer and Jeffrey Gottfried, "News Use across Social Media Platforms 2017," Pew Research Center, September 7, 2017, www.journalism.org/2017/09/07/NEWS-USE-ACROSS-SOCIAL-MEDIA-PLATFORMS-2017/ (accessed 5/21/18).

46. Michael Barthel et al., "The Evolving Role of News on Twitter and Facebook."

47. Jason Gainous and Kevin Wagner, *Tweeting to Power: The Social Media Revolution in American Politics* (New York: Oxford University Press, 2013).

48. Gainous and Wagner, *Tweeting to Power*, 1.

49. Politifact, "Donald Trump's File," www.politifact.com/personalities/donald-trump/ (accessed 1/22/18).

50. Greg Sargent, "This Brutal New Poll Shows That Trump's Safe Space Is Shrinking," *Washington Post,* August 8, 2017, www.washingtonpost.com/blogs/plum-line/wp/2017/08/08/this-brutal-new-poll-shows-that-trumps-safe-space-is-shrinking/?utm_term=.744ad3651728 (accessed 3/8/18).

51. Erin McCann, "United's Apologies: A Timeline," *New York Times*, April 14, 2017, www.nytimes.com/2017/04/14/business/united-airlines-passenger-doctor.html (accessed 5/21/18).

52. Richard Davis, "Interplay: Political Blogging and Journalism," in *iPolitics: Citizens, Elections, and Governing in the New Media Era*, ed. Richard L. Fox and Jennifer M. Ramos (Cambridge: Cambridge University Press, 2012), 76–99.

53. Pew Research Center Publications, "State of the News Media 2010," March 15, 2010, http://pewresearch.org/pubs/1523/state-of-the-news-media-2010 (accessed 9/11/12); West, *The Next Wave*.

54. Karen Mossberger and Caroline J. Tolbert, "Digital Democracy: How Politics Online Is Changing Electoral Participation," in *Oxford Handbook of American Elections and Political Behavior*, ed. Jan E. Leighley (New York: Oxford University Press, 2010), 200–18.

55. Caroline Tolbert and Ramona McNeal, "Unraveling the Effects of the Internet on Political Participation," *Political Research Quarterly* 56, no. 2 (2003): 175–85.

56. Karen Mossberger, Caroline Tolbert, and Ramona McNeal, *Digital Citizenship: The Internet, Society, and Participation* (Cambridge, MA: MIT Press, 2008). See Richard L. Fox and Jennifer M. Ramos, eds., *iPolitics: Citizens, Elections, and Governing in the New Media Era* (Cambridge: Cambridge University Press, 2011).

57. W. R. Neuman, M. R. Just, and A. N. Crigler, *Common Knowledge: News and the Construction of Political Meaning* (Chicago: University of Chicago Press, 1992).

58. A. Healy and D. McNamara, "Verbal Learning and Memory: Does the Modal Model Still Work?" in *Annual Review of Psychology*, vol. 47, ed. J. Spense, J. Darley, and D. Foss (Palo Alto, CA: Annual Reviews, 1996), 143–72.

59. Cass Sunstein, *Republic.com* (Princeton, NJ: Princeton University Press, 2001). See also Mossberger and Tolbert, "Digital Democracy."

60. Michael Margolis and David Resnick, *Politics as Usual: The Cyberspace "Revolution"* (Thousand Oaks, CA: Sage, 2000).

61. West, *The Next Wave*; McChesney and Nichols, *Death and Life of American Journalism*.

62. Hannah Roberts, "This Is What Fake News Actually Looks Like—We Ranked 11 Election Stories That Went Viral on Facebook," *Business Insider*, November 17, 2016, www.businessinsider.com/fake-presidential-election-news-viral-facebook-trump-clinton-2016-11 (accessed 5/21/18).

63. Krysten Crawford, "Stanford Study Examines Fake News and the 2016 Presidential Election," *Stanford News*, January 18, 2017, www.news.stanford.edu/2017/01/18/stanford-study-examines-fake-news-2016-presidential-election/ (accessed 5/21/18).

64. Matthew A. Baum, "Preaching to the Choir or Converting the Flock: Presidential Communication Strategies in

the Age of Three Medias," in *iPolitics: Citizens, Elections, and Governing in the New Media Era*, ed. Richard L. Fox and Jennifer M. Ramos (Cambridge: Cambridge University Press, 2012), 183–205.

65. Eli Pariser, *The Filter Bubble: What the Internet Is Hiding from You* (New York: Penguin Press, 2011).

66. Markus Prior, "News vs. Entertainment: How Increasing Media Choice Widens Gaps in Political Knowledge and Turnout," *American Journal of Political Science* 49, no. 3 (2005): 577–92.

67. Delli Carpini and Keeter, *What Americans Know about Politics*; Sunstein, *Republic.com*.

68. Mossberger, Tolbert, and Stansbury, *Virtual Inequality*.

69. Jonathan M. Ladd, *Why Americans Hate the Media and How It Matters* (Princeton, NJ: Princeton University Press, 2012).

70. Pew Research Center, "Trust in the News Media," May 9, 2017, www.journalism.org/2017/05/10/americans -attitudes-about-the-news-media-deeply-divided-along -partisan-lines/pj_2017-05-10_media-attitudes_a-05/[0] (accessed 3/20/18).

71 Amy Wong, "'That's How Dictators Get Started': McCain Criticizes Trump for Calling Media 'the Enemy,'" *Washington Post*, February 8, 2017, www.washingtonpost .com/news/the-fix/wp/2017/02/18/thats-how-dictators -get-started-mccain-criticizes-trump-for-calling-media -the-enemy/?noredirect=on&utm_term=.90e929b9948d (accessed 5/21/18).

72. David J. Garrow, *Protest at Selma: Martin Luther King, Jr., and the Voting Rights Act of 1965* (New Haven, CT: Yale University Press, 2001).

73. See Todd Gitlin, *The Whole World Is Watching* (Berkeley: University of California Press, 1980).

74. Tim Groseclose, *Left Turn: How Liberal Media Bias Distorts the American Mind* (New York: St. Martin's Press, 2011).

75. Pew Research Center, "How Journalists See Journalists in 2004: Views on Profits, Performance and Politics," May 2004, http://people-press.org/files/legacy-pdf/214 .pdf (accessed 9/7/12).

76. "Fake News," Lies and Propaganda: How to Sort Fact from Fiction," University of Michigan Library Research Guides, 2018, http://guides.lib.umich.edu/c .php?g=637508&p=4462444 (accessed 3/20/18).

77. Doris Graber, ed., *Media Power in American Politics*, 5th ed. (Washington, DC: CQ Press, 2006).

78. Amber E. Boydstun, Stefaan Walgrave, and Anne Hardy, "Two Faces of Media Attention: Media Storms vs. General Coverage," *Political Communication* 31, no. 4 (2014): 509–31.

79. Larry M. Bartels, *Presidential Primaries and the Dynamics of Public Choice* (Princeton, NJ: Princeton University Press, 1988).

80. David P. Redlawsk, Caroline J. Tolbert, and Todd Donovan, *Why Iowa? How Caucuses and Sequential Elections Improve the Presidential Nominating Process* (Chicago: University of Chicago Press, 2011).

81. Larry Bartels, *Unequal Democracy: The Political Economy of the New Gilded Age* (Princeton, NJ: Princeton University Press, 2008).

82. Pew Research Center, "Public Has Mixed Expectations for New Tax Law," January 24, 2018, www.people-press .org/2018/01/24/public-has-mixed-expectations-for-new -tax-law/ (accessed 5/21/18).

83. Robert Entman, "Framing: Toward Clarification of a Fractured Paradigm," *Journal of Communication* 43, no. 4 (1993): 51–58.

84. Shanto Iyengar and Donald R. Kinder, *News That Matters: Television and American Opinion* (Chicago: University of Chicago Press, 1987), 63.

85. *New York Times v. United States*, 403 U.S. 713 (1971).

86. United Nations General Assembly, "Report of the Special Rapporteur on the Promotion and Protection of the Right to Freedom of Opinion and Expression," 2011, www.ohchr.org/EN/Issues/FreedomOpinion/Pages/ OpinionIndex.aspx (accessed 3/14/16).

87. Andrew Chadwick, *Internet Politics: States, Citizens, and New Communication Technologies* (Oxford: Oxford University Press, 2006).

88. See Martin Linsky, *Impact: How the Press Affects Federal Policymaking* (New York: W. W. Norton, 1986).

CHAPTER 8

1. Richard Fry, "Millennials and Gen-Xers Outvoted Boomers and Older Generations in 2016 election," July 31, 2017, www.pewresearch.org/fact-tank/2017/07/31/ millennials-and-gen-xers-outvoted-boomers-and-older -generations-in-2016-election/ (accessed 1/31/18).

2. Gregory S. Schneider, "Historic Turnout of Young Voters in Virginia Election Poses Problem for Republicans," *Washington Post*, November 24, 2017, www.washingtonpost .com/local/virginia-politics/historic-turnout-of-young -voters-in-virginia-election-hints-at-national-problem -for-republicans/2017/11/24/8e90d978-cf03-11e7-9d3a -bcbe2af58c3a_story.html?utm_term=.4e20eb4f3eeb (accessed 1/31/18).

3. Gregory S. Schneider, Laura Vozzella, and Fenit Nirappil, "In the Final Spring to Election Day, a Historical Push to Turn Out Voters in Va.," *Washington Post*, November 4, 2017, www.washingtonpost.com/ local/virginia-politics/in-the-final-sprint-to-election-day -an-historic-push-to-turn-out-voters-in-va/2017/11/04/ ea833a58-bff6-11e7-97d9-bdab5a0ab381_story .html?utm_term=.3c809dcb4021 (accessed 1/31/18).

4. U.S. Census Bureau, "Voter Turnout Increases by 5 Million in 2008 Presidential Election, U.S. Census Bureau Reports," Newsroom Archive, www.census.gov/ newsroom/releases/archives/voting/cb09-110.html (accessed 2/29/16).

5. Michael McDonald, "2016 November General Election Turnout Rates," United States Elections Project, www .electproject.org/2016g (accessed 11/11/16).

6. U.S. Census Bureau, "Table 10. Reasons for Not Voting, by Selected Characteristics: November 2012," Voting and Registration, www.census.gov/hhes/www/socdemo/voting/publications/p20/2012/tables.html.

7. National Conference of State Legislatures, "Same Day Voter Registration," March 27, 2018, www.ncsl.org/research/elections-and-campaigns/same-day-registration.aspx (accessed 6/12/18).

8. Catherine E. Shoichet, "Is Racism on the Rise? More in U.S. Say It's a 'Big Problem,' CNN/KFF Poll Finds," CNN, Race & Reality in America, November 25, 2015, www.cnn.com/2015/11/24/us/racism-problem-cnn-kff-poll/ (accessed 2/29/16).

9. Sidney Verba, Kay Lehman Schlozman, and Henry E. Brady, *Voice and Equality: Civic Voluntarism in American Politics* (Cambridge, MA: Harvard University Press, 2005), chap. 3, for kinds of participation; 66–67 for prevalence of local activity.

10. Michael P. McDonald, "American Voter Turnout in Historical Perspective," in *The Oxford Handbook of American Elections and Political Behavior*, ed. Jan Leighley (New York: Oxford University Press, 2010), 125–43.

11. Todd Donovan and Shaun Bowler, *Reforming the Republic: Democratic Institutions for the New America* (Upper Saddle River, NJ: Pearson Education, 2004).

12. For a discussion of the decline in voter turnout over time, see Ruy A. Teixeira, *The Disappearing American Voter* (Washington, DC: Brookings Institution Press, 1992). See also Michael McDonald and Samuel Popkin, "The Myth of the Vanishing Voter," *American Political Science Review*, 95 (2001): 963–74; and Michael McDonald, "2012 November General Election Turnout Rates," *United States Election Project*, www.electproject.org/2012g (accessed 9/14/12).

13. McDonald, "2016 November General Election Turnout Rates."

14. Elisa Shearer and Jeffrey Gottfried, "News Use across Social Media Platforms 2017," Pew Research Center, www.journalism.org/2017/09/07/news-use-across-social-media-platforms-2017/ (accessed 3/29/18).

15. Meredith Rolfe, *Voter Turnout: A Social Theory of Political Participation* (New York: Cambridge University Press, 2012).

16. Lee Rainie, et al., "Social Media and Political Engagement," Pew Research Center, Internet, Science & Tech, www.pewinternet.org/2012/10/19/social-media-and-political-engagement/ (accessed 6/24/14).

17. Helen Margetts, Peter John, Scott Hale, and Taha Yasseri, *Political Turbulence: How Social Media Shape Collective Action* (New York: Oxford University Press, 2017).

18. Philip Bump, "'60 Minutes' profiles the genius who won Trump's campaign: Facebook," *Washington Post*, October 9, 2017, www.washingtonpost.com/news/politics/wp/2017/10/09/60-minutes-profiles-the-genius-who-won-trumps-campaign-facebook/?utm_term=.ad2bd8d8194a (accessed 3/29/18).

19. Caroline J. Tolbert and Ramona S. McNeal, "Unraveling the Effects of the Internet on Political Participation," *Political Research Quarterly* 56, no. 2 (2003): 175–85; see also Bruce Bimber, "Information and Political Engagement in America: The Search for Effects of Information Technology at the Individual Level," *Political Research Quarterly* 54 (2001): 53–67; Bimber, *Information and American Democracy: Technology and the Evolution of Political Power* (Cambridge: Cambridge University Press, 2009); J. Thomas and G. Streib, "The New Face of Government: Citizen-Initiated Contacts in the Era of E-Government," *Journal of Public Administration Theory and Research* 13, no. 1 (2003): 83–102; D. V. Shah et al., "Information and Expression in a Digital Age: Modeling Internet Effects on Civic Participation," *Communication Research* 32, no. 5 (2005): 531–65; K. Kenski and N. J. Stroud, "Connections between Internet Use and Political Efficacy, Knowledge, and Participation," *Journal of Broadcasting and Electronic Media* 50, no. 2 (2006): 173–92.

20. Sasha Issenberg, *The Victory Lab: The Secret Science of Winning Campaigns* (New York: Broadway Books, 2013); Andrew Chadwick, *The Hybrid Media System: Politics and Power* (New York: Oxford University Press, 2017).

21. Open Secrets, "Hillary Clinton (D)," www.opensecrets.org/pres16/candidate?id=N00000019 (accessed 6/20/18).

22. Open Secrets, "Donald Trump (R)," www.opensecrets.org/pres16/candidate?id=N00023864 (accessed 6/20/18).

23. Jason Gainous and Kevin Wagner, *Tweeting to Power: The Social Media Revolution in American Politics* (New York: Oxford University Press, 2013).

24. Gainous and Wagner, *Tweeting to Power*.

25. Karen Mossberger and Caroline J. Tolbert, "Digital Democracy: How Politics Online Is Changing Electoral Participation," in *Oxford Handbook of American Elections and Political Behavior*, ed. Jan E. Leighley (New York: Oxford University Press, 2010), 200–218.

26. Philip Bump, "'60 Minutes' Profiles the Genius Who Won Trump's Campaign: Facebook," *Washington Post*, October 9, 2017, www.washingtonpost.com/news/politics/wp/2017/10/09/60-minutes-profiles-the-genius-who-won-trumps-campaign-facebook/?utm_term=.ad2bd8d8194a (accessed 3/29/18).

27. W. R. Neuman, M. R. Just, and A. N. Crigler, *Common Knowledge: News and the Construction of Political Meaning* (Chicago: University of Chicago Press, 1992).

28. David P. Redlawsk, "Hot Cognition or Cool Consideration: Testing the Effects of Motivated Reasoning," *Journal of Politics* 64 (2002): 1021–44.

29. Caroline J. Tolbert, David P. Redlawsk, and Kellen J. Gracey, "Racial Attitudes and Emotional Responses to the 2016 Republican Candidates," *Journal of Election, Public Opinion and Parties* 28, no. 2 (2018): 245–62.

30. Manuel Castells, *The Rise of the Network Society: The Information Age: Economy, Society, and Culture* (Oxford: Blackwell, 1997).

31. Bruce Bimber and Richard Davis, *Campaigning Online: The Internet in U.S. Elections* (Cambridge: Cambridge University Press, 2003).

32. Robert Putnam, *Bowling Alone: The Collapse and Revival of American Community* (New York: Simon and Schuster, 2000).

33. Karen Mossberger, Caroline J. Tolbert, and Allison Hamilton, "Measuring Digital Citizenship: Mobile Access and Broadband," *International Journal of Communication* 6 (2012): 2492–528; Pippa Norris, *Digital Divide: Civic Engagement, Information Poverty, and the Internet Worldwide* (New York: Cambridge University Press, 2001); Benjamin Barber, "The New Telecommunications Technology: Endless Frontier or the End of Democracy?" *Constellations* 4, no. 2 (2011): 208–28; Tolbert and McNeal, "Unraveling the Effects of the Internet."

34. Russell Dalton, *The Good Citizen: How a Younger Generation Is Reshaping American Politics* (Washington, DC: CQ Press, 2008).

35. "Same-Sex Marriage Tweets Takeover the Internet," *USA Today*, June 27, 2015, www.usatoday.com/story/news/nation-now/2015/06/27/same-sex-marriage-scotus-gay-marriage-twitter-love-wins-trending/29389167/ (accessed 1/7/16).

36. Russell Dalton, "Citizenship Norms and the Expansion of Political Participation," *Public Choice* 56 (2008): 76–98.

37. Anamitra Deb, Stacy Donohue, and Tom Glaisyer, "Is Social Media a Threat to Democracy?" The Omidyar Group, October 1 2017, www.omidyargroup.com/wp-content/uploads/2017/10/Social-Media-and-Democracy-October-5-2017.pdf (accessed 3/29/18).

38. David S. Cloud, "Facebook Tells Congress 126 million Americans May Have Seen Russia-Linked Ads," *LA Times*, October 31, 2017, www.latimes.com/nation/la-na-russia-tech-20171031-story.html (accessed 3/29/18).

39. Josh Constine, "120K Instagrams by Russian Election Attackers Hit 20M Americans," Tech Crunch, November 1, 2017, techcrunch.com/2017/11/01/instagram-election-interference (accessed 3/29/18).

40. Julian Borger, Lauren Gambino, and Sabrina Siddiqui, "Tech Groups Face Congress as Showdown over Russian Election Meddling Looms," *The Guardian*, October 27, 2017, www.theguardian.com/technology/2017/oct/22/facebook-google-twitter-congress-hearing-trump-russia-election (accessed 3/29/18); Deb, Donohue, and Glaisyer, "Is Social Media a Threat to Democracy?"

41. Anthony Downs, *An Economic Theory of Democracy* (New York: Harper and Row, 1957); William H. Riker and Peter C. Ordeshook, "A Theory of the Calculus of Voting," *American Political Science Review* 62, no. 1 (1968): 25–42.

42. Julianna Pacheco and Jason Fletcher, "Incorporating Health into Studies of Political Behavior: Evidence for Turnout and Partisanship," *Political Research Quarterly* 68, no. 1 (2014): 104–16; Gustova López and Antonio Flores, "Dislike of Candidates or Campaign Issues Was Most Common Reason for Not Voting in 2016," Pew Research Center, June 1, 2017, www.pewresearch.org/fact-tank/2017/06/01/dislike-of-candidates-or-campaign-issues-was-most-common-reason-for-not-voting-in-2016/ (accessed 4/17/18).

43. Angus Campbell et al., *The American Voter* (New York: Wiley, 1960); Steven Rosenstone and John Mark Hansen, *Mobilization, Participation, and Democracy in America* (New York: Macmillan, 1993); Kay Lehman Scholzman, Sidney Verba, and Henry E. Brady, *The Unheavenly Chorus: Unequal Political Voice and the Broken Promise of American Democracy* (Princeton, NJ: Princeton University Press, 2012).

44. U.S. Census Bureau, "Table 7. Reported Voting and Registration of Family Members, by Age and Family Income: November 2016," Voting and Registration, www.census.gov/data/tables/time-series/demo/voting-and-registration/p20-580.html (accessed 3/29/18).

45. Sidney Verba and Norman H. Nie, *Participation in America: Political Democracy and Social Equality* (New York: Harper and Row, 1972); and www.census.gov/data/tables/time-series/demo/voting-and-registration/p20-580.html (accessed 3/15/18).

46. U.S. Census Bureau, "Voting and Registration in the Election of November 2016," May 2017, www.census.gov/data/tables/time-series/demo/voting-and-registration/p20-580.html (accessed 3/29/18).

47. Adam Hughes, "5 Facts about U.S. Political Donations," Pew Research Center, May 17, 2017, www.pewresearch.org/fact-tank/2017/05/17/5-facts-about-u-s-political-donations/ (accessed 3/29/18).

48. Julia Glum, "Youth Turnout for 2014 Midterm Election Lowest in 40 Years: Report," *International Business Times*, July 22, 2015, www.ibtimes.com/youth-voter-turnout-2014-midterm-election-lowest-40-years-report-2019813 (accessed 11/14/16); U.S. Census Bureau, "Voting and Registration in the Election of November 2016"; "Young People Dramatically Increase Their Turnout to 31%, Shape 2018 Midterm Elections," The Center for Information and Research on Civic Learning and Engagement, November 7, 2018 https://civicyouth.org/young-people-dramatically-increase-their-turnout-31-percent-shape-2018-midterm-elections/ (accessed 11/9/18).

49. Shiva Maniam and Samantha Smith, "A Wider Partisan and Ideological Gap between Younger, Older Generations," Pew Research Center, March 20, 2017, www.pewresearch.org/fact-tank/2017/03/20/a-wider-partisan-and-ideological-gap-between-younger-older-generations (accessed 3/29/18); Richard Frey, "Millennials and Gen Xers Outvoted Boomers and Older Generations in 2016 Election," Pew Research Center, July 31, 2017, www.pewresearch.org/fact-tank/2017/07/31/millennials-and-gen-xers-outvoted-boomers-and-older-generations-in-2016-election/ (accessed 3/29/18); Gary Langer, Christine Filer, Sofi Sinozich, and Allison De Jong, "Key Exit Poll Takeaways: Voters Negative on Trump, Most Interested

in Health Care, Immigration," *ABC News*, November 7, 2018, https://abcnews.go.com/Politics/negative-trump-divided-issues-voters-reshuffle-cards-washington/story?id=59025819 (accessed 11/9/18).

50. Julianna Pacheco, "Political Socialization in Context: The Effect of Political Competition on Youth Voter Turnout," *Political Behavior* 30, no. 4 (2008): 415–36.

51. Tyler Kingkade, "Youth Vote 2012 Turnout: Exit Polls Show Greater Share of Electorate than in 2008," *Huffington Post*, www.huffingtonpost.com/2012/11/07/youth-vote-2012-turnout-exit-polls_n_2086092.html (accessed 5/24/14).

52. Jennifer Lawless and Richard Fox, *Running from Office: Why Young Americans Are Turned Off to Politics* (New York: Oxford University Press, 2015).

53. Emily Hoban Kirby, Karlo Barrios Marcelo, and Kei Kawashima-Ginsberg, "Volunteering and the College Experience," Center for Information and Research on Civic Learning and Engagement, August 2009, www.civicyouth.org (accessed 11/25/09).

54. Rene Rocha et al., "Race and Turnout: Does Descriptive Representation in State Legislatures Increase Minority Voting?" *Political Research Quarterly* 63, no. 3 (2010): 890–907.

55. Susan Banducci, Todd Donovan, and Jeffrey Karp, "Minority Representation, Empowerment and Participation," *Journal of Politics* 66, no. 2 (2004): 534–56.

56. Mark Hugo Lopez and Paul Taylor, "Dissecting the 2008 Electorate: Most Diverse in U.S. History," Pew Research Center, Hispanic Trends, April 30, 2009, www.pewhispanic.org/2009/04/30/dissecting-the-2008-electorate-most-diverse-in-us-history/ (accessed 9/14/12).

57. Thom File, "The Diversifying Electorate—Voting Rates by Race and Hispanic Origin in 2012 (and Other Recent Elections)," U.S. Census Bureau, Current Population Survey, May 2013, www.census.gov/prod/2013pubs/p20-568.pdf (accessed 4/11/16).

58. Jens Manuel Krogstad and Mark Hugo Lopez, "Black Voter Turnout Fell in 2016, Even as a Record Number of Americans Cast Ballots," Pew Research Center, May 12, 2017, www.pewresearch.org/fact-tank/2017/05/12/black-voter-turnout-fell-in-2016-even-as-a-record-number-of-americans-cast-ballots/ (accessed 3/29/18).

59. See William Julius Wilson, *The Truly Disadvantaged: The Inner City, the Underclass, and Public Policy* (Chicago: University of Chicago Press, 1987); and Douglas Massey and Nancy Denton, *American Apartheid: Segregation and the Making of the American Underclass* (Cambridge, MA: Harvard University Press, 1993).

60. Jan E. Leighley and Jonathan Nagler, "Individual and Systemic Influences on Turnout: Who Votes? 1984," *Journal of Politics* 54 no. 3 (1992): 718–40.

61. Michael Dawson, *Black Visions: The Roots of Contemporary African-American Political Ideologies* (Chicago: University of Chicago Press, 2003).

62. File, "The Diversifying Electorate."

63. Matt Barreto and Gary Segura, *Latino America: How America's Most Dynamic Population Is Poised to Transform the Politics of the Nation* (New York: Public Affairs, 2014).

64. Matt Barreto, Gary Segura, and Nathan Woods, "The Mobilizing Effect of Majority–Minority Districts on Latino Turnout," *American Political Science Review* 98 (2004): 65–75, and authors' update.

65. Barreto and Segura, *Latino America*; Langer, Filer, Sinozich, and De Jong, "Key Exit Poll Takeaways: Voters Negative on Trump, Most Interested in Health Care, Immigration."

66. John Griffin and Brian Newman, *Minority Report: Evaluating Political Equality in America* (New York: Cambridge University Press, 2008); Rodney R. Hero, *Latinos and the U.S. Political System: Two-Tiered Pluralism* (Philadelphia: Temple University Press, 1992); Daniel Bowen and Christopher Clark, "Revisiting Descriptive Representation in Congress: Assessing the Effect of Race on the Constituent–Legislator Relationship," *Political Research Quarterly* 67, no. 3 (2014): 695–707.

67. Adrian Pantoja and Gary Segura, "Does Ethnicity Matter? Descriptive Representation in the Statehouse and Political Alienation Among Latinos," *Social Science Quarterly* 84 (2003): 441–60.

68. File, "The Diversifying Electorate."

69. Thom File, "Voting in America: A Look at the 2016 Presidential Election," *Census Blogs*, May 10, 2017, www.census.gov/newsroom/blogs/random-samplings/2017/05/voting_in_america.html (accessed 3/29/18).

70. "Election 2016: Exit Polls," *New York Times*, November 8, 2016, www.nytimes.com/interactive/2016/11/08/us/politics/election-exit-polls.html (accessed 11/11/16).

71. "Election 2016: Exit Polls."

72. Kira Sanbonmatsu, "Political Parties and the Recruitment of Women to State Legislatures," *Journal of Politics* 64, no. 3 (August 2002): 791–809; Jennifer L. Lawless and Richard L. Fox, *Why Are Women Still Not Running for Public Office?* (Washington, DC: Brookings Institution Press, 2008).

73. Center for American Women and Politics, *The Impact of Women in Public Office: Findings at a Glance* (New Brunswick, NJ: Rutgers University Press, 1991); Lawless and Fox, *Why Are Women Still Not Running for Public Office?*

74. See Richard A. Brody, "The Puzzle of Political Participation in America," in *The New American Political System*, ed. Anthony King (Washington, DC: American Enterprise Institute, 1978), chap. 8.

75. Rosenstone and Hansen, *Mobilization, Participation, and Democracy*, 59.

76. Alan S. Gerber and Donald P. Green, "The Effects of Canvassing, Telephone Calls, and Direct Mail on Voter Turnout: A Field Experiment," *American Political Science Review* 94, no. 3 (September 2000): 660.

77. Rolfe, *Voter Turnout*.

78. Robert M. Bond et al., "A 61-Million-Person Experiment in Social Influence and Political Mobilization," *Nature* 489 (2012): 295–98.

79. Bond et al., "A 61-Million-Person Experiment."

80. Katerina Eva Matsa and Kristine Lu, "10 Facts about the Changing Digital News Landscape," Pew Research Center, September 14, 2016, www.pewresearch.org/fact-tank/2016/09/14/facts-about-the-changing-digital-news-landscape/ (accessed 10/16/16).

81. Eitan D. Hersh, *Hacking the Electorate: How Campaigns Perceive Voters* (New York: Cambridge University Press, 2015); Sasha Issenberg, *The Victory Lab: The Secret Science of Winning Campaigns* (New York: Crown Publishers, 2012).

82. Theda Skocpol, *The Tea Party and the Remaking of Republican Conservatism* (New York: Oxford University Press, 2013).

83. Michael P. McDonald and John Samples, eds., *The Marketplace of Democracy: Electoral Competition and American Politics* (Washington, DC: Brookings Institution Press, 2006).

84. Mark N. Franklin, "Electoral Participation," in *Comparing Democracies: Elections and Voting in Global Perspective*, ed. Lawrence LeDuc, Richard G. Niemi, and Pippa Norris (Thousand Oaks, CA: Sage, 1996), 216–35; G. Bingham Powell, "American Voter Turnout in Comparative Perspective," *American Political Science Review* 80, no. 1 (1986): 17–43.

85. Todd Donovan, "A Goal for Reform: Make Elections Worth Stealing," *PS: Political Science and Politics* 40, no. 4 (2007): 681–6.

86. Donovan, "A Goal for Reform"; Gary W. Cox and Michael C. Munger, "Closeness, Expenditures, and Turnout in the 1982 U.S. House Elections," *American Political Science Review* 83, no. 1 (1989): 217–31; James G. Gimpel, Karen M. Kaufmann, and Shanna Pearson-Merkowitz, "Battleground States versus Blackout States: The Behavioral Implications of Modern Presidential Campaigns," *Journal of Politics* 69, no. 3 (2007): 786–97.

87. Gimpel, Kaufmann, and Pearson-Merkowitz, "Battleground States versus Blackout States"; Julianna Sandell Pacheco, "Political Socialization in Context: The Effect of Political Competition on Youth Voter Turnout," *Political Behavior* 30, no. 4 (2008): 415–36; Keena Lipsitz, "The Consequences of Battleground and 'Spectator' State Residency for Political Participation," *Political Behavior* 31, no. 2 (2009): 187–209.

88. David P. Redlawsk, Caroline J. Tolbert, and Todd Donovan, *Why Iowa? How Caucuses and Sequential Elections Improve the Presidential Nominating Process* (Chicago: University of Chicago Press, 2011).

89. Caroline J. Tolbert, Daniel C. Bowen, and Todd Donovan, "Initiative Campaigns: Direct Democracy and Voter Mobilization," *American Politics Research* 37, no. 1 (2009): 155–92.

90. Caroline J. Tolbert, John A. Grummel, and Daniel A. Smith, "The Effects of Ballot Initiatives on Voter Turnout in the American States," *American Politics Research* 29, no. 6 (2001): 625–48; Mark A. Smith, "The Contingent Effects of Ballot Initiatives and Candidate Races on Turnout," *American Journal of Political Science* 45, no. 3 (2001): 700–706; Caroline J. Tolbert and Daniel A. Smith, "The Educative Effects of Ballot Initiatives on Voter Turnout," *American Politics Research* 33, no. 2 (2005): 283–309; Frederick Boehmke and Daniel Bowen, "Direct Democracy and Individual Interest Group Membership," *Journal of Politics* 72, no. 3 (2010): 659–71.

91. Stephen Nicholson, *Voting the Agenda: Candidates, Elections, and Ballot Propositions* (Princeton, NJ: Princeton University Press, 2005).

92. John Myers, "That Blockbuster California Ballot Will Be a $452-Million Battle," *Los Angeles Times*, February 18, 2016, www.latimes.com/local/california/la-pol-sac-november-ballot-500-million-20160215-story.html (accessed 10/18/16).

93. Daniel A. Smith and Caroline J. Tolbert, *Educated by Initiative: The Effects of Direct Democracy on Citizens and Political Organizations in the American States* (Ann Arbor: University of Michigan Press, 2004).

94. Bruce E. Cain, Todd Donovan, and Caroline J. Tolbert, *Democracy in the States: Experiments in Election Reform* (Washington, DC: Brookings Institution Press, 2008).

95. U.S. Census Bureau, "Table 10. Reasons for Not Voting, by Selected Characteristics: November 2012," Voting and Registration, www.census.gov/hhes/www/socdemo/voting/publications/p20/2012/tables.html.

96. National Conference of State Legislatures, "Same Day Voter Registration."

97. Domenico Montanaro, "Would Automatic Voter Registration Increase Turnout?" NPR, March 18, 2015, www.npr.org/sections/itsallpolitics/2015/03/18/393645667/would-automatic-voter-registration-increase-turnout (accessed 11/14/16).

98. National Conference of State Legislatures, "Voter Identification Requirements," www.ncsl.org/research/elections-and-campaigns/voter-id.aspx (accessed 10/12/18).

99. Michael D. Regan, "What Does Voter Turnout Tell Us about the 2016 Election?" November 20, 2016, PBS News Hour, www.pbs.org/newshour/politics/voter-turnout-2016-elections (accessed 4/17/18); and "Oppose Voter ID Legislation—Fact Sheet," ACLU, www.aclu.org/other/oppose-voter-id-legislation-fact-sheet (accessed 4/17/18).

100. Michael Wines, "Wisconsin Strict ID Law Discouraged Voters, Study Finds," *New York Times*, September 25, 2017, www.nytimes.com/2017/09/25/us/wisconsin-voters.html (accessed 3/29/18).

101. National Conference of State Legislatures, "Voter Identification Requirements."

102. E. Ann Carson, "Prisoners in 2013," U.S. Department of Justice, Bureau of Justice Statistics, September 30, 2014, www.bjs.gov/content/pub/pdf/p13.pdf (accessed 4/11/16); National Conference of State Legislatures, "Felon Voting Rights," April 30, 2017 www.ncsl.org/research/elections-and-campaigns/felon-voting-rights.aspx (accessed 10/12/18).

103. Justin Wolfers, David Leonhardt and Kevin Quealy, "1.5 Million Missing Black Men," The Upshot, *New York Times*, April 20, 2015, www.nytimes.com/interactive/2015/04/20/upshot/missing-black-men.html?_r50&abt50002&abg51 (accessed 1/6/16).

104. Jean Chung, *Felon Disenfranchisement: A Primer* (Washington, DC: The Sentencing Project, 2016), www.sentencingproject.org/wp-content/uploads/2015/08/Felony-Disenfranchisement-Primer.pdf (accessed 10/12/16).

105. National Conference of State Legislatures, "Same Day Voter Registration."

106. Robert A. Jackson, Robert D. Brown, and Gerald C. Wright, "Registration, Turnout and the Electoral Representativeness of U.S. State Electorates," *American Politics Quarterly* 26, no. 3 (July 1998): 259–87. See also Benjamin Highton, "Easy Registration and Voter Turnout," *Journal of Politics* 59, no. 2 (April 1997): 565–87.

107. Stephen Knack and James White, "Election-Day Registration and Turnout Inequality," *Political Behavior* 22, no. 1 (2000): 29–44; Craig Leonard Brians and Bernard Grofman, "When Registration Barriers Fall, Who Votes? An Empirical Test of a Rational Choice Model," *Public Choice* 99 (1999): 161–76; Michael J. Hanmer, *Discount Voting: Voter Registration Reforms and Their Effects* (New York: Cambridge University Press, 2009); Mary Fitzgerald, "Greater Convenience but Not Greater Turnout: The Impact of Alternative Voting Methods on Electoral Participation in the United States," *American Politics Research* 33, no. 6 (2005): 842–67.

108. National Conference of State Legislatures, "Absentee and Early Voting," September 20, 2018, www.ncsl.org/research/elections-and-campaigns/absentee-and-early-voting.aspx (accessed 10/10/18).

109. Paul Gronke, Eva Galanes-Rosenbaum, and Peter Miller, "Early Voting and Turnout," *PS: Political Science and Politics* 40, no. 4 (October 2007): 639–45; Fitzgerald, "Greater Convenience but Not Greater Turnout"; Adam J. Berinsky, "The Perverse Consequences of Electoral Reform in the United States," *American Politics Research* 33, no. 4 (2005): 471–91.

110. Jeffrey Karp and Susan Banducci, "Going Postal: How All-Mail Elections Influence Turnout," *Political Behavior* 22, no. 3 (2000): 223–39.

111. Michael J. Hamner, *Discount Voting: Voter Registration Reforms and Their Effects* (New York: Cambridge University Press, 2009).

112. John Griffin and Michael Keane, "Are Voters Better Represented?" *Journal of Politics* 67, no. 4 (2005): 1206–27.

113. Larry Bartels, *Unequal Democracy: The Political Economy of the New Gilded Age* (Princeton, NJ: Princeton University Press, 2008).

CHAPTER 9

1. Taxdayteaparty.com, "Meet Keli Carender, Tea Party Organizer in Seattle, Washington," March 15, 2009, http:// taxdayteaparty.com/2009/03/meet-keli-carender-tea-party-organizer-in-seattle-washington/ (accessed 1/26/18).

2. Walter Dean Burnham, *Critical Elections and the Mainsprings of American Politics* (New York: W. W. Norton, 1970).

3. E. E. Schattschneider, *The Semisovereign People: A Realist's View of Democracy in America* (New York: Holt, Rinehart & Winston, 1960).

4. Larry Bartels, *Unequal Democracy: The Political Economy of the New Gilded Age* (Princeton, NJ: Princeton University Press, 2008).

5. Kathleen Bawn et al., "A Theory of Political Parties: Groups, Policy Demands and Nominations in American Politics." *Perspectives on Politics* 10, no. 3 (2012): 571–97.

6. Morris Fiorina, Samuel Abrams, and Jeremy Pope, *Culture War? The Myth of a Polarized America* (New York: Pearson Longman, 2004).

7. Todd Donovan and Shaun Bowler, *Reforming the Republic: Democratic Institutions for the New America* (Upper Saddle River, NJ: Prentice Hall, 2003).

8. James Madison, *The Federalist Papers*, no. 10, http://thomas.loc.gov/home/histdox/fed_10.html (accessed 11/11/12).

9. John H. Aldrich, *Why Parties? A Second Look* (Chicago: University of Chicago Press, 2011).

10. Raymond J. La Raja, "Political Parties in the Era of Soft Money," in *The Parties Respond: Changes in American Parties and Campaigns*, 4th ed., ed. Sandy L. Maisel (Boulder, CO: Westview Press, 2002), 163–88.

11. For an excellent analysis of the parties' role in recruitment, see Paul Herrnson, *Congressional Elections: Campaigning at Home and in Washington* (Washington, DC: CQ Press, 1995).

12. Marty Cohen et al., *The Party Decides: Presidential Nominations before and after Reform* (Chicago: University of Chicago Press, 2008).

13. Seth E. Masket, *No Middle Ground: How Informal Party Organizations Control Nominations and Polarize Legislatures* (Ann Arbor: University of Michigan Press, 2011).

14. Sasha Issenberg, *Victory Lab: The Secret Science of Winning Campaigns* (New York: Crown, 2012).

15. Glen Justice, "F.E.C. Declines to Curb Independent Fund Raisers," *New York Times*, May 14, 2004, A16.

16. See Harold Gosnell, *Machine Politics: Chicago Model*, rev. ed. (Chicago: University of Chicago Press, 1968).

17. For a useful discussion, see John Bibby and Thomas Holbrook, "Parties and Elections," in *Politics in the American States*, ed. Virginia Gray and Herbert Jacob (Washington, DC: CQ Press, 1996), 78–121.

18. John Gramlich, "Far More Americans Say There Are Strong Conflicts between Partisans Than between Other Groups in Society," Pew Research Center, December 19, 2017, www.pewresearch.org/fact-tank/2017/12/19/far-more-americans-say-there-are-strong-conflicts-between-partisans-than-between-other-groups-in-society/ (accessed 5/12/18).

19. Tara Golshan, "'Reckless, Outrageous, and Undignified Behavior': Sen. Flake Quits the Senate Over Trump," Vox, October 24, 2017, www.vox.com/2017/10/24/16536756/flake-retirement-over-trump-announcement (accessed 5/12/18).

20. "Election 2016: Exit Polls," *New York Times*, November 8, 2016, www.nytimes.com/interactive/2016/11/08/us/politics/election-exit-polls.html (accessed 11/11/16).

21. Alex Leary, "Hispanics Voting in Record Numbers in Florida, Other States, Boosting Hillary Clinton," *Miami Herald*, November 6, 2016, www.miamiherald.com/news/politics-government/election/article112958953.html (accessed 11/11/16).

22. "Election 2016: Exit Polls."

23. "Behind Trump's Victory: Divisions by Race, Gender and Education," November 9, 2016, Pew Research Center," www.pewresearch.org/fact-tank/2016/11/09/behind-trumps-victory-divisions-by-race-gender-education/ (accessed 5/12/18); Gary Langer, Christine Filer, Sofi Sinozich, and Allison De Jong, "Key Exit Poll Takeaways: Voters Negative on Trump, Most Interested in Health Care, Immigration," ABC News, November 7, 2018, https://abcnews.go.com/Politics/negative-trump-divided-issues-voters-reshuffle-cards-washington/story?id=59025819 (accessed 11/9/18).

24. Pew Research Center, Religious Landscape Study, www.pewforum.org/religious-landscape-study/ (accessed 12/16/15).

25. Gregory Smith, "A Growing Share of Americans Say It's Not Necessary to Believe in God to Be Moral," Pew Research Center, October 16, 2017, www.pewresearch.org/fact-tank/2017/10/16/a-growing-share-of-americans-say-its-not-necessary-to-believe-in-god-to-be-moral/ (accessed 5/12/18).

26. "Election 2016: Exit Polls."

27. Christopher Shea, "Who Are You Calling Working Class?" *Boston Globe*, February 12, 2006, www.boston.com/news/globe/ideas/articles/2006/02/12/who_are_you_calling_working_class/ (accessed 2/24/08).

28. Pew Research Center, "Beyond Red vs. Blue: The Political Typology," U.S. Politics & Policy, June 26, 2014, www.people-press.org/2014/06/26/the-political-typology-beyond-red-vs-blue (accessed 2/28/16).

29. Shaun Bowler, Gary Segura, and Stephen Nicholson, "Earthquakes and Aftershocks: Race, Direct Democracy, and Partisan Change," *American Journal of Political Science* 50 (January 2006): 146–59.

30. "Election 2016: Exit Polls."

31. Jeffrey A. Karp and Caroline J. Tolbert, "Support for Nationalizing Presidential Elections," *Presidential Studies Quarterly* 40, no. 4 (2010): 771–93.

32. Jeffrey M. Jones, "Democratic, Republican Identification Near Historical Lows," Gallup, January 11, 2016, www.gallup.com/poll/188096/democratic-republican-identification-near-historical-lows.aspx (accessed 8/3/16).

33. Alexa Mikalaski, "9 States Where Registered Independents Outnumber Both Major Political Parties," Independent Voter Network, August 8, 2018, https://ivn.us/2018/08/08/9-states-registered-independents-outnumber-major-political-parties/ (accessed 11/9/18).

34. See Morris Fiorina, "Parties and Partisanship: A Forty Year Retrospective," *Political Behavior* 24, no. 2 (2002): 93–115.

35. On the limited polarization among ordinary voters, see Fiorina, Abrams, and Pope, *Culture War?*; on growing partisan attachment among a subset of voters, see Alan Abramowitz and Kyle Saunders, "Why Can't We Just Get Along? The Reality of a Polarized America," *The Forum* 3, no. 2 (2005): 1–22.

36. "CQ Roll Call's Vote Studies—2013 in Review," February 3, 2014, http://media.cq.com/votestudies/ (accessed 7/25/16).

37. David Hawkings, "Ahead, the First Pure Party-Line Modern Tax Cut?" Roll Call, October 31, 2017, www.rollcall.com/news/hawkings/party-line-tax-cut (accessed 8/15/18).

38. Benjamin Page and Martin Gilens, *Democracy in America: What Has Gone Wrong and What We Can Do about It* (Chicago: University of Chicago Press, 2017).

39. Donovan and Bowler, *Reforming the Republican*. See also Marty Gilen, *Affluence and Influence: Economic Inequality and Political Power in America* (Princeton, NJ: Princeton University Press, 2014).

40. For a discussion of third parties in the United States, see Daniel Mazmanian, *Third Parties in Presidential Elections* (Washington, DC: Brookings Institution Press, 1974).

41. See Maurice Duverger, *Political Parties* (New York: Wiley, 1954).

42. Donovan and Bowler, *Reforming the Republic*.

43. Andri Blais, *To Keep or to Change First Past the Post? The Politics of Election Reform* (New York: Oxford University Press, 2008).

44. Todd Donovan, Caroline J. Tolbert, Kellen Gracey, "Campaign Civility under Preferential and Plurality Voting," *Electoral Studies* 42 (2016): 157–163.

45. Stanley Kelley, Jr., Richard E. Ayres, and William Bowen, "Registration and Voting: Putting First Things First," *American Political Science Review* 61 (June 1967): 359–70.

CHAPTER 10

1. BBC Newsbeat, "'I'm One of the Young Voters Who Backed Donald Trump,'" November 12, 2016, www.bbc.co.uk/newsbeat/article/37961355/im-one-of-the-young-voters-who-backed-donald-trump (accessed 1/26/18).

2. Emily Richmond, Mikhail Zinshteyn, and Natalie Gross, "Dissecting the Youth Vote," *The Atlantic,* November 11, 2016, www.theatlantic.com/education/archive/2016/11/dissecting-the-youth-vote/507416/ (accessed 1/26/17).

3. Richmond et al., "Dissecting the Youth Vote."

4. Thom File, "Voting in America: A Look at the 2016 Presidential Election," *Census Blogs*, May 10, 2017, www.census.gov/newsroom/blogs/random-samplings/2017/05/voting_in_america.html (accessed 1/26/18).

5. Amber Phillips, "Is Split-Ticket Voting Officially Dead?" *Washington Post*, November 17, 2016, www.washingtonpost.com/news/the-fix/wp/2016/11/17/is-split-ticket-voting-officially-dead/?utm_term=.ace9dff09c60 (accessed 5/14/18).

6. Sarah Zimmerman, "Illinois Protecting against Russian Election Tampering," February 28, 2018, *U.S. News and World Reports*, www.usnews.com/news/best-states/illinois/articles/2018-02-28/illinois-protecting-against-russian-election-tampering (accessed 5/14/18).

7. *Baker v. Carr* 369 U.S. 186 (1962); *Gray v. Sanders*, 372 U.S. 368 (1963); *Wesberry v. Sanders*, 376 U.S. 1 (1964); *Reynolds v. Sims*, 377 U.S. 533 (1964).

8. *Thornburg v. Gingles*, 478 U.S. 613 (1986).

9. Christopher Ingraham "This Is the Best Explanation of Gerrymandering You Will Ever See. How to Steal an Election: A Visual Guide," *Washington Post*, March 1, 2015, www.washingtonpost.com/news/wonk/wp/2015/03/01/this-is-the-best-explanation-of-gerrymandering-you-will-ever-see/?utm_term=.97e9bcf9a627 (accessed 7/25/18).

10. "Reelection Rates over the Years," Center for Responsive Politics, www.opensecrets.org/overview/reelect.php (accessed 11/9/18).

11. Christopher Ingraham, "'Sprawling,' Rorsarchian,' 'Corrosive' to Democracy: Pennsylvania's Top Court Condemns State Gerrymandered District," *Washington Post*, February 8, 2018, www.washingtonpost.com/news/wonk/wp/2018/02/08/sprawling-rorschachian-corrosive-to-democracy-pas-top-court-condemns-states-gerrymandered-districts/?noredirect=on&utm_term=.a009cd0645f9 (accessed 7/25/18).

12. *Shaw v. Reno*, 509 U.S. 630 (1993).

13. David Redlawsk, Caroline J. Tolbert, and Todd Donovan, *Why Iowa? How Caucuses and Sequential Elections Improve the Presidential Nomination Process* (Chicago: University of Chicago Press, 2011).

14. Redlawsk, Tolbert, and Donovan, *Why Iowa?*

15. State legislatures determine the system by which electors are selected. Almost all states use this "winner-take-all" system. Maine and Nebraska, however, provide that one electoral vote goes to the winner in each congressional district and two electoral votes go to the winner statewide.

16. *Bush v. Gore*, 531 U.S. 98 (2000).

17. Jeffrey Karp and Caroline J. Tolbert, "Polls and Elections: Support for Nationalizing Presidential Elections." *Presidential Studies Quarterly*, 40, no. 4 (2010): 771–93.

18. Todd Donovan and Shaun Bowler, *Reforming the Republic: Democratic Institutions for the New America* (Upper Saddle River, NJ: Pearson Press, 2003).

19. André Blais, *To Keep or to Change First Past the Post? The Politics of Electoral Reform* (Oxford: Oxford University Press, 2008).

20. Adam Nagourney, "Court Strikes Down Ban on Gay Marriage in California," *New York Times*, February 7, 2012, www.nytimes.com/2012/02/08/us/marriage-ban-violates-constitution-court-rules.html (accessed 8/21/12).

21. Daniel Smith and Caroline J. Tolbert, *Educated by Initiative: The Effects of Direct Democracy on Citizens and Political Organizations in the American States* (Ann Arbor: University of Michigan Press, 2004).

22. Shaun Bowler, Todd Donovan, and Caroline J. Tolbert, *Citizens as Legislators: Direct Democracy in the United States* (Columbus: Ohio State University Press, 1998).

23. BallotPedia, "2018 Ballot Measures," www.ballotpedia.org/2018_ballot_measures (accessed 11/8/18).

24. Stephen Nicholson, *Voting the Agenda: Candidates, Elections, and Ballot Propositions* (Princeton, NJ: Princeton University Press, 2005).

25. Ryan Grim and Sabrina Siddiqui, "Call Time for Congress Shows Dominates Bleak Work Life," Huffington Post, January 9, 2013, www.huffingtonpost.com/2013/01/08/call-time-congressional-fundraising_n_2427291.html (accessed 8/8/16).

26. "Most Expensive Races," Center for Responsive Politics, November 9, 2018, www.opensecrets.org/overview/topraces.php (accessed 11/9/18).

27. Stephen Ansolabehere and James Snyder, "Campaign War Chests and Congressional Elections," *Business and Politics* 2 (2000): 9–34.

28. Gary W. Cox and Eric Magar, "How Much Is Majority Status in the U.S. Congress Worth?" *American Political Science Review* 93 (1999): 299–309.

29. "Two-Thirds of Presidential Campaign Is in Just 6 States," Nationalpopularvote.com, www.nationalpopularvote.com/campaign-events-2016 (accessed 5/14/18); Daron Shaw, *The Race to 270: The Electoral College and the Campaign Strategies of 2000 and 2004* (Chicago: University of Chicago Press, 2006).

30. John Geer, *In Defense of Negativity: Attack Ads in Presidential Campaigns* (Chicago: University of Chicago Press, 2006).

31. Nicholas Confessore, Karen Yourish, "$2 Billion of Free Media for Donald Trump," *New York Times*, March 16, 2016, www.nytimes.com/2016/03/16/upshot/measuring-donald-trumps-mammoth-advantage-in-free-media.html (accessed 7/25/18).

32. Brian Stelter, "Debate Breaks Record as Most-Watched in U.S. History," CNN Money, September 27, 2016, www.money.cnn.com/2016/09/27/media/debate-ratings-record-viewership/ (accessed 10/17/16).

33. D. Sunshine Hillygus and Todd G. Shields, *The Persuadable Voter: Wedge Issues in Political Campaigns* (Princeton, NJ: Princeton University Press, 2009).

34. Sasha Issenberg, *The Victory Lab: The Secret Science of Winning Campaigns* (New York: Crown, 2012).

35. Alan S. Gerber and Donald P. Green, "The Effects of Canvassing, Telephone Calls, and Direct Mail on Voter Turnout: A Field Experiment," *American Political Science Review* 94, no. 3 (2000): 660.

36. M. Ostrogorski, *Democracy and the Organization of Political Parties* (New York: Macmillan, 1902).

37. For discussions of the consequences of this, see Thomas Edsall, *The New Politics of Inequality* (New York: W. W. Norton, 1984). See also Thomas Edsall, "Both Parties Get the Company's Money—but the Boss Backs the GOP," *Washington Post*, National Weekly Edition, September 16, 1986, 14; and Benjamin Ginsberg, "Money and Power: The New Political Economy of American Elections," in *The Political Economy*, ed. Thomas Ferguson and Joel Rogers (Armonk, NY: M. E. Sharpe, 1984).

38. Center for Responsive Politics, "Cost of Election," www.opensecrets.org/overview/cost.php (accessed 11/9/16); and Christopher Ingraham, "Somebody Just Put a Price Tag on the 2016 Election. It's a Doozy," *Washington Post*, April 14, 2017, www.washingtonpost.com/news/wonk/wp/2017/04/14/somebody-just-put-a-price-tag-on-the-2016-election-its-a-doozy/?utm_term=.6ecccc4dc35f (accessed 6/5/18).

39. *Buckley v. Valeo*, 424 U.S. 1 (1976).

40. *Citizens United v. Federal Election Commission*, 558 U.S. 50 (2010).

41. *Citizens United*.

42. Martin Gilens, *Affluence and Influence: Economic Inequality and Political Power in America* (Princeton, NJ: Princeton University Press; New York: Russell Sage, 2012).

43. *McCutcheon et al. v. Federal Election Commission*, 572 U.S. __ (2014).

44. OpenSecrets.org, Sen. Bernie Sanders, www.opensecrets.org/politicians/summary.php?cid=N00000528 (accessed 6/23/16).

45. *Buckley v. Valeo*.

46. Steve Phillips, "What about White Voters?" *Center for American Progress*, February 5, 2016, www.americanprogress.org/issues/race/news/2016/02/05/130647/what-about-white-voters/ (accessed 11/14/16).

47. Jonathan Martin, Dalia Sussman, and Megan Thee-Brenan, "Voters Express Disgust over U.S. Politics in New Times/CBS Poll," *New York Times*, November 3, 2016, www.nytimes.com/2016/11/04/us/politics/hillary-clinton-donald-trump-poll.html (accessed 11/11/18).

48. GDELT Project, "Presidential Campaign 2016: Candidate Television Tracker," television.gdeltproject.org/cgi-bin/iatv_campaign2016/iatv_campaign2016 (accessed 11/11/16).

49. "Election 2016: Exit Polls," *New York Times*, November 8, 2016, www.nytimes.com/interactive/2016/11/08/us/politics/election-exit-polls.html (accessed 11/11/16).

50. Nancy Scola, "Massive Twitter Data Release Sheds Light on Russia Trump Strategy," *Politico*, October 17, 2018, www.politico.com/story/2018/10/17/twitter-foreign-influence-operations-910005 (accessed 11/11/8).

51. Devlin Barrett, Sari Horwitz and Rosalind S. Helderman, "Russian Troll Farm, 13 Suspects Indicted in 2016 Election Interference," *Washington Post*, February 16, 2018, www.washingtonpost.com/world/national-security/russian-troll-farm-13-suspects-indicted-for-interference-in-us-election/2018/02/16/2504de5e-1342-11e8-9570-29c9830535e5_story.html?noredirect=on&utm_term=.1d49970b3df7 (accessed 11/9/18).

52. "One in Five Adults Have Attended a Political Protest, Rally, or Speech," *Washington Post*–Kaiser Family Foundation Survey (Jan. 24–Feb. 22, 2018), April 21, 2018, www.washingtonpost.com/page/2010-2019/WashingtonPost/2018/04/06/National-Politics/Polling/release_516.xml (accessed 11/9/18).

53. Ryan Sit, "More Than 2 Million in 90 Percent of Voting Districts Joined March for Our Lives Protests," *Newsweek*, March 26, 2018, www.newsweek.com/march-our-lives-how-many-2-million-90-voting-district-860841 (accessed 11/9/18).

54. Michelle Ye Hee Lee and Anu Narayanswamy, "Democratic Candidates for Congress Have Raised a Record-Shattering $1 Billion This Election," *Washington Post*, October 17, 2018, www.washingtonpost.com/politics/democratic-candidates-for-congress-have-raised-a-record-shattering-1-billion-this-election/2018/10/17/afedfe66-d231-11e8-8c22-fa2ef74bd6d6_story.html?utm_term=.350602226c5b (accessed 11/9/18).

55. Tim Craig, "Democrats' Gains in State Capitols Mark a Significant Turnaround for Party," *Washington Post*, November 8, 2018, A27.

56. Brady Dennis and David Weigel, "Progressive Ballot Measures Win over Even Red-State Voters," *Washington Post*, November 8, 2018, A33.

CHAPTER 11

1. Matt Miller, "Young Americans Get the Shaft," *Washington Post*, June 13, 2012, www.washingtonpost.com/opinions/young-americans-get-the-shaft/2012/06/13/gJQAeHp4ZV_story.html?utm_term=.4a68ebb3076f 9 (accessed 1/26/18).

2. This account drawn from Araz Hachadourian, "Who's Lobbying for Millennial Interests? Meet the 'AARP for Young People,'" *Yes! Magazine*, May 19, 2016, www.yesmagazine.org/people-power/millennials-have-the-numbers-to-move-our-politics-and-theyre-about-to-get-their-own-lobbyists-20160519 (accessed 1/26/18); and Association of Young Americans, joinaya.com/ (accessed 1/26/18).

3. Alexis de Tocqueville, *Democracy in America*, ed. J. P. Mayer and trans. George Lawrence (New York: Harper Collins, [1835–40] 1988), 513.

4. Alexander Hamilton, James Madison, and John Jay, *The Federalist Papers*, ed. Clinton L. Rossiter (New York: New American Library, 1961), no. 10, 83.

5. *The Federalist Papers*, no. 10.

6. The best statement of the pluralist view is in David Truman, *The Governmental Process* (New York: Knopf, 1951), chap. 2.

7. Martin Gilens and Benjamin I. Page, "Testing Theories of American Politics: Elites, Interest Groups, and Average Citizens," *Perspectives on Politics* 12, no. 3 (Sept. 2014):

564–81; Martin Gilens, *Affluence & Influence: Economic Inequality and Political Power in America* (Princeton, NJ: Princeton University Press, 2012); Benjamin I. Page and Martin Gilens, *Democracy in America? What Has Gone Wrong and What We Can Do about It* (Chicago: University of Chicago Press, 2017).

8. Beth L. Leech, National Survey of Governmental Relations, 2012; Center for Responsive Politics, "Political Action Committees," www.opensecrets.org/pacs/.

9. Megan R. Wilson, "Lobbying's Top 50: Who's Spending Big," The Hill, February 7, 2017, www.thehill.com/business-a-lobbying/business-a-lobbying/318177-lobbyings-top-50-whos-spending-big (accessed 4/5/18).

10. Center for Responsive Politics, "Interest Groups," www.opensecrets.org/industries/ (accessed 11/11/18).

11. Frank Baumgartner et al., *Lobbying and Policy Change: Who Wins, Who Loses, and Why* (Chicago: University of Chicago Press, 2009).

12. Baumgartner et al., *Lobbying and Policy Change.*

13. Erika Falk, Erin Grizard, and Gordon McDonald, "Legislative Issue Advertising in the 108th Congress: Pluralism or Peril?" *Harvard International Journal of Press/Politics* 11, no. 4 (Fall 2006): 148–64.

14. Truman, *Governmental Process.*

15. For an exploration of lower-class interest groups and social movements, see Frances Piven and Richard Cloward, *Poor People's Movements* (New York: Vintage, 1978).

16. E. E. Schattschneider, *The Semisovereign People: A Realist's View of Democracy in America* (New York: Holt, Rinehart and Winston, 1960).

17. The Tax Cuts and Jobs Act: Preliminary Economic Analysis, December 18, 2017, www.taxfoundation.org/tax-cuts-and-jobs-act-preliminary-analysis/ (accessed 4/5/18).

18. Kay Lehman Schlozman and John T. Tierney, *Organized Interests and American Democracy* (New York: Harper and Row, 1986), 60.

19. Clay Shirky, *Here Comes Everybody: The Power of Organizing without Organizations* (New York: Penguin Press, 2008).

20. Mancur Olson, *The Logic of Collective Action* (Cambridge, MA: Harvard University Press, 1965).

21. David Karpf, *The MoveOn Effect: The Unexpected Transformation of American Political Advocacy* (New York: Oxford University Press, 2012).

22. Christine Day, *AARP: America's Largest Interest Group and Its Impact* (Westport, CT: Praeger, 2017).

23. John Herbers, "Special Interests Gaining Power as Voter Disillusionment Grows," *New York Times*, November 14, 1978.

24. Jack Walker, "The Diffusion of Innovations among the American States," *American Political Science Association* 63, no. 3 (1969): 880–99; Thomas Dye, *Understanding Public Policy*, 15th ed. (Boston: Pearson, 2017).

25. Center for Responsive Politics, "Lobbying Database," www.opensecrets.org/lobby/ (accessed 5/15/18).

26. For discussions of lobbying, see Allan J. Cigler and Burdett A. Loomis, eds., *Interest Group Politics* (Washington, DC: CQ Press, 1983). See also Jeffrey M. Berry, *Lobbying for the People* (Princeton, NJ: Princeton University Press, 1977).

27. Marie Jojnacki, "Interest Groups' Decisions to Join Alliances or Work Alone," *American Journal of Political Science* 41 (1997): 61–87; Kevin W. Hula, *Lobbying Together: Interest Groups Coalitions in Legislative Politics* (Washington, DC: Georgetown University Press, 1999).

28. Andrew Chin, "A Case of Insecure Browsing," Newsobserver.com, September 30, 2004, www.unclaw.com/chin/scholarship/nando.pdf (accessed 3/30/16).

29. For an excellent discussion of the political origins of the Administrative Procedure Act, see Martin Shapiro, "APA: Past, Present, Future," *Virginia Law Review* 72, no. 477 (March 1986): 447–92.

30. David Kirkpatrick, "Congress Finds Ways of Avoiding Lobbyist Limits," *Washington Post*, February 11, 2007, 1.

31. *Brown v. Board of Education of Topeka, Kansas*, 347 U.S. 483 (1954).

32. *Obergefell v. Hodges*, 576 U.S. __ (2015).

33. *Roe v. Wade*, 410 U.S. 113 (1973).

34. *Webster v. Reproductive Health Services*, 492 U.S. 490 (1989).

35. E. Pendleton Herring, *Group Representation before Congress* (New York: McGraw-Hill, 1936).

36. National Rifle Association, www.home.nra.org (accessed 5/15/18).

37. Robert Maguire, "Audit Shows NRA Spending Surged $100 Million amidst Pro-Trump Push in 2016," Center for Responsive Politics, November 15, 2017, www.opensecrets.org/news/2017/11/audit-shows-nra-spending-surged-100-million-amidst-pro-trump-push-in-2016/ (accessed 7/27/18).

38. Martin Gilens, *Economic Inequality and Political Power in America* (New York: Oxford University Press, 2012).

39. *Citizens United v. Federal Election Commission*, 558 U.S. __ (2010).

40. Center for Responsive Politics, "Behind the Candidates: Campaign Committees and Outside Groups," www.opensecrets.org/pres16/raised-summ (accessed 4/6/18).

41. Center for Responsive Politics, "2016 Outside Spending, by Super PAC," www.opensecrets.org/outsidespending/summ.php?chrt=V&type=S (accessed 11/10/16).

42. Center for Responsive Politics, "2016 Outside Spending, by Super PAC," www.opensecrets.org/outsidespending/summ.php?chrt=V&type=S (accessed 1/15/18).

43. Center for Responsive Politics, "2018 Outside Spending, by Super PAC," November 8, 2018, www.opensecrets.org/outsidespending/summ.php?chrt=V&type=S (accessed 11/8/18).

44. Elisabeth R. Gerber, *The Populist Paradox* (Princeton, NJ: Princeton University Press, 1999).

45. Gerber, *Populist Paradox.*

46. *The Federalist Papers*, no. 10.

47. Olson, *Logic of Collective Action.*

CHAPTER 12

1. "Small Business Owners Praise GOP Tax Bill," Fox Business, December 20, 2017, www.foxbusiness.com/politics/2017/12/20/small-business-owners-praise-gop-tax-bill.html (accessed 2/3/18).

2. Erin Dooley and Meridith McGraw, "Program That Provides Low-Cost Health Care to 9M Children Set to Expire," ABC News, September 29, 2017, abcnews.go.com/US/program-low-cost-health-care-9m-children-set/story?id=50188069 (accessed 2/4/18).

3. Juliette Cubanski and Tricia Neuman, "The Facts of Medicare Spending and Financing," Kaiser Family Foundation Issue Brief, July 18, 2017, www.kff.org/medicare/issue-brief/the-facts-on-medicare-spending-and-financing/ (accessed 2/4/18).

4. Jennifer E. Manning, *Membership of the 113th Congress: A Profile* (Washington, DC: Congressional Research Service, October 31, 2013), www.senate.gov/CRSReports/crs-publish.cfm?pid=%260BL%2BR%5CC%3F%0A (accessed 12/1/13).

5. "Growing Racial and Ethnic Diversity in Congress," Pew Research Center, January 24, 2017, www.pewresearch.org/fact-tank/2017/01/24/115th-congress-sets-new-high-for-racial-ethnic-diversity/ft_17-01-23_congressdiversity/ (accessed 3/22/18).

6. Manning, *Membership of the 113th Congress.*

7. Jennifer E. Manning, *Membership of the 114th Congress: A Profile* (Washington, DC: Congressional Research Service, June 11, 2015), www.fas.org/sgp/crs/misc/R43869.pdf (accessed 9/14/15).

8. Manning, *Membership of the 113th Congress.*

9. For a discussion, see Benjamin Ginsberg, *The Consequences of Consent* (New York: Random House, 1982), chap. 1.

10. See Kristen D. Burnett, *Congressional Apportionment,* U.S. Census Bureau, November 2011, www.census.gov/prod/cen2010/briefs/c2010br-08.pdf (accessed 1/23/12). For some interesting empirical evidence, see Angus Campbell et al., *Elections and the Political Order* (New York: Wiley, 1966), chap. 11; for more recent considerations about the relationship between members of Congress and their constituents, see Lawrence Jacobs and Robert Y. Shapiro, *Politicians Don't Pander: Political Manipulation and the Loss of Democratic Responsiveness* (Chicago: University of Chicago Press, 2000); and Larry M. Bartels, *Unequal Democracy: The Political Economy of the New Gilded Age* (Princeton, NJ: Princeton University Press, 2008).

11. Norman J. Ornstein et al., *Vital Statistics on Congress* (Washington, DC: Brookings Institution Press, 2017), Tables 5–3 and 5–4, www.brookings.edu/,/media/Research/Files/Reports/2013/07/vital-statistics-congress-mann-ornstein/Vital-Statistics-Full-Data-Set.pdf?la5en (accessed 3/22/18); Norman J. Ornstein, Thomas E. Mann, and Michael J. Malbin, *Vital Statistics on Congress 2008* (Washington, DC: Brookings Institution Press, 2009), 111–12.

12. Ashley Parker, "Spotlighting Constituents to Buoy Congressional Candidates," *New York Times* (October 8, 2014), www.nytimes.com/2014/10/09/us/politics/out-of-the-mouths-of-constituents-candidates-find-a-message.html (accessed 9/14/15); Juana Summers, "Constituent Services Give Voters Something to Remember," National Public Radio, www.npr.org/2014/10/28/359615965/constituent-services-give-voters-something-to-remember (accessed 9/14/15).

13. Linda Fowler and Robert McClure, *Political Ambition: Who Decides to Run for Congress* (New Haven, CT: Yale University Press, 1989); and Alan Ehrenhalt, *The United States of Ambition: Politicians, Power, and the Pursuit of Office* (New York: Three Rivers Press, 1992).

14. Center for Responsive Politics, "Reelection Rates over the Years," www.opensecrets.org/bigpicture/reelect.php (accessed 11/9/18).

15. Author's calculations from Ballotpedia.org

16. Michael Leahy, "House Rules," *Washington Post,* June 10, 2007, W12. Simone Pathé, "Democrats Identify Vulnerable Incumbent Members for 2018," Roll Call, March 6, 2017, www.rollcall.com/politics/democrats-identify-vulnerable-members-2018 (accessed 3/22/18).

17. Barbara C. Burrell, *A Woman's Place Is in the House: Campaigning for Congress in the Feminist Era* (Ann Arbor: University of Michigan Press, 1994); and David Broder, "Key to Women's Political Parity: Running," *Washington Post,* September 8, 1994, A17.

18. Dan Balz, "Dodd, Dorgan, and Ritter to Retire as Democrats Face a Difficult Mid-Term Year," *Washington Post,* January 7, 2010.

19. Mark Hugo Lopez and Paul Taylor, "The 2010 Congressional Reapportionment and Latinos," Pew Research Center, www.pewhispanic.org/2011/01/05/the-2010-congressional-reapportionment-and-latinos/ (accessed 2/24/14).

20. Greg Giroux, "Republicans Win Congress as Democrats Get Most Votes," Bloomberg, March 18, 2013, www.bloomberg.com/news/2013-03-19/republicans-win-congress-as-democrats-get-most-votes.html (accessed 12/2/13).

21. Eric McGhee, "Are the Democrats Still at a Disadvantage in Redistricting?" *The Monkey Cage* (blog), July 9, 2013, themonkeycage.org/2013/07/09/are-the-democrats-still-at-a-disadvantage-in-redistricting/ (accessed 12/2/13).

22. Royce Crocker, *Congressional Redistricting: An Overview* (Washington, DC: Congressional Research Service, November 21, 2012), www.fas.org/sgp/crs/misc/R42831.pdf (accessed 12/2/13).

23. Adam Liptak, "Supreme Court Rebuffs Lawmakers over Independent Redistricting Plan," *New York Times,* June 29, 2015, www.nytimes.com/2015/06/30/us/supreme-court-upholds-creation-of-arizona-redistricting-commission.html?_r50 (accessed 9/14/15).

24. *Gill v. Whitford*, 585 U.S. __ (2018).

25. R. E. Cohen, "Did Redistricting Sink the Democrats?" *National Journal*, December 17, 1994, 2984.

26. *Miller v. Johnson*, 515 U.S. 900 (1995).

27. Bernie Becker, "Reapportionment Roundup," *New York Times*, December 24, 2009, http://thecaucus.blogs .nytimes.com/2009/12/24/reapportionment-roundup/ (accessed 1/31/10).

28. *Shelby County v. Holder*, 570 U.S. __ (2013); L. Paige Whitaker, *Congressional Redistricting and the Voting Rights Act: A Legal Overview* (Washington, DC: Congressional Research Service, August 30, 2013), www.fas.org/sgp/crs/ misc/R42482.pdf (accessed 12/2/13).

29. Chris Cillizza, "What the Supreme Court's Voting Rights Act Decision Means for Politics," *Washington Post*, June 25, 2013, www.washingtonpost.com/blogs/the -fix/wp/2013/06/25/what-the-voting-rights-act-decision -means-for-politics/ (accessed 12/2/13).

30. Tarini Parti, "High Court Reasserts Voting Rights Act in Alabama Decision," *Politico*, March 25, 2015, www.politico.com/story/2015/03/supreme -court-alabama-redistricting-ruling-116384 (accessed 9/14/15).

31. Tom Hamburger and Richard Simon, "Everybody Will Know if It's Pork," *Los Angeles Times*, January 6, 2007, A1.

32. Don Seymour, "House Republicans Renew Earmark Ban for 113th Congress," website of the Speaker of the House, November 16, 2012, www.speaker.gov/general/house -republicans-renew-earmark-ban-113th-congress (accessed 12/1/13).

33. Aaron Blake, "Trump Wants to Bring Earmarks Back," *Washington Post*, January 10, 2018, www.washingtonpost .com/news/the-fix/wp/2018/01/10/trump-wants-to -bring-earmarks-back-heres-why-its-not-so-crazy/?utm _term=.5748db2288a1 (accessed 3/22/18).

34. Martin Frost and Tom Davis, "How to Fix What Ails Congress: Bring Back Earmarks," *Los Angeles Times*, February 8, 2015, www.latimes.com/opinion/op-ed/ la-oe-frost-earmark-spending-20150209-story.html (accessed 9/14/15).

35. Richard Fenno, Jr., *Home Style: House Members in Their Districts* (Boston: Little, Brown, 1978).

36. Edward Epstein, "Dusting Off Deliberation," *CQ Weekly*, June 14, 2010, 1436–42. Sarah Binder, "Where Have All the Conference Committees Gone?" *The Monkey Cage* (blog), December 21, 2011, themonkeycage .org/blog/2011/12/21/where-have-all-the-conference -committees-gone/ (accessed 2/7/12).

37. Derek Willis, "Republicans Mix It Up When Assigning House Chairmen for the 108th," *Congressional Quarterly Weekly*, January 11, 2003, 89.

38. Rebecca Kimitch, "CQ Guide to the Committees: Democrats Opt to Spread the Power," *Congressional Quarterly Weekly*, April 16, 2007, 1080.

39. Richard E. Cohen, "Crackup of the Committees," *National Journal*, July 31, 1999, 2210–16.

40. See, for example, the announcement of an agreement on the Agricultural Act of 2014, House Committee on Agriculture, "House–Senate Negotiators Announce Bipartisan Agreement on Final Farm Bill," press release, http://agriculture.house.gov/news/documentsingle. aspx?DocumentID51220 (accessed 9/21/15).

41. Norman J. Ornstein, et al., *Vital Statistics on Congress* (Washington, DC: Brookings Institution and American Enterprise Institute, July 2013), chap. 5, www.brookings .edu/research/reports/2013/07/vital-statistics-congress -mann-ornstein (accessed 6/13/16).

42. H.R. 1111: Department of Peacebuilding Act of 2015, govtrack.us, www.govtrack.us/congress/bills/114/hr1111 (accessed 9/21/15).

43. "Statistics and Historical Comparisons: Bills by Final Status," govtrack.us, www.govtrack.us/congress/bills/ statistics (accessed 9/21/15).

44. U.S. Senate, "Senate Actions on Cloture Motions," www .senate.gov/pagelayout/reference/cloture_motions/ clotureCounts.htm (accessed 11/29/13).

45. Jeremy W. Peters, "Senate Vote Curbs Filibuster Power to Stall Nominees," *New York Times*, November 22, 2013, A1.

46. Jonathan Weisman, "House Votes 411–18 to Pass Ethics Overhaul," *Washington Post*, August 1, 2007, A1.

47. Leigh Munsil, "Graham Won't Lift Nominee-Hold Threat over Benghazi," Politico, November 11, 2013, www.politico.com/blogs/politico-live/2013/11/graham -wont-lift-nomineehold-threat-over-benghazi-177154 .html (accessed 11/30/13).

48. Sean Sullivan and Mike DeBonis, "Congress Averts Homeland Security Shutdown with One-Week Extension," *Washington Post*, February 28, 2015, www .washingtonpost.com/politics/house-gop-hopes -to-pass-stopgap-dhs-funding-before-midnight -shutdown/2015/02/27/22021530-be88-11e4-b274 -e5209a3bc9a9_story.html (accessed 9/21/15).

49. John W. Kingdon, *Congressmen's Voting Decisions* (New York: Harper and Row, 1973), chap. 3; and R. Douglas Arnold, *The Logic of Congressional Action* (New Haven, CT: Yale University Press, 1990).

50. Ben Jacobs and David Smith, "Donald Trump Blames Democrats for Stunning Failure to Repeal Obamacare," *Guardian*, March 25, 2017, www.theguardian.com/us -news/2017/mar/24/republican-healthcare-plan-bill-vote -pulled-obamacare-trump (accessed 3/22/18).

51. Jane Fritsch, "The Grass Roots, Just a Free Phone Call Away," *New York Times*, June 23, 1995, A1.

52. Eric Lipton and Ben Protess, "Banks' Lobbyists Help in Drafting Financial Bills," *New York Times*, May 23, 2013, dealbook.nytimes.com/2013/05/23/banks -lobbyists-help-in-drafting-financial-bills/ (accessed 9/21/15); Michael Corkery, "Citigroup Becomes the Fall Guy in the Spending Bill Battle" *New York Times*, December 12, 2014, dealbook.nytimes .com/2014/12/12/citigroup-becomes-the-fall-guy-in-the -spending-bill-battle/ (accessed 9/21/15).

53. Eliza Newlin Carney, "For Ethics Hawks, Congress Could Be Next," *National Journal Online*, February 17, 2009, http://freerepublic.com/focus/f-new/2187821/posts (accessed 2/5/10); Center for Responsive Politics, "Top Individual Contributors: All Federal Contributions (2018)," OpenSecrets, www.opensecrets.org/overview/topindivs.php (accessed 10/12/18).

54. Holly Idelson, "Signs Point to Greater Loyalty on Both Sides of the Aisle," *Congressional Quarterly Weekly Report*, December 19, 1992, 3849.

55. Norman J. Ornstein and Thomas E. Mann, *Vital Statistics on Congress* (Washington DC: Brookings Institution, 2018), www.brookings.edu/multi-chapter-report/vital-statistics-on-congress/ (accessed 7/25/18).

56. Center for Responsive Politics, "Contributions to Federal Candidates, 2016," www.opensecrets.org/pacs/pacgot.php?cmte=C00525600&cycle=2016 (accessed 10/13/16).

57. Kimitch, "CQ Guide to the Committees," 1080.

58. Leahy, "House Rules," W12; Marin Cogan, "Freshmen Jump Line for Floor Speeches," *Politico*, January 18, 2011, www.politico.com/news/stories/0111/47791.html (accessed 2/9/12).

59. Daniel Newhauser, "Three Booted from GOP Whip Team as Leaders Crack Down," *National Journal*, June 16, 2015, www.nationaljournal.com/congress/2015/06/16/Three-Booted-From-GOP-Whip-Team-Leaders-Crack-Down (accessed 9/21/15).

60. James J. Kilpatrick, "Don't Overlook Corn for Porn Plot," *Chicago Sun-Times*, January 3, 1992, 23.

61. Dennis McDougal, "Cattle Are Bargaining Chip of the NEA," *Los Angeles Times*, November 2, 1991, F1.

62. Mann and Ornstein, "Vital Statistics," 2017, Table 6-4.

63. "115th Congress (2017–2018)," www.congress.gov (accessed 11/9/18).

64. Thomas Kaplan, "Congress Approves $1.3 Trillion Spending Bill, Averting a Shutdown," *New York Times*, March 22, 2018, www.nytimes.com/2018/03/22/us/politics/house-passes-spending-bill.html?login=email&auth=login-email (accessed 7/30/18).

65. Geoffrey C. Layman, Thomas M. Carsey, and Juliana Menasce Horowitz, "Party Polarization in American Politics: Characteristics, Causes, and Consequences," *Annual Review of Political Science*, no. 9 (2006): 83–110.

66. For example, Fredreka Schouten, "Club for Growth Plans New Push in House Races," *USA Today*, August 17, 2015, http://onpolitics.usatoday.com/2015/08/17/club-for-growth-plans-new-push-in-house-races/ (accessed 9/21/15).

67. Elizabeth Williamson, "Revival of Oversight Role Sought; Congress Hires More Investigators, Plans Subpoenas," *Washington Post*, April 25, 2007, A1.

68. Susan Milligan, "Congress Reduces Its Oversight Role; Since Clinton, a Change in Focus," *Boston Globe*, November 20, 2005, A1; Bill Shaikin, "Clemens Is Star Attraction at Hearing," *Los Angeles Times*, February 12, 2008, D1.

69. Eric Lipton and Sheryl Gay Stolberg, "Health Law Rollout Provides Rich Target for Oversight Chief," *New York Times*, November 12, 2013, www.nytimes.com/2013/11/13/us/politics/health-law-rollout-provides-rich-target-for-oversight-chief.html?_r50 (accessed 12/12/13).

70. Michael S. Schmidt and Maggie Haberman, "Aides for Hillary Clinton and Benghazi Committee Dispute Testimony Plan," *New York Times*, July 25, 2015, www.nytimes.com/2015/07/26/us/clinton-to-testify-publicly-before-house-committee-investigating-benghazi-attacks.html (accessed 9/21/15).

71. Gregory Krieg, "FBI Boss Comey's 7 Most Damning Lines on Clinton," CNN, July 5, 2016, www.cnn.com/2016/07/05/politics/fbi-clinton-email-server-comey-damning-lines/ (accessed 9/21/16).

72. *United States v. Pink*, 315 U.S. 203 (1942). For a good discussion of the problem, see James W. Davis, *The American Presidency* (New York: Harper and Row, 1987), chap. 8.

73. U.S. House, "Impeachment," http://history.house.gov/Institution/Origins-Development/Impeachment/ (accessed 4/18/14).

74. Carroll J. Doherty, "Impeachment: How It Would Work," *Congressional Quarterly Weekly Report*, January 31, 1998, 222.

CHAPTER 13

1. This account is drawn from Amy Nixon, "Community Raises Funds to Support Hartley Family after Son Dies in Work Accident," *Tennessean*, May 4, 2017, www.tennessean.com/story/news/local/cheatham/2017/05/04/community-raises-funds-support-hartley-family-after-son-dies-work-accident/101283588/ (accessed 3/2/18); Eric Lipton, "Why Has the E.P.A. Shifted on Toxic Chemicals? An Industry Insider Helps Call the Shots," *New York Times*, October 21, 2017, www.nytimes.com/2017/10/21/us/trump-epa-chemicals-regulations.html (accessed 3/2/18); and Jamie Smith Hopkins, "EPA Wants to Restrict Sometimes-Deadly Paint Stripped Chemical," The Center for Public Integrity, January 12, 2017, www.publicintegrity.org/2017/01/12/20589/epa-wants-restrict-sometimes-deadly-paint-stripper-chemical (accessed 3/2/18).

2. These statutes are contained mainly in Title 10 of the U.S. Code, Sections 331, 332, and 333.

3. The best study covering all aspects of the domestic use of the military is that of Adam Yarmolinsky, *The Military Establishment* (New York: Harper and Row, 1971). Probably the most famous instance of a president's unilateral use of the power to protect a state "against domestic violence" was President Grover Cleveland's dealing with the Pullman strike of 1894. The famous Supreme Court case that ensued was *In re Debs*, 158 U.S. 564 (1895).

4. In *United States v. Pink*, 315 U.S. 203 (1942), the Supreme Court confirmed that an executive agreement is the legal equivalent of a treaty, despite the absence of Senate

approval. This case approved the executive agreement that was used to establish diplomatic relations with the Soviet Union in 1933. An executive agreement, not a treaty, was used in 1940 to exchange "fifty over-age destroyers" for 99-year leases on some important military bases.

5. *United States v. Nixon*, 418 U.S. 683 (1974).

6. For a different perspective, see William F. Grover, *The President as Prisoner: A Structural Critique of the Carter and Reagan Years* (Albany: State University of New York Press, 1988).

7. A third source of presidential power is implied from the provision for "faithful execution of the laws." This is the president's power to impound funds—that is, to refuse to spend money Congress has appropriated for certain purposes. One author referred to this as a "retroactive veto power" (Robert E. Goostree, "The Power of the President to Impound Appropriated Funds," *American University Law Review* 11 [January 1962]: 32–47). This impoundment power has been used freely and to considerable effect by many modern presidents, and Congress has occasionally delegated such power to the president by statute. But in reaction to the Watergate scandal, Congress adopted the Congressional Budget and Impoundment Control Act of 1974, which was designed to circumscribe the president's ability to impound funds by requiring that the president must spend all appropriated funds unless both houses of Congress consented to an impoundment within 45 days of a presidential request. Therefore, since 1974, the use of impoundment has declined significantly. Presidents have had either to bite their tongues and accept unwanted appropriations or to revert to the older and more dependable but politically limited method of vetoing the entire bill.

8. For more on the veto, see Robert J. Spitzer, *The Presidential Veto: Touchstone of the American Presidency* (Albany: State University of New York Press, 1989).

9. Dan Eggen, "Bush Announces Veto of Waterboarding Ban," *Washington Post*, March 8, 2008, www.washingtonpost.com/wp-dyn/content/article/2008/03/08AR2008030800304.html (accessed 6/10/10).

10. *Myers v. United States*, 272 U.S. 52 (1926). In the later case of *Humphrey's Executor v. United States*, 295 U.S. 602 (1935), the Court ruled that the executives of independent commissions could only be removed for cause.

11. John Yoo, *The Powers of War and Peace* (Chicago: University of Chicago Press, 2003). See also Dana D. Nelson, "The 'Unitary Executive' Question," *Los Angeles Times*, October 11, 2008, www.latimes.com/opinion/la-oe-nelson11-2008oct11-story.html (accessed 4/20/18).

12. See Eric Posner and Adrian Vermeule, *The Executive Unbound: After the Madisonian Republic* (Chicago: University of Chicago Press, 2011).

13. "Unchecked Abuse," *Washington Post*, January 11, 2006, www.washingtonpost.com/wp-dyn/content/article/2006/01/10/AR2006011001536.html (accessed 3/25/18).

14. Elena Kagan, "Presidential Administration," *Harvard Law Review* 114 (June 2001): 2262.

15. Kenneth F. Warren, *Administrative Law*, 3rd ed. (Upper Saddle River, NJ: Prentice-Hall, 1996), 250.

16. National Industrial Recovery Act, 48 Stat. 200 (1933).

17. Theodore J. Lowi, *The End of Liberalism*, 2nd ed. (New York: W. W. Norton, 1979), 117.

18. Jerry L. Nashaw, *Greed, Chaos, and Governance: Using Public Choice to Improve Public Law* (New Haven, CT: Yale University Press, 1997), 106.

19. Louis Fisher, "The Unitary Executive and Inherent Executive Power," *Journal of Constitutional Law*, 12, no. 1 (February 2010): 586.

20. 10 Annals of Cong. 613 (1800).

21. Louis Fisher, "Presidential Inherent Power: The 'Sole Organ' Doctrine," *Presidential Studies Quarterly* 37, no.1 (March 2007): 139.

22. *United States v. Curtiss-Wright Corp.*, 299 U.S. 304 (1936).

23. Clement Fatovic, *Outside the Law: Emergency and Executive Power* (Baltimore: Johns Hopkins University Press, 2009).

24. Louis Fisher, "Invoking Inherent Powers."

25. John Gramlich, "Holder Sees Constitutional Basis for Obama's Executive Actions," *Roll Call*, January 29, 2014, www.rollcall.com/news/holder_sees_constitutional_basis_for_obamas_executive_actions-230528-1.html?pg=1 (accessed 4/20/18).

26. Harold C. Relyea, "National Emergency Powers," Congressional Research Service, 2007, http://fas.org/sgp/crs/natsec/98-505.pdf (accessed 3/27/18).

27. Matthew Crenson and Benjamin Ginsberg, *Presidential Power: Unchecked and Unbalanced*, New York: W. W. Norton, 2007, pp. 341–342.

28. Andrew Reeves, "Political Disaster: Unilateral Powers, Electoral Incentives, and Presidential Disaster Declarations," *Journal of Politics* 73, no. 4 (October 2011): 1142–51.

29. William G. Howell and David E. Lewis, "Agencies by Presidential Design," *Journal of Politics* 64, no. 4 (November 2002): 1095–114.

30. A substantial portion of this section is taken from Theodore J. Lowi, *The Personal President* (Ithaca, NY: Cornell University Press, 1985), 141–50.

31. The actual number is difficult to estimate because, as with White House staff, some EOP personnel, especially in national security work, are detailed to the EOP from outside agencies.

32. Article I, Section 3, provides that "The Vice-President . . . shall be President of the Senate, but shall have no Vote, unless they be equally divided." This is the only vote the vice president is allowed.

33. Samuel Kernell, *Going Public: New Strategies of Presidential Leadership*, 3rd ed. (Washington, DC: CQ Press, 1997); also Jeffrey K. Tulis, *The Rhetorical Presidency* (Princeton, NJ: Princeton University Press, 1987).

34. Tulis, *Rhetorical Presidency*, 91.

35. Sidney M. Milkis, *The President and the Parties* (New York: Oxford University Press, 1993), 97.

36. James MacGregor Burns, *Roosevelt: The Lion and the Fox* (New York: Harcourt, Brace, 1956), 317.

37. Burns, *Roosevelt*, 317.

38. Kernell, *Going Public*, 79.

39. Claire Cain Miller, "How Obama's Internet Campaign Changed Politics," *New York Times*, November 7, 2008, bits.blogs.nytimes.com/2008/11/07/how-obamas-internet-campaign-changed-politics/?_php5true&_type5blogs&_r5o (accessed 4/7/14); David Plouffe, *The Audacity to Win: The Inside Story and Lessons of Barack Obama's Historic Victory* (New York: Viking, 2009).

40. "Presidential Job Approval Center," Gallup, www.gallup.com/poll/124922/presidential-approval-center.aspx (accessed 3/14/14).

41. Lowi, *Personal President*.

42. Lowi, *Personal President*, 11.

43. Gallup, "Trump Job Approval (Weekly)," July 22, 2018, https://news.gallup.com/poll/203207/trump-job-approval-weekly.aspx (accessed 7/27/18).

44. Milkis, *President and the Parties*, 128.

45. Milkis, *President and the Parties*, 160.

46. Kagan, "Presidential Administration," 2265.

47. John M. Broder, "Powerful Shaper of U.S. Rules Quits, with Critics in Wake," *New York Times*, August 4, 2012, A1.

48. Nadja Popovich, "67 Environmental Rules on the Way Out under Trump," *New York Times*, January 31, 2018, www.nytimes.com/interactive/2017/10/05/climate/trump-environment-rules-reversed.html (accessed 2/20/18).

49. Terry M. Moe and William G. Howell, "The Presidential Power of Unilateral Action," *Journal of Law, Economics and Organization* 15, no. 1 (January 1999): 133–34.

50. Todd F. Gaziano, "The Uses and Abuses of Executive Orders and Other Presidential Directives," *Texas Review of Law and Politics* 5 (Spring 2001): 267–315.

51. Kenneth R. Mayer, *With the Stroke of a Pen: Executive Orders and Presidential Power* (Princeton, NJ: Princeton University Press, 2001), 71–73.

52. Harold C. Relyea, "Presidential Directives: Background and Overview," Congressional Research Service, November 26, 2008, http://fas.org/sgp/crs/misc/98-611.pdf (accessed 3/25/18).

53. Vivian S. Chu and Ted Garvey, "Executive Orders: Issuance, Modification, and Revocation," Congressional Research Service, April 16, 2014, http://fas.org/sgp/crs/misc/RS20846.pdf (accessed 3/25/18).

54. Adam L. Warber, *Executive Orders and the Modern Presidency* (Boulder, CO: Lynne Rienner Publishers, 2006), 118–120.

55. Chu and Garvey, "Executive Orders."

56. Chu and Garvey, "Executive Orders," 10.

57. *Dames & Moore v. Regan*, 453 U.S. 654 (1981).

58. Philip Cooper, *By Order of the President* (Lawrence: University Press of Kansas, 2002), 201.

59. Edward S. Corwin, *The President: Office and Powers*, 5th ed. (New York: NYU Press, 1984), 283.

60. Alexander Hamilton, James Madison, and John Jay, *The Federalist Papers*, ed. Clinton Rossiter (New York: New American Library, 1961), no. 70, 423–30.

61. Terry Moe, "The Presidency and the Bureaucracy: The Presidential Advantage," in *The Presidency and the Political System*, ed. Michael Nelson (Washington, DC: CQ Press, 2002), 416–20.

62. Louis Fisher, *Congressional Abdication on War and Spending* (College Station: Texas A&M Press, 2000).

63. Letter from Thomas Jefferson to James Madison (September 6, 1789), in *The Papers of Thomas Jefferson*, ed. Julian P. Boyd (Princeton, NJ: Princeton University Press, 1958), 392, 397.

CHAPTER 14

1. This account draws from Abby Goodnough, Monica Davey, and Mitch Smith, "When the Water Turned Brown," *New York Times,* January 23, 2016; Amy Davidson, "The Contempt That Poisoned Flint's Water," *The New Yorker,* January 22, 2016; and Lindsey Smith, "This Mom Helped Uncover What Was Really Going on With Flint's Water," Michigan Public Radio, December 4, 2015, michiganradio.org/post/mom-helped-uncover-what-was-really-going-flint-s-water (accessed 8/11/17).

2. Flint Water Advisory Task Force, Final Report, March 2016, www.michigan.gov/documents/snyder/FWATF_FINAL_REPORT_21March2016_517805_7.pdf (accessed 8/11/17).

3. Amy B. Zegart, *Spying Blind: The CIA, The FBI, and the Origins of 9/11* (Princeton, NJ: Princeton University Press, 2009).

4. Paul C. Light, "A Cascade of Failures: Why Government Fails, and How to Stop It," Brookings Institution, July 14, 2014, www.brookings.edu/research/a-cascade-of-failures-why-government-fails-and-how-to-stop-it/ (accessed 8/5/17).

5. Environmental Protection Agency, "Regulations and Standards: Light Duty," www3.epa.gov/otaq/climate/regs-light-duty.htm#new1 (accessed 7/9/16).

6. Lisa Friedman and Brad Plumer, "E.P.A. Announces Repeal of Major Obama-Era Carbon Emissions Rule," *New York Times,* October 9, 2017, www.nytimes.com/2017/10/09/climate/clean-power-plan.html (accessed 10/24/17).

7. Thanks to Andy Rudalevige for this formulation.

8. Juliet Eilperin, "EPA Needed More Data before Ruling on Greenhouse Gas Emissions, Report Says," *Washington Post*, September 28, 2011, www.washingtonpost.com/national/health-science/epa-needed-more-data-before-ruling-on-greenhouse-gas-emissions-report-says/2011/09/28/gIQABs2X5K_story.html (accessed 1/2/12).

9. Margaret Cronin Fisk, Kartikay Mehrotra, Alan Katz, and Jeff Plungis, "Volkswagen Agrees to $15 Billion Diesel-Cheating Settlement," Bloomberg News, June 28, 2016, www.bloomberg.com/news/articles/2016-06-28/volkswagen-to-pay-14-7-billion-to-settle-u-s-emissions-claims (accessed 7/8/16).

10. Gary Bryner, *Bureaucratic Discretion* (New York: Pergamon Press, 1987).

11. "Federal Employees by State," *Governing,* www.governing.com/gov-data/federal-employees-workforce-numbers-by-state.html (accessed 8/10/17).

12. Congressional Budget Office, "Comparing the Compensation of Federal and Private-Sector Employees, 2011–2015," April 2017, www.cbo.gov/system/files/115th-congress-2017-2018/reports/52637-federalprivatepay.pdf (accessed 12/20/17).

13. U.S. Office of Personnel Management, "Women in Federal Service," www.fedview.opm.gov/2014files/2014_Womens_Report.pdf (accessed 8/10/17); Office of Personnel Management, "Profile of Federal Civilian Non-Postal Employees," September 30, 2017, www.opm.gov/policy-data-oversight/data-analysis-documentation/federal-employment-reports/reports-publications/profile-of-federal-civilian-non-postal-employees/ (accessed 10/13/18).

14. The President's Budget FY18, Analytical Perspectives, www.whitehouse.gov/omb/budget (accessed 8/10/17).

15. President Barack Obama, First Inaugural Address, January 21, 2009, https://obamawhitehouse.archives.gov/blog/2009/01/21/president-barack-obamas-inaugural-address (accessed 8/5/17).

16. Office of Personnel Management, "Federal Civilian Employment," September 2017, www.opm.gov/policy-data-oversight/data-analysis-documentation/federal-employment-reports/reports-publications/federal-civilian-employment/ (accessed 10/13/18); George M. Reynolds and Amanda Shendruk, "Demographics of the U.S. Military," Council on Foreign Relations, April 24, 2018, www.cfr.org/article/demographics-us-military (accessed 10/13/18).

17. Bureau of Labor Statistics, Current Employment Statistics, "Table B-1. Employees on Nonfarm Payrolls by Industry Sector and Selected Industry Detail," www.bls.gov/webapps/legacy/cesbtab1.htm (accessed 7/15/16).

18. There are historical reasons that American Cabinet-level administrators are called "secretaries." During the Second Continental Congress and the subsequent confederal government, standing committees were formed to deal with executive functions related to foreign affairs, military and maritime issues, and public financing. The heads of those committees were called "secretaries" because their primary task was to handle all correspondence and documentation related to their areas of responsibility.

19. Lauren Camera, "DeVos Outlines Vision for 'American Education,'" *U.S. News and World Report,* October 11, 2017, www.usnews.com/news/education-news/articles/2017-10-11/betsy-devos-outlines-vision-for-american-education (accessed 12/20/17).

20. Morgan Chalfant, "Homeland Security Sees Power Grow under Trump," The Hill, October 19, 2017, http://thehill.com/policy/national-security/356131-homeland-security-sees-power-grow-under-trump (accessed 11/10/17); Department of Homeland Security, "Budget Will Advance DHS Priorities," February 12, 2018, www.dhs.gov/news/2018/02/12/department-homeland-security-statement-president-s-fiscal-year-2019-budget (accessed 10/13/18).

21. Laura Koran, Elise Labott, and Nicole Gaouette, "Tillerson Visits Russia as Tensions over Syria Flare," CNN.com, April 11, 2017, www.cnn.com/2017/04/11/politics/rex-tillerson-putin-russia-g7/index.html (accessed 8/11/17).

22. U.S. Department of State, "Department Organization Chart: November 2016," www.state.gov/r/pa/ei/rls/dos/99484.htm (accessed 8/5/17); Robbie Gramer, "Lawmakers Slam Tillerson's Bungled State Department Reforms," *Foreign Policy,* November 15, 2017, http://foreignpolicy.com/2017/11/15/lawmakers-slam-tillersons-bungled-state-department-reforms-diplomacy-foreign-service-trump-administration-redesign-congress-corker-cardin/ (accessed 1/5/18).

23. For more details, consult John E. Harr, *The Professional Diplomat* (Princeton, NJ: Princeton University Press, 1972), 11; and Nicholas Horrock, "The CIA Has Neighbors in the 'Intelligence Community,'" *New York Times,* June 29, 1975, sec. 4, 2. See also Morton H. Halperin and Priscilla Clapp, *Bureaucratic Politics and Foreign Policy,* 2nd ed., with Arnold Kanter (Washington, DC: Brookings Institution Press, 2007).

24. In 2017 the Department of Defense had over 1.3 million active duty personnel and nearly 750,000 civilian employees. U.S. Department of Defense, "About the Department of Defense," www.defense.gov/About/ (accessed 12/20/17).

25. Congressional Research Service, "Defense Primer: The Department of Defense," December 13, 2016, https://fas.org/sgp/crs/natsec/IF10543.pdf (accessed 8/10/17).

26. The 5 percent reduction is compared to a 2012 baseline. Congressional Budget Office, "The U.S. Military's Force Structure: A Primer," July 29, 2016, www.cbo.gov/publication/51535 (accessed 8/10/17).

27. Louise Osborne, "Europeans Outraged over NSA Spying, Threaten Action," *USA Today,* October 29, 2013, www.usatoday.com/story/news/world/2013/10/28/report-nsa-spain/3284609/ (accessed 1/24/14).

28. Warren Strobel and Mark Hosenball, "White House Review Panel Proposes Curbs on Some NSA Programs," Reuters, December 18, 2013, www.reuters.com/article/2013/12/18/us-usa-surveillance-obama-idUSBRE9BG1AQ20131218 (accessed 1/24/14).

29. David Cole, "Here's What's Wrong with the USA Freedom Act," *The Nation,* May 6, 2015, www.thenation

.com/article/heres-whats-wrong-usa-freedom-act/ (accessed 11/10/17).

30. U.S. Department of the Treasury, "The Debt to the Penny and Who Holds It," www.treasurydirect.gov/NP/debt/current (accessed 3/27/18).

31. Financial Stability Oversight Council, "Designations," www.treasury.gov/initiatives/fsoc/designations/Pages/default.aspx (accessed 1/23/14).

32. Lisa Rein, "IRS Conference in Anaheim Featured Gifts, Other Excesses Approved by Top Officials, Report Says," *Washington Post*, June, 6, 2013, www.washingtonpost.com/blogs/federal-eye/wp/2013/06/04/irs-conference-in-anaheim-featured-gifts-other-excesses-approved-by-top-officials-report-says/ (accessed 1/31/14).

33. Alan Rappeport, "Under Trump, An Already Depleted I.R.S. Could Face Deep Cuts," *New York Times* March 2, 2017, www.nytimes.com/2017/03/02/us/politics/trump-mnuchin-irs.html (accessed 8/5/17); Joe Davidson, "IRS Chief Says Trump's Budget Would Sharply Cut Taxpayer Service," *Washington Post*, June 1, 2018, www.washingtonpost.com/news/powerpost/wp/2018/06/01/irs-chief-says-trumps-budget-would-sharply-cut-taxpayer-service/?utm_term=.5c64e7ca25e9 (accessed 10/13/18).

34. U.S. Department of Health and Human Services, Office of the Inspector General, "CMS Management of the Federal Marketplace: A Case Study," February 2016, https://oig.hhs.gov/oei/reports/oei-06-14-00350.pdf (accessed 8/6/17).

35. U.S. Department of Veterans Affairs, "Veterans Access, Choice, and Accountability Act of 2014 Fact Sheet," www.va.gov/opa/choiceact/documents/choice-act-summary.pdf (accessed 8/6/17).

36. Vice President Gore's National Partnership for Reinventing Government, "Appendix F, History of the National Partnership for Reinventing Government: Accomplishments, 1993–2000, A Summary," http://govinfo.library.unt.edu/npr/whoweare/appendixf.html (accessed 3/28/08).

37. Social and Behavioral Sciences Team 2016 Annual Report, September 2016, https://sbst.gov/download/2016%20SBST%20Annual%20Report.pdf (accessed 8/6/17).

38. Andy Rudalevige, "Trump Wants to Reorganize the Executive Branch. Good Luck with That." *The Monkey Cage* (blog), March 16, 2017, www.washingtonpost.com/news/monkey-cage/wp/2017/03/16/trump-wants-to-reorganize-the-executive-branch-good-luck-to-him/?utm_term=.8b1417c138a2 (accessed 8/6/17).

39. Mick Mulvaney, Office of Management and Budget, "Comprehensive Plan for Reforming the Federal Government and Reducing the Federal Civilian Workforce" memorandum, April 12, 2017, www.whitehouse.gov/sites/whitehouse.gov/files/omb/memoranda/2017/M-17-22.pdf (accessed 8/6/17); Eric Katz, "Transferring Responsibility and Consolidating Offices Highlight Trump Reorganization Plan," Government Executive, February 12, 2018, www.govexec.com/management/2018/02/transferring

-responsibilities-and-consolidating-offices-highlight-trump-reorganization-plan/145936/ (accessed 3/27/18).

40. Nicole Ogrysko, "Omnibus Spending Bill Complicates Administration's Reorg Plans," Federal News Radio, March 22, 2018, https://federalnewsradio.com/budget/2018/03/omnibus-complicates-administrations-reorganization-plans-as-congress-begins-votes/ (accessed 3/27/18).

41. Public Law 101-510, Title XXIX, Sections 2,901 and 2,902 of Part A (Defense Base Closure and Realignment Commission); see the 2005 commission's website, Defense Base Closure and Realignment Commission, www.brac.gov (accessed 1/3/12).

42. Walter Pincus, "For Pentagon, It's Always a Tough Battle to Get Congress to Close Military Bases, Facilities," *Washington Post*, March 17, 2014, www.washingtonpost.com/world/national-security/for-pentagon-its-always-a-tough-battle-to-get-congress-to-close-military-bases-facilities/2014/03/17/a7eda064-a887-11e3-8599-ce7295b6851c_story.html (accessed 9/30/15).

43. Dylan Mathews, "Everything You Could Possibly Need to Know," *Washington Post,* February 20, 2013, www.washingtonpost.com/news/wonk/wp/2013/02/20/the-sequester-absolutely-everything-you-could-possibly-need-to-know-in-one-faq/?utm_term=.6785d26f55af (accessed 8/6/17).

44. Eric Katz, "Social Security Offers Nearly Its Entire Workforce Early Retirement," *Government Executive,* August 4, 2017, http://m.govexec.com/pay-benefits/2017/08/social-security-has-sent-early-out-offers-nearly-its-entire-workforce/140008/?oref=govexec_today_pm_nl (accessed 8/11/17); Louis Jacobson, "Taking the Measure of the Federal Workforce under Donald Trump," Politifact, January 22, 2018, www.politifact.com/truth-o-meter/article/2018/jan/22/taking-measure-federal-workforce/ (accessed 3/27/18).

45. Lenny Bernstein, "Arizona Becomes Last State to Provide Health Insurance to Low-Income Children," *Washington Post,* July 25, 2016, www.washingtonpost.com/news/to-your-health/wp/2016/07/25/arizona-becomes-the-last-state-to-provide-health-insurance-to-low-income-children/?utm_term=.8c9293c169f2 (accessed 8/5/17).

46. Sheila R. Zedlewski, Pamela J. Loprest, and Erika Huber, "What Role Is Welfare Playing in This Period of High Unemployment?" Urban Institute, Fact Sheet 3, August 17, 2011, www.urban.org/UploadedPDF/412378-Role-of-Welfare-in-this-Period-of-High-Unemployment.pdf (accessed 7/4/12).

47. Sabrina Tavernise, "Food Stamps Helped Reduce Poverty Rate, Study Says," *New York Times*, April 10, 2012, A16.

48. John J. Dilulio, Jr., *Bring Back the Bureaucrats: Why More Federal Workers Will Lead to Better (and Smaller!) Government* (West Conshohocken, PA: Templeton Press, 2014); Kimberly J. Morgan and Andrea Louise Campbell, *The Delegated Welfare State* (New York: Oxford University Press, 2011).

49. Paul C. Light, "The New True Size of Government," Organizational Performance Initiative, Research Brief no. 2, Wagner School of Public Service, New York University, 8, https://wagner.nyu.edu/files/performance/True%20Size%20Research%20Brief.pdf (accessed 3/11/08); OMB Watch, "Total Spending by Year," FedSpending.org, www.fedspending.org/fpds/chart_total.php (accessed 1/2/12).

50. Scott Shane and Ron Nixon, "In Washington, Contractors Take On Biggest Role Ever," *New York Times*, February 4, 2007, A1.

51. Daniel Patrick Moynihan, "The Culture of Secrecy," *Public Interest* (Summer 1997): 55–71.

52. Thomas E. Mann and Norman J. Ornstein, *The Broken Branch: How Congress Is Failing America and How to Get It Back on Track* (New York: Oxford University Press, 2006), 155.

53. For the estimates on waste, see Commission on Wartime Contracting in Iraq and Afghanistan, *Transforming Wartime Contracting: Controlling Costs, Reducing Risks: Final Report to Congress*, 18, August 2011, www.wartimecontracting.gov (accessed 1/4/12).

54. Neil Gordon, "Move over FCMD, Make Way for FAPIIS," *POGO* (blog), September 11, 2009, http://pogoblog.typepad.com/pogo/2009/09/move-over-fcmd-make-way-for-fapiis.html (accessed 2/26/10).

55. Government Accountability Office, *Federal Contractors: Better Performance Information Needed to Support Agency Contract Award Decisions*, April 2009, GAO-09-374, www.gao.gov/new.items/d09374.pdf (accessed 2/26/10); Tom Lee, "FAPIIS May Be the Worst Government Website We've Ever Seen," Sunlight Foundation, April 19, 2011, sunlightfoundation.com/blog/2011/04/19/fapiis-may-be-the-worst-government-website-weve-ever-seen/ (accessed 1/23/14).

56. Joe Davidson, "OMB Moves to Cut Outside Contractors," Federal Diary, *Washington Post*, July 29, 2009, www.washingtonpost.com/wp-dyn/content/article/2009/07/28/AR2009072802812.html (accessed 2/18/10).

57. Joe Davidson, "Deficit-Cutters Must Also Weigh the Cost of Contractors," Federal Diary, *Washington Post*, February 4, 2011, www.washingtonpost.com/wp-dyn/content/article/2011/02/03/AR2011020306809.html?nav5emailpage (accessed 1/2/12).

58. Charlie Savage, "U.S. to Phase Out Use of Private Prisons for Federal Inmates," *New York Times,* August 18, 2016, www.nytimes.com/2016/08/19/us/us-to-phase-out-use-of-private-prisons-for-federal-inmates.html?_r=0 (accessed 11/8/17).

59. Marjorie Censer, "Five Provisions in the New Defense Policy Legislation for Contractors to Watch," *Washington Post*, January 5, 2014, www.washingtonpost.com/business/capitalbusiness/five-provisions-in-the-new-defense-policy-legislation-for-contractors-to-watch/2014/01/0/f6d-d00ec-6c10-11e3-a523-fe73f0ff6b8d_story.html (accessed 1/24/14).

60. Dan Egan, "Democrats Proposing New Limits on Corporate Campaign Donations," *Boston Globe*, February 12, 2010, www.boston.com/news/nation/washington/articles/2010/02/12/democrats_proposing_new_limits_on_corporate_campaign_donations/ (accessed 2/27/10).

61. Peter Baker, "Obama Orders Federal Contractors to Provide Workers Paid Sick Leave," *New York Times*, September 7, 2015, www.nytimes.com/2015/09/08/us/politics/obama-to-require-federal-contractors-to-provide-paid-sick-leave.html?_r50 (accessed 9/30/15).

62. Gregory Korte, "Trump Signs Four Bills to Roll Back Obama-Era Regulations," *USA Today,* March 27, 2017, www.usatoday.com/story/news/politics/2017/03/27/trump-signs-four-bills-roll-back-obama-era-regulations/99690456/ (accessed 11/8/17).

63. The title of this section was inspired by Peri Arnold, *Making the Managerial Presidency* (Princeton, NJ: Princeton University Press, 1986).

64. Daniel P. Gitterman, *Calling the Shots: The President, Executive Orders, and Public Policy* (Washington, DC: Brookings Institution Press, 2017).

65. Paul C. Light, *A Government Ill Executed: The Decline of the Federal Service and How To Revive It* (Cambridge, MA: Harvard University Press, 2008).

66. For more details and evaluations, see David Rosenbloom, *Public Administration* (New York: Random House, 1986), 186–221; Charles H. Levine, *The Quiet Crisis of the Civil Service: The Federal Personnel System at the Crossroads*, with the assistance of Rosslyn S. Kleeman (Washington, DC: National Academy of Public Administration, 1986).

67. John Micklethwait, "Managing to Look Attractive," *New Statesman* 125, November 8, 1996, 24.

68. Robert M. Gates, *Duty: Memoirs of a Secretary at War* (New York: Alfred A. Knopf, 2014); Leon Panetta, *Worthy Fights: A Memoir of Leadership in War and Peace* (New York: Penguin, 2014).

69. Michael J. Glennon, *National Security and Double Government* (New York: Oxford University Press, 2015).

70. Michael Crowley, "The Deep State Is Real. But It Might Not Be What You Think," *Politico Magazine,* September/October 2017, www.politico.com/magazine/story/2017/09/05/deep-state-real-cia-fbi-intelligence-215537 (accessed 11/10/17).

71. David Epstein and Sharyn O'Halloran, *Delegating Powers: A Transaction Cost Politics Approach to Policymaking under Separate Powers* (Cambridge: Cambridge University Press, 1999).

72. Robert J. McGrath, "Congressional Oversight Hearings and Policy Control," *Legislative Studies Quarterly* 38, no. 3 (2013): 349–76.

73. Mann and Ornstein, *The Broken Branch.*

74. Linette Lopez and Lydia Ramsey, "'You Asked for It'— Congress Railed on the Maker of EpiPen," *Business Insider*, September 21, 2016, www.businessinsider.com/mylan

-ceo-heather-bresch-house-oversight-committee-hearing
-epipen-2016-9 (accessed 11/9/17); see Mathew D.
McCubbins and Thomas Schwartz, "Congressional Oversight Overlooked: Police Patrols versus Fire Alarms," *American Journal of Political Science* 28, no. 1 (1984): 165–79.

75. Douglas Kriner and Liam Schwartz, "Divided Government and Congressional Investigations," *Legislative Studies Quarterly* 33, no. 2 (2008): 295–321.

76. Michael D. Shear and Michael S. Schmidt, "Benghazi
Panel Engages Clinton in Tense Session," *New York Times*,
October 22, 2015, www.nytimes.com/2015/10/23/us/
politics/hillary-clinton-benghazi-committee.html?_r50
(accessed 10/29/15).

77. Thomas E. Mann and Norman J. Ornstein, *It's Even
Worse Than It Looks: How the American Constitutional
System Collided with the New Politics of Extremism* (New
York: Basic Books, 2012); Francine Kiefer, "Comey Hearing: Why Congressional Oversight Has Broken Down,"
Christian Science Monitor, July 7, 2016, www.csmonitor
.com/USA/Politics/2016/0707/Comey-hearing-Why
-congressional-oversight-has-broken-down (accessed
11/9/17).

78. The Office of Technology Assessment was a fourth research agency serving Congress until 1995. It was one
of the first agencies scheduled for elimination by the
104th Congress. Until 1983, Congress had still another
tool of legislative oversight: the legislative veto. Each
agency operating under such provisions was obliged to
submit to Congress every proposed decision or rule,
which would then lie before both chambers for 30 to
60 days. If Congress took no action by one-house or
two-house resolution explicitly to veto the proposed
measure during the prescribed period, the measure
became law. The legislative veto was declared unconstitutional by the Supreme Court in 1983 on the
grounds that it violated the separation of powers—the
resolutions Congress passed to exercise its veto were not
subject to presidential veto, as required by the Constitution. See *Immigration and Naturalization Service v.
Chadha*, 462 U.S. 919 (1983).

CHAPTER 15

1. This account draws from Austin Berg, "Meet the Man
Who Could End Forced Union Fees for Government
Workers," Illinois Policy, 2018, www.illinoispolicy
.org/story/meet-the-man-who-could-end-forced-union
-fees-for-government-workers/ (accessed 3/3/18); and
P. R. Lockhart, "What the Latest Union Case Before
the Supreme Court Could Mean for Workers of Color,"
Vox, February 26, 2018, www.vox.com/policy-and
-politics/2018/2/26/17053328/janus-afscme-supreme
-court-unions-minorities (accessed 3/3/18).

2. *Abood v. Detroit Board of Education,* 431 U.S. 209
(1977).

3. Celine McNicholas and Janelle Jones, "Black Women
Will Be Most Affected by *Janus*," Economic Policy
Institute, Economic Snapshot, February 13, 2018, www
.epi.org/publication/black-women-will-be-most-affected
-by-janus/ (accessed 3/3/18); and Kayla Patrick, "Public
Sector Unions Promote Economic Security and Equality
for Women," National Women's Law Center Fact Sheet,
January 2018, https://nwlc.org/resources/public-sector
-unions-promote-economic-security-and-equality-for
-women/ (accessed 3/3/18).

4. U.S. Courts Statistical Tables, www.uscourts.gov/
statistics-reports/analysis-reports/statistical-tables-federal
-judiciary (accessed 9/19/2015).

5. Michael A. Fletcher, "Obama Criticized as Too Cautious, Slow on Judicial Posts," *Washington Post*, October
16, 2009, www.washingtonpost.com/wp-dyn/content/
article/2009/10/15/AR2009101504083.html (accessed
3/1/10).

6. John Bowden, "Timeline: Brett Kavanaugh's Nomination to the Supreme Court," The Hill, October 6, 2018,
https://thehill.com/homenews/senate/410217-timeline
-brett-kavanaughs-nomination-to-the-supreme-court
(accessed 10/16/18).

7. *Marbury v. Madison*, 5 U.S. 137 (1803).

8. *National Federation of Independent Business v. Sebelius*,
567 U.S. __ (2012).

9. Acts of Congress held unconstitutional in whole
or in part by the Supreme Court of the United States,
General Printing Office, www.gpo.gov/fdsys/pkg/
GPO-CONAN-2013/pdf/GPO-CONAN-2013-11.pdf
(accessed 4/20/14).

10. *Federal Election Commission v. Wisconsin Right to Life*, 551
U.S. 449 (2007); *McCutcheon v. Federal Election Commission*, 572 U.S. __ (2014).

11. This review power was affirmed by the Supreme Court in
Martin v. Hunter's Lessee, 14 U.S. 304 (1816).

12. *Brown v. Board of Education*, 347 U.S. 483 (1954).

13. *Lawrence v. Texas*, 539 U.S. 558 (2003).

14. *Paven v. Smith*, 582 U.S. __ (2017).

15. *Alabama Legislative Black Caucus v. Alabama*, 575 U.S.
__ (2015).

16. *Arizona State Legislature v. Arizona Independent Redistricting Commission*, 576 U.S. __ (2015).

17. *Cooper v. Harris,* 581 U.S. __ (2017).

18. *United States v. Jones*, 565 U.S. __ (2012).

19. *Riley v. California*, 573 U.S. __ (2014).

20. Theodore J. Lowi, *The End of Liberalism*, 2nd ed. (New
York: W. W. Norton, 1979); also David Schoenbrod,
*Power without Responsibility: How Congress Abuses the
People through Delegation* (New Haven, CT: Yale Univer-
sity Press, 1993).

21. Kenneth Culp Davis, *Discretionary Justice*
(Baton Rouge: Louisiana State University Press,
1969), 15–21.

22. Emergency Price Control Act, 56 Stat. 23 (1942).

23. *Hamdi v. Rumsfeld*, 542 U.S. 507 (2004).

24. *Hamdan v. Rumsfeld*, 548 U.S. 557 (2006).

25. *Boumediene v. Bush*, 553 U.S. 723 (2008).

26. *National Labor Relations Board v. Noel Canning*, 573 U.S. — (2014).

27. *Trump v. Hawaii*, 585 U.S. __ (2018).

28. *Roe v. Wade*, 410 U.S. 113 (1973).

29. *Schuette v. Coalition to Defend Affirmative Action*, 572 U.S. __ (2014).

30. *Fisher v. University of Texas*, 579 U.S. __ (2016).

31. Robert Scigliano, *The Supreme Court and the Presidency* (New York: Free Press, 1971), 162. For an interesting critique of the solicitor general's role during the Reagan administration, see Lincoln Caplan, "Annals of the Law," *New Yorker*, August 17, 1987, 30–62.

32. Edward Lazarus, *Closed Chambers* (New York: Times Books, 1998), 6.

33. *NAACP v. Button*, 371 U.S. 415 (1963). The quotation is from the opinion in this case.

34. *Smith v. Allwright*, 321 U.S. 649 (1944).

35. *Obergefell v. Hodges*, 576 U.S. __ (2015).

36. Charles Krauthammer, "Why Roberts Did It," *Washington Post*, June 29, 2012, www.washingtonpost.com/opinions/charles-krauthammer-why-roberts-did-it/2012/06/28/gJQA4X0g9V_story.html (accessed 4/22/14).

37. *Griswold v. Connecticut*, 381 U.S. 479 (1965).

38. *McCutcheon v. Federal Election Commission*, 572 U.S. __ (2014).

39. R. W. Apple, Jr., "A Divided Government Remains, and with It the Prospect of Further Combat," *New York Times*, November 7, 1996, B6.

40. For limits on judicial power, see Alexander Bickel, *The Least Dangerous Branch* (Indianapolis, IN: Bobbs-Merrill, 1962).

41. *Worcester v. Georgia*, 31 U.S. 515 (1832).

42. Walter Murphy, *Congress and the Court* (Chicago: University of Chicago Press, 1962).

43. Robert Dahl, "The Supreme Court and National Policy Making," *Journal of Public Law* 6 (1958): 279.

44. Martin Shapiro, "The Supreme Court: From Warren to Burger," in *The New American Political System*, ed. Anthony King (Washington, DC: American Enterprise Institute, 1978).

45. *Citizens to Preserve Overton Park v. Volpe*, 401 U.S. 402 (1971).

46. Toni Locy, "Bracing for Health Care's Caseload," *Washington Post*, August 22, 1994, A15.

47. See "Developments in the Law—Class Actions," *Harvard Law Review* 89 (1976): 1318.

48. *In re Agent Orange Product Liability Litigation*, 100 F.R.D. 718 (E.D.N.Y. 1983).

49. Donald Horowitz, *The Courts and Social Policy* (Washington, DC: Brookings Institution Press, 1977).

50. *Morgan v. McDonough*, 540 F2d 527 (1 Cir., 1976; *cert. denied*, 429 U.S. 1042 [1977]).

51. Alexander Hamilton, James Madison, and John Jay, *The Federalist Papers*, ed. Clinton Rossiter (New York: New American Library, 1961), no. 10, 78.

CHAPTER 16

1. Maureen Hayden, "Prohibition-Era Laws Keep Cap on Craft Beer Industry," *Indianapolis Tribune Star*, February 5, 2015, www.tribstar.com/news/local_news/prohibition-era-laws-keep-cap-on-craft-beer-industry/article_35917c72-5072-5f2d-8b7a-ab829eb48390.html (accessed 10/31/17).

2. Matthew Mitchell and Christopher Koopman, "Bottling Up Innovation in Craft Brewing: A Review of the Current Barriers and Challenges," Mercatus Center, George Mason University, June 2014, www.mercatus.org/system/files/MitchellKoopman-CraftBrewing-MOP.pdf (accessed 10/31/17).

3. Compare with Gabriel Kolko, *The Triumph of Conservatism* (New York: Free Press, 1963), chap. 6.

4. Bureau of Economic Analysis, "Gross Domestic Product: Percent Change from Preceding Period" (gdpchg.xls), October 27, 2017, www.bea.gov/national (accessed 11/1/17).

5. U.S. Securities and Exchange Commission, Implementing the Dodd-Frank Wall Street Reform and the Consumer Protection Act, www.sec.gov/spotlight/dodd-frank.shtml (accessed 7/10/16).

6. Alan Rappeport and Emily Flitter, "Congress Approves First Big Dodd-Frank Rollback," *New York Times*, May 22, 2018, www.nytimes.com/2018/05/22/business/congress-passes-dodd-frank-rollback-for-smaller-banks.html (accessed 7/27/18).

7. See David M. Hart, *Forged Consensus: Science, Technology and Economic Policy in the United States, 1921–1953* (Princeton, NJ: Princeton University Press, 1998).

8. See Margaret Weir, *Politics and Jobs: The Boundaries of Employment Policy in the United States* (Princeton, NJ: Princeton University Press, 1992).

9. Adam Andrzejewski, "Meet America's Elite Farm Subsidy Club," RealClear Politics, August 8, 2018, www.realclearpolitics.com/articles/2018/08/08/meet_americas_elite_farm_subsidy_club_137745.html (accessed 10/12/2018).

10. The act of 1955 officially designated the interstate highways as the National System of Interstate and Defense Highways. It was indirectly a major part of President Dwight Eisenhower's defense program.

11. Small Business Administration, Agency Financial Report: Fiscal Year—2016, p. 13, www.sba.gov/sites/default/files/aboutsbaarticle/SBA_2016_AFR.pdf (accessed 10/6/17).

12. The members included AMD, Digital, Hewlett-Packard, IBM, Intel, Lucent, Motorola, National Semiconductor, Rockwell, and Texas Instruments.

13. Molly Sherlock and Jeffrey M. Stupak, "Energy Tax Policy: Issues in the 114th Congress," Congressional Research Service, June 15, 2016, www.fas.org/sgp/crs/misc/R43206.pdf (accessed 7/9/16).

14. Timothy Cama, "Trump Eyes 70 Percent Cut to DOE's Renewables Office, The Hill, May 17, 2017, thehill.com/policy/energy-environment/333816-trump-eyes-70-percent-cut-to-does-renewables-office (accessed 10/25/17); U.S. Department of Energy, "DOE Hails Passage of FY 2018 Omnibus Bill," Energy.gov, March 23, 2018, www.energy.gov/articles/doe-hails-passage-fy-2018-omnibus-bill (accessed 3/29/18).

15. Drew DeSilver, "5 Facts about the Minimum Wage," Pew Research Center, Fact Tank, January 4, 2017, www.pewresearch.org/fact-tank/2017/01/04/5-facts-about-the-minimum-wage/ (accessed 10/6/17).

16. U.S. Consumer Product Safety Commission, Letter to Manufacturers, Importers, and Retailers of Self-Balancing Scooters, February 18, 2016, www.cpsc.gov/Global/Business-and-Manufacturing/Business-Education/SelfbalancingScooterLetter.pdf (accessed 10/23/17).

17. Ronald Reagan, Inaugural Address, January 20, 1981, www.presidency.ucsb.edu/ws/?pid543130 (accessed 4/27/14).

18. Gallup, Taxes, news.gallup.com/poll/1714/taxes.aspx (accessed 10/6/17).

19. Gallup, Taxes.

20. Tax Policy Center, "Analysis of the Tax Cuts and Jobs Act," December 22, 2017, www.taxpolicycenter.org/feature/analysis-tax-cuts-and-jobs-act (accessed 3/29/18).

21. Pew Research Center, "With Budget Debate Looming, Growing Share of Public Prefers Bigger Government," U.S. Politics & Policy, April 24, 2017, www.people-press.org/2017/04/24/with-budget-debate-looming-growing-share-of-public-prefers-bigger-government/ (accessed 10/6/17).

22. Pew Research Center, "As Sequester Deadline Looms, Little Support for Cutting Most Programs," U.S. Politics & Policy, February 22, 2013, www.people-press.org/2013/02/22/as-sequester-deadline-looms-little-support-for-cutting-most-programs/ (accessed 4/27/14).

23. See, for example, Paul Krugman, "The Bankruptcy Boys," *New York Times*, February 21, 2010, www.nytimes.com/2010/02/22/opinion/22krugman.html?_r50 (accessed 4/27/14).

24. Robert Greenstein, "Budget Deal, Though Imperfect, Represents Significant Accomplishment and Merits Support," Center on Budget and Policy Priorities, October 27, 2015, www.cbpp.org/press/statements/greenstein-budget-deal-though-imperfect-represents-significant-accomplishment-and (accessed 12/16/15).

25. Pew Research Center, "Section 2: Government, Regulation, and the Social Safety Net," U.S. Politics & Policy, October 5, 2017, www.people-press.org/2017/10/05/2-government-regulation-and-the-social-safety-net/ (accessed 10/6/17).

26. Politico/Harvard School of Public Health, "The Public's Views of Tax Reform and Other Domestic Issues," Social Science Research Solutions, September 2017 www.politico.com/f/?id=0000015e-a4d7-d873-adfe-bdd740140000 (accessed 10/12/18).

27. DeSilver, "5 Facts about the Minimum Wage."

28. DeSilver, "5 Facts about the Minimum Wage."

29. DeSilver, "5 Facts about the Minimum Wage."

30. Bureau of Labor Statistics, "Union Members Summary," January 8, 2016, www.bls.gov/news.release/union2.nr0.htm (accessed 7/9/16).

31. National Right to Work Legal Defense Foundation, "Right to Work Frequently Asked Questions," 2017, www.nrtw.org/right-to-work-frequently-asked-questions (accessed 10/24/17).

32. David E. Sanger, David M. Herszenhorn, and Bill Vlasic, "Bush Aids Detroit, but Hard Choices Await Obama," *New York Times*, December 19, 2008, www.nytimes.com/2008/12/20/business/20auto.html?r53&hp (accessed 3/7/10).

33. Reuters, "CBO Raises TARP Cost Estimate to $34 Billion," December 16, 2011, www.reuters.com/article/2011/12/16/us-usa-tarp-cost-idUSTRE7BF1W920111216 (accessed 7/3/12).

34. Bureau of Labor Statistics, "United States Unemployment Rate," www.tradingeconomics.com/united-states/unemployment-rate (accessed 7/3/12).

35. Congressional Budget Office, "Estimated Impact of the American Recovery and Reinvestment Act on Employment and Economic Output from January 2012 through March 2012," Table 1, May 2012, www.cbo.gov/sites/default/files/cbofiles/attachments/05-25-Impact_of_ARRA.pdf (accessed 7/10/16).

36. Ben Pershing, "House Passes $15 Billion Jobs Bill," *Washington Post*, March 5, 2010, www.washingtonpost.com/wp-dyn/content/article/2010/03/04/AR2010030402757.html (accessed 3/5/10).

37. Natalie Sherman, "Fed Nominee Jerome Powell Shares Views with Congress," BBC News, November 28, 2017, www.bbc.com/news/business-42156529 (accessed 3/29/18).

38. Federal Reserve Board, *Policy Tools: Open Market Operations,* March 21, 2018, www.federalreserve.gov/monetarypolicy/openmarket.htm (accessed 3/29/18).

39. Binyamin Appelbaum, "Jerome Powell Is Sworn in as Federal Reserve Chairman," *New York Times,* February 5, 2018, www.nytimes.com/2018/02/05/us/politics/jerome-powell-federal-reserve-chairman-sworn-in.html (accessed 3/29/18).

40. ATTOM Data, "U.S. Foreclosure Activity Drops to 12-Year Low in 2017," January 16, 2018, www.attomdata.com/news/foreclosure-trends/2017-year-end-u-s-foreclosure-market-report/ (accessed 3/29/18).

41. Steven R. Weisman, "Bernanke Faces Bear Stearns Queries," *New York Times*, April 2, 2008, C1.

42. Federal Reserve, "Why Did the Federal Reserve Lend to Banks and Other Financial Institutions during the Financial Crisis?" www.federalreserve.gov/faqs/why-did-the-Federal-Reserve-lend-to-banks-and-other-financial-institutions-during-the-financial-crisis.htm (accessed 12/7/15).

43. Executive Office of the President of the United States, GPO Access, "Budget of the United States Government: Historical Tables Fiscal Year 2009," Table 2.2—Percentage Composition of Receipts by Source: 1934–2013, www.gpo.gov/fdsys/pkg/BUDGET-2009-TAB/pdf/BUDGET-2009-TAB-4-2.pdf. (accessed 5/9/08).

44. There is an additional 1.45 percent tax on all income without limit that funds Medicare benefits, and an additional 0.9 percent Medicare tax for high earners (individuals earning over $200,000 and couples earning over $250,000) that was introduced by the Affordable Care Act.

45. For a systematic account of the role of government in providing incentives and inducements to business, see C. E. Lindblom, *Politics and Markets* (New York: Basic Books, 1977), chap. 13. For a detailed account of the dramatic Reagan tax cuts and reforms, see Jeffrey Birnbaum and Alan Murray, *Showdown at Gucci Gulch: Lawmakers, Lobbyists, and the Unlikely Triumph of Tax Reform* (New York: Random House, 1987).

46. Benjamin H. Harris and Adam Looney, "The Tax Cuts and Jobs Act: A Missed Opportunity to Establish a Sustainable Tax Code," Urban/Brookings Tax Policy Center, May 24, 2018, www.brookings.edu/wp-content/uploads/2018/05/es_20180524_harris-looney_taxreform.pdf (accessed 7/28/18).

47. Eric Toder, "Explaining the TCJA's International Reforms," Tax Policy Center, TaxVox: Business Taxes, February 2, 2018, www.taxpolicycenter.org/taxvox/explaining-tcjas-international-reforms (accessed 7/28/18).

48. See Tax Foundation, "U.S. Federal Individual Income Tax Rates History, 1862–2013 (Nominal and Inflation-Adjusted Brackets)," http://taxfoundation.org/article/us-federal-individual-income-tax-rates-history-1913-2013-nominal-and-inflation-adjusted-brackets (accessed 3/30/14).

49. Glen Kessler, "Revisiting the Costs of the Bush Tax Cuts," *Washington Post*, May 10, 2011, www.washingtonpost.com/blogs/fact-checker/post/revisiting-the-cost-of-the-bush-tax-cuts/2011/05/09/AFxTFtbG_blog.html (accessed 12/7/15).

50. Center on Budget and Policy Priorities, "Tax Cuts: Myths and Realities," November 16, 2007, www.cbpp.org/9-27-06tax.htm (accessed 6/1/16).

51. Jay Heflin, "House Dems Want Bush Tax Cuts to Expire, but Say It's Tough Sell," The Hill, February 8, 2010, http://thehill.com/homenews/house/80133-democrats-supporting-ending-tax-cut-but-see-it-as-tough-sell (accessed 3/8/10).

52. Jackie Calmes, "Demystifying the Fiscal Impasse That Is Vexing Washington," *New York Times*, November 15, 2012, www.nytimes.com/2012/11/16/us/politics/the-fiscal-cliff-explained.html; Jonathan Weisman, "Answers to Questions on Capital's Top Topic," *New York Times*, February 21, 2013, www.nytimes.com/2013/02/22/us/politics/questions-and-answers-about-the-sequester.html (accessed 4/26/14).

53. David Espo, "Shutdown Orders Issued as Congress Misses Deadline," Associated Press, October 1, 2013, bigstory.ap.org/article/health-law-challenge-threatens-government-shutdown (accessed 4/26/14).

54. For an account of the relationship between mechanization and law, see Lawrence Friedman, *A History of American Law* (New York: Simon and Schuster, 1973), 409–29.

55. The *Federal Register* is the daily publication of all official acts of Congress, the president, and the administrative agencies. A law or executive order is not legally binding until it is published in the *Federal Register*.

56. Renae Merle, "Trump Administration Strips Consumer Watchdog Office of Enforcement Powers in Lending Discrimination Cases," *Washington Post*, February 1, 2018, www.washingtonpost.com/news/business/wp/2018/02/01/trump-administration-strips-consumer-watchdog-office-of-enforcement-powers-against-financial-firms-in-lending-discrimination-cases/?utm_term=.4ca043ab46f0 (accessed 3/29/18).

57. Michael B. Tanner, "No to Coal Subsidies, No to Corporate Welfare," Cato Institute, August 16, 2017, www.cato.org/publications/commentary/no-coal-subsidies-no-corporate-welfare (accessed 10/25/17); and Tad DeHaven, "Corporate Welfare in the Federal Budget," Cato Institute, July 25, 2012, object.cato.org/sites/cato.org/files/pubs/pdf/PA703.pdf (accessed 10/25/17).

58. James Dao, "The Nation; Big Bucks Trip Up the Lean New Army," *New York Times*, February 10, 2002, www.nytimes.com/2002/02/10/weekinreview/the-nation-big-bucks-trip-up-the-lean-new-army.html?pagewanted5all (accessed 9/26/12).

59. See Samuel P. Hays, *Beauty, Health, and Permanence: Environmental Politics in the United States, 1955–1985* (Cambridge: Cambridge University Press, 1987).

60. U.S. Department of the Interior, "Interior Department Releases Final Well Control Regulations to Ensure Safe and Responsible Offshore Oil and Gas Development," April 14, 2016, www.doi.gov/pressreleases/interior-department-releases-final-well-control-regulations-ensure-safe-and (accessed 10/24/17).

61. Pew Center on Global Climate Change, "Climate Change 101: The Science and Impacts," www.pewclimate.org/docUploads/101_Science_Impacts.pdf (accessed 3/21/08).

62. See the discussion in Peter R. Orszag, director Congressional Budget Office, "Issues in Climate Change" (presentation for the CBO Director's Conference on Climate Change, November 16, 2007), www.cbo.gov/sites/default/files/cbofiles/ftpdocs/88xx/doc8819/11-16-climatechangeconf.pdf (accessed 3/21/08).

63. World Resources Institute Climate Analysis Indicators Tool, 2014, http://cait.wri.org/historical/ (accessed 10/27/17).

64. Pew Research Center, U.S. Politics & Policy, Section 7, "Global Warming and Environmental Regulation, Personal Environmentalism," October 5, 2017, www.people-press.org/2017/10/05/7-global-warming-and

-environmental-regulation-personal-environmentalism/ (accessed 10/9/17).

65. Lisa Friedman and Brad Plumer, "E.P.A. Announces Repeal of Major Obama-Era Carbon Emissions Rule," *New York Times,* October 9, 2017, www.nytimes .com/2017/10/09/climate/clean-power-plan.html (accessed 10/24/17).

66. Michael D. Shear, "Trump Will Withdraw U.S. from Paris Climate Agreement," *New York Times,* June 1, 2017, www.nytimes.com/2017/06/01/climate/trump-paris -climate-agreement.html (accessed 10/24/17).

67. Michael Austin, "Breaking Down the New 2016 Fuel Economy Standards," *Car and Driver,* April 2, 2010, http://blog.caranddriver.com/breaking-down-the-new -2016-fuel-economy-standards/ (accessed 9/26/12).

68. Dino Grandoni, "Trump Officials Begin Review of Obama Emissions Standards for Cars," *Washington Post,* August 10, 2017, www.washingtonpost.com/news/ energy-environment/wp/2017/08/10/trump-officials -begin-review-of-obama-emissions-standards-for -cars/?utm_term=.e0811d78344e (accessed 10/24/17).

69. Some research has shown that when taxes are linked to specific projects, public opinion is more favorable. See Department of Transportation, Office of Research and Technology, *UTC Spotlight,* "Will Americans Support Fuel Tax Increases? The Answer Could Be Surprising," March 2014, www.rita.dot.gov/utc/sites/rita.dot.gov.utc/ files/utc_spotlights/pdf/spotlight_0314.pdf (accessed 7/10/16.)

70. Steve Mufson, "Coalition Agrees on Emissions Cuts," *Washington Post,* January 15, 2009, www.washingtonpost .com/wp-dyn/content/article/2009/01/14/ AR2009011403850.html (accessed 7/10/16).

71. Hendrik Hertzberg, "Cooling on Warming," *New Yorker,* February 7, 2011, 21.

72. White House, Office of the Press Secretary, "White House Announces Commitments to the American Business Act on Climate Pledge," October 19, 2015, obamawhitehouse .archives.gov/the-press-office/2015/10/19/fact-sheet -white-house-announces-commitments-american -business-act (accessed 10/25/17).

73. Orszag, "Issues in Climate Change," 6–7.

74. Joe Palca, "California Turns to Holland for Flood Ex- pertise," National Public Radio, January 14, 2008, www .npr.org/templates/story/story.php?storyId518080442 (accessed 3/21/08).

75. Steven Greenhouse, "Our Economic Pickle," *New York Times,* January 12, 2013, www.nytimes.com/2013/01/13/ sunday-review/americas-productivity-climbs-but-wages -stagnate.html?_r50 (accessed 5/2/14).

CHAPTER 17

1. See Andrea Louise Campbell, *Trapped in America's Safety Net* (Chicago: University of Chicago Press, 2014).

2. "Americans' Views on Income Inequality and Workers' Rights," *New York Times,* June 3, 2015, www.nytimes .com/interactive/2015/06/03/business/income-inequality -workers-rights-international-trade-poll.html (accessed 10/31/15).

3. Fay Lomax Cook and Edith Barrett, *Support for the American Welfare State* (New York: Columbia University Press, 1992).

4. A good source of pre-1930s welfare history is James T. Patterson, *America's Struggle against Poverty, 1900–1994* (Cambridge, MA: Harvard University Press, 1994), chap. 2.

5. Patterson, *America's Struggle against Poverty,* 27.

6. This figure is based on a Works Progress Administra- tion study by Ann E. Geddes, reported in Merle Fainsod et al., *Government and the American Economy,* 3rd ed. (New York: W. W. Norton, 1959), 769.

7. Social Security Administration, "OASDI and SSI Pro- gram Rates & Limits, 2018," www.ssa.gov/policy/docs/ quickfacts/prog_highlights/RatesLimits2018.html (accessed 4/15/18).

8. Nikki Graf, Anna Brown, and Eileen Patten, "The Nar- rowing, But Persistent, Gender Gap in Pay," Pew Research Center Fact Tank, April 9, 2018, www.pewresearch.org/ fact-tank/2018/04/09/gender-pay-gap-facts/ (accessed 4/16/18); Dan Caplinger, "Social Security Benefits: The Striking Gap Between Women and Men," Motley Fool, September 21, 2014, www.fool.com/retirement/general/ 2014/09/21/social-security-benefits-the-striking-gap -between.aspx (accessed 4/16/18); C. Eugene Steuerle, Adam Carasso, and Lee Cohen, *How Progressive Is Social Security and Why?* (Washington, DC: Urban Insti- tute, 2004), www.urban.org/research/publication/how -progressive-social-security-and-why (accessed 5/3/14).

9. John R. Kearney, "Social Security and the 'D' in OASDI: The History of a Federal Program Insuring Earners against Disability," *Social Security Bulletin* 66, no. 3 (2006); and www.ssa.gov/policy/docs/ssb/v66n3/ v66n3p1.html (accessed 6/7/17).

10. Social Security Administration, "Social Security Fact Sheet," June 2018, www.ssa.gov/news/press/factsheets/ basicfact-alt.pdf (accessed 8/15/18).

11. Workers must have lost their job through no fault of their own. For a full description of the program, see Chad Stone and William Chen, "Introduction to Unemploy- ment Insurance," Center on Budget and Policy Priorities, July 30, 2014, www.cbpp.org/research/introduction-to -unemployment-insurance (accessed 11/18/15).

12. *Goldberg v. Kelly,* 397 U.S. 254 (1970).

13. Ife Floyd and Liz Schott, "TANF Cash Benefits Have Fallen by More Than 20 Percent in Most States and Continue to Erode," Center on Budget and Policy Pri- orities, October 15, 2015, www.cbpp.org/research/family -income-support/tanf-cash-benefits-have-fallen-by-more -than-20-percent-in-most-states (accessed 10/31/15).

14. This poverty threshold is for a household of three persons that includes two children. Department of Health and Human Services, Office of the Assistant Secretary for Planning and Evaluation, Poverty Guidelines, January 25, 2016, http://aspe.hhs.gov/poverty-guidelines (accessed 7/10/16).

15. Center on Budget and Policy Priorities, "Policy Basics: How Many Weeks of Unemployment Compensation Are Available?" May 23, 2016, www.cbpp.org/research/economy/policy-basics-how-many-weeks-of-unemployment-compensation-are-available (accessed 6/1/16).

16. Centers for Medicare and Medicaid Services, "Eligibility for Non-Citizens in Medicaid and CHIP," www.medicaid.gov/medicaid-chip-program-information/by-topics/outreach-and-enrollment/downloads/overview-of-eligibility-for-non-citizens-in-medicaid-and-chip.pdf (accessed 10/31/15).

17. Suzanne Mettler, *The Submerged Welfare State* (Chicago: University of Chicago Press, 2011); Christopher Faricy, *Welfare for the Wealthy* (New York: Cambridge University Press, 2015).

18. U.S. Congress, Joint Committee on Taxation, "Estimates of Federal Tax Expenditures for Fiscal Years 2016–2020," January 30, 2017, www.jct.gov/publications.html?func=startdown&id=4971 (accessed 5/29/17). Note that there are tax breaks in the corporate tax code as well, but the tax breaks for individuals and households account for about 80 percent of the total.

19. Office of Management and Budget, Historical Tables, "Table 2.2—Percentage Composition of Receipts by Source: 1934–2023," www.whitehouse.gov/omb/historical-tables/ (accessed 4/16/18).

20. Office of Management and Budget, Historical Tables, "Table 11.3, Outlays for Payments for Individuals by Category and Major Program: 1940–2023," and "Table 10.1, Gross Domestic Product and Deflators Used in the Historical Tables, 1940–2023," www.whitehouse.gov/omb/historical-tables/ (accessed 8/19/18); Congressional Budget Office, Long-Term Budget Projections (June 2018), "Table 1. Summary Data for the Extended Baseline," www.cbo.gov/about/products/budget-economic-data#2 (accessed 8/19/18).

21. Social Security Administration, "A Summary of the 2015 Annual Reports: Social Security and Medicare Boards of Trustees," www.ssa.gov/oact/trsum/ (accessed 11/14/15).

22. President's Commission to Strengthen Social Security, "Strengthening Social Security and Creating Personal Wealth for All Americans," December 21, 2001, www.ssa.gov/history/reports/pcsss/Final_report.pdf (accessed 3/26/08).

23. Jason Barabas, "Rational Exuberance: The Stock Market and Public Support for Social Security Privatization," *Journal of Politics* 68, no. 1 (February 2006): 50–61.

24. President's Commission, "Strengthening Social Security."

25. Christian E. Weller, "Undermining Social Security with Private Accounts," Economic Policy Institute Issue Brief, December 11, 2001, www.epi.org/content.cfm/issuebriefs_ib172 (accessed 4/3/18); Robert Greenstein, "Social Security Commission Proposals Contain Serious Weaknesses but May Improve the Debate in an Important Respect," Center on Budget and Policy Priorities, December 26, 2001, www.cbpp.org/archives/12-11-01socsec.htm (accessed 3/26/08).

26. Quoted in Jill Quadragno, "Social Security Policy and the Entitlement Debate," in *Social Policy and the Conservative Agenda*, ed. Clarence Y. H. Lo and Michael Schwartz (Malden, MA: Blackwell, 1998), 111.

27. "Full Text: Donald Trump Announces a Presidential Bid," *Washington Post,* www.washingtonpost.com/news/post-politics/wp/2015/06/16/full-text-donald-trump-announces-a-presidential-bid/?tid=a_inl&utm_term=.074bad8f73a2 (accessed 5/28/17).

28. Kathleen Romig, "Budget Agreement Funding Could Reduce Social Security Disability Backlog," *Off the Charts* (blog), February 15, 2018, www.cbpp.org/blog/budget-agreement-funding-could-reduce-social-security-disability-backlog (accessed 4/15/18).

29. Juliette Cubanski and Tricia Neuman, "The Facts on Medicare Spending and Financing," Henry J. Kaiser Family Foundation, July 18, 2017, www.kff.org/medicare/issue-brief/the-facts-on-medicare-spending-and-financing/ (accessed 4/16/18).

30. A Better Way, "A Better Way to Fix Healthcare," https://abetterway.speaker.gov/ (accessed 5/28/17).

31. Congressional Budget Office, "Long Term Analysis of a Budget Proposal by Chairman Ryan," April 5, 2011, www.cbo.gov/publication/22085 (accessed 7/6/12); see also the discussion in Kaiser Family Foundation Program on Medicare Policy, "Proposed Changes to Medicare in the 'Path to Prosperity': Overview and Key Questions," April 14, 2011, www.kff.org/medicare/upload/8179.pdf (accessed 3/1/12).

32. Kaiser Family Foundation, Kaiser Health Care Tracking Poll, February 2012, https://kaiserfamilyfoundation.files.wordpress.com/2013/01/8281-c.pdf (accessed 5/29/17).

33. See Martin Gilens, *Why Americans Hate Welfare* (Chicago: University of Chicago Press, 1999), chaps. 3, 4.

34. Gilens, *Why Americans Hate Welfare.*

35. U.S. Government Accountability Office, "Temporary Assistance for Needy Families," December 2012, www.gao.gov/assets/660/650635.pdf (accessed 10/31/15).

36. Center on Budget and Policy Priorities, Chart Book TANF at 19, March 29, 2016, www.cbpp.org/research/family-income-support/chart-book-tanf-at-19 (accessed 7/10/16).

37. LaDonna Pavetti and Liz Schott, "TANF's Inadequate Response to Recession Highlights Weakness of Block-Grant Structure," Center on Budget and Policy Priorities, July 14, 2011, www.cbpp.org/research/family-income-support/tanfs-inadequate-response-to-recession-highlights-weakness-of-block (accessed 6/1/16).

38. Center for Budget and Policy Priorities, "Chartbook: SNAP Helps Struggling Families Put Food on the Table,"

April 18, 2012, www.cbpp.org/research/food-assistance/chart-book-snap-helps-struggling-families-put-food-on-the-table (accessed 6/1/16); U.S. Department of Agriculture, Food and Nutrition Service, "National and/or State Level Monthly and/or Annual Data," April 6, 2018, https://fns-prod.azureedge.net/sites/default/files/pd/34SNAPmonthly.pdf (accessed 4/15/18).

39. Jill Colvin, "Trump Signs Executive Order Pushing Work for Welfare," *Washington Post,* April 10, 2018, www.washingtonpost.com/business/trump-signs-executive-order-pushing-work-for-welfare/2018/04/10/6bea20d4-3d29-11e8-955b-7d2e19b79966_story.html?utm_term=.ce3c7603dfd6 (accessed 4/15/18).

40. President's Advisory Panel on Federal Tax Reform. https://govinfo.library.unt.edu/taxreformpanel/ (accessed 5/29/17); see James C. Gould, "Tax Reform, Congress, and Politics," *Tax Notes,* February 23, 2015.

41. There were a couple of minor precedents. First was the Smith-Hughes Act of 1917, which made federal funds available to the states for vocational education at the elementary and secondary levels. Second, the Lanham Act of 1940 made federal funds available to schools in "federally impacted areas;" that is, areas with an unusually large number of government employees and/or where the local tax base was reduced by large amounts of government-owned property.

42. New America Foundation, "Federal, State and Local K–12 School Finance Overview," June 29, 2015, http://atlas.newamerica.org/school-finance (accessed 7/10/16).

43. David K. Cohen and Susan L. Moffitt, *The Ordeal of Equality: Did Federal Regulation Fix the Schools?* (Cambridge, MA: Harvard University Press, 2009).

44. For a positive view of the standards, see Sonja Brookins Santelises, "Abandoning the Common Core Is Taking the Easy Way Out," *The Equity Line,* March 31, 2014, https://edtrust.org/the-equity-line/abandoning-the-common-core-is-taking-the-easy-way-out/ (accessed 4/3/18); for a critique see Valerie Strauss, "The Coming Common Core Melt-down," *Washington Post,* January 23, 2014, www.washingtonpost.com/blogs/answer-sheet/wp/2014/01/23/the-coming-common-core-meltdown (accessed 5/11/14).

45. Department of Education, "Fundamental Change: Innovation in America's Schools under Race to the Top," November 2015, www2.ed.gov/programs/racetothetop/rttfinalrptexecsumm.pdf (accessed 7/11/16).

46. Elaine Weiss, "Mismatches in Race to the Top Limit Educational Improvement: Lack of Time, Resources, and Tools to Address Opportunity Gaps Puts Lofty State Goals Out of Reach," Economic Policy Institute, September 12, 2013, www.epi.org/publication/race-to-the-top-goals/ (accessed 5/11/14).

47. Valerie Strauss, "The Successor to No Child Left Behind Has, It Turns Out, Big Problems of Its Own," *Washington Post*, December 7, 2015, www.washingtonpost.com/news/answer-sheet/wp/2015/12/07/the-successor-to-no-child-left-behind-has-it-turns-out-big-problems-of-its-own/ (accessed 7/11/16).

48. Philip Bump, "Why It Was So Easy for '60 Minutes' to Rebut Betsy DeVos's Charter-School Arguments," *Washington Post,* March 12, 2018, www.washingtonpost.com/news/politics/wp/2018/03/12/why-it-was-so-easy-for-60-minutes-to-rebut-betsy-devoss-charter-school-arguments/?utm_term=.035ec0dce3ba (accessed 4/16/18).

49. One of the most vocal proponents of this viewpoint is former assistant secretary of education Diane Ravitch, *The Life and Death of the Great American School System* (New York: Basic Books, 2011).

50. Pew Research Center, "The Rising Cost of Not Going to College," February 11, 2014, www.pewsocialtrends.org/2014/02/11/the-rising-cost-of-not-going-to-college/ (accessed 7/14/17).

51. The College Board, "Trends in Student Aid 2017," 24, https://trends.collegeboard.org/sites/default/files/2017-trends-student-aid_0.pdf (accessed 4/15/18).

52. The College Board, "Trends in Student Aid 2017," 20.

53. U.S. Agency for Healthcare Research and Quality, *2011 National Healthcare Quality Report,* chap. 9, "Access to Health Care," www.ahrq.gov/research/findings/nhqrdr/nhqr11/chap9.html (accessed 7/14/17).

54. Susan Scutti, "How Does Nutrition Affect Children's School Performance?" CNN, March 21, 2017, www.cnn.com/2017/03/21/health/school-nutrition-program-benefits/index.html (accessed 7/18/17).

55. Office of Management and Budget, Historical Tables, "Table 12.3, Total Outlays for Grants to State and Local Governments, by Function, Agency, and Program: 1940–2019," www.whitehouse.gov/omb/historical-tables/ (accessed 4/16/18).

56. Henry J. Kaiser Family Foundation, *Medicaid: A Primer—Key Information on the Nation's Health Coverage Program for Low-Income People,* March 1, 2013, https://kaiserfamilyfoundation.files.wordpress.com/2010/06/7334-05.pdf (accessed 6/2/16) (see p. 26).

57. Henry J. Kaiser Family Foundation, "Total Monthly Medicaid and CHIP Enrollment," http://kff.org/health-reform/state-indicator/total-monthly-medicaid-and-chip-enrollment/ (accessed 11/4/15).

58. Henry J. Kaiser Family Foundation, "Health Insurance Coverage of Non-Elderly, 0–64," www.kff.org/other/state-indicator/nonelderly-0-64/?curentTimeframe=0&sortModel=%7B%22colId%22:%22Location%22,%22sort%22:%22asc%22%7D (accessed 4/15/18).

59. Henry J. Kaiser Family Foundation, "The Coverage Gap: Uninsured Poor Adults in States that Do Not Expand Medicaid—An Update," January 21, 2016, kff.org/health-reform/issue-brief/the-coverage-gap-uninsured-poor-adults-in-states-that-do-not-expand-medicaid-an-update/ (accessed 6/2/16).

60. *National Federation of Independent Businesses v. Sebelius,* 567 U.S. __ (2012).

61. Henry J. Kaiser Family Foundation, "The Coverage Gap."

62. Jennifer Steinhauer, "House Votes to Send Bill to Repeal Health Law to Obama's Desk," *New York Times*, January 6, 2016, www.nytimes.com/2016/01/07/us/politics/house-votes-to-send-bill-to-repeal-health-law-to-obamas-desk.html (accessed 7/11/16).

63. Amy Goldstein, "ACA Enrollment for 2018 Nearly Matches Last Year's, Despite Trump Administration Efforts to Undermine It," *Washington Post,* December 21, 2017, www.washingtonpost.com/news/to-your-health/wp/2017/12/21/aca-enrollment-for-2018-nearly-matches-last-years-despite-trump-administration-efforts-to-undermine-it/?utm_term=.71fd6fc2204e (accessed 4/15/18).

64. James Krieger and Donna L. Higgins, "Housing and Health: Time Again for Public Health Action," *American Journal of Public Health* 92, no. 5 (May 2002): 758–68.

65. John E. Schwarz, *America's Hidden Success*, 2nd ed. (New York: W. W. Norton, 1988), 41–2.

66. Congressional Budget Office, "Federal Housing Assistance for Low-Income Households," September 2015, www.cbo.gov/sites/default/files/114th-congress-2015-2016/reports/50782-lowincomehousing-onecolumn.pdf (accessed 5/29/17).

67. See, for example, Lawrence Vale, "Housing Chicago: Cabrini-Green to Parkside of Old Town," *Places Journal*, February 2012, https://placesjournal.org/article/housing-chicago-cabrini-green-to-parkside-of-old-town/ (accessed 3/1/12).

68. Edward R. Goetz, *New Deal Ruins: Race, Economic Justice, and Public Housing Policy* (Ithaca, NY: Cornell University Press, 2013).

69. Congressional Budget Office, "Federal Housing Assistance for Low-Income Households," September 2015, www.cbo.gov/sites/default/files/114th-congress-2015-2016/reports/50782-lowincomehousing-onecolumn.pdf (accessed 5/29/17).

70. ATTOM Data, "U.S. Foreclosure Activity Drops to 12-Year Low in 2017," January 16, 2018, www.attomdata.com/news/foreclosure-trends/2017-year-end-u-s-foreclosure-market-report/ (accessed 3/29/18).

71. U.S. Census Bureau, "Income and Poverty in the United States: 2016" Table 3, www.census.gov/content/dam/Census/library/publications/2017/demo/P60-259.pdf (accessed 4/16/18).

72. See, for example, Theodore R. Marmor, Jerry L. Mashaw, and Philip L. Harvey, *America's Misunderstood Welfare State* (New York: Basic Books, 1990), 156.

73. U.S. Census Bureau, "Income and Poverty in the United States: 2016," www.census.gov/content/dam/Census/library/publications/2017/demo/P60-259.pdf (accessed 4/16/18).

74. U.S. Census Bureau, "Income and Poverty in the United States: 2016," Table B-2.

75. U.S. Census Bureau, "Annual Estimates of the Resident Population for Selected Age Groups by Sex, Age, Race, and Hispanic Origin for the United States and States: 2017 Population Estimates," https://factfinder.census.gov/faces/tableservices/jsf/pages/productview.xhtml?src=bkmk (accessed 8/8/18)." www.census.gov/popest/data/national/asrh/2015/index.html (accessed 7/17/16).

76. AARP, Annual Report 2016, www.aarp.org/content/dam/aarp/about_aarp/about_us/2017/2016-annual-report-aarp.pdf (accessed 4/15/18); Center for Responsive Politics, "Lobbyists Representing AARP, 2017," www.opensecrets.org/lobby/clientlbs.php?id=D000023726&year=2017 (accessed 4/15/18); AARP, Public Policy Institute Experts Guide, 2017, www.aarp.org/content/dam/aarp/ppi/2017/09/public-policy-institute-experts-guide.pdf (accessed 4/15/18).

77. See Andrea Louise Campbell, *How Policies Make Citizens: Senior Political Activism and the American Welfare State* (Princeton, NJ: Princeton University Press, 2005).

78. Christopher Howard, *The Hidden Welfare State: Tax Expenditures and Social Policy in the United States* (Princeton, NJ: Princeton University Press, 1999); Jacob S. Hacker, *The Divided Welfare State: The Battle over Public and Private Benefits in the United States* (New York: Cambridge University Press, 2002).

79. U.S. Congress Joint Committee on Taxation, "Estimates of Federal Tax Expenditures for Fiscal Years 2016–2020," www.jct.gov/publications.html?func=startdown&id=4971 (accessed 5/29/2017).

80. Center on Budget and Policy Priorities, "A Quick Guide to SNAP Eligibility and Benefits," Februrary 7, 2018, www.cbpp.org/research/food-assistance/a-quick-guide-to-snap-eligibility-and-benefits (accessed 4/15/18).

81. "Panera CEO: On Food Stamps, I Can't Eat in My Own Restaurant," September 25, 2013, http://eatocracy.cnn.com/2013/09/25/panera-ceo-on-food-stamps-i-cant-eat-in-my-own-restaurant (accessed 5/12/14).

82. Samantha Artiga, Anthony Damico, and Rachel Garfield, "The Impact of the Coverage Gap for Adults in States Not Expanding Medicaid by Race and Ethnicity," October 26, 2015, kff.org/disparities-policy/issue-brief/the-impact-of-the-coverage-gap-in-states-not-expanding-medicaid-by-race-and-ethnicity/ (accessed 11/11/15).

83. Frances Fox Piven and Richard Cloward, *Poor People's Movements* (New York: Pantheon, 1977), chap. 5.

84. U.S. Department of Agriculture, Food and Nutrition Service, "National and/or State Level Monthly and/or Annual Data," April 6, 2018, https://fns-prod.azureedge.net/sites/default/files/pd/34SNAPmonthly.pdf (accessed 4/15/18).

85. U.S. Census Bureau, "Income and Poverty in the United States: 2016," Tables 1 and 3, www.census.gov/content/dam/Census/library/publications/2017/demo/P60-259.pdf (accessed 4/16/18).

86. See, for example, Sharon Hayes, *Flat Broke with Children: Women in the Age of Welfare Reform* (New York: Oxford University Press, 2004).

87. U.S. Census Bureau, "Income and Poverty in the United States: 2016," Table B-2.

88. For an argument that children should be given the vote, see Paul E. Peterson, "An Immodest Proposal," *Daedalus* 121, no. 4 (Fall 1992): 151–74.

89. John W. Kingdon, *Agendas, Alternatives and Public Policies*, 2nd edition (New York: Harper Collins, 1995).

90. On the history and politics of the Family and Medical Leave Act, see Anya Bernstein, *The Moderation Dilemma: Legislative Coalitions and the Politics of Family and Medical Leave* (Pittsburgh: University of Pittsburgh Press, 2001).

91. This account is from Bernstein, *The Moderation Dilemma*, chap. 5.

92. Eileen Appelbaum and Ruth Milkman, "Leaves That Pay: Employer and Worker Experiences with Paid Family Leave in California," Center for Economic and Policy Research, 2011, http://cepr.net/documents/publications/paid-family-leave-1-2011.pdf (accessed 5/14/18).

93. See L. Free and Hadley Cantril, *The Political Beliefs of Americans* (New York: Simon and Schuster, 1968); and Benjamin I. Page and Lawrence R. Jacobs, *Class War? What Americans Really Think about Economic Inequality* (Chicago: University of Chicago Press, 2009).

94. See Fay Lomax Cook and Edith Barrett, *Support for the American Welfare State* (New York: Columbia University Press, 1992); and Hugh Heclo, "The Political Foundations of Antipoverty Policy," in *Fighting Poverty: What Works and What Doesn't*, ed. Sheldon H. Danziger and Daniel H. Weinberg (Cambridge, MA: Harvard University Press, 1986), 312–40.

CHAPTER 18

1. Lyric Lewin, "In Support of a Travel Ban," CNN Politics, March 2017, www.cnn.com/interactive/2017/03/politics/travel-ban-supporters-cnnphotos/ (accessed 2/1/18).

2. Vivian Yee, "Meet the Everyday People Who Have Sued Trump. So Far, They've Won," *New York Times*, March 29, 2017, www.nytimes.com/2017/03/29/us/trump-travel-ban.html (accessed 4/12/18).

3. *Trump v. Hawaii*, 585 U.S. __ (2018).

4. Rupert Smith, *The Utility of Force: The Art of War in the Modern World* (New York: Vintage, 2008).

5. D. Robert Worley, *Shaping U.S. Military Forces: Revolution or Relevance in a Post–Cold War World* (Westport, CT: Praeger Security International, 2006).

6. Colin S. Gray, "The Implications of Preemptive and Preventive War Doctrines," Strategic Studies Institute, July 2007, www.strategicstudiesinstitute.army.mil/pdffiles/pub789.pdf (accessed 8/1/14).

7. U.S. Department of State, "U.S. Humanitarian Assistance in Response to the Syrian Crisis," September 21, 2017, www.state.gov/r/pa/prs/ps/2017/09/274360.htm (accessed 7/20/18).

8. U.S. Department of State, "U.S. Relations with Haiti," March 2018, www.state.gov/r/pa/ei/bgn/1982.htm (accessed 4/15/18).

9. Kurt M. Campbell and James B. Steinberg, *Difficult Transitions: Foreign Policy Troubles at the Outset of Presidential Power* (Washington, DC: Brookings Institution Press, 2008).

10. U.S. Senate, "Treaties," www.senate.gov/artandhistory/history/common/briefing/Treaties.htm (accessed 4/15/18).

11. P. D. Miller, "Organizing the National Security Council: I Like Ike's," *Presidential Studies Quarterly*, 43, no. 3 (2013): 592–606.

12. Ivo H. Daalder and I. M. Destler, *In the Shadow of the Oval Office: Profiles of the National Security Advisers and the Presidents They Served* (New York: Simon and Schuster, 2009).

13. Department of Defense, "About," January 27, 2017, www.defense.gov/About/ (accessed 7/23/18).

14. John J. McGrath, *The Other End of the Spear: The Tooth-to-Tail Ratio (T3R) In Modern Military Operations* (Fort Leavenworth, KS: Combat Studies Institute Press, 2007), www.cgsc.edu/carl/download/csipubs/mcgrath_op23.pdf (accessed 7/15/18).

15. D. Robert Worley, *Shaping U.S. Military Forces* (Westport, CT: Praeger, 2006), chap. 3.

16. Harold Seidman, *Politics, Position, and Power*, 5th ed. (New York: Oxford University Press, 1998), 209.

17. Mark Riebling, *Wedge: From Pearl Harbor to 9/11* (New York: Touchstone, 2002).

18. Benjamin Ginsberg, *The Worth of War* (New York: Prometheus Books, 2014), chap. 5.

19. Clinton Rossiter, ed., *The Federalist* (New York: Signet, 1961), 418.

20. Steven Lee Myers, "U.S. Move to Give Egypt $450 Million in Aid Meets Resistance," *New York Times*, September 28, 2012, www.nytimes.com/2012/09/29/world/middleeast/white-house-move-to-give-egypt-450-million-in-aid-meets-resistance.html?_r=0 (accessed 4/27/18).

21. Bill Gertz, "Congress: U.S. Military Highly Vulnerable to Cyber Attacks," *Washington Free Beacon*, June 1, 2015, www.freebeacon.com/national-security/congress-u-s-military-highly-vulnerable-to-cyber-attacks/ (accessed 4/12/18).

22. "Sleeve-Rolling Time: IMF," *The Economist*, May 2, 1992, 98–9.

23. James Dao and Patrick E. Tyler, "U.S. Says Military Strikes Are Just a Part of Big Plan," *The Alliance*, September 27, 2001; and Joseph Kahn, "A Nation Challenged: Global Dollars," *New York Times*, September 20, 2001, B1.

24. Bessma Momani, "The IMF, the U.S. War on Terrorism, and Pakistan," *Asian Affairs*, 31, no. 1 (2004), www.tandfonline.com/doi/abs/10.3200/AAFS.31.1.41-51?journalCode=vasa20 (accessed 4/15/18).

25. For information on current U.S. sanctions programs, visit U.S. Department of the Treasury, "Sanctions Programs and Country Information," www.treasury.gov/resource-center/sanctions/Programs/Pages/Programs.aspx (accessed 6/1/14).

26. Loveday Morris, "Yazidis Who Suffered Genocide Are Fleeing Again," *Washington Post*, March 21, 2017, www.washingtonpost.com/world/middle_east/yazidis-who-suffered-genocide-are-fleeing-again-but-this-time-not-from-the-islamic-state/2017/03/21/6392fe26-0353-11e7-9d14-9724d48f5666_story.html?noredirect=on&utm_term=.c2dbf2c8c6a1 (accessed 4/15/18).

27. Eleanor Albert, "China in Africa," Council on Foreign Relations, July 12, 2017, www.cfr.org/backgrounder/china-africa (accessed 4/15/18).

28. Graham T. Allison, *Destined for War: Can America and China Escape Thucydides's Trap?* (New York: Houghton Mifflin Harcourt, 2017).

29. Scott Shane and Mark Mazzetti, "Inside a Three-Year Russian Campaign to Influence U.S. Voters," *New York Times*, Febuary 16, 2018, www.nytimes.com/2018/02/16/us/politics/russia-mueller-election.html (accessed 4/15/18).

30. Shane and Mazzetti, "Inside a Three-Year Russian Campaign to Influence U.S. Voters."

31. Elias Groll, "Feds Quietly Reveal Chinese State-Backed Hacking Operation," *Foreign Policy*, November 30, 2017, www.foreignpolicy.com/2017/11/30/feds-quietly-reveal-chinese-state-backed-hacking-operation/ (accessed 4/15/18).

32. Jonathan Watts and Kate Connolly, "World Leaders React after Trump Rejects Paris Climate Deal," *Guardian*, June 1, 2017, www.theguardian.com/environment/2017/jun/01/trump-withdraw-paris-climate-deal-world-leaders-react (accessed 4/15/18).

33. Benjamin Ginsberg, *The American Lie: Government by the People and Other Political Fables* (Boulder, CO: Paradigm, 2007), 3.

Answer Key

Chapter 1
1. d
2. c
3. c
4. c
5. d
6. e
7. a
8. d
9. b
10. e
11. c
12. a
13. a
14. d
15. b

Chapter 2
1. b
2. a
3. b
4. c
5. e
6. c
7. c
8. d
9. b
10. e
11. e
12. b
13. d
14. a

Chapter 3
1. c
2. c
3. b
4. e

5. a
6. c
7. d
8. b
9. b
10. b
11. a
12. d
13. d
14. b

Chapter 4
1. a
2. e
3. b
4. e
5. b
6. e
7. b
8. b
9. d
10. a
11. e
12. c
13. a
14. d

Chapter 5
1. b
2. e
3. a
4. c
5. b
6. d
7. a
8. a
9. d
10. a

11. d
12. a
13. c
14. c

Chapter 6
1. c
2. c
3. a
4. d
5. e
6. d
7. e
8. a
9. c
10. b
11. a
12. b

Chapter 7
1. b
2. a
3. b
4. c
5. e
6. c
7. a
8. b
9. b
10. c
11. b
12. c
13. c

Chapter 8
1. e
2. a
3. d

4. e
5. e
6. c
7. d
8. d
9. c
10. d
11. d
12. c

Chapter 9
1. a
2. c
3. b
4. d
5. e
6. a
7. d
8. e
9. e
10. e
11. d
12. e
13. a

Chapter 10
1. c
2. e
3. e
4. c
5. c
6. b
7. c
8. b
9. d
10. a
11. d
12. c

13. c
14. a
15. a
16. b

Chapter 11
1. a
2. b
3. e
4. c
5. d
6. b
7. d
8. a
9. e
10. c
11. a
12. d

Chapter 12
1. b
2. a
3. d
4. c
5. d
6. c
7. a
8. a
9. d
10. d
11. e
12. c
13. a
14. a

Chapter 13
1. a
2. c

3. b
4. e
5. b
6. b
7. b
8. a
9. a
10. c
11. c
12. b
13. b
14. a

Chapter 14

1. d
2. c
3. c
4. b
5. b

6. e
7. c
8. d
9. d
10. e
11. b
12. a
13. d
14. a

Chapter 15

1. a
2. c
3. a
4. c
5. d
6. d
7. e
8. e

9. c
10. a
11. b
12. a
13. a
14. c

Chapter 16

1. a
2. b
3. c
4. e
5. a
6. c
7. c
8. d
9. d
10. b

11. e
12. a
13. c
14. d

Chapter 17

1. c
2. d
3. b
4. c
5. a
6. c
7. e
8. d
9. d
10. a
11. d
12. c

13. b
14. c
15. b

Chapter 18

1. b
2. a
3. e
4. c
5. b
6. d
7. c
8. b
9. c
10. d
11. a
12. b
13. e

Credits

PHOTOGRAPHS

Chapter 10: Page 378: Shutterstock; p. 379: Courtesy The Texas Young Republicans; p. 381: Bettmann Archive/Getty Images; p. 383 (left): Marc Serota/Reuters/Newscom; (right): Nicholas Kamm/AFP/Getty Images; p. 385 (left): Granger, NYC—All rights reserved; (right): OpenStreetMap contributors; p. 387: Port Gifford/Getty Images; p. 389: Chip Somodevilla/Getty Images; p. 394: Brendan Smialowski/AFP/Getty Images; p. 398 (left): Andrew Lichtenstein/Corbis via Getty Images; (right): Hillary for America, Campaign; p. 397 (left): Bettmann/Getty Images; (right): Yin Bogu Xinhua/eyevine/Redux; p. 400: Matthew Cavanaugh/Getty Images; p. 402 © G92, MJ3, F31/Zuma Press; p. 409: Robyn Beck/AFP/Getty Images; p. 410: Richard Ellis/Alamy Stock Photo; p. 412: AP Photo/Richard Drew; p. 413: Mike Segar/Reuters/Newscom; p. 418: Visions of America/UIG via Getty Images; p. 419: Whitney Curtis/Getty Images; p. 420: Michael B. Thomas/Getty Images.

Chapter 11: Page 428: Shutterstock; p. 429: American Benefits Council; p. 432: AP Photo/Sue Ogrocki; p. 433: AP Photo/Robert F. Bukaty; p. 437: Brandon Sloter via AP; p. 438: Amanda Cowan/The Columbian via AP; p. 439 (left): Matthew Busch/Bloomberg via Getty Images; (right): AP Photo/Bloomington Herald-Times, Jeremy Hogan; p. 440: Tasos Katopodis/Getty Images for MoveOn.org; p. 444: Karl Sonnenberg/Shutterstock; p. 445: Net Photos/Alamy Stock Photo; p. 447: Alex Wong/Getty Images; p. 450 (left): AP Photo/Alex Brandon, File; (right): AP Photo/Jacquelyn Martin; p. 451: Scott McIntyre/Bloomberg via Getty Images; p. 453: U.S. Food and Drug Administration; p. 454 (left): Steve Schapiro/Corbis via Getty Images; (right): © North County Times/ZUMAPRESS.com/Alamy Stock Photo; p. 455 (left): Tomas Abad/Alamy Stock Photo; (right): Justin Sullivan/Getty Images; p. 459: Theresa McCracken/www.CartoonStock.com.

Chapter 12: Page 466: Shutterstock; p. 467 (left): Courtesy Guy Berkebile; (right): Scott Olson/Getty Images; p. 470: Bettmann/Getty Images; p. 474: Chip Somodevilla/Getty Images; p. 479: AP Photo/Ross D. Franklin; p. 486: Brendan Smialowski/AFP/Getty Images; p. 487: Scott J. Ferrell/Getty Images; p. 492: Senate TV via AP; p. 494: Rachel Mummey for The Washington Post via Getty Images; p. 499: DPA Picture Alliance/Alamy Stock Photo; p. 500: Tom Williams/CQ Roll Call/Getty Images; p. 504 (left): Olivier Douliery/Abaca/Sipa via AP Images; (right): AP Photo/Andrew Harnik; p. 505 (left): Science History Images/Alamy Stock Photo; (right): William Philpott/Getty Images.

Chapter 13: Page 512: Shutterstock; p. 513: Cheriss May/ZUMA Press/Newscom; p. 515: Bettmann/Getty Images; p. 517 (left): AP Photo/File; (right): U.S. Army photo by Capt. Tyson Friar; p. 518: Anthony Wallace/AFP/Getty Images; p. 519: AP Photo/File; p. 521: The Asahi Shimbun via Getty Images; p. 525: Joe Raedle/Getty Images; p. 528: Jim Watson/AFP/Getty Images; p. 532: Bill Pugliano/Getty Images; p. 533: Chip Somodevilla/Getty Images; p. 535 (top): Bettmann/Getty Images; (bottom): Twitter/@realDonaldTrump; p. 541: T.J. Kirkpatrick/Bloomberg via Getty Images.

Chapter 14: Page 550: Shutterstock; p. 551: © G92, MJ3, F31/Zuma Press; p. 555: Michael Williamson/The Washington Post via Getty Images; p. 556: U.S. Department of State; p. 561: NG Images/Alamy Stock Photo; p. 563: Richard T. Nowitz/Science Source; p. 565: Timothy A. Clary/AFP/Getty Images; p. 568: Yasin Ozturk/Anadolu Agency/Getty Images; p. 569 (left): Yasin Ozturk/Anadolu Agency/Getty Images; (right): Robert Nickelsberg/Getty Images; p. 570: Department of Justice/FOIA.gov; p. 572: Saul Loeb/AFP/Getty Images; p. 573 (left): Tom Williams/CQ Roll Call/Getty Images; (right): Joe Raedle/Getty Images; p. 574: Alan Singer/CBS via Getty Images; p. 575: AP Photo/Ben Chrisman; p. 577: Jeffrey MacMillan/For The Washington Post via Getty Images; p. 582: Andrew Harrer/Bloomberg via Getty Images.

Chapter 15: Page 590: Shutterstock; p. 591: AP Photo/Andrew Harnik; p. 593: AP Photo/Michael Tarm; p. 601: Cheriss May/NurPhoto via Getty Images; p. 602: The Asahi Shimbun via Getty Images; p. 607: Michael Hibblen/KUAR News; p. 609: Mark Wilson/Getty Images; p. 612: Mark Wilson/Getty Images; p. 613: Jonathan Ernst/REUTERS/Newscom; p. 617 Dana Verkouteren via AP Photo; p. 618: Bill O'Leary/The Washington Post via Getty Images; p. 623: Alex Wong/Getty Images.

Chapter 16: Page 630: Shutterstock; p. 631: © Lindsay Gallup Photography; p. 633: Robert Mullan/Incamerstock/Corbis via Getty Images; p. 634: Cameron Davidson/Getty Images; p. 636 (left): Courtesy of Gwen Bell/Computer Museum; (right): Chip Somodevilla/Getty Images; p. 637: Jeff Kowalsky/EPA/Shutterstock; p. 638

(left): Granger, NYC—All rights reserved; (center): Bettmann/Getty images; (right): Dania Maxwell/Bloomberg via Getty Images; p. 639: Bloomberg via Getty Images; p. 640 (left): Zbigniew Bzdak/Chicago Tribune/TNS via Getty Images; (right): Timothy A. Clark/AFP/Getty Images; p. 643: AP Photo/Scott Stewart; p. 649: Norma Jean Gargasz/Alamy Stock Photo; p. 651: Drew Angerer/Getty Images; p. 660: Library of Congress; p. 662: Cameron Davidson/Corbis via Getty Images; p. 663: Scott Peterson/Getty Images; p. 665: Luke Sharrett/Bloomberg via Getty Images image p. 666: Dennis McDonald/Getty Images; p. 667: Ethan Miller/Getty Images.

Chapter 17: Page 674: LEOcrafts/iStock/Getty Images; p. 675: AP Photo/Record Searchlight, Andreas Fuhrmann; p. 678: Joseph Barnell/SuperStock; p. 681: Derek Davis/Portland Press Herald via Getty Images; p. 686: Saul Loeb/Getty Images; p. 689: Jim West Image Broker/Newscom; p. 692: Chip Somodevilla/Getty Images; p. 694: Education & Exploration 1/Alamy Stock Photo; p. 697: Jewel Samad/AFP/Getty Images; p. 699 (left): Lee Balterman/The LIFE Images Collection/Getty Images; (right): J.B. Forbes/St Louis Post Dispatch/Polaris; p. 700: Bryan R. Smith/AFP/Getty Images; p. 704: ©John Birdsall/The Image Works.

Chapter 18: Page 714: Shutterstock; p. 715: Jerry Holt/Star Tribune/ZUMA Press; p. 719: Bettmann/Getty Images; p. 724: Pete Souza/The White House via AP; p. 726: Mikhail Metzel/TASS via Getty Images; p. 729: B Christopher/Alamy Live News; p. 730: Matt McClain/The Washington Post via Getty Images; p. 732: Kena Betancur/AFP/Getty Images; p. 733 (left): Michele Eve Sandberg/Corbis via Getty Images; (right): Nicholas Kamm/Getty Images; p. 734: Korean Central News Agency/Korea News Service via AP, File; p. 735: Don Emmert/AFP/Getty Images; p. 736: Bay Ismoyo/Getty Images; p. 738: Adek Berry/Stringer/Getty Images; p. 742: Delil Souleiman/Stringer/Getty Images.

TEXT

Figure 3.7: State Marijuana Laws in 2018 Map, originally published by Governing.com, March 30, 2018. Reprinted by permission of Governing.

Figure 6.1: Graph from "Large Majorities See Checks and Balances, Right to Protest as Essential for Democracy," Pew Research Center, Washington, DC (May 2017) http://www.people-press.org/2017/03/02/large-majorities-see-checks-and-balances-right-to-protest-as-essential-for-democracy/democracy_11/. Reprinted with permission.

Figure 9.7: Figure from "Key Takeaways on Americans' Growing Partisan Divide over Political Values," Pew Research Center, Washington, DC (October, 2017) http://www.pewresearch.org/fact-tank/2017/10/05/takeaways-on-americans-growing-partisan-divide-over-political-values/. Reprinted with permission.

Table 11.1: Table: "Top Spending on Lobbying Activities by Industry, 1998–2018" from OpenSecrets.org. Reprinted by permission of Center for Responsive Politics.

Figure 14.3: "Iron Triangles" republished with permission of Wadsworth, a division of Cengage Learning from *Incomplete Conquest: Governing America*, 2nd ed. by Theodore J. Lowi (New York: Holt, Rinehart and Winston, 1981), p. 139. © 1981 by CBS College.

Figure 14.4: "Number of Federal, Contract, and Grant Employees (in millions)," from *The True Size of Government: Tracking Washington's Blended Workforce, 1984–2015* (New York: The Volcker Alliance, 2017), p. 4. Reprinted by permission.

Table 16.1: Tax Brackets and Rates, 2018. Originally published by Tax Foundation, January 2, 2018. Reprinted by permission.

Glossary/Index

Page numbers in *italic* refer to figures or photos.

Alaska, 83, 360, 481
Alcohol and Tobacco Tax and Trade Bureau (TTB), 631
alcohol testing, 140
Aldrich, John, 340
Alien and Sedition Acts, 127, 361
Aliste, Ethan, 379
Alito, Samuel, 601
Al Jazeera, 273
Allison, Graham, 741
alternative technologies, 666–67
Al Thani, Mohammed bin Abdulrahman, 568
Alvarez, Maximo, 451
Amazon, 259, 262, 450

Amendment, 6, 66–68   a change added to a bill, law, or constitution
   to the Constitution, 58, 65–69; *see also* Bill of Rights; *individual Amendments*
   Civil War Amendments, 163–64
   list of, 67
   methods for passage/incorporation, 65–66, 66
   and the Supreme Court, 68–69
   in lawmaking process, 492–93

American Civil Liberties Union (ACLU), 135, 454, 614
American Conservative Union, 447
American Family Association, 447
American Federation of State, County, and Municipal Employees (AFSCME), 590
American Israel Public Affairs Committee (AIPAC), 733
American Medical Association, 695
American National Election Studies (ANES), 241
American people
   in the 21st century, 17–22
   changes in, 13–22
   dependence on government, 6, 29–30
American Recovery and Reinvestment Act of 2009 (ARRA), 637, 639, 649, 649, 666–67, 688, 692
American Reinvestment and Recovery Act, 692
American Revolution, 8, 43–46
Americans for Prosperity (Super PAC), 294–95, 443
Americans with Disabilities Act of 1990 (ADA), 99, 104–5, 191
AM/FM radio, 266

amicus curiae, 613, 615, 625   literally, "friend of the court"; individuals or groups who are not parties to a lawsuit but who seek to assist the Supreme Court in reaching a decision by presenting additional briefs

Amnesty International, 732, 733
Andrus, Ethel Percy, 444
Annapolis Convention, 48
Anthony, Susan B., 163, 300

Antifederalists   those who favored strong state governments and a weak national government and who were opponents of the Constitution

proposed at the American Constitutional Convention of 1787
   and bill of rights, 118
   defined, 62
   and ratification of the Constitution, 62, 62–64
   and states' powers amendment, 81

antitrust policy, 659–61   government regulation of large businesses that have established monopolies

anti–Vietnam War demonstrations, 224
ANZUS (Australian, New Zealand, United States Security) Treaty, 737

appeasement, 718   the effort to forestall war by giving in to the demands of a hostile power

appellate courts, federal, 590, 596–99, 610
Apple, 24, 141, 259, 262
appointments, by president, 514, 518–19, 522, 542

apportionment, 477   the process, occurring after every decennial census, that allocates congressional seats among the 50 states

appropriations, 502   the amounts of money approved by Congress in statutes (bills) that each unit or agency of government can spend

arbitration, 740–41
Arizona
   congressional seats of, 478–79
   immigration law, 188
   public assistance in, 576
   redistricting in, 478–79
   SCHIP program in, 576
   voter ID law, 177
Arkansas, 126, 168, 168–69, 516–17
arms race, 718–19, 719
Army, U.S., 727
Army Corps of Engineers, 553
ARPA (Advanced Research Projects Agency), 552, 555–56
Arpaio, Joe, 517
ARPANET, 555–56, 636, 636
ARRA. *See* American Recovery and Reinvestment Act of 2009
Arthur, John, 40–41

Articles of Confederation, 46, 53, 54   America's first written constitution; served as the basis for America's national government until 1789

Asaei, Ali, 715
Ashcroft, John, 93–94
Asia, immigrants from, 16–17
Asian Americans
   civil rights for, 189–91
   in Congress, 471
   dance-rock band, 114–16
   party affiliations of, 354
   political participation by, 316
   voter turnout, 316
Assad, Bashar al-, 566, 742

assembly, right of, 132
Associated Press, 260
Association of Young Americans (AYA), 428–29, 460
Astroturf lobbying, 456, 495

attitude (or opinion), 207   a specific preference on a particular issue

Australian, New Zealand, United States Security (ANZUS) Treaty, 737

authoritarian government, 7   a system of rule in which the government recognizes no formal limits but may nevertheless be restrained by the power of other social institutions

autocracy, 7   a form of government in which a single individual—a king, queen, or dictator—rules

auto industry, 648
automatic voter registration, 295, 324
Ayotte v. Planned Parenthood of Northern New England, 148–49

B
background checks, 138
bailouts, 648
Baker v. Carr, 384
Bakke, Allan, 195
balance of power, federal and state governments, 47–48

ballot initiative, 9, 322, 392–93, 459   a proposed law or policy change that is placed on the ballot by citizens or interest groups for a popular vote

Ballot Initiative Strategy Center (BISC), 459
ballots, 383, 383–84

bandwagon effect, 245   a shift in electoral support to the candidate whom public opinion polls report as the front-runner

bank bailouts. *See* bailouts
Bank of the United States, 650
banks, 642, 648–52
Barreto, Matt, 315
Bartels, Larry, 223, 230, 328, 338
battleground states
   and electoral college, 320, 322, 396
   and exit polls, 319
   and media attention, 386
   and voter turnout, 319
BCRA. *See* Bipartisan Campaign Reform Act of 2002
Beard, Charles, 49
Bear Stearns, 652
Beck, Nancy, 513
Bedford, Gunning, 50
Beer distribution, 630–32
beliefs, 207
Benghazi, Libya, consulate attack and congressional investigation, 484, 493, 502–3, 582, 582
Benton, John, 142
Benton v. Maryland, 142

Berinsky, Adam, 242–43
Berkebile, Guy, 466
Bernanke, Ben, 651, 652
Bezos, Jeffrey, 262, 263

bicameral, 53, 469   having a legislative
assembly composed of two chambers or
houses; distinguished from *unicameral*

bicameral legislature, 53, 469–70
"big data," 245–47, 344

bill, 489–94   a proposed law that has been
sponsored by a member of Congress and
submitted to the clerk of the House or
Senate; *see also* lawmaking

Bill and Melinda Gates Foundation, 273
"bill of information," 142

Bill of Rights, 59, 69, *119*   the first 10
amendments to the U.S. Constitution,
ratified in 1791; they ensure certain rights
and liberties to the people
    First Amendment, 118, 120, 123–36, 255,
        285, 287, 401, 402, 449, 605; *see also*
        freedom of religion; freedom of speech
    Second Amendment, 136–38
    Third Amendment, 146
    Fourth Amendment, 139–41, 146
    Fifth Amendment, 68, 119–20, 141–43, 146
    Sixth Amendment, 144
    Eighth Amendment, 144–45
    Tenth Amendment, 56, 81, 94–95
    addition of, 54
    defined, 54, 118
    due process of law, 138–46
    freedoms in, 23
    history of, 117–18
    incorporation into Fourteenth Amendment,
        118–22, *121–22*
    nationalization of, 118–22
    personal liberties and rights in, 23
    and right to die, 150
    and right to privacy, 146–49

Bimber, Bruce, 307
bin Laden, Osama, 724, *724*
Bipartisan Campaign Reform Act of 2002
    (BCRA; McCain-Feingold Act), 128,
    346, 458, 605
birth control, 146
"birther" controversy, *274*
BISC (Ballot Initiative Strategy Center), 459
Bismarck, Otto von, 8
Black Lives Matter, 170, 218, *272*, 282, 298,
    354, *455*
Blackmun, Harry, 614, 620
BlackPAC, 295
Blades, Joan, 439
Blair, Saira, 2–4

block grants, 96, 98   federal grants-in-aid that
allow states considerable discretion in how
the funds are spent

blogs, 271, 272
Bloomberg News, 264
blue states, 354

Bodine, Brian, 378–79, *379*
Boehner, John, *450*, *499*, 506, 658
Boeing, 727
Boggess, Chris, 630, *631*, 668
Booker, Cory, *233*
Bork, Robert, 602
Boston, Massachusetts, *173*, 174
Boston Massacre, 44
Boston Tea Party, 44–45, *45*
Boumediene v. Bush, 608
bourgeoisie, 8
Bowers v. Hardwick, 149, 192
Boyd, Wes, 439
Boydstun, Amber, 280
BRAC (Defense Base Closure and Realignment
    Commission), 575
Brady Handgun Violence Prevention Act, 95
Brandeis, Louis, 94, 146
Brandenburg, Charles, 128
Brandenburg v. Ohio, 128
branding, 340
BRCA. *See* Bipartisan Campaign Reform Act of
    2002
Brennan, William, 135, 600
Bretton Woods conference, 735
Breyer, Stephen, 125

briefs, 615   written documents in which
attorneys explain, using case precedents, why
the court should find in favor of their client

British Broadcasting Company (BBC), 273, 285

broadcast media, 265–66   television, radio, or
other media that transmit audio and/or video
content to the public

Brookings Institution, 272
Brown, Ben, 428, 460
Brown, Linda, 167
Brown, Michael, 218, 536
Brown, Oliver, 167
Brown University, 182

***Brown v. Board of Education*, 26, 167–70,
186, 453, 605**   the 1954 Supreme Court
decision that struck down the "separate but
equal" doctrine as fundamentally unequal;
this case eliminated state power to use race
as a criterion of discrimination in law and
provided the national government with
the power to intervene by exercising strict
regulatory policies against discriminatory
actions

Brown v. Entertainment Merchants Association,
    136
Bryan, William Jennings, 362, 365
Buckley v. Valeo, 128, 405
budget, federal, 655–58, *659*
Budget Control Act (2011), 568, 575–76, 657
budget crisis (2011), 575

budget deficit, *657*, 657–58   amount by which
government spending exceeds government
revenue in a fiscal year

budget surplus, *240*, *657*
burden of proof, 195–97

bureaucracy, 550–85   the complex structure
of offices, tasks, rules, and principles of
organization that is employed by all large-
scale institutions to coordinate the work of
their personnel
    agencies of executive branch, 563
    defined, 553
    in a democracy, 583–84
    employment figures (2015), *557*
    FOIA requests, *585*
    goals of, 563–73
    for maintaining a strong economy, 571–73
    managing, 579–83
    organization of the executive branch, 559–62
    for promotion of the public welfare, 563–65
    for providing national security, 565–70, *567*
    reformation of, 573–79, *575–79*
    size in various countries, 562, *562*
    size of federal service, 558, *559*

bureaucrats, 556–58
Burger, Warren, 181
Burnham, Walter Dean, 337
Bush, George H.W., and administration
    attempts to shrink bureaucracy`, 575
    education policies, 690
    executive order of, 540
    judicial appointments, 602, 620
    State Department, 725
    Supreme Court nominees of, 602
    tax brackets under, 655
    war powers of, 525
Bush, George W., and administration
    administrative directives, 537
    antiterrorism initiatives, 608–9
    approval ratings, 536
    as "compassionate conservative," 215
    congressional scrutiny of, 502
    courting of religious groups, 356
    economic policies, 648
    education policies, 690
    election of 2000, 245, 364, 368–69, 384, 390
    emergency declaration following terror
        attacks, 528
    EPA under, 513
    executive orders of, 538
    and financial crisis of 2008, 648
    foreign policy, 722, 724
    foreign policy after 9/11 attacks, 232–34
    growth of government under, 102
    immigration law enforcement, 188
    inherent powers, 525, 526
    and Iraq War, 722, 724
    judicial appointments, 620
    management strategy, 581
    and micro-targeting, 398–99
    military spending, 639
    Pentagon budget under, 663
    presidential initiatives, 521
    preventive war policy, 719–20
    privatization under, 577
    public opinion of tax cuts, 223, 230
    public relations by, 535
    and religious conservatives, 319
    SCHIP regulation under, 98
    and Social Security reform, 685–86
    taxation reviews under, 689

tax brackets under, 655
tax cuts, 281, 650, 655
unitary executive theory and, 522
and United Nations, *735*
veto power used by, 520
voter mobilization in 2004 election, 320
White House Communications Office, 535
Bush, Jeb, 281

Bush Doctrine, 724 foreign policy based on the idea that the United States should take preemptive action against threats to its national security

Bush v. Gore, 390
business development, promoting, 637–39
business interest groups, 433
business organizations, 646
Business Roundtable, 646
busing, school desegregation via, 173–74
butterfly ballots, *383*

C

cabinet, 529, 530, *529* the secretaries, or chief administrators, of the major departments of the federal government; Cabinet secretaries are appointed by the president with the consent of the Senate

Cable News Network (CNN), 260, 265, *278*
cable television, 265
Calhoun, John C., 94–95, *95*
California
    Asian Americans, 189–91, 316
    electoral college votes from, 389
    federal employees in, 558
    gun laws, 136
    immigration and voter demographics, 354
    initiative campaigns in, 9, 392
    migrant workers in, 186
    Proposition 30, 323
    Proposition 62, *323*
    Proposition 187, 187
    recall of Gray Davis in, 393
    redistricting rules, 478–79
    Sacramento Delta, 667
    shifting political demographics, 224–25
    smoking bans in, 98
    unauthorized immigrants in, 187
California Paid Family Leave, 707
campaign activism, 459
campaign consultants, 393–94, *394*
campaign finance reform. *See* Bipartisan Campaign Reform Act of 2002
campaign laws, in various countries, 403, *403*
campaign strategy, 340, 395–400
Campbell, Andrea, 675–76
Canada, 606, 721
candidates
    for Congress, 476
    recruitment of, 340
    for vice president, 531
Cantwell v. Connecticut, 126
cap-and-trade system, *666*
capitalism, 23, 86, 642–43
capital punishment, 144–45
Cardozo, Benjamin, 120

Carender, Keli, 334–35, *335*
Carlson, Tucker, *276*
Carter, Aston, 158
Carter, Jimmy, 528, 574, 580, 641
Case Act of 1972, 503–4
caseloads, *598*
cash assistance, 687–88, *688*

categorical grants, 91, 638–39 congressional grants given to states and localities on the condition that expenditures be limited to a problem or group specified by law

Catholics, 14, 18, 220, 234, 355–56
Cato Institute, 272
Catt, Carrie Chapman, 300

caucus (political), 342, 343, *373*, 386–88, 482, 489 a normally closed political party business meeting of citizens or lawmakers to select candidates, elect officers, plan strategy, or make decisions regarding legislative matters

CBN (Christian Broadcasting Network), 234
CBO (Congressional Budget Office), 649, 656
CBS News, 260, 265, *278*
CDA (Communications Decency Act), 135, 285
CDC (Centers for Disease Control and Prevention), 694
CEA (Council of Economic Advisers), 531, 637
Center for Medicare and Medicaid Services, 573
Centers for Disease Control and Prevention (CDC), 694
Central Intelligence Agency (CIA), 639, 717, 726
certiorari. *See* writ of certiorari
Chairman of the Joint Chiefs of Staff, 568
Chamber of Commerce, U.S., 646
Chamber of Commerce of the United States v. EPA, 615
Charlotte bathroom bill. *See* Public Facilities Privacy and Security Act
Charlotte City Council, 107
Charlottesville white nationalist rally, 208, *208*, *272*, 298
charter schools, 692–93
Chàvez, César, 186

checks and balances, 53, *60* mechanisms through which each branch of government is able to participate in and influence the activities of the other branches; major examples include the presidential veto power over congressional legislation, the power of the Senate to approve presidential appointments, and judicial review of congressional enactments; *see also* separation of powers

Cheney, Dick, 746
Chicago Daily Tribune, 243
Chicago Tribune, 263

chief justice, 600, 616 justice on the Supreme Court who presides over the Court's public sessions and whose official title is "chief justice of the United States"

child labor, 88, *88*

children
    political socialization of, *216*, 217
    social policy for, 704
Children's Defense Fund, 706
Children's Health Insurance Program (CHIP), 467
China, 285, 287
    cyberattacks from, 717
    and human rights, 721–22
    human rights violations by, 721–22
    manufacturing in, 668
    and U.S. foreign policy, 742–45
Chinese Exclusion Act of 1882, 16, 190
Christian Broadcasting Network (CBN), 234
Christian Coalition, 459
Christian right, 318
Chrysler, *637*
church and state. *See* separation of church and state
CIA. *See* Central Intelligence Agency
Citadel military college, 182–83
Citigroup, 495
citizen groups, 435

citizen journalism, 271–72 news reported and distributed by citizens, rather than professional journalists and for-profit news organizations

citizenship, 10–13 informed and active membership in a political community; *see also* digital citizen

    African American rights, 161
    defined, 11
    digital, 11
    and political efficacy, 12
    and political knowledge, 10–13, *12*, 228–29
    and undocumented immigrants, 120
Citizens United, 447
Citizens United v. Federal Election Commission, *128*, 128–29, 397, 401–2, 458

civil law, 594 the branch of law that deals with disputes that do not involve criminal penalties

civil liberties, 114–53 areas of personal freedom constitutionally protected from government interference

    Bill of Rights; *see also specific amendments*, *e.g.*: First Amendment
    Constitution, 117–22
    defined, 118, 160
    freedom of religion, 123–26
    freedom of speech, 127–33
    freedom of the press, 133–36
    rights of the criminally accused, 138–46
    right to bear arms, 136–38
    right to privacy, 146–49
    and USA PATRIOT Act, 570
    in various nations, *150*
Civil Liberties Act of 1988, 190

civil rights, 158–99, *168* obligation imposed on government to take positive action to protect citizens from any illegal action of government agencies and of other private citizens

D

DACA (Deferred Action for Childhood Arrivals), 105, 187–88, 350
Daily Show, The, 266
Dalton, Russell, 307
DAPA (Deferred Action for Parents of Americans), 105
dark money, 404–5
Dasari, Anooha, 255
Daschle, Tom, 497
databases, 321, 343–44
data mining, 246
Davids, Sharice, 419, *419*
Davie, William R., 53
Davis, Gray, 393
Dawson, Michael, 314
DEA (Drug Enforcement Administration), 530

dealignment, 358 a movement away from the major political parties; a decline in partisan attachment

death penalty, 144–45
debates, *399*
  campaign, 398
  congressional, 491–93
de Blasio, Bill, 141
decision making
  by Congress, 494–502
  by Supreme Court, 618–24
  by voters in elections, 406–8
Declaration of Independence, 23, 25, 45–46
Declaration of Sentiments and Resolutions, 162

de facto literally, "by fact"; refers to practices that occur even when there is no legal enforcement, such as school segregation in much of the United States today
  segregation, 168

defendant, 593 the one against whom a complaint is brought in a criminal or civil case

Defense, Department of, 530, 558, 566, 725, 727–28
Defense Base Closure and Realignment Commission (BRAC), 575
Defense of Marriage Act of 1996 (DOMA), 40–42, 80–81, 180, 192
Deferred Action for Childhood Arrivals (DACA), 105, 187–88, 350
Deferred Action for Parents of Americans (DAPA), 105
deficits, 644, 649

de jure literally, "by law"; refers to legally enforced practices, such as school segregation in the South before the 1960s
  segregation, 168

Delaware, 167
DeLay, Tom, 452, 657

delegate a representative who votes according to the preferences of his or her constituency
  congressional, 470
  to political conventions, 388

delegated powers, 515, 523, 525 constitutional powers that are assigned to one governmental agency but that are exercised by another agency with the express permission of the first

democracy, 28–29 a system of rule that permits citizens to play a significant part in the governmental process, usually through the election of key public officials
  as basic political value, 23
  and Congress, 505–6
  in the Constitution, 69
  constitutional, 7–8
  core values of, 210
  defined, 7, 209–10
  functioning of, 10, 11
  function of political parties in, 337–38
  function of the press in, 257–58
  ideal of vs. practice of, 28
  interest groups as challenge to, 460
  and the judiciary, 624
  and the media, 288
  and national security, 569–70
  and opinions based on inadequate knowledge, 230–32
  and political culture, 28–29
  and presidential power, 514
  and public opinion, 247–48
  responsible bureaucracy in, 583–84

Democracy in America (Tocqueville), 460
Democratic National Committee (DNC), 346
Democratic National Convention (1972), 345
Democratic National Convention (2012), *346*
Democratic National Convention (2016), 210–11, 389, *409*
Democratic Party, 339; *see also* political parties
  and 2009 economic stimulus package, 648–49
  and ACA, 697–98
  and Affordable Care Act, 282
  anti-incumbent sentiment, 477
  Asian American voters, 316
  characteristics of, 353
  and civil rights of African Americans, 163
  conference committees, 483–84
  conflict with Republican Party, 348
  congressional party unity, 496–98, *497*
  data mining, 246–47
  demographics of, 339, 353–58
  distrust in government among members of, 31
  and economic policy, 641
  factions within, 351
  and Federal Reserve, 652
  fund-raising activities of, 346
  and gender gap, 316
  gerrymandering, 478
  and health care reform, 695, 697–98
  ideology, 356
  immigration stance, 348
  key policy positions of, 348
  and labor groups, 646
  and laissez-faire economics, 642–43
  Latino voters, 314–15, 353–54
  and leadership PACs, 498
  and lower-income voters, 356
  members' characteristics, 221–22

  and minimum wage, 645
  origins of, 361–63
  party identification, 352–53
  and polarization, 276–77, 366, 367–68
  and primary delegates, 388
  and Progressive Party reforms, 369–70
  and proportional representation voting, 345, 388
  and public works financing, 89
  recruitment of candidates by, 476
  and redistricting, 479–80
  and regulation, 644, 646
  religious affiliations of members, 221
  responsiveness of, 338
  and social programs, 31
  tax and social spending views of, 356, 643–44
  and voter ID laws, 324, 326
  voter mobilization, 320
  and white southerners, 224–25
  and young Americans, 358, *358*
  and youth vote, 358
democratic socialism, 214
demonstrations, 455
Denmark, 259
Dennis v. United States, 129

department, 559 the largest subunit of the executive branch; the secretaries of the 15 departments form the Cabinet

deportation policies, 105–7, 120

deregulation, 661 a policy of reducing or eliminating regulatory restraints on the conduct of individuals or private institutions

descriptive representation, 315
desegregation, 516–17

deterrence, 719 An effort to prevent hostile action by promising to retaliate forcefully against an attacker
devolution, 96, 100–102, 576–77 a policy to remove a program from one level of government by delegating it or passing it down to a lower level of government, such as from the national government to the state and local governments

DeVos, Betsy, 565, 683
Dewey, John, *243*, 257
DHS. *See* Homeland Security, Department of
digital advertising, 267

digital citizen a daily internet user with broadband (high-speed) home internet access and the technology and literacy skills to go online for employment, news, politics, entertainment, commerce, and other activities; *see also* internet
  defined, 11, 268
  offline political participation of, 304–7

digital divide, 268, 309 the gap in access to the internet among demographic groups based on education, income, age, geographic location, and race/ethnicity

digital media, 267–71; *see also* internet

digital political participation, 303–10 activities designed to influence politics using the internet, including visiting a candidate's website, organizing events online, and signing an online petition

digital revolution, 261–63
digital subscription models, 264

diplomacy, 734 the representation of a government to other governments

diplomatic power (president), 517–18
diplomatic recognition, 517, 725
direct-action politics, 10

direct democracy, 9, 392–93 a system of rule that permits citizens to vote directly on laws and policies

direct lobbying, 449–52
direct mail campaigns, 400
Director of National Intelligence (DNI), 728
direct patronage, 480–82
Disability Rights Education and Defense Fund, 191–92
disabled Americans, civil rights for, 191–92

discretionary spending, 658, *658, 659* federal spending on programs that are controlled through the regular budget process

discrimination the use of any unreasonable and unjust criterion of exclusion; *see also* segregation
    against African Americans, 95
    against Asian Americans, 189–91
    based on sexual orientation, 192–93
    against citizens of other states, 83
    defined, 161
    against disabled Americans, 99, 191–92
    employment, 171, 174–75, 195
    gender, 180–85
    in housing, 177–78
    against Latinos/Hispanics, 184–89, *186*
    in lending, 177–78
    against Native Americans, 191–92
    positive, 198
    racial, 161–79, 678
    against white Americans, 198
    against women, 171

Disney, 260

dissenting opinion, 617 a decision written by a justice in the minority in a particular case in which the justice wishes to express his or her reasoning in the case

district courts, federal, *596*, 596–97, 598, 599
district judges, appointment of, 599
District of Columbia, 82, 143, 167, 326, 327
District of Columbia v. Heller, 136–38
diversity, news media and, 273

divided government, 365 the condition in American government wherein the presidency is controlled by one party while the opposing party controls one or both houses of Congress

DNA testing, 140–41
DNC. *See* Democratic National Committee
Dodd–Frank Act, 495–96, 661
Doha Amendment to the Kyoto Protocol, 745
Dole, Bob, 95
domestic military power, 516–17
domestic social spending, 500
donations (political campaigns). *See* fund-raising
Donovan, Todd, 245, 321
"Don't Ask, Don't Tell," 192
double government, 581

double jeopardy, 120, 142 the Fifth Amendment right providing that a person cannot be tried twice for the same crime

Douglas, William O., 146
Douglass, Frederick, 162
DREAM Act, 187, *229*
Dreamers. *See* DACA (Deferred Action for Childhood Arrivals)
Dred Scott v. Sandford, 162
Druckman, James, 229
Drudge Report, 264
Drug Enforcement Administration (DEA), 76, 530
drug testing, 140

dual federalism, 85–86, *91* the system of government that prevailed in the United States from 1789 to 1937 in which most fundamental governmental powers were shared between the federal and state governments

Du Bois, W.E.B., 165
due process clause, 120

due process of law, 138–46 the right of every individual against arbitrary action by national or state governments
    cruel and unusual punishment, 144–45
    defined, 597
    double jeopardy, 142
    eminent domain, 143
    grand juries, 142
    right to counsel, 144
    and same-sex marriage ruling, 193
    searches and seizures, 139–41
    self-incrimination, 142–43

Duke Power Company, 175

E

Early, Stephen, 535

early voting, 327 the option in some states to cast a vote at a polling place or by mail before the election

earmarks, 480–81
Earned Income Tax Credit (EITC), 702, 703
East India Company, 44, 45, *45*
e-commerce, 105
economic aid and sanctions, 736–37
economic class, public opinion and, 222–24
economic crisis of 2008. *See* financial crisis and recession of 2008

economic development agencies, 572–73
economic equality/inequality, 20, *21*, 25–26
economic freedom, 24–25
economic growth
    environmental policy vs., 238
    measuring, 634–36
economic inequality. *See* income equality/inequality
Economic Opportunity Act, 91–92
economic policy, 630–69
    for business development, 637–39
    for economic prosperity, 634–37
    and the environment, 663–67
    fiscal policies, 652–58
    goals of, 633–41
    government spending, 643–44
    monetary policies, 649–52
    politics of, 641
    to protect employees and consumers, 639–41
    regulation, 644–46
    regulation and antitrust policy, 659–61
    and special interest groups, 646
    for stable markets, 633–34
    subsidies and contracting, 661–63
    taxation, 643
economic populism, 356
economic power, political power and, 28
economic prosperity
    economic policy for, 634–37
    foreign policy for, 720–21
economic stimulus package (2009). *See* American Recovery and Reinvestment Act of 2009
economy
    bureaucracy for maintaining, 571–73
    as campaign influence, 407
    and federal control, 88
education
    of Congress members, *473*, 474
    elementary and secondary, 690, 692–93
    and gender discrimination, 182–83
    government relief for student loans, *709*
    higher, 693–94
    party affiliation and, *359*
    and political participation, 310–11, *311*
    for a productive workforce, 636
    and public opinion, 217
    public policies for, 689–94
    school segregation/desegregation, 25–26, 167–70, 623
    state laws on, 86
Education, Department of, 530, 552, 564–65
Education Act of 1972, 182
EEOC. *See* Equal Employment Opportunity Commission
Eighth Amendment, 144–45
Eisenhower, Dwight D., 168–69, 363, 516–17, *517*, 662
EITC (Earned Income Tax Credit), 703

elastic clause, 56, 64 The concluding paragraph of Article I, Section 8, of the Constitution (also known as the "necessary and proper clause"), which provides Congress with the authority to make all laws "necessary and proper" to carry out its enumerated powers

FactCheck.org, 275, *277*
Fair Housing Act, 177–78
Fair Housing Amendments Act, 177
Fair Labor Standards Act of 1938, 640, 645
fairness doctrine, 286
fake news, 274, 275, *275, 277*
Fallon, Brian, *394*
family, political socialization by, 216–17
Family and Medical Leave Act, 104–5, 706–7
farm subsidy program, 638
Farook, Syed, 141
Faubus, Orval, 168, 516–17
FBI. *See* Federal Bureau of Investigation
FCC (Federal Communications Commission), 254, 255, 285, 286
FDA. *See* Food and Drug Administration
FDIC (Federal Deposit Insurance Corporation), 651
FEC (Federal Election Commission), 404
Fed, the. *See* Federal Reserve Board
federal agencies, 523, 525, 530
   created by executive order, 538
   implementation of laws by, 537
federal agencies, judicial review of, 608
federal aid, *92*
Federal Aviation Administration, 552
Federal Bureau of Investigation (FBI), 24, 141, 273, 280, *280*, 284, 503, 566, 725, 728
Federal Communications Commission (FCC), 254, 255, 285, 286
federal courts, *595*, 604–24; *see also individual courts, e.g.:* Supreme Court
   appellate courts, 599
   caseloads, *598*
   court cases, 593–94
   and judicial revolutions, 622–24
   and the legal system, 593–97
   traditional limitations on, 621–22
   transformation of role and power of, 621–24
   trial courts, 599
   types of courts, 594–97
Federal Deposit Insurance Corporation (FDIC), 651
Federal Election Campaign Act of 1971, 404, 456
Federal Election Commission (FEC), 404
Federal Election Commission v. Wisconsin Right to Life, 128
Federal Emergency Management Agency (FEMA), 528, 530, 553

federal funds rate, 650   the interest rate on loans between banks that the Federal Reserve Board influences by affecting the supply of money available

federal government; *see also* bureaucracy; federalism; government(s)
   Constitutional limits on power of, 58, 59
   Constitutional provisions on power of, 57–58, 59
   and dual federalism, 85–86
   effect on daily life at state universities, *80*
   growth in power of, 87–88
   role as defined in Articles of Confederation, 46
   spending by, *560*
   traditional system of, 84–95
federal grants, *90*, 91, *92*, 96

federalism, 76–109   a system of government in which power is divided, by a constitution, between a central government and regional governments
   and business, 88
   and changing role of states, 94–95
   in the Constitution, 54, 59, 79–84
   cooperative, 89–93, *91*, 91–93
   defined, 54, 79
   and devolution, 100–102
   dual, 85–86
   dual vs. cooperative, *91*
   federal grants, *90*, 91
   and growth of national government's power, 87–88
   in modern era, 89–99
   New Deal, 89
   politics of, 102–7
   public spending, *103*
   regulated, 93–99, *96, 100*
   traditional system of, 84–95

Federalist Papers, **62, 730**   a series of essays written by Alexander Hamilton, James Madison, and John Jay supporting ratification of the Constitution

Federalists   those who favored a strong national government and supported the Constitution proposed at the American Constitutional Convention of 1787
   and bill of rights, 117–19
   defined, 60
   and electoral realignment, 365
   origin of, 339
   and ratification of the Constitution, 60–65, *62*
   and states' powers amendment, 82
   and two-party system, 339, 360–61

federal judges, 600–603, *603*
Federal Labor Relations Authority (FLRA), 580
Federally Funded Research and Development Centers (FFRDCs), 727
Federal Meat Inspection Act of 1906, 660, *660*
Federal Register, 537, 661
Federal Regulation of Lobbying Act of 1946, 449
Federal Reserve Act, 650–51
Federal Reserve banks, 650
Federal Reserve Board (the Fed), 571, *572*, 650–51, *651*

Federal Reserve System, 571, 650–51   a system of 12 Federal Reserve banks that facilitates exchanges of cash, checks, and credit; regulates member banks; and uses monetary policies to fight inflation and deflation

federal service, 558, *559; see also* bureaucracy
federal system, 79, *85, 97*, 381; *see also* federalism
Federal Trade Commission (FTC), 660
Federal Trade Commission Act of 1914, 660
Feeding America, 703
fee shifting, 622
Feingold, Russell, 404
felons, voting rights of, 326
Ferguson, Missouri, 170, 218, 536

Fifteenth Amendment, 28, 163, 299–300   one of three Civil War amendments; it guaranteed voting rights for African American men

Fifth Amendment, 141–43
   double jeopardy, 142
   eminent domain, 143
   grand juries, 142
   incorporated in Fourteenth Amendment, 120
   provisions of, 119–20
   rights of the accused, 68
   right to privacy, 146
   self-incrimination, 142–43
"Fight for Fifteen" campaign, 646

fighting words, 129   speech that directly incites damaging conduct

filibuster, 368, 492, 506   a tactic used by members of the Senate to prevent action on legislation they oppose by continuously holding the floor and speaking until the majority backs down; once given the floor, senators have unlimited time to speak, and it requires a vote of three-fifths of the Senate to end a filibuster

filter bubble, 275
financial crisis and recession of 2008 (Great Recession), 28, 576, *637*, 688
   and federal deficit, 657
   Federal Reserve's response to, 650
   and financial industry regulation reform, 661
   foreclosure crisis, 651, 699–700
   government response, 648
   and public opinion, 226
   and SNAP benefits, 704
   stimulus package, 637
financial industry reform, 661
Financial Stability Oversight Council, 571–73
Fiorina, Morris, 221–22

"fire alarm" oversight, 582   episodic, as-needed congressional hearings on bureaucratic agency operations, usually prompted by media attention or advocacy group complaints

firearms. *See* gun control
First Amendment, 118–19, 123–36, *124*
   and campaign contribution limits, 401, 402, 605
   case with the Slants, 114–15
   and freedom of religion, 123–26; *see also* freedom of religion
   and freedom of speech, 127–33; *see also* freedom of speech
   and freedom of the press, 133–36
   incorporated in Fourteenth Amendment, 120
   and lobbying, 449
   and media, 257, 285
   and net neutrality, 255
   and press freedom around the world, 287
First Continental Congress, 45
First Founding, 43–46
"first past the post," 340, 341
first spouse, 532–33
fiscal agencies, 571–73

fiscal policy, 571, 652–58   the government's use of taxing, monetary, and spending powers to manipulate the economy

Fisher, Louis, 526, 543
Fisher v. University of Texas, 180, 197, 611

501(c)(4) committees (dark money), 404–5
politically active nonprofits; under federal
law, these nonprofits can spend unlimited
amounts on political campaigns and not
disclose their donors as long as their activities
are not coordinated with the candidate
campaigns and political activities are not their
primary purpose

**527 committee (Super PAC), 346, 404–5,
458** a nonprofit independent political
action committee that may raise unlimited
sums of money from corporations, unions,
and individuals but is not permitted to
contribute to or coordinate directly with
parties or candidates

FiveThirtyEight.com, 246
flag burning, 132
Flint drinking water disaster, 246, 550–52
Flint Water Advisory Task Force, 551
Florida
    congressional seats of, 478
    election of 2000, 176, *383*, 384, 390
FLRA (Federal Labor Relations Authority), 580
Flynn, Michael, 531
FOIA. *See* Freedom of Information Act
Food and Drug Administration (FDA), 93, 552,
    640, 660
Ford, Gerald, 517, 532
foreclosure crisis, 699–700
foreclosures, 651
foreign aid, 721–22, 736–37
Foreign Intelligence Surveillance Act (FISA), 729
foreign policy, 526, 714–47
    after 9/11 attacks, 234
    and America's role in the world, 746
    arbitration, 740–41
    with China and Russia, 741–43
    for collective security, 737–38
    diplomacy, 734
    for economic aid and sanctions, 736–37
    for economic prosperity, 720–21
    and global environmental policy, 745
    goals of, 717–22
    human rights, 721–22
    instruments of, 733–41
    international humanitarian policies, 722
    and international monetary structure, 735–36
    with Iran and North Korea, 743–44
    makers of, 722–33
    and military force, 738–40
    for security, 717–20
    and trade policy, 744–45
    and the United Nations, 734–35
Foreign Service, U.S., 725
foreign service officer, *556*
formula grants, 91
foundations, as media revenue source, 272–73
Founding, 64–65
    American demographics at time of, 13
    Articles of Confederation, 46
    and British taxes, 43–44
    and colonists' political strife, 44–45

and Constitution, 40–53
    Declaration of Independence, 45–46
    First, 43–46
    Second, 47–53

Fourteenth Amendment, 83, 618 one of three
Civil War amendments; it guaranteed equal
protection and due process

    citizenship for freed slaves, 16
    civil rights, 161
    and double jeopardy, 142
    due process clause, 119–20
    equal protection, 163, 164, 193
    first definitive interpretation of, 198
    incorporation of Bill of Rights into, 118–22,
        121–22
    levels of scrutiny under equal protection
        clause, 179–80
    Obergefell v. Hodges, 41, 193
    and voting rights, 170–71
Fourth Amendment, 139–41, 146
Fourth of July (Independence Day) celebration,
    46
Fox News, 265, 276, *278*
Frahm, Stephen, *568*

framing, 234, 282 the power of the media
to influence how events and issues are
interpreted

France, 19, 43, 79, 259, 524
Franken, Al, 258
Frankfurter, Felix, 600, 616–17, 619
Franklin, Benjamin, 45
Franklin v. Gwinnett County Public Schools, 182
Francisco, Noel, *612*
Frederick, Joseph, 130
Freedom of Information Act (FOIA), 569–70,
    570, 583, *585*
freedom of religion, 123–26
    free exercise clause, 126
    separation of church and state, 123–25
freedom of speech, 114–16, 127–33, 401, 402,
    605
freedom of the press, 257, 287, *287*
free elections, as essential to democracy, 210

free exercise clause, 126 the First Amendment
clause that protects a citizen's right to believe
and practice whatever religion he or she
chooses

free markets, 23

free riders, 441 those who enjoy the benefits
of collective goods but did not participate in
acquiring or providing them

Free Soil Party, 162
French and Indian War, 43
FTC (Federal Trade Commission), 660

full faith and credit clause, 82 provision from
Article IV, Section 1 of the Constitution
requiring that the states normally honor the
public acts and judicial decisions that take
place in another state

Fulton, Robert, 87

fund-raising (election campaigns), 304, 328,
    371–72, 394–95, *395*, 400–405,
    403, 422, *423*; *see also* Bipartisan
    Campaign Reform Act of 2002

G

Gadsden, Christopher, 45
Gainous, Jason, 269, 270
Gallup polls, 243
Gannett, 260
GAO (Government Accountability Office), 579
Garland, Merrick, 602
Garner, Eric, 218
Garrity, W. Arthur, Jr., 174, 623
gas crisis of 1973, *101*
Gates, Bill, 273, 450
Gates, Rick, 284
Gates Foundation, 273
GATT (General Agreement on Tariffs and Trade),
    518, 721
gay marriage. *See* same-sex marriage
gay rights, 192–93; *see also* same-sex marriage
GDP. *See* gross domestic product
Geer, John, 397
gender
    and party affiliation, 355, *359*
    and political opinions, 220, *222*
    and political participation, 316–17
    public opinion questions of, 242–43
gender discrimination, 180–85, *182*

gender gap, 220, *222*, 355 a distinctive
pattern of voting behavior reflecting the
differences in views between women and men

**General Agreement on Tariffs and Trade
(GATT), 518, 721** international trade
organization, in existence from 1947 to
1995, that set many of the rules governing
international trade

general election, 382 a regularly scheduled
election involving most districts in the nation
or state, in which voters select officeholders;
in the United States, general elections for
national office and most state and local
offices are held on the first Tuesday after the
first Monday in November in even-numbered
years (every four years for presidential elections)

General Motors, 550

general revenue sharing, 96 the process
by which one unit of government yields a
portion of its tax income to another unit
of government, according to an established
formula; revenue sharing typically involves
the national government providing money to
state governments

genetics, political beliefs and, 216
Georgia, 149, 188, 478, 621
Gerber, Alan, 319
Gerber, Elizabeth, 459
Germany, 259
    cooperative federalism in, 97
    term limits for judges in, 606
Gerry, Elbridge, 385

Hersh, Eitan, 321
HHS. *See* Health and Human Services, Department of
higher education, 693–94
Higher Education Act (HEA), 693
highway system, 638–39
Hill, Anita, 602
Hispanic Americans. *See* Latinos/Hispanics
Hispanic Caucus, 188
Hispanics. *See* Latinos/Hispanics
HIV/AIDS, 694
Hoffman, Hazel, 466
Holder, Eric, 181, 519, 526
holds, 492
Holmes, Oliver Wendell, 127
Holt, Gregory, 126
Holt v. Hobbs, 126
Homeland Security, Department of (DHS), *567*, 211, *565*, 565–66
   congressional battle over funding, 493
   creation of, 102, 523, 525, 552
   immigration enforcement, 188
   and NSC, 728–29
   oversight of, 581–83
   in Trump administration, 558, 566

home rule, 84 power delegated by the state to a local unit of government to manage its own affairs

homosexuality, 149, 192–93; *see also* same-sex marriage
Honest Ads Act, 309
Honest Leadership and Open Government Act (2007), 492–93
Hoover, Herbert, 89, 363
Hoovervilles, 89
HOPE VI program, 698–99
House Armed Services Committee, 731
House Committee on Foreign Affairs, 731
House Intelligence Committee, 731, 732
House Judiciary Committee, *486*
House of Representatives; *see also* Congress
   ACA repeal votes, 696
   allocation of floor time, 498
   campaign funding for, 394, *395*
   conference committees, 493
   constituency service time in, 475
   Constitutional provision for, 55–56
   costs of campaigning for seat in, 342
   differences between Senate and, *469*, 469–70
   domestic social spending (2018), 500
   ethics law of, 480
   and foreign policy, 731
   gerrymandering, 478
   Great Compromise provision for, 50, *51*
   and impeachment, 504–5
   majority party structure, *483*
   majority rule through, 28–29
   number of representatives in, 22
   party leadership in, 482
   polarization in, 367–68
   political parties' function in, 351–52
   redistricting, 384
   Three-Fifths Compromise, 52–53
   women serving in, 317

House Rules Committee, 484
House Select Committee on Benghazi, 484, 502–3
House Select Committee on Homeland Security, 484
housing, *699*
   as civil right, 177–78
   social policies for, 698–700
Housing and Urban Development, Department of (HUD), 178, 651
housing bubble, 699
housing crisis (2007–2008), 651, 699
housing market, 651
hoverboards, *640*, 641
Howes, Will, 254
HUD. *See* Housing and Urban Development, Department of
Hull, Cordell, 725
Human Genome Project, 636
humanitarian policies, 722
human rights
   internet access as, 286
   policy for, 721–22
Human Rights Campaign, 193
human rights policies, 721–22
Hungary, 287
Hunt, Ward, 163–64
Hupp, Suzanna, 204–5
Hurricane Katrina, 553
Hussein, Saddam, 746

I

ICC (Interstate Commerce Commission), 660
Idaho, 165–66, 479, 576
ideas, marketplace of, 232
ideological groups, 435
ideology. *See* political ideology
"I Have a Dream" speech (King), 170
Illinois, 384, *385*, 677
IMF (International Monetary Fund), 735–36
immigrants, *16*
   civil rights of, 187–89
   impact of languages/customs of, 22–23
   and Medicaid, 682
   undocumented, 18, *18*, 102, 105–7, 187
immigration, 13–22, *15*
   Congressional Hispanic Caucus and, *474*
   by continent of origin, *17*
   and ethnic diversity, 14–16, *15*
   Kamala Harris and, *229*
   as issue in 2016 presidential election, 189
   Latino public opinion on, 219–20
   and race, *15*, 16
   state and local policies for, 102, 105–7
Immigration Act of 1965, 189, 190
Immigration and Customs Enforcement (ICE), 188, 729
immigration reform, 315
Immigration Reform and Control Act of 1986, 188

impeachment, 504–5, 542 the formal charge by the House of Representatives that a government official has committed "Treason, Bribery, or other high Crimes and Misdemeanors"

implementation, 553 the efforts of departments and agencies to translate laws into specific bureaucratic rules and actions

implied powers, 79, 515, 526 powers derived from the necessary and proper clause of Article I, Section 8 of the Constitution; such powers are not specifically expressed but are implied through the expansive interpretation of delegated powers

inalienable rights, 23, 46
incarceration rates, 147
income equality/inequality, 20, *21*, 27–28, 668
   and economic populism, 356
   Latino public opinion on, 219–20
   and political influence of the affluent, 236–37
   and public opinion, 222–23, *231*, 236
income levels; *see also* poverty; socioeconomic status
   internet access and, 268
   political opinion expression and, *249*
income taxes, 652, 655
increased defense, 500

incumbency, 476–77 holding the political office for which one is running

incumbency advantage, 367, 385, 394, 395, 476–77, *477*

incumbent, 393, 394, 395 a candidate running for re-election to a position that he or she already holds

Independence Day celebration, *46*

independent agency, 560 agency that is not part of a Cabinet department

independent regulatory commissions, 561
independent voters, *358*, *359*

indexing, 680 periodic process of adjusting social benefits or wages to account for increases in the cost of living

Indiana, 177, 188
Indiana Beverage Alliance, 630
Indian Self-Determination and Education Assistance Act, 191
individual mandate, 696
Indivisible Oregon, *233*

inflation, 637, 650 a consistent increase in the general level of prices

informational benefits, 442 special newsletters, periodicals, training programs, conferences, and other information provided to members of groups to entice others to join

inherent powers, 515, 525–26 powers claimed by a president that are not expressed in the Constitution but are inferred from it

initiatives (ballot measures), 9, 322

in-kind benefits, 680 noncash goods and services provided to needy individuals and families by the federal government

judicial review, 57, 69, 604–10   the power of the courts to review and, if necessary, declare actions of the legislative and executive branches invalid or unconstitutional; the Supreme Court asserted this power in *Marbury v. Madison* (1803)
   of acts of Congress, 604–5
   of federal agency actions, 608
   and presidential power, 608–9
   of state actions, 605–7
   in various countries, *606*

judicial revolutions, 622–24
Judiciary Act of 1789, 605
Juneau-Douglas High School, 130
Jungle, The (Sinclair), 640, 660

jurisdiction, 595   the sphere of a court's power and authority

Justice Department, 198
   immigration law challenges, 188–89
   and internal security, 566
   job discrimination cases, 174–75
   and LBGT rights, 182
   private prison use, 579
   school desegregation, 172–73
   and school desegregation, 690

K

Kagan, Elena, 602, 606
Kaine, Tim, *389*
Kansas, 167
Karpf, David, 443
Kavanaugh, Brett, 500, 592, 600–601, 602, 619
Keating-Owen Child Labor Act of 1916, 88
Kelo v. City of New London, 144
Kennedy, Anthony, 140, 592, 600, 601, 602, 618
Kennedy, John F.
   civil rights supported by, 364
   media use by, 535
   tax cut by, 637
   in televised debates, 398, *399*
   vice president for, 531
Kentucky, 125, 326
Kerry, John, *504*, 725, 727, 734
Keynes, John Maynard, 637

Keynesians, 637, 642, 644   followers of the economic theories of John Maynard Keynes, who argued that the government can stimulate the economy by increasing public spending or by cutting taxes

Keystone XL pipeline, 520–21
Kibby, Regan, 158–60
Kim Jong-un, 518, *518*, 720, 725, *734*, 743–44
King, Martin Luther, Jr., 170, 177, 300, *454*, 454–55
King Caucus method, 388
Kingdon, John, 706
King v. Burwell, 107, 619
Kissinger, Henry, 531
knowledge, political, 10–13, 11–13, *12*, 228–32
Knowledge Networks (KN), 241
Koch, Charles, *236*
Korean War, 525, 719, 740
K Street Project, 496

Ku Klux Klan, 128
Kushner, Jared, 530
Kyoto Protocol, 745

L

labor (unions). *See* organized labor
Labor, Department of, 640
labor interest groups, 433, 435, 646
labor relations, 640, 660
Ladd, Jonathan, 276

laissez-faire capitalism, 24, 642   an economic system in which the means of production and distribution are privately owned and operated for profit with minimal or no government interference

Lambda Legal Defense and Education Fund, 193
Landon, Alf, 243
Land Ordinance of 1785, 689
Landrieu, Mary, *450*
Lanham Act of 1946, disparagement clause of, 115
Lansing, John, 50
Lasswell, Harold, 9
Late Show, The, 266
Latin America, immigrants from, 18
Latinos/Hispanics
   and 2012 election, 243
   child poverty rate, 705–6
   civil rights of, 184–89, *186*
   in Congress, 471, *472*
   and Democratic Party, 353–54
   and digital divide, 309
   elderly poverty rate for, 700
   immigration of, 17–18
   lending discrimination against, 178, *178*
   news sources for, 269
   party affiliations of, 353–54
   policy attitudes of, 219–20
   political participation by, 314–15, 353–54
   population demographics, 13, 16–17
   poverty rate for, 700, 704
   racial classification, 16–17
   and states' refusal of Medicaid expansion, 703
   trust in government, 31
   voter discrimination in Texas, 176–77
   voting rights of felons, 326
Lau, Richard, 229
Lau v. Nichols, 190, 191
Lavrov, Sergei, 727
law(s)
   implementation of, 537
   presidential nonenforcement of, 540–41
law clerks, *613*, 613–14
law enforcement, judicial review of, 605–7
lawmaking
   committee deliberation, 489–91
   conference committee, 493
   debate, 491–93
   presidential approval, 494
   rules of, 489–94, *490*
Law of the Sea Treaty (LOST), 730–31
Lawrence v. Texas, 149, 192
Lead and Copper Rule, 552
leadership PACs, 498

League of United Latin American Citizens (LULAC), 186
leaks, media, 283
Ledbetter, Lily, 184
Ledbetter v. Goodyear Tire and Rubber Co., 184
Lee, Barbara, 491
Lee, Richard Henry, 62
Legal Defense and Educational Fund (NAACP), 166–67
legal system, 593–97; *see also* federal courts
legislative branch; *see also* Congress; House of Representatives; Senate
   Constitutional provisions for, 55–56
   separation of powers, 58, *59*

legislative initiative, 521   the president's inherent power to bring a legislative agenda before Congress

legislative power (president), 519–21
Lehman Brothers, 652

Lemon test, 124   a rule articulated in *Lemon v. Kurtzman* that government action toward religion is permissible if it is secular in purpose, neither promotes nor inhibits the practice of religion, and does not lead to "excessive entanglement" with religion

Lemon v. Kurtzman, 124
LePage, Paul, *433*
lesbian, gay, bisexual, transgender, and queer (LGBTQ) movement, 192–93
lesbian marriage, 80–81; *see also* same-sex marriage
Lewinsky, Monica, 505
LGBTQ (lesbian, gay, bisexual, transgender, and queer) movement, 192–93

libel, 134   a written statement made in "reckless disregard of the truth" that is considered damaging to a victim because it is "malicious, scandalous, and defamatory"

liberal governments, 7
liberalism, 30, 212, *213*, 234, 368, 619–20

liberals, 356   today this term refers to those who generally support social and political reform, governmental intervention in the economy, more economic equality, expansion of federal social services, and greater concern for consumers and the environment

Libertarian Party, 369

libertarians, 214   someone who emphasizes freedom and believes in voluntary association with small government

liberty, 26–27, 33–34   freedom from governmental control; *see also* civil liberties
   central underpinnings of, 8
   in the Constitution, 69
   defined, 23, 209
   and political culture, 24–25
   as political value, 23, 209

Liberty Displaying the Arts and Sciences, *52*
Liberty Party, 162

Libya attack. *See* Benghazi, Libya, consulate attack and congressional investigation
life expectancy, and health spending, 691, *691*
Lily Ledbetter Fair Pay Act of 2009, 182, *182*, 184
Limbaugh, Rush, 265
limited government, 23, 64   a principle of constitutional government; a government whose powers are defined and limited by a constitution
limits of presidential power, 541–43
Lincoln, Abraham
   debating skill of, 398
   election of 1860, 362, 365, 390
   executive orders of, 533
   inherent powers of, 525, 526
   oath of office, 515, *515*
   writ of habeas corpus, 515
linked fate, 218, 314
LinkedIn, *270*
literacy tests, 300
Literary Digest poll, 243
Little Rock Central High School, 168–69
living Constitution concept, 69
Livingston, Robert, 45
lobbies, 433; *see also* interest groups
lobbying, *450*, 614   a strategy by which organized interests seek to influence the passage of legislation by exerting direct pressure on government officials
   corporate, 450
   defined, 461
   direct, 449–52
   regulation of, 452–53
   spending, by industry, *434*
Lobbying Disclosure Act of 1995, 449, 453
local districts, third parties in, 369
local governments
   categorical grants to, 638
   and the Constitution, 84
   effect on daily life at state universities, *80*
   election administration by, 381–82
   and labor relations, 640
Locke, John, 8, *8*
logrolling, 499   a legislative practice whereby agreements are made between legislators in voting for or against a bill; vote trading
loophole, 653   incentive to individuals and businesses to reduce their tax liabilities by investing their money in areas the government designates
Louisiana, 162
Love Canal, 664
Loving v. Virginia, 82, 179, *179*
LULAC (League of United Latin American Citizens), 186

M
machine politics (party machines), 347, *347*
machine politics, voter mobilization and, 320
Maddow, Rachel, *276*

Madison, James
   on division of power, 64
   and *Federalist Papers*, 60
   and Great Compromise, 50
   and internal improvements, 86
   on legislative branch, 55
   on liberty, 69, 431, 460
   and *Marbury v. Madison*, 604
   and political conflict, 339
   on representation, 63
   on states' interests, 50
mail-in ballots, 327
Maine, 9, 326, 392
majority leader, 482, 498   the elected leader of the majority party in the House of Representatives or in the Senate; in the House, the majority leader is subordinate in the party hierarchy to the Speaker of the House
majority-minority district, 386   an electoral district, such as a congressional district, in which the majority of the constituents belong to racial or ethnic minorities
majority party, 351   the party that holds the majority of legislative seats in either the House or the Senate
majority rule, minority rights, 28–29   the democratic principle that a government follows the preferences of the majority of voters but protects the interests of the minority
majority system, 382   a type of electoral system in which, to win a seat in the parliament or other representative body, a candidate must receive a majority of all the votes cast in the relevant district
MALDEF (Mexican American Legal Defense and Education Fund), 187
Malik, Tashfeen, 141
Malkin, Michelle, 335
Manafort, Paul, 284
managerial presidency, 581
mandatory spending, 658, *658*   federal spending that is made up of budget items that cannot be controlled through the regular budget process, such as interest on the national debt, Social Security and Medicare benefits, and certain programs in the Departments of Agriculture and Veterans Affairs, among others
Manning, Bradley, 134
manufacturing, 668
Mapp, Dollree (Dolly), 139
Mapp v. Ohio, 139
Marbury, William, 604
Marbury v. Madison, 604
March for Our Lives, 456
March on Washington (1963), 170
margin of error, 239
marijuana, 9, 76–78, 104, 108, 224, 420
Marine Corps, 568
Marjory Stoneman Douglas High School shooting, 204–5, 208
Marketplace Fairness Act, 105

marketplace of ideas, 232   the public forum in which beliefs and ideas are exchanged and compete
markets
   federal support for, 638
   stable, 633–34
marriage
   interracial, 82, 179, *179*
   same-sex. *See* Defense of Marriage Act of 1996; same-sex marriage
Married Women's Property Act (New York), 162
Marshall, John, 87–88, 526, 621
Marshall, Thurgood, 167
Martin, Lockheed, 662
Maryland, 479
Maryland v. King, 140
Massachusetts, 48–49, 98, 131, 365, 392
"massive resistance," 168
mass media. *See* media
mass shootings, 137–38, *138*, 208–9
Matal v. Tam, 605
material benefits, 442   special goods, services, or money provided to members of groups to entice others to join
Mattis, James, *568*, 725
McCain, John, 277, 351, 404, 522
   campaign financing legislation. *See* Bipartisan Campaign Reform Act of 2002
   election of 2000, 245
   election of 2008, 405
McCain–Feingold Act. *See* Bipartisan Campaign Reform Act of 2002
McCarthy, Kevin, *500*
McClatchy, 260
McConnell, Mitch, 351
McConnell v. Federal Election Commission, 128
McCreary County v. American Civil Liberties Union of Kentucky, 125
McCulloch v. Maryland, 87–88
McCutcheon et al v. FEC, 404, 620
McDonald v. Chicago, 137
McIver, John, 235
McKinley, William, 363, 365
means testing, 680   a procedure by which potential beneficiaries of a social assistance program establish their eligibility by demonstrating a genuine need for the assistance
meatpacking industry, 660, *660*
media, 253–88   print and digital forms of communication, including television, newspapers, radio, and the internet, intended to convey information to large audiences
   advertising revenue, *264*
   defined, 257
   and democracy, 288
   distrust of, 276–77
   influence of, 277–82
   Iowa caucus coverage, 387, 388
   news coverage, 283–85
   ownership of mass media, 260
   print, 263–65

and profit motive, 259–60
and public knowledge, 265
and public opinion, 232, 234, 247–48
regulation of, 285–87
traditional, 263–66

media monopoly, 260 the ownership and control of the media by a few large corporations

Medicaid a federally and state-financed, state-operated program providing medical services to low-income people
and Affordable Care Act, 9, 99, 698
beneficiaries of, *701*
costs of, 694–95
defined, 680
expansion of, 108
expansion under ACA, 695, 696
federal grants to states for, 695
government spending on, 686–87
as grant-in-aid, 90, 91
and health care reform, 106, 686
as in-kind benefit, 680
for the middle class, 702
for the poor, 703
for poor women, 705
and public welfare, 563
as social policy, 674–76
spending on, 683–87, *685*
state implementation of, 92–93, 420–21
state variation in eligibility, 682
state variations in, 682
and undocumented immigrants, 98
as unfunded mandate, 99

medical care. *See* health care
medical marijuana, 76–78, 108

Medicare, *700* a form of national health insurance for the elderly and the disabled
costs of, 683, *685*, 687, 694–95
creation of, 680
defined, 680
and elderly, 700–702
government spending on, 686–87
HHS and, 563
as portion of GDP, 683
proposed changes to, 687, 697–98
public support for, 644
as social policy, 675–76
taxes for, 653, 679

membership association, 440 an organized group in which members play a substantial role, sitting on committees and engaging in group projects

Mendez v. Westminster, 186
Menendez, Robert, *233*

merit system, 556 a product of civil service reform, in which appointees to positions in public bureaucracies must objectively be deemed qualified for those positions

Merit Systems Protection Board (MSPB), 580
Merrill, Nick, *394*
Me Too movement, 217, *217*, 417

Mexican American Legal Defense and Education Fund (MALDEF), 187
Mexican American political movement, 184, 186
Mexican Americans, 16–17, *186*, 186–87
Mexican border, *186*, *187*
Mexico, 721
Michigan, 107, 246, 392
Michigan Department of Environmental Quality, 551
Michigan Department of Health and Human Services, 551
Microsoft, 273, 450, 661

micro-targeting, 344, 398–99 when political campaigns tailor messages to individuals in small homogenous groups based on their group interests to support a candidate or policy issue

middle class, social policy for, 702
Middle East, 742–43; *see also individual countries*
Middle East wars, 525

midterm elections, 302, *302*, 381 congressional elections that do not coincide with a presidential election; also called *off-year elections*; *see also specific midterm elections, e.g.:* election of 2010

military
base closures, 575, *575*
contracting for, 662–63, *663*
demographics of U.S. forces, *739*
differing views of, 224–25
homosexuals in, 192
privatization of operations, 577–79
sexual harassment in, 183–84
women in, 182–83, *183*
Military Commissions Act of 2006, 609
military force, foreign policy and, 738–40
military power (of president), 516–17, 525–26
military spending, 639, 662–63, *720*, 738
militias, 136
Mill, John Stuart, 8, *8*
Miller v. Johnson, 479
minimum wage, *26*, 236, 640, 645, *645*, 646, *647*, 668, 703
Minnesota, 98, 100, 323, 668
minorities, 704–6; *see also specific minority groups*

minority leader, 482 the elected leader of the minority party in the House or Senate

minority party, 351 the party that holds the minority of legislative seats in either the House or the Senate

minority rights, 28
Miranda, Ernesto, 142–43

Miranda rule, 143 the requirement, articulated by the Supreme Court in *Miranda v. Arizona*, that persons under arrest must be informed prior to police interrogation of their rights to remain silent and to have the benefit of legal counsel

Mississippi, 98, 163, 176, 323–24
Missouri, 107, 166, 170, 392
Missouri Compromise, 162

mixed regime, 58
Mnuchin, Steven, 572, *572*
mobile devices, as news source, 268

mobilization the process by which large numbers of people are organized for a political activity
data analysis for, 321
defined, 319
in early days of American elections, 371–72
in formation of parties, 339
for political participation, 319–21
of public opinion by interest groups, 454–55
of voters, 343–44
modern era, federalism and, 89–99
Moe, Terry, 542
momentum, 282, 387
monetary agencies, 571–73

monetary policies, 649–52 efforts to regulate the economy through the manipulation of the supply of money and credit; America's most powerful institution in this area of monetary policy is the Federal Reserve Board

monetary structure, international, 735–36
money, politics and, 29, *395*, 400–405, 422; *see also* fund-raising
"money bills," 489

monopoly, 659 a single firm in a market that controls all the goods and services of that market; absence of competition

Monroe, James, 718
Monroe Doctrine, 718
Montana, 479
Montesquieu, Baron de la Brède et du, 58
Montgomery bus boycott, 169–70, *170*
Montreal Protocol, 745
Moonves, Les, 260
Moore, Roy, 258

mootness, 610 a criterion used by courts to screen cases that no longer require resolution

Moral Majority, 318
Morrill Act of 1862, 689–90
Morse v. Frederick, 130
mortgage lending crisis, 651, 699
Mott, Lucretia, 162
MoveOn.org, 215, *233*, 270, 439, 440, *440*, 443–45, 444, *444*
MSNBC, 265, 276, *278*
MSPB (Merit Systems Protection Board), 580
Mueller, Robert, 284, 351
multi-party systems, *341*
Mulvaney, Mick, 661
Murdoch, Rupert, *262*, 278
Muslims, 18
Muslim travel ban, 526, 528, 538
Myers v. United States, 522

N

NAACP. *See* National Association for the Advancement of Colored People
NAACP Legal Defense and Educational Fund, 166

Nader, Ralph, 368–69, *369*, 641
Nashaw, Jerry L., 525
National Aeronautics and Space Administration (NASA), 561, *561*
National American Woman Suffrage Association (NAWSA), 165–66
National Association for the Advancement of Colored People (NAACP), 146, 165, 453, 614
National Association of Evangelicals, *348*
National Association of Manufacturers, 646
national bank, 87–88
national committees, 346

national convention, 345–46, *346*, 388–89
convened by the Republican National Committee or the Democratic National Committee to nominate official candidates for president and vice president in the upcoming election, establish party rules, and adopt the party's platform

national debt, 658
National Defense Education Act of 1958 (NDEA), 690, 693
National Emergencies Act of 1976, 528
National Endowment for the Arts (NEA), 499
National Environmental Policy Act of 1969 (NEPA), 622, 663
national government. *See* federal government
National Industrial Recovery Act of 1933, 525
National Institutes of Health (NIH), 553, 563, *563*, 636, *636*, 694
National Labor Relations Act of 1935, 640
National Labor Relations Board (NLRB), 609, 640
National Opinion Research Center, 240
National Organization for Women (NOW), 180–81
National Origins quota system, 16
National Park Service, 563
National Performance Review (NPR), 574, *574*, 575
National Public Radio (NPR), 259, 265, 266, 273, *278*
National Restaurant Association, 646
National Review, 264
National Rifle Association (NRA), 209, 294–95, 429, 432, 456, 459
National Science Foundation, 635–36
national security
bureaucracy for providing, *567*, 565–70
and green technologies, 667
technological innovation for, 640
national security advisor (NSA), 725
National Security Agency (NSA), 24, 134, 141, 145, 283, 526, 570
cyberattacks of 2016 campaign, 211
electronic surveillance by, 151, *729*
national security alliances, 737
National Security Archive, 569–70

National Security Council (NSC), 531, 725 a presidential foreign policy advisory council composed of the president, the vice president, the secretary of state, the secretary of defense, and other officials invited by the president

national security directives, 540

national standards
regulation and, 93–99
and unfunded mandates, 99
National Traffic and Motor Vehicle Safety Act of 1966, 641
national unity
Constitutional provisions for, 57–58
and obligations among states, 82, 83
National Welfare Rights Organization, 703–4
National Woman's Party, 166
National Women's Political Caucus, 317

nation-states, 719 political entities consisting of a people with some common cultural experience (nation) who also share a common political authority (state), recognized by other sovereignties (nation-states)

Native Americans, 13, *14*, 16, 115
and civil rights, 191
in Congress, 419
NATO. *See* North Atlantic Treaty Organization
natural disaster response, *528*, 528–29
NAWSA (National American Woman Suffrage Association), 165–66
NBC News, 265, *278*
NDEA (National Defense Education Act of 1958), 690, 693
NEA (National Endowment for the Arts), 499
Near v. Minnesota, 133

necessary and proper clause, 79, 87–88
Article I, Section 8 of the Constitution, which provides Congress with the authority to make all laws "necessary and proper" to carry out its expressed powers

negative campaign advertising, 397, *397*
Negotiated Rulemaking Act of 1990, 450–51
NEPA (National Environmental Policy Act of 1969), 622, 663
Netanyahu, Benjamin, *733*
Netherlands, 341
net neutrality, 254–56
Nevada, 392, 478
Never Again MSD, 205
New Deal, 84, 89, *89*, 363, 369–70
and African American voters, 353–54
and Democratic Party, 224–25
and employment, 637
and government expansion, 87, 89
and income-based voting, 356
and Jewish voters, 355–56
and judicial review of federal agency actions, 608
and middle class, 20
and party affiliation, 356
and Supreme Court, 594, 619, 622
Newdow, Michael A., 124–25

New Federalism, *96* attempts by presidents Nixon and Reagan to return power to the states through block grants

New Hampshire primaries, 322, 387, 388
New Jersey, 479

New Jersey Plan, 50 a framework for the Constitution, introduced by William Paterson, that called for equal state

representation in the national legislature regardless of population

Newman, Brian, 236
new media, 372
New Politics movement, 447
news; *see also* media
in broadcast media, 265–66
"fake," 274, 275, *275*
followers by age, income, and education, 268
online, 273–76, 306
in print media, 263–65
types of coverage, 283–85

news aggregator, 267 an application or feed that collects web content such as news headlines, blogs, podcasts, online videos, and more in one location for easy viewing

News Corporation, *262*, 278
newspapers, 263–65, 272–73
New York, 162
New York City
Eric Garner incident, 218
stop and frisk, 141
New York Convention, 741
New York Times, 180–81
circulation, 263
digital subscriptions to, 263
online presence of, 261
Pentagon Papers, 133, 234, 283, 284
revenue for, 263
Vietnam coverage, 283, 284
Watergate coverage, 284
New York Times v. Sullivan, 134
New York Times v. United States, 133; *see also* Pentagon Papers
New Zealand, 737
Next Gen, 295, 311
niche journalism, 288
NIH. *See* National Institutes of Health
9/11 attacks. *See* September 11, 2001 attacks
Nineteenth Amendment, 28, 166, *302*
Nixon, Richard, and administration, *399*, 574
and block grants, 96
and budget process, 537
bureaucratic reform, 574
and election of 1968, 363
electronic surveillance by, 730
and employment discrimination, 175
on Keynesians, 642
and media coverage, 277
pardon of, 517
in presidential debates, 398, *399*
regulatory review by, 537
resignation of, 532, 542
and school segregation, 174
"southern strategy" of, 364, *364*
vice president of, 532
Watergate, 264, 284, 456, 484, 519, *519*, 602
NLRB (National Labor Relations Board), 609, 640
No Child Left Behind Act of 2001, 102, 690, 692
"no excuse" absentee voting, 327
nominating conventions. *See* national convention

nomination, 342, 382, 386–89 the process by which political parties select their candidates for election to public office

noncontributory programs, 680–81, 687–89 social programs that provide assistance to people on the basis of demonstrated need rather than any contribution they have made

nonenforcement of laws, 540–41
nonprofit journalism, 259, 272–73

non-state actors, 717 groups other than nation-states that attempt to play a role in the international system; terrorist groups are one type of non-state actor

nonworking poor, social policy for, 703–4, *704*
North
    Republican Party in, 362
    slavery in, 162
    and Three-Fifths Compromise, 52–53
Northam, Ralph, 294
North Atlantic Treaty Organization (NATO), 716, 737–38, 742–43
North Carolina, 107, 181
North Dakota, voter registration in, 323
North Korea, 518, *518*, 719–20, 724–26, 743–44
Northwest Ordinance of 1787, 689
NOW. *See* National Organization for Women
NPR (National Performance Review), 574, *574*, 575
NPR (National Public Radio), 259, *278*
NRA. *See* National Rifle Association
NSA. *See* National Security Agency
NSC. *See* National Security Council
"nuclear option," 492
nuclear proliferation, 743–44
nullification, 94–95

O

OAS (Organization of American States), 737
oaths of office, 57–58
Obama, Barack, and administration, 574
    and 2009 economic stimulus package, 648–49
    administrative directives of, 537–38
    Affordable Care Act, 99
    and African American voters, 314
    approval rating of, 536
    background checks for gun owners, 137–38
    "big data" use in election campaigns, 245
    "birther" controversy, *274*
    branding, 340
    bureaucratic reform, 573, 574
    campaign funding of, 405
    campaign strategies, 396
    charter schools supported by, 692
    on *Citizens United*, 129
    classified information leak cases, 134
    climate change focus of, 666–67
    and congressional Democrats, 534
    congressional foreign relations committees, 730, 731
    continuation of George W. Bush's policies, 215
    debating skill of, 398

Deferred Action for Childhood Arrivals program, 105, 187–88
diplomatic power, 517, 734
"Don't Ask, Don't Tell" repeal, 192
on earmarks, 480–81
economic development, *572*
economic policies of, 648, 657–58
and economic recession of 2008, 637
education policies, 692, *692*
election campaign of 2008, 281, 314, 344, 364, 388, 399, 401
election campaign of 2012, 243, *315*, 401, 459
on energy and climate change, 666–67
establishment of Consumer Financial Protection Bureau, *639*
Every Student Succeeds, 104
executive orders of, 538
executive privilege, 519
farewell address of, 2
on federal contractors, 579
and federal deficit, 652–53
and federal regulation of state laws, 94
and financial crisis of 2008, 648
foreign policy of, 720, 724, 726, 742
on function of government, 558
on government programs, 644
on government secrecy, 570
and greenhouse gas emissions, 554
and Guantánamo Bay prison camp, 746
health care, 534, 541, 695–98
holds on nominees of, 493
immigration law, 105–7
internet used by, 535, 536
and Israel, 733
issues focus in campaigns of, 407
judicial appointments, 602
and Latino voters, *315*, 353–54
and LBGT rights, 181
liberalism under, 213
Lily Ledbetter Fair Pay Act, 182, *182*, 184
and limits of presidential power, 537
managerial presidency of, 581
on medical marijuana legalization, 77
and military powers, 526
minimum wage under, 646
and net neutrality, 254
net neutrality and, 254
and No Child Left Behind Act, 692
and nonenforcement of laws, 541
NSA investigation, 570
and political polarization in Congress, 368
presidential initiatives, 521
pro-choice voter support for, 459
on prosecution of marijuana use, 104
public opinion shaping by, 232
public relations by, 535
raid on bin Laden's compound, 724, *724*
recess appointments, 609
Secure Communities program, 105–7, 187
signing statements of, 540
Social and Behavioral Sciences, 574
social media use by, 232, 233, 312
State Department, 725
and states' rights, 106
surveys during 2012 election, 241

tax brackets under, 655
tax cuts, 281–82
and tax cuts, 230, 656
and Tea Party movement, 368
Toxic Substances Control Act reform, 512, *513*
use of online fundraising, 304
veto power used by, 520–21
voter mobilization in 2008 and 2012 elections, 320
and voter turnout in 2008, 301
White House Communications Office, 535
Obamacare, 11, 282, 695–98; *see also* Affordable Care Act of 2010
Obergefell, Jim, 40–42
Obergefell v. Hodges, 41–42, 83, 193, 618
obscenity, 135–36
Occupational Safety and Health Administration (OSHA), 661
Occupy movement, 10, 297, 455
OCR (Department of Education's Office of Civil Rights), 183
OECD (Organization for Economic Cooperation and Development), *654*, 691
Office of Civil Rights (OCR), 183
Office of Energy Efficiency and Renewable Energy, 639
Office of Information and Regulatory Affairs (OIRA), 537
Office of Management and Budget (OMB), 531, 537, 579, 656, 661
Office of Personnel Management (OPM), 580
Office of Secretary of Defense (OSD), 568
Office of the U.S. Trade Representative (USTR), 728
Off the Sideline, 498
Off the Sidelines, 498
Ohio, 128
OIRA (Office of Information and Regulatory Affairs), 537
Oklahoma, 392
older Americans
    and political culture, 33
    political participation by, 311
    social policy for, 700–702

oligarchy, 7 a form of government in which a small group—landowners, military officers, or wealthy merchants—controls most of the governing decisions

OMB. *See* Office of Management and Budget
Omidyar, Pierre, 262
online advocacy groups, 440, 443–45, 455
online media. *See* internet
online news, 273–76, 306
online political participation, 303–10
online-processing model of political opinion formation, 235
online purchases, 105
Online surveys, 240–41

open primary, 382 a primary election in which the voter can wait until the day of the primary to choose which party to enroll in to select candidates for the general election

open rule, 491 a provision by the House Rules Committee that permits floor debate and the addition of new amendments to a bill

Operation Fast and Furious, 519

opinion the written explanation of the Supreme Court's decision in a particular case; *see also* public opinion
defined, 207
dissenting, 617–18
forming of, 216–25
and political knowledge, 228–32
stability of, 225–32, *227*
of the Supreme Court, 616–17

OPM (Office of Personnel Management), 580
opportunity, equality of, 25–28, 209–10, 689

oral argument, 616, *617* the stage in the Supreme Court procedure in which attorneys for both sides appear before the Court to present their positions and answer questions posed by justices

Oregon, 93, 105, 327, 576, 668
Oregon Music News, 114
Organization for Economic Cooperation and Development (OECD), *654*, 691
Organization of American States (OAS), 737
organized labor, 433, 646
"originalist" judges, 602

original jurisdiction, 596–97 the authority to initially consider a case; distinguished from appellate jurisdiction, which is the authority to hear appeals from a lower court's decision

OSHA (Occupational Safety and Health Administration), 661
outsourcing, *578*, 583, 720; *see also* privatization

oversight, 502–3, 581–83 the effort by Congress, through hearings, investigations, and other techniques, to exercise control over the activities of executive agencies

P

PAC. *See* political action committee; Super PACs
packing, 385, 607
Page, Benjamin, 235
Pahlavi, Reza, 743
Pai, Ajit, 254, 255
paid media time, 397
Pakistan, 736
Palko, Frank, 120, 142
Palko v. Connecticut, 120, 122, 142
Parents Involved in Community Schools v. Seattle School District No. 1, 175
Paris Agreement, 227, 733, 745
Parks, Rosa, 169, *170*
parliaments, 8
participation, political. *See* political participation

partisan gerrymandering, 385–86 occurs when politicians from one party intentionally manipulate the boundaries for drawing legislative election districts to disadvantage

their political opponents' chance of winning an election and advantage their own political party

partisan loyalty, 406
partisan media, 276
partisan politics, 339, 500–501, 668; *see also* party polarization

partisanship, 207, 337 identification with or support of a particular party or cause

and health care policies, 697–98
over economic policy, 668
in policymaking, 706–7
and social policy variations, 682

party activists, 352–53 partisans who contribute time, energy, and effort to support their party and its candidates

party affiliation, 221–22

party identification, 352–60, *353, 359, 406* an individual voter's psychological ties to one party or another

party leadership, in Congress, 482–83, 496–500
party-line voting, 366, 367

party machines, 320, 347, *347* strong party organizations in late nineteenth- and early twentieth-century American cities; these machines were led by often corrupt "bosses" who controlled party nominations and patronage

party organization, 344 the formal structure of a political party, including its leadership, election committees, active members, and paid staff

party platform a party document, written at a national convention, that contains party philosophy, principles, and policy positions

party polarization, 276–77, 339, *367, 367–68, 500–501, 501, 682* the division between the two major parties on most policy issues, with members of each party unified around their party's positions with little crossover

party systems, 360–61, *366*

party unity vote, 496, *497* a roll-call vote in the House or Senate in which at least percent of the members of one party take a particular position and are opposed by at least 50 percent of the members of the other party

Paterson, William, 50
Patient Protection and Affordable Care Act of 2010. *See* Affordable Care Act of 2010
Patrick, Amanda, 714
Patriot Act. *See* USA PATRIOT Act
"patrol mode," 280, 281

patronage, 347, 480 the resources available to higher officials, usually opportunities to make partisan appointments to offices and

to confer grants, licenses, or special favors to supporters

pattern-of-cases strategy, 614
Paul, Rand, 214, *492*
Pavan v. Smith, 605
Paxton, Ken, 83
pay, congressional, 68
payroll taxes, Social Security and, 685
PBS, 259
peacekeeping efforts, 722, 735
Pearl Harbor, 718
Pell grants, 693
Pelosi, Nancy, 472, 498, *500*
Pence, Mike, 531, *532*
Pennsylvania, 47, 148, 322, 386

penny press, 267 cheap, tabloid-style newspaper produced in the nineteenth century, when mass production of inexpensive newspapers first became possible due to the steam-powered printing press; a penny press newspaper cost one cent compared with other papers, which cost more than five cents

Pentagon Papers, 133, 234, 283, 284

permanent absentee ballots, 327 the option in some states to have a ballot sent automatically to your home for each election, rather than having to request an absentee ballot each time

permanent committees. *See* standing committee
Perot, Ross, 368, 405
Persian Gulf War, 525
personal freedom, 23
Personal Responsibility and Work Opportunity Reconciliation Act, 687
petition, right of, 132, 133
petitions, 536
Pew Research Center, 226, 272
Phillip, Celeste, *694*
phone banks, 400
photo IDs, 324
physician-assisted suicide, 93, 105, 149–50
PIRG (Public Interest Research Group), *447*

plaintiff, 593 the individual or organization that brings a complaint in court

Planned Parenthood of Southeastern Pennsylvania v. Casey, 148–49

platform, 345, 389 a party document, written at a national convention, that contains party philosophy, principles, and positions on issues

plea bargain, 595 a negotiated agreement in a criminal case in which a defendant agrees to plead guilty in return for the state's agreement to reduce the severity of the criminal charge or prison sentence the defendant is facing

Pledge of Allegiance, 124–25, 146
Plessy v. Ferguson, 26, 164

pluralism, 9, 431 the theory that all interests are and should be free to compete for influence in the government; the outcome of this competition is compromise and moderation plurality system, 382 a type of electoral system in which, to win a seat in the parliament or other representative body, a candidate need only receive the most votes in the election, not necessarily a majority of the votes cast

Plyler v. Doe, 18

pocket veto, 494, 520 a presidential veto that is automatically triggered if the president does not act on a given piece of legislation passed during the final 10 days of a legislative session

polarization. *See* party polarization
police brutality, 170

"police patrol" oversight, 581–82 regular or even preemptive congressional hearings on bureaucratic agency operations

police power, 82 power reserved to the state government to regulate the health, safety, and morals of its citizens

policy entrepreneur, 350 an individual who identifies a problem as a political issue and brings a policy proposal into the political agenda

policy feedback, 226
policymaking process, 706–7
policy preferences, 407

political action committee (PAC), 404, 432, 456–58, *457*, 498 a private group that raises and distributes funds for use in election campaigns; *see also* Super PACs

political culture, 2–39 broadly shared values, beliefs, and attitudes about how the government should function; American political culture emphasizes the values of liberty, equality, and democracy
   Americans' view of government, 29–33
   and changes in American people, 13–22
   citizenship, 10–13
   defined, 23
   and democracy, 28–29
   and equality, 25–28
   and ethnic diversity, 14–16, *15*
   future of, 33–34
   government, 5–10
   and immigration, 13–22
   and liberty, 24–25
   and race, *15*, 16
   thinking critically about, 22–29

political efficacy, 12 the ability to influence government and politics

political environment
   ballot measures, 322–23
   electoral competition, 321–22
   mobilization, 319–21
   and political participation, 319–23
   and public opinion, 224–25
   state electoral laws, 323–27, *325*

political equality, 25 the right to participate in politics equally, based on the principle of "one person, one vote"

political ideology, a cohesive set of beliefs that forms a general philosophy about the role of government
   conservatism, 213, *214*
   current American state of, 215, *215*
   defined, 207
   liberalism, 211, *213*
   libertarianism, 214
   and party identification, 356, *359*
   and public opinion, 211–15
   and Supreme Court decisions, 620–21

political knowledge, 10–13, 11–13, *12*
   possessing information about the formal institutions of government, political actors, and political issues
   costs to democracy, 230, 232
   defined, 10
   digital media's effect on, 230
   necessity of, 11–13
   and public opinion, 228–32
   shortcuts and cues, 229–30

political participation, 297–328, *300*; *see also* turnout; voting
   and access to government, 8–9
   by African Americans, 313–14
   age and, 311, *311*, 311–13
   by Asian Americans, 316
   and beliefs about political efficacy, 12–13
   citizenship and, 10–13
   democracy and, 28–29
   digital, 303–10
   forms of, 297–310
   gender and, 316–17
   influencing government through, 9–10
   by Latinos, 314–15
   online vs. offline, 304–7
   and political environment, 319–23
   political equality and, 25
   religious identity and, 318–19
   socioeconomic status and, 310–11
   and state electoral laws, 323–27, *325*
   through voting, 299–300, *311*; *see also* voting
   traditional, 297–302

political parties, 334–73, *341, 366* organized groups that attempt to influence the government by electing their members to important government offices; *see also specific parties*
   and campaign funding, 404–5
   congressional party unity, 496–98
   defined, 337
   in election of 2012, *370*
   and elections, 340–44
   electoral alignments and realignments, *366*
   factions within, 350–51
   formation of, 339
   function of, 337–38
   functions of, 339, 340
   in government, 348–52
   House steering committees of, 482
   influence of money on, 29
   influence of the wealthy on, *236*
   interest groups vs., 334, 438–39
   as organizations, 344–48
   party identification, 352–60

party polarization, 339, 367–68
party systems, 360–61
   and political socialization, 221–22
   and presidential powers, 534
   recent affiliation trends, 358–60, *359*
   as source of power for the presidency, 534
   third parties, 368–71
   two-party system, 339

political power, economic power and, 28

political socialization, 216–17 the induction of individuals into the political culture; learning the underlying beliefs and values on which the political system is based

political speech, 127–29
political values, public opinion and, 209–11
Politico, 264

politics, 9–10 conflict over the leadership, structure, and policies of governments
   defined, 5, 9
   of economic policy, 641
   media's influence on, 278, 280–82
   and monetary policy, 650
   and money, 400–405
   retail, 387

PolitiFact, 271, 275
polling, 236–37, 237–47, 398–400; *see also* public-opinion polls
poll taxes, 300
Pompeo, Mike, *440*, 567, *568*, 725, *734*
poor, the. *See* poverty
popular mobilization, expansion of presidential power through, 534

popular sovereignty, a principle of democracy in which political authority rests ultimately in the hands of the people

population demographics
   in the 21st century, 17–22
   changes in, 13–22
   and representation, 22
populism, 356
Populist Party, 362–63, 368

pork barrel (or pork), 480–82 appropriations made by legislative bodies for local projects that are often not needed but that are created so that local representatives can win re-election in their home districts

Porkulus Protest, 334–35
pornography, 135–36
positive discrimination, 198
Postal Service, U.S., 552
poverty, *704*, 704–6, *705*; *see also* socioeconomic status
   and African American voter turnout, 314
   civil rights of those in, 193, 195
   education policies concerning, 693
   "feminization of," 705
   and political influence, 328
   social policy for the nonworking poor, 703–4
   social policy for the working poor, 702–3
   and voter influence, 338

Powell, Jerome, *572*, 650, *651*
Powell, Lewis F., 197

power(s)   influence over a government's leadership, organization, or policies; *see also* separation of powers
   centralization of government's power, 84
   concurrent, 82
   of Congress, 543
   congressional, 55, 502–5, 649
   contracting, 662
   defined, 9
   economic, 28
   expressed, 56, 79
   of federal courts, 621–24
   with federalism, 85–88
   Federalist vs. Antifederalist views on, 64
   growth of national government's power, 87–88
   implied, 79
   judicial, 610
   limits of president's, 541–43
   nonenforcement of laws as, 540–41
   police, 82
   political, 28
   of the presidency, 514–29, 533–44, 608–9
   of the presidency in various countries, *524*
   reserved, 82

prayer, in public schools, 318–19

precedent, 594   prior case whose principles are used by judges as the basis for their decision in a present case

predatory lending, 699

preemption, 93, *93–99*, 106, 724   the principle that allows the national government to override state or local actions in certain policy areas; in foreign policy, the willingness to strike first in order to prevent an enemy attack; *see also* preventive war

presidency, 512–45; *see also* president(s)
   administrative strategies of, 536–42
   and budget process, 656
   and Cabinet, 530
   Constitutional powers of, 515–29
   Constitutional provision for, 56
   contemporary bases of power for, 533–44
   delegated powers of, 515, 523
   and democracy, 514
   demographics of U.S. presidents, *527*
   emergency powers, 528
   establishment of, 515
   Executive Office of the President, 530–31
   expressed powers of, 515–21
   first spouse, 532–33
   and foreign policy, 722–30
   going public as source of power for, 534–36
   implied powers of, 515, 522–23, 526
   influence of, 514
   inherent powers of, 515, 525–26, 528–29
   as institution, *529*, 529–33
   judicial power of, 522
   managerial, 581
   nonenforcement of laws as power, 540–41

party as source of power for, 534
   and party lines in Congress, 500
   and separation of powers, 58, *59*
   signing or vetoing bills, 494
   unitary executive theory, 522–23
   veto power of, 519–21, *520*
   vice presidency, 531–32
   White House staff, 530, 537
president(s)
   appointments by, 514, 518–19, 522
   as chief executive, 580
   demographics of, *527*
   economic responsibility of, 642
   expansion of powers by, 534
   as head of state, 515, 517–19, *518*
   impeachment of, 542
   lobbying of, 450
   regulatory review by, *513*, 523, 537–38
   removal of appointed officials by, 522
presidential elections, 386–92; *see also* specific election years, e.g.: election of 2016
   electoral college, 322, 389–90, 392
   party conventions, 388–89
   primaries and caucuses, 386–88
   steps in process, *391*
presidential findings, 540
presidential memoranda, 540
presidential primaries. *See* primary elections
presidential proclamations, 540
Presidential Succession Act of 1947, 532
President's Commission on Civil Rights, 166
press, freedom of, 133–36
press releases, 283

preventive war, 718   policy of striking first when a nation fears that a foreign foe is contemplating hostile action

primary elections, 32, 260, 281, 322, 342, 345, 367, *373*, 381–82, 386–88   elections held to select a party's candidate for the general election

priming, 226, 282   process of preparing the public to bring specific criteria to mind when evaluating a politician or issue

print media, 263–65; *see also* newspapers
Printz v. United States, 95
Priority Enforcement Program, 106

prior restraint, 133   an effort by a governmental agency to block the publication of material it deems libelous or harmful in some other way; censorship; in the United States, the courts forbid prior restraint except under the most extraordinary circumstances

PRISM surveillance program, 728
prison inmates, 147, 326
Prison Litigation Reform Act, 621
privacy, 68–69, 146–49

private bill, 481   a proposal in Congress to provide a specific person with some kind of relief, such as a special exemption from immigration quotas

private property, 23, 68, 82, 86, 143

privatization, *577*, 577–79, *578*   a formerly public service that is now provided by a private company but paid for by the government

privileges and immunities clause, 83   provision, from Article IV, Section 2 of the Constitution, that a state cannot discriminate against someone from another state or give its own residents special privileges

probability sampling, 237
procedural limits, 7
productivity, for economic growth, 636
professional association lobbies, 435
professional politicians, 488
Progressive movement, 347
Progressive Party, 368, 370

progressive taxation, 652   taxation that hits upper-income brackets more heavily

promotion of the public welfare, 563–65
property, private, 23, 68, 82, 86, 143
property rights, for women, 162

proportional representation, 340, 341, 345, 369, 370–71, 382–83   a multiple-member district system that allows each political party representation in proportion to its percentage of the total vote

Proposition 30 (California), 323
Proposition 187 (California), 187

prospective voting, 407   voting based on the imagined future performance of a candidate or political party

prosperity. *See* economic prosperity
PROTECT Act of 2003, 135

protest, 297–99, *298*, *418*, 454, 455   participation that involves assembling crowds to confront a government or other official organization
   health care, *226*
   Porkulus, 334–35
   against Trump, 297–98

Protestants, 14, 18, 221, 234, 356
Pruitt-Igoe public housing project, *699*
public accommodations, as civil right, 171–72
public campaign funding, 405
Public Facilities Privacy and Security Act (HB2), 107

public goods, 5, 634   goods or services that are provided by the government because they either are not supplied by the market or are not supplied in sufficient quantities

public health agencies, 694–98

public interest groups, 435, 447, *447*   groups that claim they serve the general good rather than only their own particular interests

Public Interest Research Group (PIRG), *447*
public investment, 635

public opinion, 204–49   citizens' attitudes about political issues, leaders, institutions, and events

and "big data," 245–47
on climate change, 664–65
definition of term, 207
and democracy, 247–48
disapproval of Congress, 500–502
elements of, 207–15
on equality, *27*
errors in polling, 242–45
formation of, 216–25
government policy and, 235–37
government responsiveness to, 235–36
interest groups and, 233–34
measuring, 237–47; *see also* surveys, public
    opinion
media's influence on, 234
and political ideology, 211–15
and political knowledge, 228–32
political leaders' influence on, 232–33
and political socialization, 216–17
and political values, 209–11
social groups and, 218–25
of social policies, 707–8
stability of, 225–32, *226*
survey construction, 237–47; *see also* surveys,
    public opinion
trust in government, 6, 31, 32, 33–34
view of government, 29–33

public-opinion polls, 237, 237–47 scientific
instruments for measuring public opinion
representative samples, 237–38
sources of error in, 242–45
survey design, 240

public policy, 633 a law, rule, statute, or
edict that expresses the government's goals
and provides for rewards and punishments
to promote those goals' attainment; *see also
specific types of policy, e.g.:* economic policy
and public opinion, 235–37
voters' policy preferences, 407

public relations, 534–35
public-sector groups, 435, 437
public spending, *103*, 643–44
public welfare, promotion of, 563–65

purposive benefits, 442 selective benefits
of group membership that emphasize the
purpose and accomplishments of the group

push poll, 245 a polling technique in which
the questions are designed to shape the
respondent's opinion

Putin, Vladimir, 210, 284, 720, 724, *726*, 727,
    742
Putnam, Robert, 307

Q
questions, public opinion survey, 240

R
race
    and death penalty, 145
    and electoral districts, 479–80
    and immigration, 16

and internet access, 309
and party affiliation, 353–54, *359*
and perception of fair treatment, *219*
and political culture, 16
and political participation, *311*
and political socialization, 218–19
public opinion on, 218–19, 242–43
race relations, *208*
Race to the Top, 692–93
racial categories/categorization, 18, 618–19; *see
    also* affirmative action
racial discrimination, 161–79, 678; *see also*
    discrimination; segregation
racial equality, 197–98
racial profiling, 141, 170, 188–89
racial segregation. *See* segregation
racism, public opinion on, 218–19
radio, 265–66
railroad subsidies, 638, *638*
Ramos, Jorge, *269*
Randolph, Edmund, 50, 53

random digit dialing, 237–38 a polling
    method in which respondents are selected
    at random from a list of 10-digit telephone
    numbers, with every effort made to avoid bias
    in the construction of the sample

random sample public-opinion polling, 399
ranked choice voting (RCV), 371, 392
Rankin, Jeanette, *470*
Ratification of U.S. Constitution, 58,
    60–65, *63*
rational basis test, 180
R.A.V. v. City of St. Paul, 130
RCV (ranked choice voting), 371, 392
Reagan, Ronald, and administration, *348*
    attempts to shrink bureaucracy`, 575
    on big government, 558
    block grants of, 96
    bureaucracy under, 558
    as California governor, 224
    children's political affiliations, 217
    on Department of Education, 564–65
    deregulation by, 661
    education policies, 690
    judicial appointments of, 620
    and religious conservatives, 318
    as Republican Party leader, 364
    and strikes, 640
    Supreme Court nominees of, 602
    and taxation, 643
    tax brackets under, 655
RealClear Politics, 267

recall, 393 a procedure to allow voters to
    remove state officials from office before their
    terms expire by circulating petitions to call
    a vote

recess appointments, 542, 609
recession of 2008. *See* financial crisis and
    recession of 2008
Recovery Act of 2009. *See* American Recovery
    and Reinvestment Act of 2009
Red Cloud, *14*
Reddit, 267, *270*

redistribution, 653 a policy whose objective is
to tax or spend in such a way as to reduce the
disparities of wealth between the lowest and
the highest income brackets

redistributive programs, 100 economic policies
designed to transfer income through taxing and
spending, with the goal of benefiting the poor

redistricting, 367, 384–86, 477–80 the
process of redrawing election districts and
redistributing legislative representatives; this
happens every 10 years, to reflect shifts in
population or in response to legal challenges
in existing districts

Redlawsk, David, 229

redlining, 178 a practice in which banks refuse
to make loans to people living in certain
geographic locations

Redskins (NFL), 115
red states, 353–54
Reed, Stanley, 617

referendum the practice of referring a proposed
law passed by a legislature to the vote of the
electorate for approval or rejection; *see also*
ballot initiative

Reform Party, 369
Regents of the University of California v. Bakke,
    195–97
region, party affiliation and, 357, *359*

regressive taxation, 652 taxation that hits
lower-income brackets more heavily

regular concurrences (Supreme Court), 617

regulated federalism, 96, 100 a form of
federalism in which Congress imposes
legislation on states and localities, requiring
them to meet national standards

regulation, 659–61
    costs of, 99
    and economic policy, 644–46
    environmental, 663–67
    by the Fed, 650–51
    of lobbying, 452–53
    of media, 285–87
    in the name of public protection, 24–25
    national policies for, 633–34
    opposition to, 646

regulatory agency, 563 department, bureau, or
independent agency whose primary mission
is to impose limits, restrictions, or other
obligations on the conduct of individuals or
companies in the private sector

regulatory review, by presidents, *513*, 514, 523,
    537–38
Rehabilitation Act of 1973, 99, 191
Reid, Harry, 492
religion/religious affiliation; *see also specific
    religious groups*
    of American population, 18
    of congresspersons, 471, *473*

freedom of. *See* freedom of religion
of immigrants, 14–16
and Latino vote, 314–15
and party affiliation, 355–56
and political opinion, 220–21
and political participation, 318–19
religious symbols, 125–26
removal power, of presidents, 522
renewable energy, 639
Reno v. ACLU, 135
representation
by Congress, *481*
descriptive, 315
Federalist vs. Antifederalist views on, 62
of minorities, 479
sociological vs. agency, 471–75, 474–75

representative democracy (republic), 9 a
system of government in which the populace
selects representatives, who play a significant
role in governmental decision-making

representative samples, 237–38
Republican National Committee (RNC), 346
Republican National Convention (1984), 132
Republican Party; *see also* political parties
and 2009 economic stimulus package,
648–49
and ACA, 282, 696, 697–98
Asian Americans' support for, 316
black citizens in, 163
characteristics of, 353
climate change views, 664
conference committees, 483–84
conflict with Democratic Party, 348
congressional party unity, 496–98, *497*
data mining, 246
demographics of, 339, 353–58
distrust in government among members of, 32
and economic policy, 641
election of 2016, 339
electoral realignments, 365
evangelical Christians, 319
factions within, 351
and Federal Reserve, 652
fund-raising activities of, 346
gender gap, 316
gerrymandering, 175–76, 478
health care reform, 696, 697–98
ideology, 356
K Street Project, 496
and laissez-faire economics, 642–43
Latino voters and, 314–15
and leadership PACs, 498
in Massachusetts, 365
members' characteristics, 221–22
and minimum wage, 645
origins of, 361–63
party-building by, 352
party identification, 352–53
and polarization, 276–77, 366, 367–68
and preemption power, 93
primary debates in 2016, 398
and primary delegates, 388
and proportional representation voting, 345,
388
recruitment of candidates by, 476

and redistricting, 479–80
and regulation, 644, 646
religious affiliations of members, 221
responsiveness of, 338
and slavery issue, 362
and social programs, 31
tax and social spending views of, 356, 643–44
and upper-income voters, 356
and voter ID laws, 324
voter mobilization, 320
and white southerners, 224–25
and young Americans, *358*

reserved powers, 82 powers, derived from the
Tenth Amendment to the Constitution, that
are not specifically delegated to the national
government or denied to the states

restraint, judicial, 619–21

retail politics, 387 a style of campaigning
where candidates connect to voters at
intimate gatherings and local events

retrospective voting, 407 voting based on the
past performance of a candidate or political
party

revenue, advertising, *264*

revenue agency, 572 an agency responsible
for collecting taxes. Examples include the
Internal Revenue Service for income taxes;
the U.S. Customs Service for tariffs and other
taxes on imported goods; and the Bureau of
Alcohol, Tobacco, Firearms and Explosives
for collection of taxes on the sale of those
particular products

Revolutionary War, 47
Reza Shah Pahlavi, 743
Rhode Island, 47–48, 53
Rice, Condoleezza, 725
Richardson, Susan, 714
right(s); *see also* civil rights
of assembly, 132
to bear arms, 119, 136–38
to counsel, 144
of the criminally accused, 138–46
to die, 150
of petition, 132, 134
to privacy, 146–49
of rebuttal, 286
to vote. *See* voting rights

right of rebuttal a Federal Communications
Commission regulation giving individuals the
right to have the opportunity to respond to
personal attacks made on a radio or television
broadcast

"right to die" law, 105; *see also* physician-assisted
suicide
right-to-life movement, 233

right to privacy, 146–51, 192–93 the right to
be left alone, which has been interpreted by
the Supreme Court to entail individual access
to birth control and abortions

"Right to work" provisions, 646
Rio Treaty, 737
ripeness, 610–11
RNC. *See* Republican National Committee
Roberts, John, 130, 601, 618, 619, 697
Roberts, Owen, 619
Roberts, Pat, 492
Robertson, Pat, 318
Rock the Vote, 311
Roe v. Wade, 148–49, 233, 453–54, 610, 620
Rogers Act of 1924, 732
rogue states, 719–20
Rolf, Meredith, 303

roll-call vote, 496 a vote in which each
legislator's yes or no vote is recorded as
the clerk calls the names of the members
alphabetically

Roman Catholics. *See* Catholics
Romer v. Evans, 192
Romney, Mitt, 243
Roosevelt, Eleanor, 533
Roosevelt, Franklin Delano, 725
and African American voters, 353–54
economic initiatives, 641
election of 1932, 363, 365
election of 1936, 242–43
executive orders of, 538
"fireside chats," 232, 284
and first spouse's role, 533
and internment camps, 190
and New Deal, 89, 363, 369–70
and partisan loyalty, 406
public appeals of, 534–35, *535*
as strong president, 534
and Supreme Court, 608, 619, 622
war powers of, 525
and World War II, 718
Roosevelt, Theodore, 284, 534
Rothstein, Barbara, 622
Rubio, Marco, 28, 489, *732*, 733
rules
issued by government agencies, 554–55
of lawmaking, 489–94

runoff election, 382 a "second-round" election
in which voters choose between the top two
candidates from the first round

rural areas, American population in, 20
Russia, 210–11, 284, 308–9, 718, 719–20,
724–26, 737, 741–42
Rutledge, John, 64
Ryan, Paul, 213, *214*, 481, *500*, 506, 687

S
"safe" districts, 367
Safe Drinking Water Act of 1974, 552, 663–64
sales taxes, 105

same-day registration (SDR), 295, 327 the
option in some states to register on the day of
the election, at the polling place, rather than
in advance of the election

same-sex marriage; *see also* Defense of Marriage
Act of 1996

simple random sample (or probability sample), 237–39 a method used by pollsters to select a representative sample in which every individual in the population has an equal probability of being selected as a respondent

Simpson, Alan, 428
Sinclair, Betsy, 216–17
Sinclair, Upton, 640, 660
Sixteenth Amendment, 652
Sixth Amendment, 144
Skimm, The (newsletter), *230*
slacktivism, 307

slander, 134 an oral statement made in "reckless disregard of the truth" that is considered damaging to the victim because it is "malicious, scandalous, and defamatory"

Slants, The, 114–16
slavery, 161, 162
    and abolitionist movement, 161–62
    Three-Fifths Compromise, 52–53
    at time of Founding, 13
    and value of liberty, 23
Small Business Administration (SBA), 573, 638
smartphones, 268, 271
Smith, Adam, 642–43
Smith v. Allwright, 616–17
smoking bans, 98, 235
SNAP. *See* Supplemental Nutrition Assistance Program
Snopes.org, 275
Snowden, Edward, 24, *133*, 134, 283, *283*, 570, 579, 728
Snyder, Rick, 551
Snyder v. Phelps, 132–33
Social and Behavioral Sciences of 2015, 574

social desirability effect, 242 the effect that results when respondents in a survey report what they expect the interviewer wishes to hear rather than what they believe

social equality, 25
social groups, public opinion and, 218–25
    economic class, 222–24
    ethnicity, 219–20
    gender, 220, *222*
    party affiliation, 221–22
    political environment, 224–25
    race, 218–19
    religion, 220–21
    self-interest, 222–24

socialist, 214 someone who generally believes in social ownership, strong government, free markets, and reducing economic inequality

socialization, political, 211–12, 216–17

social media, 267–71 web- and mobile-based technologies that are used to turn communication into interactive dialogue among organizations, communities, and individuals; social media technologies take on many different forms including text, blogs, podcasts, photographs, streaming video, Facebook, and Twitter

as clicktivism, 304
defined, 268
and fake news, 228–29
and interest groups, 443
for measuring public opinion, 245–47
Obama's use of, 232–33, 312, 535
partisan, 276, 307–8
and political participation, 303–4, 306
politicians' use of, 303–4
and presidential campaigns, 397–98
and public interest groups, 447
public opinion shaping by, 217
and Supreme Court same-sex marriage decision, 307, *307*
Trump's use of, *226*, 233, 535, 536
social networks, 216–17, 319–21
social policy
    beneficiaries of programs, *701*
    contributory welfare programs, 679–80
    education policies, 689–94
    for the elderly, 700–702
    and equality, 708
    and equality of opportunity, 689–700
    health policies, 694–98
    history of social welfare system, 677–79
    housing policies, 698–700
    for the middle and upper class, 702
    for minorities, women, and children, 704–6
    noncontributory welfare programs, 680–81
    for the nonworking poor, 703–4
    paying for the welfare state, 683–87
    for the working poor, 702–3

Social Security, 31, 40, 643, 680, 683–87, 685, 702 a contributory welfare program into which working Americans contribute a percentage of their wages and from which they receive cash benefits after retirement or if they become disabled

Social Security Act of 1935, 679, 705
Social Security Administration, 530, 576
Social Security Commission, 685–86
Social Security Disability Insurance (SSDI), 679, 686
Social Security taxes, 653
Social Security Trust Fund, 685
social welfare. *See* social policy; welfare programs

socioeconomic status, 310 status in society based on level of education, income, and occupational prestige; *see also* poverty
    and interest group membership, *438*, 438–39, 447, 449
    and party affiliation, 356, *359*
    and political culture, 20
    and political participation, 310–11, *312*
    and voter influence, 338, *338*

sociological representation, 471–75, *474* a type of representation in which representatives have the same racial, gender, ethnic, religious, or educational backgrounds as their constituents; it is based on the principle that if two individuals are similar in background, character, interests, and

perspectives, then one can correctly represent the other's views

soft money, 346, 404 money contributed directly to political parties and other organizations for political activities, such as voter mobilization drives, that is not regulated by federal campaign spending laws

soft power, 721, 740
sole executive agreements, 518

solicitor general, 612 the top government lawyer in all cases before the Supreme Court where the government is a party

solidary benefits, 442 selective benefits of group membership that emphasize friendship, networking, and consciousness-raising

Solove, Daniel, 151
Sotomayor, Sonia, 602, 606
sound bites, 265
South
    black voter registration, 175–77, *176*
    black voting rights in, 299–300, 313–14
    Democratic Party in, 362
    post–Civil War, 362
    school desegregation in, 167–70
    slavery in, 162
    and Three-Fifths Compromise, 52–53
South Carolina, 167, 188, 478
Southeast Asia Treaty Organization (SEATO), 737
Southern Christian Leadership Conference (SCLC), 455
Southern Manifesto, 95
Soviet Union, 717–19, 737

Speaker of the House, 482, 498, 532 the chief presiding officer of the House of Representatives; the Speaker is the most important party and House leader and can influence the legislative agenda, the fate of individual pieces of legislation, and members' positions within the House

special concurrences (Supreme Court), 617
speech, freedom of. *See* freedom of speech
SpeechNow v. FEC, 401–2

"speech plus," 134 speech accompanied by conduct such as sit-ins, picketing, and demonstrations; protection of this form of speech under the First Amendment is conditional, and restrictions imposed by state or local authorities are acceptable if properly balanced by considerations of public order

speed limit, national, 101–2
spending, federal, 655–58
Spicer, Sean, 495
Spirit of the Laws, The (Montesquieu), 58
split-ticket voting, 383
spoiler effect, 340
spoils system, 556
SSI (Supplemental Security Income) program, 680

staff agencies, 487 legislative support agencies responsible for policy analysis

Stafford Act of 1988, 528

staff organization, 441 a type of membership group in which a professional staff conducts most of the group's activities

staff system (Congress), 487, *487*
Stamp Act, 44

standing, 610 the right of an individual or organization to initiate a court case, on the basis of having a substantial stake in the outcome

standing committee, 483–84, *485* a permanent committee with the power to propose and write legislation that covers a particular subject, such as finance or agriculture

Stanford University, 275
Stanton, Elizabeth Cady, 162, 300

stare decisis, 594 literally, "let the decision stand"; the doctrine that a previous decision by a court applies as a precedent in similar cases until that decision is overruled

State Children's Health Insurance Program (SCHIP), 576, 695, 696
state courts, 594–95, *595*
State Department, 566, 567, *568*, 725–27
state governments; *see also* federalism
    control on policy areas, 86
    and cooperative federalism, 91–93
    and dual federalism, 85–86
    effect on daily life at state universities, *80*
    election administration by, 381–82
    and gridlock of national government, 105
    legislative races, 406
    powers of, 57–58, 79, 82
    preemption of local policy, 107
    spending cuts by, 576
state insurance exchanges, 696
state legislatures, redistricting and, 384–86
State of the Union address, 519, *521*
states
    ballot access in, 371
    ballot measures in, 322–23
    categorical grants to, 638–39
    changing role of, 94–95
    children's benefits from, 576
    comity among, 57–58
    electoral laws of, 323–27, *325*
    fiscal constraints of, 98–99
    judicial review of actions by, 605–7
    obligations among, 82
    party organizations in, 347–48
    role as defined in Articles of Confederation, 46
    third parties in, 369
    voter identification requirements, 324, 326
    voter registration requirements, 324
    voting and registration reforms, 327

states' rights, 94–95 the principle that the states should oppose the increasing authority of the national government; this principle was most popular in the period before the Civil War

statutes, 594
Stein, Jill, 215
Stevens, John Paul, 135–36
Stewart, Potter, 135
Steyer, Tom, 215, 295
stimulus package (2009). *See* American Recovery and Reinvestment Act of 2009
Stone, Harlan F., 95, 616
Stonewall riots (1969), 192
stop and frisk, 141, *141*

straight-ticket voting, 383 selecting candidates from the same political party for all offices on the ballot

strategic voting, 340, 369
streaming video, 267, 273

strict scrutiny, 127, 167–68, 180 a test used by the Supreme Court in racial discrimination cases and other cases involving civil liberties and civil rights that places the burden of proof on the government rather than on the challengers to show that the law in question is constitutional

strikes, 639
structural remedies (judicial), 623
student loans, 209
student loans, government relief for, *709*
student speech, 130–31

subsidies, 638, *638*, 661–62, *662* government grants of cash or other valuable commodities, such as land, to an individual or an organization; used to promote activities desired by the government, reward political support, or buy off political opposition

substantive limits, 7

suffrage, 165–66, 299 the right to vote; also called *franchise*; *see also* voting rights

Sugar Act of 1764, 44
Sundquist, James, 91
"Supercommittee," 657
superdelegates, 389
Super PACs, 338, 346, 397, 402, 404–5, 458, 496
"Super Tuesday," 322

Supplemental Nutrition Assistance Program (SNAP), 680, *681*, *685*, 688, 703, 704 the largest antipoverty program, which provides recipients with a debit card for food at most grocery stores; formerly known as food stamps

Supplemental Security Income (SSI) program, 680

supply-side economics, 643 an economic theory that posits that reducing the marginal rate of taxation will create a productive economy by promoting levels of work and investment that would otherwise be discouraged by higher taxes

supremacy clause, 57, 64, 605 Article VI of the Constitution, which states that laws passed by the national government and all treaties are the supreme law of the land and superior to all laws adopted by any state or any subdivision

Supreme Court, 604–24 the highest court in a particular state or in the United States; this court primarily serves an appellate function
    on AFDC benefits, 680
    and Affordable Care Act, 697
    amicus briefs per case (average), *625*
    on campaign contributions, 401, 402, 404, 405, 422
    campaign spending, 422
    cases filed in, *612*
    cases heard by, 598–99
    on civil rights, 165–66, 179–97
    Clean Power Plan ruling, 554
    on congressional inaction on presidential orders, 540
    constitutional interpretation by, 68–69
    Constitutional provision for, 56–57
    controlling flow of cases to, 612–14
    and due process of law, 138–46
    on education of undocumented students, 18
    and election of 2000, 384
    and expansion of federal power, 87–88
    explaining decisions of, 618–24
    on federal preemption, 93
    and Fourteenth Amendment, 118–22
    on freedom of religion, 126
    on freedom of speech, 127–33
    on freedom of the press, 133–36
    and Gun-Free School Zones Act, 95
    on health insurance subsidies, 106
    influences on decisions of, 618–21
    and interest group litigation, 453
    on interstate commerce, 88
    judicial review by, 604–10
    justice appointment process, 601–2
    on legislative districts, 384, 386
    limiting of congressional powers by, 95
    lobbying for access, 614
    on Medicaid expansion, 99, 682
    on medical marijuana legalization, 77
    on national standards, 93
    and party polarization in Congress, 367–68
    procedures of, 614–18
    pro-national stance of, 87–88
    on racial redistricting, 479–80
    redistricting rulings, 384
    Republican obstruction of confirmation hearings, 467–68
    rights of the accused, 68
    right to privacy, 145, 148–49
    rules of access, 610–11
    same-sex marriage, 83, 193, 226–27, 307, *307*
    school prayer decision, 318–19
    on separate but equal accommodation, 26
    on slavery, 162
    on states' return of fugitives, 83
    term limits for justices of, 606
    time-line of a case, *615*
    and travel ban, 189, *189*, 207, 538
    on union dues, 590–92, *591*
    on voter ID laws, 177
    writs, 611–12

supreme courts (state), 595
surveillance, *151*, 570
surveys, public opinion, 237–47
    design of, 240
    online, 240–41
    question wording, 240
    representative samples, 237–38
    sample size, 239–40
survivor benefits, of Social Security, 679
suspect classifications, 180
swing states, 396
symbolic speech, 132–33
Syria, 722, 738, 742, *742*, 743
Syrian refugees, 189

T

"take care clause" (U.S. Constitution), 515
Taliban, 608–9, 736
talk show interviews, 396
Tam, Simon, 114
TANF. *See* Temporary Assistance for Needy
    Families

tariff, 571, 637, 652, 716, 721   a tax on
    imported goods

TARP (Troubled Asset Relief Program), 648
Tauzin, Billy, 450
taxation, 652–55
    648, 644
    British, *43*, 43–44
    collection of, 572
    and Democratic Party, 356
    demographics of taxpayers, *669*
    e-commerce, 105
    income, 652, 655
    and income inequality, 27–28
    influence of the wealthy on policy, 236
    public opinion on, *240*
    rates in various countries, *654*
    revenues by type of, *653*
    as social policy, 682–83
    Social Security, 653, 679, 686–87
    and supply-side economics, 643
    taxable income brackets/rates, *656*
    tax cuts, 230–32, 281–82, 637, 643–44, 655
    tax policy, 572
tax brackets, 655
Tax Cuts and Jobs Act of 2017, 107, 437, 438,
    466, 643, 655, 698

tax expenditure system, 682–83, 689
    subsidies in the tax code that achieve social
    goals by lowering the cost of homeownership,
    child raising, employer-provided health
    insurance and retirement pensions, etc.,
    through reduced taxation

tax reform, 28, 521, 534
Tax Reform Act of 1986, 689
Tea Act, 45
teachers, as interest group, *432*
Tea Party movement, 270, 334–36, *335*, *368*
    and 2010 midterm elections, 455
    candidate recruitment by, 342
    origin of, 455
    and polarization, 368

and proportional representation voting, 345
    as protest, 215, *454*
    in the South, 224–25
technological innovation, 640
technologies, alternative, 666–67
Telecommunications Act of 1996, 135–36, 260,
    285, 286
Temporary Assistance for Needy Families
    (TANF), 563, 680, 681, *681*, *682*,
    687, 688, 703, 705
Ten Commandments, 125
Tennessee, 668
Tenth Amendment, 56, 81, 94–95
termination of agencies, 575

term limits   legally prescribed limits on the
    number of terms an elected official can serve
    congressional, 477
    Supreme Court, 606

terrorism, 24, *224*, 234, 719–20, 727; *see also*
    September 11, 2001, attacks
terrorism prevention, 24; *see also* war on terror/
    terrorism
Terry v. Ohio, 141
Texas, 107
    congressional seats, 478
    discrimination in, 166–67, 184
    education funding, 18, 26
    executions, 145
    federal employees in, 558
    flag desecration statute, 132
    freedom of religion, 125
    gerrymandering, 175–76, 479–80
    redistricting, 479–80
    same-sex marriage opposition, 83
    sexual conduct statute, 192–93
Texas Young Republican Federation, 378, *379*
"textualist" judges, 602
think tanks, 272
Third Amendment, 146

third parties, 340, 368–71, *369*, 390–91
    parties that organize to compete against the
    two major American political parties

Thirteenth Amendment, 163   one of three Civil
    War amendments; it abolished slavery 163

Thomas, Clarence, 601, 602, 616, 618, 619

Three-Fifths Compromise, 52–53   the
    agreement reached at the Constitutional
    Convention of 1787 that stipulated that
    for purposes of the apportionment of
    congressional seats only three-fifths of slaves
    would be counted

Three Floyds Brewing Co., 630–32
Thucydides Trap, 741
Tilden, Samuel, 390
Tillerson, Rex, 566, 567, 725, *730*, 731
Title IX, Education Act of 1972, 182
Title VII, Civil Rights Act of 1964, 175, 179–85,
    185
Tocqueville, Alexis de, 429, 460

tort case, 609   a lawsuit by one individual (the
    plaintiff) demanding compensation for harm

allegedly caused by the actions of another (the
    defendant)

To Secure These Rights (President's Commission
    on Civil Rights report), 166

totalitarian government, 7   a system of rule in
    which the government recognizes no formal
    limits on its power and seeks to absorb or
    eliminate other social institutions that might
    challenge it

town hall meeting, 396   an informal public
    meeting in which candidates meet with
    ordinary citizens; allows candidates to deliver
    messages without the presence of journalists
    or commentators

Toxic Substances Control Act of 1976, 512
toxic substances regulation, 512–14
trade, international, 721, 723, *744*
trade associations, 433
trade policy, 721, 744–45
traditional media, 263–66

traditional political participation, 297–302
    activities designed to influence government,
    including voting, campaign contributions and
    face-to-face activities such as volunteering
    for a campaign or working on behalf of a
    candidate or political organization

traditional system, 85, *85*, 86
transgender individuals, 158–60, 181
Trans-Pacific Partnership, 723, 744
Transportation, Department of, 552, 572, 641
travel ban, 189, *189*, 207, 609, *609*, 714–15
Treasury Department, 571, 572, *572*, 575, 648,
    728
Treaty of Guadalupe Hidalgo, 184

trial court, 594, 599   the first court to hear a
    criminal or civil case

Troubled Asset Relief Program (TARP), 648
Truman, David, 437
Truman, Harry S., 166, *243*, 500, 525
Trump, Donald, and administration, *31*, *226*,
    338, *726*
    in 2016 debates, 389, *399*
    and ACA, 698
    administrative directives of, 538
    adversarial journalism under, 284
    branding, 340
    bureaucratic reform, 574
    campaign spending, 401, 405
    Clean Power Plan, 554
    Hillary Clinton emails, 280, 282
    Consumer Financial Protection Bureau
        under, 661
    cyberattacks of 2016 campaign, 210, 308–9
    Defense and Homeland Security, 558, 568, 569
    Deferred Action for Childhood Arrivals
        program, 105
    digital communication strategy, 396
    diplomatic power, 517–18, *518*, 734
    on earmarks, 493
    Education Department, 565
    education under, 693

U.S. Court of Appeals, 599
U.S. Court of Appeals for the Federal Circuit, 597
U.S. Court of Appeals for Veterans Claims, 597
U.S. Court of Federal Claims, 596–97
U.S. Court of International Trade, 596
U.S. Court of Military Appeals, 597
U.S. Patent and Trademark Office, 115
U.S. Public Health Service, 694
U.S. Public Health Service (USPHS), 694
USA Freedom Act, 570
USA PATRIOT Act, 102, 570
USCAP (U.S. Climate Action Partnership), 666
USMCA (United States–Mexico–Canada Agreement), 721
USPHS (U.S. Public Health Service), 694
Utah, 98, 165–66, 188, 478

V

Valdes, Jessica, 379

values (or beliefs) basic principles that shape a person's opinions about political issues and events
consensus on, 210, *212*
in the Constitution, 69
defined, 207
democracy, 28–29
equality, 25–28
immigration and, 22–23
liberty, 24–25
political, 209–11

Van Ordern v. Perry, 125
Varnum v. Brien, 226
Verizon, 254–55, 259
Vermont, voting rights of felons in, 326
vesting clause (U.S. Constitution), 515, 522
Veterans Affairs, Department of, 552, 564, 573
Veterans Health Administration, 573

veto, 494, 519–21, *520, 520* the president's constitutional power to turn down acts of Congress; a presidential veto may be overridden by a two-thirds vote of each house of Congress

vice presidency, 531–32
video, streaming, 267, 273
Vietnam War, *284*
deterrence policy, 719
domestic repercussions, 740
media coverage, 277
and New Deal coalition, 363
Pentagon Papers case, 133, 283, 284
and public interest groups, 447
secret presidential agreements, 503–4
shaping of political environment by, 224
and Twenty-Sixth Amendment, *68*, 300
veterans with Agent Orange exposure, 565, 622–23
Vilarino, Irina, *451*
Virginia, 82, 167, *208*, 294–95, 326
Virginia, Karena, *412*
Virginia League of Conservation Voters, 295
Virginia Military Institute (VMI), 182

Virginia Plan, 50 a framework for the Constitution, introduced by Edmund Randolph, that called for representation in the national legislature based on the population of each state

VMI (Virginia Military Institute), 182
Volcker, Paul, 650–51
Volkswagen diesel emissions scandal, 555
voter ID laws, 177, 324
voter mobilization, 343–44
voter registration
automatic, 295
same-day, 295, 324
state requirements, 324
voters
demographics in 2016, *55*, 355–58
election decision making by, 406–8
emotions of, 306
voting, 8, 294–96, 299–302, 310–19
in Congress, 493, 497
for congressional representatives, *507*
in election of 2008, *29*
in election of 2016, *29*
formal barriers to, 326
by mail, 327
and political knowledge, 226
political participation through, 299–300
split-ticket, 358, 383
state electoral laws, 323–27, *325*
straight-ticket, 383
turnout. *See* turnout
voting rights, 29, 175–77, *176*, 299–300
for African Americans, *161*, 163, 299–300, 313–14
Amendments regarding, 71
for felons, 326
Twenty-Sixth Amendment, *68*
and voter turnout, 301
for women, 29, 161, *163*, 164–66, *165*, 300–301, *301*
Voting Rights Act of 1965 (VRA), 29, 175–77, *176*, 190–91, 300, 364, *381*, 479, 480
VRA. *See* Voting Rights Act of 1965

W

wage inequality, 183–84, *185*, 703; *see also* minimum wage
Wagner, Kevin, 269, 270
Wagner, Marcella, 674–76, *675*
Wagner-Steagall National Housing Act of 1937, 698
Wales, Jimmy, 288
Walker, Scott, 393
Wallace, George, 92
Wall Street Journal
digital subscriptions to, 263
online presence of, 261
Walters, Lee Ann, 550, *551*
War on Poverty, 91
war on terror/terrorism, 232, 569–70, 719–20, 738
war power (president), 525–26, 543
War Powers Resolution, 525–26
Warren, Earl, 142, 600, 619–20

Warren, Elizabeth, *213*, *639*
Warsaw Pact, 737
Washington, George, 339, 519, 718
Washington Post
investigative journalism by, 262
online presence of, 261
Pentagon Papers, 283, 284
profitability of, 263–64
Watergate coverage, 284
Washington State, 104, 105, 115, 478, 479
Watergate, 264, 284, 456, 484, 519, *519*
Watson, Gregory, 68
WEAL (Women's Equity Action League), 181
wealth, political influence and, 236–37
wealth inequality. *See* income equality/inequality
Weather Service, U.S., 552
Webster v. Reproductive Health Services, 148, 453–54
wedge issues, 398–99
welfare programs
beneficiaries of, *701*
caseload for, *688*
contributory, 679–80
noncontributory, 680–81
public opposition to, 687
state variation in benefits, 681–82
welfare reform, 98, 100
welfare state, 677–89
costs of, *684*
foundations of, 679–83
history of social welfare system, 677–79
paying for, 683–87
size of, *685*
Westboro Baptist Church, *123*, 132–33
West Virginia, 2
West Virginia State Board of Education v. Barnette, 125
Whig Party, *361*, 362

whip, 482, 499 a party member in the House or Senate responsible for coordinating the party's legislative strategy, building support for key issues, and counting votes

white Americans
as naturalized citizens, 16
party affiliation of, 356, 357
poverty rate for, 704
and racism, 218–19, *219*
and Republican Party, 356
trust in government, 31
White House Communications Office, 535
Whitehouse.gov website, 535

White House staff, 530, *529, 537* analysts and advisers to the president, each of whom is often given the title "special assistant"

white nationalists, *208*, *272*, 298
WikiLeaks, 134, 283
Wikipedia, 288
Wilcox County, Alabama, *381*
Wilson, Daren, 218
Wilson, James, 50, 52–53
Wilson, Woodrow, 166, 284, 300, 534
Windsor v. U.S., 83, 180
winner-take-all system, 340, 388
Wisconsin, 322, 326, 386, 479

Wolfowitz, Paul, 746
women
    in abolitionist movement, 162, *163*
    civil rights for, 180–85, *185*
    in Congress, 472, *472*, *473*, 474, 476–77, 488, *488*
    in elective office, 317, *317*
    gender discrimination, 180–85
    gender gap, 220, *222*, 316–17
    in military, 182–83, *183*
    and political opinion, 220, *222*
    political participation, 316–17
    and private inequalities, 27
    recruited for Congress, 476–77
    social policy for, 704–6
    in social reform, 161
    Title IX, *182*
    voting rights for, 29, 161, *163*, 164–66, *165*, 300, *301*
    women's issues partisanship, 317
Women's Campaign, 317
Women's Equity Action League (WEAL), 181
Women's March, 297, *298*
women's organizations, 165–66
women's rights movement, 162, 180–85
workers' compensation, 677

working-class voters, 356, *414*
working poor, social policy for, 702–3, *704*
work requirements, for social policy programs, 689
Works Progress Administration (WPA), *89*, 637
World Bank, 735, *736*

World Trade Organization (WTO), 721
    international organization promoting free trade that grew out of the General Agreement on Tariffs and Trade

World War I, 718
World War II, 525, 533
    civil rights following, 166–67
    Defense Department in, 568
    internment camps, 190, 569
    isolationism in early years of, 718
    Pearl Harbor, 718
WPA (Works Progress Administration), *89*, 637
Wright, Gerald, 235

writ of certiorari, 611–12   a decision of at least four of the nine Supreme Court justices to review a decision of a lower court; *certiorari* is Latin, meaning "to make more certain"

writ of habeas corpus, 118, 597, 609   a court order that the individual in custody be brought into court and shown the cause for detention; habeas corpus is guaranteed by the Constitution and can be suspended only in cases of rebellion or invasion

WTO (World Trade Organization), 721
Wyoming, 136, 165–66

Y
Yates, Robert, 50, 62
Yellen, Janet, 651
YouGov, 241
Young, Don, 481
youth vote, 295
YouTube, 267, *270*, 312, 535

Z
Zaller, John, 225–26
zero-based budgeting, 580
Zika virus outbreak, *694*

Governing California in the Twenty-First Century

THE POLITICAL DYNAMICS OF THE GOLDEN STATE

J. Theodore Anagnoson
California State University, Los Angeles

Gerald Bonetto
Vice President, Government Affairs, Printing Industries of California

J. Vincent Buck
California State University, Fullerton

Jolly Emrey
University of Wisconsin–Whitewater

James J. Kelleher
College of the Canyons

Nadine Koch
California State University, Los Angeles

Melissa Michelson
Menlo College

W. W. NORTON & COMPANY
INDEPENDENT PUBLISHERS SINCE 1923

W. W. Norton & Company has been independent since its founding in 1923, when William Warder Norton and Mary D. Herter Norton first published lectures delivered at the People's Institute, the adult education division of New York City's Cooper Union. The firm soon expanded its program beyond the Institute, publishing books by celebrated academics from America and abroad. By midcentury, the two major pillars of Norton's publishing program—trade books and college texts—were firmly established. In the 1950s, the Norton family transferred control of the company to its employees, and today—with a staff of four hundred and a comparable number of trade, college, and professional titles published each year—W. W. Norton & Company stands as the largest publishing house owned wholly by its employees.

Printed in Canada.

The text of this book is composed in Berlin with the display set in Interstate.

Book design: Lissi Sigillo

Composition: Achorn International

Manufacturing: Transcontinental

Editor: Laura Wilk

Editorial Assistant: Chris Howard-Woods

Project Editor: Laura Dragonette

Managing Editor, College: Marian Johnson

Managing Editor, College Digital Media: Kim Yi

Production Manager, College: Ashley Horna

Media Editor: Spencer Richardson-Jones

Associate Media Editor: Michael Jaoui

Media Project Editor: Marcus Van Harpen

Media Editorial Assistant: Tricia Vuong

Design Director: Jillian Burr

Marketing Manager, Political Science: Erin Brown

Director of College Permissions: Megan Schindel

Permissions Specialist: Bethany Salminen

Photo Editor: Ted Szczepanski

Library of Congress Cataloging-in-Publication Data

Names: Anagnoson, J. Theodore, editor.

Title: Governing California in the twenty-first century : the political dynamics of the Golden State / J. Theodore Anagnoson, California State University, Los Angeles, Gerald Bonetto, Vice President, Government Affairs, Printing Industries of California, J. Vincent Buck, California State University, Fullerton, Jolly Emrey, University of Wisconsin-Whitewater, James J. Kelleher, California State University, Dominguez Hills, Nadine Koch, California State University, Los Angeles, Melissa Michelson, Menlo College.

Description: Seventh Edition. | New York : W.W. Norton & Company, [2019] | Previous edition: 2017. | Includes bibliographical references and index.

Identifiers: LCCN 2018053633 | ISBN 9780393664881 (paperback)

Subjects: LCSH: California—Politics and government—21st century—Textbooks.

Classification: LCC JK8716 .G67 2019 | DDC 320.4794—dc23 LC record available at https://lccn.loc.gov/2018053633

W. W. Norton & Company, Inc., 500 Fifth Avenue, New York, N.Y. 10110

www.wwnorton.com

W. W. Norton & Company Ltd., Castle House, 75/76 Wells Street, London W1T 3QT

1 2 3 4 5 6 7 8 9 0

Contents

Preface

In 2017 and 2018, California assumed a new role: the epicenter of resistance to the Trump administration. Ever since Trump became president, California has been at odds with his administration over many of its policy directives, including immigration, the environment, trade, and numerous social issues, among others. While these conflicts demonstrate federalism in action, and underscore what makes California politics unique, the state is far from homogenous. The same issues that challenged the country heading into the 2018 midterm elections divided the state along demographic, geographic, and economic lines. In this new edition, we explore California's new role as well as the political history that brought us to this point.

The Seventh Edition features updated scholarship throughout the book, building on the foundation that has made *Governing California* a success. We began this project over a decade ago with a working title asking whether California's political system and its politics were simply "broken." That is, politicians were caught within a system that was so contradictory in its rules, norms, and mores that budgets couldn't be passed on time or balanced, programs and departments couldn't be managed under the existing set of rules, and citizen expectations were so out of line with the ability of the political system to satisfy them that the level of negativism and cynicism was as bad as could be found anywhere in the nation.

We think after a decade of false and halting starts that the picture needs some modification. California has begun to repair its infrastructure. The state has new incentives for politicians to be less ideologically extreme on the right or the left, in particular the "top two" primary system and the commission that is now drawing new districts for the Assembly, the state Senate, and congressional districts every 10 years after the census. Decision rules in Sacramento still leave much to be desired, but at least a budget can be passed with majority rule instead of a two-thirds vote, a rule that necessitated some votes from the minority party and, unfortunately, some pork projects or other incentives to gain those votes. And the nation's strictest term-limit rules have been modified to allow members of the Assembly or state Senate to serve 12 years in a single house before being "termed out" and forced to seek another office outside the state legislature. Hopefully, this will increase the level of expertise available among legislators.

The Seventh Edition of *Governing California* offers a ray of hope but also the reality of a long distance to go. We hope you enjoy our analysis of California's politics as not quite "broken" but as not yet "fixed" either.

Highlights of this revision include the following:

- NEW co-author Melissa Michelson (Menlo College) brings fresh scholarship to Chapters 2, 6, and 9. In Chapter 2, a new discussion of California's complicated legacy of discrimination provides deeper insight into the evolution of the state constitution. Additionally, Chapter 6 provides an overview of the new governor and administration, while Chapter 9 provides new data on the housing crisis.

- NEW coverage of the 2018 midterm elections (Chapter 4) explores the issues that were at stake and the propositions that were on the ballots, and provides a thorough analysis of the election results and what they say about where California is heading as the country looks toward the next presidential election in 2020.

- NEW "Who Are Californians?" features by contributing author R. Allen Bolar (Bakersfield College), explore diversity in the legislature (Chapter 5) and the growing population of uninsured in the state (Chapter 10). In addition, all of the other features have been thoroughly updated to help students understand the data behind big questions about state government.

- NEW information on California's political landscape provides points of comparison and contrast on divisive issues across the country, including the WeSaidEnough movement (Chapter 4) in the state capitol, which echoed the sentiments of the national #MeToo movement against sexual harassment.

- A thoroughly revised InQuizitive course helps reinforce the key topics and concepts in each chapter by quizzing students on what they still need to learn, not on what they've already mastered. InQuizitive is customizable to align the chapters and sections that you assign to your students. In addition, a test bank is available for all your assessment needs.

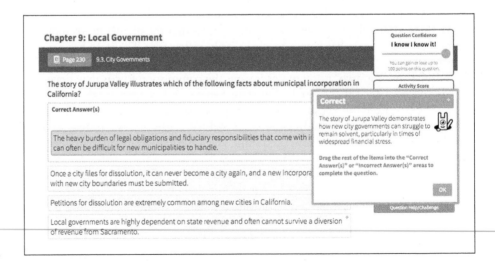

In order to provide the most knowledgeable analysis of the diverse topics in the table of contents, we divided the writing of this book as follows:

1. California Government: Promise and Practice—Anagnoson (tanagno@calstatela.edu)
2. The Constitution and the Progressive Legacy—Michelson (melissa.michelson@menlo.edu)
3. Interest Groups and the Media in California—Bonetto (gbonetto@roadrunner.com)
4. Parties and Elections in California—Koch (nkoch@calstatela.edu)
5. The California Legislature—Buck (vbuck@fullerton.edu)
6. The Governor and the Executive Branch—Michelson
7. The California Judiciary—Emrey (emreyj@uww.edu)
8. The State Budget and Budgetary Limitations—Anagnoson (tanagno@calstatela.edu)
9. Local Government—Michelson
10. Public Policy in California—Emrey

We would like to acknowledge the helpful recommendations from professors who have reviewed the book. Their comments have assisted us in updating events and materials. For the Seventh Edition, we thank the following reviewers:

John Vento, Antelope Valley College
Betty Chan, American River College, Sierra College
James E. Starkey, College of the Canyons
Anthony O'Regan, Los Angeles Valley College
Cameron Billeci, California State University, Sacramento
Janice Shiu, California State University, Sacramento
Allen K. Settle, California Polytechnic State University
Christopher Arns, California State University, Sacramento

We also thank the several students who have communicated their comments.

We would be glad to hear from you about the book. Please use the email addresses above to communicate with us.

J. Theodore Anagnoson
Professor of Political Science
California State University, Los Angeles

1 California Government: Promise and Practice

WHAT CALIFORNIA GOVERNMENT DOES AND WHY IT MATTERS

In the morning you drive to work on the freeway, stopping first at the gas station on the corner to fill up, then at the corner grocery store to buy an apple for a midday snack. Next you drive across a bridge to get to the university where you are currently taking general education courses. You are already considering what will follow after graduation. Perhaps you'll work for the California Highway Patrol (CHP), a private security guard service, or for a technology company. In the evening you are ready to relax after a full day of school, so you go out to a restaurant.

How is the government of California relevant to your day? Let's start at the beginning. Your car is built to conform to government safety standards. The freeways are built by the state government, with a mixture of federal and state money, to conform to federal and state standards. Traffic is monitored by the CHP. The gas station has to meet local safety regulations—it uses gasoline that conforms to federal standards for automobiles. Additionally, you paid a gas tax of 41.7 cents per gallon, which was increased by 12 cents on November 1, 2017 (to pay for increased construction and maintenance on the state's roads), and was the subject of a referendum on the November 2018 ballot to repeal the 12 cent increase. The grocery store relies on scales that are certified by county government; both imported and domestic fruit must meet U.S. and state Department of Agriculture standards. The bridge was built by government and is maintained by government (although a large proportion of the bridges nationally and in California are behind on their scheduled maintenance). If you attend a K-12 school, the school must comply with state standards for curriculum at each grade level and administer tests to determine whether it is meeting those standards. If you are in higher education, the public university you attend must have a general education program that conforms to state regulations. If you are enrolled in a community college, California State University, or the University of California, the cost of your education is partially subsidized by state funds. If you attend a private college, you might be receiving federal student aid. If you eventually go to work for the CHP, you will work under state laws and regulations. The private security service is regulated by the state as well, and the tech industry must conform to state and federal privacy regulations. The restaurant in which you enjoy your evening meal is inspected periodically by the local government health department, and in some locations the department will post the summary score (A, B, or C).

The California Dream?

For almost 200 years the **California dream** has attracted residents from other parts of the United States as well as immigrants from abroad. Former governor Arnold Schwarzenegger, in his 2004 State of the State address, said that California represents "an empire of hope and aspiration," a place where "Californians do great things." To some, the California dream is sun and surf; to others, the warm winter season and a house on the coast amid redwoods and acres of untrammeled wilderness, and to still others, the luxury of three or four cars per family.

The core of the dream is the ability to live a middle-class lifestyle in the most congenial climate in the nation, but that lifestyle is becoming increasingly difficult to attain in California. A 2018 analysis of the California dream posted on CalMatters.org shows that by 2014, median California families made only 8 percent more than they did in 1980. The median U.S. family made 22 percent more.[1] The modern conception of the California dream seems to have become finding a way to stick it out here. "California is a struggle, so we dream of the good struggle, of finding our footing, of figuring out some way to beat the statistics and buy a house and educate our kids."[2]

No matter what the conception, some of the dream is attainable for many— California's winter weather is the envy of most of the nation—but much of it is not. One of the themes of this book is the conflict between dreams and reality, between the ideals that we set for ourselves and the reality of our everyday lives. Particularly vivid for politicians is the conflict between our expectations of them and the constraints we place upon them.

Why Study California Politics?

The obvious answer is that you have to: your California history course meets some requirement for graduation or your major, since the state of California decided that every college student should know something about the California Constitution and California government and politics. But more important—why *care* about California politics?

- You are **the residents and voters of the present and future**. The policies and political trends occurring today will impact your lives, affecting everything from university tuition fees to the strength of the job market.

- California politics is plagued by **low levels of participation and turnout**, so much so that the electorate is older, more conservative, wealthier, more educated, and less ethnically diverse than would be the case if every eligible adult voted. So your vote and participation really can make a difference.

- California politics also suffers from **too much interest-group participation and not enough citizen participation**. The general interests of large groups of citizens need to be represented at the table.

That's the narrow answer. The broad answer is that California's government and politics are distinctive and worthy of study. How is California different from other states?

- We have much more **cultural diversity** than other states, including a much higher proportion of Latino and Asian residents. By some measures, we are the country's multicultural trendsetter. Our diversity affects our politics, and our solutions to multicultural issues have become an example for other states.

- We are **one of the five largest economies in the world**. The California economy in 2017, according to the federal Bureau of Economic Analysis, is the fifth largest in the world, surpassing Russia, Italy, Brazil, the United Kingdom, and India. Only the United States without California, and China, Japan, and Germany have larger economies. California's large and diverse economy means that we are able, in theory, to weather economic downturns more easily than other states. The fact that budget crises continue to plague California indicates that our taxing and spending system has fundamental problems (see below and Chapter 8).

- We are **the most populous state, with about 39.5 million people, and we have grown more quickly than other states**. In 1960, New York had 41 members in the U.S. House of Representatives; California had 38. The 2010 census gave California 53 seats, followed by Texas with 36 and Florida and New York with 27 each. In the past, California was forced to develop creative solutions to the problems engendered by high growth—problems such as uneven population distribution among various regions of the state and the need for housing and schools. However, California is currently losing more people to other states than it is gaining, and in recent years the exodus has grown as a result of high housing costs, taxes, and other costs of living. (The most popular destination for those leaving is Texas.) California's population is still slowly increasing on account of our having more births than deaths in recent years, but internally the population changes mean that the average age is growing and that the state has more senior citizens than it has had in the past. In the near future, we could even see California's population decline slightly each year. Current projections show the number of congressional seats staying at 53 after the 2020 Census, or even declining by a seat if the undercount is significant.

- We are **more majoritarian than other states**, meaning that we rely more on the measures for direct democracy—the initiative, the referendum, and

The initiative was added to the California Constitution by the Progressive movement in 1911 as a way to promote the involvement of the people in public policy and affairs. In November 2018 there were 11 propositions on the ballot, including Proposition 6, on which Californians had to decide whether or not to repeal a gas tax enacted in 2017. This proposition ultimately failed.

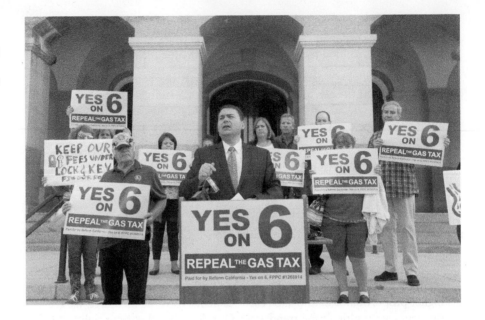

the recall—that were added to the state constitution by the Progressive movement in 1911. Every state uses majority rule for most decisions, but in a majoritarian state the public is more likely than elected representatives to make important policy decisions.

Consider the following continuum:

majoritarian   republican

A **majoritarian** government is one that is highly influenced by the public at large, through public-opinion polls and measures such as the initiative, the referendum, and the recall that enable voters to decide government policies directly.

A **republican** government is one in which we elect representatives to make our decisions for us, based on the Madisonian model for the federal government.

California government has moved much more toward the majoritarian model than other states. Initiatives to amend the constitution are routine, and interest groups often collect signatures for an initiative in order to pressure the legislature into voting in their favor. By voting directly on public policies and constitutional amendments that are placed on the ballot, California voters can influence policy in their state more than voters can in other states.

And Californians like being majoritarian. Surveys show that most don't want to restrict use of the initiative in spite of its extensive use and manipulation by interest groups as well as other problems. Ballotpedia lists 364 initiatives from 1912 through 2016, and we had another eleven in November 2018, for a total of 373.[3] California's number of initiatives historically is second only to Oregon's. Twenty-seven states do not have the initiative at all, and the top five states account for more than half of all initiatives considered from 1904 to 2012.[4] In other words, interest in and use of the initiative is highly concentrated in just a few states, one of which is ours.

What Determines the Content and Character of California's Politics?

Three factors shape the content and character of California's politics:

- the underlying demographic and sociopolitical trends that affect California and the other states;
- the rules of the game, as set out in the federal and state constitutions and in state laws;
- and the decisions of voters and politicians.

In Chapters 1 and 2 we will discuss the underlying demographic and sociopolitical trends and the rules of the game. The decisions of voters and politicians, and the way they shape California politics, will be discussed later in the text.

Who Are Californians?

The preamble to the California State Constitution begins, "We, the People of the State of California, . . . " This is fitting for a democratic form of government, which seeks to give voice to the people in the governing of their community affairs. So, who are Californians? Do the demographic characteristics of California differ from those of the United States as a whole? And how have changing demographic and socioeconomic trends contributed to the political challenges that face California voters and politicians? (See the "Who Are Californians?" feature.)

RACE AND ETHNICITY In many respects, California's population has a notable degree of **racial and ethnic diversity** compared with the U.S. population. **Latino or Hispanic** is not a racial category in the official census, but a separate census question asks about Hispanic or Latino origin. Answers to this question reveal that about 17 percent of the United States is Latino but that Latinos make up about 39 percent of California's population.[5] Almost 60 percent of that population is of Mexican heritage.

AGE California's population is relatively young, mostly because of immigration. Immigrants tend to be younger and have larger families than those who have been residents for longer periods. However, in recent decades the proportion of senior citizens has been increasing, from 10.6 percent in 2000 to 11.4 percent in 2010 and to an estimated 13.6 percent in 2017. California is therefore still a relatively young state. Nevertheless, because of the increase in the number and proportion of senior citizens, there has been an increased need for caregivers. Issues regarding the quality of care in nursing homes in the state have persisted for many years.

EDUCATION Californians are relatively well educated, with a greater proportion having gone to college or completed a bachelor's degree or higher than in the

How Is the California Population Changing?

California's demographics are changing rapidly. The state used to be predominately comprised of non-Latino whites (Anglos), but since 2000 the state has had a majority minority population. Latinos and Asians in particular are fast-growing populations, while whites and blacks are an increasingly small proportion. If these trends continue, by 2060, less than 31 percent of Californians will be white, while close to half (45 percent) will be Latino.

At the same time, the total size of the state's population is expected to continue to grow rapidly, from 40 million people in 2019 to 51 million in 2060. Population density will increase in the state's urban areas as well as inland areas, particularly in the Central Valley and Inland Empire, where housing is substantially less expensive.

Projected population growth by demographic group

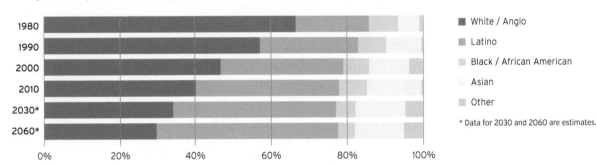

- White / Anglo
- Latino
- Black / African American
- Asian
- Other

* Data for 2030 and 2060 are estimates.

Projected population growth between 2019 and 2060 by county

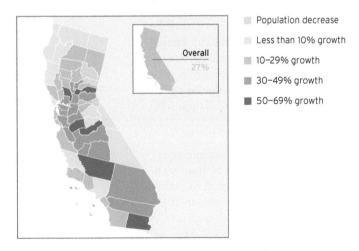

- Population decrease
- Less than 10% growth
- 10–29% growth
- 30–49% growth
- 50–69% growth

Overall
27%

SOURCE: Frank Hobbs and Nicole Stoops, "Demographic Trends in the 20th Century," U.S. Census Bureau, www.census.gov/prod/2002pubs/censr-4.pdf (accessed 7/26/18); Jonathan Vespa, David M. Armstrong, and Lauren Medina, "Demographic Turning Points for the United States: Population Projections for 2020 to 2060," U.S. Census Bureau, https://www.census.gov/content/dam/Census/library/publications/2018/demo/P25_1144.pdf (accessed 7/26/18); and "Projections," State of California Department of Finance, www.dof.ca.gov/Forecasting /Demographics/projections/ (accessed 7/26/18).

forcriticalanalysis

1. What impact are these shifting demographics likely to have on politics? Will they change the issues that the state government focuses on? Will they change the issues that are the subject of citizen-driven initiatives?

2. California's coastal regions have traditionally been more densely populated, but rapid population growth and rising housing costs are increasingly driving populations to settle further inland. How will this change California politics in the inland counties, particularly in areas traditionally dedicated to agriculture?

United States as a whole. Fewer, however, have graduated from high school in recent years (83 percent from 2015 to 2016 versus 84 percent for the United States as a whole from 2015 to 2016). About three-quarters of California's two million college students attend a UC, CSU, or community college campus, with 44 percent of the total attending community colleges. Even with those numbers, analysts anticipate the state in 2030 will face a long-term shortage of college-educated workers, with about 33 percent of the state's workers having a college education in 2030 but with over 38 percent of all jobs requiring a college education.[6]

MOBILITY AND FOREIGN-BORN RESIDENTS About 60 percent of all Americans live in the state in which they were born, but only 50 percent of all Californians were born in California. In fact, 27.0 percent are **foreign-born**, more than twice the percentage of foreign-born residents in the United States as a whole (13.2 percent). "About half (49%) of California's immigrants are naturalized US citizens, and another 26% have . . . legal status."[7] As one might expect with such a large foreign-born population, only 61 percent of those over age five speak English at home in California, as opposed to 82 percent nationwide. That is a substantial difference by the standards of social science. Many political issues have arisen from this, ranging from debates over whether local store signs should be written in foreign languages to the "English as the official state language" movement.

INCOME The U.S. Census Bureau has estimated California's median household income at $63,783 for 2012–16, $8,461 higher than the national figure of $55,322. The state poverty rate is almost the same as the national figure: 14.3 percent (California) compared to 12.7 percent (United States). The official poverty line does not account for California's costs, particularly housing costs. A California-based poverty line calculated by the respected Public Policy Institute of California (PPIC) and the Stanford Center on Poverty and Inequality puts the 2016 poverty line at 19.4 percent, about 7.4 million people. Another 19 percent of Californians live within 1.5 times of the poverty line, which means that 38.2 percent of state residents were poor or near-poor.[8]

Income inequality in California has increased in the last 35 years. A study by the PPIC found that pretax cash incomes of top earners in California are 40 percent higher than they were in 1980, but middle incomes are only 5 percent higher and low incomes 19 percent lower. Bay Area incomes are twice those in the Central Valley, on average. The report did find that California's safety net, including tax credits as well as nutrition, cash, and housing assistance, had played a significant role in lessening inequality in the state. When local, state, and federal safety net programs are included, the amount of inequality shrinks by about 40 percent.[9]

GEOGRAPHY AND POLITICS Over the last 40 years, the population of California has shifted so that the coastal regions have become significantly more liberal and aligned with the Democratic Party than have the inland regions, which in turn have become more conservative and aligned with the Republican Party. These liberal coastal regions include every county on the coast from Del Norte County near Oregon to Los Angeles County. The Central Valley and Inland Empire (Riverside and San Bernardino counties) are disproportionately Republican. Orange and San Diego counties have been very Republican in the past but less so in recent elections. Local politics, on the other hand, are quite different even among Democratic- or

Republican-leaning cities (for example, San Francisco's local politics are very liberal compared with Los Angeles's more moderate politics).

POPULATION GROWTH Except for the four years from 1993 to 1996, California's population has grown by about 450,000 people per year for more than two decades until the early 2000s. The 2010 census listed California's population as 37,691,912; at the end of 2015 the state Department of Finance estimated the population at 39.5 million. California's current rate of growth has slowed: the rate for the 10 years preceding 2016 was 310,000 per year. Regardless of this slowdown, which includes outmigration, many of the problems that have plagued the state in the past will continue to raise issues in the future. The following are some of these issues:

- **Housing and Transportation**   Even with the decline brought on by the recession of 2008–09, housing prices and rents in many areas have skyrocketed in recent years. Many lower- and middle-class people who work in San Francisco's Bay Area must live in the Central Valley, while many of those who work in the Los Angeles area must live in Riverside and San Bernardino counties. Commutes of one to two hours each way are common for residents of these areas. Housing costs in 2018 have risen so much that many younger families are leaving the state for other states. And our transportation systems, built for a much smaller population, have not kept pace with this growth.

- **Schools**   Population growth means more schoolchildren and thus a higher demand for teachers across the state. In recent years, California has lacked enough fully qualified or credentialed teachers to meet this demand, particularly in many urban areas. Projections of the educational requirements of the future job market indicate that approximately 38 percent of jobs will require a college degree in 2030. The University of California, California State University, and community college systems do not produce sufficient numbers of graduates to meet this goal, which means that well-educated workers from other states will move in to fill these positions. The proportion of students who receive a college degree should be rising to meet future job requirements; instead, it is falling. More evidence on the inadequacy of California's degree production comes from data on high school graduates and where they go to college. The numbers who go out of state are up markedly from just a decade ago, with data from the U.S. Department of Education showing that about 40,000 high school graduates left the state for college in 2016, compared with the 22,000 who did so in 2006.[10]

- **Immigration**   California has experienced high levels of immigration since the 1950s—so high in some areas that candidates for Mexico's presidency have campaigned here. Between 1970 and 2016 the number of immigrants in California's population increased from 1.8 million to about 10.2 million; 27 percent of the state's population in 2016 was foreign-born, a much higher proportion than the 13 percent nationwide. Most of California's immigrants were born in either Latin America (51 percent) or Asia (39 percent); 4.3 million come from Mexico alone, composing some 43 percent of the total immigrant population in California. Immigrants live in all parts of the state,

TABLE 1.1 ● Leading Countries of Origin of Immigrants in California, 2016

Country	Number of Immigrants in California
Mexico	4,200,000
China (including Taiwan)	936,000
Philippines	813,000
Vietnam	534,000
India	482,000

SOURCE: Public Policy Institute of California, "Just the Facts: Immigrants in California." ppic.org/publication/immigrants-in-california/ (accessed 10/23/18).

with those from Latin America more likely to live in Southern California and those from Asia more likely to live in Northern California. Immigrants are younger than nonimmigrant Californians and are more likely to be poor, and although some have relatively high levels of education, most are less educated than the native population.[11] Table 1.1 shows the five largest countries of origin for immigrants in California in 2016.

As of 2014 there were approximately 2.35 million **undocumented immigrants** in California, according to the Urban Institute and the Public Policy Institute of California, which used the census figures on the foreign-born population and subtracted the numbers of people who are naturalized or here on legal visas and work permits.[12] Undocumented immigrants are a continuing political issue, with politicians arguing over the public services to which they should have access: Should they be treated in hospital emergency rooms? Should they be allowed to buy insurance on the state exchange under the federal Affordable Care Act? As of January 1, 2015, one issue was decided: California residents who cannot establish legal presence in the United States can apply for a California driver's license if they can establish proof of identification and state residency. As of March 31, 2018, 1,001,000 such licenses had been issued. Table 1.2 lists the number of undocumented immigrants by state, along with the share they compose of that state's total population. California and Texas have the highest numbers of undocumented immigrants, at 2.3 and 1.6 million respectively.

Reflecting the controversies over both documented and undocumented immigration in recent years, a number of demonstrations have taken place in California on the immigration issue. These demonstrations have represented different views: against more immigration, in favor of closing the borders, in favor of a "path to citizenship," both for and against the Arizona immigration law of 2010, against housing undocumented children who have been taken into custody before their court hearings, and so forth. At least one of the demonstrations involved more than 1 million people, the largest ever seen in Southern California to date. But aside from the 2013 law that allowed undocumented immigrants to obtain driver's permits starting in 2015 (see above), little policy action has taken place at the state level.

TABLE 1.2 ● Undocumented Immigrants by State, 2014

State	Number of Undocumented Immigrants	Share of State's Total Population (%)
California	2,350,000	6.0%
Texas	1,650,000	6.1
Florida	850,000	4.2
New York	775,000	3.9
New Jersey	500,000	5.4
Illinois	450,000	3.5
Georgia	375,000	3.6
North Carolina	350,000	3.4
Arizona	325,000	4.9
Virginia	300,000	3.5
Other States	3,175,000	2.0
All states	11,100,000	3.5

SOURCE: Pew Research Center, Hispanic Trends, "U.S. Unauthorized Immigration Population Estimates." www.pew hispanic.org/interactives/unauthorized-immigrants/ (accessed 10/23/18).

The Crisis of California Politics

Is California government capable of making the decisions needed for the state to thrive and preserve its standard of living through the twenty-first century? The general sentiment among informed observers is that California is hamstrung by voter-approved rules and regulations, some of which are admirable on an individual level but make for a collective nightmare. However, some progress toward effective decision making began during the 2003–11 Schwarzenegger administration and continued under Governor Jerry Brown, who left office in 2019:

- Proposition 11, approved in November 2008, took the power to apportion the districts of the Assembly and state Senate (**redistricting**) away from those bodies and gave it to a citizens' commission. Later, the voters added apportioning congressional districts to the duties of the new citizens' commission. In the first years the new districts have been used, they seem to be fair (that is, not gerrymandered). Future years will establish whether unbiased districts will produce more moderate legislators who are willing to compromise for the good of the state as a whole, which was the goal of changing the reapportionment method. So far, elections have been more competitive.

- In 2010 the voters opted to change the state's party primary elections to a new **top-two primary** system, used for the first time in June 2012. Under the new system, there is no party primary. Instead, the election system is like a swim meet or a track meet, in which there are preliminary heats and finals. Following the preliminary election, the top two candidates advance to the finals in November, even if they are from the same party or are not in a major party. Third parties such as the Green Party are strongly opposed to the new system, since they rarely finish in the top two candidates in the primary election and thus have no access to the general election ballot during the two months when voter attention is highest. Two problems have arisen recently with the new system. First, if a party wishes to replace its candidate on the ballot, there are no provisions for that action or even for a candidate to withdraw—once on the ballot, the candidate is on for good. And second, no write-ins are allowed on the November ballot, so the two candidates approved in the June primary are the ones the voters are stuck with in November, no matter what.

- In 2010 the voters also approved of a change in the legislative process for approving the state budget. The previous requirement was a **two-thirds vote** of the total number of legislators in each chamber (the Assembly and the state Senate). It is now a simple majority (50 percent plus one). The budget approved in June 2011 was the first to use the new system. In order to raise or lower taxes, however, the state constitution still requires a two-thirds majority of both houses of the state legislature, plus the governor's signature.

After the election of Governor Jerry Brown in November 2010, California's frustrating budget stalemate initially continued in spite of the new majority rule, largely because the taxation system had not changed. In June 2012 the budget gap was $16 billion—more than the total revenues received for the general fund in 40 of the 50 states. By mid-2014, however, the budget had a surplus almost as large as the deficit from two years before, and this surplus has lasted into the 2018–19 budget year. The California taxation system is highly dependent on its **capital gains tax**—income taxes paid on capital gains (funds received from selling stock). It produced a huge surplus in 2013 and 2014 when the stock market rose, inducing many investors to sell shares. The governor and legislature agreed to use the surplus to build up a "rainy day" fund and to pay off many old bonds issued when the budget was in deficit.

In contrast to the decade beginning in 2010, the first decade of the 2000s was one long downward trend, the result of difficult and tough decisions. The budgets of all three segments of public higher education deteriorated substantially in the face of ever rising numbers of entering students. Other budget reductions included rates and services of Medi-Cal (California's medical program for the poor), many cost-containment measures in state programs for the developmentally disabled, and the elimination of local government redevelopment agencies and their state funding (see Chapter 9). Prisoners were sent from the state prisons to local jails, and many state responsibilities were passed to the local level of government. The fiscal years around 2014 show that California can have budget-surplus years as well as deficits, but no one should think that a permanent era of plenty has arrived. California's budget is unduly responsive to the economy and especially to capital gains. When the next recession arrives, and it *will* arrive, revenues will dive again. As Governor Jerry Brown said after delivering his 2018 budget (a budget with a strong surplus) message: "What's out there is darkness, uncertainty, decline and recession," meaning that the problem is that no one knows when the next recession will begin or how severe it will be.

California state government thus faces a series of paradoxes. On the one hand, we see progress in cutting the deficit and in making the hard decisions necessary to weather the national economic storm. On the other hand, the difficulty of those decisions and the fact that taxes can be raised only by a two-thirds majority has meant that a budget crisis occurred every year from 2000 to 2012 and to a lesser extent through 2016. Every decision in the state government became—and still is—a budget decision, a decision made solely, or almost solely, on the basis of whether there is enough money and a budget source for the considered activity.

Let us take a closer look at some reasons for the recurring crises despite the promise of California state government.

The Ease of Passing Initiatives

One factor in these recurring crises is certainly the ease with which **special interests** collect signatures to propose, campaign for, and sometimes pass initiatives to help their own causes. The initiative was added to the California Constitution by the Progressive movement in 1911 as a way to promote the involvement of the people in public policy and affairs. One recent example of a special interest using the initiative for its own gain was Proposition 15 on the June 2010 ballot, which ostensibly allowed taxpayers to have more control over their government but was in fact designed to keep local public utilities from competing against Pacific Gas and Electric (PG&E). Similarly, Proposition 33 on the November 2012 ballot ostensibly allowed insurance companies to give longevity discounts to drivers who had continuous insurance coverage from another insurance company; in fact, this initiative was designed to give one insurance company the ability to raise rates on drivers who had lapses in insurance coverage. Another example was the November 2016 referendum on the law banning single-use plastic bags statewide. The sponsors of the referendum, opposed to the law, made—you guessed it—plastic bags. In general, the initiative has ceased to promote direct democracy for at least the last two decades. Instead, it has mostly become just another method by which special interests convince voters who are paying little attention to government and politics to enact rules, laws, and constitutional amendments that benefit a particular interest at the expense of the public as a whole. While there are exceptions, far too many initiatives fall into this category.

To place an initiative on the ballot requires 5 percent of the votes at the last gubernatorial election for an initiative statute and 8 percent for initiative constitutional amendments. With the number of votes cast for governor in 2014 at 7,317,581 (only 42.2 percent of registered voters and 29.9 percent of voter-eligible adults), the number of signatures was lowered to 365,880 for an initiative statute and 585,407 for an initiative constitutional amendment, the lowest number since the 1975–78 period. It is thus easier to place an initiative on the ballot today than it has been in some time.

Term Limits

The **term limit** movement found fertile ground in California in the 1980s and 1990s. Proposition 140 in 1990 imposed what were then the severest term limits in the nation on the legislature and the elected officials of the executive branch. The voters in many California cities instituted term limits on their local leaders as well. Part of the statewide anger and consequent push for term limit legislation was directed against Willie Brown, then speaker of the California Assembly, whose flamboyant lifestyle and prolific fund-raising provoked the ire of voters.

The term limits movement's theory is that term limits will encourage members of the Assembly and state Senate to pay more attention to their jobs and spend less time raising money for future campaigns, and that the limits will make the legislative bodies more welcoming to minority and female candidates. Since term limits have been imposed, the proportion of Latino legislators has indeed risen; however, members now have much less expertise on the matters they vote on, and by the time they acquire this expertise they are term-limited out. Additionally, many—perhaps most—members of the legislature spend a good deal of their time in office worrying about their next job and raising funds for future campaigns. Most observers believe that term limits have worsened the legislature, not bettered it, and increased the power of lobbyists and interest groups as inexperienced legislators rely on them for expertise.

While voters strongly support term limits, they recently took a step to address some of the institutional problems that have resulted from them. In June 2012 the voters approved Proposition 28, which allows legislators to serve as many as 12 years in the legislature, as long as those 12 years are served in one house. (The previous total service time was actually higher—14 years—but was capped at 6 years in the Assembly and 8 in the Senate.) Currently, the term limits are 12 years (six terms) for the Assembly, 12 years (three terms) for the state Senate, and 8 years (two terms) for all statewide officials (governor, lieutenant governor, attorney general, controller, secretary of state, treasurer, superintendent of public instruction, insurance commissioner, and the four elected members of the Board of Equalization).

The Two-Thirds Requirement for Raising Taxes

As noted earlier, until the voters passed Proposition 25 in November 2010, California's constitution required a two-thirds vote of the total membership—not just those present and voting—in each house of the legislature to pass the budget. Only three states, Arkansas, California, and Rhode Island, required such a strong **supermajority** to pass the budget. Proposition 25 lowered the required vote to 50 percent plus one. So far, all the budgets passed under the new rules, which financially penalize legislators if the budget is not passed on time, have been passed around June 15, the constitutional deadline.

However, a two-thirds vote of the absolute number of legislators in both houses of the state legislature is still necessary to raise or lower any tax level. With a Republican Party that refuses to countenance tax increases of any kind (plus the taxpayer groups that promise to sue the instant any tax increase is passed), the burden of balancing the state budget has fallen on low- and moderate-income state residents, who benefit disproportionately from the state programs that have been cut. For higher-income state residents, state services are at least partially irrelevant—their major "service" is a low tax rate, as well as exemptions and deductions that enable some of their income to be taxed at a lower rate.

The Democratic Party has had a two-thirds majority in the legislature three times during the last several years. The 2012 elections saw the Democrats win a short-lived supermajority of seats in the legislature, which meant they had enough votes to raise taxes without any Republican support (see Chapter 5). Raising taxes, however, requires the approval of the governor, and former governor Jerry Brown had consistently wanted a balanced budget without additional tax increases beyond those instituted by Proposition 30, approved by voters in November 2012. This proposition enacted a four-year increase in the state sales tax and seven-year increases in the tax rates for citizens making over $250,000 in income (see Chapter 8). The supermajority lasted a little over a year, until early 2014 when three Democrats in the state Senate were suspended over corruption allegations. In 2017 the Democrats again had a two-thirds supermajority, and they did indeed raise a tax: the gas tax, in order to fund highway development and repair, long considered to be sorely needed. Repealing the gas tax increase was a referendum item on the November 2018 ballot, which did not pass. The basic structure of California's tax system, however, has been frozen since the 1960s.

Lack of Consensus on Fundamental Questions

Another reason for California's perpetual state of crisis is the inability of legislators to unify on matters of policy and principle. In order to be effective, a political system must overcome the inertia generated by narrow interests to make decisions that benefit the broader public interest. This is a persistent issue in a large, complex state such as California, but in the past, California politicians have been able to overcome the lack of **consensus** to make progress on significant questions. Has California changed? Why do interest groups cause impasse in the 2000s, when their influence was relatively minimal back in the 1970s and 1980s? After all, we have always had interest groups, and we had the two-thirds decision rule for adopting the budget or raising taxes in the legislature from 1935 until 2010.

Journalist Dan Walters suggests that the blame heaped on the legislature is inappropriate:

> In fact, California's governance maladies stem from the complex, often contradictory nature of the state itself. With its immense geographic, economic, and cultural diversity, California has myriad policy issues, but those same factors also have become an impediment to governance. The state lost its vital consensus on public policy issues, and without that civic compass, its politicians tend to ignore major

Passing a balanced state budget is a perennially contentious issue in California. However, the budget surplus in early 2014 allowed Governor Jerry Brown—shown here breaking down certain state expenditures—to propose budgets for 2014-17 that increased state funding for education and paid off some of the debt that the state had accrued over previous years.

issues and pursue trivial ones. . . . The real issue is whether the public's anger at Gray Davis will morph into a new sense of civic purpose or whether California is destined to be . . . ungovernable.[13]

If you combine the lack of consensus with the swift-moving news cycle typified by Twitter and other social media, you can get a sense of the problem. So far, the events following the recall of Governor Gray Davis in 2003 have indicated very slow progress, with no "new sense of civic purpose." The same old problems seem to vex California's political class over and over.

A recent example concerns the legislature declaring California to be a **sanctuary state**, meaning that the state limits its cooperation with the federal government in accelerating deportations for violations of the immigration laws. SB (Senate Bill) 54 limits state and local law enforcement in helping the federal government enforce the immigration laws, unless the individual concerned has been convicted of one of several hundred serious or violent crimes (in the latter situation, state and local officials cooperate with the federal government in deporting the person concerned). For incarcerated inmates, the state fully cooperates with the federal government. AB (Assembly Bill) 450 generally prohibits both public and private employers from giving federal immigration workers access to the nonpublic areas of a business or government agency unless the federal workers have a warrant. AB 103, the third bill in this area, prevents local governments from contracting with the federal Immigration and Customs Enforcement agency to house immigrant detainees in local jails.

Within a few months, at least six counties and 13 California cities passed resolutions voicing their opposition to the laws or have joined the U.S. Department of Justice lawsuit filed against California. One question is the extent to which a state can refuse to cooperate with the federal government. Another is the extent to which state law can compel local cities and counties to comply. The traditional rule has been "Dillon's Rule" (see Chapter 9), under which subgovernmental units within states lack the rights of a federal state and can be governed as a state wishes, subject to the state's own constitution and laws. Whether that will apply in this case we shall have to see.

Reform Ideas

In addition to the steps already taken (as discussed earlier), numerous reforms have been suggested over the years to address the institutional hindrances to effective California governance. Some of the standard ones are listed below. See how many you agree with as you begin reading this book. You might check this section at the end of your course to see if you still have the same opinion. You might not!

On the liberal side:

- **Instituting public financing of election campaigns. Public financing** would reduce the impact of money on Assembly, state Senate, and congressional campaigns because all or most campaign funding would come from the state, not from interests who want something in return for these donations. It would also lessen the impact of fund-raising on members of the legislature, some of whom spend up to half their time in Sacramento raising money. However, it would be difficult to devise a system that would not unduly benefit incumbents, who are typically better known than their challengers.

- **Lowering the required supermajority to raise taxes** from two-thirds to some lower, more achievable, percentage, such as 55 or 60 percent. This proposal would require an amendment to the state constitution, probably impossible on a tax issue such as this unless it is proposed as part of a broad package of tax relief and reform.

- **Restricting the initiative process** to allow more citizen participation and lessen the need to hire professional firms to collect signatures and run initiative campaigns. This would require lengthening the time allowed to collect signatures even more than the recent change from 150 days to 180. Changing an initiative process that California's citizens hold in high regard would be a tough sell, and the industry that sponsors initiatives and makes money from them might well oppose it, making the campaign expensive.

- **Realigning the tax structure** to match the state's shift from a manufacturing economy to a service-based one (see Chapter 8). The most powerful method for doing this would be to change the sales tax to make it apply to services such as medical care and automobile repair. In order to pass, this would have to be sold as decreasing the sales-tax rate. Several recent commissions have indicated interest, but few politicians want to be associated with the cause.

On the conservative side:

- **Changing the legislature from full time to part time.** This idea is popular in Tea Party circles, reflecting their nostalgia for an earlier era and their desire for a less expensive government, not to mention the typical Californian's distrust of the legislature. However, it would weaken the legislature's level of expertise on the programs it is expected to enact and oversee. Term limits, another measure taken to limit the legislature, have clearly weakened the average legislator's knowledge of the subject areas the legislature oversees.

- **Lowering California's tax rates**, making the system less progressive in the process. This is popular among conservatives but is a tough sell for liberals and Democrats.

- **Improving California's business climate** with lower taxes and fewer regulations. Almost everyone agrees that this goal is laudable, but there is little agreement on what taxes to lower (or how to make up the difference financially) and what regulations to simplify or abolish.

Most of these ideas involve so much controversy that they have little chance of being enacted, at least in the short run. Enacting major reforms such as those just listed is much easier through the ballot box (that is, via an initiative) than it is through the legislature, where constitutional changes require a two-thirds vote of the Assembly and the Senate before being placed on the ballot for ratification.

Conclusion

In this book we are going to consider the real world of California politics and the possibilities, both fascinating and frustrating, of the present, as well as changes that might make the future more positive for both politicians and the public. We will investigate what makes California different from other states and examine its unique political problems, which include the following:

- the inability to balance the budget year after year (the most recent years under Governor Jerry Brown are an exception)

- the malapportioned districts for the California legislature that, in combination with the primary system, produce legislators who are more liberal than the public on the Democratic side and more conservative than the public on the Republican side (we shall see whether the new top-two primary system and the non-gerrymandered legislative districts make any difference in this area)

- the public's attachment to the strict term limits

- the public's attachment to extreme majoritarianism, which produces the longest ballots in the nation as well as low turnout rates

Our coverage includes subjects that newspapers and bloggers discuss in great detail, as well as some subjects, such as the California tax system and the impact of Proposition 13, that receive little coverage in the media. Welcome to the journey.

A Guide to This Book

Chapter 2, "The Constitution and the Progressive Legacy," deals with California's state constitution and the Progressives, the two crucial factors that define the shape and direction of today's California government.

Chapters 3 and 4 consider the bodies outside government that influence what government can accomplish. Chapter 3, "Interest Groups and the Media in California," takes a look at the groups that are as prevalent and influential in California as they are in our nation's capital. Chapter 4, "Parties and Elections in California," examines how both parties and voters influence government through elections and campaigns.

Chapters 5, 6, and 7 cover the institutions of government. Chapter 5, "The California Legislature," discusses the legislature, the body we love to hate. We try in this book to understand the legislature and why it functions as it does rather than simply to condemn it. Chapter 6, "The Governor and the Executive Branch," asks whether California has become ungovernable. Chapter 7, "The California Judiciary," deals with judges and the criminal justice system.

Chapters 8, 9, and 10 provide an in-depth guide to policy problems and governmental structures that are particularly relevant today. Chapter 8, "The State Budget and Budgetary Limitations," addresses taxes, spending, and the California budget, asking whether the budget can be controlled in today's political and policy environment with the tools we have available to us. Chapter 9, "Local Government," considers local government and its dependency on the state, a dependency that localities are taking action to eliminate in part through the initiative process. Chapter 10, "Public Policy in California," delves into several contemporary public policy problems, illustrating how the institutions and voters have acted in these areas.

Study Guide

FOR FURTHER READING

Bonn, Sarah, and Caroline Danielson. *Income Inequality and the Safety Net in California*. Public Policy Institute of California, May 2016. http://ppic.org/main/publication.asp?i=1190. Accessed 7/1/18.

Davis, Mike. *City of Quartz: Excavating the Future in Los Angeles*. New York: Vintage, 1990.

Hill, Laura, and Joseph Hayes. "Just the Facts: Undocumented Immigrants." Public Policy Institute of California, March 2017. http://www.ppic.org/publication/undocumented-immigrants-in-california/. Accessed 7/1/18.

Horwitz, Sasha. *Termed Out: Reforming California's Term Limits*. Center for Governmental Studies, October 2007. www.policyarchive.org/handle/10207/2047. Accessed 7/1/18.

Lewis, Michael. "California and Bust." *Vanity Fair*, November 2011.

Mathews, Joe, and Mark Paul. *California Crackup: How Reform Broke the Golden State and How We Can Fix It*. Berkeley: University of California Press, 2010.

McGhee, Eric, and Daniel Krimm. *California's Political Geography*. Public Policy Institute of California, February 2012. www.ppic.org/main/publication_quick.asp?i=1007. Accessed 7/1/18.

Mejia, Marisol Cuellar, and Hans Johnson. "Just the Facts: Immigrants in California." Public Policy Institute of California, May 2018. http://www.ppic.org/publication/immigrants-in-california/. Accessed 7/1/18.

Olin, Spencer C. *California's Prodigal Sons: Hiram Johnson and the Progressives, 1911–1917*. Berkeley: University of California Press, 1968.

Skelton, George. "California's Capitol—The Long View. A Columnist Looks Back on 50 Years Covering the Ups and Downs of Sacramento." *Los Angeles Times*, December 1, 2011.

ON THE WEB

California Choices. www.californiachoices.org. Accessed 7/1/18.

California Forward. "How to Fix CA's Government." www.cafwd-action.org/pages/how-to-fix-CA-government. Accessed 7/1/18.

Los Angeles Times. www.latimes.com. Accessed 7/1/18.

Public Policy Institute of California. www.ppic.org. Accessed 7/1/18. A think tank devoted to nonpartisan research on how to improve California policy.

Sacramento Bee. www.sacbee.com. Accessed 7/1/18.

San Francisco Chronicle. www.sfgate.com. Accessed 7/1/18.

SUMMARY

I. California politics are important for several reasons.
   A. California is the most populous state, has the fifth largest economy in the world, and has a population more multicultural and diverse than the rest of the nation.
   B. California is strongly majoritarian, and its citizens like it that way.
   C. California is younger than many states, has a greater percentage of college-educated citizens, and is richer than most states.
   D. California has experienced some of the strongest population growth of any state, resulting in a number of political conflicts over the years. The high price of housing, in particular, has been difficult to solve.
   E. California has more immigrants, and more undocumented immigrants, than any other state, although Texas has almost the same proportion of undocumented immigrants.

II. Progress in dealing with California's problems has occurred in the last decade, in spite of the fact that the state is generally considered to be hamstrung by voter-approved rules and regulations.
   A. Redistricting, once the province of the legislature, is now done by a citizens' commission. The new districts (used from 2012 forward) seem to have considerably less gerrymandering than the old.
   B. The party primary election system has been changed to the new "top-two" system, in which the two top vote-getters from the primary election, regardless of party, move to the general election for a runoff.
      1. The new system is more like a swim meet or track meet, with a preliminary heat and final, than a party primary.
   C. In 2010 the voters approved a change to the state constitution so that the legislature could approve the state budget by a majority vote, instead of the prior rule of two-thirds of the total membership of each house of the legislature.
      1. The state constitution still requires any tax increase to be approved by a two-thirds vote of

each house of the legislature, plus the governor's signature.
   D. These changes have not resolved the underlying problems with the state's taxation system, which result in soaring surpluses when the stock market is high and the opposite during recessions.
III. Some reasons for the continual crisis in California state government include the following:
   A. The ease of passing initiatives. Special interests find that the state has a congenial atmosphere in which they can spend several million dollars to collect signatures and fund a campaign to pass a law or change the state constitution in order to benefit the initiative's proposer.
   B. Term limits, in spite of the 2012 change that lengthened the maximum time to 12 years in either the Assembly or the state Senate, still hamper the legislature. By the time legislators learn their jobs, they are often looking for new ones.
   C. The two-thirds vote requirement in the Assembly and state Senate to raise taxes has meant that the only realistic way to balance declining budgets has been to cut services disproportionately used by the lower-middle class and the poor.
   D. The lack of consensus on fundamental questions among both politicians and citizens has made it difficult to build the broad consensus that major change requires.
IV. Reform ideas are abundant but few have the political support necessary for enactment in the short run. Several ideas from both sides of the political spectrum are listed in the text.

PRACTICE QUIZ

1. The budget must be passed by a majority of those present and voting in both chambers of the legislature.
   a) true
   b) false

2. Most states require a two-thirds majority to pass their budgets each year.
   a) true
   b) false

3. According to the text, California's total population, its foreign-born population, and the approximate number of undocumented immigrants living in the state are
   a) 50 million, 5 million, and 2 million.
   b) 34 million, 8.8 million, and 2.4 million.
   c) 25 million, 20 million, and 18 million.
   d) 39.5 million, 10.2 million, and 2.35 million.

4. "Latino" or "Hispanic" is one of the racial categories in the U.S. Census, which is taken every 10 years.
   a) true
   b) false

5. Compared to the proportion of immigrants who speak English at home in the U.S. population, the proportion of immigrants in California who speak English at home is
   a) greater.
   b) lesser.
   c) the same.

6. According to this book, the inability of the California legislature to make decisions that benefit the state as a whole is due to
   a) the influence of interest groups.
   b) the two-thirds requirement to raise taxes.
   c) California's size and diversity.
   d) all of the above

7. California's current term limits are
   a) 8 years for the governor, 4 years for the Assembly, and 6 years for the state Senate.
   b) 6 years for the governor, 6 years for the Assembly, and 8 years for the state Senate.
   c) 8 years for the governor, 12 years for the Assembly, and 12 years for the state Senate.
   d) 8 years for the governor, 8 years for the Assembly, and 12 years for the state Senate.

8. Undocumented immigrants were able to obtain a driver's permit in California as of 2015.
   a) true
   b) false

9. "Majoritarian" as applied to California government means that
   a) the state requires majority rule in all major decisions.
   b) the state does not have a "republican" form of government; it has a "majoritarian" form.
   c) the state makes many important decisions through direct democracy and the initiative process.
   d) the California legislature uses majority rule for all decisions.

10. California's institutions of higher education produce sufficient numbers of graduates to meet the the state's workforce needs in the foreseeable future.
    a) true
    b) false

11. California's "top-two" primary is more like an athletic event with preliminary heats and finals than it is a political party primary.
    a) true
    b) false

CRITICAL-THINKING QUESTIONS

1. How distinctive is California compared with other states? Are we really that different from citizens in the rest of the country?

2. California's population differs from that of other states on several levels. What are the two or three that are most significant, and why are they significant?

3. What are the advantages and disadvantages of the "majoritarian" form of government? Of the "republican" form of government?

4. Consider the disparity between the number of college-educated workers required for the California economy in the future compared with the number that the state will be producing. What happens to a state when it doesn't produce enough college-educated workers for its needs? When it doesn't have housing that workers can afford?

KEY TERMS

California dream (p. 2)
capital gains tax (p. 11)
consensus (p. 14)
cultural diversity (p. 3)
foreign-born (p. 7)
Latino or Hispanic (p. 5)

majoritarian (p. 4)
public financing (p. 15)
racial and ethnic diversity (p. 5)
redistricting (p. 10)
republican (p. 4)
sanctuary state (p. 15)

special interests (p. 12)
supermajority (p. 13)
term limit (p. 12)
top-two primary (p. 10)
two-thirds vote (p. 11)
undocumented immigrants (p. 9)

2 The Constitution and the Progressive Legacy

WHAT CALIFORNIA GOVERNMENT DOES AND WHY IT MATTERS

The purpose of a constitution is to define the rules under which political actors and citizens interact with each other to fulfill their goals as individuals, as members of a group, and as a population as a whole. The California Constitution is long and very detailed, with numerous amendments added over the years that deal with both the fundamental principles and power of government as well as commonplace issues such as the right to fish on government property, English as the state's official language, and grants for stem cell research. Today, California has the second highest number of constitutional amendments (over 500 by some counts), behind Alabama, and the second longest state constitution, behind Louisiana.

One distinctive feature of the California Constitution is that it allows the people to enact both constitutional amendments and legislation through a majority vote without going through the legislature. The process through which citizens make legislation at the ballot box is called the initiative. The initiative developed out of a political movement called Progressivism, which opposed the influence of moneyed special interests in politics and called for political power to be returned to the people. Any individual or group can propose a statute or an amendment to the California Constitution. In 2018 there were five statewide propositions on the June primary ballot and eleven statewide propositions on the November ballot.[1]

However, the initiative process has not always lived up to its progressive ideals. Today, wealthy individuals and special interest groups spend hundreds of millions of dollars on campaigns for and against initiatives. In the November 2016 general election, more than $485 million was spent by both sides on 17 propositions; in 2018, initiative spending topped $379 million. Although the initiative does put legislative power in the hands of the general public, it does not eliminate the influence of money in politics, and—ironically—it bypasses the more careful debate and compromise that might take place in the legislature.

The most expensive ballot proposition battle in 2016 was over Proposition 61, a high-profile initiative to limit state spending on prescription drugs. Supporters of the measure, led by the Los Angeles-based AIDS Healthcare Foundation, spent over $19 million, while pharmaceutical industry opponents, led by Merck, Pfizer, and Johnson & Johnson, spent $109 million. Just two years later, spending on Proposition 8 broke a new record with spending of over $131 million. Proposition 8 would have added new regulations for outpatient kidney dialysis clinics, requiring those clinics to limit the amounts they could charge (and thus to limit their profits). Supporters, led by local unions including the Service Employees International Union-United Healthcare Workers West, spent over $20 million; opponents, led by health care companies specializing in dialysis care clinics, DaVita and Fresenius, spent more than $111 million.

The impetus behind Proposition 8 was a failed effort by the unions to pressure those two companies, who control 70 percent of the dialysis clinics in the state, to allow workers at those clinics to unionize. In short, a labor dispute led to the most expensive ballot initiative battle in California history, and asked regular voters to make a decision that, if the campaign commercials on both sides were to be believed, would endanger the lives of dialysis patients. Many voters were left confused by the competing claims, emphasizing a major weakness of the modern use of the initiative process: it often asks voters to make decisions about issues on which they lack reliable information and expertise.

In the end, Proposition 8 was defeated, losing by a vote of 38.9 percent to 61.1 percent. Overall spending on Proposition 8 was not a record—that distinction falls to the $156 million spent in 2006's battle over Proposition 87, which proposed to reduce petroleum consumption. In that instance, supporters contributed $69.9 million, and opponents contributed $94.4 million. Yet, while spending on Proposition 8 was lower overall, it marks a record spent in opposition to a state ballot proposition. These are just a few examples of an overall pattern: initiative battles in California often are waged with television commercial battles funded by multimillion-dollar donations, a far cry from the return of power to the people that the Progressives intended.

In Chapter 1 we discussed some of the demographic differences between California and other states. We also mentioned that the institutional design of California's government prevents it from solving critical state issues. Here are some of the unique features of the state's political process:

- The **sheer size of the state** increases the cost of political campaigns and media outreach programs.

- The **competing networks of interest groups** cause groups to jockey for position and influence.

- The **increasing use of the initiative** significantly affects state and local governance and policy.

- The **divided executive branch**, composed of nine separately elected officials, each with their own area of authority and responsibility, leads to overlapping responsibilities and fragmentation in the execution of state policy.

- The **widespread, almost universal use of nonpartisan elections at the local level of government** eliminates a valuable clue that helps voters identify the policy positions of the candidates on the ballot.

Aside from the size of the state and its interest-group network, the other characteristics listed above are a result of the **Progressive movement**, which flourished in California from 1900 to 1917. The leaders of this movement focused on one goal: making government more responsive to the political, social, and economic concerns of the people. Their reforms continue to shape California's government and politics in ways that sharply differentiate it from other states. To some, these features hamper the political process and should be changed. To others, they form part of the essence of California. Were they to be changed, that essence would be destroyed.

California's political history is also heavily influenced by the extreme diversity that resulted from the Gold Rush, which took place before the Civil War, from 1848 to 1855. Forty-niners, as the miners were called, came from around the world to make their fortunes—by wagon train across the county or by ship from the west, either sailing around Cape Horn or crossing by canoe and donkey train through the jungles of Panama (the Panama Canal did not exist until half a century later). Canadian merchant William Perkins described the mining town of Sonora in 1849: "Here were to be seen people of every nation in all varieties of costume, and speaking 50 different languages, and yet all mixing together amicably and socially."[2]

At the same time, this diversity, combined with competition over mining claims and other resources, also led to significant racism and discrimination. The vigilante justice of the Gold Rush included violence against Mexicans, South Americans, Chinese, and other foreigners, as well as against the few free Blacks in the area, whom white miners did not believe were entitled to "their" gold. Cycles of violence against Native Americans reduced the state's native population from 150,000 in 1848 to just 30,000 by 1870. As we will see, this racism was often institutionalized in early California's laws and constitutions.

The Rules of the Game: California's Constitution

The California Constitution has a long and storied history that can be divided into four stages:

- **The 1849 Constitution** Written by residents of the territory in anticipation of statehood, this constitution contains many of the basic ideas underlying California's government today.

- **The 1879 Constitution** Written by a constitutional convention in 1878, this is the basic governing document, with amendments, that is in force today.

- **From 1900 to 1917** During this period, the Progressives amended the constitution and passed laws to temper the power of special interests and make government responsive to the people's desires and needs. The most prominent reforms of this period are the initiative, referendum, and recall.

- **From 1918 to the present** Amendment after amendment lengthened the state's constitution, resulting in a document that at one point was almost 100,000 words long. Several commissions proposed substantive changes, but only two commissions, one in the 1960s and the other in the 1990s, saw their proposals realized: the constitution's language was shortened and clarified, but no substantial changes were made to its provisions.

The 1849 Constitution

Gold was discovered in California in January 1848; news spread slowly until President James Polk mentioned it in his State of the Union message to Congress on December 5, 1848. In 1849, 80,000 fortune seekers from around the world moved to California, tripling the area's non-native population past the minimum needed to apply for statehood and also increasing the need for a formal government to impose order.[3] Yet, since the start of the Mexican-American War, Americans had been bitterly divided over whether to allow slavery in any new acquired territories. During congressional debate on a bill sought by President Polk to fund treaty negotiations, Pennsylvania congressman David Wilmot proposed the Wilmot Proviso, an amendment to eliminate slavery within any land acquired as a result of the Mexican-American War. Although the amendment was killed in the Senate, it enflamed the growing controversy over slavery, as the South understood that slavery was now seriously under attack. In 1849 newly elected president Zachary Taylor proposed that California and New Mexico be admitted as free states (states, unlike formal territories, had the power to decide for themselves whether to allow slavery). As Congress debated over what to do with the newly acquired lands, including border disputes between Texas and New Mexico, California citizens elected delegates to a constitutional convention. These included famous pre-1846 settlers such as John Sutter, as well as eight *Californios*, among them General Mariano Guadalupe Vallejo.

Meeting in Monterey, the 48 elected delegates met for 37 days between September 1 and October 13, 1849. They drafted a constitution that relied heavily on the Iowa Constitution and to a lesser degree on the New York Constitution. The

California electorate ratified the constitution in November 1849, and on December 15 California formally petitioned Congress for admission to the Union.

The basic provisions of the 1849 Constitution are still in force:

- The framework of the government rests on a separation of powers—executive, legislative, and judicial—interacting through a system of checks and balances, like the federal government.

- Executive power is divided, with the separate election and jurisdiction of the governor, lieutenant governor, comptroller, treasurer, attorney general, surveyor general, and superintendent of public instruction. This division weakens the governor, who cannot appoint—or remove—senior members of his or her own administration. Moreover, each of these statewide officials is a potential competitor for the governor's office, and each can release statements that contradict what the governor is saying.

- An extensive bill of rights begins the constitution.

- The legislature is elected and consists of two houses, one called the Senate, the other the Assembly.

However, there are notable differences between the 1849 Constitution and the framework that exists today:

- The right to vote at that time was limited to white (including white Mexican) males 21 years of age or older who had lived in California for at least six months. Another provision denied citizenship to African Americans, Chinese Americans, and Native Americans; they were also prohibited from testifying against whites in court. The legislature could, by a two-thirds vote, enfranchise Native Americans "in such special cases as such proportion of the legislative body may deem just and proper."

- The judiciary was elected, as judges are today, but they were organized into four levels—as Mexico's judiciary was at the time.

- All laws and other provisions were to be published in both English and Spanish, since California was a bilingual state.

The nativism and racism in the 1849 Constitution reflected the competitive greed of the Gold Rush. Miners overran Native American territories and organized themselves into gangs to drive natives away. Volunteer infantries attacked and massacred villages. As mining became more difficult and fortunes more elusive, white miners increasingly believed they were entitled to the gold and that people of color were not. They defended this privilege with violence, as well as with laws and constitutional provisions. Mexican Americans, whose claims to citizenship and property ownership had been promised in the Treaty of Guadalupe Hidalgo, were victims of state-sanctioned violence and claim jumping, and lost their land to white settlers.

In July 1850 the sudden death of President Taylor, who wanted to exclude slavery from the Southwest, and the accession of Vice President Millard Fillmore, who was anxious to resolve the border dispute between Texas and New Mexico, paved the way for the federal government to pass a series of five bills that together composed the Compromise of 1850. The package balanced the interests of slave owners and abolitionists, allowing California admission to the Union as a free state on September 9, 1850.

California's 1849 Constitution quickly proved to be problematic. Its framers had neglected to include provisions for the financial stability of the new government; within the first five years, California was in deficit. There were few provisions for taxation but no limits on spending, legislative salaries, or the governor's pardon power.[4] Four times between 1859 and 1873 the legislature called for a new constitutional convention to fix obvious defects; each time, too many voters left their ballots blank to achieve the necessary majority to approve the convention.

Additionally, the provision that California was a free state was not immediately successful. Proslavery lawmakers and judges worked to undermine the constitution and cement the rights of slave owners, culminating in the California Fugitive Slave Law of 1852. Slaves and free Blacks found themselves dragged before state courts and remanded to their self-professed owners, even if they had earned or purchased their emancipation. The law expired in 1855, but proslavery sentiment (and legal victories) continued until 1858, coinciding with the rise of the free soil Republican Party.

The 1879 Constitution

The call for a new constitutional convention finally succeeded in 1877, as California suffered from the worst recession in the brief history of the nation. The Panic of 1873 began in September 1873 with a series of bank failures and the closing of the New York Stock Exchange. As railroads went bankrupt and businesses failed, wages were cut and unemployment spiked, leading to the Great Railroad Strike of 1877. Although the depression technically ended in the spring of 1879, the tension in the labor market persisted. This included increased resentment of Chinese railroad workers, who were often willing to work for much lower wages. For example, in 1870, Union Pacific in Wyoming hired Chinese laborers for $32.50 a month, while whites were asking for $52 a month.

At a July 1877 rally in San Francisco meant to organize support for striking railroad workers in the East, a mob of hundreds broke away from the meeting and charged through the center of the city, sparking a riot that lasted for three nights and spread throughout the city. Rioters attacked Chinese homes and businesses, mostly laundries, and threatened establishments that employed Chinese workers. Several people died over the course of the riots and dozens were injured.

The riots created a movement determined to settle "the Chinese question" and workers' grievances. Called the Workingmen's Party of California, the movement was led by Irish immigrant Denis Kearney. Under Kearney's leadership, the party adopted a platform to break up monopolies, redistribute wealth, and remove Chinese residents from California. His rallying cry was, "The Chinese must go!"[5] The Workingmen became a force in Bay Area politics, winning a seat in the state Senate in early 1878 and electing officials in San Francisco, Oakland, and Alameda. The Kearneyites also won almost all of the San Francisco delegate seats for the 1878 constitutional convention, where they worked to include their anti-Chinese demands in the new constitution.

Article XIX of the 1879 Constitution banned private and public employment of Chinese workers. The laws enacting these provisions were swiftly struck down in federal courts that ruled they violated the Fourteenth Amendment's guarantee of equal protection, infringed on rights due to Chinese immigrants under treaty, and trampled upon corporate rights. However, anti-Chinese sentiment persisted. (The voters of California formally repealed Article XIX in 1952.)

Anti-Chinese sentiment didn't suddenly appear in the 1870s; it had been brewing for decades. In the peak year of gold rush immigration in 1852, 20,000 Chinese immigrants came to San Francisco in search of gold. Mirroring the racist attitudes that stripped Mexicans of their claims, white miners also believed Chinese immigrants were not entitled to "their" gold. Anti-Chinese prejudice led to a ruling that Chinese miners could only work claims that white miners had abandoned as worthless, and white prospectors often attacked Chinese miners. In 1850 the California legislature adopted a Foreign Miners License Law, charging all non-U.S. citizens $20 per month. The exorbitant fee led many Chinese (and others, including thousands of Mexicans) to abandon the mining camps and move to San Francisco, where they created America's first Chinatown, before the law was repealed in 1851. A new foreign miners' tax of $4 per month soon followed, and anti-Chinese feeling persisted in the mining camps.

In the 1840s and 1850s most of the country saw the rise of the American Party (the "Know Nothing" Party), which focused on protecting Americans from the influx of Catholic immigrants. The San Francisco chapter of the Know Nothings, founded in 1854, focused instead on opposing Chinese immigration. The party enjoyed sweeping victories in the state election of 1855, including that of 30-year-old gubernatorial candidate James Neely Johnson (the youngest governor in California history), and large majorities in both houses of the legislature. While the party soon faded, xenophobia and racism persisted.

In 1863 work began on the Central Pacific railroad line, to run from Sacramento to the East, and Chinese workers had the physical courage and intellectual

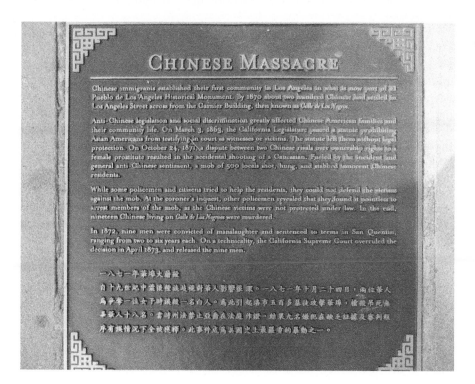

Decades of xenophobia and racism against Chinese immigrants in California culminated in the largest mass lynching in American history. The lives lost in the Chinese Massacre are memorialized here in this bilingual plaque in Los Angeles.

resourcefulness to lay the track and blast routes through the Sierras. They were also willing to work for lower wages, as noted above. When the railroads were completed in the early 1870s, Chinese workers moved into new jobs, including in agriculture as farm workers. As the economy worsened in the 1870s, white Californians blamed Chinese residents for their economic woes. Newspaper editorials attacked Chinese residents as inferior and immoral. Calls for an end to Chinese immigration grew louder, and incidents of anti-Chinese violence became more frequent. White mobs attacked Chinese communities throughout California in the 1870s. On October 24, 1871, a mob in Los Angeles massacred at least 17 Chinese men and boys in the largest mass lynching in American history, and looted the Chinese section of town.

It was in this context of economic anxiety and hostility toward Chinese immigrants that delegates met to decide how best to reorganize the government of California. The delegates at the 1878–79 constitutional convention adopted a large number of diverse provisions. Among these were the shifting of responsibility for the debts of a corporation to stockholders and various new rules regarding the railroads: the railroads could not give free passes to those holding political office, they could not raise rates on one line to compensate for reductions made to compete on alternative lines, and they would be regulated by a railroad commission.

These provisions added words—almost doubling the constitution's size—and policies that read very much like a series of laws rather than a fundamental framework within which laws could operate. In this way, the California Constitution differs greatly from the federal U.S. Constitution, whose articles and amendments deal strictly with institutional procedures and rules that construct a governmental framework. The Eighteenth Amendment stands as the only experiment in establishing a substantive policy in the U.S. Constitution; it prohibits the manufacture, sale, import, or export of alcohol and was repealed with the Twenty-First Amendment just 14 years later.

At the time, however, the many specific, substantive policies in the drafted California Constitution were viewed as beneficial, and it was approved by a vote of 54 to 46 percent in May 1879, with 90 percent of those eligible to vote participating. Most of the reform measures were not put into practice right away, as corporate and railroad power continued to dominate the state and sued to block their implementation. These setbacks were temporary, however. In a matter of three decades the broad reforms of the Progressive movement gained passage, weakening the grip of these special interests in the legislature and reshaping the landscape of California politics.

One notable feature of the 1879 Constitution is the procedures it established for amendment. The federal Constitution and every state constitution in the United States include procedures for their own amendment, but these procedures vary considerably. The U.S. Constitution is one of the most difficult to amend in the world, requiring a two-thirds majority vote in the House and Senate followed by ratification by three-fourths of the states.[6] This very high hurdle explains in part why the U.S. Constitution has only been amended 27 times since 1789. In contrast, the California Constitution is much easier to amend. (See Figure 2.1 for an overview of the different paths through which the constitution can be amended.) Convening a constitutional convention is a more dramatic method of reform and has rarely been used. It is not particularly difficult, however, to get 8 percent of voters in the most recent gubernatorial election to sign a petition adding an amendment to the next ballot; the amendment then needs a simple majority vote to

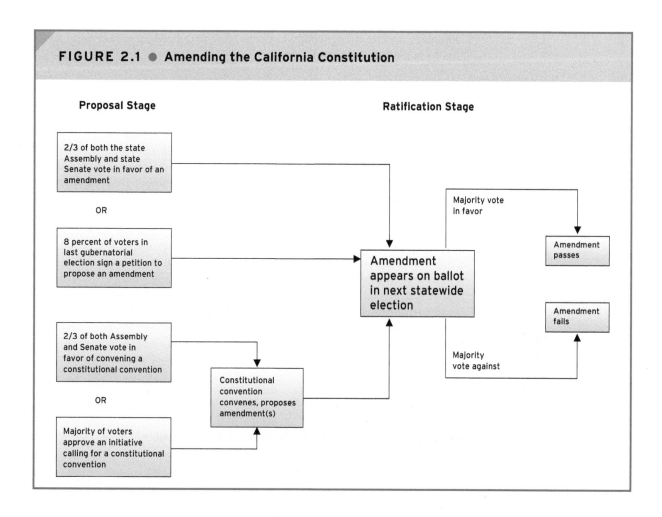

FIGURE 2.1 ● Amending the California Constitution

Proposal Stage

Ratification Stage

2/3 of both the state Assembly and state Senate vote in favor of an amendment

OR

8 percent of voters in last gubernatorial election sign a petition to propose an amendment

2/3 of both Assembly and Senate vote in favor of convening a constitutional convention

OR

Majority of voters approve an initiative calling for a constitutional convention

Constitutional convention convenes, proposes amendment(s)

Amendment appears on ballot in next statewide election

Majority vote in favor

Majority vote against

Amendment passes

Amendment fails

pass. This method has been used more than any other to amend the California Constitution.

You can get a sense of the California Constitution and how different it is from the U.S. Constitution by examining California's bill of rights, called the "Declaration of Rights." The federal Bill of Rights consists of the first 10 amendments to the U.S. Constitution, and while other amendments may be passed, the first 10 will remain the Bill of Rights as they were written. California's bill of rights, meanwhile, can be expanded or rewritten as times change, and it therefore reflects the political changes and conflicts that have occurred over time, with some of the rights described in much greater specificity than the corresponding federal rights. You can see an example of this specificity in the provisions for freedom of speech as they apply to a newspaper. The federal Constitution has the familiar First Amendment:

> Congress shall make no law respecting an establishment of religion, or prohibiting the free exercise thereof; or abridging the freedom of speech, or of the press; or the right of the people peaceably to assemble, and to petition the Government for a redress of grievances.

California's corresponding section has both more detail and more specificity, since it has been amended over time.

> SEC. 2. (a) Every person may freely speak, write and publish his or her sentiments on all subjects, being responsible for the abuse of this right. A law may not restrain or abridge liberty of speech or press.
>
> (b) A publisher, editor, reporter, or other person connected with or employed upon a newspaper, magazine, or other periodical publication, or by a press association or wire service, or any person who has been so connected or employed, shall not be adjudged in contempt by a judicial, legislative, or administrative body, or any other body having the power to issue subpoenas, for refusing to disclose the source of any information procured while so connected or employed for publication in a newspaper, magazine, or other periodical publication, or for refusing to disclose any unpublished information obtained or prepared in gathering, receiving, or processing of information for communication to the public. Nor shall a radio or television news reporter or other person connected with or employed by a radio or television station, or any person who has been so connected or employed, be so adjudged in contempt for refusing to disclose the source of any information procured while so connected or employed for news or news commentary purposes on radio or television, or for refusing to disclose any unpublished information obtained or prepared in gathering, receiving, or processing of information for communication to the public.

Note the use of modern language, such as *wire service* and *television*.

From 1900 to 1917: The Progressive Movement

Pressure for political reform did not end with the 1879 Constitution. Beginning at the turn of the twentieth century, the Progressives pursued three goals: reduce corporate political influence, eliminate the political corruption that accompanied such influence, and democratize the political process.[7]

The Progressives understood that these goals had to be accomplished before they could address equally pressing but more mundane concerns of the time. They accomplished all of their goals—and much more. Beginning with the 1911 legislative session, these reformers passed dozens of constitutional amendments and statutes that changed the face of California government and politics.[8] The most prominent of the political reforms were the following:

- **Nonpartisanship**   This is the norm in local elections and means that no party label is affixed to the candidates' names on the ballot. Of the more than 19,000 elected public officials in California, fewer than 300 are elected in partisan races.

- **Primary elections**   Before the institution of primary elections, political parties chose their candidates in party conventions (the stereotypical smoky back room) or caucuses—meetings of party members at the local level. In a primary election, each prospective party nominee has to obtain more votes than any other prospective nominee in order to run as the party's candidate in the November general election. (This system was changed again in 2010; see next section.)

- **The office block ballot**   This is the ballot that we vote on today, with a "block" for each office and the candidates listed for that office. Before this reform, in some elections, voters cast ballots for their preferred party, not for individual candidates.

- **Direct democracy**   These grassroots processes—the initiative, referendum, and recall—give citizens the ability to exert some control over both the legislative and executive branches. In this way, citizens can rein in the abuse of power by elected officials or reignite officials who have become paralyzed by inaction and partisan bickering. These processes will be examined in detail later in the chapter.

- **The civil service**   An essential element of the Progressive reform movement was the implementation of a civil service in which government employees are selected on the basis of merit, replacing the spoils system in which employees are selected based on their personal connections to the party in power. In California, the 1913 Civil Service Act created a Civil Service Commission to eliminate politics and the spoils system among the state's public employees.

During this period, the California Constitution grew substantially as the legislature enacted dozens of constitutional amendments and statutes. In the first three months of 1911 alone, the legislature passed more than 800 statutes and 23 constitutional amendments.

From 1960 to the Present: Late Revisions

In 1963 the legislature created a constitution revision commission as a result of a 1962 initiative. The commission, composed of 50 citizens, 3 state senators, and 3 Assembly members, submitted two major reports containing recommended revisions to the state constitution. The legislature incorporated these into 14 constitutional amendments and submitted them to the voters for approval between 1966 and 1976; the voters approved 10. These amendments simplified, shortened, and reorganized the constitution but made few substantive changes to it.

In 1993 the legislature again established a constitution revision commission, which proposed a number of substantial changes, some of which reformers had discussed for generations. For a variety of reasons, including the difficulty of achieving the two-thirds vote in the Assembly and Senate required to place the proposed changes on the ballot, they were never submitted to the voters.

In 2010 the voters implemented a change to the primary election system that echoed the effort of many Progressive Era reforms to further democratize the political process. This change replaced the party primaries with a "top-two" primary election, in which the top two candidates from a list of all candidates, regardless of party, proceed to the November runoff. The new system is no longer a party primary; instead it is like a swim meet or track meet, with preliminary and final races.

Despite its numerous amendments, the California Constitution is not well suited to a state that is 25 times larger than it was in 1900. The legislature is the same size, with 40 state senators and 80 Assembly members, but each state Senate district has grown from just over 60,000 persons to almost 1 million; legislators are able to offer far less individualized attention to their constituents than they could in an earlier era (see the "Who Are Californians?" feature on the facing page). In the early twentieth century, small amateur groups could utilize the initiative, but well-funded interest groups are now uniquely able to take advantage of it. Unfortunately, serious efforts to modernize state government have been few and far between, and when they have occurred, as with the constitutional revision commission of the 1990s, the results have been subject to partisan voting and have not achieved the majorities necessary to send them to the people for a final decision.

The Progressive Movement and Its Impact on California Politics

The development of California's distinctive constitution has been influenced by many different groups over the course of the state's history. One group whose influence is still deeply felt in California politics is the Progressives. The Progressive movement had roots in the economic and political changes that swept the United States after the Civil War. It was foreshadowed by the Populist movement, which dominated American politics from 1870 to 1896.

Some of the political concerns and much of the moral indignation expressed by the Populists about the changes taking place in the United States were subsequently reflected in the Progressive movement. From the Civil War on, the country rapidly industrialized, and wealth became concentrated in the hands of a new breed of corporate entrepreneurs. *Monopoly* was the word of the day. These corporate giants dictated economic policy, with significant social and political consequences. One huge corporation, the Southern Pacific Railroad, held a monopoly on shipping in California and could charge producers and retailers exorbitant prices. Its vast wealth and power gave it undue influence not only economically but also politically; along with a web of associated interests, it ruled the state to a degree previously unparalleled in the nation. Bribing public officials was not unusual, nor was handpicking candidates for the two major political parties.[9]

The Progressives countered the powerful corporations, specifically the Southern Pacific Railroad, by prosecuting the corrupt politicians who served them. Eventually, this tactic led to a series of regulatory reforms that loosened the choke hold of the railroad, corrupt politicians, and interest groups on state and local politics.

Local Politics

Progressive reforms began at the local level. The battle against the Southern Pacific Railroad and corporate influence in general started in San Francisco in 1906, with the reform movement fighting to rid city government of graft and bribery. President Theodore Roosevelt stepped in to help. Working hand in hand with James D. Phelan, the former mayor of San Francisco, Roosevelt sent in federal agents led by William J. Burns to investigate bribery and corruption charges.[10] Public officials were put on trial for bribery, bringing to the public's attention the extent of graft and political corruption in municipal government, and 17 supervisors and a number of corporate leaders were indicted.[11] The mayor was forced to resign, and his henchman, Abraham Reuf, who implicated officials of the Southern Pacific Railroad and several utility companies, was convicted and sentenced to 14 years in jail. Although the graft trials largely failed to convict those indicted (Reuf was an

Who Draws the Lines in California?

The Constitution of 1879 provided for 80 Assembly and 40 Senate districts based on population, and after each U.S. Census the lines were supposed to be redrawn by the state legislature (to account for births, deaths, and people moving). This procedure was followed until 1910, when conflict between urban and rural areas led to the Reapportionment Act of 1911, which shortchanged the growing urban areas of Los Angeles and San Francisco. In 1926, a constitutional amendment made representation in the California Senate even more unequal. In 1964, this unequal representation was declared unconstitutional by the U.S. Supreme Court (in Reynolds v. Sims), leading to new districts of roughly equivalent populations.

In 2008, California voters approved a constitutional amendment that placed redistricting in the hands of the new Citizens Redistricting Commission. The new districts took effect for the June 5, 2012 primary. The commission drew new districts that followed a set of nonpartisan rules, such as creating geographically compact districts that kept existing cities and communities intact, and they are not allowed to take into consideration where incumbents live or the partisan tilt of district voters. How do the most recent changes compare to the districts in 1961 and 2001, before the amendment that assigned restricting to the Citizens Redistricting Commission?

Population per district

■ 50,000 or less   ■ 50,001 – 99,999   ■ 100,000 – 199,999   ■ 200,000 – 499,999   ■ 500,000 – 999,999   ■ 1,000,000 or more

State Senate Districts, 1961	**State Senate Districts, 2001**	**State Senate Districts, 2016**
		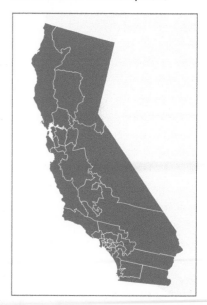

SOURCES: Join California, "Election History for the State of California" www.joincalifornia.com/; Don A. Allen Sr., Legislative Sourcebook (1965); California Citizens Redistricting Commission, www.wedrawthelines.ca.gov (accessed 12/07/18).

forcriticalanalysis

1. Does the large population size of current Assembly and State Senate districts make it difficult for Californians to truly be represented in the legislature?

2. If the plan adopted by California in 1926 is unconstitutional because representation is unequal, why is it that the representation in the U.S. Senate is not invalid?

This cartoon from 1882 depicts the Southern Pacific Railroad as a destructive octopus with farmers, miners, lumber dealers, and other victims of the company's monopoly on shipping entangled in its tentacles. The faces of Mark Hopkins and Leland Stanford, two of the railroad's founders, form the creature's eyes.

THE CURSE OF CALIFORNIA.

exception), they were nonetheless an important step in breaking the power of the Southern Pacific Railroad and its political allies.

In 1906 the Southern Pacific Railroad also dominated local politics in Los Angeles.[12] During this time, a group dedicated to good government, the Non-Partisan Committee of One Hundred, was formed. They selected a reform candidate for mayor who was opposed by the two major parties, labor groups, and the *Los Angeles Times*. While the reform candidate lost his bid for the mayoralty, 17 of 23 reform candidates for other city positions were elected.[13] The nonpartisan reformers were on their way to ridding the city of the Southern Pacific machine.

State Politics

The 1907 legislative session was one of the most corrupt on record, heavily controlled by the political operatives of the Southern Pacific Railroad. At the end of the session, the editor of the *Fresno Republican*, Chester Rowell, wrote, "If we are fit to govern ourselves, this is the last time we will submit to be governed by the hired bosses of the Southern Pacific Railroad Company."[14]

At the same time, Rowell and Edward Dickson of the *Los Angeles Express* began to organize a statewide movement to attack Southern Pacific's power. At Dickson's invitation, a group of lawyers, newspaper publishers, and other political reformers met in Los Angeles. They founded the Lincoln Republicans, later to become the League of Lincoln-Roosevelt Republican Clubs (also known as the Lincoln-Roosevelt League), dedicated to ending the control of California politics by the Southern Pacific Railroad and linking themselves to the national Progressive movement.

The Lincoln-Roosevelt League participated in the statewide legislative elections of 1908 and managed to elect a small group of reformers to the legislature. Two years later it fielded a full-party slate, from governor down to local candidates.

STATEHOUSE VICTORY In 1910, Hiram Johnson became the Lincoln-Roosevelt League candidate for governor. He campaigned up and down the state, focusing on one issue: the Southern Pacific Railroad. He claimed that the company, acting in concert with criminal elements, had corrupted the political process in California. He defined the battle as one between decent, law-abiding citizens and a few corrupt, powerful individuals who were determined to run the state in their own best interests.

Johnson won the election and met with leading national Progressives—Theodore Roosevelt, Robert La Follette, and Lincoln Steffens—to discuss a reform program for California. The new administration in Sacramento set out to eliminate every special interest from the government and to make government solely responsive to the people and Johnson. Through a series of legislative acts and constitutional amendments, they made significant progress in that direction. In 1911 the voters passed the initiative, the referendum, and the recall. These three reforms, widely known as **direct democracy**, placed enormous power and control over government in the hands of the voters. Now citizens could write their laws or amend the constitution through the initiative, approve or reject constitutional amendments through the referendum, and remove corrupt politicians from office through the recall.

In addition to these reforms, a new law set up a railroad commission that had power to fix rates beginning in 1911. Other reforms included the direct primary, which gave ordinary citizens the power to select the candidates of the political parties for national and state offices. Women obtained the right to vote in California in 1911. Legislation was also enacted that limited women to an eight-hour workday, set up a workmen's compensation system, put into practice a weekly pay law, and required employers to inform strikebreakers that they were being hired to replace employees on strike (and therefore might face verbal abuse and physical violence). These reforms were in part a reaction to what were viewed as harsh employment practices by Southern Pacific Railroad.

The Progressives in California made significant headway in limiting the influence of corporations and political parties in politics. In its first two years in office, the Johnson administration succeeded in breaking the power of the Southern Pacific Railroad.[15]

LAST HURRAH The national Progressive Party lost its bid to capture the White House in 1912 with Theodore Roosevelt on the ticket for president and Hiram Johnson for vice president. The failure to win an important national office weakened the party by lessening the enthusiasm of its supporters. It also meant that the party had no patronage with which to reward its followers between elections. Electoral failure was just one of several major problems that plagued the Progressives. Several other factors also contributed to the decline of the party: the public grew tired of reform; there was a major falling out among the leadership in California; the Progressives generally opposed World War I, which was supported by the overwhelming majority of the American public once the country got into the war; and the party failed to support reforms that labor badly wanted.

When the Progressives learned that the Republican Party would not nominate Roosevelt in 1916, they offered him the nomination. Roosevelt declined. At a dinner in San Francisco in July 1916, the California Progressive Party disbanded and Hiram Johnson urged his followers to join either the Republican or the Democratic Party. Later that year Johnson, now a Republican, was elected to the U.S. Senate, where he served for 28 years.

Despite the success of the Progressive reforms mentioned above, one major flaw in Progressive thinking was the belief in an active, informed citizenry willing to participate in politics. Progressives believed that, given the opportunity, citizens would be happy to support the democratic process and spend whatever time and effort was needed to participate in politics. Since the late 1940s, however, a host of studies have shown that many people neither vote nor pay attention to politics. Nevertheless, the Progressives left behind the significant legacy of having gained tremendous political power for the people of California, if and when they choose to use it. As noted later in this chapter, however, many of these powers are most often used by moneyed interests rather than by members of the general public.

Another flaw was that although Progressives wanted to increase political participation, that support applied only to white citizens. Many Progressives were racists, believing Blacks and immigrants from Eastern and Southern Europe to be genetically inferior to immigrants from Western Europe. Federal immigration policies of the era, including the Immigration Act of 1917 and the National Quota Law of 1921, were designed to increase immigration from Western and Northern Europe, to decrease immigration from Southern and Eastern Europe, and to exclude immigration from Asia.

Progressives particularly discriminated against Japanese Americans. In 1913 state legislators passed the California Alien Land Law of 1913, prohibiting "aliens ineligible from citizenship" from owning land or possessing long-term leases. The law applied to all Asian immigrants but was mainly aimed at Japanese farmers, with the further aim of reducing Japanese immigration. Japanese immigration had surged beginning in 1900, with many Japanese immigrants settling in rural areas of southern California to work in agriculture and fishing. Anti-Japanese sentiment soon followed; the California legislature in January 1901 urged Congress to protect American labor by restricting Japanese immigration; a second resolution was approved in March 1905. In 1920 voters approved by a 75–25 percent margin a ballot proposition to close loopholes in the 1913 measure, stoked by fears that Japanese people could not assimilate and that their birth rate was so high that they would eventually replace white people. While the two laws failed to have much effect, and were eventually struck down as unconstitutional, their passage reflects the era's hostility.

The Progressives' strategies to gain power for the people were appropriate for 1910, when California had a population of 2.4 million. Since then, however, California has grown so much and so quickly that its constitution has been unable to catch up. In a state of 39.5 million people, reforms that allowed "the people" to propose initiatives and recall public officials cannot now be exercised on a statewide[16] level without a great deal of money, organization, and professional help. The last initiative that did *not* use paid, professional signature gatherers was introduced in 1990, and it relied on a paid campaign coordinator. An initiative organized completely by volunteers has not been successful since 1984.

Direct Democracy

The Progressives established civil service reforms, nonpartisan commissions to control key state regulatory functions, nonpartisan elections to cripple local machines, office block voting, and primary elections. Even if these innovations have failed to check the power of special interests, they have given voters the power of direct action through the initiative, referendum, and recall. Citizens can activate these three mechanisms by circulating petitions to gather a required number of signatures and bring the measure to statewide vote. The number of signatures, as we shall see, varies depending on the mechanism.

Initiative

THE PROCESS Of the three direct voices in government, the **initiative** is the most well known and most frequently used. The process, also known as direct legislation, requires the proponent to obtain a title (for example, "Farm Animals Confinement Standards") and summary of the proposed initiative from the state attorney general. Upon obtaining the title and summary, the proponents have 150 days to circulate a petition to gather the required number of signatures to qualify for the ballot—5 percent of voters in the last gubernatorial election for statutes, and 8 percent for constitutional amendments. The secretary of state submits the measure at the next general election held at least 131 days after it qualifies or at any special election held before the next general election. The governor may call a special election for the measure.

Before 1960 initiatives appeared only on the general election ballot, thus limiting their use to the two-year election cycle. From 1960 to 2012 they appeared on the primary, general, and special election ballots. In 2012 a new law, propelled by the Democratic majority in the legislature, again required that ballot propositions appear only on the general election ballot in November, motivated by the general consensus that the smaller and more conservative primary electorates disadvantage more liberal initiatives.

FREQUENCY OF USE Initiatives have become indispensable to California's political fabric. From 1912 to 2018 over 2,000 initiatives were titled and summarized for circulation. Of this number, 397 qualified for the ballot, 4 were removed by court order, and 142 were approved by the voters—for an overall passage rate of 36 percent. Of the 142 initiatives approved, 42 were constitutional amendments and 13 were constitutional/stationary changes.[17]

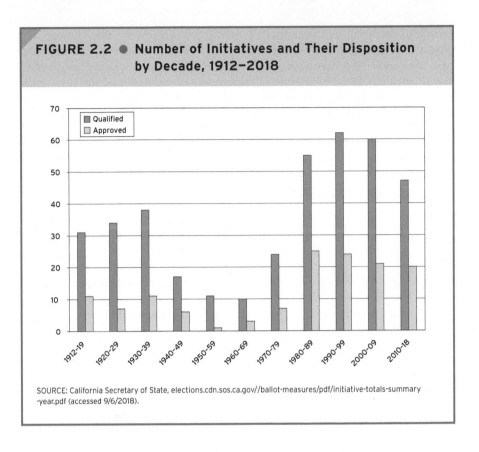

FIGURE 2.2 ● Number of Initiatives and Their Disposition by Decade, 1912–2018

SOURCE: California Secretary of State, elections.cdn.sos.ca.gov//ballot-measures/pdf/initiative-totals-summary
-year.pdf (accessed 9/6/2018).

Figure 2.2 presents the use of initiative by decade. Note these two points: the increasing frequency of initiatives since 1970, and the varying, but generally low level of success for the measures that made it to the ballot.

For discussion purposes, we can compress the 100-year history of initiatives into four time periods: 1912–39, 1940–69, 1970–99, and 2000–18.

1912–39 From the beginning, various individuals and special interests understood that the initiative could be used to forward their special causes. Social and cultural issues, such as outlawing professional fighting, prostitution, gambling on horse races, and land ownership by Asian Americans, drew the highest voter turnout during this period. Labor issues (closed versus open shops) and tax propositions were also volatile issues.

No single issue, however, dominated the initiative process during this period more than the so-called "liquor question."[18] These initiatives were among the most controversial, and they drew high voter turnouts. Twelve measures related to liquor control appeared on the ballot between 1914 and 1936: measures for and against full prohibition, anti-saloon measures, and measures related to state regulation versus local control. Voting was consistent throughout this period, with the anti-Prohibition forces generally prevailing on every measure. The issue, however, wouldn't go away—until 1948 when, after many failures to qualify an initiative, the anti-liquor forces qualified another local option measure, which was rejected by 70 percent of the voters. After this vote, the issue lost its appeal, never to appear on the ballot again.

1940–69 In this time period use of the initiative declined markedly. Compared to the previous 27 years, a higher percentage of proposed measures failed to gather enough signatures to qualify for the ballot. The subject matter of the initiatives also varied from those of 1912–39. Newer issues came to the forefront: race and civil rights, property taxes, and labor and welfare.

Proposition 14 (1964) was the most prominent of a number of initiatives that dealt with fair housing. The initiative was drafted to nullify the Rumford Fair Housing Act, which prohibited discrimination in the rental, lease, or purchase of housing on the basis of race and national origin. The Rumford Act, supporters of Proposition 14 claimed, interfered with their private property rights. Real estate and homeowners' associations led the efforts in support of the proposition; a coalition of Democratic Party leadership, organized labor, churches, and a variety of other groups led the forces against it. The broader issue of race, specifically regarding treatment of and biases toward African Americans, lingered in the background of the campaign; by all accounts, race was the deciding factor in how people voted. Proposition 14 passed by a 2-to-1 margin in November 1964. Its victory was a major impetus for the Watts riots during the summer of 1965, which lasted six days, resulted in 34 deaths, and damaged almost 1,000 buildings.[19] Over the next two years, Proposition 14 was overturned, first by the California Supreme Court and then by the U.S. Supreme Court, for violating the Fourteenth Amendment.

1970–99 In this period initiatives abounded, with over 1,000 initiatives receiving titles, 141 qualifying for ballot, and 56 approved by the voters. The subjects involved social, cultural, and economic issues, including the death penalty, gun control, busing, the property tax, nuclear power, water resources, air quality, coastal preservation, English as the official language, affirmative action, undocumented immigrants, and gay marriage.

The most controversial initiative of this period was Proposition 13, titled the "People's Initiative to Limit Property Taxation" (1978). Sponsored by longtime antitax activists Howard Jarvis and Paul Gann, Proposition 13 was a reaction to the spiraling appreciation of property throughout the 1970s. In just one year, some properties were reassessed at a value 50 to 100 percent higher, and their owners' tax bills jumped accordingly. Proposition 13 included several provisions, one of which dramatically reduced residential property taxes and another that required a two-thirds supermajority in both houses of the legislature to approve tax increases.

Proposition 13 was a grassroots effort, opposed by nearly every state employee and labor union and most Democratic leaders. The pro side raised $2.2 million, and the con side raised $2 million. On June 6, 1978, nearly two-thirds of California's voters passed the proposition, reducing property tax rates by about 57 percent.

Now, almost 40 years later, Proposition 13 is still hotly debated. Critics argue that it creates tax inequities by treating residential and commercial property as equivalent and by assessing similar properties in different ways based solely on when a homeowner bought a house. Supporters argue that pegging property taxes to the value of the property, assessed yearly, exposes homeowners to accelerated yearly property taxes, which leaves them vulnerable to losing their homes. In 2020, California voters will decide whether to revise Proposition 13 to split the rolls.

2000–18 During this period, California voters decided on 105 initiatives in 19 separate elections, 3 of which were special elections, including the special election to recall Governor Gray Davis. Initiatives that passed included measures on farm animal confinement practices, redistricting the state legislative boundaries, victims' rights, and parole procedures. (See Table 2.1 for a list of the top contributors for this period.)

The most controversial and long-lasting ballot issue deals with same-sex marriage, an issue that has been publicly debated for some 35 years. In 1977 the state legislature passed a law stating that marriage was a "personal relation arising out of a civil contract between a man and a woman." This was reaffirmed in 2000 when the voters passed Proposition 22, a statutory—not constitutional—amendment that revised the California Family Code to define marriage as between a man and a woman. However, in May 2008, the California Supreme Court ruled Proposition 22 invalid. At about the same time, fearing such a decision, proponents of Proposition 8 ("Eliminates Right of Same-Sex Couples to Marry") had already begun to qualify the initiative for the ballot, relying on a **constitutional amendment**, not a **statute**, to end debate on the issue.

The campaign over Proposition 8 was fiercely contested. In the end, the initiative passed by a margin of 52.3 to 47.7 percent. Both sides raised significant amounts of money: those supporting Proposition 8 contributed $39 million, while those opposing contributed $44 million, making it one of the most expensive initiative campaigns in state history and the highest expenditure on a same-sex marriage initiative campaign in the nation. After the election, six lawsuits were filed with the California Supreme Court by same-sex couples and government bodies challenging the constitutionality of Proposition 8. The court consented to hear three of the six jointly, but it denied the request to stay the enforcement of

TABLE 2.1 ● Top Contributors to Initiative Ballot Committees, 2000–18

Contributor	Amount ($)
California Teachers Association	$159,281,213
Philip Morris	107,037,384
Pharmaceutical Research & Manufacturers of America	71,159,206
DaVita Inc	66,974,313
California State Council of Service Employees	65,023,920
RJ Reynolds Tobacco Company	64,475,932
Pacific Gas & Electric Company	62,718,850
California Association of Hospital and Health Systems	61,195,522
Charles Munger, Jr.	59,123,466
Stephen L. Bing	51,066,372
Thomas Steyer	49,434,000
Pechanga Band of Luiseno Mission Indians	48,931,480
Morongo Casino Resort Spa	46,660,977
AIDS Healthcare Foundation	46,397,012
Chevron Corporation	44,777,500

SOURCE: National Institute on Money in State Politics, www.followthemoney.org/show-me?s=CA&y=2018,2017,2016, 2015,2014,2013,2012,2011,2010,2009,2008,2007,2006,2005,2004,2003,2002,2001,2000&m-exi=1#[{3|(1|gro=d -eid,d-ad-st,d-ins (accessed 11/12/18).

Two same-sex couples— Paul Katami and Jeffrey Zarrillo, and Kristin Perry and Sandra Stier—pictured here outside the U.S. Supreme Court, were the plaintiffs in *Hollingsworth v. Perry*. The Court held that the sponsors of Proposition 8 "lacked standing" to appeal the federal court ruling that upheld same-sex marriage under the Equal Protection Clause of the federal Constitution and thus paved the way for same-sex marriage in California.

Proposition 8. On May 26, 2009, the court ruled that Proposition 8 was valid but allowed existing same-sex marriages to stand (in *Strauss v. Horton*).

Opponents of Proposition 8 then took their fight to federal court, which, on August 4, 2010, declared the ban unconstitutional in *Perry v. Schwarzenegger* (renamed *Perry v. Brown* to reflect the changing governorship). This decision was upheld by the Ninth Circuit in February 2012. The supporters of Proposition 8 (but not the state government) then appealed to the U.S. Supreme Court. The Court ruled in *Hollingsworth v. Perry* in June 2013 that the proposition's supporters could not appeal the case; only the state government could defend a proposition approved by the voters, and the state had declined to do so. As a result of this decision, same-sex marriage became legal in California. Two years later, same-sex marriage became legal throughout the United States as a result of the U.S. Supreme Court decision in *Obergefell v. Hodges*.

How can we account for the increase in initiatives over the past four decades? The simplest explanation is that it is a consequence of several factors, including the complexity of modern society and the increased willingness of the government to regulate decisions previously left to citizens. Additionally, the legislature went from part to full time in 1968, which had a number of significant effects on California politics: more politicians made a career in the field, more legislation was passed, the budget grew, and decision making and power shifted to Sacramento.

These shifts, coupled with the other Progressive reforms designed to rid the capital of political corruption and an unresponsive legislature—direct primaries, term limits, regulation of campaign contributions, and various tactics to weaken political parties—undermined voters' influence on elected officials. Frustrated by the action or inaction of the legislature, voters have turned to the initiative to get what they want.

In addition to voters, special interests frequently turned to initiatives during this period to promote policies they could not get through the legislature. Money has increasingly become the only requirement for a successful initiative campaign. As a result, an industry of professional campaign managers and signature gatherers is flourishing. These so-called policy managers identify hot issues and then search for clients who will pay for the privilege of sponsoring the initiative.

Referendum

THE PROCESS The referendum allows voters to approve or reject constitutional amendments or statutes proposed or passed by the state legislature. There are two types of referendum: the legislative referendum and the popular referendum.[20]

The **legislative referendum** exists when the legislature proposes a constitutional amendment or revision, or the issuing of the majority of bonds (long-term borrowing to finance capital projects such as construction of buildings and infrastructure). This type of referendum must be approved by a two-thirds vote of both houses of the legislature before it appears on the ballot. In contrast to other direct democracy measures, legislative referenda are brought before the voters automatically, without the need for qualifying petitions.

The **popular referendum** is employed when voters are displeased with a law that was passed by the legislature. The requirements are the same as those for the initiative, and the two are sometimes confused. The process is as follows: the measure may be proposed by presenting to the secretary of state a petition with signatures equal to 5 percent of the voters in the last gubernatorial election. The filing of the signatures must take place within a 90-day period after the enactment of the statute. If the measure qualifies to be on the ballot, the law in question may not take effect until the electorate decides whether it should become a law.

FREQUENCY OF USE The referendum is used infrequently. In fact, it has almost faded from use. Between 1912 and 2016, 50 referenda have appeared on the ballot. Voters rejected 29 laws and approved 21. Of the seven approved since 1982, five dealt with Indian gaming. Proposition 29 (2000) rejected repeal of the Pala Indian tribe compact that authorized the operation of "video lottery terminals" if operated as lotteries, not slot machines. Propositions 94, 95, 96, and 97 (2008) allowed four individual tribes to operate additional slot machines and revised the environmental impact procedures. In 2012 voters rejected a veto referendum funded by Charles Munger, Jr., keeping intact the state Senate districts drawn by the Citizens Redistricting Commission.[21] In the 2016 general election, voters upheld a law passed by the state legislature that prohibited grocery and other retail stores from providing single-use plastic or paper carryout bags at point of sale and placed a 10-cent charge on reusable paper bags. The referendum to repeal the plastic bag fee, Proposition 65, was mostly funded by the plastics industry; environmental groups and grocers supported the fee.

Recall

THE PROCESS The **recall** allows voters to determine whether to eject an elected official from office before his or her term expires. Proponents first submit a petition alleging the reason for recall. They then have 150 days to present to the secretary of state a petition with the required number of signatures to qualify for the ballot. If the sitting official is recalled, a successor is elected. Most recalls are of school board or city council members at the local level.

For statewide offices, the number of signatures must be equal to 12 percent of the last vote for the office, with signatures from at least five counties equal to 1 percent of the last vote for the office in the county. For the Senate, Assembly, members of the Board of Equalization, and judges, the number of signatures must be equal to 20 percent of the last vote for the office. Upon receiving the petitions, an election must be held between 60 and 80 days from the date of certification of sufficient signatures.

FREQUENCY OF USE Recall of statewide offices or the state legislature are rare. There have been eight recall elections out of 118 filings against state officeholders. Seven of the eight were state legislators; Governor Gray Davis in 2003 was the other. Four of the state legislators were expelled from office. The recall was put into use against three state legislators almost immediately after its passage—twice in 1913, against Senator Marshall Black for involvement in a banking scandal, which succeeded, and against Senator James Owen for corruption, which failed. The next year, Senator Edwin Grant, who represented the red-light district in San Francisco, was successfully recalled for opposing prostitution.

Four other state legislators faced a recall vote in 1994 and 1995. The National Rifle Association failed in its attempt to recall Senator David Roberti for his position on gun control legislation. Two Republican members of the Assembly, Doris Allen and Paul Horcher, were voted out of office for supporting Democrat Willie Brown for speaker in a battle between the parties for control of the Assembly. Similarly, an attempt to recall Democratic Assemblyman Mike Machado for backing Republicans failed.[22]

The most notorious recall was that of Governor Davis. He is the only California governor to have been recalled, although there have been over two dozen previous attempts, including three against Ronald Reagan in the 1960s and one against Pete Wilson in the 1990s. During the 2002 campaign for governor, Davis, the incumbent governor, had claimed that the budget deficit was $18 billion, but a week after his election he revealed it was actually $35 billion. Proponents of the recall immediately accused Davis of misleading voters about the severity of the state's budget crisis during his reelection campaign. Other actions prompting the recall included the governor's efforts to prevent the anti-immigrant Proposition 187 from being appealed to the U.S. Supreme Court and his approval of two gun control measures. The public also held Governor Davis partially responsible for the electricity crisis, during which some people's electricity bills doubled and even tripled. Supporters of the recall also blamed Davis for California's generally weak economy. After Representative Darrell Issa, who hoped to run for governor, funded the signature collection effort with a contribution of $2 million, the recall took off on its own momentum. Because the filing requirements to run as Davis's successor were relatively low, 135 candidates filed to replace him. Arnold Schwarzenegger's candidacy quickly gained the most attention, and he easily won the two-part election, in which voters were asked to decide whether Davis should be recalled and to choose his successor. Only 4 of the 135 candidates received more than 1 percent of the vote.

Debating the Merit of Direct Democracy

The debate about the merits of direct democracy has been ongoing since its adoption in the early twentieth century. As we have seen, the initiative has been employed more than the referendum or recall and is generally the focus of the debate on the value of direct democracy.

Many scholars believe that the initiative blurs the complexity of many issues and reduces them to clichés or sound bites for the voter. Large donors with deep pockets dominate the initiative process, undermining the efficacy of representative government with its built-in system of checks and balances. Only millionaires and billionaires, not average citizens, can afford to qualify their ideas for the ballot; once qualified, no contribution limits apply. Single elections often feature competing ballot measures, such as the contest between competing income tax measures Proposition 30 and 38 on the November 2012 ballot. If both had been approved, the one with the most votes would have prevailed (but only Proposition 30 was approved by voters). Similarly, in November 2016 voters were asked to either repeal the death penalty (Proposition 62) or speed up executions (Proposition 66). If both had been approved, only the one receiving more votes would have taken effect, but voters only approved Proposition 66.

Most who have studied the initiative believe it to be a flawed method of forming public policy. Many initiatives are poorly drafted and are difficult to understand even for judges and legislators. The process is complex, proponents cannot correct errors once circulation of petitions has begun, and many are later declared unconstitutional. The legislature is discouraged from participating in the process at all. Reflecting the strong historic bias of its citizens against the legislature, California is the only state that prohibits the legislature from amending initiatives unless permission is written into the initiative itself. Even then, it usually requires a supermajority of two-thirds of the legislature to approve changes, a level of support difficult if not impossible to obtain on significant amendments. Qualifying initiatives by signature is too easy for a signature-gathering firm and too difficult in the five months allowed for those without one, meaning that a large amount of money is necessary in order to qualify an initiative.

Supporters of the initiative, on the other hand, claim that it is a more effective means of serving the majority in California than the legislative process. Therein lies the catch-22 that largely defines California politics: the legislature is supposedly hamstrung by the zealous use of direct democracy, while direct democracy is supposedly necessary to overcome an unproductive legislature.

A 2013 Public Policy Institute of California (PPIC) poll (see Figure 2.3) showed continued strong support for the initiative process, with 72 percent of likely voters viewing as positive the initiative's power to change public policy, and only 40 percent agreeing that major reforms are needed to the initiative process. At the same time, 60 percent said that public policies made through the initiative are superior to those made by the governor and legislature. Likely voters supported several reforms of the initiative process: more public disclosure of funding sources on initiatives; giving the legislature and the initiative's sponsors more time to seek a compromise before the initiative goes on the ballot; and increased public engagement, such as a citizens' commission to hold hearings on initiatives and make ballot recommendations. Oregon established such a program in 2011.

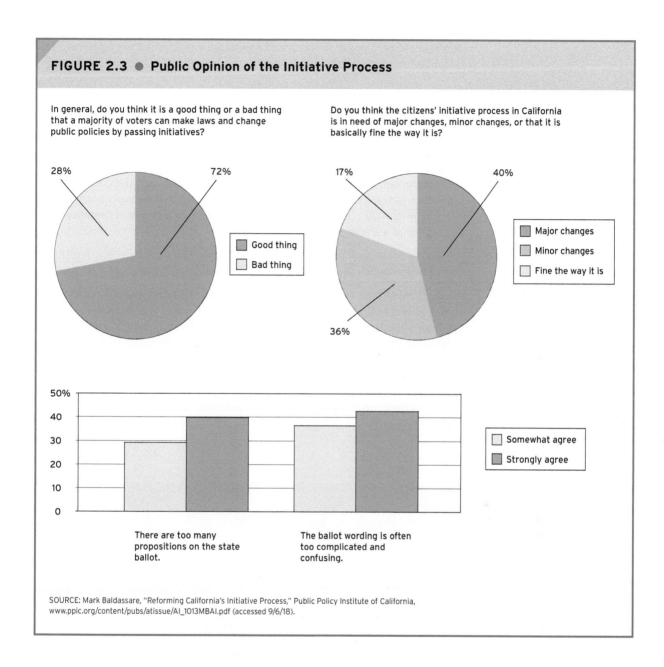

FIGURE 2.3 ● **Public Opinion of the Initiative Process**

In general, do you think it is a good thing or a bad thing that a majority of voters can make laws and change public policies by passing initiatives?

28%   72%

- Good thing
- Bad thing

Do you think the citizens' initiative process in California is in need of major changes, minor changes, or that it is basically fine the way it is?

17%   40%

36%

- Major changes
- Minor changes
- Fine the way it is

There are too many propositions on the state ballot.

The ballot wording is often too complicated and confusing.

- Somewhat agree
- Strongly agree

SOURCE: Mark Baldassare, "Reforming California's Initiative Process," Public Policy Institute of California, www.ppic.org/content/pubs/atissue/AI_1013MBAI.pdf (accessed 9/6/18).

California's Constitution: Where Are We Now?

California's constitution has been through three stages—establishment in the mid-1800s, rewriting in 1879, and extensive amendment during the Progressive Era. Since then, a fourth, ongoing stage has been defined by political scientists and others, in which numerous suggestions have been made to update the constitutional framework. Most notably, the 1996 California Constitutional Revision Commission made many suggestions to strengthen the governor and make state government less susceptible to interest-group influence. These suggestions included the following:

- Having the governor and lieutenant governor run as a team. Because the governor and lieutenant governor currently are elected separately, their political agendas may diverge.

- Having the other elected members of the executive branch appointed by the governor. The governor currently has no supervisory responsibility over the lieutenant governor, the secretary of state, the treasurer, the controller, the attorney general, the insurance commissioner, and the state superintendent of public instruction. The lack of supervisory authority significantly weakens the governor as a leader (see Chapter 6).

- Merging the several tax administration agencies. The state currently has three tax administration agencies; merging them would save money (see Chapter 6).

- Lengthening term limits for legislators. In 2012 the term limit for state Assembly members was lengthened from 6 years to 12 and for state senators from 8 years to 12, provided the total time in both chambers is limited to 12 years. This is an improvement over the stricter limits enacted in 1990, but the term limits still increase the likelihood that major, complex state legislation will be enacted by inexperienced legislators (see Chapter 5).

Most of these proposals have never come before the voters.

Study Guide

FOR FURTHER READING

Broder, David. *Democracy Derailed: Initiative Campaigns and the Power of Money.* New York: Harcourt, 2000.

California Secretary of State. "History of California Initiatives." www.sos.ca.gov/elections/ballot-measures/resources-and -historical-information/history-california-initiatives/. Accessed 6/19/18.

Donovan, Todd, S. Bowler, D. McCuan, and K. Fernandez. "Contending Players and Strategies: Opposition Advantages in Initiative Elections." In *Citizens as Legislators: Direct Democracy in the United States,* edited by S. Bowler, T. Donovan, and C. Tolbert, 133–52. Columbus: Ohio State University Press, 1998.

Gerber, Elisabeth. *The Populist Paradox: Interest Group Influence on the Promise of Direct Legislation.* Princeton, NJ: Princeton University Press, 1999.

Hofstadter, Richard. *The Age of Reform.* New York: Washington Square Press, 1988.

HoSang, Daniel Martinez. *Racial Propositions: Ballot Initiatives and the Making of Postwar California.* Berkeley: University of California Press, 2010.

Hui, Iris and David O. Sears. "Reexamining the Effect of Racial Propositions on Latinos' Partisanship in California." *Political Behavior* 40, 1 (March 2018): 149–174.

Johnson, Hiram. "First Inaugural Address." January 3, 1913. http://governors.library.ca.gov/addresses/23-hjohnson01 .html. Accessed 6/20/16.

Levy, JoAnn. *They Saw the Elephant: Women in the California Gold Rush.* Norman: University of Oklahoma Press, 2014.

Lustig, R. Jeffrey, ed. *Remaking California: Reclaiming the Public Good.* Berkeley: Heyday, 2010.

Madley, Benjamin. *An American Genocide: The United States and the California Indian Catastrophe, 1846–1873.* New Haven: Yale University Press, 2017.

Matthews, Joe, and Mark Paul. *California Crackup, How Reforms Broke the Golden State and How We Can Fix It.* Berkeley: University of California Press, 2010.

Romero, Mindy, and Greg Keidan. 2018. "California's 2014 Ballot Initiative Transparency Act (BITA) and Its Impact on Public Involvement in the Ballot Initiative Process." *California Journal of Politics and Policy* 9, 2. DOI: 10.5070 /P2CJPP9234891

Starr, Kevin. *Inventing the Dream: California through the Progressive Era*. New York: Oxford University Press, 1985.
———. *California: A History*. New York: The Modern Library, 2005.

Smith, Daniel A. and Caroline J. Tolbert. "The Initiative to Party: Partisanship and Ballot Initiatives in California," *Party Politics* 7, 6 (November 2001): 739–57. DOI: 10.1177/13 54068801007006004
———. *Educated by Initiative: The Effects of Direct Democracy on Citizens and Political Organizations in the United States*. Ann Arbor: University of Michigan Press, 2004.

ON THE WEB

Baldassare, Mark. *At Issue, Reforming California's Initiative Process*. Public Policy Institute of California, 2013. www.ppic .org/main/publication.asp?i=1071. Accessed 6/20/16.

Baldassare, Mark, Dean Bonner, Sonja Petek, and Jui Shrestha. *The Initiative Process in California*. Public Policy Institute of California, 2013. www.ppic.org/main/publication_show .asp?i=1072. Accessed 6/20/16.

Bruno, Carson. "Is it time to reconsider California's initiative system?" *Eureka: California's Policy, Economics, and Politics*. The Hoover Institution, Aug. 30, 2016, https://www.hoo ver.org/research/it-time-reconsider-californias-initiative -system. Accessed 6/19/18.

California Secretary of State. *Ballot Measures*. www.sos.ca.gov /elections. Accessed 6/20/16.

California State Constitution. www.leginfo.ca.gov/const.html. Accessed 6/20/16. This site makes the California State Constitution searchable by keyword.

Center for Governmental Studies. *Democracy by Initiative*. May 2008. www.policyarchive.org/collections/cgs/index ?section=5&id=5800. Accessed 6/20/16. Search for "Democracy by Initiative."

Initiative & Referendum Institute. www.iandrinstitute.org. Accessed 7/20/16.

Southern Pacific Historical & Technical Society. www.sphts.org. Accessed 6/20/16.

KQED. "Boomtown, 1870s: Decade of Bonanza, Bust and Unbridled Racism." *KQED News*. https://www.kqed.org/news /10413670/draft-boomtown-history-2a. Accessed 6/19/18.

KQED. "The California Gold Rush." *The American Experience*. https://www.pbs.org/wgbh/americanexperience/features /goldrush-california/. Accessed 6/19/18.

SUMMARY

I. The history of the California Constitution comprises four stages.
   A. 1849: basic structure of government established. Includes separation of powers, bicameralism, federalism, and popular election of most state offices.
   B. 1879: a constitutional convention adds nine new articles and 8,000 words to respond to the reform needs of the time.
   C. 1910–17: the Progressive Era adds the initiative, referendum, and recall, as well as hundreds of reform laws.
   D. 1960–present: California voters have authorized a few significant reforms.

II. Proposing an amendment to the California Constitution is easy.
   A. Amendments can be proposed in three ways:
      1. Through a constitutional convention. The legislature can convene the convention by a two-thirds vote, or it can be convened by a majority vote of the electorate from an initiative. A Bay Area business group tried to collect sufficient signatures for a new constitutional convention in 2009–10 but gave up because professional signature-gathering firms refused to work with the group, feeling that the effort would imperil their future existence.
      2. Amendments may be proposed by collecting signatures through the initiative process.
         a) Signatures totaling 8 percent of the vote in the last gubernatorial election are required, collected over a five-month period.
         b) Most amendments are proposed this way. The cost is approximately $1 million to $2 million, mostly for signature gathering.
      3. The legislature may propose an amendment by a two-thirds vote.
   B. Amendments must go through a ratification stage. Regardless of the way in which an amendment is proposed, the electorate must then ratify the amendment before it goes into the constitution. A majority vote is required.

III. The Progressive reformers had several key goals.
   A. Ending the dominance of big business, especially the Southern Pacific Railroad, over the state.

B. Reforming the corrupt political process.

C. Removing from office corrupt political officials at the state and local levels of government.

D. Returning political power to the people.

IV. Progressive laws and constitutional amendments wrought many significant changes.

A. Enacted protections for working people

B. Established nonpartisan elections

C. Instituted primary elections

D. Created office block voting

E. Set in motion the process of direct democracy—the initiative, referendum, and recall

F. Resulted in the great number of Progressive reforms that are still in operation today

V. Direct democracy is a vital aspect of California politics.

A. The initiative is the most popular of the three direct democracy mechanisms.

1. Proponents need to gather signatures equal to 5 percent of voters in the last gubernatorial election for statutes and 8 percent of the voters for constitutional amendments.

2. Since 1912 roughly 36 percent of initiatives that have been voted on have passed.

3. The initiative has increasingly become a mechanism by which special interests or wealthy individuals can pass legislation by circumventing the legislature.

B. The referendum refers legislation to the voters for a direct decision. There are two types of referendum: legislative and popular.

1. Legislative referendum allows voters to decide on statutes or constitutional amendments as well as most bond measures proposed by the legislature; it takes a two-thirds vote of the legislature to place a referendum on the ballot.

2. Popular referendum allows voters to approve or repeal an act of the legislature. If the legislature passes a law that voters do not approve of, they may gather signatures to demand a popular vote on the law. Proponents need to gather signatures equal to 5 percent of voters in the last gubernatorial election.

3. The referendum is infrequently used and has appeared on the ballot 50 times since 1912.

C. The recall allows voters to remove a public official from elected office before his or her term is up.

1. The number of signatures that needs to be gathered depends on the office: 12 percent of the last vote for statewide office from at least five counties equal to 1 percent of the last vote in the county; 20 percent of the last vote for office for Senate, Assembly, and Board of Equalization.

2. Since 1912 there have been only eight recalls of statewide officials and legislative members.

3. Governor Gray Davis is the only statewide official to have been recalled.

PRACTICE QUIZ

1. The popular direct-democracy process by which citizens can place a constitutional amendment or statute on the ballot is called a(n)
   a) referendum.
   b) initiative.
   c) recall.
   d) nonpartisan election.

2. The individual who served as governor during much of the Progressive Era was
   a) Chester Rowell.
   b) Edward Dickson.
   c) Hiram Johnson.
   d) Samuel P. Huntington.

3. The process by which a petition signed by a specific percentage of those who cast votes in the last gubernatorial election enables voters to approve or reject a law enacted by the legislature is a(n)

   a) popular referendum.
   b) initiative.
   c) recall.
   d) nonpartisan election.

4. The process by which an elected official is removed from office before his or her term expires is called a(n)
   a) referendum.
   b) initiative.
   c) recall.
   d) nonpartisan election.

5. Progressive reformers pointed to this company whenever they spoke about machine politics and corporate privilege in Sacramento.
   a) Standard Oil Company
   b) Bank of America
   c) Southern Pacific Railroad
   d) Northern Securities Company

6. The only sitting California governor to be recalled from office was
   a) Ronald Reagan.
   b) Jerry Brown.
   c) Gray Davis.
   d) Pete Wilson.

7. Which of the following direct-democracy devices allows voters to approve or reject constitutional amendments or statutes and the majority of bond measures put on the ballot by the legislature?
   a) initiative
   b) direct primary
   c) legislative referendum
   d) recall

8. In which historical block was the greatest number of initiatives titled?
   a) 1912–39
   b) 1940–69

c) 1970–99
d) 2000–16

9. Which of the following is not a Progressive Era reform?
   a) nonpartisan elections
   b) primary elections
   c) the office block vote
   d) party caucuses

10. Which of the following is *not* a legal way to amend the California Constitution?
    a) The legislature can convene a constitutional convention by a two-thirds vote.
    b) The governor can sign into law a proposed amendment passed by the legislature.
    c) The legislature may propose a constitutional amendment by a two-thirds vote.
    d) The electorate can propose a constitutional amendment through the initiative process.

CRITICAL-THINKING QUESTIONS

1. The California Constitution has gone through a series of revisions. Identify the periods of those revisions and discuss the contributions that each made to the state's political structure.
2. How did the extreme diversity of the state, which began with the Gold Rush, shape the California Constitution?
3. Suppose you worked for a coalition of interest groups supporting legislation to increase the state sales tax to fund a state-run health care system. The coalition is frustrated by the lack of action in the legislature. They come to you for advice about the initiative process and the possibility of success. What would you tell them, based on what you've learned in this chapter?
4. Some people argue that direct democracy provides citizens with another way to correct the behavior and decision

making of public officials. Others argue that it is merely the instrument of those special interest groups that have enough money to manipulate the political process. Present an argument for each position. Where do you stand in this debate?
5. California is the model Progressive state. The key components of the Progressive agenda, however, greatly weakened the role of political parties in the state. Identify and discuss how some of these Progressive reforms have weakened the state's party system. Is this a good or a bad thing? Do you think there are any correlations between weak parties and the increasing use of the initiative process?

KEY TERMS

constitutional amendment (p. 40)
direct democracy (p. 35)
initiative (p. 37)

Progressive movement (p. 23)
recall (p. 42)
legislative referendum (p. 42)

popular referendum (p. 42)
statute (p. 40)

4 Parties and Elections in California

WHAT CALIFORNIA GOVERNMENT DOES AND WHY IT MATTERS

In 2017 and 2018 California assumed a new role: the epicenter of resistance to the Trump administration. Ever since Donald Trump became president, California has been at odds with his administration over many of its policy directives. Many federal policies either passed by Congress or implemented through Trump's signing of executive orders—which do not require approval from both houses of Congress—are in direct conflict with California laws. California's attorney general, Xavier Becerra, has filed over 30 lawsuits against the Trump administration, claiming that specific federal policies violate California law or the U.S. Constitution. Examples of these lawsuits demonstrate the environmental, immigration, and social policies pitting California against the Trump administration:

- California cities have taken on "sanctuary" status to limit how they will cooperate with federal immigration officials.
- California has sued the Environmental Protection Agency for rolling back the requirement that agricultural companies train California workers about the hazards of pesticides.
- California has backed a Planned Parenthood court motion against the Trump administration's plan to withhold funding for women's reproductive health services to any organization that provides abortions or makes referrals for the procedure.
- Along with more than a dozen other states, California has sued the federal government over the lowering of federal automobile emission standards.

- California has sued the federal government over plans to reintroduce a citizenship question for the 2020 Census, arguing this will discourage undocumented individuals from participating.
- California has sued the federal government for ending the Deferred Action for Childhood Arrivals (DACA) program.

These lawsuits demonstrate what many analysts and political observers believe is only natural—that California has taken on the leading role of the anti-Trump resistance. California is dominated by the Democratic Party, its voters favor progressive candidates and policies, and it has historically been on the cutting edge politically, culturally, economically, and socially. The state has the fifth largest economy in the world, is the most populated and diverse state in the country, and is home to some of the most powerful and influential high-tech industries in the world. Other states watch what California does; we are an influential trendsetter.

Political Parties

A political party is an organization of people with roughly similar political or ideological positions who work to win elections in order to gain greater control of the government and change public policy. Political parties perform many valuable functions in a democratic society. One of their most important roles is to mobilize voters at election time. They are directly involved in political campaigns: providing workers, raising money, and identifying important political issues. In theory, parties help bring about consensus on important political issues and serve as two-way communication channels between government and the people. Consequently, most political scientists consider them vital to the health of a democratic state.

California has a **winner-take-all system** of voting in which the candidate receiving the highest number of votes wins the election. Political scientists have long known that such a system promotes two dominant political parties, and, as expected, the Republicans and the Democrats dominate the political process in California. But as you will discover below, California has what is considered a weak political party system, a consequence of the reforms brought about by the Progressive movement, which took a considerable amount of power away from organized political parties.

The Progressive Impact on Political Parties

The Progressive movement (1890s–1920s) viewed political parties as corrupt organizations operating in concert with big corporations to control and manipulate the political system for their own benefit. Historian Spencer Olin describes the attitude of Progressives toward political parties:

> Accompanying their democratic faith in the wisdom of the individual voter was a distrust of formal party organizations, which were viewed as the media of special-interest power. . . . Furthermore, it was argued by progressives that science and

efficient management would solve the problems of government; parties were irrelevant and unnecessary.[1]

The Progressives attacked the power of the political parties with reforms such as party primaries. **Primary elections** are used to select the party candidate who will run for office against other candidates in the **general election**. Before primaries were established, party leaders typically selected their candidates in proverbial "smoke-filled rooms," outside of public view. Primaries were designed to allow voters, not parties, to select candidates for office. The primary system also opened up the opportunity to run for office to anyone capable of meeting the basic qualifications, which included age and residency requirements. Historically, the party leadership and their corporate allies had selected candidates and subsequently manipulated them while they held office; with the Progressive reforms, the people could participate in a whole new class of elections, forcing candidates to direct their political messages and loyalty to the average voter.

The Progressives also introduced a new type of ballot, the **office block ballot**. This type of ballot made it difficult to vote the straight party ticket, a method popular in many other states where ballots list all the candidates running for each office by party. Political parties preferred this party column ballot because it made it easy for voters to select only candidates from their party. The use of the office block ballot in California discourages such behavior by listing each office separately and has resulted in more split-ticket voting, where people vote for candidates from different parties.

Another Progressive reform was the introduction of nonpartisan elections, which further weakened parties by preventing party designations from appearing on the ballot for most local contests (city councils, board of supervisors, school boards, and judges). Instead, voters were given only the current occupational status of the candidate and thus could no longer use their party loyalties to make voting decisions at the county and city level on Election Day. The Progressives wanted the electorate to research the candidates by reading up on them or attending forums.

Political scientists believe that the weakening of political parties through nonpartisan elections at the county and city levels has an impact on voters. Despite the hopes of the Progressives, most voters do not devote a lot of time to conducting research on each candidate to determine how to cast their vote. County and city races are typically low profile; therefore, forbidding party labels on ballots further diminishes the voters' already limited information. Voters who identify with a political party view the party affiliation of candidates as important and rely on it to make their voting decisions. As political scientists Brian Schaffner, Matthew Streb, and Gerald Wright describe it, "Party identification is a, or even the, central component of voter decision making. As an effective attachment, it motivates individuals to participate as a display of party support."[2] Therefore, nonpartisan elections may have lower turnout rates than partisan ones.

The Democratic and Republican Parties in California

Currently, California is considered a very Democratic state. Democratic candidates running for the presidency are fairly confident they will win the popular vote in California (for example, Hillary Clinton won 62 percent of the vote in 2016), and they visit our state not to sway voters but to hold expensive fund-raisers. Republican candidates don't spend too much time campaigning in California, as they are certain they will lose the popular vote—although, like Democrats, they do visit to collect campaign contributions. For over 20 years, our state has had two Democratic U.S. senators, and for over 20 years the Democratic Party has controlled the state legislature.

But California has not always been in the Democratic camp. From 1952 to 1988, Republican presidential candidates won every presidential vote in California except for one (Democrat Lyndon Johnson defeated Republican Barry Goldwater in 1964). Richard Nixon and Ronald Reagan were both hugely popular in California: Nixon represented California in both the U.S. House and Senate before being elected president, and Reagan served two terms as governor of California before serving in the White House.

What caused the Republican Party to lose support? A couple of reasons may help explain this shift. Some scholars point to a series of anti-immigrant initiatives, beginning with Proposition 187 in 1994, which were embraced by the Republican Party. Proposition 187, a ballot measure that prohibited undocumented individuals from receiving nonemergency medical care, public education, and other services, was strenuously supported by Republican Governor Pete Wilson in his re-election bid. Shortly after the passage of Proposition 187 (which was ultimately invalidated), Propositions 209 and 229 sought to outlaw affirmative action and bilingual education. As Figure 4.1 illustrates, there was a spike in Latinos registering with the Democratic Party and voting for Democratic candidates after these propositions were introduced. And Latinos have apparently not forgotten the anti-immigrant positions of the Republican Party. A 2010 survey found that Latino voters had negative views when asked about former governor Pete Wilson's involvement in the campaign of a Republican gubernatorial candidate—this was nearly 20 years after Proposition 187.[3]

Many experts also believe that demographic changes in the state help explain the ascendancy of the Democratic Party. White and older voters, an important part of the Republican Party coalition, are declining in numbers. As of July 2014, Latinos are the largest ethnic group in California, just edging out the white population. It is projected that by 2060, Latinos will make up 49 percent of the state's population. The Asian population has also increased in California. Overall, the Asian population in the United States has grown 72 percent since 2000 and about one-third of the Asian population resides in California.[4] Young and ethnically diverse voters prefer the Democratic Party. Nonwhites now amount to a majority in the state, and these voters have not supported some of the more conservative and strident anti-immigrant policies touted by Republican candidates. Conservative, right-wing Republicans do not do well in statewide elections; California voters largely prefer centrist leaders who advocate moderate policies. And California appears to be a harbinger of national trends. "Where L.A. goes is where the rest of the state goes and where the rest of the country goes," proclaimed one analyst. "We announce, demographically speaking, the future for the rest of the country."[5]

Third Parties in California

The American political system, which is a federal system, delegates power to three levels of government: national, state, and local. One of the powers that states retain is to determine how political parties may organize and gain access to the ballot. By dominating the legislature in California, Republicans and Democrats have not made it easy for third parties to qualify for the ballot, and consequently the two parties

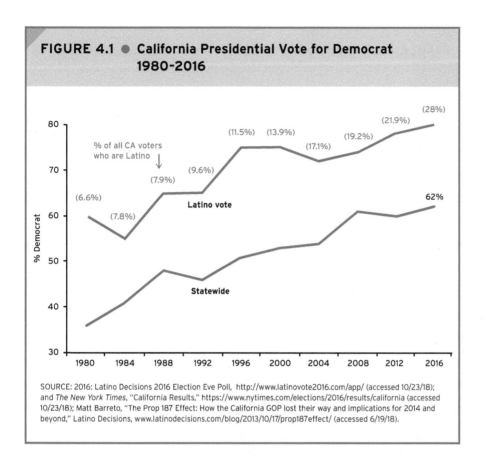

FIGURE 4.1 ● California Presidential Vote for Democrat 1980-2016

% of all CA voters who are Latino ↓

(6.6%) (7.8%) (7.9%) (9.6%) (11.5%) (13.9%) (17.1%) (19.2%) (21.9%) (28%)

Latino vote

Statewide

62%

% Democrat

30 40 50 60 70 80

1980 1984 1988 1992 1996 2000 2004 2008 2012 2016

SOURCE: 2016: Latino Decisions 2016 Election Eve Poll, http://www.latinovote2016.com/app/ (accessed 10/23/18); and *The New York Times*, "California Results," https://www.nytimes.com/elections/2016/results/california (accessed 10/23/18); Matt Barreto, "The Prop 187 Effect: How the California GOP lost their way and implications for 2014 and beyond," Latino Decisions, www.latinodecisions.com/blog/2013/10/17/prop187effect/ (accessed 6/19/18).

dominate California politics. Third parties then are defined as any party other than Republican or Democratic.

Traditionally, third-party candidates do not win in a winner-take-all system, a fact that both major parties emphasize to warn voters against throwing their votes away. However, a significant percentage of voters continue to vote for third-party candidates anyway.

There are two ways in which political parties can qualify to get on the ballot in California. The first method is by registration; the second is by petition. To qualify a new party by the registration method, the law requires that one-third of the total number of voters registered on the 154th day before the primary election or the 123rd day before the presidential general election are registered with the new party. The petition method is just as difficult and tedious. New political parties must petition to be included in the upcoming election; the party must collect signatures equal to 10 percent of those who voted in the last gubernatorial election. In 2018 approximately 12 million votes were cast in the governor's race, so the law mandates that over one million signatures must be collected to qualify a new party. Qualifying as a new political party clearly is not an easy task and requires time, personnel, expertise, and resources. In 2018, California had six qualified parties (see Table 4.1): the American Independent

TABLE 4.1 ● Qualified Political Parties in California, 2018	
AMERICAN INDEPENDENT PARTY	www.aipca.org
DEMOCRATIC PARTY	www.cadem.org
GREEN PARTY	www.cagreens.org
LIBERTARIAN PARTY	www.ca.lp.org
PEACE AND FREEDOM PARTY	www.peaceandfreedom.org
REPUBLICAN PARTY	www.cagop.org

Party, the Democratic Party, the Green Party, the Libertarian Party, the Peace and Freedom Party, and the Republican Party. So what is the role of third parties in politics, particularly in California? One theory is that third parties act as spoilers, drawing enough votes from one or the other of the two major parties to alter the election outcome. Third parties also help focus public attention on important political issues. Once an issue attracts enough public attention, it will be taken over by one or both of the two major political parties. Sometimes, third parties can motivate people who do not usually vote to turn up at the polls because the third-party candidate better represents their views than do the established Democratic or Republican candidates.

Party Affiliation of California Voters

A plurality of California voters identify with the Democratic Party. As of October 2018 about 44 percent of voters are registered with the Democratic Party compared to 24 percent registered with the Republican Party. A substantial 28 percent of voters have **no party preference**, and 5 percent identify with one of the minor third parties. It should be noted that the name of one of these minor third parties, the American Independent Party, has confused voters who thought they actually were registering as independent voters (no party preference). Because the word *independent* appears in the party's name, tens of thousands of Californians mistakenly registered with this party, a party that was formed in the 1960s by a segregationist and that espouses ultraconservative, antigay, and antiabortion positions. After the *Los Angeles Times*[6] brought to light this confusion on the part of voters, nearly 32,000 voters who had previously registered with the American Independent Party changed their political party registration. The American Independent Party, however, still attracts over half a million voters, the most of any of the minor parties, and because of this the party meets the requirements of California law for ballot access.

Party affiliation is fairly easy to determine because people are asked to declare **political party affiliation** when registering to vote (one of the options, however, is no party preference). As Figure 4.2 illustrates, since 1998 registration in the two major political parties has declined. The percentage of voters registering with the Democratic Party fell by 3 percentage points, while the percentage registering with the Republican Party fell by 12 points. The most dramatic change has been among those who have no political party preference (also referred to as independent voters). This group has more than doubled in size over the past 20 years; more than one in four voters now claim no party preference when they register to vote.

Now let us look at political-party affiliation and some demographic factors. Figure 4.3 presents the results of a California statewide survey conducted in October 2018 that asked respondents about their party affiliation, age, gender, race, educational level, and place of birth. The results suggest that young, middle-aged, and older Californians prefer the Democratic Party over other parties. The survey also found that the Republican Party is becoming the party of senior citizens. Currently, those 55 years of age or older make up the majority of the party, and this number is growing annually as the population ages. Many are questioning what the Republican Party of the future will look like in California with the passing of these older Republicans. Will the party be able to survive this demographic trend? Another important trend is young voters' movement away from organized parties to register instead as independent voters; no party preferences (30 percent) has the second highest affiliation.

We also observe a sizeable gender difference in party affiliation, with many more women affiliating with the Democratic Party (52 percent of women versus 37 percent of men). Also of note is that more men than women are registering as independents. The Democratic Party has more support than the Republican Party regardless of educational level. Race is also a key predictor of party identification, with Latinos preferring the Democratic Party at a much higher rate than do whites (55 percent compared to 40 percent). Similarly, 51 percent of immigrants identify with the Democratic Party compared to 43 percent of those native born. Some of these demographic trends suggest that politics in our state will change in the future. Older white males' proportionate decline in the population will continue to have an impact on the Republican Party as it loses a large segment of its support.

Another important demographic change is the increasing Latino population. Data from the U.S. Census Bureau demonstrate that from 2000 to 2017 the Latino population grew by nearly 30 percent to 15 million, whereas the white population

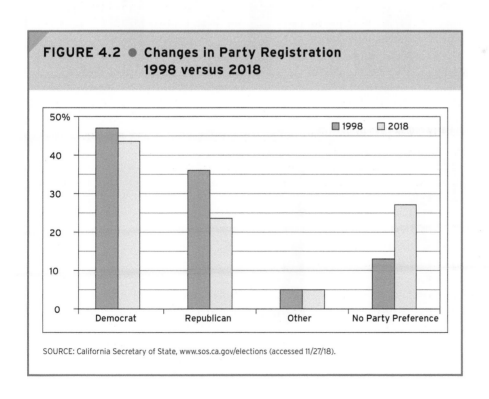

FIGURE 4.2 ● Changes in Party Registration 1998 versus 2018

SOURCE: California Secretary of State, www.sos.ca.gov/elections (accessed 11/27/18).

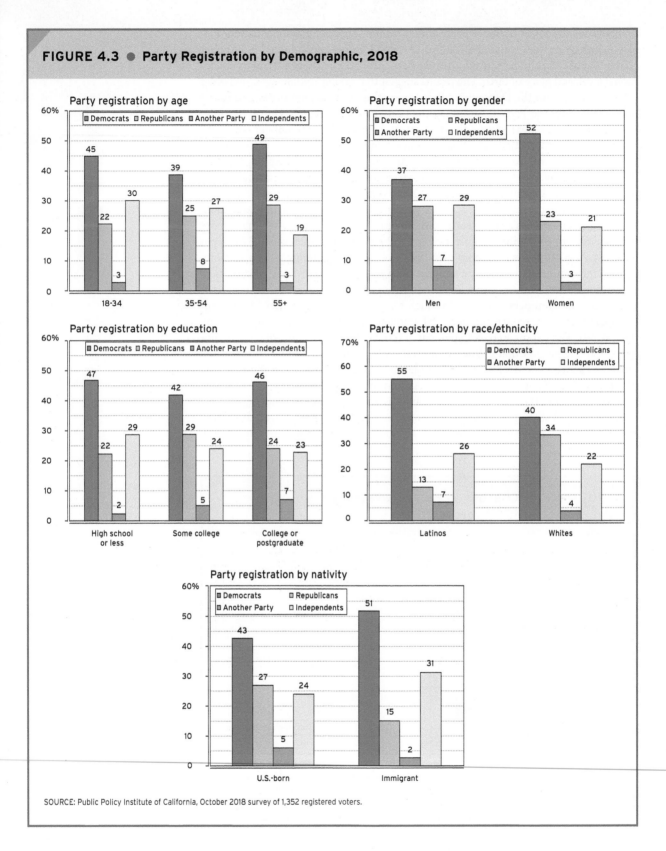

FIGURE 4.3 ● Party Registration by Demographic, 2018

Party registration by age

Legend: Democrats, Republicans, Another Party, Independents

- 18-34: 45, 22, 3, 30
- 35-54: 39, 25, 8, 27
- 55+: 49, 29, 3, 19

Party registration by gender

Legend: Democrats, Republicans, Another Party, Independents

- Men: 37, 27, 7, 29
- Women: 52, 23, 3, 21

Party registration by education

Legend: Democrats, Republicans, Another Party, Independents

- High school or less: 47, 22, 2, 29
- Some college: 42, 29, 5, 24
- College or postgraduate: 46, 24, 7, 23

Party registration by race/ethnicity

Legend: Democrats, Republicans, Another Party, Independents

- Latinos: 55, 13, 7, 26
- Whites: 40, 34, 4, 22

Party registration by nativity

Legend: Democrats, Republicans, Another Party, Independents

- U.S.-born: 43, 27, 5, 24
- Immigrant: 51, 15, 2, 31

SOURCE: Public Policy Institute of California, October 2018 survey of 1,352 registered voters.

declined by more than 5 percent to just under 15 million. The California Department of Finance projects that in the next 20 years whites will make up 35 percent of the population and Latinos will make up 43 percent of the population. Currently, Latinos favor the Democratic Party over the Republican Party by a sizable percentage, and there is no reason to expect this to change in the future. Thus, many are predicting an even stronger Democratic Party presence in the state in the future.

THE RED AND THE BLUE IN CALIFORNIA You may recall that most television programs focusing on the 2016 presidential election exhibited a color-coded map of the United States, which represented the states that voted Republican as red and the states that voted Democratic as blue. The map nicely illustrated the national split between urban areas and rural, agricultural, and suburban areas; the West Coast, most of the Northeast, and the major urban areas of the United States were blue; the South, the agricultural regions, and the Great Plains states were red.

As the map in Figure 4.4 illustrates, the same geographic split appears within the state of California, between the coastal counties and the inland counties. Most of the Democratic counties are coastal and encompass major urban areas, whereas most of the Republican counties are inland and rural.

As reported by the *Los Angeles Times*:

> Over the last decade, Republican influence has grown more concentrated in conservative inland California—largely the Central Valley and Inland Empire but also the Antelope Valley, the Sierra and rural north. . . . At the same time Democrats have strengthened their domination of counties along California's coastline, building overwhelming advantages in the San Francisco and Los Angeles areas as Latino voters have expanded the party's base. And from San Diego's beachfront suburbs to the Central Coast, Democrats have eroded Republican support among moderates, especially women.[7]

What does this split mean politically? Overall, the Democratic Party has an electoral advantage in California; nearly 70 percent of the state's population resides in Democratic-leaning coastal regions. Republicans have an uphill battle to win statewide elections and are more likely to succeed if they nominate ideologically moderate candidates who are able to gain the support of Democratic voters. The fact that the urban and coastal population centers are largely Democratic and moderate to liberal, coupled with the tendency of the majority of independent voters to lean toward the Democratic Party, suggests that California will remain a distinctly blue state. However, this ideological split has potentially negative consequences. As described by Mark Baldassare, president of the Public Policy Institute of California, before the 2016 election,

> California seems poised to maintain its blue status this fall (2016). However, the geo-political segregation of the state—with Republican pockets of strength in California's northern, inland, and rural regions—means that federal and state legislators will be elected to represent the views of voters who are worlds apart. Indeed, the political polarization and antipathy of this year's election may result in a California Congressional delegation that will contribute to Washington gridlock and a California Legislature that will struggle to find common ground on solutions to the many challenges facing California's future.[8]

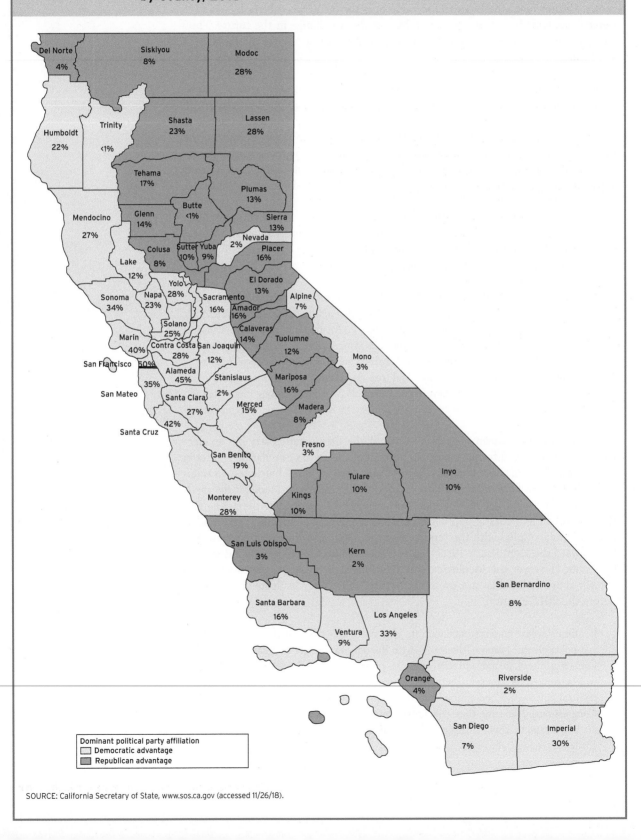

FIGURE 4.4 ● Percent Difference between Democratic and Republican Registration by County, 2018

Del Norte
4%

Siskiyou
8%

Modoc
28%

Humboldt
22%

Trinity
<1%

Shasta
23%

Lassen
28%

Mendocino
27%

Tehama
17%

Plumas
13%

Glenn
14%

Butte
<1%

Sierra
13%

Lake
12%

Colusa
8%

Sutter
10%

Yuba
9%

Nevada
2%

Placer
16%

Sonoma
34%

Yolo
28%

Napa
23%

Sacramento
16%

El Dorado
13%

Alpine
7%

Amador
16%

Marin
40%

Solano
25%

Calaveras
14%

Tuolumne
12%

Mono
3%

San Francisco 50%

Contra Costa
28%

San Joaquin
12%

San Mateo
35%

Alameda
45%

Stanislaus
2%

Mariposa
16%

Santa Clara
27%

Merced
15%

Madera
8%

Santa Cruz
42%

San Benito
19%

Fresno
3%

Inyo
10%

Monterey
28%

Kings
10%

Tulare
10%

San Luis Obispo
3%

Kern
2%

San Bernardino
8%

Santa Barbara
16%

Los Angeles
33%

Ventura
9%

Riverside
2%

Orange
4%

San Diego
7%

Imperial
30%

Dominant political party affiliation
☐ Democratic advantage
☐ Republican advantage

SOURCE: California Secretary of State, www.sos.ca.gov (accessed 11/26/18).

This is not to imply, however, that all populated coastal regions are the same politically and ideologically. As the next section illustrates, there are some interesting variations.

California's Local Political Cultures from Left to Right

Political culture is difficult to define and to quantify. However, we can offer at least a few statistics to show how three of the state's most populous counties differ in terms of political partisanship, political ideology, political activism, political tolerance, and voting tendencies on important issues. Table 4.2 compares and contrasts the city of San Francisco and counties of Los Angeles and San Diego on these selected indicators of local political culture.

POLITICAL PARTY REGISTRATION As of October 2018, registered Democrats outnumber Republicans in San Francisco by eight to one and by three to one in Los Angeles County. In San Diego County, however, Democrats slightly outnumber Republicans 35 percent to 28 percent.

TABLE 4.2 ● Regional Political Cultures: Three California Counties Compared from Left to Right

Indicator	San Francisco (%)	Los Angeles (%)	San Diego (%)
1. Democrats (2018)	57%	50%	35%
2. Republicans (2018)	7	17	28
3. Very liberal (2000)	21	8	6
4. Very conservative (2000)	4	15	14
5. High protest activity (2000)	47	30	30
6. Voter turnout (Nov. 8, 2016)	38	23	33
7. Voter turnout (Nov. 6, 2012)	57	52	56
8. Yes on Proposition 13 (1978)	47	67	60
9. Yes on Proposition 187 (1994)	29	56	68
10. Yes on Proposition 209 (1996)	29	45	63
11. Yes on Proposition 8 (2008)	25	50	54
12. Yes on Proposition 30 (2012)	77	60	46
13. Yes on Proposition 47 (2014)	79	63	55
14. Yes on Proposition 62 (2016)	71	52	44
15. Yes on Proposition 64 (2016)	74	58	56
16. Yes on Proposition 6 (2018)	17	39	51
17. Vote Brown for governor (2014)	88	66	50
18. Vote Obama for president (2012)	83	69	51
19. Vote for Clinton for president (2016)	85	72	56

SOURCE: Indicators 1–2, 6–19: California Secretary of State, various official statements of vote. Indicators 3–5: Analysis of sample survey data obtained from the Social Capital Benchmark Survey 2000.

POLITICAL IDEOLOGY Based on community surveys conducted in late 2000, 21 percent of San Franciscans identify themselves politically as "very liberal" and only 4 percent as "very conservative." In both Los Angeles County and San Diego County, conservatives outnumber liberals by about two to one.[9]

POLITICAL PROTEST AND VOTER TURNOUT Those same surveys show that San Franciscans are much more inclined to engage in political protest than are their counterparts in the southland. Specifically, 47 percent of San Francisco citizens scored "high" on a nationally normed political-protest-activity index, as compared with only 30 percent of citizens in both Los Angeles and San Diego counties. In terms of more conventional forms of political participation, the 2016 presidential election saw San Francisco voters turning out at a slightly higher rate than San Diego voters, with Los Angeles lagging somewhat behind. In November 2018 voter turnout skyrocketed nationally (especially considering this was a non-presidential election year), and a similar turnout pattern held with San Francisco voters leading the way with an historically high turnout rate of 75 percent. San Diego and Los Angeles voters followed with turnout rates slightly higher than the 2016 presidential election.

SUPPORT FOR PROPOSITION 13 Proposition 13, the 1978 initiative that rolled back property tax rates and limited the government's ability to raise local property taxes in the future, is regarded by some observers "as one of the most significant political events in California's history."[10] It won by a landslide vote nearly everywhere in the state, including a 67 percent vote in favor in Los Angeles County and a 60 percent vote in favor in San Diego County. In San Francisco, however, it mustered only a 47 percent vote in favor, not even a majority.

SUPPORT FOR PROGRESSIVE POLICIES AND RACIAL AND CULTURAL DIVERSITY Table 4.2 reports county voting results on different statewide ballot propositions over the period 1994–2018. All results can be viewed as indicators of California voters' political tolerance and level of support for racial and cultural diversity and progressive policies.

- Proposition 187 was a 1994 initiative constitutional amendment that made undocumented immigrants ineligible for various public social services. The state's voters approved it by a wide margin, with 56 percent voting yes in Los Angeles County and 68 percent voting yes in San Diego County. Only 29 percent voted for it in San Francisco. After passage, Proposition 187 was challenged in the courts and was ultimately invalidated.

- Proposition 209 was a 1996 initiative constitutional amendment that prohibited state and local government agencies from giving preferential treatment to any individual or group on the basis of race, sex, color, ethnicity, or national origin. Widely viewed by friends and foes alike as an attack on affirmative action, this measure passed in the statewide vote, with 63 percent support in San Diego County. It received only 45 percent support in Los Angeles County, however, and a mere 29 percent support in San Francisco.

- Proposition 8 was a 2008 initiative constitutional amendment that eliminated the right of same-sex couples to marry. Backers of the proposition placed it on the ballot as a direct challenge to the California Supreme Court's ruling in

May 2008 affirming the constitutionality of same-sex marriage. The measure was approved 52 to 48 percent in the statewide vote. Only 25 percent of San Francisco County's voters voted yes, however, compared with 50 percent in Los Angeles County and 54 percent in San Diego County. In June 2015 the U.S. Supreme Court ruled in favor of same-sex marriage nationwide, declaring Proposition 8 unconstitutional.

- Proposition 30 was a 2012 initiative constitutional amendment that would temporarily raise taxes to fund education. Personal income taxes would increase for those earning over $250,000 for seven years, and the sales tax would increase by 25 cents for four years. This increased state revenue would be used to fund education at the K–12, community college, and university levels, which otherwise faced budget cuts. Teacher unions and Governor Brown campaigned aggressively for the passage of this initiative. Failure of the proposition would result in extensive budget cuts to the already struggling public school and university systems. Proposition 30 was approved statewide by a vote of 54 to 46 percent. Over 75 percent of San Francisco voters approved of the measure, as did 60 percent of Los Angeles County voters. In San Diego County, however, only 46 percent voted yes. Proposition 55 on the November 2016 ballot sought to extend by 12 years the temporary personal income tax increases enacted in 2012. This proposition passed with 62 percent of the statewide vote. San Francisco voters approved it by 72 percent, Los Angeles voters by 67 percent, and San Diego voters by 60 percent.

- Proposition 47 was a 2014 initiative that would reform the state's three strikes law. This law resulted in harsh prison sentences for those convicted of a third felony offense. However, the "third strike" for many was a nonviolent crime. Research has found that the three strikes law has disproportionately affected minority populations; over 45 percent of those serving life sentences under this law are African Americans.[11] Under the law as reformed by the initiative, those convicted of certain drug and property crimes would receive a misdemeanor sentence instead of a felony sentence if they had no prior convictions for serious or violent crimes such as rape, murder, or child molestation. Additionally, this measure would allow offenders currently serving felony sentences for nonviolent crimes to petition to have their felony sentences reduced to misdemeanor sentences. The measure passed with a statewide vote of 59 percent. It passed 79 percent to 21 percent in San Francisco and 63 percent to 37 percent in Los Angeles County. In San Diego County it passed by only 55 percent to 45 percent.

- Proposition 62 was a November 2016 initiative asking voters to approve the repeal of the death penalty and replace it with life imprisonment without the possibility of parole. This measure would apply retroactively to those inmates currently on death row. A very similar measure failed to pass in 2012 with a statewide vote of only 47 percent. November 2016 was no different: 54 percent of voters disapproved of this measure. San Francisco voters were very supportive of repealing the death penalty, with 71 percent voting in favor of the initiative. A slim majority (52 percent) of Los Angeles voters supported repeal. In contrast, only 44 percent of San Diego County voters were in favor of this measure.

- Proposition 64 on the November 2016 ballot legalizes marijuana and hemp under state law. With the support of 56 percent of the voters, this measure passed. Nearly 75 percent of San Francisco voters supported legalization, with

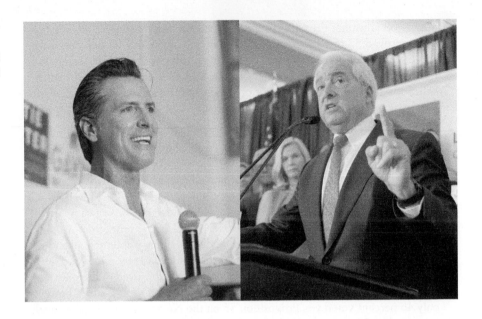

In 2018, Democratic candidate Gavin Newsom (left) and Republican candidate John Cox (right) ran to replace outgoing Governor Jerry Brown.

Los Angeles and San Diego voters supporting passage at 58 and 56 percent respectively.

- Proposition 6 on the November 2018 ballot asked voters to repeal fuel and vehicle tax increases that were enacted in 2017. The law mandated that the funds (about $5 billion per year) be used for road repairs and public transportation. Proposition 6 failed to pass and the fuel and vehicle taxes remain law. Not surprisingly, 83 percent of San Francisco voters were against the repeal of the fuel tax. Sixty percent of Los Angeles voters and only 49 percent of San Diego voters were against the repeal. Again, this exemplifies the progressive character of San Francisco and the comparatively more conservative leanings of San Diego.

THE GUBERNATORIAL ELECTION OF 2018 In the 2018 race for governor, the winner, Democrat Gavin Newsom, easily beat Republican John Cox with 86 percent of the vote in San Francisco and 71 percent in Los Angeles County. In San Diego County, however, support for Newsom stood at only 56 percent.

THE PRESIDENTIAL ELECTION OF 2016 In the November 8, 2016, presidential election, California voters preferred Hillary Clinton over Donald Trump 62 to 33 percent. San Francisco County overwhelmingly voted for Clinton with a resounding 85 percent; voters in Los Angeles County supported her at 72 percent, and San Diego County at 56 percent.

TO SUM UP The statistics in Table 4.2 demonstrate that political life varies dramatically in California from region to region. If you happen to reside in San Francisco, you live in one of the nation's most liberal, tolerant, and activist political cultures.[12] The political environment in San Diego, on the other hand, is more conservative, less tolerant, and more passive. Los Angeles falls somewhere in between. These three regions reflect the range of political cultural differences that exist across the state. You can easily see why local representatives in the state legislature fight so much and so fiercely and why they have such a hard time agreeing on anything.

Elections in California

The Battle over the Primary

The past decade has seen considerable controversy and upheaval and a number of court challenges regarding the type of primary system used in California. In primary elections, voters select their party's nominee for the general election. In the United States, there are three general types of primary-election systems, and states have the authority to determine the system under which they will operate.

- **Closed primary system**   Only voters who declare a party affiliation when they register to vote are permitted to vote in their party's primary election. Each party has its own ballot, listing the names of those who are competing to be the party's candidate in the general election. Voters receive the ballot of the party for which they are registered. Voters who decline to state a party affiliation when they register are not eligible to receive a party ballot; only party members can elect the party's nominees. Approximately 25 states use this system.

- **Open primary system**   Registered voters, regardless of their party affiliation, can vote in the party primary of their choice on primary election day. For example, a registered Democrat can decide if he or she would like to vote in the Republican Party primary and request that ballot. The choice of party ballot on primary election day does not affect the voter's permanent party affiliation. Approximately 20 states operate under this system.

- **Blanket primary system**   One ballot lists all candidates from all of the parties. All registered voters, including those not affiliated with any party, are permitted to vote, and all voters receive the same ballot. For instance, a voter who is not affiliated with a party may vote for a Democrat to run as the nominee for governor and a Republican to run as the nominee for the U.S. Senate. Under this system, voters who are not affiliated with a party help to choose that party's nominees. Alaska, Louisiana, Washington State, and California all use this primary system.

California operated under the closed primary system until the passage of Proposition 198 in 1996. Proposition 198 instituted a blanket primary system in which all voters received a single ballot containing the names of all candidates from all parties. California held two blanket primaries—in June 1998 and March 2000—before the U.S. Supreme Court (in the case of *California Democratic Party v. Jones*) invalidated Proposition 198. The Court ruled that, based on the First Amendment's guarantee of freedom of association, California's political parties have the right to exclude nonparty members from voting in party primaries. In an effort to include the growing number of nonaffiliated voters, California adopted a **modified closed primary system**. Beginning with the March 2002 primary election, political parties still had their own ballots but now had the option of adopting a party rule that would allow unaffiliated voters to vote in their party primary. If an unaffiliated voter was not allowed to request a party's ballot, he or she was given a ballot containing only the names of candidates for nonpartisan races and ballot measures.

Proponents of the blanket primary were not satisfied with the modified closed primary system, arguing that the blanket primary system is more inclusive and would result in more moderate candidates running in primary elections, thus producing more competitive races. The logic is that if independent, ideologically moderate voters participate in the primary election, they will bring a counterbalance to the more extreme and ideological views of traditional primary-party voters, the party loyalists. Primary candidates would, therefore, need to moderate their positions to attract the votes of independent voters. Therefore, in June 2010 voters once more passed a proposition that changed California's primary-election system.

Proposition 14 mandates a form of a blanket primary system known as the "top-two vote getters" or "jungle primary" system. This primary system only applies to state legislative and U.S. congressional elections as well as to the election of statewide officials such as governor and attorney general. (This system does not apply to candidates running for U.S. president, county central committees, or local offices. Presidential primaries continue to use closed or semi-closed primaries.) All registered voters, even those stating no party preference, receive a ballot listing all candidates from all qualified political parties. The two candidates who win the most votes for each office then participate in a runoff in November's general election. An interesting feature of this new primary election system is the possibility that the top two candidates can belong to the same political party.

The June 5, 2012, primary election was the first statewide election held under this new system, and the results were quite interesting. As a result of this new primary system, the November 2012 election saw 29 same-party runoffs for Congress, the state Assembly, and state Senate. This trend continued for the June 2014 and 2016 primaries. The June 2014 primary produced 24 same-party runoffs, and the June 2016 primary resulted in 28 same-party contests. The June 2016 primary made history as it produced the first same-party runoff for a statewide office, the U.S. Senate seat replacing long-term senator Barbara Boxer. Kamala Harris, California's Democratic attorney general, faced off against Democratic House member Loretta Sanchez in the November 2016 election. History repeated itself again in the June 2018 U.S. Senate primary, in which two Democrats were the top two vote getters: long-serving incumbent Diane Feinstein and Democrat Kevin de León. The June 2018 primary garnered national attention as Democrats hoping to win control of the House of Representatives worried that their chances would be greatly diminished because of our top-two primary system. California was home to seven House seats held by vulnerable Republicans, and the Democratic Party needed to flip those seats in their quest to win majority status in the House (we will discuss these contests in more depth later in this chapter).

For statewide races only, this new primary system also allows candidates to designate whether they have a political party preference and how it should be stated on the ballot. According to California law, "a candidate for nomination to a voter-nominated office shall have his or her party preference, or lack of party preference, stated on the ballot, but the party preference designation is selected solely by the candidate." This means that candidates can state the party with which they identify or they can state that they don't have a party preference. In this age of voter frustration directed at party politics and legislative gridlock, electing to have the ballot state "Party Preference: None" appears to be a strategy adopted by some candidates. This is what happened in a race for a hotly contested congressional seat in Ventura County in 2012. The redrawing of the state's congressional district boundaries created a new swing district in the area. A swing district is one in which there are near equal numbers of Republican and Democratic voters and a significant number of independent voters—who often decide the winner. This new district consisted of 41 percent Democrats, 35 percent Republicans, and 19 percent independent voters. There were four Democrats, one Republican, and one independent running in this primary. The "independent" candidate was actually a Republican who switched her party registration to "no party preference" just before filing her papers to run, hoping to win the support of enough independent and moderate voters to be one of the top two winners. A number of candidates have used this strategy, hoping voters won't remember or even know that they have been party loyalists before the campaign. Unfortunately for this candidate, the only Republican on the ballot and the better-known Democrat captured the top two positions and competed against each other in the November general election.

Will this new primary system have the intended result of encouraging more moderate candidates to run in primaries and ensuring their success? Louisiana and Washington operate under similar primary systems, and analyses of their election outcomes found that these states have not seen more moderate candidates elected. It has been found that Democrats in the state legislature have become slightly more moderate, but no similar ideological change has been found among Republican state lawmakers or among Democrats and Republicans in California's congressional delegation.[13] However, some argue that blanket primaries can boost voter turnout by 3 to 6 percent because they attract voters with no party preference. The June 2014 primary election in California did not meet these expectations. Neither did the June 2016 primary, whose exceptionally high turnout of 48 percent (with many voting for the first time) was largely a result of an exciting presidential primary and not the blanket primary. Although the June 2018 primary did see a substantial increase over the June 2014 turnout rate, it was only about 3 percent higher than the typical primary turnout prior to the adoption of the top-two system. One possible explanation for this higher turnout was the national attention focused on a number of California races as well as voters being more engaged and mobilized in this anti-Trump state.

Presidential Primaries: Maximizing California's Clout?

Until 2000 California held its presidential primaries in June of election years and was one of the last states to cast its votes for the parties' nominees. States holding earlier primaries and caucuses often determined the presidential nominees before Californians had a chance to go to the polls. To have more influence in the nomination process, California changed its presidential primary election date to March for the 2000 and 2004 presidential primaries.

Many believed it fitting that the most populous state should have an early primary date. However, this earlier primary date did not give California voters more clout in the presidential nomination process, because other states moved their primaries to even earlier dates. Hence, for the 2008 presidential primaries California changed the date once again, to February 5, the earliest permissible date under national party rules.

Many political analysts and journalists heralded the early February presidential primary date. But did this move really have the intended effect, as reflected in a hopeful 2007 *Los Angeles Times* article titled "Earlier Primary Gives California a Major Voice"? Many who had argued for the 2008 presidential primary in early February believed that candidates would have to campaign early and hard in the Golden State and win support from a racially and ethnically diverse population, especially the growing number of Latino voters. To win voters' support, the candidates would need to address issues important to Californians, and all this would result in California's greater prominence in presidential campaign politics. Or so the theory went.

One of the unanticipated consequences of California's adoption of an early primary date was that a number of states with long-standing early primaries set their election dates even earlier, not wanting to be overshadowed by the most populous state in the nation. Twenty-three other states also moved their primaries to February 5, resulting in something akin to a national primary. California's dream of being in the electoral limelight quickly faded.

Another consequence of the early February presidential primary was additional cost for the state, as the primaries for statewide offices continued to be held in June. The June 2008 primary election for statewide offices cost the state and counties $100 million and resulted in a historically low voting turnout rate of less than 25 percent of the registered voters. Including the November 2008 general election, California voters were asked to vote in three elections in less than 10 months. California's presidential primary went again back to the June date. However, the June 2012 California primary (which included primaries for presidential and statewide candidates) saw a record low turnout of only 22 percent of registered voters. Some believe that the frequent date changes for primary elections confuse voters and thereby contribute to California's less than spectacular voting turnout rates. We witnessed a slight improvement in June 2016, with 33 percent of registered voters casting ballots in the primary, and again in 2018, with a 37 percent turnout rate. To further confuse voters, California's 2020 presidential primary will be on March 3.

Initiative Campaigns: Direct Democracy or Tool of Special Interests?

One legacy of California's early-twentieth-century Progressive reform movement is the **ballot initiative** process. Californians can completely bypass the state legislature and their elected representatives and place proposed policies on the ballot for direct vote by the people. As the name suggests, the electorate *initiates* initiatives. Most people think of the initiative process as direct democracy in action—concerned citizens circulating petitions to qualify their issue for the ballot and then holding an election for the public to state its preference for or against the proposed policy. In reality, only a small number of ballot initiatives emerge as a result of grassroots efforts. Initiatives are largely a political tool used by special-interest groups to achieve their policy goals. Depending on the issue, interest groups sometimes find it politically expedient to bypass the legislature altogether, believing they have a better chance of achieving their policy goals if they take the issue directly to the voters.

For example, many members of the California legislature would find it politically unwise to introduce legislation to legalize marijuana, abolish the death penalty, or raise taxes. Positions on these issues are sure to outrage some voters, making re-election more difficult. That is why these types of issues find their way onto our ballots as initiatives or referendums. Likewise, legislation that would curb the power of special interests, interests that make sizable campaign contributions to legislators, also are unlikely to be dealt with by our elected representatives. Recently, some local ballot measures have passed that reduce retirement benefits for public employees. If an elected official introduced this type of proposal, he or she would be targeted for re-election defeat by unions representing public employees. Therefore, for many of these types of issues, interest groups realize that the most productive route is to go directly to the voters via the initiative process. In addition, citizen groups have found the initiative process to be the only avenue for policy change in the areas of legislative term limits, nonpartisan redistricting, and the blanket primary system. These changes would never have been proposed or approved by legislators, whose power and that of their political party would be curbed.

Since 1912, the first year initiatives were permitted, nearly 400 statewide initiatives have appeared on the California ballot. These ballot initiatives have dealt with a wide range of issues, such as legalization of marijuana, campaign-finance reform, same-sex marriage, taxation policy, legalization of gambling casinos, the establishment of a state lottery, environmental regulations, affirmative action policy, the criminal justice system, and labor issues. Of these hundreds of initiatives, only about one-third have been approved by the voters. In the past three decades, there has been a dramatic surge in the number of initiatives that have been proposed and that have qualified for the ballot. Many surmise that the reason for this increase is that special interests have become more sophisticated in their use of the initiative process to achieve their policy goals.

QUALIFYING FOR THE BALLOT For initiatives creating new laws (statutes) to qualify for the ballot, the state requires signatures of registered voters equal to 5 percent of the number of people who voted in the previous governor's race. For propositions aiming to amend the state constitution, the state requires 8 percent— about 600,000 for initiatives and 1 million for constitutional amendments. Signatures are gathered on petitions, which are then submitted to the secretary of state's office for verification. Collecting hundreds of thousands of signatures of registered voters is a daunting task. Rarely is this a grassroots movement in which ordinary citizens fan out across the state, knock on doors, and stand in front of supermarkets, asking strangers to support their initiative by signing a petition. More common is the hiring of professional signature gatherers, such as political consulting firms that hire people to go to college campuses, supermarkets, malls, and other places where voters congregate. Typically they are paid an average of $1.50 for every signature they acquire. However, the November 2018 election, with 11 ballot measures and many big-money donors, saw the average price of a signature rise to $6. All total, to qualify for the November 2018 ballot, campaigns spent over $20.5 million just on signature-gathering activities.[14]

CAMPAIGNING To wage a successful campaign either in support of or in opposition to a more controversial initiative, one needs ample political resources, particularly money. Not only must a statewide initiative campaign hire political consultants, but it must also plan and implement a sustainable media campaign. Such campaigns are very costly because of California's size and expensive media markets. Therefore, it is not surprising that the more high-profile and controversial initiative campaigns cost tens of millions of dollars. In 2008 slightly over $80 million was spent on the highly controversial initiative Proposition 8, a constitutional amendment to eliminate same-sex marriage in California. Proposition 8 was put on the ballot in response to the state Supreme Court's May 2008 ruling (in a 4-to-3 decision) declaring that the state constitution protects a fundamental "right to marry" that extends equally to same-sex couples. Both sides of the issue collected near equal contributions, with the majority of the contributions in support of Proposition 8 coming from members of the Mormon Church throughout the United States.[15] As expensive as Proposition 8 was, it did not break the record for the most expensive initiative campaign. In 2006 both sides combined spent more than $150 million on Proposition 87, the alternative energy initiative, which was soundly defeated by a 55 percent vote. Breaking that spending record was a series of initiatives in 2008 (Propositions 94–97) that sought to expand the number of Native American casinos in the state. According to a recent report by the *Washington Post*, the two sides combined spent over $170 million on those campaigns.[16] This was, by far, the most expensive proposition campaign not only in California history but in U.S. history.

It should be noted that spending more money than the opposing side does not always guarantee victory. Case in point: Proponents of Proposition 34, an initiative to repeal the death penalty on the November 2012 ballot, spent over $8 million on the yes campaign, whereas the opposition spent only a paltry $400,000 to defeat the measure.

Political savvy is another important resource. The chances of winning an initiative campaign increase if one understands how the game is played. For example, the naming of the proposition can increase its chance of passage. In the November 1996 election, Proposition 209, officially titled "Prohibition against Discrimination or Preferential Treatment by State and Other Public Entities," appeared on the ballot. Its supporters referred to the proposition as the "California Civil Rights Initiative." Considering these titles alone, it would be difficult to imagine this proposition failing; in these progressive times, it is fair to say that most voters are opposed to discrimination and are supportive of civil rights. In reality, however, Proposition 209 was not what most would consider a civil rights statute. The proposition proposed to eliminate affirmative action programs in California for women and minorities in public employment, education (college admissions, tutoring, and outreach programs), and contracting. But the clever naming worked: Proposition 209 passed and is now state law.

CRITICISMS OF DIRECT DEMOCRACY Critics of the initiative process believe that too many complicated issues are presented to the voters as ballot propositions. In some recent elections, voters have had to vote for candidates for federal, state, county, and city elective offices as well as cast their votes for more than a dozen important state propositions and numerous county and city measures. Case in point—the November 2016 election had 17 ballot propositions, and the Official California Voter Information Guide was 224 pages, the longest ever. It was estimated that it would take about 14 hours to read the guide. Not surprisingly, few voters will spend this amount of time educating themselves on the ballot propositions. David Redlawsk, co-author of *How Voters Decide: Information Processing in Election Campaigns*, describes the situation as follows: "People want to do what we would call a good job—that is make what they think is the right decision—but they want to do it essentially with the least amount of effort necessary."[17]

Some argue that many of the issues that appear as ballot initiatives are best suited for debate and deliberation by our elected representatives and should not be represented by misleading television ads aimed at the public. Sometimes the propositions are very confusing in name and in substance, and some question whether we are asking too much of the electorate to wade through all this information. Another problem with the initiative process is that the constitutionality of many propositions approved by the voters is later challenged. It takes years for the courts to render a decision, and it is not uncommon for the courts to declare the law based on the passage of the proposition to be unconstitutional, null, and void. Not only does this complicate the process, it also frustrates the public to see the courts invalidate its will.

The legislature understands some of the problems associated with the initiative and has created state commissions to investigate and reform the process. Some of these suggested reforms aim to accomplish the following: prohibit the use of paid signature gatherers, which only well-funded interest groups can afford; increase the number of signatures required, with the goal of reducing the number of initiatives; restrict the types of issues that can appear as ballot initiatives; and review the constitutionality of initiatives prior to placing them on the ballot. In September 2014 the legislature enacted two bills that reform the initiative process. One bill provides for a 30-day public review period that commences when the initiative is first proposed. Reformers hope that public input during this time will result in constructive modifications to propositions before they appear on the ballot, and that such input may motivate supporters of the proposed initiative to work with lawmakers to find a legislative solution to the issue. The other bill requires that the secretary of state post online and continuously update the top 10 donors contributing to both sides of an initiative. This provision creates more transparency by revealing exactly who is contributing big money in support of or in opposition to an initiative.

The 2003 Gubernatorial Recall Election: A Perfect Political Storm

On October 7, 2003, Governor Gray Davis made history. Only 11 months after he successfully won his re-election bid, he was recalled from office. He was the first and only governor in the state of California and the second governor in the nation's history to be recalled. The recall movement and election of Arnold Schwarzenegger were in every sense dramatic, historic, and stunning.

Davis was re-elected in November 2002, thanks in part to a very weak challenger, even though just before the election a majority of voters disapproved of his overall performance as governor.[18] Voters held Governor Davis responsible for the 2000–01 energy crisis, during which Californians were forced to reduce their energy consumption and pay more for their electricity while experiencing or being threatened by blackouts. News reports focused on this issue for many months, which had a negative impact on Davis's popularity. Compounding the problem was a dramatic decrease in state revenues. The governor had to announce that the state was short $23.6 billion and that the 2003–04 budget shortfall would rise to nearly $35 billion. The state legislature could not produce a budget on time, and voters were very uneasy about the economic future of the state. Davis entered his second term as a wounded, unpopular governor, viewed as distant, too beholden to special interests, and ineffectual.

Darrell Issa, a multimillionaire Republican member of Congress from the San Diego area, was a dominant force in the movement to recall Davis. He injected nearly $2 million into the recall effort and had hopes of running for governor if the recall succeeded. Nearly 1.5 million voter signatures were collected on recall petitions, meeting the state requirement for an October 2003 recall election. Unfortunately for Representative Issa's hopes of capturing the governorship, a well-known, charismatic, moderate Republican anti-politician, anti-establishment actor/businessman appeared on the scene: Arnold Schwarzenegger. In the summer of 2003 Schwarzenegger announced his candidacy and immediately became the front-runner among Republican candidates, making national and international headlines with his decision to run.[19] Politically, it was a perfect storm: a weak and unpopular governor, an unhappy electorate, and an internationally known celebrity. On the day of the election, 9.4 million Californians cast ballots, 11 percent more than the turnout in Davis's

2002 re-election. Fifty-five percent voted to remove Davis from office. Schwarzenegger was elected governor in his place with 48.6 percent of the votes cast. Schwarzenegger's adoption of moderate positions—pro-choice on abortion, moderate on the environment, and cooperative with the Democratically controlled state legislature—placed him in sync with voters, resulting in his re-election victory in 2006.

The 2008 Election: Demographic and Ideological Shifts

The 2008 election was somewhat unusual, even by California standards. A very popular, young, charismatic candidate, Barack Obama, topped the ticket as the Democratic candidate for the presidency, winning 61 percent of the popular vote compared to John McCain's 37 percent, the biggest margin in the state of California since 1964.

The *Los Angeles Times*, in an article aptly titled "State's Shifting Political Landscape," described the election results:

> Those unpredictable decisions by voters, however, were accompaniments to the election's main theme: the demographic and ideological shifts that have delivered the state into Democratic hands and demonstrated anew the tough road ahead for the Republican minority.[20]

The Democratic Party was hopeful that it could continue to win the support and allegiance of the overwhelming number of voters who had cast their votes for Obama, including 83 percent of first-time voters. Seventy-six percent of those 18–29 years of age voted for Obama compared to only 48 percent of those 65 and older. However, some analysts were not confident that future elections would see high percentages of young voters turning out to vote or substantial increases in support for the Democratic Party.

By November 2, 2010, the evidence was in. The lead headline from Scott Fahey's Elections 2010 blog from Southern California Public Radio read, "Low youth voter turnout hurts Democrats." As he described it, "In California, one of every five voters in 2008 was between the ages of 18 and 29, compared with about 1 in 10 on Tuesday." California reflected the overall national trend with fewer young, liberal, and black voters casting votes in the November 2010 general election.

The 2010 General Election

While the nation witnessed a historic "shellacking" of the Democratic Party, as President Obama called it, with an unprecedented loss of Democrat-held seats in Congress, Californians voted to the beat of a different drummer. All of the Democratic candidates running for statewide elective office won, and nearly all of them won by respectable margins. The *Los Angeles Times*, in an analysis of the vote based on exit poll data, concluded that the strength of the Latino vote was a key factor in the success of Democratic candidates. Latino voters made up 22 percent of the California voter pool, a record tally that sunk the election hopes of many Republicans.

THE GOVERNOR'S RACE The costliest statewide race in the nation's history pitted novice politician and billionaire Meg Whitman against political insider Jerry Brown. Whitman spent a record-breaking $160 million on her general election campaign (see Table 4.3 on p. 112), with over $140 million from her own personal wealth. Of this total, she poured nearly $110 million into TV and radio advertising.

Californians quickly became aware of her candidacy, and voters easily recognized her name. In contrast, Jerry Brown, who had served two terms as governor (1975–83), had been mayor of Oakland (1999–2007), and most recently had served as state attorney general, spent only $25 million on his campaign. In the end, Brown won by a very comfortable margin, 54 percent to 41 percent. Furthermore, Brown's cost per vote was only $1.24, whereas Whitman spent a whopping $51.82 per vote!

THE U.S. SENATE RACE Barbara Boxer, a liberal Democrat running for her fourth term in the U.S. Senate, had a tough re-election challenge, the toughest of her political career. Boxer, a career politician, ran against outsider and novice campaigner Carly Fiorina, a Republican and former CEO of Hewlett-Packard (HP). Typically, incumbents such as Boxer, running for re-election in a state where their political party dominates, have a relatively easy time keeping their seat. The situation was different this time around. California's economy was in shambles, Boxer's popularity had been declining, and Fiorina was a formidable opponent. In the end, Boxer prevailed, winning re-election with 52 percent of the vote compared to Fiorina's 43 percent. Many pundits believe that Fiorina's failure to moderate her position on social issues (she was ardently antiabortion and anti-illegal immigration), along with Boxer's stinging ads highlighting the layoff of 30,000 HP workers under Fiorina's stewardship, was responsible for Fiorina's loss.

PROPOSITION 20: REDISTRICTING CONGRESSIONAL DISTRICTS VS. PROPOSITION 27: ELIMINATING THE STATE REDISTRICTING COMMISSION Propositions 20 and 27 were actually competing initiatives. Proposition 20 is an extension of Proposition 11, which passed in November 2008. Proposition 11 created the 14-member Citizens Redistricting Commission that would be in charge of drawing the boundaries of state Assembly and state Senate districts after each U.S. Census. November 2010's Proposition 20 asked voters to remove the authority for congressional redistricting from the legislature and give this power to the newly created Citizens Redistricting Commission. The commission would then be responsible for drawing congressional district lines as well as continuing to exercise the power to draw state Assembly and state Senate district boundaries. The competing initiative, Proposition 27, on the other hand, would have eliminated the Citizens Redistricting Commission and returned to the legislature the power to draw state district boundaries (essentially repealing Proposition 11). California voters soundly endorsed the Citizens Redistricting Commission (defeating Proposition 27 with a 59 percent vote against it) and gave the Commission the power to determine congressional districts as well (Proposition 20 passed with a 61 percent vote in favor).

PROPOSITION 25: SIMPLE MAJORITY VOTE TO PASS BUDGET Proposition 25 changed the legislative vote requirement to pass the budget from two-thirds to a simple majority. In addition, all members of the legislature must permanently forfeit reimbursement for salary and expenses for every day the budget is late. At the time that Proposition 25 was introduced, California had not passed a state budget by the mandatory June 15 deadline in 23 years. Budget negotiations in 2010 extended 100 days past the deadline, just close enough to Election Day for it to be fresh in voters' minds. Californians passed Proposition 25 with a 55 percent affirmative vote. Supporters of this initiative were labor unions (especially teachers who received layoff notices when the budget was not passed on time), the League of Women Voters, groups representing retirees, and others who were able to devote resources to the "Yes on Prop 25" campaign. Since passage of this proposition, the state budget has been passed on time.

The 2012 Primary Election

The June 2012 primary was an interesting one. Usually, the major contest in the primary during a presidential election year is between the candidates competing for their party's nomination for the presidential race. But, as typically happens when states hold their primary late in the political season, Mitt Romney already had won enough delegates to secure his party's nomination, and President Obama had no Democratic challenger and was, by default, his party's nominee. Perhaps this explains why only one in three registered voters participated in this election, with one of the lowest turnout rates in Los Angeles County, at less than 22 percent. As mandated by the passage of Proposition 14, this was the first statewide blanket primary using the new top-two candidates system. It was also the first election since the adoption of the newly drawn congressional and state legislative districts. The ballot looked different, all voters regardless of party affiliation were given the same ballot, the results were calculated differently, and some candidates found themselves running in new or very different districts. A very interesting election, indeed.

The 2012 General Election: More Demographic and Ideological Shifts

THE PRESIDENTIAL RACE The outcome of the November 2012 presidential election looked similar to that of the 2008 presidential election, with young and minority voters favoring President Obama and older and white voters supporting Romney. Statewide, Obama won 59 percent of the vote, slightly less than the 61 percent he won in 2008. He received 71 percent of the votes cast by 18- to 29-year-old Californians, which is close to the 76 percent he received in 2008. Of those 65 years of age and older, 48 percent voted for Obama, the same percentage as did in 2008. Other notable demographic results were based on race, marital status, and place of residence. While only 45 percent of whites supported Obama, 79 percent of Asian Americans and 72 percent of Latinos voted for him. Marital status also made a difference, with Obama receiving 67 percent of the votes of unmarried Californians and 51 percent of the votes of married voters. Voters living in urban areas chose to re-elect the president by 65 percent compared to rural voters at 50 percent.

The 2012 election was interesting in terms of voter turnout rates. Although 5 percent fewer Californians voted in 2012 than in 2008, more young voters turned out to vote in 2012. The youth vote accounted for 20 percent of all votes cast in 2008 and 28 percent of all votes in 2012. That is a 40 percent increase in turnout among 18- to 29-year-old California voters. Nationwide, there was only a slight increase in the youth vote, which grew from 17 percent in 2008 to 19 percent in 2012. What accounted for this dramatic increase in the turnout of young California voters?

According to political scientist Peter Levine, California's new online voter registration system (described later in this chapter), made available shortly before the 2012 election, registered nearly 700,000 new voters, many of whom were young people.[21] Also, Proposition 30 (the initiative to fund higher education) was a salient issue for young voters. If the measure did not pass, college students would face another round of tuition increases, crowded classes, and cuts in enrollment to the California State University and University of California systems. This combination of an accessible online voter registration system and an important initiative impacting higher education motivated young voters.

CONGRESSIONAL RACES As mandated by the U.S. Constitution, all House members serve two-year terms in office. California has 53 House members, and in the November 2012 election, 11 new members were elected, the most in 20 years. Democrats won 38 of the 53 seats, and the number of seats held by Latinos increased. These changes were a result of the recent remapping of House districts and changing demographics. A number of incumbent House members retired when their districts were redrawn after the 2010 U.S. Census, and some found themselves in competitive districts where their re-election was not assured. Prior to the 2012 election, only one House seat had changed between the parties during the last five congressional elections. In 2012, Democratic candidates won four more House seats than they had in 2010. A second factor related to the strong showing by Democratic candidates is the growing number and clout of Latino voters, especially in Southern California. As reported in the *Los Angeles Times*, "Voters in Riverside and San Bernardino counties elected three Democrats to Congress— two Latinos and a gay Asian American—after having sent only two Democrats to Washington in the last four decades."[22]

CALIFORNIA LEGISLATIVE RACES The *Los Angeles Times* headline on November 8, 2012, read, "Blue reign in Sacramento: Democrats' historic gains position them for unchecked power." Prior to the November 6 election, Democrats had controlled both the state Assembly and the state Senate. Amazingly, this election not only allowed the Democratic Party to maintain its majority status, it also gave it *supermajority* status. Having a supermajority means there are enough Democratic votes in each chamber to raise taxes without needing any votes from Republicans. The last time a party had supermajority power in California was in 1933 when the Republicans were in charge. The Democrats last had this power in 1883. This supermajority status was short-lived, however—three Democratic state senators were suspended in March 2014 after being indicted on felony criminal charges.

PROPOSITIONS There were 11 measures on the November 2012 ballot. Voters were asked to weigh in on a number of issues ranging from increased taxes to funding for educational programs to the repeal of the death penalty. A record-breaking amount of money was spent on these campaigns. George Skelton, a *Los Angeles Times* columnist, wrote, "It's almost unfathomable that $372 million was spent to promote or attack the 11 measures. To put it in perspective, that amount of money could pay for the annual tuitions of 31,000 undergrads at the University of California. The top 20 donors provided 69 percent of all initiative funding."[23] What follows is a description of some of the more high-profile measures:

- **Proposition 30: Taxes to Fund Education versus Proposition 38: Tax to Fund Education and Early Childhood Programs** These two competing propositions dealt with ways to raise revenue to fund education. Proposition 30, backed by the governor, would temporarily raise the state sales tax for 4 years and increase taxes on the wealthy for 7 years. Proposition 38 would raise taxes on earnings for all Californians for 12 years. Since these were competing measures, if both passed, the one receiving the most votes would prevail. Proposition 30 passed with 55 percent of the vote. Proposition 38 received only 28 percent of the vote even though its sponsor, Molly Munger, spent $44 million of her own money on the measure. In addition, an outside political group from Arizona spent over $11 million to defeat both Propositions 30 and 38.

- **Proposition 34: Death Penalty**   This initiative statute would repeal the death penalty and replace it with life in prison without possibility of parole. Those currently on death row would have their sentences commuted to life imprisonment. Proponents of this measure spent over $8 million. Opponents spent a small fraction of that amount. The measure was defeated with a 52 percent "no" vote.

- **Proposition 36: Three Strikes Law: Repeat Felony Offenders**   This measure would revise the existing three strikes law to impose life sentences only when the offender is convicted of a new violent felony. Those previously convicted under this law for nonviolent felonies may have their sentences reviewed. The measure easily passed with 69 percent of the vote.

- **Proposition 37: Genetically Engineered Foods Labeling**   This proposition would require the labeling of food that is made from plants or animals containing genetically altered material. Agroscience opponents, including DuPont, Dow Agro, and Monsanto, spent over $15 million to defeat this measure. The proposition failed, receiving only 48 percent of the vote.

The 2014 Election

Nationally, the contest between Democrats and Republicans over control of the U.S. Senate was the most important issue of the 2014 midterm elections. If the Republican Party gained six Senate seats, they would then control both chambers of Congress. The Democratic Party hoped to maintain control of the Senate but faced an uphill battle in a number of important U.S. Senate contests. The Republican Party prevailed, and both chambers of Congress were controlled by the Republican Party. In California, however, 2014 was a rather subdued election year, evidenced by the fact that fewer than three in 10 voters participated in this election. California's two U.S. senators were not up for re-election, the governor's race was not very competitive, and only a few ballot initiatives engaged in media campaigns.

THE GOVERNOR'S RACE Governor Jerry Brown, a popular incumbent, was re-elected by a comfortable margin. His opponent, Neel Kashkari, never stood much of a chance to win. Unlike Brown's 2010 challenger, Meg Whitman (who raised over $176 million), Kashkari was virtually unknown to the public and was seriously underfunded. Six weeks prior to the election his campaign had less than $700,000 to spend compared to Governor Brown's nearly $24 million. Brown agreed to only one 60-minute televised debate, which did not enjoy a large audience and did little to boost Kashkari's popularity. Kashkari's weeklong stint as an undercover homeless person in Fresno also failed to generate support for his campaign. Kashkari even gave away $25 cash cards to the first 100 people who showed up at one of his campaign events (most likely violating the state's election code that prohibits candidates from giving gifts to win votes). Brown beat Kashkari 54 percent to 41 percent and was re-elected to serve a historic fourth and final term as governor.

PROPOSITIONS Six propositions appeared on the ballot, comparatively few by California standards. Below is a description of the initiatives that passed:

- **Propositions 1 and 2: Water Bond and State Budget**   These two measures were publicized as companion initiatives ("Save Water, Save Money") and had virtually no opposition. These propositions dealt with the water crisis in California and ensured stricter enforcement of the state's "rainy day" surplus money fund. Both propositions passed overwhelmingly with 67 percent and 69 percent of the vote respectively.

- **Proposition 47: Criminal Sentences; Misdemeanor Penalties**   As described earlier in this chapter, crimes such as drug possession, shoplifting, petty theft, and forgery would qualify as misdemeanor, not felony, crimes under this measure. The result would be lesser penalties for those with no prior convictions for serious, violent crimes. As reported in the *Los Angeles Times*, it is believed that 20 percent of criminals would face more lenient sentences and more than 7,000 current inmates could petition the courts to reduce their sentences.[24] Most law enforcement organizations were opposed to this measure, arguing that thousands of dangerous criminals would be released from prison and that our criminal justice system would be overwhelmed with petitions for reduced sentences. However, pre-election polling found the public to be overwhelmingly in favor of this measure. The proposition passed with 59 percent of the vote.

The 2016 Primary Election

Many believed that California would finally have a June presidential primary that mattered. California's impact, however, was not as great as had been anticipated. All but one of the Republican candidates vying for the presidential nomination had dropped out prior to the June primary: Donald Trump was the last man standing on the Republican side and won the California Republican primary with over 75 percent of the vote. On the Democratic side, in the Clinton versus Sanders contest, Clinton had surged far enough ahead of Sanders in the delegate count that her nomination was a foregone conclusion prior to the California primary. Her victory in the California Democratic primary (winning nearly 56 percent of the vote to Sanders 43 percent) technically put her in the position where she could officially declare that she was her party's presidential nominee.

One positive consequence of this primary was that it engaged the public. As previously mentioned, the 2016 presidential primary motivated people to register to vote. From May 2012 to May 2016 California voter registration numbers had increased by over 760,000 people, with 650,000 people registering in the few weeks prior to the June 2016 primary.

The contest to fill retiring Democratic U.S. senator Barbara Boxer's seat saw two Democrats win the top-two primary, out of a field of 34 candidates. Kamala Harris, the twice-elected California attorney general, trounced Loretta Sanchez, a 20-year House member, in the primary. Harris, a daughter of Jamaican and Indian immigrants, and Sanchez, a daughter of Mexican immigrants, ensured that the next U.S. senator from California would be a woman of color.

The 2016 General Election

THE PRESIDENTIAL RACE The outcome of the November 2016 presidential race was a stunner. Virtually all the polls and predictions had Hillary Clinton winning the presidency. Surprisingly, on election night as the state by state results were coming in, it gradually became apparent that Clinton was losing the electoral college vote. Donald Trump exceeded the necessary 270 electoral college votes needed to win the presidency, in the end winning over 300 electoral college votes. Clinton, however, won the popular vote count by more than two million votes. To say this was an upset victory would be an understatement: the nation was shocked. Young people across the country protested in the streets (a number of the larger protests were in California). It was calculated that if 1 out of every 100 Trump voters had shifted their vote to Clinton, she would have won the presidency with 307 electoral college votes. That's how close of an election it was. California, not surprisingly, voted overwhelming for Clinton by a nearly 2-to-1 margin (62 percent Clinton; 33 percent Trump). Statewide, Clinton beat Obama's margin over Romney in 2012 by 6 percentage points. This was the widest margin in a presidential election in the past 80 years. In fact, southern California's Orange County, birthplace of the reactionary John Birch Society and historic Republican stronghold, voted for a Democratic candidate for the first time in 88 years. Clearly, California was out of step with the rest of the nation.

In the 2012 presidential election, Obama won 71 percent of the 18- to 29-year-old vote. Clinton fell slightly short of that number, winning 66 percent of the youth vote. Those 45 to 64 years of age had the highest turnout of any age group, contributing 38 percent of the total vote count in the state. This age group voted for Trump at a higher percentage (39 percent) than any other age group. Minority voters were overwhelming in favor of Clinton but fell short of their support of Obama in 2012. Seventy percent of Asian Americans, 71 percent of Latinos, and 88 percent of African American voters supported Clinton. White voters voted for Clinton at a lower rate: 50 percent of white men and 57 percent of white women voted for Clinton. Similar to the national trend, whites with no college degree were more likely to vote for Trump. In California this group supported Trump at 59 percent, compared to 67 percent of this group nationally. Religion was another differentiating factor. Protestants were more likely to vote for Trump than any other religious group (51 percent). Slight regional differences were noted in this election. The areas that were the most supportive of Clinton were the Bay Area (79 percent), coastal communities (67 percent), and Los Angeles (71 percent). Trump drew support from inland and central California (45 percent) and parts of southern California (45 percent).[25]

Nationwide, voting turnout rates were the lowest in about 20 years. Of those eligible to vote, only about 57 percent went to the polls. In California even fewer eligible voters participated (approximately 50 percent), with the exception of Latino voters, who flocked to the polls. This group mobilized in California most likely due to Trump's anti-immigrant positions. The Latino vote comprised nearly one-third of all votes cast, an increase of nearly 10 percent from the 2012 election. African American turnout was slightly below the 2012 turnout. White turnout fell by about 7 percent, and Asian American turnout remained about the same. The youth vote declined by about 7 percent from 2012 and mirrored the national youth turnout, where 18- to 29-year-olds made up about 20 percent of all those voting.

CONGRESSIONAL RACES In 2016, California sent its first new senator in 24 years to Washington. Kamala Harris, California's attorney general, won the seat vacated by Senator Barbara Boxer. Harris also made history as the first African American to represent California in the U.S. Senate as well as the second African American woman ever to be elected to the Senate. In our new top-two primary system, Harris ran against another Democrat, Representative Loretta Sanchez. Overshadowed by the more media-driven presidential race, this race received scant attention and was not competitive. Harris easily beat Sanchez, winning 63 percent of the vote.

California's House delegation saw few changes in the 2016 election. No seats switched party, and California sent 39 Democrats and 14 Republicans to the House of Representatives. A handful of Republican incumbents narrowly won re-election. One of the most watched contests was between six-term Republican House member Darryl Issa, representing a district that straddles Orange and San Diego counties, and newcomer retired colonel Doug Applegate. Issa had fended off challengers before with double-digit leads, but Applegate made this contest highly competitive. Issa eked out a win by a very slim margin.

CALIFORNIA LEGISLATIVE RACES The Democratic Party again had firm control over both the state Assembly and the state Senate. Three Republican Assembly incumbents lost their seats to Democrats. Two Democratic Assembly incumbents lost their seats to fellow Democratic challengers (remember, we now have a top-two vote-getter primary system that makes it possible for the top two candidates running against each other in the general election to be from the same political party). Democrats had a supermajority in the state Assembly with 55 seats; Republicans had 25 Assembly seats. Incumbent state senators all won their re-election bids. The Democrats also won a supermajority in the state Senate and had 27 seats to the Republicans' 13 seats.

PROPOSITIONS There were 17 measures on the November 2016 ballot, the largest number of initiatives on a ballot since March 2000. Voters were asked to consider issues such as legalization of marijuana (again), repeal of the death penalty (again), background checks on purchases of ammunition, a ban on plastic grocery bags, caps on health care costs, and workplace rules for adult movie actors, to name a few. Let's look at some of the more high-profile, controversial initiatives:

- **Proposition 58: Repeal English-Only Education**   This proposition repealed Proposition 227, the initiative passed in 1998 that made California public schools English-only. Proposition 58 requires school administrators to solicit input from parents in developing language acquisition programs and allows schools to offer dual immersion language programs. This proposition had overwhelming support and passed with more than 72 percent of the vote. Proposition 227 passed in 1998 with more than 60 percent of the vote. The dramatic reversal in 20 years most likely reflects the demographic changes in the state and the growing Latino population and its strength at the ballot box.

- **Proposition 61: Drug Price Standards**   This initiative would require that the state of California pay no more than prices paid by the U.S. Department of Veterans Affairs for prescription drugs. Over $125 million was spent on this campaign, with most of the money coming from major drug companies hoping to defeat this measure. Most experts agreed this was a poorly crafted measure that would not bring about the desired outcome of lower prescription drug costs. The measure failed with a 54 percent "no" vote.

- **Proposition 62: Repeal the Death Penalty and Proposition 66: Death Penalty Procedures** These were competing initiatives. Proposition 62 sought to end the death penalty in California. Prisoners already on death row would have their sentences commuted to life in prison with no chance of parole. Proposition 66 was an opposing measure that would retain the death penalty and speed up the appeals process, mandating that all appeals be completed within five years of the death penalty sentence. Proposition 62 failed with 54 percent of voters not wanting to repeal the death penalty. Proposition 66 passed by a slim major- ity of 51 percent. It is interesting to note that Los Angeles County and virtually all of the northern California coastal counties voted to repeal the death penalty and voted against speeding up the appeals process, whereas most of the inland counties voted against repeal and for the expedited appeals process.

- **Proposition 63: Background Checks for Ammunition Purchases and Ban on Large-Capacity Magazines** This measure requires individuals to have a permit to purchase ammunition, closes the loophole on allowing exemptions to the ban on large-capacity magazines, strengthens enforcement prohibiting felons from owning firearms, and makes the theft of firearms a felony. This initiative passed with a 63 percent vote. Proponents outspent opponents by a 5-to-1 margin. Surprisingly, the National Rifle Association, which opposed this measure, spent less than $100,000 on efforts to defeat it. And again we see a regional split, with most inland counties voting against this measure and coastal and near-coastal counties supporting it.

- **Proposition 64: Legalization of Marijuana** California, along with Massachusetts, Maine, and Nevada, voted to legalize the recreational use of marijuana. In addition, Arkansas, Florida, North Dakota, and Montana all passed initiatives to make medical marijuana legal. Proposition 64 passed with 56 percent of the vote. Many of the counties voting against this measure are solidly Republican (as indicated in Figure 4.4 on page 88).

- **Proposition 65: Disposable Bag Sales Revenue to Wildlife Conservation Fund and Proposition 67: Plastic Bag Ban** These two competing measures dealt with the legislative ban on plastic bags (Senate Bill 270). Proposition 65 was supported by the plastic bag industry and, if passed, would essentially kill Senate Bill 270. Proposition 67 would ratify SB (Senate Bill) 270, which outlaws single-use plastic bags and mandates that stores make available recyclable bags for a minimum cost of 10 cents. Revenue from the sale of these bags would be used to cover their costs and to educate consumers about sustainability. Proposition 65 failed to pass with a 55 percent "no" vote while SB 270 was ratified with 52 percent of the vote.

The 2018 Election

California was home to seven Republican House seats that the Democratic Party had targeted as vulnerable, and they needed to flip those seats in their quest to gain control of the House of Representatives. Democrats worried that their chances of winning these House seats might be diminished because of our top-two primary. There was a possibility that in some of the highly competitive House districts the top two candidates receiving the most votes would end up being two Republicans who would compete in November's election, thereby making it impossible for Democrats to win those seats.

How could this happen: two Republican candidates running against each other in November 2018? The problem was that too many Democratic candidates had entered these races. Some races had a total of 16 or more candidates on the ballot! The concern was that Democratic voters would split their votes amongst their party's numerous candidates, and that Republican voters would not splinter their votes (five of the seven targeted districts had an incumbent Republican on the ballot with few if any Republican challengers). In the end, all congressional primaries resulted in both a Democratic and a Republican candidate competing in the November 2018 general election. However, as mentioned earlier, the competition for the U.S. Senate resulted in two Democrats winning the top-two primary: Dianne Feinstein, the incumbent, and her fellow Democratic challenger, Kevin de León. It is interesting to note that there were 31 candidates running against the incumbent Feinstein.

The November 2018 midterm election was historic. Nationwide, an estimated 113 million people went to the polls, breaking the record for the most number of people voting in a non-presidential election in U.S. history. Over 49 percent of eligible voters participated in this midterm election, the largest percentage in a midterm election in over 100 years. In California, a whopping 62.5 million people cast votes, a 20 percent increase over the 2014 midterm election. Analysts believe one reason for these historically high turnout rates was voters' displeasure with President Trump. As political scientist Michael McDonald, head of the University of Florida's Elections Project, describes it:

> In a typical midterm election, where the President's party is overseeing an economy that is on sound footing, you would not expect high turnout. So clearly, something has changed here in our politics. The only logical explanation for the thing that has changed is Donald Trump.[26]

And as with June's primary election, California was in the spotlight once again. Democrats needed to flip 23 seats in the U.S. House of Representatives to gain control of that chamber. Gaining control of at least one chamber of Congress would result in a divided government where there would be a check on the Republican Party's power over the legislative and executive branches of government. The Democratic Party had identified seven Republican House seats located in California that they needed to flip in their quest to win majority status in the House. In the end, Democrats won control of the House, winning 40 seats nationwide previously held by Republicans. And, all of the seven targeted House races in California were won by Democratic candidates, providing nearly one-third of the needed 23 seats.

CONGRESSIONAL RACES It would be an understatement to say that the 2018 midterm congressional election in California was historic. As described above, voting turnout rates were exceptionally high. Over 12 million ballots were cast in California. However, it was the House of Representatives contests that were the focus of national attention. Control of the House depended on a number of House seats in California flipping from Republican control to Democratic control. This was not an easy feat as many of these House seats were in congressional districts that historically voted Republican. Case in point was four Republican-held House seats in Orange County, one of the most Republican counties in California. Former president Ronald Reagan once quipped "Orange County is where all good Republicans go to die." It is the home of one of the most right-wing conservative groups, the John Birch Society, and the birthplace of Richard Nixon and home to his presidential library. This previously reliable Republican stronghold saw all four of these targeted seats turn from Republican to Democratic control, leaving Orange County with no Republican House members, a first since the 1930s. Stuart Spencer, a veteran Republican strategist, commented "this election is one hell of a wake-up call for the Republican Party in California."[27] Of California's 53 House seats, only seven are now held by Republicans. This is the lowest number in the California House delegation since 1883.

As mentioned earlier, as a result of our top-two primary system, the U.S. Senate race pitted two Democrats against each other: long-term incumbent Senator Dianne Feinstein versus state senator Kevin de León. Feinstein, representing the moderate wing of the Democratic Party, did not receive the endorsement of the California Democratic Party, who instead supported the candidacy of the more left-leaning de León. However, Feinstein was endorsed by Governor Jerry Brown, Los Angeles mayor Eric Garcetti, and the *Los Angeles Times*. The 85-year-old Feinstein campaigned on her experience and seniority in the Senate, outspent her rival, and won her re-election bid with 54 percent of the vote.

THE GOVERNOR'S RACE Jerry Brown, the popular two-term Democratic governor, was prohibited by state law from running for office again. The 2018 governor's race saw Democratic Lieutenant Governor Gavin Newsom run against Republican John Cox, a San Diego businessman. In California, Republican candidates in statewide races typically need to run as moderates in order to win enough independent voters to propel them to victory. Cox was not a centrist Republican and lost the governor's race to Newsom, winning only 38 percent of the vote.

CALIFORNIA LEGISLATIVE RACES The blue wave extended to the California state house races. Democrats won enough seats in the state Assembly and the state Senate to maintain their supermajority status in both chambers. A supermajority (two-thirds votes) is needed to pass tax increases and to place constitutional amendments on the ballot. Democrats won enough seats to accomplish this without Republican support. In the state Assembly Democrats won 59 seats, nearly three-quarters of the 80 seats open. Republicans hold a paltry 21 seats in this chamber. This is the largest Democratic advantage in 40 years. The state Senate will now have 29 Democrats and only 11 Republicans serving, the largest Democratic advantage since 1962 (with one exception in 2012).

PROPOSITIONS There were 11 propositions on the ballot, three of which were bond measures. Voters were asked to weigh in on issues such as housing programs for the mentally ill, repeal of the state fuel tax, regulation of kidney dialysis treatment centers, change to daylight savings time, rent control, and the humane treatment of farm animals.

Propositions 6 and 8 were two of the more high-profile propositions. Proposition 6: Repeal of the Gas Tax, which was discussed earlier (see p. 92), ultimately failed. Proposition 8: Regulate Kidney Dialysis Treatment Charges was the most expensive proposition in 2018, and it also failed. This law would require dialysis clinics to issue refunds to patients or insurance companies for revenue above 115 percent of the costs of direct patient care and health care improvements. More than $130 million was spent by both sides. The "No" on Proposition 8 side raised over $111 million while the supporters raised only $18 million with most of the funds contributed by the Service Employees International Union (SEIU), who sponsored this ballot initiative. The SEIU, a labor union, had an ongoing conflict with the state's two largest dialysis companies concerning alleged retaliation against workers at these clinics trying to unionize. The proposition was defeated 60 percent to 40 percent.

Campaigning in California

California politics presents many challenges to those seeking elective office or the passage of a ballot measure. First, the immense size of the state means that groups hoping to pass or defeat statewide propositions, candidates running for statewide office, and candidates vying for the U.S. Senate or the presidency must plan campaigns that reach voters throughout the entire state. California has 13 distinct media markets, making it very expensive to communicate to its 39 million residents about politics. Second, California's population is very diverse, with many ethnicities, racial groups, cultures, professions, occupations, and interests represented. Successful campaigns must find ways to effectively communicate their platform and messages to all of the state's 19 million registered voters. And third, California has passed a number of political campaign reform acts in an attempt to regulate campaign spending and to provide public information on contributions and expenditures. These laws have proved beneficial to some and not as helpful to others.

Whatever the challenges of campaigning in California, one thing is certain: California's campaign politics are watched by the nation. We are a campaign trendsetter.

Money and Politics: California Style

As the record-breaking spending in the campaigns of 2010 demonstrated, campaigning in California requires money, and lots of it. In fact, California is one of the most expensive states in which to conduct a political campaign. Table 4.3 illustrates how the candidates in the 2010 governor's race spent nearly $200 million, making it the most expensive governor's race in U.S. history.

Running for the California legislature is also very expensive. Citing a Pew Center on the States study, blogger and researcher D. P. Osorio notes that California is the costliest state in which to win a state Senate seat ($938,522). The least expensive state is North Dakota where it costs $5,713; in Arizona it costs $36,696; in Wisconsin, $140,287; and in North Carolina, $234,031.[28] The prohibitive cost of campaigning in California limits those who can realistically run for office, another factor contributing to the state's governance challenges. Incumbents far outspend challengers, and incumbents' spending has increased over time while challengers' spending has not. On average, challengers spend only a fraction of what incumbents spend. This discrepancy helps to explain the high re-election rates of those elected to the California legislature. Some competitive races for the California legislature cost in excess of $1 million.

The following are some reasons that California campaigns are so expensive:

MEDIA-DOMINATED CAMPAIGNS Because of the state's size and its 13 different **media markets**, candidates must run **media-dominated campaigns**, spending

TABLE 4.3 ● Spending in California's Gubernatorial Election: How the Money Was Spent, 2010

Expenditure	Whitman ($)	Brown ($)
Television and radio advertising	$106,930,505.28	$21,259,408.00
Campaign consultants	11,693,547.95	167,200.00
Campaign literature and mailings	10,582,303.93	2,532,801.36
Campaign workers' salaries	5,918,110.80	157,870.01
Radio airtime and production costs	5,472,228.17	0
TV or cable airtime and production costs	4,139,919.07	182,103.12
Information technology costs (Internet, email)	3,177,977.76	23,345.51
Office expenses	2,321,340.46	132,023.40
Meetings and appearances	1,772,342.56	0
Polling and survey research	1,410,893.36	93,728.30
Staff/spouse travel, lodging, and meals	1,260,616.12	2,618.30
Fund-raising events	1,241,158.66	70,626.38
Candidate travel, lodging, and meals	950,890.17	12,071.76
Professional services (legal, accounting)	880,044.13	39,310.00
Postage, delivery, and messenger services	668,059.56	2,117.00
Campaign paraphernalia/miscellaneous	633,946.72	65,129.65
Phone banks	549,904.75	0
Contribution	252,500.00	0
Print ads	153,440.00	0
Voter registration	66,710.00	0
Civic donations	16,383.00	0
Returned contributions	0	99,364.14
Candidate filing/ballot fees	0	3,579.74
TOTAL	**160,092,822.45**	**24,843,296.67**

SOURCE: Lance Williams, "Meg Whitman Spending: Where did $160 Million Go?" *Huffington Post*, November 2, 2010, www.huffingtonpost.com/2010/11/02/meg-whitman-spending-wher_n_777644.html (accessed 11/2/10).

enormous amounts of money producing political ads and buying the broadcast time to air them. During the 2003 gubernatorial recall election, it cost approximately $2 million a week to run political ads statewide.[29] In the 2006 governor's race, Schwarzenegger's campaign alone spent $9 million on TV ads in the short time span between July 1 and September 30. As is shown in Table 4.3, an astounding $128 million was spent in the November 2010 governor's race just on TV, cable, and radio airtime and production. This cost is in addition to the $57 million spent on media during the primary campaign. As one media consultant described it, "There's a lot to be said for traditional politicking, kissing babies and shaking hands, but you have to get on TV to reach voters."[30]

POLITICAL CONSULTANTS Professional campaign managers and various **political consultants**—media consultants, pollsters, fund-raisers, direct-mail experts, and voter mobilization professionals—cost money. Because of California's love for direct democracy, especially the initiative process, many well-known political consultants have established offices in California. There is money to be made in California politics, and candidates and supporters of ballot initiatives know that to win elections you must hire the costly services of top-notch political consultants.

WEAK POLITICAL PARTIES California has comparatively **weak political parties**. The Progressive reform movement of Governor Hiram Johnson (served 1911–17) implemented many rules that reduced the organizational strength and clout of political parties within the state, as described earlier. Because of California's weak party system, the party organizations are minimally involved in organizing and conducting the campaigns of candidates running for office. In addition, California has a relatively large number of registered voters who decline to affiliate with any political party and consider themselves politically independent. These unaffiliated, independent voters compose nearly one-quarter of all registered voters. The combination of weak party structure and less party attachment means that candidates themselves have to work harder—raise and spend more money—to reach these voters.

Campaign-Finance Reform in California

To create more transparency in the electoral process and to make public the flow of money in political campaigns, several **campaign-finance reform** laws have been enacted in California over the past 100 years. Brief descriptions of the most recent laws follow.

1974: POLITICAL REFORM ACT In 1974 a group of reform-minded Californians crafted a statewide proposition that would require the most detailed campaign-finance reporting in the nation. Proposition 9 appeared on the ballot during the Watergate scandal and passed with an overwhelming majority of votes. This act created the Political Reform Division within the office of the secretary of state to administer and oversee key provisions of the law. A new independent state agency, the Fair Political Practices Commission, was also created for the purposes of interpreting and enforcing the act.

1988: PROPOSITION 73 In 1988, California voters overwhelmingly passed Proposition 73, which limited contributions to legislative and statewide candidates to $1,000 per donor, including individuals, labor unions, and corporations. A federal judge struck it down in 1990.

1996: PROPOSITION 208 Voters approved Proposition 208 by a 61 percent vote in 1996. Contributions to candidates from individuals, political parties, committees, corporations, unions, and political action committees (PACs) were limited. Spending limits also were imposed on candidates, although these were voluntary. Candidates who abide by the spending limits are allowed to collect larger contributions, whereas candidates who do not abide by them have lower contribution limits. Proposition 208 was being challenged in the courts when Proposition 34 was proposed and passed.

2000: PROPOSITION 34 Proposition 34 was placed on the ballot by the legislature. Spending limits were substantially increased, as were contribution limits. For example, under Proposition 208, individuals were permitted to contribute $1,000 to gubernatorial candidates—$500 if the candidate decided not to abide by the voluntary spending limits. Proposition 34 increased individual contributions

While Latinos in California currently vote at a significantly lower rate than whites, the Latino population is poised to exert great influence over California's electoral outcomes as it increases in size and clout.

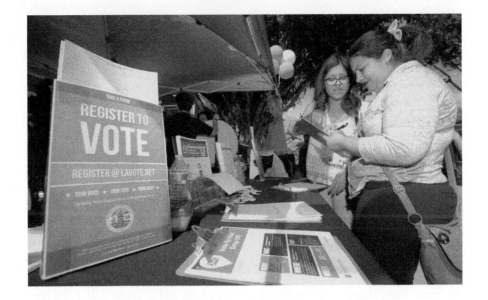

to $21,200. Many reform-minded organizations that had supported Proposition 208, such as the League of Women Voters and Common Cause, were opposed to Proposition 34. They saw Proposition 34 as an attempt by the legislature to replace the more stringent Proposition 208 that was then under review in the courts. Nevertheless, in November 2000, Proposition 34 passed with close to 60 percent of the popular vote and has replaced the provisions of Proposition 208.

Although it could be argued that Proposition 34 has resulted in less control of campaign financing, California does receive high marks when it comes to laws requiring public disclosure of campaign contributions and expenditures. The Campaign Disclosure Project conducted by UCLA in 2008 studied the campaign disclosure laws in all 50 states and ranked the states accordingly. California received a grade of A for its disclosure laws and ranked second in the nation; Washington State ranked first.

Voting in California

Of California's 39 million residents, slightly more than 25 million are eligible to vote. Seventy-eight percent of those eligible (nearly 20 million) are registered. Contrary to some beliefs, registering to vote does not put one at higher risk of being selected for jury duty, nor does one receive more income tax scrutiny. To register to vote in the state of California, you must meet the following criteria:

- You will be 18 years of age on or before Election Day.
- You are a citizen of the United States.
- You are a resident of California.
- You are not in prison or on parole for a felony conviction.
- You have not been judged by a court to be mentally incompetent to register and to vote.

How You Can Register to Vote

The law mandates that you must register to vote at least 15 days before an election. In California, 16- and 17-year-olds are allowed to preregister to vote, and will be automatically registered at age 18. Since this law was passed in September 2016, more than one-quarter of a million young people have preregistered to vote! Here are the options for doing so:

- **Obtain a voter registration form** from any U.S. post office or library. Forms are usually available on counters. Fill out the preaddressed, stamped form and mail it in.

- **Visit a branch of the California Department of Motor Vehicles.** The National Voter Registration Act of 1993 (also known as "**Motor Voter**") permits persons conducting business at a DMV office to register to vote or to update their voter registration information while at the office. Since 1995 more than 12.5 million people have registered or reregistered in conformance with this law. California passed a new voter registration law, effective January 1, 2016. Now, at the DMV office, individuals will be asked if they are eligible to vote and, if so, their information will automatically be transmitted to the secretary of state's office where citizenship will be verified and names added to the voter registration rolls. An individual may opt out of this automatic registration.

- **Register online.** Go to the secretary of state's website and use the new online voter registration system (registertovote.ca.gov). The process is very simple and can be completed entirely online if you have a California driver's license or identification card. Because voter registration applications must be signed by the individual, the online system retrieves your signature from your driver's license or ID card and electronically transfers it to your online registration application. This new system has proven to be extremely popular: of the record 1.4 million newly registered voters for 2012, over half of them registered online. As of October 2018, California, along with 36 other states and the District of Columbia, offers electronic voter registration.

You will need to reregister to vote if:

- you move,
- you change your name, or
- you change your political party affiliation.

Who Votes in California?

There are demographic differences between those adults who are likely to vote and those who vote infrequently or who are not registered to vote. Table 4.4 also clearly illustrates this. Of the individuals who are very likely to vote, 59 percent are white, 21 percent are Latino, 11 percent are Asian American, and 6 percent are African American. Likely voters live in urban areas, are older, are college educated, are U.S. born, and earn higher incomes. Over the decades, the composition of the eligible voting population has changed and now there are more minority voters.

TABLE 4.4 ● California's Likely Voters, 2018

	Percentage of registered voters likely to vote in California's next statewide election (%)
Race/Ethnicity	
White	59%
Latino	21
Asian	11
Black	6
Other/Multirace	3
Region	
Los Angeles County	26
San Francisco Bay Area	23
Orange/San Diego Counties	17
Central Valley	16
Inland Empire	9
Other	9
Age	
18 to 34	18
35 to 54	34
55 and older	48
Education	
No college	19
Some college	42
College graduate	39
Nativity	
U.S.-born	84
Immigrant	16

SOURCE: Eight PPIC Statewide Surveys from September 2017 to July 2018, including 13,669 adults and 7,999 likely voters. California Secretary of State, Report of Registration, May 2018. US Census Bureau, 2012-16 American Community Survey.

But overall the same pattern has held: whites vote at a higher rate. Three factors help explain this discrepancy:

- **Eligibility**   A significant proportion of the Latino and Asian populations are not eligible to vote because they are not citizens.

- **Youth**   The Latino and Asian populations are both younger, and younger people are much less likely to vote than are older people.

- **Education**   The probability of voting increases significantly for those with college or advanced degrees.

Research shows that if you control for these three factors, Latinos vote at rates comparable to whites.[31]

The 2016 presidential election saw a decline in voter turnout nationally. According to an analysis by political website FiveThirtyEight, a smaller percentage of eligible voters participated in the 2016 presidential election than in the previous two elections.[32] Only about 57 percent of voters went to the polls, down from about 59 percent in 2012 and nearly 62 percent in 2008.

As Figure 4.5 illustrates, California fits in with this national trend. Fifty-six percent of eligible voters turned out in 2012, and about 54 percent voted in 2016. It is interesting to note that, nationwide, the decline in turnout was more prevalent in states that voted for Clinton, as evidenced in California. Although overall turnout declined in California, Latino turnout in the 2016 election substantially increased from previous years. Over 30 percent of voters self-identified as Latino compared to the 2012 election when that number was 22 percent. Latino voters were probably mobilized to vote in 2016 because of the anti-Latino, anti-immigrant campaign of Donald Trump. Midterm elections typically have low voter turnout, but the 2018 midterms broke voting turnout records. In California, there was about a 50 percent increase in early voting and requests for absentee ballots among Latinos compared to the 2014 midterms. (See the "Who Are Californians?" feature for a breakdown of California's voting population in 2018.)

THE EVER-EXPANDING GROUP OF VOTERS: VOTING BY MAIL California now has very liberal vote-by-mail laws. Before 1978 voters could only receive a mail ballot if they signed a sworn statement affirming that they would be away

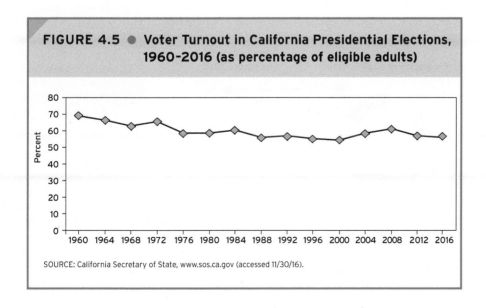

FIGURE 4.5 ● **Voter Turnout in California Presidential Elections, 1960–2016 (as percentage of eligible adults)**

SOURCE: California Secretary of State, www.sos.ca.gov (accessed 11/30/16).

Who Votes in California?

Gender

■ Male ■ Female

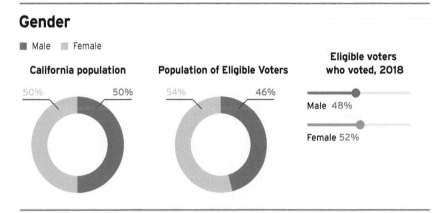

California population
50% 50%

Population of Eligible Voters
54% 46%

Eligible voters who voted, 2018
Male 48%
Female 52%

Age

■ Youth (Under 18) ■ Young Adults (18-29) ■ Older Adults

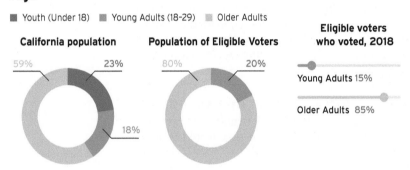

California population
59% 23% 18%

Population of Eligible Voters
80% 20%

Eligible voters who voted, 2018
Young Adults 15%
Older Adults 85%

Race*

■ White ■ Latino ■ African American ■ Asian American

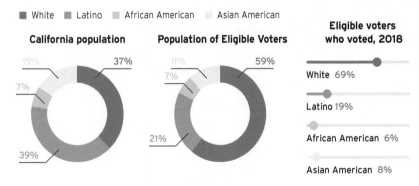

California population
15% 37% 7% 39%

Population of Eligible Voters
11% 59% 7% 21%

Eligible voters who voted, 2018
White 69%
Latino 19%
African American 6%
Asian American 8%

* Percentages do not sum to 100 because some people identify with another race or as multiracial.

SOURCES: U.S. Census Bureau, Quick Facts: California, https://www.census.gov/quickfacts/ca (accessed 10/2/18); Public Policy Institute of California, California's Likely Voters, http://www.ppic.org/publication/californias-likely-voters/ (accessed 10/2/18); State of California Department of Finance, Projections,http://www.dof.ca.gov/Forecasting/Demographics/projections/ (accessed 10/2/18). CNN Exit Polls, www.cnn.com/elections/2018/exit-polls/California/governor (accessed 11/12/18).

The active voting population in California is not reflective of general population demographics. Compared to their proportion of the population, white non-Latinos (Anglos) and older voters were overrepresented among active voters in the 2018 midterm election. Despite the large size of the Latino population, they are a relatively small share of the electorate. Latinos have long been considered the "sleeping giant" of California politics, because they have yet to fully participate at a level proportional to their size.

forcriticalanalysis

1. What do you think might account for the differences in turnout rates among different groups in California? Why is turnout among whites and African Americans so much higher than among Latinos and Asians? Why is turnout among older voters higher than among young voters?

2. Looking ahead, what impact will the shifting electorate have on California politics, when the percentage of Latinos in the population increases and percentage of whites decreases, as discussed in Chapter 1?

from their home precincts on Election Day or that they were infirm or bedridden and physically unable to cast a vote in person. All this changed in 1978 when California eliminated the requirement that voters present a valid excuse in order to vote absentee. Now, mail ballots are available to any voter who wants one. You are permitted to request a mail ballot for a particular election, or you may request permanent vote-by-mail status, meaning that a mail ballot is sent automatically to your home before each election.

From 1962 to 1978 the percentage of those voting by mail in primary and general elections averaged slightly under 4 percent of all votes cast. After the change in the law, voting by mail increased substantially. Of the over 11 million votes cast in November 2016, over 5 million were cast by mail ballots. Compared to the rest of the country, California's approach is fairly distinctive: 29 states allow voting by mail without an approved excuse, but only 3 other states allow for permanent voting by mail.

EARLY VOTING There is a special type of voter in California: the early voter. In fact, in the November 2016 general election, nearly 60 percent of all voters were early voters. There are several ways in which Californians can vote early (casting votes before official Election Day).

Most early voters voluntarily request **vote-by-mail ballots**. Virtually all of these voters are classified as "permanent vote-by-mail" voters, which means they have requested to automatically receive a vote-by-mail ballot for every election. Otherwise, one needs to request such a ballot for each election. These ballots must be received by the county registrar's office no later than Election Day, often making it necessary to mail in the completed ballot at least a few days before this deadline. In fact, a number of voters fill out and mail their ballots weeks before Election Day because state law permits voting as early as 29 days before an election. A number of sparsely populated rural precincts in California, where staffing a traditional polling place makes little sense, have moved entirely to mail-in ballots for all voters. And in an attempt to lighten the volume of voters on Election Day, some counties have permitted "early voting," in which voters can go to various publicized locations (such as shopping malls, registrars' offices, and civic centers) to cast their votes as early as 29 days before an election.

In 2016 California passed the California Voter's Choice Act, which allows counties to provide more flexibility and convenience to voters. For those counties opting in, mail ballots will automatically be mailed to all registered voters, in-person early voting will be expanded, and voters can vote at any vote center throughout their county (rather than having to vote only in their precinct). In 2018, 14 counties were permitted to conduct elections under the Voter's Choice Act; by 2020 all remaining counties will be permitted to conduct Voter's Choice Act elections.

Nationally, states' approach to early voting is varied: early voting that requires no special excuse is permitted in 37 states.

Many view these developments as positive changes, in the belief that making voting more convenient will increase participation in this important civic activity. However, as with many reforms, there are unintended consequences. One major consequence is that early voting has had a direct impact on campaign strategy. Traditionally, political campaigns approach the weekend before the election as their last opportunity to communicate with voters. Candidates spend an enormous amount of money in the last days of their campaigns trying to convince people to vote for them or their initiative (or at least not to vote for their opponent or opposing side) by bombarding them with TV ads and messages. By this point in the election cycle, however, nearly half of California voters have most likely already voted by mail or at an early-voting location. Therefore, candidates must now spend money earlier in the campaign cycle in order to reach these early voters before they cast their votes. As an example, state senator Tom McClintock lost a race for state controller by less than one-half of a percentage point because he did not have enough money to buy TV ads until the final days of the campaign. Many absentee voters had already mailed in their ballots and did not see his campaign ads until after they had cast their vote. Earlier campaigning means more expensive campaigning in a state that is already prohibitively expensive.

HOW YOU CAN VOTE BY MAIL To apply for a mail ballot, you may use the application form contained in the sample ballot mailed to your home before the election, or you may apply in writing to your county elections official. Ballots can be returned by mail or in person to a polling place or elections office within your county on Election Day.

What Reforms Are Needed?

It is fascinating to observe electoral politics in California. We live in a state where ballot initiatives are frequently used to make law, bypassing our duly elected representatives and the deliberative process of the legislature. In recent elections voters have been asked to weigh in on important policy matters such as same-sex marriage, abortion and parental notification, renewable energy, legalization of marijuana, the state budget process, tax issues, and the process by which state and congressional district boundaries are determined. Many people question whether the initiative process is the best way to make public policy.

Although the recall, referendum, and initiative originally were established as Progressive reforms, during the past few decades these tools of direct democracy have been taken over by special-interest groups. Some believe that reforms are needed to make it more difficult to recall an elected official or to bypass the legislative branch through the initiative process. Suggested reforms have included the prohibition of paid signature gatherers, a judicial review of the proposed initiative before placement on the ballot, and a higher requirement for the number of signatures needed to qualify a recall or initiative for the ballot. For a recall to qualify for the ballot, California law currently requires the number of signatures to equal 12 percent of the votes cast in the last gubernatorial election. Other states require 25 to 40 percent. While progress has been made with the reforms recently signed into law, many serious issues with the initiative process remain.

Candidates and initiative campaigns spend enormous amounts of money in hopes of electoral victory. Proposition 34, the campaign-finance initiative passed in 2000, substantially increased spending and contribution limits. California's limits on contributions to gubernatorial candidates are far more liberal than federal limits on contributions to presidential candidates. In fact, Californians can contribute more than 10 times the amount to gubernatorial candidates than they are permitted to contribute to presidential candidates ($25,900 versus $2,500). Many fear that these high limits will lead to spiraling campaign costs in a state where it is already expensive to campaign. The amounts of money spent in the 2010 governor's race seems to indicate that these fears are becoming reality.

Study Guide

FOR FURTHER READING

Barabak, M. "California's Not Goofy, It's Really Big. That's Why Counting the Vote Takes So Long." *Los Angeles Times*, November 9, 2018. www.latimes.com/politics/la-me-pol -midterm-california-ballots-20181109-story.html#nws =mcnewsletter. Accessed 11/30/18.

Blume, H. "Push for Young Minority Voters Reaches into High School." *Los Angeles Times*, October 24, 2018. www.latimes .com/local/education/la-me-edu-youth-voter-registration -20181024-story.html. Accessed 11/30/18.

Cain, B. "The California Recall." Interview, Brookings Institution, October 8, 2003.

Cain, Bruce E., and Elisabeth R. Gerber. *Voting at the Political Fault Line: California's Experiment with the Blanket Primary.* Berkeley: University of California Press, 2002.

California Fair Political Practices Commission. "Proposition 34." www.fppc.ca.gov. Accessed 12/03/14.

California Secretary of State's History of Political Reform Division. www.sos.ca.gov/campaign-lobbying/history-political -reform-division/. Accessed 9/26/16.

Cohen, Micah. "Over the Decades, How States Have Shifted." FiveThirtyEight, October 15, 2012. www.fivethirtyeight .com/features/over-the-decades-how-states-have-shifted/. Accessed 9/26/16.

Douzet, Frédérick, Thad Kousser, and Kenneth P. Miller, eds. *The New Political Geography of California.* Berkeley: Berkeley Public Policy Press, 2008.

Lubenow, Gerald C., ed. *California Votes: The 2002 Governor's Race and the Recall That Made History.* Berkeley: Berkeley Public Policy Press, 2003.

Marinucci, C. "RIP California GOP: Republicans Lash Out After Midterm Election Debacle." *Politico*, November 18, 2018. www.politico.com/story/2018/11/17/rip-california -gop-republicans-lash-out-after-midterm-election-debacle -1000481. Accessed 11/30/18.

Meyers, John. "California's Major Political Parties Feared the Top Two Primaries But Emerged as Powerful as Before." *Los Angeles Times*, June 6, 2018. www.latimes.com/poli tics/la-pol-ca-california-primary-rules-election-analysis -20180606-story.html. Accessed 9/17/18.

Meyers, John. "GOP on verge of being third choice of state voters. No-party voters nearly pass GOP." *Los Angeles Times*, May 11, 2018. enewspaper.latimes.com/infinity/article_share .aspx?guid=4aaa86a9-5fea-431d-9afb-72436bb8caa5. Accessed 9/17/18.

Peterson, Pete. "Why Californians Don't Vote." *Business Insider.* www.businessinsider.com/why-californians-dont-vote -2014-6. Accessed 6/24/14.

Pastor, Manuel. *State of Resistance: What California's Dizzying Descent and Remarkable Resurgence Means for America's Future.* New York: The New Press, 2018.

Rarick, E. *California Votes: The 2010 Governor's Race.* Berkeley: Institute of Governmental Studies, 2012.

Rasky, Susan. Introduction to "An Antipolitician, Anti-establishment Groundswell Elected the Candidate of Change." In *California Votes: The 2002 Governor's Race and the Recall That Made History*, edited by G. Lubenow. Berkeley: Berkeley Public Policy Press, 2003.

UCLA School of Law, Center for Governmental Studies, and the California Voter Foundation. "Grading State Disclosure 2008: A Comprehensive, Comparative Study of Candidate Campaign Finance Disclosure Laws and Practices in the 50 States." 2008. campaigndisc.calvoter.org/grading state/index.html. Accessed 9/17/18.

Warren, M. "Can the News for Republicans in California Get Any Worse?" *The Weekly Standard*, November 26, 2018. www.weeklystandard.com/michael-warren/midterms -postmortem-the-gop-cant-even-win-in-orange-county -california. Accessed 11/30/18.

ON THE WEB

Baldassare, Mark, Dean Bonner, David Kordus, and Lunna Lopes. "PPIC Statewide Survey: Californians and Their Government." www.ppic.org/main/publication.asp?i=1218. Accessed 11/11/2016.

California Elections and Voter Information. www.sos.ca.gov /elections. Accessed 11/11/16. The California secretary of state offers a comprehensive guide to California elections, including information on how to register to vote.

California General Election Results. http://vote.sos.ca.gov. Accessed 12/3/14. Detailed breakdowns of California election results.

The California Voter Foundation. http://calvoter.org. Accessed 7/25/12.

Fair Political Practices Commission. www.fppc.ca.gov. Accessed 12/3/14.

Join California. www.joincalifornia.com. Accessed 12/3/14.

Los Angeles Times. "Did Your Neighborhood Vote to Elect Donald Trump?" www.latimes.com/projects/la-pol-ca-cali fornia-neighborhood-election-results. Accessed 11/12/16.

SUMMARY

I. Introduction.
   A. California as an epicenter of anti-Trump movement.
      1. California challenges federal laws and Trump's executive orders.
      2. Expected role for California as a political, social, economic trendsetter.

II. Political parties.
   A. An important function of parties is to mobilize voters at election time.
   B. The Progressives' (1890s–1920s) impact on parties was sizable.
      1. They disliked corrupt parties and passed legislation to weaken the power of parties.
      2. They created many nonpartisan elective offices.
      3. They introduced direct primary elections to select the party candidate who will run for office against candidates of opposing parties in the general election.
   C. California has two dominant political parties: the Democratic Party and the Republican Party.
      1. California is considered a very Democratic state.
   D. Third parties struggle to compete.
      1. There are six certified minor parties.
      2. Third parties can impact the political agenda by raising issues the major parties ignore.

III. Party affiliation of California voters varies by region and demographics.
   A. The Democratic Party represents a plurality of voters.
   B. Historic shift from Republican Party to Democratic Party largely due to anti-immigration positions of Republican candidates (Prop. 187) and changing demographics.
   C. There has been an increase in the number of independents ("no party preference").
   D. Demographics and party affiliation.
      1. Whites tend to vote Republican; Latinos tend to vote Democratic.
      2. Younger and middle-aged voters compose the highest percentage of independents.
      3. Women tend to prefer the Democratic Party, as do non–U.S.-born citizens.
   E. The blue and red in California. Similar to the nation overall, areas of California are either distinctly Democratic or Republican.
      1. Coastal and urban areas tend to be Democratic.
      2. Inland and rural areas tend to be Republican.

IV. Elections in California.
   A. There have been many changes in the primary system.

1. California operated under a *closed* primary system until Proposition 198 in 1996.
2. Then a *blanket* primary system was in place from 1998 to 2000. In *California Democratic Party v. Jones* (2002), the California Supreme Court ruled this form of the *blanket* primary unconstitutional.
3. A *modified closed* primary system was adopted from 2002 to 2010. "Decline to state" voters (also known as "no party preference") were permitted to vote in party primaries if the party granted permission.
4. Proposition 14, passed in 2010, replaced the *modified closed* primary system with another version of the *blanket* primary.
   B. Presidential primaries.
      1. California has changed the date of its presidential primaries in order to allow voters to have more of an impact in the selection process.
      2. The 2008 presidential primary was moved to an early February date. Unfortunately, the increase in clout for the state was unrealized.
      3. In 2012, it was moved back to June. In 2020, the primary is scheduled for early March.
   C. Initiative campaigns.
      1. Typically, initiatives are tools of special-interest groups or grassroots movements. Such groups find it easier to bypass the state legislature and take their issue directly to the people. Often, initiatives deal with controversial issues that legislators would rather avoid.
      2. From 1912 to 2018 there were approximately 400 ballot initiatives.
      3. How to qualify an initiative for ballot.
         a) Nearly 600,000 signatures of registered voters are needed for an initiative to qualify for the ballot, and nearly 1 million are needed to place a constitutional amendment on the ballot.
         b) For an initiative to be successful requires millions of dollars and highly paid political professionals. As an example, the cost of collecting petition signatures for the 17 ballot propositions in the November 2016 elections exceeded $45 million.
      4. Criticisms of direct democracy.
         a) Critics say that issues presented as ballot propositions are often too complicated or confusing and should be decided through legislative deliberation rather than a popular vote.

b) Recent reforms have provided for a 30-day public review process for all proposed initiatives as well as more transparency regarding donations to initiative campaigns.

D. The 2003 gubernatorial recall election of Gray Davis.
1. Only 11 months after he won his re-election bid, Davis was recalled from office. He was the first and only governor in the state of California and the second governor in the nation's history to be recalled.
2. Voters held Governor Davis responsible for the 2000–01 energy crisis and for the fiscal struggles of the state.
3. Arnold Schwarzenegger, an actor and a moderate Republican, was elected governor.

E. The 2008 election: ideological and demographic shift to Democratic side.
1. Obama won 61 percent of the popular vote compared to John McCain's 37 percent, the biggest margin in California since 1964.
2. Young people voted in historic numbers, solidifying the Democratic Party's dominance in the state.

F. The 2010 election was the most expensive governor's race in history.
1. Brown, the former governor, beat a wealthy billionaire, Meg Whitman.
2. Initiatives passed that have an important impact on state budget process and political representation and party politics.

G. The 2012 election: results similar to 2008 but more of a Democratic shift.
1. The Democratic Party gained supermajority status in the state legislature (lost it in 2014).
2. Young voters' turnout increased, but overall turnout declined.
3. California adopted a new online voter registration system.
4. Proposition 30 passed, increasing the state sales tax and taxes on the wealthy to fund education.

H. The 2014 election: a noncompetitive governor's race.
1. Incumbent Jerry Brown easily beat underfunded challenger Neel Kashkari.
2. For the more controversial ballot measures (Propositions 45, 46, and 48), the well-funded "no" campaigns were successful because the proponents were absent from the airwaves.

I. The 2016 election: Democratic Party remains strong.
1. Decline in Republican Party registration and increase in number of "no party preference" voter registrations.

2. Hillary Clinton won California by a 2–1 margin but lost the presidential contest.
3. Kamala Harris elected as first African American U.S. senator from California and second ever female African American elected to Senate.
4. Democratic Party won supermajority in state Assembly and state Senate.
5. Proposition 58 repealed English-only in public schools. Proposition 62 to repeal death penalty failed while Proposition 66 to expedite death penalty appeals passed. Proposition 64 legalized marijuana. Proposition 67 banned plastic shopping bags.
6. Overall voter turnout declined, but Latino turnout surged from 22 percent in 2012 to 33 percent in 2016.
7. Voting by mail continued to be very popular.

J. The 2018 Election:
1. There were historic voting turnout rates for a midterm election.
2. California congressional races attracted national attention as Democrats targeted vulnerable seats to win a majority in the House of Representatives.
3. Democrats won all targeted House seats leaving Orange County (historically conservative stronghold) with no Republican House members.
4. Democrats maintained their supermajority status in both the state Assembly and the state Senate.

V. Running for elective office in the largest state is expensive.
A. The size of the state requires candidates to spend a lot of money on campaigns. California often attracts wealthy candidates with personal fortunes.
B. Because of the size of the state, candidates need to spend a lot of money on TV ads in order to reach voters. Statewide campaigns are very expensive because of the need to broadcast political ads throughout the state.
C. Numerous state laws have been passed to reform political campaigns and to minimize the influence of big money and create transparency.
1. 1974: Proposition 9, Political Reform Act created the Political Reform Division and established the Fair Political Practices Commission.
2. 1988: Proposition 73 passed, limiting campaign contributions, but was later declared unconstitutional in 1990.
3. 1996: Proposition 208 passed, limiting campaign contributions.
4. 2000: Proposition 34 passed, increasing spending and contribution limits and invalidating Proposition 208.
5. 2008: in a study of 50 states California gets an A for campaign-finance disclosure laws.

VI. Voting in California.
   A. With a population of 39 million, there are 19 million registered voters in the state. Since September 2016, more than 250,000 16- to 17-year-olds have preregistered to vote.
   B. How to register to vote:
      1. Obtain a voter registration form from any post office or library.
      2. Visit the California DMV.
      3. Register online.
   C. Who votes?
      1. Whites are overrepresented in the voting population; Latinos and Asians are underrepresented; African Americans vote in equal proportion to their percentage of population.
      2. About 60 percent of all registered voters cast their votes by mail.
      3. California Voter's Choice Act of 2016 makes voting more flexible and convenient.

VII. Reforms may be necessary.
   A. Is the initiative process the best way to make policy?
   B. Need for campaign-finance reform to limit contributions and candidate spending.

PRACTICE QUIZ

1. In the 2016 general election, 18- to 29-year-olds voted at a lower rate than they did in 2012.
   a) true
   b) false

2. In running for the state legislature, incumbents and challengers spend nearly the same amount of money on their political campaigns.
   a) true
   b) false

3. Political campaigns are so expensive in California because
   a) campaigns need to hire political consultants.
   b) campaigns need to spend a substantial amount of money on media advertising.
   c) political parties are not very involved in the planning and running of campaigns.
   d) all of the above

4. Special-interest groups often use the initiative process to achieve their policy objectives.
   a) true
   b) false

5. Which of the following is *not* true about Proposition 34, which deals with campaign finance?
   a) The League of Women Voters and Common Cause supported Proposition 34.
   b) Proposition 34 increased allowable individual contributions to candidates to $21,200.
   c) Proposition 34 has resulted in less control of campaign financing.
   d) Proposition 34 replaced the stricter campaign-finance law enacted through Proposition 208.

6. Of California's 39 million people, approximately how many are registered to vote?
   a) 30 million
   b) 25 million
   c) 5 million
   d) 20 million

7. Democrats are the plurality party in California.
   a) true
   b) false

8. The number of voters who decline to state a party affiliation at the time they register is declining.
   a) true
   b) false

9. Most of the Democratic counties encompass major urban areas, whereas most of the Republican counties are more rural in nature.
   a) true
   b) false

10. California presently operates under which of the following primary election systems?
   a) open primary
   b) blanket primary
   c) modified closed primary
   d) fully closed primary

CRITICAL-THINKING QUESTIONS

1. How might the cost of campaigning be reduced in California? Because incumbents spend much more money than challengers do, what reforms might level the playing field of campaign politics?
2. What do you think have been the successes and failures of campaign-finance laws in California? Do you think that additional reforms are needed? Why or why not?
3. How do you think the increase in unaffiliated voters and the increase in mail voters will affect campaigns and elections in the future?
4. Why do you think so many states follow California's lead in the areas of ballot propositions and recall efforts? Do you think this is a good or bad development? Explain why.

KEY TERMS

ballot initiative (p. 96)
blanket primary system (p. 93)
campaign-finance reform (p. 113)
closed primary system (p. 93)
general election (p. 81)
media-dominated campaigns (p. 111)
media markets (p. 111)

modified closed primary system (p. 93)
Motor Voter (p. 115)
no party preference (p. 84)
office block ballot (p. 81)
open primary system (p. 93)
political consultants (p. 112)

political culture (p. 89)
political party affiliation (p. 84)
primary elections (p. 81)
vote-by-mail ballots (p. 119)
weak political parties (p. 113)
winner-take-all system (p. 80)

5 The California Legislature

WHAT CALIFORNIA GOVERNMENT DOES AND WHY IT MATTERS

Californians give little if any thought to their legislature. We have a general sense that it is made up of a group of elected individuals who write laws, but beyond that our knowledge is limited.

Our lack of knowledge is related to the minimal media coverage that legislatures receive. The media find it difficult to cover institutions that have multiple members who are doing many different things and have no single voice. They find it much easier to focus on a chief executive who has a press office that provides news-ready stories. Moreover, media coverage of state politics is minimal. Prior to the election of Governor Arnold Schwarzenegger, no Los Angeles television station had a Sacramento bureau. But even the interest in a movie-star governor did not carry over to the legislature, and since the arrival of Governor Jerry Brown, who made only a minimal effort to feed the news establishment, media interest in Sacramento has sharply declined. The last Los Angeles TV news bureau in Sacramento closed in 2013.

Accompanying our lack of knowledge is the general belief that the legislature does not work well. According to Public Policy Institute of California (PPIC) polls, a low was reached in 2010 when only 14 percent of Californians approved of the job that the state legislature was doing (72 percent disapproved). Among likely voters only 9 percent approved. Our dissatisfaction with the legislative process stems in part from a lack of understanding of how it works, but it has several other sources as well.

First, Americans dislike and distrust politics in general. They also like harmony and are turned off by conflict between the governor and the legislature and between parties. Since the legislature is the most transparent and thus most observable political arena, conflict here is more obvious.

Second, the dysfunction that so often characterizes state government negatively affects attitudes toward the legislature. While the legislature is not the principal cause of this dysfunction, term limits and voting rules have, at times, led to gridlock and to elevated partisan conflict, which makes it difficult for the legislature to function well.

Third, while voters want their legislators to work together, these same citizens want their individual interests forcefully represented against competing ones. We have conflicting expectations of legislatures, and legislators' attempts to balance these expectations often contribute to our dissatisfaction. "Laws are like sausages; it is better not to see them being made." This quote, often attributed to the nineteenth-century German statesman Otto von Bismarck, has a point in suggesting that, like in the making of sausages, respect for the making of laws decreases with our awareness of how they are made.

Finally, the occasional bad behavior of individual legislators brings the entire institution into disrepute. During the spring of 2014 three Democratic senators facing criminal charges were suspended by their colleagues. And in 2017-18, after the WeSaidEnough movement focused attention on sexual harassment in the state capitol, three legislators resigned under pressure. These events were followed by dips in the public's evaluation of the legislature. However, according to PPIC polls, the trend in public opinion since 2010 has been toward increased approval of the legislature, to the point where since July of 2018 more Californians approve than disapprove of the job it is doing. A Fall 2016 Field Poll found 50 percent of voters approved of the legislature, the highest in 28 years. (A July 2018 PPIC poll of all adults showed a favorable view of the legislature by an 8 percent margin.)[1]

Several factors have contributed to the legislature's improved reputation: redistricting by a nonpartisan commission, new primary election rules, removal of the two-thirds vote requirement to pass budgets, and changes in term limits. (Each of these factors will be discussed later in this chapter.) But perhaps most important, in 2010 a Democrat was elected governor, and in subsequent elections the Democrats gained a two-thirds majority in each legislative house, greatly reducing both gridlock and conflict. The legislature became more harmonious not because Democrats and Republicans began to work together but rather because Republicans became marginalized. At the same time, the public's approval rating of the U.S. Congress—where power is closely divided and gridlock is common—dropped to a historic low of 9 percent in November 2013 and has generally been in the teens since then.[2]

In spite of Californians' distrust of and lack of interest in their legislature, the influence it has on our lives is significant. In the 2017-18 session alone, the legislature considered (and in some cases passed) legislation dealing with internet privacy, affordable housing, gasoline taxes, bail bonds, gender identification, net neutrality, community college tuition, housing for the homeless, and climate change. The range of issues could hardly be greater. In addition, the legislature funds all state government agencies, including parks, the highway patrol, and universities.

Legislatures, although poorly understood, play a critical role in our government. The framers of the U.S. Constitution, fearing a powerful executive, gave Congress the most significant and most explicit powers, including control over taxation and spending and the authority to write all laws. Today the president gets the most media attention, and some congressional powers have gravitated to the executive branch; Congress, however, remains a very powerful body.

Most state legislatures, including California's, have been modeled on the U.S. Congress in structure, process, and function. California has a **bicameral** (two-house) legislature consisting of the 40-member Senate (sometimes called the upper house) and the 80-member Assembly. As in the U.S. Congress, members of both houses represent geographically determined districts and are elected in winner-take-all elections. As in Congress, bills become law by being approved by both houses and signed by the chief executive. The bulk of the work of each house is done in committees. Each house is organized by party, and party leaders determine committee membership. Despite these similarities, significant differences—such as the role of seniority in committee assignments—do exist. These differences will be addressed in more detail later in the chapter.

The recent history of the California legislature has been remarkable in its extremes. In the 1960s, under the leadership of Assembly Speaker Jesse Unruh, the legislature was transformed from an often corrupt, amateur body into a well-paid, well-staffed professional organization regarded by many as the best state legislature in the country. Then in 1990 California voters passed **Proposition 140**, imposing **term limits** on legislators. Although this did not change the basic structure of the legislature, it did change the collective knowledge, effectiveness, and power of the legislature by reducing the time that legislators were permitted to serve to 14 years, and by reducing the size of the staff that makes legislative work possible.

In 2012 term limits were slightly modified when voters passed Proposition 28, which further reduced the time that legislators could serve to 12 years. However, unlike Proposition 140, which limited members to 6 years in the Assembly and 8 in the Senate, Proposition 28 allowed for all 12 years to be served in one house. The principal result, in time, should be to increase the effectiveness of the Assembly by giving members and leaders more time to become knowledgeable in their jobs and thus become more competent players in the policy game.

Functions

Legislatures have two principal functions: **representation** and policy making. The tensions between these functions make it difficult for a legislature to perform as effectively as citizens might wish.

Representation

The legislature is the principal representative institution in our society, although the executive branch and interest groups also lay claim to this function. It is the duty of legislators (also called members, representatives, assemblypersons, or senators) to represent the voters and other residents (collectively known as **constituents**) within their districts, as well as to represent the dominant district interests. This is easier said than done. In the first place, the term *representation* has many meanings. Here we will simplify it to mean that our representative is our counterpart in Sacramento and that he or she will do what we would do if we were there, especially when it comes to influencing legislation or voting. Of course, there are many more constituents than there are legislators, and rarely do all people see things the same way. Some are wealthy and educated; others, destitute. Some see government as the means to solve society's problems; others see it as the main problem.

Furthermore, representatives face many different and difficult issues: same-sex marriage versus traditional marriage, lower taxes versus improved services, new highways versus neighborhood preservation, higher spending on prisons versus lower college tuition. How one approaches these issues depends in part on the way in which one understands the goal of representation: Is it to give constituents what they want or what they need?

Political scientists talk about two poles of representation style: the delegate who tries to find out what constituents want and then act according to their wishes, and the trustee who believes that he or she has been chosen to act based on his or her own best judgment. Delegates most often try to provide what constituents want, whereas trustees are more inclined to provide for their districts' needs *as they perceive them*. Both types of representation are difficult to achieve in practice. It is often impossible to know what constituents want because they do not communicate with their representatives very well, if at all. It is no easier to determine district needs, which are often diverse, conflicting, and influenced by ideology or other subjective factors.

In theory, a representative should act based on the wants and needs of each member of his or her district equally. But in practice, certain groups wield more influence than others. For instance, some legislators identify closely with a particular group—such as women, small business owners, or immigrants—and they view themselves as representatives of that group. In addition, some groups are better organized and funded than others and are particularly adept at gaining the representative's attention. These would include chambers of commerce, large employers, labor unions, and environmental organizations. Large campaign contributors do not give their donations without expecting something in return, so the legislator is unable to ignore them. Ultimately, it is the constituents who have the vote, and this should force representatives to pay attention to the needs of the entire district. However, even this principle has been weakened in recent years by big money and term limits. Rarely do voters have a realistic chance of keeping favored representatives in power or "throwing the rascals out."

In addition to representing our policy views, representatives try to look out for us when we have specific problems with government, whether it's not getting a disability check, being treated unfairly by an inspector, worrying that a new highway will be built through our property, or opposing the sale of liquor near our kids' school. This ombudsman function is called *constituency service* or *casework*, and it involves intervening with the bureaucracy to resolve specific problems. Representatives also try to get favorable treatment for economic interests in their districts—when a restaurant owner wants a liquor license that he or she believes is

It is easy to stay on top of what is happening in the legislature on the internet. Both houses have web pages. The Senate page is www.sen.ca.gov; the Assembly page is www.assembly.ca.gov. From these sites you can find out about the legislative process and about the status of individual bills. You can also find out how to stay in touch with your legislators. If you type in your address, the site will tell you who your legislators are and how you can contact them. Another useful site is that of the legislative counsel: http://leginfo.legislature.ca.gov.

State legislators are surprisingly accessible, especially in the district. If you have an issue for which you want to contact your legislator, be informed, call for an appointment, and be brief and forthright. Information is helpful, and a good anecdote is always useful! Thoughtful letters are also helpful. Email is used too much, and staff can recognize form mail as soon as it is opened.

Of course, working through a lobby is also effective, and you may belong to an organization that lobbies. Environmental groups, unions, and student organizations are just a few of the many organizations that write, track, and try to influence legislation in their area of concern. Many of these organizations maintain websites discussing the status of legislation in which they have a stake.

being unfairly denied, for instance, or when a construction company wants to build more buildings at the local state university. Representatives will also take stands on issues that are largely symbolic but still important to their constituents, such as flag burning or prayer in schools.

Another important part of representation is being available to constituents. People want to see their representative, and representatives accordingly spend much of their time in their districts attending functions, speaking to groups about the activities of government, distributing commendations and certificates, and listening to constituents. Individual constituents as well as leaders of organized groups also visit with their representatives in Sacramento. See Box 5.1 for information on contacting your state representatives.

Policy Making

Representatives come together to make policy, most obviously through the complex process of making laws, which involves writing bills, holding committee hearings, conducting legislative debates, and adding amendments. These steps will be described in more detail later in the chapter.

Policy making also involves ensuring that legislation is carried out by the bureaucracy as the legislature intended and looking out for potential problems in the implementation of policy. This function, called **oversight**, is carried out through a variety of means, including staff follow-up on constituents' concerns, legislative hearings, budgetary hearings, and confirmation hearings. Legislators do not have much appetite for holding hearings that might make a governor of their own party uncomfortable, but any scandal involving a public agency almost automatically triggers such hearings. In recent years the state legislature has held hearings on construction flaws in the new Bay Bridge, progress of the high-speed rail project, private (ex parte) meetings between coastal commissioners and developers, sexual harassment, and the unnecessarily cumbersome college transfer process. Congressional oversight hearings at the federal level gain far more attention, sometimes due to divided government, but more recently because the strong ideological stances of some of the political appointees in government departments often conflict with congressional expectations. While these hearings most often have a valid administrative or legislative purpose, they are also used to embarrass or damage the members of the opposite party. If they can do both, so much the better. Perhaps the most notable recent examples have been the hearings on Hillary Clinton's role in Benghazi and on her email servers, which were, at the very least, difficult to deal with in her presidential campaign and likely contributed to her loss.

Members and Districts

Unlike Congress, in which each state has two seats in the Senate regardless of population, both houses of the California legislature are apportioned by population. The state is divided into 80 Assembly districts and 40 state Senate districts. In each of these districts a single representative is elected by local voters, which means that these representatives will give serious attention to local interests. As former Speaker of the U.S. House of Representatives Tip O'Neill once said, "All politics is local." Our legislative system is designed to favor local interests (and interests with money), and for representatives, these local interests often take precedence over statewide interests.

State Senator Richard Pan (D-Sacramento) meeting with constituents after his bill requiring nearly all schoolchildren to be vaccinated was signed by Governor Jerry Brown.

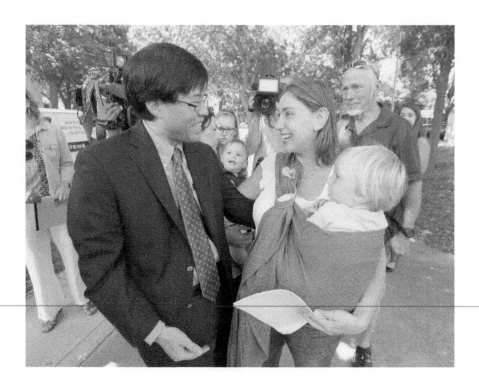

Legislators have offices in both Sacramento and in their districts. Mail, email, and phone messages are answered from both places. When representatives are in their districts, they listen to the concerns of their constituents and tell them about government activities, policy, and politics (e.g., they try to explain what life is like in the capital). In Sacramento they interact with those constituents who travel to the capital as well as with representatives of interest groups. In addition, they work on framing policy, primarily in committees. Legislators often spend Monday through midday Thursday in Sacramento and return to their districts for the remainder of the week; however, this varies with the time of the year, and special events often bring them back to their districts. It is essential to keep a high profile in the district to discourage potential election opponents. Being accused of ignoring one's district could be fatal in an election. Since minority party members often have little say in policy making, they may emphasize their availability to constituents to demonstrate that they have value in Sacramento.

Elections

Every member of the California Senate and Assembly must be elected by voters from a single geographic district. Most members with previous elective experience have served on school boards, city councils, or county boards of supervisors. Many are self-selected. Others are tapped to run for office by party leaders or interests who see them as viable candidates and friendly to their policies. Assembly members serve two-year terms while senators serve for four years.

Legislative elections are **winner-take-all** elections, which means that minor or third parties are generally excluded from the legislature even if they have substantial support statewide. Without a majority of votes in any single district, they cannot place a representative in Sacramento.

The process by which candidates are elected changed significantly in 2010 with the passage of Proposition 14. Prior to 2010, the primary elections were structured to select one candidate from each party to run in the general election. Candidates ran as Republicans, Democrats, or as representatives of a third party in separate contests against members of their own party only. Voters could choose one of those contests in which to vote. The winners faced off against each other in the general election in November. In districts where the voters were overwhelmingly of one party—typical of many California districts—the real contest was in the primary, and election was all but assured to the candidate of the majority party. Many believed that this resulted in the election of extremist legislators who were beholden only to the majority of the voters in their party, not to the majority of the voters in their district.

Proposition 14 instituted a single blanket primary, or top-two primary, in which all candidates run and all voters take part. Voters in the primary or preliminary election vote for the candidate of their choice for each office from a single list of all candidates, and the top two candidates go on to the November election regardless of party. Candidates need not state their party identification on the ballot. The expectation is that, even if both of the winning candidates are in the same party, the more moderate candidate will win the general election by appealing to voters in the minority parties (see Chapter 4). It is not uncommon for there to be more than two dozen contests (out of more than 150 legislative races) in which the top two candidates belong to the same party. In 2018 there were 13 in the state legislature and four for congressional seats. Even the race for the U.S. Senate was between two Democrats, as it was in 2016.

If there are only two candidates in the preliminary election, they will have to run against each other for a second time in the general election. While this may seem redundant, the electorate in November is almost always larger (and therefore less Republican) than in June, which can affect the outcome of the election. In 2012 the 65th Assembly District in Orange County provided an excellent example of an incumbent challenged by a single opponent—in this case, a Republican challenged by a Democrat. When they ran against each other in June, the Republican incumbent won with over 58 percent of the vote. In the runoff in November, the Democratic challenger won with about 52 percent of the vote, helping the Democrats gain a two-thirds majority in the Assembly. Contributing to this victory was a significant increase in voter turnout: about 50,000 people voted in June while over 120,000 voted in November. The new incumbent lost to a different Republican two years later when only 77,000 people voted and regained the seat in 2016 when there were over 140,000 voters.

Two other key features of California politics have a significant influence on who gets elected. First, the large size of each district means that campaigns are expensive and fund-raising is necessary. Second, the manner in which district boundaries are drawn influences the role of political parties and the strength of incumbents.

Fund-raising

Campaigns can easily cost millions of dollars (see Chapter 4), and campaign expenditures are likely to be much higher in the future because of the Supreme Court ruling in *Citizens United* (see Chapter 3), which rejected corporate spending limits, and because the California Citizens Redistricting Commission has created more competitive legislative districts. Fund-raising is one of the most significant obstacles to winning an election. The nature of California and the size of the districts make election victories unlikely through old-fashioned precinct work. Use of TV and radio advertising is also impractical in the larger media markets because of cost. Most candidates have campaign consultants and engage in polling, which help them come up with strategies for targeted distribution of literature, internet advertising, and social media outreach.

Districting

Because of the relatively small size of the state legislature, its districts are among the largest in the country. Senate districts have over 950,000 constituents, and Assembly districts over 475,000. (For comparison, U.S. House districts in California have approximately 715,000 constituents.) Historically, district lines were drawn by the legislature, often leading to charges of **gerrymandering**. This term dates to the early 1800s, when Massachusetts governor Elbridge Gerry oversaw a redistricting that benefited his party and resulted in district lines that resembled, in a famous cartoon of the day, a salamander. To *gerrymander* means to draw district lines in a manner that favors one party over another, generally by packing most of the opponent's voters into a few districts and spreading the remainder thinly over the remaining districts. To date, the courts have generally accepted this practice, saying only that districts must be equal in population and must not be drawn to diminish the voting strength of any minority.

Redistricting is done following each census and until 2012 had to pass both houses and be signed by the governor, like any other piece of legislation. However, after the 2000 census, despite Democratic control of both houses and the governor's office, the party did not create more gerrymandered Democratic districts. Instead, endeavoring (successfully) to avoid a lawsuit, they approved a set of maps known as the "incumbency protection plan," which maintained safe seats for both parties. Thus, the power of voters to hold their legislators accountable was diminished, as incumbents throughout the state were unlikely to lose a future election.

Therefore, before 2012 most action took place in the primaries, though incumbents rarely faced a serious challenge there either following the advent of term limits in 1992. Knowing that an incumbent assemblyperson would be out of office in no more than four years, the astute challenger waited for that vacancy to occur rather than engaging in an expensive, divisive challenge. Term limits had the unintended consequence of inhibiting voters from "throwing the rascals out," and thus the legislature was more immune from direct electoral challenge than ever before.

Since 2012 the situation that created safe districts with highly partisan incumbents has significantly changed. As a result of their continued frustration with the legislature, the voters approved two measures—Proposition 11 in November 2008 (followed by Proposition 20 in 2010) and Proposition 14 in June 2010—that have had an impact on who gets elected to the legislature.

The consequences of Proposition 14, the top-two primary law described above, have been overwhelmingly overshadowed by those of Propositions 11 and 20, both redistricting initiatives that unexpectedly resulted in a two-thirds Democratic majority in both houses. Proposition 11 took the task of drawing legislative districts away from the legislature and replaced it with a 15-person Citizens Redistricting Commission. This commission created districts with a closer partisan balance.

The expectation was that Proposition 11 would result in fewer safe seats and in the election of moderate legislators more willing to engage in bipartisan compromise. It will take several election cycles before these results can be assessed because the large Democratic majorities currently in the state legislature make bipartisan compromise largely unnecessary. However, some observers believe that the smaller Republican minority is less moderate and less inclined to compromise while the larger Democratic majority is more moderate—not a surprising result as the minority shrinks towards its base while the majority becomes larger and more inclusive of different viewpoints.

The Democratic two-thirds supermajority has wavered in recent years. In 2014 it was lost after three state senators were suspended. It was recouped in 2017, only to disappear again after the recall election discussed below. In 2018 the supermajority was regained, allowing Democrats to carry out business with little regard for their Republican colleagues. Thus, gridlock has been reduced, and the public's regard for the legislature has become correspondingly more favorable.

Still, the large majority of Democrats have not proven to be radical. They did raise taxes, but those taxes were narrowly focused on the transportation infrastructure (still, it resulted in a successful recall election of a single state senator and a defeated ballot initiative to repeal the taxes, both discussed below). Yet most actions have been moderate and have not resulted in drastic or excessive new laws or regulations. This is partially because the legislature has had to work with a moderate and fiscally conservative Democratic governor who would probably veto such measures. More important, many of these new Democratic legislators are from marginal seats that have many Republican voters (such as the 65th Assembly District in Orange County and the 32nd Assembly District in Bakersfield) and are reluctant to take bold actions that might endanger their chances of re-election.

In addition, when contests in the general election are between two Democrats, big corporations (such as Chevron Oil) often spend large sums of money backing the candidate who is more supportive of their interests. While these candidates may or may not be moderates, they are definitely supportive of the corporations that have funded them.

There are enough business-oriented Democrats to form a loosely structured caucus that has designated leaders, as well as a PAC, and that holds fund-raisers. Membership is not published but is probably around 20, more or less, depending on the issue. As the Democratic tent has grown bigger, the new members are most often from more conservative districts, and big business with big money has taken advantage of the top-two primaries to aggressively support friendly Democratic candidates. One Assembly member, Cheryl Brown (D-San Bernardino), who was key to helping gut climate control bills in 2015, received over $1 million from Chevron in independent spending supporting her 2016 primary campaign, leading her opponents to label her "Chevron Cheryl." Brown was ultimately defeated in November 2016 in a race that cost $6.1 million in independent spending, mostly from the oil companies.

If the Democrats in the Assembly have 52 members, as was the case in 2015 (in 2018 there were 55 Democrats), then it takes only 12 "moderates" to join 28 Republicans to defeat legislation, as they did in 2015. In 2016, at the end of the two-year session, the governor and the Democratic leadership through intense politicking were able to pass meaningful climate control legislation with the minimum number of needed votes, over the opposition of the oil companies. Although the governor and the Democratic leadership made a comeback, overcoming the opposition in 2016 to pass strong climate change legislation was a struggle. Business-oriented Democrats have demonstrated that they are an important third force in the legislature. A new chapter in California politics has begun, and no one knows exactly how it will be written.[3]

Organization

The process of policy making is complex, involving many steps and many actors. Over time, both the Senate and Assembly have, for reasons both practical and political, adopted principles of organization that structure how the legislature works.

Leadership

The leader of the Assembly is the **speaker**, and he or she has a remarkable array of powers (although these were diminished by the 6-year term limit on members of the Assembly). In an attempt to increase the power of the speaker by lengthening his or her time in the position, in 2003 and 2009 the Democrats elected a first-term legislator to the speakership. In 2014 they elected a member, Toni Atkins, in her second term (well regarded, she is now the president pro tempore of the

Assembly speaker Anthony Rendon, center, was elected to the position in only his second term, but new rules on term limits may allow him to serve longer than any speaker in recent history and offer some stability to a legislature lacking experience and institutional memory.

state Senate). In 2016 she was replaced by another member in his second term, Anthony Rendon. Rendon, however, was elected to the legislature under new rules that allow him to serve 12 years in the Assembly. If he serves as speaker for the remainder of his allotted time—until 2024—he will have been one of the longest-serving speakers in recent history. This is a game changer that should increase the speaker's effectiveness and thus the effectiveness of the legislature.

The Assembly speaker's powers are considerably more extensive than those of the Speaker of the U.S. House of Representatives. Beginning with control over assigning parking spaces and offices, these powers include almost complete control over establishing committees, assigning members to serve on them, and, if the speaker chooses, removing members from these committees. Because the bulk of legislative work is done in committees, members depend on the speaker to provide them with a meaningful role in the legislature. The speaker can also assign floor leadership of high-profile or popular bills to legislators of his or her choice, enhancing their reputations both inside and outside the Assembly.

When the full Assembly meets, the speaker acts as presiding officer and thereby controls the debate; when not presiding, he or she designates the person who does. The speaker also appoints the majority floor leader, who assists in running legislative sessions. It is difficult to overstate the speaker's power, which can move bills, help supporters, and hurt opponents. Speakers can raise money as well, which in turn allows them to solidify support. Members find it advantageous to cooperate with the speaker. The speaker is elected by the entire membership of the Assembly, but in most cases the outcome is determined in advance by the majority party caucus, which consists of all of the members of the majority party meeting together. Only when the majority is split does the full Assembly vote become significant.

The minority caucus elects the Assembly minority leader, who is the public voice of the minority party and who works with the speaker to determine minority party assignments on committees. The speaker, however, has the final say.

The other important element of the leadership is the **Assembly Rules Committee**, which is made up of nine members, four elected by each party's caucus, plus a chair appointed by the speaker. The committee's responsibilities include hiring staff, assigning bills to committees, and reviewing legislative rules. Rarely does this committee operate independently of the speaker's wishes.

The organization of the Senate is similar to that of the Assembly, but the Senate leader, the **president pro tempore** (sometimes shortened to president pro tem), does not have the absolute power of the Assembly speaker. Many of the speaker's powers in the Assembly rest with the Rules Committee in the Senate. Yet for a time the president pro tempore—most notably John Burton—was the most influential legislator in Sacramento, largely because of the impact of term limits. Prior to 2012 senators often served 6 years in the Assembly first, and their time in the Senate could last up to 8 years. Senate leaders could accrue 10 to 12 years of experience in Sacramento before assuming leadership roles. In contrast, Assembly leaders might have had only two or three years of experience. John Burton, who was the last of his breed, had far more experience than that, including experience in the U.S. Congress.

This pattern is now changing thanks to the passage of Proposition 28 in June 2012. Legislators elected in 2012 and after may now serve no more than 12 years in the state legislature, but those years can be spent entirely in one house or in a combination of both houses. Thus, Speaker Rendon may remain in his position for up to 8 years, potentially having greater influence than his immediate predecessors did. Senators will no longer be able to serve 14 years, which will level the playing field and provide members and leaders of the Assembly the opportunity to attain the same level of experience.

Committees

The bulk of legislative work is done in **committees**. Committees allow for greater specialization, greater expertise of those involved, and greater attention to detail. In 2017–18 there were 32 standing or permanent committees in the Assembly and 22 in the Senate (see Table 5.1). Each member sits on several standing committees. In addition to standing committees, there are many select committees that exist to study specific issues and joint committees to look at issues that concern both houses. Members may serve on a dozen or more of these less important committees.

Committees are at the heart of groups of players often referred to as **issue networks**. These networks consist of committee members and **staff**, senior members of the respective executive branch agency, and interest groups concerned with issues in a committee's jurisdiction. The bulk of policy details are worked out in these networks. Lobbyists and bureaucrats involved in issue networks tend to be specialists who spend their entire careers in a single subject area. It would be unusual for someone who has spent a career in transportation to move to education. Previously, legislators would spend their careers in specific issue areas as well. Term limits have changed that, or rather have shortened the length of careers. While policy is still worked out within these networks, the power to shape the policy has shifted to those who have greater permanency, experience, and expertise—namely, lobbyists and bureaucrats. The less experienced and less knowledgeable legislator is now

TABLE 5.1 ● Standing Committees of the California Legislature, 2017–18

State Senate

Agriculture	Health
Appropriations	Human Services
Banking and Financial Institutions	Insurance
Budget and Fiscal Review	Judiciary
Business, Professions and Economic Development	Labor and Industrial Relations
Education	Natural Resources and Water
Elections and Constitutional Amendments	Public Employment and Retirement
Energy, Utilities, and Communications	Public Safety
Environmental Quality	Rules
Governance and Finance	Transportation and Housing
Governmental Organization	Veterans Affairs

Assembly

Accountability and Administrative Review	Human Services
Aging and Long-Term Care	Insurance
Agriculture	Jobs, Economic Development, and the Economy
Appropriations	Judiciary
Arts, Entertainment, Sports, Tourism, and Internet Media	Labor and Employment
Banking and Finance	Local Government
Budget	Natural Resources
Business and Professions	Privacy and Consumer Protection
Communications and Conveyance	Public Employees, Retirement and Social Security
Education	Public Safety
Elections and Redistricting	Revenue and Taxation
Environmental Safety and Toxic Materials	Rules
Governmental Organization	Transportation
Health	Utilities and Commerce
Higher Education	Veterans Affairs
Housing and Community Development	Water, Parks, and Wildlife

more dependent than before on these individuals for policy details. Experienced staff can help, but since the severe staff reductions required by Proposition 140 in 1990, staff members are often no more experienced than legislators.

Staff

Without staff, the legislature cannot effectively do its job. Staff members are crucial in both the policy-making and the representative functions of the legislature. All legislators have staff in both their Sacramento and district offices to help with constituency contacts, including handling casework, scheduling appearances, and answering mail and phone calls from constituents. In addition, committees have staff, called consultants, to help with the policy work of that committee, and consultants are also critical components of the issue networks. Some of the best consultants will take their hard-earned experience and move on to become lobbyists, where the pay is often far higher and the job more secure. Each legislator is allotted an office budget for staffing. Legislators are permitted additional staff depending on whether they occupy a committee leadership role and on the generosity of the party leadership. In addition, the house leaders and caucuses have staff that may number more than 150 for the majority party. This staff helps with bill analysis for individual members and public relations for both individual members and the party.

There are over 2,000 legislative aides. It is not unusual for majority legislators to have 13 or 14 staff members. Minority members may have only 4 or 5. While most aides are modestly paid, some—especially highly-valued committee consultants—make over $150,000 a year. The total personnel budget for legislative workers in 2015 was $216 million. The median salary for staff members is about $55–65,000. These aides often work alongside members of the prestigious Assembly and Senate Fellows program as well as many college interns.

There are three important and well-regarded groups of staff who are nonpartisan and who work for the entire legislature. The first is the Legislative Analyst's Office, which analyzes budget proposals and the fiscal impact of ballot propositions. The second is the Legislative Counsel, which helps write bills, analyze ballot propositions, and provide legal advice. The third is the State Auditor's Office, which handles management and fiscal audits of the executive branch.

Before Proposition 140 passed in 1990, the staff of the California legislature was considered the best in the nation. However, that proposition required a staff cut of 40 percent and resulted in layoffs and the departure of many of the most experienced staffers, especially the highly-paid experts on which the committees relied. Staff is still a significant factor in the legislature, and over the years it has inched back toward its previous size and influence.

Legislative Process

There are three types of items that may pass the legislature: bills, which if successful become laws; constitutional amendments, which require a two-thirds vote of both houses and a referendum by the voters; and resolutions, which are largely symbolic expressions of opinion. The remainder of this section is concerned primarily with bills.

Bills are introduced only by legislators, even if the content was originally proposed by someone as politically important as the governor. Indeed, bills are often written by someone other than the person who introduces them. Many bills may be written by, or in conjunction with, lobbyists; and the nonpartisan Legislative Counsel's office may help in drafting language. An individual senator may introduce no more than 40 bills in a two-year session, whereas Assembly members may introduce 50 bills. Legislators may have a variety of motives for introducing a bill, such as impressing constituents or paying off a political favor, and most go nowhere. In the 2017–18 legislative session, 2,511 bills were introduced in the Senate and 2,264 in the Assembly for a total of 4,775. Of these, 2,214 reached the governor's desk. He signed 1,895 of them and vetoed 319, including some that were strongly supported by his allies. In his 16 years as governor, Brown signed nearly 20,000 bills into law.

Once a bill is introduced, the rules committee of the appropriate house assigns the bill to a standing committee or even two committees, depending on its content.

There may be a political or strategic component to this assignment. The bill is also numbered and printed. Committees cannot act on a bill until it has been in print for 30 days to allow comment from interested parties. Committees hold hearings, scrutinize the language to make sure that it clearly and accurately states what members intend, add amendments, and pass or reject bills. An absolute majority of the committee must vote favorably to report a bill out. If a bill is reported out of committee, it may go to the floor for discussion by the entire house; or bills with major fiscal impact may end up in the "suspense file" of the appropriations committee of either house to die, be amended, or be advanced without public vote and without explanation. These committees substantially reduce the number of bills reaching the floor and may significantly change others. In the closing weeks of a legislative session, these committees may report out hundreds of bills in a single day, which adds to the end-of-session logjam. Once a bill reaches the floor, amendments may be added and require only a majority vote. Bill passage requires an absolute majority (41 in the Assembly, 21 in the Senate). Once a bill has passed one house, it goes to the other house for similar consideration. Bills must pass both houses with identical language before they are forwarded to the governor for his signature. If the governor vetoes a bill, a two-thirds vote in each house is required to override the veto. This rarely happens.

Most bills pass through each house with different wording. In this case one house may acquiesce to the wording of the other house, or a conference committee will be established to work out the differences. A conference committee is a joint committee consisting of three members from each body. Assembly members are appointed by the speaker, and Senate members are appointed by the Senate Rules Committee. They suggest compromise language that must pass both houses. If this attempt fails, two additional attempts may be made before the bill is put to rest. See Figure 5.1 for an illustration of how a bill becomes a law in the California legislature.

SHORTCUTS The process described above is the textbook approach, but much legislation is able to bypass some of these steps, especially near the end of a legislative session when bills tumble over one another and deals are made in back rooms in a rush to adjourn. (In the last weeks of the 2015–16 session the legislature dealt with over 1,500 bills.) Many bills reappear as amendments to other bills, attracting even less public attention than they would have in the normal process. At this time, the influence of party leaders is greater because they are able to grease the skids for compromises and logrolling. **Logrolling** is vote trading, the process by which members exchange votes: "You vote for my bill, and I will vote for yours." Another common end-of-session legislative tactic is to hijack a bill and then **"gut and amend"** it. An issue that may have been presumed dead suddenly reappears, without warning, in a procedurally alive bill that previously dealt with an entirely different topic. In an editorial denouncing the practice, the *Sacramento Bee* describes how "gut and amend" works:

> A bill on air pollution morphs into a bill on immigration. A bill on college tuition becomes a bill on shark fins. In the last three weeks of the 2011 session, legislators gutted and amended 48 bills, passing 22 of them. Gov. Jerry Brown signed 19 of them.[4]

Efforts to reform this procedure in the legislature by requiring bills to be in print for several days before coming up for a vote never gained traction; so in 2016 wealthy Republican Charles Munger solely funded a successful ballot proposition

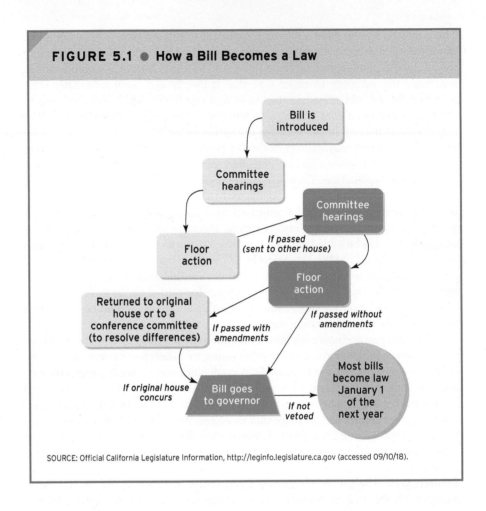

FIGURE 5.1 ● How a Bill Becomes a Law

Bill is introduced

Committee hearings

Floor action

If passed (sent to other house)

Committee hearings

Floor action

If passed without amendments

Returned to original house or to a conference committee (to resolve differences)

If passed with amendments

If original house concurs

Bill goes to governor

If not vetoed

Most bills become law January 1 of the next year

SOURCE: Official California Legislature Information, http://leginfo.legislature.ca.gov (accessed 09/10/18).

that prohibits the legislature from passing a bill until it has been in print and published on the internet for 72 hours (Proposition 54). Attempts have been made to lessen the impact of this initiative by defining "bill" narrowly and by limiting "passing" to mean only the final vote in the legislature before the bill goes to the governor, not earlier votes.

End-of-session periods in Sacramento reflect quintessential American politics: a system that favors insiders, corporations, and those with big money. While this goes on throughout the year, these backroom strategies work best when time is compressed and the media and other outsiders cannot follow what is going on or cannot do anything about it.

At the end of the session there is intense pressure to get things done. As noted earlier, 2,214 bills passed in 2017–18, and many others were in play. Insiders and lobbyists focus their attention on a single bill or a small number of bills that are important to their clients. Large corporations and other interest groups hire full-time lobbyists and lawyers, sometimes a full platoon of them, to follow their important bills, develop strategy, and take the necessary actions to ensure the desired outcome, all of which can be written off as business expenses.

These insiders work out deals behind the proverbial closed doors, and provisions to bills are added and removed at the last minute. Often the junior members voting on the floor have no idea of what they are voting on. Before the legislature was term-limited, members were extremely well-versed about their policy interests and had long memories about what tricks lobbyists and other legislators had pulled in previous sessions. This meant that it was more difficult to make unnoticed changes in legislation to benefit a special interest. Institutional memory is much more limited now among legislators. Experience, knowledge, and skills rest disproportionately with lobbyists and agency representatives.

Differences from U.S. Congress

While the California legislature is modeled closely on the national legislature, there are important differences that, collectively, make the California legislature a weaker body.

Term Limits

Unlike members of Congress, who can serve as long as they are re-elected, California legislators are limited to a total of 12 years, which can be served in one or both houses. Term limits enacted by the passage of Proposition 140 in 1990 limited members to three 2-year terms in the Assembly and two 4-year terms in the Senate for a maximum total of 14 years. Proposition 28 in 2012 instituted the current 12-year limit.

There were numerous reasons for the success of Proposition 140. First, it was a reaction to the highly effective Assembly Speaker Willie Brown, a flamboyant African American politician from San Francisco who was immensely unpopular with conservative voters. Second, it was an effect of public aversion to **gridlock** and divided government (generated by partisan conflict between the Republican governor and the Democratic legislature). Third, voters were protesting against the large fund-raising efforts of incumbents. Fourth, it was a reflection of the national trend against entrenched incumbents. Finally, it was the product of a belief among some Republicans that term limits could overthrow the Democratic majority. However, these term limits did not end divided government, gridlock, or large fund-raising (campaign-related spending has vastly increased), and they only briefly suspended the Democratic majority and in only one house, the 1994 Assembly. The proposition did reduce the ability of the legislature to act effectively. It is still too early to know if Proposition 28 will ultimately make the legislature more effective.

Item Veto

In Washington, D.C., the president has to sign or reject bills passed by Congress in their entirety. The president cannot approve parts that he or she likes and reject those that he or she dislikes. In California, as in most states, the governor has a **line-item veto** on appropriations, including those in the budget. This power allows the governor to reduce or eliminate a specific spending item, although he or she cannot increase items. This means that the legislature cannot force the governor's hand by including an item that the governor opposes in a large spending bill that he or she mostly supports. In 2016, for the first time in over 40 years, the governor did not use the line-item veto when signing the budget. A line-item veto can be overridden by an absolute two-thirds vote in both houses.

Apportionment and District Size

Both houses of the California legislature are apportioned by population, called **apportionment**; in Congress, the Constitution allots two senators to each state, regardless of size. California has a population about equal to the populations of the 22 smallest states combined. While these states have 44 senators between them, California has the same number of senators as the smallest of these states, Wyoming. In fact, there are four states that have fewer residents than are in each of California's 53 congressional districts.

Because California is so populous (about 39 million people) and because its legislature is relatively small, its legislative districts are among the largest in the nation. Senate districts have over 950,000 constituents, while Assembly districts contain over 475,000 residents. Compare this to New Hampshire, with a population of about 1.3 million and with 400 members in its lower house, which results in one representative for about every 3,000 residents. While New Hampshire's representatives are very accessible and elections are not expensive, most representatives do not wield much influence in their very large chamber. California senators, unlike any other U.S. legislative body, represent more constituents than members of Congress and more than the U.S. senators of seven states. This means that they are considerably less accessible than their counterparts in other states and that their elections are considerably more expensive.

The fact that both legislative houses are apportioned by population has led some informed observers to suggest that a unicameral legislature of 120 members would make more sense. This would result in smaller districts and increased accessibility to legislators.

Media Visibility

In Washington, D.C., the media interpret the national government's actions by focusing on the president, who consequently dominates the news. The comments of members of Congress are generally used to give more depth to a presidential story. Most often, these are party leaders, committee chairs, or the occasional legislator who has managed to make a name for himself or herself on a given issue.

The same is true in California's capital, but the statewide media, especially television, rarely cover news in Sacramento. Only the four party leaders receive air time, and because they hold their positions for so few years, the public has difficulty keeping track of who they are. The former Speaker of the U.S. House of Representatives from 2015–18, Paul Ryan, was practically a household name, but California Assembly Speaker Anthony Rendon is not. Consequently, most of what happens in Sacramento occurs out of the spotlight.

Court Appointments

Some of the greatest legislative battles in Congress have occurred during the Senate's hearings to confirm judicial appointments, especially to the Supreme Court. In contrast, many judges in California are elected. Those who are appointed by the governor are approved by the Commission on Judicial Appointments. The Senate does get to approve many other gubernatorial appointments to executive positions and regulatory boards and commissions, including the governing boards of both the California State University and the University of California. In both the U.S.

Senate and the California Senate, legislators have rejected recent nominees over policy differences.

Filibusters

In the U.S. Senate, a body that is not apportioned on the basis of one person, one vote, 41 members (potentially representing slightly more than 33 million people—about 10 percent of the country's population) can block the passage of most legislation through use of the filibuster. California has no such provision. Indeed, in most cases the majority rules. The principal exceptions are tax increases and constitutional amendments, which require a two-thirds vote.

Initiatives

Unlike the U.S. Constitution, the California Constitution provides several means of taking issues directly to the voters. Of these, the most significant is the initiative. The initiative is important in the legislative context because those who are thwarted in their attempts to get legislation passed can always threaten to take it—or an even more extreme version of it—to the voters. This tactic is often used to persuade legislators to vote for measures that they would otherwise oppose, and it significantly weakens the legislature (see discussion on the soda tax initiative later in this chapter).

Seniority

In the U.S. Congress, seniority is used as an informal rule in appointing members to committees and in choosing each committee's majority and minority leaders; once members are appointed to their committee positions, they are almost never removed. In the California legislature, both the appointment and removal power resides with the Assembly speaker and Senate majority leadership. Seniority plays a much smaller role (with term limits, seniority is of course limited). Both the speaker and the Senate majority leadership in recent years have removed members of both parties from committee leadership roles for disagreeing with them over various issues and because of financial and sexual harassment scandals.

Challenges Facing the California Legislature

When voters pay attention to the legislature, complaints and criticism of its actions often result. At times these objections are on target, at times not. State government tends to be perceived as dysfunctional, and the legislature is an easy target. It is easy to be repulsed by the contentious process of arriving at legislative agreements. Moreover, individual members often run for the legislature by running against it, emphasizing the legislature's shortcomings and foibles in order to play up their own importance as an agent of change.

Scandal also gets the public's attention. In 2014 three senators were suspended for misbehavior ranging from lying about living in their district to international gunrunning. Another was fined for misuse of campaign funds. A fifth was removed from his committee positions as a result of claims of domestic violence. During the 2017–18 session over 140 women working in or around the capitol went public about incidents of sexual harassment that they had experienced or witnessed from legislators, staff, or lobbyists. As a result, two Assembly members and one senator resigned under pressure. All were replaced by women.

The misbehavior of any one of the 120 legislators is often generalized to reflect badly on the whole institution. To have several legislators in the news at the same time for improper behavior is especially damaging, and these latest scandals may have contributed to the marginal decline in the legislature's approval rating. While the Senate had the authority to suspend the three senators in 2014, it did not have the authority to cut off pay and benefits. As a consequence, Proposition 50, which would allow a house of the legislature to suspend a member's pay and privileges with a two-thirds vote, was passed in June 2016. The threat of these powers has since been used in forcing the resignation of at least one legislator.

Among the most common criticisms of the legislature are the following:

Money

In the California legislature, as is the case throughout American politics, money carries a great deal of clout. Elections are expensive, and the money for elections comes from many sources, including the candidate's personal wealth, small contributions from many individuals, and larger contributions from business, unions, and other special interests. Large contributions are generally given to ensure support for a particular interest. Although legislators claim that their vote cannot be bought and that contributors are buying access and nothing else, that claim is difficult to support. Moreover, simply having access that the ordinary voter does not have is a significant advantage for these contributors. We have the best legislature that money can buy, and short of moving to public financing of campaigns—an idea rejected by the voters in June 2010—those who have money will always have an advantage over those who do not. With increasing social inequality and more money available to big industries and a few very wealthy individuals (and less available to the rest of us), and with the Supreme Court having loosened the restrictions on campaign spending, this advantage is growing.

Money is usually distributed to legislators who support the position of a given interest or to those who might be swayed by an offer of monetary support. It also goes to party leaders, who then distribute it to other legislators or candidates to solidify their support both within their party and against the other party. Indeed, the amassing of a large war chest contributed to the distrust and dislike of Speaker Willie Brown and led to the passing of Proposition 140, setting term limits. However, term-limited legislators, having little background in fund-raising, have become more dependent than their predecessors on large donations from special interests. Jesse Unruh once said, "If you can't take their money, eat their food, drink their booze . . . and then vote against them, you don't belong here."[5] On this basis, there are probably more legislators now than before that "don't belong here."

Term Limits (and Insufficient Knowledge and Expertise)

When Proposition 140 was passed in 1990, many believed that term limits would remove a remote professional class of legislators and bring in a new breed with closer ties to their districts. The ballot argument said that term limits "would remove the grip that vested interests have over the legislature" and create a "government of citizens representing their fellow citizens."[6] The expectations for this proposition were too high, and the results were unfortunate.

Legislative politics works best as an ongoing game among a relatively stable group of experienced players. Many of the aphorisms about politics, such as "Politics makes strange bedfellows" and "Don't burn your bridges" are based on ongoing relationships played out over a period of years. With a short, fixed term limit, the players change too rapidly for legislators to learn whom they can trust, with whom they can work, and whom they should avoid. This knowledge could facilitate cooperation across party lines as legislators come to learn that not all good is on their side of the aisle and that not all evil is on the other side. But in a short six years, legislators cannot learn that well; the players change too rapidly. The people who can work out effective compromises seldom emerge, and even if capable negotiators materialized, they would not know with whom to work.

Nor can effective leadership emerge with term limits as short as six years. In recent years, to give leaders more time in office, Assembly Democrats have often chosen freshmen legislators as committee chairs and as speaker. But a freshman legislator, no matter how talented, cannot effectively lead a large collegial body.

Nor in six short years is there time to develop expertise in process or subject matter, which are the ordinary skills of a good legislator. This dilemma was summed up by a lobbyist:

> I feel sorry for the first-term members who faced the energy crisis. They don't know who's smart; they don't know who knows what they're doing; they don't know the policy; they don't know the politics. And they are faced with a crisis.[7]

Real power has shifted from the legislature to the permanent establishment—the bureaucracy and interest groups. Members in these institutions may spend a career in Sacramento outlasting three or four generations of Assembly members. Much as they were dissatisfied with the legislature, it is doubtful that the voters wanted to shift power to either of those two groups. In June 2012 voters made a change in term limits, which on balance may have shifted *some* power back to the legislature. Proposition 28 reduced the time a legislator could serve in Sacramento from 14 years (6 in the Assembly and 8 in the Senate) to 12 years, but now those years can all be served in one house. When this change is fully played out, it will give each house more stability and should result in more experienced leaders. Senators may be a little less experienced than they were previously, but whatever is lost in that body will be gained by the much greater experience that Assembly members will achieve before being forced to leave.

The result could be a more knowledgeable and effective legislature that is at least marginally better able to deal with lobbyists and bureaucrats. But we have not yet reached this point. Only those legislators elected in 2012 and after operate under the new term limits, and change is not likely to be significant until sometime after 2018. Speaker Rendon, the first speaker chosen under the new limits, may serve for up to eight years in that position. In the previous eight years there were three different speakers.

If there has been a positive aspect to term limits, it is the increased diversity in the legislature. The percentage of Latino legislators rose from 6 percent in 1990 to 25 percent in 2009, before declining to 19 percent in 2015. In 2017 the percentage of Latinos rose slightly to 22.5 percent. In the 2017–18 session the Assembly membership was 54 percent nonwhite minority. The percentage of women in the legislature increased from 17.5 percent in 1990 to 32 percent in 2008 before dropping to 21.6 percent in 2017 (see "Who Are Californians?" on p. 149). Toni Atkins, the speaker of the Assembly prior to Anthony Rendon, was the first openly lesbian politician to hold that office (in 2018 she was elected president pro tempore of the state Senate). Her immediate predecessor as speaker was John Pérez, an openly gay Latino, and before that by Karen Bass, an African American woman. Women and members of nonwhite ethnic groups regularly occupy positions in the Democratic leadership of both houses.[8]

Partisanship

Many believe that **partisanship** has increased in the legislature in recent years. This trend has often been attributed to safe districts, in which representatives who couldn't lose in a general election were elected by their party's—often extremist—majority. In these safe districts the general election is determined by the primary election outcome and results in representatives who are more extreme than average voters. According to the common interpretation, safe districts have resulted in increased partisanship and legislators who are less willing to compromise.

As usual, the issue is more complex than this, although the new, more competitive general elections that began in 2010 may have resulted in the election of more moderates—at least in the Democratic Party. The problem with partisanship is not that there are strong partisans in the legislature—this has always been so. It is that in recent years the quality of public discourse has become less civil, and the participants have come to have less regard for their opponents and less willingness to work with them. Part of this incivility is a reflection of the increasing homogeneity and polarization of the national parties and their leaders (epitomized by the in-your-face style of the president). Term limits may play a role as well. Recognizing that they will not have to live with and deal with their opponents for years into the future, legislators make less effort to develop civil working relationships with them.

But legislators should be partisan. We elect representatives on a partisan basis. If we vote for Republicans rather than Democrats, then the Republicans should deliver on their partisan promises. Even those who rail against partisanship still want their interests to be forcefully proposed and protected.

Some of the greatest legislatures in the world, such as the British Parliament, are fiercely partisan and yet manage to govern. The difference is that in those bodies, the majority is permitted to rule. In our system, which permits a minority veto on taxation, bipartisan cooperation is essential; when it is not forthcoming, the system functions badly. If the California legislature appears to function better in recent years, it is not because of a reduction in partisanship; rather it's because the Democrats' overwhelming majority makes cross-party cooperation less necessary. Proposition 25, passed in 2010, which removed the requirement for a two-thirds vote on the annual budget, also reduced the need for cross-party cooperation.

Gridlock, Minority Rule, and Lack of Accountability

While California does not have the filibuster that thwarts majority rule in the U.S. Senate, it does have two major checks on effective majority governance. The first is that the legislature and the governor are elected separately and may represent different parties. The second is that a **two-thirds vote** is required to raise taxes, necessitating, in the absence of an overwhelming one-party majority, that the two parties work together to produce realistic fiscal policy.

How Diverse Is the State Legislature?

California's demographic changes are changing the electorate and the state legislature. White Californians now make up less than half of the representatives in the State Assembly (46 percent), but still make up the vast majority of the State Senate (78 percent). Women account for just under 21 percent of the state legislature, which is the lowest percentage since 1991–92.

How does this compare to the population of California? Look at the infographics below. The United States Census Bureau survey in 2017 found the population of California to be 37 percent white, 39 percent of Latino descent, 6 percent black or African American, and 15 percent Asian. What groups are overrepresented? Which groups are underrepresented?

By Race

	1	2	3
● White	37%	46%	78%
● Latino	39%	28%	12%
● Black or African American	6%	10%	5%
● Asian-Pacific Islander	15%	14%	5%
● Multi-Racial	2%	2%	0%

Key

1 2 3

1. Total population

2. Assembly distribution*

3. Senate distribution*

By Gender

	1	2	3
● Male	49.7%	79%	77%
● Female	50.3%	21%	23%

*Note: The Legislature of California has 40 state Senators and 80 Assembly members.

SOURCES: "Demographics in the California Legislature," California Research Bureau: California State Library, www.library.ca.gov/Content/pdf/crb/reports/LegDemographicsNov16.pdf (accessed 07/27/2018); United States Census Bureau, "Quick Facts: California, 2017", https://www.census.gov/quickfacts/fact/table/ca/PST045217 (accessed 07/27/2018).

forcriticalanalysis

1. Thinking back to the projected population growth by demographic group in the Chapter 1, Who Are Californians? feature, what changes would you expect to see in terms of diversity in the state legislature in the next ten years?

2. In addition to the demographic trends outlined in this feature, what political issues—both at the state and national level—do you think will influence the composition of the state legislature in the future?

Perhaps no other provision of governance has contributed more to the dysfunctional state of California and to the **lack of accountability** that characterizes the legislature than the two-thirds vote needed to raise taxes. Californians may elect a majority in the legislature and even a governor of the same party, but unless that party controls two-thirds of each house, it cannot control fiscal policy. Voters blame the majority party for gridlock when in fact control rests with the minority party, a political dynamic known as **minority rule**. This provision is even more restrictive than the filibuster, which can only work with 41 percent of the U.S. Senate actively backing it; California fiscal policy is held hostage to a one-third minority sitting on its collective hands, ensuring gridlock. As Peter Schrag describes it:

> More than any other structural flaw, it [the two-thirds rule] diffused accountability and brought on much of the budgetary gridlock that California became notorious for in the 1980s and early 1990s.[9]

This structural flaw has been in place for several decades, and in recent years the minority party has relied on it to refuse to compromise on the most critical issue before the state: the need for adequate and stable sources of revenue. The power of the minority to block taxation measures and the unwillingness of Republicans to vote for any tax increase can lead to harmful gridlock. If this has been less noticeable in recent years, it is partly because of the passage of Proposition 30 in 2012, which temporarily increased taxes and revenues, and partly because of an improving economy. Together, these have reduced the need for new or increased taxes. While the provisions of Proposition 30 expire in 2018, Proposition 55 on the November 2016 ballot extended these tax provisions for 12 years. But at some point, the economy will turn sour and, if anything, the Republicans have hardened their opposition to any tax increase (see discussion below on the 2018 tax repeal initiative). Gridlock will return.

Even Governor Jerry Brown, a political moderate, a skilled negotiator, and one of the most experienced individuals to serve as governor of California, was at first unable to find negotiating partners in the legislature's minority leadership. If he were governing amid the political culture of the 1970s, when he first served, he would have been very successful. According to a long-time associate of the governor, Jodie Evans, "He is aghast. He reports on some of his conversations like he couldn't believe the narrowness or lack of comprehending by public officials. . . . He said, 'Some of my old tools are not going to work.'"[10] Brown himself said that the Republicans have a "perverse fidelity to each point in the Republican gospel."[11] These points are reinforced in the party caucuses.

The Republicans, of course, saw it differently. Senator Bob Dutton stated, "He's all talk and no go. He throws a few scraps out there . . . let's demonize the Republicans, and that's supposed to fix a problem?"[12] *Los Angeles Times* columnist George Skelton wrote, "The entire legislative system has been corrupted by Democrats' fear of angering labor unions and Republicans' subservience to a few antitax opportunists and entertainers."[13] But while the governor has shown a willingness to oppose the unions (an important Democratic constituency) on pensions and organizing child care workers, the Republicans seem unwilling to agree to increasing revenues, going so far as to place a repeal initiative on the ballot in 2018 when taxes were raised for transportation infrastructure improvements—a widely recognized need.

Change began in 2010 when enacting budgets with a simple majority vote became permitted. Budgetary gridlock tapered off further after the Democrats' overwhelming electoral victory in 2012 and the passage that same year of Proposition 30, which raised taxes and lessened the need for further immediate tax increases. These changes together greatly lessened the need for Republican cooperation on legislative action. Although the Democrats temporarily lost their two-thirds margin in the Senate in 2014, their overwhelming majorities still allowed them to largely ignore the minority. However, when Governor Brown decided to put a "rainy day fund" constitutional measure on the ballot for November of 2014 (ACA 4), he needed and—in a rare demonstration of bipartisanship—gained Republican support. Brown also secured bipartisan support for a $7.5 billion water bond for the same election. Both measures passed by healthy margins.

Initiatives

A further complication to effective policy making in California is the initiative, which is often used to bypass the legislative process. If an interest group has the money and believes that it can get an initiative proposition with a populist appeal on the ballot, then it has little incentive to submit legislation for careful consideration by committees in each house of the legislature or to engage in legislative bargaining. Taking a page from the interest groups' playbook, Governor Brown in 2016 threatened to place an initiative on the ballot if adequate progress was not made on climate change legislation. In spite of his ultimate success in passing that legislation, the possibility of an initiative to achieve far-reaching climate control regulations remains.

Moreover, initiatives have passed that have weakened the legislature or weakened the legislature's ability to make responsible policy. Proposition 140, which instituted term limits, greatly weakened the ability of the legislature to function effectively by ensuring that there were rarely any experienced legislators in Sacramento. Propositions 13 (1978) and 98 (1988) each limited legislators' ability to make responsible fiscal policy, the first by limiting the use of a stable tax tool (property taxes), the second by locking up a huge chunk of the available funds for a single purpose—education.

In 2014 modest changes were made to the initiative process through the passage of SB (Senate Bill) 1253, which provided a public review period for initiatives (see Chapter 4). Of most significance to the legislative process is the bill's provision that after 25 percent of the needed signatures for an initiative proposition are obtained, the Senate and Assembly must hold a joint hearing on the issue. These hearings could possibly result in compromise legislation that would make the initiative unnecessary. The process envisioned by SB 1253 worked in 2016 to help get a minimum pay bill enacted after labor unions had started the initiative process. However, it was not until June of 2018 that the real potential of this legislation was demonstrated. On June 28, facing a deadline for removing initiatives from the fall ballot, four issues were in play, all of which had qualified for the ballot and most of which had substantial corporate money behind them: rent control, lead paint cleanup, internet privacy, and soda taxes.

No deal was reached on rent control, and the issue went on the ballot, where it failed. The paint issue, in which paint companies wanted a subsidy to clean up lead paint, also fell short of a deal, but the measure was pulled (legislators threatened drastic action if it passed), and legislators promised to keep trying to seek a solution. A compromise was worked out between the supporters and opponents of internet privacy, which resulted in a bill that was less objectionable to the opponents than was the initiative.

The most controversial of the four issues was the one on taxing soft drinks. The industry wanted legislation to prevent local governments from raising taxes on soft drinks, something the legislature did not favor. To move the legislature to action, the industry qualified an initiative, a constitutional amendment, that would prevent local governments from raising any taxes without a public, extra-majoritarian vote, an almost impossible achievement. Faced with that draconian possibility, the legislature passed and the governor signed a bill banning local governments from raising soda taxes until 2030.

While some saw this flurry of activity resulting in legislative compromise and the removal of three issues from the 2018 fall ballot as evidence of a successful reform, others saw chaos, frenzy, and extortion.[14] Few, however, could disagree with Speaker Rendon's understatement that "it can spur the Legislature to act on issues that challenge us."[15] We will probably see many more propositions in the future: in 2016 there were 17 (resulting in a voter information guide of over 200 pages), and in 2018 there were 11. Already in a reaction to the soda tax deal, major health care groups announced they would pursue a soda tax initiative in 2020, which would put in the constitution the right of local governments to impose soda taxes.[16] Live by the sword, die by the sword. It is often easier to sway a majority of the voters than a majority of the legislature, and there are increasingly large amounts of money available to do just that.

Californians have done a lot of damage to effective legislative governance through the initiative process. Voters feel dissatisfied with the legislature and consequently, though not intentionally, pass propositions that result in the legislature working less effectively. That makes voters more dissatisfied, and they vote for more propositions. Since 2008 there has been a modest reversal in this trend, and at the moment the state government is functioning more effectively.

The 2017-18 Session of the Legislature

In 2017–18 the legislature faced a unique set of issues: it became a key player in resisting federal policies that were at odds with California culture and policy; it passed a gas tax increase that subsequently resulted in an unsuccessful referendum on the law itself on the November ballot and a successful recall election against one member who voted for it; and it faced a massive protest by many women working in the legislature and other Sacramento organizations against a culture of rampant sexual harassment.

CONFRONTATION WITH THE FEDERAL GOVERNMENT With the election of 2016 the Republican Party took complete control of the federal government. This was not the traditional, elite, business-oriented Republican Party, but one led by Donald Trump drawing on the most populist elements of the party. As defined by Trump, the party emphasizes opposition to immigration—legal and illegal—and the rolling back of much of the progressive policies of the past 85 years. This runs counter to the culture and policies of California, which remain in that progressive tradition. Among the areas of conflict, in addition to immigration, are climate change and reducing greenhouse gasses, protecting national parks and monuments, supporting the Affordable Care Act, opposing vote suppression, and more.

Along with the governor and the attorney general (and many private groups including the ACLU, Planned Parenthood, Common Cause, and the Environmental Defense Fund) the legislature is a key player in these battles that have led the state to be viewed as a center of anti-Trumpism (Trump received less than a third of the vote in California in the 2016 election). Perhaps the one battle that has gained the most attention has been that over California's status as a so-called sanctuary state. In 2017 alone the legislature passed (and the governor signed) bills that would prohibit the police from detaining crime victims or witnesses on immigration violations (AB [Assembly Bill] 493); require colleges and universities that offer Cal Grants to create policies that safeguard their campuses from immigration officials (AB 21); prohibit landlords from reporting tenants' immigration status (AB 291); and limit assistance with federal immigration enforcement and prohibit detaining immigrants for federal immigration enforcement (unless they have committed violent crimes, are repeat offenders, or committed one of 800 other crimes) (SB 54, The California Values Act).

These laws do not make the state a sanctuary state in the traditional meaning of the word but rather spell out noncooperation with the federal government within the constitutional structure of federalism. These battles, which began in 2017–18, are sure to intensify, especially with the restructuring of the already conservative U.S. Supreme Court.

GAS TAX, RECALL, AND AN INITIATIVE In the 2016 election, Democratic state Senate candidate Josh Newman won a close election (by fewer than 2,500 votes) in a traditionally Republican district, helping to give Democrats a two-thirds majority in both houses. Taking advantage of those large numbers—and using a lot of good old-fashioned political horse trading—the Democrats, with one defection and one Republican vote from a termed-out member, passed a narrowly focused tax increase (mostly on fuel and automobile registration) to improve the badly deteriorated and outdated transportation infrastructure in the state—a widely recognized need.

Subsequently, a Republican-funded campaign spearheaded by a talk radio host and a former San Diego councilman was launched against Newman, saying (erroneously) that he cast the critical vote for the tax increase. In fact, that honor would more accurately go to the termed-out Republican Anthony Cannella, who in return for his vote got important transportation projects for his district.

Cynically, the proponents called this the "gazelle strategy," an attack on the weakest member of the group. Newman's "crime" had been to vote as a Democrat along with 81 other Democrats, thereby gaining a narrow victory for the tax. The point of the recall was to eliminate the two-thirds Democratic majority and to send a message to all legislators, Republicans and Democrats alike, that voting for tax increases is risky even in a liberal state. With fewer than half the number of voters that voted in the general election turning out, Newman was recalled by a margin of about 58–42 percent. Though the two-thirds majority was regained in 2018, the recall's message—we can take you out in a low-turnout recall—is unlikely to be forgotten.

In addition, the Republican Party successfully placed an initiative issue on the 2018 November ballot repealing the infrastructure tax and prohibiting the legislature from enacting any future gas tax without a vote of the electorate. Again cynically, proponents of this effort—funded in large part by the national Republican establishment—stated that this was largely a means to draw Republican voters to the polls in November with the hopes of preserving the seats of several endangered Republican U.S. Representatives.[17] The initiative failed by 13 points.

SEXUAL HARASSMENT The state legislature has many different employers (each legislator hires his/her own staff) who hire a mix of experienced and inexperienced workers (most without civil service protection). Many of the latter are young interns or staff members in their first jobs. There are also lobbyists with lots of money and booze who throw receptions nightly. And many of the legislators and lobbyists are far from home and families. These conditions can contribute to a culture of sexual harassment.

While the #MeToo movement did not start in Sacramento, it got a huge boost when in October of 2017 a group called WeSaidEnough, consisting of over 140 women with jobs in the state capitol or related to government (including legislators, senior staff, and lobbyists), sent a letter to the *Los Angeles Times* detailing the sexual harassment they had experienced or witnessed. Theirs was the ". . . first open statement by women working in politics calling for an end to the pervasive culture of harassment and assault within a Capitol community."[18]

The impact was immediate and reached to political centers far beyond Sacramento. Hundreds of media articles were written, many interviews were given, and dozens of bills were introduced into the legislature. Ultimately Governor Brown signed at least four into law, including those that would expand anti-harassment provisions in state law and limit non-disclosure agreements. Under some pressure two Assembly members (Raul Bocanegra and Matt Dababneh) and one senator (Tony Mendoza) resigned, ultimately to be replaced by women. Another legislator, Sebastian Ridley-Thomas, facing harassment charges, resigned for "health" reasons and was also replaced by a woman. Assemblywoman Cristina Garcia was stripped of her committee assignments after accusations of groping. And another legislator, John Moorlach was reprimanded for putting women in headlocks and giving them "noogies." A subcommittee chaired by Assemblywoman Laura Friedman on Sexual Harassment Prevention and Response was established under the Joint Committee on Rules, and in June of 2018 it recommended, among other actions, that a special investigative unit be set up in the Legislative Counsel's office and that a panel of five outside experts be established to examine the findings of that unit.[19]

This is only a start, and what we have heard to date is probably only the tip of the iceberg. Policies, however far-reaching and while essential, are not enough. Assemblywoman Friedman has said, "This is about culture change. It's not about voting on a set of policies and saying that you're done."[20] The change required is huge, and it will not happen overnight.

California Legislature: Where Are We Now?

The legislature serves two principal functions: policy making and representation. The different requirements of these two functions create tensions. Legislators are also pressured by the needs versus the wants of their districts; state versus local interests; and the demands of interest groups, campaign contributors, party leaders, and the governor. California is a large state with many competing wants and needs. Legislative districts are among the largest anywhere. These factors turn policy making into a complex and often unseemly process, a process moved by humans who will always be imperfect. Even before term limits were imposed, the once highly regarded legislature passed some bad legislation and left problems unaddressed.

Yet the legislature could work better than it does, and it is valid to ask if the legislature is the creator or the victim of this impaired system. In large part, problems of inefficacy have been generated by outside forces. Term limits, big money for campaigns and elections, and the two-thirds vote requirement for passing tax legislation are the most notable outside factors. The declining level of civility in the legislature is a reflection of the impact of term limits and of the increasing political polarization in the nation. But individuals are responsible for their own behavior. Regardless of outside forces, individual legislators of goodwill could make a difference.

Since 2008 a series of changes have taken place (mostly via the initiative process, ironically) that appear to have strengthened the legislative process and reduced gridlock, at least for the time being.

- **Proposition 11 (November 2008), Proposition 20 (November 2010), and Proposition 27 (November 2010, defeated)** Proposition 11 took redistricting of the legislature away from the legislature and put it in the hands of a Citizens' Redistricting Commission. It passed by only 50.9 percent of the vote. It was strengthened by the passage (by 61 percent) of Proposition 20, which extended the jurisdiction of the commission to congressional districts, and by the corresponding defeat (by 59.5 percent) of Proposition 27, which would have eliminated the commission. As a result of the commission's redistricting, which took effect in 2012, districts became more evenly balanced, and Democrats gained a two-thirds margin in both legislative houses.

- **Proposition 14 (June 2010)** Proposition 14 created the top-two primary system, with the expectation that more moderate legislators would be elected. It is too early to tell if that result was accomplished, and whatever impact this has is overshadowed by the impact of Propositions 11, 20, and 27. But in the first election following this change, in 19 districts two members of the same party ended up winning the primary election and running against each other in the general election. In 2018, thirteen of the same party—all Democrats—ran against each other for state legislative seats. This kind of primary system offers an opportunity for minority party members to help select the more moderate of the opposing candidates. It also provides an opportunity for big businesses to put a lot of money behind the candidate who is most friendly to their goals, which has resulted in the rise of "business-friendly" Democrats in the legislature.

- **Proposition 25 (November 2010)** The requirement for a two-thirds majority to pass the annual budget was eliminated by this measure, which has ended the ability of the minority—whose involvement in this fiscal measure was required every year—to block this required legislation. Thus, the influence of the minority in the legislative process has been substantially reduced.

- **Proposition 28 (June 2012)** This proposition reduced the term limits in the legislature from 14 to 12 years, but it allowed members to serve all that time in a single house. This allows legislators the opportunity to gain more experience, especially in the Assembly, and presumably to achieve greater knowledge and effectiveness. However, it is too early to make a judgment of whether that is actually happening.

- **Proposition 30 (November 2012)** Proposition 30 temporarily increased taxes, giving the state greater fiscal stability and reducing the need for the minority party's help in passing tax legislation. Proposition 55 in 2016 extended the tax provisions for 12 years.

The two-thirds Democratic majority did not reappear until 2017. During this off-year election—as is usually the case—Republicans were more likely to vote than Democrats, resulting in some marginal districts switching to Republicans.

It is too early to make a long-term assessment of the impacts of these propositions on the legislature. The current trend is promising, and on the positive side, both houses currently have experienced leaders. But the power of big money and the threat of dominating interests are always there to skew the process.

While the skilled moderate leadership of Governor Brown has been an important factor in creating the current favorable situation, there is about to be a sea change in California politics. For eight years the Democrats have ruled the state under an experienced, highly respected—if not much loved—governor. Those who may have had doubts about the overwhelming Democratic membership of the legislature could still look to the governor as "the adult in the room" who would keep the legislature in line and not let it spend too much money or veer too far to the left.[21] Or at least that was the image. The new governor, Gavin Newsom, does not have that gravitas or stature, and the public may begin to view the legislature and the Sacramento governing structure with a more skeptical eye. The legislature's approval rating tends to follow that of the governor, and if his is low, that of the legislature will likewise decline.

In addition, American politics tends to have a self-correcting nature. The Democrats have been in control with huge majorities, and yet many problems remain unsolved, most notably the creation of a stable financial base. Other unsolved problems include: the homeless, a lack of affordable housing, crime, traffic, water, air, and many more. Moreover, many feel that the Democrats, using their exceptional majorities, have overreached themselves with policies such as the gas tax increase and laws protecting illegal immigrants.

The attitude of the public towards the government is affected by how people feel about life in general. The current favorable economic climate will predictably cycle downwards. Major disasters are inevitable. The Democrats have had a reasonably favorable climate in which to work (created in no small part by having changed a budget deficit of $27 billion when Governor Brown came into office to a surplus of about $6 billion when he left). At some point it will end, and the Democrats will face a more hostile public that will be demanding change.

Given the challenging national mood, the diverse nature of the state, and an electorate that is itself divided, positive change cannot be ensured. Moreover, the public has little understanding of legislative functions or processes, making further positive change through the initiative process unlikely. In the past, ill-advised measures such as a part-time legislature have often been suggested. As the cartoonist Walt Kelly's character Pogo said, "We have met the enemy and he is us."

But not always. We should be thankful for the current hiatus in gridlock that has permitted the legislature to address many of the issues that face our state.

Study Guide

FOR FURTHER READING

Cain, Bruce E., and Roger G. Noll, eds. *Constitutional Reform in California: Making State Government More Effective and Responsive*. Berkeley: Institute of Governmental Studies Press, 1995.

California Journal and State Net. *Roster and Government Guide*. Sacramento: California Journal, 2004.

de Sá, Karen. "How Our Laws in California Are Really Made." *San Jose Mercury News*, July 10, 2010. www.mercurynews .com/politics-government/ci_15452125. Accessed 8/15/16.

Institute of Governmental Affairs. "IGS Goes to Sacramento to Assess Ten Years of Term Limits." *Public Affairs Reports* 42, no. 3 (Fall 2001).

Mathews, Joe, and Mark Paul. *California Crackup: How Reform Broke the Golden State and How We Can Fix It*. Berkeley: University of California Press, 2010.

Muir, William K., Jr. *Legislature: California's School for Politics*. Chicago: University of Chicago Press, 1982.

Schrag, Peter. *California: America's High-Stakes Experiment*. Berkeley: University of California Press, 2006.

———. *Paradise Lost: California's Experience, America's Future*. New York: New Press, 1998.

Wilson, E. Dotson. *California's Legislature*. Sacramento: Office of the Chief Clerk, California State Assembly, 2016.

ON THE WEB

California Choices. http://californiachoices.org. Accessed 8/16/16.

California Legislative Analyst's Office. www.lao.ca.gov/. Accessed 8/16/16. The LAO is a nonpartisan fiscal and policy adviser to the legislature.

California State Assembly. http://assembly.ca.gov/. Accessed 8/16/16.

California State Assembly Democratic Caucus. www.asmdc .org. Accessed 8/16/16.

California State Assembly Republican Caucus. http://asmrc .org. Accessed 8/16/16.

California State Senate. http://senate.ca.gov/. Accessed 8/16/16.

CALmatters. https://calmatters.org/. Accessed 8/16/16.

Legislative Counsel. www.leginfo.legislature.ca.gov/. Accessed 8/16/16. The Legislative Counsel of California's official site, maintained by law.

Los Angeles Times. "Essential Politics." www.latimes.com/poli tics/essential/la-pol-sac-essential-politics-updates-147146 0386-htmlstory.html. Accessed 8/16/16. A daily news feed on California government and politics.

Rough & Tumble. www.rtumble.com. Accessed 8/16/16. Daily summary of California news.

Sacramento Bee. www.sacbee.com/news/politics-government/. Accessed 8/16/16.

Senate Democrats. http://democrats.senate.ca.gov/. Accessed 8/16/16.

Senate Republicans. http://cssrc.us/. Accessed 8/16/16.

University of California, Berkeley, Institute of Governmental Studies Library. http://igs.berkeley.edu/library. Accessed 8/16/16.

SUMMARY

I. Legislatures are not well understood, but they are critical to a democratic form of government. Indeed, a working legislature is practically the definition of a democratic government.

II. The California legislature is, for the most part, modeled on the U.S. Congress.
    A. It is bicameral.
    B. Members are elected from single-member, geographically based districts.
    C. Unlike the U.S. Congress, both houses of the California legislature are apportioned by population.

III. Legislators must both represent their constituents and make policy.
    A. These two items are not always compatible.
    B. In representing their districts, members must decide whether to follow the wants or the needs of their constituents and whether to follow directions from the district or use their own best judgment.
    C. Poor communication from constituents makes these actions difficult.
    D. Legislators have offices both in Sacramento and in their districts.

IV. Members of both the California Senate and Assembly are elected through a blanket or top-two primary followed by a general election. Two key features of California politics influence who gets elected:
  A. Candidates must engage in extensive fund-raising to increase their chances of getting elected.
  B. Redistricting, which follows each census, has a significant impact on who is elected. For example, redistricting by a Citizens Redistricting Commission in 2012 resulted in a Democratic supermajority in the legislature.

V. The leader of the Assembly is the speaker; the leader of the Senate is the president pro tempore.
  A. Each leader is elected by all of the members in that body, but the majority party caucus usually determines the outcome.
  B. The speaker controls most of the resources and is very powerful.
  C. The speaker and the president pro tempore are term-limited.
  D. The president pro tempore shares powers with the Senate Rules Committee.

VI. The bulk of legislative work is done in committees.
  A. Bills are read and amended here.
  B. Issue networks are made up of a group of individuals—lobbyists, staffers, members, and bureaucrats—who make and control policy in a given substantive area.

VII. Professional staff members make the legislature possible.
  A. Some of them work in districts, some in members' offices, some for committees, and some for the leadership.
  B. The best-paid staff members are usually subject-matter experts working for committees.

VIII. The legislative process has several steps.
  A. Bills are first introduced by members and sent to committees.
  B. Bills must pass the floors of both houses (with identical wording) before they are sent to the governor for his or her signature.
  C. If the governor vetoes a bill, it takes a two-thirds vote in each house to override it.

D. Tax bills also require a two-thirds vote, giving the minority party important power in the legislature and making it difficult for the majority party to govern.

IX. The state legislature is different from the U.S. Congress in several ways.
  A. Members are term-limited.
  B. The governor has line-item veto power (he can cut or eliminate any item in a budget bill, while still approving the entire bill).
  C. Both houses are apportioned by population.
  D. Very little media attention is given to the California legislature.
  E. The legislature does not have a role in judicial appointments.
  F. The legislature does not have a filibuster, unlike the U.S. Senate. However, the two-thirds requirement for increasing taxes has a similar effect in thwarting the majority.
  G. California also has the initiative process, which allows the legislative process to be bypassed, most often by special-interest groups with deep pockets.

X. The effectiveness of the California legislature is limited
  A. by the power of big money;
  B. by term limits and members' lack of experience;
  C. by intense partisanship;
  D. by the two-thirds-vote rule on taxes, which limits the majority party's decision-making ability and makes accountability difficult; and
  E. by the initiative, which is often used to bypass the legislative process.

XI. Propositions passed since 2008 have reduced gridlock and made the legislature more effective by increasing the size of the majority party and by eliminating the two-thirds vote required for the budget.
  A. Propositions 11 and 20 took districting away from the legislature.
  B. Proposition 14 created the top-two primary system.
  C. Proposition 25 removed the two-thirds-vote requirement for passing budgets.
  D. Proposition 28 increased the amount of time that legislators can serve in one house.
  E. Proposition 30 temporarily increased taxes, and therefore state revenues.

PRACTICE QUIZ

1. A line-item veto allows
   a) the governor to reject any single item in an appropriations or budget bill.
   b) the speaker or the president pro tempore to pull any single item from the agenda.
   c) a single member to block a single piece of legislation by signing a written objection.
   d) a petition by a group of 10 legislators to block any single piece of legislation.

2. Proposition 140
   a) limits the time that legislators can serve in Sacramento.
   b) limits the power of the legislature to raise property taxes.
   c) sets aside 40 percent of the budget for education purposes.
   d) requires the speaker to assign staff to the minority party.

3. The legislature is composed of
   a) 80 members in the Senate and 40 in the Assembly.
   b) 120 members in a single body.
   c) 60 members in each body.
   d) 80 members in the Assembly and 40 in the Senate.

4. A two-thirds vote is needed to pass
   a) appropriation bills.
   b) budget bills.
   c) tax bills.
   d) all of the above

5. Partisanship in the legislature
   a) has declined because of apportionment.
   b) has declined because of the blanket primary now in effect.
   c) has led to greater ease in getting budgets improved.
   d) has increased in recent years.

6. The powers of the speaker of the California Assembly include all of the following *except*
   a) the power to assign parking spaces.
   b) the power to assign office space.
   c) the power to assign members to committees but not to remove them during the current term.
   d) the power to assign a member to a committee against both the member's wishes and the wishes and needs of his or her constituency.

7. Proposition 140 resulted in all of the following *except*
   a) an increase in office budgets.
   b) the establishment of term limits.
   c) a reduction of committee staff and personal staff.
   d) layoffs of some of the most knowledgeable staff experts from committees.

8. The legislative process is biased in favor of
   a) issues favored by the public.
   b) the status quo.
   c) change that interest groups favor.
   d) legislation proposed by the governor, who can introduce a limited number of bills directly to both houses, bypassing some of the steps of the legislative process.

9. California has some of the largest legislative districts in the nation. This means that
   a) elections in California tend to be expensive.
   b) citizen access to legislators is unusually good because legislators need to face the voters so often.
   c) legislators appear in the media more often because they represent so many people.
   d) California has an unusually large number of legislators.

10. Term limits have resulted in which of the following:
    a) an increase in expertise among legislators, who have only a few years to make a name for themselves.
    b) an increase in citizen legislators, people with little or no political experience who are able to run because seats are open.
    c) an increase in staff members, who are needed to help legislators lacking experience.
    d) a decline in the knowledge needed to pass good-quality legislation.

CRITICAL-THINKING QUESTIONS

1. Should a legislator vote for what his or her constituents want or what his or her constituents need?
2. Who should apportion the legislature?
3. What criteria should be used to apportion a legislature?
4. Should a legislator take orders from constituents or use his or her own best judgment, even if it is unpopular?
5. How much access should lobbyists have to legislators?
6. When should a legislature have rules that allow a minority to block legislation?

KEY TERMS

apportionment (p. 144)
Assembly Rules Committee (p. 138)
bicameral (p. 129)
committees (p. 138)
constituents (p. 130)
gerrymandering (p. 134)
gridlock (p. 143)
"gut and amend" (p. 141)

issue networks (p. 138)
lack of accountability (p. 150)
line-item veto (p. 143)
logrolling (p. 141)
minority rule (p. 150)
oversight (p. 131)
partisanship (p. 148)
president pro tempore (p. 138)

Proposition 140 (p. 129)
representation (p. 129)
speaker (p. 136)
staff (p. 138)
term limits (p. 129)
two-thirds vote (p. 148)
winner-take-all (p. 133)

6 The Governor and the Executive Branch

WHAT CALIFORNIA GOVERNMENT DOES AND WHY IT MATTERS

Consider the following activities that recently took place in the executive branch of our state government:

- Governor Brown's administration initiated an investigation of Caltrans after receiving reports of shoddy work on a segment of the Bay Bridge and learning that Caltrans had transferred or ended the contracts of the "whistle-blowing" project managers.

- In June 2018 Governor Brown signed a budget creating a $13.8 billion cash reserve, the largest in state history, a result of the increase in taxes approved by the voters in 2012 and extended in 2016.

- After President Trump withdrew from the Paris climate accord in 2017, Governor Brown traveled to China to discuss global warming with President Xi Jinping. In 2018 Governor Brown signed an executive order to boost the state's supply of zero-emission vehicles and charging and refueling stations.

- Caltrans decided to replace high-occupancy vehicle lanes with toll lanes on an Orange County freeway over the objections of local governments and agencies.

- Attorney General Xavier Becerra sued the Trump administration after it was announced in March 2018 that the 2020 Census would include a question on citizenship status. Becerra argued that this would make noncitizens reluctant to participate, generating an undercount that would allow the federal government to direct resources away from California, which has the largest immigrant population of any state.

- In August 2018 Attorney General Becerra led an 18-state coalition seeking legal protections against potential deportation for hundreds of thousands of people in the United States who hold Temporary Protected Status (TPS), including individuals from El Salvador, Haiti, Nicaragua, and Sudan.

If you think you know little about the executive branch of California, you are not alone. The media rarely pay much attention to state government, and in 2013 the last out-of-town TV bureau in Sacramento closed. California government operates largely out of the public view. The governor's reputation is based mainly on his interactions with the legislature, which are often public and may be contentious—and therefore newsworthy. Barring major scandal, the governor's actions as the executive head of a huge bureaucracy are off the press's radar. Few reporters would be able to locate Caltrans or the Natural Resources Agency either physically or on an organization chart. Most of California's 500,000-plus state employees are known to the public only as friends and neighbors.[1] Other members of California's plural executive tend only to make headlines when their actions relate to President Trump— as when Attorney General Xavier Becerra filed various lawsuits in 2017 and 2018 to block the president's policies on immigration, the U.S. Census, and other issues.

When Governor Brown came into office in 2011, it was not uncommon to hear that the state was ungovernable. Now, government is said to be working well, and many credit Brown's widely acknowledged political skills with helping to increase the state's productivity. However, the government's recent successes are a result not only of Brown's abilities but also of the overwhelming Democratic majorities in the California legislature and unified Democratic control of other executive branch positions.

Recent changes in the state constitution that have made it possible to pass budgets on a majority vote have made a difference as well. When Brown had to deal with a larger Republican minority in the legislature, he was less successful. Governor Gavin Newsom, who took over as governor in 2019, similarly presides over a unified Democratically controlled legislature and a uniformly Democratic executive branch. While political conflicts always exist, the party is relatively unified and currently focused more on opposing the Trump administration than on intra-party disagreements. While Trump's approval rating in the state is below 30 percent, both the governor and legislature have recently enjoyed approval from strong majorities of the California public.

The Invisible Governor?

While the governor is the most visible political figure in the state, his visibility pales in comparison to that of the president of the United States. There are a number of reasons for this lack of visibility. We depend on the media for most of what we know about our government, and for the most part the media in California are not interested in state politics or governance. The media, after all, are a business, responding to the desires of their consumers and advertisers. For many Californians, and thus for the media, Sacramento does not capture much attention; it is a long way from the major population centers of the state, and what happens there just does not captivate an audience the way a good car chase does. The media have found that their business model works best by focusing on well-known or riveting personalities. For California, this generally means a focus more on U.S. Senators Dianne Feinstein and Kamala Harris, and, except in election seasons, less so on state politicians such as Governor Gavin Newsom or Attorney General Xavier Becerra. Media-wise, what happens in Sacramento stays in Sacramento.

The governor's job is divided analytically into two roles: **head of government** and **head of state**, mirroring the dual roles held by the president of the United States. As the leader of the California state government, the governor's role is to govern—that is, to develop policy and get it passed through the legislature and implemented via the bureaucracy. The governor's approach to these various tasks is often divisive. For example, when Governor Jerry Brown signed a bill into law in October 2017 making California a sanctuary state, critics reiterated their concerns that the measure was a danger to public safety and would cause the Trump administration to withhold federal funds from the state. Governor Brown's lobbying on behalf of the California high-speed rail project, even in the face of massive price overruns and multi-year delays, contributed to growing opposition over time.

In contrast, the governor's role as head of state—attending groundbreaking ceremonies, lighting the capitol Christmas tree, attending memorial ceremonies—are less visible. Often the events are so insignificant that not many people care. Few dignitaries of note visit Sacramento, and the media simply do not warm to filming the governor talking to teachers or highway patrol officers. Because he was a showman able to generate his own buzz, Governor Arnold Schwarzenegger made as

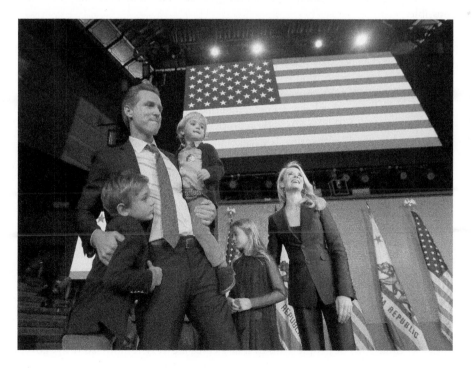

In 2018, Californians elected former lieutenant governor Gavin Newsom as governor of the state. Throughout his campaign, he emphasized California values that were being challenged in Washington, among them immigration rights, civil rights, and environmental protections.

much as he could of the head-of-state role; Governor Brown simply had no interest in it. Instead, that role was filled more by other members of the California executive branch, such as Attorney General Becerra and Alex Padilla, the California secretary of state. Governor Newsom has a stronger history of seeking the media limelight; his administration is likely to bring more overt attempts to highlight his role as head of state.

Also, as with the presidency, the governor's role is one of limited power. In fact, the state's plural executive and the federal government's sovereignty over state government mean that the governor of California is significantly weaker than the public might expect. The governor does not run the state of California any more than the president runs the United States. Our nation's founders feared a strong executive, having experienced such rule under a king and under capricious colonial governors. Consequently, they created a system in which the powers of all institutions were strictly limited, and in which the powers of the executive were secondary to those of the legislature. The California state government mirrors the federal government's system of separation of powers and limits on the **formal powers** of the executive branch.

As with the president, people have many incomplete, incorrect, and conflicting views about the governor. Political scientists Tom Cronin and Michael Genovese compiled a list of what they call the paradoxes of the presidency:

- We want the president to be an effective politician while being above politics.

- We want the president to be a common person and an extraordinary person at the same time.

- We want the president to be powerful but not too powerful.[2]

In sum, we want the president to be all things at all times, and, of course, this is not possible.

The governor is not burdened with as much symbolic baggage as the president, yet many misperceptions carry over to this office as well. These misperceptions are amplified by the fact that people think they understand the office. After all, it is an executive office, a position with which all of us who work in organizations have some familiarity. But the governorship is a *political* executive office, in an organization that often does not have a single, identifiable chain of command and which does not respond well, if at all, to direct orders.

Our greatest misperception is exaggerating the amount of power wielded by the governor. The governor does not control the legislature and has trouble making policy without the cooperation, or at least acquiescence, of legislators who may have little reason to support the governor. The governor can win legislative cooperation only through persuasion—perhaps hardball persuasion, but persuasion nonetheless. The governor is one of multiple independently elected members of the plural executive and does not control the attorney general, secretary of state, or other executive officers—individuals with their own constituencies, their own political ambitions, and their own policy goals. Although all of these executives are currently Democrats, sometimes the plural executive has included officials from opposition political parties, which further limits the governor's influence.

Within the bureaucracy of the executive branch, it is possible for the governor to exert influence more directly. But the executive branch is large, employing hundreds of thousands of people who in many cases are very remote from the governor. How does the governor get a Caltrans engineer in San Diego or a park ranger in Marin County to follow his wishes? Some organizations, such as the University of California, are governed by boards that can be influenced only by appointments, budgetary threats, or strongly voiced public opinion. The lack of formal powers and direct accountability mean that gubernatorial power is less reliant on formal powers than on political skills and an ability to bargain, a long political memory, and friends and allies in important positions. A good economy, an absence of natural disasters, and luck can also be important.

Arnold Schwarzenegger came into office in 2003 on a wave of popularity that initially gave him a substantial amount of informal power. By sheer dint of personality and the threat to go to the public with initiatives, he managed a series of impressive victories in the early days of his tenure. His success did not last, however. He overreached, and he antagonized the members of his own party with his moderate positions on many issues. His attempt to pass four initiatives in a special—and costly—election in November 2005 was a disaster. Near the end of his time in office, his approval ratings had reached a low of 23 percent in a Public Policy Institute of California (PPIC) poll.[3]

Schwarzenegger's successor, Jerry Brown, was the polar opposite of Arnold Schwarzenegger. Due in part to his previous stints as governor from 1975 to 1983 and his long career of public service, he came into office in 2011 as one of the most knowledgeable governors that California has ever had. He loved the details of policy making, knew the intricacies of governing, and did not crave or need the limelight. He knew how to bargain and make deals. In 2011 he was faced with a bad economy, huge revenue shortfalls, and an opposition party that would not bargain on revenue issues. But things turned around with the emergence of favorable political and economic situations. Republican opposition became less important after new redistricting and primary laws provided the Democrats with overwhelming majorities in both houses of the legislature. Along with the improved economy and the passage of tax-raising Proposition 30—thanks in large part to the governor's political acumen and skills—and the earlier elimination of the two-thirds vote requirement for approving budgets, governing suddenly became much easier. In a PPIC poll during May of 2018, 48 percent of California adults approved of the job he was doing.[4]

In November 2018, Californians elected Lieutenant Governor Gavin Newsom to succeed Jerry Brown. Unlike Brown, Newsom enjoys being in the media spotlight and is working to move California to the left and away from Brown's policies of fiscal conservatism. While he came into office with a strong victory and robust approval ratings, it remains to be seen if his style will be effective at generating significant policy changes and how those public approval ratings will change as his administration moves from promises to action.

Formal Powers of the Governor

The formal powers of the governor, while limited, are still significant. The governor has powers—the most important of which is the **line-item veto**—that are denied to the president. The true value of these powers, however, is as vantage points from which the governor bases his or her **informal powers**, or powers to persuade. (See Box 6.1 for a summary of the governor's formal and informal powers.) A governor who expects to use only formal powers to govern will not accomplish much. Those powers must be leveraged to persuade other political actors to support the governor's goals. For example, in 2017, to get Republican support for his cap-and-trade bill, Governor Brown agreed to a proposal from the state Assembly's Republican minority leader, Chad Mayes, to a vote in the legislature in 2024 on how to spend the cap-and-trade revenues. In 2018, Governor Brown was seeking Republican support in the legislature for a massive ($52.4 billion) infrastructure bill. In a last-minute meeting with state Senator Anthony Cannella (R-Merced), Brown agreed to add $500 million to the bill for a commuter rail and expressway connecting Merced to the Bay Area; in exchange, Cannella voted for the governor's bill.[5]

The state constitution vests supreme executive power in the governor, a phrase that conveys both more and less than it seems. Less, because the governor's office is an office of limited powers in which nothing is supreme. More, because executives often push established constitutional limits. However, given a supportive legislature that views most executive requests positively—as is true currently—most of the executive's goals can be reached.

Appointments

Making appointments is one of the governor's most significant powers. The governor appoints four distinct groups of individuals: **personal staff**, heads of major administrative divisions, some judges, and members of a number of **boards and commissions**. Some of these appointments require confirmation by other bodies, while others do not. Some appointees work at the governor's pleasure, while others serve for fixed terms. Some answer directly to the governor, while others are several steps removed or protected from executive intervention. Over the course of an administration, a governor can make more than 2,500 appointments, including about 500 positions that will be filled at the start of the term.

The governor's personal staff consists of about 100 individuals who craft policy recommendations, work with the legislature, or handle all the details to make the governor's life run smoothly, including providing structure, and packaging and presenting him or her to the public. Governors hire, fire, and move these individuals about at will. No confirmation is required.

Next closest to the governor are the members of the **cabinet**. The governor determines who will serve in the cabinet and what role, if any, the cabinet will play in policy development. The heads of the **superagencies** of state government (large organizations similar to federal departments, which contain a number of related bureaus and agencies) are in the cabinet, as are the director of finance and others whose presence the governor finds useful and appropriate. These positions require confirmation by the Senate, but the governor has the ability to remove them at will.

The governor also appoints the heads of the major bureaus or departments, which are mostly located within the superagencies. These individuals have the responsibility of overseeing the organizations and the more than 230,000 state employees (not including employees of California's public universities) that do the real work of government.

In addition, the governor appoints members to more than 325 boards and commissions, important and unimportant, visible and invisible. Once appointed, individuals do not have to answer to the governor, although the governor can apply political pressure, including threatening to cut the budget of the institution that the individuals administer.

Stating that "the state's bureaucracy is a labyrinth of disjointed boards, commissions, agencies and departments,"[6] Governor Brown in 2012 proposed a restructuring and consolidation of agencies, having eliminated 25 boards and commissions the previous year. There was no political payoff in this. Few outside of the government would notice. Not surprisingly, little came of this proposal.

Independent Executive Actions

The governor's powers are constitutionally restricted by the legislature, but in some cases he or she is able to act independently of it. Independent executive actions are permitted by the constitution or under laws passed by the legislature. They are most significant in times of an emergency.

Few laws passed by the legislature are self-implementing; most require positive action on the part of the administration. This process of implementation involves clarification of the law (e.g., what does the language used by the legislature imply?) and the assembling of finances and an administrative structure to allow action to take place. All of this requires prioritization and fund requests by the governor's appointees or the governor. This allows the governor considerable influence; using the line-item veto or failing to request adequate funds, for example, can effectively kill a program. Governor Brown has used these powers several times, in one instance eliminating both the California Postsecondary Education Commission and the duplicative office of the secretary of education, neither of which he found useful.

The governor also has the power to issue executive orders. This can be fairly noncontroversial orders, such as declaring a state of emergency due to a wildfire, but can also be used to make public policy, such as when Governor Brown in January 2018 ordered the creation of more zero-emission vehicle charging stations and worked to get more zero-emission vehicles on California's roads.[7]

Commander in Chief

The governor is the commander in chief of the California National Guard. This role is of little significance until times of civil disorder or natural disaster, when the governor has the power to call out the guard, though not to direct its actions. In April 2018, in response to an order from President Donald Trump that National Guard troops be sent to control the U.S.–Mexico border, Governor Jerry Brown ordered the mobilization of 400 members of the California National Guard to fight transnational criminal gangs, human traffickers, and illegal firearm and drug smugglers, but declined to order them to aid in enforcing federal immigration law.[8]

Organizing and Managing the Executive Branch

The governor is empowered to organize and manage the executive branch. *Organize* means that he or she can make a number of administrative appointments. *Manage* means that many of these appointees must report to the governor, at least indirectly, and the governor can remove them from office. Again, the limits of this power should be recognized.

First, the functions of the state government are not boundless. Much of the money that it collects is passed on to local government and school districts to spend.

Second, the rest of the elected executive branch, most notably the attorney general, limits the governor's actions, and some state employees report to these elected officials—over 4,500 report to the attorney general alone.

Third, some of the appointments made by the governor are to boards that can, and do, act independently of the governor. These appointments may be for fixed terms. The best known of these independent boards is the Regents of the University of California. This 26-member board consists of 7 ex officio members (members, including the governor, who sit on the board because they occupy another office), one student, and 18 members appointed by the governor for 12-year terms—terms that are longer than the governor's. Control over this board, if the governor wishes to exert it, is possible only through new appointments, the loyalty of previously appointed members, persuasion (including threats to cut the budget), and, in extreme cases, working with the legislature to restructure the body.

Fourth, the governor must make appointments to agencies about which he or she knows little, often appointing individuals about whom he knows little. Information coming out of these agencies is limited; hence, the governor is often in the dark about what is happening until something goes terribly wrong and it appears in the press.

The controversy over Caltrans' management of the rebuilding of the eastern span of the Bay Bridge mentioned earlier provides a case in point. In 2006, Caltrans, perhaps the most visible of California's government agencies, hired a Chinese company with limited bridge-building experience to build key elements of the new span. According to the *Sacramento Bee*, numerous flaws and cost overruns followed, leading to questions of whether the bridge will meet its planned 150-year lifespan. The governor's public stance was that "stuff happens" (or words to that effect), but his administration initiated investigations, legislative and external, into the entire operation and culture of Caltrans. Were it not for aggressive reporting on the issue by California newspapers in the north of the state, the governor might never have acted to address long-standing issues within Caltrans.[9]

Intense public scrutiny over actions (or inactions) by the California Public Utilities Commission (CPUC) also led to a flurry of activity by the governor and the legislature (the governor appoints all five members of the CPUC). The handling of the Aliso Canyon (Porter Ranch) gas leak, the San Bruno gas pipeline explosion, and the closure of the San Onofre nuclear power plant with public utility customers picking up most of the cost were all major scandals. In the latter case, the chair of the CPUC—a former Edison president—had an ex parte (secret) meeting with top Edison executives in Warsaw during which a settlement favorable to the utility was discussed. Subsequently, Edison donated $25 million to a program at UCLA favored by the chair. This meeting remained secret until the state Justice Department raided the chair's home on another matter.

In September 2016, Governor Brown signed a set of five reform bills aimed at increasing transparency and accountability at the CPUC. Commissioners must now disclose and report ex parte communications with utility executives and other interested parties in rate-setting cases. The new laws also required more information to be made publicly available, established the position of safety advocate, and authorized the attorney general's office to bring enforcement actions in Superior Court against commission employees who violate ex parte rules.[10]

Also, ex parte meetings between developers and members of the California Coastal Commission (the governor shares appointments to the 12-member board with the legislature) and the firing of its well-regarded executive director by more development friendly commissioners drew intense public scrutiny that led to proposed—but as of yet unsuccessful—legislation that would limit such meetings.[11] The issue remains alive in the courts and media. Not only will the governor and the legislature ultimately have to deal with the ex parte issue, it will also be a factor in future appointments to the commission.

Budget

Perhaps the governor's most significant power is that of preparing the budget, coupled with the power to exercise a line-item veto of budget provisions. At the federal level, the president presents Congress with a budget proposal—but it is only a proposal; the House of Representatives has constitutional authority over fiscal matters. The California Constitution gives the power of preparing the budget to the governor. This means that all budget requests from executive branch agencies must pass through the governor. It is at this point that the governor has life-or-death power over a program and can have a critical impact on the policy that a program implements. The actual work on this process of preparing the budget is done by the Department of Finance.

The budget is prepared and sent to the legislature by January 10, with revisions following later in the spring (called the May Revise) as the financial picture becomes clearer. The governor then lobbies for his or her budget, negotiating with members of the legislature as they make final changes. Until the 2011–12 budget, a supermajority of two-thirds was required to approve a budget, and impasses and late budgets were common while marginal votes were rounded up. Now only a simple majority in both houses of the legislature is needed, and budgets come in on time.

Although a supermajority vote is no longer needed to pass a budget, it is still required to raise new revenues. Because budgets may not have adequate revenues, in the absence of a supermajority the support of the minority party can be important, requiring expensive trade-offs with recalcitrant legislators who withhold their support until they receive an offer they cannot refuse. There are, in effect, five major players in the budget game: the governor and the leaders of both parties in both houses of the legislature. Because of his or her role at both ends of the budgetary process, and because one person needs to broker the deal, the governor usually has the key role. But even the governor can be held hostage by stubborn legislators. Although in recent years Republican legislators have been adamant in opposing any and all tax increases, the passage of the tax-raising Proposition 30 along with the improving economy has marginalized their influence. While neither the Republican Schwarzenegger nor the Democrat Brown were able to persuade the two parties to work together to shape revenue legislation, the Democratic majorities in the legislature make bipartisan cooperation largely unnecessary at present. Proposition 30 expired in 2018, but an extension on the 2016 ballot (Proposition 55) successfully extended the tax provisions for 12 years.

Veto and Line-Item Veto

The second most significant power of the governor is the **veto**. Just as in Congress, all bills passed by the legislature can be vetoed by the governor. The legislature passes about 1,000 bills each year, and since 1967 the governor has vetoed 13 percent of them on average. Veto rates vary considerably, however; Governor Schwarzenegger holds the record for the highest veto rate—over 35 percent in 2008—while Governor Brown holds the record for the lowest veto rate—less than 2 percent in 1982, a record he attributed to his behind-the-scenes work to change or kill proposals he doesn't like.[12] The veto can be overridden by a two-thirds majority of each house of the legislature, but that has happened only seven times since 1946 (and four of those were against Jerry Brown in the 1970s). The most recent veto override attempt was on a 2012 bill that would have permitted local governments to take over the management of some state parks to keep them open during the fiscal crisis.

Equally important, and unlike the president, the governor has a line-item veto, which permits him or her to reduce or delete any appropriation in a spending bill. Consequently, legislators cannot force the governor to accept funding for a program that he or she does not like by burying it inside a large spending bill that the governor must sign. The governor cannot add items, but the ability to reduce or eliminate the favorite programs of legislators is a powerful tool. It is a key item in the governor's box of bargaining tools, and one that no other player has (although it is impossible to tell how often governors use it).

In recent years line-item vetoes have been minor, often correcting technical errors. However, they have also been used to kill programs that the governor feels are unnecessary or ineffective, such as Brown's 2011 veto of funding for the California Postsecondary Education Commission, a body that provided policy advice to the governor on the three branches of higher education. In the state budget for 2014–15, Governor Brown used the line-item veto only 10 times for cuts totaling $37.9 million (out of a budget of $156 billion).[13] Large majorities in the legislative houses that support the governor make the line-item veto less necessary, and in 2016, for the first time in over three decades, the line-item veto was not used.

Legislative Powers

Much of the governor's success depends on having the ability to persuade the legislature to go along with specific programs. This is a difficult task because legislators owe little to the governor, who does not help elect them. Legislators represent smaller and different constituencies and often look out for local rather than statewide issues. They are on different career paths with different time constraints. Because they are term limited, they are relatively inexperienced in bargaining and do not have a long-term commitment to the Sacramento governing process. Their next jobs may be in the private sector, perhaps as lobbyists. If so, they may be more interested in pleasing potential employers (special interests) than in cooperating with the governor.

The governor's ability to persuade legislators depends on political skill as well as on many factors beyond his or her control, including the partisan makeup of the legislature and the political and economic environment. Although much of this influence depends on informal and other formal powers, the governor does have several specific powers that are directed primarily toward influencing the legislature. These include preparing the budget, vetoing bills or provisions of bills, and making legislative recommendations.

Rather than twisting arms to get legislators to support his programs, Governor Brown was in the enviable—and nearly unique—position of having to persuade the Democratic legislature not to overreach and antagonize the electorate by passing too much legislation, spending too much money, or attempting to raise taxes.[14] However on some issues, especially the complex one of climate control, he did at times run into resistance from a group of moderate or business-friendly—some say petroleum-friendly—Democrats, especially in the Assembly. In 2015 they were able to gut his climate control bill, which would have reduced oil use by 50 percent by the year 2030; but in 2016 through astute politicking, the governor and the Democratic leadership made a successful comeback, persuading 17 Assembly members to change their votes (some agreed to the change only when the outcome was not in doubt) from the previous year.[15] As *Los Angeles Times* columnist George Skelton has pointed out, "Dominant Democrats in Sacramento hang together more often than not. . . ."[16] Still, this group is an emerging third force in the legislature.

Legislative Recommendations

At the beginning of a legislative session, as required by the constitution, the governor presents a State of the State address to the legislature. This speech may be short or long, general or specific. It is normally not covered in detail by the media, unlike the president's State of the Union address. Whether or not the State of the State address contains the governor's legislative program, most governors have such a program, which addresses the state's problems as they see them and which they hope to get passed through the legislature.

The governor cannot introduce legislation but has allies who will introduce specific proposals. As the most prominent political figure in the state, the governor is in a position to press for action on these proposals. Success once again depends on a variety of factors, including political skills. Because of his star power, Governor Schwarzenegger had greater access to the public through the media and, more than most governors, could bring outside pressure to bear on the legislature through public appearances. But Schwarzenegger's governorship is widely considered to have been filled with wasted opportunities, partly because of his support for ill-advised initiatives. Jerry Brown preferred to work on the inside, using his significant personal political skills. But he too needed public support for tax increases, and his successful public appearances to lobby for Proposition 30 may have had more impact simply because previously they had been so rare. Former state librarian Kevin Starr feels that the governor's reputation is enhanced by "everything he chooses not to say"—by staying, for the most part, out of the press.[17]

Judicial Powers

The governor has the power to grant pardons and commute or shorten sentences for state crimes. He or she can also reverse parole decisions or delay a death sentence. While these are significant powers, governors tend to use them with extreme care and caution, because appearing "soft on crime" can have serious political consequences. Among other judicial powers of the governor is the power to nominate justices to the Supreme Court and appellate courts, as well as the power to appoint other judges if positions are opened by retirement or resignation.

Public Roles of the Governor

While the governor's role as head of state does not provide as much access to the public as the president enjoys, the governor still is occasionally seen cutting a ribbon, bestowing an honor upon some citizen, leading an international trade delegation or, most often, signing a bill into law. These and other ceremonial and symbolic appearances may have little policy content, but they keep the governor in the public eye. Because of his—and the state's—longtime leadership on global warming, Jerry Brown received notable attention in Paris when he attended the important 2015 UN Conference on Climate Control.

While far less visible than the president, governors do not underestimate these appearances, which remind people that the governor is on the job and cares about their concerns, and that, in case of a disaster, the governor and the resources of the state will be available.

Occasionally issues arise of such overwhelming importance—the budget crises are prime examples—that the media are willing to give the governor significant air time. On other occasions the governor can stage policy-related events such as showing up at a school to emphasize his or her education policies (or to mask opposition to certain education policies). Finally, disasters such as earthquakes, droughts, and fires require the governor to be publicly active, and during these crises the media will broadcast every statement he or she makes.

The governor also moves into the public spotlight during elections, and not only when campaigning for re-election. California governors often think they have a chance to become president, in that governors of far less populous or attention-getting states have been elected. However, only one governor of the state, Ronald Reagan, has successfully moved on to the presidency. Nevertheless, when governors sense a chance for the presidency they try to get into the national media as much as possible. Jerry Brown ran for president twice during his first two terms in office (and once afterward), to the detriment of his performance as governor. Speculation that Gavin Newsom has his eyes on the presidency has circulated for years, leading him to vow during the 2018 campaign that he would not run for president in 2020 or 2024, having learned from Brown's mistakes.

Governors also campaign for political allies, including candidates for president or loyal legislators, although their influence in the latter cases is probably marginal at best. Additionally, they may take an active role in an initiative or referendum campaign, either to bolster the chances of an initiative that they support or to gain more public attention. In spite of his mixed success in this arena, Governor Schwarzenegger continued to be involved right through the elections of 2010, endorsing the successful Proposition 14 in June of that year and leading the successful effort in November to defeat Proposition 23, which would have suspended an air pollution control law (AB (Assembly Bill) 32). Governor Brown's campaign for Proposition 30, which greatly enhanced his political reputation and helped put the state on a firmer financial footing, provides a critically important recent example. In 2014 Governor Brown also campaigned vigorously and successfully for Proposition 1, the water bond, and Proposition 2, the Rainy Day Budget Stabilization Fund Act. In 2016 Brown campaigned successfully against Proposition 53, which would require a public vote on public works projects of over $2 billion before bonds could be issued. This would make some of Brown's projects—especially the Delta tunnels—difficult to implement. The governor's extensive fundraising appearances may also receive public attention, which is useful because it shows the opposition that the governor has a formidable war chest and convinces the party faithful that the governor is out there stumping on their behalf.

Gavin Newsom as Governor

Gavin Newsom was elected governor in November 2018, easily defeating his Republican Challenger John Cox. The true battle was earlier that year, in June 2018, when Newsom and Cox were chosen in the state's unique Top Two Vote Getter (TTVG) system to continue to the November election. Polls taken before the June primary suggested that two Democrats might instead be the finalists, as was the case for many other elected offices that year. In fact, Newsom faced criticism in the primary season for his campaign advertisements, which seemed to encourage turnout in favor of Cox and to the detriment of challenger Antonio Villaraigosa—former mayor of Los Angeles, and who would likely have presented a tougher head-on challenge in the November run-off.

Newsom began his political career in 1997, when he was appointed to fill a vacancy on the San Francisco Board of Supervisors. After winning several re-election campaigns, he successfully ran for Mayor of San Francisco in 2003. Just a month into his term in 2004, he rose to national prominence when he directed the city-county clerk to begin issuing marriage licenses to same-sex couples, in violation of state law. While those marriages were later annulled by the California Supreme Court, the move cemented his popularity in the city.

In early 2009 he launched a run for governor of California but consistently lagged behind front-runner Jerry Brown. He dropped out later that year and instead filed paperwork to run for Lieutenant Governor, winning that election in November 2010 and re-election in 2014. In 2017 Newsom again launched a gubernatorial bid (as Jerry Brown would now be termed out of office). This time he was a consistent favorite in the polls; he won the multicandidate June primary with a comfortable 33.8 percent of the vote (John Cox won 26.2 percent), and in November he won the general election with 61.6 percent of the vote to Cox's 38.4 percent.

As Lieutenant Governor, Newsom served under his predecessor, Jerry Brown. Jerry Brown was the son of Pat Brown, one of California's most popular governors, who in the 1960s helped develop the education system and infrastructure that made California the envy of the nation. In 1974, seven years after his father left office, Jerry Brown was elected governor for two consecutive terms.

During his first term as governor, in the 1970s, Brown was given the nickname "Governor Moonbeam," a moniker reflecting his youth, idealism, and eccentricity. His advocacy of fiscal restraints (which reflected his personal lifestyle) did not go over well in a state that still remembered his father, who had presided over an era of seemingly unlimited promise.

After his first two terms of office ended in 1983, Brown, still in his early 40s, was adrift. During the next 16 years he studied Buddhism, ran for president (again), and chaired the California Democratic Party. In 1999 he reestablished his career as an elected official by starting at the local level as mayor of the economically troubled city of Oakland (1999–2007), and he held the position of attorney general from 2007 to 2011. In the 2010 governor's race, voters had the opportunity to select between Brown, an experienced if unpredictable Democratic politician, and Meg Whitman, a billionaire Republican internet entrepreneur. The voters chose political experience over business acumen. Whitman had little political experience but a lot of money, and her self-financed campaign (see Chapter 4) was the most expensive in California history. Brown spent far less and won by emphasizing his political experience and ability to work with the opposition Republicans.

Jerry Brown's predecessor in office, Arnold Schwarzenegger, was elected in the October 2003 recall of Governor Gray Davis. Davis was recalled partly because of the state's inadequate response to a manipulated energy crisis, legislative budgetary stalemates, fund-raising scandals, and his own remoteness. Hoping for change, the voters turned to the inexperienced but flamboyant movie actor who stood out in a weak field of possible replacements.

Most of Schwarzenegger's years in office were characterized by extreme state budget deficits that the governor and legislature were unable to close on a long-term basis. There were annual standoffs lasting for months with Republicans unwilling to raise taxes and revenues under any circumstances (a two-thirds vote was needed for a budget or for tax increases). In the end, the Schwarzenegger governorship failed to resolve the crises in California politics. Schwarzenegger's failures as a political outsider likely contributed to the decision by California voters in 2010 to elect an experienced politician, Jerry Brown, rather than yet another outsider candidate.

The 2012 election resulted in the passage of the tax-raising Proposition 30 and in overwhelming Democratic majorities in both legislative houses. Along with an improved economy and the elimination of the supermajority vote requirement for passing a budget, these results set a far more positive tone for state politics. Overnight, gridlock became a thing of the past; rather than encouraging the legislature to act, Governor Brown had to caution Democrats about overreaching—advice they appeared to take to heart. Journalists who a few years before had viewed California as a disaster area began talking about Jerry Brown's "political reboot," "turnaround," and "revenge."[18]

But California's problems, especially its fiscal problems, have not disappeared. While Brown engineered a change from a $25 billion budget deficit when he took office to a $14.8 billion surplus projected for 2019–20, the Proposition 30 tax increase is temporary. Although Proposition 55 in 2016 extended the tax provisions for 12 years, substantial long-term debts remain, along with vexing issues concerning water, transportation, income inequality, climate change, and infrastructure deficiencies. Because the California Constitution still requires a two-thirds vote on tax measures, the minority party has a veto so long as the majority does not enjoy a supermajority; without the minority's support, approving the increased revenues needed for significant infrastructure repairs or creating an adequate and stable source of revenue will not happen. Moreover, there are times when a coalition of Republicans and moderate Democrats will thwart attempts to pass environmental legislation or to regulate businesses and developers, as they did in 2015 when, in response to heavy lobbying by oil companies, they killed a provision that would have reduced gasoline use by 50 percent by 2030. Governors also face ongoing battles with well-funded private industry. For example, in 2018, Governor Brown reluctantly agreed to a law banning new local taxes on sodas and sugary drinks for 12 years in order to get beverage industry backers to pull away from a proposed ballot initiative that would have made it harder for local governments to raise taxes of any kind.

See the "Who Are Californians?" feature on p. 177 for more information on how California's governorship compares to other states' governorships.

Structure of the Executive Branch

The executive branch of California has several significant divisions: the governor's personal staff; the appointed cabinet and other department heads; the other elected officials of the executive branch (the plural executive); the appointed boards and commissions; and the more than 500,000 state employees (including those in state universities), who are divided into more than 85 agencies and 30 educational institutions. Not all of these agencies and employees are under the control of the governor. Figure 6.1 provides a graphic representation of the executive branch.

Personal Staff

Closest to the governor is the personal staff. The members of this staff include schedulers, speechwriters, and press officers. In addition, some staff members oversee the appointment process and the general development of policy, and act as liaisons with the legislature. They structure the governor's day, develop statements for the press and the public, arrange relations with various groups, and set up appearances throughout the state. Members of this staff tend to be young and transient and are expendable. Their positions depend on staying in the governor's good graces.

Governor Brown, preferring a flatter administrative structure, did not appoint a chief of staff. His principal (unpaid) aide, with the title "special counsel," was his wife, Anne Gust Brown, a former lawyer with Gap, Inc. She was credited with having strong political and personal skills and with softening many of the rough edges that Brown demonstrated during his first stint as governor in the 1970s. She was even suggested as a possible successor to Governor Brown.[19]

The Cabinet and Agency Heads

The governor uses the cabinet as he or she sees fit. It has no official policy function as a body but can be used to help formulate policy. The cabinet is often more

FIGURE 6.1 ● Executive Branch of the California State Government

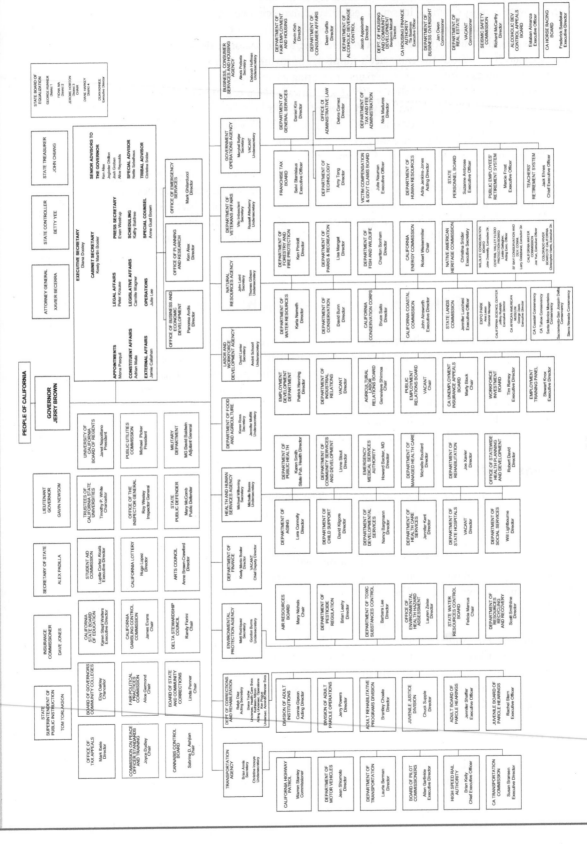

SOURCE: California Online Directory, https://cold.govops.ca.gov/File/OrganizationalChart (accessed 7/5/2018).

How Does California's Governorship Compare?

The powers of the governorship vary considerably from state to state. In California, governors can serve a total of two four-year terms. They have full budget-making power as well as the power to veto line items in appropriations bills. How do the powers of California's governor compare to the powers of governorships in other states?

	Can serve unlimited terms	Budget making power	Line-item veto?
AK		Full	Appropriations only
AL		Full*	Yes
AR		Shared	Appropriations only
AZ		Full*	Appropriations only
► CA		Full*	Appropriations only
CO		Shared	Appropriations only
CT	Yes	Shared	Yes
DE		Full*	Yes
FL		Shared	Appropriations only
GA		Full	Appropriations only
HI		Shared	Appropriations only
IA	Yes	Shared	Appropriations only
ID	Yes	Shared	Yes
IL	Yes	Shared	Yes
IN		Full	
KS		Full	Appropriations only
KY		Full*	Appropriations only
LA		Shared	Appropriations only
MA	Yes	Full	Yes
MD		Full	Yes
ME		Shared	Appropriations only
MI		Full	Appropriations only
MN	Yes	Shared	Appropriations only
MO		Full*	Appropriations only
MS		Shared	Appropriations only

	Can serve unlimited terms	Budget making power	Line-item veto?
MT		Full	Appropriations only
NC		Shared	
ND	Yes	Full	Appropriations only
NE		Shared	Appropriations only
NH	Yes	Full*	Appropriations only
NJ		Full*	Appropriations only
NM		Full	Appropriations only
NV		Full	
NY	Yes	Shared	Yes
OH		Full	Appropriations only
OK		Shared	Appropriations only
OR		Shared	Appropriations only
PA		Full	Appropriations only
RI		Shared	
SC		Shared	Appropriations only
SD		Full	Appropriations only
TN		Shared	Appropriations only
TX	Yes	Shared	Appropriations only
UT	Yes	Shared	Appropriations only
VA		Full	Appropriations only
VT	Yes	Full	
WA	Yes	Full	Yes
WI	Yes	Full*	Appropriations only
WV		Full	
WY		Shared	Appropriations only

Key

Can serve unlimited terms
✓ Yes

Budget making power
✓ Full   ✓ Shared

Line-item veto?
✓ Yes   ✓ Appropriations bills only

*Governor proposes budget; legislature amends; governor then signs or vetoes.

SOURCE: The Council of State Governments, http://knowledgecenter.csg.org/kc/content/book-states-2017-chapter-4-state-executive-branch (Accessed 10/22/18).

forcriticalanalysis

1. What are the advantages or disadvantages of having term limits? What effect might a term limit have on a governor's actions?

2. What are the advantages or disadvantages of having a governor with full versus shared budget-making power? What about the ability to veto line items?

a symbolic body than an integral structure of governing. The executive branch is divided into seven superagencies, and the heads of these agencies, called secretaries, are generally in the cabinet. These are State and Consumer Services; Youth and Adult Corrections; Environmental Protection; Health and Human Services; Labor and Workforce Development; Business, Transportation, and Housing; and Resources. These superagencies contain most of the executive branch's agencies. It is the individual agencies, not the umbrella superagencies, that carry out functions, and they may act independently of the superagency secretaries. The governor appoints these agency heads, although he or she often does not have a free choice. Someone with expertise in the area needs to be appointed, and sometimes the qualifications are spelled out in law. These agencies and superagencies are called *line agencies*, the term used to describe organizations that have their own statutory authority to carry out functions and provide services.

In addition, the governor has several staff advisory agencies, including the Department of Finance, the Office of Planning and Research, and the Department of Personnel Administration. Perhaps the most important of these is the Department of Finance, which prepares the governor's budget.

The Plural Elected Executive

One of the most notable features of California government is the number of statewide *elected* administrative offices. There are seven of these positions, plus the Board of Equalization, which oversees the administration of property, sales, and excise taxes (see Box 6.2). This means there are eight elected independent bases of power that do not report to the governor or need to adhere to gubernatorial wishes. This differs from other states that have a single elected leader who appoints lesser state executives. While California government's distribution of power may limit the governor's freedom to make or implement policy, most of these elected positions do not deal with substantial policy issues. The attorney general is usually the governor's only real policy competitor. A vacancy in most of the plural executive offices, such as the attorney general, is filled by the governor, subject to the approval within 90 days of both houses of the legislature.

Let's take a closer look at each of these seven elected administrative offices.

THE LIEUTENANT GOVERNOR The lieutenant governor sits on many of California's regulatory commissions and executive agencies, and takes up the role of acting governor if the sitting governor dies, resigns, or is otherwise unable to fulfill the duties of the office or is out of the state. Since he or she is occasionally from a different party, this provides occasions for great mischief. In 1979, while Governor Jerry Brown was traveling, lieutenant governor Mike Card signed bills, issued vetoes and executive actions, and even created commissions and made judicial appointments, leading to a battle in the state Supreme Court over the limit of those powers.[20]

The lieutenant governor can also preside over the Senate, breaking tie votes. Perhaps more than others, this position captures the imagination of those who would restructure government, either by eliminating the office or by linking the election of the lieutenant governor to that of the governor, as is the case in other states, such as Illinois. The lieutenant governor serves on several important boards, including the governing boards of both the University of California and the California State

BOX 6.2 ● The Plural Executive

In addition to the selected duties listed below, all these officeholders sit ex officio on various state boards.

Governor: Organizes the executive branch, prepares the budget and legislation, signs or vetoes bills.

Lieutenant Governor: Replaces the governor if he or she is out of the state, incapacitated, or leaves office for any reason.

Attorney General: Enforces laws, oversees and assists district attorneys.

Secretary of State: Holds elections and oversees the records and archives of the state.

Treasurer: Manages state money, including investments and bond sales.

Insurance Commissioner: Regulates insurance companies.

Controller: Monitors collection of taxes, provides fiscal controls for receipts and payments.

Superintendent of Public Instruction: Administers the state role in public education, sits on the state board of education.

Board of Equalization: Oversees the assessment and administration of property taxes, the collection and distribution of sales taxes, and the collection of excise taxes. The controller is a member of this body.

University system, and the State Lands Commission. The current lieutenant governor, first elected in 2018, is Democrat Eleni Kounalakis. Kounalakis is the first woman to be elected to the position in California history. In 2009–2010, Mona Pasquil served briefly as acting Lieutenant Governor when John Garamendi was elected to the U.S. House of Representatives. Prior to her candidacy, Kounalakis worked in her family's housing development firm and as U.S. ambassador to Hungary under President Barack Obama.

THE ATTORNEY GENERAL The attorney general (AG) oversees the Department of Justice, which employs more than 4,500 people and is responsible for ensuring that the laws are enforced. The attorney general is free to determine which areas and which issues will receive the most attention and resources and has oversight responsibilities for local district attorneys and county sheriffs. The AG is legal counsel to the state and defends the state in lawsuits. There is no obligation to cooperate with the governor, and the AG is often viewed as a rival. In 2004 Governor Schwarzenegger ordered the attorney general to intercede with the state supreme court to stop gay marriages in San Francisco. The governor had no statutory basis for giving such an order, and although the attorney general ultimately followed the order, it was done on the AG's own authority. This office is very powerful, second only to the governor of California, and incumbents often see themselves as leading candidates for governor. Although few have successfully made this transition, Jerry Brown used this office to launch his successful campaign for governor in 2010. The attorney general's office is able to set its own agenda, which may run counter to the governor's agenda. It can also use its substantial powers to counter or even embarrass the governor.

The most recently elected attorney general is Xavier Becerra (appointed in 2017 and re-elected in 2018). He is the first Latino attorney general, the child of immigrants from Mexico. Prior to serving as attorney general, Becerra served in the U.S. House of Representatives from 1993 to 2017, representing downtown Los Angeles. Becerra grabbed headlines in 2017 and 2018 with a series of 44 lawsuits filed against the Trump administration, including legal action involving environmental protection, health care, reproductive rights, education, transgender military troops, immigration, and the 2020 U.S. Census. Becerra's predecessor, Kamala Harris, first elected in 2010, was the state's first female African American state attorney general, as well as the nation's first Asian American state attorney general. Harris was elected to the U.S. Senate in 2016.

THE SECRETARY OF STATE The secretary of state is the chief elections officer, responsible for maintaining a database of registered voters, for overseeing all federal and state elections in the state, and for disclosure of campaign and lobbyist financial information. The secretary of state is also responsible for corporate filings

In 2018, Alex Padilla was re-elected as secretary of state. His campaign focused on his accomplishments during his first term, which included increasing voter registration and turnout, as well as protecting voter rights.

and other filings related to businesses operating in the state, for registries including the Safe at Home confidential address program, and for safeguarding the state archives. The current secretary of state, Alex Padilla, was first elected in 2014 and re-elected in 2018. The son of Mexican immigrants, Padilla has served in public office since 1999, when at age 26 he was elected to the Los Angeles City Council.

THE CONTROLLER The controller is the chief fiscal officer of California, responsible for accountability and disbursement of the state's financial resources. The controller also safeguards many types of property until claimed by the rightful owners, independently audits government agencies that spend state funds, and administers the payroll system for state government employees and California State University employees. The controller serves on 70 boards and commissions with authority, ranging from state public land management to crime victim compensation, and is a member of numerous financing authorities and fiscal and financial oversight entities including the Franchise Tax Board and Board of Equalization. The current controller, Betty Yee, was first elected in 2014 and re-elected in 2018. She is the daughter of Chinese immigrants and is the first woman of color to hold the position. Prior to running for controller, Yee served on the Board of Equalization from 2004 to 2015.

THE TREASURER The treasurer manages the state's money after it comes in and before it is spent. He or she manages the investment of money and the sale of bonds. The current Treasurer, Fiona Ma, was elected in 2018. The child of Chinese immigrants, Ma won her first election in 2002, when she was elected to the San Francisco Board of Supervisors. She then served in the California State Assembly from 2006 to 2012 and on the Board of Equalization from 2015 to 2019.

THE SUPERINTENDENT OF PUBLIC INSTRUCTION The superintendent is the chief administrator of the Department of Education. Unlike the other elected statewide officers, the superintendent is elected on a nonpartisan basis. Education administration is a confusing policy area: the superintendent shares power with an appointed board of education. This arrangement ensures controversy and was even more confusing before Governor Brown eliminated the parallel position of the appointed secretary of education in 2011. The current superintendent, Afro-Latino Tony Thurmond, was first elected in 2018.

THE INSURANCE COMMISSIONER The insurance commissioner's office was made elective by Proposition 103 in 1988, making it the newest plural executive in the state. It is the only position of the plural executive created by an initiative. The commissioner regulates the insurance industry, and Proposition 103 passed because the public felt that the appointed commissioner was not doing his job. It is not clear that making this an elective post has improved matters, because most of the contributions to the campaigns for this position come from the insurance industry. The state's current insurance commissioner, Ricardo Lara, was first elected in 2018 and is the state's first openly gay statewide office holder.

In addition to these positions, voters elect by district four members to the Board of Equalization (BOE), which is chaired by the state controller. Created with the 1879 Constitution, the BOE is the only elected tax collection agency in the nation, and until 2017 was responsible for administering more than 30 tax and fee programs, and for hearing appeals to assessments and other tax decisions. In 2017 the agency came under fire for inappropriate behavior regarding tax assessment appeals and misallocation of funds. A set of legislative reforms signed by Governor Jerry Brown in June 2017 stripped the BOE of much of its power and moved it to two new unelected entities: the Department of Tax and Fee Administration (to handle most tax and fee programs) and the Office of Tax Appeals. Of the 4,800 BOE employees, 4,400 were transferred to the new organizations, leaving a much smaller BOE retaining only the few tax administration responsibilities originally given to it in the state constitution.

Agencies and the Bureaucracy

Most of the work of California state government is carried out by more than 200,000 state employees (not counting employees in higher education) housed in over 85 agencies. Most of these agencies are located within the seven superagencies, and most are invisible to the general public, which tends to sustain the impression that state government runs by itself. A few agencies, such as the California Highway Patrol and Caltrans, are well known if not well understood. Others, such as the Office of Small Business Development or the Department of Aging, rarely make it into the news or the public consciousness. Few Californians could name anyone in the executive branch up to and including department heads; few governors could name more than a handful. Many of these individuals are professional experts on policy subjects who are quietly doing their jobs.

Most California employees have civil service protection. Many are also represented by unions. A few of these unions, notably the CCPOA (discussed in Chapter 3), are very powerful and politically well connected to the point where the wishes and desires of the unions are more likely to become state policy than are, for instance, the wishes and desires of the governor, the head of the relevant administrative agency, or the administration of the department in which the employee works.

There are more than 325 state boards and commissions. Positions on these boards are mostly filled by the governor and subject to the approval of another body, most often a legislative body (some are appointed by the legislature; some are ex officio). These boards and commissions include the Air Resources Board, the Public Utilities Commission, the California Coastal Commission, and the Gambling Control Commission. Probably the most visible are the Board of Regents of the University of California and the Trustees of the California State University, which together are responsible for more than 100,000 employees. On the other hand, boards such as the Board of Chiropractic Examiners and the Apprenticeship Council are probably known only to those with a direct interest in that area. Most members of these boards and commissions serve for fixed terms, some as long as 12 years, and, once appointed, do not have to respond to the governor's wishes.

The California bureaucracy does not enjoy a particularly positive reputation with the public, in part in response to various news stories revealing unethical and illegal behavior by various state employees. For example, a 2009 internal investigation found that Stockton Caltrans employees were operating a porn-exchange ring using government computers. Recent reports from the state auditor have documented other misconduct by state employees, including misuse of state vehicles, unauthorized disclosure of confidential information, and wrongly received excess pay and leave time. In 2015 the auditor shared details about a Caltrans engineer who played dozens of rounds of golf during work hours.[21] There is also concern over looming retirement costs for state employees. The California Public Employees' Retirement System (CalPERS) and the California State Teachers' Retirement System (CalSTRS) do not have enough funds to pay for the retirement benefits they have promised. Increasing spending on public employee pensions and medical benefits over the next few years is expected to put enormous pressure on city budgets, requiring either increased taxes, reduced services, or negotiated changes to existing compensation packages.

California Executive Branch:
Where Are We Now?

In recent years several tentative steps have been taken toward tackling the biggest long-term structural problems facing the state and providing the governor with a greater capacity to lead. First, Proposition 25 removed the two-thirds vote requirement to pass a budget. Although this loses some of its force because revenues cannot be similarly raised, its impact has been greater than expected. Even in the absence of a supermajority in the legislature, Governor Brown was able to largely ignore Republican legislators and work out legislative deals with the more accommodating Democrats. (This may come back to haunt the Democrats if someday the Republicans should control all parts of the state government and have the ability to cut programs at will.)

Second, Proposition 11, approved in November 2008, took the power to draw the state legislative districts away from the legislature and gave it to a citizens' commission. This commission created new districts that have a closer partisan balance and that initially pitted some incumbents of the same party against one another. The hope was to gain a legislature that was willing to cooperate and compromise both internally and with the governor. The result of Proposition 11 was different than expected, however: the overwhelming Democratic majorities that resulted made cooperation and compromise between parties largely unnecessary.

Along similar lines, Proposition 14, approved in June 2010, created a system of preliminary and final elections for the party primary (see Chapter 4). Again, the ambition was to create a less partisan legislature. As a result of these two measures, the reduced number of Republicans appear to be no less conservative than before, but the policies of the heavily Democratic legislature have not been as extreme as some feared. Even during the supermajority period following the 2012 election, for instance, there was no push to raise taxes, as might have been expected. Five years later, however, Democrats used their majorities to pass a significant increase to state gasoline taxes. The bill, approved in April 2017, passed without any Republican support in the state Assembly and with only one Republican yes vote in the state Senate. The gas tax went on to survive an attempted repeal by statewide initiative on the November 2018 ballot, which voters rejected by a 55–45 percent margin. The Democrats are held in check in part by having to work with a moderate governor who would veto extreme bills, as well as by some Democrats who were elected from marginal districts or who are backed by big business money and who are more likely to share some values with Republicans. While these changes have resulted, unfortunately, in a marginalized minority party, they have also given rise to an executive (and legislative) branch that is more effective, productive, and popular with the electorate.

However, nothing has been done to fix the distortions caused by Proposition 13 (the 1978 proposition that limited property tax increases) and the series of other initiatives that have locked in certain parts of the budget and have made it close to impossible to create a stable and adequate revenue stream for the state. California's revenues are far more volatile than those of other states, and Californians' willingness to govern by initiative remains undaunted. Given this situation, it is difficult to see how the state's revenue problems will be solved in the near future. And while the government seems to be functioning smoothly at the moment, there are many unfunded needs in the state—infrastructure, the homeless, and the costs of education, among others—that are not being addressed.

Study Guide

FOR FURTHER READING

Cain, Bruce E., and Roger G. Noll, eds. *Constitutional Reform in California: Making State Government More Effective and Responsive*. Berkeley: Institute of Governmental Studies Press, 1995.

California Performance Review. *Prescription for Change, Report of the California Performance Review*. Vols. I–IV. California Performance Review, 2004. https://www.ucop.edu/acadinit/mastplan/cpr/Commission_Perspective.pdf. Accessed 8/31/18.

Gerston, Larry N., and Terry Christensen. *Recall! California's Political Earthquake*. Armonk, NY: M. E. Sharpe, 2004.

Lubenow, Gerald C., ed. *Governing California: Politics, Government, and Public Policy in the Golden State*. 2nd ed. Berkeley: Institute of Governmental Studies Press, University of California, 2006.

Mathews, Joe. *The People's Machine: Arnold Schwarzenegger and the Rise of Blockbuster Democracy*. New York: Public Affairs Press, 2006.

Schrag, Peter. *California: America's High-Stakes Experiment*. Berkeley: University of California Press, 2006.

——. *Paradise Lost: California's Experience, America's Future*. New York: New Press, 1998.

Simmons, Charlene Wear. *To Faithfully Execute the Law: California Executive Branch Agencies 1959–2003*. Sacramento: California Research Bureau, California State Library, 2004.

ON THE WEB

Around The Capitol. www.aroundthecapitol.com. Accessed 8/25/16. Includes a daily blog, *The Nooner*.

California Choices. www.californiachoices.org. Accessed 8/25/16.

California Department of Finance. www.dof.ca.gov. Accessed 8/25/16.

California State Library. www.library.ca.gov. Accessed 8/25/16.

CALmatters. https://calmatters.org. Accessed 8/25/16.

Governor of California. www.gov.ca.gov/home.php. Accessed 8/25/16. The official site of the Office of the Governor, where you can find background information and up-to-date news and even send an email to the governor.

Public Policy Institute of California. www.ppic.org. Accessed 8/25/16.

Rough & Tumble. www.rtumble.com. Accessed 8/25/16. A daily summary of California news.

University of California, Berkeley, Institute of Governmental Studies Library. http://igs.berkeley.edu/library. Accessed 8/25/16.

SUMMARY

I. The office of the governor is modeled on that of the U.S. president, but there are significant differences between the two offices, mostly having to do with visibility.

II. Each job has two analytical roles.
   A. Head of state, which is largely ceremonial, symbolizing the unity of the state or country. In this role, the governor or president makes public appearances doing activities that bring people together. The president, in this role, is on TV almost every evening. The governor has less opportunity to play this role, and even when he does, the state TV stations seem uninterested.
   B. Head of government, which involves making policy and trying to get it passed by the legislature and implemented by the executive branch. This role is partisan and divisive. It is also an almost invisible role, especially on the implementation side.

III. The formal powers of the office are greater for the governor than for the president.
   A. The governor's formal powers include making appointments and organizing the executive branch; conducting independent executive actions that are permitted by law; being commander in chief; proposing the budget; making legislative recommendations; and exercising the veto, including the line-item veto.
   B. The governor has powers similar to those of the president in domestic policy but also can use the line-item veto, which gives the governor more control over the political process of constructing the budget.
   C. California has an initiative process that a popular governor can use to pressure the legislature into action.

IV. The governor's public roles as head of state include cutting ribbons, signing bills, and leading the response to natural disasters. Non–head-of-state public roles include campaigning and fund-raising as well as advocating for initiatives.

V. Like the presidency, the office of governor is one of limited powers, which are restricted by the legislature, the judiciary, the plural elected executive, and the permanent executive branch.

VI. The structure of the state government includes the following:
   A. The governor's personal staff.
   B. The governor's cabinet, which includes the heads of major departments (superagencies).
   C. The plural elected executive, which includes the lieutenant governor, the attorney general, the secretary of state, the controller, the treasurer, the superintendent of public education, the insurance commissioner, and the State Board of Equalization.
   D. The 85 or more agencies that comprise the major departments.
   E. More than 325 boards and commissions, including the Public Utilities Commission and the Regents of the University of California.

VII. California employs the equivalent of more than 300,000 full-time employees to staff the government, including more than 100,000 in higher education, who are not under the direct control of the governor.

PRACTICE QUIZ

1. Which of the following is *not* part of the plural executive?
   a) the chancellor of the California State University
   b) the secretary of state
   c) the attorney general
   d) the controller

2. Which of these powers does the governor have that the president does *not* have?
   a) legislative veto
   b) line-item veto
   c) power to appoint the secretary of state
   d) power to appoint judges

3. Which of the following activities of the governor would be considered part of his or her role as head of government?
   a) proposing a budget
   b) vetoing legislation
   c) proposing new air quality standards
   d) all of the above

4. Which of the following groups of employees are under administrative control and report ultimately to the governor?
   a) legislative aides
   b) supreme court clerks
   c) highway patrol
   d) professors at California State University, Fullerton

5. How many state boards and commissions are there?
   a) fewer than 50
   b) between 50 and 150
   c) between 150 and 300
   d) more than 300

6. The California governor is "invisible" under normal conditions for all of the following reasons *except*:
   a) California's governors appear in events where they are visible to the public, but for the most part there is little public interest in those events.
   b) For almost every recent governor, there has been little media interest in Sacramento.
   c) The governor splits his or her power with other state executives, who are also trying to attract the media.
   d) The governor's star power is only of interest to those who like superhero movies.

7. The governor manages the executive branch, but this power is limited by all of the following *except*:
   a) There are many appointees of the governor, many of whom belong to agencies the governor doesn't know much about.
   b) Some of California government is outside the governor's power to supervise, such as the University of California and California State University.

c) The boards and commissions whose members the governor appoints are mostly, except in extreme cases, outside of his or her power.

d) The attorney general must approve appointments to many boards and commissions, and that appointment approval is difficult for the governor to obtain.

8. The line-item veto allows the governor to adjust any appropriations item up or down, including reducing it to zero.
   a) true
   b) false

9. All of the following are true of the governor's appointments to the cabinet *except*:
   a) Most cabinet appointments are routine, usually given to the governor's political supporters and campaign contributors.

b) The cabinet as a whole has no official policy function, unless the governor wants to give it a role.

c) Some cabinet and subcabinet positions require an appointment of someone with qualifications that are spelled out in law.

d) The superagency heads are usually considered part of the governor's cabinet.

10. The job of the lieutenant governor, one columnist wrote not entirely in jest, consists of getting up in the morning, checking that the governor is still alive, and then making arrangements for lunch!
    a) This statement is probably true.
    b) This statement is probably false.

CRITICAL-THINKING QUESTIONS

1. Is the state government too large?
2. Does the plural elected executive contribute to effective or efficient government?
3. What is the value of having independent boards such as the Regents of the University of California that employ large numbers of people?

4. Which is more important for governing: the formal or informal powers of the governor? Think about this question in terms of "necessary" versus "sufficient" powers.

KEY TERMS

boards and commissions (p. 166)
cabinet (p. 167)
formal powers (p. 164)
head of government (p. 163)

head of state (p. 163)
informal powers (p. 165)
line-item veto (p. 165)
personal staff (p. 166)

superagencies (p. 167)
veto (p. 170)

7 The California Judiciary

WHAT THE CALIFORNIA JUDICIARY DOES AND WHY IT MATTERS

State courts are an integral and necessary component of state government. They ensure that a state's citizenry is guaranteed due process of law and that the other branches and levels of government within the state uphold state statutes, codes, and the provisions in the state constitution. Therefore, judges play a much larger role than simply punishing criminals or imposing fines on a polluting company. Courts make decisions that are often political and sometimes controversial, with the potential to affect more individuals than just those directly involved in the cases. Court rulings can have far-reaching consequences that not only ignite political debate but that also have an iterative effect. This is especially true in California, a state that witnesses a high rate of litigation and where politics can be very contentious. And while some cases that come before the California courts gain a significant amount of statewide and national media attention, many cases that remain under the radar still have an impact on citizens' daily lives.

California court decisions on immigration policy, for example, have the potential to influence national debates on immigration reform and are particularly salient in a state with a high population of undocumented immigrants. Questions of state policy regarding undocumented immigrants who entered the United States as children were tested in the case of Sergio Garcia, who came with his family to California only months after his first birthday. Garcia and his family moved back to Mexico when he was nine years old, but they returned to the United States eight years later, in 1994. This time, Garcia's father attained lawful permanent resident status for himself and filed a petition seeking the same for his family. But, because of limits on the number of visas distributed each year, Garcia graduated from high school, college, and law school while still undocumented. After obtaining his law degree, Mr. Garcia passed the California Bar Examination and applied for admission to the bar, at which point his undocumented status came under scrutiny from the Committee of Bar Examiners. The committee asked the California Supreme Court to determine whether state law or public policy banned Garcia's admittance. The court ruled that it did not, and it held that the intent of the legislature and the governor clearly indicated that Garcia's status should not be an impediment to his application. Garcia's case effectively illustrates the complexity of contemporary immigration issues in the United States. It also serves as a good example of what it means to be an undocumented person versus a person with legal immigration status.

Immigration and immigrants are very important to California. Immigration is a political topic that receives considerable media attention. It is also a political topic that often gets vetted through the courts. Recently, and as discussed in Chapter 4, California has become actively involved in a number of lawsuits challenging the federal government and President Trump's administration's policies. The *Los Angeles Times* reported on July 22, 2018, that "California has sued the Trump administration 38 times."[1] While these cases involve a range of policy issues, it is very important to note that immigration is a key area of conflict between California and the current administration. The state is at odds with federal positions on undocumented children and seeks to continue to protect them. California sought a preliminary injunction (an injunction is a court order telling an official to either stop or start doing a specific act) to prevent undocumented children from being deported.

The California case regarding these children centers on family separation/reunification policies, which have been well-documented in the media in 2018. A federal judge in San Diego had earlier ruled that the separation policy was invalid. The state has also been at odds with the Trump administration's position on sanctuary cities. On July 5, 2018, a federal judge ruled that the Trump administration could not compel local government officials to enforce immigration policies. The judge did state, however, that California could not prohibit private employers from working with immigration agents.[2] Another controversy included a suit against the Trump administration's plan to build a wall on the U.S.-Mexico border. In a lawsuit, California Attorney General Xavier Becerra challenged the construction of the wall, claiming that it violated California environmental protection laws. The state, however, lost.

It is important to note that these immigration issues, though they involve the state, are federal controversies that have been decided by federal courts or are pending in federal courts. They are significant illustrations of federalism and how a state and the national government can use the courts when their policy preferences conflict. We will focus primarily on California state courts for the remainder of this chapter, including a discussion of how California courts and federalism are involved in the case of medical marijuana.

Organizers of this Los Angeles rally in 2017 called for an immediate stop to the Immigration and Customs Enforcement (ICE) raids, demonstrating how the policies of the Trump administration have been at odds with California's values. California has used the courts during these conflicts.

Structure of the California Judicial System

To understand the role that courts play in California politics, consider the following: from 2015 through 2016, approximately 6,200,000 cases were filed in California **superior courts** (trial courts of general jurisdiction).[3] Of these, almost 80 percent were criminal in nature (crimes against the state or society; for instance, failing to pay state taxes or stealing a car), and the remaining 20 percent were civil cases (disputes between individuals). Each one of these 6.2 million cases had to be handled individually in one way or another by the appropriate state court until it was resolved. To put this into context, let's consider the number of people living in the state. According to the U.S. Census Bureau, as of July 2018 California's population was estimated at almost 40 million (39.78 million), which puts the case-to-person ratio at 1 to 6. While this is obviously a very significant statistic, it is worth noting that the California court system actually witnessed a 9 percent decline in case filings from the previous two years.

To adjudicate both criminal cases and civil cases, the state's courts comprise three levels: superior courts (trial courts), California Courts of Appeal, and the California Supreme Court.

The Lower Courts

Superior courts adjudicate cases that involve violations of state and local criminal and civil law. These are the trial courts of California. We often refer to these courts as "courts of first instance" because this is the first time that a case is heard in a court of law. When cases come before the superior courts, a jury or judge reviews the facts of the case and determines guilt or innocence in a criminal proceeding. If it is a civil case, the jury or judge determines which side presents the best case and awards damages accordingly. There are 58 state trial courts (one in each county), with approximately 2,000 judicial officers presiding. This number includes judges, commissioners, and referees. The superior courts are the busiest courts of the state court system.

The California Courts of Appeal are intermediate courts with **appellate jurisdiction**; those who lose their cases at the superior court can appeal first to the California Courts of Appeal. The purpose of this intermediate appellate court is to review the trial or the superior court records for error. The California Courts of Appeal are divided into six districts across the state. Ninety-seven justices preside over these courts, and the judges sit on three-judge panels to review cases.[4]

The Supreme Court

The California Supreme Court is the highest court in the state. Like the California Courts of Appeal, it is an appellate court that reviews decisions for reversible error, submitted by losing parties in the lower courts. When a party to a case is unhappy with the ruling of the California Courts of Appeal, the next step is to appeal to the California Supreme Court. In California, the supreme court has what is known as **judicial discretion**. Discretion allows the justices on the state supreme court to decide which cases they wish to review. Therefore, appeals filed with the California Supreme Court are not automatically reviewed. This is the only court in California with discretionary authority. Discretion is valuable because it provides the high court with a tool to moderate its workload. However, this discretion is not absolute: all death-penalty sentences are automatically appealed and go directly to the California Supreme Court for review (see Figure 7.1). The supreme court

FIGURE 7.1 ● Flow of Cases Through the California State Judicial System

SOURCE: Copyright 2014, Judicial Council of California, used by permission.

TABLE 7.1 ● Membership of the California State Supreme Court (as of November 2018)

Tani Gorre Cantil-Sakauye, chief justice, appointed by Governor Arnold Schwarzenegger in 2010

Ming W. Chin, appointed by Governor Pete Wilson in 1996

Carol A. Corrigan, appointed by Governor Arnold Schwarzenegger in 2005

Goodwin H. Liu, appointed by Governor Edmund G. Brown in 2011

Mariano-Florentino Cuéllar, appointed by Governor Edmund G. Brown in 2014

Leondra R. Kruger, appointed by Governor Edmund G. Brown in 2014

is also required to hear disciplinary cases involving judges or attorneys. The court includes one chief justice and six associate justices (see Table 7.1). Currently, the court has one seat vacant. Kathryn Werdegar retired from the bench in 2017. Governor Brown did not announce an appointment to fill her seat. Judges from other courts have been filling in to help with the workload. Four out of the seven justices must agree in order for a party to win the case.

While the supreme court may seem remote, it often makes decisions that have an impact on Californians' daily lives. For example, on July 26, 2018, the California Supreme Court announced its ruling in *Troester v. Starbucks*. The issue in this case centered on whether or not employers were obligated to pay employees for work they performed off the clock. In a unanimous ruling, the California Supreme Court stated that "California labor law 'contemplates that employees will be paid for all work performed.'"[5] While the opinion of the court stressed that employers were not required to pay employees for off the clock work that was performed from time to time, they did determine that if employees regularly performed work off the clock, they were to be compensated. Why is this decision so important? First, because people should be paid for their work. Consider how many people live and work in the state who are paid hourly wages, then think about how ten minutes or more each day could add up in wages over a week or month. Second, it's important because of what the California Supreme Court did: a *state* court of last resort set a precedent that other states may follow. Finally, the decision is important because it demonstrates that state courts can offer more protections than the federal government or United States Supreme Court may require. Over sixty years ago the United States Supreme Court ruled that employers were not required to pay employees wages if employees had to work a few minutes off the clock. States could, however, decide to compel employers to pay for time worked off the clock if they chose.[6] As those of us who teach law and courts often tell our students, "The United States Supreme Court sets the floor, and states set the ceiling." In this instance, the state of California has raised the ceiling.

When individual citizens or groups of citizens believe that private entities or government has trampled on state law or on their civil liberties or civil rights, they turn to the courts. The judges serving on California's courts must decide if the state's laws or the rights of Californians have been violated.

Jurisdiction

Both criminal and **civil courts** in California are limited as to the cases and controversies they handle because of jurisdiction. Jurisdiction refers to the kind of law handled by a court. For example, there are criminal courts that deal with violations of state and local laws, and there are civil courts that hear cases involving disputes between individuals or classes of individuals. Civil courts may rule on cases involving breach of contract, tort liability, and wrongful-death suits, to name a few. Jurisdiction also refers to geographic boundaries. There are 58 superior court divisions in California, with at least one superior court in each county. Cases are assigned to these courts depending on where the parties in civil suits reside or where alleged crimes have been committed in criminal cases.

It is easier for an individual to go to criminal court (just drive over the speed limit and get caught) than to civil court. Civil courts have rules about the types of cases they can hear. In civil disputes, parties must also have what is known as "standing to sue." To bring a case to court, an individual must suffer personal and real injury. Typically, an individual cannot sue on behalf of someone else. As well as requiring standing to sue, California courts, like the federal courts, will not handle collusive suits. Collusive suits are lawsuits in which both parties want a similar or the same outcome. Our legal system is an adversarial one, in which it is presumed that parties want opposite outcomes, and when one party wins, the other loses.

Both civil and criminal courts have rules that guide how they proceed. Civil cases are typically classified by the dollar amounts that plaintiffs (the party or parties initiating the case) are seeking. In California, a plaintiff who is not represented by an attorney and is seeking a dollar amount of $10,000 or less is filing a "small claim" and goes to small claims court. Cases in which plaintiffs are seeking more than $10,000 but no more than $25,000 are called "limited civil filings." Finally, cases in which plaintiffs are seeking more than $25,000 in damages are called "unlimited civil cases." In 2015–16 almost 50 percent of the civil actions filed were limited civil cases (individuals suing other individuals for more than $10,000 but less than $25,000).

Criminal cases are also divided into different classifications: felonies, misdemeanors, and infractions. Felonies are serious crimes. The punishment if a person is convicted of a felony is incarceration in state prison or, if it is a capital offense, the death penalty. Examples of felonies in California include murder, rape, burglary, and robbery. Misdemeanors are far less serious crimes, and the punishment for committing a misdemeanor ranges from county jail time (up to one year) and/or a fine. Prosecutors do have discretion in this state to charge people who may have been arrested for committing a misdemeanor with a felony. Cases where prosecutors may choose to do this are called "wobblers," and they typically involve something like the use of a weapon during the act of committing the misdemeanor offense. Finally, we have infractions. Infractions are typically offenses that come with citations or tickets. Traffic violations are a form of infraction. Other infractions in California include possession of less than one ounce of marijuana and fishing without a license. Here too, prosecutors can use their discretion to raise an infraction to a misdemeanor. An example of an infraction "wobbler" would be if a person had a number of other outstanding traffic violations or a record of other criminal activity at the time they received their ticket. Infractions constitute an overwhelming amount of the California criminal court system's workload. For example, in 2015–16, 80 percent of criminal cases were infractions. By contrast, misdemeanors accounted for 17 percent, while felonies only made up 4 percent of criminal court filings.[7]

Access to the Court

The California Constitution and its statutes provide rights to the people of California regarding access to the courts. For example, Californians have:

- the right to sue for money owed and for other relief,
- the right to defend oneself against a lawsuit,
- the right to be presumed innocent if charged with a crime,
- the right to defend oneself against all criminal charges,
- the right to a public and speedy trial by jury if charged with a misdemeanor or a felony, and
- the right to an attorney at public expense if one is charged with a felony or misdemeanor and cannot afford an attorney.

These rights apply to citizens and noncitizens of the state alike. However, they do not mitigate concerns about quality of legal representation for indigent persons. The lack of resources in some local court jurisdictions, especially in smaller localities, and the impact of the current budget crisis on the state's judiciary as a whole will affect access to the courts.

Federalism and the California Courts:
The Case of Medical Marijuana

The California court system must occasionally negotiate discrepancies between federal law and state law in a particular policy area. For example, California's laws permitting medicinal marijuana use are at odds with federal laws that classify marijuana as a controlled substance. In 1996, through use of the initiative, voters in California approved Proposition 215, the Compassionate Use Act (CUA). This act provides for the medical use of marijuana for seriously ill persons. It requires that a physician recommend that a patient's health would benefit from using marijuana to alleviate symptoms of serious illness. In addition, the act also shields patients and their caregivers from criminal prosecution for cultivating or possessing marijuana for use approved under the act.

More recently, voters approved Proposition 64, the California Marijuana Legalization Initiative, which allows persons 21 years or older to use and grow marijuana for personal use. The sale and taxation of marijuana went into effect in January 2018. The passing of Proposition 64 expanded the legalization of marijuana and may lead to future conflict between the federal government and the state. The Department of Justice under the Trump administration has made statements that it would revert to enforcing federal law involving the regulation of controlled substances, including enforcing it in states that permit medical and recreational use of marijuana. As you read below the accounts of the conflict over this controversial issue, think about the significance of Proposition 64 with respect to growing one's own marijuana and the facts and ruling in the U.S. Supreme Court case, *Gonzales v. Raich*.

Confusion ensued shortly after the CUA was implemented. First, there were many (successful) attempts at expanding the scope of the law. And second, the state law came directly into conflict with federal law, which makes the cultivation, possession, sale, and consumption of marijuana illegal.

Seven years after the CUA was passed, Governor Gray Davis signed Senate Bill 420, the Medical Marijuana Program Act (MMPA), into law. The MMPA was designed to flesh out the parameters of the CUA. Among other things, the MMPA sought to create collective cooperatives in the state where marijuana could be cultivated and sold to qualified patients and caregivers. The cooperatives would be regulated by state and local agencies, and the patients and caregivers would be issued identification cards that would help law enforcement more easily determine whether persons were covered by the CUA and, therefore, not subject to criminal prosecution under state law. The MMPA also allows for persons who can be classified as cooperatives, caregivers, or patients to raise a defense if they are charged with violating state laws involving the cultivation, possession, sale, or consumption of medical marijuana.

The MMPA had immediate implications regarding federalism. Although both the CUA and the MMPA are technically "good law" (meaning they are still current and enforceable), the national government has made various attempts to exercise preemption—a practice in which the government claims to have authority over a particular policy area when it comes to legislation, thus preempting state and local regulations. In 2005, for example, the U.S. Supreme Court reviewed the case *Gonzales v. Raich*. At issue was whether Congress's power to regulate the manufacture and possession of marijuana under the Controlled Substances Act (21 U.S.C. § 801) allowed the national government to preempt California's laws governing the medicinal use of marijuana. The Supreme Court ruled in a 6–3 decision that the Commerce Power gives Congress the authority to regulate and to punish the manufacture and cultivation of marijuana despite California law allowing for compassionate use. The dissenting Supreme Court justices argued that to preempt these laws was a violation of federalism and that, because the issue involved purely local or *intrastate*, rather than interstate, commerce, the state law should prevail.

Since this ruling in 2005, many local California governments have seized the opportunity to create new zoning ordinances to limit the expansion of marijuana dispensaries. In fact, one tactic commonly used by local governments to close down dispensaries involves calling the U.S. attorney's office. The U.S. attorney has the authority to order these shops to discontinue their operations under the threat of having their property forfeited or seized, as well as other criminal sanctions under federal law.

Despite the U.S. Supreme Court's ruling in *Gonzales v. Raich*, California courts have continued to try medical marijuana cases according to state law. For example, a 2009 case, *People v. Colvin*, involved a co-owner (William Frank Colvin) of two nonprofit medical marijuana dispensaries: Holistic I (in Santa Monica) and Holistic 2 (in Hollywood). The dispensaries are registered with the city of Los Angeles and have been incorporated for several years. In addition, they are often reviewed by local law enforcement to ensure that they meet the requirements and restrictions of the MMPA. Like other similar dispensaries, and in compliance with the MMPA, Holistic 1 and Holistic 2 grow some of their marijuana on-site but also belong to a cooperative that includes growers in Los Angeles and Humboldt. In March 2009, Colvin was less than a block from Holistic 2 en route to Holistic 1. He was stopped by police, taken into custody, and charged with violating state laws for possession of cocaine, sale or transportation of marijuana, and possession of marijuana. He was carrying an identification card for medicinal use and showed it to the arresting officer at the time. He also presented evidence to the trial court that he was registered to run the Holistic dispensaries.

The trial court judge agreed that Colvin's dispensaries seemed to be in compliance with both the CUA and the MMPA, which are still California law despite the *Raich* decision. Colvin's attorneys argued that he was only transporting the marijuana (one pound) from one dispensary to another. However, the trial court judge disagreed and ruled that the MMPA did not cover the transportation of marijuana. Colvin was found guilty of all three charges, placed on probation, and given community service. Colvin appealed this conviction, and the court of appeal determined that the transportation of marijuana from one dispensary to another fell within the scope of the MMPA, reversing the trial court's decision with respect to two of Colvin's convictions (transportation and possession; the cocaine conviction was not appealed).

However, both parties to a case have the right to appeal, and the state appealed the decision of the court of appeal. The California Supreme Court had to determine whether it would take the case and rule on its merits or if it would choose not to hear the case and allow the court of appeal decision to stand (remain in effect). In May 2012 the California Supreme Court denied review, noting that medicinal marijuana remains an issue that has important implications for local, state, and federal law. It also cited the many cases dealing with this policy issue that continue to be filed in the courts. This is an interesting case study in the principle of federalism, particularly in those circumstances in which state and national law clearly conflict over a very controversial issue.[8]

In January 2014 the U.S. Court of Appeals for the Ninth Circuit disposed of a number of cases involving medical marijuana use. In their "unpublished" memorandum, the court wrote that states have no special protection from federal law when it comes to use, including medicinal, of marijuana.[9] One month later, the Ninth Circuit disposed of the case *Sacramento Nonprofit Collective v. Holder*. Here, the plaintiffs argued that because nine western states permit the use of marijuana for medicinal purposes, it should be recognized as a fundamental right. The court chose to dismiss the case in favor of the federal government. In fact, it dismissed with prejudice: the plaintiffs in this legal action are prohibited from ever bringing the case back to the court.

In a federal system, like ours, what may seem to be the end of a story isn't necessarily so. In October 2015, Governor Brown signed the California Medical Marijuana Regulation Safety Act (MMRSA) into law. This new law puts into place several state regulations of medical marijuana that had not existed in the past. Various state and local level agencies are given oversight authority with respect to the cultivation of medical marijuana, the operations of dispensaries, and the licensing and practices of prescribing physicians.[10] Given all of the state and federal court cases involving this issue, it might seem as if California were picking a fight with the federal government. This is not the case. In December 2014, Congress passed the "Consolidated and Further Continuing Appropriations Act of 2015," which includes Section 538 that basically prohibits the U.S. Department of Justice from spending any funds to interfere with California's laws regarding medical marijuana, including cultivation, dispensing, and possession.[11]

Judicial Selection

California's court system is the largest in the nation. Serving on the bench requires (1) qualifications and (2) having been selected to serve. The qualifications for

The members of the California State Supreme Court are (from left to right) Mariano-Florentino Cuéllar, Kathryn M. Werdegar (retired August 2017), Carol A. Corrigan, Chief Justice Tani Gorre Cantil-Sakauye, Goodwin H. Liu, Ming W. Chin, and Leondra R. Kruger.

judges are the same for all three court levels. In California, potential judges must have at least 10 years of experience practicing law in the state of California or service as a judge of a court of record.

The selection process for judges to serve on the California Supreme Court and California Courts of Appeal is the same. Judges are initially nominated by the governor to serve on the appellate bench and are then approved by the Commission on Judicial Appointments. The Commission on Judicial Appointments consists of the chief justice of the supreme court, the attorney general, and a presiding judge on the California Courts of Appeal. In addition, all nominees for California's appellate courts are reviewed by the State Bar of California's Commission on Judicial Nominees Evaluation. This body evaluates the nominees by conducting thorough background checks on their qualifications as judges and as citizens. The governor may use the commission's decision as a source of information when making his or her selections but is not bound by the commission's findings. After a judge's appointment is confirmed, the judge holds office until the next **retention election**. To remain on the appellate courts in California, judges must win their retention elections. These elections are noncompetitive; the voters are simply asked whether the judge should remain on the appellate bench. If a judge does not receive a majority of affirmative votes, he or she is removed and the governor will appoint a new judge.

Likewise, judges serving on California's superior courts must face their non-partisan retention elections. However, their electoral process is different from the retention elections of sitting supreme court and courts of appeal judges. While appellate court judges run uncontested, simply against their own records, judges serving on California's superior courts can be challenged in their retention races. In addition, superior courts may have open seat races from time to time. These occur when a judge decides to retire close to an election. Finally, if an incumbent is up for retention and has no challengers, he or she may simply be declared re-elected; thus, no retention election is held.

Governors take advantage of opportunities to appoint judges to the courts by placing qualified jurists on the bench whose political beliefs most closely resemble their own. From time to time, a governor may be quite transparent about his or her preferences for those serving on the state supreme court. In the 1980s former governor George Deukmejian spoke out to the press and public about his desire to put more conservatives on the state supreme court because the liberals serving on the bench at the time were making decisions he vehemently disliked.

In addition, governors may have other political goals for the bench. They may, for example, seek to place more women and minorities on the supreme court so that it is more representative of the state's diverse population. Today's supreme court is diverse in regard to gender, race, and ethnicity; as of 2018 four of the justices are women, and five identify as persons of color or of more than one race. (See the "Who Are Californians?" feature on p. 198 for more on the diversity of California's justices.)

However, the court is not so diverse ideologically. Three of the six justices seated on the court were appointed by Republican governors. Generally, Republicans are more conservative than Democrats on issues of ideological preference, such as civil rights or civil liberties. For example, a liberal judge is more likely than a conservative judge to uphold laws that involve regulating business. This expectation, that ideology or party identification translates into differences in judicial decision making, is even more important when we consider issues such as same-sex marriage/LGBTQ rights, affirmative action, voting rights, freedom of expression, and capital punishment. Because the decisions of the California Supreme Court are binding on all persons residing in the state, the composition and dominating political ideology of the state's high court can be very important.

We may start to see some ideological shifts in the court. Since 2011, Governor Brown, a Democrat, has had the opportunity to appoint three justices, who will likely be more liberal than their predecessors. He has also demonstrated a commitment to diversifying the high court through his appointments. For example, in 2014 the governor announced his nomination of Mariano-Florentino Cuéllar to replace Justice Marvin R. Baxter, and the California Commission on Judicial Appointments unanimously confirmed the nomination. Cuéllar, who took office on January 5, 2015, is the first Latino immigrant appointed to the California Supreme Court.[12] Governor Brown has brought additional diversity to the bench by appointing an African American attorney, Leondra Kruger, who replaced Justice Joyce L. Kennard. Ms. Kruger was previously a deputy attorney general in President Obama's administration. Kruger is the first African American to hold a seat on the court since 2005.[13]

Judicial Elections

Unlike the federal judiciary, which consists of appointed judges who serve life terms with good behavior, many states, including California, have some form of election system for selecting their judges. Federal judges are appointed to allow for **judicial independence**. Theoretically, appointed judges are less likely to be influenced by politics in their decision making because they do not have to rely on the electorate to maintain their positions on the bench. Most states, however, have adopted some kind of election system for selecting or retaining their judges in order to secure **judicial accountability**. Elections allow voters to select members of the courts and to remove them for decisions contrary to the public's preferences.

Justices Corrigan and Kruger were on the November 6, 2018, ballot seeking retention. Both were re-elected. Justices Werdegar (retired), Liu, and Cuéllar faced elections in November 2014, and all successfully retained their seats on the bench. Over 70 percent of California voters supported Werdegar's retention, while Liu and Cuéllar received approximately 67 percent of all votes. Although the voters rarely pay much attention to competitive judicial races or retention elections, there have been instances when judges have lost their seats on the bench because of voters' perceptions about judicial rulings. For example, in the November 1986 election, six justices serving on the California Supreme Court were seeking retention. Governor George

Who Are California's Judges?

Since 2006, the Judicial Council of California has produced an annual report with information about the demographic characteristics of the state's justices and judges. Over time, increasing proportions of the judiciary have been women and people of color, although the proportions do not yet reflect the general population. The ethnoracial composition of the California bar (lawyers who are qualified to practice law in California) is heavily white, at 80.3 percent and just 5.9 percent Asian, 4.6 percent Latino, and 1.9 percent black; the bar is 40.6 percent female.

Justices and Judges in California, 2018

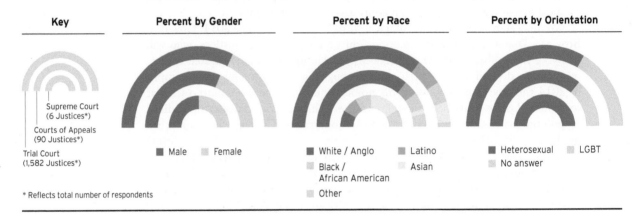

Key

Supreme Court
(6 Justices*)

Courts of Appeals
(90 Justices*)

Trial Court
(1,582 Justices*)

* Reflects total number of respondents

Percent by Gender
- ■ Male
- ■ Female

Percent by Race
- ■ White / Anglo
- ■ Black / African American
- ■ Other
- ■ Latino
- ■ Asian

Percent by Orientation
- ■ Heterosexual
- ■ No answer
- ■ LGBT

Gubernatorial Appointments, 1975–Present

- ■ Female
- ■ Latino
- ■ Black / African American
- ■ Asian
- ■ Democratic governor

Governor	0%	10%	20%	30%	40%	50%
Jerry Brown (2011–2018)						
Arnold Schwarzenegger (2003–2010)						
Gray Davis (1999–2003)						
Pete Wilson (1991–1998)						
George Deukmejian (1983–1990)						
Jerry Brown (1975–1982)						

forcriticalanalysis

1. Is it important for the judiciary to reflect the diversity of the California population? Why or why not?

2. Besides gender, ethnicity, race, and sexual orientation/gender identity, what other dimensions of diversity are important to consider and why?

SOURCES: "Demographic Data Provided by Justices and Judges Relative to Gender, Race/Ethnicity, and Gender Identity/Sexual Orientation," As of December 31, 2017, http://www.courts.ca.gov/documents/2018-JO-Demographic-Data.pdf (accessed 7/30/2018); The State Bar of California, "2017 Demographic Survey," http://www.calbar.ca.gov/Portals/0/documents/reports/ORIA/Survey-2017.pdf (accessed 7/30/18); and "Governor Brown Releases 2017 Judicial Appointment Data," Office of Governor Edmund G. Brown Jr., https://www.gov.ca.gov/2018/03/01/governor-brown-releases-2017-judicial-appointment-data/ (accessed 7/30/18).

Deukmejian spoke out against the retention of three of the six judges for their rulings on death-penalty cases and was especially critical of Rose Bird, the chief justice of the California Supreme Court at the time. While she served on the court, Bird participated in 61 death-penalty cases and voted every time to vacate the death sentence—an especially notable choice during a time of widespread public support among Californians for the death penalty. In fact, her appointment as chief justice occurred the same year that the death penalty was reinstated by a legislative override of a gubernatorial veto. One year later (1978), an initiative was adopted that expanded the number of special circumstances allowed for death-penalty cases. While she had many supporters, her decision making went against the tide of moneyed interests and those supportive of capital punishment.[14]

Governor Deukmejian warned Bird and two associate justices, Cruz Reynoso and Joseph Grodin, that he would oppose their retention elections if they did not change their rulings in death-penalty appeals and uphold the death-penalty sentences. Numerous interest groups and political action committees joined the governor's campaign against Rose Bird and her two colleagues. Political advertisements against the retention of Bird, Grodin, and Reynoso aired on radio and television. In response, Chief Justice Rose Bird produced a television ad explaining her decision-making record. Her explanations did not satisfy voters, however, and on November 4, 1996, Bird, Grodin, and Reynoso lost their seats on the California Supreme Court. Shortly thereafter, Governor Deukmejian appointed three justices to replace them, including Malcolm Lucas, who was nicknamed "Maximum Malcolm" for his rulings that sentenced convicted criminals to the maximum penalties, including death.

Despite their low visibility, judicial elections have many political scientists and jurists concerned, particularly over the amount of money being spent by candidates in them. A 1995 study of contested elections in Los Angeles County Superior Court reported that campaign spending by trial court judges had risen a great deal in the years between 1976 and 1994. In 1976 the median cost of a judicial campaign for a Los Angeles County Superior Court seat was approximately $3,000. By 1994 the median had skyrocketed to $70,000. Meanwhile, incumbents running for re-election spent, on average, $20,000 more than the median challenger, or $90,000. Compare that to the $1,000 median campaign expenditure of an incumbent in 1976.

The Civil Justice Association of California (CJAC), a group of citizens, taxpayers, and professionals, reviewed campaign contributions to the California judiciary from 1997 to 2000 and found the following:

- From 1997 to 2000, contributions to candidates in contested superior court elections totaled over $3 million for four counties.

- In a single race in Sacramento County, over $1 million was raised.

- Attorneys are the largest contributors to most judicial races.

- Two supreme court justices seeking retention in 1998—in uncontested elections—received contributions of $887,000 and $710,000.

The escalation of campaign spending in judicial elections is controversial because it usually requires judicial candidates to seek funding support from outside sources. Like candidates seeking election to state legislative or executive offices, judges now receive and even solicit financial support from organized interests. This phenomenon has even spilled over into retention elections for the state supreme court, even though these elections are noncompetitive. Judges must solicit campaign contributions to retain their seats on the bench. Contributors often include trial lawyers associations and other special interests. This connection has raised concern: financial contributions by interest groups to a judge's campaign increase the potential for influence over judicial decision making. The original intent by lawmakers in instituting elections for judicial candidates was to ensure judicial accountability to voters, not to the narrow preferences of an organized interest group. This concern has mobilized a national movement for reform. One of the most active reform advocates is former associate justice of the U.S. Supreme Court Sandra Day O'Connor. Retired justice O'Connor has been a vocal critic of state judicial elections because of the amounts that judicial candidates are soliciting and spending and because of the public perception that money buys influence.

Most people consider the judiciary to be the least political of all branches of government, yet the increased spending in competitive and noncompetitive elections for judgeships compromises this assumption. Even judges are expressing concern. In 2001 an opinion survey, "Justice at Stake Campaign," revealed that 53 percent of California judges are dissatisfied with the current climate of judicial campaigning in the state. Over 80 percent of the judges surveyed believed that voters knew little about candidates for the bench and were electing judges based on criteria other than qualifications for office. The majority of judges polled agreed that reform of campaign financing for judicial elections is necessary and that public financing of these elections would be an appropriate alternative.

In response to stories in the media—including a series of articles published in the *Los Angeles Times*—and the concerns of the public, judges, public officials, and others, the Judicial Campaign Task Force for Impartial Courts was established in 2007. It consists of 14 members appointed by former California Supreme Court chief justice Ronald M. George, and it investigates several issues, including the structure of California judicial elections as well as the filing, reporting, and accessibility of judicial campaign contributions and spending. The findings of this commission to date were reported in a 408-page volume in December 2009.[15] Many problems with respect to judicial campaigns and elections were documented, most notably the amount of money spent by candidates for judicial elections and, ironically, the poor quality or low level of information disseminated by judicial candidates to the public. In 2012 the commission released an update on the implementation of these 2009 recommendations. The following reforms have so far been successfully implemented:

- Judicial candidates are prohibited from making statements that commit or appear to commit them with respect to cases, controversies, or issues that could come before the courts.

- Judicial candidates may not knowingly misrepresent certain facts, including the identity, qualifications, or present position of themselves or an opponent.

- Any contributions to or expenditures of $100 or more by judicial candidates must be itemized.

- Judicial candidates for superior court may file a candidate statement to be included in the voter's pamphlet. These statements are very expensive, however, and the cost is prohibitive for most candidates.

There is one further caveat that should be mentioned. Whenever limits or rules are placed on campaign spending, the rights of freedom of expression and freedom of association guaranteed by both the California and U.S. constitutions may be abridged. Campaigning for political office is guaranteed by the right to speak freely, and in today's political contests, it is becoming increasingly expensive. It is almost impossible to impose limits on campaign spending. Therefore, judges running for retention on the California Supreme Court or running to serve on the state's trial courts must exercise their own restraint—not an easy task if your opponent or opposing forces are spending a lot of money to keep you off the bench. Added to this are concerns about the impact of the U.S. Supreme Court's 2010 ruling in *Citizens United v. FEC*. This decision allowed corporations and unions substantial freedom to spend money during elections through "independent expenditures." As long as corporations and unions do not coordinate their campaign advertising expenditures with candidates, they can spend practically without limits. In a 2011 report, "Spending in Judicial Elections: State Trends in the Wake of *Citizens United*," researchers suggested that California judicial politics may not be as influenced by this ruling as judicial elections in other states. The authors noted that the unions and corporations were already influential in the state's campaigns and elections.[16] Retention elections for the high court are uncontested and, therefore, spending remains relatively low. Moreover, most vacancies on all other state courts, including trial, are filled by gubernatorial appointment. Finally, campaign spending in trial court races is likely suppressed (compared with other states) because judicial incumbents are automatically re-elected if they are unopposed.

Removing Judges from the Bench

As we have already discussed in this chapter, voters may remove judges from the bench during an election. In addition, there are other means for removing judges in the case of public concern regarding judicial misconduct or judicial competency:

- **Impeachment** California's judges may be impeached by the Assembly and convicted by a two-thirds majority of the state Senate.

- **Recall election** Like the governor, California judges are subject to recall election petitioned by voters.

- **Regulatory commission investigation** The Commission on Judicial Performance may, after investigation of complaints regarding misconduct or incapacity, punish, censure, or remove a judge from office.

Contemporary Issues in the Judiciary

Change in the Court

The new justices appointed by Governor Brown influenced the court's patterns of decision making. The California Supreme Court had a conservative majority for a significant period of time, and Governor Brown appointed justices who are more liberal than their predecessors. This shifted the ideological direction of the state high court from a conservative majority to a liberal one.

Legislative Redistricting

Every term, judges serving on the California bench across all court levels (trial, intermediate appellate, and supreme) are confronted with cases that require them to make political decisions or decisions that have political consequences. One example of this is political redistricting. The redrawing of electoral districts is always a political process. Political parties seek either to maintain or to increase their odds of getting candidates re-elected through the redrawing of district lines. It is common for redistricting plans to end up contested in the courts by political parties, elected officials, candidates seeking political office, or organized special interests.

Since the 1980s the California courts have been involved in many cases and controversies regarding redistricting. Perhaps the most controversial occurred in 2005 when Governor Schwarzenegger and others proposed an initiative, Proposition 77, which would reform redistricting procedures in the state. Rather than having legislators redraw district lines after each census, the responsibility would be given to a panel of three retired judges (selected by legislative officials). This ballot measure was contested in the California Courts of Appeal before it even appeared on the ballot. Those opposed to the measure argued that judges should not have the power to redraw or create new political districts. Although there was some success with procedural challenges to the initiative in the courts of appeal, attempts to block the initiative from the ballot finally failed, and in November 2005 the voters vetoed the measure by a margin of approximately 19 percent, prohibiting retired judges from redrawing the state's electoral district lines.

Judicial Review and the Statewide Initiative

Another issue of concern regarding the judiciary in California is the relationship between direct democracy and judicial review. California is one of 26 states that allow citizens to propose and enact their own legislation through the initiative. Like any piece of legislation coming out of the state legislature, the initiative is subject to judicial interpretation and review. When the initiative is used to enact controversial policies—such as anti–affirmative action laws, a temporary tax to fund education, the decriminalization of marijuana, or term limits for elected officials—it is usually debated in the press and often contested in the courts. In fact, the constitutional validity of each of the initiatives mentioned above has been challenged in at least one court of law. The outcomes of these court cases have been varied. But most central to the controversy is the ability of state court judges, like judges on federal courts, to conduct judicial review. Judicial review is the power of a judge, on a state or federal court, to determine whether or not a law, agency policy, or some action of government is valid. When judges invalidate or overturn laws and policies they are often referred to as activists. We have already covered examples of judicial review in the beginning of this chapter when we briefly explored the legal battles between California and the Trump administration. We also witness judicial review in our discussion of California's policies on the use of marijuana. Judicial review and the statewide initiative puts this power in a starker contrast. When state judges have the power to overturn laws enacted by the people as well as laws composed by state legislators, the tension between lawmaking and law reviewing is heightened.

Is this tension all that important? Many scholars and many voters would argue that it is. In fact, the common opinion among the electorate in California is that the initiative as an alternative policy-making tool has become an exercise in futility, precisely because of legal intervention. The consensus among California voters is that once an initiative passes at the ballot box, it ends up in a court of law. In truth, courts are reactive bodies. Judges must wait until a case comes to their courtrooms to make a legal decision. So why do so many initiatives end up in the California courts? The answer is simply *politics*. California is a very diverse state, and our diversity can be measured in a number of ways. We are diverse in race and ethnicity, we are diverse in culture, we are diverse economically, we are even diverse in terrain and climate. Given so many dimensions of diversity, there is no dearth of conflict in our state regarding which political problems are important and which solutions to these problems should be adopted. Hence, California courts also function as an arena for the continuation of political debate.

For example, the United States Supreme Court's landmark ruling in *Obergefell v. Hodges* determined that the Fourteenth Amendment requires states to permit same-sex couples to obtain marriage licenses and to recognize the marriages of same-sex couples from other states. Although this case did not originate in California, the issue of same-sex marriage has been a subject of California politics for over a decade. It began in February 2004, when the county and city of San Francisco began to issue marriage licenses to same-sex couples. The following month, the California Supreme Court issued an injunction ordering San Francisco to stop issuing these licenses. Several pending cases regarding same-sex marriage were consolidated and some traveled through the courts separately. Groups organized in support of and in opposition to same-sex marriage as the cases percolated up to the California Supreme Court.

In May 2008 the California high court ruled in favor of gay and lesbian couples, finding that denying them the right to civil marriage violated the state constitution. Meanwhile, opponents to same-sex marriage drafted an initiative, "Prop. 8," which was adopted by 52 percent of the voters. Proposition 8 amended the California Constitution to exclude same-sex marriage. All of these events, which occurred over a relatively short period of time, were part of the broader national debate regarding rights of same-sex couples to legally marry.

Legal challenges to Proposition 8 were brought very quickly. A federal district court found Proposition 8 unconstitutional. There were subsequent appeals, and the case went all the way to the United States Supreme Court in *Hollingsworth v. Perry*. At issue was whether or not Proposition 8 violated the United States Constitution's Fourteenth Amendment rights to due process and equal protection. The Supreme Court did not decide these constitutional questions, however, because they determined that the petitioners, Hollingsworth and others, did not have standing and therefore couldn't bring this suit before the Court. The effect of the Supreme Court's ruling, even though it did not answer the questions on the merits, left lower-court decisions in place. Same-sex couples had the right to marry in California. Two years later this right was extended to gay and lesbian couples in all states in the *Obergefell* decision.

Caseload

While the caseload for all court levels in California has recently begun to decline after increasing over a period of several years, it remains very high when compared with other state court caseloads. And while the superior courts and appellate courts have managed this load fairly efficiently, there are legitimate concerns about the system's ability to continue to do so, given the state's continued fiscal crisis. As noted earlier, from 2015 to 2016 approximately 6.2 million cases were filed in California superior courts (trial courts of general jurisdiction).[17] There are many reasons for the high caseloads in the state court system. Following are a few examples: California, like many other states, has modified its laws to allow juveniles to be tried as adults in some criminal cases. Although the intent of this law may have been to let juveniles know that California has little tolerance for certain types of crime, regardless of the defendant's age, the effect has been to shift cases from the courts of judges who deal exclusively with juveniles to the already overburdened courts handling crimes involving adults. In addition, victims' rights legislation, which has elevated some misdemeanors (nonserious crimes) to felonies (serious crimes), increases not only the severity of the penalties for the accused but also the workload for the courts. California's three strikes law, originally enacted to punish repeat offenders, has had a similar impact. Keep in mind that these are just a few reasons for the high number of court cases in California.

To be sure, most of the cases filed in California's civil courts will be resolved through negotiation between the parties and their attorneys. For example, in 2015–16 almost 80 percent of unlimited jurisdiction civil cases were resolved without trial, while 92 percent of limited jurisdiction civil cases were disposed of before trial.[18] However, the courts must still process the paperwork and deal with the other administrative issues that each civil case may involve.

Similarly, most of the cases in the state's criminal courts will be resolved through plea bargaining, despite what we see in film or on television. Full court trials for the prosecution of high-profile crimes, like that of Conrad Murray, the personal physician found guilty in 2011 of involuntary manslaughter of his patient, singer Michael Jackson, are rare. A plea bargain is the norm. Even so, the courts are still involved in the process. Even if a criminal case never goes beyond the formal filing of charges against a defendant, judges are part of a plea bargain. As a referee, the judge's job is to determine if the plea bargain is appropriate and if the defendant entered into the plea bargain knowingly. If the judge decides that the terms of the plea bargain are inappropriate, that the defendant's ability to comprehend the terms of the plea was compromised, or that the plea was not entered into voluntarily, then a new plea may have to be negotiated, or the case may actually go to trial. Regardless, a single case in the criminal courts involves many people, from clerks to administrators and, of course, a judge.

Despite this incredible workload, California's criminal courts typically resolve cases involving felonies within 12 months (85 percent were resolved in 2015–16). Civil cases are also resolved fairly quickly; on average, 75 percent of civil cases filed in a given year are resolved within 12 months. Most recently, California superior courts reported disposing of 95 percent all civil cases within the 2015–16 fiscal year.

While these are impressive figures, problems remain. The lack of resources in some local court jurisdictions, especially in smaller localities, and the impact of the current budget crisis on the state's judiciary as a whole affect access to the courts and can compromise the quality of legal representation for indigent persons.

California Courts: Where Are We Now?

A number of issues currently confront California's courts. As discussed earlier, chief among these issues is the court system's ability to manage its caseload as the state continues to face a tenuous fiscal situation. Courts are subject to constraints similar to those that affect state agencies. It is fairly easy to argue that the greatest of these constraints, aside from jurisdiction, is the state's economy and budget. In recent years, the court system in California has found itself constrained by the extraordinary challenges of the state's budget. Chapter 8 discusses the budgetary process and its political implications in greater detail, but here we can examine the impact of this budgetary crisis on the courts.

Taken at face value, a discussion about budgets and courts may not appear all that interesting. However, when Governor Brown signed the budget on June 27, 2012, it included $6 billion of automatic cuts—hundreds of millions to the court system—severely affecting both day-to-day operations and future construction plans. It is important to note that these cuts come on top of other actions that have been taken to reduce the size of court administration throughout the state. Because most courts are located at the local level, counties and municipalities have taken the brunt of these budget cuts. Responses to the ramifications of these cuts have included threatened strikes by state court administrative personnel and the elimination of some innovative, albeit controversial, programs at the local level. One such program focuses on nonviolent misdemeanor crimes by juvenile offenders in the Los Angeles area. This program is part of a relatively recent legal movement known as "problem-solving justice," or the good courts movement. It served as an alternative to traditional, more punitive, forms of addressing juvenile low-level crime. The nontraditional court served more than 100,000 children each year, but it has been shut down by the county because of budget cuts.[19]

In addition, Chief Justice Tani Gorre Cantil-Sakauye has had to respond to some criticisms by organized interests and other parties about wasteful spending on projects and the growth of the state's Administrative Office of the Courts (AOC). The Alliance of California Judges, established in 2009, has been pressuring the chief justice and the judicial council to respond to past and present budget cuts more proactively and to pay closer attention to wasteful spending, predicting (accurately) that, like his predecessors, Governor Brown would include more cuts to the state courts' budgets in the new fiscal year. More specifically, this organization targeted the now defunct electronic Court Case Management System. According to the *Courthouse News Service*, "Even as trial courts were closing, the [Judicial] Council voted repeatedly, with only one or two dissenting votes, to continue pouring hundreds of millions into that now failed IT project. That money came primarily from trial court funds." The same article claims that over half a billion dollars was spent before the Court Management Case System was terminated.[20]

On top of this, Chief Justice Cantil-Sakauye released a report "prepared by a committee of state judges" in late May 2012 criticizing the AOC for understating the number of its employees and for paying "hundreds" of its personnel six-figure salaries. The report noted that this growth in both size and salaries paid was taking place during a hiring freeze. The investigation concluded, among other things, that the AOC had circumvented the hiring freeze and had violated some of its own personnel rules; it recommended significant cuts to the staff and organizational consolidation to allow for more oversight and, presumably, more efficiency.[21]

Additionally, reforming judicial campaigns in the state is also a critical agenda item. Some attempts at reform, such as campaign finance reporting, have been implemented and have not been found unconstitutional. However, when voters amended the state constitution in 1986 to prohibit political parties from endorsing judges who run in nonpartisan elections, the California Supreme Court found the initiative unconstitutional because it violated Californians' rights to freedom of expression and freedom of association. Obviously, judges have a lot of say when it comes to these reforms, and it is up to the individual judge to decide how much is too much when it comes to campaign spending.

Finally, there is the vacancy that remains on the court since Justice Werdegar's 2017 retirement. The court has been able to manage its workload by having judges from the lower appellate courts sit in. As of March 2018, 56 judges from California's intermediate courts of appeals served as "pro tem justices" (pro tem means temporarily) on the high court. Before leaving office Governor Brown did not announce an appointment to this vacant seat.[22]

Study Guide

FOR FURTHER READING

Bonneau, Chris W., and Damon Cann. "Campaign Spending, Diminishing Marginal Returns, and Campaign Finance Restrictions in Judicial Elections." *Journal of Politics* 73 (October 2011): 1267–80.

Bonneau, Chris W., and Melinda Gann Hall. *In Defense of Judicial Elections.* New York: Routledge Press, 2009. This book is a critique of previous empirical studies of judicial elections. Bonneau and Hall argue that elections as a selection method for judges are actually beneficial to democratic society.

California Courts. "Guide to California Courts." www.courtinfo.ca.gov/courts. Accessed 9/27/12.

Civil Justice Association of California. "Campaign Contributions to the California Judiciary 1997–2000." http://cjac.org/assets/finalrept2000.pdf. Accessed 8/16/12.

Hall, Melinda Gann, and Chris W. Bonneau. "Attack Advertising, the *White* Decision, and Voter Participation in State Supreme Court Elections." *Political Research Quarterly* 66 (March 2013): 115–26.

The National Center for State Courts (NCSC). www.judicialselection.us. Accessed 10/3/16.

Streb, Matthew J., ed. *Running for Judge: The Rising Political, Financial and Legal Stakes of Judicial Elections.* New York: New York University Press, 2007. This book is a collection of contemporary research conducted by professors who study state courts and judicial elections. Each chapter examines current issues and controversies that are confronted by state courts and state court judges.

Streb, Matthew J., and Brian Frederick. "When Money Can't Encourage Participation: Campaign Spending and Rolloff in Low-Visibility Judicial Elections." *Political Behavior* 33 (2011): 665–84.

ON THE WEB

California Courts. www.courts.ca.gov. Accessed 11/27/18. This is the official website of the California court system.

The California Supreme Court Historical Society (CSCHS). http://cschs.org. Accessed 11/27/18. CSCHS catalogs and archives information about the history of the California Supreme Court.

Institute for the Advancement of the American Legal System. http://iaals.du.edu/. Accessed 11/27/18.

The National Center for State Courts (NCSC). www.ncsc.org. Accessed 11/27/18. NCSC is an organization that provides services for court administrators, practitioners, and others interested in state courts. The website includes information, data sets, and articles about state courts and court-related topics.

SCOTUSblog (Supreme Court of the United States blog). www.scotusblog.com. Accessed 7/30/18. SCOTUSblog is a website that provides legal analysis of pending and decided cases of the United States Supreme Court. It also includes hyperlinks to case materials such as litigant briefs, amicus briefs, oral argument, and opinions.

SUMMARY

I. Structure of the California courts.
  A. Court rulings, such as the recent rulings on undocumented immigrants, can affect all Californians.
  B. Superior courts are the trial courts of the California court system. They are courts of "first instance" and triers of fact. The California Courts of Appeal are intermediate appellate courts. They are divided into six districts across the state. All cases except for death-penalty cases are first appealed to the California Courts of Appeal.
  C. The supreme court is the highest court in the state. It is composed of seven justices and, like the courts of appeal, is an appellate court—that is, it reviews cases that were first heard in lower state courts such as the courts of appeal or a superior court.
  D. Jurisdiction limits the types of cases that civil courts and criminal courts can hear. Criminal courts deal with violations of state and local laws, and civil courts hear cases involving disputes between individuals or classes of individuals.
  E. Access to California courts is widely available. However, there is concern about the cost of litigation and legal representation.
  F. Federalism and California courts.
    1. Legal challenges to Proposition 215, the Compassionate Use Act (CUA), illustrate the tension between state and federal government. California permits the use of medical marijuana under certain conditions, but the federal government does not. There have been frequent attempts by federal law enforcement to close marijuana dispensaries that are operating legally under the CUA.
    2. Some local governments are adopting ordinances to regulate or even prohibit dispensaries from operating in their communities. At times, local governments will call on federal law enforcement to assist them in closing dispensaries.
    3. The California courts currently have a number of cases across all levels examining this policy.

II. Judicial selection.
  A. Methods of selection for the California courts include nonpartisan elections for superior court and merit selection for appellate courts.
  B. The California courts are diverse in terms of gender, race, and ideology. Governor Brown has appointed three justices to the court: Goodwin Liu, Mariano-Florentino Cuéllar, and Leondra Kruger. These appointments may give him the opportunity to shape the decision making of the California Supreme Court for years to come.
  C. There are two competing theories regarding judicial selection—appointment and election. Those who favor judicial independence argue that appointment is a better method for selecting judges because it insulates judges from politics. Conversely, those who favor accountability argue that election as a method of selection is essential in a democracy and that judicial elections allow citizens to hold judges accountable for their decision making, similar to the way other elected officials are held accountable for their actions in office.
  D. Controversies about judicial campaigning and campaign finance have led to some high-profile jurists (for example, retired U.S. Supreme Court associate justice Sandra Day O'Connor) and others to call for reforms. The most radical reforms proposed would eliminate judicial elections entirely. The increasing cost of judicial campaigns, which are low-saliency and low-turnout elections, have many members of the bar and legal community concerned.
  E. Methods of removal from the bench include recall elections and impeachment. In addition, because all judges in California face some sort of election (direct or retention), voters may choose to vote for another judicial candidate or they may choose to vote against retaining an appellate court judge.

III. Contemporary issues in the judiciary.
  A. Governor Brown's appointments of Goodwin Liu, Mariano-Florentino Cuéllar, and Leondra Kruger to the bench has shaped and influenced the court's decision making.
  B. Justice Werdegar's seat on the bench remains vacant.
  C. Judges serving across all court levels are confronted with cases that require them to make political decisions and often exercise the power of judicial review.
  D. State judges have the power to overturn laws enacted by the people through the initiative as well as laws composed by state legislators. There is a very strong likelihood that contested initiatives will end up in the courts, and the courts serve as an arena for continued political debate.
  E. California courts have a very high caseload, though they remain fairly efficient and are able to dispose of a significant percentage of their criminal and civil caseload at all court levels.

PRACTICE QUIZ

1. All death-penalty sentences are automatically appealed directly to the California Supreme Court for review.
   a) true
   b) false

2. The California Supreme Court is similar to the U.S. Supreme Court in that it has nine justices.
   a) true
   b) false

3. Most civil cases in California are resolved before going to trial.
   a) true
   b) false

4. Voters in California are highly informed about the candidates running in judicial elections.
   a) true
   b) false

5. Initiatives passed in California are not subject to either judicial interpretation or judicial review.
   a) true
   b) false

6. In recent years, campaign spending in judicial elections
   a) has increased.
   b) has decreased.
   c) has remained the same.
   d) cannot be determined.

7. Chief Justice Rose Bird and associate justices Cruz Reynoso and Joseph Grodin were voted out by citizens who were angry about the judges' decisions concerning
   a) same-sex marriage.
   b) the death penalty.
   c) Proposition 13.
   d) term limits.

8. Judges selected by the governor to serve on the supreme court and the courts of appeal in California must be approved by
   a) the state legislature.
   b) the attorney general.
   c) the Commission on Judicial Appointments.
   d) none of the above

9. Superior courts in California adjudicate which of the following types of actions?
   a) civil and criminal cases
   b) only civil cases
   c) only criminal cases
   d) only appeals

10. One method of removing judges in the state of California is
    a) removal by the governor.
    b) censure by the state legislature.
    c) agreement between the speaker of the Assembly and the attorney general.
    d) a recall election.

CRITICAL-THINKING QUESTIONS

1. Given the concern on the part of lawmakers and the public over the role of money in judicial elections, what kinds of reforms might be implemented that would still allow for accountability? Is it possible to keep money and special interests out of judicial elections?

2. What factors do you believe are responsible for the tremendous criminal caseload in the California superior courts?

3. Is judicial independence important for state court judges?

4. What kinds of checks have been placed on the California judiciary? How do the other branches and political actors hold the state courts accountable?

KEY TERMS

appellate jurisdiction (p. 190)
civil courts (p. 192)
judicial accountability (p. 197)
judicial discretion (p. 190)
judicial independence (p. 197)
retention election (p. 196)
superior courts (p. 189)

8 The State Budget and Budgetary Limitations

WHAT CALIFORNIA GOVERNMENT DOES AND WHY IT MATTERS

Why does student tuition keep rising? The answer is simple: higher education is a major category of the state budget, the third or fourth largest in most years, and charts circulating among politicians in Sacramento made it look as if California students until recently paid relatively low tuition and fees by national standards. The charts came from the Legislative Analyst's Office and the California Postsecondary Education Commission (CPEC), a research agency created by the legislature to be independent of the three systems of higher education. Everyone involved in higher education policy saw these charts: the governor's department of finance; the legislative committees and their staff; the bureaucracy; and two of this book's authors, who were members of the California State University (CSU) statewide academic senate for several years. After seeing these charts, legislators on the hunt for an extra several hundred million dollars to cut from the budget felt justified in saying, "Well, the students are paying relatively little by U.S. standards; just increase the university's fees to cover the difference."

And that was the process that occurred, year after year, for about a decade. Meanwhile, the inequalities have increased. University of California (UC) students pay for more than half their education cost; California Community College (CCC) students cover 15 percent. The Legislative Analyst's Office found that "UC's tuition and fees are higher than all but 10 of the 65 largest public research universities in other states. By contrast, tuition and fees at the CSU are lower than all but 42 universities among a group of 244 masters-level public universities in other states. CCC tuition and fees are the lowest in the country. . . ."[1] As the legislative analyst has stated several times, the "state currently does not have a tuition policy." Instead, when economic times are good, tuition and fees are frozen, but when the inevitable downturn comes, fees and tuition rise sharply. What kind of budget process produces such inequalities over time?

Ultimately, over the four years from 2008 to 2012, higher education lost $2.8 billion in funding (about 22 percent of its total), and by 2018, despite limited increases granted by the governor, the CSU had 19 percent less money to spend than it had in 2007-08.[2] Similar statements can be written about the University of California.

Figure 8.1 contrasts state spending on higher education with state spending on prisons and corrections. Forty years ago the state spent almost 18 percent of the state general fund on higher education and less than 4 percent on corrections. By 2008-09, the shares were almost equal at 11.1 percent on higher education and 10.7 percent on corrections. Since then, higher education spending has increased a bit and corrections spending has fallen, in part because the state has shifted inmates from state prisons to locally funded jails.

Students aren't the only citizens heavily affected by California's budget woes. With a budget of over $169 billion, plus almost $100 billion in federal funds, California represents one of the largest economies in the world. Its *deficit* in recent years has been larger than the entire budgets of all but the 10 largest states. Over

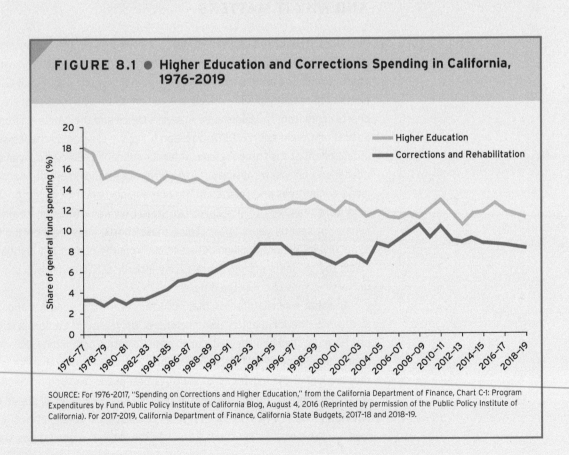

FIGURE 8.1 ● Higher Education and Corrections Spending in California, 1976-2019

SOURCE: For 1976-2017, "Spending on Corrections and Higher Education," from the California Department of Finance, Chart C-1: Program Expenditures by Fund. Public Policy Institute of California Blog, August 4, 2016 (Reprinted by permission of the Public Policy Institute of California). For 2017-2019, California Department of Finance, California State Budgets, 2017-18 and 2018-19.

2.5 million workers in California (1 out of 6) work for the federal, state, or local governments, and a number of other workers are indirectly funded by the public sector.[3]

It is therefore unsurprising that the process to approve a budget that controls the livelihood of so many people is controversial. The public itself is split—most Californians are opposed to spending cuts in public programs as well as to increases in taxes or fees. They are also distrustful of state government and disapprove of the job their politicians are doing. One political party in the state legislature—the Republicans—won't increase taxes under any circumstances; indeed, some Republicans consider the entire budget so illegitimate that they won't vote for it under any realistic set of circumstances (one legislator didn't vote for a budget for over a decade). In 2002 the legislature came within one vote of increasing the sales tax, but that vote was impossible to obtain. The amount and intensity of political controversy over the state budget, a document that embodies the values and decisions of the citizens, its legislature, and its leaders, is truly remarkable.

Passing the budget is at the center, both in difficulty and in scope, of what the state government does each year. Since the passage of Proposition 13 in 1978, the state government has received less revenue than it would have otherwise, and that revenue has become more volatile, rising and falling with the economy. The state constitution mandates that the legislature pass the budget by June 15. Since 1990 the legislature has met this deadline in only 12 of 29 years. Two of those were budget surplus years, when it is always easier to pass a budget. Eight others occurred after the passage of Proposition 25 in 2010. Proposition 25 requires only a majority vote to pass the budget and penalizes legislators by cutting their salaries when the budget is overdue.

How Is the Budget Formed?

The process of forming a budget has four steps. Most governments today follow a similar process—proposal by the executive branch, enactment by the legislature, approval by the governor, and implementation by the executive branch. Note that the preparation, enactment, and implementation of the budget for a single fiscal year takes almost three calendar years. See Box 8.1 for a summary of the budget process and Box 8.2 for the constitutional requirements for California's budget. The four steps of the budget process are discussed in detail below.

Executive Proposal

Each fall, state agencies send their budget proposals to the governor through the state **Department of Finance**. The governor formulates a proposal and sends it to the legislature in January. In late spring, he or she revises the proposal in what is called the **May revise**.

Before 1922, agencies proposed their budgets directly to the legislature; there was no **unified budget** proposed by the governor or anyone else. Instead, "budgeting

BOX 8.1 ● California's Budget Process

CALENDAR YEAR 1

JULY–SEPTEMBER

- Agencies prepare requests and make proposals.
- Requests sent to Department of Finance.

OCTOBER–DECEMBER

- Department of Finance reviews requests and consults governor.

CALENDAR YEAR 2

JANUARY–MARCH

- California Constitution requires governor to send a balanced budget to the legislature by January 10.
- Governor's budget proposal is introduced in both houses as identical budget bills.
- Legislative Analyst's Office prepares extensive analysis.
- Budget hearings held in both houses.

APRIL–JUNE

- May: Governor sends revised and updated projections of revenues and expenditures to legislature (the May revise).
- June 15: California Constitution requires legislature to pass (by a majority vote) a balanced budget by this date. As of 2010, all members of the legislature permanently forfeit salary and expenses every day until the budget is passed.
- Governor signs budget, using line-item veto, if desired, to lower any appropriation items. Legislature can override by a two-thirds vote.

JULY–SEPTEMBER

- July 1: California's fiscal year begins. This is the first quarter. (The federal fiscal year, in contrast, begins October 1.)

OCTOBER–DECEMBER

- Second quarter of California's fiscal year.

CALENDAR YEAR 3

JANUARY–MARCH

- Third quarter of California's fiscal year.

APRIL–JUNE

- Fourth quarter of California's fiscal year.

was the domain of interest groups, department heads, and ranking committee members."[4] In 1911, upon finding little or no justification for the amounts contained in the appropriations bills sent to him, Progressive governor Hiram Johnson created the Board of Control to advise him on the fiscal justification for each appropriation.

In 1922, California adopted its own version of new federal legislation that had been passed the previous year, thus *unifying* the budget process. The legislation called for a consolidated administration proposal in the form of a **governor's budget** that must be balanced, contain justifications for the amounts proposed, and be accompanied by bills introduced by legislative leaders in each house, thus providing a starting point for the negotiations and decisions each year. The existence of a governor's budget was an improvement over the situation before 1900, when "government structures . . . hid more than they revealed to the public."[5]

Legislative Adoption

The legislature adopts a balanced budget based on the governor's proposal. As of 2011 both the Assembly and the state Senate must adopt the budget by a majority of the entire membership. The Assembly and Senate budget committees and their subcommittees hold hearings on the budget bills, during which they receive testimony and input from individuals and groups, including the affected departments and agencies, the Department of Finance, the **Legislative Analyst's Office**, committee staff, and interest groups.

The Legislative Analyst's Office provides nonpartisan and independent review of the entire budget, including alternative ways to accomplish the same goals and objectives. The reviews are so nonpartisan that former legislative analyst Elizabeth

Hill was called the "Budget Nun" because of her "incorruptible" fiscal reports. Respected columnist George Skelton of the *Los Angeles Times* said about the reports that "They're the bible. The one source of truth. . . . She's the most influential non-elected official in the Capitol."[6] The current legislative analyst, Mac Taylor, was appointed in 2008 and has 30–plus years of experience in the Legislative Analyst's Office.

Before 2011 a **Budget Conference Committee** was appointed to work out the differences between the Assembly and Senate budget bills. Since the passage of Proposition 25 in 2010, however, a majority vote is now the sole requirement to pass the budget; the endless compromising with the Republican Party that used to occupy Sacramento through the summers of the 1990s and 2000s is over. The "Big 5" group, consisting of the governor, Assembly speaker, Senate president pro tempore, and Assembly and Senate minority leaders, used to be instrumental in soliciting a few Republican votes to pass the budget under the old two-thirds requirement. Their influence in the budget process is now largely irrelevant, or at least it has been in the first few years under the new system. From 2011 to 2018 the budget was passed by June 15, the official deadline in Proposition 25; if legislators miss this deadline they lose their salaries for every day that the budget is late.

Raising a tax, however, still requires a two-thirds vote of both the Assembly and the state Senate (or the approval of the majority of the voters through an initiative). While the Democrats achieved majorities of over two-thirds in both the Assembly and Senate in 2012, the voters approved Jerry Brown's initiative proposal on the November 2012 ballot, Proposition 30, to raise the state sales and income taxes in the same year. Because of this new source of revenue, Governor Brown strongly urged the legislature not to pass any additional tax increases in 2013. The two-thirds supermajority disappeared in early 2014 after three Democratic state senators were suspended for their involvement in various scandals. In 2017 the Democratic party again had a two-thirds majority in the Assembly and state Senate and passed an increase in the gas tax and related fees to repair roads and bridges and accomplish other transportation-related tasks. Proposition 6 on the November 2018 ballot was a referendum on the increases, and it failed by a vote of 43 percent to 57 percent.

Gubernatorial Action

The governor may use the **line-item veto** to lower any line-item appropriation in the budget, including lowering it to zero. The legislature may override the governor's veto by a two-thirds majority in each of the two houses and replace the lowered number with its own amount, although doing so is rare. Because of the line-item veto, the final budget is usually very close to the governor's May revise proposal.

Implementation

Agencies implement the budget as passed, with the fiscal year beginning July 1. The Department of Finance states explicitly that agencies and departments are expected to operate within their budgets and comply with any provisions enacted by the legislature: There is some flexibility in implementation, but, compared to other states, the governor's flexibility is limited, as we shall see.

Other Groups Involved in the Budget Process

In addition to the governor and legislature, the agencies mentioned earlier—the Department of Finance on the executive side and the Legislative Analyst's Office on the legislative side—are closely involved in the budget process, as are two other groups:

- The courts have sometimes ruled on the constitutionality of particular budget actions, particularly on proposed administrative actions to be taken when the legislature has been late submitting a budget. They have also had to decide on the constitutionality of various budget provisions, such as the limits on property taxes established by Proposition 13 in 1978.

- **Moody's, Fitch Ratings, and Standard & Poor's** rate the ability of the states to repay their bonds. A "bond" is a loan in which the investor is lending the government a certain amount of money for a certain length of time at a certain rate of interest. The rating is one of several factors that influence the cost of selling a bond issue. The lower the credit rating, the higher the interest rate that must be paid to induce investors to purchase the bonds. In 2003, Moody's rating of California's bonds was the lowest rating given for any state, but since then California's credit rating has risen. Standard & Poor's raised California's credit rating in 2015, reflecting the budget discipline imposed by Governor Jerry Brown during his administration. However, 27 of the 39 states rated in 2018 still have a higher credit rating than California's. The 2018 ratings have come up to the AA level, meaning the state's bonds are of high quality but with more fluctuation or long-term risk than bonds at the AAA level. Of more significance perhaps was Moody's test in early 2016 of the four most populous states and their ability to withstand a potential recession in the next two years. Of the four (Texas, Florida, New York, and California), California was the least able because of revenue volatility and inadequate reserves.[7]

What Is in the Budget?

Every state budget contains the following information:

- economic assumptions—how the economy should respond during the forthcoming fiscal year, and what that response means for revenues and expenditures
- revenues expected in the various categories
- expenditures broken down by department and program

Revenues

The **general fund** includes all state revenues that are *not* **federal funds**, special funds, or bond funds. (See Box 8.3 for more on federal funds.) The state budget is usually assumed to consist of either just the general fund or the general fund plus special funds and bond funds. The general fund receives over 90 percent of its

BOX 8.3 ● Federal Funds

The 2018-19 budget included $106 billion in federal funds, almost three-fourths of which was intended for use in the health and human services category. Most of this was for Medi-Cal, California's Medicaid program (medical care for the poor). About $7 billion of the total was for labor and workforce development, mostly federal funds to supplement the Unemployment Insurance program. Another large portion was for education. None of the $106 billion included the additional $290 billion the federal government spent in California on wages and benefits for California-based federal employees, Social Security payments, Medicare payments to doctors, hospitals, and other providers (for those 65 and over, and some of those with disabilities), procurement contracts (defense and others), grants to universities and nonprofits, and so forth.[a]

Federal dollars are important to states during economic downturns, when states often cut back their budgets to meet balanced budget requirements. Federal money for unemployment insurance and stimulus packages typically increases substantially during recessions. Federal money received in California increased from $52.9 billion in 2006-07, just before the great recession of 2008-09, to $91.5 billion in 2010-11, according to the California Budget Project.[b]

Reports from the state controller's office indicate that cities in California received about 4 percent of their total income in 2016 from federal funds, and counties received some 16 percent, about $11 billion. Counties receive more because in California they are responsible for administering state and national health and welfare programs.[c]

Does California receive more from the feds than it pays in taxes? In spite of the large amounts discussed above, the answer is "no," because no wealthy state gets back more from the federal government than it pays in taxes. Federal funds, in general, redistribute money from wealthier states to poorer ones.

Many federal programs are based on population counts, and in 2018 the U.S. Census Bureau proposed asking whether respondents of the 2020 Census were citizens, a factor certain to reduce California's population count, since an estimated 2.5 million of California's 40 million citizens are undocumented. The results could affect both California's representation in the U.S. House of Representatives, based on the census, and the funds received from various federal programs.

[a]Legislative Analyst's Office, "Federal Spending in California," Sacramento: Legislative Analyst's Office, 2017.
[b]California Budget Project, "How Are Federal Dollars Spent in California?" https://calbudgetcenter.org/wp-content/uploads/111117_How_Are_Federal_Dollars_Spent_pb.pdf (accessed 7/25/2018).
[c]Controller's Office, State of California, 2014a, "Cities Financial Data," https://cities.bythenumbers.sco.ca.gov/#!/year/default; and Controller's Office, State of California, "Counties Financial Data," https://counties.bythenumbers.sco.ca.gov/#!/year/default (accessed 7/25/18).

$100 billion–plus revenues from the sales tax, the income tax, and corporate taxes and consists of all state money that is not allocated to a special fund or a bond fund. **Special funds** are funds that are allocated for a specific purpose; thus, there is a beverage container recycling fund, a fish and game fund, and almost 500 more, totaling some $58 billion in the 2018–19 budget. As well as a specific use for which the fund is designated, each also has a specific source of income. **Bond funds** come from bonds that are repaid over spans of a few years to a few decades, though some of them substitute for current expenditures.

Looking at all sources of revenue—both general funds and special funds—we see the revenue sources are as follows, according to the 2018–19 enacted budget (see Figure 8.2).

PERSONAL INCOME TAX Figure 8.2 shows that the **personal income tax** provides 50 percent of California's state budget, some $97 billion. California's personal income tax ranges from 0 to 13.3 percent of income, with a substantial credit per child or dependent. The income tax is considered highly **progressive**, with the top 1 percent of taxpayers paying about half of the income tax most years. The wealthiest 10 percent paid 80.4 percent of the income tax in 2012.[8] This is one of the most progressive personal income taxes in the nation. (See the "Who Are Californians?" feature on the next page for more on how California's income tax figures into its total revenue as compared to other states.) Regular income (salaries and wages) does not vary that much from year to year, but **capital gains** income (income from selling stock that has appreciated in value, for example) varies considerably from one year to the next, making revenues from the income tax fluctuate a great deal. Proposition 30 established three new brackets for taxpayers who make more than $305,100 per year: at 11.3, 12.3, and 13.3 percent of income. They make the California state income tax even more progressive. Proposition 55 on the November 2016 ballot extended those "temporary" brackets for 12 years.

SALES TAX Figure 8.2 shows that the **sales tax** provides about 20 percent of California's state budget, almost $39 billion. The baseline state sales tax rate is 7.25 percent. Counties or taxing districts are allowed to add between 0.13 and 0.5 percent per local district for local services. In some areas there is more than one district tax in effect. The average sales tax in California is 8.5 percent. The minimum in any area is 7.5 percent. The maximum is in eight cities at about 10 percent. Economists consider the sales tax **regressive**—that is, as individual or household income increases, the proportion of income paid through the tax decreases because lower-income households spend a higher proportion of their incomes on consumption goods that are taxed compared with higher income households. In California, the state refunds 1.25 percent of its share to the local city and county; this feature

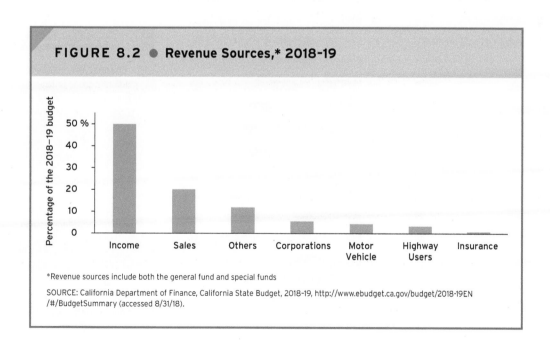

FIGURE 8.2 ● Revenue Sources,* 2018–19

*Revenue sources include both the general fund and special funds

SOURCE: California Department of Finance, California State Budget, 2018-19, http://www.ebudget.ca.gov/budget/2018-19EN/#/BudgetSummary (accessed 8/31/18).

Where Does California Get Its Revenue?

There is wide variation in how states fund their programs and activities. Sources of state revenue usually include individual income taxes, sales taxes, property taxes, and corporate taxes; most states also collect a variety of smaller taxes, including gasoline and cigarette taxes. Fifteen states don't levy property taxes at all, while four states (Nevada, Texas, Washington, and Wyoming) don't levy taxes on individual incomes.

Share of State Tax Revenue

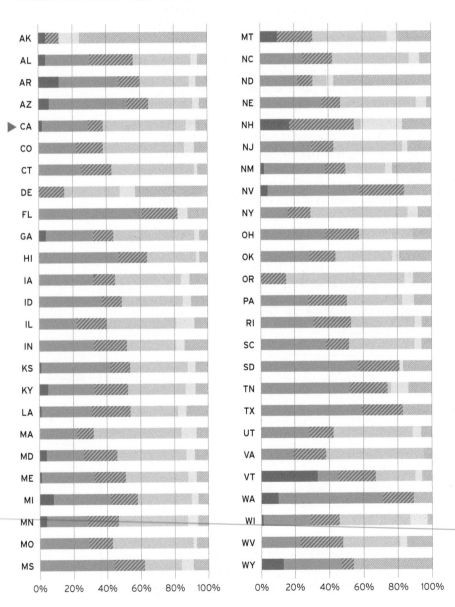

Legend:
- Property tax
- Sales tax (general)
- Sales tax (selective)
- Individual income tax
- Corporate net income tax
- License tax and other

SOURCE: Ben Casselman and Allison McCann, "Where Your State Gets Its Money," FiveThirtyEight, www.fivethirtyeight.com/features/where-your-state-gets-its-money/ (accessed 8/17/18).

forcriticalanalysis

1. How does the distribution of different types of taxes in California compare to the distribution of taxes in other states? For example, why do you think property tax makes up a smaller share of revenue in California than in New Hampshire?

2. California's largest revenue source, individual income taxes, is structured as a progressive tax: those with larger incomes pay larger percentages. Is this the best system, or would the state be better served by a flat income tax?

has led many cities to search for businesses that are both clean industries and have a high sales volume (thus increasing sales-tax revenue), such as **big-box shopping centers and automobile dealerships**. A "clean industry" is one that produces little air or water pollution. The process has been called the **fiscalization of land use**.

A state sales tax has existed in California since 1933, with the rate raised on average every five years. In 2013, Proposition 30 temporarily raised the state sales tax one-quarter of 1 percent. The increase would have expired in 2016 but was extended by Proposition 55 on the November 2016 ballot.

The sales tax was developed over 75 years ago and is based on an older conception of the economy consisting mostly of goods that are manufactured, bought, and sold. Services make up over half of the modern economy, but these are not taxed in California. In many states, at least some services are taxed. Having a broader base on the sales tax would enable the rate to be lowered from its current high level, but finding a two-thirds majority in the legislature to pass a tax reform act is close to impossible. Even in recent years, when the Democratic Party at some points had a two-thirds majority in both the Assembly and the state Senate, the Democrats were unwilling and not unified enough to modernize the tax code. As a result, every year the proportion of the state revenue total composed of the sales tax goes down slightly. In 2016–17 the sales tax was 23 percent of revenues; in 2018–19 it was 20 percent.

PROPERTY TAX Property tax revenues go to the local level of government, so they are not included in Figure 8.2. All property owners pay California's property tax, limited under Proposition 13 to 1 percent of the assessed value in 1975 or the value of a more recent sale. Once acquired, annual tax increases are limited to 2 percent or the amount of inflation, whichever is smaller. Proposition 13 passed overwhelmingly in 1978 and contains provisions requiring special majorities greater than 50 percent for legislators and voters to raise taxes. Proposition 13 rolled back property taxes in California by more than half, and the state has endeavored to make up the difference ever since. Local property tax revenue available for cities, counties, and school districts has been substantially reduced. As a result, all local government entities are more reliant on the state for revenue, and decision-making power has substantially shifted, in the eyes of virtually all observers, from the local level to the state level.

School districts are an excellent example of the effects of this shift. Whereas California once had some of the best-quality and best-funded schools in the nation, its expenditures per pupil have fallen in comparison to the rest of the nation. Its staff-per-student ratio is now 70 percent of the average for other states. Its student achievement levels lag behind the rest of the nation, and a greater proportion of high-income families send their children to private schools compared to the pre-1978 period. At the same time, teacher salaries are relatively high to accommodate California's cost of living and housing prices, and to attract good-quality recruits to the profession.

Compared to other states, California's overall tax structure depends more on taxes that are volatile, rising and falling with the economy (income tax, sales tax), and less on taxes that don't vary with the economy (property tax) because of Proposition 13's limits. The average state obtains 31 percent of its total state and local tax funds from the property tax, but because of Proposition 13's limits, California obtains only 25 percent.[9] (See Box 8.4 for a more detailed explanation and assessment of Proposition 13.)

California's public schools have suffered since the passage of Proposition 13, which decreased local property tax revenues and effectively transferred the responsibility for funding school districts from the local to the state level. Overcrowded classrooms have been one result of this shift.

CORPORATION TAX The corporation tax is levied on corporate profits and provides about 6 percent of state revenues, some $12 billion. The corporation tax structure is cited favorably by *Governing* magazine in its appraisal of the state's tax system as "tough on the creation of tax-dodge subsidiaries, and the law covers a firm's property and assets, not just its sales."[10] Like the income tax, the corporation tax is mostly paid by corporations earning high profits; the top 1,000 or more pay 70 percent or more of the total.[11]

INDIAN CASINOS Governor Schwarzenegger attempted to increase the amount of revenue received for the general fund from Indian gambling operations in California. In 2005–06 the state received only $27 million for the general fund of the $301 million from the tribal–state gambling compacts negotiated by the governor and ratified by the legislature. In 2008–09 the governor's budget projected $430 million in revenues, but much less was actually received. More recent budgets have no information on Indian gambling revenues, as they are so small as to be insignificant (less than one-tenth of one percent) in a budget of more than $200 billion.

STATE LOTTERY Lottery monies received by the state and allocated to education, approximately $1.6 billion in 2016–17, would be meaningful if the state added them to the education budget. Instead, research shows that in California, as in other states, "lottery funds have merely substituted for normal levels of appropriations, despite the fact that lotteries had been promoted as boosting spending for education," according to the North Carolina Center for Public Policy Research.[12]

Why Do Revenues Vary So Much?

California's budget rises and falls each year, soaring when the economy is healthy and plunging in even the mildest recessions. Here is why:

- Revenues from the sales tax and the personal income tax depend directly on how the state economy performs each year.

BOX 8.4 ● What Exactly Is Proposition 13?

What is it? Proposition 13, passed overwhelmingly by the voters in June 1978, contained the following provisions:

- All property taxes were rolled back to a maximum of 1 percent of the value of the property in 1975–76.

- The value of the property, and thus the tax paid, was allowed to increase by the rate of inflation, but the inflation rate was capped at 2 percent per year.

- When ownership changed, property would be revalued at the current market value.

- No new property taxes could be imposed, either by the state or by local governments.

- Any "special taxes" could be imposed only by a two-thirds margin of the voters in the particular area (the state legislature was already under a two-thirds approval rule for raising taxes, a rule in force since 1933).

- All property taxes collected were to be distributed "according to law," but because no such laws existed, the legislature had to create them.

THE EFFECTS OF PROPOSITION 13

Proposition 13 immediately affected local governments. Before 1978, local governments and agencies each established their own property tax rate, designed to produce sufficient revenues to accomplish the particular function of the agency. Now, each agency's property tax rate was irrelevant; the state would decide "according to law" how much money to apportion to each local jurisdiction. The total property tax collected decreased by over half. The state, however, had a $55 billion surplus, which helped bridge the gap in funds for several years.

The single biggest change set in motion by Proposition 13 is that the state assumed considerable authority over issues formerly handled by local government.[a] Local governments used to set the local tax rate to produce sufficient funds for public services necessary to the locality. Instead, those decisions are now made by the state, and "clearly, the property tax is now really a state tax."[b]

Another consequence stems from the provision that requires a two-thirds vote of the local area to impose or raise a tax. Many localities have seen election results of 60 to 66 percent in favor, just short of the required two-thirds, and have been powerless to initiate local projects, such as acquiring land for parks. Bond issues for the repair and construction of school facilities, however, were authorized by Proposition 39 in 2000 to require the approval of only 55 percent of local voters.

One of the most important consequences is called "the fiscalization of land use"–that is, the tendency of local governments not only to evaluate land use changes in terms of how much money will be brought to the local government but to make decisions on that basis. Because localities receive a share of the state sales tax, land use changes that produce a lot of sales tax revenues are preferred. Many cities favor big-box shopping centers and auto malls over housing developments, and rely increasingly on development fees and other ways to obtain revenue not available through the property tax.

Finally, we have seen the development of many "arcane" financing techniques, those so intricate that no one understands them except the few who developed them. These are also designed to help obtain revenues and replace property taxes.

(continued)

A Legislative Analyst's Office (LAO) study[c] completed in 2016 debunks some common claims about Proposition 13 and provides the best evidence on its current effects. Following the enactment of Proposition 13 and its 1 percent of assessed value property tax limit in 1978, property tax payments fell by 60 percent in California. The LAO study confirms that similar properties purchased at different times pay vastly different property taxes, depending on when the owner purchased the property. Higher-income Californians tend to own more homes and homes of greater value, and they therefore receive the majority of the tax relief dollars provided by Proposition 13. Property turnover has declined considerably since 1978, with Proposition 13 appearing to play some, but not the total, role in this decline.

One of the most significant findings was that homeowners pay only a slightly higher share of property taxes now compared to the period before 1978, and that residential properties do not turn over more than commercial properties. One of the justifications for the proposed split roll reform of Proposition 13, in which commercial properties would be taxed at different and presumably higher rates than residential properties, was that residential properties were thought to be sold and resold at faster rates than commercial properties.

[a]The best description of Proposition 13 and its implications is Jeffrey I. Chapman, "Proposition 13: Some Unintended Consequences," Public Policy Institute of California, www.ppic.org (accessed 7/27/12).
[b]Chapman, "Proposition 13," p. 22.
[c]Legislative Analyst's Office, "Common Claims About Proposition 13," www.lao.ca.gov/Publications/Report/3497 (accessed 7/31/18).

- Compared to other states, the budget relies more on the personal income tax, the capital gains portion of which soars when stock options are cashed out, than on the property tax, which was limited in 1978 by Proposition 13 and is roughly constant every year.

How Well Does the Tax System Function?

The tax system seems to be functioning poorly. Little has changed since *Governing* magazine published "The Way We Tax" in 2003, comparing tax policy in all 50 states. The report gave California one star out of four in the category "Adequacy of Revenue," two out of four in "Fairness to Taxpayers," and two out of four in "Management of System."[13] Only Tennessee received a lower overall rating, and four other states were tied with California.

A more recent study of tax administration, conducted by the Council on State Taxation (COST) and published in December 2013, ranked California's tax administration in 49th place, tied with Louisiana, and graded it a D–. The study cited errors such as permitting the same people to serve on the boards at different levels of tax appeal and allowing officials unqualified in tax administration onto those boards.[14]

Is California Overtaxed?

THE CONSERVATIVE VIEW Conservatives think California is overtaxed. The California Taxpayers Association makes the case that "the extraordinary level of taxation in California can provide more than enough in tax revenue to fund police and fire services, education for our children, and public works projects and health and welfare services for California's poor."[15] Taxes are so high, in their view, that the state is no longer economically competitive with other states. The Washington, D.C.–based Tax Foundation, which calculates the total tax burden, including taxes paid out of state (for vacation property, for example), found California's state and local tax burden for fiscal year 2012 to be the sixth highest in the nation.[16]

THE LIBERAL VIEW Liberals often argue *not* that California's taxes are low, but that they are moderate in comparison with California's income, ranked 15th to 20th among the states. The California Budget & Policy Center, for example, stated in 2014 that California was a "moderate" tax state, ranking 20th among the 50 states "with respect to total 'own source' revenues raised by state and local governments." California ranked 11th in the percentage of state taxes compared with personal income in the state in 2010–11. Personal and corporate income tax collections are relatively high in California, but the tobacco and alcoholic beverage taxes are relatively low.[17]

THE REALITY California is a relatively rich state, but one with significant numbers of relatively poor citizens. Its household and median family incomes are some $8,000 higher than the U.S. averages, but 14.3 percent of Californians are poor by the official statistics, and the Stanford Center on Poverty and Inequality calculates that almost two-fifths of Californians are poor or near-poor. The income and sales tax rates are among the higher tax rates of all American states, although there are numerous exemptions that bring the total tax rate lower.

The critical challenge to California's tax structure is not that taxes are high but that the tax structure is outmoded. It reflects the economy of the 1950s and Proposition 13 decisions made in the 1970s. The property tax collects less money proportionally than other wealthy states because of Proposition 13. The sales tax is based on the purchase of goods (with food exempted), not of services. Lower- and middle-class families with children are largely exempted from the personal income tax. The bottom line is that, like so many areas of the state's governmental structure, California's tax structure needs to be reformed.

Betty Yee, California state controller, established a Council of Economic Advisors on Tax Reform in 2015 to discuss the problems of California's present tax structure. Since Proposition 13 was approved in 1978, policy makers have adopted incremental changes to California's taxes, but no comprehensive restructuring has been adopted. Meanwhile, revenues from the sales tax, the corporation tax, and the property tax have diminished relative to the size of the economy, and the resulting increasing emphasis on the personal income tax has led to greater unpredictability of state tax revenue and increasing challenges for budget policy makers. The commission found that comprehensive reform of the state's tax structure was long overdue and sought in its findings to discuss the underlying principles and tradeoffs that would be necessary in any legislation, without discussing actual proposals.[18]

Without comprehensive tax reform, California will continue to be a battleground for both liberals and conservatives, with conservatives seeking to lower the highest rates, and liberals seeking exemptions for the poor and middle class.

Technology company Google has its global headquarters in Mountain View. Despite talk of California's unfriendly business climate, California ranks second for the number of Fortune 500 companies located in the state, with 53, exceeded only by New York's 54.

Conservative groups rate California's business climate as one of the worst of any state because of the high levels of taxes; the taxation of capital gains at regular tax rates; and the number of regulations and permits affecting citizens' ability to establish, run, and expand a business.[19] Nevertheless, many large corporations are located in California, particularly in Silicon Valley (the area between San Francisco and San Jose) because of the wealth of skilled talent in the area's labor market.

One question is whether California's tax levels hold down the state's economic growth. An analysis of the growth rates of nine states with high personal income taxes compared to the nine states that lack any personal income tax indicates no conclusive relationship. In fact, the states that grow the most seem to be those with high rates of population growth, and several of the non-income-tax states have economic resources (such as oil, which obviates the need for a state income tax) not available to other states.[20] Many observers point to the healthiness of California's recovery from the 2008 recession, especially compared with other states, as evidence that high tax rates do not correlate with low economic growth.

Expenditures

Figure 8.3 depicts the 2018–19 state budget, including the general fund, special funds, and bond funds.

It indicates that the largest spending category is health and human services (HHS), at 32 percent of the budget and some $64 billion. This category includes the state (but not the federal) contribution for Medi-Cal, California's Medicaid program, which provides health coverage for the poor as well as for senior citizens in nursing homes. It also includes the public health system; Healthy Families, California's state children's health insurance program; welfare, including Temporary Assistance for Needy Families; and the state contribution to food stamps and to the Women, Infants, and Children (WIC) supplemental food program, among many others.

The second largest expenditure category in Figure 8.3 is elementary and secondary education, at $57 billion and 28 percent of total expenditures. With the passage of Proposition 13 in 1978, a gradually increasing proportion of the state general fund has been spent on K–12 education. The money in this category supplements property tax revenues for education, collected by each county.

Higher education is the third largest category at $17 billion and 8 percent of total expenditures. Higher education in 2018 includes funding for the community college system (115 campuses, 2.1 million students), the CSU system (23 campuses, 484,000 students), and the UC system (10 campuses, 5 medical centers, 3 national labs, 238,000 students).

Since 1980–81 there has been a downward trend in the proportion of the budget devoted to higher education, as discussed in the beginning of this chapter. In the late 2000s and early 2010s, state funding for higher education was cut severely. A

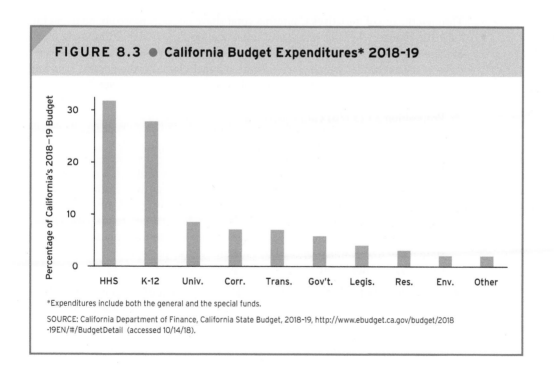

FIGURE 8.3 ● California Budget Expenditures* 2018-19

*Expenditures include both the general and the special funds.

SOURCE: California Department of Finance, California State Budget, 2018-19, http://www.ebudget.ca.gov/budget/2018 -19EN/#/BudgetDetail (accessed 10/14/18).

report from the Public Policy Institute of California demonstrates that funding for higher education composed more than 17 percent of the state budget as recently as 1975, but since then the proportion has declined to between 11 and 13 percent.[21] Another report, from the Center on Budget and Policy Priorities in Washington, D.C., compares spending-per-student cuts and tuition increases in all states from fiscal years 2008 to 2013.[22] All but two of the states cut their expenditures per student during this time period, and California is in the middle of the pack with a 29.5 percent cut. California's tuition increase percentage for the same time period, at 72 percent, is the second largest among the states. Governor Jerry Brown has recently augmented the higher education budgets, partially restoring the millions that were cut from higher education in the 2000s.

The fourth largest category is corrections and rehabilitation, which includes funding for state prisons and youth authorities. At $15 billion and 7 percent of the budget, this category increased steadily from 1980–81 through the mid-1990s as the public demanded the three strikes law and similar measures. It has since leveled off.

The fifth largest category is transportation, at $15 billion and 7 percent of the budget. It includes money for Caltrans, mass transit projects, and subsidizing Amtrak.

The balance of the categories in Figure 8.3 are all 6 percent or less of the budget, including general government administration; the legislative, executive, judicial category; the natural resources category (e.g., state parks); and areas covering state expenditures for the environment. The last category is "other," covering everything else.

Budgetary Limitations

Through the use of initiatives California voters have not only passed bond issues but have also limited what the state government can do in very significant areas. Many of these initiatives, such as Propositions 99, 111, 49, and 71, have placed money into various "special funds," which is why Figure 8.3 includes both the general fund and special funds. Here are a few of the most significant initiatives, by date.[23]

- **Proposition 13 (1978)** cut property taxes to 1 percent of the assessed valuation of the property in 1975 and allows reassessment only when the property is sold. If justified by inflation, the tax can rise a maximum of 2 percent between assessments.

- **Proposition 4 (1979)** limited the state government's growth from one year to the next to the percentage growth in the cost of living and the percentage increase in population. Any excess funds are to be returned to taxpayers. The state must also reimburse local governments for the cost of complying with state mandates. It was proposed by Howard Jarvis's partner, Paul Gann, and called "The Gann Limit."

- **Proposition 98 (1988)** requires that at least 40 percent of the general fund be devoted to K–14 education, including community colleges; annual increases are to be at least equal to the increase in school enrollment and the cost of living.

- **Proposition 99 (1988)** mandated a 25-cent tax on cigarettes, with the proceeds to be spent on antismoking campaigns and medical research.

- **Proposition 111 (1990)** increased the gas tax and trucking fees; the proceeds must be spent on transportation projects.

- **Proposition 218 (1996)** requires voter approval before local tax increases and prohibits property-related fees for general government services.

- **Proposition 49 (2002)**, supported by then potential Republican candidate for governor Arnold Schwarzenegger, requires that several hundred million dollars be spent on after-school programs.

- **Proposition 71 (2004)** authorizes the sale of $3 billion in bonds to fund stem-cell research in the state.

- **Proposition 22 (2010)** banned the state government from balancing the state budget by borrowing or taking money raised by local governments in California. The state had taken some $5 billion the previous fiscal year.

Of these, the two that have had the most effect are Propositions 13 and 98. Proposition 13 has made the state budget more reliant on taxes that vary with the economy and less reliant on sources of income that don't vary with the economy, particularly the property tax. Proposition 98 dictated that a certain proportion of the budget, almost half when higher education is included, must be devoted to one policy area.

Because the initiative requires only a majority vote, it is relatively easy to authorize expenditures through the initiative compared with doing so through the legislature. California has become a state in which it is easy to lower taxes or budget items through the legislature or to authorize expenditures through the initiative, but in which it is increasingly difficult to raise the funds to pay for basic state functions, including higher education and health. Voters in recent public opinion surveys find most items in the budget to be popular (except welfare), but they strongly resist paying extra for any of them.

Recent California Budgets and the Budget Process

In recent years, California lawmakers and the governor have closed the budget gap with the standard techniques used in other states—incremental (small) tax or fee increases; cuts in education, health, and social services (which make up the largest portions of the budget); and borrowing through bond issues that are repaid over a 5- to 10-year period to cover a portion of the yearly deficit. The capital gains tax produced extra funds for the budgets of 2013–14 through 2018–19, making the process easier, although Governor Jerry Brown strongly resisted legislators' push to make agencies that had been cut substantially in the previous decade "whole" again. Governor Brown also insisted that the state begin repaying the funds borrowed during the last decade to close budget gaps.

California Forward, a bipartisan group aimed at fixing some of California's perennial budget process problems, stated in 2008 that

> the current budget process is largely a relic of the mid-20th century, with the focus on how much to increase spending (or how much to cut), rather than the value that

public services bring to Californians over time. The ongoing and chronic imbalance between revenues and expenditures is one indicator of system failure. Changing how budget process decisions are made could enable public leaders to deal with the more intractable and complex problems involving the revenue system and the state–local relationship.[24]

They identify, as we have, the key problems of budgeting:

> The costs of operating state programs are growing faster than the revenue base that supports them. The revenue system is highly sensitive to changes in the economy, producing significant volatility. The single-year budgeting horizon encourages short-term fixes, rather than long-term solutions. The budget does not take a strategic approach to ensure a return on public investments and there is a lack of public and legislative review of how money is spent.[25]

Many commentators noted the cumulative effect of the fees and caps that have been proposed more and more frequently in recent years.[26] Traditionally, California tried to supply sufficient services for all, on the principle that "if you're eligible, we'll serve you." The community colleges guarantee, for example, that any high school graduate can go to college. That principle has been shifting though. The Schwarzenegger budget for 2004–05 included caps on the number of individuals who could be served in various programs; immigrants in Medi-Cal and the program that supplies drugs for those with HIV/AIDS were both capped at the level of January 1, 2004. Both the CSU and UC have limited admissions in significant ways in the twenty-first century. California's fees for students attending CSU and community colleges used to be among the lowest in the nation, but they have increased substantially in recent years. Measures are often proposed as emergency measures, but few emergency measures have been repealed in the past.

In short, the lowered expectation for services has become particularly apparent in the Arnold Schwarzenegger and Jerry Brown eras but has been in the background for the last two decades or more.

The California Budgetary Process: Where Are We Now?

We retain some optimism about California's fiscal prospects, but we temper it by concurring with Governor Brown's forecast that more recessions will come in the future, and at a time that cannot be forecast. Brown has insisted that California live within the means that the voters have provided. Now that budgets are easier to balance, the governor has insisted that the budget surpluses from the capital gains tax be used to provide the state with a rainy day fund (Proposition 44 on the November 2014 ballot) and to repay some of the bonds that were floated to pay for the deficits of the 2000s under Governor Schwarzenegger. Unfortunately for all of us, tax revenue still retains its tendency to soar in good times and plunge deeply in bad ones. It would be better to reform California's tax system, but this possibility is remote; any meaningful reform would engender substantial opposition.

The biggest fiscal problem facing the state is the voters' willingness to approve propositions (initiatives) that allocate money from the general fund or establish a special fund without having a funding source. Some of these are self-serving; others have more merit. While some initiatives divert money from the general fund by setting up special funds, others simply state that the money for a certain purpose shall be a specific amount to be paid from the general fund; this reduces the funds available for existing programs. Higher education in particular has been hurt by these actions.

Study Guide

FOR FURTHER READING

Barrett, Katherine, Richard Greene, Michele Mariani, and Anya Sostek. "The Way We Tax." *Governing*, February 2003.

California Budget & Policy Center. "2018–19 State Budget Invests in Reserves and an Array of Vital Services, Sets Course for Future Advances." June 2018. https://calbudget center.org/resources/2018-19-state-budget-invests-in -reserves-and-an-array-of-vital-services-sets-course-for -future-advances. Accessed 7/25/18.

———. "An Incomplete Vision: Putting the Governor's Proposed 2014–15 Budget in Context." California Budget & Policy Center, February 2014. https://calbudgetcenter.org /blog/new-from-the-cbp-an-incomplete-vision-putting -the-governors-proposed-2014-15-budget-in-context. Accessed 9/27/18.

———. "Principles and Policy: A Guide to California's Tax System." California Budget & Policy Center, April 2013. https://calbudgetcenter.org/wp-content/uploads/0902 _Californias_Tax_System.pdf. Accessed 9/27/18.

———. "Who Pays Taxes in California?" California Budget & Policy Center, April 2015. https://calbudgetcenter.org/wp -content/uploads/Who-Pays-Taxes-in-CA_Issue-Brief _04.14.2015.pdf. Accessed 9/27/18.

California Taxpayers Association. "Cal-Tax: Taxes Are a Heavy Burden in California." http://digital.library.ucla.edu/web sites/2004_999_003/dynamic/downloads/individual _download_file_link_1_english_10.pdf. Accessed 7/25/18.

Johnson, Hans. "Defunding Higher Education. What Are the Effects on College Enrollment?" Public Policy Institute of California, May 2012. www.ppic.org/main/publication.asp ?i=988. Accessed 7/25/18.

League of Women Voters of California. *Guide to California Government*. 16th ed. Sacramento: League of Women Voters of California, 2015.

Legislative Analyst's Office. "California's Tax System: A Primer." April 2007. https://lao.ca.gov/2007/tax_primer/tax_primer _040907.pdf. Accessed 7/25/18.

———. "Federal Spending in California." January 18, 2017. https://lao.ca.gov/Publications/Report/3531/1. Accessed 7/25/18.

Oliff, Phil, Vincent Palacios, Ingrid Johnson, and Michael Leachman. "Recent Deep State Higher Education Cuts May Harm Students and the Economy for Years to Come." Washington, DC: Center on Budget and Policy Priorities, May 2013.

Public Policy Institute of California. "Just the Facts: California's State Budget: The Enacted 2018–19 Budget." Public Policy Institute of California, July 2018. www.ppic.org. Accessed 7/25/18.

———. "Just the Facts: Proposition 13, 40 Years Later." Public Policy Institute of California, June 2018. www.ppic.org. Accessed 7/25/18.

ON THE WEB

California Budget & Policy Center. http://calbudgetcenter.org. Accessed 7/31/18.

California Forward. www.cafwd.org. Accessed 7/31/18.

Howard Jarvis Taxpayers Association. www.hjta.org. Accessed 7/31/18.

Legislative Analyst's Office. www.lao.ca.gov. Accessed 7/31/18.

Public Policy Institute of California. www.ppic.org. Accessed 7/31/18.

State of California, Department of Finance, Budget Update Site. www.ebudget.ca.gov. Accessed 7/31/18.

State of California, Department of Finance. http://dof.ca.gov /Reports/Demographic_Reports. Accessed 7/31/18. California statistics and demographic information.

SUMMARY

I. How is the budget formulated?
   A. Agencies send their requests to the governor each fall.
   B. The governor sends a balanced budget request to the legislature each January for the fiscal year starting the next July 1.
   C. The legislature adopts a balanced budget by June 15 each year for the fiscal year to start July 1.
      1. In recent years, the volatility of the state's revenues has caused the budget to be substantially readjusted during the fiscal year.
      2. If the budget is not passed by June 15, members of the legislature forfeit their pay and travel reimbursements for each day until it is passed. As a result, budgets have been on time since 2010, when this condition was enacted.
   D. The governor has a line-item veto, allowing him or her to reduce any line-item dollar amount downward, even to zero. However, the governor may not raise any line item.
   E. The legislature is assisted by its own neutral budget office—the Legislative Analyst's Office.
   F. If the Assembly and state Senate versions of the budget differ, a "budget conference committee" will attempt to iron out the differences.
   G. Agencies then implement the approved budget, including specific policy or budget studies to be carried out and presented to the legislature.

II. What is the California budget?
   A. The budget is the governor's and legislature's views of the future.
      1. The future of the state's economy (economic assumptions).
      2. The future income of the state (revenues).
      3. The future spending of the state (expenditures).
   B. The budget is at the center of the state's activities each year.

III. Revenues.
   A. Personal income tax—the largest source of income for the general fund, highly progressive, and subject to extreme volatility because of its dependence on taxes derived from capital gains.
   B. Sales tax—the next largest source of income. Local governments can add a small amount to the state sales tax. A portion of the tax, in addition, is refunded to them. Many localities have added businesses to their communities that produce sales tax, such as big-box shopping centers and automobile dealerships, specifically because of the revenues they then receive from the state.

   C. Corporate tax—the third-largest source of revenue. Most corporate taxes are paid by the larger corporations in the state.
   D. Property tax—severely limited by Proposition 13, composes only 22 percent of California's state and local total tax revenues.
   E. The California tax system is volatile compared to the tax systems of other states. It depends on the ups and downs of the economy and produces surges in revenue when the economy booms and precipitous falls when a recession takes place.

IV. Expenditures.
   A. Health and Human Services is the largest budget category, driven by state expenditures for Medi-Cal and other health programs.
   B. Education (K–12) is the second-largest single expenditure and second-largest budget category. Proposition 98 requires that 40 percent of the state general fund be designated for K–12 expenditures.
   C. Higher education is the third-largest budget category; it includes expenditures for the community colleges, the California State University, and the University of California.
   D. The fourth largest category is corrections, followed closely by transportation.

V. Box 8.4 describes Proposition 13 and its restrictions on how property is taxed in California. Among the effects of Proposition 13 was an increased power for the state over local government and the "fiscalization of land use." Conservative groups supporting Proposition 13 strongly resist change, and legislators and interest groups seeking to change it have had little success. A proposal to split the tax roll and place a higher rate on commercial property has faced great opposition from the business community.

VI. Limitations on the budget.
   A. The most substantial limitations have come from initiatives passed by the voters.
   B. Proposition 13, which limits the property tax to 1 percent of the value of one's house, and Proposition 98, which guarantees a certain amount to K–12 education, are the most important of these limitations.
   C. Cumulatively, these budget limitations have limited well over half the general fund and at least half of all expenditures, giving the governor and legislature less flexibility than they would have in other states. This is precisely the intended goal of initiatives—to limit the powers of the governor and legislature. The level of distrust the voters have for the governor and legislature is high in California.

VII. Recent state budgets have been characterized by huge and fluctuating gaps between revenues and expenditures.
  A. These gaps have made it difficult to find the middle ground necessary to obtain a two-thirds vote in the legislature for a budget. But starting in 2011, with only a majority required, the budget has been passed more or less on time. The last six years, 2013–14 to 2018–19, had surpluses because of a surge in income tax (capital gains) revenues. Governor Brown insisted that some of this money be set aside for a rainy day fund, to be used when revenues inevitably turn downward, and that some of the money should repay the bonds used to balance the budget during the 2000s.

VIII. What is the future of budgeting in California?
  A. California seems to have turned a corner, with several budgets in a row passed on time and more or less balanced. The surge in revenues from the capital gains tax is being used to pay back old debt and to create a rainy day fund for the future.
  B. The biggest fiscal problems facing the state continue to be the willingness of the voters to approve propositions (initiatives) that allocate money from the general fund or establish a special fund without having a funding source, and the volatile mix of revenue sources.

PRACTICE QUIZ

1. Both the governor and the legislature are obliged by the California Constitution to pass a balanced budget.
   a) true
   b) false

2. The state of California cannot pass its budget in 2019–20 unless the Assembly and state Senate pass the budget by
   a) 50 percent plus one vote.
   b) 55 percent.
   c) 66.7 percent.
   d) 75 percent.

3. The state of California cannot raise state taxes unless the Assembly and state Senate pass the relevant law by
   a) 50 percent plus one vote.
   b) 55 percent.
   c) 66.7 percent.
   d) 75 percent.

4. Proposition 13 requires
   a) property taxes to be lowered to the level when the property was last sold. Property tax values can rise 2 percent per year.
   b) property taxes to be set at 1975 levels; property is reassessed when it is sold. Property tax values can rise as much as 2 percent per year.
   c) property taxes to be lowered to 1945 levels; property is reassessed when it is sold. The level of the tax can rise 3 percent per year.
   d) Property taxes to be raised to the appropriate level when the properties on both sides of a house or business have been sold—all the property is then reassessed at current values. The level of the tax can rise 2 percent per year if the properties are not sold.

5. Proposition 98 requires education spending to be at least
   a) 50 percent of the entire state budget.
   b) 50 percent of the general fund.
   c) 33.3 percent of the general fund.
   d) 40 percent of the general fund.

6. What is the general fund?
   a) The general fund includes all revenues that are not otherwise allocated into special or bond funds.
   b) The general fund includes all tax revenue.
   c) The general fund includes all state revenue, including special and bond funds.
   d) The general fund includes all state revenue except bond funds, because these are used to construct state facilities and are paid back over a period of several decades.

7. The governor's line-item veto allows
   a) the governor, if desired, to lower any appropriation item.
   b) the governor, in conjunction with an agency, to veto any bill in its entirety.
   c) the governor to "pencil out" any line or sentence in any bill.
   d) the governor to raise or lower any appropriation item, including lowering the item to zero.

8. The governor's line-item veto may be overridden by a 50 percent plus one vote in both houses of the legislature.
   a) true
   b) false

9. The credit rating assigned to the state of California by Moody's, Fitch Ratings, or Standard & Poor's is important because
   a) the credit rating influences the size of California's deficit or surplus in any given fiscal year.
   b) when the credit rating goes down, the interest rate that the state pays to float its bonds goes up.
   c) when the credit rating goes up, the amount of interest the state pays goes down.
   d) all of the above

10. Indian gambling revenues have become a significant source of income for the state of California.
    a) true
    b) false

11. The lottery is a significant source of income for K–12 education.
    a) true
    b) false

CRITICAL-THINKING QUESTIONS

1. How might California's tax system be made more predictable and less dependent on the economy than it is now? How might *Governing* magazine rate your proposed changes?
2. How should the budget process in California be reformed, assuming it should be reformed? What goals are important in reforming the process, and what changes in the process might achieve those goals?
3. Should the governor have more authority in the budget process? What reforms might help with the long-term budget process in California?
4. The other major player in the budget process is the legislature. How might the legislature's consideration of the budget be changed to make California's budget more predictable and timely?
5. How might the tax system be reformed to make it less volatile from year to year?

KEY TERMS

big-box shopping centers and automobile dealerships (p. 219)
bond funds (p. 216)
Budget Conference Committee (p. 214)
capital gains (p. 217)
Department of Finance (p. 211)
federal funds (p. 215)

fiscalization of land use (p. 219)
general fund (p. 215)
governor's budget (p. 213)
Legislative Analyst's Office (p. 213)
line-item veto (p. 214)
May revise (p. 211)
Moody's, Fitch Ratings, and Standard & Poor's (p. 215)

personal income tax (p. 217)
progressive (p. 217)
regressive (p. 217)
sales tax (p. 217)
special funds (p. 216)
unified budget (p. 211)

9 Local Government

WHAT CALIFORNIA'S LOCAL GOVERNMENTS DO AND WHY THEY MATTER

Governing California would be hard to imagine without the more than 5,000 local governments that help run the state. Local officials and workers in cities, counties, school districts, special districts, and regional bodies all play an essential role. The complexity of the state's local government system makes it difficult to generalize about what local governments do. But a short list would include the following:

- General-purpose local governments, such as cities and counties, do everything from putting out fires to cleaning the streets and ensuring that the buses run on time. They protect the health, safety, welfare, and overall quality of life of all who live within their jurisdictions.

- Limited-purpose governments, such as school districts and other special districts, deliver specific public services such as public education, pest abatement, and irrigation to meet particular needs within defined territorial boundaries.

- Regional governments address problems such as air pollution and population growth that affect broad areas across many jurisdictions and that require comprehensive study and planning to solve.

- Many local governments do the actual work involved in implementing state and federal laws, from controlling water quality and producing affordable housing to carrying out duties related to homeland security.

- Most local governments provide citizens with opportunities to learn about public problems, express their opinions, practice hands-on democracy, and collectively exercise some degree of popular control on issues close to home that they really care about.

- Some local governments experiment and innovate to pioneer new ways of better serving citizens or improving the democratic process. Often these local initiatives spread and can have major impacts on how government works at the state and national levels.

California's local governments have been subjected to a severe stress test over the last few years, thanks to both the Great Recession and the political responses to it both inside and outside the system—a system that has evolved over decades to help different levels and facets of local government fit and work together. This chapter offers a description and analysis of the essential parts of that system and discusses its capacity to solve problems and function effectively in serving the public. The goal is to give the reader a basic knowledge and appreciation of California's local governments in all their variety, including what they do and why they matter.

The Legal Framework: Dillon's Rule, Home Rule, and Local Powers of Governance

The U.S. Constitution assigns power and authority to the national and state governments, but it says nothing about local governments. **Counties, cities, special districts**, and other forms of local government have no inherent rights or powers. What rights and powers they do have are conferred on them by the state constitution or state legislature.

The constitutional doctrine that gives state governments ultimate authority over local governments is known as **Dillon's Rule**. In 1868, Iowa judge John F. Dillon ruled that "municipal corporations" such as counties and cities were mere "creatures of the state" and could exercise only those powers delegated to them by the state.[1] Upheld by the U.S. Supreme Court in 1903 and again in 1923, Dillon's Rule is firmly established, at least in theory, as the basic legal framework for relations between state and local governments. In practice, however, only a few states, including Alabama, Idaho, and Nebraska, demand strict obedience to Dillon's Rule and require local governments to seek their permission in order to act. California, like most states, has passed government codes and **home-rule** laws that allow significant local discretion and autonomy. Within broad limits, county and city residents can select their own form of government, manage their own elections, raise their own revenues, and choose what kinds of functions to perform and at what levels of service.[2]

In California, under the provisions of Article 11, Section 5, of the state constitution and because of various court rulings,[3] most of the more populous cities and counties have adopted home-rule charters. The others are designated as general-law cities and counties that fall more directly under state authority and control.

A more practical restraint on state meddling in local government is based on the maxim that all politics is local. State legislators, after all, are elected by local constituencies to protect their local interests, and legislators won't last long if they forget who brought them to the dance. These political realities have kept state power over local governments in check.[4] Finally, as part of the so-called devolution revolution that began in the 1970s, federal and state authorities have increasingly delegated responsibility to local governments to solve their own problems, using their own money.

In sum, Dillon's Rule is very liberally construed in California. The state's constitutional and legal framework confers broad formal powers of local governance, especially in charter cities and counties. Home rule on paper, however, does not necessarily translate into home rule in reality. In recent years, for example, the state's budget crises, public employee pensions, and other financial stresses have seriously limited the capacity of some local governments to govern effectively and serve the public well. Formal authority minus needed resources weakens home rule and diminishes local autonomy.

County Governments

At the first meeting of the California legislature in 1850, lawmakers divided the state into 27 counties for the purpose of administering state laws. Since then many new counties have been created, mostly by subdivision. The state's current 58 counties have been with us since 1907, when the last addition, Imperial County, was carved out of the old San Diego County (see Figure 9.1). Political movements have arisen from time to time that attempted to split an existing county to make a new one. An 1894 amendment to the state constitution, however, made it virtually impossible to do so by requiring a favorable majority vote in both the entire county affected and the territory of the proposed new county.[5]

California's 58 counties vary greatly in their territory, population, and demographic characteristics.

TERRITORY Just in terms of size, the differences are vast. You could fit 427 areas the size of San Francisco County (at just 47 square miles, the smallest county in California) within the borders of San Bernardino County (the largest county in California, at 20,053 square miles). The differences in physical geography are also striking, ranging from deserts to rain forests, flat farmlands to tall mountains. Some counties are densely urban and covered with cities, whereas others are so rural that coyotes outnumber people.

POPULATION Alpine County's grand total of 1,120 residents could all live comfortably in one San Francisco precinct. Los Angeles County, at the other extreme, is bursting with more than 10 million people, representing over 26 percent of the state's entire population. The lowest-ranking 29 counties combined contain only about 5 percent of the state's total population, while the 5 most populous counties (Los Angeles, Orange, San Diego, San Bernardino, and Riverside) hold about 54 percent of the state's total population.

DEMOGRAPHY If you tour the state's 58 counties, you'll discover vastly different social and economic worlds. The populations of some counties are relatively poor, while those of others are relatively rich. Some counties are mostly white, others are mainly nonwhite. Some are dominated by homeowners, others—for example, San Francisco—by renters.

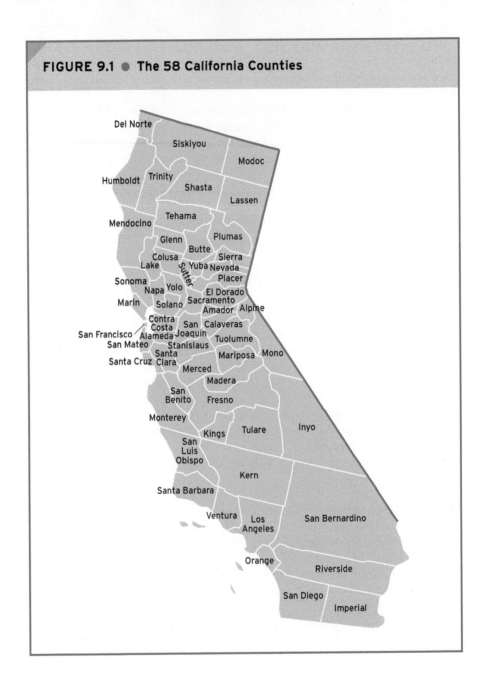

FIGURE 9.1 ● The 58 California Counties

The "Who Are Californians?" feature reports the lowest- and highest-ranking counties on these and other indicators to illustrate the extremes that exist among California's counties.

Legal Framework

The state constitution provides a general legal framework for the governing of most counties, which are known as **general-law counties**. It prescribes the number and functions of elected county officials, how they are selected, and what they may or

Who Lives in California's Counties?

Total Population

- Under 50,000
- 50,000–249,999
- 250,000–499,999
- 500,000–999,999
- 1,000,000 or more

Lowest
Alpine County
1,154

Highest
Los Angeles County
10,283,729

Non-Latino White Population

- Under 30%
- 30–44.9%
- 45–59.9%
- 60–74.9%
- 75% or more

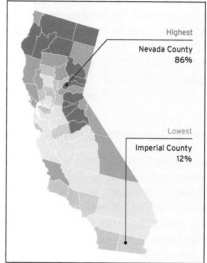

Highest
Nevada County
86%

Lowest
Imperial County
12%

Bachelor's Degree or Higher

- Under 15%
- 15–24.9%
- 25–34.9%
- 35–44.9%
- 45% or more

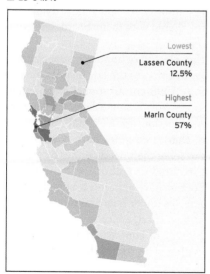

Lowest
Lassen County
12.5%

Highest
Marin County
57%

Median Household Income

- Under $40,000
- $40,000–$49,999
- $50,000–$59,999
- $60,000–$69,999
- $70,000 or more

Lowest
Trinity County
$35,270

Highest
Santa Clara County
$101,173

California's 58 counties are extremely diverse in terms of their population size, ethnoracial composition, and economic conditions. Los Angeles, for instance, has the largest population, at nearly 10.3 million residents, and the second smallest white population, at 27 percent. In other ways, Los Angeles falls roughly in the middle: about 38 percent of its residents have a bachelor's degree and the median household income is $58,000.

SOURCES: Population Estimates for Cities, Counties, and the State – January 1, 2017 and 2018, California Department of Finance, http://www.dof.ca.gov/Forecasting/Demographics/Estimates/E-1/ (accessed 09/01/2018); Statistical Atlas, Race and Ethnicity in California, https://statisticalatlas.com/state/California/Race-and-Ethnicity#data-map/county; Statistical Atlas, Educational Attainment in California, https://statisticalatlas.com/state/California/Educational-Attainment#top; Statistical Atlas, Household Income in California, https://statisticalatlas.com/state/California/Household-Income (accessed 10/2/18).

forcriticalanalysis

1. Why are the counties of California so different from one another? Are the four variables considered here related to each other, or to other factors not included here?

2. How do you think this range of ethnoracial diversity, educational attainment, and economic conditions affects California politics? How might this diversity affect local politics vs. state politics?

may not do as they raise revenue, spend money, and deliver services. Fourteen counties have adopted a home-rule charter, which gives voters greater control over the selection of governing bodies and officers, more flexibility in raising taxes and revenues, and broader discretion in organizing to deliver services. All of the state's most populous counties and one small county—Tehama, with 64,000 residents—are now **charter counties**. Voters can adopt a charter for their county government by a majority vote.

Long content to live without a charter, the voters of Orange County adopted one in March 2002. They did so mainly to prevent the governor from filling a vacancy on the county board of supervisors with his own choice of representative, an act within his authority under the general-law provisions.

San Francisco is an unusual case. It is governed under a single charter as a consolidated county and city, an arrangement that is unique in the state but more common in other areas of the country, particularly the Midwest and Upper South. Other consolidated city-county governments include Philadelphia, Pennsylvania; Nashville, Tennessee; and Jacksonville, Florida. County charters vary widely in content and in the range of powers claimed for local control. Anything that goes unmentioned within a charter is governed by the general law.

County Government Organization

In all counties except San Francisco, an elected five-member board of supervisors exercises both legislative and executive authority. Given the extremes in the size of county populations, this yields huge disparities in political representation. For example, each board member in tiny Alpine County represents, on average, only 224 residents. In mammoth Los Angeles County, on the other hand, each board member represents more than 2 million people.

County boards of supervisors, whose members are elected by districts for staggered four-year terms, not only pass laws, called **ordinances**, at the local level, but also control and supervise the departments charged with administering these ordinances. This combination of legislative and executive authority gives county supervisors great power.

In the consolidated city and county government of San Francisco, an elected 11-member board of supervisors has legislative authority. An independently elected mayor has executive authority and some control, shared with many boards and commissions, over the bureaucracy.

In addition to the board of supervisors, other elected or appointed county officers required by general law include a sheriff, who enforces the law in areas outside the cities; a district attorney; and an assessor. A 1998 constitutional amendment consolidated municipal and superior trial courts into a single layer of superior court judges who are elected by county voters. Elections for all county offices are nonpartisan. In terms of appointed positions, charter counties have considerable latitude in creating departments and agencies to serve their needs, either by charter provision or by ordinance. Other offices are required or authorized by state law. Some charter counties, such as Los Angeles County, have appointed a chief executive officer to manage their sprawling bureaucracies under board supervision.

Figure 9.2 shows Placer County's organizational chart, which is very simple and typical of counties with small populations. By way of contrast, Figure 9.3 shows Los Angeles County's organizational chart. The latter illustrates the complexity of

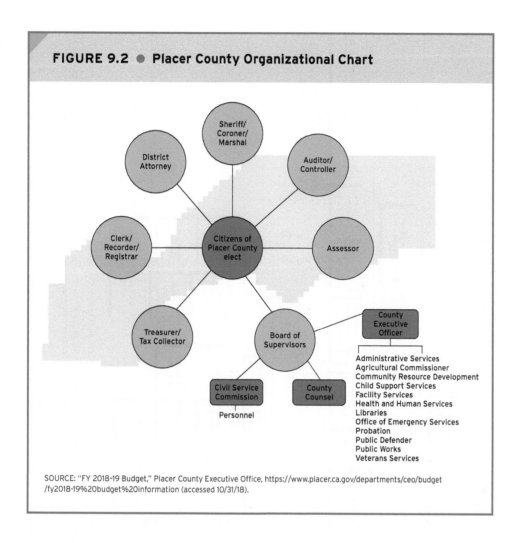

FIGURE 9.2 ● Placer County Organizational Chart

- Sheriff/Coroner/Marshal
- District Attorney
- Auditor/Controller
- Clerk/Recorder/Registrar
- Citizens of Placer County elect
- Assessor
- Treasurer/Tax Collector
- Board of Supervisors
- County Executive Officer
- Civil Service Commission
  - Personnel
- County Counsel

County Executive Officer:
- Administrative Services
- Agricultural Commissioner
- Community Resource Development
- Child Support Services
- Facility Services
- Health and Human Services
- Libraries
- Office of Emergency Services
- Probation
- Public Defender
- Public Works
- Veterans Services

SOURCE: "FY 2018-19 Budget," Placer County Executive Office, https://www.placer.ca.gov/departments/ceo/budget/fy2018-19%20budget%20information (accessed 10/31/18).

local government authority and responsibility that can be found in counties with large and diverse populations.

County Government Functions and Responsibilities

County governments have major functions and responsibilities, most of them mandated by state or federal law, especially outside the jurisdictions of cities. County responsibilities include bridges and highways, public safety, public health, employment, parks and recreation, welfare and public assistance, public records, tax collection, general government, court administration, and land use. In the largest counties, the public workforce required to manage these responsibilities and the budget needed to pay for them can be truly massive. In 2018, for example, Los Angeles County had 111,392 employees and an adopted budget of $31.4 billion.[6]

Decisions on land-use policy are perhaps the most important and controversial ones a county board of supervisors can make. If you're ever in the mood to watch a good political fight, attend a county board of supervisors meeting in a place like Napa County or San Diego County. Areas like these still have plenty of open land

FIGURE 9.3 ● Los Angeles County Organizational Chart

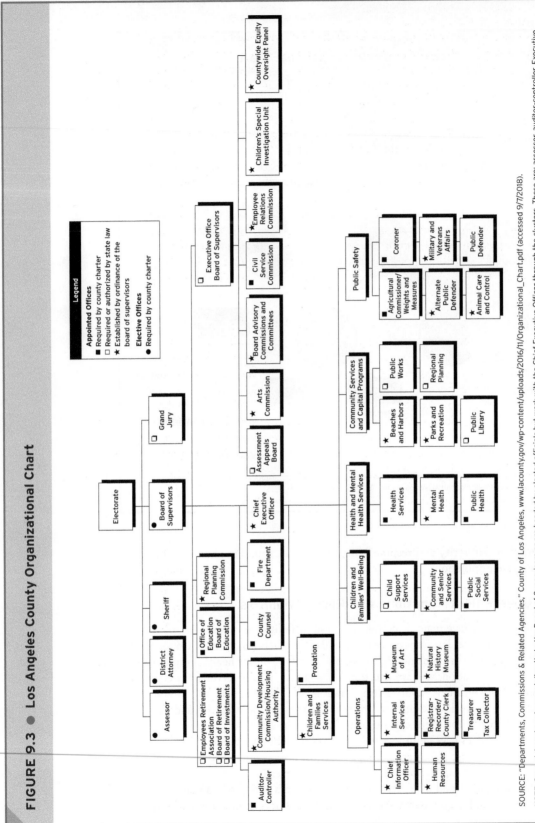

SOURCE: "Departments, Commissions & Related Agencies," County of Los Angeles, www.lacounty.gov/wp-content/uploads/2016/11/Organizational_Chart.pdf (accessed 9/7/2018).

NOTE: Several departments report directly to the Board of Supervisors or are headed by elected officials but work with the Chief Executive Officer through the clusters. These are: assessor, auditor-controller, Executive Office of the Board of Supervisors, County Counsel (operations); Community Development Commission (community services and capital programs); Children and Family Services (Children and Families' Well-Being); sheriff, district attorney, fire, probation (public safety).

outside the cities and fast-growing populations that fuel a demand for new housing construction, schools, and public infrastructure (sewers, highways, etc.). Landowners and developers typically pressure the county board of supervisors to allow them to build, while conservationists, environmentalists, and other groups mobilize in opposition to push them back. Housing developments are further complicated by the reality that homeowners are usually opposed to new housing in their neighborhoods, whether they are Democrats or Republicans, conservatives or liberals.

For example, on July 31, 2012, the Riverside County Board of Supervisors met to decide whether to "fast-track" approval of Granite Construction's application to build a surface mine known as Liberty Quarry near the small town of Temecula. Fast-tracking would allow the project to skip the county planning commission's standard review and thus expedite the board's final decision. The debate at the crowded public meeting was impassioned on both sides. Orange-shirted opponents faced off against green-shirted supporters. Representatives of the chamber of commerce, labor unions, and other groups backed the proposal, arguing that the quarry would stimulate the local economy and create badly needed jobs. Temecula city officials, environmentalists, and leaders of the Pechanga Band of Luiseño Indians contended that the quarry would pollute the air, wreck the economy, and destroy a nearby sacred tribal site. One supervisor called Liberty Quarry "the most divisive project in county history." The board voted 3-to-2 to fast-track approval, prompting cheers from the green shirts and cries of outrage from the orange shirts. Then, on November 15, 2012, just days before the board was scheduled to give its final approval, leaders of the Pechanga Band announced that they had reached an agreement with Granite Construction to purchase the Liberty Quarry site for $3 million and to pay the firm an additional $17.35 million to cover its project costs. Granite was permitted to build its mine elsewhere, miles from Temecula and the sacred tribal lands. The Pechanga Band promised to preserve the original site as it was.[7]

As California's population continues to grow and spread from the cities into the state's remaining farmlands and rural areas, you can expect to see more land-use battles of this sort erupting in the political arenas of county governments.

Local Agency Formation Commissions

All 58 California counties have a **local agency formation commission (LAFCo)**, whose members are appointed by the county board of supervisors. These commissions play a critical role in resolving conflicts among the many local governments that often compete with one another for power and resources within their county jurisdictions. A county's LAFCo has the following responsibilities:

- reviewing and approving the incorporations of new cities, the formation of new special districts, and any proposed changes of jurisdictional boundaries, including annexations and detachments of territory, **secessions**, consolidations, mergers, and dissolutions

- reviewing and approving contractual service agreements between local governments and between local governments and the private sector

- defining the official spheres of influence for each city and special district

- initiating proposals for consolidation, dissolution, mergers, and reorganizations if such changes seem necessary or desirable

These powerful commissions are especially busy in counties that are rocked by large-scale land-use battles, such as Riverside County, or that teem with masses of people and a multitude of governments, such as Los Angeles County.[8]

City Governments

Legal Framework

Like counties, California's cities derive their powers as municipal corporations from the state constitution and state legislature. Within that legal framework, as of September 2018, the state's 482 incorporated cities fell into three categories: **general-law cities** (361), **charter cities** (120), and the unique case of San Francisco's consolidated city and county.[9] The California Government Code, enacted by the legislature, specifies the general powers and structure of general-law cities. Broader home-rule powers are granted to charter cities, giving citizens more direct control over local affairs. Under these different arrangements, all cities have the power to legislate, as long as their local policies don't conflict with state or federal law. They have the power to raise revenues, levy taxes, charge license and service fees, and borrow. They may also hire personnel as needed; exercise police powers to enforce local, state, and federal laws; and condemn property for public use.

Incorporation and Dissolution

The state grants powers to cities, and in that sense cities are indeed creatures of the state. But cities themselves are created only by the request, and with the consent, of the residents in a given area. In California, this process of **municipal incorporation** is typically initiated by a citizen petition or by a resolution of the county board of supervisors. Landowner petitions are also possible but rare. The following are some of the more important reasons that motivate residents to seek incorporation:

- to limit or accelerate population growth
- to provide more or better-quality services than those provided by the county
- to prevent annexation by a nearby city
- to create a unit of government more responsive to local needs and concerns
- to escape the tax and spending burdens imposed by county government rule

A petition for municipal incorporation must be submitted to the county's LAFCo. The LAFCo panel reviews the proposed plans for the new city, its boundaries, its service provisions, its governing capacity, and its financial viability. The LAFCo also studies the likely financial and other impacts of the proposed incorporation on neighboring local governments, including the county itself. If the petition for incorporation survives this initial review and a later public hearing and possible protests, it moves to an election. If a majority of voters living within the boundaries of the proposed new city approve, a new city is legally born.[10] The rate of incorporation of new cities has fallen dramatically in recent years. Only 9 have incorporated since 1999 and only two in the last decade, raising the total number of cities to 482 in 2018.[11]

The heavy burden of legal obligations and fiduciary responsibilities that come with incorporation can be difficult for municipalities to handle, particularly in times of widespread financial stress. The trials and tribulations of Jurupa Valley, the state's youngest city, illustrate this point. Jurupa Valley, a community of about 100,000 people located in Riverside County, formally became an incorporated, general-law city in July 2011. The community thereby gained home-rule powers and greater local control over land use and service provision within its borders. The summer of 2011 proved an unfortunate time for the city of Jurupa Valley to be born, however, as the governor and state legislators faced yet another budget crisis. Only days after the community's incorporation, the state government diverted all of its vehicle license fee revenues away from local governments to bolster budgets for prisons and other law enforcement programs at the state level. This sudden diversion of funds hurt all California cities, but it hit Jurupa Valley especially hard; city officials had counted on their share of that money, which was several millions of dollars, to make ends meet. On January 16, 2014, after months of cutting staffing and services to the bone while searching in vain for state financial support, Jurupa Valley's city council members voted unanimously to petition Riverside County's LAFCo for municipal dissolution and a return to county rule.

It was the first such petition received by a LAFCo in more than 40 years, and it triggered a legal process of disincorporation that could have taken up to two years to complete.[12] A local reporter warned her readers of some of the implications: "If home rule goes away, decision-making on land-use and other issues like code enforcement, public works and road repairs will revert to Riverside County. Traffic enforcement will be handled by the California Highway Patrol."[13]

This story, however, has a happy ending. On September 22, 2015, with the economy now booming and his budget balanced, Governor Brown signed a bill authored by State Senator Richard Roth (D-Riverside) that restored funding to Jurupa Valley and three other recently born cities in Riverside County. On October 1, Jurupa Valley's city council members joyfully passed a resolution rescinding the earlier dissolution request.[14] Thus did the new city of Jurupa Valley survive its near-death experience.

City Government Functions and Responsibilities

City governments provide a wide range of services and facilities that directly affect the lives of their residents: fire and police protection; street construction and maintenance; sewage and waste disposal; health, social, and recreational programs; and planning and zoning to determine land use that is consistent with the community's needs and values. Most city governments provide water, and some run public transit systems. A few, such as Los Angeles and Sacramento, own and manage municipal electricity or natural gas utilities.

Residents in most cities are content if basic services such as police, fire, and waste management are provided reliably and efficiently, either directly by the municipality itself or, as in many smaller cities, by contracting services from other local governments and the private sector.[15] In some places, however, residents demand more from their city government than just the basics. For example, in some cities, business leaders and entrepreneurs pressure city hall to promote rapid economic growth and development. In other cities, community activists pressure city hall to limit growth and development and to pursue ambitious social agendas on the world stage.

City Government Revenues and Expenditures

As shown in Figure 9.4, the typical city budget in California relies most heavily on current service charges and taxes for most of its revenues. Most of what it spends goes toward public safety, community development and health, public utilities,

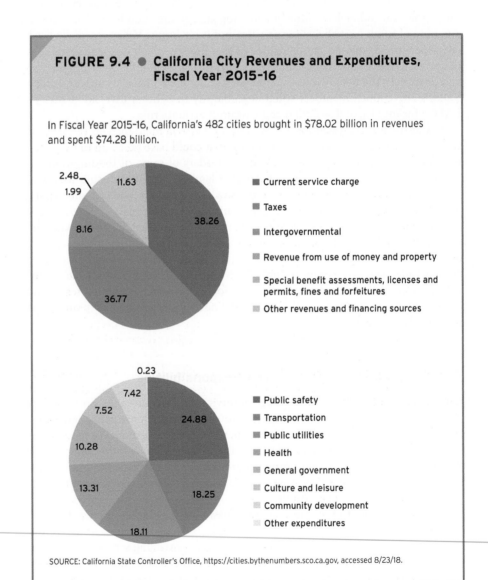

FIGURE 9.4 ● California City Revenues and Expenditures, Fiscal Year 2015-16

In Fiscal Year 2015-16, California's 482 cities brought in $78.02 billion in revenues and spent $74.28 billion.

2.48
1.99
11.63
8.16
38.26
36.77

■ Current service charge
■ Taxes
■ Intergovernmental
■ Revenue from use of money and property
■ Special benefit assessments, licenses and permits, fines and forfeitures
■ Other revenues and financing sources

0.23
7.42
7.52
24.88
10.28
13.31
18.25
18.11

■ Public safety
■ Transportation
■ Public utilities
■ Health
■ General government
■ Culture and leisure
■ Community development
■ Other expenditures

SOURCE: California State Controller's Office, https://cities.bythenumbers.sco.ca.gov, accessed 8/23/18.

and transportation. We will have more to say about city finances later in this chapter in the context of the state's continuing budget crisis.

Forms of City Government and the Legacy of Progressive Structural Reforms

The overall vision and structural reforms advanced by the Progressives nearly a century ago have had an enduring impact on the form of municipal government in California. Progressive reformers sought to replace the corrupt bosses running partisan, ward-based, big-city political machines with government by reputable civic leaders and nonpartisan experts managing local affairs in the public interest. To implement that vision, the following structural reforms were necessary:

- strong managers and weak mayors
- nonpartisan elections
- at-large council elections
- the tools of direct democracy (the initiative, referendum, and recall)

Other Progressive reforms included civil service (merit-based) systems of municipal employment and, especially in the larger cities, professionally run city planning commissions and departments.[16] Reformers were particularly successful in the southwestern states, where populations were growing fast and new cities were popping up everywhere, isolated from the influence of eastern-style partisanship and urban machine politics.[17] Municipalities that have all or most of these institutional features are known as **reform governments**. Most medium-size American cities and nearly all of California's cities qualify for that label.

COUNCIL-MANAGER PLAN VERSUS MAYOR-COUNCIL SYSTEM Under the council-manager form of government, the voters elect a city council, which in turn appoints a professionally trained city manager to run the administration. The city manager directly controls the bureaucracy and supervises the performance of department heads. The council restricts itself to legislative policy making, while retaining the ultimate authority to fire or replace the appointed manager. Nearly all small- and medium-sized California cities, as well as San Jose and Sacramento, are governed by the **council-manager plan**.[18] Mayors are directly elected in about a third of these cities, but they perform mainly ceremonial duties and have no independent executive powers, such as the veto or budget control. (A partial exception is San Jose, whose mayor has very limited control of the budget and bureaucracy.)

The rest of California's cities are governed by **mayor-council systems**. Most are very small cities that can't afford a professional city manager and have weak mayors of the purely ceremonial type. Most of the state's largest cities, however, have strong mayor-council systems in which the mayor is elected independently of the council and serves as the city's overall chief executive. These are often called strong-mayor systems because the mayor proposes the city's budget, appoints department heads, and has veto power over council legislation. The council (or, in the case of San Francisco, the board of supervisors) is responsible for legislative policy making. Typically, as in Los Angeles and San Francisco, various appointive boards and commissions set overall policy and supervise administration of important city departments such as police and fire, thus limiting the mayor's direct control of the bureaucracy.

In recent years, the voters in some council-manager cities have approved the switch to a strong-mayor system to make local government decision making more accountable, nimble, and responsive to changing political environments. When former governor Jerry Brown ran for mayor of Oakland in 1998, he insisted that the voters support Measure X, which he had helped to draft, that would give the mayor the veto, control over budget preparation, and extensive appointment powers while reducing the then-powerful city manager to an administrator under mayoral authority. Oakland's voters approved the measure by a 3-to-1 margin and elected Brown as the city's new mayor. In 2004, San Diego's voters followed suit, changing one of the nation's largest council-manager systems into a strong-mayor system on a trial-run basis, and voted again in 2010 to make that new system permanent. In contrast, on November 4, 2014, Sacramento's voters soundly rejected (57-to-43 percent) Measure L, a proposed charter amendment that would have changed the city's current council-manager plan to a strong-mayor system. Sacramento and San Jose remain the state's two largest cities still sticking with the council-manager system.

In practice, formal and informal power arrangements vary widely across both the council-manager and mayor-council systems. Personal ambition, political skill, and leadership style are key factors that influence the degree of power accorded to a given mayor or manager to run local government and shape public policy.[19]

NONPARTISAN ELECTIONS California law requires that all local elections be officially **nonpartisan**. The Progressive Era reformers had pushed for nonpartisan elections as a means to insulate the important business of local government from what they saw as the distracting and corrupting influence of partisan politics. In nonpartisan elections, no information about a candidate's political party membership is shown on the ballot. In practice, of course, many local contests are fiercely partisan, even if the voters do not see a "D" or an "R" next to the candidates' names. They can infer partisanship through statements about other elected officials (for example, about President Trump or members of his administration) or from endorsements from local party organizations and other local officials.

AT-LARGE VERSUS DISTRICT COUNCIL ELECTIONS More than 90 percent of California cities conduct at-large council elections, in which voters elect council members citywide rather than by districts or wards.[20] Under the **at-large elections** system, for example, if a number of candidates compete for one of the three vacant seats on the council, all of the city's voters have the opportunity to vote for any three of them, and the top three vote-getters are declared the winners. About 5 percent of cities use the **district elections** method, which divides the city into districts and requires the voters in each district to elect one of the candidates running in that district to represent them on the council. The remaining cities—Oakland is an example—use some hybrid combination of at-large and district elections to elect their councils.

Local governments change their election systems infrequently, if at all, and they usually do so only after being pressured by political reform movements or lawsuits. (As an illustration of how lawsuits can force such change, see the discussion of the California Voting Rights Act on the next page.) In 2000, for example, San Francisco switched from at-large to district elections for electing its board of supervisors in response to voter demand for greater representation of neighborhoods and minority groups, reduced influence of big money on elections, and a wider field of candidates who otherwise could not afford to run citywide campaigns.[21] Of course, the district system by itself doesn't guarantee a more neighborhood-oriented council, less costly campaigns, or political life on a smaller scale. The 15 members of the Los Angeles City Council, for example, are elected by districts. But each council member represents nearly a quarter of a million residents on average and must run expensive campaigns over vast territories to get elected.

The major trend in the past two decades has been a shift to district elections to allow for better representation of historically marginalized groups, especially Latinos. The first city to make the switch, in 1989, was Watsonville. Attorney Joaquin Avila and the Mexican American Legal Defense and Educational Fund sued Watsonville in federal court, arguing that the increasingly-Latino town's at-large system of electing city council members was diluting the Latino vote in violation of the federal Voting Rights Act of 1965 (VRA). The victory made national news, but few cities or counties chose to follow suit. Instead, many were forced to follow Watsonville's lead as various legal groups filed charges of vote dilution. Avila worked to help draft the California Voting Rights Act of 2001 (CVRA), which made it easier to prove minority vote dilution.

The CVRA expanded on the VRA by eliminating the need for minority plaintiffs to identify a particular geographic district in their city in which a minority is sufficiently concentrated to result in a majority of voters. This crucial distinction makes it easier for plaintiffs to claim that at-large elections dilute their votes. CVRA-based lawsuits by minority groups in Modesto, Compton, Anaheim, Escondido, Whittier, Palmdale, and other cities have been successful, and more are coming. Local governments using at-large elections in racially diverse communities have been put on the defensive, and it's not hard to see why. Consider the egregious case of Palmdale, whose mayor, according to the *Los Angeles Times*, could not "explain why Palmdale, whose population is almost 55% Latino and nearly 15% black, has elected only one Latino and no African Americans to its council."[22]

The state's rapidly surging Latino population has been a major driver of CVRA lawsuits.[23] The Southwest Voter Registration Project, a Latino voting rights organization, has been particularly aggressive in suing local governments that have at-large systems and an underrepresentation of Latinos as a legally protected minority class. If such jurisdictions fight in court and lose, as they almost always do, they often must pay large settlements and fees. Palmdale, for example, fought such a lawsuit, lost, and had to pay about $4.6 million in attorneys' fees. Fearing expensive lawsuits, officials in many jurisdictions have taken steps proactively to change from at-large to district systems. An example is the city of San Marcos, in which Latinos make up 37 percent of the population but have elected no Latinos to the city council in two decades.[24] Under the threat of such lawsuits, according to one report, more than 100 school and college districts throughout the state have also proactively decided to change their election systems.[25] Some advocates, like law professor Richard Hasen, see the CVRA as a "bright spot" in an era when other states are erecting barriers to minority voter participation. "In California, you have a large Latino population that's growing," Hasen told a reporter. "And you couple that with a Democratic majority in a state legislature that is willing to protect minority voting rights, then you get a very different situation than in Texas, where Republican legislators are making it harder for Latinos to vote."[26]

Most recently, the city of Santa Clara adopted district elections in response to a lawsuit brought on behalf of Asian American residents, who noted in their 2017 filing that all members of the council were white, despite a population that is just 34 percent non-Hispanic white and more than 40 percent Asian.

DIRECT DEMOCRACY At the local level of government, just as at the state level, ordinary citizens have access to the tools of **direct democracy** (the initiative, referendum, and recall) bequeathed to them by Progressive Era reformers. Specifically, if citizens gather the required number of valid signatures on formal petitions, they can accomplish the following:

- initiate direct legislation, including proposed ordinances and charter amendments, by placing such measures on the ballot for voter approval

- suspend implementation of council legislation until the voters approve it at a referendum election

- subject incumbent elected officials to a recall vote and possible dismissal before the next scheduled regular election

Local referenda are quite rare. Local recall elections are also rare, but they occur more often than do statewide recalls. For example, in the politically contentious town of Pacifica, voters have successfully petitioned for five recall elections over the last 40 years. The use of local ballot initiatives, however, is much more frequent and widespread, although not nearly to the extent observed at the state level. Direct legislation by citizen ballot initiative has become common in a few cities, especially larger and more diverse cities such as San Francisco, especially around land-use and housing issues. Citizen initiatives appear on ballots less frequently in most other cities, but they are not uncommon. A 2012 study found that there were only 212 city initiatives and 62 county initiatives in the 2001–08 period, an average of just half an initiative per jurisdiction over eight years.[27] A replication of that survey in 2018 would probably show a higher rate of citizen initiatives, given the rise of contentious politics and anti-establishment movements at all political levels.

Legal scholars Matthew Melone and George Nation III offer an important insight into the relationship between direct democracy and representative government:

> The importance of direct democracy is not diminished by the fact that representative democracy is the primary form of government because the importance of direct democracy is not determined by the frequency of its use. . . . [T]he mere fact that the tools of direct democracy are readily available in a state prevents many of the abuses associated with representative government despite the fact that such tools are actually used infrequently. . . . The institutions of representative democracy and the representatives themselves function better due to the possibility of the voters' resort to direct democracy.[28]

Some of the cases discussed later in this chapter will illustrate this point.

Also see Box 9.1 on the Brown Act, the "open meetings law" that gives citizens yet another tool of direct democracy to help them become more informed about the decision-making process and to hold their local government officials accountable.

The Ralph M. Brown Act of 1953 required that "all meetings of the legislative body of a local agency shall be open and public, and all persons shall be permitted to attend any meeting of the legislative body of a local agency, except as otherwise provided in this chapter." The intent of the Brown Act, also known as the "open meetings law," was to support transparency and prevent secret meetings and backroom dealings of local government officials conducting public business. (The Bagley-Keene Act of 1967 later extended the same open-meetings requirement to state government agencies.) The Brown Act allows closed meetings for personnel decisions and the like to protect community and individual rights. This also includes 1) city council or board of supervisors meetings discussing litigation, 2) labor relations, 3) disciplinary action, and 4) property acquisitions such as use of eminent domain. These meetings must be noticed and results reported out after a decision is made, but the public can be excluded from the discussion in an executive session.

The rules were further broadened in the 1990s to include meetings negotiating local collective-bargaining agreements, which the public may see only after they are signed—often too late to raise hard questions and objections about the financial implications. Further extensions were approved in 2008 and 2009 in order to ban serial meetings (in which Official A conveys a view privately to Official B who conveys it to Official C to reach a majority consensus). A majority of members of an elected body cannot communicate via any means outside a public meeting.

The Little Hoover Commission, the state's independent oversight agency, noted in a 2015 report that the state's open meeting acts have "hindered government decision-making processes and created less transparency instead of more." They further noted that the rules have isolated decision makers, "reduced their collective understanding of issues and opened them to greater manipulation out of public view." In 2017 columnist Joe Mathews opined, "The act's requirements of advance notice before local officials hold a meeting has mutated into strict limitations on the ability of local officials to have frank conversations with one another. Brown Act requirements that we, the public, can weigh in at meetings have been turned against us, by way of a standardized three-minute-per-speaker limit that encourages rapid rants and discourages real conversation with our representatives."

SOURCE: League of California Cities, *Open & Public IV: A Guide to the Ralph M. Brown Act* (2007); Peter Scheer, "Public Employee Unions: Losing the Image Battle," *San Francisco Chronicle*, June 13, 2010, p. N5; www.lhc.ca.gov /sites/lhc.ca.gov/files/Reports/227/Report227.pdf; www.sacbee.com/opinion/op-ed/article140151118.html (accessed 8/24/18).

LOCAL VOTER TURNOUT AND POLITICAL REPRESENTATION Despite the surge in voter turnout in the 2008 presidential election, with 62.2 percent of eligible voters going to the polls, the overall trend in voter participation since 1960 has been gradually downward in national elections (see Chapter 4). That trend continued in the 2016 presidential election, with just 60.2 percent of eligible voters going to the polls—an improvement from the 58.6 percent turnout in 2012. Turnout in California mirrors national trends, with 61.7 percent turnout in 2008, 55.7 percent turnout in 2012, and 58.4 percent turnout in 2016.[29] Voter turnout rates in California's local elections tend to be much lower. A study by Melissa Marschall and John Lappie of mayoral elections between 1995 and 2014 found that turnout was only 21 percent, decreasing to just over 16 percent if a single candidate for mayor was running unopposed (of the mayoral elections they examined, nearly a quarter were uncontested).[30] Boosting turnout in these elections thus to a certain extent depends on the candidates and whether they are running unopposed; however, rescheduling local nonconcurrent elections to coincide with high-turnout presidential and midterm congressional elections would likely result in significantly higher participation rates.

Similar reasoning lies behind one of the arguments for ranked-choice voting, also known as the alternative vote or "instant runoff voting," which San Francisco adopted in 2002 (soon followed by Berkeley, Oakland, and San Leandro). Under ranked-choice voting, voters in the November general election rank the candidates for an office by order of preference (first choice, second choice, and so on). When all the ballots are counted, if no candidate receives a majority of first-choice preferences, the candidate receiving the fewest is dropped from the list and his or her ballots are transferred to the remaining candidates according to voters' rankings. (If a voter's lower-ranked candidates aren't among the survivors, his or her ballot is classified as "exhausted" and removed from the transfer flow of "continuing" ballots to be counted again in the next round.) Another tally is taken of continuing ballots, and if there is still no majority winner, the process is repeated until a majority winner is declared.

This system presents an alternative to the typical local election in California, in which the top two vote-getters face off in a typically low-turnout, low-interest runoff election in December if no candidate receives a majority of the votes cast in November. Under the ranked-choice system, these December runoff elections can be avoided.

Some critics of ranked-choice voting argue that many voters actually prefer December runoffs because they winnow the field of candidates and sharpen the voter's focus on only two choices. Further, voter turnout for mayoral elections and other high-profile local contests is sometimes even higher in the December runoff than in the November general election. These kinds of debates about the merits of ranked-choice voting and other proposed electoral reforms will continue.[31] This is considered a benefit by scholars who view local governments as ideal "laboratories of democracy" where innovations like ranked-choice voting can be tried and tested before being recommended to a wider public.[32]

California has implemented a number of reforms to its voter registration and electoral processes in recent years with the aim of increasing participation among eligible voters. In 2017, California began to allow 16- and 17-year olds to preregister to vote, although they cannot actually participate in elections until they are 18 years old. In 2018 the state rolled out an automatic voter registration policy that automatically registers eligible citizens when they go to the DMV for their drivers license. Also in 2018 selected counties (Madera, Napa, Nevada, Sacramento, and San Mateo) began to implement the California Voter's Choice Act of 2016, which replaces traditional community polling places with mailed ballots and vote centers. Instead of requiring registered voters to only vote by mail or at their local polling place, the VCA allows citizens within a participating county to vote at any of the county's vote centers.[33]

Finally, and more controversially, a case can be made for greater political representation of noncitizens in local government. Noncitizens are not only tolerated but respected in many California cities, and their voices are heard and heeded by local officials. Leaders of immigrant-serving nonprofit agencies, community-based organizations, and worker centers are highly politically active in self-declared sanctuary cities such as San Francisco, where their efforts have led to assured equal access to city services regardless of immigrant status, the provision of municipal identification cards, and passage of wage-theft legislation to deter the economic exploitation of this vulnerable population. In 2004 advocacy groups and a broad coalition of supporters advanced a ballot measure giving noncitizen parents of children enrolled in public schools the right to vote in the city's school board elections. That measure failed, just barely, and it failed again in 2010 by a slightly larger margin. The third time was a charm, however. In the November 8, 2016, election, the city's voters approved the measure by an 8-point margin, 54-to-46 percent.[34] The measure was then unanimously adopted by the San Francisco Board of Supervisors in May 2018, paving the way for noncitizen parents to vote in November 2018 school board elections. According to Hong Mei Pang, director of advocacy at the San Francisco–based nonprofit Chinese for Affirmative Action, about one-third of the students in the district come from immigrant households, so the measure will give many parents a rightful voice.[35] That said, few noncitizens chose to take advantage of the opportunity to vote in November 2018.

Special Districts

Special districts are limited-purpose local governments. They fill the need or desire for services that general-purpose governments such as counties and cities cannot or will not provide. If residents or landowners desire new or better services, they can take steps to establish a special district to pay for them. As a popular guide to special districts notes: "Special districts *localize* the costs and benefits of public services. Special districts allow local citizens to obtain the services they want at a price they are willing to pay."[36] Examples of special districts include fire protection districts, cemetery districts, water districts, recreation and park districts, storm water drainage and conservation districts, irrigation districts, and mosquito abatement districts.

School and Community College Districts

California's **school and community college districts** are a unique type of special district. As of 2017–18 there were 1,026 K–12 school districts in the state, serving over 6.2 million students.[37] School districts derive their authority from the California Education Code and are governed by locally elected school boards. Each board sets general policies and appoints a superintendent as chief executive officer, who serves at the pleasure of the board. The superintendent has overall responsibility for managing the system and its various schools and programs. In 2018 the state's community college system of two-year public institutions comprised 114 colleges organized into 72 districts. Serving more than 2.1 million students, it is the largest system of higher education in the nation.[38] In 1988 the California legislature enacted Assembly Bill 1725, giving community colleges status as institutions of higher education. AB 1725 also strengthened the advisory role of local academic senates and of the Student Senate for California Community Colleges in working with state government officials to make higher-education policy. Each community college district is governed by a locally elected board of trustees that sets general policies and appoints a chancellor as chief executive officer. As discussed elsewhere in this book, the state of California's K–14 public education system, and especially the financial crises that surround it, continue to be a major focus of policy debate and political battle.

In recent years, community colleges in California have come under fire for their poor graduation rates. A 2010 report by the Institute for Higher Education Leadership & Policy at Cal State Sacramento found that 70 percent of students seeking degrees at California community colleges did not attain them or transfer to four-year universities within six years. In 2018 new rules went into effect that tie each college's funding to how well it serves students (as measured by graduation and transfer rates), and especially to how well it serves poor students.[39]

Nonschool Special Districts

Excluding the school districts, the state had 4,884 special districts in 2017.[40] These special districts can be classified in three different ways: single-purpose versus multiple-purpose, enterprise versus nonenterprise, and independent versus dependent.

- About 85 percent of the state's special districts perform a single function, such as sewage management, water management, fire protection, or mosquito abatement. The others are multifunctional, such as the state's more than 800 County Service Areas (CSAs), which provide two or more services, such as enhanced recreation services and extended police protection.

- About one in four special districts are **enterprise districts**, which are run like businesses and charge **user fees** for services. Nearly all airport, harbor and port, transit, water, waste, and hospital districts are enterprise districts of this sort. In fiscal year 2015–16, the state's enterprise districts generated a total of $21.98 billion in user fees.[41] The state's many nonenterprise districts provide public services such as fire protection and pest control that benefit the entire community, not just individual residents. Typically, property taxes rather than user fees pay the costs.

- About two-thirds of the state's special districts are **independent districts**. An independent district is governed by its own separate board of directors appointed by an authorizing agency or elected directly by the district's voters. Dependent districts are governed by existing legislative bodies. Nearly all CSAs, for example, are governed by a county board of supervisors.

These three ways of classifying special districts are not mutually exclusive, and examples of all possible combinations exist.

Legal Framework

Like all local governments in the state, special districts must conform to the state constitution and to the legislature's government code. Statutory authority for special districts derives from either a principal act or a special act of the state legislature. A *principal act* is a general law that applies to all special districts of a given type. For example, the Fire Protection District Law of 1987 in the California Health and Safety Code governs all 386 fire districts. About 60 of these principal law statutes are on the books and can be used to create a special district anywhere in the state. Another 120 or so *special acts* have been passed by the legislature to adapt a special district's structure, financing, and authority to unique local circumstances. The Alameda County Flood Control and Water District, for example, was formed under such a special act.

How Special Districts Are Created

To form a special district, the voters in the proposed district must apply to their county's LAFCo. After the LAFCo reviews and approves the proposal, it moves to an election in which only the voters residing inside the proposed district boundaries may vote. A simple majority is required for approval in most cases. A two-thirds majority is required if new special taxes are involved. As of August 2018 there were 3,776 special districts in California.

The Advantages and Disadvantages of Special Districts

The advantages of special districts include the following:

- the flexibility that such districts allow in tailoring the level and quality of service to citizen demands

- the linking of costs to benefits, so that those who don't benefit from a district's services don't have to pay for them

- the greater responsiveness of special districts to their constituents, who often reside in smaller geographic areas of larger city and county jurisdictions

The disadvantages of special districts include the following:

- the overlapping of jurisdictions and the resulting duplication of services already provided by cities and counties or by other special districts

- the reduced incentives for needed regional planning, especially in providing water, sewer, and fire protection services, which are typically offered by a host of special districts governed by independent boards without any central coordination

- the decreased accountability that results from the sheer multiplicity of limited special districts, which overwhelms the average citizen's ability to find out who is in charge of delivering specific services

Some critics think special districts should be abolished, their functions redistributed to established general-purpose city and county governments. One contends that special districts "make a mockery of the natural connections that people have with a specific place. Special districts lie beyond the commonsense experience of most citizens; their very purpose is to divorce a narrow element of policy from the consideration of those charged with the maintenance of the common interest."[42] Advocates for special districts counter that special districts "focus on providing one service, or sometimes a small suite of services, to a community. It is this focused service that leads to efficiency and effectiveness. By focusing on doing one thing really well, special districts excel at innovation. It also allows them to plan ahead, think long-term, and practice sustainable decision-making."[43]

Regional Governments

A number of **regional governments** have formed in California to cope with problems such as air pollution, waste management, growth control, affordable housing production, and transportation gridlock—problems that affect large geographical areas and millions of people living in many different city and county jurisdictions. Some of these regional bodies have strong regulatory powers. Others are mainly advisory in function.

Regulatory Regional Governments

Examples of state **regulatory regional governments** include the California Coastal Commission, the South Coast Air Quality Management District, and the San Francisco Bay Conservation and Development Commission.

CALIFORNIA COASTAL COMMISSION (CCC) Appointed by the governor and the state legislature, the 12-member CCC has state-empowered regulatory authority to control all development within the 1,000-yard-wide shoreline zone along the entire California coast. Exercising its powers to grant or withhold permits for development, the CCC has succeeded over the years in opening public access to beaches, protecting scenic views, and restoring wetlands. Sometimes, the commission's mission to protect public access to California's coast brings prolonged legal battles. In 2008, Sun Microsystems cofounder Vinod Khosla bought an 89-acre

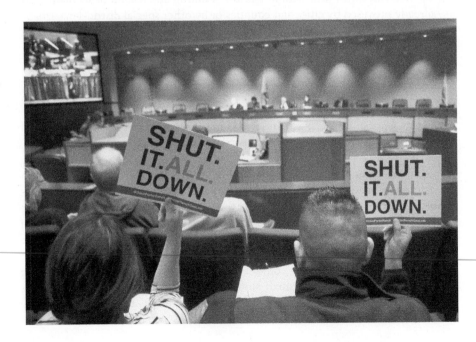

The South Coast Air Quality Management District, one of California's regional regulatory governments, uses its rule-making authority to promote the welfare of citizens like those here, who supported the closure of a well that leaked massive amounts of gas into the atmosphere outside LA.

property south of Half Moon Bay that included public Martins Beach. Khosla closed access to the beach and posted "do not enter" signs, launching what became a 10-year battle with the CCC to force him to restore public access, which they eventually won. Similarly, in 2005 music producer David Geffen lost a 22-year fight with the commission to unlock access to an area of beach next to his Malibu home.[44]

SOUTH COAST AIR QUALITY MANAGEMENT DISTRICT (SCAQMD) The 12-member SCAQMD board has state-granted regulatory authority to control emissions from stationary sources of air pollution such as power plants, refineries, and gas stations in the state's south coast air basin. This region encompasses all of Los Angeles and Orange Counties and parts of Riverside and San Bernardino Counties, an area of 12,000 square miles and home to more than 12 million people, nearly half the state's total population. This area also has the worst smog problem in the nation. Over the years, the board, which is appointed by city governments in the basin area, has conducted many studies, monitored air pollution levels, developed regional pollution abatement plans, and vigorously enforced federal and state air pollution laws. Thanks in large part to its efforts, the maximum level of ozone in the basin has been cut to less than half of what it was in the 1950s, despite the tripling of the population and quadrupling of vehicles in the region over that same period.

SAN FRANCISCO BAY CONSERVATION AND DEVELOPMENT COMMISSION (BCDC) The 27-member BCDC was created by the state legislature in 1965 in response to growing public concern about the future of San Francisco Bay, which was being dredged and polluted at an alarming rate by landfill projects. The commission includes members appointed by the governor, legislature, and various state and federal agencies; four city representatives appointed by the Association of Bay Area Governments; and nine county supervisors—one from each of the nine Bay Area counties. The commission is charged with regulating all filling and dredging in the bay; protecting the Suisun Marsh, the largest wetlands in California; regulating proposed new development within the first 100 feet inland from the bay to ensure maximum public access; enforcing the federal Coastal Zone Management Act; and other regulatory functions. By exercising its permit powers, BCDC not only stopped development that could have reduced the bay to a pond but also added hundreds of acres of new open water.

TAHOE REGIONAL PLANNING AGENCY (TRPA). The TRPA is a unique bistate compact between California and Nevada, formed in 1969 with the mandate to protect the environment of the Lake Tahoe Basin. It includes seven members from California, seven from Nevada, and a fifteenth nonvoting member chosen by the president of the United States. Working in cooperation with other organizations, agencies, and private property owners, the TRPA works to heal past damage to the area's ecosystem through restoration projects and to minimize the impact of developed properties on the Lake Tahoe watershed. Board members work to maintain and expand recreational use of the lake and it's 72-mile shoreline, while also protecting air and water quality and minimizing the introduction of invasive species.[45]

Advisory Regional Governments

In addition to regional regulatory bodies, the state also has a number of regional planning, research, and advisory institutions called **advisory regional governments**.

The most important are various regional **councils of government (COGs)**. COGs are assemblies of delegates representing a region's counties and cities who join voluntarily and meet regularly to discuss common problems and regional issues. The state's two most prominent COGs are the Southern California Association of Governments (SCAG), which is the nation's largest COG, and the Association of Bay Area Governments (ABAG).

SCAG's regional jurisdiction encompasses 15 million people living in an area of more than 38,000 square miles, while ABAG's boundaries include 6 million people living in an area of 7,000 square miles. Both SCAG and ABAG have general assemblies that represent the broad membership of counties and cities located in each region. In both COGs, the serious work is done by smaller executive committees, a 75-member regional council in the case of SCAG and a 38-member executive board in the case of ABAG. Like most COGs, both SCAG and ABAG have professional staffs that conduct extensive research and planning studies of regional problems. Both regularly host regional conferences and forums on a range of substantive issues. And both have been designated by the federal government as metropolitan planning organizations for their regions, with the mandate to draw up plans for regional transportation, air quality, growth management, hazardous waste management, and production of affordable housing.

Both SCAG and ABAG have raised public awareness of regional problems and issues. They have also encouraged more regional planning and collaborative decision making. Neither COG, however, has the effective power or authority to enforce its policy recommendations on other local governments in their regions. Many Bay Area local officials, for example, pay lip service to ABAG's recommended fair-share quotas for production of affordable housing but then routinely ignore them when making decisions. Recent research has found that members of both political parties, and both conservatives and liberals, oppose new housing in their own neighborhoods.

Occasionally, a serious organized effort is made to create a truly comprehensive regional government with broad regulatory authority and strong enforcement powers. In the early 1990s, for example, an attempt was made to establish a powerful Bay Area regional government under the banner of BayVision 2020.[46] That proposal failed, like all the others, because most of the region's local governments were unwilling to surrender local autonomy and delegate some of their powers to a new, higher authority.

Local Government: Where Are We Now?

Ten years after the Great Recession of 2008, California's local governments have survived a gauntlet of economic and political crises. The Great Recession had severely weakened local economies and hit most of the state's city and county governments hard as tax revenues plummeted, which resulted in austerity in the form of slashed budgets, staff layoffs, and cutbacks in services. The cities of Vallejo (in 2008), Stockton (in 2012), and San Bernardino (in 2012) had been forced to declare bankruptcy, and other cities had teetered on the brink. As discussed earlier in this chapter, the state's newest city, Jurupa Valley, had barely survived a near-death experience. No financial rescue had come from the federal government, nor had the state government been of much help during the worst of it. Faced with its own budget crisis, the state had abolished California's 435 redevelopment agencies to extract new revenues to help make ends meet.

Today, California's finances have shifted dramatically thanks to the improving economy and to an increase in taxes that voters approved in 2012 (Proposition 30) and reauthorized in 2016. From a low point in 2011 when the state carried a $25 billion deficit, the state since 2013 has enjoyed surpluses, peaking in 2018 to a $14.8 billion surplus. The surplus funds allowed former governor Brown and the state legislature to give back to the cities and other local governments rather than taking from them. Funding was restored for public schools, health care, and social services. Plans for creating sustainable communities, improving transportation infrastructure, producing more affordable housing, and controlling greenhouse gas emissions—all of which had been placed on hold during hard times—were reactivated. Brown also set aside significant amounts from the surplus years into a rainy day fund, to help mitigate the need for another round of cuts the next time the economy hits a downturn.

At the local government level, post-recession economic recovery continues in most cities, especially in the San Francisco Bay Area and Los Angeles metropolitan region. In some cities, such as San Francisco, the tech-driven economic boom has created the problem of too much growth too fast, which has resulted in a housing affordability crisis, evictions and displacement, and growing political protest. In other cities, however, recovery from the recession still lags. The cities of Vallejo, Stockton, and San Bernardino are now released from bankruptcy, but all three continue to struggle with the same kinds of problems that forced them into bankruptcy in the first place: underfunded pension plans; limited tax revenues from slowly recovering businesses; and growing demands from citizens for better services, security, and employment opportunities. While cities in the state's coastal regions are once again thriving, many in the Central Valley and Inland Empire regions are still striving to attain prerecession levels of financial stability and economic well-being.

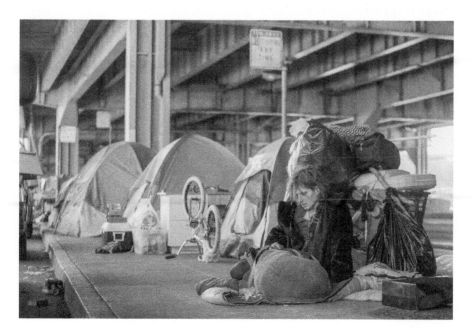

Illustrating the problems of the housing crisis and income inequality, San Francisco's homeless resorted to tent camps while the median price of homes in the city reached over $1,000,000 in 2018.

The Housing Crisis

Housing is perhaps the biggest crisis now facing California local governments. The median price of a home sale in June 2018 was over $600,000, double the U.S. median home price and a price only 30 percent of Californians can afford.[47] The upward pressure on prices is caused by a major shortage of housing supply, particularly lower-priced houses. From 2017 to 2018, the availability of homes priced below $200,000 fell by nearly 29 percent, while the supply of homes priced at $1 million or more increased by more than 18 percent. The housing shortage is particularly acute in the San Francisco Bay Area, where the median price of homes hit $1,088,000 in May 2018. The pace of new building is simply not keeping up with demand. Between 2008 and 2017, an average of 24.7 new housing permits were filed for every 100 new residents in California, well below the national average of 43.1 permits per 100 people.[48] See Figure 9.5 for details on this trend in recent years. At least 30 percent of people in every metropolitan area of the state cannot afford local rents, and that proportion increases to nearly 60 percent in some areas, as shown in Figure 9.6. The crisis has led to increased housing insecurity and homelessness. In the impacted areas of Silicon Valley and Los Angeles, more and more residents are living in trucks and RVs, parked along public streets, or in tents.

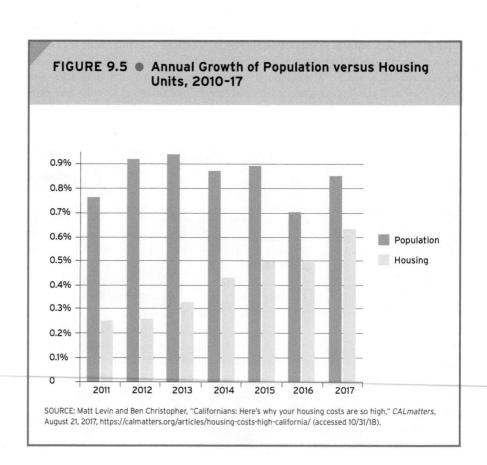

FIGURE 9.5 ● Annual Growth of Population versus Housing Units, 2010-17

SOURCE: Matt Levin and Ben Christopher, "Californians: Here's why your housing costs are so high," *CALmatters*, August 21, 2017, https://calmatters.org/articles/housing-costs-high-california/ (accessed 10/31/18).

FIGURE 9.6 ● Percentage of People Who Cannot Afford Local Rents by Metropolitan Area

In one report, it was shown that in every metropolitan area included in the study at least 30 percent of people were unable to afford local rent, with that figure being in some areas almost as high as 60 percent.

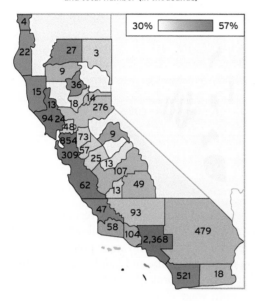

Households unable to afford rent as percent and total number (in thousands)

SOURCE: Data from U.S. Census Bureau; Zillow; McKinsey Global Institute analysis, and graph from www.artplusmarketing .com/california-needs-a-housing-first-agenda-my-2018-housing-package-1b6fe95e41da (accessed 9/7/2018).

NOTE: Shaded regions represent 98 percent of state population; unshaded regions represent 2 percent of state population and lacked sufficient data for analysis.

In September 2017, Governor Brown signed a set of 15 bills meant to ease the housing crunch, including a new tax on real estate transactions and a $4 billion bond that was approved by the voters in November 2018. Yet even the 14,000 new homes to be built each year with those funds will not put much of a dent in the problem, as shown in Figure 9.7. Developers would need to build well over 100,000 new homes more than planned each year to keep pace with California's population growth.[49]

Given simple economic rules of supply and demand, why don't developers simply build more housing? Part of the answer is that there is not enough affordable land to build on, particularly in the most impacted areas such as the San Francisco Bay Area. There is also a shortage of construction labor; California's unemployment rate in July 2018 was just 4.2 percent, the lowest rate since 1976.[50] Finally, there is the challenge of NIMBYism (Not In My Back Yard). Existing homeowners don't want new housing built near them, especially lower-priced housing, and this is true across political lines.[51]

FIGURE 9.7 ● **New Homes Built Each Year in California**

180,000

200,000

150,000

100,000

50,000

0

'90   '95   '00   '05   '10   '15

To keep up with a growing population, California needs 180,000 new homes each year. New legislation could add about 14,000 new homes each year.

SOURCE: Liam Dillon, "Gov. Brown just signed 15 housing bills. Here's how they're supposed to help the affordability crisis," *Los Angeles Times*, Sept 29, 2017, http://www.latimes.com/politics/la-pol-ca-housing-legislation-signed-20170929-htmlstory.html (accessed 10/31/18).

Another pressing issue faced by many local governments is the issue of growing income inequality and economic injustice. Following the lead of many local governments who adopted a $15 minimum wage policy, including San Francisco, Oakland, San Jose, Los Angeles County, and San Diego, in April 2016, Governor Brown signed a bill that made California the first state government in the country to adopt the $15 minimum wage along with the most generous paid-sick-leave policy in the United States. The increased minimum wage rules will take effect gradually, increasing $.50 to $1 each year for small and large businesses, and reaching $15 by 2022 for larger businesses and 2023 for smaller businesses.[52]

Conflict between California and the federal government has increased during the Donald Trump administration. Led by Attorney General Xavier Becerra, California has pushed back against Trump administration policies to roll back greenhouse gas emissions regulations. The state has also sought to protect marijuana markets, immigrants, and voting rights. As of October 2018, California has filed 44 lawsuits against the federal government. In September 2018, Governor Brown signed a bipartisan bill to block Trump's plan to expand offshore oil drilling off the California coast.[53] Battles between the state and federal government are also being waged over the 2020 Census and immigration.

Of all the lessons learned from the Great Recession, perhaps the most important is that local governments cannot solve economic and housing problems alone. Empowered business leadership, public-private partnerships, and market-based initiatives have the potential to help, but the private sector also is limited in its capacity to solve public problems. Local governments and their business partners require the power and resources of the federal and state governments to cope with such issues effectively. The years immediately ahead are certain to be politically turbulent and contentious, especially at the national level, and the future of California's state and local governments under the Trump administration is as yet unclear.

Study Guide

FOR FURTHER READING

Baldassare, Mark. *A California State of Mind: The Conflicted Voter in a Changing World*. Berkeley: University of California Press, 2002.

Bridges, Amy. *Morning Glories: Municipal Reform in the Southwest*. Princeton, NJ: Princeton University Press, 1997.

DeLeon, Richard Edward. *Left Coast City: Progressive Politics in San Francisco, 1975–1991*. Lawrence, KS: University Press of Kansas, 1992.

Hajnal, Zoltan L., Paul G. Lewis, and Hugh Louch. *Municipal Elections in California: Turnout, Timing, and Competition*. San Francisco: Public Policy Institute of California, 2002.

Rodriguez, Daniel B. "State Supremacy, Local Sovereignty: Reconstructing State/Local Relations under the California Constitution." In *Constitutional Reform in California: Making State Government More Effective and Responsive*, edited by Bruce E. Cain and Roger G. Noll, 401–29. Berkeley: Institute of Governmental Studies Press, University of California, 1995.

Sonenshein, Raphael J. *Politics in Black and White: Race and Power in Los Angeles*. Princeton, NJ: Princeton University Press, 1993.

ON THE WEB

California Department of Finance. www.dof.ca.gov. Accessed 8/24/18. The Department of Finance produces detailed and up-to-date statistical reports and studies on local government finances, the state budget process and its impacts on localities, and a wide range of demographic and economic information on cities and counties.

California Employment Development Department. www.edd.ca.gov. Accessed 8/24/18. Valuable source of up-to-date statewide and county-level information on employment and labor market conditions.

California Secretary of State. www.sos.ca.gov/elections. Accessed 8/24/18. Excellent source of information on county-level election results for statewide candidate races and ballot propositions.

California Special Districts Association. www.csda.net. Accessed 8/24/18.

California State Association of Counties. www.csac.counties.org. Accessed 8/24/18. Useful source of wide-ranging news and information on California's counties, with a main focus on policy and administration.

Institute for Local Government. www.ca-ilg.org. Accessed 8/24/18. The research arm and affiliate of the League of California Cities and the California State Association of Counties. Good source for in-depth studies of key policy issues facing the state's local governments.

League of California Cities. www.cacities.org. Accessed 8/24/18. An excellent source of news, information, and data on all aspects of governing California's cities.

U.S. Conference of Mayors. www.usmayors.org. Accessed 8/24/18.

SUMMARY

I. Overview of California local governments.
   A. California has more than 5,000 local governments of various types, including general-purpose governments such as those in counties and cities, specific-purpose governments such as those for school districts and special districts, and regional governments.
   B. Local governments provide essential services, ranging from law enforcement and fire protection to waste management and street maintenance to air- and water-quality control.

II. Legal framework for local government: the state has ultimate authority over local governments.
   A. Under Dillon's Rule, local governments are "creatures of the state" and have no inherent rights or powers except those given to them by the state constitution or legislature.
   B. California, like most states, gives counties and cities significant powers to govern themselves, make policies, enforce laws, raise revenues, borrow, and generally control local affairs as long as their decisions don't conflict with state or federal laws.
   C. The more populous cities and counties have adopted home-rule charters, which allow maximum local autonomy in self-governance.
   D. The other cities and counties operate as general-law counties and cities, which have to abide more strictly by the state legislature's local government code.

III. County governments.
   A. California's 58 counties are extremely diverse in terms of territorial extent, population size, demographic characteristics, and political culture.

B. Except for the unique case of San Francisco's consolidated county/city government, all counties are governed by five-member boards of supervisors that exercise both legislative and executive powers.

C. Counties perform important functions, many of them required by state government laws and mandates.

D. Counties also provide essential services, especially in unincorporated areas outside the cities and other jurisdictions, and they are major arenas for making large-scale land-use and development policies.

E. Each county also has a local agency formation commission (LAFCo), which plays a critical role in creating, merging, or dissolving new local governments, such as those in cities and special districts, and resolving disputes among competing jurisdictions.

IV. City governments.

A. The state has 482 cities, most of them general-law cities; the rest are charter cities with significant home-rule powers and local autonomy.

B. Cities are legally created through a process of municipal incorporation that requires LAFCo review and approval as well as a final majority vote of the community seeking formal city status.

C. Nearly all cities have a form of government modeled on the vision of Progressive Era reformers. Called reform cities, most of them have strong city managers, weak mayors, nonpartisan elections, at-large council elections, nonconcurrent elections, and direct democracy procedures (the initiative, referendum, and recall). Important exceptions to such reform cities are cities such as Los Angeles and San Francisco, which have strong mayors and district elections.

V. Citizen participation in local government.

A. The Brown Act of 1953, known as the "open meetings law," requires that all meetings of local legislative bodies be open and public unless specifically exempted, and that all citizens be permitted to attend such meetings.

B. Voter turnout in city elections has been steadily declining in recent years.

1. Those who do vote in city elections tend to be whiter, older, richer, and more educated than those who don't.

2. In particular, the state's growing population of noncitizens has little political voice or formal representation in local government.

3. Certain electoral reforms, such as a shift from nonconcurrent to concurrent elections, could markedly increase voter turnout levels.

VI. Special districts.

A. Special districts are limited-purpose local governments.

B. Excluding the state's 1,028 K–12 school districts and 72 community-college districts, California has nearly 5,000 special districts.

C. Special districts provide a range of services—for example, irrigation, pest abatement, parks and recreation, water, and fire protection—which are not provided at all (or in insufficient amounts) by general-purpose governments such as those for counties and cities.

D. Special districts are created by a LAFCo-approved citizen petition and a majority vote.

E. Most special districts are independent agencies that provide one type of service received and paid for by residents in smaller territories of larger jurisdictions, like counties.

F. Some special districts are enterprise districts that charge individual user fees for service.

G. Most special districts are funded by taxes or special assessments from service recipients.

H. The advantages of special districts include greater flexibility and responsiveness in tailoring service and requiring only the beneficiaries to pay the costs.

I. The disadvantages of special districts include duplication of services, lack of coordination, and unclear structures of authority and accountability.

VII. Regional governments.

A. The state's regional governments address problems such as air pollution and population growth that affect large areas and multiple local government jurisdictions.

B. Some regional governments, such as the San Francisco Bay Conservation and Development Commission and the California Coastal Commission, have strong regulatory authority and enforcement powers.

C. Other regional governments, such as the Southern California Association of Governments, the Association of Bay Area Governments, and other councils of government (COGs), mainly perform research, planning, and advisory functions and have little or no power or authority to impose their decisions on local jurisdictions.

VIII. The housing crisis.

A. Higher-priced homes have been increasing while more affordable homes are scarcer.

B. Building more housing has been impeded by increasing land costs, a shortage of construction labor, and homeowner obstruction.

C. Income inequality in cities has been addressed by a $15 minimum wage first instituted by localities then by the state.

PRACTICE QUIZ

1. Cities and counties that have home-rule charters have the authority to make their own laws even if they violate state and federal laws.
   a) true
   b) false

2. The U.S. Constitution gives local governments inherent rights and powers that cannot be taken away by state governments.
   a) true
   b) false

3. County boards of supervisors have both legislative and executive authority.
   a) true
   b) false

4. Most cities are governed by council-manager systems.
   a) true
   b) false

5. At the local government level, citizens cannot petition for a referendum or recall election.
   a) true
   b) false

6. Which of the following is *not* a characteristic of reform government at the local level?
   a) at-large council elections
   b) nonpartisanship

   c) city manager plan
   d) concurrent elections

7. Which of the following counties operates under a single charter as a consolidated city and county?
   a) Los Angeles
   b) Sacramento
   c) San Francisco
   d) Orange

8. Which of the following elected officials can be found only in county governments?
   a) sheriff
   b) mayor
   c) council member
   d) manager

9. ABAG is an example of a COG.
   a) true
   b) false

10. Despite decreasing availability of affordable homes in California's urban areas, the pace of new building has kept up with demand, averting a housing shortage.
    a) true
    b) false

CRITICAL-THINKING QUESTIONS

1. Do you think the Progressive Era reform vision for local governments is still a good one today? Should the state's local governments continue to be run by professional managers and insulated as much as possible from state and national party politics? Why or why not?

2. Should local governments, such as cities, be given more home-rule powers and greater local autonomy free of state interference? Test case: Would you support all California cities asserting their home-rule powers and local autonomy to the extent that San Francisco has? Why or why not?

3. Do you agree with some critics that most special districts should be abolished and their functions centralized un-

der the control of county and city governments? Why or why not?

4. Do you agree with some observers that California needs more and stronger regional governments? Why or why not? If you agree, what are some of the problems facing those who seek to form such governments, and what steps would you take to create them? How would you balance your recommendations with the principles of home rule and local autonomy?

5. Do you support or oppose the rebellion of local governments against the state as a response to the state's attempt to use local government property tax revenues to solve its budget deficit problems? Why or why not?

KEY TERMS

10 | Public Policy in California

WHAT CALIFORNIA GOVERNMENT DOES AND WHY IT MATTERS

California's housing crisis has been one of economics throughout its history. The climate and the state's abundance have drawn people to California since before its statehood. By the late twentieth century, the effects of housing costs were still mostly felt by those who were low-income or living in densely populated areas where property values had skyrocketed and Proposition 13's effects were deeply rooted. The impact of this problem has shifted in recent years and now affects many more groups in the population and many more areas within the state.

Recent problems in Riverside County, east of Los Angeles, illustrate the complexity of this problem well. The county has over 300 trailer parks, many inhabited by migrant agricultural workers who pick the vegetables and fruit that grow abundantly in the county's irrigated valleys. In 1999 the county accused several trailer parks that catered to migrant workers of substandard and dangerous conditions and subsequently shut them down. Harvey Duro, Sr., a member of the Torres Martinez Desert Cahuilla Indian Reservation, spread the word of a new trailer park on reservation land where the displaced workers could reside. Many farmworkers moved in, paying about $500 a month per trailer to live there.[1]

The conditions weren't good. The trailer park, officially called Desert Mobile Home Park but unofficially known as Duroville or Duros, was located next to a dump that burned from time to time. Heaps of tires and construction debris littered the area, the streets were dusty (and muddy when it rained), and the area's sewage flowed into a pond next door. In 2002 the teachers in the local schools noticed that many of their students who lived in the park were suffering from asthma and rashes, and they determined that the dump was the likely cause. The Bureau of Indian Affairs, which had jurisdiction because the trailer park was on the reservation, moved to close the park because of the unsanitary conditions. In 2009 the local U.S. attorney cited in court the park's "leaking sewage, 800 feral dogs, piles of debris and fire hazards," as well as 5,000 tenants. The cost of bringing it into compliance would be more than $4 million, which the owner could not afford.

After several years of litigation, in 2009 a federal judge decreed that since there was no other place for the residents to go, the park could stay open. The population of the park numbered between 2,000 to 6,000 people, depending on the time of year and economic conditions. Many residents were undocumented. Many earned less than $10,000 per year. And many of them were Purépechas, an indigenous people from Michoacán, Mexico. Many, in fact, were from a single town in Michoacán.

By 2010 most of the people who sold drugs in the park were gone, the feral dog problem was substantially reduced, and the rotting garbage had been cleared. But there was still no place for the residents to move, and the quality of the trailers was also still no better. Riverside County then completed a public housing project for the residents, Mountain View Estates, six miles away from Duroville and composed of 181 units.[2] Duroville finally closed in June 2014, 15 years after it opened. Public housing projects require that residents be in the United States legally, so many undocumented former residents of Duroville moved to other trailer parks in the area.

While Duroville was open, articles about the community occasionally appeared in the *New York Times* and the *Los Angeles Times* as well as in the local newspapers. It even had its own Wikipedia entry. And although Duroville had new-resident councils and representatives to help ensure residents' adherence to the rules and was eventually cleaned up because of legal intervention, a lack of quality housing and living conditions persisted and continues to persist for many farmworkers, particularly the undocumented. For example, the *Los Angeles Times* reported in October 2015 that some families who work in the Coachella Valley have "pooled resources" to create livable trailer parks. Given their limited resources, the end result is that "they [have] jury-rigged almost everything. Electricity was tapped from a post meant to power one well, the dirt road was covered in rugs to keep down the choking dust." Similar trailer parks dot the area, and most are vulnerable to power outages, storm damage, and sewage overflow. Residents are sometimes left with no option but to sleep in tents because of the heat index during the summer. Riverside County has responded to this problem by proposing $3.4 million dollars to pave dirt roads in a number of the trailer parks, and the county has "authorized the use of temporary construction power lines to return power."[3]

Duroville is one of many extremes that illustrate how the least enfranchised in the state have been among those most affected by this problem. But as stated in the beginning of this chapter, in the twenty-first century the housing crisis has impacted many groups. The state has attempted to respond to this crisis. In 2017, former governor Jerry Brown signed 15 bills that were created by the legislature to address housing issues in the state. Some of the bills included incentives for developers who dedicated a proportion of their projects to low-income housing, and one bill was a bond measure proposing fees, including real estate transaction fees. While these kinds of policies are intended to help ameliorate the housing crisis, the *Los Angeles Times* has reported that they likely will be insufficient. The problem is such that the supply cannot possibly meet the demand given the severity of the shortage.[4] The legislature is aware of this and recently proposed several additional bills. One of these, SB 1227, is aimed at student housing. It provides incentives to developers who build housing dedicated to students and, more importantly, set aside 20 percent of the units for students who are very low-income or homeless.[5]

The issue of housing, along with many other policy areas in California politics, exemplifies the challenges posed throughout this book—challenges related to California's enormous diversity and unique institutions. Sites such as Duroville can exist on Indian reservations, which have jurisdiction over most governmental areas except law enforcement. If not for this jurisdiction, the zoning and other laws in effect in most areas of California would have shut Duroville down much sooner.

You may have concluded by now that California is a land of contrasts. The same state that includes Beverly Hills and Silicon Valley also has its Durovilles. Public policy in California governs areas that are like Duroville—that is, areas that are not doing so well—and other areas that are in better shape. California's high degree of heterogeneity is evident in the proposal to divide California into six states, an initiative that failed to collect enough signatures in 2014 to make the ballot. It was attempted again in 2018. This plan would have created the richest state in the United States (the state that would have encompassed Silicon Valley), as well as the poorest (the state that would have included the Central Valley).

We know from earlier chapters in this book that California has come close to being ungovernable during the last two decades. We have a public that demands a high level of services but consistently refuses to pay for them. Many members of the public feel that the free tuition and low fees in higher education during the Pat Brown era are still possible at a time when the state's people and politics have changed profoundly. Proposition 30, passed in November 2012, is one of the few exceptions—a small sales tax increase and larger temporary income tax increases on the wealthy (these increases were set to expire in 2018, but were extended by Proposition 55 until 2025). The public is sometimes willing to approve initiatives to undertake new projects that lack funding. It is also willing to pass special taxes earmarked for special purposes, many of which benefit the interests sponsoring the relevant initiative.

The lack of consensus among the public is reflected in our institutions, which in some cases barely function. However, major steps have been taken to improve the quality of the political process in California. While the legislature has been unable to change the state's tax structure, now over 50 years old, some new institutional changes—most notably the top-two primary system and the new nonpartisan legislative redistricting system—are designed to improve the functioning of our political system. The 50 percent majority now necessary to pass a budget has ended the budget haggling that used to paralyze Sacramento all summer and for part of the fall, but the cost of limited revenues in 2011 and 2012 was a substantial reduction in funds for the state's public schools. The top-two primary, the 50 percent rule for passing the state's budget in the legislature, and the commission to handle redistricting every 10 years in a neutral and nonpartisan fashion may be just the beginning of a wave of reform, though these reforms will take years to assess.

Meanwhile, our focus in this chapter is on the current state of public policy in California. The term **public policy** means what government actually does or "produces" in various policy areas such as health, welfare, education, higher education, water, and the like. The policies in each of these areas are different in each state. For the California of the 1950s and 1960s, education and water policy were proud, if politically difficult, achievements, and the state was one of the nation's leaders in solving its problems and supporting its schools and colleges. For the California of the 2000s, these are areas of profound disappointment.

For example, even with Proposition 98 (1988) "guaranteeing" the public schools some 40 percent of the general fund, California's finances have been so tight that K-12 spending is below average, sometimes ranking in the bottom 40 percent of states.[6] *Education Week*, a national newspaper that covers issues in K-12 public education, gave California a C− for its "overall quality" of education. The grade includes evaluations of financial support, probabilities of success, and measures of student achievement. Only 10 other states received lower marks in early 2016.[7] Like 46 other states and the District of Columbia, California has adopted the Common Core Standards. Although the state adopted these standards in 2010, they were not implemented until 2012-13, so it is a bit soon to evaluate whether the Common Core Standards have improved student learning and achievement. According to Tom Torlakson, the State Superintendent of Public Instruction, it is hopeful that the Common Core Standards will improve college readiness. Results of the 2018 statewide standardized testing of students across all grades found that 49.83 percent met or exceeded the English language arts/literacy standard. Eleven percent fewer (38.65 percent) met or exceeded the standard for mathematics.[8] It is obvious from these measures that there is significant need for improvement. Advocates of the Common Core argue that over time the scores should improve because of the rigorous curriculum. One of the biggest problems facing public education in California is the achievement gap. It remains to be seen whether the Common Core will help narrow this gap given the many factors that need to be addressed, especially funding.

Likewise, the University of California, the California State University, and the state's extensive community college system have all seen cutbacks in faculty pay and course offerings as well as substantially higher costs for tuition and fees. How much higher these can go is a major, unanswered question, but there were few alternatives in the severe recession of 2009-10.

One could write several books about California public policy, so in this chapter we have confined ourselves to three areas of interest. They are typical in the sense that they show some of the best and worst areas in which the state is involved. The first of these is water policy. The second is health insurance. The third is the state's infrastructure, which has experienced spending issues similar to those endured by K-12 education.

Water Policy

Of the water used in California, 20 percent is for households, business, and industry, while 80 percent is for agricultural purposes, including irrigation. Farm production and food processing compose about 2 percent of the California economy, down from 5 percent in 1960. Over the past decade or more, higher revenue perennial crops that require annual watering, such as grapes, nuts, and other fruits, have increased as a proportion of California's total agricultural output (as compared to annual crops, which enable land to be left fallow in times of drought). As a consequence, **agricultural water use** has been creeping up.

Household water use is dominated by the two megalopolises of California: the San Francisco Bay region and Southern California. Residential and commercial water use is split 50–50 between use inside the house and landscaping outside. Total urban water usage has declined significantly in recent years. For example, 2013–15 witnessed an additional reduction of 25 percent in residential use according to the Public Policy Institute of California (PPIC).[9] Water districts have instituted water conservation programs that have aided in this effort despite increases in the state's population. Some of these are tiered pricing programs, so that large users pay more per unit, and some incorporate legal requirements to install low-flow toilets and showerheads. Even so, substantial differences among similar cities exist, depending on their closeness to the Pacific coast, density of the population, typical climate, and amount of industry. Coastal cities use less water; a dense population means smaller yards. Hot weather means more watering, and more industry can skew statistics because some industries may use a lot more water than others. A 2004 law requires that water meters be installed statewide by 2025. As of 2018 there were still cities with some unmetered customers; generally they are billed a flat rate each month.[10]

The major **2013–14 drought** exposed the problems of water rights and uses in the existing system. Governor Jerry Brown proclaimed a statewide water emergency in January 2014, and local water agencies, depending on their particular situations, gradually imposed measures to restrict the use of water.

The drought has also highlighted problems in the water supply. A study by several University of California researchers released in 2014 pinpointed the central problem: California's freshwater runoff in an average year is about 70 million acre-feet, but since 1914 the state has handed out water rights totaling 370 million acre-feet. That's five times more water than nature, on average, produces.[11] An acre-foot of water (one foot of water in depth on an acre of land) is sufficient for two average households for a year. There is tension here, however, between what are known as *riparian* vs. *appropriative* water rights. **Riparian rights** are water rights that people have because they own property on a lake or stream, for example. There are restrictions on exercising these rights such as "natural flow" of the water source and requirements that the water source be adjacent to the smallest piece of the property. California and Oklahoma are the only "western" states to recognize riparian rights. Granting water rights to private persons obviously makes California's water problems more complex. In addition, there are what are known as *appropriative* rights. These rights are given to persons who use water that is not on riparian land or to persons who are on riparian land but do not have riparian rights. People are given permits by the State's Division of Water Rights.[12] If this sounds a bit confusing, it is. And it exacerbates the state's water problems because the number of permits issued under **appropriated rights** exceeds the amount of water available.[13]

Many solutions have been proposed, among them the following: building two 35-mile tunnels around the Sacramento–San Joaquin Delta to bring water to the California aqueduct, importing water from new sources, increasing water conservation efforts, and using rainwater or gray water at home. Four practical solutions were suggested in major studies released in June 2014 by Oakland's Pacific Institute, the Natural Resource Defense Council, and researchers from UC Santa Barbara. Taken together, these four solutions, listed below, point to the future of water supply.[14]

1. Increasing efficiency in homes and industries by replacing or improving inefficient appliances, reducing waste and leaks, and replacing traditional landscapes with low-water-use plants and gardens. The potential savings are 2.9 to 5.2 million acre-feet per year.
2. Increasing efficiency in agriculture through better irrigation techniques and practices, with potential savings of 5.6 to 6.6 million acre-feet per year.
3. Reusing treated wastewater for irrigation, landscapes, industry, and recharging groundwater basins. Savings here could total 1.2 to 1.8 million acre-feet per year.
4. Capturing storm water at homes and businesses, using it locally or to recharge groundwater basins. Savings could total 0.4 to 0.6 million acre-feet per year.[15]

At a minimum, the new sources over time could add 10 million acre-feet of water.

The other side of the water quantity problem is the water *quality* problem, involving problems of **groundwater management**, naturally occurring minerals such as arsenic in California's water, and, in the eyes of many Californians, hardness. (The latter isn't a water quality issue, but many feel that it is.)

Thirty-five percent of the total water used in California in an average year is groundwater. In a drought year, pumping groundwater increases as users attempt to compensate for the lack of rain. While surface water is regulated in California, until September 2014 groundwater was largely unregulated. Some groundwater basins have been so heavily used that the amount taken out each year exceeds what can reasonably be replenished, even in El Niño years with relatively heavy rainfall totals. When groundwater declines, the energy costs of pumping water from deeper wells increase, and the additional pumping can cause land to sink, damaging surface infrastructure such as roads and canals.[16]

Contamination of groundwater is a growing problem in California. Some basins are contaminated from fertilizers and manure, and others suffer because of salinity. Changes in water-use practices will help in the future, but some existing basins will need to be cleaned up.

Until 2014, California was the only western state in the United States without some level of state regulation of groundwater. The state took a major step in this direction as a result of the 2013–14 drought: the Assembly and state Senate passed three bills to compel water-basin managers in certain areas of the state to design groundwater management plans that would prevent overdrafting. All three bills were signed into law by Governor Brown. Together, they make up the Sustainable Groundwater Management Act (SGMA). The SGMA includes not only guidelines and regulations for the management of groundwater, but also regulatory language for areas that may not have groundwater basin managers.

In addition, a water bond issue of more than $7 billion was placed on the November 2014 ballot, as the drought provided the catalyst for the legislature to agree on a series of projects in the water policy area. The bond issue had previously been stalled in the legislature for several years. The water bond was approved by almost 67 percent of the voters.

Health Insurance

While many Californians are still without health insurance coverage, President Obama's Affordable Care Act (ACA) has already had a significant impact in California. During the first six months of enrollment, 1.4 million people purchased a policy on Covered California, the state's health insurance exchange.[17] Another 1.9 million people enrolled in Medi-Cal, now open to single adults and couples without children who qualify on the basis of poverty. These enrollments should reduce the number of people without health insurance in California by about 3 million; the exact number is unclear because some new enrollees replaced their private insurance plans with insurance through the exchange or Medi-Cal. Gallup polls taken in 2013 and in mid-2014 showed a reduction in those without health insurance in California from 21.6 percent to 16.3 percent, which is "in the ballpark" of what can reasonably be expected—a good start toward reducing the very high proportion of people in California without health insurance. More recently, a 2015 Gallup poll indicated that the trend has continued—only 11.8 percent of Californians were uninsured.

While the number of uninsured has declined steadily since the ACA's adoption and implementation, there are three major reasons why the number of uninsured has been so high in California. One is that many people in California, more than the national average, work in small firms, and small firms tend not to offer health insurance nearly as often as large firms do. The second is that the state's population has a large proportion of immigrants, and immigrants are much less likely to have health insurance than are native-born Americans. The third reason is that undocumented immigrants are not eligible to enroll in Medicaid (Medi-Cal is California's Medicaid program, discussed later in this section), nor are they eligible to purchase health insurance through the ACA exchanges. (See the "Who Are Californians?" feature on p. 275 for more information on who is uninsured in the state.) About 2.5 million people are undocumented in California, a figure that has remained constant for over a decade. These statistics are unlikely to improve given the 2016 presidential election outcome. Donald Trump called for the repeal of the ACA in his campaign, and this position was a very popular one for many of his supporters and other conservatives. In 2017 he attempted to replace the ACA with his own health care reform plan. Trump's plan would have significantly impacted those who are eligible to participate as well as those who will remain uninsured because of their undocumented status. One proposed change was a tax deduction for the insured. The working poor or those who have a lower income would have been unlikely to benefit from a tax deduction in the way that wealthier Californians would, however.

After a bill proposing single payer health care stalled in the California Assembly, members of the California Nurses Association rallied at the Capitol in June 2017 to bring the bill to a vote.

Employer-Sponsored Insurance

In 2015 about 50 percent of Californians under age 65 had **employer-sponsored insurance (ESI)**—that is, they obtained their insurance through their employer, who typically subsidized some of the cost. ESI has been declining nationally, and the recession of 2008–09 accelerated the process. In California, ESI has historically been lower than in other states because of the size and structure of California's employers and the number of undocumented workers in the state. After the first round of enrollment in the ACA, there was some decline in ESI numbers for eligible lower-income workers with families, who may have chosen not to enroll in ESIs given the more affordable alternatives under the ACA.[18]

Single Payer Proposal

SB 562, known as the Healthy California Act, was proposed in the state Senate in 2017. The scope of the act was very broad. It included health care as a right to California residents and guaranteed universal health care with substantial government subsidies and potentially no out-of-pocket expenses for all Californians. The Healthy California Act became very controversial very quickly. A report issued by the state projected the cost of SB 562 to be approximately 400 billion dollars per year. Proponents of the bill argued that at least half of the cost would be offset by funds from other existing plans at the federal, state, and local levels. Paying for the other 200 billion per year became a larger sticking point. A proposed increase in payroll taxes would have helped to cover this, but the percentage of the necessary increase became an issue of political debate.[19]

In June 2017 the bill hit a roadblock in the state Assembly. The state Assembly shelved the bill because of what members thought were significant problems with funding and implementing the legislation. **Single payer health care** remains an important political issue despite the fact that SB 562 was stalled in the Assembly. In fact, it was one of the most important issues in the 2018 governor's race, dividing candidates and the electorate alike along party lines. Democrats are in support, and Republicans are in opposition. According to a May 2018 survey conducted by the Public Policy Institute of California, 41 percent of likely voters in the gubernatorial race favored single payer while 41 percent opposed it. Another 12 percent responded that they favored single payer as long as it didn't increase taxes.[20] Political support among Democratic candidates for single payer, as well as public support for such plans, means that single payer will remain on the public policy agenda in California for the near future.

Individual Health Insurance Marketplace

In California's state **individual insurance marketplace**, people purchase a health insurance policy directly from the insurance company. This is the market expected to be most directly affected by the ACA. Several provisions in the act reformed this market, which has been characterized in the past by extremely large price increases from year to year (one large insurer asked for a 39 percent price increase from 2010 to 2011) and by **rescissions**, cases in which insurers have dropped policyholders who have become sick and filed large claims, on the grounds that their applications were not truthful. The extent of these price increases and rescissions enabled by California's pre-ACA marketplace meant that it was a model other states would not want to emulate. The ACA now prohibits companies that provide insurance on the marketplace from charging higher rates for preexisting conditions, rescinding policies after policyholders file insurance claims, rating users by health status so that those with fair or poor health pay a higher rate, and enforcing lifetime limits on policies. In 2016 about 1.5 million Californians participated in this market. Most of the people in the market should eventually be receiving their health insurance through Covered California, the state's health insurance exchange.

Medi-Cal

Medi-Cal is California's version of the federal Medicaid plan for the poor. The federal government sponsors two large federal health insurance programs, **Medicare** and **Medicaid**. Medicare, aimed primarily at senior citizens, is paid for with federal funds, a tax on workers and their employers, and beneficiary premiums, deductibles, and co-pays. Medicaid, in contrast, is aimed at low-income people, and the financing is split between the federal government and the states. The federal government provides an average of 57 percent of the funding and some national standards, and the states provide the other 43 percent of the funding plus basic program administration and decision making. The proportion of the funding that each state provides is determined by a formula based on state per-capita income, and because California is a relatively rich state, it receives 50 percent federal funding, the minimum rate. Mississippi received the maximum federal funding rate at 73.6 percent in fiscal year 2015.

Under the ACA, Medicaid/Medi-Cal will expand by dropping requirements that excluded single individuals and couples without children and by accepting Medi-Cal enrollees solely on the basis of their income. These changes resulted in 1.9 million people signing up for Medi-Cal during the first enrollment period for the ACA, from November 2013 to March 2014. Medi-Cal now covers more than 13 million Californians, one-third of the population.[21]

The downside to this expansion is that California's average cost per Medi-Cal recipient is the lowest of any state, mostly because provider payments—the payment to each hospital and doctor for providing a service covered by Medi-Cal—are the lowest in the country. Consequently, access to doctors, particularly specialists, is limited for Medi-Cal beneficiaries in many parts of the state. This is because, for financial reasons, many medical practices either will not take Medi-Cal beneficiaries at all or limit the number of Medi-Cal patients they will see.[22]

Medicare

Approximately 12.5 percent of Californians are over 65, and almost all of the 4.5 million people in that category are on Medicare. In addition, 2.4 percent of Californians under 65 also qualify for Medicare. All those under 65 who are on Medicare have a disability of some kind (although not all those with disabilities are eligible for Medicare): anyone with ALS (Lou Gehrig's disease) or end-stage renal disease is immediately eligible for Medicare, and those who are on Social Security disability are eligible for Medicare after a two-year wait. The Medicare numbers are not expected to be affected by the ACA.

TRICARE

TRICARE and other military-related programs are the health care programs for military retirees and their dependents, including some members of the military reserves, with some civilian health benefits for military personnel as well. The category also includes those who receive their health care from the U.S. Department of Veterans Affairs (VA). About 2.4 percent of those under 65, some 800,000 Californians, are on TRICARE. The ACA does not affect TRICARE.

The Uninsured

The California Health Care Foundation, using census data from the federal government, calculated the proportion of uninsured Californians under age 65 at 21.2 percent in 2010 to 2012. Gallup, using its own surveys and a much simpler question, calculated the proportion as 21.6 percent in 2013 and 16.3 percent in mid-2014, and less than 9 percent in 2016.[23] See the "Who Are Californians?" section on the facing page about who the 3 million uninsured Californians were in 2018. Clearly, the implementation of the ACA in early 2014 has resulted in a major drop in the number and proportion of the uninsured. Just as surely, there is still a long way to go. Basic information about those without insurance follows, although any specific numbers cited are from *before* the ACA.

- Some 23 percent of workers lacked insurance in California, compared with 19 percent in the nation.

- Most heads of household without insurance have a job, and most of those jobs are full-time.

Who Are California's 3 Million Uninsured?

California has a large degree of income inequality, and it has struggled with providing equal access to health insurance. While American citizens and permanent residents have access to government-provided health insurance through Medicare at the age of 65, many Californians under that age are unable to gain insurance either through employer-based, individual, or public programs. Before the passage of the Affordable Care Act in 2010, California had one of the highest uninsured rates in America for people between the ages of 0–64 (24.3 percent in 2009), but since then the uninsured rate has dropped significantly (7 percent in 2018) across the state.

Though coverage has expanded, approximately 3 million Californians under the age of 65 remain uninsured. For those who qualify for one of these government heath care programs but chose not to apply, it may be for a variety of reasons including they do not want to enroll in a government program, they do not know they are eligible for one of these programs, or the programs, despite subsidies, are still cost prohibitive.

Why are Californians Uninsured?

■ Immigration Status   ■ Eligible for Covered CA WITH Subsidies

■ Eligible for Medi-Cal   ■ Eligible for Covered CA with NO Subsidies

ἱ = 2% of total population

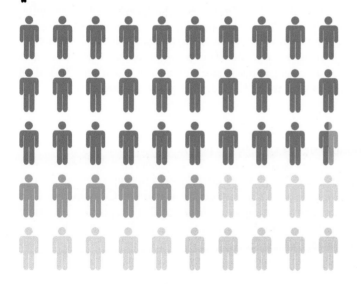

Percentage of Uninsured by County

▢ Less than 1% uninsured   ▨ 6–10% uninsured

▨ 1–5% uninsured   ■ Greater than 10% uninsured

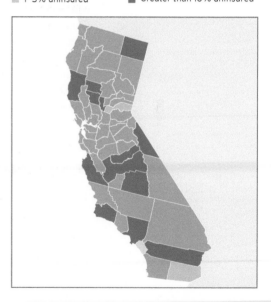

SOURCE: http://healthpolicy.ucla.edu/publications/Documents/PDF/California%27s%20 Uninsured%20by%20County2.pdf (accessed 07/27/2018); "2008–2016 Small Area Health Insurance Estimates (SAHIE) using the American Community Survey (ACS)," United States Census Bureau, www.census.gov/data/datasets/time-series/demo/sahie/estimates-acs.html (accessed 07/27/2018); "How Many in Your Area Are Uninsured–and Why?," California Health Care Foundation, www.chcf.org/publication/how-many-area-uninsured-why/ (accessed 07/27/2018); "Child Uninsured Rate In California Ranks Lowest In Nation," Georgetown University Health Policy Institute: Center for Children and Families, ccf.georgetown.edu/2016/11/01/child-uninsured-rate-in-california-ranks-lowest-in-nation/ (accessed 07/27/2018).

forcriticalanalysis

1. Why do some regions of California have higher rates of uninsured than others? What drives the different rates shown in the map?

2. What other strategies might California use to lower the uninsured rate further?

- It is estimated that most *children* without insurance are eligible for Medi-Cal or Healthy Families, California's State Children's Health Insurance Program (SCHIP, which is a federal program aimed at those whose incomes are just above the Medicaid/Medi-Cal eligibility levels).

- 25- to 34-year-olds are the largest age group represented among the uninsured (26 percent), but every age group under 65 is represented. So-called pre-retirees, 55- to 64-year-olds, make up 9 percent of the total.

- In terms of ethnicity, of those without health insurance in California most are Latino (about 58 percent). Whites represent the next most frequent group, at 24 percent. Asians compose 11 percent of the total, and African Americans 5 percent.

- Of those without health insurance, 63 percent are American citizens and 37 percent are not.

California's Infrastructure

Infrastructure is the part of government with which citizens come into contact the most—highways, schools, universities, commuter buses, and railways. California's infrastructure deteriorated significantly from the 1970s into the 2000s, although recently the state has made some progress toward improving the system. One factor complicating the successful maintenance of the state's infrastructure is what Bruce Cain of UC Berkeley's Institute of Governmental Studies calls California's "infrastructure ambivalence." On the one hand, Californians want modern facilities and infrastructure, but "we don't want what often comes with those things. There are, for instance, unavoidable environmental costs. Water projects can endanger fisheries in the Delta. New roads and housing can separate and destroy ecosystems."[24] And, of course, we don't want to pay for them. Consider the following examples.

Highways

California's highway system was close to the best in the nation after World War II and into the 1950s and 1960s. Beginning in the 1970s, however, it declined severely. The "California Infrastructure Report Card 2018," issued by the American Society of Civil Engineers, gave California's infrastructure a grade of C–, which is a bit better than the D grade for the nation as a whole.[25] A 2011 report on pavement conditions in the United States found 37 percent of California's roads to be "poor," with only 21 percent "good," making California the state ranked sixth from the bottom of the list.[26] A study of the structural quality of California's bridges found an improvement overall from 2007 to 2013. In 2007, 3,249, or 13.4 percent, of California's 24,189 bridges were structurally deficient; this number declined to 2,769, or 11.1 percent, in 2013.[27] There has been progress, partly the result of bond issues that were approved by the voters during the Schwarzenegger administration, but there is still much to be done.

The rebuilding of the Bay Bridge connecting San Francisco and Oakland is an extreme example of the substantial problems that have plagued the California state government's management of infrastructure projects. A 2014 report published in the *Sacramento Bee* indicated that the state agency responsible for the bridge construction chose a Chinese contractor who had never built parts for a bridge before to fabricate the steel structure of the bridge. The contractor ignored quality requirements built into the contract and fell behind schedule, necessitating the expenditure of hundreds of millions of dollars above the contract level. The result was a bridge built years behind schedule, costing more than twice the original price, and inspiring significant doubts about its quality.[28]

The management of California's transportation funds is clearly an issue. Dan Walters, who has been writing about California politics and management issues for the *Sacramento Bee* for several decades, points to "the labyrinth of interlocking transportation accounts" that direct money to infrastructure projects as the root of the mismanagement.[29] Others locate the problem in the increase in hybrid automobiles that use less gasoline, resulting in less income for the state from the gasoline tax. Another factor is the politicians who find few political benefits from maintaining infrastructure compared with building new projects. Additionally, there are governance problems. In a recent op-ed piece for the *Los Angeles Times*, George Skelton identified Proposition 13 as another factor that has affected potential revenues for California's highways and bridges. As noted in earlier chapters, Proposition 13 requires a two-thirds vote in both houses of the state legislature for any statewide tax increases. Governor Brown called for a special session of the legislature to address infrastructure problems. Representatives from Northern California, Senator Jim Beall and Assemblyman Jim Frazier, both Democrats, co-sponsored a bill that would increase the gas tax on regular fuel by 17 cents a gallon and on diesel fuel by 30 cents a gallon. The bill would also require zero-emission vehicles to pay an annual fee of $165. Skelton noted that it is unlikely for this 7.4 billion-dollar plan to pass, however, because of the two-thirds vote requirements and because of the current majorities in the state legislature.[30] But despite these obstacles, it did pass in 2017 (see related discussion of Proposition 6, an attempt to reverse this increase, in Chapter 4). One bright note in all of this is a change in California's car culture. As noted in the "Who Are Californians?" feature on p. 278, recent survey results from the state's department of transportation show that increasing numbers of Californians are choosing public transportation, biking, and walking to get around over driving personal cars. Transportation is not the only persistent infrastructure problem that is confronted with political obstacles. When a water main broke in Los Angeles in 2014, it turned out that the main was 100 years old and that water rates were too low to keep up with the cost of maintenance. This was because the city council, not a water agency, set the rates. Although California's infrastructure is clearly beset by numerous problems, few people consider the maintenance of California's infrastructure, so critical to the movement of citizens, to be a top priority.

Levees

In 1986 a levee along the Yuba River broke and inundated the small town of Linda in the Central Valley, causing several hundred million dollars' worth of damage. In 2004, 18 years later, the state Supreme Court ratified a court of appeal decision that found the state of California liable because it had not repaired the broken stretch of levee. While the state resisted liability for the break and its consequences, the courts have determined that the state must pay for the consequences of its neglect.[31]

The *Sacramento Bee* published a series of articles detailing several governmental agencies that were responsible for flood control and maintenance of the levees

How Do Californians Get Around?

Every 10 years, the California Department of Transportation conducts the California Household Travel Survey. The most recent survey covers the 2010–12 period and includes responses from 42,431 California households. Though the average household owns 1.8 cars, nearly 8 percent of California residents said that they don't own a car. When comparing the most recent survey data to the previous survey, conducted in 2000, we see that the percentage of people driving a car dropped by 11 percentage points, while the percentage of people walking, biking, and taking public transit doubled to 23 percent.

Percentage of All Trips by Travel Mode

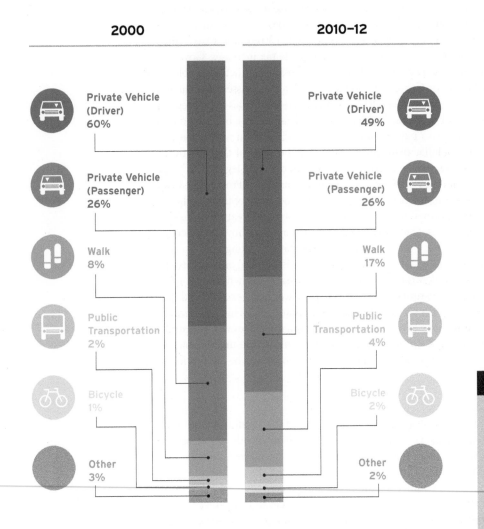

2000

- Private Vehicle (Driver) 60%
- Private Vehicle (Passenger) 26%
- Walk 8%
- Public Transportation 2%
- Bicycle 1%
- Other 3%

2010–12

- Private Vehicle (Driver) 49%
- Private Vehicle (Passenger) 26%
- Walk 17%
- Public Transportation 4%
- Bicycle 2%
- Other 2%

SOURCE: U.S. California Department of Transportation, Statewide Travel Analysis Branch, www.dot.ca.gov/hq/tpp/offices/omsp/statewide_travel_analysis/ (accessed 10/31/18).

for critical analysis

1. How do you travel to school? What role does the government play in your commute?

2. What, if anything, should government do to encourage people to use methods other than private cars to get where they need to go?

along the Sacramento River. Although the agencies have not been able to find the funds to repair more than 150 sites where the levees could fail during a major flood, builders and developers have continued to construct large developments in the Central Valley near Sacramento in areas where levees hold back rivers that are capable of flood damage to thousands of homes and businesses.[32]

In mid-2004, just after the publication of the *Sacramento Bee* series, a dirt levee broke suddenly in the Delta region, instantly changing 12,000 acres of farmland into a 12,000-acre lake. Officials found that a second levee was in danger of breaking, and a third needed to be shored up to prevent a road from being flooded and cutting off the only connection to two islands housing 178 residents.[33] The total damage amounted to $35 million in damages to buildings and crops, plus another $36.5 million to fix the levees. Some of this changed when California lawmakers prioritized levee reconstruction after the destruction wreaked by Hurricane Katrina on the Gulf Coast and the subsequent failure of government in many places to fulfill its emergency responsibilities. The public-works package of bond issues approved by the voters in November 2006 included Proposition 1E, the Disaster Preparedness and Flood Prevention Act, which authorized $4.1 billion in bonds to rebuild flood-control structures, including the Delta levees. The authorized money has provided a starting point for rebuilding the eroding facilities.

In late 2013, Governor Jerry Brown proposed a $25 billion plan to build two 35-mile-long tunnels to carry water under and around the Delta and to rebuild the Delta levees, with construction starting in 2017. The plan would restore wetlands and, in the eyes of supporters, would provide a more reliable source for the 25 million Californians who use the Delta's water. Opponents, however, are concerned about the cost of the tunnels, the possible ecological damage from the additional water pumped out of the Delta, and the project's questionable financing. In April 2016 the *Los Angeles Times* reported that the previously projected impact of this project, now called California WaterFix, may have been overstated. According to the article, some federal agencies that have reviewed the plan are skeptical about its ability to do more than sustain the status quo of water delivery.[34] This skepticism is predicated on factors such as the complicated irrigation and other water delivery systems that currently exist in and adjacent to the Delta, as well as the existing federal regulatory policies that protect endangered fish species that would be affected by the proposed tunnel system. Water is obviously essential to California in myriad ways. It is a public policy problem that deserves to be at the top of the state's agenda. It illustrates, however, the challenges to solving critical public problems even when there is a consensus to act.[35]

In April 2018 the Delta tunnels or "twin tunnels" project was given a major boost with a $10.8 billion funding commitment from the Metropolitan Water District of Southern California. The project still faces other obstacles, according to the *Sacramento Bee*. These include water rights and access, and legal challenges. It is estimated that the project won't begin until 2019, even if these hurdles are overcome, and that it will still take at least 15 years to complete it.[36]

The Future of California's Infrastructure

In addition to the Delta tunnels, Governor Brown's second long-term infrastructure priority is the high-speed rail system that would connect San Francisco, Sacramento, and Los Angeles. A ground-breaking ceremony was held in Fresno on January 6, 2015. Construction has been delayed by numerous lawsuits over the system's funding and other design and implementation problems. The plan was projected to cost $68 billion, and the voters have authorized about $10 billion in bonds for the first phase of construction, along with federal stimulus funds from the 2009 recession. However, in March 2018 the state revealed that the projected cost would now be at least $77.3 billion and may even exceed $98 billion by its completion. Moreover, it was expected that it wouldn't be fully operational until 2033.[37] In April, California High-Speed Rail Authority's chief executive, Jeff Morales, resigned. His departure and those of others in this agency have reinforced concerns that the project is too problematic to be realized.[38] Since its inception, many have argued that the state cannot afford a project this large on top of its other needs.

The neglect of the state's infrastructure over time is obvious. There are many reasons why infrastructure repair and upkeep are not more pressing concerns, but the priorities of both politicians and the public are clearly part of the problem. Infrastructure is a long-term problem, and our political system, based on two- and four-year terms of office, thinks short-term. This factor is magnified by the term limits imposed on the legislature, traditionally a body in which legislators spend several decades of their careers and can think in longer terms than the governor and the executive-branch officials, who are elected for only one or two four-year terms. Now with term limits, the members of the legislature are subject to the same short-term time constraints.

Conclusion

The Duroville case study illustrates the problems that arise in California because of fractured interests, complications of land (Indian reservations) that the state cannot control or regulate, and problems resulting from the number of undocumented immigrants. That a disgraceful trailer park finally closed after many years of dysfunction is good. That it took so many years to find a substitute location for the people who lived in the park is not good. That some families who work in this area are still residing in inadequate housing and lack basic amenities that are widely available to most Californians remains a problem. One characteristic of contemporary California is that years or decades can pass before even modest starts are made on solving problems.

Water policy and health insurance are two issues that illustrate how external changes, such as climate fluctuations or new federal policy, can dramatically affect state policy. When these kinds of catalysts do not exist, California is often slow or unable to make headway. For example, the health insurance situation only worsened in the two decades before the passage of the ACA, and the last great pieces of legislation affecting water policy were decided upon during the administration of Governor Edmund G. "Pat" Brown, from 1959 to 1967. Recent external events have finally prompted movement in both policy areas. The 2013–14 drought stimulated California's state government to pass path breaking legislation in August 2014, making it the last western state to enact groundwater regulations. Regarding health insurance, the passage of the federal Affordable Care Act gave California the opportunity to insure a substantial proportion of its uninsured population at the minimum cost. California was wise to take advantage of this opportunity. Single payer was an important issue in the gubernatorial race. How to fund it without increasing existing taxes and fees will determine public support for single payer plans in the future.

Water policy has become immensely more complicated with the growth of the environmental movement since the first Earth Day in 1969. But even under the senior Governor Brown in the early 1960s, the decisions made on water were not easy and involved prolonged political conflict. We often hear commentators discussing the "cultural breakup" of the old political consensus in the state, but the truth is that we are better for the multiplicity of voices that continually debate the best course of action for California to pursue. These differing voices make it more difficult to achieve public policy consensus and to make decisions, some long overdue, but water policy and health insurance are two important interests that need to be considered in the present day. We have begun the long road to reform on many issues discussed in this chapter and the book as a whole, and there is hope that California will be more governable in the future. But more steps have to be taken, and we need both visionary leadership and voters who pay attention and are interested in change. We hope the readers of this book will be those voters.

A federal judge ordered the closure of Duroville, a mobile park residence in Thermal, California, where a large population of undocumented immigrants resided.

Study Guide

FOR FURTHER READING

"Arnold's Big Chance: A Survey of California." *The Economist*, May 1, 2004, pp. 1–16.

Barrera, E. A. "A Firestorm of Controversy—Still No County Fire Department Five Years after Cedar Blaze." *East County Magazine*, August 2008. www.eastcountymagazine.org. Accessed 8/17/12.

"The Drying of the West." *The Economist*, February 22, 2014, pp. 22–23.

Gleick, Peter H. "Solving California's Water Problems." *Huffington Post*, June 10, 2014. www.huffingtonpost.com/peter-h-gleick/solving-californias-water_b_5479569.html. Accessed 9/3/14.

Hanak, Ellen, Jeffrey Mount, and Caitrin Chappelle. "Just the Facts: California's Latest Drought." Public Policy Institute of California, February 2014. www.ppic.org. Accessed 9/3/14.

Hill, Laura E., Magnus Lofstrom, and Joseph M. Hayes. "Immigrant Legalization: Assessing the Labor Market Effects." Public Policy Institute of California, 2010. www.ppic.org/content/pubs/report/R_410LHR.pdf. Accessed 8/17/12.

Johnson, Hans, and Laura Hill. "At Issue: Illegal Immigration." Public Policy Institute of California, July 2011. www.ppic.org/content/pubs/atissue/AI_711HJAI.pdf. Accessed 8/17/12.

Khazan, Olga, "Are You Sure You Want Single Payer?" *The Atlantic*, August 21, 2017. https://www.theatlantic.com/health/archive/2017/08/are-you-sure-you-want-single-payer/537456. Accessed 9/18/18.

Lustig, R. Jeffrey. *Remaking California, Reclaiming the Public Good*. Berkeley: Heyday Books, 2010.

Matthews, Joe, and Mark Paul. *California Crack-Up, How Reform Broke the Golden State and How We Can Fix It*. Berkeley: University of California, 2010.

Pear, Robert. "Lacking Papers, Citizens Are Cut from Medicaid." *New York Times*, March 12, 2007, p. A1.

Piller, C. "Bay Bridge's Troubled China Connection," *Sacramento Bee*, June 8, 2014.

Rogers, Paul. "Is Jerry Brown's Delta Tunnels Plan Repeating the Errors of High-Speed Rail?" *San Jose Mercury-News*, December 9, 2013.

Schrag, Peter. *California: America's High-Stakes Experiment*. Berkeley: University of California Press, 2006.

Simmons, Charlene Wear. *Gambling in the Golden State, 1998 Forward*. Sacramento: California Research Bureau, California State Library, May 2006.

"Special Report: Democracy in California, The People's Will." *The Economist*, April 23, 2011.

State of California, Legislative Analyst's Office. *A Primer: The State's Infrastructure and the Use of Bonds*. Sacramento: Legislative Analyst's Office, January 2006.

Walters, Dan. "Politicians Often Ignore California's Aging Infrastructure." *Sacramento Bee*, August 9, 2014.

ON THE WEB

American Association of State Highway and Transportation Officials. www.transportation.org. Accessed 10/17/16.

American Society of Civil Engineers (ASCE). https://www.asce.org/report_cards (accessed 9/28/18).

California Health Care Foundation. www.chcf.org. Accessed 9/3/14.

Huffington Post. www.huffingtonpost.com. Accessed 9/3/14.

Kaiser Family Foundation. http://kff.org. Accessed 9/3/14. Health insurance information.

Pacific Institute. http://pacinst.org/ or www.californiadrought.org. Accessed 9/3/14.

Public Policy Institute of California. www.ppic.org. Accessed 9/3/14.

State of California, Legislative Analyst's Office. www.lao.ca.gov. Accessed 9/3/14.

SUMMARY

I. Duroville was a trailer park located on an Indian reservation in Riverside County. Many of its residents were agricultural workers, and they experienced particularly squalid conditions during the 12 years of the park's existence.

   A. The federal government filed suit to close Duroville, but federal and state efforts to do so were stymied by the lack of an alternative location that the park's several thousand residents could afford.

   B. The state and county have constructed a new trailer park/public housing complex using redevelopment funds, and the Duroville trailer park was finally closed in 2014.

II. The 2013–14 drought worsened California's water supply problem.

   A. Twenty percent of the water used in California is for household and business consumption, half of which is used for landscaping. The other 80 percent is for agriculture.

   B. Urban water use has been constant despite increases in population, evidence of the conservation programs implemented in water districts in California.

   C. California water agencies have vastly overpromised the average amount of water that runs off each year in California.

   D. Practical solutions to increase the amount of water available for people to use in California include increased efficiency at home or in industry, increased efficiency in agriculture, reusing treated wastewater on landscapes and recharging groundwater basins, and capturing storm water.

   E. Water quality is also an issue in California because of pollution and naturally occurring minerals such as arsenic in the groundwater.

   F. Groundwater makes up 35 percent of the water used in an average year, and the percentage is higher in drought years. Until 2014, California was the only western state that did not regulate its groundwater. In August of that year, the legislature passed a bill that allows the state to review groundwater management plans to be produced by many water districts in the state.

III. The lack of health insurance among Californians is a major problem, but President Obama's Affordable Care Act has had a major impact in the state, with 1.4 million people purchasing health insurance policies and another 1.9 million enrolling in Medi-Cal, California's Medicaid program during the first six months of enrollment.

   A. Employers insure a lower proportion of people in California compared with other states because there are more small firms in California and the state is home to many noncitizens.

   B. Proportionally, more people in California buy their own health insurance than people in other states do. The California health insurance market has been characterized by large price increases from year to year and by "rescissions," the cancellation of policies because of inaccurate applications (from the perspective of the insurance companies) or because high claims have been filed (from the perspective of the state). These are the areas that the Affordable Care Act will affect the most, by more closely standardizing policies and eliminating rescissions.

C. Medi-Cal covers 30 percent of Californians, a larger proportion than are covered by Medicaid in other states. California's average cost per beneficiary is among the lowest of the states because provider payments are so low. As a result, access to providers is a major problem in some areas of the state.

D. In California, Medicare covers some 600,000 persons under 65 with disabilities. A similar number is covered by TRICARE or the Department of Veterans Affairs (VA).

E. Although we do not have good quality data on the statistics at this point, it appears that because of the Affordable Care Act, the percentage of uninsured adult Californians under 65 has fallen to 16 percent or less, down from 21 percent.

IV. California's infrastructure has noticeably deteriorated in the last 50 years.

A. The state's highways were in poor condition but are being gradually upgraded through bond issues passed in 2006 at Governor Schwarzenegger's urging and through federal Recovery Act funds.

B. The management of transportation funds is an issue, with the major contemporary example being the problems with the new San Francisco–Oakland Bay Bridge.

C. The levees in the Delta and the Central Valley of California are the subject of a major and controversial plan that Governor Jerry Brown pushed for in 2014. Some levee work is being attended to by state funds provided in bond issues passed in 2006.

PRACTICE QUIZ

1. Medicaid is
   a) a national program, administered by the federal government, with little state input.
   b) a state program, administered with little federal government guidance or funds.
   c) a federal/state program, with over half the money coming from the federal government.
   d) a federal/state program, with over half the money coming from the states.

2. Duroville was a particularly difficult public policy problem because
   a) the trailer park was located on an Indian reservation, where the state has little jurisdiction.
   b) many of the residents were undocumented, meaning they will have a difficult time qualifying for public housing.
   c) the many other trailer parks in Riverside County indicate that the problems symbolized by Duroville may be widespread.
   d) all of the above

3. In California, employer-sponsored health insurance or ESI
   a) has historically been higher proportionately than in other states because of the size and structure of California's employers and the number of noncitizens in the state.
   b) has historically been about the same as in other states.
   c) has historically been lower than in other states because of the size and structure of California's employers and the number of noncitizens in the state.
   d) has historically been higher than in other states because of the generosity of the state's medical programs.

4. The individual health insurance market in California, prior to the implementation of the Affordable Care Act, was a model that other states might emulate.
   a) true
   b) false

5. California's basic water allocation is as follows:
   a) Most is used for households and businesses, and only a small amount for agriculture. The water for household and business use is divided roughly 50–50 between inside and outside use.
   b) About half is used for households and businesses, with the other half for agriculture. The household and business portion is dominated by inside use, which is the greater proportion.
   c) Most is used in agriculture. The portion used for households and businesses is divided about 50–50 between inside and outside use.
   d) Most is used in agriculture. The portion used for households and businesses is mostly used outside for landscape watering.

6. The most likely solution for increasing California's water supply relies on
   a) reusing treated wastewater.
   b) capturing storm water.
   c) increased efficiency at homes, businesses, and in agriculture.
   d) all of the above

7. California's infrastructure has been neglected for all *except* which of the following reasons?
   a) Most recent budgets have had to cut expenses, and infrastructure is among the easier items to cut.

b) The state legislature does not put a high priority on infrastructure issues.

c) Most politicians in California have long-term horizons.

d) California's transportation funds are often mismanaged.

8. The amount of groundwater pumped during a drought is higher than the average amount pumped in most years.
   a) true
   b) false

9. The example of the new San Francisco–Oakland Bay Bridge illustrates the following problem:
   a) Not nearly enough money was spent on the bridge.
   b) The management of bridge construction is a major problem for California state government.
   c) The bridge was built far too quickly, although by competent construction workers.
   d) The governor of the state should not be involved in constructing major projects such as the new Bay Bridge.

CRITICAL-THINKING QUESTIONS

1. Discuss the condition of California's highways, both in your experience and as presented in the book. What do you think is the nature of the problem at the most fundamental level?

2. Issues such as housing scarcity and health care costs continue to be significant problems for California's residents. Do you think these are solvable problems?

3. What future reforms of California state government might help with the public policy problems illustrated in this chapter?

KEY TERMS

2013–14 drought (p. 269)
agricultural water use (p. 269)
appropriated rights (p. 270)
employer-sponsored insurance (ESI) (p. 272)
groundwater management (p. 270)

household water use (p. 269)
individual insurance marketplace (p. 273)
infrastructure (p. 276)
Medicaid (p. 273)
Medi-Cal (p. 273)

Medicare (p. 273)
public policy (p. 268)
riparian rights (p. 269)
rescissions (p. 273)
single payer health care (p. 273)

Answer Key

Chapter 1
1. a
2. b
3. d
4. b
5. b
6. d
7. c
8. a
9. c
10. b
11. a

Chapter 2
1. b
2. c
3. a
4. c
5. c
6. c
7. a
8. c
9. d
10. b

Chapter 3
1. c
2. b
3. a
4. c
5. b
6. c
7. a
8. d
9. b
10. b

Chapter 4
1. a
2. b
3. d
4. a
5. a
6. d
7. a
8. b
9. a
10. b

Chapter 5
1. a
2. a
3. d
4. c
5. d
6. c
7. a
8. c
9. a
10. d

Chapter 6
1. a
2. b
3. d
4. c
5. d
6. d
7. d
8. b
9. a
10. b

Chapter 7
1. a
2. b
3. a
4. b
5. b
6. a
7. b
8. c
9. a
10. d

Chapter 8
1. a
2. a
3. c
4. b
5. d
6. a
7. a
8. b
9. d
10. b
11. b

Chapter 9
1. b
2. b
3. a
4. a
5. b
6. d
7. c
8. a
9. a
10. b

Chapter 10
1. c
2. d
3. c
4. b
5. c
6. d
7. c
8. a
9. b

Notes

Chapter 1

1. Joe Matthews, "What Is the California Dream? Commentary," Zocalo Public Square, January 14, 2015, http://curious.kcrw.com/2015/01/what-is-the-california-dream (accessed 7/7/16). Matt Levin, "Digging Into the Data: How Attainable is the 'California Dream' Today?" Calmatters, February 15, 2018, https://goo.gl/iSfqAA (accessed 6/18/18).
2. James Q. Wilson, "A Guide to Schwarzenegger Country," Commentary (December 2003): 45–49. Field Institute, "Legislation by Initiative vs. through Elected Representatives," November 1999, https://web.archive.org/web/20160306150856/ (accessed 9/10/18).
3. Ballotpedia, "History of the Initiative and Referendum in California," https://ballotpedia.org/History_of_Initiative_and_Referendum_in_California (accessed 6/29/18).
4. Initiative and Referendum Institute, "Initiative Use," University of Southern California Gould School of Law, September 2010, www.iandrinstitute.org (accessed 7/2/18).
5. United States Census Bureau, "Quick Facts, California," www.census.gov/quickfacts/table/PST045215/06 (accessed 7/2/18).
6. United States Census Bureau, "Quick Facts, California; United States," https://www.census.gov/quickfacts/fact/table/CA,US/EDU685216 (accessed 7/2/18). Public Policy Institute of California, "Higher Education in California, 2016, http://www.ppic.org/content/pubs/report/R_0416HEBKR.pdf (accessed 6/14/18).
7. Public Policy Institute of California (PPIC), "Just the Facts, Immigrants in California," San Francisco, PPIC, May 2018, http://www.ppic.org/publication/immigrants-in-california/ (accessed 7/2/18).
8. Public Policy Institute of California, "Just the Facts: Poverty in California," San Francisco, PPIC, July 2018, http://www.ppic.org/publication/poverty-in-california/ (accessed 9/10/18).
9. Sarah Bonn and Caroline Danielson, "Income Inequality and the Safety Net in California," Public Policy Institute of California, May 2016, http://ppic.org/main/publication.asp?i=1190 (accessed 7/2/18).
10. Philip Reese, "California high school grads increasingly leave state for college. Here's where they go," Sacramento Bee, June 16, 2018, https://www.sacbee.com/news/local/education/article212922549.html (accessed 6/18/18).
11. Public Policy Institute of California, "Just the Facts: Immigrants in California," May 2018, http://www.ppic.org/publication/immigrants-in-california/ (accessed 7/2/18).
12. Jeffrey S. Passel, Randy Capps, and Michael Fix, "Undocumented Immigrants: Facts and Figures," Urban Institute Immigration Studies Program, January 12, 2004, www.urban.org/UploadedPDF/1000587_undoc_immigrantsfacts.pdf (accessed 7/2/18). Public Policy Institute of California, "Just the Facts: Undocumented Immigrants," March 2017, http://www.ppic.org/publication/undocumented-immigrants-in-california/ (accessed 7/2/18).
13. Dan Walters, "Ex-Governors Miss Chance to Discuss Complexities," Santa Barbara News-Press, February 21, 2004, p. A11.

Chapter 2

1. California Secretary of State, Ballot Measures, "Qualified Statewide Ballot Measures," http://www.sos.ca.gov/elections/ballot-measures/qualified-ballot-measures/ (accessed 9/6/2018).
2. Paddison, Joshua, "1848–1865: Gold Rush, Statehood, and the Western Movement," Calisphere, https://calisphere.org/exhibitions/essay/4/gold-rush/ (accessed 6/1/2018).
3. In March 1848 there were about 157,000 people in the California territory; fewer than 800 were non-native Americans, 150,000 were California Indians, and 6,500 were Californios of Spanish/Mexican descent. Congress required 60,000 residents to apply for statehood. http://users.humboldt.edu/ogayle/hist383/GoldRush.html.
4. Joe Matthews and Mark Paul, California Crackup: How Reform Broke the Golden State and How We Can Fix It (Berkeley: University of California Press, 2010), 21.

5. Carl Brent Swisher, *Motivation and Political Technique in the California Constitutional Convention: 1878–79* (New York: Da Capo Press, 1969).
6. The U.S. Constitution can also be amended by passage in a constitutional convention called by two-thirds of the states, followed by ratification by three-fourths of the states. This method has never been used, however. See Article V of the U.S. Constitution.
7. Spencer C. Olin, Jr., *California's Prodigal Sons: Hiram Johnson and the Progressives, 1911–1917* (Berkeley: University of California Press, 1968), 70.
8. John M. Allswang, *The Initiative and Referendum in California, 1898–1998* (Stanford, CA: Stanford University Press, 2000), 15.
9. George Mowry, *The California Progressives* (Chicago: Quadrangle Paperbacks, 1963), 9, 12–13.
10. Kevin Starr, *Inventing the Dream: California through the Progressive Era* (New York: Oxford University Press, 1985), 242–43.
11. Dean R. Cresap, *Party Politics in the Golden State* (Los Angeles: The Haynes Foundation, 1954), 12.
12. Mowry, *The California Progressives*, 12.
13. Mowry, *The California Progressives*, 15.
14. Quoted in Mowry, *The California Progressives*, 65.
15. Starr, *Inventing the Dream*, 254.
16. Many recalls take place at the local level; volunteer groups organize recalls of city council or school board members because they feel strongly about a particular issue. Statewide recalls, however, are rare.
17. California Secretary of State, "History of California Initiatives," www.sos.ca.gov/elections/ballot-measures/resources-and-historical-information/history-california-initiatives/ (accessed 11/15/16).
18. Allswang, *The Initiative and Referendum in California*, 33.
19. Allswang, *The Initiative and Referendum in California*, 75.
20. National Conference of State Legislatures, "Initiative, Referendum, and Recall," www.ncsl.org/research/elections-and-campaigns/initiative-referendum-and-recall-overview.aspx (accessed 6/23/16).
21. California Secretary of State, "Referendum," www.sos.ca.gov/elections/ballot-measures/referendum/ (accessed 11/15/16).
22. Jim Puzzanghera, "History of Recall Adds Fuel to Both Sides," *San Jose Mercury News*, June 18, 2003, http://digital.library.ucla.edu/websites/2003_999_022/latest.news/94/index.htm (accessed 6/23/16).

Chapter 3

1. Jay Michael, Dan Walters, and Dan Weintraub, *The Third House: Lobbyists, Power, and Money in Sacramento* (Berkeley: Berkeley Public Policy Press, 2002), 13.
2. Sam Delson, "Some Call Spending Money to Get Money Regrettable but Necessary for Inland Cities and Schools," *Riverside Press Enterprise*, July 6, 1997, A2.
3. California Secretary of State, "Employers of Lobbyists, 2015–16," http://cal-access.sos.ca.gov/Lobbying/Employers/list.aspx?session=2015 (accessed 6/7/18).
4. Mark Sappenfield, "Why Clout of Lobbyists Is Growing," Christian Science Monitor, July 23, 2003, www.csmonitor.com/2003/0722/p01s02-uspo.html (accessed 6/7/18).

5. Benjamin Ginsberg, Theodore J. Lowi, Margaret Weir, and Caroline J. Tolbert, *We the People, An Introduction to American Politics*, 11th ed. (New York: Norton, 2016), 424–25.
6. California Secretary of State, The Lobbying Directory 2015–2016, http://prd.cdn.sos.ca.gov/pdf/2015-2016-lobbying-directory.pdf (accessed 6/7/18).
7. Stephen Ansolabehere, James Snyder, Jr., and Mickey Tripathi, "Are PAC Contributions and Lobbying Linked? New Evidence from the 1995 Lobby Disclosure Act," *Business and Politics* 4, no. 2 (2002): 131–55, www.tandfonline.com/doi/abs/10.1080/1369525022000015586#preview (accessed 6/7/18).
8. National Institute on Money in State Politics, "California 2016 Elections," www.followthemoney.org/tools/election-overview?s=CA&y=2016 (accessed 6/7/18).
9. National Institute on Money in State Politics, "Independent Spending in California 2016, Offices," www.followthemoney.org/show-me?dt=2&is-s=CA&is-y=2016#[{1|gro=is-r-ot; Independent Spending in California 2016, Ballot Measures, www.followthemoney.org/show-me?dt=2&is-s=CA&is-y=2016#[{1|gro=is-t-beid (accessed 6/7/18).
10. National Institute on Money in State Politics, "California 2016 Elections, Parties," www.followthemoney.org/tools/election-overview?s=CA&y=2016 (accessed 6/7/18).
11. National Institute on Money in State Politics, "Ballot Measures," www.followthemoney.org/show-me?s=CA&y=2016&m-exi=1#[{1|gro=y (accessed 6/7/18).
12. The discussion of incumbent and open elections is based on data from the National Institute on Money in State Politics, Senate, www.followthemoney.org/show-me?s=CA&y=2016&c-exi=1&c-r-ot=S#[{1|gro=c-t-ico,c-t-sts; Assembly, www.followthemoney.org/show-me?s=CA&y=2016&c-exi=1&c-r-ot=H#[{1|gro=c-t-ico,c-t-sts (accessed 6/7/18).
13. National Institute on Money in State Politics, "Incumbency Status 2015–16," www.followthemoney.org/research/institute-reports/money-incumbency-in-2015-and-2016-state-legislative-races (accessed 6/7/18).
14. Robert Salladay, "Why Money Is Important," *Los Angeles Times*, September 11, 2006.
15. National Institute on Money in State Politics, www.followthemoney.org/entity-details?eid=3286 and www.followthemoney.org/show-me?dt=3&lby-f-fc=2#[{1|gro=lby-f-eid (accessed 6/7/18).
16. Maria Lagos, "Result of Furloughs—$1 Billion Liability," *San Francisco Chronicle*, April 23, 2011, www.sfgate.com/cgi-bin/article.cgi?f=/c/a/2011/03/07/MNSQ1I2ASB.DTL&ao=all (accessed 6/7/18).
17. Steven Malanga, "The Beholden State," *City Journal* 20 (Spring 2010), www.city-journal.org/2010/20_2_california-unions.html (accessed 6/7/18).
18. Mark Baldassare et al., "The Initiative Process in California," October 2013, Public Policy Institute of California, http://www.ppic.org/publication/the-initiative-process-in-california/ (accessed 6/7/18).
19. Elisabeth R. Gerber, "Interest Group Influence in the California Initiative Process," Public Policy Institute of California, 1998, www.ppic.org/main/publication.asp?i=49 (accessed 6/7/18).
20. Carey McWilliams, *California: The Great Exception* (Berkeley: University of California Press, 1999), 213.
21. Arthur H. Samish and Bob Thomas, *The Secret Boss of California* (New York: Crown Publishers, 1971), 13.

22. California Secretary of State, "History of the Political Reform Division," 2004, http://ss.ca.gov/campaign-lobbying/history-political-reform-division (accessed 6/7/18).

23. Patrick McGreevy and Nancy Vogel, "Senate Travel Perks for Sale," *Los Angeles Times*, March 16, 2008.

24. Pew Research Center for the People and the Press, "State of News Media 2016," http://assets.pewresearch.org/wp-content/uploads/sites/13/2016/06/30143308/state-of-the-news-media-report-2016-final.pdf (accessed 6/7/18).

25. Susan F. Rasky, "Covering California: The Press Wrestles with Diversity, Complexity, and Change," in *Governing California: Politics, Government, and Public Policy in the Golden State*, ed. Gerald C. Lubenow and Bruce E. Cain (Berkeley: Institute of Governmental Studies Press, University of California, 1997), 157–88.

26. Amy Mitchell et al., "The Modern News Consumer," July 7, 2016, Pew Research Center, http://assets.pewresearch.org/wp-content/uploads/sites/13/2016/07/07104931/PJ_2016.07.07_Modern-News-Consumer_FINAL.pdf (accessed 6/7/18).

27. Rasky, "Covering California," 182.

28. Kristen Bialik and Katerina Eva Matsa, "Key trends in social and digital news media," Pew Research Center, http://www.pewresearch.org/fact-tank/2017/10/04/key-trends-in-social-and-digital-news-media/, October 4, 2017 (accessed 6/7/18).

29. David Pricco, "How Political Crowdfunding Killed Traditional Campaign Financing," http://crowdexpert.com/articles/crowdfunding-in-politics/ (6/7/18).

30. Assemblyman Mike Gatto, press release, January 6, 2015, http://asmdc.org/members/a43/news-room/press-releases/assemblyman-mike-gatto-continues-groundbreaking-wiki-bill-project-invites-public-to-directly-draft-privacy-legislation (access 6/7/18).

31. Innovate Your State, "Prop 54: The Online Crowdsourced Initiative, http://www.innovateyourstate.org/crowdsourced_initiative_approved_by_californians (accessed 6/7/18).

32. Joe Garofoli, "Labor Beat Prop. 32 via Social Media," *SFGate*, December 25, 2012, www.sfgate.com/politics/joegarofoli/article/Labor-beat-Prop-32-via-social-media-4145607.php (accessed 6/7/18).

33. Jim Rutenberg, "Distrust of Media Takes a Role in Campaigns," *New York Times*, October 12, 2003, http://209.157.64.201/focus/f-news/999985/posts (accessed 6/7/18).

Chapter 4

1. Spencer C. Olin, *California's Prodigal Sons: Hiram Johnson and the Progressives, 1911–1917* (Berkeley: University of California Press, 1968).

2. Brian F. Schaffner, Matthew Streb, and Gerald Wright, "Teams without Uniforms: The Nonpartisan Ballot in State and Local Elections," *Political Research Quarterly* 54, no. 1 (2001): 7–30.

3. Matt Barreto, "The Prop 187 Effect: How the California GOP lost their way and implications for 2014 and beyond," Latino Decisions, October 17, 2013, www.latinodecisions.com/blog/2013/10/17/prop187effect/.

4. Lopez, Gustavo, Neil G. Ruiz, and Eileen Patten, "Key facts about Asian Americans, a diverse and growing population," http://www.pewresearch.org/fact-tank/2017/09/08/key-facts-about-asian-americans/ (accessed 10/18/18).

5. Javier Panzar, "It's Official: Latinos Now Outnumber Whites in California," *Los Angeles Times*, July 8, 2015, www.latimes.com/local/california/la-me-census-latinos-20150708-story.html (accessed 9/26/16).

6. John Myers, "Tens of Thousands Have Left California's American Independent Party in the Last Month," *Los Angeles Times*, May 20, 2016, www.latimes.com/politics/la-pol-ca-american-independent-voters-registration-20160520-snap-story.html (accessed 9/26/16).

7. Michael Finnegan, "The Race for the White House," *Los Angeles Times*, September 8, 2004, p. A1.

8. Mark Baldassare, "World Apart: California's Partisan Divide and the 2016 Election," *Viewpoints* (blog), Public Policy Institute of California, June 14, 2016, www.ppic.org/main/blog_detail.asp?i=2073#.V32JZcEPuII.email (accessed 9/26/16).

9. Roper Center for Public Opinion Research, *Social Capital Community Benchmark Survey: Methodology and Documentation*, February 17, 2001, http://ropercenter.cornell.edu/2000-social-capital-community-benchmark-survey/ (accessed 9/26/16).

10. Mark Baldassare, *A California State of Mind: The Conflicted Voter in a Changing World* (Berkeley: University of California Press, 2002), 47.

11. Stanford Law School Justice Advocacy Project, "Three Strikes Basics," law.stanford.edu/stanford-justice-advocacy-project/three-strikes-basics/ (accessed 9/26/16).

12. Richard Edward DeLeon, *Left Coast City: Progressive Politics in San Francisco, 1975–1991* (Lawrence: University Press of Kansas, 1992).

13. Eric McGhee, "Political Reform and Moderation in California's Legislature: Did Electoral Reforms Make State Representatives More Moderate?" Public Policy Institute of California, May 2018, http://www.ppic.org/publication/political-reform-and-moderation-in-californias-legislature-did-electoral-reforms-make-state-representatives-moderate/.

14. Christine Mai-Duc, "Get signatures, make money: How some gatherers are making top dollar in this year's flood of ballot initiatives," *Los Angeles Times*, August 10, 2016, www.latimes.com/politics/la-pol-ca-signature-gatherers-ballot-initiatives-california-20160627-snap-htmlstory.html (accessed 12/5/16).

15. "The Mormon Money behind Proposition 8," *The Atlantic*, October 23, 2008, www.theatlantic.com/daily-dish/archive/2008/10/the-mormon-money-behind-proposition-8/209748/ (accessed 8/13/12).

16. Reid Wilson, "The Most Expensive Ballot Initiatives," *GovBeat* (blog), *Washington Post*, May 17, 2014, www.washingtonpost.com/blogs/govbeat/wp/2014/05/17/the-most-expensive-ballot-initiatives/?utm_term=.4f950116984b (accessed 12/5/16).

17. Carla Javier, "California's biggest ever election guide might not actually help voters decide," *Fusion*, September 22, 2016, fusion.net/story/349469/california-voter-guide-decide/?utm_source=emailshare&utm_medium=email&utm_campaign=socialshare&utm_content=theme_bottom_mobile (accessed 9/25/16).

18. Susan Rasky, "Introduction to 'An Antipolitician, Antiestablishment Groundswell Elected the Candidate of Change,'" in *California Votes: The 2002 Governor's Race and the Recall That Made History*, ed. Gerald Lubenow (Berkeley: Berkeley Public Policy Press, 2003).

19. Rasky, "Introduction."
20. Catherine Decker, "State's Shifting Political Landscape," *Los Angeles Times*, November 6, 2008, p. A1.
21. "Young Voters Help Secure Obama Victory, Passage of Progressive Ballot Measures," *Huffington Post*, November 7, 2012, http://www.huffingtonpost.com/2012/11/07/young-voters-2012-obama_n_2089789.html (accessed 9/26/16).
22. Phil Willon, "GOP Loses Grip on Inland Empire," *Los Angeles Times*, November 11, 2012, p. A37.
23. George Skelton, "Time for Initiative Reforms," *Los Angeles Times*, November 15, 2012, p. A2.
24. P. St John, "Prop. 47 would cut penalties for 1 in 5 criminals in California," *Los Angeles Times*, October 11, 2014, www.latimes.com/local/politics/la-me-ff-pol-proposition47-2014 1012-story.html (accessed 9/26/16).
25. "Exit Polls," *CNN*, November 9, 2016, www.cnn.com/election/results/exit-polls/california/president (accessed 11/17/2016).
26. A. Vesoulis, "The 2018 Elections Saw Record Midterm Turnout," *Time*, November 13, 2018, http://time.com/5452258/midterm-elections-turnout (accessed 11/30/18).
27. Jorge L. Ortiz, "Orange Is the New Blue: California Democrats Sweep 7 House Seats in Former GOP Stronghold," *USA Today*, November 18, 2018, www.usatoday.com/story/news/politics/elections/2018/11/18/california-democrats-sweep-house-seats-orange-county/2048696002/ (accessed 11/30/18).
28. D. P. Osorio, "The Cost of Winning a Senate Race," https://dposorio.com, May 9, 2012, http://dposorio.com/blog/822/the-cost-of-winning-a-senate-race (accessed 7/20/12).
29. Rasky, "Introduction."
30. William Booth, "In Calif. Governor's Race, It's Ads Infinitum," *Washington Post*, May 29, 1998, p. A1.
31. Carol A. Cassel, "Hispanic Turnout: Estimates from Validated Voting Data," *Political Research Quarterly* 55, no. 2 (June 2002): 391–408. Michael A. Jones-Correa and David L. Leal, "Political Participation: Does Religion Matter?" *Political Research Quarterly* 54, no. 4 (2001): 751–70.
32. Carl Bialik, "Voter Turnout Fell, Especially in States that Clinton Won," FiveThirtyEight, November 11, 2016, http://fivethirtyeight.com/features/voter-turnout-fell-especially-in-states-that-clinton-won (accessed 11/11/2016).

Chapter 5

1. Field Research Corporation, "California Voter Views of the State Legislature Turn Negative after the Arrest of State Senator Leland Yee," Poll release #2464, April 10, 2014, https://www.scribd.com/document/217499631/Field-Poll-California-Views-Of-The-State-Legislature (accessed 7/9/2018). Field Research Corporation, "Mixed View of the State Legislature . . . ," Poll release #2500, February 25, 2015, https://www.sacbee.com/site-services/newsletters/capitol-alert-newsletter/article11125130.ece/BINARY/Field%20Poll%20results:%20Legislature%20job%20performance%20and%20program%20funding (accessed 7/9/2018). Field Research Corporation, "Californians Hold Divergent Views . . . ," Poll release #2552, September 29, 2016, https://www.politico.com/states/f/?id=00000157-72c9-d370-addf-73cf03460000 (accessed 7/9/2018).

Mark Baldassare et al., "Californians and the Environment," Public Policy Institute of California, July 2018, http://www.ppic.org/wp-content/uploads/ppic-statewide-survey-july-2018.pdf (accessed 9/7/2018). Information on previous PPIC polls can be found at http://www.ppic.org/wp-content/uploads/timetrends-alladults0518.pdf (accessed 7/10/2018).
2. Andrew Dugan, "Congressional Approval Rating Languishes at low Level," Gallup Politics, July 15, 2014, www.gallup.com/poll/politics.aspx?ref=b (accessed 8/11/14). Gallup, "Congress and the Public," www.gallup.com/poll/1600/congress-public.aspx (accessed 7/9/2018).
3. Jeremy B. White, "Chevron Spends $1 Million to Boost Assembly Democrat Cheryl Brown," *Sacramento Bee*, April 14, 2016, www.sacbee.com/news/politics-government/capitol-alert/article71852047.html (accessed 7/9/2018). Patrick McGreevy and Chris Megerian, "With a record $24 million spent on the election so far, are special interests trying to buy their way into the Legislature?" *Los Angeles Times*, May 30, 2016, www.latimes.com/politics/la-pol-sac-california-independent-spending-20160530-snap-story.html (accessed 8/24/2016). Laurel Rosenhall, "Money Rains from Perfect Storm of Politics," *CALmatters*, June 16, 2016, https://calmatters.org/articles/money-rains-from-perfect-storm-of-politics/ (accessed 7/9/2018).
4. Editorial Board, "Editorial: Stop Disgrace of 'Gut and Amend' in Legislature," *Sacramento Bee Capitol Alert*, April 30, 2013, https://www.dailynews.com/2013/05/01/another-view-stop-disgrace-of-gut-and-amend-in-legislature/ (accessed 9/15/16).
5. Lou Cannon, *Governor Reagan: His Rise to Power* (New York: Public Affairs, 2003), 166.
6. Peter Schrag, *Paradise Lost: California's Experience, America's Future* (New York: New Press, 1998), 244.
7. Institute of Governmental Studies, "IGS Goes to Sacramento to Assess Ten Years of Term Limits," *Public Affairs Report* 42, no. 3 (Fall 2001).
8. National Association of Latino Elected and Appointed Officials Education Fund, *National Directory of Latino Elected and Appointed Officials 2017*, https://d3n8a8pro7vhmx.cloudfront.net/naleo/pages/1402/attachments/original/1512779367/2017_National_Directory_of_Latino_Elected_Officials.pdf#page=16 (accessed 7/9/2018). The National Conference of State Legislatures, 2015 Latino Legislators, http://www.ncsl.org/research/about-state-legislatures/latino-legislators.aspx (accessed 7/9/2018). The National Conference of State Legislatures, Women in State Legislatures for 2018, http://www.ncsl.org/legislators-staff/legislators/womens-legislative-network/women-in-state-legislatures-for-2018.aspx (accessed 7/9/2018). Leadership California Institute, *Women: The Status of Women in California State and Local Government*, http://www.leadershipcaliforniainstitute.org/ (accessed 7/9/2018).
9. Schrag, *Paradise Lost*, 143.
10. Adam Nagourney, "Political Shift in California Trips Brown," *New York Times*, September 20, 2011, www.nytimes.com/2011/09/21/us/politics/brown-says-california-gop-is-harder-to-work-with-decades-later.html?pagewanted=all (accessed 7/9/2018).
11. Anthony York, "Brown and Obama Find Bipartisanship a Difficult Goal to Reach," *Los Angeles Times*, February 24, 2012, http://articles.latimes.com/2012/feb/24/local/la-me-jerry-brown-20120224 (accessed 7/9/2018).
12. Nagourney, "Political Shift in California Trips Brown."

13. George Skelton, "California's Capitol—the Long View: A Columnist Looks Back on 50 Years Covering the Ups and Downs of Sacramento," *Los Angeles Times*, December 1, 2011, p. A2.
14. John Meyers, Melanie Mason and Liam Dillon, "Chaos Helps Avert Ballot Battles," *Los Angeles Times*, July 1, 2018, p. B1. George Skelton, "Voters Spared 3 Ballot Battles," *Los Angeles Times*, July 2, 2018, p. B1.
15. Laurel Rosenhall, "Special Interests Win As Lawmakers Cut Last-Minute Deals To Pull Initiatives Off Your Ballot," *CALmatters*, June 29, 2018, https://calmatters.org/articles/special-interests-win-as-lawmakers-cut-last-minute-deals-to-pull-initiatives-off-your-ballot/ (accessed 7/8/2018).
16. Melanie Mason, "Hard View on Soft Drinks," *Los Angeles Times*, July 3, 2018, p. B1.
17. Adam Nagourney, "How Control of Congress Could Hinge on a 12-Cent Tax on Gasoline," *New York Times*, July 8, 2018, p. A18.
18. We Said Enough, "The Silence Breakers," https://www.wesaidenough.com/silence-breakers/ (accessed 7/8/2018); for more on this issue visit https://wesaidenough.com.
19. Melanie Mason, "Panel OKs New Policy on Capitol Harassment Complaints," *Los Angeles Times*, June 27, 2018 p. B3.
20. Melanie Mason, "Panel OKs New Policy on Capitol Harassment Complaints."
21. John Meyers, "Jerry Brown's Budget Legacy," *Los Angeles Times*, July 1, 2018, p. A1.

Chapter 6

1. This figure is calculated from 154,000 employees from the UC system, 150,000 from the California State University system, and 230,000 other state employees. www.universityofcalifornia.edu/infocenter/employee-fte; www2.calstate.edu/csu-system/about-the-csu/facts-about-the-csu; www.sco.ca.gov/ppsd_empinfo_demo.html (accessed 7/5/18).
2. Thomas E. Cronin and Michael A. Genovese, *The Paradoxes of the American Presidency* (New York: Oxford University Press, 1998).
3. Public Policy Institute of California, "PPIC Statewide Survey: Time Trends for Job Approval Ratings for Governor Schwarzenegger," http://www.ppic.org/data-set/ppic-statewide-survey-time-trends-for-job-approval-ratings/ (accessed 8/30/18).
4. Public Policy Institute of California, "Californians and Their Government," May 2018, www.ppic.org/wp-content/uploads/crosstabs-alladults0518.pdf (accessed 7/5/18).
5. Andy Kroll, "The Last Days of Jerry Brown," *The California Sunday Magazine*, March 18, 2018, https://story.californiasunday.com/jerry-brown-last-days (accessed 7/5/18).
6. Mark Truppner, "Brown's Plan to Streamline State Government," MyMotherlode.com, https://www.mymotherlode.com/news/local/63810/browns-plan-to-streamline-state-government.htm (accessed 10/29/18).
7. Office of Governor, "Governor Brown Takes Action to Increase Zero-Emission Vehicles, Fund New Climate Investments," January 26, 2018, www.gov.ca.gov/2018/01/26/governor-brown-takes-action-to-increase-zero-emission-vehicles-fund-new-climate-investments/ (accessed 7/5/18).
8. John Myers, "Gov. Jerry Brown agrees to National Guard border efforts, but not 'a mission to round up women and children,'" *Los Angeles Times*, April 11, 2018, www.latimes.com/politics/la-pol-ca-jerry-brown-national-guard-20180411-story.html (accessed 7/5/18).
9. Joshua Stark, "New Report Calls for Radical Reform of Caltrans," *TransForm*, February 4, 2014, www.transformca.org/trblogpost/report-calls-radical-reform-caltrans (accessed 8/24/16). Debra J. Saunders, "Jerry Brown on Bay Bridge: Don't Worry, Be Happy," *SFGate*, May 16, 2014, https://blog.sfgate.com/djsaunders/2014/05/16/jerry-brown-on-bay-bridge-dont-worry-be-happy/ (accessed 8/30/18).
10. Jeff McDonald, "Brown signs bills to reform CPUC, urges administrative fixes too," *San Diego Union-Tribune*, September 29, 2016, www.sandiegouniontribune.com/news/watchdog/sd-me-watchdog-cpuc-20160929-story.html (accessed 7/5/2018).
11. Dan Weikel and Kim Christensen, "How a Ban on Ex Parte Communications by the Coastal Commission Could Change the Balance of Power," *Los Angeles Times*, May 14, 2016, www.latimes.com/local/california/la-me-adv-coastal-commission-20160515-story.html (accessed 8/24/16). Steve Lopez, "Cover Your Ears: Coastal Commissioner Martha McClure's on the Phone," *Los Angeles Times*, May 14, 2016, www.latimes.com/local/california/la-me-lopez-commission-sleepover-20160514-column.html (accessed 8/24/2016).
12. California Senate Office of Research, "How Often Do Governors Say No?" October 16, 2017, https://sor.senate.ca.gov/sites/sor.senate.ca.gov/files/Governors%20Vetoes%202017_Senate%20Office%20of%20Research.pdf (accessed 8/31/18). John Meyers, "Political Roadmap: There's a Reason Why Jerry Brown Signs so Many Bills," *Los Angeles Times*, October 2, 2016, http://www.latimes.com/politics/la-pol-sac-roadmap-jerry-brown-signs-bills-20161002-snap-story.html (accessed 8/31/2018).
13. Eric McGhee and Paul Warren, "The Vanishing Line-Item Veto," *Viewpoints: The PPIC Blog*, Public Policy Institute of California, June 26, 2014, www.ppic.org/main/blog_detail.asp?i=1551 (accessed 8/24/16).
14. Steven Harmon, "Gov. Brown Warns Democratic Lawmakers Not to Overreach, Overspend," *Vallejo Times-Herald*, January 24, 2013, www.timesheraldonline.com/ci_22439612/gov-brown-warns-democratic-lawmakers-not-overreach-overspend (accessed 8/24/16).
15. Liam Dillon, "More than a Dozen Assembly Members Flipped Their Votes from Last Year to Support Climate Change Bill," *LA Times Essential Politics*, August 23, 2016, www.latimes.com/politics/essential/la-pol-sac-essential-politics-updates-more-than-a-dozen-assemblymembers-1471987788-html-story.html (accessed 9/24/16). Jessica Calefati, "California Climate Change Law: Extension of Greenhouse Gas Goals OK'd by Assembly," *The Mercury News*, August 23, 2016, www.mercurynews.com/2016/08/23/california-climate-change-law-extension-of-greenhouse-gas-goals-okd-by-assembly/ (accessed 9/24/16).
16. George Skelton, "Governor Hits Back at Big Oil," *Los Angeles Times*, August 25, 2016, p. B1.
17. James Fallows, "Jerry Brown's Political Reboot," *The Atlantic Monthly*, June 2013, https://www.theatlantic.com/magazine/archive/2013/06/the-fixer/309324/ (accessed 10/20/18).
18. Fallows, "Jerry Brown's Political Reboot." Egan, "Jerry Brown's Revenge." Lou Cannon, "Calif. Comeback: Jerry Brown Leads a Turnaround," *Real Clear Politics*, June 25, 2013, www.real

clearpolitics.com/articles/2013/06/25/calif_comeback_jerry
_brown_leads_a_turnaround_118943.html (accessed 8/24/16).

19. Dan Walters, "Could Anne Gust Brown Be the Next Governor," *Sacramento Bee*, March 8, 2015, www.sacbee.com/news/politics-government/politics-columns-blogs/dan-walters/article13044824.html (accessed 8/24/16).

20. Times Editorial Board, "Designating an active governor when the actual governor leaves California is an archaic and pointless tradition," *Los Angeles Times*, July 29, 2006, http://www.latimes.com/opinion/editorials/la-ed-acting-governor-20160728-snap-story.html.

21. Reports can be viewed at www.auditor.ca.gov.

Chapter 7

1. Patrick McGreevy, "California has sued the Trump administration 38 times. Here's a look at the legal challenges," *Los Angeles Times*, July 22, 2018, www.latimes.com/politics/la-pol-ca-california-sues-trump-20180722-story.html (accessed 8/20/18).

2. Massoud Hayoun, "A Judge Ruled Against Trump's Challenge to California's Sanctuary Law. But That Doesn't Mean the Immigration Battle Is Over," *Pacific Standard*, July 6, 2018, psmag.com/news/judge-ruled-against-trump-challenge-to-california-sanctuary-law (accessed 8/20/18).

3. Court Statistics Report (2017), "Statewide Caseload Trends, 2006–2007 Through 2015–2016," www.courts.ca.gov/documents/2017-Court-Statistics-Report.pdf (accessed 8/20/18).

4. www.courts.ca.gov.

5. Bob Egelko, "In Starbucks case, California court says workers owed for off-the-clock time," July 26, 2018, www.sfchronicle.com/bayarea/article/in-suit-against-starbucks case (accessed 8/20/18).

6. See *Anderson v. Mt. Clemons Pottery Co*, 328 U.S. 680 (1946).

7. Court Statistics Report (2017).

8. *People v. Colvin*, 203 Cal.App.4th 1029 (2012).

9. *Unpublished* means that the memorandum may not be used for purposes of legal citation or precedent. gpo.gov/fdsys/pkg/USCOURTS-caed-2_11-cv-02939. The memorandum can be found here: U.S. Government Printing Office, *11-2939—Sacramento Nonprofit Collective et al v. Holder et al.*, cdn.ca9.uscourts.gov/datastore/memoranda/2014/01/15/12-15991.pdf (accessed 8/20/18).

10. "SB-643 Medical marijuana," California Legislative Information, https://leginfo.legislature.ca.gov/faces/billNavClient.xhtml?bill_id=201520160SB643 (accessed 9/7/18).

11. The act can be found here: www.congress.gov/bill/113th-congress/house-bill/83/text (accessed 8/20/18).

12. Bob Egelko, "California Supreme Court Nomination a 'Statement' to U.S.," *SF Gate*, July 22, 2014, www.sfgate.com/politics/article/Brown-nominates-Stanford-professor-to-state-high-5638237.php (accessed 8/20/18).

13. David Siders, "Gov. Jerry Brown Names Obama Administration Lawyer to California Supreme Court," *Sacramento Bee*, November 24, 2014, www.sacbee.com/news/politics-government/capitol-alert/article4123447.html (accessed 8/20/18).

14. Prebloe Stolz, *Judging Judges: The Investigation of Rose Bird and the California Supreme Court* (New York: Free Press, 1981).

15. California Courts, "Judicial Council," www.courts.ca.gov/policyadmin-jc.htm?genpubtab (accessed 8/20/18).

16. Carmen Lo, Katie Londenberg, and David Nims, "Spending in Judicial Elections: State Trends in the Wake of *Citizens United*," http://gov.uchastings.edu/public-law/docs/judicial-elections-report-and-appendices-corrected.pdf (accessed 8/20/18).

17. 2017 Court Statistics Report.

18. Unlimited jurisdiction civil cases are disputes that involve more than $25,000. Limited jurisdiction civil cases are disputes that involve amounts from $10,000 to $25,000. See Court Statistics Report (2017), "Statewide Trends," 2017.

19. "California Courts Wrestle with Budget Cuts Old and New," *Los Angeles Times*, June 19, 2012, latimesblogs.latimes.com/california-politics/2012/06/california-court.html (accessed 8/20/18).

20. Maria Dinzeo, "IT Project Sinks in Sea of Criticism," *Courthouse News Service*, March 27, 2012, www.courthousenews.com/2012/03/27/45079.htm (accessed 8/20/18).

21. Cheryl Miller, "Judges Criticize Court Bureaucracy in Blistering Report," inlandpolitics.com/blog/2012/05/30/the-record-judges-criticize-court-bureaucracy-in-blistering-report/ (accessed 8/20/18).

22. Cheryl Miller, "What's Taking Jerry Brown So Long to Pick a Supreme Court Justice?" *The Recorder*, March 5, 2018, www.law.com/therecorder/2018/03/05/whats-taking-jerry-brown-so-long-to-pick-a-supreme-court-justice/.

Chapter 8

1. Legislative Analyst's Office, "2016–17 Budget: Higher Education Analysis," February 25, 2016, www.lao.ca.gov (accessed 7/31/18).

2. Rosanna Xia, "State Funding Cuts During the Recession Still Shortchanging Cal State Students, Officials Say," *Los Angeles Times*, July 21, 2016, www.latimes.com/local/lanow/la-me-cal-state-executive-compensation-20160719-snap-story.html (accessed 7/31/18).

3. Marla Dickerson, "State Fiscal Woes Threaten Cities' Budgets and a Leading Job Engine," *Los Angeles Times*, January 17, 2003, pp. C1+.

4. California Department of Finance, "Historical Budget Publications," February 24, 1998, www.dof.ca.gov (accessed 7/31/18).

5. California Department of Finance, "Historical Budget Publications."

6. George Skelton, "The 'Budget Nun' Earns Her Pay and Bipartisan Respect," *Los Angeles Times*, May 26, 2003, p. B5.

7. Public Finance Division, "California's Current Credit Ratings," California State Treasurer, www.treasurer.ca.gov/ratings/current.asp (accessed 7/31/18). Dan Walters, "Moody's Raises California's Credit Rating," *Sacramento Bee*, June 25, 2014, https://inlandpolitics.com/blog/2014/06/26/sacbee-moodys-raises-californias-bond-credit-rating (accessed 9/22/18). Moody's Investors Service, "Moody's Fiscal Test of Most Populous States Show Texas Best Prepared for Next Recession, California Least Ready," April 21, 2016, www.moodys.com/research/Moodys-Fiscal-test-of-most-populous-states-show-Texas-best—PR_347649, April 21, 2016 (accessed 7/31/18).

8. William Chen, "Who Pays Taxes in California?" April 2015, calbudgetcenter.org/wp-content/uploads/Who-Pays-Taxes-in-CA_Issue-Brief_04.14.2015.pdf (accessed 7/31/18). Justin Garosi and Jason Sisney, "'Top 1 Percent' Pays Half of State Income Taxes," Legislative Analyst's Office, December 4, 2014, lao.ca.gov/LAOEconTax/Article/Detail/7 (accessed 7/31/18).

9. Tax Foundation, "Facts & Figures, How Does Your State Compare?" Washington, DC: Tax Foundation, 2018, files.taxfoundation.org/20180411102900/Facts-Figures-2018-How-Does-Your-State-Compare.pdf (accessed 7/20/18).

10. Katherine Barrett, Richard Greene, Michele Mariani, and Anya Sostek, "The Way We Tax," *Governing*, February 2003, p. 20.

11. Franchise Tax Board, State of California, "2012 Annual Report," Table C-8, Corporation Tax, Tax Liability by Net Income Class, Franchise Tax Board, 2011, www.ftb.ca.gov/aboutFTB/Tax_Statistics/Reports/2012/2012_C-8.pdf (accessed 7/31/18). See also Chen, "Who Pays Taxes in California?"

12. Oliver Libaw, "Where Does Lottery Revenue Go?" ABC News, August 26, 2001, abcnews.go.com/US/story?id=92595&page=1 (accessed 7/31/18). See also Valerie Strauss, "Mega Millions: Do Lotteries Really Benefit Public Schools?" *Washington Post*, March 30, 2012, www.washingtonpost.com/blogs/answer-sheet/post/mega-millions-do-lotteries-really-benefit-public-schools/2012/03/30/gIQAbTUNlS_blog.html (accessed 7/31/18).

13. Barrett et al., "The Way We Tax."

14. Council on State Taxation, "The Best and Worst of State Tax Administration," December 2013, www.cost.org (accessed 7/31/18).

15. California Taxpayers Association, "Cal-Tax: Taxes Are a Heavy Burden in California," digital.library.ucla.edu/websites/2004_999_003/dynamic/downloads/individual_download_file_link_1_english_10.pdf (accessed 7/31/18).

16. Tax Foundation, "State-Local Tax Burden Rankings FY 2012," taxfoundation.org/article/state-local-tax-burden-rankings-fy-2012 (accessed 7/31/18).

17. Chen, "Who Pays Taxes in California?"

18. Betty T. Yee and the Controller's Council of Economic Advisors on Tax Reform, "Comprehensive Tax Reform in California: A Contextual Framework," June 2016, www.sco.ca.gov/eo_cea_contextual_framework.html (accessed 7/31/18).

19. Carson Bruno, "California: CEOs Rate It Worst U.S. Business Climate for 8 Years Running," March 21, 2014, www.realclearmarkets.com/articles/2014/03/21/california_ceos_rate_it_worst_us_business_climate_for_8_years_running_100963.html (accessed 7/31/18).

20. Institute for Taxation and Economic Policy, "'High Rate' Income Tax States Are Outperforming No-Tax States," February 2012, www.itepnet.org (accessed 7/31/18).

21. Hans Johnson, "Defunding Higher Education" (San Francisco: Public Policy Institute of California, 2012), 4.

22. Phil Oliff, Vincent Palacios, Ingrid Johnson, and Michael Leachman, "Recent Deep State Higher Education Cuts May Harm Students and the Economy for Years to Come" (Washington, DC: Center on Budget and Policy Priorities, May 2013).

23. James D. Savage, "California's Structural Deficit Crisis," *Public Budgeting and Finance* 12, no. 2 (Summer 1992): 82–97.

24. California Forward, "Curing Deficits and Creating Value: Principles for Improving State Fiscal Decisions," s3.amazonaws.com/zanran_storage/www.caforward.org/ContentPages/1903423.pdf (accessed 7/31/18).

25. California Forward, "Curing Deficits and Creating Value."

26. Peter Nicholas and Virginia Ellis, "Budget Signals Narrowed Ambitions," *Los Angeles Times*, February 18, 2004, p. A1.

Chapter 9

1. Bernard H. Ross and Myron A. Levine, *Urban Politics: Power in Metropolitan America*, 6th ed. (Itasca, IL: F.E. Peacock, 2001), p. 90.

2. Dale Krane, Platon N. Rigos, and Melvin B. Hill Jr., *Home Rule in America: A Fifty-State Handbook* (Washington, DC: CQ Press, 2001).

3. Daniel B. Rodriguez, "State Supremacy, Local Sovereignty: Reconstructing State/Local Relations under the California Constitution," in *Constitutional Reform in California: Making State Government More Effective and Responsive*, eds. Bruce E. Cain and Roger G. Noll (Berkeley: Institute of Governmental Studies Press, University of California, 1995), pp. 401–29; Krane, Rigos, and Hill, *Home Rule in America*; Melvin B. Hill, *State Laws Governing Local Government Structure and Administration* (Washington, DC: U.S. Advisory Commission on Intergovernmental Relations [ACIR], 1993).

4. Ross and Levine, *Urban Politics*, p. 91.

5. John Taylor, "What Happened to Branciforte County?" in California State Association of Counties, *Introduction to California Counties*, www.counties.org/sites/main/files/file-attachments/tab_1_intro_to_california_counties.pdf (accessed 9/7/18).

6. County of Los Angeles, *2018–19 Recommended Budget*, April 10, 2018, https://www.lacounty.gov/budget (accessed 9/22/16).

7. Aaron Claverie and David Downey, "Pechanga to Buy Quarry Site," *The Californian*, November 15, 2012, www.sandiegouniontribune.com/sdut-region-pechanga-to-buy-quarry-site-2012nov15-story.html (accessed 9/7/18).

8. For an excellent study of the 1963 Knox-Nisbet Act, which created LAFCos to impose order and control on the post–World War II explosion of new cities and annexations in California, see Tom Hogen-Esch, "Fragmentation, Fiscal Federalism, and the Ghost of Dillon's Rule: Municipal Incorporation in Southern California, 1950–2010," *California Journal of Politics & Policy* 3, no. 2 (2011): 1–22.

9. California Senate Governance and Finance Committee, "City Fact Sheet," September 2016, https://sgf.senate.ca.gov/sites/sgf.senate.ca.gov/files/city_facts_2016.pdf (accessed 11/30/18).

10. Voters in these elections may, of course, choose not to incorporate as a city and run their own show. The prospect of rapid growth and development, for example, scared many of the 57,000 residents of Castro Valley. In November 2002 they voted three to one against incorporation, opting to remain Northern California's largest unincorporated community and governed locally by the Alameda County Board of Supervisors.

11. League of California Cities, "California Residents and Basic Geography," http://www.cacities.org/Resources/Learn-About-Cities (accessed 10/30/18).

12. See John H. Knox and Chris Hutchinson, "Municipal Disincorporation in California," *Public Law Journal* 32, no. 4 (Fall 2009), californiacityfinance.com/DisincorporationKnox2010.pdf (accessed 8/23/14).

13. Sandra Stokley, "Understanding the Disincorporation Issue," *The Press Enterprise*, September 18, 2013, www.pe.com/2013 /09/18/jurupa-valley-understanding-the-disincorporation -issue (accessed 10/7/16). For more background on Jurupa Valley's tribulations, see Rick Rojas, "For Jurupa Valley, Cityhood Isn't What It Expected," *Los Angeles Times*, December 1, 2013, http://articles.latimes.com/2013/dec/01/local/la-me-jurupa -valley-20131202 (accessed 8/25/14); Sandra Stokley, "'Bitter' Announcement on Disincorporation," *The Press Enterprise*, December 18, 2013, www.pe.com/articles/city-682062-valley -jurupa.html (accessed 8/21/14); Irvin Dawid, "Puff! There Goes California's Newest City," *Planetizen*, January 18, 2014, www.planetizen.com/node/66954 (accessed 10/7/16).

14. Sandra Stokley, "Jurupa Valley: City Says It Will Survive, After All," *The Press Enterprise*, September 29, 2015, www .pe.com/articles/county-781898-city-jurupa.html (accessed 10/12/15).

15. Zoltan L. Hajnal, Paul G. Lewis, and Hugh Louch, *Municipal Elections in California: Turnout, Timing, and Competition* (San Francisco: Public Policy Institute of California, 2002), pp. 23–24.

16. Ross and Levine, *Urban Politics*, pp. 165–78.

17. Amy Bridges, *Morning Glories: Municipal Reform in the Southwest* (Princeton, NJ: Princeton University Press, 1997).

18. International City/County Management Association (ICMA), "Officials in U.S. Municipalities 2,500 and Over in Population," in *The Municipal Year Book 2003* (Washington, DC: ICMA, 2003), pp. 195–200.

19. Bruce E. Cain, Megan Mullin, and Gillian Peele, "City Caesars? An Examination of Mayoral Power in California," presented at the 2001 annual meeting of the American Political Science Association, August 29–September 2, San Francisco.

20. Hajnal et al., *Municipal Elections in California*, p. 25.

21. Richard DeLeon, *Left Coast City: Progressive Politics in San Francisco, 1957–1991* (Lawrence, KS: University Press of Kansas, 1992). A recent study of over 7,000 U.S. cities found that district systems were better than at-large systems at achieving diverse city councils only in areas where underrepresented groups were highly concentrated geographically and constituted a sizable share of the population. See Jessica Trounstine and Melody Ellis Valdini, "The Context Matters: The Effects of Single-Member Versus At-Large Districts on City Council Diversity," *American Journal of Political Science* 52, no. 3 (July 2008): 554–69.

22. Jean Merl, "Voting Rights Act Leading California Cities to Dump At-Large Elections," *Los Angeles Times*, September 14, 2013, www.latimes.com/local/la-me-local-elections-20130915 -story.html#axzz2tt5grBf9 (accessed 8/27/14).

23. Javier Panzar, "It's Official: Latinos Now Outnumber Whites in California," *Los Angeles Times*, July 8, 2015, www.latimes .com/local/california/la-me-census-latinos-20150708-story .html (accessed 5/4/16).

24. Teri Figueroa, "City Poised to Shake Up Voting System," *San Diego Union-Tribune*, June 21, 2016, www.sandiegouniontri bune.com/news/2016/jun/21/san-marcos-considering-district -elections (accessed 6/30/16).

25. Austin Walsh, "Redwood City Elementary School District Looking at Shifting Election System," *San Mateo Daily Journal*, January 13, 2016, https://www.smdailyjournal.com/news /local/redwood-city-elementary-school-district-looking-at -shifting-election-system/article_ff79167d-2b6c-58d9-b6e3 -f8e6046a058f.html (accessed 6/30/16).

26. Spencer Woodman, "How California Is Solving Its Voting Rights Problem," *VICE Magazine*, May 26, 2016, www.vice .com/read/how-california-is-solving-its-voting-rights-problem (accessed 6/30/16). For a critical perspective on the CVRA as a boondoggle for lawyers at taxpayers' expense, see Carolyn Schuk, "California Voting Rights Act: $14 Million Legal Bill for Taxpayers," *Santa Clara Weekly*, December 2, 2015, www.santaclaraweekly.com/2015/Issue-49/city-observer.html (accessed 6/30/16).

27. Brian E. Adams. "Citizens, Interest Groups, and Local Ballot Initiatives" *Politics & Policy* 41, 1 (2012): 43–68. '

28. Matthew A. Melone and George A. Nation III, "'Standing' on Formality: *Hollingsworth v. Perry* and the Efficacy of Direct Democracy in the United States" (unpublished paper), March 2014, p. 289, http://works.bepress.com/matthew_melone/2 (accessed 5/3/14).

29. "Voter Turnout," United States Election Project, www.elect project.org/home/voter-turnout/voter-turnout-data (accessed 9/7/18).

30. Melissa Marschall and John Lappie. "Turnout in Local Elections: Is Timing Really Everything?" *Election Law Journal: Rules, Politics, and Policy* (July 2018).

31. FairVote, a nonprofit advocacy group that promotes ranked-choice voting and other electoral reforms, provides useful background research and discussion of the pros and cons on its website at www.fairvote.org.

32. For example, see Richard Briffault, "Home Rule and Local Political Innovation," *Journal of Law and Politics* 22 (Winter 2006): 1–32, which uses San Francisco's ranked-choice voting system as a case study exemplifying the idea that local government can act as "laboratories of democracy."

33. California Secretary of State, "About California Voter's Choice Act," www.sos.ca.gov/elections/voters-choice-act/about-vca (accessed 9/7/18).

34. These are the unofficial results reported November 23, 2016. For more background on this measure and the outcome, see the Ballotpedia entry for "Local Measure N–Non-Citizen Voting in School Board Elections," https://ballotpedia.org/San _Francisco,_California,_Non-Citizen_Voting_in_School_Board _Elections_Amendment,_Proposition_N_(November_2016) (accessed 11/23/16).

35. Kimberly Yam, "San Francisco Now Allows Noncitizens to Vote in School Board Elections," *Huffington Post*, July 18, 2018, www.huffingtonpost.com/entry/san-francisco-now-allows -non-citizens-to-vote-in-school-board-elections_us_5b4e301 ee4b0de86f48775d0 (accessed 9/7/18).

36. Senate Local Government Committee, *What's So Special about Special Districts? A Citizen's Guide to Special Districts in California*, 3rd ed. (Sacramento: California State Senate, 2002), p. 3.

37. California Department of Education, "Fingertip Facts on Education in California," www.cde.ca.gov/ds/sd/cb/ceffingertipfacts .asp (accessed 9/7/18).

38. California Community Colleges, www.cccco.edu (accessed 9/7/18).

39. David Kirp, "California to Community Colleges: Graduate More Students or Lose Your Funding," *Los Angeles Times*, August 22, 2018, www.latimes.com/opinion/op-ed/la-oe-kirp

-california-community-college-graduation-rates-20180822
-story.html (accessed 9/7/18).

40. California State Controller, "Special Districts Listing," https://
bythenumbers.sco.ca.gov/Special-Districts-Other/Special
-Districts-Listing/fv6y-3v29 (accessed 9/7/18).

41. California State Controller's Office, *Special Districts Annual
Report 2011–2012*, p. vii, www.sco.ca.gov/Files-ARD-Local
/LocRep/1112_special_districts.pdf (accessed 10/7/16).

42. Brian P. Janiskee, "The Problem of Local Government in California," *Nexus* (Spring 2001): 219–33.

43. Neil McCormick, Chief Executive Officer, and Kyle Pack-
ham, Advocacy and Public Affairs Director, California Special Districts Association, written testimony to Little Hoover
Commission Review of Special Districts, August 8, 2016,
lhc.ca.gov/sites/lhc.ca.gov/files/Reports/239/WrittenTestimony
/CSDAAug2016.pdf (accessed 9/22/18).

44. Rosanna Xia, "With Supreme Court challenge, tech billionaire could dismantle beach access rights—and a landmark
coastal law," *Los Angeles Times*, March 6, 2018, www.latimes
.com/local/lanow/la-me-martins-beach-supreme-court-2018
0306-story.html (accessed 9/7/18).

45. Tahoe Regional Planning Agency, www.trpa.org (accessed
9/7/18).

46. Gabriel Metcalf, "An Interview with Joe Bodovitz," SPUR
report no. 378 (September 1999).

47. California Association of Realtors, "Market at a Glance,"
www.car.org/en/marketing/chartsandgraphs/marketglance
(accessed 9/7/18).

48. Andrea Riquier, "California exodus gathers strength, as home
prices continue upward march," *Market Watch*, June 1, 2018,
www.marketwatch.com/story/with-no-letup-in-home-prices
-the-california-exodus-surges-2018-05-03 (accessed 9/7/18).

49. For more about the CA housing crisis, go to calmatters.org
/articles/housing-costs-high-california.

50. California Employment Development Department, "July
2018 California Employment Highlights," www.labormarket
info.edd.ca.gov/file/lfmonth/Employment-Highlights.pdf (accessed 9/7/18).

51. Emily Badger, "The Bipartisan Cry of 'Not in My Backyard,'"
New York Times, August 21, 2018, www.nytimes.com/2018
/08/21/upshot/home-ownership-nimby-bipartisan.html
(accessed 9/7/18).

52. California Department of Industrial Relations, "Minimum
Wage," www.dir.ca.gov/dlse/faq_minimumwage.htm (accessed
9/7/18).

53. Paul Rogers, "Jerry Brown signs new laws to block Trump's
California offshore oil drilling plans," *Mercury News*, September 8, 2018, www.mercurynews.com/2018/09/08/jerry-brown
-signs-new-laws-to-block-trumps-california-offshore-oil-drill
ing-plans.

Chapter 10

1. Dan Barry, "Beside a Smoldering Dump, a Refuge of Sorts,"
New York Times, October 21, 2007, www.nytimes.com/2007
/10/21/us/21land.html?_r=1 (accessed 9/17/18).

2. David Olson, "Duroville: Slum Mobile Home Park Finally
Closes," *Riverside Press-Enterprise*, June 26, 2014, www.pe.com
/articles/duroville-678572-park-mobile.html (accessed 9/17/18).

See also Phil Willon, "Farmworkers' New Home Is Near Duroville, Yet a World Away," *Los Angeles Times*, March 25, 2013,
www.latimes.com/news/local/la-me-duroville-20130325
,0,5395710.story (accessed 9/17/18).

3. Paloma Esquivel, "Farmworkers Find a Bumper Crop of
Squalor in Coachella Valley Trailer Parks," *Los Angeles Times*,
October 5, 2015, www.latimes.com/local/california/la-me
-farmworker-trailers-20151006-story.html (accessed 9/17/18).

4. Liam Dillon, "Gov. Brown just signed 15 housing bills. Here's
how they're supposed to help the affordability crisis," *Los
Angeles Times*, September 29, 2017, www.latimes.com/poli
tics/la-pol-ca-housing-legislation-signed-20170929-htmlstory
.html (accessed 9/17/18).

5. This bill can be found at: leginfo.legislature.ca.gov/faces/bill
TextClient.xhtml?bill_id=201720180SB1227.

6. California Budget Project, "School Finance Facts, a Decade
of Disinvestment: California Education Spending Nears the
Bottom," October 2011, calbudgetcenter.org/wp-content
/uploads/111012_Decade_of_Disinvestment_%20SFF.pdf
(accessed 9/17/18). See also National Education Association, "Rankings and Estimates, Rankings of the States 2013
and Estimates of School Statistics 2014," NEA Research
(March 2014), www.nea.org/home/rankings-and-estimates-2013
-2014.html (accessed 9/17/18).

7. "Quality Counts 2016: State Report Cards Map," *Education Week*, www.edweek.org/ew/qc/2016/2016-state-report
-cards-map.html (accessed 9/17/18).

8. California Department of Education, "State Schools Chief
Tom Torlakson Announces Results of California Assessment
of Student Performance and Progress Online Tests," October 2, 2018, https://www.cde.ca.gov/nr/ne/yr18/yr18rel62
.asp (accessed 10/31/18).

9. "Managing Droughts," Public Policy Institute of California
Water Policy Center, www.ppic.org/wp-content/uploads/cali
fornias-water-managing-droughts-november-2018.pdf
(accessed 11/30/18).

10. Paul Rogers and Nicholas St. Fleur, "California Drought:
Database Shows Big Difference Between Water Guzzlers
and Sippers," *Mercury News*, February 7, 2014, www.mercury
news.com/2014/02/07/california-drought-database-shows
-big-difference-between-water-guzzlers-and-sippers (accessed
9/17/18).

11. Matt Weiser, "California Allocates Vastly More Water Than
Supplies Allow, Study Shows," *Sacramento Bee*, August 19,
2014, www.sacbee.com/news/local/article2607102.html
(accessed 9/17/18).

12. "Water Rights: Frequently Asked Questions," California Water
Boards, www.waterboards.ca.gov/waterrights/board_info/faqs
.html#toc178761090 (accessed 9/17/18).

13. George Skelton, "In California, rights to water exceed the
supply," *Los Angeles Times*, April 12, 2015, www.latimes.com
/local/politics/la-me-cap-drought-water-20150413-column
.html (accessed 9/17/18).

14. Peter H. Gleick, "Solving California's Water Problems," *Huffington Post*, June 10, 2014, www.huffingtonpost.com/peter
-h-gleick/solving-californias-water_b_5479569.html (accessed
9/17/18).

15. Gleick, "Solving California's Water Problems."

16. Caitrin Chappelle and Ellen Hanack, "Just the Facts: Groundwater in California," Public Policy Institute of California,

May 2017, www.ppic.org/publication/groundwater-in-california (accessed 9/17/18). Chappelle, Hanack, and Mount, "Just the Facts: California's Latest Drought," Public Policy Institute of California, July 2016, www.ppic.org/publication/californias -latest-drought (accessed 9/17/18).

17. "Lessons Learned: Covered California Open Enrollment 2013–2014," Covered California, October 2014, www.coveredca .com/PDFs/10-14-2014-Lessons-Learned-final.pdf (accessed 9/17/18).

18. Ken Jacobs, "Employer-Sponsored Insurance in California," UC Berkeley Labor Center, October 23, 2017, healthcare.assembly .ca.gov/sites/healthcare.assembly.ca.gov/files/employer-based coverage_kenjacobs_chair_ucberkeley.pdf (accessed 9/17/18).

19. Tracy Seipel, "Healthy California Act annual price tag: $400 billion," *Mercury News*, May 22, 2017, www.mercurynews.com /2017/05/22/healthy-california-act-annual-price-tag-400-billion (accessed 9/17/18).

20. Alyssa Dykman, "Single-Payer Health Care and the Governor's Race," Public Policy Institute of California, June 4, 2018, http://www.ppic.org/blog/single-payer-health-care-and-the -governors-race (accessed 9/17/18).

21. California Health Care Foundation. "Medi-Cal Facts and Figures: An Evolving Program," December 21, 2017, www.chcf .org/publication/medi-cal-facts-and-figures-a-program-trans forms (accessed 9/28/18).

22. For more information about Medi-Cal, see the many publications of the California Health Care Foundation at their website, www.chcf.org (accessed 9/17/18), or the Kaiser Family Foundation, www.kff.org (accessed 9/17/18).

23. California Health Care Foundation, "California's Uninsured: Progress Toward Universal Coverage," August 6, 2018, https:// www.chcf.org/publication/californias-uninsured-progress-uni versal-coverage (accessed 9/28/18).

24. Bruce E. Cain, "Searching for the Next Pat Brown: California Infrastructure in the Balance," in "California's Future in the Balance," *California Policy Issues Annual*, special edition (Los Angeles: Edmund G. "Pat" Brown Institute of Public Affairs, November 2001).

25. "Report Card for California's Infrastructure 2018," The American Society of Civil Engineers, October 2018, http://asceca reportcard.org/wp-content/uploads/2018/10/2018-ASCE -California-Surface-Transportation-Report-Card.pdf (accessed 10/31/18).

26. Gary Stoller, "U.S. Roads, Bridges Are Decaying Despite Stimulus Influx," *USA Today*, July 29, 2013.

27. Daniel C. Vock, "Under Scrutiny, States Trim List of Bad Bridges," *Governing Magazine*, June 4, 2014.

28. C. Piller, "Bay Bridge's Troubled China Connection," *Sacramento Bee*, June 8, 2014.

29. Dan Walters, "California's Hefty Fuel Tax Buys Poor Roads," *Sacramento Bee*, July 2, 2013, www.sacbee.com/news/politics -government/politics-columns-blogs/dan-walters/article2577 987.html (accessed 9/17/18).

30. George Skelton, "On Road Repairs, Legislators Still in the Driveway," *Los Angeles Times*, August 22, 2016.

31. Stuart Leavenworth, "Logjam May Break on Mending Levees," *Sacramento Bee*, April 2, 2004.

32. Stuart Leavenworth, "Defenses Decayed: Neglected Levees Pushed Past Limits," *Sacramento Bee*, March 28, 2004.

33. Sara Lin and William Wan, "Crews Shore Up Levees as Concerns Rise over Upkeep," *Los Angeles Times*, June 10, 2004, pp. B1+.

34. Bettina Boxall, "A Delta Tunnel Project's Lofty Ambitions Have Been Scaled Back," *Los Angeles Times*, April 4, 2016, www.la times.com/science/la-me-delta-pumps-20160404-story.html (accessed 9/17/18).

35. Denny Walsh, "State Supreme Court Rules in State's Favor on Delta Property Rights," *Sacramento Bee*, July 21, 2016, www .sacbee.com/news/state/california/water-and-drought/delta /article91048507.html (accessed 9/17/18).

36. Ryan Sabalow and Dale Kasler, "Massive Delta tunnels project took a giant step forward—here's what you need to know," *Sacramento Bee*, April 11, 2018, www.sacbee.com/news/state /california/water-and-drought/delta/article208576299.html (accessed 9/17/18).

37. Ryan Sabalow and Dale Kasler, "Massive Delta tunnels project."

38. Ralph Vartabedian, "Leadership Turnover at the California High-Speed Rail Authority Could Signal Shakeup," *Los Angeles Times*, May 1, 2017, www.latimes.com/local/california/la -me-bullet-turmoil-20170428-story.html (accessed 9/17/18).

Credits

Chapter 1

Page 4: AP Photo/Rich Pedroncelli; **Pg. 14:** Max Whittaker/Reuters/Newscom.

Chapter 2

Pg. 27: Joy Jia-Shiuan Boston. **Pg. 34:** The Wasp, F850. W18, Volume 9, Number 316, pp 520–521. Courtesy of The Bancroft Library, University of California, Berkeley. **Pg. 41:** AP Photo/J. Scott Applewhite.

Chapter 3

Pg. 57: Monte Wolverton/Cagle Cartoons/PoliticalCartoons.com. **Pg. 65:** AP Photo/Rich Pedroncelli.

Chapter 4

Pg. 83: Figure from "The Prop 87 Effect: How the California GOP lost their way and implications for 2014 and beyond," by Matt Barreto. Latino Decisions, October 17, 2013. Reprinted by permission of Latino Decisions. **Pg. 92:** left: AP Photo/Chris Carlson, right: K.C. Alfred/San Diego Union-Tribune/ZUMA Wire/Alamy Live News. **Pg. 114:** Lucy Nicholson/Reuters/Newscom.

Chapter 5

Pg. 132: AP Photo/Rich Pedroncelli. **Pg. 137:** AP Photo/Rich Pedroncelli.

Chapter 6

Pg. 163: AP Photo/Rich Pedroncelli. **Pg. 180:** AP Photo/Rich Pedroncelli.

Chapter 7

Pg. 189: Sipa USA via AP. **Pg. 190:** "Flow of Cases through the California State Judicial System." Copyright © 2014, Judicial Council of California, used by permission. **Pg. 196:** Courtesy of the Supreme Court of California. Photo by Bob Knapik.

Chapter 8

Pg. 210: "Spending on Corrections and Higher Education" from the California Department of Finance, Chart C-1: Program Expenditures by Fund. Public Policy Institute of California Blog, August 4, 2016. Reprinted by permission of the Public Policy Institute of California. **Pg. 220:** Ben Margot/AP Photo. **Pg. 224:** Ken Wolter/Alamy Stock Photo.

Chapter 9

Pg. 254: Mark Boster/Los Angeles Times via Getty Images. **Pg. 257:** Gabrielle Lurie/The New York Times/Redux. **Pg. 258:** Figure from "Californians: Here's why your housing costs are so high," by Matt Levin and Ben Christopher. CALmatters, Aug. 21, 2017. Reprinted with permission. **Pg. 259:** Exhibit from "A Tool Kit to Close California's Housing Gap: 3.5 Million Homes by 2025," October 2016, McKinsey Global Institute, www.mckinsey.com. Copyright © 2018 McKinsey & Company. All rights reserved. Reprinted by permission. **Pg. 260:** Figure from "Gov. Brown just signed 15 housing bills. Here's how they're supposed to help the affordability crisis," by Liam Dillon. Los Angeles Times, Sep. 29, 2017. Copyright © 2017. Reprinted by permission of the Los Angeles Times.

Chapter 10

Pg. 272: AP Photo/Rich Pedroncelli. **Pg. 281:** AP Photo/Damian Dovarganes.

Index

Page numbers followed by *b*, *f*, or *t* refer to boxes, figures, and tables respectively. Italic page numbers refer to photos.

influence of government via, 265–69
  on infrastructure, 276–80
  on water use, 269–71

Quimby, John P., Sr., 54–55

race and ethnicity
  of Californians, 5
  of judges, 198
  of legislature members, 149
  political party affiliation and, 85, 86f
  of voters, 115–17, 116t, 118
racial and ethnic diversity, 5, 90–92
Rainy Day Budget Stabilization Fund Act, 173
rainy day fund, 11, 105, 151, 173, 228, 258
Ralph M. Brown Act of 1953, 248, 249b
ranked-choice voting, 250
Reagan, Ronald, 43, 71, 82, 110, 172
Reapportionment Act of 1911, 33
recalls, 4, 24, 31, 42, 44, 55, 120
  in city governments, 248
  establishment of, 35
  frequency of use, 43
  of government officials, 15, 39, 43, 99–100, 153, 174
  of judges, 201
  process, 42–43
redistricting, 10, 101, 155
  court cases on, 202
  impact of on legislature, 134–36
  responsibility for, 33
Redlawsk, David, 98
referenda, 3–4, 24, 31, 44, 55, 120, 140
  city governments and, 248
  establishment of, 35
  legislative, 42
  popular, 42
  process and frequency of use, 42
reform. *See also* Progressive movement
  campaign-finance, 15, 113–14
  of electoral politics, 120
  ideas for, 15–16
  of the judiciary, 200
  in voting process, 250
reform governments, 245
Regents of the University of California, 168, 182
regional governments, 233, 254–56
registration method (for qualifying as new party), 83
regulatory commission investigations, 201
regulatory regional governments, 254–55
Rendon, Anthony, 137, *137*, 138, 144, 147, 148, 152
rent control initiatives, 151
rents, lack of affordable, 258, 259f
representation
  by legislature, 129–31
  local voter turnout and, 249–51
republican government, 4
Republican Party
  elections of 2018 and, 108–10
  federal government controlled by, 152–53
  status of in California, 81–82

voter affiliation with, 7–8, 84, 85–87
  voter registration by county, 88f, 89
rescissions, 273
resolutions, 140
retention elections, 196, 197–99, 200, 201
Reuf, Abraham, 32–34
revenues, 215–22
  of city governments, 244–45, 244f
  sources of, 215–20, 217f
  variation in, 220–22
Reynolds v. Sims, 33
Reynoso, Cruz, 199
Ridley-Thomas, Sebastian, 154
riparian rights, 269–70
Riverside County, 235, 241, 265–66
Robbins, Alan, 64
Roberti, David, 43
Romney, Mitt, 102, 106
Roosevelt, Theodore, 32, 35–36
Roth, Richard, 243
Rowell, Chester, 35
Rumford Fair Housing Act, 39
runoff elections, 250
Ryan, Paul, 144

Sacramento, 245, 246
Sacramento Nonprofit Collective v. Holder, 195
Sacramento River levees, 279
sales tax, 13–14, 16, 103–4, 217–19, 223
same-sex marriage, 40–41, 63, 90–91, 97, 173, 180, 203. *See also*
    Proposition 8 (2008)
Samish, Arthur, 64
San Bernardino, 235, 256
San Bruno gas pipeline explosion, 169
Sanchez, Loretta, 94, 105–6, 107
sanctuary cities, 250–51
sanctuary states, 15, 79, 153, 163
Sanders, Bernie, 105
San Diego County
  political culture of, 89, 89t, 90, 91, 92
  population of, 235
San Francisco
  city government of, 242
  county government of, 238
  district elections in, 246–47
  housing crisis in, 257, *257,* 258, 259
  political culture of, 89, 89t, 90, 91, 92
  in Progressive era, 32
  ranked-choice voting in, 250
  sanctuary city status of, 251
  water use in, 269, 271
San Francisco Bay Conservation and Development Commission
    (BCDC), 255
San Leandro, 250
San Marcos, 247
San Onofre nuclear power plant, 169
Santa Clara, 248
Schaffner, Brian, 81
school and community college districts, 251–52
Schrag, Peter, 150

Voter Registration Information

State	Registration Deadline before Election*	Early Voting Permitted?**	Identification Required to Vote?**	More Information
Alabama	14 days	No	Photo ID requested	alabamavotes.gov
Alaska	30 days	Yes	ID requested; photo not required	elections.alaska.gov
Arizona	29 days	Yes	ID required; photo not required	azsos.gov/election
Arkansas	30 days	Yes	Photo ID requested	sos.arkansas.gov
California	15 days; election-day registration permitted	Yes	No	sos.ca.gov
Colorado	8 days by mail or online; no in-person deadline	Yes (all voting by mail)	ID requested; photo not required	sos.state.co.us
Connecticut	14 days by mail; 7 days in person; election-day registration permitted	No	ID requested; photo not required	ct.gov/sots
Delaware	24 days	No	ID requested; photo not required	elections.delaware.gov
District of Columbia	30 days by mail or online; no in-person deadline	Yes	No	dcboee.org
Florida	29 days	Yes	Photo ID requested	dos.myflorida.com/elections
Georgia	28 days	Yes	Photo ID required	sos.ga.gov
Hawaii	30 days; no in-person deadline	Yes	Photo ID requested	hawaii.gov/elections
Idaho	25 days; election-day registration permitted	Yes	Photo ID requested	idahovotes.gov
Illinois	27 days; 16 days online	Yes	No	elections.il.gov
Indiana	29 days	Yes	Photo ID required	in.gov/sos/elections
Iowa	10 days; election-day registration permitted	Yes	Photo ID required	sos.iowa.gov
Kansas	21 days	Yes	Photo ID required	kssos.org
Kentucky	27 days	No	ID requested; photo not required	elect.ky.gov
Louisiana	30 days; 20 days online	Yes	Photo ID requested	sos.la.gov
Maine	21 days by mail; no in-person deadline	Yes	No	maine.gov/sos
Maryland	21 days	Yes	No	elections.state.md.us
Massachusetts	20 days	No	No	www.sec.state.ma.us
Michigan	30 days	No	Photo ID requested	michigan.gov/sos
Minnesota	21 days; election-day registration permitted	Yes	No	mnvotes.org
Mississippi	30 days	No	Photo ID required	sos.ms.gov
Missouri	Fourth Wednesday prior to election	No	ID requested; photo not required	sos.mo.gov
Montana	30 days by mail; no in-person deadline	Yes	ID requested; photo not required	sos.mt.gov

State	Registration Deadline before Election*	Early Voting Permitted?**	Identification Required to Vote?**	More Information
Nebraska	Third Friday prior to election by mail; second Friday prior to election in person	Yes	No	www.sos.ne.gov
Nevada	31 days by mail; 21 days in person	Yes	No	nvsos.gov
New Hampshire	10 days; election-day registration permitted	No	ID requested; photo not required	sos.nh.gov
New Jersey	21 days	Yes	No	njelections.org
New Mexico	28 days	Yes	No	sos.state.nm.us
New York	25 days	No	No	www.elections.ny.gov
North Carolina	25 days	Yes	No	ncsbe.gov
North Dakota	No voter registration required	Yes	ID required; photo not required	vote.nd.gov
Ohio	30 days	Yes	ID required; photo not required	sos.state.oh.us
Oklahoma	24 days	Yes	ID requested; photo not required	ok.gov/elections
Oregon	21 days	Yes (all voting by mail)	No	sos.oregon.gov
Pennsylvania	30 days	No	No	votespa.com
Rhode Island	30 days; election-day registration permitted	No	Photo ID requested	www.elections.state.ri.us
South Carolina	30 days	No	ID requested; photo not required	scvotes.org
South Dakota	15 days	Yes	Photo ID requested	sdsos.gov
Tennessee	30 days	Yes	Photo ID required	tn.gov/sos/election
Texas	30 days	Yes	Photo ID requested	votetexas.gov
Utah	30 days by mail; 7 days in person; election-day registration permitted	Yes	ID requested; photo not required	elections.utah.gov
Vermont	Wednesday before the election; no in-person deadline	Yes	No	www.sec.state.vt.us/elections
Virginia	22 days	Yes	Photo ID required	sbe.virginia.gov
Washington	30 days by mail and online; 8 days in person	Yes (all voting by mail)	ID requested; photo not required	sos.wa.gov/elections/
West Virginia	21 days	Yes	ID requested; photo not required	sos.wv.gov
Wisconsin	20 days by mail; election-day registration permitted	Yes	Photo ID required	www.sos.state.wi.us
Wyoming	14 days; election-day registration permitted	Yes	No	soswy.state.wy.us

* Information collected from Project Vote Smart, votesmart.org/elections/voter-registration (accessed 11/1/18).
** Information collected from National Conference of State Legislatures, www.ncsl.org (accessed 11/1/18). In states where an ID is "requested," voters who do not bring ID to the polls may be required to sign an affidavit of identity, vote on a provisional ballot, have a poll worker vouch for their identity, or take additional steps after Election Day to make sure their vote is counted.
Note: In November 2018, Arkansas and North Carolina passed ballot measures requiring a photo ID to vote. Michigan passed ballot measures to implement same-day and automatic voter registration.